Rise of the Hyksos

Egypt and the Levant from the Middle Kingdom to the Early Second Intermediate Period

Anna-Latifa Mourad

Archaeopress Egyptology 11

Archaeopress Publishing Ltd
Gordon House
276 Banbury Road
Oxford OX2 7ED

www.archaeopress.com

ISBN 978 1 78491 133 1
ISBN 978 1 78491 134 8 (e-Pdf)

JSESH v.6.3.3 was used to create the Egyptian hieoglyphic font in this book

Printed in England by Oxuniprint Ltd, Oxford
This book is available direct from Archaeopress or from our website www.archaeopress.com

For Mum and Dad

Preface and Acknowledgements

Egypt and the Levant: two areas that have continually shaped societies and the advancement of civilisation in both the past and the present. Throughout the last few years, I have been lucky enough to delve into their ancient cultures, searching for hints of intercultural contact. I offer this body of work as a small contribution to their histories and their people, with the hope that it will inspire many more.

This study is based on a doctoral dissertation submitted in 2014 at Australia's Macquarie University. As its title suggests, it concentrates on the rise of the Hyksos, exploring relations between Egypt and the Levant from the Middle Kingdom to the early Second Intermediate Period. This period is characterised by the destabilisation of the Egyptian state, when the *ḥḳꜣ.w ḫꜣs.wt* 'rulers of foreign lands', or 'Hyksos', extended their control over parts of Egypt. Investigations into how the Hyksos gained such control was dependent on Manetho's affirmation of an Asiatic invasion until recent excavations at Tell el-Dab'a revealed new and significant data on their dynasty. Since then, much debate has circulated on the rise of the Hyksos, with scholars advocating one of three models: (1) invasion; (2) gradual infiltration and peaceful takeover; or (3) gradual infiltration and violent takeover. The Hyksos have also been argued to be from either the Northern or Southern Levant, the confusion partly due to the lack of an up-to-date study assessing Levantines, their growing influences on Egypt, and whether this influence helped the Hyksos establish their rule.

The present work is a response to this need. It outlines the development of the status of Levantines in Egyptian society, and reassesses the changing nature of Egyptian-Levantine relations. The approach is holistic, gathering archaeological, textual and artistic evidence that reveals intercultural contact. Special focus is placed on archaeological ethnic markers to identify the presence of Levantines in Egypt as well as the Egyptian concept of ethnicity.

This book would never have been possible without the generosity and advice of several individuals. As a doctoral student at Macquarie University, I was supervised by Professor Naguib Kanawati, who has been a valuable source of guidance and counsel. I also thank my associate supervisor, Associate Professor Boyo Ockinga, for his insights and constructive comments, especially on some of my translations, and Dr Ann McFarlane for proofreading the manuscript. Inherent errors are, however, my own. I would also like to extend my sincerest gratitude to the following for their support and encouragement: Dr Susanne Binder; Dr Linda Evans; Dr Jana Jones; Dr Miral Lashien; Dr Joyce Swinton; Dr Alexandra Woods; Robert and Kathy Parker; and to Archaeopress for publishing this work, particularly Dr David Davison for his support.

There are also researchers whom I greatly thank for kindly taking the time to provide helpful comments on the examined material evidence. This, in particular, includes the dissertation's examiners as well as a number of researchers who not only offered their thoughts on the topic but also discussed unpublished excavation material: Professor Hélène Sader (Tell el-Burak and Tell Hizzine, American University of Beirut), Associate Professor Hermann Genz (Tell Fad'ous, American University of Beirut), Dr Claude Doumet-Serhal (College Site, Sidon, British Museum), and Professor Youssef Hourany, now retired. A number of expedition members and researchers commented on their work: Natasha Ayers (Tell Edfu, Oriental Institute at the University of Chicago); Kathryn Bandy (Tell Edfu, Oriental Institute at the University of Chicago); Dr Vanessa Boschloos (College Site, Sidon, Royal Museum of Arts and History, Brussels); Dr Anat Cohen-Weinberger (Tell el-Dab'a, Israel Antiquities Authority); Dr Irene Forstner-Müller (Tell el-Dab'a, Austrian Archaeological Institute in Cairo); Dr Karin Kopetzky (College Site, Sidon, Austrian Academy of Sciences, Institute for Oriental and European Archaeology); Dr Günther Karl Kunst (Tell el-Dab'a, Vienna Institute for Archaeological Science); Dr Nadine Moeller (Tell Edfu, Oriental Institute at the University of Chicago); Dr Mary Ownby (Kom Rabi'a, Research Petrographer, Desert Archaeology Inc.); Chiara Reali (Tell el-Dab'a, University of Vienna); and Aaron de Souza (Macquarie University). To them all, I wish to express my thanks and gratitude.

Unless noted, all images were photographed, inked or redrawn by the author. Thanks are due to Professor Naguib Kanawati for permission to include images of wall scenes from the Australian Centre for Egyptology's work at Beni Hassan and Meir, Professor Hélène Sader for permission to include images of Tell el-Burak's wall scenes, and the National Museums Scotland for copyright approval for Plate 3.

Last, but definitely not least, I am wholeheartedly grateful for the incredible patience and support of my family who unceasingly encouraged me throughout my research into the Hyksos: my father, Toufic Mourad, who fervently offered his expertise as a wood sculptor and artist; my mother, Lama Mourad, for patiently reading through my work, for countless discussions on the topic and many warm inspirations; my sisters, Zena, Nada and Rima, and brothers-in-law, George and Giuliano, whose support, sense of humour and close friendship kept me calm and sane. Rima also spent many hours editing and proofreading my work, to which I am extremely grateful. Without such a family, this work would not have come to fruition. I love you all from the depths of my heart and sincerely thank you for always being there for me. This work is dedicated to you.

Contents

List of Figures and Plates

CHAPTER 5

CHAPTER 6

CHAPTER 7

Appendix B

Plates

List of Abbreviations

Books, journals, publication series and institutions

AAALiv	*Liverpool Annals of Archaeology and Anthropology*
AAS	*Annales archéologiques de Syria*
AASOR	*Annual of the American Schools of Oriental Research*
ÄA	Ägyptologische Abhandlungen
ÄAT	Ägypten und Altes Testament
ABSA	*The Annual of the British School at Athens*
ACE: Reports	Australian Centre for Egyptology: Reports
ACE: Studies	Australian Centre for Egyptology: Studies
ADAJ	*Annual of the Department of Antiquities of Jordan*
AHL	*Archaeology and History in the Lebanon*
AJA	*American Journal of Archaeology*
AJBA	*Australian Journal of Biblical Archaeology*
AJSL	*The American Journal of Semitic Languages and Literatures*
Akk	*Akkadica*
ANES	*Ancient Near Eastern Studies*
AOAT	Alter Orient und Altes Testament
AOF	*Altorientalische Forschungen*
ARCE	American Research Centre in Egypt
ArOr	*Archiv orientálni*
ASAE	*Annales du service des antiquités de l'Égypte*
ASOR	American Schools of Oriental Research
AsPn	*Asiatische Personennamen* (T. Schneider, *Asiatische Personennamen in ägyptischen Quellen des Neuen Reiches*, OBO 114 [Gottingen, 1992])
AV	Archäologische Veröffentlichungen
BA	*The Biblical Archaeologist*
BAAL	*Bulletin d'archéologie et d'architecture Libanaises*
BACE	*Bulletin of the Australian Centre for Egyptology*
BAR	British Archaeological Reports
BASOR	*Bulletin of the American Schools of Oriental Research*
BdE	Bibliothèque d'Étude
BES	*Bulletin of the Egyptological Seminar*
BIA	*Bulletin of the Institute of Archaeology*
BiAe	Bibliotheca Aegyptiaca
BIES	*Bulletin of the Israel Exploration Society*
BiOr	*Bibliotheca Orientalis*
BIFAO	*Bulletin de l'Institut français d'archéologie orientale du Caire*
BMB	*Bulletin du Musée de Beyrouth*
BMMA	*Bulletin of the Metropolitan Museum of Art*
BSEG	*Bulletin de la société d'égyptologue, Genève*
BSFE	*Bulletin de la société Française d'égyptologie*
CAH	*The Cambridge Ancient History*
CASAE	*Cahiers. Supplement aux Annales du service des antiquités de l'Égypte*
CCE	*Cahiers de la céramique Égyptienne*
CCEM	Contributions to the Chronology of the Eastern Mediterranean
CdE	*Chronique d'Égypte*
CRAIBL	*Comptes-rendus des séances de l'académie des inscriptions et belles-lettres*
CRIPEL	*Cahiers de recherches de l'Institut de papyrologie et d'egyptologie de Lille*
DAIAK	Deutsches Archäologisches Institut, Abteilung Kairo
DE	*Discussions in Egyptology*
DFIFAO	Documents de fouilles de l'Institut français d'archéologie orientale du Caire

E&L	*Ägypten und Levante/ Egypt and the Levant*
EA	*Egyptian Archaeology*
FIFAO	Fouilles de l'Institut français d'archéologie orientale du Caire
GM	*Göttinger Miszellen*
IEJ	*Israel Exploration Journal*
IOS	*Israel Oriental Society*
JAC	*Journal of Ancient Civilizations*
JAEI	*Journal of Ancient Egyptian Interconnections*
JAIGB	*Journal of the Anthropological Institute of Great Britain and Ireland*
JAOS	*Journal of the American Oriental Society*
JANER	*Journal of Ancient Near Eastern Religions*
JARCE	*Journal of the American Research Center in Egypt*
JAS	*Journal of Archaeological Science*
JBL	*Journal of Biblical Literature*
JBS	*Journal of Black Studies*
JCS	*Journal of Cuneiform Studies*
JEA	*The Journal of Egyptian Archaeology*
JEH	*Journal of Egyptian History*
JEOL	*Jaarbericht van het vooraziat-egyptisch Genootschap, Ex Oriente Lux*
JESHO	*Journal of the Economic and Social History of the Orient*
JMA	*Journal of Mediterranean Archaeology*
JNES	*Journal of Near Eastern Studies*
JÖAI	*Jahreshefte des Österreichischen Archäologischen Instituts*
JPOS	*Journal of the Palestine Oriental Society*
JPR	*Journal of Prehistoric Religion*
JRAS	*Journal of the Royal African Society*
JSA	*Journal of Social Archaeology*
JSS	*Journal of Semitic Studies*
JSSEA	*Journal of the Society of the Studies of Egyptian Antiquities*
JSOT–Suppl.	*Journal of the Study of the Old Testament Supplement Series*
LÄ	*Lexikon der Ägyptologie*
MDAIK	*Mitteilungen des deutschen archäologischen Instituts Kairo*
MIFAO	Mémoires publiés par les membres de l'Institut français d'archéologie orientale du Caire
MMA	Metropolitan Museum of Art, New York
MMJ	*Metropolitan Museum Journal*
NARCE	*Newsletter of the American Research Center in Egypt*
NEA	*Near Eastern Archaeology*
ÖAW	Österreichische Akademie der Wissenschaften
OBO	Orbis Biblicus et Orientalis
OIMP	Oriental Institute Museum Publications
OIP	Oriental Institute Publications
OIS	Oriental Institute Seminars
OLA	Orientalia Lovaniensia Analecta
OLP	Orientalia Lovaniensia Periodica
PAM	*Polish Archaeology in the Mediterranean*
PEFA	The Palestine Exploration Fund Annual
PEQ	*Palestine Exploration Quarterly*
PM	B. Porter and R. Moss, *Topographical Bibliography of Ancient Egyptian Hieroglyphic Texts, Reliefs and Paintings* (Oxford, 1927-52; 2nd edition J. Málek, 1960-)
PT	A. B. Mercer, *The Pyramid Texts* (New York, London and Toronto, 1952)
QDAP	*Quarterly of the Department of Antiquities in Palestine*
RdE	*Revue d'égyptologie*
RT	*Recueil de traveaux relatifs à la philologie et à l'archéologie ègyptiennes et assyriennes*
SAGA	Studien zur Archäologie und Geschichte Altägyptens
SAHL	Studies in the Archaeology and History of the Levant
SAK	*Studien zur Altägyptischen Kultur*
SAOC	Studies in Ancient Oriental Civilization
SBAW	Sitzungsberichte der Bayerischen Akademie der Wissenschaften
SMA	Studies in Mediterranean Archaeology

SSEA	Society for the Study of Egyptian Antiquities
TeD	*Tell el-Dab'a* (series)
UF	*Ugarit-Forschungen. Internationales Jahresbuch für die Altertumskunde Syrien-Palästinas*
Urk	K. Sethe, *Urkunden des Alten Reichs* (Leipzig, 1933)
VA	*Varia aegyptiaca*
VT	*Vetus Testamentum*
Wb	A. Erman and H. Grapow, *Wörterbuch der Aegyptischen Sprache*, 7 vols (Berlin, 1926-1971)
ZÄS	*Zeitschrift für ägyptische und allgemeine Kunstwissenschaft*
ZBA	Zaberns Bildbände zur Archäologie
ZDPV	*Zeitschrift des deutschen Palästina-Vereins*

Other terms

Chron.	Chronology
EBA	Early Bronze Age
Lat.Lon.	Latitude and Longitude
LBA	Late Bronze Age
MBA	Middle Bronze Age
NAA	Neutron Activation Analysis
Ref(s)	Reference(s)

Section 1: Studying the Hyksos

1. Introduction

'... unexpectedly, from the regions of the East,
invaders of obscure race marched
in confidence of victory against our land.
By main force they easily seized it,
without striking a blow.'
Manetho, *Aegyptiaca*, frg. 42, 1.75-1.76.

1.1 Introduction

Manetho's obscure reference to a race of invaders has been a constant source of debate and controversy. But who are they and where did they come from? They are named the 'Hyksos' – a Greek modification of the Egyptian expression *ḥḳ3 ḫ3s.wt* 'ruler of foreign lands'. The Hyksos are correlated with the Fifteenth Dynasty of the Second Intermediate Period, a time characterised by the destabilisation and regionalisation of the Egyptian state. Several scholars have pondered over their victory and rule in Egypt, from the manner in which they entered Egypt and the means with which they claimed the throne to their final expulsion from the land. The present work assesses their rise to power, exploring the preliminary stages that enabled the Hyksos to gain control over a portion of Egyptian territory and thus to merit a small mention in Manetho's history.

1.2 Research Problems

The Fifteenth Dynasty has provoked much discussion on the role of foreigners in Egypt. Manetho's account originally led historians to search for traces of northeastern warriors violently succeeding the Egyptian regime.[1] Over the past few decades, excavations in the Delta have caused scholars to propose that the Hyksos takeover may not have been wholly violent, but that it was partly or even completely facilitated by a northeastern population already living in Egypt.[2] Archaeological evidence from Tell el-Dab'a (Avaris) has revealed that the population largely derived from a Levantine ethnic group, one which is represented in the Egyptian corpus as that of the 'Asiatics'. A study on the rise of the Hyksos must therefore entail an assessment of Levantines in Egypt during the period before their rule, that is, the Middle Kingdom and the early Second Intermediate Period.

This exercise is well reflected in the available literature but is marked by a lack of a thorough and recent examination of the varying representations of northeasterners within Egyptian society. A few attempts have been made in tracing their presence in Egypt, yet the studies mostly focus on a particular body of evidence, such as textual references to Asiatics or specific forms of archaeological data. Often, the representations are removed from their context and utilised to support circumstantial evidence, with an inherent disregard for the influence of the Egyptian concept of the *other* that permeates representations and incorporates ideological affirmations of Egyptian supremacy. Consequently, a land in the Levant is equated to one with 'fuzzy-wuzzies in some godforsaken outback'[3] while depictions of Asiatics in the Middle Kingdom become scenes of wandering nomadic tribes. With such conclusions, scholars have discounted the nature of the evidence, its purpose and the context in which it appears.

In addition, many researchers have concentrated on developments within a specific category of evidence, effectually omitting data that can significantly alter their findings.[4] The reliance on scarab analysis, for instance, has led some to assert that the Hyksos and their people originated from the Southern Levant. While this may be correct, correlating the distribution of scarabs and seals with ethnic origins is subject to error, much like the equation of particular ceramics at a site with the presence of the people behind its production (i.e. the 'pots equal people' contention). The presence or absence of these finds may instead be related to commercial activities.

Another research problem is that the literature is primarily concentrated on evidence from one specific area, namely the Delta or the Southern Levant. Although of utmost significance, such areas should not overshadow the equally important regions of Middle Egypt, Upper Egypt, the Northern Levant and the Eastern Desert.

A further research dilemma is the reliance on finds from unclear contexts and/or later periods. An example is the use of the aforementioned history of Manetho which should instead be utilised as supporting data. Scholars' dependence on such evidence has resulted in misinterpretations in the chronology, ethnic origins, and nature of the Fifteenth Dynasty that still resonate in current scholarly literature.

Evidently, the research problems highlight the need for a new study that examines the rise of the Hyksos through a reappraisal of various forms of evidence across Egypt and the Levant. Such a study would surely advance

1 For example, Winlock, *Rise and Fall*, 96-97; Redford, *Egypt, Canaan, and Israel*, 98-106. For more on past scholarship, see Chapter 2.2.

2 For example, see Bietak, *Avaris*; Bietak, in *Second Intermediate Period*, 139-181.

3 Redford, *Egypt, Canaan, and Israel*, 85.

4 Baines, in *Study of the Ancient Near East*, 344.

our knowledge of the ambiguous Fifteenth Dynasty in Egyptian history and address the 'warm and ongoing debate'[5] surrounding the Hyksos's emerging reign.

1.3 Research Goals

In an attempt to shed new light on the socio-political developments associated with Asiatics and the accession of the Fifteenth Dynasty, this study aims to examine the rise of the Hyksos by tracing Egyptian-Levantine contact from the Middle Kingdom to the early Second Intermediate Period via a holistic approach of the evidence.

The primary objective is to investigate how the Hyksos were able to form an independent state in the north of Egypt. The nature and development of Egyptian-Levantine relations is assessed to examine the validity of proposed theoretical models explaining the rise of the Hyksos, including: (1) the invasion model; (2) the gradual infiltration and peaceful takeover; and (3) the gradual infiltration and violent takeover.

The study secondarily aims to explore the origins of the Fifteenth Dynasty. Scholarly consensus agrees that the Hyksos are from West Asia. However, a more precise area of origin has been fervently debated. This aim is linked with that of the rise of the Hyksos and is largely dependent on which of the aforementioned models is supported by the evidence.

The third aim entails a reanalysis of Egyptian relations with the Levant. Changes in the status and role of foreigners from the northeast are to be examined with a reassessment of developments in the Egyptian concept of and reaction to foreigners. The latter further encompasses an investigation into the influence of context and genre on the collected data.

1.4 Research Methodology

The main method is to trace elements of a West Asiatic ethnic group(s) and culture in Egypt and the Eastern Desert. These markers may be revealed through:

1. *Archaeological evidence*, gathered from sites featuring non-Egyptian elements encompassing: (a) secular and sacral architecture; (b) burial customs; (c) characteristic non-Egyptian vessels; and (d) small material goods. The evidence is compared to and supplemented by archaeological finds from the Levant;

2. *Textual evidence*, including contemporary texts preserved on (a) stelae, (b) royally-instigated inscriptions, (c) tomb inscriptions, (d) scarabs, seals and seal impressions, (e) papyri, and (f) graffiti. Asiatics can be identified by the use of terms designating Asiatic groups, Levantine toponyms and non-Egyptian names. Literary and linguistic perspectives are utilised, the former of which is used to assess the influence of genre and style while the latter focuses on terminology; and

3. *Artistic evidence*, which embraces depictions of Asiatics on (a) wall scenes in funerary contexts; (b) scarabs, seals, and seal impressions; (c) stone, ceramic and wooden three-dimensional figures; and (d) small material goods. These are evaluated according to their context and aspects of composition. The contextual study includes an artefact's overall decorative scheme, immediate context as well as its contemporary socio-political and religious circumstances, whereas aspects of composition embrace artistic details such as posture, colour and clothing.

The second method is to examine the development of Egyptian-Levantine relations as expressed by evidence in the Levant. The same three abovementioned bodies of data are collected, focussing on that which displays contact with the Egyptian culture. Results are then compared with evidence from Egypt and the Eastern Desert.

All forms of evidence are presented geographically and, where possible, chronologically. Such an analysis helps identify the development of Egyptian-Levantine relations for each particular site and region, as well as the progression of foreigners' status in Egyptian society. It further provides a holistic approach to help determine how the Hyksos emerged as a dominant power in Egypt and the Mediterranean.

1.5 Research Parameters

1.5.1 Geographical scope and terminology

Three areas are investigated: (1) Egypt; (2) the Eastern Desert; and (3) the Levant (Figure 1.1). Sites considered in each area are those which bear traces of Egyptian-Levantine relations and/or are heavily featured in the literature. Egypt is divided into four regions of the Delta, the Memphite region, Middle Egypt and Upper Egypt. The Eastern Desert has been selected as a peripheral zone frequented by Egyptian expeditions and includes the Sinai Peninsula. Contacts with the Libyans to the west,[6] the Nubians and Puntites to the south,[7] as well as the civilisations further north[8] are only discussed in relation to Egyptian-Levantine relations.

5 Redford, *Egypt, Canaan, and Israel*, 101.

6 See Booth, *Role of Foreigners*, 9-10, 38-44; Forbes, *KMT* 16/1 (2005), 73.

7 See Booth, *Role of Foreigners*, 9, 45-53; Bourriau, in *Studien zur altÄgyptischen Keramik*, 25-41; Bourriau, in *Egypt and Africa*, 129-144; Bourriau, in *Ancient Egypt*, 194-197; Liszka, *Medjay and Pangrave*; Schneider, *Ausländer in Ägypten* 2, 82-104, 110-111, 179-181; Lacovara, in *Hyksos*, 69-86.

8 For example, the Minoan and Cypriote cultures. See Schneider, *Ausländer in Ägypten* 2, 183-184; Merrillees, *Trade and Transcendence*; Kemp and Merrillees, *Minoan Pottery*; Maguire, *TeD* 21; Warren, in *Egypt, the Aegean and the Levant*, 1-18.

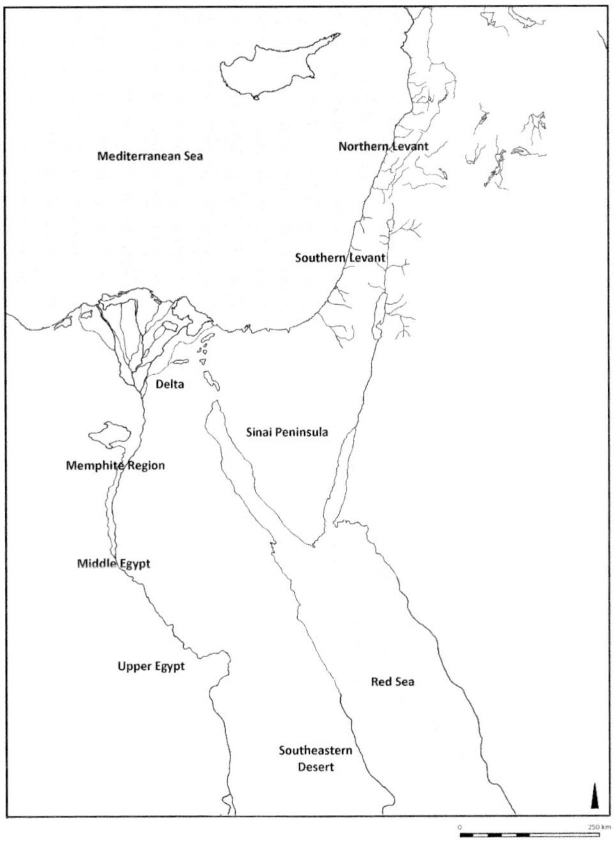

FIGURE 1.1. GEOGRAPHICAL SCOPE: EGYPT, THE EASTERN DESERT AND THE LEVANT.

The Levant is presented as two main geographical regions (Figure 1.1): (1) the Northern Levant, including modern western Syria and Lebanon; and (2) the Southern Levant, including present-day Israel, the Palestinian occupied territories and Jordan. The division is simply a geographical differentiation that is commonly found in the literature. Levantine cultural traits were often shared across the region, but can appear in the archaeological record at slightly different periods, especially following the collapse of the Early Bronze Age (EBA) and the rise of the Middle Bronze Age (MBA). Thus, the terms used in this work are derived from geographical terminology rather than ethnic identifiers (e.g. Amorite or Canaanite). The expression 'Syria-Palestine' is only utilised to refer to a type of Levantine vessel typically classified as the 'Syro-Palestinian store-jar'.

1.5.2 Chronological scope and terminology

A detailed investigation into chronological correlations between Egypt and the Levant would be too vast to explore in the present work. As such, the monograph is dependent on other chronological analyses and does not aim to offer revisions of synchronised chronologies. Instead, the study sheds new insights on the socio-political changes that may have led to an independent Fifteenth Dynasty in Egypt. Further discussion into chronological correlations that are adopted in the study may be found in Chapter 2.3.

The Egyptian period under examination is the Twelfth to early Fifteenth Dynasties, the sequence of dynasties and rulers cited here adhering to Ryholt (Figure 1.2).[9] Due to the unclear nature of the absolute chronology of the Middle Kingdom, and the absolute and relative chronology of the Second Intermediate Period, absolute dating is not utilised or discussed.[10] While the Middle Kingdom includes Dynasty 12, the Thirteenth Dynasty has been proposed to belong fully or partially to the Second Intermediate Period, the beginning of which remains conjectural. The present work follows Ryholt's division of the Second Intermediate Period into two stages: (1) a weakened Egyptian state and its disintegration into two main kingdoms, the Fourteenth Dynasty in the north and the Sixteenth Dynasty in the

DYNASTY	NOMEN	PRENOMEN
12	Amenemhat I	Sihotepibra
	Senwosret I	Kheperkara
	Amenemhat II	Nebkaura
	Senwosret II	Khakheperra
	Senwosret III	Khakaura
	Amenemhat III	Nimaatra
	Amenemhat IV	Maakherura
	Sobeknofru	Sobekkara
13*	Sobekhotep I	Sekhemrakhutawy
	Amenemhat V	Sekhemkara
	ꜥꜣmw/Qemau	-
	Sihornedjheritef	Hotepibra
	Siwesekhtawy	Sihotepibra
	Hor	Awibra
	Khendjer	Weserkara
	Noferhotep I	Khasekhemra
	Sihathor	Menwadjra
	Sobekhotep IV	Khaneferra
	Sobekhotep V	Merhotepra
	Sobekhotep VI	Khahotepra
	Ibiaw	Wahibra
	Aya	Mernoferra
	Sobekhotep VII	Merkaura
14*	*Ykbm*	Sekhaenra
	Yꜣꜥmw	Nebweserra
	Ḳꜣrḥ	Khaweserra
	ꜥꜣmw	Aahotepra
	Šši (Sheshi)	Maaibra
	Nehsy	Aasehra
15*	*Smḳn*	-
	ꜥpr-ꜥnti	-
	Skrhr	-
	Ḫyꜣn (Khayan)	Siweserenra
	Ỉppi (Apophis)	Aaweserra
	Ḫꜣmwdi	Hotepibra

FIGURE 1.2. KINGS OF DYNASTY 12 AND SELECTED RULERS OF DYNASTIES 13-15. AFTER RYHOLT, *POLITICAL SITUATION*.
* The sequence of rulers is not fixed.

[9] Ryholt, *Political Situation*.
[10] For a brief overview of chronological issues, see Chapter 2.3.

Present Work	Southern Levant (old)	Southern Levant (New)	Northern Levant
EBIV/MBI	Intermediate BA or MBI	EBIVA	EBIVa
		EBIVB	EBIVb
		EBIVC	
MBIIA	MBIIA	MBI	MBIa
			MBIb
MBIIB	MBIIB	MBII	MBIIa
MBIIC	MBIIC	MBIII	MBIIb

Figure 1.3. Terminology of divisions in EBA-MBA Levantine chronology. After Burke, *MBA Fortification Strategies*, 19, table 1.

south; and (2) the rise of the Fifteenth Dynasty in the north, with its capital at Avaris, and the Seventeenth Dynasty in the south, with its capital at Thebes.[11] Overlap between Dynasties 13-17 is not unfeasible.

Correlating with the Egyptian period is the Levantine MBA, for which a number of terminologies exist. The traditional tripartite division, namely MBIIA-C, is employed in this work.[12] It is recognised that this terminology is not commonly applied by researchers studying the Northern Levant, who typically divide the MBA into MBI (MBIIA) and MBII (MBIIB-C). However, for continuity's sake, the tripartite division is utilised in discussion to finds from the north. The various terminologies for describing Levantine chronology and their correlations can be found in Figure 1.3.

Synchronisations of the MBA with the Egyptian chronology follow Bietak's low chronology.[13] The MBIIA would thereby generally correlate with the Twelfth Dynasty and the first half of the Thirteenth Dynasty, the MBIIA-B to the third quarter of the Thirteenth Dynasty, the MBIIB to the end of the Thirteenth and first half of the Fifteenth Dynasty, and the MBIIC to the late Fifteenth and possibly early Eighteenth Dynasty (Figure 1.4). Based on these correlations, only Levantine material from the MBIIA to MBIIB period is examined. Evidence from the MBIIC is only included in the clarification or reassessment of traditional relative dates.

1.5.3 Evidential scope

The translation of titles and epithets predominantly follow Ward's study on Middle Kingdom terms, unless otherwise specified.[14] For emphasis, toponyms and personal names of postulated non-Egyptian origin, including those of Fourteenth and Fifteenth kings,[15] are left untranslated. Pottery fabrics are classified according to the Vienna System.[16] The typology of Tell el-Yahudiyah ware is reliant on its most recent study by Aston and Bietak[17] and scarab seal typology adheres to Ben-Tor's classifications.[18]

Evidence of clear provenance and context is selected, relying on the basis that only such provenanced artefacts can securely reflect contemporaneous Egyptian-Levantine contact. Examples of material of uncertain provenance or date of deposition include scarabs bought from antiquity dealers and surface finds. Some are included to signal possible intercultural contact but are clearly marked as questionable pieces or are only given a general chronological attribution. Exceptions are a few unprovenanced artefacts, such as the Tale of Sinuhe or the Berlin Execration Bowls, that justifiably reflect a Middle Kingdom date or Middle Kingdom Egyptian-Levantine relations. Non-contemporary sources, however, are not analysed. These include the Kamose 'victory' stela, the Turin King-List, Manetho's history, as well as Canaanite and Biblical stories, such as those of Io, Joseph, and the Exodus, which have been related to the Fifteenth Dynasty.

Lastly, it is important to note the fragmented nature of the evidence itself, particularly as a small percentage of it survives.[19] The presence of variability and the possibility that the evidence only concerns a small percentage of the population should be recognised.[20] Moreover, the collected evidence is dependent upon the methodologies followed by excavation teams in preliminary surveys, consequent excavations and the final publication of data.[21] Many sites have also been subjected to looting and mutilation in both ancient and modern times.

11 Ryholt, *Political Situation*.
12 Albright, *Archaeology of Palestine*; Mazar, *Land of the Bible*.
13 See Chapter 2.3.
14 Ward, *Index*.
15 The origin of the name *ỉppỉ* 'Apophis' is uncertain and could be either Egyptian or foreign in origin. For more, see von Beckerath, *Zweiten Zwischenzeit*, 127, n. 2; Ryholt, *Political Situation*, 129; Schneider, *Ausländer in Ägypten* 1, 36-39.
16 Nordström and Bourriau, in *Ancient Egyptian Pottery*, 147-190.
17 Aston and Bietak, *TeD* 8
18 Ben-Tor, *IEJ* 47/3 (1997), 162-189; Ben-Tor, *Scarabs*.
19 Clarke, *Antiquity* 47 (1973), 16; Renfrew and Bahn, *Archaeology*, 54-72.
20 O'Connor, in *Population Growth*, 81-83; Baines and Eyre, *GM* 61 (1983), 65-67; Baines and Lacovara, *JSA* 2 (2002), 12.
21 For more on problems in excavations and publications of Egyptian material, see Richards, *Society and Death*, 67-69.

EGYPTIAN DYNASTY	BC*	TELL EL-DAB'A	LEVANT*
A I	1980	N/2-3	
		N/1	
S I	1950	HIATUS	EBIV/MBI
	1920	M	
A II			
12	1890	L	
S II			
S III	1860	K	
A III		I	
	1830		
A IV	1800	H	MBIIA
SOBEK.			
	1770	G/4	
	1740	G/1-3	
	1710		
13		F	MBIIA-B
14 (?)	1680		
		E/3	
	1650		
		E/2	MBIIB
	1620		
		E/1	
15	1590		
		D/3	
	1560		
		D/2	MBIIC
18	1530		
		D/1	

FIGURE 1.4. CHRONOLOGICAL CORRELATIONS BETWEEN EGYPT, TELL EL-DAB'A AND THE LEVANT. AFTER BIETAK, IN *CITIES AND URBANISM*, FIG. 7.
* Following Bietak's low chronology.

1.5.4 *Other limitations*

The scope of the present work has been specifically tailored to provide the best results for its aims. Therefore, some topics could not be examined in detail, despite their significance for the study of the Hyksos. These include: absolute and relative dating methods determining the chronological point when the Hyksos took over; the genealogy of Hyksos rulers and the etymology of the names of Fourteenth and Fifteenth Dynasty kings; shifts in the ceramic sequence across Egypt; and developments in scarab typology. Such studies deserve entirely different research projects and have, in some form, been dealt with in other works.[22]

Any reflection on the names and sequence of Fourteenth and Fifteenth Dynasty kings is limited by evidential scope. Much of the evidence for these kings is from non-contemporaneous sources like the Turin King-List or unprovenanced scarabs. Therefore, the study only refers to Dynasty 14 if an item from a selected site clearly relates to a Fourteenth Dynasty king.

As a final note it should be stressed that some regions have been more favoured by archaeological researchers than others. Such regions as the Egyptian western Delta or the Beqa' Valley of Lebanon, for instance, have not been adequately explored. The current political situation in all examined areas also continues to restrict personal inspection of sites and artefacts. Thus, future archaeological and historical research will only help clarify and contribute to the present work's findings, enriching our general understanding of the Second Intermediate Period.

1.6 Research Outline

The study is divided into three sections: (1) *Studying the Hyksos*, with three chapters offering introductory information on previous scholarship and current understandings; (2) *Evidence for Contact*, investigating the data for Egyptian-Levantine relations from the regions of Egypt, the Eastern Desert and the Levant, each explored in a separate chapter; and (3) *Observations and Findings*, with two chapters, one on Asiatic representations in text and art, and the other on the origins and rise of the Hyksos. Appendices include *Ambiguous Data from the Levant* which could not be featured in Section 2 due to its questionable nature, as well as *Translations* of lengthy texts examined in the present work.

[22] See, for example, von Beckerath, *Zweiten Zwischenzeit*; Helck, *Die Beziehungen Ägyptens*; Schneider, in *Ancient Egyptian Chronology*, 168-196; Schneider, *Ausländer in Ägypten* 1; Ben-Tor, *Scarabs*; Ryholt, *Political Situation*.

2. Previous Scholarship

'In Egyptian memory the Hyksos episode
clearly stands out as a unique phenomenon,
previously unparalleled,
a time when foreign lords
imposed their rule on Egypt.'
Oren, in *Hyksos*, xix.

2.1 Introduction

For over a century, scholars of Egyptology and Near Eastern history have mused on Middle Kingdom and Second Intermediate Period relations with the Levant. From the events culminating in the defragmentation of Middle Kingdom rule to the establishment of the New Kingdom, the period has attracted much attention and debate. The focus of the present work, the rise of the Hyksos, has not escaped the scholarly gaze. This chapter presents an overview of scholarly contributions. It first outlines the literature on the origins and rise of the Hyksos and then offers a brief discussion on the chronological issues inherent in the examination of the Second Intermediate Period.

2.2 The Origins and Rise of the Hyksos

Before the discovery of Tell el-Dab'a, few sources were available to discern the origins and rise of the Hyksos. Often utilising the term 'Hyksos' for the rulers of the Fifteenth Dynasty as well as their people, scholars relied on mostly non-contemporaneous evidence in their discussion of a so-called 'Hyksos culture', traces of which were seemingly found in Egypt, the Levant and, in a few cases, further east.

The most well-known non-contemporaneous text on the Hyksos is Manetho's history. In Josephus's *Contra Apionem*, Manetho is quoted writing about an 'obscure race' of invaders from the east who 'unexpectedly' overpowered the Egyptian rulers 'without striking a blow'.[1] They destroyed cities and temples, massacred the local population and then appointed one of their own as a pharaoh who reigned from Memphis. He then levied tribute from the Egyptians, installed garrisons across the land and built the fortified Avaris.[2] The king and his successors were Hyksos, which was translated by Josephus to read 'shepherd kings' or 'captive kings'.[3] Josephus then mentions that some called them 'Arabs'.[4] Africanus and Eusebius contrarily note that the Hyksos were from 'Phoenicia' and, after founding Avaris, 'subdued' Egypt.[5]

Other references in non-contemporaneous texts come from Egypt's Pharaonic history. The first stela of Seventeenth Dynasty Kamose mentions Avaris's king and people as a *ꜥ3m* group who had desecrated Egypt.[6] Kamose's second stela adds that the Hyksos king was a *ḥḳ3 n(.y) Rtnw* 'ruler of *Rtnw*', his city at Avaris holding 300 ships of *ꜥš*-wood filled with 'all the fine products of *Rtnw*'.[7] The Eighteenth Dynasty inscription of Hatshepsut at Speos Artemidos, Egypt, records that the queen had restored the ruins caused by the Hyksos *ꜥ3m.w* in Avaris.[8] The Nineteenth Dynasty literary Quarrel between Apophis and Seqenenra also associates the Hyksos with *ꜥ3m.w* who worshipped Seth at Avaris.[9] The mention of Seth complements the Stela of the Year 400 that commemorates the worship of the god as a king in the Delta.[10] Set up in Dynasty 19, the stela has been used to support Dynasty 15's reverence to Seth.[11] Combined, the Pharaonic texts agree on the identification of the Hyksos with a *ꜥ3m* or Asiatic ethnic group who had controlled the city of Avaris. The Kamose stela also hints at some relations to the region of *Rtnw*. Such evidence thereby provides justification for linking the Hyksos with Asiatics or individuals from the east.

Maspero and Tomkins were among the first scholars to question the origins of these foreign rulers.[12] They looked to the Elamite region east of Babylon for the invaders and analysed the names of Manetho's kings to identify their ethnicity.[13] Tomkins additionally proposed some relations between the Levantines and the Hyksos.[14] Petrie utilised the archaeological findings at Tell el-Yahudiyah as proof of a 'Hyksos culture' in the Delta, offering the site as a possible location for Avaris.[15] The topic was again addressed by Labib, who grouped the available Egyptian textual sources.[16] He was followed by Engberg, who

1 Manetho, *Aegyptiaca*, frg. 42, 1.75-1.76 (Josephus, *Contra Apionem*, I.14.75-76). Translation in Waddell, *Manetho*, 77-79.
2 Manetho, *Aegyptiaca*, frg. 42, 1.76-1.79 (Josephus, *Contra Apionem*, I.14.78-79). Translation in Waddell, *Manetho*, 79-83.
3 Manetho, *Aegyptiaca*, frg. 42, 1.82-1.83 (Josephus, *Contra Apionem*, I.14.82-83). Translation in Waddell, *Manetho*, 82-85.
4 Manetho, *Aegyptiaca*, frg. 42, 1.83 (Josephus, *Contra Apionem*, I.14.83). Translation in Waddell, *Manetho*, 84-85.
5 Manetho, *Aegyptiaca*, frgs 43 (Syncellus, 113), 48 (Syncellus, 114; Eusebius, *Chronica* 1, 99). Translation in Waddell, *Manetho*, 90-97.
6 Gardiner, *JEA* 3 (1916), 95-110; Lacau, *ASAE* 39 (1939), 245-271, pls 37-38; Smith and Smith, *ZÄS* 103 (1976), 48-76.
7 Habachi, *Second Stela of Kamose*.
8 Sethe, *Urkunden der 18. Dynastie* 2, 390 [35-39].
9 Papyrus Sallier I, recto 1.1-3.3, verso 2-3. Gardiner, *Late Egyptian Stories*, 85-89; Goedicke, *Quarrel*.
10 Montet, *Kêmi* 4 (1933), 191-215.
11 Van Seters, *Hyksos*, 97-103; Redford, *Orientalia* 39 (1970), 1-52; Redford, *Egypt, Canaan, and Israel*, 117-118.
12 Maspero, *History of Egypt*, 161; Tomkins, *JAIGB* 19 (1890), 182-199.
13 Maspero, *History of Egypt*, 161; Tomkins, *JAIGB* 19 (1890), 182-199.
14 Maspero, *History of Egypt*, 161; Tomkins, *JAIGB* 19 (1890), 182-199.
15 Petrie, *Man* 6 (1906), 113-114; Petrie, *Hyksos and Israelite Cities*.
16 Labib, *Hyksos*.

contributed his study of archaeological sources from the Levant to assess Hyksos 'life and habits'.[17]

Engberg argued that the Fifteenth Dynasty rulers were Hurrian or 'Indo-Aryan' despite the 'clearly recognised Semitic element enmeshed in what is called the Hyksos movement'.[18] The Hurrian group would have been part of the last phase of a migration across the Near East, their strength in archery and chariotry assisting their victorious outcome in Egypt. This Hurrian element was later favoured by Ward,[19] von Beckerath[20] and Helck,[21] but has since been refuted on chronological grounds, with the Hurrian power emerging after the establishment of Dynasty 15.[22] Van Seters also asserted that Helck's association of Hyksos names with Hurrian personal names was not justified by the evidence.[23]

Van Seters's study was one of the first to offer a detailed examination on the Hyksos. Not only recognising the errors caused by searching for a 'Hyksos culture', he attempted to balance the archaeological evidence with textual sources.[24] His investigation was not without faults, with an over-reliance on the Admonitions of Ipuwer[25] as well as an assertion that the MBA Levant was under Hyksos control. Nevertheless, van Seters rightly contended that Manetho's history should be approached cautiously.[26] He theorised that the Hyksos did not invade Egypt, but that they gained power through 'a fifth-column movement' of Amorites who eventually affected a political or violent coup d'état.[27] Säve-Söderbergh took a similar approach, debunking Manetho's invasion and arguing for a peaceful takeover by Levantines.[28] He contended that Levantines had migrated to the Delta during the Thirteenth Dynasty when political unrest led to lax border control.[29] Following the fall of the Thirteenth Dynasty, they were then able to form their own dynasty.[30]

Evidently, the literature before Tell el-Dab'a's excavations had formulated varying arguments. The eastern Hyksos could be Hurrian, Indo-European or Levantine, and the three basic models for their rise to power had been theorised as: (1) the invasion model; (2) the gradual infiltration and peaceful takeover; and (3) the gradual infiltration and violent takeover.

The discoveries at Tell el-Dab'a have since greatly refined theories on the Hyksos. Scholarly consensus now agrees that the site marks the location of Avaris.[31] Its material culture supports the presence of a large Levantine population and vindicates that the origins of the Hyksos should be sought in the Levant. The exact point of origin remains a matter of debate. Scholars are typically split in opinion with those favouring a Southern Levantine origin and those looking to the Northern Levant.

Bietak, the director of Tell el-Dab'a's excavations, argues for both in different publications. At first, following McGovern's analysis of Tell el-Dab'a's ceramics,[32] he asserted that the Hyksos rose to power after a 'massive movement of population out of southern Canaan'.[33] McGovern also supports a Southern Levantine origin.[34] Disregarding the problems in his pottery analysis,[35] his relation between trade commodities and the origins of Tell el-Dab'a's rulers, like the 'pots equal people' contention, is highly problematic, especially as it is used as the sole basis of his argument. Nonetheless, a peaceful rise to power by Southern Levantine rulers is similarly advocated by Kempinski, based on the Hyksos's apparent Semitic names,[36] Tubb, who identifies a cultural continuum with Southern Levantine sites,[37] and Gardiner.[38]

Weinstein notes that the Hyksos were 'simply southern and inland Palestinian princes'.[39] He maps the geographical spread of Second Intermediate Period scarabs and observes that the majority are located south of the Carmel Ridge.[40] With little supporting evidence, he remarks that the early New Kingdom kings focussed their military efforts on this southern region following the expulsion of the Hyksos.[41] These two points lead him to infer a Southern Levantine origin for the Hyksos.[42] Yet, the nature of early New Kingdom rulers' campaigns remains unclear and the very notion of a Hyksos expulsion deserves reconsideration. Furthermore, the geographical spread of scarabs, many of which are from unclear or non-contemporaneous contexts, does not necessarily correlate to the spread of Hyksos control or to their ethnicity. Instead, it is more suggestive of access to Dynasty 15 commodities.[43]

Employing scarab seal typology, Ben-Tor additionally favours a Southern Levantine origin.[44] She writes that the beginning of Dynasty 15 is marked by the termination of commercial relations with the north and the commencement

17 Engberg, *Hyksos Reconsidered*.
18 Engberg, *Hyksos Reconsidered*, 42.
19 Ward, *Orientalia* 30 (1961), 137-138.
20 Von Beckerath, *Zweiten Zwischenzeit*.
21 Helck, *Die Beziehungen Ägyptens*.
22 Van Seters, *Hyksos*, 181-190; Oren, in *Hyksos*, xxi.
23 Van Seters, *Hyksos*, 181-190.
24 Van Seters, *Hyksos*.
25 See Chapter 4.6.4.
26 Van Seters, *Hyksos*, 192.
27 Van Seters, *Hyksos*, 192-193.
28 Säve-Söderbergh, *JEA* 37 (1951), 53-71.
29 Säve-Söderbergh, *JEA* 37 (1951), 53-71.
30 Säve-Söderbergh, *JEA* 37 (1951), 53-71.
31 See Chapter 4.2.2; Bietak *Avaris and Piramesse*; Bietak, *BASOR* 281 (1991), 27-72; Bietak, *Avaris*; Oren, in *Hyksos*, xx.
32 See Chapter 4.2.2.8.
33 Bietak, in *Hyksos*, 113.
34 McGovern, *Foreign Relations*.
35 See Chapter 4.2.2.8.
36 Kempinski, in *Pharaonic Egypt*, 129-137.
37 Tubb, *Canaanites*, 56-64.
38 Gardiner, *Egypt of the Pharaohs*.
39 Weinstein, *BASOR* 241 (1981), 10.
40 Weinstein, *BASOR* 241 (1981), 1-28; Weinstein, *Levant* 23 (1991), 107-108.
41 Weinstein, *BASOR* 241 (1981), 1-28.
42 Weinstein, *BASOR* 241 (1981), 1-28.
43 As also argued by Bietak, in *Second Intermediate Period*, 150.
44 Ben-Tor, *Scarabs*, 190-192; Ben-Tor, in *Synchronisation of Civilisations* 2, 246; Ben-Tor, in *Scarabs of the Second Millennium BC*, 27-42; Ben-Tor, *JAEI* 1/1 (2009), 1-7; Ben-Tor, in *Second Intermediate Period*, 92-93; Ben-Tor, in *Egypt, Canaan and Israel*, 23-43.

of significant relations with the Southern Levant.[45] Accordingly, the resurgence of contact with the latter is indicative of the origins of Tell el-Dab'a's settlers, while the absence of MBIIB-C scarabs in the Northern Levant and their presence in the south supports kin relations between the Southern Levantines and the Hyksos.[46] A few problems are apparent with this argument: Ben-Tor's corpus of analysed scarabs is largely, if not wholly, derived from the Southern Levant, thereby skewing the data in favour of relations with the south; the remark that the north has no evidence for contact with Egypt during the Second Intermediate Period ignores recent findings from Tell el-Dab'a as well as modern Lebanon;[47] and the premise of relating scarab seal production with the origins of Fifteenth Dynasty rulers is the same as the 'pots equal people' theory which, alone, does not make a strong argument for ethnic origins.

In recent years, Bietak has shifted his stance in favour for the Hyksos's Northern Levantine origin. He uses the architectural, ceramic and burial elements at Tell el-Dab'a to show close cultural influences from the Northern Levant.[48] Uniquely, he combines the artistic data with the archaeological evidence to support his claim, yet few textual sources are utilised. This is also the case with Kopetzky, who supports close relations with the Northern Levant based on the MBIIB ceramic corpus at Tell el-Dab'a. She does not make assertions on the origins of the Hyksos, simply observing that 'the northern regions of Palestine and Lebanon were more closely connected to Hyksos Empire than to southern Palestine'.[49] Hourany's study utilises toponomy and classical Arab histories to reach the same conclusion, further suggesting that the Hyksos originated in the south of modern Lebanon.[50]

While publications over the past two decades have evidently altered in focus on Hyksos origins to either the Northern or Southern Levant, the mechanisms behind the Hyksos's accession still encompass the three aforementioned models. Scholars such as Bietak[51] and Booth[52] maintain that the Hyksos rulers gradually and peacefully took control of Egypt, others such as Quirke[53] and Knapp[54] argue for a gradual increase in a Levantine population that forcibly took control over the Thirteenth Dynasty through, for instance, a bucolic (pastoralist) revolt, and Redford[55] and Ryholt[56] advocate an invasion into Egypt. Redford asserts that the invasion was caused by weakened border control and the sudden appearance of urban communities in the Delta.[57] He also relies on stelae of questionable or later date.[58] Ryholt, on the other hand, notes Redford's circumstantial and non-contemporaneous evidence.[59] He argues that the transition in material culture at Tell el-Dab'a between the Fourteenth and Fifteenth Dynasties is marked by major changes in ceramic typology, cylinder seal use and a new imperialistic outlook.[60] Such developments are employed to justify an invasion by a 'Canaanite chieftain' who took advantage of an Egypt severely affected by famine and political unrest.[61]

The many theories regarding the origin and rise of the Hyksos clearly favour one form of evidence or one site analysis over another. This study seeks to address the problems in scholarly literature by providing a more holistic examination of the evidence across Egypt and the Levant. Such a task will surely contribute to our knowledge on the Hyksos, further clarifying their predecessors' relations with the Middle Kingdom and their consequent rise to power.

2.3 Chronological Considerations

Problems in correlations between Egypt and the Levant are largely caused by inherent issues in the two regions' respective chronologies. The expression 'Second Intermediate Period' implies that it began with the fragmentation of Egypt. However, the period of transition has been a subject of much discussion, its relative and absolute dating constantly being revised.[62] Von Beckerath and Ryholt produced significant studies collating the textual and archaeological evidence for the reconstruction of Dynasties 13-17.[63] Both argue that the Second Intermediate Period began in the Thirteenth Dynasty, but Ryholt places its emergence at the beginning of the dynasty, postulating the land's possible division as early as the late Twelfth Dynasty. He also includes a dynasty in Abydos which, although firstly opposed in the literature,[64] is possible considering recent archaeological findings.[65] While Ryholt's reconstruction of the Turin King-List, which has since been refined by Allen[66] and Polz,[67] provides a significant benchmark in relative dating, his use of scarab typology as well as questionable archaeological data has received criticism.[68] The Fourteenth Dynasty, for example, is lengthened from the beginning of the Thirteenth Dynasty

45 Ben-Tor, *Scarabs*, 190-192; Ben-Tor, in *Scarabs of the Second Millennium BC*, 27-42; Ben-Tor, *JAEI* 1/1 (2009), 1-7; Ben-Tor, in *Egypt, Canaan and Israel*, 23-43.
46 Ben-Tor, *Scarabs*, 190-192; Ben-Tor, in *Scarabs of the Second Millennium BC*, 27-42; Ben-Tor, *JAEI* 1/1 (2009), 1-7; Ben-Tor, in *Egypt, Canaan and Israel*, 23-43.
47 See Chapters 4.2.2 and 6.3.3.
48 Bietak, in *Second Intermediate Period*, 151-163.
49 Kopetzky, in *Bronze Age in the Lebanon*, 227.
50 Hourany, المجهول والمهمل (*The Unknown and the Neglected*).
51 Bietak, in *Second Intermediate Period*, 151-163.
52 Booth, *Hyksos Period*, 9-20.
53 Quirke, in *Middle Kingdom Studies*, 123-139.
54 Knapp, *Ancient Western Asia and Egypt*, 168-170.
55 Redford, *Egypt, Israel, and Canaan*, 101-113.
56 Ryholt, *Political Situation*, 302-304.
57 Redford, *Egypt, Israel, and Canaan*, 101-102.
58 Redford, *Egypt, Israel, and Canaan*, 111-113.
59 Ryholt, *Political Situation*, 302, n. 1057.
60 Ryholt, *Political Situation*, 302-303.
61 Ryholt, *Political Situation*, 304.
62 For the most recent chronological summary of the period, see Schneider, in *Ancient Egyptian Chronology*, 168-196.
63 Von Beckerath, *Zweiten Zwischenzeit*; Ryholt, *Political Situation*.
64 See Ben-Tor, Allen and Allen, *BASOR* 315 (1999), 47-74; Spalinger, *JNES* 60/4 (2001), 296-300.
65 The tomb of pharaoh Senebkay was uncovered at South Abydos by the University of Pennsylvania. Studies on skeletal remains found within the burial suggest that the individual died in battle.
66 Allen, in *Second Intermediate Period*, 1-10.
67 Polz, *Der Beginn des Neuen Reiches*.
68 Ben-Tor, Allen and Allen, *BASOR* 315 (1999), 47-74; Spalinger, *JNES* 60/4 (2001), 296-300; Shirley, in *Ancient Egyptian Administration*, 521-522; Dodson, *BiOr* 57/1-2 (2000), 49.

to the Fifteenth Dynasty, the latter agreeing with Bietak's chronology at Tell el-Dab'a.[69] However, neither the Turin King-List nor the archaeological evidence inform us how the Fourteenth Dynasty kings relate to the preceding and succeeding kingdoms, the possibility of overlap being very likely.[70] Nonetheless, Ryholt's meticulous assessment of the historical data remains the most recent detailed investigation of Second Intermediate Period chronology and so his relative chronology has been adopted in the present work. Other studies, focussing on ceramic developments[71] and genealogies,[72] have also produced notable insights into the chronology of Dynasties 16 and 17.

As the beginning of the Second Intermediate Period remains unclear, chronologically identifying the beginning of the Fifteenth Dynasty and its kings is problematic. Tell el-Dab'a's excavations have identified the early Fifteenth Dynasty stratigraphically through slight changes in the material culture, but its beginning in other areas of Egypt is more difficult to assess. Similarly, the sequence of kings is hampered by their few archaeological attestations in secure and contemporary contexts. Damaged entries in the Turin King-List and a reliance on the Manethonian tradition have resulted in further discrepancies and several reconstructions.[73] The length of Dynasty 15 is also unclear: the Turin King-List lists a total of 108 years[74] while Manetho's copyists record 190-284 years.[75] Recent archaeological findings at Edfu have shed light on some aspects of the chronology. The Upper Egyptian site yielded sealings of Fifteenth Dynasty *Ḫyꜣn* alongside those of mid-Thirteenth Dynasty Sobekhotep IV in a secure context containing early Second Intermediate Period ceramics,[76] indicating that the reigns would have been close to one another. Accordingly, the length of the Fifteenth Dynasty could be altered as an overlap between the mid-Thirteenth and Fifteenth Dynasties may have existed.[77] The find also emphasises that the chronology of the Second Intermediate Period is in no way fixed, but remains to be enhanced and refined by new archaeological data.

Studies in MBA chronology are faced with a dilemma regarding the emergence of the period following the end of the EBA.[78] The MBA's absolute dating is debated by scholars advocating a high, middle or low absolute chronology, the three closely linked with Egyptian and Mesopotamian chronologies. Albright was the first to propose an ultra-low chronology for the beginning of the MBIIA which he correlated with the Twelfth Dynasty.[79] He encountered much objection due to his reliance on the finds at Byblos, many of which are of uncertain date.[80] Higher dates were supported by Gerstenblith,[81] Kenyon,[82] and Mazar,[83] and a middle chronology was advocated by Dever.[84] After excavating at Tell el-Dab'a, Bietak proposed a low chronology that synchronises the MBIIA with the Twelfth and early Thirteenth Dynasties, the MBIIA-B to the mid-Thirteenth Dynasty, and the MBIIB to the late Thirteenth and first half of the Fifteenth Dynasty (see Figure 1.4).[85] Bietak relied on hemispherical cup seriation, MBA ceramic types and scarabs, noting that the earliest MBIIA phase was not represented at Tell el-Dab'a.[86] Disagreement ensued by Levantine scholars including Dever[87] and Weinstein,[88] but many have now accepted his dating.[89] The low chronology has further been supported by the results of the SCIEM 2000 project that investigates chronological correlations between the Mediterranean, Egyptian and Near Eastern civilisations.[90] Pertinent material at, for instance, the Southern Levantine sites of Ashkelon[91] and Tel Ifshar,[92] and the Northern Levantine site of Sidon,[93] corroborates the evidence from Tell el-Dab'a (see Figure 6.26). As the SCIEM 2000 project is still underway, its final results are expected to clarify the chronology of the Hyksos dynasty. Still, recent findings of the international project 'Radiocarbon-based Chronology for Dynastic Egypt' have raised some questions regarding SCIEM's research as well as current understandings of the absolute chronologies in Egypt and the Levant.[94] However, until further scientific and archaeological data comes to light, it is the low chronology which is followed in the present work, although the reader should keep in mind that it remains contested.

---

69 Ryholt, *Political Situation*, 94-117, 299-300.

70 As Franke writes, 'the Fourteenth Dynasty seems to be chronologically "floating" and the extent and nature of its territorial power is unclear' (Franke, *JEH* 1/2 [2008], 274).

71 See, for example, Bourriau, *BES* 8 (1986/1987), 47-59; Bourriau, in *Second Intermediate Period*, 12-37; Seiler, *Tradition und Wandel*; Seiler, in *Second Intermediate Period*, 39-53.

72 See, for example, Bennett, *GM* 149 (1997), 25-32; Bennett, *JARCE* 39 (2002), 123-155; Bennett, *E&L* 16 (2007), 231-244; Dodson, *GM* 120 (1991), 33-38.

73 For more on the names of the Hyksos kings, see Schneider, *Ausländer in Ägypten* 1.

74 Ryholt, *Political Situation*, 118-119, fig. 11.

75 Manetho, *Aegyptiaca*, frgs 43 (Syncellus, 113), 44 (Syncellus, 114; Eusebius, *Chronica* 1, 99), 46 (Syncellus, 116). Translation in Waddell, *Manetho*, 90-93.

76 Moeller and Marouard, *E&L* 11 (2011), 87-121. See Chapter 4.5.4.2.

77 A reinterpretation of the Ahmose Tempest Stela correlates its events with the Thera eruption which consequently also shortens the length of the Second Intermediate Period. See Ritner and Moeller, *JNES* 73/1 (2014), 1-19.

78 For a recent treatment of the phase, see the papers in Schwartz and Nichols (eds), *After Collapse*; Parr (ed.), *Levant in Transition*. See also Cohen, *BASOR* 354 (2009), 1-13.

79 Albright, *BASOR* 176 (1964), 38-46.

80 For a discussion, see Gerstenblith, *Levant at the Beginning of the MBA*, 41, 103; Dever, in *Magnolia Dei*, 1-38. For the finds at Byblos, see Chapter 6.3.3.

81 Gerstenblith, *Levant at the Beginning of the MBA*.

82 Kenyon, *Amorites and Canaanites*, 35.

83 Mazar, *IEJ* 18 (1968), 65-97.

84 Dever, in *Magnolia Dei*, 1-38; Dever, *BASOR* 281 (1991), 73-79.

85 Bietak, *AJA* 88 (1984), 471-485; Bietak, in *High, Middle, Low* 3, 78-120; Bietak, *BASOR* 281 (1991), 27-72; Bietak, *E&L* 3 (1992), 29-37.

86 Bietak, *AJA* 88 (1984), 471.

87 Dever, *BASOR* 281 (1991), 73-79; Dever, *BASOR* 288 (1992), 1-25.

88 Weinstein, *BASOR* 288 (1992), 27-49; Weinstein, in *Egypt, the Aegean and the Levant*, 84-90.

89 See, for instance, Cohen, *Canaanites, Chronologies, and Connections*, 134-136.

90 The Synchronisation of Civilisations in the Eastern Mediterranean in the Second Millennium B.C. Project. See the website for *The Synchronization of Civilizations in the Eastern Mediterranean in the 2nd Millennium BC*.

91 See Chapter 6.2.2.

92 See Chapter 6.2.5.

93 See Chapter 6.3.7.

94 Shortland and Ramsey (eds), *Radiocarbon*.

3. Ethnicity and its Representation

'I have subjugated lions
and I have caught crocodiles.
I have suppressed the *W3w3.yw*
and I have caught the *Md3.yw*.
I caused that the *St.tyw*
do the walk of the dogs.'
Instructions of Amenemhat I, 68-70.

3.1 Introduction

A study on Egyptian-Levantine relations entails the differentiation between Egyptian elements and non-Egyptian elements. This *idea of difference* is a fundamental concept that forms a group's identity, whether self-identified or applied by others. Chapter 3 presents theories on the idea of difference as reflected through *ethnicity*. It begins with a definition of the term and discusses how the Egyptians represented the concept of otherness. This is followed by comments on determining ethnicity through the analysis of archaeological remains as well as a brief overview of various approaches to cultural mixing.

3.2 Defining Ethnicity

Although a modern term, ethnicity is not a modern phenomenon. Derived from the Greek 'ethnos' to define a group of animals or humans sharing common attributes,[1] the term is related to such concepts as *ethnic identity* and *ethnic group*. *Ethnic identity* is associated with an individual's self-identification as a member of a broader *ethnic group* of people who define themselves (the 'us'), or are defined by others (the 'them'), by a set of environmental, cultural and physical characteristics and/or common descent.[2] Accordingly, ethnicity is 'all those social and psychological phenomena associated with a culturally constructed group identity'.[3]

Ethnicity has been a subject of different anthropological approaches. The 'primordialists' distinguish it as an inherent social bond characterised by bounded ties of blood, religion, language, custom and territory.[4] As the ties are a biological and psychological part of an ethnic identity, ethnicity would be a static, uniform, and naturalistic phenomenon.[5] Primordialism has since been criticised for its simplified approach and failure to explain historical developments in ethnic groups.[6] It was ousted by the 'instrumentalists', who propose that ethnicity is mutable, dynamic, self-defining and diachronically influenced by economic and socio-political relations.[7] Individuals could display, manipulate or develop ethnicity in response to changing situations.[8] This focus on self-interest was critiqued by some scholars, who stress the importance of an ethnic group and an individual's psychological ties to it.[9] Current theories instead attempt to fuse the primordial and instrumental approaches.[10] The present work follows one such theory, namely the minimalist approach of Hutchinson and Smith that interprets an ethnic group as one featuring six main elements in varying degrees: a common name; a myth of common ancestry; shared historical memories; common cultural elements; a link with a homeland; and a sense of solidarity.[11]

3.3 Ancient Egyptians on Ethnicity

Ethnicity's inherent idea of difference, the 'us' versus 'them' concept, is well reflected in Egyptian textual and artistic representations of the *other*. The Egyptians defined themselves and the *other* by geographical borders: the Levantines were to the north and east, the Libyans were to the west, and the Nubians were to the south.[12] Each group was assigned a proper name and a phenotype that would have been immediately recognisable to the Egyptians.[13] Northeasterners were typically portrayed with yellow skin, a hooked nose, long or coiffed hair, a full beard, non-

1 Hutchinson and Smith, in *Ethnicity*, 4-5.
2 Jones, *Archaeology of Ethnicity*, xiii.
3 Jones, *Archaeology of Ethnicity*, xiii.
4 For examples, see Shils, in *Selected Papers*, 111-126; Geertz, in *Old Societies*, 105-157.
5 Shils, in *Selected Papers*, 111-126; Geertz, in *Old Societies*, 105-157; Hutchinson and Smith, in *Ethnicity*, 8.
6 Hutchinson and Smith, in *Ethnicity*, 8; Jones, *Archaeology of Ethnicity*, 68-71; Eller and Coughlan, *Ethnic and Racial Studies* 16/2 (1993), 183-201; Voss, *Archaeology of Ethnogenesis*, 27.
7 For examples, see Hutchinson and Smith, in *Ethnicity*, 8-9; Jones, *Archaeology of Ethnicity*, 72-79; Voss, *Archaeology of Ethnogenesis*, 27; Barth, in *Ethnic Groups and Boundaries*, 9-38; Cohen, in *Urban Ethnicity*, ix-xxiv.
8 Jenkins, *Rethinking Ethnicity*, 17-27; Lucy, in *Archaeology of Identity*, 96; Smith, *Wretched Kush*, 17.
9 Jones, *Archaeology of Ethnicity*, 76-79; Lucy, in *Archaeology of Identity*, 96-97; Smith, *Wretched Kush*, 6, 17-19.
10 For example, Jones contends that an ethnic group is self-defining while ethnicity is situational (Jones, *Archaeology of Ethnicity*), and Royce argues for an instrumental ethnicity but one that is consistent with its cultural context (Royce, *Ethnic Identity*). For more, see Hutchinson and Smith, in *Ethnicity*, 9-10; Lucy, in *Archaeology of Identity*, 86-109; Fearon, *Journal of Economic Growth* 8/2 (2003), 195-222; Smith, *Ethnic Revival*.
11 Hutchinson and Smith, in *Ethnicity*, 6-7. Dever has also proposed a similar set of qualities (Dever, in *Archaeology of Difference*, 53).
12 Smith, *Wretched Kush*, 21; Booth, *Role of Foreigners*; O'Connor, in *Egypt's View of its Past*, 155-185.
13 Smith, *Wretched Kush*, 21; Weeks in *Egyptology and the Social Sciences*, 50-81.

Egyptian weaponry and non-Egyptian dress. Textually, individuals were identified by their non-Egyptian names[14] or with the ethnonym *ʿꜣm*, a term which may derive from the Semitic עם *ʿm* 'people'[15] or Egyptian *ʿmʿꜣ* 'throw-stick'.[16] *ʿꜣm* was also utilised to designate an ethnic group(s) of Levantines. Other terms are concerned with environmental dispositions, such as *Ḥr.yw-šʿ* 'those who are on/across the sand', *Ḫꜣs.tyw* 'those of the foreign lands' and *Nmi.w-šʿ* 'those who traverse the sand'. A few ethnonyms are more open to interpretation due to uncertain derivation, and include *Mnṯ.tyw*, *Pḏ.tyw*, *St.tyw* and *Iwn.tyw*.[17]

Loprieno's study on Egyptian literary representations of the foreign provides a useful differentiation between *topos* (rhetoric) and *mimesis* (reality).[18] *Topos* denotes the idealised and stereotypical view of foreigners as inferior and subordinate ethnic groups.[19] It was employed in cosmic, royal and elite power assertions to emphasise Egyptian solidarity and superiority, and highlight the king's maintenance of cosmic *mꜣʿ.t* 'order' within Egypt and *isf.t* 'chaos' within and beyond Egypt.[20] *Mimesis* represents the reality and individuality of situational encounters with foreigners,[21] who, for instance, could be included in lists of Egyptian household members. Despite the dichotomy, the two representations could be manipulated according to purpose and context. When this is not identified, it could result in Liszka's so-called 'secondary ethnocentrism', where present-day scholars often and involuntarily absorb and perpetuate Egyptian views.[22]

This is apparent in instances where representations of Asiatics have been utilised to validate theories on Egyptian-Levantine relations with little reflection on their nature and context.[23] An example is Redford's selective interpretation of textual references where he notes bellicose activity rather than inherent ideological dogma to justify punitive action against the Levant.[24] This approach is largely inspired by early theories of Egyptian empirical control over the Levant,[25] as well as notions reliant on biblical patriarchal traditions.[26] The concept of the *other* was also uncritically utilised to support the notion that all Levantines were nomadic herdsmen entering Egypt as refugees or slaves.[27] Weinstein's study proposes that the Levant was 'an economic, political, and military backwater'[28] while the term 'bedouin' is still used by scholars to refer to Asiatics.[29] This particular misnomer has led Saretta to identify the *ʿꜣm.w* as nomadic, warlike, uncivilised breeders of cattle who can consequently be related to the Mesopotamian Amurru, despite her lengthy treatment on Egyptian representations of the foreign.[30] Because of such inaccuracies, this study offers a reappraisal of textual and artistic evidence by acknowledging Egyptian and modern understandings of ethnicity and its varied representations.

3.4 Ethnicity in Archaeology

If representations of Asiatics are influenced by Egyptian beliefs of the *other*, then the archaeological data may provide less subjective traces of ethnic groups. Scholars initially adhered to a culture-history and primordialist approach that identified fixed artefact assemblages as markers for the presence of the people who produced them (i.e. the pots equal people concept).[31] The assemblages were thereby used to support ethnic groups' migration, assimilation or disappearance,[32] as in the aforementioned 'Hyksos culture' of Chapter 2.2. Processual archaeologists and instrumentalists refuted this association and inferred that archaeology could not be productively used as a means to assess ethnicity: the multidimensional nature of a flexible ethnic identity would theoretically result in a qualitatively and quantitatively varied material culture that would be impossible to trace.[33] Jones contrarily proposed that ethnicity could be identified in archaeology.[34] She demonstrated that its implied cultural traits would not be randomly deposited within socio-historical contexts.[35]

14 For studies on the etymology of these names, see Helck, *Die Beziehungen Ägyptens*, 44-86; Schneider, *Ausländer in Ägypten* 2.

15 Also غلام *glm* 'people' as it is in Ugaritic and modern Arabic. Other suggestions are ערב *ʿrv* 'Arab' (the inclusion of the bet is problematic) and Akkadian *ḫammu* (utilised by Saretta to associate the group with the Amorites). See Rainey, *BASOR* 295 (1994), 81-82; Redford, *JARCE* 23 (1986), 127, n. 19; Saretta, *Egyptian Perceptions of West Semites*, 18-28.

16 For references, see Redford, *JARCE* 23 (1986), 127, n. 21.

17 For the different interpretations, see Redford, *JARCE* 23 (1986), 125; Saretta, *Egyptian Perceptions of West Semites*, 18-34.

18 Loprieno, *Topos und Mimesis*. See Quirke, *DE* 16 (1990), 89-95; Di Biase-Dyson, *Characterisation across Frontiers*, 12-16; Di Biase-Dyson, *Foreigners and Egyptians*, 18-21.

19 Loprieno, *Topos und Mimesis*, 10-13.

20 Smith, *Wretched Kush*, 21-27; Baines, in *Study of the Ancient Near East*, 339-384.

21 Loprieno, *Topos und Mimesis*, 10-13.

22 Liszka, *Medjay and Pangrave*, 76.

23 See, for example, Gardiner, *Egypt of the Pharaohs*, 88-102; Smith, *Interconnections in the Ancient Near East*; Posener, *Littérature et politique*; Warburton, *Egypt and the Near East*; Rainey, *BASOR* 295 (1994), 81-85; Aharoni, *Archaeology of the Land of Israel*, 84-94; Aharoni, *Land of the Bible*, 78-99. Notable exceptions are Liszka, *Medjay and Pangrave;* Schneider, *Ausländer in Ägypten* 2; Booth, *Role of Foreigners;* Cohen, *Canaanites, Chronologies, and Connections.*

24 Redford, *Egypt, Canaan, and Israel*, 75-76. The selectivity is apparent when, in a discussion of the Instructions of Amenemhat I and its comparison of Asiatics with dogs, Redford clearly notes that the text reflects ideological kingly duties.

25 Redford, *Egypt, Canaan, and Israel*, 76; Albright, *JPOS* 2 (1922), 110-138; Albright, *JPOS* 15 (1935), 193-234; Mazar, *IEJ* 18 (1968), 65-97; Giveon, in *Egypt, Israel, Sinai*, 23-40.

26 Genesis 12:10 and 42:1, for example, record a famine in the land of Canaan that led to the patriarchs' journey from Canaan to the powerful and more stable Egypt.

27 Albright, *JPOS* 2 (1922), 110-138; Albright, *JPOS* 15 (1935), 193-234; Wright, *Biblical Archaeology*; Albright, *BASOR* 184 (1966), 26-35.

28 Weinstein, *BASOR* 217 (1975), 9.

29 Albright, *BASOR* 184 (1966), 26-35; Redford, *Egypt, Canaan, and Israel*, 82-93; Redford, *BASOR* 301 (1996), 77-81; Rainey, *IOS* 2 (1972), 369-408; Rainey, *BASOR* 295 (1994), 81-85; Bárta, *Sinuhe, the Bible, and the Patriarchs*, 177-184; Saretta, *Egyptian Perceptions of West Semites*, 63-65, 70, 105.

30 Saretta, *Egyptian Perceptions of West Semites*, especially 65-66.

31 For an overview of culture-history, see Jones, *Archaeology of Ethnicity*, 15-29.

32 An example is Petrie's 'dynastic race' that founded the Egyptian civilisation (Petrie, *Prehistoric Egypt*). For more, see Jones, *Archaeology of Ethnicity*, 26-29; Lucy, in *Archaeology of Identity*, 86, 88, 91; Smith, *Wretched Kush*, 14-15.

33 Bursche, in *Cultural Identity*, 228-237. For more, see Jones, *Archaeology of Ethnicity*, 124.

34 Jones, *Archaeology of Ethnicity*, 119-127.

35 Jones, *Archaeology of Ethnicity*, 125. See also Kamp and Yoffee, *BASOR* 237 (1980), 85-104.

The minimalist approach to ethnicity that is favoured here acknowledges that these traits or *ethnic markers* embrace objects, their function and their contexts.[36] They can be divided into material reflecting ritual custom (e.g. temple architecture or offering pits), funerary belief (e.g. grave goods or body disposition), culinary practices (e.g. utilitarian ceramics or organic products), foreign dress (e.g. toggle-pins for one-shouldered fringed garments) and private and communal architecture.[37] In regards to the Hyksos and Asiatics in Egypt, some archaeological markers are open to various interpretations. For instance, simple or double vaulted mudbrick tombs have been identified as 'Hyksos' or MBA constructions.[38] While rare in Egypt, Schiestl has recently argued that barrel and domical vaults may be traced to Old Kingdom traditions.[39] Intra-mural burials in Egypt, including those of infants, have similarly been approached as Levantine or 'Hyksos traditions'.[40] The customs were indeed practiced in the MBA Levant; however some cases in Predynastic, Old and Middle Kingdom sites such as Merimde, Tell Basta and el-Lahun suggest that they were also created by the local Egyptian population.[41] Only when such customs occur with other MBA elements, such as an MBA funerary kit, can the burial be more definitively assessed as one of a Levantine ethnic group.

Another example is the so-called 'Hyksos tradition' of the burial of equids. These interments occur at such Fifteenth Dynasty eastern Delta sites as Tell el-Dab'a, Tell el-Maskhuta and Tell el-Yahudiyah,[42] but also at Southern Levantine sites like Tell el-'Ajjul, Jemmeh and Jericho, and the Mesopotamian Tell Brak, Kish and Ur.[43] Wapnish correctly affirms that the practice is a region-wide MBA to LBA phenomenon, with each expression being 'both a syncretism and an innovation'.[44] This explains the lack of exact parallels for equid burials in the eastern Delta, and implies other ethnic, cultic or religious associations with equids. From an Egyptian perspective, the donkey is usually connected to Seth,[45] but from a Levantine, Anatolian and Mesopotamian perspective, equids are associated with socio-economic status, particularly as they are typically represented as ridden by the elite.[46] Mari texts refer to their slaughter for treaty ratification and Ugaritic texts note their sacrificial offering to deities such as Baal and El.[47] Therefore, the equid burials, their function and their context suggest that they reflect a hybrid tradition (see below) in which Seth, possibly synonymous with Baal,[48] is honoured with equid interments that also express status and, perhaps, an association with trade.[49] The archaeological, cultic and religious elements of such a tradition thereby support its use as a marker for cultural mixing (see below) rather than the presence of Hyksos rulers. However, if it occurs with other goods such as Levantine ceramics, scarabs and weaponry, the combined assemblage may be critically used as an archaeological ethnic marker.

The burial of equids, as with other cultic, culinary or architectural traditions, can represent opportunities to reinforce ethnic identity.[50] While not all cultural elements are ethnic markers,[51] determining agent and activity can evidently help identify ethnicity. Based on its idea of difference, ethnicity becomes more pronounced in areas of intercultural contact, like the eastern Delta, and instances of environmental, economic or historical shifts,[52] such as those witnessed during the Second Intermediate Period. As such, an investigation employing archaeology for the study of ethnicity must rely on provenanced and contextual material, and take into account theories of cultural mixing.

3.5 When Ethnic Groups Interact: Theories of Cultural Mixing

Ethnic identities are not only more apparent in areas of contact, but their cultural elements are also subject to change. The nature and rate of change has been determined by several terms in the literature. Due to their vast number,[53] not all are examined here. The following instead offers a brief outline of three concepts pertinent in the present work.

36 Hutchinson and Smith, in *Ethnicity*, 6-7. See also Dever, in *Archaeology of Difference*, 52-53; Liszka, *Medjay and Pangrave*, 58-59.

37 Santley, Yarborough and Hall, in *Ethnicity and Culture*, 85-100; Smith, *Wretched Kush*, 6-7, 32-53; Bietak, in *Second Intermediate Period*, 153.

38 Van den Brink, *Tombs and Burial Customs*.

39 Schiestl, in *Bronze Age in the Lebanon*, 246-250.

40 Petrie, *Kahun*, 24; David, *Pyramid Builders*, 137-138; David, *BACE* 2 (1991), 36-37.

41 Junker, *Anzeiger der Akademie der Wissenschaften in Wien* 66 (1926), 156-248; Hansen, *JARCE* 6 (1965), 31-39; Farid, *ASAE* 58 (1964), 85-98; Petrie, *Kahun*, 24. For more, see van den Brink, *Tombs and Burial Customs*, 61-65.

42 See, respectively, Chapters 4.2.2, 4.2.9 and 4.2.13.

43 Petrie, *Gaza* 2, 40; Stiebing, *JNES* 30 (1971), 115; Zurins, in *Equids*, 164-193; Wapnish, in *Hyksos*, 337-349; van den Brink, *Tombs and Burial Customs*, 74-83.

44 Wapnish, in *Hyksos*, 360.

45 Te Velde, *Seth*, 7-9, 12-15, 26, pls 3 [2], 6 [1], 12 [2]; Ward, *JNES* 37/1 (1978), 23-34; Maeir, *DE* 14 (1989), 64; Way, *Donkeys in the Biblical World*, 37-38.

46 Way, *Donkeys in the Biblical World*, 100-101, 199-203.

47 Way, *Donkeys in the Biblical World*, 41-48, 75-82; van den Brink, *Tombs and Burial Customs*, 77.

48 Te Velde, *Seth*, 121, 127-128; van Seters, *Hyksos*, 171-173; Allon, *E&L* 17 (2007), 15-22; Bietak, *Avaris*, 29, 41; Redford, *Egypt, Canaan, and Israel*, 117-118.

49 For similar propositions, see Maeir, *DE* 14 (1989), 64; Way, *Donkeys in the Biblical World*, 39.

50 Smith, *Wretched Kush*, 7.

51 Culture is regarded as a set of cognitive and socially transmitted ideas, values and understandings that contributes to the formation of ethnicity while the latter is demarcated from culture by its idea of difference. For more, see Jones, *Archaeology of Ethnicity*, 119-120; Smith, *Wretched Kush*, 17-18; Smith, in *Egyptian World*, 218-241; Ballard, in *Sociology*, 93-124; Kamp and Yoffee, *BASOR* 237 (1980), 96-97.

52 Smith, *Wretched Kush*, 17-19; Jones, *Archaeology of Ethnicity*, 109-110, 113, 124-125; Kamp and Yoffee, *BASOR* 237 (1980), 96-97; Schneider, *E&L* 8 (2003), 155-161; Schneider, in *Egyptian Archaeology* (Oxford, 2010), 143-144, 146.

53 Other concepts include that of mestizaje, syncretism, transnationalism and diffusion. For more, see Antonaccio, in *Material Culture*, 32-53; Bader, in *Archaeological Review from Cambridge* 28/1 (2013), 257-286; Eriksen, in *Creolization*, 172-173; Stewart, *Diacritics* 29/3 (1999), 40-62; Stewart, *Portuguese Studies* 27/1 (2011), 48-55; Wade, *Journal of Latin American Studies* 37 (2005), 239-257.

3.5.1 *Acculturation*

Acculturation is a multi-faceted process through which individuals adopt cultural elements of their host country (the 'dominant' group).[54] It embraces several degrees beginning with the use of the dominant group's material goods and resulting in the assumption of its beliefs and, lastly, ethnic identity.[55] Individual and group acculturation vary: individuals may be acculturated rapidly for private gain or if isolated in a dominant group; and non-dominant groups require a willingness and ability to acculturate in a majority group that favourably receives them.[56] The non-dominant group could subsequently have two ethnic identities, choosing to express one or the other according to changing circumstances.[57] Schneider utilises the theory of acculturation to explain the growing population of Asiatics and shifts in their textual representation.[58] However, he interprets the preservation of cultural elements as 'relics' of 'symbolic ethnicity' rather than as an expression of an individual's multi-ethnic identity.[59]

3.5.2 *Hybridity*

In social sciences, hybridity refers to individuals or groups of diverse origins that are reflexively and self-consciously mixed.[60] Stockhammer suggests that the process leading to this mixed identity, or *entanglement*, results in new materially *entangled objects* reflecting elements of diverse origins, such as the possible religious and cultic affiliations discussed in the abovementioned equid burials.[61] Egyptologists favour the terms 'hybridised' or 'hybrid' objects to identify the fusion of different cultural elements as, for instance, those at Tell el-Dab'a. [62]

3.5.3 *Creolisation*

Creolisation refers to the 'social encounter and mutual influence between/among two or several groups' that result in a dynamic exchange of cultural elements and, eventually, new *creole* qualities.[63] First used to describe the cultural mixing at Carribean colonies and plantations, the *creole culture* is relatively stable and often pervasive, and is commonly based in trade zones where new allegiances are developed.[64] *Creoles*, or individuals utilising *creole cultural elements*, are of mixed origins and ethnic groups and assume the *creole identity* in a variety of ways: by birth, achievement, or force.[65] Unlike acculturation, there are no dominant groups as creolisation is the outcome of reciprocal cultural, political and commercial interactions.[66] Bader's recent study posits that hybridity and creolisation are almost synonymous and may be represented by elements at Tell el-Dab'a.[67] She infers that the process of creolisation is countered by Dynasty 15's dominance in Egypt and Avaris's role as a core rather than a periphery area.[68] Still, the concept could provide some insight into the social mechanisms that may have occurred during the period leading to Hyksos rule, when no particular dominant group held power.

The following section explores the evidence in view of these three processes and their insight into the interaction of different cultures. Worthy of note is that an ethnic group could experience all three processes at various stages, offering new perspectives on the manner in which the Hyksos assumed their reign.

54 Schneider, in *Egyptian Archaeology*, 145.
55 Schneider, in *Egyptian Archaeology*, 144-145, with references; Berry, in *Acculturation*, 17-37.
56 Schneider, in *Egyptian Archaeology*, 145; Gordon, *Assimilation*; Zane and Mal, in *Acculturation*, 39-60.
57 Phinney, in *Acculturation*, 63-81.
58 Schneider, *Ausländer in Ägypten* 2, 316-338; Schneider, *E&L* 8 (2003), 155-161; Schneider, in *Egyptian Archaeology*, 144-146.
59 Schneider, in *Egyptian Archaeology*, 145.
60 The term is a biological one referring to the cross-breeding of two different species. Bader, *Archaeological Review from Cambridge* 28/1 (2013), 261; Eriksen, in *Creolization*, 172.
61 Stockhammer, in *Cultural Hybridization*, 43-58; Bader, *Archaeological Review from Cambridge* 28/1 (2013), 261.
62 Bader, *Archaeological Review from Cambridge* 28/1 (2013), 261; Bietak, in *Second Intermediate Period*, 170.
63 Eriksen, in *Creolization*, 172-173.
64 Eriksen, in *Creolization*, 155; Abrahams, in *Creolization as Cultural Creativity* (Jackson, 2011), 285-305.
65 Eriksen, in *Creolization*, 175.
66 Eriksen, in *Creolization*, 172-175; Cohen and Toninato, in *Creolization Reader*, 1-21.
67 Bader, in *Archaeological Review from Cambridge* 28/1 (2013), 262, 277-278. For more on the similarities between hybridity and creolisation, see Abrahams, in *Creolization as Cultural Creativity*, 287-291.
68 Bader, in *Archaeological Review from Cambridge* 28/1 (2013), 279. For more on the core and periphery concept, see Wallerstein, *Critique of Anthropology* 11 (1991), 169-194; Hall and Chase-Dunn, *Journal of Archaeological Research* 1 (1993), 121-143; Rowlands, Larsen and Kristiansen, *Centre and Periphery*.

Section 2: Evidence for Contact

4. Tracing Asiatics in Egypt

'To assess the place of origin of this population, it must be asked how and why they came to Egypt in great numbers... these questions may to some extent be answered by a phenomenological study of Asiatic immigration into Egypt.'
Bietak, in *Second Intermediate Period*, 139.

4.1 Introduction

Identifying Levantine ethnic markers in a largely Egyptian context necessitates an assessment of the various sites and locations deemed by scholars to be 'Hyksos settlements' or to have a Levantine presence. To assess the spread of Levantines and their culture across Egyptian terrain, sites are divided into four geographical regions including the Delta, the Memphite region, Middle Egypt and Upper Egypt (Figures 1.1, 4.1).

Each site is examined chronologically to identify (a) the emergence of an Asiatic culture; (b) possible shifts in the number of Asiatics; (c) possible changes in the status of Asiatics; and (d) Levantine influence. A selection of unprovenanced texts, such as the Tale of Sinuhe or Papyrus Brooklyn 35.1446, are included at the end of this chapter for their unique insight into Egyptian-Levantine relations as well as their reliance by scholars.

Sites with little evidence of contact (for instance, a few Tell el-Yahudiyah vessels or scarabs with Levantine designs) are not included. Such artefacts most probably reached their destination via the flow of traded goods and therefore should not be confused with ethnic markers. A few exceptions are examined due to their frequent treatment in the literature. These include Mostagedda and Deir Rifeh, two sites theorised to be on the border between the northern and southern dynasties but with different political affiliations.

The sites are listed alphabetically, their geographical location provided in Figure 4.1. Each entry includes the location of a site by Latitude and Longitude (*Lat.Lon.*), a list of selected references (*Refs*) as well as a general temporal placement within the investigated period utilising the Egyptian chronology (*Chron.*). This is followed by a succinct description of each location with a summary of the evidence relating to possible Asiatic presence, Levantine influences and the Egyptian treatment of Levantines. Depending on both their significance and publication, some finds will be analysed in greater detail than others. This presents one major difficulty encountered during the compilation of this chapter, which was largely determined by the publication of archaeological reports. Some sites noted to have elements of a 'Hyksos culture', such as Tell el-Kabir,[1] Ghita (Tell Yehud),[2] Tell Fawziya and Tell Geziret el-Faras,[3] have no published material.

A similar case can be discerned for the Wadi Tumilat. The Wadi is situated between the Delta and the Sinai Peninsula, an area which, following an initial survey and consequent excavations by the University of Toronto, proved to be most fruitful in relation to MBA materials.[4] Out of the 21 sites recorded to have remnants dating to the Second Intermediate Period,[5] only a few have been excavated and, to the author's knowledge, only one has been reasonably published (Tell el-Maskhuta). It is useful to note that other sites may include significant remains of a non-Egyptian culture, such as Tell el-Ku'a and Qaudrant 25 at Birak el-Nazzazat.[6] Again, due to the lack of published evidence, these sites cannot be examined here.

The criteria for dating a number of artefacts and texts are not as refined as for other periods in Egyptian history. Some of the evidence investigated in the following pages could only be assigned to the general period of the late Middle Kingdom or early Second Intermediate Period which, despite the shortcomings, still provides a wealth of evidence for the circumstances influencing the rise of the Fifteenth Dynasty. To observe chronological correlations, parallels with Levantine(-influenced) artefacts from sites comprising well-excavated stratigraphic sequences, such as Tell el-Dab'a, are included where possible.

1 Hoffmeier writes of the discovery of tombs at Tell el-Kebir with 'Canaanite' materials of high quality (Hoffmeier, *Israel in Egypt*, 68, fig. 2).

2 Habachi reportedly noticed some MBA remains at the site. Bietak, *TeD* 2, 195, n. 693; van den Brink, *Tombs and Burial Customs*, 57. For later finds, see Petrie, *Hyksos and Israelite Cities*, 54-62, pls 40-49; PM 4, 56; Snape, *Tell Yehud* 2.

3 Van den Brink, van Wesemael and Dirksz, *MDAIK* 43 (1987), 20ff.

4 See Holladay, *Tell El-Maskhuṭa*, 5-9; Redmount, *On an Egyptian/Asiatic Frontier*, 15-17.

5 Redmount, *On an Egyptian/Asiatic Frontier*, 177.

6 Redmount, *On an Egyptian/Asiatic Frontier*, 139, 153.

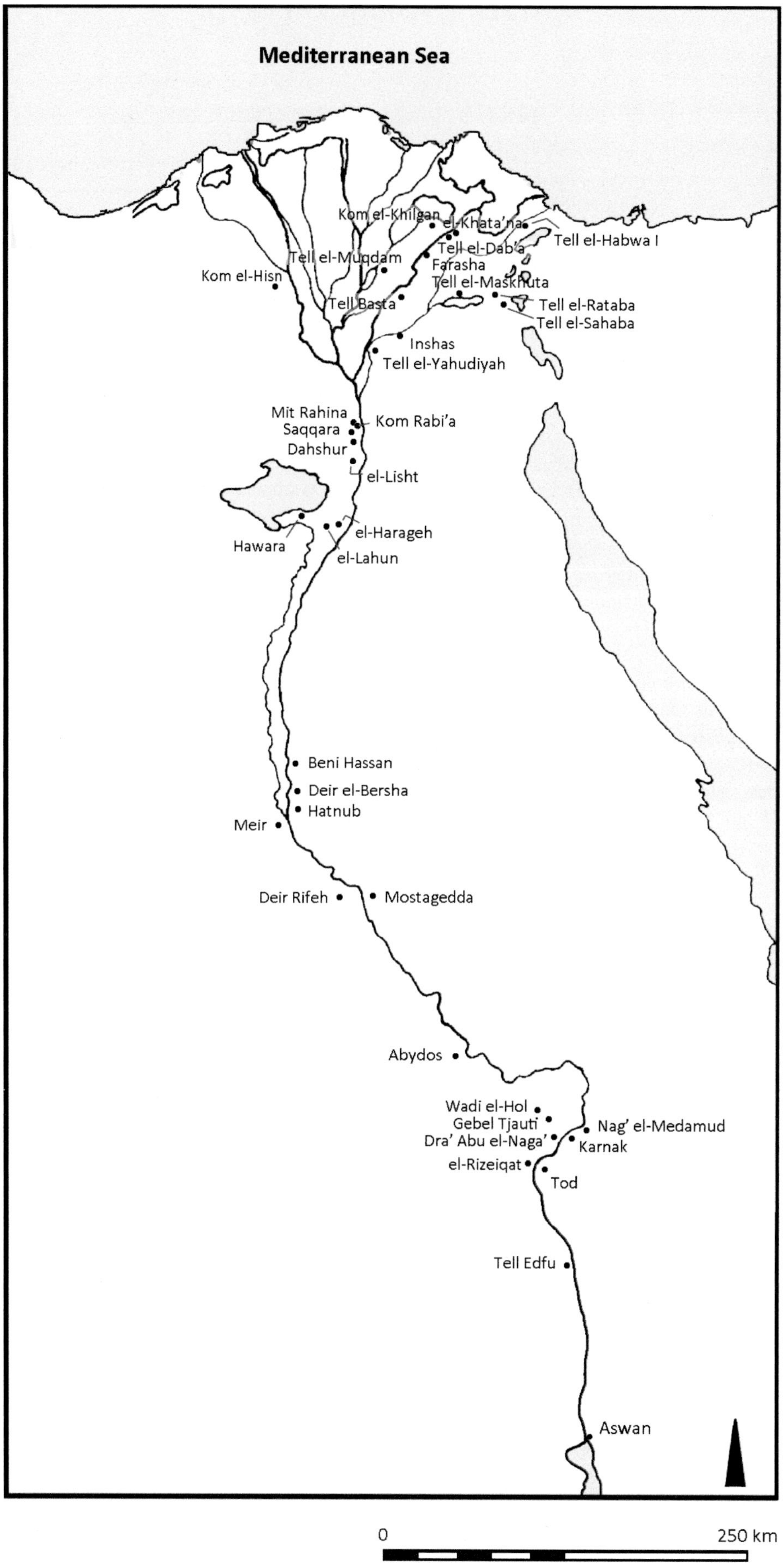

FIGURE 4.1. EXAMINED SITES IN EGYPT.

4.2 Delta Region

4.2.1 *Basta, Tell (Bubastis)*

Lat.Lon. 30°34'N 30°31'E

Refs *LÄ* 1, 873-874; PM 4, 27-35; Naville, *Bubastis*; Habachi, *Tell Basta*; Farid, *ASAE* 58 (1964), 85-98; el-Sawi, *Tell Basta*; van Siclen III, in *Akten des vierten Internationalen Ägyptologen Kongresses*, 187-194; van Siclen III, in *Haus und Palast*, 239-246; Tietze and Abd el-Maksoud, *Tell Basta*.

Chron. Thirteenth to early Fifteenth Dynasty

Tell Basta lies south of the northeastern Delta, between the Pelusiac and Tanitic branch and the beginning of Wadi Tumilat. Several excavations have been directed by Naville,[7] Habachi,[8] Farid,[9] el-Sawi[10] and, more recently, Tietze.[11] Despite being the finding location of several 'Hyksos monuments',[12] archaeological remains pointing to a foreign culture are minimal. In fact, what van Siclen has described as evidence for 'the increasing influence of and intrusion by the foreigners in the area',[13] is heavily reliant on an interpretative exploration of data. This includes: a scarab of the king's son Nehsy in the Mayoral cemetery; the name of Mayor Maheshotep's daughter, Iunisetekh, which features the element 'Seth'; the destruction of the Mayor's Residence by fire during the early Thirteenth Dynasty; and two Tell el-Yahudiyah juglets from a simple pit grave (Figure 4.2).

Firstly, the scarab of Nehsy, which remains unpublished in detail,[14] only testifies to the scarab's use as a funerary item.[15] Secondly, the name Iunisetekh and the reverence to Seth support other material from the site for the worship of Seth from at least Amenemhet III's reign.[16] Thirdly, the destruction of the largest administrative palace in the Delta following the last mayor, Maheshotep, during early Dynasty 13 can only reveal political turmoil, the instigators of which are unknown. More significant is that the palace remained deserted,[17] suggesting a power shift in the region from Tell Basta to another site, most probably Tell el-Dab'a. However, Burial 9's Tell el-Yahudiyah juglets (Figure 4.2), a globular vessel[18] and a piriform vessel,[19] point to access to Levantine(-influenced) commodities. Based on the vessels' styles, the burial may coincide with Tell el-Dab'a's Stratum E/2, or early Dynasty 15.[20] Other Second Intermediate Period tombs were unearthed at the site, but none appear to contain any indicators of a foreign populace.[21]

As such, the evidence does not definitively point to increasing foreign influences. Rather, it suggests political changes in the Delta region. Tell Basta continued in its function as a cultic centre for the worship of Bastet, but its role as administrative centre significantly altered. The shift in power may be dated to Mayor Maheshotep's rule, after which the Mayor's Residence was abandoned and the first signs of northern goods appear. In view of the political events of the time,[22] this may be interpreted as evidence of a schism between the capital Itjtawy and the Delta during the early Thirteenth Dynasty.

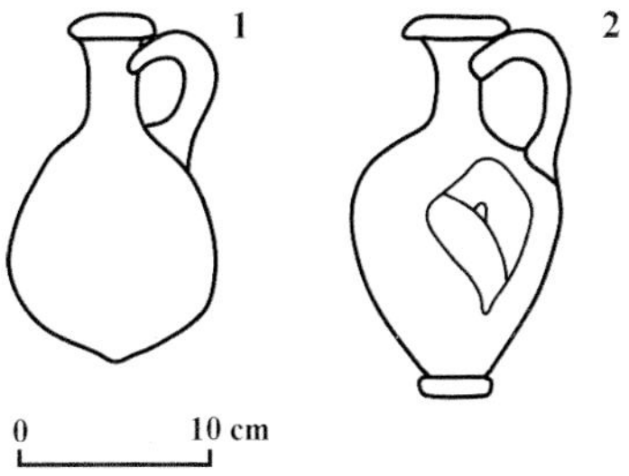

FIGURE 4.2. TELL EL-YAHUDIYAH WARE, TELL BASTA. AFTER EL-SAWI, *TELL BASTA*, FIGS 16-17.

7 Naville, *Bubastis*.
8 Habachi, *Tell Basta*.
9 Farid, *ASAE* 58 (1964), 85-98.
10 El-Sawi, *Tell Basta*.
11 Tietze and Abd el-Maksoud, *Tell Basta*.
12 The 'Hyksos monuments' of *Hy3n* and Apophis. See PM 4, 28-29; Tietze and Abd el-Maksoud, *Tell Basta*, 51.
13 Van Siclen III, in *Akten des vierten Internationalen Ägyptologen Kongresses* 4, 194.
14 Van Siclen III, in *Akten des vierten Internationalen Ägyptologen Kongresses*, 192, n. 6; van Siclen III, in *Haus und Palast*, 245.
15 Based on its find-spot in a Middle Kingdom cemetery, van Siclen has dated the scarab to the period before the fall of the Middle Kingdom, thus giving support to the argument that the king's son Nehsy belongs to this era rather than the late Second Intermediate Period (Van Siclen III, in *Haus und Palast*, 245).
16 This is evident in a lintel from the Middle Kingdom Mayor's Residence upon which a Seth animal is depicted to be offering life to Amenemhet III in celebration of his *Heb-sed* festival. Farid, *ASAE* 58 (1964), 94-95; Tietze and Abd el-Maksoud, *Tell Basta*, 19 (top figure).
17 Although some theorise that the building was intended for royalty, the architecture of the palace points to an administrative function. It includes a storage area, a colonnaded courtyard (perhaps for public use) and a private residential area. Also, the nearby cemetery with tombs of individuals holding the *ḥ3.ty-ʿ* title highly suggests that the palace was for counts, or mayors, rather than royalty. See van Siclen III, in *Akten des vierten Internationalen Ägyptologen Kongresses*, 193-194, pl. 1; van Siclen III, in *Haus und Palast*, 245-246, figs 1, 3, 5, 8; Grajetzki, *Middle Kingdom*, 131; Kemp, *Ancient Egypt*, 341, fig. 117.
18 Item Nr 1535. Aston and Bietak's Late Egyptian Group L.9. The vessel finds parallels with a globular juglet from Tomb 77 at Tell el-Yahudiyah. Aston and Bietak, *TeD* 8, 254-257, fig. 189; Kaplan, *Tell el Yahudiyeh*, 18, fig. 18 [d].
19 Item Nr 1536. The juglet is similar to others from el-Khata'na and Tell el-Dab'a (Tomb A/II-e/12-Nr 2, TD 170). Kaplan, *Tell el Yahudiyeh*, 19-22, figs 48 [a, f], 50 [f].
20 Bietak, *BASOR* 281 (1991), fig. 12; Kopetzky, in *Bronze Age in the Lebanon*, 212, figs 2, 16-17.
21 The publication of tomb finds does not provide enough detail for further examination. However, van den Brink reports that Tell Basta includes several tombs with elements of an MBA culture (Van den Brink, *Tombs and Burial Customs*, 57).
22 Ryholt, *Political Situation*; Grajetzki, *Middle Kingdom*, 66-68.

4.2.2 Dab'a, Tell el- (Avaris)

Lat.Lon. 30°47'N 31°50'E

Refs[23] *LÄ* VI, 321-323; Adam, *ASAE* 56 (1959); Bagh, *TeD* 23; van den Brink, *Tombs and Burial Customs;* Bietak, *Avaris and Piramesse;* Bietak, *BASOR* 281 (1991), 27-72; Bietak, *Avaris*; Czerny, *TeD* 9; Fuscaldo, *TeD* 10; Aston, *TeD* 12; Philip, *TeD* 15; Bietak and Forstner-Müller, *E&L* 16 (2006), 61-76; Forstner-Müller, *TeD* 16; Müller, *TeD* 17; Schiestl, *TeD* 18; Bietak and Forstner-Müller, *E&L* 19 (2009), 91-119; Sartori, *E&L* 19 (2009); Kopetzky, *TeD* 20; Aston and Bietak, *TeD* 8.

Chron. Twelfth to Fifteenth Dynasty

Tell el-Dab'a, a term used here for the tell itself as well as its surrounding district, is located north of Faqus in the northeastern Delta. Results from geological and geophysical surveys point to its position near the Pelusiac branch of the Nile[24] (Figure 4.3) and the presence of three possible harbours:[25] one located in the centre of the district; another to the south (F/II); and a third to the north near 'Ezbet Rushdi.[26] Such strategic positioning would have given the site's inhabitants access to land-based, river-based and sea-based trading routes. The site was partially excavated by Naville,[27] Habachi[28] and Adam,[29] and, since 1966, has been continuously excavated by the Austrian Archaeological Institute in Cairo and the Institute of Egyptology at the University of Vienna.[30] The excavations uncovered the remains of a city dating from at least the First to the Third Intermediate Periods and spanning an area of approximately 1200 hectares.[31] It is because of the magnitude of such a settlement, as well as its material remains, that the city's identification with Avaris, capital of the Hyksos, is now widely accepted by Egyptologists.[32]

The archaeological research at Tell el-Dab'a by the Austrian Archaeological Institute and the Institute of Egyptology is the best documented work for the Delta region between the Middle Kingdom and the Second Intermediate Period. Due to the vast number of publications and studies relating to each area, only evidence from strata dating from the Twelfth to the early Fifteenth Dynasty (i.e. N/2-3 to E/1 of the site's general stratigraphy; Figure 4.4) are summarised here. Evidence pertaining to Asiatic presence are examined for each excavated area.[33] This is then followed by a section reviewing scientific analysis on Levantine-style ceramics.

4.2.2.1 Area R/I ('Ezbet Rushdi)

'Ezbet Rushdi is situated to the northeast of Tell el-Dab'a (Figure 4.3). Remains of two Egyptian-style structures deduced to be a temple and an administrative building have been unearthed.[34] The former contained a stela of Senwosret III naming the site as  *Ḥw.t-Ỉmn-m-ḥ3.t-m3ʿ-ḫrw-n.t-r3-w3.ty* 'district of Amenemhat, justified, of the beginning of the two roads'.[35] The temple's construction is dated to Senwosret III's reign while earlier strata possibly date between the reigns of Senwosret I and Amenemhat II.[36]

The earlier remains were of structures that underwent at least four distinct phases of renovation corresponding to the first half of the Twelfth Dynasty (Strata e/1-4 and d; see Figure 4.4).[37] Within these strata are the earliest MBA ceramics from the Tell el-Dab'a district. These include locally-made holemouth cooking pots[38] and Levantine Painted Ware jugs, the earliest fragments of which occur in Stratum e/4.[39] The Levantine Painted Ware dipper juglets ascribe to the MBIIA globular shape with monochrome red horizontal band decoration.[40] Such forms find their closest parallels with those from el-Lisht, Kom el-Hisn and Byblos.[41] Syro-Palestinian store-jars contribute to 15% of the entire assemblage.[42] This figure increases to 85% with more amphorae fragments in strata contemporary with the temple (Strata c-a).[43] Levantine Painted Wares in these later strata are mostly of the slender type,[44] which similarly occur at Byblos.[45] So, the MBIIA ceramics point to trade with the Levantine coast, particularly Byblos, during the first half of Dynasty 12. In view of Senwosret III's stela, the finds agree with the site's designation as a *r3-w3.ty* or a destination of merging routes.

23 For a more extensive list of site publications, see *The Tell el-Dab'a Homepage*.
24 Bietak, *TeD* 2, 47-112; Bietak, *Avaris and Piramesse*, 227-228; Bietak, *Avaris*, 3.
25 Forstner-Müller, *EA* 34 (2009), 12; Forstner-Müller, in *Cities and Urbanism*, 117-119, fig. 12; Herbich and Forstner-Müller, *Études et travaux* 26 (2013), 258-272.
26 Forstner-Müller, in *Cities and Urbanism*, 12.
27 Naville, *Saft el-Henneh*, 21-23.
28 Habachi, *ASAE* 52 (1954), 443-448.
29 Adam, *ASAE* 56 (1959), 207-226.
30 See *The Tell el-Dab'a Homepage*.
31 Bietak, *Avaris*, 2-3.
32 Van Seters, *Hyksos*, 127-151; Bietak, *TeD* 2, 179-220; Bietak, *Avaris and Piramesse*, 271-283; Bourriau, in *Ancient Egypt*, 177-178; Kemp, *Ancient Egypt*, 41.
33 Despite extensive publications, the analyses of the repertoire of evidence from individual strata and phases are still meagre compared to general studies and publications assessing artefact developments. This examination is instead organised according to the stratigraphy.
34 Adam *ASAE* 56 (1959), 208-210, 218-219. For a different interpretation regarding the structure of the so-called temple, see Goedicke, *E&L* 12 (2002), 187-190.
35 Adam, *ASAE* 56 (1959), pl. 9.
36 Bietak and Dorner, *E&L* 8 (1998), 12-15, 28-29; Bagh, *TeD* 23, 45.
37 Bagh, *TeD* 23, 15, 28.
38 The origins of these cooking pots are disputed yet it is possible that the form was appropriated from the Levantine holemouth cooking pots. For more, see Czerny, in *MBA in the Levant*, 138, fig. 23; Aston, in *MBA in the Levant*, 46-47; Forstner-Müller, *E&L* 17 (2007), 89.
39 Bagh, *TeD* 23, 43-45, fig. 15 [a, b, q].
40 Bagh, *TeD* 23, 43, fig. 15 [c, e]; Bagh, in *MBA in the Levant*, 96, fig. 2 [1-5].
41 Bagh, in *MBA in the Levant*, 96, fig. 4.
42 Bagh, in *MBA in the Levant*, 96, fig. 3.
43 Bagh, in *MBA in the Levant*, 96.
44 Bagh, in *MBA in the Levant*, 96, fig. 2 [11-14]; Bagh, *TeD* 23, 43, fig. 15 [k].
45 Bagh, in *MBA in the Levant*, fig. 4 [8].

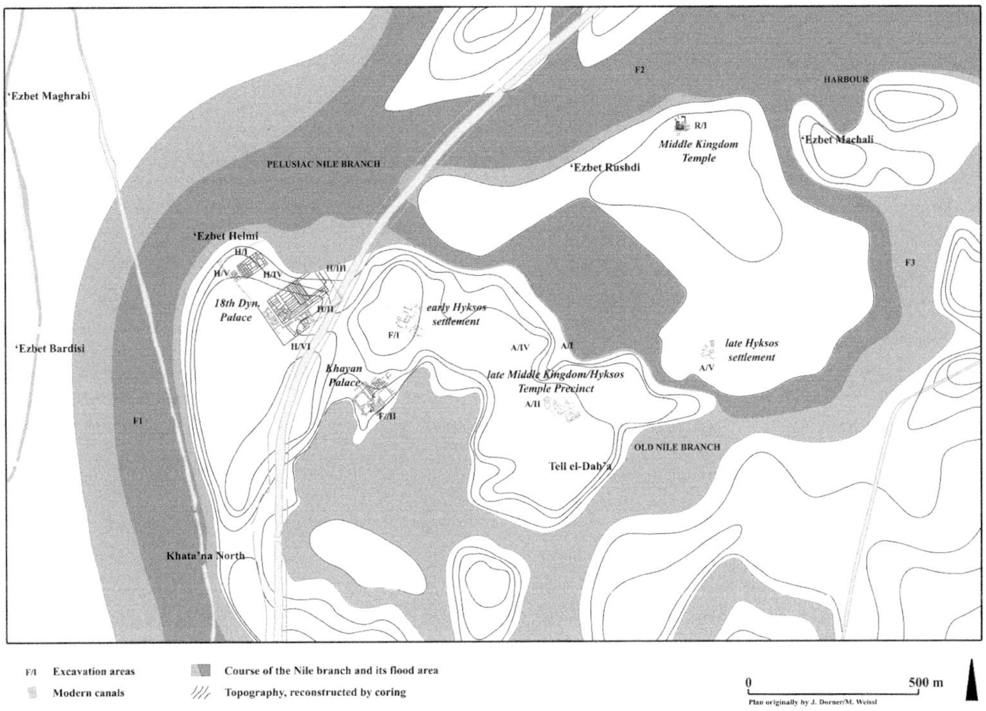

FIGURE 4.3. MAP OF TELL EL-DAB'A. AFTER BIETAK, IN *CULTURES AND CONTACTS*, FIG. 1.

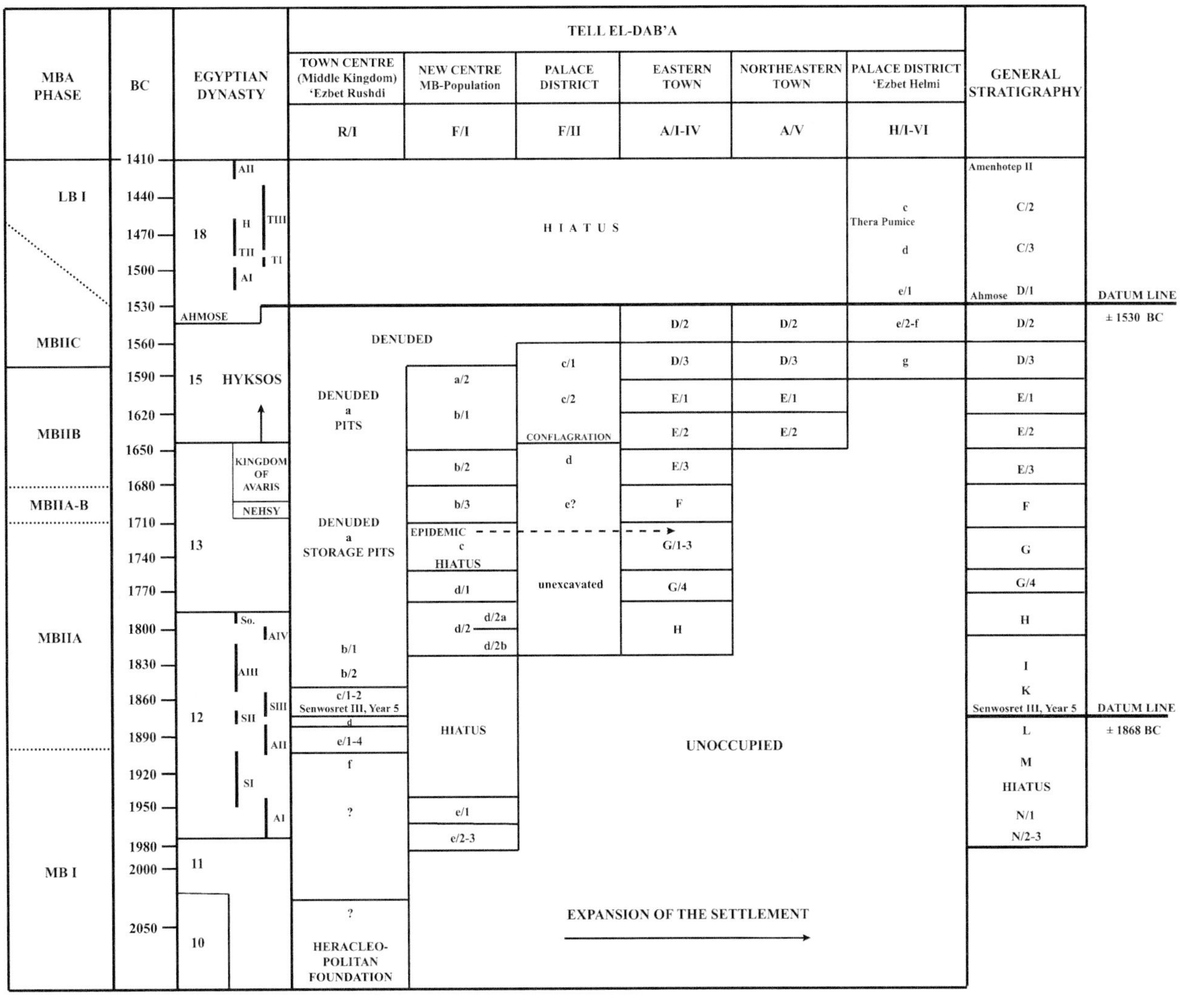

FIGURE 4.4. STRATIGRAPHY OF TELL EL-DAB'A. AFTER BIETAK, IN *CITIES AND URBANISM*, FIG. 7; BAGH, *TED* 23, FIG. 4.

4.2.2.2 *Area R/III*

Surveys and salvage excavations have been carried out in Area R/III, east of 'Ezbet Rushdi.[46] The results have so far revealed a densely settled area of the Fifteenth Dynasty with complexes consisting of burials, courtyards, silos and ovens.[47] The first occupation layers are of the early to mid-Fifteenth Dynasty (Strata d-k), from which Kerma Ware and a seal impression of *Ḫy3n* were found.[48] Other seal impressions of the late Middle Kingdom and Second Intermediate Period have also been uncovered, suggesting an added administrative function to Area R/III.[49]

4.2.2.3 *Area F/I*

Southwest of 'Ezbet Rushdi lies the partly excavated Area F/I (Figure 4.3), which yielded remains from the late Eleventh to the Fifteenth Dynasty (Figure 4.4).[50]

Strata e/1-3: Late Eleventh to early Twelfth Dynasty

A planned Egyptian settlement is found in Strata e/1-3.[51] Fragments of coarse, handmade cooking pots, possibly flat-bottomed, of MBI type occur.[52] Although comparatively rare, the presence of such cooking pots has been explained to indicate contact with bedouins in the Delta who apparently favoured the use of handmade pots over holemouth wheel-made vessels.[53] Such a designation, however, is questionable, especially as handmade cooking pots were in use by peoples in urban contexts across the

Figure 4.5. Plan of Near Eastern types of houses, Area F/I, Stratum d/2, Tell el-Dab'a. After Bietak, in *Cities and Urbanism*, fig. 12.

46 Forstner-Müller, et al., *E&L* 18 (2008), 87-106; Forstner-Müller, in *Cities and Urbanism*, 103-107; Forstner-Müller et al., 'Report on the Excavations at Tell el-Dab'a 2011', 2-4; Forstner-Müller and Rose, *E&L* 22-23 (2012/2013), 53-64.

47 Forstner-Müller et al., 'Report on the Excavations at Tell el-Dab'a 2011', 2; Forstner-Müller and Rose, *E&L* 22-23 (2012/2013), 53-64.

48 Forstner-Müller et al., 'Report on the Excavations at Tell el-Dab'a 2011', 4; Forstner-Müller and Rose, in *Nubian Pottery*, 181, 184, 201; Forstner-Müller and Rose, *E&L* 22-23 (2012/2013), 53, 58.

49 Forstner-Müller et al., 'Report on the Excavations at Tell el-Dab'a 2011', 3; Reali, *E&L* 22-23 (2012/2013), 67-74.

50 Czerny, *TeD* 9, 17-19.

51 Czerny, *TeD* 9; Bietak, *BASOR* 281 (1991), 31.

52 Bietak, *BASOR* 281 (1991), 31, n. 9.

53 Bietak, *BASOR* 281 (1991), 31; Holladay, in *Hyksos*, 184.

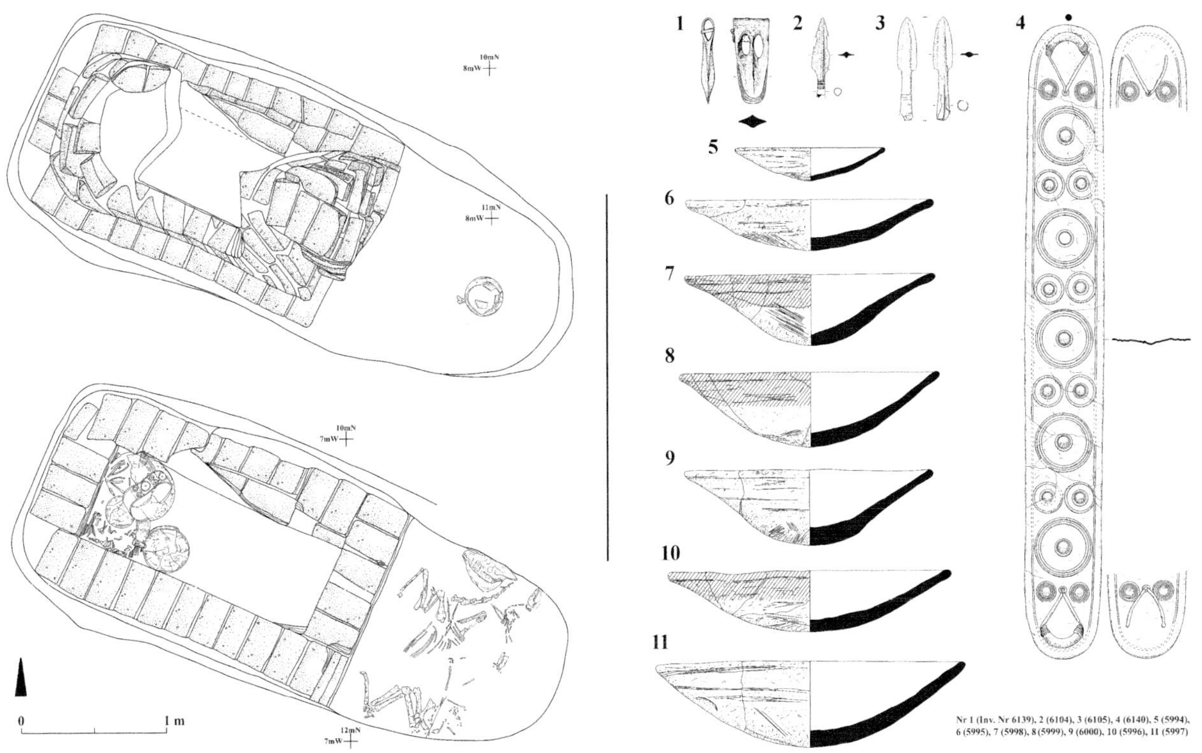

Figure 4.6. Plan of Tomb F/1-o/19-Nr 8 and its associated grave goods (not to scale), Area F/I, Stratum d/2, Tell el-Dab'a. After Schiestl, in *MBA in the Levant*, figs 2-3.

Levantine region from the EBIV period.[54] Therefore, the presence of the handmade cooking pots need not only be interpreted as evidence of bedouins but can denote the existence of a non-Egyptian MBI element in F/I.

Stratum d/2: Late Twelfth Dynasty

Following a brief hiatus, F/I was resettled and rectangular mudbrick residences were constructed.[55] Among the latter are those which follow the architecture of the Northern Levantine Breitraumhaus (broad-room house) and Mittelsaalhaus (middle-room house) (Figure 4.5).[56] The latter were constructed in such EBA settlements as Arad[57] and Meser[58] in the Southern Levant, and Titriş Höyük,[59] Tell Brak[60] and Byblos[61] in the Northern Levant, with the contemporary MBA palace at Mari bearing similar Mittelsaalhaus elements.[62] Pottery from the settlement features approximately 20% MBIIA forms[63] including Syro-Palestinian store-jars,[64] carinated bowls,[65] and a fragment of an imported ovoid Tell el-Yahudiyah jug.[66]

South of the Mittelsaalhaus are two cemeteries in which the majority of excavated tombs follow the typical Middle Kingdom types of simple or multiple brick chambers.[67] The tombs bear burial customs which appear to be non-Egyptian, including: the deposition of donkeys and caprids in pits that are either directly or indirectly related to the tombs; the contraction of bodies; silver bracelets on right forearms; and the inclusion of bronzes, particularly weapons, in 50% of adult male burials.[68] Tomb F/I-o/19-Nr 8, for example, is a mudbrick vaulted chamber with an entrance pit containing the skeletal remains of an adult female donkey, a kid and a lamb (Figure 4.6).[69] Grave goods include two socketted copper spearheads, a decorated bronze belt and a fenestrated axe, which parallel mostly MBIIA and MBIIA-B forms.[70] Pottery remains from the tomb are of local forms and fabrics, suggesting that the tomb owner is either an acculturated Asiatic,[71] or a Levantine-influenced

54 Forstner-Müller, *E&L* 17 (2007), 92; Bader, in *Intercultural Contacts in the Ancient Mediterranean*, 144.
55 Bietak, *BASOR* 281 (1991), 32.
56 Eigner, *JÖAI* 56 (1985), 19-25.
57 Amiran and Ilan, *Early Arad* 2, pl. 96.
58 Wright, *Ancient Building in South Syria and Palestine*, 286.
59 See the website for the *Titriş Höyük Archaeological Project*.
60 Akkermans and Schwartz, *Archaeology of Syria*, fig. 8 [26].
61 Bou-Assaf, in *Bronze Age in the Lebanon*, fig. 3.
62 Gates, *BA* 47/2 (1984), 73.
63 Bietak, *BASOR* 281 (1991), 32.
64 Only fragments of Syro-Palestinian store-jar rims have been identified. Aston, in *MBA in the Levant*, figs 5-6.
65 Sherds of Levantine Painted Ware were also uncovered within the area of the Mittelsaalhaus, but in secondary contexts. Aston, in *MBA in the Levant*, fig. 13 [1]; Bagh, *TeD* 23, 53-54, figs 16 [a, b], 17 [b-f], 18 [a-d], 19 [b], 21 [c].
66 Parallels are found at Afula, Byblos and Ginosar. Bagh, *TeD* 23, 51-52, fig. 17 [1].
67 Schiestl, in *Bronze Age in the Lebanon*, fig. 2.
68 Bietak, *Avaris*, 10-14, fig. 10 [5]; Schiestl, in *MBA in the Levant*, 330-331; Philip, *TeD* 15, 61.
69 Philip, *TeD* 15, 332, fig. 2.
70 Philip, *TeD* 15, 33, 138, 332-337.
71 Schiestl assigns the burial to the 'ethnic group of *ꜥ3m.w* or Asiatics'.

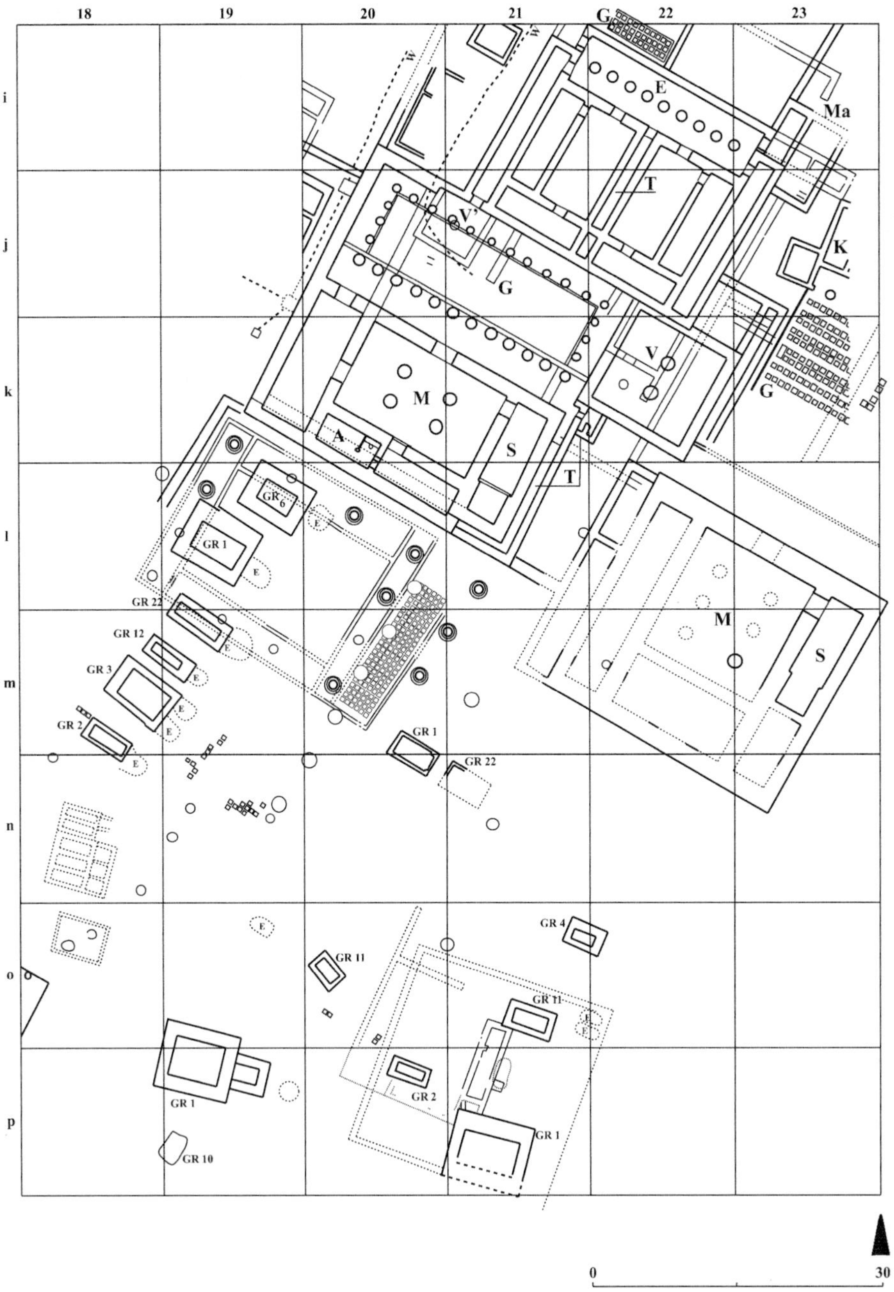

FIGURE 4.7. EGYPTIAN-STYLE COMPOUND WITH ASSOCIATED TOMBS, AREA F/I, STRATUM D/1, TELL EL-DAB'A. AFTER BIETAK, *BASOR* 28 (1991), FIG. 6.

Egyptian. The same may be the case for the majority of the stratum's inhabitants considering the combined evidence from the settlement and the cemetery. If house architecture bears witness to ethnicity, then it may be surmised that the late Twelfth Dynasty at Tell el-Dab'a featured a number of Northern Levantines living and possibly working in the region. A funerary tradition associated with Levantine weaponry is also apparent.

Stratum d/1: Early Thirteenth Dynasty

A large sand-brick compound was erected atop the Mittelsaalhaus of the preceding phase (Figure 4.7).[72] The Egyptian-style complex encompassed two residential units, a large pillared courtyard and a 'reception' room with numerous subsidiary rooms.[73] The architecture and layout of the earlier stratum's structures were evidently recognised by builders who, in an attempt to restrict structural damage to earlier interments, constructed a courtyard atop Stratum d/2 tombs.[74] Tombs of Stratum d/1

Schiestl, *E&L* 16 (2006), 173.

72 Eigner, *JÖAI* 56 (1985), 19-25.
73 Bietak, *Avaris*, 21, fig. 18, pls 5-6.
74 Bietak, *Avaris*, 21-22.

are located south of the complex but, unlike those of the former level, are positioned in the gardens of the compound in up to six parallel rows.[75] Despite this difference, a direct architectural relation between the late Twelfth Dynasty and early Thirteenth Dynasty may be surmised, indicating a plausible link between the occupants of Stratum d/2 and d/1.

The function of Stratum d/1's compound, however, may not be connected with the Mittelsaalhaus of the earlier stratum. Some have interpreted the complex's larger dimensions as evidence of its palatial function and argue for its possible use by Thirteenth Dynasty ruler Hotepibra Sihornedjheritef whose seated statue was apparently found at the site.[76] In actuality, the statue was uncovered prior to Bietak's excavations from an uncertain context.[77] Although damaged, it features inscriptions bearing the king's epithets as well as his nomen, *ꜥꜣmw/ Ḳmꜣw-Sꜣ-Ḥr.w-nḏ-ḥr-it=f* '*ꜥꜣmw/Ḳmꜣw*-Sihornedjheritef'.[78] Based on the accompanying epithet *mry Ptḥ-rs.t-inb=f* 'beloved of Ptah-South-of-his-Wall', the statue may have in fact originated from Memphis.[79] As such, it cannot conclusively indicate the date of the complex's construction or its function.

The compound is more similar to an Egyptian residence than a palace.[80] The size of the pillared courtyard and 'reception' room might indicate a political or administrative purpose,[81] the functionaries of which could have been the owners of the tombs attached to the compound's gardens.[82] The same may also be observed at the Mayor's Residence at Tell Basta.[83]

One major find from the complex's northern wing is a haematite cylinder seal (Figure 4.8).[84] The seal's design incorporates a striding figure standing with each foot placed above the crenellation of a mountain. Slightly inclined forward, the figure holds a mace in his left hand and an axe in his right. The axe, which is held directly before his

75 Bietak, *Avaris*, 21-22, fig. 18; Schiestl, in *MBA in the Levant*, 341. For more on these tombs, refer to Schiestl, *TeD* 18.
76 Bietak's 'Asiatic's Son'. Bietak, *E&L* 2 (1991), 71; Bietak, *Avaris*, 21-22; Bietak, *BASOR* 281 (1991), 34; Bietak, in *Cities and Urbanism*, 19-20; Eigner, *JÖAI* 56 (1985), 78-80.
77 Habachi, *ASAE* 52 (1954), 460, pl. 9.
78 Scholars are divided on the reading of as either *ꜥꜣmw* or *ḳmꜣw*. A few attestations of the glyphs occur at Dahshur (in a pyramid of an Imeny-*ꜥꜣmw/Ḳmꜣw*), el-Harageh (on a coffin of *ꜥꜣmw/Ḳmꜣw*), and el-Atawla (on a block with the name of the king attested on the Tell el-Dab'a piece). Due to the ambiguities, the items are not explored in this work. For more, see Schneider, *Ausländer in Ägypten* 2, 7-11, 48; Quirke, in *Middle Kingdom Studies*, 129; Bietak, *E&L* 2 (1991), 71; Scandone-Matthiae, in *Hyksos*, 418-420; Ryholt, *Political Situation*, 214; Ryholt, *BASOR* 311 (1998), 1-6; Maragioglio and Rinaldi, *Orientalia* 37 (1968), 325-338; Swelim and Dodson, *MDAIK* 54 (1998), 319; Dodson, *ZÄS* 114 (1987), 40; Engelbach, *Harageh*, 25, pl. 75 [1]; Daressy, *RT* 16 (1870), 133; Kamal, *ASAE* 3 (1902), 80; Habachi, *ASAE* 52 (1952), 461, pl. 10.
79 Matthiae, in *Hyksos*, 418-420; von Beckerath, *Zweiten Zwischenzeit*, 39, 231; Schneider, *Ausländer in Ägypten* 2, 7-11, 48.
80 O'Connor, in *Hyksos*, 53; Wegner, *JARCE* 35 (1998), 25.
81 Wegner, *JARCE* 35 (1998), 25.
82 Schiestl, in *MBA in the Levant*, 341; Bietak, *E&L* 2 (1991), 64-71.
83 See Chapter 4.2.1 and n. 17.
84 Bietak, *Avaris*, 26-29, fig. 25; Porada, *AJA* 88 (1984), 485.

FIGURE 4.8. CYLINDER SEAL IMPRESSION PICTURING A STRIDING FIGURE, AREA F/I, STRATUM D/1, TELL EL-DAB'A. AFTER PORADA, *AJA* 88 (1984), FIG. 1.

face, has a longitudinal extension with two horizontal lines possibly denoting the fenestrations of a duckbill axe-head or an earlier type of Egyptian axe.[85] Although contemporary Levantine seals indicate the widespread use of the smiting stance motif in cylinder seal designs, the figure's slightly bent stance ascribes more to Egyptian renditions.[86] Behind the figure is a bull with its head forward as if in an attacking pose. It stands on a guilloche, below which is a seated lion extending one paw towards a sinuous serpent slithering its body on a platform or dais.[87] Above the lion is a simplified cutting of a bird,[88] whereas behind it is a stylised sailboat rowed by two individuals. The area above the sailboat preserves the end of a wing, either of a sun-disc or bird,[89] with an animal[90] underneath it pointing its head downwards as if falling toward the sailboat.

All elements of this seal exert a symbolic association expressing a particular belief system. Porada and Bietak interpret the figure as the weather god Baal Saphon[91] whose proximity to the sailboat reveals his role as protector of seafarers and slayer of such enemies as the falling animal.[92] Bietak views the snake to be Yamm,[93] deity of the sea and enemy of Baal, whereas Marcus links the snake and lion with Asherah, patron goddess of mariners.[94] The seventh century BC Baal Saphon[95] could be regarded as the Bronze Age Baal who built his palace on Mount Sapan, north of Ugarit.[96] In the Ugaritic Baal Cycle, the bull god is described as a Cloud-rider who strikes down the Twisty Serpent, the

85 Porada, *AJA* 88 (1984), 485-486, n. 5.
86 Porada, *AJA* 88 (1984), pl. 65 [2].
87 For the interpretation of the platform as a dais or throne, see Porada, *AJA* 88 (1984), 487, n. 8.
88 Porada notes that the bird could be a composite mythological creature of a bird and fish (Porada, *AJA* 88 [1984], 487, n. 9).
89 Porada, *AJA* 88 (1984), 485.
90 The animal may be a goat (Porada, *AJA* 88 [1984], 485).
91 Porada, *AJA* 88 (1984), 487, n. 10; Bietak, *Avaris*, 26-29.
92 Porada, *AJA* 88 (1984), 487.
93 Bietak, *Avaris*, 26.
94 Marcus, *Timelines* 2, 188.
95 Porada, *AJA* 88 (1984), 487.
96 The construction of Baal's palace on Mount Sapan is described in the Baal Cycle of the Ugaritic tablets of 1400-1350 B.C. Another interpretation sees Sapan as the enthronement place following Baal's victory. Baal Cycle, 10:V: 35-65, VI:1-64 as translated in Parker, *Ugaritic Narrative Poetry*, 131-135. See also Geyer, *Mythology and Lament*, 88.

fleeing serpent Litan, and god of the sea Yamm.[97] The seal cutter could have employed specific symbols connected to this myth, such as the bull (the god himself), the guilloche (the winds) and the serpent (the sea) to represent Baal's power over these elements.[98] The lion motif could also be seen as an extension of this strength. Consequently, the representation would have assured safe passage for those in the pictured boat which warrants the interpretation of the seal as a means to ritualistically invoke protection for seafarers.[99] In retrospect to the item's context, it's possible to infer that seafarers and worshippers of Baal were in contact with individuals of F/I's administrative complex. If Porada is correct in identifying the item as a locally-made copy combining Egyptian and Syrian techniques, then the cylinder seal reflects a familiarity with Levantine gods and myths at Tell el Dab'a.[100]

The tombs in the complex's gardens correspondingly reflect an awareness of Levantine customs. All burials follow Egyptian architectural practices[101] and adhere to an organised layout initiated by the first six tombs positioned in clearly planned rows (Figure 4.7).[102] However, the tombs feature donkey offerings and Levantine bronze weaponry.[103] These include MBIIA and MBIIA-B forms such as socketted spearheads, globular-shaped pommels, a notched narrow-bladed axe (replacing the duckbill form), a dagger with five midribs and a curved knife.[104] Tomb F/I-m/18-Nr 3, one of the largest and earliest of this stratum, is a mudbrick-lined pit with two chambers and remnants of a superstructure for offerings.[105] The tomb, which featured two offering pits, one with two donkeys and the other with caprids, contained seven individuals.[106] Amongst the grave goods were a Levantine Painted Ware fragment,[107] a pair of silver spearheads[108] (most probably prestige items paralleling MBIIA spearheads from Megiddo),[109] a notched axe-head and a single-edged knife with a curved blade.[110] The knife's blade, which uniquely ends in a spiral tip, only has recorded parallels from Kharji, near modern-day Beirut.[111] Another item providing links with the Northern Levant is a silver bracelet, the form of which is very similar to one found in an MBIIA tomb at Sidon.[112] This apparent connection with the Northern Levantine coast may be explained by a scarab from the tomb. Mounted on a gold ring, the scarab's glyphs have been translated as either *[ỉm.y]-rꜣ ḫꜣs.wt [rn]ṯn Sbk-m-ḥꜣ.t* '[overseer] of foreign lands and caravan leader, Sobekemhat'[113] or *[ḥḳꜣ n.y R]ṯnw Di-sbk-m-ḥꜣ.t* '[ruler of] *Rṯnw*, Disobekemhat'.[114] Either translation provides evidence for elite traders exercising relations with the Levant during early Dynasty 13, justifying the occurrence of such foreign finds in the tomb.

Despite heavy looting, finds from the cemetery and palatial compound confirm this association. A few scarabs were inscribed with pseudo-hieroglyphs[115] whereas another depicts a smiting figure poised to strike a seated caprid.[116] The latter also includes two branches and a fish, elements unknown in Egyptian iconography but commonly represented in Old Syrian cylinder seals in connection with the weather god Baal.[117] Pottery forms of the MBIIA include ovoid to piriform Syro-Palestinian store-jars of diverse fabrics and sizes;[118] both unburnished combed and red burnished dipper juglets possibly imported from the northern Israeli or Lebanese coast;[119] and Levantine Painted Ware fragments, the decoration of which parallels those from Tell 'Amr in the Southern Levant and Tell 'Arqa in the north.[120] The presence of Classical Kamares Ware scattered in the gardens of the complex also points to trade with Crete.[121]

Alongside these fragments were those belonging to a limestone statue of a seated man, some of which were recovered from the plundered tombs of Strata d/2, d/1 and possibly Stratum c.[122] The statue may have been set up in a tomb's superstructure, after which it was deliberately destroyed.[123] Reconstructed, the statue would have been larger than life-size, extending to approximately 2m in height. It was styled in the fashion of Middle Kingdom statues of the late Twelfth to early Thirteenth Dynasties (Figure 4.9),[124] the head designed with the common Asiatic

97 This concept of a weather god destroying a serpentine water creature is common throughout the Near East. Contemporary with the Tell el-Dab'a seal and depicting this battle are seals from Alalakh. Baal Cycle 8:IV:1-27; 8:II:38-39; 9:III:41-42; 11:1:I-2 and 11:I:28-29; Kramer, *Sumerian Mythology*, 76-83, pl. 19; Green, *Storm-God*, 161-164; Schwemer, *JANER* 8/1 (2008), 36.

98 In a letter to Zimri-Lim at Mari, Hadad, cognate of Baal, is said to have defeated the sea. Chavalas, *Ancient Near East*, 126-127 [73].

99 For more on Baal and his function as patron deity of seafaring, see Schwemer, *JANER* 8/1 (2008), 13.

100 Bietak (*Avaris*, 28-29) asserts that the seal indicates the establishment of a Baal cult, which is refuted by Ryholt (*Political Situation*, 150, n. 545).

101 Approximately 92% have mudbrick chambers with either vaulted or barrelled roofs. Schiestl, in *Bronze Age in the Lebanon*, 245-246, fig. 3.

102 F/I-1/19-Nr 6 and Nr 1; F/I-m/19-Nr 22; and F/I-m/18-Nr 12, Nr 3 and Nr 2. Schiestl, in *MBA in the Levant*, 341; Bietak, *Avaris*, fig. 18.

103 Schiestl, in *Bronze Age in the Lebanon*, 341.

104 Schiestl, in *Bronze Age in the Lebanon*, 341-342; Bietak, *Avaris*, 26.

105 Schiestl, in *MBA in the Levant*, 343.

106 Two are male, three female, one juvenile and one infant. Schiestl, in *MBA in the Levant*, 343.

107 Bagh, *TeD* 23, 54, fig. 18 [e].

108 A fragment of a silver spearhead has also been found in Tomb F/I-I/19-Nr 6 (Philip, *TeD* 15, 67).

109 Philip, *TeD* 15, 67. Silver alloys for use in spearheads can also be found at Byblos. See el-Morr and Pernot, *BAAL* 13 (2011); el-Morr and Pernot, *JAS* 38 (2011), 2619.

110 Schiestl, *TeD* 18, 381, fig. 337 [13]; Philip, *TeD* 15, 75, fig. 34 [2].

111 Cave 4, Chamber 1. Philip, *TeD* 15, 149; Saidah, *Berytus* 41 (1993/1994), 189, pls 4-5.

112 Schiestl, *TeD* 18, fig. 336 [5], pl. 17 [b]; Doumet-Serhal, *AHL* 20 (2004), 27.

113 Bietak, *E&L* 2 (1991), 67; Hein and Mlinar, in *Pharaonen und Fremde*, 97.

114 Martin, *E&L* 8 (1998), 110.

115 TD 103 and TD 106 from F/I-k/22-Nr 69. Mlinar, in *Scarabs of the Second Millennium BC*, 118-119, fig. 6a [7, 9].

116 TD 110 from F/I-o/20-Nr 2. Mlinar, in *Scarabs of the Second Millennium BC*, 114, fig. 4 [5].

117 Mlinar, in *Scarabs of the Second Millennium BC*, 114; Bietak, in *Studies in Honor of Ali Radwan*, 202-203, fig. 5 [e].

118 Tomb F/I-m/18-Nr 3 contained at least seven Syro-Palestinian store-jars. Schiestl, in *MBA in the Levant*, 346-350.

119 Schiestl, in *MBA in the Levant*, 350, fig. 15 [6]; Kopetzky, in *MBA in the Levant*, 229, 244, figs 1-2; Kopetzky, *AHL* 26-27 (2007/2008), 28, fig. 7 [73].

120 Kopetzky, *AHL* 26-27 (2007/2008), 28, ns 64-65; Bagh, *TeD* 23, 46-52, figs 18-22.

121 Bietak, *BASOR* 281 (1991), 36; Bietak, *Avaris*, 29, pl. IA.

122 For more on the fragments and their archaeological contexts, see Schiestl, *E&L* 16 (2006), 175.

123 Schiestl dates the point of destruction to Stratum c. Schiestl, *E&L* 16 (2006), 175.

124 Schiestl, *E&L* 16 (2006), 175-176; Arnold, in *Second Intermediate*

elements of a red-coloured coiffed hairdo[125] and yellow skin. The figure's body possibly wears a long garment, the details of which have been preserved in fragments delineating its colourful texture and decoration of ornate stripes and wavy fringes.[126] Stylistically, the garment conforms to Asiatic dress as depicted in Khnumhotep II's tomb at Beni Hassan[127] or Syrian/Mesopotamian robes from, for instance, Ebla,[128] although it is questionable whether or not the garment was draped over one shoulder.[129]

The seated figure carries an object in his right-hand (Figure 4.9) which, based on Schiestl's reconstruction, could be a throw-stick[130] symbolising status[131] or the ethnicity of the *ʿ3m* Asiatic who carries it. Another interpretation, based on an Eblaite statue of a seated figure with a similar throw-stick in his left hand and an offering bowl in his right, connects the throw-stick with the statue's function as a recipient of offerings.[132] Indeed, the statue's base consists of a hieroglyph for incense, suggesting that a complete offering formula may have been inscribed on the statue's base in compliance with Egyptian religious customs.[133] Whether or not the throw-stick represents status or ritual, the connection with Ebla implies that the artist(s) embedded Northern Levantine symbolism with Egyptian elements to customise the statue for both Egyptian and Asiatic offering bearers. Therefore, the complexity of such a design that blends the Egyptian and Asiatic both physically and symbolically must be observed as a reflection of the hybridity of the direct (the seated figure)[134] and the indirect (the artists, the offering bearers and the immediate community).[135] Such a hybrid character would have necessitated the combination of Egyptian and Asiatic features not only across the artistic sphere, but also across the funerary, administrative and urban modes, which is, in fact, reflected by the aforementioned archaeological evidence.

Stratum d/1 terminates after the abandonment of the complex. While it was being renovated, building instruments were dropped and doors were sealed.[136] Such a sudden desertion could reflect momentous political and/or administrative changes in the region.

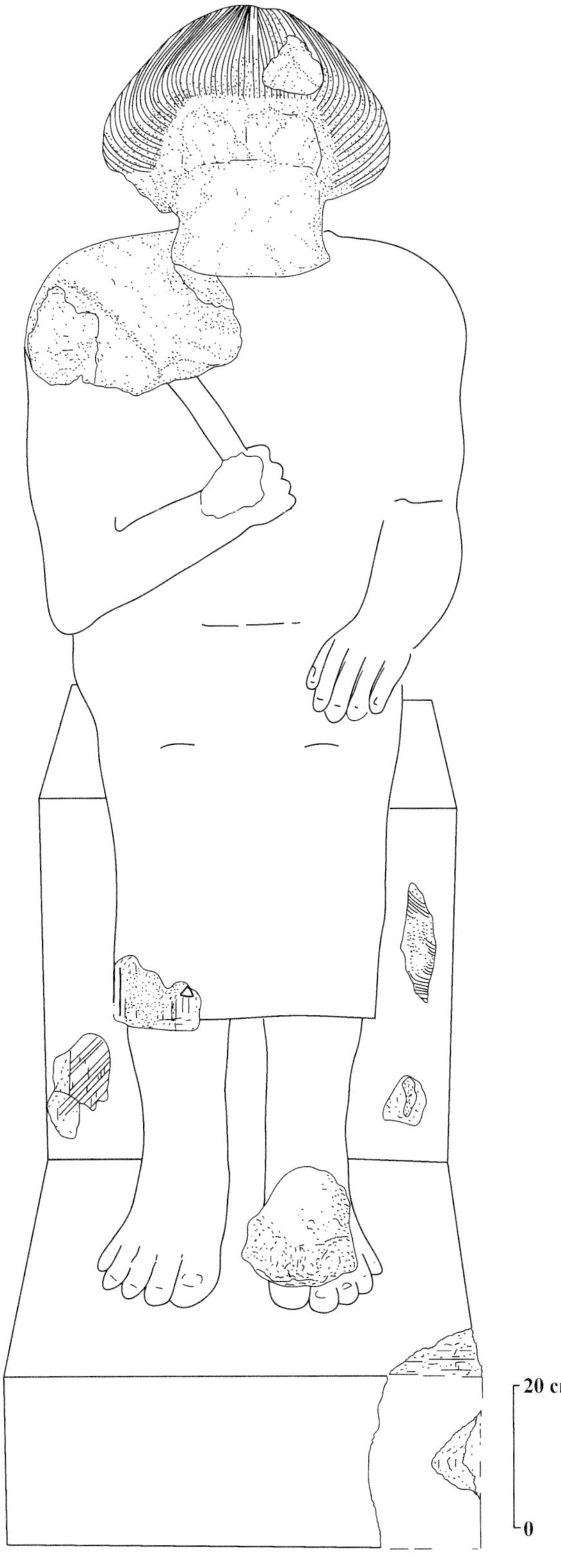

Figure 4.9. Reconstruction of a limestone statue of an official. Fragments from Tombs F/I-p/19-Nr 1, F/I-p/21-Nr 1 and F/I-p/21-Nr 1, Area F/I, Tell el-Dab'a. After Schiestl, *E&L* 16 (2006), fig. 2.

Period, 192.

125 Fragments of a dark brown-red colour have also been detected on a limestone head of a similar unprovenanced statue currently in the Egyptian Museum in Munich (Munich ÄS 7171). Arnold, in *Second Intermediate Period*, 191, n. 87, pl. 30; Wildung, *Ägypten 2000 v. Chr.*, 164-165, 186 [83].

126 Schiestl, *E&L* 16 (2006), 179-180.

127 See Chapter 4.4.1.3, Figure 4.52.

128 Matthiae, in *Von Uruk Nach Tuttul*, pl. 50.

129 Schiestl, *E&L* 16 (2006), 179; Arnold, in *Second Intermediate Period*, 199.

130 Schiestl, *E&L* 16 (2006), 175-176.

131 Arnold, in *Second Intermediate Period*, 198.

132 Matthiae, in *Von Uruk Nach Tuttul*, pl. 50. The crook is held over the left shoulder in the same manner as the Tell el-Dab'a statue. See also Figure 6.16 of a dagger from Byblos (Chapter 6.3.3.1).

133 Schiestl, *E&L* 16 (2006), 182.

134 Schiestl, *E&L* 16 (2006), 183. Schiestl proposes that the statue illustrates a dignitary of either Egyptian or Asiatic ethnicity. The noted hybridity of the statue suggests that the represented dignitary could have been both.

135 Arnold, in *Second Intermediate Period*, 200.

136 Bietak, *Avaris*, 29-30.

Stratum c: Mid-Thirteenth Dynasty

A settlement developed with uniform two-roomed houses, some of which had perimeter walls.[137] Burials were sunk either within the houses, their courtyards, or rectangular structures attached to the houses.[138] Grave goods include imported ceramics of MBIIA-B forms such as ovoid and piriform Tell el-Yahudiyah ware,[139] Syro-Palestinian store-jars,[140] amphora-jugs,[141] wheel-made holemouth cooking pots,[142] dishes,[143] carinated bowls,[144] as well as red, brown and black burnished jugs.[145] The vessels' shapes and fabrics find parallels across the Northern and Southern Levant,[146] signifying extensive trade along the Levantine coast and inland areas. Non-Egyptian manufacturing techniques were also known by local craftsmen as indicated by the Egyptian clays of such Levantine forms as dipper juglets and carinated bowls.[147] An increase in MBA ceramics from approximately 20% to 40% has also been detected. While it has been postulated to represent an influx of peoples from the Levant,[148] it can equally indicate a rise in (a) trade relations; (b) demand for MBA forms; and/or (c) population. An influx of Levantine people from other parts of Egypt, rather than the Levant, cannot be ruled out.

The end of Stratum c is characterised by numerous shallow pit graves.[149] Most bodies were buried in an extended position with little to no grave goods while some seem to have been 'thrown' into pits.[150] A few cases also present the burial of several individuals at the same time.[151] Bietak postulates the spread of an epidemic such as the 'Asiatic disease' as a reason for such hasty burials.[152] The cause of death may have indeed been a deadly disease, perhaps linked to the speculated migration of peoples into the region. Another probable explanation could be conflict in the area.

Stratum b/3-2: Mid-late Thirteenth Dynasty

Occupation at the settlement continued while the 'villa' type of tripartite houses, otherwise known in el-Lahun, was introduced.[153] Social differentiation is more recognisable with the various house sizes and the designation of quarters for servants near villas.[154] As in the previous stratum, graves were sunk in courtyards, within houses and within structures adjacent to the houses ('family cemeteries').[155] The majority were heavily plundered, although remains of such items as imported red-polished juglets, spouted brown-polished jugs, piriform Tell el-Yahudiyah ware and globular flasks, point to an elite sector with relations with an MBIIA-B and MBIIB culture. These, alongside remnants of sheep offerings and intra-mural burials, imply the presence of Levantine individuals.[156]

Like the construction of servant quarters near villas, so-called 'servant burials' were discovered alongside tombs of the elite, particularly in Stratum b/3.[157] These typically consisted of females interred in an extended position in chambers or pits before the main tomb's entrance.[158] The lack of offerings and the subsidiary positioning at the entrance of larger tombs suggest that these were lower status individuals dependent on those buried in the main chambers. As the main tomb owners were either male or female, the roles of those in the attendant burials could be as subsidiary wives.[159] One attendant burial, however, was of a seven or eight year old infant of an age regarded as too young for a wife or concubine.[160] As such, Bietak has identified the burials to be those of servants.[161] Based on the close proximity of a few attendant burials to the undamaged entrance pits of the main tombs, he proposes that they were buried at the time of, or shortly after, the interment of their masters, possibly as sacrificial victims.[162] Such practices are known to have occurred in the Early Dynastic Period[163] and the Mesopotamian Early Dynastic I-III periods,[164] although the only contemporary examples of attendant sacrifices are of the Classical Kerma Period at Kerma.[165] Here, the attendant burials of females were discovered in pits along the beds of the main burial but in numerous, irregular, burial postures.[166] Despite these differences, Bietak proposes a 'spiritual connection' between those at Tell el-Dab'a and those at Kush.[167] Lack of further evidence weakens the validity of this reasoning. The attendant burials at Tell el-Dab'a may not even be of servants but could be of individuals with some familial relationship to the main

137 Bietak, *Avaris*, 31; Bietak, *BASOR* 281 (1991), 36-38.
138 Bietak, *BASOR* 281 (1991), 38.
139 Aston, in *MBA in the Levant*, fig. 17 [4], 17 [7]. Jug 5588 is decorated with incised lines with running spirals that are possibly Minoan-influenced.
140 Aston, in *MBA in the Levant*, figs 3-4, 9.
141 Aston, in *MBA in the Levant*, fig. 10 [1].
142 Aston, in *MBA in the Levant*, fig. 11 [5]. See also above, n. 38.
143 Aston, in *MBA in the Levant*, fig. 12 [2].
144 Aston, in *MBA in the Levant*, fig. 12 [5-7].
145 Aston, in *MBA in the Levant*, figs 14 [1], 15 [1-5], 15 [11], 15 [13].
146 Aston, in *MBA in the Levant*, 47-50.
147 Aston, in *MBA in the Levant*, 48-50.
148 Bietak, *Avaris*, 31. Bietak later alters this viewpoint in Bietak, in *Second Intermediate Period*, 151.
149 Bietak, *Avaris and Piramesse*, 295.
150 Bietak, *BASOR* 281 (1991), 38.
151 Bietak, *BASOR* 281 (1991), 38.
152 Bietak, *Avaris*, 35; Bietak, *BASOR* 281 (1991), 38.
153 Bietak, *BASOR* 281 (1991), 38-39; Bietak, in *Cities and Urbanism*, 18.
154 Bietak, *BASOR* 281 (1991), 39; Bietak, in *Cities and Urbanism*, 18.
155 Bietak, *BASOR* 281 (1991), 39.
156 See Bietak, *Eretz Israel* 20 (1989), 30-43.
157 Bietak, *Eretz Israel* 20 (1989), 30-43.
158 Tomb F/I-p/19-Nr 12A included the remains of an infant of unidentifiable sex. Bietak, *Eretz Israel* 20 (1989), 30.
159 Tomb F/I-i/22-Nr 43, for example, was of a female and infant whose chamber includes a pit with a female's body across its entrance. Bietak, *Eretz Israel* 20 (1989), 35-36, 39.
160 Tomb F/I-p/19-Nr 12A. Bietak, *Eretz Israel* 20 (1989), 30.
161 Bietak, *Eretz Israel* 20 (1989), 35-36, 39.
162 Tombs A/II-m/16-Nr 2 and F/I-l/22-Nr 28A are offered as examples of burying the 'servants' at the time or shortly after the interment of their 'masters'. Bietak, *Eretz Israel* 20 (1989), 40; van den Brink, *Tombs and Burial Customs*, 48.
163 Evidence exists at the cemeteries of Abydos, Giza and Saqqara. Petrie, *Royal Tombs* 1; Reisner, *Egyptian Tomb*, 75, 108-121; Tatlock, *Human Immolation in the Eastern Mediterranean*, 112-114.
164 Attendant burials have been uncovered at Ur (Early Dynastic III) and Kish (Early Dynastic I and II). Woolley, *Ur* 2, 33-41; Watelin, *Kish* 4, 19-20, 30; Moorey, *Iraq* 46/1 (1984), 13; Tatlock, *Human Immolation in the Eastern Mediterranean*, 76-80.
165 Bietak, *Eretz Israel* 20 (1989), 40-41.
166 Bietak, *Eretz Israel* 20 (1989), 40-41; Tatlock, *Human Immolation in the Eastern Mediterranean*, 115-117.
167 Bietak, *Eretz Israel* 20 (1989), 42.

tomb owner(s), such as subsidiary/secondary wives or the children of such wives. Additionally, the sacrificial nature of the attendant burials cannot be proven by the conjectured simultaneous time of burial.[168] Nonetheless, all cases of attendant burials confirm that the practice was reserved for the elite as if to transfer status to the hereafter or probably, as Hoffman suggests, as an attempt to affirm social hierarchy during a time of dynastic emergence.[169] Perhaps it was also connected to the establishment and diversification of various social roles in a period of transition from one socio-political system to another.

Stratum b/1-a/2: Early to mid-Fifteenth Dynasty

The villa type and the small one-or-two-roomed houses continued in use in the settlement while burials remained among and within residential units,[170] with children mostly interred in Syro-Palestinian store-jars.[171] Near the settlement, foundations of a mudbrick temple with a possible tripartite sanctuary have been preserved.[172] Before this temple are large offering pits filled with ceramics and animal bones, including those of pigs and equids.[173] One pit is 2.34m x 2.0m large and contained 792 vessels,[174] some of which showed evidence of intentional burning.[175] A few vessels, like miniature bowls, had a cultic function, while the majority, including bowls, cooking pots, cups, beaker jars and dipper juglets, were used directly for consuming food and water. Thus, it is very possible that a ritual practice involving cultic meals was performed before the temple.[176] Similar rituals were practiced across the MBIIA and MBIIB Levant, with the closest contemporary parallels found in the *favissae* of Ebla.[177]

4.2.2.4 Area A/II

Area A/II represents part of the eastern district of Tell el-Dab'a (see Figure 4.3) in which significant remains of a sacred precinct have been unearthed.[178] Spanning an extensive period between the Twelfth to Eighteenth Dynasties, the site's material culture reveals the same emergence of hybrid Egyptian-Asiatic elements as in Area F/I,[179] with an added insight into the religious customs practiced in A/II's temples.

Stratum H: Late Twelfth to early Thirteenth Dynasty

A marginal settlement of huts and sand-brick enclosure walls is recognisable.[180] Finds include Egyptian and MBIIA Levantine-style pottery, such as locally-made holemouth cooking pots,[181] handmade flat-bottomed cooking pots[182] and imported Syro-Palestinian store-jars.[183] Although the origin of the first two is debatable, the presence of Syro-Palestinian jars attests to contacts with the Levant.

Stratum G/4-1: Early Thirteenth Dynasty

Stratum H's settlement continued in development though remnants of a conflagration layer of charcoal signal a short interval between it and Stratum G.[184] As in Tell el-Habwa I and Tell el-Maskhuta, houses are adjoined with round silos and surrounded by enclosure walls.[185] Tombs were dug within these enclosures and adhere to the Egyptian types of pit graves or vaulted chamber tombs.[186] Funerary goods imply an MBIIA connection with 56% of the ceramics following MBA forms compared to the 40% of MBA ceramics from the settlement area.[187] These include a high number of Syro-Palestinian store-jars,[188] a few holemouth wheel-made cooking pots,[189] burnished jugs with double-stranded handles,[190] ovoid Tell el-Yahudiyah ware,[191] dishes with internal rims[192] and the first occurrence of handmade globular juglets with simple incised decoration.[193] Parallels for the imported ceramics mostly stem from the Northern Levant, particularly coastal Lebanon.[194]

Weapons of MBIIA type feature in the funerary repertoire. Tomb A/II-m/15-Nr 9 contained a copper belt and a broad dagger positioned at a semi-contracted male's abdomen.[195] Sheep bone fragments were additionally deposited among a pile of offerings near the entrance,[196] demonstrating further links with the contemporary burials of Area F/I d/1

168 Bietak writes that 'the evidence is, however, not cogent for claiming sacrificial burials' in *Eretz Israel* 20 (1989), 40.
169 Hoffman, *Egypt Before the Pharaohs*, 279; Tatlock, *Human Immolation in the Eastern Mediterranean*, 112, 161.
170 Bietak, *BASOR* 281 (1991), 41.
171 Bietak, *BASOR* 281 (1991), 41.
172 Bietak, *Avaris and Piramesse*, 295; Bietak, *BASOR* 281 (1991), 40.
173 Müller, in *MBA in the Levant*, 277, 279-280.
174 F/I-i/22-Nr 5. Müller, in *MBA in the Levant*, 277.
175 Müller, in *MBA in the Levant*, 277.
176 Müller, in *MBA in the Levant*, 277-279, fig. 7.
177 The *favissae* at Ebla not only contained ceramic vessels, but also bore other objects such as clay figurines, jewellery, beads and weapons. Other areas across the Levant containing remnants of cultic meals include Byblos and Ugarit in the north, and Nahariya, Giv'at Sharett, Megiddo and Lachish in the south, although those in the north are of earlier date. Müller, in *MBA in the Levant*, 280-281; Marchetti and Nigro, *JCS* 49 (1997), 34-36; Marchetti and Nigro, in *Languages and Cultures in Contact*, 281-282.
178 Bietak, *Avaris*, 36-48.
179 Forstner-Müller, in *Second Intermediate Period*, 127.

180 Bietak, *Avaris and Piramesse*, 236-237.
181 See n. 38; Forstner-Müller, *E&L* 17 (2007), 89, fig. 12.
182 One cooking pot is of Levantine clay whereas the others are of Nile fabric attributed to either a Nile source or the north Sinai. Forstner-Müller, *E&L* 17 (2007), 91-92, fig. 14; Aston, in *MBA in the Levant*, 46; McGovern, *Foreign Relations of the Hyksos*, 123; Oren, in *Hyksos*, 72.
183 Forstner-Müller, *E&L* 17 (2007), 89, fig. 13.
184 Bietak, *Avaris and Piramesse*, 238; van den Brink, *Tombs and Burial Customs*, 4.
185 See Chapters 4.2.4 and 4.2.9; Bietak, *Avaris and Piramesse*, 238.
186 Forstner-Müller, *TeD* 16, 84, fig. 32.
187 The increase occurs between G/4 and G/3-1 in the settlement. Forstner-Müller, *TeD* 16, 85; Bietak, *BASOR* 281 (1991), 34-35.
188 Aston, in *MBA in the Levant*, figs 3 [3], 7 [2, 4], 9 [1, 5, 8].
189 Aston, in *MBA in the Levant*, fig. 11 [4].
190 Aston, in *MBA in the Levant*, fig. 14 [5-8].
191 Forstner-Müller, *TeD* 16, fig. 72 [3].
192 Bader, in *Intercultural Contacts in the Ancient Mediterranean*, 142-143.
193 Bietak, *BASOR* 281 (1991), 38.
194 Some cases are similar to ceramics from northern Israel and inland Syria whereas a few could originate from the Southern Levant. Bader's note that limited archaeological exploration in southern Israel may hinder conclusions is worthy of note, although the same may be said for archaeological exploration in Lebanon, particularly inland areas. Bader, in *Intercultural Contacts in the Ancient Mediterranean*, 144.
195 The dagger follows Philip's Type 13. Philip, *TeD* 15, 45, fig. 12; Forstner-Müller, *TeD* 16, fig. 72 [1-2].
196 Forstner-Müller, *TeD* 16, 129-133.

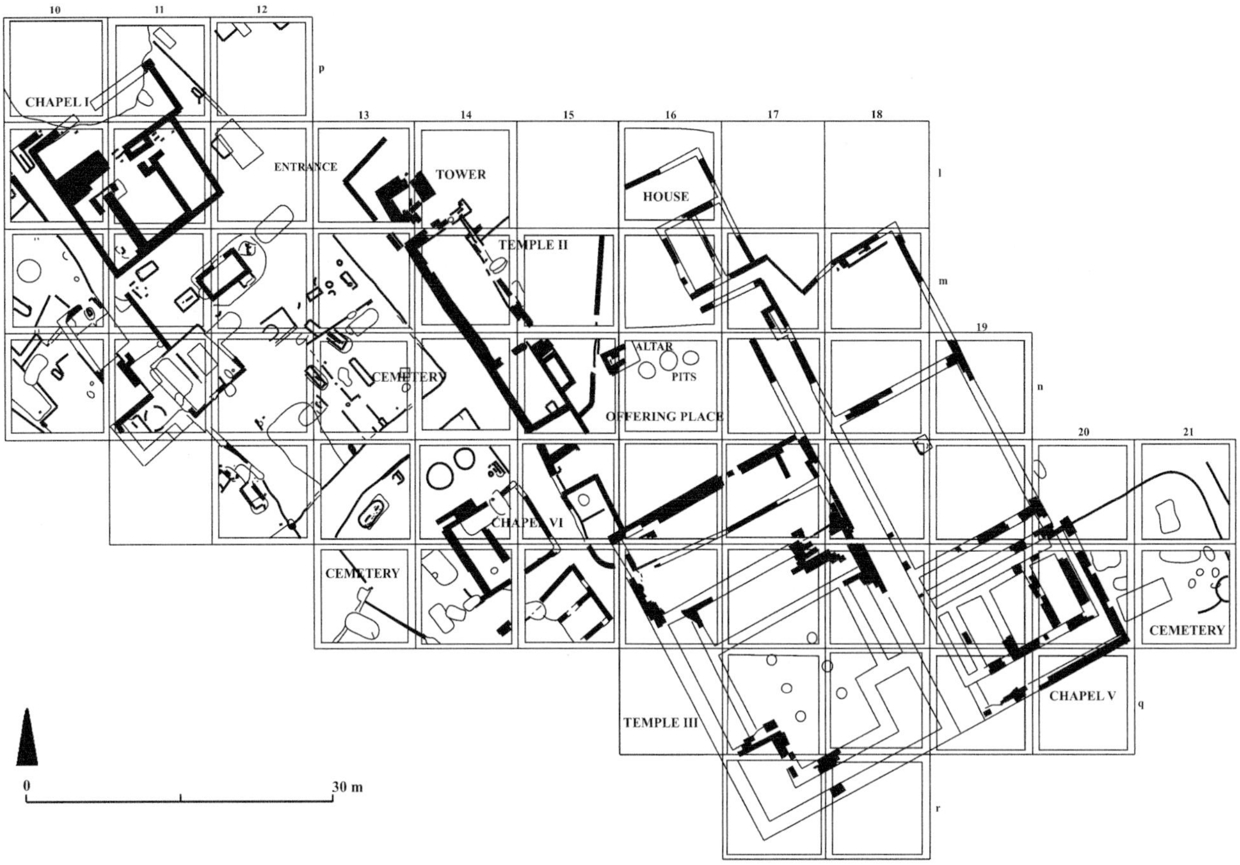

FIGURE 4.10. PLAN OF AREA A/II, TELL EL-DAB'A. AFTER BIETAK, IN *CITIES AND URBANISM*, FIG. 34.

and later tombs at Tell el-Maskhuta and Tell el-Yahudiyah. This element, combined with the location of the tombs within house enclosures, the contraction of interred bodies as well as the presence of Levantine-style weaponry and pottery, hints at an ethnic group from the Levant living at Tell el-Dab'a during the early Thirteenth Dynasty. The populace was also intermixed with Egyptians or influenced by the Egyptian culture as observed by the Egyptian-style houses, tombs, ceramics and grave goods.[197] The size of residential units and tombs, and the quality and quantity of artefacts indicates that the majority of individuals were neither of the elite nor of the lowest echelon of society.[198] Therefore, it is possible that Stratum G was represented by a common populace familiar with both Egyptian and Levantine customs, implying the spread of Levantine elements and perhaps influence across Tell el-Dab'a.

The concluding stage of Stratum G/1 is marked by numerous shallow pit graves with few to no grave goods.[199] Apparently, the crisis that affected the end of Stratum c in F/I could have extended over a wider area.

Stratum F: Mid-Thirteenth Dynasty

Major changes are discernible, especially with the function of A/II. The settlement of the previous phase was reorganised and plots were redistributed, their design slightly influenced by the earlier units but inferior in quality to the contemporary houses of F/I.[200] A precinct of temples, chapels and cemeteries was constructed at the edges of the town with its tombs orientated towards the main temple (III).[201] Described as the largest temple in the MBA,[202] Temple III is a broad-room temple with a rectangular niche in its shrine and two procellas (Figure 4.10).[203] Fragments of blue paint suggest a decorated exterior whereas a rectangular mudbrick instalment in the forecourt may have been an altar.[204] Around the altar were offering pits, one of which contained a pair of donkey burials that were perhaps linked with temple activities.[205] The architectural elements of Temple III are uncommon in Middle Kingdom Egyptian temples but are detected in contemporary Northern Levantine temples[206]

197 Forstner-Müller, *TeD* 16, 129-140; Bader, in *Egypt and the Near East*, 56.
198 Forstner-Müller, *TeD* 16, 138.
199 Bietak, *BASOR* 281 (1991), 38.

200 Bietak, *Avaris and Piramesse*, 241; Bietak, *BASOR* 281 (1991), 39.
201 Forstner-Müller, in *MBA in the Levant*, 163-164.
202 Bietak, *Avaris*, 36.
203 The style of niche is more common among Migdol-temples. Bietak, *BASOR* 281 (1991), 39; Müller, in *MBA in the Levant*, 275.
204 Bietak, *BASOR* 281 (1991), 39; Bietak, *Avaris*, 36.
205 Pit l/14-Nr 11. Müller, in *MBA in the Levant*, 271.
206 Examples of temples of the late MBA and LBA with similar architectural features are the so-called Hurrian Temple at Ugarit, the Orthostat Temple at Hazor and Temple 2048 at Megiddo. Bietak, in *Second Intermediate Period*, 156, n. 131; Yadin, *Hazor*, fig. 23; Loud, *Megiddo* 2; Warner, *Archaeology of Canaanite Cult*, 232.

such as those at Ebla[207] and Alalakh.[208] Because of this Near Eastern architecture as well as the equid burials, Bietak suspects the worship of a Levantine deity at Temple III.[209]

Within houses, house courtyards and the cemeteries of the sacred precinct were 26 tombs.[210] Three of these contained attendant burials which, as in F/I b/3-2, were of females interred outside the main burial.[211] Some also had donkey burials, usually in pairs, as well as caprid offerings.[212] Notable changes are the increase in contracted burials,[213] the first appearance of the MBIIB chisel-shaped axe[214] and the final occurrence of daggers with five midribs,[215] axes with square sections[216] and bronze belts.[217] Within A/II-p/14-Nr 18 is the only scimitar found in an undisturbed context in Egypt.[218] With a clear MBIIA form, parallels are few but derive from Byblos and Mesopotamia.[219] The scimitar's rarity may be linked with its function as a status symbol. Indeed, the adult male tomb owner appears to be of high status as inferred by his provisioning with an attendant burial, an equid burial as well as such grave goods as a dagger, a copper belt, caprid offerings, and a range of Egyptian and MBA pottery, including a rare model amphora.[220]

Levantine-style wares of the MBIIA and MBIIB amount to 53% of the entire funerary ceramic assemblage, compared to an estimated 40% from non-funerary contexts.[221] The locally-made and imported forms encompass: piriform and ovoid Tell el-Yahudiyah jugs which, for the first time, are mainly locally produced;[222] handmade globular juglets;[223] piriform and biconical red-and-brown-burnished juglets and jugs;[224] as well as unburnished and red burnished dipper juglets with parallels along the Levantine coast.[225] Syro-Palestinian store-jars are present, though in lesser quantities than those in F/I tombs and A/II settlement areas.[226]

A curious case is tomb A/II-l/12-Nr 5 of an adult male in a semi-contracted position.[227] The tomb was equipped with weaponry (a dagger and an axe), pottery (Egyptian and MBIIA forms) and a scarab seal on the tomb owner's finger inscribed with  *ỉdn.w n.y ỉm.y-r3 ḫtm.t ʿ3m* 'deputy of the overseer of the treasury, *ʿ3m*'.[228] Ryholt maintains that, because deputy treasurers did not usually have many seals, the individual buried in A/II-l/12-Nr 5 could himself be *ʿ3m*.[229] He also dates the seal stylistically to the reign of *Šši* or shortly thereafter.[230] The tomb owner was provided with an offering pit at the tomb's entrance housing the remains of cattle and the greatest number of donkey interments thus far recorded (five to six).[231] The pit additionally contained the dissevered bones of an adolescent and a mature individual,[232] a practice otherwise unattested in Egypt but similar to an EBIV/MBIIA offering pit at Ebla containing human and sheep remains.[233]

Much like the Eblaite pit, that of A/II-l/12-Nr 5 could be an indicator of status which, combined with the entire funerary assemblage, emphasises the tomb owner's elite ranking as deputy treasurer. If Ryholt is correct, then *ʿ3m*'s tomb demonstrates the use of Egyptian titles by Asiatics as well as the relation of the funerary kit with an Asiatic ethnic group.[234] It further indicates that officials were not buried near the capital but at a sacred area in Tell el-Dab'a, the location thereby hinting at growing regionalisation during the mid-Thirteenth Dynasty.[235] Based on tomb location alone, such a theory may prove to be erroneous. However, it is corroborated by the rearrangement of plots and change in function of A/II, as well as the establishment of a temple and possible temple cult following Northern Levantine customs and rituals. The inference that an invading culture fuelled this regionalisation cannot be substantiated by the available evidence. If anything, the material culture and scarab inscription signify a continued presence of Egyptian and Levantine elements, the latter exhibiting MBIIB traits towards the conclusion of Stratum F.[236]

207 Temple G3 and the temples of Ishtar and Hadad's sacred precinct (D and P2). Matthiae, *CRAIBL* 131/1 (1987), 142-149; Marchetti and Nigro, *JCS* 49 (1997), 1-3, fig. 1.

208 The temples of Strata IV and VII of the MBA and LBA. Woolley, *Alalakh*, 71-73, figs 30, 35.

209 Bietak, *Avaris and Piramesse*, 253.

210 Forstner-Müller, in *Second Intermediate Period*, 129; Forstner-Müller, *TeD* 16, 36-37.

211 Tombs A/II-m/16-Nr 2, A/II-l/12-Nr 5 and A/II-l/11-Nr 3. Forstner-Müller, *TeD* 16, 156-164; van den Brink, *Tombs and Burial Customs*, 48-49; Bietak, *Eretz Israel* 20 (1989), 31-32, 39-43.

212 Van den Brink, *Tombs and Burial Customs*, 46-51; Forstner-Müller, *TeD* 16, 177-184.

213 Bietak, *BASOR* 281 (1991), 40.

214 Bietak, *BASOR* 281 (1991), 40.

215 Forstner-Müller, *TeD* 16, 49-50; Forstner-Müller, in *MBA in the Levant*, 165.

216 Forstner-Müller, *TeD* 16, 49; Forstner-Müller, in *MBA in the Levant*, 165-166.

217 Forstner-Müller, *TeD* 16, 51-52; Forstner-Müller, in *MBA in the Levant*, 166.

218 Forstner-Müller, *TeD* 16, 50-51; Forstner-Müller, in *MBA in the Levant*, 167.

219 Forstner-Müller, *AHL* 26-27 (2007/2008), 207-211; Montet, *Byblos et l'Égypte*, 173-177.

220 Forstner-Müller, in *MBA in the Levant*, 172-174, figs 8-10; Forstner-Müller, *TeD* 16, 177-184.

221 Bietak, *BASOR* 281 (1991), 39; Forstner-Müller, in *MBA in the Levant*, 184.

222 Forstner-Müller, in *MBA in the Levant*, 167, 184; Forstner-Müller, *TeD* 16, 69-77; Bietak, *BASOR* 281 (1991), 39.

223 Forstner-Müller, in *MBA in the Levant*, 167; Bietak, *BASOR* 281 (1991), 39.

224 Forstner-Müller, in *MBA in the Levant*, 168.

225 Kopetzky, in *MBA in the Levant*, 229-231; Forstner-Müller, *TeD* 16, 76.

226 Perhaps this contrast reveals the different social status of buried individuals across the areas, or variant funerary priorities. Forstner-Müller, in *MBA in the Levant*, 169.

227 Van den Brink, *Tombs and Burial Customs*, 48-49.

228 Bietak, *MDAIK* 23 (1968), 108, pl. 32 [c]; Bietak, *Avaris*, 41; Ward, *Index*, 70 [576].

229 Ryholt, *Political Situation*, 105.

230 Ryholt, *Political Situation*, 61, 104.

231 Bietak, *Avaris*, 41; van den Brink, *Tomb and Burial Customs*, 49.

232 Van den Brink argues against their deposition as secondary burials in *Tomb and Burial Customs*, 49.

233 Pit D.6274 in the Sacred Area of Ishtar. Nigro, *JPR* 11-12 (1998), 22-36.

234 Bourriau, in *Ancient Egypt*, 178.

235 For a similar opinion, see Forstner-Müller, in *Second Intermediate Period*, 134-135.

236 Bietak, *BASOR* 281 (1991), 40; Forstner-Müller, in *MBA in the Levant*, 184.

Stratum E/3: Late Thirteenth Dynasty

Building works were carried out in the sacred precinct of A/II. Temple III was renovated and a brick altar was added in its forecourt within which were remnants of ash, charcoal, red burnt sand and animal offerings.[237] Three temples were constructed near Temple III (Figure 4.10), one of which follows the architecture of Levantine broad-room temples with a bent axis (Temple II).[238] Another, Chapel V, adheres to the typical Egyptian design but includes an altar in its open courtyard, much like Temple III with its Levantine-style altar.[239] Other Egyptian-style mortuary temples were also built,[240] signifying the presence of Egyptian funerary cults alongside an active non-Egyptian cult focussed around the Levantine-style altars.

The majority of ceramics are Egyptian while 40% are of imported and locally-made MBA shapes.[241] Piriform 1-2 and Ovoid 2-3 Tell el-Yahudiyah jugs are attested[242] along with piriform black, brown and red-polished jugs with button bases,[243] holemouth cooking pots,[244] biconical brown-polished jugs,[245] MBIIB carinated bowls[246] and burnished globular bowls with longer, slightly everted necks.[247] Syro-Palestinian store-jars are also among the repertoire, with one example bearing traces of horizontal burnishing across the rim and vertical burnishing across the body, a technique observed among Tell 'Arqa's jars.[248]

The tombs of Stratum E/3 continued in the same type, location and orientation as those of the earlier phase.[249] The stratum also marks the first occurrence of burying infants in Syro-Palestinian store-jars in A/II.[250] Compared to the overall figures for Egyptian and Levantine ceramics, 80% of the ceramics from the tombs ascribe to MBA forms, 20% of which are imported.[251] Bronzes include weapons, particularly such MBIIB styles as the chisel-shaped axe, the dagger with raised midrib and the spearhead with a tapering blade.[252] Toggle-pins[253] and single-edged knives with curved blades are also common.[254]

Overall, Stratum E/3 could be regarded as an extended phase of Stratum F. The growing discrepancy between the quantity of MBA ceramics from the settlement and those from the graves may indicate an acculturated ethnic group adhering to its Levantine customs for funerary and cultic purposes.

237 Forstner-Müller, in *MBA in the Levant*, 177.
238 Forstner-Müller, in *MBA in the Levant*, 177.
239 Bietak, *BASOR* 281 (1991), 40.
240 Bietak, *Avaris*, 45.
241 Bietak, *BASOR* 281 (1991), 40.
242 Bietak, *BASOR* 281 (1991), 40-41; Aston, *TeD* 12, 343, fig. 74 [h, k].
243 Bietak, *BASOR* 281 (1991), 40-41.
244 Aston, *TeD* 12, 168-169, 343, pls 179-180.
245 Bietak, *BASOR* 281 (1991), 40-41.
246 Aston, *TeD* 12, 342, fig. 74 [e].
247 Such bowls are found throughout the Levant. For a list of parallels, see Kopetzky, *AHL* 26-27 (2007/2008), 39-40.
248 Phase N, Level 14B. Kopetzky, *AHL* 26-27 (2007/2008), 40, fig. 31 [79].
249 Forstner-Müller, *TeD* 16, 89-93.
250 Forstner-Müller, *TeD* 16, 89.
251 Forstner-Müller, *TeD* 16, 90-91.
252 Forstner-Müller, *TeD* 16, 52, 89, fig. 312; Philip, *TeD* 15, 67, fig. 24 [1].
253 Forstner-Müller, *TeD* 16, 204, fig. 121 [1].
254 Philip, *TeD* 15, 71, fig. 31 [2]

Stratum E/2: Early Fifteenth Dynasty

A new temple (I) was built west of the sacred area (Figure 4.10).[255] Like Chapel V, the building is generally Egyptian in style but combines such foreign elements as a tripartite procella, akin to Hazor's LBA temple, and the construction of benches along the front and interior of temple walls.[256] In a niche near the entrance is a large plate around which libation channels were placed, possibly for the provision of liquid for an older burial located beneath the temple's foundations.[257] This placement could denote the continued practice of funerary obligations across at least one generation,[258] paralleling such libation channels as those appended to tombs at Ugarit[259] and Byblos.[260]

The MBA ceramic repertoire from Stratum E/2 is very similar to that of the earlier phase. A major difference distinguishing the two is that jugs are found both with candlestick and everted rims as well as bipartite and strap handles. [261] After E/2, only the candlestick rim and strap handle are recorded.[262] Piriform 2 Tell el-Yahudiyah ware with three to four zones of decoration occur towards the end of E/2 whereas biconical juglets gain popularity.[263] Other MBIIB forms include carinated bowls,[264] large globular pots with everted rims,[265] local red-slipped bowls each decorated with a burnished cross[266] and dipper juglets with pointed bases.[267] The most common imported form is the Syro-Palestinian store-jar[268] and the rarest includes the Cypriote White Painted Cross Line and White Painted Pendant Line Styles.[269] A higher percentage of MBIIB vessels is estimated to come from funerary contexts (81%).[270]

Burials were simple pit graves, mudbrick or sand brick constructions with vaulted roofs and Syro-Palestinian store-jar burials.[271] Bodies were interred either contracted or semi-contracted.[272] Burial goods other than ceramics include sheep/goat offerings,[273] silver earrings,[274] toggle-pins,[275] a copper axe,[276] a dagger,[277] as well as an undecorated

255 Bietak, *Avaris and Piramesse*, 257.
256 Bietak, *BASOR* 281 (1991), 41; Bietak, *Avaris and Piramesse*, 256-257, fig. 10; Yadin, *Hazor*, 87-95, fig. 19.
257 Bietak, *Avaris and Piramesse*, 256-257.
258 Bietak, *Avaris and Piramesse*, 257.
259 Schaeffer, Montet and Virollaud, *Syria* 15/2 (1934), 116, figs 5-6; van den Brink, *Tombs and Burial Customs*, 7.
260 Van den Brink, *Tombs and Burial Customs*, 7; Montet, *Byblos et l'Égypte*, figs 65, 67.
261 Bietak, *BASOR* 281 (1991), 41; Aston, *TeD* 12, 352.
262 Aston, *TeD* 12, 352.
263 Bietak, *BASOR* 281 (1991), 41, fig. 12.
264 Aston, *TeD* 12, 354.
265 Aston, *TeD* 12, 117-118, fig. 84 [d], pl. 99.
266 Aston, *TeD* 12, 106-107, fig. 84 [b], pl. 86.
267 Aston, *TeD* 12, 155, fig. 84 [u], pl. 148.
268 Aston, *TeD* 12, 162-165, pl. 171.
269 Aston, *TeD* 12, 359.
270 Forstner-Müller, *TeD* 16, 94.
271 Bietak, *BASOR* 281 (1991), 41; Forstner-Müller, *TeD* 16, 93, fig. 47.
272 Forstner-Müller, *TeD* 16, 93-94, 221-241.
273 Tomb A/II-p/13-Nr 15. Forstner-Müller, *TeD* 16, 234.
274 Tomb A/II-k/14-Nr 8. Forstner-Müller, *TeD* 16, 222, fig. 146.7 [7660].
275 Tombs A/II-k/14-Nr 8, A/II-k/16-Nr 24, A/II-l/17-Nr 16 and A/II-p/13-Nr 15. Forstner-Müller, *TeD* 16, 222, 226, 231, 234, fig. 146.6 [7661].
276 Tomb A/II-p/13-Nr 15. Forstner-Müller, *TeD* 16, 234-235, fig. 163a.2 [8905].
277 Tomb A/II-p/13-Nr 15. Forstner-Müller, *TeD* 16, 234-235,

silver headband placed around the head of the deceased.[278] Scarabs were also among the funerary repertoire[279] and consisted of new designs belonging to Mlinar's Type IV, the 'Palestinian Group'.[280] Such elements as the Horus falcon with the 𓊪 sign,[281] misrendered hieroglyphic symbols,[282] and the L-shaped red crown[283] are attested. Finding parallels with designs from Ben-Tor's Early Palestinian Series, the scarabs may have thus been imported from the Southern Levant. Pairs of donkey burials and remains of a horse have additionally been uncovered in front of tomb entrances.[284] Such funerary practices are highly similar to those observed in previous phases and nearby areas, indicating that the population at Tell el-Dab'a generally remained of the same Egyptian-Levantine background in the early Fifteenth Dynasty, with accentuated Northern Levantine influences on religious practices and emerging trade with areas like Cyprus and the Southern Levant.

Stratum E/1: Early to mid-Fifteenth Dynasty

Temple III was renovated, evidence of offering pits uncovered around its brick altar.[285] Pits with donkey burials were found, continuing the custom from the earlier Stratum F.[286] Round brick structures, either huts or silos, emerged in the cemetery area with adjoined storerooms.[287] Similar to those of Strata H-G/4, the construction of such structures possibly coincides with the rapid expansion of the settlement[288] which would accordingly indicate a growing population or an influx of people. Correspondingly, a sharp increase in burials is observed, particularly in the number of Syro-Palestinian store-jar burials that suggest a high infant mortality rate.[289] These were typically sunk either in houses, especially beneath doorways, or house courtyards.[290]

Mudbrick chambers, with and without vaulted roofs, and numerous simple pit graves were found in houses, house courtyards and the cemeteries of the sacred precinct.[291] Bodies were extended or semi-contracted, usually in supine position.[292] Funerary goods are much like those of E/2, comprising equid burials at the entrances,[293] caprid offerings,[294] toggle-pins,[295] gold and silver headbands,[296] as well as copper and bronze single-edged knives.[297] The last occurrence of copper weapons is also noted.[298] Approximately 87% of ceramics are MBIIB vessels,[299] again a dissimilar figure compared to an estimated 40% from the settlement.[300]

The majority of MBIIB ceramics from both funerary and non-funerary contexts were locally produced, except for the Syro-Palestinian store-jars which were mostly imported.[301] Distinct local types of pottery additionally occur, testifying to a definite regionalisation in material culture across Egypt.[302] Influences are mostly from Northern Levantine traditions and some are from the Southern Levant's inland region.[303] Tell el-Yahudiyah ware is common, especially among funerary goods, and encompasses the piriform, biconical, ovoid, quadrilobal and cylindrical shapes.[304] From E/1 onwards, incised black-burnished juglets and large, round-bottomed jugs with incised triangles are found in settlement layers, the latter paralleling those from Tell el-'Ajjul and Ashkelon.[305] Fish-shaped juglets with black-burnishing on unincised surface parts and strap handles are observed to have lumps of clay for fish eyes, a feature otherwise known from Byblos and Beirut.[306]

Stratum E/1 also marks the first appearance of local carinated dishes with ring bases and spiral handles, the style of which follows MBIIA-B dishes at Megiddo and Ain el-Samiyeh.[307] Furthermore, an increase in such Middle Cypriote pottery as White Painted Pendant Line and White Painted Cross Line styles is detected,[308] indicating continued trade relations with Cyprus.

The pottery remains of Stratum E/1 reveal the escalating separation of Tell el-Dab'a from Memphis and Upper Egypt. The increase in settlement size and burial number attests to a growing population with obviously escalating demands for

fig. 163a.1 [8906].

278 Tomb A/II-p/13-Nr 15. Forstner-Müller, *TeD* 16, 236, fig. 161; Doumet-Serhal and Kopetzky, *AHL* 34-35 (2011/2012), 34.

279 Mlinar, in *Timelines* 2, 213.

280 Mlinar states that Type IV scarabs had already developed in the Southern Levant where they are found at such sites as Megiddo, Afula, Akko, Atlit, Tel Aviv, Tell el-'Ajjul and Jericho. Mlinar, in *Scarabs of the Second Millennium BC*, 122-128, ns 69-77, figs 9-11b.

281 TD 7656 from A/II-k/14-Nr 8. Mlinar, in *Scarabs of the Second Millennium BC*, 128, fig. 11b [16].

282 TD 7656 and TD 402 from A/II-m/11-Nr 6. Mlinar, in *Scarabs of the Second Millennium BC*, 128, figs 11a [1], 11b [16].

283 TD 7657 from A/II-k/14-Nr 8. Mlinar, in *Timelines* 2, 222-232, fig. 8.

284 Bietak, *BASOR* 281 (1991), 41; van den Brink, *Tombs and Burial Customs*, 42.

285 Müller, in *MBA in the Levant*, 277.

286 Pit n/18-Nr 1. Müller, in *MBA in the Levant*, 271-275.

287 Bietak, *BASOR* 281 (1991), 42-43; van den Brink, *Tombs and Burial Customs*, 7.

288 Bietak, *BASOR* 281 (1991), 43.

289 Forstner-Müller, *TeD* 16, 99.

290 Bietak, *BASOR* 281 (1991), 41-43.

291 Bietak, *BASOR* 281 (1991), 41-43; Forstner-Müller, *TeD* 16, 99.

292 Bietak, *BASOR* 281 (1991), 42.

293 Tombs A/II-k/14-Nr 3 and A/II-l/16-Nr 2. Bietak, *BASOR* 281 (1991), 42; Forstner-Müller, *TeD* 16, 245, 272, fig. 180.

294 Tombs A/II-k/17-Nr 30, A/II-l/14-Nr 4, A/II-l/16-Nr 2, A/II-n/15-Nr 1 and A/II-s/18-Nr 1. Forstner-Müller, *TeD* 16, 249, 251, 272, 282, 293.

295 Tombs A/II-o/14-Nr 46 and A/II-o/14-Nr 43, L393. Forstner-Müller, *TeD* 16, 244, 289, figs 179 [1/8911], 209 [26/8913B], 209 [27/8913D].

296 Tomb A/II-n/15. Forstner-Müller, *TeD* 16, 279-281, figs 202 [2/2185], 203a [5/2190].

297 Tombs A/II-l/16-Nr 2 and A/II-n/15. Forstner-Müller, *TeD* 16, 268, 278-279, figs 194a [1/2147, 2/2164, 3/2170, 4/2171], 202 [3/2186].

298 Tombs A/II-l/14-Nr 5 and A/II-n/15. Forstner-Müller, *TeD* 16, 252, 277-281, figs 189a [4/1356], 189a [5/1377], 201 [4/2174], 202 [4/2187], 203a [3/2193], 203a [4/2194].

299 Forstner-Müller, *TeD* 16, 100.

300 Bietak, *BASOR* 281 (1991), 43.

301 Bietak, *BASOR* 281 (1991), 43.

302 Forstner-Müller, in *Second Intermediate Period*, 129; Forstner-Müller, *TeD* 16, 99; Bietak, Forstner-Müller and Mlinar, in *Contributions*, 171-181.

303 Kopetzky notes that forms similar to those from the Southern Levant are rare, both in the ceramic corpus at Tell el-Dab'a and the site bearing most parallels, Jericho. Kopetzky, in *Bronze Age in the Lebanon*, 225.

304 Aston, *TeD* 12, 364-372; Kopetzky, in *Bronze Age in the Lebanon*, 196-198, figs 2-3.

305 Kopetzky, in *Bronze Age in the Lebanon*, 198-201, fig. 4 [1, 3].

306 Kopetzky, in *Bronze Age in the Lebanon*, 203, fig. 6 [2]; Merrillees, *Levant* 10 (1982), 78-80.

307 A fragment was also found at Tell el-Maskhuta. Aston, *TeD* 12, 224, 361, fig. 93 [h], pl. 266; Redmount, *On an Egyptian/Asiatic Frontier*, 810, fig. 134 [10-11]; Loud, *Megiddo* 2, pl. 38.10; Dever, *BASOR* 217 (1975), 33, fig. 3 [4].

308 Aston, *TeD* 12, 372; Bietak, *BASOR* 281 (1991), 43.

ceramics as well as housing and burial sites. This offers a likely motivation for the creation and development of distinct pottery styles, the rising number of intra-mural burials and the use of necropolis areas as habitation. It has been postulated that such changes are related to the formation of a Hyksos kingdom,[309] which is possible if one considers the increase in population numbers. That is, people may have settled in Area A/II if the Hyksos administration decreed a resettlement or created an attractive, economically lucrative and politically stable environment.

4.2.2.5 Area F/II

In recent years, excavations at Area F/II (see Figure 4.3) have revealed a grand complex orientated in the same manner as the late Hyksos Palaces F and G at 'Ezbet Helmi (N-S).[310] A stratigraphical assessment of the area has uncovered at least nine phases, the earliest of which includes remains of a late Middle Kingdom building complex (late Thirteenth Dynasty, Stratum e/2-1) as well as domestic structures and large households with courtyards and ovens (Stratum d).[311] Remains of the aforementioned grand complex are found atop one of these domestic structures and have been preliminarily dated to the Fifteenth Dynasty (between E/3 and D/3 of the site's general stratigraphy; see Figure 4.4).[312]

Stratum d: Late Thirteenth to early Fifteenth Dynasty

Three main zones beneath the complex are assigned to Stratum d. The first is Pit L928 with pottery vessels such as Syro-Palestinian store-jars and Marl C ceramics.[313] As the pit is similar to those found in the later Stratum c/2, a cultural continuum could be deduced throughout the occupation phases.[314] The second zone has been interpreted to be a bath with a pipe system (L1135) and the third a workshop (L1421).[315] The latter contained red clay, various fragments of Syro-Palestinian store-jars, bowls, cooking pots and Marl C vessels, as well as substantial charcoal remains indicating either the employment of or exposure to fire.[316] Further remnants of ivory inlays, obsidian and bronze fittings, as well as faience, calcite and jasper materials denote the area's use as a workshop.[317] One seal impression from the site features the hieroglyphs  *ḥḳꜣ n(.y) Rṯnw ꜥꜣ*[...] 'ruler of *Rṯnw*, *ꜥꜣ*[...]' between two rows of seated caprids.[318] The last three glyphs may belong to *ꜥꜣm*, perhaps part of the ruler's name.[319] The left half portrays a spiral design (guilloche?) and another row of caprids impressed upon unidentifiable hieroglyphs.[320] The presence of such an object combining both the Egyptian script and Near Eastern artistic elements indicates that relations between Tell el-Dab'a and *Rṯnw* were likely active during the beginning of the Fifteenth Dynasty.

Stratum c/3: Storage and workshop quarter,[321] late Thirteenth to early Fifteenth Dynasty

Northwest of the complex's forecourt are a number of pits disturbed by a later enclosure wall (see below). Yielding pottery, the pits have been theorised to be remnants of ritual banqueting practiced prior to the complex's construction. They are perhaps contemporaneous to a group of magazines uncovered north of the complex bearing traces of severe conflagration. Although unpublished, the excavator reports several prestigious items from one store-room, such as decorated knives, amphorae filled with minerals, an ivory-handled Hathor sistrum and a large collection of locally produced Middle Cypriote pottery. Based on this description, it is likely that the magazines belonged to a palatial or elite household, the stored objects being either items for export or objects imported from another, most probably Egyptian, site. Their proximity to the pits further supports a palatial function, perhaps one which continued in the following complex's administrative links.

Stratum c/2: Building S and Compounds G and A, early Fifteenth Dynasty

Compounds A and G feature rooms with attached magazines, the former housing a high number of imported Syro-Palestinian store-jars.[322] A vestibule positioned to its northeast contained the burial of a horse.[323] The compounds likely retained an administrative function linked with trade.[324]

Stratum c/2-1: Building B, Compound E, Courtyards D and C, mid-late Fifteenth Dynasty

North of the magazines of Compound A is a large rectangular and possibly columned hall.[325] A platform or 'throne' towards the middle of the back wall suggests

309 Bietak, *BASOR* 281 (1991), 43; Forstner-Müller, in *Second Intermediate Period*, 129; Bietak, Forstner-Müller and Mlinar, in *Contributions*, 171-181.
310 Bietak, Forstner-Müller and Herbich, in *Archaeology and Art* 1, 121; Bietak et al., *E&L* 22-23 (2012/2013), 17-53.
311 Bietak and Forstner-Müller, *E&L* 16 (2006), 66-68; Bietak and Forstner-Müller, *E&L* 19 (2009), 93; Forstner-Müller, et al., 'Report on the Excavations at Tell el-Dab'a 2011', 7, 12; Bietak et al., *E&L* 22-23 (2012/2013), 19, fig. 2..
312 Bietak and Forstner-Müller, *E&L* 19 (2009), 93; Bietak and Forstner-Müller, *E&L* 16 (2006), 66; Bietak et al., *E&L* 22-23 (2012/2013), 19, fig. 2.
313 Bietak and Forstner-Müller, *E&L* 19 (2009), 108, fig. 23.
314 Bietak and Forstner-Müller, *E&L* 19 (2009), 108.
315 Bietak and Forstner-Müller, *E&L* 19 (2009), 109, fig. 24.
316 Bietak and Forstner-Müller, *E&L* 19 (2009), 109, fig. 27; Bietak, in *Proceedings of the 6th International Congress* 2, 102-103.
317 Bietak, in *Proceedings of the 6th International Congress* 2, 102-103; Bietak and Forstner-Müller, *E&L* 19 (2009), 109-111; Bietak et al., *E&L* 22-23 (2012/2013), 32-33.
318 Bietak and Forstner-Müller, *E&L* 19 (2009), 112, fig. 30.
319 Perhaps the name is associated with that of the Fourteenth Dynasty king *ꜥꜣmw*. See Figure 1.2.
320 Cylinder seals from Byblos and Cyprus (but of Northern Levantine manufacture) feature a column with a guilloche near another with seated caprids (Collon, *First Impressions*, 52-53 [200, 202, 205]).
321 Personal communication with Irene Forstner-Müller; Forstner-Müller et al., 'Report on the Excavations at Tell el-Dab'a 2011', 7, 10-12; Bietak et al., *E&L* 22-23 (2012/2013), 32-38.
322 Bietak and Forstner-Müller, *E&L* 19 (2009), 97, fig. 5; Bietak et al., *E&L* 22-23 (2012/2013), fig. 3.
323 The vestibule was later cut into by an infant burial. Bietak and Forstner-Müller, *E&L* 19 (2009), 98-100, figs 7-8; Bietak, in *Proceedings of the 6th International Congress* 2, 100.
324 Bietak and Forstner-Müller, *E&L* 19 (2009), 93.
325 Forstner-Müller et al., 'Report on the Excavations at Tell el-Dab'a 2011', 8.

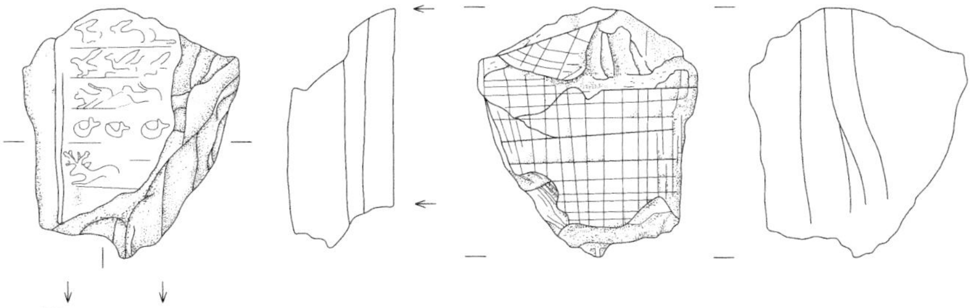

FIGURE 4.11. SEAL 9373, AREA F/II, STRATUM C/2-1, TELL EL-DAB'A. AFTER SARTORI, *E&L* 19 (2009), FIG. 13.

that it was for hosting visitors, supporting the proposed administrative or palatial nature of the complex.[326] Another four-pillared broad-room hall with an L-shaped annex was constructed along a new enclosure wall.[327] At the front of this wall were two pits with the remains of 14 severed right hands.[328] Two more pits within the four-columned hall contained a hand each.[329] The custom of severing hands is probably connected with the 'Gold of Honour' practice, where the hand of an enemy was presented in exchange for an award (gold) from an Egyptian ruler.[330] The discovery at F/II suggests (a) possible conflict in Dynasty 15; (b) an administration perhaps encouraging victorious conflicts; and (c) an administration utilising a probable Egyptian custom or a custom later adopted by the Egyptians.

Within Building B is a large courtyard with mudbrick benches along its southeast, northeast and northwest sides, as well as remnants of a sandbrick installation, possibly for storage, at its southwest.[331] At the centre of the southeast bench is a podium attached to the wall, perhaps an altar.[332] A staircase on the outside of the west wall leads to a tower which, together with the layout of the courtyard, finds close parallels with Ebla's near contemporary Palace Q.[333] The features within the courtyard also suggest that it was employed for cultic assemblies such as the *marzeah* ritual, an inference supported by the presence of a large pit (L81) thought to be a depository for remains of ritual meals.[334]

The pit was filled with approximately 1800 vessels, animal bones and a range of small objects such as beads, flints, scarabs and toggle-pins.[335] The ceramic material fits well within the period identified for E/1-D/3 and consists of both local and imported forms.[336] Among these are: cylindrical, globular, quadrilobal, piriform and biconical Tell el-Yahudiyah ware of local manufacture;[337] Marl C material possibly from the Memphis/Fayum region;[338] storage jars and lids from the Egyptian oases (Bahariyah or Khargeh);[339] White Pendant Line Style and White Painted Cypriote jugs;[340] Nubian wares;[341] and Syro-Palestinian store-jars probably imported from the Levantine coast.[342] Flint objects from L81[343] also show similarities to those from Tell el-Maskhuta,[344] Tell el-'Ajjul[345] and Tell 'Arqa[346] while beads parallel finds from Tell el-Maskhuta,[347] Tell el-Habwa I[348] and Tell el-'Ajjul.[349]

Recovered from L81 and other pits throughout the complex were 16 scarabs and 230 seal impressions.[350] Some seal impressions are inscribed with the names of Thirteenth Dynasty royals (Sobekhotep III, Noferhotep I and Sobekhotep IV)[351] and *ḥḳꜣ ḫꜣs.wt Ḫyꜣn* 'ruler of foreign lands, *Ḫyꜣn*'.[352] One seal, Nr 9373 (Figure 4.11), depicts at least five rows of animals (hares, lions, deer, etc.) in a style typical of MBA Old Babylonian and Syrian seal impressions from Kültepe, Acemhöyük, Byblos and Alalakh.[353] Creases on the seal's obverse mimic papyrus strands, indicating possibly written diplomatic correspondence.[354]

326 Bietak et al., *E&L* 22-23 (2012/2013), 30-31, fig. 3.
327 Forstner-Müller et al., 'Report on the Excavations at Tell el-Dab'a 2011', 9.
328 Forstner-Müller et al., 'Report on the Excavations at Tell el-Dab'a 2011', 9; Bietak et al., *E&L* 22-23 (2012/2013), 31-32, figs 10, 14a-c.
329 Forstner-Müller et al., 'Report on the Excavations at Tell el-Dab'a 2011', 9; Bietak et al., *E&L* 22-23 (2012/2013), 21-22.
330 Binder, *Gold of Honour*, 145-148; Bietak et al., *E&L* 22-23 (2012/2013), 32.
331 Bietak, in *Proceedings of the 6th International Congress* 2, 101.
332 Bietak et al., *E&L* 22-23 (2012/2013), 21-22.
333 The excavators also note close architectural similarities with earlier Mesopotamian palaces. Bietak et al., *E&L* 22-23 (2012/2013), 21-22, figs 3, 5-6.
334 Bietak, in *Proceedings of the 6th International Congress* 2, 103, fig. 13; Bietak et al., *E&L* 22-23 (2012/2013), 22.
335 Aston and Bader, *E&L* 19 (2009), 19-89.
336 Aston and Bader, *E&L* 19 (2009), 20.
337 Only one, 9012M, is imported. Aston and Bader, *E&L* 19 (2009), 39.
338 Aston and Bader, *E&L* 19 (2009), 40-61, figs 8-9.
339 Aston and Bader, *E&L* 19 (2009), 62-63.
340 Sherds are similar to White Painted B, White Painted Cross Line Style, White Painted Tangent, Wavy Line Style and White Painted Eyelet Style. Aston and Bader, *E&L* 19 (2009), 64.
341 Bourriau offers parallels with Nubian pottery from Diospolis Parva See Aston and Bader, *E&L* 19 (2009), 63-64; Forstner-Müller and Rose, in *Nubian Pottery*, 184, 201-210; Bietak, in *Proceedings of the 6th International Congress* 2, 101.
342 Aston and Bader, *E&L* 19 (2009), 64, n. 191, fig. 11.
343 Aston and Bader, *E&L* 19 (2009), 68.
344 Holladay, in *Hyksos*, 194, fig. 7 [7].
345 Petrie, Mackay and Murray, *Gaza* 5, pl. 21.
346 Thalmann, *Tell Arqa* 1, pls 136-142.
347 Holladay, in *Hyksos*, 197, fig. 7 [9].
348 Abd el-Maksoud, *Tell Heboua*, 260-261.
349 Petrie, *Gaza* 2, pl. 25.
350 Sartori, *E&L* 19 (2009), 281-292.
351 Sartori, *E&L* 19 (2009), 284, fig. 4.
352 Personal communication with Chiara Reali; Sartori, *E&L* 19 (2009), 284-288, figs 5-9.
353 Sartori, *E&L* 19 (2009), 288-289, n. 17, fig. 13.
354 Sartori, *E&L* 19 (2009), 289.

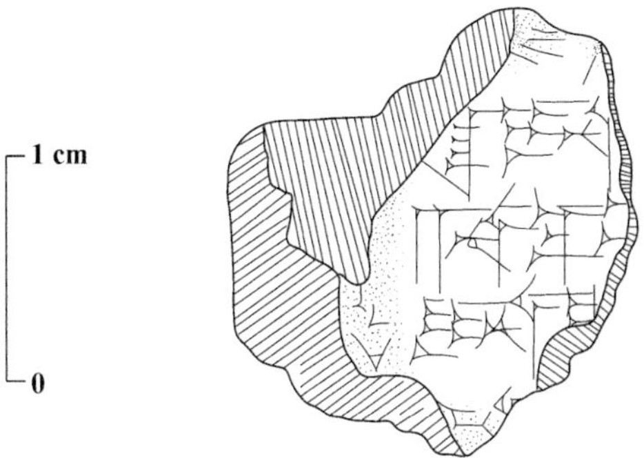

FIGURE 4.12. FRAGMENT WITH CUNEIFORM TEXT, AREA F/II, STRATUM C/2-1, TELL EL-DAB'A. AFTER BIETAK AND FORSTNER-MÜLLER, *E&L* 19 (2009), FIG. 22.

A fragment of a cuneiform tablet near L1045 supports such correspondence (Figure 4.12).[355] It was recovered from a filling with pottery of the mid-late Fifteenth Dynasty.[356] Although only a few Akkadian words remain, the style and orthography of the inscribed text has been ascribed to the last phase of the First Dynasty of Babylon, after Hammurabi's reign.[357] Thus, contact with Mesopotamia may have existed during Dynasty 15.

The remains from Stratum c/1 imply an administrative function for the complex at F/II. Trade with the Theban and Memphite districts, which is otherwise unattested in A/II and F/I strata of Dynasty 15, emphasises the structure's administrative, and perhaps even diplomatic, function which is likewise supported by imported Nubian, Cypriote and Levantine pottery. The occurrence of *Ḫy3n*'s seals signifies that this Hyksos ruler could have taken part in such trade relations. Furthermore, seal Nr 9373 and L1045's cuneiform tablet indicate the dynasty's attempts to develop relations with regions near and far.

4.2.2.6 Area A/IV

Area A/IV remains largely unpublished but has been identified as a sector for domestic housing.[358] The earliest levels have been assigned to Strata I-H of the site's general stratigraphy (see Figure 4.4), or the late Twelfth to early Thirteenth Dynasties, with remnants of simple rectangular structures with kilns and adjoined courtyards.[359]

Ceramics from these areas, specifically K4249 (a refuse in one of the courtyards) and K4236/4256 from a building in the north-northwest of A/IV, comprise 40% MBIIA and MBIIA-B shapes, 73% of which were imported.[360] The non-Egyptian shapes include red-burnished or painted bowls with incurved rims;[361] open bowls with everted rims akin to vessels from Tell Jerishe;[362] large globular bowls comparable to those from Shechem, Tell Jerishe and Megiddo;[363] globular burnished jars with parallels from MBIIA-B Lachish and Ruweise;[364] and Syro-Palestinian store-jars, some of which are of a fabric from Tell 'Arqa's 'Akkar plain.[365] Of the same fabric is a wheel-made cooking pot with a grooved, out-curved rim and grooved horizontal ridges along the body,[366] a form that is additionally attested at Tell 'Arqa.[367] Traces of burning on the vessel point to its use by individuals travelling or living at Tell el-Dab'a.[368] Therefore, the ceramic corpus from the settlement denotes the presence of a MBIIA-B culture at A/IV trading with both the Southern and Northern Levant, with a possible direct link with the area surrounding Tell 'Arqa.

Among the houses were tombs with mudbrick-lined chambers of various sizes dating from the mid-Thirteenth to early Fifteenth Dynasties (Stratum F-E/1 of the site's general stratigraphy; see Figure 4.4).[369] Reported finds include ceramics (e.g. incised piriform and ovoid Tell el-Yahudiyah ware, and burnished jugs), metallic items (e.g. a single-edged knife and a toggle-pin), seals and seal impressions (e.g. one of Amenemhat III),[370] meat offerings, as well as donkey burials in front of tombs' entrances.[371] With such elements, it is likely that Area A/IV housed the same Egyptian-Levantine hybrid culture observed in other areas at Tell el-Dab'a.

Two seal impressions worthy of note are Sealings 8314 (Figure 4.13) and 7669 (Figure 4.14).[372] Both were unearthed in later contexts, the first in Locus 62 and the second in A/IV-j/6,[373] yet both have been stylistically dated to the second half of Dynasty 13.[374] Sealing 8314 is a fragment of fine silt with impressions of four figures (Figure 4.13). The first to the right stands in a long robe

355 Bietak and Forstner-Müller, *E&L* 19 (2009), 108, figs 21-22. The surface filling between Late Period houses at Area A/II yielded another cuneiform seal impression, the text of which is typical of MBA Mesopotamia, signalling that its seal is likely of Mesopotamian origin. For more, see van Koppen and Lehmann, *E&L* 22-23 (2012/2013), 91-94.

356 Bietak et al., *E&L* 22-23 (2012/2013), 25, fig. 7.

357 Von Koppen and Radner, in Bietak and Forstner-Müller, *E&L* 19 (2009), 115-118.

358 Hein, 'Area A/IV'.

359 Hein, 'Area A/IV', fig. 2; Kopetzky, *AHL* 26-27 (2007/2008), 31, fig. 13.

360 Kopetzky, *AHL* 26-27 (2007/2008), 31-32, fig. 13.

361 Kopetzky, *AHL* 26-27 (2007/2008), 35, fig. 23 [27].

362 Kopetzky, *AHL* 26-27 (2007/2008), 35, fig. 16 [37]; Geva, *Tell Jerishe*, 32, fig. 28 [14].

363 Kopetzky, *AHL* 26-27 (2007/2008), 35, fig. 23 [30-31]; Cole, *Shechem* 1, 111, pl. 6 [e]; Geva, *Tell Jerishe*, 32, fig. 28 [19]; Loud, *Megiddo* 2, pl. 28 [2].

364 Kopetzky, *AHL* 26-27 (2007/2008), 35, figs 16 [31, 39], 18 [70-71], 24 [40]; Singer-Avitz, in *Lachish* 3, 917, fig. 16.9 [17]; Guigues, *BMB* 2 (1938), 37, fig. 57 [c].

365 Kopetzky, *AHL* 26-27 (2007/2008), 36-38, fig. 20 [99].

366 Kopetzky, *AHL* 26-27 (2007/2008), 38, fig. 25 [55], photo 1.

367 Kopetzky, *AHL* 26-27 (2007/2008), fig. 25; Thalmann, *Tell Arqa* 1, pl. 94 [11].

368 Kopetzky, *AHL* 26-27 (2007/2008), 38.

369 Hein, 'Area A/IV', fig. 2.

370 The inscribed prenomen, *Ny-m3ʿ.t-Rʿ*, may also be that of the Thirteenth Dynasty king Khendjer (*Ny-m3ʿ.t-n(.t)-Rʿ.w*). Hein, 'Area A/IV', fig. 17; von Beckerath, *Zweiten Zwischenzeit*, 49, 238-239.

371 Hein, 'Area A/IV', figs 3-18.

372 Hein, in *Timelines* 2, 135-148.

373 The contexts of the seals appear to be secondary, belonging to the earlier building levels of A/IV. Hein, in *Timelines* 2, 135-145, figs 2-3, 5, 8; Collon, in *Timelines* 2, 101.

374 Collon, in *Timelines* 2, 98, 101. A number of recently published sealings have been uncovered in Late Period or Ptolemaic strata from Tell el-Dab'a's Area A/I and A/II. Some are clearly of MBA Classical Syrian inspiration or origin. Another sealing from Area R/II was found in a late Thirteenth to early Fifteenth Dynasty context (probably Stratum E/2). Its origins, however, are uncertain. For more, see Collon, Lehmann and Müller, *E&L* 22-23 (2012/2013), 95-104.

FIGURE 4.13. SEAL 8314, AREA A/IV, TELL EL-DAB'A. AFTER HEIN, IN *TIMELINES*, FIG. 2.

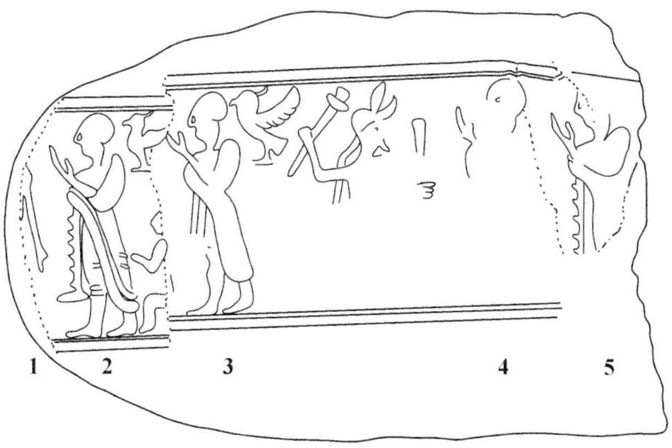

FIGURE 4.14. SEAL 7669, AREA A/IV, TELL EL-DAB'A. AFTER HEIN, IN *TIMELINES*, FIG. 3.

with a vertical fringe draped over the shoulders and left arm, and holds the end of a curved stick.[375] In a sub-register are three men with legs overlapping as if to mimic strides. They wear short kilts with horizontal ridges, much like the Asiatic men of Amenemhat's tomb (Nr 2) at Beni Hassan,[376] and raise their arms.[377] Due to the fragmentary nature of the impression, it remains uncertain whether all figures belong to the same seal or if they are Egyptian. The style of clothing, particularly for the larger figure, hints that they are Asiatics. Parallels from Kültepe, Tell Leilan, Mari and Ruweise indicate that the sealing derived from or was influenced by artistic traditions of the Northern Levant.[378]

The second sealing, 7669, is set upon a strip or tongue of clay used for administrative purposes.[379] It portrays four to five robed figures facing left and one facing right (Figure 4.14).[380] The latter wears a headdress with two short protrusions at the top (a horn and a spike), and a longer curl of hair down the back in a style typical of Northwest Syrian seals.[381] The right arm is raised and holds a mace whereas the left arm, mostly damaged, carries a staff-like object.[382] The posture indicates that the figure could be a deity, most probably a Levantine storm god who uniquely faces the right on seals.[383] The accompanying figures are depicted with long robes draped across the left shoulder with possible fringed hemlines.[384] Each raises one hand as if in praise. Other elements of the seal include two crested birds and parts of a smaller or squatting figure (a monkey?).[385] Again, such elements point to Northern Levantine art.[386]

375 Collon, in *Timelines* 2, 97, fig. 1.
376 See Chapter 4.4.1.2, Figure 4.50; Newberry, *Beni Hasan* 1, pl. 16.
377 Collon, in *Timelines* 2, 95.
378 Collon, in *Timelines* 2, 98.
379 Collon, in *Timelines* 2, 99; Collon, *First Impressions*, 119.
380 Collon, in *Timelines*, 99-100, fig. 2.
381 Collon refers to Otto's Northwestern Syrian Group 2c. Collon, in *Timelines*, 99-101, fig. 2; Otto, *Klassisch-Syrischen Glyptik* (Berlin, 1999), ns 159-160, 162.
382 This might be the shaft of an axe or a spear. Collon, in *Timelines*, 100.
383 Collon, in *Timelines* 2, 99.
384 Collon, in *Timelines* 2, fig. 2.
385 Collon, in *Timelines* 2, 100.
386 Collon, in *Timelines* 2, 100-101.

Although from later contexts, the two seals imply close artistic relations between Tell el-Dab'a and the Northern Levant. Further publication of A/IV would clarify the nature of such links; however this initial examination indicates that the area shared the same connections with the Levant as witnessed across Tell el-Dab'a.

4.2.2.7 Area A/V

Situated to the northeast of the main tell is A/V (see Figure 4.3), an area of domestic occupation dating from the early Fifteenth to the Eighteenth Dynasty (Strata E/1-D/2; see Figure 4.4).[387] The earliest stratum is represented by A/V-p/19 of a walled structure's southeast corner in which several pottery fragments of Egyptian and foreign shapes were uncovered.[388] Locally made MBIIB forms include dipper juglets;[389] red-polished bowls with incurved rims;[390] globular pots with a burnished zigzag pattern around the neck,[391] parallels of which may be found in Tell el-Maskhuta,[392] Shechem[393] and Tell 'Arqa;[394] and piriform Tell el-Yahudiyah jugs with horizontal combed grooves.[395] Imported wares, which amount to 4.6% of the total ceramic finds, consist of MBIIB vessels like Syro-Palestinian store-jars[396] and fragments of red-burnished monochrome jugs.[397] Cypriote White Painted V sherds were also uncovered.[398] The variety of wares stresses the hybrid character of A/V's settlement. Its occupational context suggests that the inhabitants were familiar with foreign materials and technology, pointing to a cultural continuance with other areas at Tell el-Dab'a.

387 Hein and Jánosi, *TeD* 11, 27-28.
388 Hein and Jánosi, *TeD* 11, 28-35, figs 3-7.
389 Kopetzky, in *TeD* 11, 251-252, fig. 178.
390 Kopetzky, in *TeD* 11, 251, figs 165, 178.
391 Kopetzky, in *TeD* 11, 251, fig. 178.
392 Redmount, *On an Egyptian/Asiatic Frontier*, 809, figs 133 [4-7].
393 Cole, *Shechem* 1, 127, pl. 14 [h-i].
394 Thalmann, *Tell Arqa* 1, pl. M05 [6].
395 Hein and Jánosi, *TeD* 11, 29-31, figs 4 [12, 15].
396 Kopetzky, in *TeD* 11, 254, fig. 182.
397 Kopetzky, in *TeD* 11, 254, fig. 182.
398 Kopetzky, in *TeD* 11, 255, fig. 183.

4.2.2.8 Scientific analysis of characteristic non-Egyptian ceramics

Two main scientific analyses on Tell el-Dab'a's Levantine ceramics have been carried out. The first examined the chemical composition of pottery utilising the Neutron Activation Analysis (NAA) process,[399] and the second probed petrographic thin sections.[400] Both assessed specimens from the Twelfth to the end of the Fifteenth Dynasties, mainly from Area A/II (Strata H-D/3) and F/I (Strata d/2-a/2) with a few samples from 'Ezbet Rushdi, but both arrived at opposing conclusions. McGovern's NAA study concluded that the majority of vessels were imported from southern Palestine, particularly the region surrounding Tell el-'Ajjul and Ashkelon.[401] Conversely, Cohen-Weinberger and Goren's petrographic analysis pointed to more varied sources for the vessels' manufacture with most specimens deriving from the coast of the Northern Levant.[402] Methodological errors in the NAA study, such as the reliance on a limited and problematic database, draw much doubt on its results.[403] Additionally, McGovern's association of a vessel's place of manufacture with ethnicity[404] is not explained or substantiated by the analysis. As such, his conclusions do not securely demonstrate trade or political connections between the people of Tell el-Dab'a and other foreign entities.

The petrographic analysis concluded that over 60% of vessels were imported from the Northern Levant across the late Twelfth to Fifteenth Dynasties.[405] 11 fabric groups were identified from over 200 petrographic sections and assigned to various areas in the Levant (Figures 4.15-16), including the northwestern Syrian coast (Groups A and E), the Lebanese coast (Groups B, C, D and E), the northern Israeli coast (Group B), Mount Carmel (Group F), the central coast of Israel (Group G), the Upper Shephelah, the Judean or Samarian Hills (Groups H, I and J) and the Negev Region (Group K).[406]

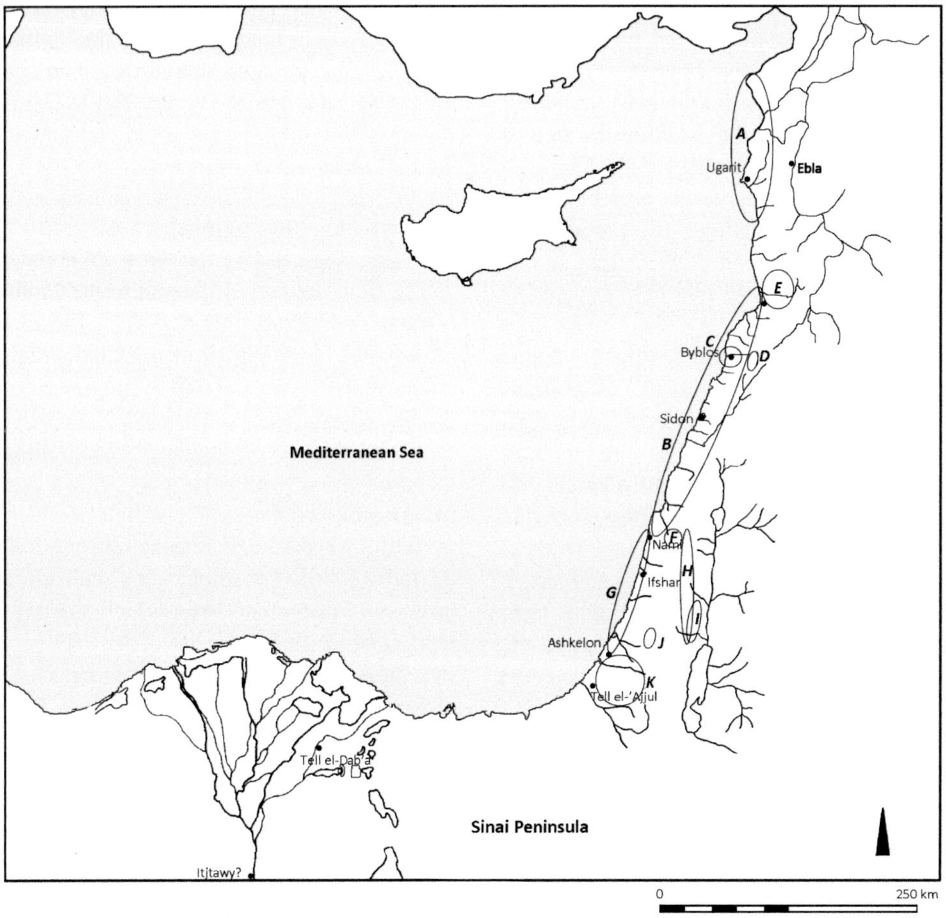

Figure 4.15. Geographical designates of petrographic groups A-K of imported vessels from Tell el-Dab'a. After Cohen-Weinberger and Goren, *E&L* 14 (2004), fig. 2.

399 McGovern, *Foreign Relations of the Hyksos*.

400 Cohen-Weinberger and Goren, *E&L* 14 (2004), 69-100.

401 McGovern, *Foreign Relations of the Hyksos*, 70-83.

402 Cohen-Weinberger and Goren, *E&L* 14 (2004), 80-85, figs 2-3, tables 1-2.

403 For more on the inherent problems in the NAA study, see Goren, *BiOr* 60/1-2 (2003), 105-109; Aston, *JEA* 90 (2004), 233-237; Ownby, *Canaanite Jars from Memphis* 8-9, 179.

404 McGovern, *Foreign Relations of the Hyksos*, 4, 80-83.

405 Cohen-Weinberger and Goren, *E&L* 14 (2004), 80-84, fig. 2.

406 Cohen-Weinberger and Goren, *E&L* 14 (2004), 71-80, fig. 1, table 2.

DYNASTY	PHASE	GROUP															
		A1	A2	B1	B2	B3	C	D	E	F	G	H	I	J	K	?	TOTAL
12	e-d	-	1	-	-	2	-	-	-	-	-	-	-	-	2	-	5
	H, d/2-e	-	-	-	-	2	-	-	1	-	-	-	-	-	-	10	13
	Sub-Total	**-**	**1**	**-**	**-**	**4**	**-**	**-**	**1**	**-**	**-**	**-**	**-**	**-**	**2**	**10**	**18**
13	G/4, d/2-d/1	3	1	6	21	20	2	19	7	5	7	-	-	-	5	1	97
	G, c	-	1	-	2	3	-	4	-	2	3	-	-	-	4	-	19
	Sub-Total	**3**	**2**	**6**	**23**	**23**	**2**	**23**	**7**	**7**	**10**	**-**	**-**	**-**	**9**	**1**	**116**
14	G-F, c-b/3	-	-	-	6	2	-	4	1	-	-	-	-	-	3	-	16
	F-E/3, b/3-b/2	-	2	-	3	1	-	-	1	2	1	1	-	-	5	2	18
	E/3, b/2	1	-	-	6	3	-	5	1	-	2	-	1	-	3	2	24
	Sub-Total	**1**	**2**	**-**	**15**	**6**	**-**	**9**	**3**	**2**	**3**	**1**	**1**	**-**	**11**	**4**	**58**
15	E/2-E/1, b/1	-	1	2	1	4	-	1	1	-	1	-	-	1	1	-	13
	E/1, b/1-a/2	-	-	1	2	2	-	1	-	-	1	-	-	1	2	-	10
	E/1-D/3, a/2	-	1	-	2	-	-	2	1	-	-	1	-	-	-	-	7
	D/3	1	1	-	4	2	-	-	1	1	2	-	1	-	-	1	14
	D/3-D/2	2	-	-	3	4	-	-	-	-	-	-	-	-	-	1	10
	Sub-Total	**3**	**3**	**3**	**12**	**12**	**-**	**4**	**3**	**1**	**4**	**1**	**1**	**2**	**3**	**2**	**54**
	TOTAL	**7**	**8**	**9**	**50**	**45**	**2**	**36**	**14**	**10**	**17**	**2**	**2**	**2**	**25**	**17**	**246**

FIGURE 4.16. NUMBER OF SAMPLES ANALYSED FROM PETROGRAPHIC GROUPS A-K OF IMPORTED VESSELS FROM TELL EL-DAB'A ACCORDING TO THE SITE'S STRATIGRAPHY (SEE FIGURE 4.4). AFTER COHEN-WEINBERGER AND GOREN, *E&L* 14 (2004), TABLES 1-2.

Notes: Samples belonging to two or more petrographic groups are not included. Vessels of undetermined stratigraphy are also not included.

A: Northern Syrian coast
B: Lebanese or northernmost Israeli coast
C: Area of Byblos, Lebanon
D: East coast between Beirut and Byblos, Lebanon
E: 'Akkar plain, Lebanon
F: Carmel region, Israel
G: Central coast between Ashdod and Carmel, Israel
H: Mediterranean mountainous region, Levant
I: Judea or Samaria
J: Shephelah region, Israel
K: Negev coastal plain, southern Shephelah
?: Unknown

As shown in Figure 4.16, Group B was identified in high quantities for vessels dating from Dynasties 12-15, thereby indicating the popular use and trade of vessels from this area at Tell el-Dab'a. Group D was common in the mid-Thirteenth Dynasty while vessels belonging to Groups A, C and H-J were rare. This suggests that maritime trade between Tell el-Dab'a and the Levantine coast, particularly along the coast of the 'Akkar Plain and Tyre, was very active in the Middle Kingdom and Second Intermediate Period.

As most specimens are derived from Dynasty 13 levels, no comment can be made on shifts in trading activity from Dynasties 12-15, except that certain groups are utilised in the Thirteenth Dynasty (Group C) or after the Fourteenth Dynasty (Groups H-J), indicating possibly new sources for ceramic manufacture and trade. If the samples are considered representative of the ceramic repertoire across the site and its stratigraphy, then figures reveal a slight decrease in imports from the Northern Levantine Groups A-E in the Fourteenth Dynasty (from 76.7% to 62%) and an increase in imports from the Southern Levantine Group K (from 7.8% to 19%). The data for the Fifteenth Dynasty, however, suggests a return to the observed numbers of the Thirteenth Dynasty with 74% of imports identified as Northern Levantine and 5.5% as of a Group K fabric. Although these results may be used to indicate political changes during the Fourteenth Dynasty, they cannot be used as a definite reflection of the situation across the site until an equal number of petrographic sections are examined from the different strata. Nonetheless, the results point to ongoing trade with particular regions before and during Hyksos rule, emphasising the continuance of foreign relations, and perhaps policies, with Levantine MBA cities.

As for expressions of ethnicity, the petrographic sections of cooking pots may shed light on the ethnic identity of people living at Tell el-Dab'a, or their culinary preferences. Three specimens were examined from F/I d/2 (late Twelfth Dynasty), A/II F (mid-Thirteenth/Fourteenth Dynasty) and E/I (Fifteenth Dynasty).[407] Accordingly, those derived from Groups F, E and J,[408] indicating the presence of individuals at Tell el-Dab'a who used wares from both the Northern and Southern Levant for their cooking requirements.

407 Cohen-Weinberger and Goren, *E&L* 14 (2004), tables 1b [21], 1d [28], 1e [17].
408 Cohen-Weinberger and Goren, *E&L* 14 (2004).

4.2.2.9 Anthropological analysis of skeletal remains

Results of an analysis of 257 skeletal remains from burials of A/II included information regarding mortality, life expectancy, gender, craniometry and osteometry.[409] Approximately half of the examined remains were of infants and neonates, leading the anthropologists to infer a high mortality rate for newborns (50%) and sub-adults (49.4%).[410] Of the remaining half, 71 burials were ascribed to be of females and 49 of males, reflecting a greater ratio of females to males at A/II.[411] As for the health of these individuals, an examination of pathological changes indicates a high rate of deficiency caused by either disease (infectious or parasitic) or poor nutrition,[412] supporting the above hypothesis that A/II featured the burials of a more common rather than elite population.

The craniometric, odontoscopic and osteometric results revealed close similarities between the A/II specimens and those from the region of the Near East and Europe.[413] These were based only on 35 sets of measurements out of the 257 samples due to the remaining sets' poor state of preservation.[414] The 35 stemmed from Strata G-D/3, providing a good sampling of A/II's population. When compared to the craniometry of other populations, the cranial measurements of primarily males at A/II reflected close affinities with the so-called 'Phoenician' group of samples from North Africa's Carthage, Algeria and Tunisia, and the Northern Levant's Kamid el-Loz.[415] This has led to suggestions that males migrated from the Levant and then married local women at Tell el-Dab'a.[416]

Although possible, such a scenario cannot be substantiated by the craniometric results alone. Firstly, the craniometric samples from surrounding regions are not from contemporary contexts, with those from North Africa and Kamid el-Loz stemming from the Iron Age.[417] Secondly, greater sampling is needed from the Delta as well as other areas of the Levant. Thirdly, the determination of ancestry based on craniometry is not an exact science but one which has been disputed in several studies.[418] Therefore, the results of the craniometric analysis cannot be used here as evidence for the origins of A/II's population.

4.2.2.10 Significance of Tell el-Dab'a

The combined evidence from Tell el-Dab'a reflects a growing community with shared Egyptian and Levantine elements across the domestic, architectural, religious and cultic spheres. From the Eleventh Dynasty, the first signs of non-Egyptian elements occur at F/I with sherds of holemouth cooking pots uncovered at a planned Egyptian settlement. Despite F/I's resettlement during the late Twelfth Dynasty, temple and tomb architecture across Tell el-Dab'a remained Egyptian. However, finds within these structures indicate a growing heterogeneity at the site. Syro-Palestinian store-jars, Levantine Painted Wares and cooking pots from 'Ezbet Rushdi's temple were predominantly derived from the Northern Levant, particularly Byblos, much like the ceramic repertoire from settlements at F/I, A/II and A/IV with the latter featuring approximately 20% more MBA pottery than F/I. Additionally, the funerary kit of burials at F/I and A/II was largely influenced by Levantine customs with the deposition of weaponry, silver jewellery and animal offerings of caprids and equids either within or before the tombs. Interestingly, a greater percentage of MBA pottery bearing influences from the Northern Levant has been uncovered in burials from A/II (56%) than F/I (20%) with objects from F/I burials suggesting that they belonged to a higher echelon, although tomb robbing may have distorted the data. If the elite were buried at F/I and the general populace was interred at A/II, the mostly Egyptian ceramic corpus at F/I tombs can be explained by greater Egyptian influences on the elite. Therefore, the elite of the late Twelfth Dynasty may have been acculturated Levantines and/or Egyptians influenced by Levantine customs. Both inferences are possible, reflecting rulers of a heterogeneous Egyptian-Levantine populace at A/II trading mostly with cities of the Northern Levantine coast. Houses containing Egyptian and Levantine features at F/I also support this heterogeneous character of the population.

Such a proposition is promising when evidence from the first half of Dynasty 13 is examined. The construction of an Egyptian-style administrative complex at F/I with tombs of, presumably, its officials, denotes Tell el-Dab'a's rising significance in the Delta, perhaps replacing Tell Basta's mayoral seat of power. Continued trade with the Northern Levant is evident alongside added artistic inspirations on, for example, the statue uncovered in the complex's courtyard and the cylinder seal's possible depiction of Baal. The prosperity of the site was short-lived as F/I's complex was suddenly abandoned, suggesting a possible political intermission. A settlement developed shortly after with graves displaying greater trade relations with the Levant and more noticeable influences from the Southern Levant. Locally and imported MBA forms in the ceramic corpus increased to 40%, signifying heightened trade, greater demand or a rise in population numbers. A possible antagonism may have existed over F/I's former ruler(s) with the deliberate smashing of its complex's hybridised statue. Additionally, a high mortality rate is witnessed by

409 Winkler and Wilfing, *TeD* 6.
410 Winkler and Wilfing, *TeD* 6, 77-78, 140, tables 11-12.
411 Winkler and Wilfing, *TeD* 6.
412 Winkler and Wilfing, *TeD* 6, 122-137, 140.
413 Winkler and Wilfing, *TeD* 6, 90-120.
414 Winkler and Wilfing, *TeD* 6, 90-120, appendix 1.
415 Winkler and Wilfing, *TeD* 6, 90-98, 120.
416 Bietak, *Avaris*, 36.
417 Winkler and Wilfing, *TeD* 6, table 25.
418 Bader, in *Egypt and the Near East*, 66; Collard and Wood, *Proceedings of the National Academy of Sciences of the United States of America* 97 (2000), 5003-5006; Strauss and Hubbe, *Human Biology* 82/3 (2010), 315-330. For a different view, see Mays, in *Human Osteology*, 277-288.

the shallow graves of F/I and A/II, possibly connected to conflict, disease and/or the influx of people.

The second half of the Thirteenth Dynasty, or the Fourteenth Dynasty as some posit, features F/I's continued settlement but with greater social differentiation. Major changes occur at A/II with a new settlement alongside a sacred precinct of Egyptian chapels, the Levantine-inspired Temple III and new burial features. The phenomenon of attendant burials is observed at F/I and A/II, representing, at the very least, a status marker of the affluential elite. Officials continued their involvement in trade as apparent from the finds of F/II's workshop and A/IV's seal impressions. Links with the Northern Levantine coast persisted but can, for the first time, be definitively associated with more than trade relations as reflected by, for instance, the scimitar of Tomb A/II-p/14-Nr 18, a cultic pit with human and animal remains, and the architecture of Temple III. Thus, it is possible to deduce that some rulers of Tell el-Dab'a belonged to a Northern Levantine ethnic group. The inhabitants of the site are likely to have been of a more heterogeneous or creole character, originating from various areas across the Levant and Egypt as evident by ceramic forms and scarabs uncovered at the settlements of F/I, A/II and A/IV.

The differences between the first and second halves of the Thirteenth Dynasty, featuring the above-mentioned high mortality rate and the abandonment of F/I's administration, indicate a possible political turnover after which an increased representation of foreign culture and religion is apparent. It is important to note that such a transition most likely affected the ruling echelon and not the general populace who seemingly continued to reside in the same type of settlement structures, expressing the same material culture as the previous phase. An influx of people from surrounding regions is, however, possible. The rulers, on the other hand, evidently had a newly enforced power to instigate and manage the construction of such public works as those of the sacred precinct, which are not only absent at such scales at Tell el-Dab'a in previous phases, but which could have also hypothetically legitimised the new regime's power and authority over an Egyptian-Levantine populace.

From the late Thirteenth to early Fifteenth Dynasties, continued developments in trade relations, administration and cultic practices are evident. A settlement developed in R/III and new temples were constructed at F/I and A/II, the latter paralleling Southern Levantine architecture. Rituals connected to these temples seem to be of non-Egyptian, possibly Northern Levantine, origins, such as the practice of cultic meals, the sacrifice of donkeys and pigs, and the use of libation pipes. The transference of ritual practices to the administrative sphere is inferred by pits filled with remnants of so-called 'ritual banqueting' near the forecourt of F/II's complex. Evidence for trading relations with Memphis/Fayum, Nubia, Cyprus and the Northern and Southern Levant can also be found. Worthy of note is the lack of direct evidence for a possible invasion or conflict, for which the only indication is circumstantial and can be found in the conflagration of F/II's magazines.

The first half of Dynasty 15 can be described as a continuation of the previous phase but with increases in burials, local ceramic production and, possibly, housing. Such data infers a rise in population which, in itself, would point to the site's growing prosperity. This may also be deduced from Temple III's renovation and the first signs of cultic rituals around its altar. In turn, the heightened prosperity signifies an efficient administration able to manage and sustain stability, consequently attracting more people into Tell el-Dab'a. The site from which the administration decreed its schemes was possibly located at the complex of F/II. Here, items such as Memphite, Cypriote, Levantine and Nubian pottery, Near-Eastern style seal impressions and an Akkadian cuneiform tablet, signify the promotion of trade relations with Tell el-Dab'a's neighbours who were possibly greeted at the complex's pillared halls. Conversely, the development and popularity of the local ceramic industry hint at further regionalisation or 'Nilotisation'.[419] The practice of ritual banqueting in administrative areas also continued, but with the added custom of burying severed hands, a tantalising hint of conflict in Dynasty 15 otherwise absent from the archaeological record at Tell el-Dab'a.

Hence, the data from Tell el-Dab'a reflects the growth of a trading hub initially controlled by the Middle Kingdom Memphite administration. Slowly, the site grew in prosperity under local officials of possible Northern Levantine ethnicity. During the second half of the Thirteenth Dynasty, a marked change occurred, possibly instigated by a political turnover, as foreign cultic rituals influenced by those of the Northern Levant became more pronounced. Tell el-Dab'a continued to flourish through to the Fifteenth Dynasty with increased contact with the Southern Levant and greater trade with Nubia and Cyprus, when complete independence from the Memphite Residence evidently secured the site's position as a major trading centre in the Mediterranean.

4.2.3 *Farasha, Tell / Maghud, Tell el-*

Lat.Lon. 30°41'N 31°43'E

Ref. Yacoub, *ASAE* 65 (1983), 175-176.

Chron. Second Intermediate Period

Tell Farasha is located between Tell Basta and Tell el-Dab'a. Excavations in 1972 uncovered 16 graves assigned to the Second Intermediate Period.[420] The burials have not been published in full, but a short report notes their similarity in architecture and funerary equipment to tombs at Tell el-Dab'a.[421]

419 Bietak, in *Second Intermediate Period*, 152; Bietak, Forstner-Müller and Mlinar, in *Contributions*, 171-181.
420 Yacoub, *ASAE* 65 (1983), 175-176.
421 Yacoub, *ASAE* 65 (1983), 175-176.

Some were rectangular graves with mudbrick walls and vaulted roofs.[422] Skeletons within were semi-contracted.[423] Burial goods included animal remains, scarabs, bronze weapons, bronze earrings and Tell el-Yahudiyah ware.[424] Based on the publication of the latter, a few may be identified as Piriform 2a[425] and small globular vessels[426] with parallels from Tell el-Dab'a E/1-D/2.[427] Other biconical and piriform shapes are also identified.[428] Therefore, the vessels assign the tombs to the Fifteenth Dynasty. Until all material is published, it is only possible to stipulate that the site may have had some access to Levantine(-influenced) commodities.

4.2.4 *Habwa I, Tell el- (Tjaru)*

Lat.Lon. 30°54'N 32°17'E

Refs Abd el-Maksoud, *ASAE* 69 (1983), 1-3; Seiler, *CCE* 5 (1997), 23-30; Abd el-Maksoud, *Tell Heboua;* Maksoud and Valbelle, *RdE* 56 (2005), 1-44.

Chron. Late Thirteenth to Fifteenth Dynasty, Second Intermediate Period

Tell el-Habwa I is positioned near a Nile distributary at the entrance of the North Sinai. The tell's strategic location and massive New Kingdom fortifications have recently led scholars to link it with Tjaru, the first pit-stop on the Ways-of-Horus.[429] Such a designation points to Tell el-Habwa's function as a merging point on the 'highway' to the Southern Levant.[430]

Abd el-Maksoud classifies the site's stratigraphy into five levels for Areas A and B and four levels for Area C, with all generally ranging from the Middle Kingdom to the Graeco-Roman period.[431] Pertinent to this study are Levels 4b, 4c, 5a and 5b (Areas A and B) of the Middle Kingdom and the first half of the Second Intermediate Period.

4.2.4.1 *Area B, Level 5b*

The level is mostly unexcavated, but Abd el-Maksoud records the discovery of a few Middle Kingdom items from Area B, including:[432] an incomplete alabaster statuette of a seated man;[433] a seal with the name of Senwosret II;[434] a *bekhen* vase with Senwosret I's Horus name;[435] and three fragments of an inscribed left door jamb. The latter were discovered scattered in an earlier layer of debris from Room C, Building I, and damaged by fire.[436] Reconstructed as one column, they read:[437]

1. 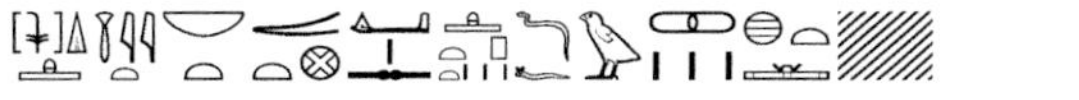
ḥtp di [nsw.t] W3ḏ.yt nb.t Im.t ḏi=s ḥtp.wt ḏf3.w iḫ.t [nb.t nfr.t]
An offering which the [king] gives and Wadjet, lady of Imet, that she may provide [every good] thing

2. 
[..t] mw... nṯr.w [3...]
[...] the gods [...]

3. 
[...] *n ir.y-pʿ.t ḥ3.ty-ʿ [ḫtm.ty bi.ty smr] wʿ.ty im.y-r3 ḫtm.t ʿpr-Bʿ3r n=i mry W3ḏ.yt*
[..] of the nobleman, count, seal-bearer of the king of Lower Egypt,[438] sole companion,[439] overseer of the treasury,[440] *ʿpr-Bʿ3r*,[441] to me, beloved of Wadjet.

The name, *ʿpr-Bʿ3r*, follows the *ʿpr*-DN pattern, where DN is typically a Levantine Deity's Name, in this case Baal. The spelling  *Bʿ3r* for Baal's name is otherwise unattested for the Middle Kingdom, but  *Bʿ3* is found on two Middle Kingdom unprovenanced scarabs, supporting Baal's worship in Egypt before Hyksos rule.[442] The acquisition of the sequential titles 'seal-bearer of the king of Lower Egypt, sole companion, overseer of the treasury' not only suggests a late Middle Kingdom date,[443] but also highlights that this Levantine was an individual of high status. Being 'beloved of Wadjet', an Egyptian god, additionally implies his assumption of Egyptian cultural traits.

Some have connected *ʿpr-Bʿ3r* with another from Apophis's reign.[444] The latter is mentioned on an offering stand in the Berlin Museum (22487) only as *im.y-r3 ḫtm.t ʿpr ...*

422 Yacoub, *ASAE* 65 (1983), 175-176, pls 1-3.

423 Yacoub, *ASAE* 65 (1983), 175-176, pls 1-2.

424 Yacoub, *ASAE* 65 (1983), 175-176, pls 4-6.

425 Aston and Bietak's Late Egyptian Group L.I.3. Yacoub, *ASAE* 65 (1983), pls 4-5 [8, 11]; Aston and Bietak, *TeD* 8, 206-211, figs 141, 147.

426 Aston and Bietak's Late Egyptian Group L.9 or Handmade Globular N.2 or N.3. Yacoub, *ASAE* 65 (1983), pls 4-5 [9, 17]; Aston and Bietak, *TeD* 8, 254-257, 302-311, figs 189, 227, 230.

427 Aston and Bietak, *TeD* 8, 206-211, 254-257, 553-556, fig. 253.

428 Yacoub, *ASAE* 65 (1983), pls 4-5.

429 See, for instance, Abd el-Maksoud, in *Delta in Pharaonic Times*, 181-184; Morris, *Architecture of Imperialism*, 46-50; Hoffmeier, in *Egypt, Israel, and the Ancient Mediterranean World*, 130-131.

430 Abd el-Maksoud, *Tell el-Heboua*, 30-33.

431 So far, the earliest excavated level at Area C dates to the transitional period between the Second Intermediate Period and the New Kingdom (Level 3). Abd el-Maksoud, *Tell el-Heboua*, 35-40.

432 Abd el-Maksoud, *Tell el-Heboua*, 39. Hoffmeier notes on-site observations of unpublished sherds possibly belonging to the Twelfth Dynasty (*BASOR* 343 [2006], 9, n. 23).

433 Item 497 from Area B/3. Abd el-Maksoud, *Tell el-Heboua*, 268, fig. 50.

434 Item 447 from Area B/3. Abd el-Maksoud, *Tell el-Heboua*, 255-259, fig. 44. As the seal was found amongst items of the late Second Intermediate Period, it is very possible that it could have been retrieved from an earlier level or a nearby site.

435 Abd el-Maksoud and Valbelle, *RdE* 56 (2005), 4, fig. 2.

436 Abd el-Maksoud, *Tell el-Heboua*, 271.

437 Transcription follows Abd el-Maksoud, *Tell el-Heboua*, 271, pl. 1. Transliteration and translation are by the author.

438 Ward, *Index*, 104-105 [864], 170 [1472].

439 Ward, *Index*, 151 [1299].

440 Quirke identifies the sequence 'seal-bearer of the king, sole companion and overseer of the treasury' to be of more 'national' significance in the administration (Quirke, *Title and Bureaux*, 48-49). For more, see Ward, *Index*, 171 [1476].

441 For more on this name form, see Ward, *OLP* 6/7 (1976), 593; Schneider, *UF* 19 (1987), 258; Schneider, *AsPN*, 66-69; Schneider, *Ausländer in Ägypten* 2, 141-142 and references.

442 Schneider, *Ausländer in Ägypten* 2, 142; Martin, *Egyptian Administrative and Private-Name Seals*, 30 [319-320], pl. 10 [14].

443 Quirke, *Titles and Bureaux*, 49.

444 Grajetzki, *Two Treasurers*, 37-38; Abd el-Maksoud and Valbelle, *RdE* 56 (2005), 11.

'overseer of the treasury, *ꜥpr...*'.[445] Due to the incomplete name[446] and lack of any similarities in titles save for one, the association of the two remains questionable. Furthermore, Abd el-Maksoud assigns the lintel fragments to Level 5b which, according to the site's stratigraphy, dates to the Middle Kingdom.[447] So, *ꜥpr-Bꜥꜣr* is considered here as evidence for the Thirteenth Dynasty presence of elite Asiatics at Tell el-Habwa.

4.2.4.2 Areas A and B, Level 5a

Excavations revealed a number of inscriptions bearing the name Nehsy.[448] Their discovery connotes the site's possible occupation during Dynasty 14.[449] Another item which may date to either this level or the following (Level 4c) is a seated statue,[450] the base of which is inscribed with  *knb.ty n Ṯꜣrw Stẖ-m-wsḫ.t wḥm ꜥnḫ* 'district councillor of Tjaru,[451] Setekhemwesekhet, repeating life'. The councillor's name may indicate reverence to Seth.

4.2.4.3 Area B, Level 4c

Level 4c is documented as the first stratum with substantial early Second Intermediate Period remains.[452] As it only has thus far been identified from one survey, the repertoire of finds is minor, but includes a varied ceramic assemblage of Egyptian and Levantine-influenced pottery.[453] The latter includes piriform and cylindrical Tell el-Yahudiyah ware manufactured from Nile silt (Figure 4.17).[454] One Piriform 2a juglet matches Levantine wares of the MBIIA-B period that are common at Tell el-Dab'a's Strata E/2-E/1 (early half of Dynasty 15).[455] The excavation report does not specify other finds belonging to this level.

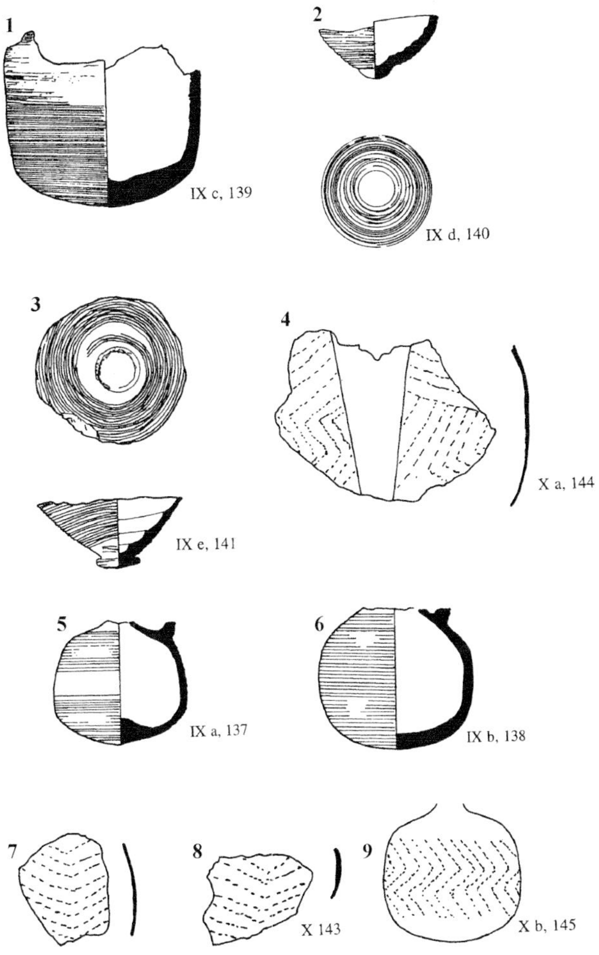

FIGURE 4.17. SELECTED CERAMICS, TELL EL-HABWA I (NOT TO SCALE). AFTER MAKSOUD, *TELL EL-HEBOUA*, FIGS 16-17.

4.2.4.4 Area B, Level 4b

Level 4b is marked by the construction of new granaries and houses while existing ones continued in use.[456] Houses are generally rectangular and constructed out of mudbrick with either two rooms (MS.II, MS.III, MS.IV and MS.V) or three (MS.I), and are mostly located in Area B's western sector (Figure 4.18).[457] MS.V is situated between this settlement area and the granaries, with its entrance positioned at the southern wall of GR.I, one of the largest mudbrick granaries of Level 4b.[458] Six silos were identified in GR.I with six inhumations on the granary floor (T.106, T.109, T.110, T.112, T.113 and T.114) and three tombs within silos (T.107 and T.108 in SI.2; T.111 in SI.6).[459] All but three (T.106, T.107 and T.112) can be ascribed to Level 4b.[460] Bodies were mostly

---

445 The complete inscription reads [...] *Ỉpepi di ꜥnḫ sn.t nsw.t Tny im.y-rꜣ ḫtm.t ꜥpr*[...] '[...] Apophis, may he give/be given life, king's sister, Tany, overseer of the treasury *ꜥpr*[...]'. The offering stand is originally from the Twelfth Dynasty. Helck, *Historisch-biographische Texte*, 57 [82]; Simpson, *CdE* 34 (1959), 237.

446 Krauss's line drawing of the inscription includes the beginning of a damaged glyph following *ꜥpr* (Krauss, *Orientalia* 62/2 [1993], 27-28, pl. 2). Krauss proposes that it is a *wr* sign whereas Ryholt indicates that it could be an *r* for *ꜥpr-r*[*šp*] or a *d* for *ꜥpr-d*[*d*] (Ryholt, *Political Situation*, 129-130). Schneider offers *ir* as another possibility for *ꜥpr-ir* (Schneider, *Ausländer in Ägypten* 2, 141-142). On the other hand, Goedicke writes that *ꜥpr* might signal the beginning of a title (Goedicke, *JSSEA* 7/4 [1977], 12, n. 6). In all cases, based on the size and shape of the damaged hieroglyph, the sign could not represent glyphs for Baal's name. Thus, it is most likely that the two inscriptions did not belong to the same treasurer.

447 Abd el-Maksoud, *Tell el-Heboua*, 39.

448 Abd el-Maksoud, *Tell el-Heboua*, 39, 271-273; Abd el-Maksoud, *ASAE* 69 (1983), figs 1-2; Abd el-Maksoud and Valbelle, *RdE* 56 (2005), 5-10, figs 3-4, 6.

449 The Dynasty 14 date for one stela is questionable as it mentions the son of Ra Nehsy and Tany together, the latter being otherwise known as Apophis's affiliate. See Abd el-Maksoud, *Tell el-Heboua*, 39; Abd el-Maksoud and Valbelle, *RdE* 56 (2005), 10-11, fig. 6, pl. V.

450 Abd el-Maksoud and Valbelle, *RdE* 56 (2005), 7-8, fig. 5, pl. 4.

451 The title is in use from the late Middle Kingdom onwards. Ward, *Index*, 179 [1546]; Quirke, *Titles and Bureaux*, 113.

452 Abd el-Maksoud, *Tell el-Heboua*, 38.

453 Abd el-Maksoud, *Tell el-Heboua*, 38; Al-Ayedi, *Tharu*, 101.

454 Group X. Abd el-Maksoud, *Tell el-Heboua*, 201-202, fig. 17.

455 Abd el-Maksoud, *Tell el-Heboua*, 201; Bietak, *BASOR* 281 (1991), 55, fig. 12; Seiler, *CCE* 5 (1997), 26, fig. 6. See also Kaplan, *Tell el Yahudiyeh*, 21-22, 42.

456 Abd el-Maksoud, *Tell el-Heboua*, 38.

457 Abd el-Maksoud, *Tell el-Heboua*, 52-62, fig. 19.

458 Abd el-Maksoud, *Tell el-Heboua*, 59-61, fig. 19, pl. 5 [a].

459 Abd el-Maksoud, *Tell el-Heboua*, 59, fig. 25.

460 Abd el-Maksoud, *Tell el-Heboua*, 37-38. Five tombs (T.110, T.111, T.112, T.113 and T.114) reportedly belong to this level in one section of the report (p. 38), but are labelled as Level 1 tombs in another (p. 96-97). Al-Ayedi, however, corroborates their classification as Level 4b tombs (*Tharu*, 100-101).

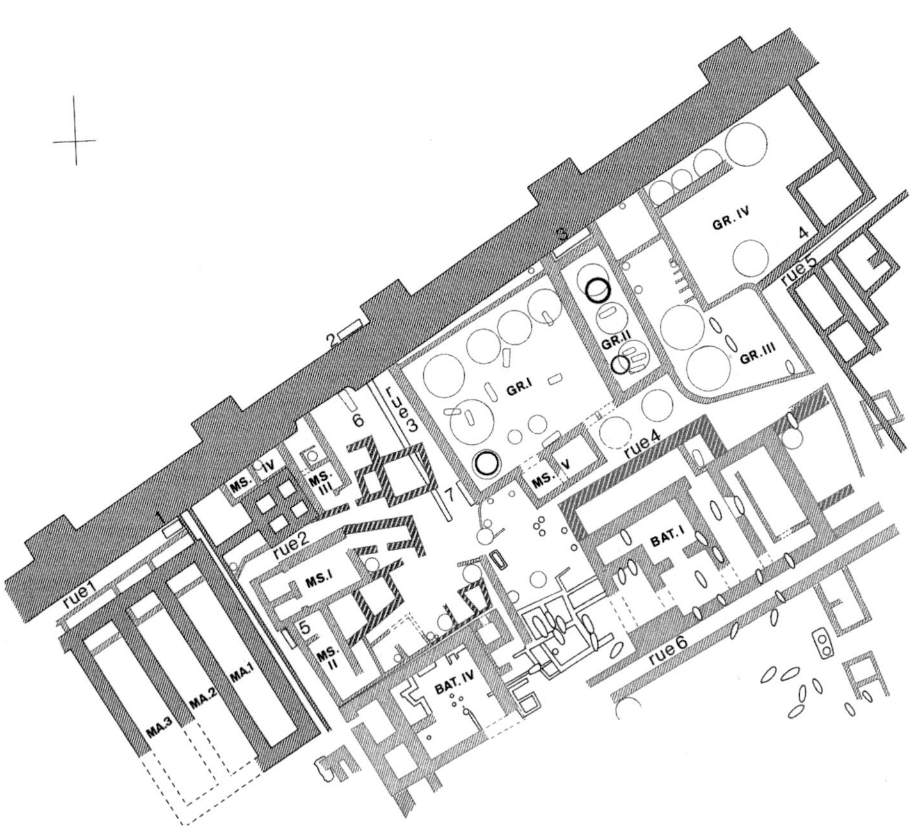

FIGURE 4.18. PLAN OF AREA B, TELL EL-HABWA I. AFTER MAKSOUD, *TELL EL-HEBOUA*, FIG. 19.

contracted with only one instance of the skeleton being in an extended position (T.113).[461] Grave goods are absent. To the east of GR.I are other granaries without burials.[462] Pertinent ceramics include two imported Levantine wares (Figure 4.19 [13]).[463] The vessels' brown-red conical form and button base parallel MBA jugs from Lachish.[464] Classic Kerma cups were also uncovered,[465] indicating possible relations with Upper Nubia.

Tell el-Habwa's function as a storage location for foodstuffs such as grain or barley becomes more evident in this level. The number of silos and their close proximity to houses denote the site's rising economic importance whereas burials with contracted individuals within the settlement hint at the non-Egyptian origin of some inhabitants. The presence of imported ceramics additionally points to trade. Nonetheless, the largely Egyptian architecture and ceramic repertoire[466] indicate that, until Level 4b, the majority of people at Tell el-Habwa were Egyptian or acculturated Levantines.

4.2.4.5 Other

Within the published corpora are ceramics that bear a high degree of similarity with those of nearby sites. Despite being catalogued as Level 4 finds, the exact sub-stratum is not clearly defined. Based on their form and style, it is possible to date the following to the Second Intermediate Period:

- Cups (Figure 4.19 [1-10]):[467] Common at Tell el-Habwa, particularly the settlement area, are cups of Nile silt, mostly red-slipped. Four forms (Groups Ia, Ib, Ig and Ih) have characteristics that are shared with MBIIB cups from Tell el-Maskhuta[468] and Tell el-Dab'a Strata E/1-D/3 (flat-bottomed bases with simple or slightly rolled lips).[469] They most likely date from Level 4b or later.
- Plates (Figure 4.19 [16-17]):[470] Three vessels of rough Nile silt with rounded bodies and flat bases (Groups XXVe and XXVf) are much like specimens from Strata E/1-D/3 at Tell el-Dab'a.[471]
- Jugs:[472] Level 4a's Tomb T.103 contained three jugs of non-Egyptian fabric, two with a fine polished

461 Abd el-Maksoud, *Tell el-Heboua*, 96-97.
462 GR.II with silos SI.7 and SI.8, GR.III with SI.9 and SI.10, and GR.IV with SI.14 and SI.15. Abd el-Maksoud, *Tell el-Heboua*, 62-66.
463 Abd el-Maksoud, *Tell el-Heboua*, 38.
464 Abd el-Maksoud, *Tell el-Heboua*, 189; Tufnell et al., *Lachish* 4, 188, pl. 76 [713].
465 Abd el-Maksoud, *Tell el-Heboua*, 38, 191.
466 For the pottery assemblage, see Abd el-Maksoud, *Tell el-Heboua*, 167-245.

467 Abd el-Maksoud, *Tell el-Heboua*, 167-171.
468 See Redmount, *On an Egyptian/Asiatic Frontier*, fig. 135 [2-8].
469 See Bietak, *BASOR* 281 (1992), fig.10.
470 Abd el-Maksoud, *Tell el-Heboua*, 228-233.
471 Bietak, *BASOR* 281 (1992), fig. 10.
472 Abd el-Maksoud, *Tell el-Heboua*, 94, 191-193. T.103 is the only

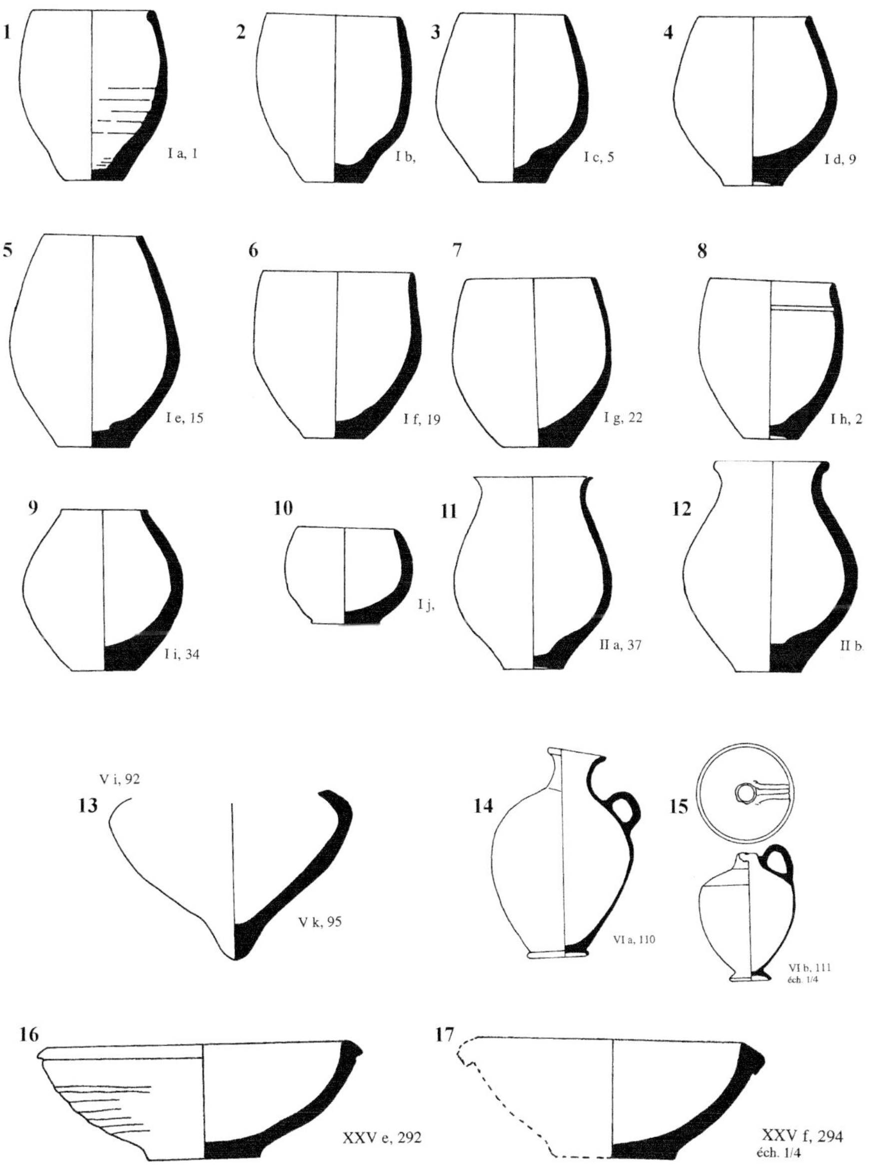

FIGURE 4.19. SELECTED CERAMICS, TELL EL-HABWA I (NOT TO SCALE). AFTER MAKSOUD, *TELL EL-HEBOUA*, FIGS 1-2, 9, 14, 29-30.

surface (Figure 4.19 [14-15]), and the third with a brown body (114/VIe). Their forms are reminiscent of MBIIB jugs from Jericho,[473] Megiddo[474] and Lachish.[475]

Another probable indicator of non-Egyptian presence is the discovery of up to five equid burials.[476] Details of their date and structure remain unpublished.

vaulted rectangular mudbrick tomb thus far uncovered at the site. A bronze dagger was found within the tomb.

473 The Jericho specimen is similar to Jug 114/VIe. See Kenyon and Holland, *Jericho* 4, pl. 7 [8].

474 Jugs 110/VIa and 111/VIb find parallel forms from Stratum XI at Megiddo. See Amiran, *Ancient Pottery*, 106, pl. 34 [7-8].

475 Jugs 110/VIa and 114/VIe are comparable to vessels from Lachish. Tufnell, *Lachish* 4, pls 74 [672], 77 [766].

476 See, for instance, Abd el-Maksoud, *ASAE* 69 (1983), 2-3, pl. 2; Al-Ayedi, *Tharu*, 115, n. 98; Hoffmeier, in *Egypt, Israel, and the Ancient Mediterranean World*, 131; Morris, *Architecture of Imperialism*, 46.

The finds from Tell el-Habwa I illustrate the site's emerging importance as a food supply point. The presence of a Levantine treasurer from its earliest levels as well as later evidence of Levantine(-influenced) products insinuate ongoing Levantine influence which, as implied by Level 4a and 3 remains, continued throughout the Second Intermediate Period and New Kingdom.[477] Although inconclusive, this influence was apparently primarily from the Southern Levant. Indeed, the site is situated at a strategic point between Tell el-Dab'a, the Sinai and the Mediterranean Sea. Therefore, it is not surprising to find an increasing number of imported goods. The high number of silos signifies a growing need or policy to store grains. Due to the lack of rich burials from the early levels at Tell el-Habwa, the tell's primary function may have been

477 See Abd el-Maksoud, *Tell el-Heboua*.

as a storage and supply facility rather than a trading point. Consequently, consumers would have included inhabitants of the surrounding region, particularly Tell el-Dab'a. This could effectually explain why 'the southern prince' of the Rhind Mathematical Papyrus purportedly attacked Tjaru before striking Avaris:[478] he employed the proven tactic of depleting a target's food supply before attacking its city.[479]

4.2.5 Inshas

Lat.Lon. 31°21'N 31°27'E

Ref. Desroches-Noblecourt, *BSFE* 1 (1949), 12-13.

Chron. Second Intermediate Period (?)

Inshas is located in the southern Delta, northeast of Tell el-Yahudiyah. The site was excavated by Habachi who reportedly uncovered at least 70 'Hyksos burials'.[480] The finds are unpublished but details of the excavation are found in Desroches-Noblecourt's two-page report.[481]

The tombs are described as rectangular mudbrick burials with vaulted roofs built in a distinctly new style (i.e. 'très nouveau').[482] Within the burials were contracted bodies,[483] and such grave goods as so-called 'Hyksos scarabs' and Tell el-Yahudiyah juglets.[484] The vessels' shape and fabric are not published, but Habachi ascribes their form to similar juglets from Tell el-Dab'a's earlier Middle Kingdom strata.[485] A probable indicator of Levantine influence are equid remains unearthed before at least a dozen burials.[486] As no chronological deductions can yet be ascertained, these burials could point to a Levantine presence at Inshas during the Second Intermediate Period or, if Habachi's analysis of the pottery is correct, possibly even the late Middle Kingdom.[487]

4.2.6 Khata'na, el-

Lat.Lon. 30°47'N 31°49'E

Refs PM 4, 9; Naville, *Saft el-Henneh*, 21-22; Naville and Griffith, *Mound of the Jew*, 56-57, pl. 19.

Chron. Second Intermediate Period

El-Khata'na lies approximately southwest of Tell el-Dab'a, near Qantir (see Figure 4.3). Several monuments attest to the site's occupation during the Middle Kingdom.[488] Pertinent to this study are finds from a Middle Kingdom to Second Intermediate Period cemetery.[489] A complete publication of material is not available, yet Naville and Griffith have elaborated upon some finds.[490] These include a burial of a seven month old infant in an oval jar, the fabric and style of which are unknown.[491] Other burials contained scarabs (Figure 4.20), pottery, small flints and two bronze items (a 15.4cm spearhead and an axe).[492] Scarabs range from Thirteenth Dynasty to Second Intermediate Period styles. Out of the 13 published scarabs, four bear foreign elements:

- Two scarabs with the Horus falcon and ╔ sign, one of which contained a 'shrine' panel (Figure 4.20 [2, 8]). All elements are of Ben-Tor's Early Palestinian Series and are similar to those from early MBIIB Megiddo;[493]
- A hollowed-out scarab with a standing falcon-headed figure holding a cobra, an artistic component popular in the late MBIIB to MBIIC period (Figure 4.20 [11]);[494] and
- A hollowed-out scarab with an L-shaped red crown, a feature common in MBIIB scarabs (Figure 4.20 [12]).[495]

478 Helck, *Historisch-biographische Texte* 2, 78 [113].
479 This view is also shared by Al-Ayedi, *Tharu*, 167-169.
480 Desroches-Noblecourt, *BSFE* 1 (1949), 12.
481 Desroches-Noblecourt, *BSFE* 1 (1949), 12-13.
482 Desroches-Noblecourt, *BSFE* 1 (1949), 12.
483 Desroches-Noblecourt, *BSFE* 1 (1949), 12.
484 Desroches-Noblecourt, *BSFE* 1 (1949), 12; Williams, *Second Intermediate Period*, 83.
485 Williams notes that he had approached Habachi regarding the juglets in 1973. Williams, *Second Intermediate Period*, 83, n. 1.
486 Desroches-Noblecourt, *BSFE* 1 (1949), 12-13.
487 Equid burials are only attested at Tell el Dab'a Strata H-E/1. If the burial custom was practiced at the same time throughout the Delta, then the interments at Inshas may similarly date between the Thirteenth to early Fifteenth Dynasty. See Forstner-Müller, in *Second Intermediate Period*, 132.

488 See PM 4, 9.
489 Naville, *Saft el-Henneh*, 21-22. Current excavations at el-Khata'na North are being conducted by the Austrian Archaeological Institute in Cairo. To the author's knowledge, only New Kingdom remains from the site have been published. For more, see Forstner-Müller et al., *E&L* 17 (2007), 97-100.
490 Naville and Griffith, *Mound of the Jew*, 56-57.
491 Other similar jars were uncovered, but it is uncertain whether or not these contained human remains. Some reportedly included charcoal and ash remnants. Naville and Griffith, *Mound of the Jew*, 56; Naville, *Saft el-Henneh*, 21-22.
492 Naville, *Saft el-Henneh*, 21; Naville and Griffith, *Mound of the Jew*, 56-57, pl. 19.
493 Ben-Tor's Design Class 3A4, 3B4 and 3E2. Naville and Griffith, *Mound of the Jew*, pl. 19 [2, 8]; Ben-Tor, *Scarabs*, 76-77, 135, pl. 52 [17, 19].
494 Ben-Tor's Design Class 10A. Similar scarabs are found at Tell el-'Ajjul, Gezer, Megiddo and Jericho. Naville and Griffith, *Mound of the Jew*, pl. 19 [11]; Ben-Tor, *Scarabs*, 179, pls 99 [15, 17, 19], 102-103.
495 Ben-Tor's Design Class 3B3d. Naville and Griffith, *Mound of the Jew*, pl. 19 [12]; Ben-Tor, *Scarabs*, 130.

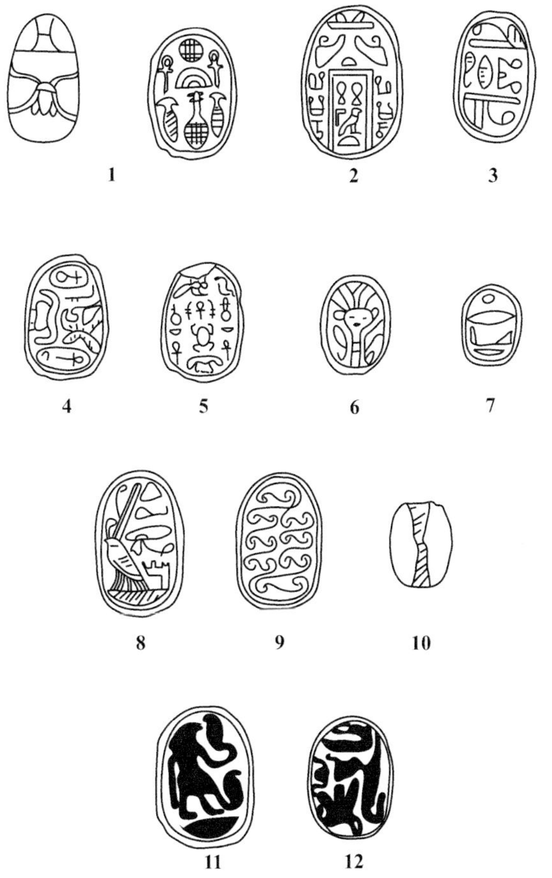

FIGURE 4.20. SELECTED SCARABS, EL-KHATA'NA (NOT TO SCALE). AFTER NAVILLE AND GRIFFITH, *MOUND OF THE JEW*, PL. 19.

Of the ceramic assemblage, cylindrical and piriform Tell el-Yahudiyah ware were collected.[496] Red polished jugs, an ovoid black polished juglet and flat-based cups were also unearthed.[497] Combined, the assemblage corresponds with that of Tell el-Dab'a's Strata E/1-D/3, or the Fifteenth Dynasty.

Little else is known of the material from el-Khata'na. The site's close proximity to Tell el-Dab'a suggests a possible function connected with its earlier Middle Kingdom occupation. Therefore, it may be surmised that el-Khata'na was visited or influenced by a culture bearing Southern Levantine MBIIB traditions during the Second Intermediate Period.

496 Aston and Bietak's Late Egyptian Group L.1 and L.12. Naville and Griffith, *Mound of the Jew*, pl. 19 [16]; Kaplan, *Tell el Yahudiyeh*, figs 6 [f], 7 [e], 48 [f]; Aston and Bietak, *TeD* 8, 206-211, 265.

497 Naville and Griffith, *Mound of the Jew*, 56-57, pl. 19 [13, 15].

4.2.7 *Kom el-Hisn*

Lat.Lon. 30°48'N 30°36'E

Refs Hamada and el-Amir, *ASAE* 46 (1947), 105-106; Hamada and Farid, *ASAE* 46 (1947), 197-198, 201-205, pl. 56; Hamada and Farid, *ASAE* 48 (1948), 301, pl. 7; Kirby, Orel and Smith, *JEA* 84 (1998), 39-40; Orel, *GM* 179 (2000), 39-49.

Chron. Twelfth Dynasty and Second Intermediate Period

Kom el-Hisn is situated at the edge of the western Delta. Excavations between 1943 and 1952 were preliminarily published by Hamada and Farid. They revealed a large necropolis of tombs originally ascribed to the Second Intermediate Period.[498] Orel's analysis of the available material has redated them between the First Intermediate Period and the early Middle Kingdom.[499] Later survey work in 1996 by the Egypt Exploration Society further recovered Second Intermediate Period material.[500]

Hamada and Farid mention a number of graves with assemblages akin to those at Tell el-Dab'a. Evidently, some individuals were provided with bronze weaponry of EBIV-MBIIA types such as D-shaped fenestrated axes (Philip's Type 2), daggers with crescent-shaped pommels and a socketted spearhead.[501] Alongside the weaponry, burials also contained meat offerings, Levantine pottery, as well as copper or silver torques and bracelets.[502] A large, ovoid Levantine Painted Ware dipper jug of uncertain context was additionally reported,[503] its decoration similar to jugs from Byblos.[504] It has been dated to the early Middle Kingdom.[505]

While such grave goods point to Levantine influences, most individuals were interred in a more typical Egyptian funerary custom, in supine deposition and in simple mud-lined graves buried in sand.[506] This suggests that they could have been acculturated Levantines or Egyptians heavily influenced by Levantine traditions, the former being more likely. Although the exact dating of the burials remains uncertain, the type of weaponry supports an early Middle Kingdom date, thereby agreeing with Orel's dating.[507] Based on this, Philips writes that the burials may represent an earlier or formative stage to those at Tell el-Dab'a, preceding its Stratum H (see

498 Hamada and el-Amir, *ASAE* 46 (1947), 101-141; Hamada and Farid, *ASAE* (1947), 195-235; Hamada and Farid, *ASAE* 48 (1948), 299-325; Hamada and Farid, *ASAE* 50 (1950), 367-390.

499 Orel, *GM* 179 (2000), 39-49.

500 Kirby, Orel and Smith, *JEA* 84 (1998), 23-43. See also Wenke et al., *JARCE* 25 (1988), 5-34.

501 Hamada and el-Amir, *ASAE* 46 (1947), 105-106; Hamada and Farid, *ASAE* 46 (1947), 201-205, pl. 56; Hamada and Farid, *ASAE* 48 (1948), 301, pl. 7; Philip, *TeD* 15, 225, 231-232.

502 Hamada and Farid, *ASAE* 46 (1947), 197-198; Philip, *TeD* 15, 231.

503 The vessel was evidently retrieved from a rubbish deposit above burials of the First Intermediate Period (Hamada and Farid, *ASAE* 46 [1947], 198, fig. 15). See also Bagh, *TeD* 23, 61-62.

504 Bagh, *TeD* 23, 61-62.

505 Bagh, *TeD* 23, 62.

506 Hamada and Farid, *ASAE* 48 (1948), 304; Philip, *TeD* 15, 231-232.

507 As also supported by Philip, *TeD* 15, 231.

Figure 4.4).[508] Indeed, the similarities with Tell el-Dab'a point to the Middle Kingdom, yet the differences in architecture and deposition could infer more localised traditions at Kom el-Hisn or even the western Delta.

Contact with Levantine elements apparently also occurs in the Second Intermediate Period. While no graves have been assigned to this date, an auger core survey yielded three Tell el-Yahudiyah sherds from Core 5.[509] Reportedly, two black polished sherds belonged to Thirteenth Dynasty piriform vessels and one brown sherd with chevrons is possibly from a Second Intermediate Period piriform or biconical juglet.[510] The three are feasibly products of trade, perhaps from Tell el-Dab'a.

Therefore, the material from Kom el-Hisn supports an early Middle Kingdom population likely constituting accculturated Levantines with links to warrior traditions, as well as Second Intermediate Period trade in Levantine(-influenced) products.

4.2.8 Kom el-Khilgan

Lat.Lon. 30°55'N 32°38'E

Ref. Ownby, *Égypte, Afrique et Orient* 65 (2012), 33-38.

Chron. Second Intermediate Period

The eastern Delta site of Kom el-Khilgan was excavated by the Institut français d'archéologie orientale between 2002 and 2005.[511] It features a Predynastic cemetery as well as a Second Intermediate Period necropolis and settlement.[512] Finds from the latter have not yet been completely published, however petrographic analysis on pottery sherds has been carried out.[513] Despite the lack of contextual information or precise dating, the analysis provides significant results on the origins of Syro-Palestinian store-jars of the Second Intermediate Period. They are provided here for comparison with other petrographic analyses of store-jars from this period.[514]

22 samples of Syro-Palestinian store-jars from the site were examined by Ownby.[515] Her findings revealed six regions from which their fabrics originated (Figure 4.21): (1) coastal Syria (4.55% of the samples); (2) the 'Akkar Plain of northern Lebanon (9.1%); (3) different areas along the Lebanese coast, (50%); (4) coastal Israel (9.1%); (5) the Egyptian Delta (9.1-13.6%); and (6) a region producing clay with plagiogranite and large inclusions of pyroxene and amphibole minerals, like Cyprus (13.6%).[516] Those of an Egyptian marl clay were not locally produced, the fabric being from another site on the outskirts of the Delta.[517]

The majority of samples (63.55%) are from the Northern Levant, predominantly from sites along the coast of Lebanon. This corresponds with findings of petrographic analyses on Syro-Palestinian store-jars from Tell el-Dab'a as well as Kom Rabi'a, in which Southern Levantine fabrics are similarly not as common and those from Syria are rare.[518] The local manufacture of Levantine vessels is also attested at Tell el-Dab'a but not Kom Rabi'a, signifying a Delta site producing Syro-Palestinian store-jars for local Second Intermediate Period consumers. The possibly Cypriote fabric has not been found elsewhere,[519] indicating either another unknown origin for its fabric, or a unique flow of traded goods across the Delta and the Mediterranean region.

The results thereby highlight the Lebanese coast as a popular source of fabric(s) for Syro-Palestinian store-jars imported into Kom el-Khilgan. Trade evidently existed between the Northern Levant and the site in the Second Intermediate Period, with the Delta site also gaining access to products from other Mediterranean coastal regions, as well as locally-made Syro-Palestinian store-jars.

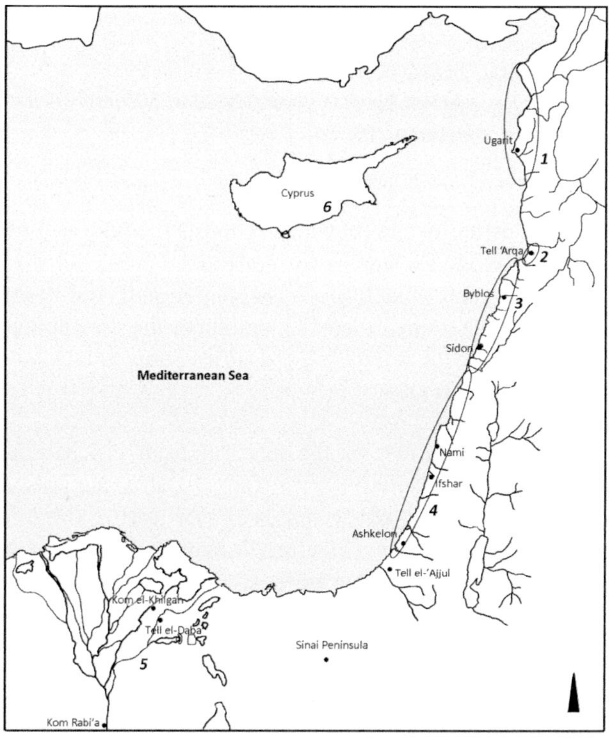

Figure 4.21. Geographical designates of petrographic groups 1-6 of imported vessels from Kom el-Khilgan. After Ownby, *Égypte, Afrique et Orient* 65 (2012), 36, fig. 1.

[508] Philip, *TeD* 15, 232.
[509] Kirby, Orel and Smith, *JEA* 84 (1998), 39.
[510] Kirby, Orel and Smith, *JEA* 84 (1998), 39-40.
[511] Midant-Reynes et al., in *Egypt at its Origins*, 467-486.
[512] Midant-Reynes et al., in *Egypt at its Origins*, 467-486.
[513] Ownby, *Égypte, Afrique et Orient* 65 (2012), 33-38.
[514] See Chapter 4.2.2.8 and 4.3.4, Figures 4.15-16, 436.
[515] Ownby, *Égypte, Afrique et Orient* 65 (2012), 33-38; Ownby, *JAEI* 4/3 (2012), 26.
[516] Ownby, *Égypte, Afrique et Orient* 65 (2012), 36, fig. 1; Ownby, *JAEI* 4/3 (2012), 26.
[517] Ownby, *Égypte, Afrique et Orient* 65 (2012), 36-37.
[518] See Chapter 4.2.2.8 and 4.3.4, Figures 4.15-16, 4.36.
[519] Ownby, *Égypte, Afrique et Orient* 65 (2012), 36.

4.2.9 Maskhuta, Tell el- (Tjeku)

Lat.Lon. 30°33'N 32°06'E

Refs *LÄ* 6, 351; PM 4, 53-55; Naville, *Story-city of Pithom;* MacDonald, *BA* 43/1 (1980), 49-58; Holladay, *Tell El-Maskhuṭa;* Redmount, *On an Egyptian/Asiatic Frontier;* Redmount, *BA* 58/4 (1995), 182-190; Redmount, *JMA* 8/2 (1995), 61-89; Paice, Holladay and Brock, in *Haus und Palast*, 159-173; Holladay, in *Hyksos*, 183-247.

Chron. Second Intermediate Period

Located in the eastern Wadi Tumilat and spanning an area of approximately two hectares is Tell el-Maskhuta, the largest site in the Wadi and the second most excavated Second Intermediate Period mound in the Delta.[520] The site is strategically situated upon high ground at a point where the valley constricts, enabling settlers to better control and/or discern movement along the valley floor.[521] Following investigations by Naville,[522] Petrie[523] and Clédat,[524] Holladay directed a team from the University of Toronto between 1978-1985, uncovering six phases of 'Hyksos occupation'.[525] Based on the pottery assemblage, Holladay and Redmount correlate these phases between the end of Tell el-Dab'a's Stratum E/1 and the beginning of Stratum D/3 (see Figure 4.3).[526]

As the relative chronology for the individual phases is yet to be ascertained, data from all six phases has been included in this examination.[527] Furthermore, the ceramic assemblage remains unpublished and, where investigated, is only done so as a complete corpus.[528] The following phases thus only include the 'temporal modifications noted'[529] by excavators, with a subsequent section detailing Levantine influences on the pottery.

520 Redmount, *On an Egyptian/Asiatic Frontier*, 145-148; Redmount, *BA* 58/4 (1995), 183-184.

521 Holladay notes that the valley floor provides the easiest route for transportation through the Wadi. Another constriction at the western end of the valley bears the location of Tell el-Retaba (Chapter 4.2.11), which similarly offers a good vantage point for detecting movement in the Wadi. Holladay, *Tell El-Maskhuṭa*, 11-12; Redmount, *On an Egyptian/Asiatic Frontier*, 106, 111, figs 13-14.

522 Naville possibly uncovered a Second Intermediate Period burial (Naville, *Pithom*, 11). For more on Naville's excavations, see also Holladay, *Tell El-Maskhuṭa*, 3; Redmount, *On an Egyptian/Asiatic Frontier*, 150-151.

523 Petrie, *Tanis* 1, 28.

524 Clédat, *RT* 32 (1910), 40-42.

525 Holladay, *Tell El-Maskhuṭa;* Redmount, *JMA* 5/2 (1995), 67.

526 Holladay, in *Hyksos*, 188; Paice, Holladay and Brock, in *Haus und Palast*, 159-160. Redmount, however, notes the sketchy relationship between Tell el-Dab'a and Tell el-Maskhuta, which she cautiously dates to 1700-1600 BC (Redmount, *On an Egyptian/Asiatic Frontier*, 265; Redmount, *JMA* 8/2 [1995], 68, 81).

527 The grouping of Phase 1 with 2 is after Redmount's classification of the findings. Thus far, her dissertation presents the most detailed examination of the site. Redmount, *On an Egyptian/Asiatic Frontier*.

528 Holladay, *Tell El-Maskhuṭa*, 50, pl. 1; Redmount, *JMA* 8/2 (1995), 68-78; Redmount, *BA* 58/4 (1995), 184-188; Holladay, in *Hyksos*, pl. 7 [1-18]. A more thorough investigation of the assemblage may be found in Redmount, *On an Egyptian/Asiatic Frontier*, 770-901, figs 126-149.

529 Redmount, *On an Egyptian/Asiatic Frontier*, 770.

4.2.9.1 Phases 1 and 2

Remains from Phases 1 and 2 are scarce and scattered.[530] The settlement included rectangular houses, with perimeter walls in Phase 2.[531] Between two of these structures is Locus 6116, an area defined by a small circular pit filled with intact pottery vessels connected with drinking (mostly cups, juglets, ringstands and bowls), suggesting a link with the Levantine *marzeah* ritual.[532] Circular structures resembling silos are also scattered across the site, some within house courtyards.[533]

Tombs can be found within Areas L, H and the excavated settlement.[534] Vaulted mudbrick roofs atop rectangular pits are the norm, with four dating to Phase 1 and three to Phase 2.[535] Adults and/or infants were usually buried in individual tombs, with the majority lying flexed on one side.[536] Body orientation varied.[537] Caprid bones were discovered within the tombs whereas equid skeletons were found outside two tombs, one from each phase.[538] Grave goods include ceramics (juglets, bowls, beakers, cups and ringstands), a gold earring, silver adornments (headbands, bracelets, earrings, chokers, a ring and armband fragments) and bronze items (toggle-pins, daggers and an axe).

13 scarabs have also been discovered within these tombs, with another unearthed in the settlement. Of pertinence are:

- One scarab with a convoluted coil pattern, possibly from the Levant (Figure 4.22 [4]);[539]
- One scarab with the figure of a man wearing a short, possibly striped, kilt holding a flower in his right hand and another unidentified item in his left. Other signs around the figure may also be present (Figure 4.22 [5]);[540]
- One scarab with two cobras flanking a kneeling figure with a probable mythical head (Figure 4.22 [2]);[541] and
- One scarab with two cobras wearing red crowns.[542]

530 Redmount, *On an Egyptian/Asiatic Frontier*, 231.

531 Paice, Holladay and Brock, in *Haus und Palast*, 162-164, fig. 5.

532 Redmount, *On an Egyptian/Asiatic Frontier*, 234; Holladay, in *Hyksos*, 196.

533 Redmount, *On an Egyptian/Asiatic Frontier*, 231-234; Holladay, in *Hyksos*, 162-164.

534 Redmount, *On an Egyptian/Asiatic Frontier*, 234; Holladay, *Tell El-Maskhuṭa*, 44.

535 Redmount, *On an Egyptian/Asiatic Frontier*, table 39.

536 Redmount, *On an Egyptian/Asiatic Frontier*, table 39.

537 Redmount, *On an Egyptian/Asiatic Frontier*, table 39.

538 Equid remains were discovered south of Tomb L12.12321 from Phase 1, and at the head of L12.12317 from Phase 2. Redmount, *On an Egyptian/Asiatic Frontier*, table 39.

539 Ben-Tor's Design Class 6C3. Ben-Tor suggests a Levantine origin. Ben-Tor, *Scarabs*, 90-91.

540 Ben-Tor's Design Class 10A. Ben-Tor, *Scarabs*, 98-100.

541 Ben-Tor's Design Class 9C and 10C. Ben-Tor, *Scarabs*, 95-97, 100-101.

542 Weinstein, *BASOR* 288 (1992), 33, 39-40, n. 17.

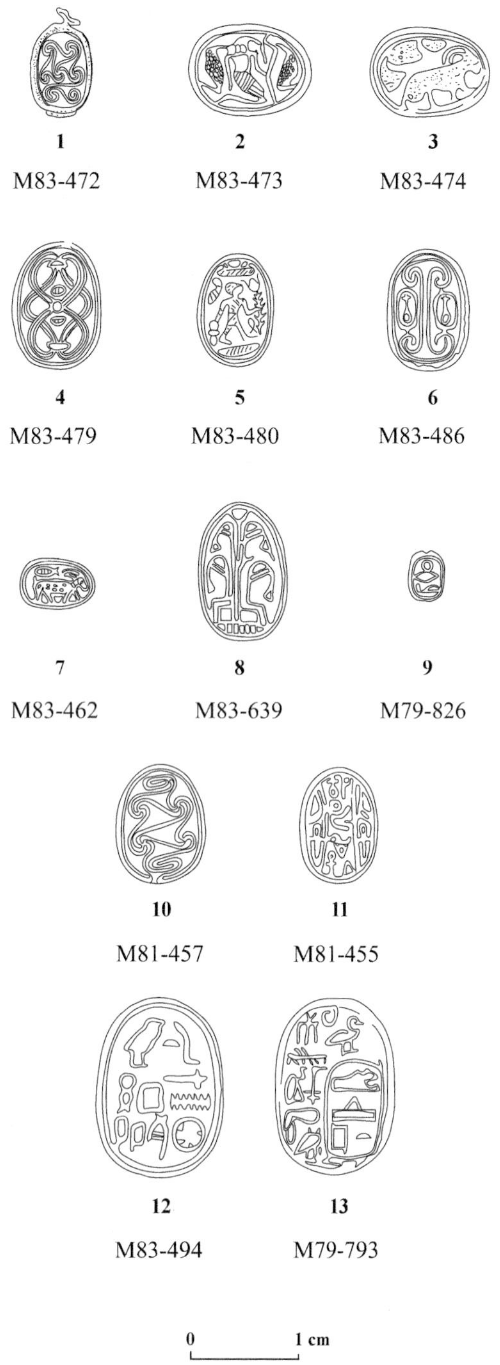

FIGURE 4.22. SELECTED SCARABS, TELL EL-MASKHUTA. AFTER BEN-TOR, *SCARABS*, APPENDIX PLS 1-2.

Overall, most scarabs stylistically belong to the late Thirteenth Dynasty. Designs such as the horned animal, the two cobras either flanking a mythical figure or wearing red crowns, and the standing figure carrying a flower, all point to Levantine influences.[543]

Of the pottery corpus, Holladay notes the dominance of handmade flat-bottomed cooking pots (38%) against wheel-made holemouth cooking pots (0%) in Phase 1.[544]

543 See Ben Tor, *Scarabs*, 66-68.

544 See above n. 38; Holladay, in *Hyksos*, 190, n. 18.

By Phase 2, the handmade cooking pots still dominated the corpus (36%), yet more wheel-made holemouth cooking pots are attested (4%).[545] The flat-based cooking pots are typical of the MBIIA period in both the Northern and Southern Levant,[546] while the holemouth cooking pots are characteristic of the MBIIB and MBIIC, their bulbous rims finding parallels with those from EBA Ebla.[547] The majority of both types are of Nile silt,[548] indicating that local manufacturers had some knowledge in Levantine pottery-making techniques.

4.2.9.2 Phase 3

Phase 3 features the first signs of substantial building activity with the construction of well-built houses and larger, more common, silos.[549] The custom of filling a round pit with drinking vessels continued and is evident in two pits in Area R6 with neatly arranged cups, bowls and cup-stands.[550]

At least three tombs were discovered in front of houses,[551] one of which consisted of a simple burial of a newborn infant outside House B in Area R7/R8.[552] The neonate was buried in an extended position in an imported MBIIA or MBIIA-B Syro-Palestinian store-jar, a clear ethnic marker for the presence of Levantines.[553]

Redmount notes a possible occupational break between Phases 3 and 4. This is based on Pit 1184, which cuts into a Phase 3 house and was sealed by Phase 4 structures, and Pit 12256 which also cuts into a previous perimeter wall.[554]

4.2.9.3 Phase 4

The site's layout remained the same except for the addition of a perimeter wall along a north-south axis delineating the excavated area into two sections:[555] (1) the eastern compound in which Phase 3's R1 structures were replaced with boundary walls and courtyard structures; and (2) the western compound of R7/R8 with House B and a large courtyard.[556]

The southwestern room of House B yielded large quantities of sickle blades and pottery with other luxury materials, notably a decorated spindle-whorl of donkey bone and bone slips of a Levantine-style inlaid box.[557] A shed along

545 Holladay, in *Hyksos*, 190.

546 Holladay, in *Hyksos*, 190; Redmount, *On an Egyptian/Asiatic Frontier*, 831.

547 Holladay, in *Hyksos*, 195, pl. 7 [18]; Redmount, *On an Egyptian/Asiatic Frontier*, 831.

548 Redmount, *On an Egyptian/Asiatic Frontier*, 820.

549 Redmount, *On an Egyptian/Asiatic Frontier*, 234; Paice, Holladay and Brock, in *Haus und Palast*, 164; Holladay, in *Hyksos*, 190-192.

550 Redmount, *On an Egyptian/Asiatic Frontier*, 237; Paice, Holladay and Brock, in *Haus und Palast*, 165.

551 Holladay, in *Hyksos*, 192.

552 Burial R8.8112. Paice, Holladay and Brock, in *Haus und Palast*, 164; Redmount, *On an Egyptian/Asiatic Frontier*, table 39.

553 Redmount, *On an Egyptian/Asiatic Frontier*, 847, fig. 179; Redmount, *JMA* 8/2 (1995), 77.

554 Redmount, *On an Egyptian/Asiatic Frontier*, 237.

555 Redmount, *On an Egyptian/Asiatic Frontier*, 237, fig. 42.

556 Redmount, *On an Egyptian/Asiatic Frontier*, 237, fig. 42.

557 Paice, Holladay and Brock, in *Haus und Palast*, 167.

the northern face of the house, along with findings of, for instance, red-ochre mottles across its floor, ochre-stained red palettes, grinders and leather dressings, denote a possible workshop-function for the house. The product is postulated to be 'some sort of composite apparatus or adornment, such as red-dyed leather goods with locally made metal ornaments and fittings'.[558] Within Section R6 of the courtyard, a circular pit filled with drinking vessels indicates the continuance of the custom witnessed in earlier phases.[559]

Only one tomb has been assigned to Phase 4. The burial was uncovered in the northeastern corner of the eastern compound, built beneath a wall of a structure in the courtyard.[560] It features a vaulted mudbrick roof covering the interment of a sub-adolescent lying flexed on one side.[561] Grave goods include a flat-based cup, a bronze toggle-pin and a cylindrical Tell el-Yahudiyah juglet similar to those from Tell el-Dab'a's E/2-D/3 strata of Dynasty 15.[562]

Redmount postulates another hiatus between Phases 4 and 5. She writes that Pit 12311 is indicative of an occupational interruption as it cuts into a perimeter wall from Phase 4 and is sealed by Phase 5 structures.[563]

4.2.9.4 Phase 5

An increase in the quantity of structures is observed within the excavated area, signalling a possible rise in population.[564] House B in Area R7/R8 continued in use as a possible workshop but was renovated with a third room's addition to the east.[565] Several new structures were built with rooms more square in plan and with attached courtyards, two features noted in the Northern Levantine MBA site of Hama (Level H4).[566] To the north of House B,[567] House D contained a courtyard with three silos along its boundary wall.[568] A neonate burial was unearthed in this courtyard, with the infant interred within a MBIIA or MBIIA-B Syro-Palestinian store-jar of possible Levantine fabric.[569]

Another tomb from Phase 5, R2.2054, was built as a rectangular pit with mudbrick lining and capping.[570] The skeleton was found flexed on one side with ceramic vessels (rims of a holemouth cooking pot, a carinated bowl and a jar) as well as two scarabs.[571] One is incised with *nṯr nfr M3ʿ-ib-Rʿ.w ḏi ʿnḫ* 'the good god, Maaibra, may he give/be given life' (Figure 4.22 [11]), offering a *terminus post quem* for the tomb.[572]

One other burial belonging to either this phase or the next (R8.8060) contained five beads and a scarab (Figure 4.22 [8]).[573] On the base of the latter are two out-curved papyrus plants, a motif regarded as a Levantine design.[574] As no similar scarab is yet to be found in Egypt dating to the Second Intermediate Period, the item is most probably from the Levant.[575]

4.2.9.5 Phase 6

Phase 6 is marked by continuous settlement growth with signs of renovation.[576] Remnants of a reddish-brown substance ascertained to be donkey dung were found on the floors of House D in Area L12 suggesting the unit's use as a donkey stable.[577] Between House D and B (i.e. the 'stable' and the 'workshop'), two silos were utilised for simple inhumations of individuals.[578] Assigned to the end of Phase 6,[579] they belong to an elderly female, tightly flexed and possibly wrapped in a mat, and an adolescent male with evidence of a wound to his skull reminiscent of a duckbill axe injury.[580] The female was laid on her right and the male on his left, paralleling burial traits recorded in the Southern Levantine EBIV/MBI site of Jericho.[581]

Burial L2.2178 may additionally be assigned to Phase 6.[582] The tomb has a vaulted mudbrick roof and housed the interment of an adolescent.[583] Grave goods include pottery (a juglet, a flat-based cup, a bowl and a jar rim), a possible silver bracelet and a *rḏi-rʿ* scarab (Figure 4.22 [9]).[584]

4.2.9.6 Characteristic non-Egyptian ceramics

Along with the two aforementioned Syro-Palestinian store-jars utilised for neonate burials, several fragments of the ceramic type were unearthed across all phases.[585] Their fabrics' calcite inclusions point to their Levantine production whereas their bulbous rims and the addition of handles ascribe to MBIIA or MBIIA-B forms.[586] Regardless of the minor quantity of store-jar fragments in comparison with other ceramics, their presence indicates

558 Paice, Holladay and Brock, in *Haus und Palast*, 167.
559 Redmount, *On an Egyptian/Asiatic Frontier*, 237.
560 Burial R1.1138. Paice, Holladay and Brock, in *Haus und Palast*, 167.
561 Redmount, *On an Egyptian/Asiatic Frontier*, table 39.
562 Aston and Bietak's Late Egyptian L.12.2a. Aston and Bietak, *TeD* 8, 265, 513, 553-556, figs 196, 201, 253; Redmount, *On an Egyptian/Asiatic Frontier*, table 39.
563 Redmount, *On an Egyptian/Asiatic Frontier*, 239.
564 Redmount, *On an Egyptian/Asiatic Frontier*, 239, 764-765.
565 Redmount, *On an Egyptian/Asiatic Frontier*, 239; Paice, Holladay and Brock, in *Haus und Palast*, 169, fig. 10.
566 Redmount, *On an Egyptian/Asiatic Frontier*, 169.
567 Redmount, *On an Egyptian/Asiatic Frontier*, 169, fig. 12.
568 Redmount, *On an Egyptian/Asiatic Frontier*, 169.
569 Burial L12.12170. Redmount, *On an Egyptian/Asiatic Frontier*, 847, table 39, fig. 177; Redmount, *JMA* 8/2 (1995), 77.
570 Redmount, *On an Egyptian/Asiatic Frontier*, table 39.
571 Redmount, *On an Egyptian/Asiatic Frontier*, table 39.
572 For more on the scarabs of this king see Ben-Tor, *Scarabs*, 107, pls 44-45; Ryholt, *Political Situation*, 366-76.
573 Redmount, *On an Egyptian/Asiatic Frontier*, table 39.
574 Ben-Tor's Design Class 1E. Ben-Tor, *Scarabs*, 72-74.
575 Parallels from Harageh, Aniba and Semna date to the early Eighteenth Dynasty. Ben-Tor, *Scarabs*, 72, n. 359.
576 Paice, Holladay and Brock, in *Haus und Palast*, 170.
577 Paice, Holladay and Brock, in *Haus und Palast*, 170; Holladay, in *Hyksos*, 192.
578 Paice, Holladay and Brock, in *Haus und Palast*, 170.
579 Redmount, *On an Egyptian/Asiatic Frontier*, 239, 256, table 39; Paice, Holladay and Brock, in *Haus und Palast*, 170.
580 Paice, Holladay and Brock, in *Haus und Palast*, 170.
581 Paice, Holladay and Brock, in *Haus und Palast*, 170; Palumbo, *BASOR* 267 (1987), 45.
582 Redmount, *On an Egyptian/Asiatic Frontier*, 256, table 39.
583 Redmount, *On an Egyptian/Asiatic Frontier*, table 39.
584 Redmount, *On an Egyptian/Asiatic Frontier*, table 39.
585 Redmount, *On an Egyptian/Asiatic Frontier*, 847, fig. 143 [1-15]; Redmount, *JMA* 8/2 (1995), 77.
586 Redmount, *JMA* 8/2 (1995), 77; Redmount, *On an Egyptian/Asiatic Frontier*, 847.

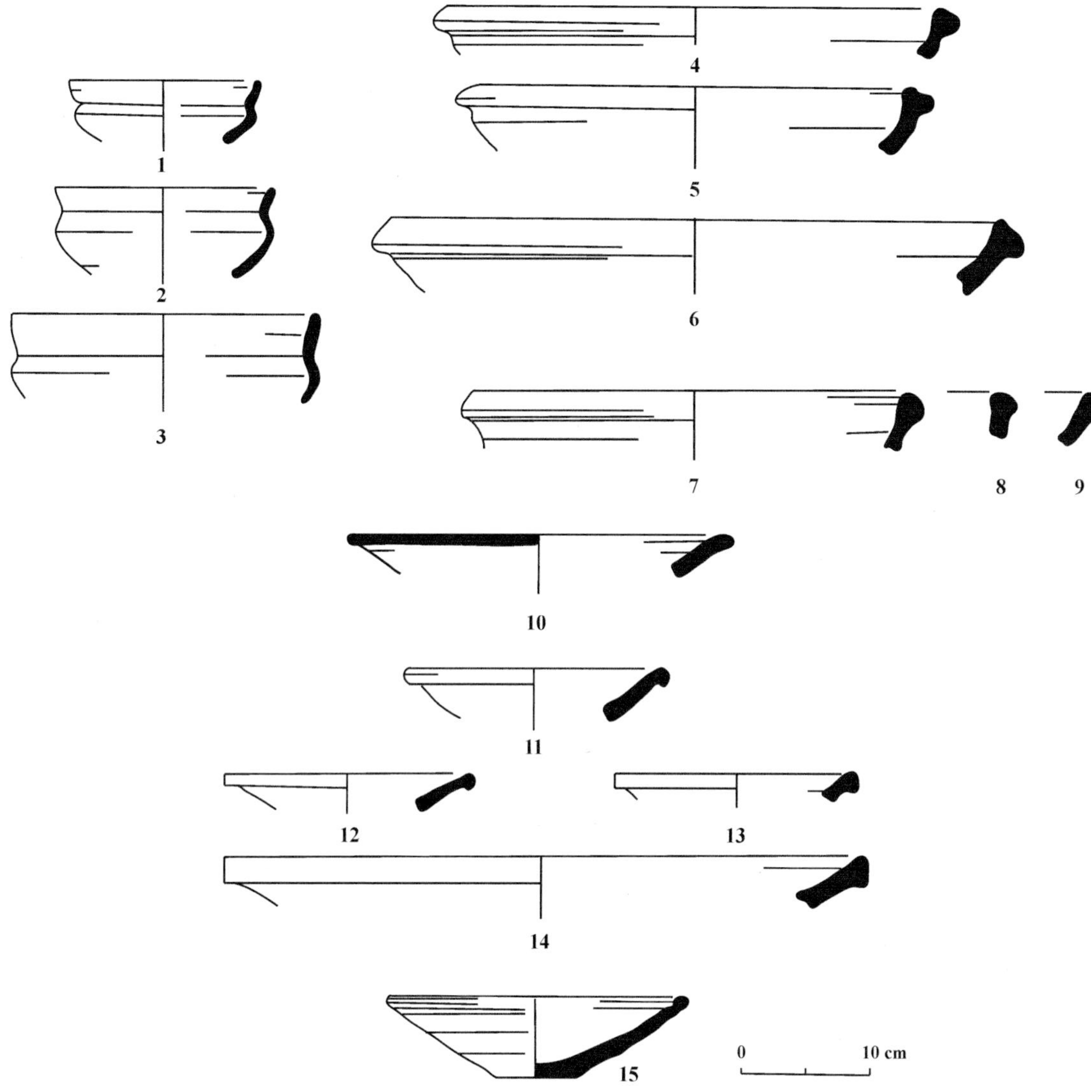

FIGURE 4.23. PLATTER BOWLS, THIN-WALLED AND THICK-WALLED CARINATED BOWLS, TELL EL-MASKHUTA. AFTER REDMOUNT, *ON AN EGYPTIAN/ASIATIC FRONITER*, FIGS 129, 131-132.

some trade with the Levant.[587] The MBIIA or MBIIA-B style presents a conundrum in dating as it is spread across all phases yet is of the same typological sequence. Perhaps the decrease in the number of sherds from the early to late phases[588] indicates a reduction in popularity or a decline in trade. It may also point to the reuse of store-jars across successive periods.

Other distinguishable Levantine styles include punctate or grooved Tell el-Yahudiyah ware of the globular, piriform, cylindrical and biconical forms,[589] as well as piriform or biconical red or black polished juglets.[590] Found in all six phases, the juglets are characteristic of Aston and Bietak's Levanto-Egyptian group and can be found in both settlement and burial contexts.[591] They parallel forms from Tell el-Dab'a's Fifteenth Dynasty Strata E/2-D/1.[592] With the exception of a few red polished vessels, all juglets are reportedly of Nile silt.[593]

Carinated and platter bowls are also of local fabrics (Figure 4.23).[594] Some platter bowls have radial and pattern burnishing typical of EBA pottery (Figure 4.23 [15]).[595] Other platter bowl types with straight or rounded lips are known from the MBA period (Figure 4.23 [10-14]).[596] For the carinated bowls, two types may be distinguished: (1) the rare thin-walled bowls with straight, everted lips and rounded or angular body profiles similar to Southern Levantine forms (Figure 4.23 [1-3]); and (2) the more

587 Redmount, *JMA* 8/2 (1995), 77.

588 Almost twice the amount of Syro-Palestinian store-jar sherds are recorded for the early phases. Redmount, *JMA* 8/2 (1995), 77.

589 Respectively, Aston and Bietak's Type Groups N, L.1, D.6 and L.2. Redmount, *JMA* 8/2 (1995), 74, fig. 9; Redmount, *On an Egyptian/Asiatic Frontier*, 877, fig. 146; Kaplan, *Tell el Yahudiyeh Ware*, 15-29, figs 2-3; Aston and Bietak, *TeD* 8, 120, 206-221, 302.

590 Redmount, *On an Egyptian/Asiatic Frontier*, 877-886.

591 Redmount, *On an Egyptian/Asiatic Frontier*, 874-876.

592 Aston and Bietak's Late Egyptian L.1.4, L.4, L.5.3 and L.12.2. Aston and Bietak, *TeD* 8, 211, 221, 231, 265, 553-554, figs 142, 147, 159, 162-164, 167, 176-201, 253

593 Redmount, *On an Egyptian/Asiatic Frontier*, 876.

594 Redmount, *JMA* 8/2 (1995), 74-77.

595 Redmount, *JMA* 8/2 (1995), 74-77.

596 Redmount, *On an Egyptian/Asiatic Frontier*, 791-797, fig. 129.

common thick-walled carinated bowls (Figure 4.23 [4-9]) with either sharp carinations, low points of carination or a small protrusion at points of carination, all of which find parallels from the Northern Levant.[597]

It is, therefore, apparent that the ceramic repertoire was influenced by Levantine traditions, indicating that the inhabitants of Tell el-Maskhuta most likely had access to both Northern and Southern Levantine-inspired ceramics. The full extent of relations is uncertain as the complete pottery assemblage remains unpublished. Redmount reports that the assemblage exhibits only direct points of contact for particular ceramic types, with the overall repertoire being atypical by having no close correspondence to any Levantine site and only a few of the most common MBA pottery forms.[598]

4.2.9.7 Other

Five burials cannot be assigned to particular phases.[599] Significant grave goods include silver adornments (chokers, earrings and toggle-pins), bronze items (toggle-pins and daggers), faience amulets, beads (faience, carnelian, gold and amethyst), pottery (cups, juglets and ringstands) and MBIIB scarabs, including M79-793 naming Dynasty 13's Sobekhotep IV (Figure 4.22 [13]).[600] One tomb, L2.2029, included a donkey burial in its forecourt[601] while another, L2.2040, has been noted to belong to a transhuman Levantine pastoralist. The interpretation is based on the presence of a sheep at the head and a dog at the feet of a female interred flexed on her right side, as well as cattle skulls before the tomb.[602] However, the individual's mode of subsistence cannot be determined solely on the buried animals. In fact, their burial is common in the settlement[603] as well as other sites in the Delta, suggesting that the female could equally belong to a settled population. The skulls of the female and dog are pierced with wounds similar to, like the abovementioned individual buried in a Phase 6 inhumation, those inflicted by duckbill axes.[604]

Grave goods, especially those of silver, signify that some inhabitants were wealthy. Settlement finds suggest a poorer class involved in such industries as weaving, spinning, pottery-making, sickle-making and bronze-work.[605] The mixture of artefacts delineates social stratification across all six phases with the high possibility that the elite, based on their tombs' goods, controlled trade relations. House B's workshop suggests a growing industry linked with adornments whereas House D's stable implies an increasing need to accommodate donkeys, a most common mode of transport along the Egyptian-Levantine land-based route. Palaeobotanical studies report the absence of summer weed seeds which, when considered with the amount of hearths in houses and the growing number of silos, insinuates the site's usage as a winter residence.[606] Hence, it is possible that Tell el-Maskhuta functioned as a trading settlement, a 'reception and supply point for winter caravans',[607] on a very strategic corridor between the Sinai and the Delta. This might explain the eclectic combination of Northern and Southern Levantine features across the site's architectural, ceramic and burial traditions.

The scarab designs and pottery forms range in date from the late MBIIA to early MBIIC periods and the late Thirteenth to Fifteenth Dynasties, with only two rulers (Sobekhotep IV and *Šši*) represented by scarabs. Excavators note that the architectural development from Phases 1 to 6 spans 50-100 years,[608] but it is feasible to add a further 10-20 years to take into account the possible seasonal occupation activity as well as the two postulated hiatus periods. Tell el-Maskhuta could then be assigned an occupation history between 60-110 years in the Second Intermediate Period, witnessing the rise and rule of the Hyksos Dynasty. Consequently, the site's location, foundation and trading function could be linked to new initiatives by the Hyksos to control and officiate the land-based route between Egypt and the Levant.

4.2.10 Muqdam, Tell el- (Leontopolis)

Lat.Lon. 30°41'N 31°21'E

Refs *LÄ* 6, 351-352; PM 4, 37-39; Naville, *Ahnas el Medineh*, 28, pl. 4b; Borchardt, *Statuen und Statuetten* 2, 87-88, pl. 89 [538].

Chron. Fourteenth Dynasty (reign of Nehsy)

The base of a black granite statue was discovered at Tell el-Muqdam.[609] The statue's seated figure most probably represented a Twelfth Dynasty king, but was later usurped by Nehsy and then Dynasty 19's Merenptah.[610] Some posit that the statue was originally set up at Tell el-Dab'a.[611] On both sides of the feet are traces of parallel inscriptions, reading 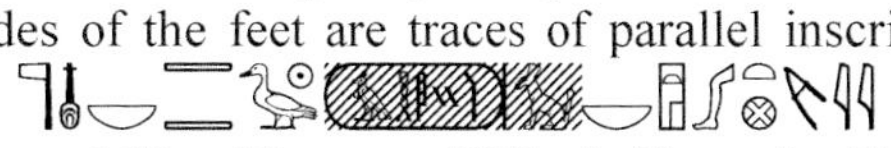 *nṯr nfr [nb] t3.wy s3 Rˁ.w Nḥsy mry [Sṯḫ] nb Ḥw.t-wˁr.t* 'the good god, [lord] of the two lands, son of Ra, Nehsy, beloved of [Seth], lord of Avaris'. Bietak writes that this marks the first use of the epithet 'beloved of Seth' and the first attestation of the name Avaris.

597 Redmount, *On an Egyptian/Asiatic Frontier*, 801-806, figs 131-132.
598 Redmount, *On an Egyptian/Asiatic Frontier*, 250-251; Redmount, *JMA* 8/2 (1995), 77; Redmount, *BA* 58/4 (1995), 186-187; Holladay, in *Hyksos*, 195.
599 Redmount, *On an Egyptian/Asiatic Frontier*, table 39.
600 Redmount, *On an Egyptian/Asiatic Frontier*, table 39; Holladay, *Tell El-Maskhuṭa*, 45, fig. 75. For more, see Ben-Tor, *Scarabs*, appendix pls 1-2.
601 MacDonald, *BA* 43/1 (1980), 57; Holladay, *Tell El-Maskhuṭa*, 46-47.
602 Holladay, *Tell El-Maskhuṭa*, fig. 72.
603 Redmount, *On an Egyptian/Asiatic Frontier*, 195.
604 Holladay, *Tell El-Maskhuṭa*, 47, figs 73-74.
605 Holladay, in *Hyksos*, 195-196.
606 Holladay, in *Hyksos*, 195; Paice, Holladay and Brock, in *Haus und Palast*, 172.
607 Paice, Holladay and Brock, in *Haus und Palast*, 172.
608 Paice, Holladay and Brock, in *Haus und Palast*, 171; Redmount, *On an Egyptian/Asiatic Frontier*, 265; Redmount, *JMA* 8/2 (1995), 68.
609 Naville, *Ahnas el Medineh*, 28.
610 Ryholt, *Political Situation*, 150, n. 545.
611 Von Beckerath, *Zweiten Zwischenzeit*, 83, 262.

4.2.11 *Retaba, Tell el-*

Lat.Lon. 30°33'N 31°58'E

Refs *LÄ* 6, 353-354; PM 4, 55; Naville, *Saft el-Henneh*; Petrie, *Hyksos and Israelite Cities*; Redmount, *On an Egyptian/Asiatic Frontier*, 124-131, fig. 19; Rzepka et al., *E&L* 19 (2009), 241-280; Rzepka et al., *E&L* 24 (2014), 39-120.

Chron. Second Intermediate Period

Tell el-Retaba is situated in the Wadi Tumilat at a strategic point above the westerly valley constriction.[612] Several excavations and surveys have unearthed remains of the Old Kingdom to the Ptolemaic Period.[613] Finds dating to the Middle Kingdom and Second Intermediate Period from early excavations are generally unstratified.[614] Minor artefacts of this period, such as scarabs and ceramic sherds, were also primarily collected from surface surveys and the 'town rubbish'.[615] Of the scarabs, Petrie includes:[616]

- One royal-name scarab of a Sihotepibra, either Dynasty 12's Amenemhat I or Dynasty 13's Sewesekhtawy (Figure 4.24 [1]);[617]

- One scarab with two horizontal panels and the signs for *Ptḥ ḏi wꜣs nfr ꜥnḫ* 'Ptah, may he give/be given strength and good life' (Figure 4.24 [2]). The design and inclusion of Ptah's name indicate a late Thirteenth to Fifteenth Dynasty date;[618]

- One scarab with two red crowns flanking *nfr* signs (Dynasty 13-15) (Figure 4.24 [3]);[619]

- Three scarabs, each with a confronting pair of cobras flanking a *ḫpr* beetle with either a *nbw* or *nb* sign underneath (Figure 4.24 [4-6]).[620] Their style finds the closest parallels from late MBIIB to MBIIC Jericho, Tell el-'Ajjul and Megiddo;[621] and

FIGURE 4.24. SELECTED SCARABS, TELL EL-RETABA (NOT TO SCALE). AFTER PETRIE, *HYKSOS AND ISRAELITE CITIES*, PL. 32.

- One scarab bearing two crocodiles as a figurative rather than hieroglyphic motif akin to late MBA Levantine scarabs, especially those from Tell el-'Ajjul (Figure 4.24 [7]).[622]

Petrie also mentions the discovery of a 'Hyksos fortification wall' (Petrie's Wall 1), remnants of which were unearthed during recent salvage excavations.[623] He additionally notes an infant's burial within a rectangular 'arched' mudbrick pit beneath Wall 1, near a triangular stack of bricks.[624] While the structures have been dated to the Second Intermediate Period,[625] newly discovered Nineteenth Dynasty infant burials across the site and in proximity to Wall 1 indicate that the wall, as well as Petrie's structures, should instead be assigned to a later date.[626]

Nonetheless, recent excavations by the Polish-Slovac Archaeological Mission and the Ministry of Antiquities report the discovery of other Fifteenth Dynasty tombs, as well as domestic layers with Levantine ceramics.[627] One tomb, for instance, shares architectural similarities with vaulted tombs at Tell el-Dab'a's Stratum D/3, its finds also pointing to the MBIIB/C period.[628] Despite the dating of this

612 Redmount, *On an Egyptian/Asiatic Frontier*, 124.

613 Naville, *Saft el-Henneh*, 24-25; Petrie, *Hyksos and Israelite Cities*, 28-35; Holladay, *Tell El-Maskhuṭa*, 3-9; Redmount, *On an Egyptian/Asiatic Frontier*, 125-131; Rzepka et al., *PAM* 19 (2007), 143-151; Wodzińska, *PAM* 19 (2007), 152-160; Rzepka et al., *E&L* 19 (2009), 241-280; Wodzińska, *JAEI* 4/4 (2012), 45-46; Rzepka et al., *E&L* 24 (2014), 39-120. For more on the excavations at the site, see Rzepka et al., *E&L* 19 (2009), 241-245.

614 Rzepka et al., *E&L* 19 (2009), 267; Holladay, *Tell El-Maskhuṭa*, table 1; Redmount, *On an Egyptian/Asiatic Frontier*, 125-131. A Tell el-Yahudiyah vessel has been linked to the site, although its provenance is disputed (Myres, *Journal of Hellenic Studies* 17 [1897], 145, n. 6; Kaplan, *Tell el Yahudiyeh*, 92, 101)

615 Redmount, *On an Egyptian/Asiatic Frontier*, 127; Petrie, *Hyksos and Israelite Cities*, 32.

616 Petrie, *Hyksos and Israelite Cities*, pl. 33.

617 Petrie, *Hyksos and Israelite Cities*, pl. 33 [2]; Ryholt, *Political Situation*, 338-339, table 17.

618 Ben-Tor's Design Class 3B8. The scarab is not included in Ben-Tor's study, yet it finds parallels with those from Tell el-Dab'a and her Late Palestinian Series. Petrie, *Hyksos and Israelite Cities*, pl. 32 [2b]; Ben-Tor, *Scarabs*, 132-133, 165, pl. 81.

619 Ben-Tor's Design Class 3B3e. Petrie, *Hyksos and Israelite Cities*, pl. 32 [3]; Ben-Tor, *Scarabs*, 19, 80-81, 131, 163, pls 8, 34, 54, 79.

620 Petrie, *Hyksos and Israelite Cities*, pl. 32 [5, 5a, 63].

621 Ben-Tor's Design Class 9C1. Ben-Tor, *Scarabs*, 175, pl. 97.

622 Ben-Tor's Design Class 9D. Petrie, *Hyksos and Israelite Cities*, pl. 32 [32]; Ben-Tor, *Scarabs*, 177, pl. 99 [24].

623 Petrie, *Hyksos and Israelite Cities*, 29, pl. 35a; Redmount, *On an Egyptian/Asiatic Frontier*, 128-129; Rzepka et al., *E&L* 19 (2009), 247; Górka and Rzepka, *MDAIK* 67 (2011), 93-94, figs 1-2.

624 Petrie, *Hyksos and Israelite Cities*, 29, pl. 35a. Redmount also notes that the spacing between the infant burial and the stack of bricks is odd, suggesting either a second burial or an error in Petrie's plan (Redmount, *On an Egyptian/Asiatic Frontier*, 128-129).

625 Petrie, *Hyksos and Israelite Cities*, 29; Redmount, *On an Egyptian/Asiatic Frontier*, 128-129, fig. 19.

626 Górka and Rzepka, *MDAIK* 67 (2011), 93-100.

627 Rzepka et al., *E&L* 24 (2014), 39-120; Wodzińska, *JAEI* 4/4 (2012), 45-46.

628 Rzepka et al., *PAM* 23/1 (2011), 93-97, figs 6-7; Rzepka et al., *E&L* 24 (2014), 39-120; Wodzińska, *PAM* 23/1 (2011), 109-110,

and other similar tombs between the mid and late Fifteenth Dynasty,[629] the evidence suggests that further data on the early Hyksos period may yet be discovered at Tell el-Retaba.

Overall, the known finds signify that a material culture with some Levantine influences and links with the eastern Delta was occupying Tell el-Retaba in the latter half of the Second Intermediate Period. The site's close proximity to Tell el-Maskhuta and similar tactical placement on a ridge in the Wadi Tumilat would support some connection to Fifteenth Dynasty trade. Future excavations will surely clarify the nature of this connection.

4.2.12 Sahaba, Tell el-

Lat.Lon. 30°32'N 32°06'E

Refs PM 4, 22ff; Leclant, *Orientalia* 44 (1975), 202; Redmount, *On an Egyptian/Asiatic Frontier*, 162, fig. 56 [7-12].

Chron. Second Intermediate Period (?)

Southeast of Tell el-Maskhuta lies Tell el-Sahaba, a site previously excavated by Abd el-Haq Ragab[630] and surveyed by Holladay's Wadi Tumilat project.[631] The results are yet to be published, but secondary references note two possible spheres of Levantine influence: (1) tombs with grave goods such as MBA bronze daggers and Levantine-style scarabs; and (2) Levantine-style pottery, including thick-walled platter bowls, a red-polished jar, Tell el-Yahudiyah juglets and possibly imported Syro-Palestinian store-jars.[632] If correct, the evidence suggests some contact with Levantine cultural elements at Tell el-Sahaba, perhaps akin to those observed at Tell el-Maskhuta.

4.2.13 Yahudiyah, Tell el-

Lat.Lon. 30°17'N 31°19'E

Refs *LÄ* 6, 331-335; PM 4, 56-57; Naville and Griffith, *Mound of the Jew*; Petrie, *Hyksos and Israelite Cities;* du Mesnil du Buisson, *BIFAO* 29 (1929), 155-178; Adam, *ASAE* 55 (1958), 305, 308-312; Tuffnell, in *Archaeology in the Levant*, 76-101; Ashmawy Ali, *E&L* 20 (2010), 31-42.

Chron. Late Thirteenth to Fifteenth Dynasty

Situated between Memphis and Wadi Tumilat is Tell el-Yahudiyah. The site was excavated and marginally published by Naville and Griffith,[633] Petrie,[634] du Mensil du Buisson,[635] Adam,[636] Abd el-Fatah[637] and, most recently, Ashmawy Ali,[638] all of whom describe various, and often contradictory, elements of Tell el-Yahudiyah's topography.[639] Reports agree that the site extends approximately 29.82 hectares, encompassing both the southern Tell el-Kabir (the 'Great Tell') and the northeastern Tell el-Soghier (the 'Small Tell').[640]

4.2.13.1 The 'Hyksos camp'

Petrie was the first to identify Tell el-Kabir's earthen embankment as the fortification walls of a so-called 'Hyksos camp' (Figure 4.25).[641] He also interpreted them as evidence for the nomadic, archery-based, culture of the Hyksos.[642] Scholars followed his interpretation in studies on Hyksos origins and Near Eastern fortification systems.[643] Ricke and Wright, however, viewed the earthwork as an Egyptian artificial mound built for cultic rather than defensive purposes.[644] Indeed, the stepped walls of the mound are constructed at an inclination varying between 27° to 55° which, as Petrie himself wrote, 'greatly detract(s) from the inaccessibility of the slope'.[645] Because they are plastered, the perimeter walls may have also functioned as retaining walls to either protect the tell from erosion or counterbalance the pressure of the fill laid within the enclosure.[646] Combined with the lack of a defensible gateway or any other noticeable protective/ defensive elements atop the enclosed area,[647] the sloping perimeter walls would strongly suggest that the structure was not primarily built for defensive purposes.

A cultic rationale behind the earthwork's construction necessitates the presence of cultic elements within the area of the enclosure. Thus far, statues and inscriptions from Dynasties 19 and 20 point to the presence of a temple,[648] but earlier remains are absent. Another suggestion may be offered through Veblen's theory of conspicuous consumption, or the socio-political reasoning behind public works.[649] Constructing the artificial tell likely necessitated an organised bureaucratic system which could have utilised the building activity as a means to

fig. 1.

629 Rzepka et al., *PAM* 23/1 (2011), 93-97, figs 6-7; Rzepka et al., *E&L* 22-23 (2012/2013), 253-288.

630 Bietak, *TeD* 2, 90, n. 319.

631 Holladay, *Tell El-Maskhuṭa*, 6; Redmount, *On an Egyptian/Asiatic Frontier*, 162.

632 Redmount, *On an Egyptian/Asiatic Frontier*, fig. 56 [7-12]; van den Brink, *Tombs and Burial Customs*, 56.

633 Naville and Griffith, *Mound of the Jew*.

634 Petrie, *Hyksos and Israelite Cities*.

635 Du Mensil du Buisson, *BIFAO* 29 (1929), 155-178.

636 Adam, *ASAE* 55 (1958), 305, 308-312.

637 See Ashmawy Ali, *E&L* 20 (2010), 31-42, n. 3.

638 Ashmawy Ali, *E&L* 20 (2010), 31-42.

639 For an overview, see Wright, *ZDPV* 84 (1968), 3-10.

640 Ashmawy Ali, *E&L* 20 (2010), 31.

641 Petrie, *Hyksos and Israelite Cities*, 1-2.

642 The same inference was applied to explain a similar earthwork uncovered by Petrie at Heliopolis. Petrie, *Hyksos and Israelite Cities*, 1-10; Petrie, *Man* 75 (1906), 113-114; Petrie, *Heliopolis*.

643 See, for instance, Albright, *JPOS* 2 (1922), 110-138; Albright, *JPOS* 15 (1935), 224; Kenyon, *Amorites and Canaanites*, 70.

644 Ricke, *ZÄS* 71 (1935), 107-111; Wright, *ZDPV* 84 (1968), 16-17.

645 Petrie, *Hyksos and Israelite Cities*, 5.

646 Ricke, *ZÄS* 71 (1935), 108; Wright, *ZDPV* 84 (1968), 17.

647 Reports note the depredation of the earthwork and its structures due to *sebbakhin* activities, although parts remain despite the damage. See Naville and Griffith, *Mound of the Jew*, 6-7; du Mensil du Buisson, *BIFAO* 29 (1929), 158.

648 Naville and Griffith, *Mound of the Jew*, 7-12; Petrie, *Hyksos and Israelite Cities*, 3.

649 Veblen, *Theory of the Leisure Class*. See also Bagwell and Bernheim, *The American Economic Review* 86/3 (1996), 349-373; Trigg, *Journal of Economic Issues* 35/1 (2001), 99-115.

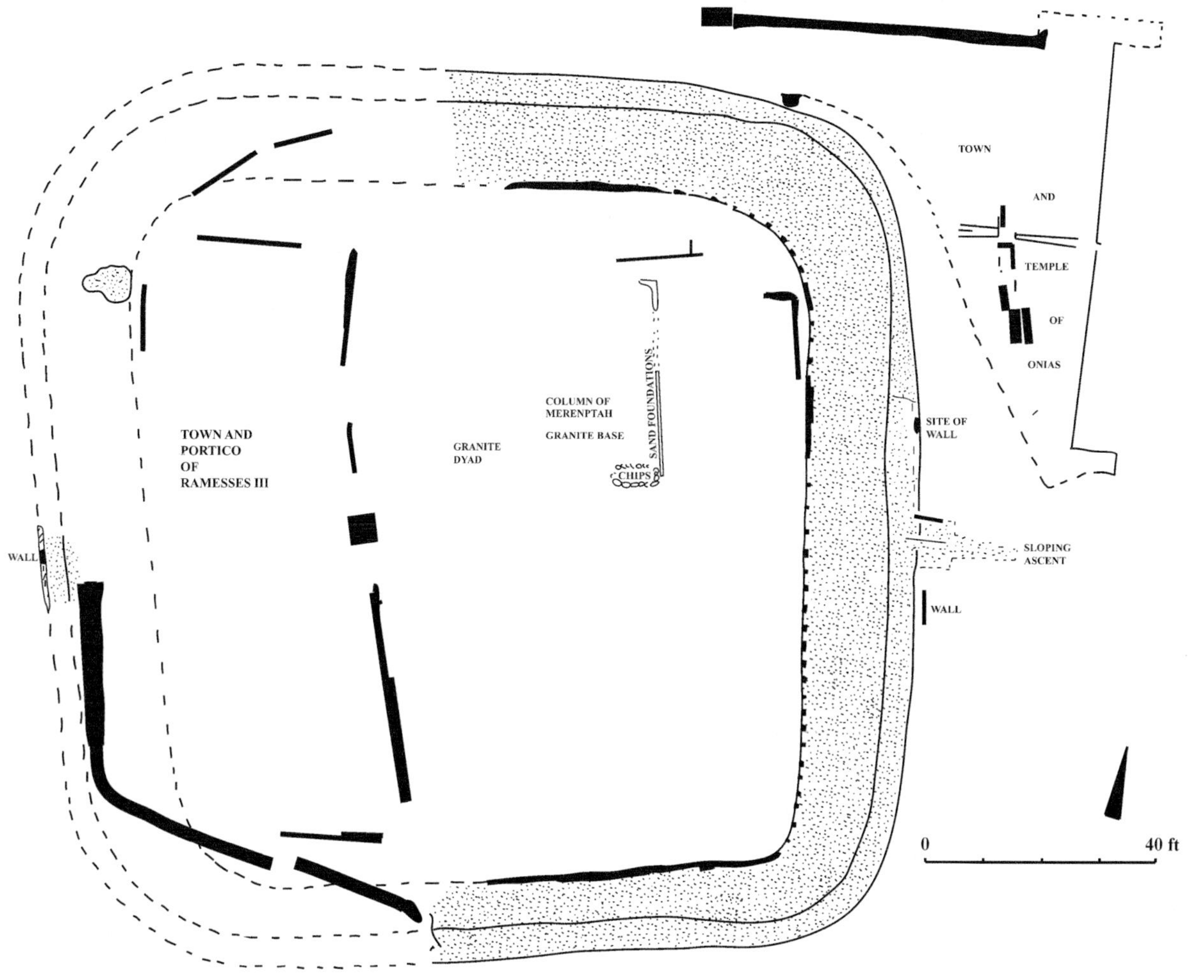

FIGURE 4.25. PLAN OF THE SO-CALLED 'HYKSOS CAMP', TELL EL-YAHUDIYAH. AFTER PETRIE, *HYKSOS AND ISRAELITE CITIES*, PL. 2.

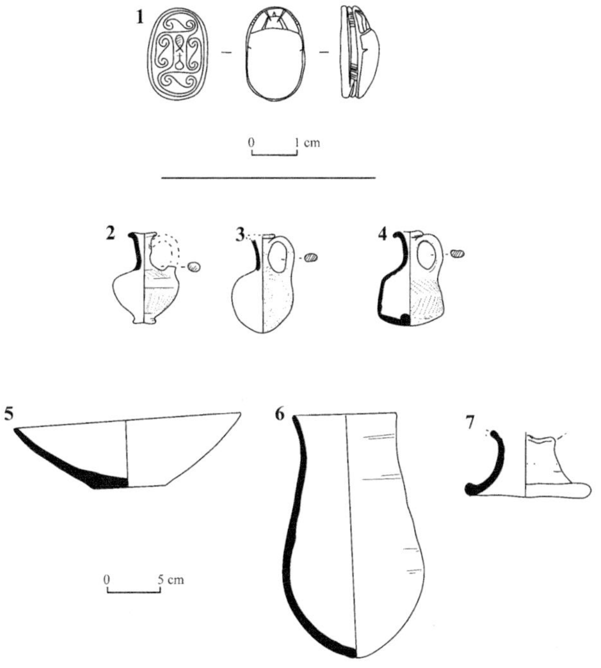

FIGURE 4.26. ITEMS FROM GRAVE 2, TELL EL-YAHUDIYAH. AFTER TUFNELL, IN *ARCHAEOLOGY IN THE LEVANT*, FIGS 3, 5-7.

establish, legitimise and/or enhance prestige and power.[650] The result of this activity would consequently present an impressive symbol of authority.[651] In this case, when the Tell el-Yahudiyah earthwork was built is as significant as by whom. If its construction is dated to the earliest discovered remains in the enclosure which, as discussed below, belong to the late Thirteenth or early Fifteenth Dynasty, then the structure may be viewed as evidence of either a weakened political system searching for a means to strengthen its reign, or a newly-established bureaucracy attempting to stabilise its rule.[652]

Thus, the instigator of the building activity could have been either the existing rulers of the Thirteenth Dynasty or an emerging power in the eastern Delta. Both were surely likely to benefit from Tell el-Yahudiyah's strategic location between Memphis, Wadi Tumilat and Tell el-Dab'a. Until further excavations are completed on the earthwork and its enclosed area, no firm conclusions can be made

650 For similar cases in the Southern Levant, see Finkelstein, *Tel Aviv* 19 (1992), 201-220; Bunimovitz, *Tel Aviv* 19 (1992), 221-234.

651 Bunimovitz, *Tel Aviv* 19 (1992), 225.

652 Examples from the Southern Levant indicate that the need to demonstrate such power and prestige was stronger in either the formative or transitional phases of administrations. See Bunimovitz, *Tel Aviv* 19 (1992), 225; Finkelstein, *Tel Aviv* 19 (1992), 213-214.

regarding its construction. However, applying the theory of conspicuous consumption provides a tantalising glimpse into the activities of the elite.

4.2.13.2 Burial customs

Tombs have been discovered at three different areas at Tell el-Yahudiyah: (1) within the earthwork; (2) to the northeast of the earthwork near the temple of Onias; and (3) to the northeast of Tell el-Soghier.[653] The majority are rectangular mudbrick pits without superstructures. A few cases are of burials with vaulted roofs or 'projecting bricks'.[654] No particular orientation or positioning of skeletal remains has been observed,[655] but infants tend to be contracted with their knees drawn up.[656] Both single and double burials occur.[657]

Petrie and Tufnell have both provided a sequence for the tombs based on the stylistic development of the graves' scarabs.[658] Petrie was reliant on the rule of degradation by which artefacts develop from well-executed forms to poorly executed items, whereas Tufnell compared scarab base designs and lengths with those of the Southern Levant.[659] Despite the limitations of both approaches,[660] the two attributed the tombs to the Hyksos period and agreed on a sequence for the graves (Graves 2, 407, 3, 5, 19, 4, 16, 20, 37, 1, 6 and 43). The following presents a revised sequence based on specific scarab base designs as well as Egyptian pottery forms and characteristic non-Egyptian ceramics.[661]

Late Thirteenth to early Fifteenth Dynasty: Graves 2, 3 and 407 (Figures 4.26-27)

The tombs contained biconical, globular and cylindrical Tell el-Yahudiyah ware. Also unearthed were a buff globular juglet with red wavy lines and flat-based bowls. Grave 2 contained a copper toggle-pin at the blade-bone of a skeleton and scarabs (Figure 4.26 [1]).[662] A Levantine origin is argued for two scarabs from Grave 407 which feature the so-called Canaanite *k3* form (Figure 4.27 [1, 3]).[663] The assemblages of these graves fit well within the late Middle Kingdom to early Fifteenth Dynasty period, with parallels from Tell el-Dab'a's Strata E/2-E/1.

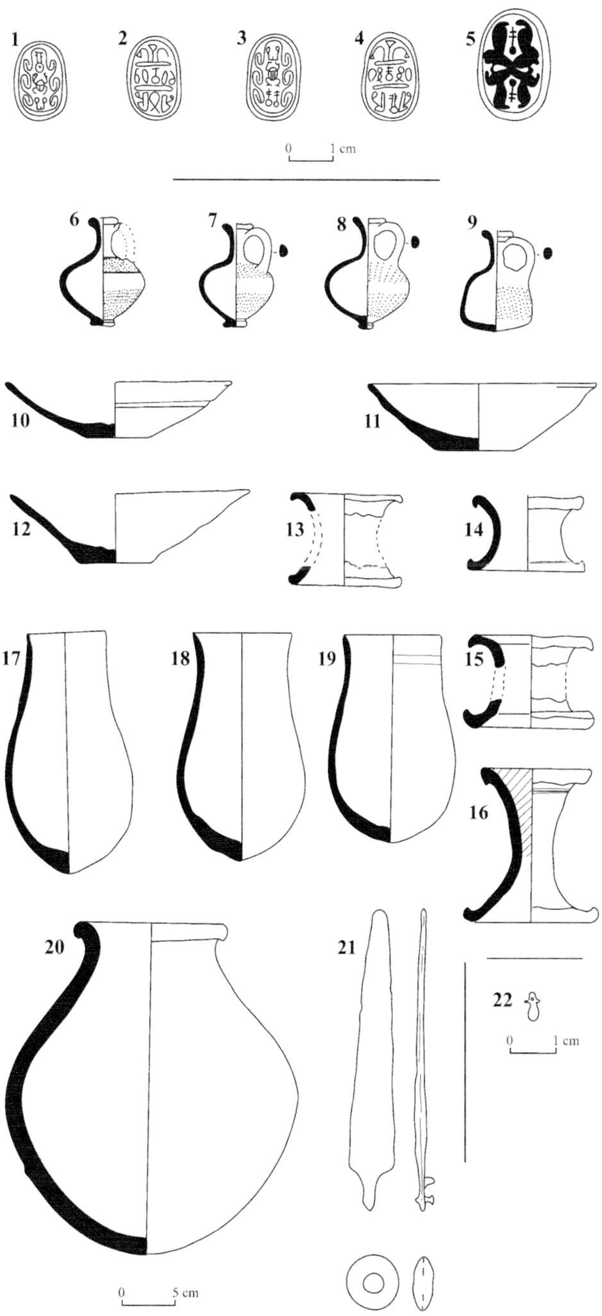

FIGURE 4.27. ITEMS FROM GRAVE 407, TELL EL-YAHUDIYAH. AFTER TUFNELL, IN *ARCHAEOLOGY IN THE LEVANT*, FIGS 1, 3, 5-9.

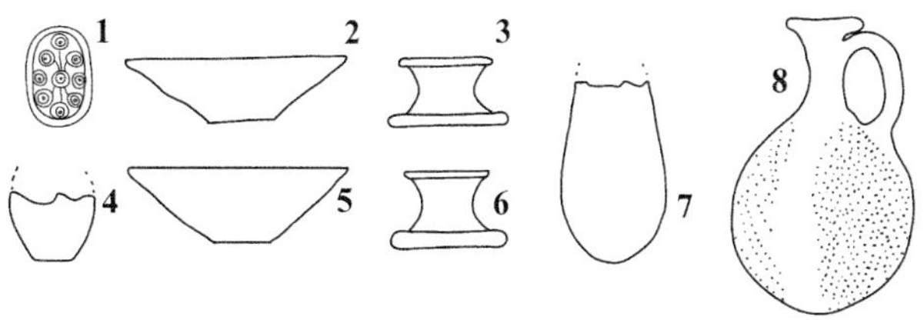

FIGURE 4.28. ITEMS FROM GRAVE 4, TELL EL-YAHUDIYAH (NOT TO SCALE). AFTER PETRIE, *HYKSOS AND ISRAELITE CITIES*, PLS 7, 10.

653 Petrie, *Hyksos and Israelite Cities*, 10; Adam, *ASAE* 55 (1958), 309-310; Ashmawy Ali, *E&L* 20 (2010), fig. 1.
654 Graves 5 and 37 excavated by Petrie and an unspecified number unearthed by Abd el-Fatah. Petrie, *Hyksos and Israelite Cities*, 12-13; Ashmawy Ali, *E&L* 20 (2010), 33, 38-39.
655 Tufnell, in *Archaeology in the Levant*, 76.
656 Petrie, *Hyksos and Israelite Cities*, 12-13; Ashmawy Ali, *E&L* 20 (2010), 33.
657 Petrie, *Hyksos and Israelite Cities*, 12-13.
658 Petrie, *Hyksos and Israelite Cities*, 11-12; Tufnell, in *Archaeology in the Levant*, 81.
659 Petrie, *Hyksos and Israelite Cities*, 11-12; Tufnell, in *Archaeology in the Levant*, 77-79.
660 For more, see Ben-Tor, *Scarabs*, 63-66.
661 Further details on the material may be found in Tufnell's inventory list. Tufnell, in *Archaeology in the Levant*, 92-100.
662 Ben-Tor's Design Class 2B2. Ben-Tor, *Scarabs*, 13-14, pl. 4 [25].
663 Ben-Tor's Design Class 7B2. Ben-Tor, *Scarabs*, 29.

Early Fifteenth Dynasty: Grave 4 (Figure 4.28)

A globular Tell el-Yahudiyah juglet and flat-based bowls were uncovered alongside a flat-based incurved cup, its form being similar to those from Tell el-Maskhuta.[664] One scarab with concentric circles bears an almost identical pattern to another from the MBIIA period at Jericho.[665] An early Fifteenth Dynasty date is offered for this tomb.

Mid-Fifteenth Dynasty: Graves 19, 16, 20 and 37 (Figure 4.29)

Levantine-style pottery includes globular, piriform, biconical and grooved Tell el-Yahudiyah juglets. Lamb bones were uncovered in Grave 19 and a goose egg was found in Grave 37.[666] The skeleton in the latter also had a bronze toggle-pin at its neck (Figure 4.29 [7]). Of the scarabs, only one may be of Levantine origin as implied by its design of confronted cobras flanking a *ḫpr* sign (Figure 4.29 [6]). Such elements are among Ben-Tor's Late Palestinian Series and find parallels with those on scarabs from Tell el-'Ajjul.[667]

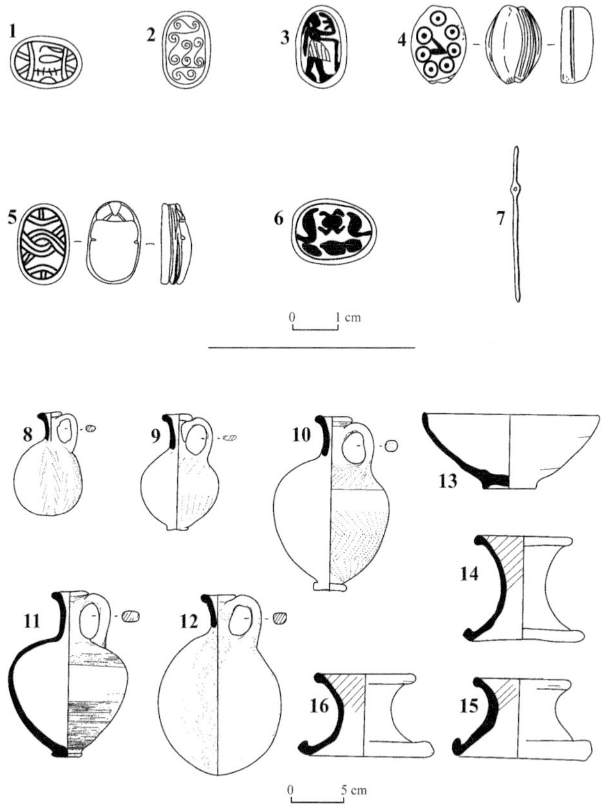

FIGURE 4.29. ITEMS FROM GRAVE 37, TELL EL-YAHUDIYAH. AFTER TUFNELL, IN *ARCHAEOLOGY IN THE LEVANT*, FIGS 2, 4-5, 7, 9.

664 Redmount, *JMA* 8/2 (1995), fig. 3 [5].
665 Ben-Tor's Design Class 4B. Ben-Tor, *Scarabs*, pl. 58 [32].
666 Petrie, *Hyksos and Israelite Cities*, 13.
667 Ben-Tor's Design Class 9C1. Ben-Tor, *Scarabs*, 96, 175, pl. 97 [12-13].

Mid-late Fifteenth Dynasty: Grave 5 (Figure 4.30)

The grave was constructed as a vaulted rectangular tomb with an additional vaulted room annexed to its west.[668] The chamber contained two skulls buried after decomposition while the annex consisted of caprid bones.[669] Grave goods included bronze weapons (a dagger and a knife), two bronze toggle-pins, Egyptian-style pottery, animal offerings, pendants and scarabs. One scarab displays a mythical figure paralleling another from MBIIB Tell el-Farah.[670] Also contemporary with the MBIIB period is the shape of the discovered dagger, which ascribes to Philip's Type 18 and is akin to those from Tell el-Dab'a's Strata E/2-D/3.[671] Interestingly, a burial from Tell el-Dab'a's Stratum D/2-3 (A/II-n/15-Nr 1) not only contains a similar assemblage and weaponry to Grave 5, but was also used as a double burial[672] with a small chamber annexed to its west containing supplementary offerings.[673] Therefore, Grave 5 should not be placed in the beginning of the grave sequence at Tell el-Yahudiyah, but should be regarded as a mid to late Fifteenth Dynasty burial.

Late Fifteenth Dynasty: Graves 1, 6 and 43

The Tell el-Yahudiyah juglets from Graves 6 and 43 are not incised. A biconical juglet from Grave 43 is painted with horizontal lines, a feature which occurs only in the late Fifteenth Dynasty at Tell el-Dab'a.[674] Although Grave 1 did not consist of any ceramics, its assemblage included a dagger of Philip's Type 18[675] and a scarab with an antelope, pointing to its late date.[676]

Although revised, the above sequence is heavily dependent upon Petrie's publication. Further archaeological exploration will refine the postulated dates, particularly for Graves 3, 6, 16 and 20. Views on observed customs may also alter as revealed by, for instance, Abd el-Fatah's recent excavations at Tell el-Soghier which have unearthed a round pit containing one donkey.[677] Dated to the Second Intermediate Period,[678] the donkey burial attests to other funerary traditions that may yet be discovered at Tell el-Yahudiyah. It is evident that the occupation spans the late Thirteenth to Fifteenth Dynasty, with Southern Levantine scarab designs more popular in the latter half of the Fifteenth Dynasty. Despite this, there are no other noticeable developments in tomb architecture and burial assemblages, thereby suggesting a presence of Levantine individuals or Levantine influence rather than an invasion of Levantine peoples into Tell el-Yahudiyah.

668 Petrie, *Hyksos and Israelite Cities*, 12.
669 Petrie, *Hyksos and Israelite Cities*, 12-13.
670 Ben-Tor's Design Class 10B and 10C. Ben-Tor, *Scarabs*, 100-101, 180, pls 103 [44], 105 [7].
671 Philip, *TeD* 15, 142.
672 Van den Brink, *Tombs and Burial Customs*, 34-35.
673 Van den Brink, *Tombs and Burial Customs*, 34-35.
674 Aston and Bietak's Late Egyptian Group L.5.3. Kopetzky, in *Bronze Age in the Lebanon*, 205, fig. 8; Aston and Bietak, *TeD* 8, 231, fig. 167.
675 Philip, *TeD* 15, 142.
676 Ben-Tor's Design Class 9B. Ben-Tor, *Scarabs*, 95.
677 Ashmawy Ali, *E&L* 20 (2010), 34.
678 Ashmawy Ali, *E&L* 20 (2010), 38.

4.2.13.3 Other

Over 132 scarabs were found across Tell el-Yahudiyah or were bought from local workers.[679] Utilised as evidence of Hyksos rule, the scarabs include three with Middle Kingdom royal names,[680] as well as the Second Intermediate Period names of Sekhaenra, *Ḫy3n* and Apophis.[681] Other scarab seals purportedly from the site are inscribed with the names of *Šši*,[682] *Yʿḳbhr*,[683] *ḥḳ3 ḫ3s.wt Smḳn* 'ruler of the foreign lands, *Smḳn*'[684] and *ḥḳ3 ḫ3s.wt Ḫy3n* 'ruler of the foreign lands, *Ḫy3n*'.[685] Other scarabs display MBIIA-B Levantine features such as a Horus bird wearing a red crown[686] and a cross pattern.[687] Scarabs with MBIIB-C Levantine designs are also found.[688] The scarabs' unknown contexts, however, restrict analysis concerning date of deposition, function and trade relations.

Nonetheless, the pottery and scarab forms uncovered in the graves support Tell el-Yahudiyah's conjectured occupation in Dynasty 15. Although Weinstein has argued for its abandonment prior to the fall of the Hyksos,[689] the evidence points to the site's use until at least late Dynasty 15.[690] The site's function, marked especially by the so-called 'Hyksos camp', appears to be as a funerary, cultic and/or socio-political centre for gathering. From the earliest remains, it is evident that the occupants were most likely heavily influenced by a Levantine culture or were themselves of Levantine ethnicity as implied by the following customs: the placement of toggle-pins at the neck; the burial of bodies after decomposition; the inclusion of a goose egg and caprids in tombs; and the donkey interment. Such burials alongside the fine juglets and metal weaponry indicate that they did not belong to poor shepherds,[691] but neither were all of the elite. Furthermore, the incorporation of Egyptian ceramics and pendants within the tomb owners' funerary repertoire points to knowledge and appreciation of the Egyptian culture. Therefore, it is possible to conclude that some of Tell el-Yahudiyah's occupants were acculturated Levantines who received imports from the Levant, particularly the Southern Levant, after the establishment of Hyksos rule in the eastern Delta.

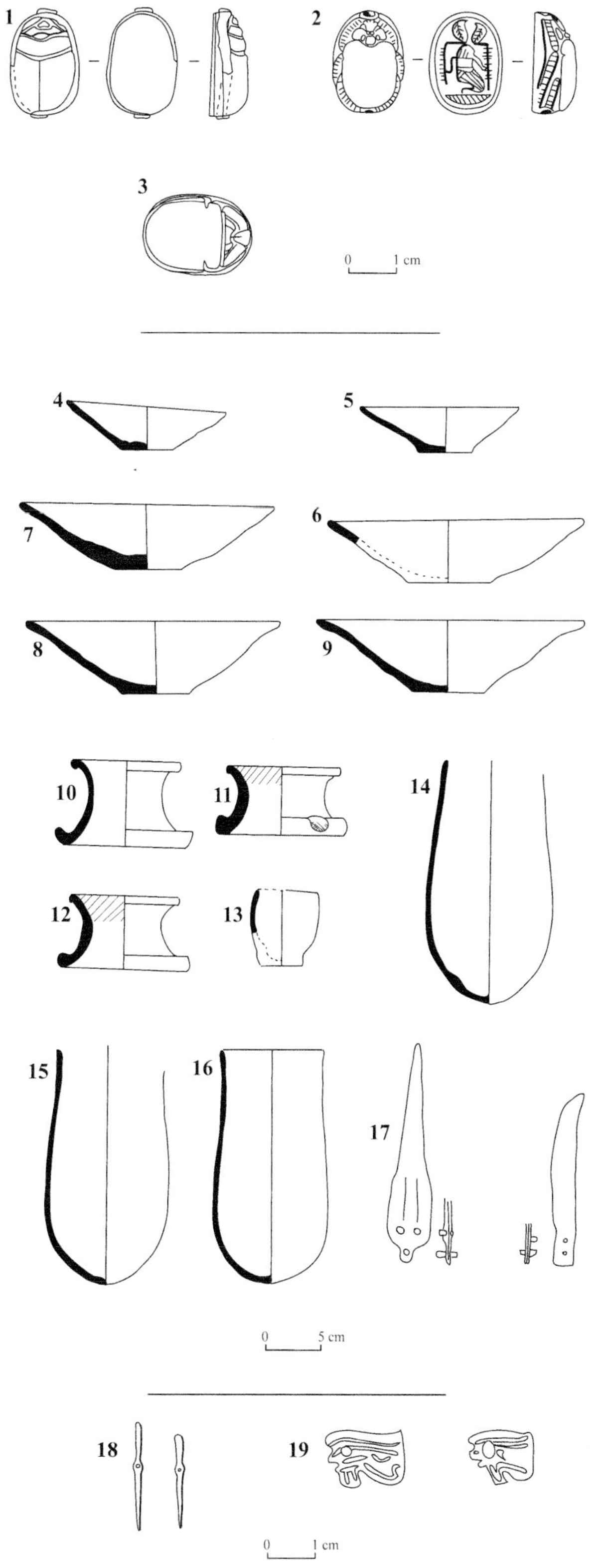

Figure 4.30. Items from Grave 5, Tell el-Yahudiyah. After Tufnell, in *Archaeology in the Levant*, figs 2, 5-9.

679 Naville and Griffith, *Mound of the Jew*, 39, pl. 10; Petrie, *Hyksos and Israelite Cities*, 3-4, 10-15, pls 6-9; Adam, *ASAE* 55 (1958), 310, pl. 20.

680 Naville and Griffith, *Mound of the Jew*, 39.

681 Petrie, *Hyksos and Israelite Cities*, 10, pl. 9 [116, 124, 143-144].

682 Ryholt, *Political Situation*, 368.

683 Ryholt, *Political Situation*, 382.

684 Ryholt, *Political Situation*, 383; Newberry, *Scarabs*, 152, pl. 23 [10].

685 Newberry, *Scarabs*, 151, pl. 22 [22]; Ryholt, *Political Situation*, 383.

686 Design class 3A4. Similar Levantine scarabs are from Megiddo and Beth Shemesh. Ben-Tor, *Scarabs*, pl. 52 [21, 28].

687 Design class 5. Similar Levantine scarabs are from Sidon and Jericho. Ben-Tor, *Scarabs*, pl. 52 [24, 29, 32]; Loffet, *AHL* 34-35 (2011/2012), 122.

688 For example, one scarab depicts a standing lion, another presents Hathor being flanked by red crowns, and a third bears a branch. Naville and Griffith, *Mound of the Jew*, pl. 10 [10, 34, 41]; Ben-Tor, *Scarabs*, 97, 102, 158, 177, pls 100 [3, 36], 105 [35], 74 [52].

689 Weinstein, *BASOR* 288 (1992), 28; Weinstein, in *Egypt, the Aegean and the Levant*, 87-88.

690 See also Aston, in *Synchronisation of Civilisations* 2, 137-138, 140-142.

691 Tufnell, in *Archaeology in the Levant*, 87.

4.3 Memphite Region

4.3.1 Dahshur

Lat.Lon. 29°48'N 31°14'E

Refs *LÄ* 1, 984-987; PM 3, 229-240; de Morgan, *Dahchour* 1, 19-23, 116, figs 23-26, 270; vol. 2, *Dahchour* 2, 38, fig. 90; Borchardt, *Statuen und Statuetten* 2, 78, pl. 88 [515]; Maragioglio and Rinaldi, *Orientalia* 37 (1968), 325-338; Swelim and Dodson, *MDAIK* 54 (1998), 319-334; Arnold, *Senwosret III*, 42-43, pls 24-27a; Allen, *BASOR* 352 (2008), 29-39.

Chron. Mid-Twelfth to Thirteenth Dynasty

Almost 30km south of modern Cairo is the necropolis of Dahshur. Featuring both Old and Middle Kingdom burials, the site has been explored by de Morgan[692] and, more recently, by the German Archaeological Institute and the Metropolitan Museum of Art.[693] Among the finds are pertinent material pointing to Egyptian-Levantine relations from the reign of Amenemhat II to the Thirteenth Dynasty.

4.3.1.1 Mid-Twelfth Dynasty, reign of Amenemhat II

A fragment uncovered at the pyramid of Amenemhat II relates to the possible burial of an Egyptian-Asiatic official.[694] The top of the fragment features remnants of torus-moulding and a cavetto-cornice, suggesting that it belonged to a false door. Two columns of text are preserved: (1)  *mty n(.y) sꜣ Sꜣ-Ip* 'controller of a phyle,[695] Sa-Ip';[696] (2)  *msi n ꜥꜣm.t nb(.t) imꜣḫ* 'born to *ꜥꜣm.t*, possessor of reverence'.[697] The official was the son of an Asiatic woman but held an Egyptian title concerned with religious duties, thereby pointing to his employment within Amenemhat II's administration. Furthermore, and especially if the fragment belongs to a tomb's false door, the inscription represents the adoption of Egyptian burial customs by Asiatics as well as their allotment of tombs surrounding the king's pyramid, indicating the administration's positive treatment of acculturated Asiatics.

4.3.1.2 Mid-late Twelfth Dynasty, reign of Senwosret III

Pyramid complex of Senwosret III

Five or six boats were uncovered in two caches interred south of Senwosret III's pyramid.[698] Scientific analyses on two boats revealed that they are of cedar (*Cedrus sp.*)[699] and it is highly likely that the remaining ships are also of the same timber.[700] The type of wood points to trade with the Northern Levant[701] and, considering the boats' royal and ritualistic function, was most probably directly imported by the state for shipbuilding.

Tomb of Khnumhotep III

Located north of Senwosret III's pyramid and linking Beni Hassan with the Memphite capital is the tomb of vizier Khnumhotep, the possible son of Khnumhotep II, 'who brings what is useful' to the king.[702] Like Khnumhotep II's tomb,[703] the mastaba of Khnumhotep III contains significant evidence for relations with Asiatics. Fragments of an inscription positioned on the mastaba's exterior niches were first published by de Morgan[704] and more recently reconstructed by Allen following the Metropolitan Museum of Art's expedition in 2001.[705] Allen posits that the remaining inscription only amounts to around 40% of the original text.[706] A translation of pertinent passages may be found in Appendix B.1.

The text's literary style, along with the use of the third person, sets it apart from typical autobiographies. Closer to such works as the Story of the Shipwrecked Sailor or that of Sinuhe,[707] the inscription stands as a rare example of the amalgamation of textual genres, providing a scenario in which the latter two pieces of literature may have been based on or inspired by true events. Khnumhotep III is not mentioned in the narrative by name but may be identified as one of the major characters frequently represented: the *im.y-rꜣ mšꜥ n(.y) sḳd.w* 'overseer of the expedition of sailors'. Another rare feature of the inscription is its positioning on the exterior of the tomb, indicating its public literate audience. Such a location could denote the text's significance in the public and 'international' career of Khnumhotep III, which is reflected in his title *mḥ-ib nsw.t m ḏr St.t m ptpt Mnṯ.tyw* 'confidant of the king in obstructing *St.t* and trampling the *Mnṯ.tyw*'.[708] If so, then the suppression of his name cannot only be explained by his 'extraordinary devotion... to the kings'[709] but also by royal control over the foreign. That is, the decorum of the time may have restricted the extent to which Khnumhotep III attributed his personal success in international politics.[710] Thus, a *topos* representation of Asiatics is to be expected.

692 De Morgan, *Dahchour*, 2 vols.
693 Arnold, *Senwosret III*; Arnold, *MDAIK* 38 (1982), 25-65.
694 De Morgan, *Dahchour* 2, 38, fig. 90.
695 Ward, *Index*, 96 [803].
696 Ranke, *Personennamen* 1, 22 [4].
697 Schneider, *Ausländer in Ägypten* 2, 31; Doxey, *Egyptian Non-Royal Epithets*, 321.
698 De Morgan, *Dahchour* 1, 81-83, fig. 105.
699 Now located at the Carnegie Museum of Natural History, Pittsburgh, and the Field Museum of Natural History, Chicago. Ward, *Ancient Egyptian Ships*, 84.
700 Two ships are at the Cairo Museum (CG 4925 and CG 4926) and one is at an unknown location. Creasman, *Cairo Dahshur Boats*, 9, 30, 36-37, n. 89.
701 Creasman suggests that the timbers may have also been war booty, yet no Middle Kingdom evidence exists for the import of cedar via this method. Creasman, *Cairo Dahshur Boats*, 37.
702 See Chapter 4.4.1.3.
703 For a discussion on the familial relationship, see Franke, in *Middle Kingdom Studies*, 51-65.
704 De Morgan, *Dahchour* 1, 19-23, figs 23, 26.
705 Allen, *BASOR* 352 (2008), 29-39.
706 Allen, *BASOR* 352 (2008), 32.
707 Allen, *BASOR* 352 (2008), 32, 36-37. See Chapter 4.6.9.
708 2H.
709 Allen, *BASOR* 352 (2008), 38.
710 The same may be the case in private tombs' battle scenes of the Old and Middle Kingdoms in which the tomb owner never explicitly represented his involvement. See Mourad, *BACE* 22 (2011), 148.

Figure 4.31. Pectoral, tomb of Mereret, Dahshur. After de Morgan, *Dahchour* 1, pl. 19 [1] (drawn from photograph).

Figure 4.32. Pectoral, tomb of Mereret, Dahshur. After Grajetzki, *Tomb Treasures*, fig. 69 (drawn from photograph).

When viewed from this perspective, the portrayal of events in the Levant becomes clearer. The inscription follows a maritime expedition to *Kbny* (Byblos) and *Wꜣti/Wꜣiṯ* (Ullaza) for ꜥš-wood.[711] Docking at Byblos, the overseer of the expedition meets with the city's ruler, called *Mꜣki*, either his personal name or the hieroglyphic transcription of the Semitic *malku* 'king',[712] and informs him of a previous trading arrangement between the two lands.[713] After ascertaining the Egyptian's desire to trade with Ullaza,[714] the Byblite ruler arranges another expedition. *Mꜣki*'s son, along with 100 *ꜥꜣm.w* and Egyptian-speakers, perhaps becomes involved in both a land and sea voyage to Ullaza.[715] The Egyptian-speakers arrive first via ship, delivering *Mꜣki*'s message to Ullaza's nameless ruler to not let the ships return (empty?) to Byblos. Afterwards, *Mꜣki*'s son and his *ꜥꜣm.w* combine forces with the maritime contingent and make a plan to fight with Ullaza's ruler.[716] At this juncture, letter correspondence takes place between the Egyptian pharaoh, *Mꜣki* and Ullaza's sovereign, after which the text hints at the pharaoh's possible militaristic intervention.[717] The outcome is gleaned from a fragment mentioning the continuance of maritime contact with Byblos.[718]

If, as Allen suggests, Egypt had originally been trading with Ullaza and sided with it against Byblos,[719] then one must question why Egyptian ships continued to dock at Byblos. Allen infers that the pharaoh had toppled the regime at Byblos causing the change from a *Mꜣki* '*malku*' kingship to a *ḥꜣ.ty-ꜥ* leadership,[720] thereby opening a new trading channel under Egyptian control. It is also viable that the Egyptian expedition initially arrived at Byblos to seek assistance in establishing relations with Ullaza.

Regarding the inscription's context, it is more feasible that the text exaggerates the pharaoh's involvement as a regulator of peace, perhaps signalling the expedition's timely observance of two cities competing for trading power, with Byblos emerging as the victor. Here, Khnumhotep III's roles as overseer of the expedition and king's confidant in Asiatic matters would have surely been vital, leading to the inscription's placement in his tomb while glorifying the *topos* of the superlative Egyptians and the abysmal Asiatics who are determined literally as *pf* and figuratively as tied up, kneeling, figures with coiffed hair. Despite such a stereotypical representation, the remaining text signifies Egyptian commercial and political involvement in the coastal Northern Levant during Dynasty 12. It further signals the Egyptians' knowledge of their neighbours' political frameworks and geography.

4.3.1.3 Late Twelfth Dynasty, reign of Amenemhat III

Among the pottery types uncovered within Amenemhat III's first pyramid complex at Dahshur are sherds of Syro-Palestinian store-jars.[721] The fragments of two bases and a rim ascribe to MBIIA forms and signify trade with the Levant.[722]

Presenting more hostile relations are two well-preserved pectorals buried in the tomb of Amenemhat III's sister, Mereret (Figures 4.31-32). The first pectoral depicts a cartouche of Senwosret III beneath which are opposing,

711 The expedition's destination is not specified in the remaining text. The following outline is dependent on Allen's reconstruction of the fragments in Allen, *BASOR* 352 (2008), 29-39.

712 Allen, *BASOR* 352 (2008), 33.

713 2A4-2B4.

714 2A2-3.

715 2P8-10, 2C1-D3, 3A5-B5.

716 The preposition *ḥnꜥ* 'with' rather than r 'against' is used.

717 3P4, 3P6-10, 3C1-D2, 3D2-4.

718 ON4-5.

719 Allen, *BASOR* 352 (2008), 36-37.

720 Allen, *BASOR* 352 (2008), 37. See Chapter 6.3.3 for this title's use by the Byblite elite.

721 Arnold, *MDAIK* 38 (1982), 41-42.

722 De Morgan, *Dahchour* 1, 73-74, figs 164-165; Allen, in *Pottery* 2, 188-190, 194.

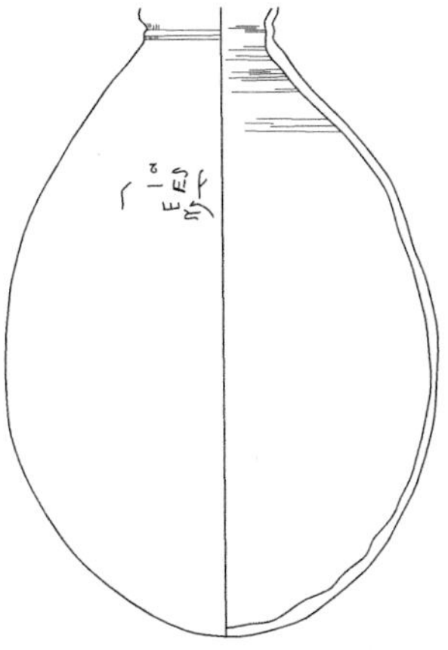

FIGURE 4.33. MARL C JAR WITH HIERATIC TEXT, BURIAL OF SITWERET, TOMB OF HORKHERTI, DAHSHUR. AFTER ALLEN, IN *ARCHAISM AND INNOVATION*, FIG. 1 [11].

kneeling figures of Asiatics with yellow skin, shoulder-length hair and pointed beards. Each raises his arm towards the face and has his hair grasped by a griffin that additionally tramples a darker-skinned figure, probably another foreigner (Figure 4.31).[723] The second pectoral portrays two facing and identical smiting scenes, each featuring the king and a yellow-skinned Asiatic captive with a coiffed hairstyle, short beard and decorated kilt (Figure 4.32).[724] Each Asiatic is armed, carrying a probable dagger in one hand and a throw-stick in the other, lifting it up before his face as if to stop the smiting king. Surrounding glyphs read *nṯr nfr nb tȝ.wy ḫȝs.wt nb.(w)t N(.y)-mȝʿ.t-Rʿ.w* 'the good god, lord of the two lands and all foreign lands, Nimaatra (Amenemhat III)'. Between the king's legs are *sḳr St.tyw* 'smiting the *St.tyw*', verifying the kneeling figures' Asiatic identity and affirming the continuity of the smiting scene as a *topos* representation of kingly control over Egypt's enemies.

A different reference to the Levant occurs in the burial of Sitweret in the tomb of Horkherti (Nr 31). Recently excavated and yet to be completely published, the burial probably belonged to a member of an elite family of viziers and officials.[725] Its assemblage includes a cedar coffin as well as a Marl C jar with a label apparently reading *ỉrp n(.y) Kṯ* 'wine of *Kṯ*', the toponym identified as a site near Homs in modern Syria (Figure 4.33).[726] Evidently, Levantine commodities were distributed in Egyptian vessels likely via an Egyptian trading centre. Along with the cedar coffin, this highlights the demand for Northern Levantine products by the capital's elite.

723 De Morgan, *Dahchour* 1, 64, pl. 19 [1].
724 Gee, *JARCE* 41 (2004), 27.
725 Arnold, 'Private Tombs'; Allen, in *Archaism and Innovation*, 327.
726 Allen, in *Archaism and Innovation*, 327, fig. 1 [11]; Arnold, 'Private Tombs'.

4.3.1.4 Thirteenth Dynasty

Shaft-tomb of Nebhoteptikhered

Another princess whose shaft-tomb contained a representation of an Asiatic is Nebhoteptikhered. Located within Amenemhat III's pyramid complex, the tomb's contents bear closer affinities to those of Awibra Hor's nearby shaft-tomb.[727] The location and burial goods support the ascription of Nebhoteptikhered to the Thirteenth Dynasty, with a possible familial relation to Awibra, perhaps as his and, as some theorise, Queen Nebhotepti's daughter.[728] The tomb yielded a wooden statuette of a standing male described as 'un sémite'.[729] Wearing a short kilt with one arm preserved by his side, the figure's black hair is near shoulder-length (Figure 4.34). The presence of a short pointed beard covering the figure's lower jaw from ear to ear is akin to Asiatic beards, such as that of Khnumhotep II's *Ỉbšȝ*, suggesting that the statuette is of an Asiatic.[730] Other elements absent from de Morgan's sketch but pictured in Borchardt's publication[731] are possible hieroglyphs on the figure's chest[732] and a broken nose. As Nebhoteptikhered's statuette does not depict the Asiatic in a submissive position, it presents a less bellicose representation of Levantines.

Graffiti, pyramid of Senwosret III

Beneath Senwosret III's pyramid is a system of underground apartments and tunnels accessible via a vertical shaft dug into the pyramid's inner court.[733] An unblocked corridor leads to an antechamber, devoid of obstacles, with an easterly door opening into a serdab.[734] Here, the walls are covered with the graffiti of figures bearing foreign features (Figure 4.35). Although the subterranean complex was likely constructed during Senwosret III's reign,[735] the graffiti may date to a later period. De Morgan originally attributed them to the complex's builders, yet it is doubtful whether workers would have been permitted to deface a royal structure during or immediately following construction.[736] Finds dating between the late Twelfth Dynasty and Second Intermediate Period indicate that individuals could have entered the chambers at this time.[737] Pyramid blocks were also quarried near the end

727 De Morgan, *Dahchour* 1, 91-117; Ryholt, *Second Intermediate Period*, 217-218, n. 750.
728 Some have dated the tomb to the late Twelfth Dynasty, identifying Nebhoteptikhered as Amenemhat III's daughter. Ryholt, *Second Intermediate Period*, 217-218, n. 750; Hari, *BSEG* 4 (1980), 45-48; Wastlhuber, *Die Beziehungen zwischen Ägypten und der Levante*, 94; Schmitz, *Titel sȝ-njswt 'Königsohn'*, 195, n. 5.
729 De Morgan, *Dahchour* 1, 116-117, figs 270, 274.
730 See Chapter 4.4.1.3, Figure 4.52. See also Wastlhuber, *Die Beziehungen zwischen Ägypten und der Levante*, 94.
731 Borchardt, *Statuen und Statuetten* 2, 78, pl. 88 [515].
732 Cautiously identified as two hieroglyphs in the centre of the chest, the one above being similar to .
733 Arnold, *Senwosret III*, 33-34.
734 Arnold, *Senwosret III*, 34-35.
735 Arnold, *Senwosret III*, 41.
736 De Morgan explains that the graffiti was created for 'le simple désir de passer leur temps pendent que leurs camarades travaillent au fond de la mine'. De Morgan, *Dahchour* 2, 95; Arnold, *Senwosret III*, 42.
737 Arnold, *Senwosret III*, 41-42; Arnold, in *Second Intermediate*

of the Ramesside period, leading Di. Arnold to distinguish the foreigners as northerners from the Aegean.[738] An examination of the graffiti, however, points to a Thirteenth Dynasty date, agreeing with Do. Arnold's proposition.[739]

The graffiti includes several profile portraits of males (Figure 4.35), most of whom have hairdos with a tuft above the forehead. The style at the back varies from voluminous yet straight to round and coiffed. The closest parallels are found in the Asiatic warriors' hairstyles from the fragment of Senwosret I's pyramid (see Figure 4.43) and Amenemhat's tomb, Beni Hassan (see Figure 4.50). Two complete figures of individuals are depicted with this distinctive hairstyle. That on the south wall (Figure 4.35D) wears a garment draped over his shoulders with a fringed edge partially hanging loose beneath the left shoulder, and the other on the east wall (Figure 4.35B) is dressed in similar attire with fringed/dotted detailing on the left shoulder. The clothing and hairstyles support the two's identification as Asiatics.[740] As for when they were drawn, the stance and apparel of the only typical portrayal of an Egyptian on the south wall (Figure 4.35D) points to the Thirteenth Dynasty.[741] This period also presents the most likely date when visitors could have entered the subterranean complex with ease and without attracting punishment.

The Egyptian-like figure on the south wall provides a point of comparison with the Asiatic portraits,[742] as the artists clearly differentiated the two's phenotype. It is also likely that the individuals who drew them were themselves Asiatic, as the graffiti mostly focus on these non-Egyptians. The purpose of the graffiti cannot be positively ascertained. Do. Arnold suggests a connection between the south wall's falcon and the worship of chthonic Sokar, positing that the visitors had a religious experience in the subterranean complex and 'left the sketches as a token of their visit'.[743] Conversely, they could be tomb robbers or explorers who chose to draw familiar images on the walls of a former ruler's complex. In any case, the graffiti portray a certain freedom to express ethnic identity, indicating awareness of what physically distinguished such an identity during the late Middle Kingdom.

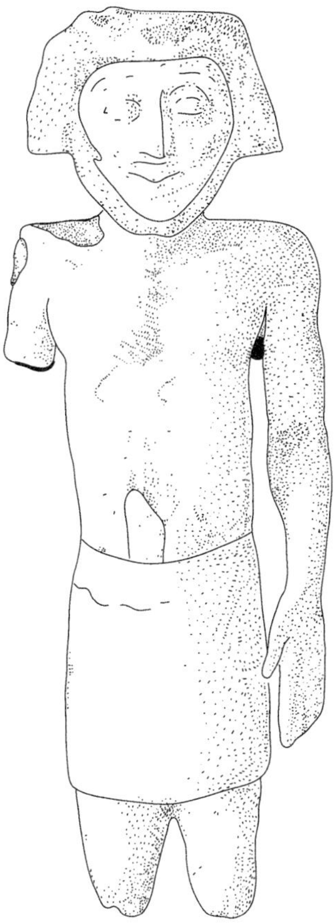

FIGURE 4.34. WOODEN STATUETTE, TOMB OF NEBHOTEPTIKHERED, DAHSHUR. AFTER DE MORGAN, *DAHCHOUR* 1, FIG. 270.

4.3.2 *Harageh, el-*

Lat.Lon. 29°13'N 31°02'E

Refs PM 4, 105-107; Engelbach, *Harageh*; Grajetzki, *Harageh*.

Chron. Twelfth to early Fifteenth Dynasty

Opposite el-Lahun lies el-Harageh, where a number of Predynastic to New Kingdom cemeteries were uncovered. The cemeteries include approximately 300 burials of the Middle Kingdom, primarily of the late Twelfth to early Thirteenth Dynasties.[744] Due to the cemeteries' proximity to el-Lahun, scholars have proposed that the nearby cultivated lands were estates owned by the elite of el-Lahun, who were buried at el-Harageh.[745] Although not proven, the size and quality of finds from el-Harageh's tombs suggest that they belonged to higher status individuals, some possibly

Period, 204, n. 165.

738 Arnold, *Senwosret III*, 42, 42-43.

739 Arnold, in *Second Intermediate Period*, 204.

740 Arnold, in *Second Intermediate Period*, 202-204, n. 159. The fringed edge of the garment depicted on the south wall is similar to those of Asiatics in the Beni Hassan tombs of Khnumhotep I and Khnumhotep II (Figures 4.49, 4.52).

741 Arnold, in *Second Intermediate Period*, 204.

742 This is also suggested in Arnold, in *Second Intermediate Period*, 204-205.

743 Arnold, in *Second Intermediate Period*, 205-206.

744 See n. 78; Engelbach, *Harageh*; Grajetzki, *Harageh*, 21-22.

745 Engelbach, *Harageh*, 9; David, *Pyramid Builders*, 178. Kemp and Merrillees argue that the almost 4km distance between el-Lahun and el-Harageh reduces the chance that el-Lahun's workers were buried at el-Harageh. Instead, el-Harageh's cemeteries were probably associated with a nearer settlement constructed for a yet undiscovered royal building project (Kemp and Merrillees, *Minoan Pottery*, 15).

A.

B.

C.

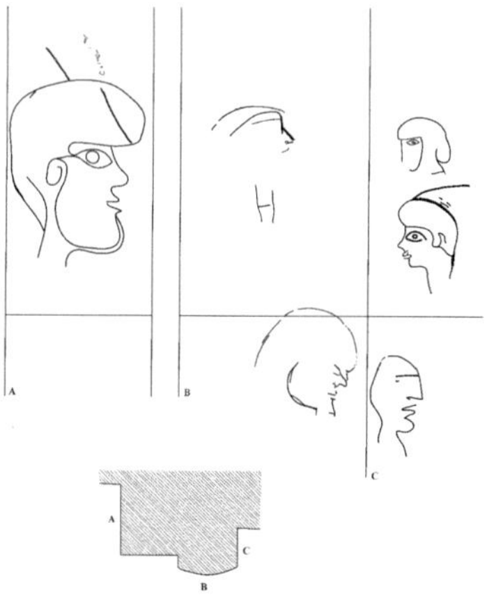

D.

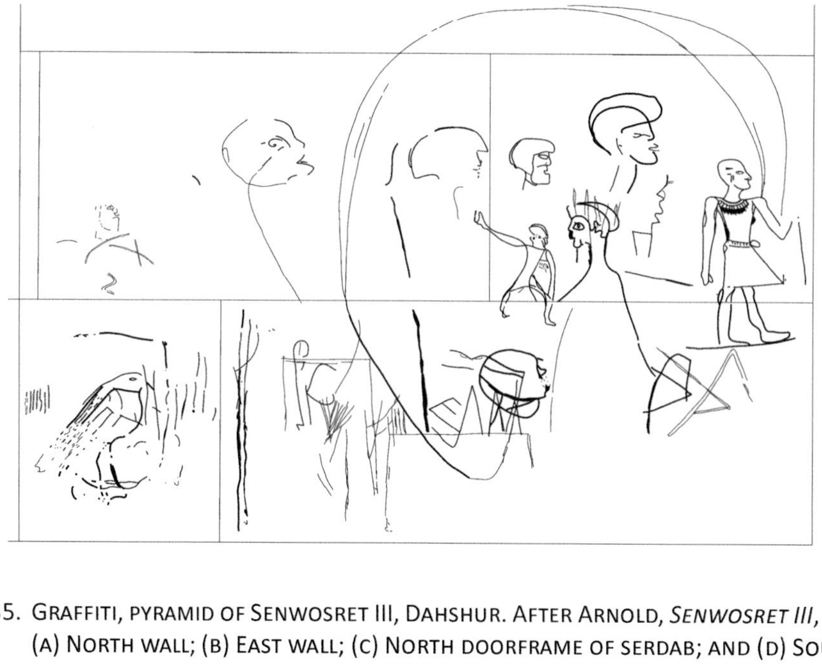

Figure 4.35. Graffiti, pyramid of Senwosret III, Dahshur. After Arnold, *Senwosret III*, pls 24-26. (a) North wall; (b) East wall; (c) North doorframe of serdab; and (d) South wall.

GROUP	PLACE OF ORIGIN	LEVEL	DYNASTY
1	Lebanese 'Akkar Plain and Tripoli	VIc-b	Mid-late 15
2	Inland Lebanon, between Sidon and Tripoli	VII-VIc	Early 13 to mid-15
3	Lebanese coast, between Sidon and Tripoli	VII-VIa	Early 13 to late 15
4	Northern Israeli coast, possibly around the Haifa Bay	VII-VIa	Early 13 to late 15
OTHER	Inland Levant, including Ashkelon region	VII-VIa	Early 13 to late 15

FIGURE 4.36. PETROGRAPHIC GROUPS IDENTIFIED FROM A PETROGRAPHIC ANALYSIS OF IMPORTED VESSELS FROM KOM RABI'A. AFTER OWNBY, *CANAANITE JARS FROM MEMPHIS*, 120-178.

of the royal family.[746] Pertinent data from the cemetery includes:

- Tell el-Yahudiyah ware,[747] including two piriform jugs from Tomb 297 with parallels from the early Thirteenth Dynasty,[748] two wheel-made globular jugs with parallels from the early Fifteenth Dynasty,[749] and fragments of unknown shape;[750] and

- A tall ovoid dipper juglet from Tomb 297, decorated in red and white horizontal bands.[751] The shape is very similar to locally made dipper juglets from Tell el-Dab'a's Stratum D/3,[752] although no parallels for its decoration can be found. Based on form, a Fifteenth Dynasty date is favoured.

These finds indicate that some elite individuals buried at el-Harageh had access to Levantine(-influenced) products during the Middle Kingdom and Second Intermediate Period.

4.3.3 *Hawara*

Lat.Lon. 20°16'N 30°54'E

Refs Petrie, *Kahun*, 18, pl. 11 [2-4]; Marochetti, *JEA* 86 (2000), 44, pl. 7 [1].

Chron. Mid-Thirteenth Dynasty

Approximately 9km northwest of el-Lahun is Hawara, the location of the second pyramid and mortuary complex of Amenemhat III. Excavated by Petrie, the site contains tombs of Dynasties 12-13,[753] one of which belongs to the 'controller of a phyle' Imenysenebnebwy. Possibly dating to the reign of Khendjer,[754] the tomb owner is shown on one fragment before an offering table, next to which are remnants of two horizontal registers probably showing offering bearers.[755] Between the two is a row with the inscription  *ꜥ3m wdp.w Mnw-nfr* 'ꜥ*3m*, butler,[756] Menunofer',[757] identifying a foreigner with an Egyptian name and thus his assumption of local customs. The term 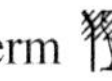 *ꜥ3m* may similarly be inscribed at the beginning of a partially preserved column of text above the seated Imenysenebnebwy. Overall, then, the block provides evidence for the employment of Asiatics by middle class Egyptians in the region of Hawara during the mid-Thirteenth Dynasty.

4.3.4 *Kom Rabi'a*

Lat.Lon. 29°50'N 31°15'E

Refs Bader, *TeD* 19; Ownby, *Canaanite Jars from Memphis*.

Chron. Late Twelfth to Fifteenth Dynasty

Kom Rabi'a, a mound 300m south of Mit Rahina, was first excavated by the Egypt Exploration Society between 1984 and 1990.[758] Within the 500m^2 area examined at the northwest section of the mound (Kom Rabi'a Area AT/RAT) is a stratified sequence dating between Dynasties 12 and 26.[759] Pertinent to this study are Levels VIII to VI of the Middle Kingdom strata, in which foreign pottery was uncovered (Figures 4.36-37).[760]

Over 98% of the ceramic repertoire is Egyptian in style,[761] providing chronological points of comparison

746 For instance, court type Tombs 280 and 608 contained remnants of beaded flagellums while silver pectoral fragments decorated with such royal symbols as the bee and the falcon were found in Tomb 124. Engelbach, *Harageh*, 15-16, pl. 15 [2]; Grajetzki, *Harageh*, 23-26, 31; Richards, *Society and Death*, 104-124.

747 Engelbach dates the vessels to Dynasty 12 (*Harageh*, 10).

748 Aston and Bietak's Levanto-Egyptian Group I.3.2a with contemporaneous finds from Tell el-Dab'a's Strata F-E/2. Engelbach, *Harageh*, pl. 41 [99f, j]; Kaplan, *Tell el Yahudiyeh*, fig. 37a-b; Aston and Bietak, *TeD* 8, 169, 553, figs 105, 110.

749 Aston and Bietak's Late Egyptian IX Groups L.9.1 and L.9.4 with contemporaneous finds from Tell el-Dab'a's Stratum E/3. Engelbach, *Harageh*, pls 41 [99d], 52; Kaplan, *Tell el Yahudiyeh*, fig. 19c; Aston and Bietak, *TeD* 8, 257, 556, figs 183, 186, 189.

750 Engelbach, *Harageh*, 10, pl. 10 [15].

751 Engelbach, *Harageh*, 11, pls 10 [12], 41 [99s]; Kemp and Merrillees, *Minoan Pottery*, 34, fig. 16.

752 The shape of the neck and the ovoid body find close parallels with Juglet 2619 from Tell el-Dab'a's A/II-m/16-Nr 1. Kopetzky, in *MBA in the Levant*, 234, 242, fig. 6.

753 Petrie, *Kahun*, 18.

754 Fiore-Marochetti, *JEA* 86 (2000), 43.

755 Block 1889.1021 at the Ashmolean Museum, Oxford. Fiore-Marochetti, *JEA* 86 (2000), 44, pl. 7 [1]; Petrie, *Kahun*, 18, pl. 11 [2].

756 Ward, *Index*, 90 [755].

757 Ranke, *Personennamen* 1, 152 [5].

758 Bourriau and Gallorini, in *Pottery* 2, 107; Giddy, *Memphis* 2, 1.

759 Giddy, *Memphis* 2, 1-4.

760 Giddy and Jeffreys, *JEA* 77 (1991), 4. The discovery of late Middle Kingdom seals has also been mentioned in preliminary reports. Richards lists two bearing the *ꜥnrꜥ* formula from, apparently, an Eighteenth Dynasty context (Richards, *Anra Scarabs*, 132) whereas Ben-Tor, in reference to these two *ꜥnrꜥ* scarab seals, writes that they were 'among a late Middle Kingdom group of discarded sealings' (Ben-Tor, *Scarabs*, 46). Due to such discrepancies regarding their context and the lack of the excavation's publication, they are not included here. However, if the seals are of late Middle Kingdom date, then they corroborate the ceramic evidence by indicating Memphite access to Levantine imports.

761 Bourriau, in *Ancient Egypt*, 184.

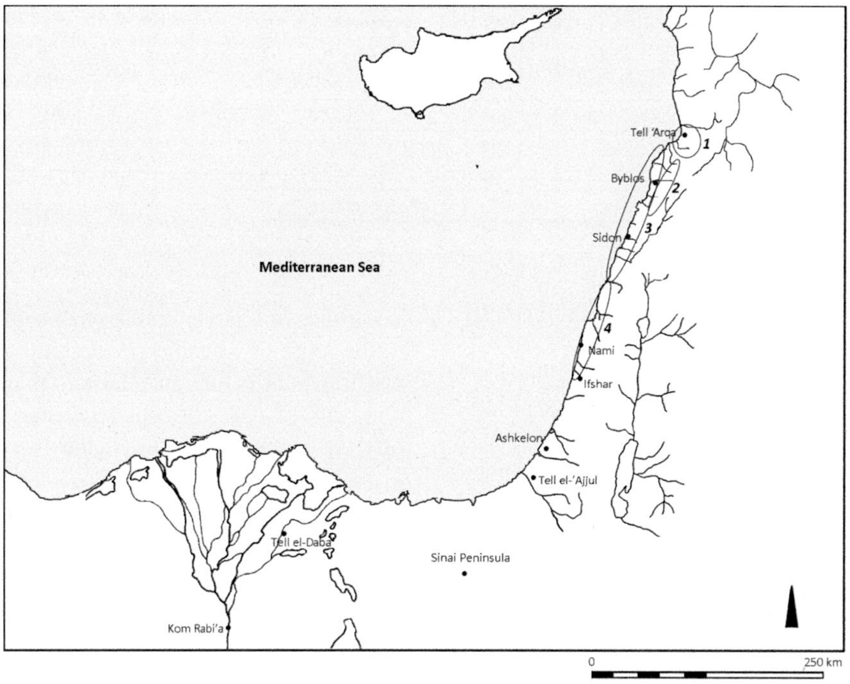

FIGURE 4.37. GEOGRAPHIC DESIGNATES OF PETROGRAPHIC GROUPS 1-4 OF IMPORTED VESSELS FROM KOM RABI'A. AFTER OWNBY, *CANAANITE JARS FROM MEMPHIS*, FIG. 5.9.

with sites further north. Bader's studies on Kom Rabi'a's ceramic association with Tell el-Dab'a have revealed a synchronisation between Tell el-Dab'a's G/4 and Kom Rabi'a's Level VIII; G/3-1 with Level VII; F-E/3 with Level VIe-d; and D/3 with Level VIb.[762] The studies also report that distinct regional variations are first attested in the ceramics of Strata F-E/3 and Level VIe-d (the late Thirteenth Dynasty), with evidence of continued albeit limited contact until at least the mid-Fifteenth Dynasty.[763] Evidently there was growing regionalisation,[764] but it remains unclear whether a complete cultural or political border existed between the two cities from the late Thirteenth Dynasty. Still, it is apparent that middle to lower class individuals were not under complete control by a non-Memphite hegemony. Additionally, no evidence exists for a takeover by a foreign race.

The same may be deduced from the non-Egyptian pottery at the site.[765] Fragments of Tell el-Yahudiyah ware were discovered,[766] including an imported Piriform 1a juglet attributed to Dynasty 13 with parallels from el-Lahun, Byblos and Tell el-Dab'a.[767] The majority of foreign wares were of Syro-Palestinian store-jar sherds, most of which occur in Level VId.[768] Petrographic and chemical analyses of 51 jar samples from Levels VI and VII deduced four areas for the sherds' fabrics (Figures 4.36-37), including: (1) the 'Akkar Plain of northern Lebanon (13.7% of the 51 samples); (2) inland Lebanon (11.7%); (3) the Lebanese coast (39.2%); and (4) the northern Israeli coast (25.4%).[769] Remaining sherds could not be classified to a particular Levantine region, although one sample was probably from southern Israel, near Ashkelon.[770]

The findings agree with petrographic tests on Tell el-Dab'a's Syro-Palestinian store-jars,[771] demonstrating that such vessels were primarily imported from the Northern Levant, specifically the modern Lebanese coast. Fabrics at Tell el-Dab'a suggest wider trading patterns as well as greater demand, an expected outcome considering Tell el-Dab'a's extensive stratigraphy, larger excavation area and more varied social classes. These same reasons restrict the analysis of Kom Rabi'a, a much smaller site, as a representation of the city of Memphis.[772] Nonetheless, Kom Rabi'a provides a sampling of the material culture

762 Bader, in *Synchronisation of Civilisations* 3, 249-267; Bader, in *Proceedings of the 5th International Congress*, 207-223; Bader, *TeD* 19.

763 Bader, in *Synchronisation of Civilisations* 3, 265; Bader, in *Proceedings of the 5th International Congress*, 214-216.

764 Bader, in *Synchronisation of Civilisations* 3, 265; Bader, in *Proceedings of the 5th International Congress*, 216-217.

765 These include a Cypriote Base Ring juglet and several sherds of Nubian ware akin to the Pan-Grave tradition. Jeffreys and Giddy, *JEA* 75 (1989), 2; Bourriau, in *Egypt and Africa*, 132.

766 Bader, *TeD* 19, 383-387, 497-498.

767 Aston and Bietak's Levanto-Egyptian Type Group I.1.5. Bader, *TeD* 19, 496 [6094]; Aston and Bietak, *TeD* 8, 144, 552, figs 85-86; Kaplan, *Tell el Yahudiyeh*, fig. 29 [b].

768 Bourriau, *Eretz Israel* 21 (1990), 19; Ownby, *Canaanite Jars from Memphis*, 61-62, fig. 3 [9].

769 Samples from late Second Intermediate Period and early New Kingdom levels are not included here but are listed as residual MBA samples in Ownby, *Canaanite Jars from Memphis*, 120-178; Ownby and Bourriau, in *Petrographic Approaches to Archaeological Ceramics*, 175-184, fig. 2; Ownby and Smith, in *Intercultural Contacts in the Ancient Mediterranean*, 269-273, fig. 2.

770 Ownby, *Canaanite Jars from Memphis*, 141-149.

771 See Chapter 4.2.2.8 and 4.2.8; Figures 4.15-16, 4.21.

772 Further excavation of the mound and surrounding regions would provide a more complete portrait of Memphis during the Middle Kingdom and Second Intermediate Period. Until then, the name 'Memphis' should only be used cautiously.

of the more average Memphites who still had continued access to and demand for Levantine commodities well into the Fifteenth Dynasty.

4.3.5 *Lahun, el-*

Lat.Lon. 29°13'N 30°59'E

Refs PM 4, 107-112; Petrie, *Illahun;* Petrie, *Kahun;* Petrie, Brunton and Murray, *Lahun* 2; Griffith, *HieraticPapyri;* Kaplony-Heckel, *Handschriften* 1; Merrillees, *AJBA* 2 (1973), 51-53; Luft, *Archiv*; Luft, in *Sesto Congresso* 2, 297-297; David, *Pyramid Builders;* Quirke, *Lahun;* Collier and Quirke, *Letters;* Collier and Quirke, *Religious, Literary;* Collier and Quirke, *Accounts.*

Chron. Mid-Twelfth to early Fifteenth Dynasty

El-Lahun is located at the entrance of the Fayum and was founded by Senwosret II as his final resting place. A cemetery of the Middle Kingdom royal family and administrative officials was established around the north and west of the king's pyramid.[773] Further east, a settlement, also known as Kahun,[774] was developed for pyramid workers and personnel who administered the cultic activities of funerary temples in the area. First excavated by Petrie, several finds in the settlement aroused suspicion of a resident immigrant population.[775] This was reinforced after the translation of hieratic papyri pointed to a number of Asiatics amidst the Egyptian population.[776] As findings from renewed excavations are not yet published,[777] archaeological details are largely reliant on Petrie's monographs. Settlement data prior to the New Kingdom is generally assigned between the reigns of Senwosret II and the end of Dynasty 13 with the last king attested being Ibiaw,[778] whereas temple papyri date to the reigns of Senwosret III and Amenemhat III.[779]

4.3.5.1 *The settlement*

Petrie's plan lays out a standard, orthogonal, settlement,[780] indicating its purpose-built construction during Senwosret II's reign.[781] The town includes an 'Acropolis' with a sizeable, possibly mayoral, complex,[782] large houses with granaries, and small units. According to the granaries' capacities, a population density between 5000 (maximum rations) and 9000 (minimum rations) has been estimated[783] while the spatial capacity of houses suggests a population of 8000 people.[784] Finds linked to trade and the presence of Levantines are presented below.

Characteristic non-Egyptian ceramics

Imported and local imitations of foreign ceramics occur, including Cypriote, Minoan, Pan-Grave and Levantine pottery.[785] The latter includes at least four Levantine Painted Wares with decorative band-zones, including a dipper juglet similar in form to those from Tell el-Dab'a's Strata d/1 (G/4) and b/3 (F);[786] a handle-less(?) piriform jug;[787] two fragments of a shoulder;[788] and a vessel's neck.[789] Remains of Syro-Palestinian store-jars may have also been discovered in recent excavations but remain unpublished.[790]

Around 21 specimens of Tell el-Yahudiyah vessels have been recorded.[791] These include a piriform juglet with a ring base and three zones of decoration paralleling a juglet from MBIIA Kafr el-Jarra,[792] and three other fragments, possibly of piriform juglets, comparable to a vessel from Mirgissa.[793] The assemblage additionally contains MBIIB forms such as a wheel-made globular juglet paralleling those from Tell el-Dab'a's Strata E/1-D/2,[794] a cylindrical juglet,[795] and two fragments of a vessel(s) with a naturalistic design.[796] Thus, the Tell el-Yahudiyah juglets reflect MBIIA and MBIIB styles with Egyptian parallels dating between Dynasties 13 and 15. The variety

773 Quirke, *Lahun*, 7-10.
774 For more on the ancient Egyptian toponyms for the site and its complexes, see Quirke, *Administration of Egypt*, 157, 178, n. 10; Luft, in *Lahun Studies*, 1-41; Horváth, in *Archaism and Innovation*, 171-203.
775 Petrie, *Kahun*, 25-26, 40-45; Petrie, *Illahun*, 9-11, 14-15.
776 Petrie, *Kahun*, 45-46; Petrie, *Illahun*, 47-49; Griffith, *Hieratic Papyri*.
777 See Quirke, *Lahun*, 133; David, *Pyramid Builders*, 113; Horváth, *Bulletin du Musèe Hongrois des Beaux-Arts* 110-111 (2009), 186-190.
778 Petrie, *Kahun*, 31, pl. 10 [72]; David, *Pyramid Builders*, 112-113, 195-197; Kemp and Merrillees, *Minoan Pottery*, 88-102; Gallorini, in *Under the Potter's Tree*, 410-411.
779 Quirke, *Lahun*, 32.
780 Petrie, *Illahun*, pl. 14; Petrie, Brunton and Murray, *Lahun* 2, pls 2, 33-34a; Kemp, *Ancient Egypt*, 211-213, fig. 76.
781 Petrie, *Kahun*, 23.
782 Petrie, *Illahun*, 6; Quirke, *Lahun*, 47, 55.
783 Kemp, *Ancient Egypt*, 215-216, table 1.
784 Badawy, *JARCE* 6 (1967), 108. For another estimate see Kemp, *Ancient Egypt*, 217.
785 Foreign wares include the neck of a Cypriote White Painted III-IV Pendant Line Style jug, Classical Kamares ware and other Minoan sherds of closed and open vessels, as well as an incised sherd of a bowl paralleling those from Pan-Grave burials at Hu and Mostagedda. Petrie, *Illahun*, 9-10, pl. 1; Kemp and Merrillees, *Minoan Pottery*, 57-86, 98-99, figs 22-23, table 1; Merrillees, *BASOR* 326 (2002), 3, figs 1-2; Gallorini, in *Under the Potter's Tree*, 410-411; Fitton, Hughes and Quirke, in *Lahun Studies*, 112-140; Kemp, *JNES* 36/4 (1977), 289-292.
786 Petrie, *Illahun*, pl. 1 [16]; Merrillees, *AJBA* 2 (1973), 51-53, fig. 2; Bagh, in *MBA in the Levant*, 92-93; Bagh, *TeD* 23, 63, fig. 30 [g]; Kopetzky, in *MBA in the Levant*, 229-231, 240, fig. 2 [7280, 4761].
787 Petrie, *Illahun*, pl. 1 [22]; Merrillees, *AJBA* 2 (1973), 51-53, fig. 2; Bagh, in *MBA in the Levant*, 92-93; Bagh, *TeD* 23, 63, fig. 30 [h].
788 Petrie, *Illahun*, pl. 1 [11]; Merrillees, *AJBA* 2 (1973), 51, fig. 1; Bagh, *TeD* 23, 63, fig. 30 [f].
789 Petrie, *Illahun*, pl. 1 [19]; Bagh, *TeD* 23, 63, fig. 30 [e].
790 They are noted in Petrik, in *From Illahun to Djeme*, 218.
791 Petrie, *Illahun*, pl. 1 [17, 20-2]; Petrie, *Kahun*, pl. 27 [199-202]; Merrillees, *Trade and Transcendence*, 64; Kemp and Merrillees, *Minoan Pottery*, 98, n. 256; Kaplan, *Tell el Yahudiyeh*, figs 8 [b], 13 [d].
792 Aston and Bietak's Early Levantine V Group F.3. Petrie, *Illahun*, 10, pl. 1 [21]; Contenau, *Syria* 1 (1920), 127-128, pl. 11; Aston and Bietak, *TeD* 8, 128-137, fig. 74.
793 Aston and Bietak's Levanto-Egyptian Group I.3.2. Petrie, *Illahun*, 10, pl. 1 [17, 20]; Petrie, *Kahun*, 25, pl. 27 [202]; Kaplan, *Tell el Yahudiyeh*, fig. 32 [b]; Aston and Bietak, *TeD* 8, 169, figs 106, 108.
794 Aston and Bietak's Late Egyptian IX Group L.9.4. Kaplan, *Tell el Yahudiyeh*, fig. 18 [b]; Aston and Bietak, *TeD* 8, 257, 499-507, figs 186, 189, pls 97-102.
795 Aston and Bietak's Late Egyptian XII Group L.12.1. Kaplan, *Tell el Yahudiyeh*, fig. 8 [b]; Aston and Bietak, *TeD* 8, 265, figs 195, 201.
796 Aston and Bietak's Levanto-Egyptian Group J. Petrie, *Kahun*, pl. 27 [199-200]; Aston and Bietak, *TeD* 8, 193.

FIGURE 4.38. INSCRIPTIONS ON A HEDDLE-JACK, EL-LAHUN. AFTER QUIRKE, *LAHUN*, 95.

of non-Egyptian pottery attests to trade and a demand for Levantine(-influenced) products. Such demand, as well as the domestic context, perhaps indicates the presence of individuals of foreign ancestry.

Adornment

A house in the town's western sector contained a copper torque with flattened, coiled ends.[797] NAA on the copper verified that it was not sourced from an area in or near Egypt.[798] As a common Near Eastern adornment, it has been proposed that the torque belonged to a foreign woman living at el-Lahun.[799] However, figurines of males and females from Byblos specify that both sexes wore the torque.[800] If belonging to a foreigner, then the torque would suggest that he/she could wear customary dress in an Egyptian town. If worn by an Egyptian, then the torque represents the rising influence of Levantine culture on local fashion. At the very least, its appearance in a domestic setting signifies contact with the Levant.

Weaving and spinning

Spindle whorls and a heddle-jack of imported hard wood (see below) denote contact with northerners.[801] One cylindrical heddle-jack features five signs incised around its side (Figure 4.38).[802] Linked to a linear script, possibly Semitic,[803] the signs have been interpreted as *'ḥṭb*,[804] *'ḥṭwb*,[805] *'ḥi'ṣb'*[806] or *'d'ṣb.*[807] As Petrie did not record the artefact's exact context,[808] it could date to a later period. However, the type of loom is horizontal, which is the only form known in the Middle Kingdom and the less common loom type in the New Kingdom, indicating that the heddle-jack could be assigned to the earlier occupation of the site.[809] A palaeographic analysis of the linear script also points to the MBA period.[810] As such, a date between the Thirteenth and Fifteenth Dynasties for the creation of the heddle-jack is favoured here, its presence thereby implying trade with the Levant or, based on its domestic use, the presence of literate Near Eastern weavers in the area.

Organic products[811]

Plants not indigenous to Egypt but native to the Mediterranean and Levantine region were among the botanical remains at el-Lahun.[812] These include the carob plant (*Ceratonia siliqua*), black cumin (*Nigella sativa* L.), juniper berries (*Juniperus oxycedrus*) and safflower fruits (*Carthamus tinctorius* L.).[813] The remnants of carob, black cumin and safflower offer the earliest archaeological instances of the plants in Egypt. If a Middle Kingdom date is accepted, it is highly likely that they, along with the juniper berries, were imported from the Levant.[814]

The hard wood used for the spindle whorls and heddle-jack (see above) was also imported. Belonging to the *Pinacaea* family, the wood, perhaps of pine or fir,[815] was either recycled[816] or imported into el-Lahun.

4.3.5.2 The papyri

The papyri from el-Lahun can be divided into two collections: (1) mostly unpublished papyri retrieved from the rubbish deposit north of the valley temple, consisting of lists and account papyri for Senwosret II's cult and dating between Senwosret III and Amenemhat III's reign;[817] and (2) manuscripts from across the settlement,[818] which was occupied from the Twelfth to at least the early Second Intermediate Period. Foreigners are represented either by an ethnonym (e.g. *ꜥꜣm(.t)* or *Mḏꜣ.w/y*) and/or their non-Egyptian names. Appendix B.2 includes translations of published papyri, with dated documents arranged first

797 Petrie, *Illahun*, 12, pl. 13 [18].

798 Gilmore, in *Science in Egyptology*, 451.

799 David, *Pyramid Builders*, 135-136.

800 Seeden, *Standing Armed Figurines*, 97, pls 96 [1676], 128 [4-6].

801 Quirke, *Lahun*, 93; Gallorini, *Incised Marks*, 241; Cartwright, Granger-Taylor and Quirke, in *Lahun Studies*, 92-111.

802 Petrie, *Kahun*, pl. 27 [85].

803 Sass, however, writes that 'the signs do not resemble Proto-Canaanite letters of any date' (*Genesis of the Alphabet*, 104).

804 Eisler, *Die Kenitischen Weihinschriften der Hyksoszeit*, 172.

805 Driver, *Semitic Writing*, 103.

806 Dijkstra, *ZDPV* 106 (1990), 55-56.

807 Hamilton, *Origins of the West Semitic Alphabet*, 330-331.

808 Reportedly, the context was not recorded in his field books (Gallorini, *Incised Marks*, 248, n. 14).

809 Gallorini, *Incised Marks*, 248-249; Quirke, *Lahun*, 95-96.

810 Dijkstra proposes a MBIIC or Fifteenth Dynasty date (Dijkstra, *ZDPV* 106 [1990], 55-56).

811 Petrie found dyed wool (blue strands, blue with red and green ends, and red unspun dyed wool) which Saretta uses as evidence for contact with Levantines. The fleece type of the 'weaver's waste' suggests a *terminus post quem* of the Roman period and its radiocarbon dating points to the Medieval Age. Although wool has been found in other Egyptian contexts, the el-Lahun fabric cannot be positively ascertained as Middle Kingdom wool nor as an import until further tests are carried out. Petrie, *Kahun*, 28; Saretta, *Egyptian Perceptions of West Semites*, 146-151; Quirke, *Lahun*, 95; Jones, *Textiles in Early Egyptian Funerary Contexts*, 158, 171-173, 179, 234, 314, 317-320; Cooke, *Archaeological Textiles Newsletter* 17 (1993), 13-14; Cartwright, Granger-Taylor and Quirke, in *Lahun Studies*, 101; Kemp and Vogelsang-Eastwood, *Ancient Textile Industry*, 34-55.

812 Gale et al., in *Ancient Egyptian Materials and Technology*, 338; Germer, in *Lahun Studies*, 88-89; Battle and Tous, *Carob tree*, 20-21; Zohary, *Israel Journal of Plant Sciences* 50/1 (2002), 141-145.

813 Germer, in *Lahun Studies*, 88-89; Petrie, *Kahun*, 47, 50.

814 Also suggested in Germer, in *Lahun Studies*, 88-89; Szpakowska, *Daily Life*, 96. See Chapter 4.4.1.2-4.4.1.3 and Figure 4.54 for possible artistic representations of carob at Beni Hassan.

815 Cartwright, Granger-Taylor and Quirke, in *Lahun Studies*, 92-111; Quirke, *Lahun*, 93.

816 Cartwright, Granger-Taylor and Quirke, in *Lahun Studies*, 97; Gallorini, *Incised Marks*, 241.

817 Quirke, *Lahun*, 31-33.

818 Griffith, *Hieratic Papyri;* Collier and Quirke, *Letters*, v-ix; Collier and Quirke, *Accounts*.

and in chronological order. Further information on the manuscripts and their respective bibliographic references are provided in Figure B.1.

The papyri specify that male and female Asiatics were employed in temple activities and non-cultic duties. These references, which mostly occur in papyri uncovered near the temple, include such occupations as temple door-keepers, attendants, retainers, singers, dancers and *d̠ꜣi*-priests. Singers, male and perhaps female,[819] could perform at the Residence (P Berlin 10002) while dancers performed at local, regional and national festivals for Egyptian deities (UC 32191). Asiatics seem to have some association with those who recorded temple activities; they are noted as letter deliverers, a position requiring reliability, efficiency and a good knowledge of the town's layout and inhabitants. Foreigners participating in non-cultic duties were evidently employed as butchers, stone-haulers, workmen and house-servants. The latter could work for the same household across generations or could be transferred from one to another in legal documents such as UC 32058 or UC 32167. The inheritor would additionally be legally responsible for Asiatic youths, perhaps the house-servants' children. As for administrative tasks, UC 32143E suggests that an Asiatic was hired as a staff member to the vizier while Papyrus Berlin 10004 consists of an Asiatic phyle leader. Foreigners could also be attached to an administrative district, as in UC 32201 and UC 32286. Both Papyrus Berlin 10004 and UC 32151B also note Asiatic soldiers led by an 'overseer of the expedition of *ꜥꜣm(.w)*'. The title, as well as Papyrus Berlin 10010's 'scribe of the *ꜥꜣm.w*', points to a structured managerial hierarchy specifically for the Asiatic milieu.

The unpublished Papyrus Berlin 10002 evidently lists 50 singers performing at the Residence, many of whom are Asiatic.[820] Dating to Year 36 of Amenemhat III's reign, the papyrus includes such names as *ꜥꜣm* Senwosret's son Khakheperraseneb (nickname Ityihor), Senwosret (nickname *Bꜥri*), Senet (nickname Itni), *ꜥꜣm* Iqeq's son Khakheperrawah (nickname *ꜥꜣ*), Khakhereperraseneb (nickname *Mki*) and Senet (nickname Khayti).[821] Also unpublished is Papyrus Berlin 10004 from Amenemhat III's Year 21 listing *ꜥꜣm.w*, including an 'overseer of the expedition of *ꜥꜣm.w*',[822] the singer Khaaye and 'the great *wꜥb*-priest Nofrit's son *S-n-ꜣ-h-r*'. Such non-Egyptian names as *Bꜥri* (Baaliya?),[823] *Mki* (Malku?)[824] and *S-n-ꜣ-h-r*,[825] and their correlations with Egyptian appellations, reflect the individuals' Asiatic origins as well as their acculturation. The same case is observable in the translated papyri, where the majority classified as *ꜥꜣm* have Egyptian names. A common designation is 'Senwosret' or Senwosret II's throne name 'Khakheperra', obviously relating to el-Lahun's founder. Perhaps, then, the foreigners were given common local names when they migrated into the area. Papyrus Berlin 10021 offers a clue that Asiatics were collected to work from a *wn.t*. Despite Larkman's tenuous suggestion that this was a 'special prison' where war captives were kept,[826] the location is given a  determinative and could refer to a designated area where Asiatics lived or (were) gathered for vocational opportunities. Again, this would point to an organised conglomeration for Asiatics at el-Lahun.

The papyri suggest that the number of Asiatics increased between the reigns of Senwosret III (Year 6) and Amenemhat IV.[827] Their adoption of Egyptian names, employment as Egyptian temple priests and performance at festivals demonstrates their close affinity with Egyptian traditions. This acculturation perhaps attracted their positive treatment by the Egyptians which, in fact, is supported by several instances, including those where Egyptians are listed alongside Asiatics. Similarly, Papyrus Berlin 10047 presents a case where the scribe saw fit to write Initef's occupation before his designation as *ꜥꜣm*, and UC 32127 records a female servant, seemingly Egyptian, under an Asiatic's responsibility. One letter which Luft finds to be discriminatory, Papyrus Berlin 10228E with fragments from 10323A and 10111Aa, could be taken as a preference for Egyptian rather than Asiatic workers.[828] The Hymns to Senwosret III (UC 32157) additionally present a hostile view of Levantines, with the king slaughtering the *Pd.tyw*, striking the *Ꞽwn.tyw* and restraining the *St.tyw*. The hymns, however, denote a *topos* representation of foreigners intended to depict the king as protector. Still, the evidence attests that the Egyptians, maybe even as children in households with foreign servants, were well-accustomed to Asiatics. It is, therefore, no surprise that Hathor is mentioned as 'lady of Byblos' during Amenemhat IV's reign (UC 32196).

The papyri correspond with the archaeological data. Clearly, a Levantine community was thriving at el-Lahun and was involved in vocational ventures from at least Senwosret III's reign. Although the pottery features Cypriote, Minoan and Pan-Grave forms, the papyri only reveal that the *ꜥꜣm.w* and *Mḏꜣ.w/y* were at el-Lahun.[829]

819 Papyrus Berlin 10391 a-e suggests that a female Asiatic singer could feature in the temple papyri (Kaplony-Heckel, *Handschriften* 1, 227 [576]). See, however, Petrik, in *Illahun to Djeme*, 213.

820 Schneider, *Ausländer in Ägypten* 2, 26-27; Luft, in *Sesto Congresso* 2, 292-296; Kaplony-Heckel, *Handschriften* 1, 2 [2].

821 Luft, in *Sesto Congresso* 2, 292-295.

822 Transcribed by Kaplony-Heckel as  *im.y-rꜣ mšꜥ ꜥꜣm.w* (Kaplony-Heckel, *Handschriften* 1, 3 [4]). See Chapter 4.5.5.1 for the title's usage at Wadi el-Hol.

823 Luft, in *Sesto Congresso* 2, 294; Schneider, *Ausländer in Ägypten* 2, 146; Schneider, *AsPN*, 87. See also the inscription of *ꜥpr-Bꜥꜣr* at Tell el-Habwa I (Chapter 4.2.4.1).

824 Luft, in *Sesto Congresso* 2, 294. This is similar to the names attested for a ruler in Khnumhotep III's biography, Dahshur (see Chapter 4.3.1.2), a territory and ruler in the Levant (E37 and E62 of the Saqqara Execration Texts, Chapter 4.3.8) and a foreign ruler in the region of Sinuhe's *Ꞽꜣꜣ* (Chapter 4.6.9). See also Figure 7.10.

825 Luft, in *Sesto Congresso* 2, 297; Schneider, *Ausländer in Ägypten* 2, 161.

826 Larkman, *JSSEA* 34 (2007), 110.

827 Also observed by Luft in *Sesto Congresso* 2, 297.

828 Luft, in *Sesto Congresso* 2, 297. Interestingly, the name of the nomarch given this request, Senwosret's son Khakheperraseneb, matches that of *ꜥꜣm* Senwosret's son Khakheperraseneb mentioned a year earlier in Papyrus Berlin 10002. If they are the same person, then one could question why the overseer of sealers did not wish the nomarch to send Asiatics when his father was one. Perhaps the matter concerned Egyptians and thus necessitated native workers.

829 For the *Mḏꜣ.w/y* see UC 32191 and UC 32143A (Collier and

Foreign weavers and spinners are not mentioned in the papyri,[830] yet such activities may have been carried out by house-servants. Trade in organic products is substantiated by the many attestations of cedar (ʿš),[831] which was evidently used in temple architecture.[832] As the archaeological evidence suggests that trade persisted into Dynasty 15, it is likely that Asiatics continued to reside in el-Lahun. The data confirms the Egyptian population's exposure to Levantine ethnic groups, their religion, dress, language, commerce and possibly food. Organised and hierarchical institutions were possibly set up to coordinate relations between Egyptians and Asiatics, and a certain degree of mutual respect and appreciation appears to have presided. None of the evidence indicates an Asiatic invasion or disregard for the foreign population, but the absence of royal-name seals of the Hyksos suggests that relations with the Fifteenth Dynasty were meagre. Until further archaeological work is carried out, it is only possible to surmise that el-Lahun reached its peak as a hub of cultic and commercial activity during the late Twelfth Dynasty, when a Levantine population became well-integrated into the Egyptian settlement but was still among the lower to middle class of society.

4.3.6 Lisht, el-

Lat.Lon. 24°34'N 31°13'E

Refs Merrillees, *AJBA* 2 (1973), 53-57; Kemp and Merrillees, *Minoan Pottery*, 1-6; Arnold, Arnold and Allen, *E&L* 5 (1995), 13-32; Arnold, in *Haus und Palast*, 13-21; Bourriau, in *Studies in Honour of William K. Simpson*, 101-116; Saretta, *Egyptian Perceptions of West Semites*, 77, 155-157, 171-180, pls 20, 32-33, 38, 40; Arnold, *Tomb Architecture*; Martin, in *Scarabs of the Second Millennium BC*, 103-106; Bietak and Kopetzky, in *Exploring the Longue Durée*, 7-34.

Chron. Early Twelfth to Fifteenth Dynasty

Approximately 65km south of Cairo, near the Middle Kingdom capital of Itjtawy, is el-Lisht. The site features the pyramid complexes of the first two kings of Dynasty 12, Amenemhat I (el-Lisht North) and Senwosret I (el-Lisht South). These were surrounded by a necropolis for officials, as well as quarters for funerary cult priests that later developed into a Thirteenth Dynasty settlement (el-Lisht North).[833] Investigations at the site were recorded by Lepsius, Maspero and the Institut français d'archéologie orientale.[834] Recently, the Metropolitan Museum of Art has re-excavated the Middle Kingdom remains.[835]

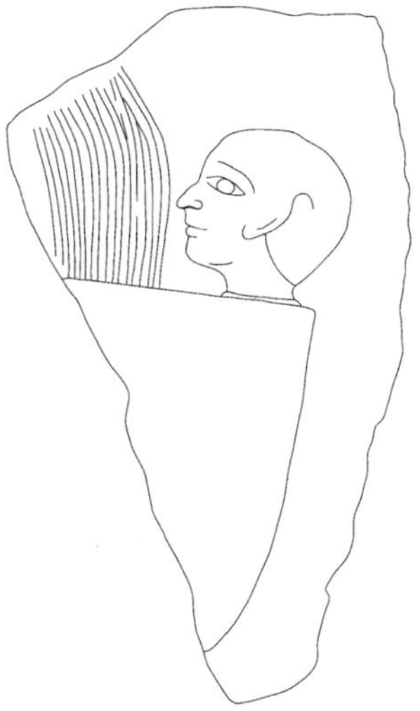

FIGURE 4.39. FRAGMENT MMA 13.235.1, MORTUARY TEMPLE OF AMENEMHAT I, EL-LISHT. AFTER 'FRAGMENT OF RELIEF', *MMA COLLECTION ONLINE* (DRAWN FROM PHOTOGRAPH).

4.3.6.1 Early Twelfth Dynasty

Pyramid complex of Amenemhat I

One fragment from Amenemhat I's mortuary temple portrays a child carried in a brownish-red garment wrapped around the back of a female with long hair (Figure 4.39).[836] Such a carrying position is rarely attributed to Egyptians before the New Kingdom and is more reminiscent of those of unprovenanced Middle Kingdom figurines from the Museum of Fine Arts and the Metropolitan Museum of Art,[837] a Beni Hassan statuette[838] and the Libyans of Khnumhotep I's tomb at Beni Hassan.[839] The female's hair shows greater similarity with an earlier fragment from Nebhepetra Montuhotep's temple at Deir el-Bahri.[840] This Eleventh Dynasty fragment pictures two Asiatic men accompanying an Asiatic woman with an infant wrapped at her back. So, the portrayal of a child on a female's back could be attributed to a range of foreigners from the Middle Kingdom. More on the identity of the el-Lisht figures is revealed through the child's yellow skin colour and hooked nose, features equivalent to the Asiatic children of Khnumhotep II's tomb at Beni Hassan.[841] Hence, it is probable that the decorative programme of Amenemhat I's pyramid temple originally included Asiatics.

Quirke, *Accounts*, 92-93, 176-177).

830 See, however, those of Papyrus Brooklyn 35.1446, Chapter 4.6.3.

831 Collier and Quirke, *Accounts*, 68-69 (UC 32125), 116-117 (UC 32310), 170-171 (UC 32104), 260-261 (UC 32152A).

832 UC 32125 and UC 32152A (Collier and Quirke, *Accounts*, 68-69). The latter includes, alongside the cedar, *ḥm.t mȝ* 'new copper' and a *mnb* 'axe', and could therefore be a list of imported commodities.

833 Arnold, Arnold and Allen, *E&L* 5 (1995), 14-15.

834 Arnold, *Tomb Architecture*, 11; Gautier and Jéquier, *Licht*.

835 Arnold, *Tomb Architecture*, 11.

836 MMA 13.235.1 in the Metropolitan Museum of Art; Goedicke, *Re-Used Blocks*, 146-147.

837 Wildung, *Le Moyen Empire*, 182, fig. 159; Hayes, *Scepter of Egypt* 2, 35, fig. 16.

838 See Chapter 4.4.1.4, Plate 3. Arnold, in *Offerings to the Discerning Eye*, figs 1-3.

839 See Chapter 4.4.1.1, Figure 4.48; Goedicke, *Re-Used Blocks*, n. 387.

840 Naville, *Deir el-Bahari* 1, pl. 15f.

841 'Fragment of Relief', *MMA Collection Online*. See Chapter 4.4.1.3, Figure 4.52.

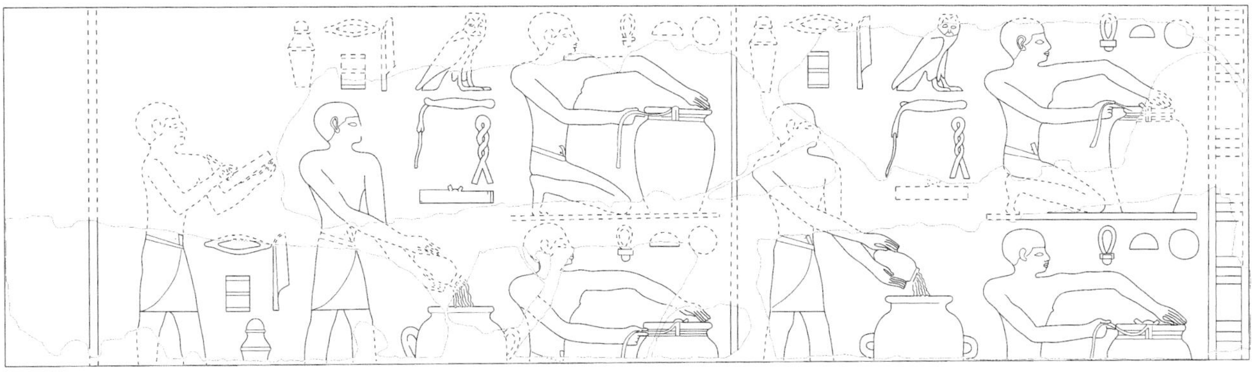

FIGURE 4.40. RECONSTRUCTED WALL SCENE DEPICTING SYRO-PALESTINIAN STORE-JARS, EL-LISHT. AFTER ARNOLD, *TOMB ARCHITECTURE*, PL. 25[A-B].

Depiction of characteristic non-Egyptian ceramics

At the southwest corner of Amenemhat I's pyramid complex is Pit 614 in which blocks from the tombs of Sobeknakht and Rehuerdjersen were uncovered.[842] Dating to Amenemhat I's reign, the tombs belong to high officials, the former a royal chief steward and the latter a treasurer and royal sealer.[843] One tomb scene, of which eight fragments remain, illustrates Egyptian scribes recording the activities of workers filling with wine and sealing jars (Figure 4.40).[844]

The vessels being filled greatly resemble Syro-Palestinian store-jars with their handles, large ovoid shape and wide, thickened rims. Parallels include an EBIV/MBI jar from Byblos's Baalat temple and a MBIIA jar from the Byblite Chamber of Offerings.[845] The vessels point to the (re)use of Levantine jars by Egyptians and for, apparently, Egyptian commodities.[846] As for indications of trade, the possibility of the jars' reuse from earlier periods cannot be disproved, especially as Egyptians are filling them. Contrarily, the tomb owner's high office could have granted him access to imported products. Nonetheless, the scene implies the use of Syro-Palestinian store-jars during early Dynasty 12.

Pyramid complex of Senwosret I

Fragments from Senwosret I's mortuary temple portray the royal subjugation of foreigners. Hayes comments on a scene in which Senwosret I is illustrated in a smiting stance, grasping the hair of nine captives, or the Nine Bows, before rows of bound and kneeling individuals.[847] The scene includes a Nubian, Puntite, Asiatic, Libyan and two other unidentified foreigners.[848] The kneeling posture of one individual is ascertained from the upper register of an associated relief picturing Seshat recording the event and its spoils (Figure 4.41).[849] The top of the column to the left of the relief's central panel illustrates a seated individual carrying an unknown item in his hand.[850] His hairstyle is slightly bulbous then angular at the back, shaved almost straight to the neck. Such a hairstyle is akin to that of an Asiatic in the tomb of Amenemhat at Beni Hassan (see Figure 4.50, figure to the left), thereby suggesting that the

FIGURE 4.41. SESHAT RECORDING A POSSIBLE SMITING SCENE, PYRAMID COMPLEX OF SENWOSRET I, EL-LISHT. AFTER HAYES, *SCEPTER OF EGYPT* 1, 188 (DRAWN FROM PHOTOGRAPH).

842 Arnold, *Tomb Architecture*, 67.

843 Arnold, *Tomb Architecture*, 64, 66-67, 85.

844 MMA 16.3.1 in the Metropolitan Museum of Art. Arnold, *Tomb Architecture*, 66-67, pls 125-126.

845 Thalmann, in *Bronze Age in the Lebanon*, 64-67, figs 2 [4], 3 [1-4].

846 As the jars being sealed have no handles and are more Egyptian in shape, perhaps the scene depicts the transfer of Levantine wine from imported vessels to Egyptian storage jars. The existence of such local jars with Levantine wine is evident from the hieratic text painted on a sherd of a Marl C jar neck from the burial of Sitweret (see Chapter 4.3.1.3, Figure 4.33).

847 The description, particularly of the smiting scene, is reliant on Hayes, *Scepter of Egypt* 1, 188.

848 Hayes, *Scepter of Egypt* 1, 188. A southerner and a Libyan are identified in fragment MMA 13.235.4 from the causeway. Other foreigners from the pyramid temple are also depicted in MMA 09.180.74. Both fragments are in the Metropolitan Museum of Art.

849 The theme is also featured in Pepy II's smiting scene at his mortuary temple at Saqqara. Such a commonality supports a reliance on the Old Kingdom decorative programme for pyramid complexes. See Berman, *Amenemhet I*, 72; Grajetzki, *Middle Kingdom*, 44, n. 161.

850 The individual underneath with protruding elements in his hair at the fore and back is similar to that of MMA 11.151.12, a faience fragment probably of the Middle Kingdom from el-Lisht (North) that illustrates a foreigner (northeasterner?). The fragment is in the Metropolitan Museum of Art.

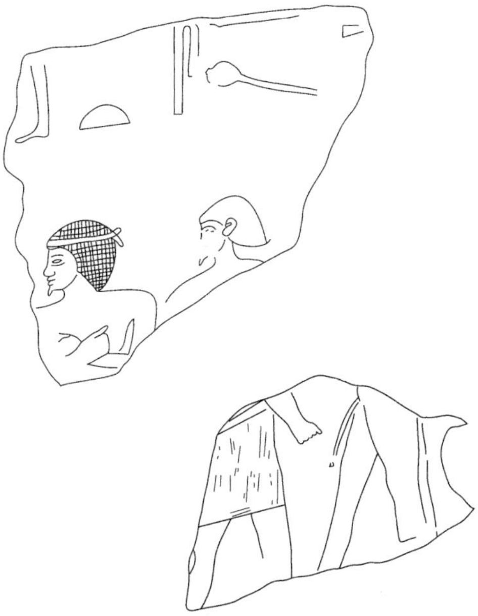

FIGURE 4.42. FRAGMENTS MMA 09.180.54 AND 09.180.50, PYRAMID COMPLEX OF SENWOSRET I, EL-LISHT. AFTER 'BLOCK OF RELIEF', *MMA COLLECTION ONLINE* (DRAWN FROM PHOTOGRAPH).

FIGURE 4.43. FRAGMENT MMA 13.235.3, PYRAMID TEMPLE OF SENWOSRET I, EL-LISHT. AFTER 'FRAGMENT FROM A BATTLE SCENE', *MMA COLLECTION ONLINE* (DRAWN FROM PHOTOGRAPH).

individual is Asiatic and amongst Senwosret I's enemies. If, as proposed here, the hairstyle is of Asiatic individuals, then a figure in a procession of foreigners from another fragment discovered in the altar court could also feature an Asiatic with a pointed beard (Figure 4.42).[851] Remaining hieroglyphs at the top of the block read 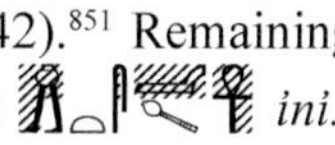 *ini.t sḳr(.w)-ꜥnḫ* 'bringing of captives'.

The battle that could have brought such prisoners may have been preserved in a relief from the pyramid temple, probably positioned in the causeway, that portrays a bearded man with yellow-brown skin (Figure 4.43).[852] His hair is characterised by its thick red strands and a tuft at the front. The tuft is analogous to those of the early Twelfth Dynasty Asiatics of Khnumhotep I's tomb at Beni Hassan,[853] the early Thirteenth Dynasty statue from Tell el-Dab'a's F/I d/1[854] and the Asiatics of Mereret's pectoral.[855] The red hair colour is also observed for the foreigners at Beni Hassan.[856] The individual seemingly carries in his left hand a spear that is aimed downwards at an unknown enemy, signalling that the foreigner could be positioned at the top of a fortress. Another object with a pointed end at the bottom left is perhaps associated with a type of Asiatic shield pictured in the Beni Hassan tomb of Khety.[857] The combination of elements indicates that the figure is an Asiatic warrior. It is, therefore, very possible that Senwosret I's pyramid complex consisted of a battle scene concerned with fighting and capturing Asiatics.[858]

4.3.6.2 Late Twelfth to Fifteenth Dynasty

Other evidence from el-Lisht can be generally assigned to the late Twelfth to Fifteenth Dynasty. They are used here only as signs for Asiatics living in the region and as examples of Egyptian representations of Asiatics.

Execration Texts

Execration Texts painted on mud figurines were collected from the surface debris west of the tomb of Senwosretankh of Senwosret I's reign.[859] Due to the uncertain context, the texts can only be attributed to Dynasty 12 or 13. They reportedly begin with 'the deceased, the rebel, ...'.[860]

[851] MMA 09.180.54. The fragment has been reconstructed with MMA 09.180.50 showing the lower half of two individuals, with the Asiatic of MMA 09.180.54 connected with the lower half of a body, hands bound behind back and wearing a short kilt. The skin is yellow. Both fragments are at the Metropolitan Museum of Art.

[852] Fischer, *Kush* 9 (1961), 44-56, 71, n. 57, fig. 10; Hill, in *American Discovery of Ancient Egypt*, 153 [59]. The fragment is in the Metropolitan Museum of Art.

[853] See Chapter 4.4.1.1, Figure 4.48.

[854] See Chapter 4.2.2.3, Figure 4.9.

[855] See Chapter 4.3.1.3, Figure 4.32.

[856] See Chapter 4.4.1, Figure 4.55. The red colour is also used for the hair of Asiatics depicted in the Eleventh Dynasty tomb of Intef (Jaroš-Deckert, *Asasif* 5, folding pls 1-3). For more on the colour, see Saretta, *Egyptian Perceptions of West Semites*, 98-99, 115.

[857] See Chapter 4.4.1, Figure 4.47. The shield may also be shown in the Eleventh Dynasty tomb of Intef (Jaroš-Deckert, *Asasif* 5, pl. 17, folding pls 1-3).

[858] For an earlier royal battle scene, see that of Montuhotep II at Deir el-Bahri (Naville, *Deir el-Bahari* 1, 68-69, pls 14-15; Smith, *Interconnections in the Ancient Near East*, 152, fig. 184).

[859] MMA 33.1.66-147. The 96 figurines were found alongside a mud coffin-shaped container. A manuscript by Posener regarding these tablets is reportedly to be published in the near future while a publication on the mastaba of Senwosretankh including the tablets is also forthcoming. See Lansing and Hayes, *BMMA* 28/11.2 (1933), 23-25, fig. 32; Hayes, *Scepter of Egypt* 1, 329, fig. 217; Redford, *Egypt, Canaan, and Israel*, 89, n. 103; Saretta, *Egyptian Perceptions of West Semites*, 173, n. 482; Arnold, *Tomb Architecture*, 13-16, n. 11.

[860] Hayes, *Scepter of Egypt* 1, 329; Saretta, *Egyptian Perceptions of*

Saretta notes that, while the majority of names listed are Egyptian, three can be 'qualified as Asiatic *ꜥ3mw*'.[861] This, along with the reported lack of toponyms and rare inclusion of titulary, has led Redford to identify the foreigners as possible fugitives.[862] Yet, until the texts are published, it is only possible to surmise that the Egyptians were resorting to a known magical ritual to guarantee either protection against foreigners[863] or the submission of Asiatic enemies within and beyond Egypt.

Statue base of Imeny

An unpublished diorite statue base was unearthed in the debris of Tomb 499 at el-Lisht North, near Amenemhat I's pyramid.[864] Four rows of hieroglyphs are inscribed at the feet and evidently include *'Imny im.y-r3 iḥ.w msi n ꜥ3m.t* 'Imeny, overseer of cattle,[865] born to *ꜥ3m.t*'.[866] The inscription indicates that the official, Imeny, was of Asiatic descent. His assumption of an Egyptian name and title points to the assimilation of Asiatics within the Middle Kingdom bureaucracy. Additionally, the material used for the statue hints at a royal commission, signalling the administration's acknowledgement and rewarding of Asiatic officials.[867]

Statuette of a Levantine cultic figure

A statuette was found at el-Lisht North within the surface debris west of Amenemhat I's pyramid.[868] Possibly discarded from the nearby Thirteenth Dynasty settlement, the figurine has been described as a portrayal of a crowned king;[869] however, particular details warrant an alternative identification. Made from unbaked clay, it measures 21cm in height and portrays a standing figure wearing a conical crown, the top of which is no longer preserved,[870] as well as a close-fitting dress identified by the remains of a greenish colour across the torso and right shoulder.[871] The left arm, right hand and right foot are missing. The head is elongated, ears long and protruding, eyes large and round, and chin raised. The body is heavyset with small modelled breasts, a delineated waist and the possible etching of a bellybutton. Such features, particularly those of the face and chin, are more akin to cultic figurines uncovered in the Levant, specifically those from MBIIA and MBIIB Byblos.[872] As for the crown, the angle at which it is positioned is more similar to the crowns of Levantine statuettes related to a 'warrior' function.[873] One bronze female figurine found in a hoard of weapons at Byblos features this crown along with a line across the upper décolletage and right shoulder indicating dress.[874] Perhaps the piece of clothing can be linked to that of el-Lisht's statuette, supporting its portrayal of a Levantine divinity.[875] In any case, the el-Lisht statuette's facial characteristics follow Levantine rather than Egyptian artistic trends, indicating its non-Egyptian craftsmanship. Due to the lack of fabric analysis, the statuette's place of manufacture cannot be ascertained. However, its discovery near el-Lisht's Middle Kingdom settlement not only signifies that Levantine individuals were in the region, it also highlights their involvement in a non-Egyptian cult in an area that was largely devoted to the worship of Egyptian royals.

4.3.6.3 Characteristic non-Egyptian ceramics

Remains of vessels of MBA shape were discovered at the cemetery and settlement of el-Lisht (Figure 4.44). The northern pyramid of Amenemhat I yielded one sherd of a non-Egyptian clay fabric possibly belonging to the shoulder of a bowl or beaker (Figure 4.44 [1]).[876] Two bands of clay mimicking ropes are moulded onto the sherd, paralleling a decorative element found on Northern and Southern Levantine EBIII-MBIIA vessels.[877] The fragment was retrieved from a sand filling between stones located behind the casing blocks of the main burial chamber's passageway.[878] The context was not sealed and was susceptible to contamination by tomb robbers, but other flint objects uncovered in the sand indicate a deposition during the complex's construction.[879] Thus, excavators date the sherd to the MBIIA and Amenemhat I's reign.[880] However, if from the MBIIA, the sherd presents a

West Semites, 172.

861 Saretta, *Egyptian Perceptions of West Semites*, 172-174.

862 Redford, *Egypt, Canaan, and Israel*, 89, n. 103.

863 Di. Arnold suggests that the magical figurines acted as protective defences against those who could harm the mastaba (Arnold, *Tomb Architecture*, 16). Texts with a similar function are known from the Teti cemetery, Saqqara. See Chapter 4.3.8.

864 The statue base is discussed by Saretta (*Egyptian Perceptions of West Semites*, 155-156, pl. 31) and mentioned by Schneider, relying on Saretta (*Ausländer in Ägypten* 2, 62). It was accessioned by the Metropolitan Museum of Art as MMA 15.3.585. Museum curators note that they had sold it to The American Museum of Natural History (personal communication). Despite the author's efforts, the artefact could not be tracked further and so the information here follows Saretta's examination. The black and white facsimile from Saretta's thesis is unfortunately not clear enough for a personal assessment.

865 Ward, *Index*, 11 [41].

866 Saretta, *Egyptian Perceptions of West Semites*, 156.

867 Saretta further notes the discovery of two small MBA jars in Tomb 499, one of which appears to be a miniature jar with one handle and a bulbous body (Saretta, *Egyptian Perceptions of West Semites*, 156, pl. 32). Without further data on the size, fabric and other features of the vessels, they cannot be definitively classified as MBA pottery.

868 Mace, *BMMA* 17/12.2 (1922), 13.

869 As Mace writes, 'it has a crown, and is certainly meant to represent a king, but what a queer figure it is... it may have been fashioned in an idle moment by one of the craftsmen... it certainly cannot have been made as a serious piece of work' (Mace, *BMMA* 17/12.2 [1922], 13).

870 Recent images of the statuette, now in the Metropolitan Museum of Art, show the damaged crown.

871 For a colour photograph, see 'Statuette of King', *MMA Collection Online*.

872 Seeden, *Standing Armed Figurines*, pls G [230, 308], 86 [1511], 96 [1681, 1682].

873 Seeden, *Standing Armed Figurines*, 135-137. See also Figure 6.16B.

874 Seeden, *Standing Armed Figurines*, 94-95, pls K [1682], 96 [1682].

875 Saretta, *Egyptian Perceptions of West Semites*, 77, n. 499.

876 Arnold, Arnold and Allen, *E&L* 5 (1995), 16, figs 6 [1], 7.

877 Arnold, Arnold and Allen, *E&L* 5 (1995), 16-17. Parallels include those at EBIV Byblos, Tell 'Arqa (Phase P) and Jericho, MBIIA Tell Aphek and Tell Ifshar, as well as MBIIB-C Baalbek and Lachish (Area P-4). For Byblos, see: Bou-Assaf, in *Bronze Age in the Lebanon*, fig. 7 [6]. Tell 'Arqa: Thalmann, in *Bronze Age in the Lebanon*, 64, fig. 2 [9, 18]. Jericho: Kenyon and Holland, *Jericho* 4, 255-258, fig. 97 [4, 28]. Tell Aphek: Beck, *Tel Aviv* 2 (1975), 45, figs 1 [4], 2 [12]. Tell Ifshar: Marcus, Porath and Paley, *E&L* 18 (2008), 233, fig. 9 [5]. Baalbek: Genz, in *Baalbek/Heliopolis*, 144, pl. 7 [2]. Lachish: Singer-Avitz, in *Lachish*, 919, fig. 16.26 [6].

878 Arnold, Arnold and Allen, *E&L* 5 (1995), 16.

879 Arnold, Arnold and Allen, *E&L* 5 (1995), 16.

880 Arnold, Arnold and Allen, *E&L* 5 (1995), 16-17.

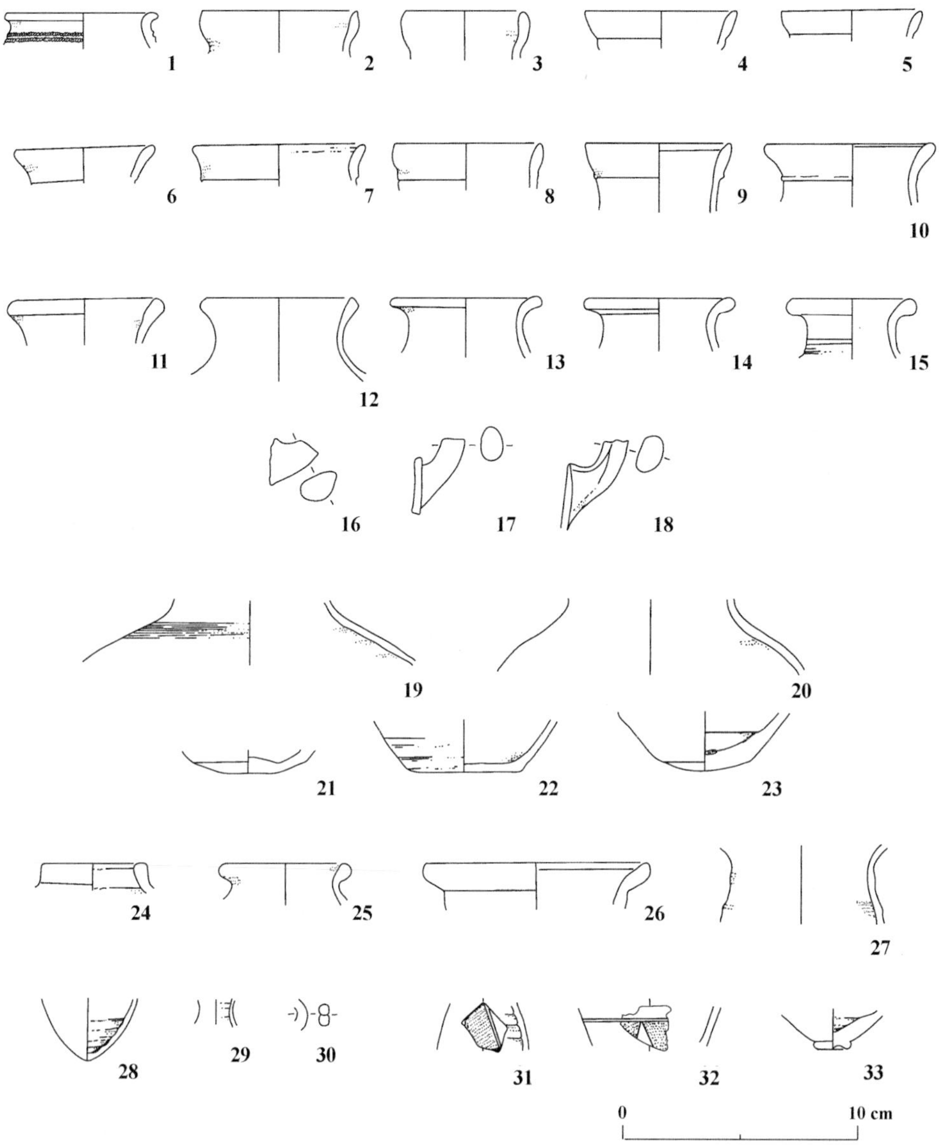

FIGURE 4.44. SELECTED CERAMICS, EL-LISHT. AFTER ARNOLD, ARNOLD AND ALLEN, *E&L* 5 (1995), FIG. 6.

chronological conundrum as the period is thought to have commenced after Amenemhat I's reign. Nevertheless, it could be an heirloom or a reused vessel from the EBA, a traded item from the near contemporary EBIV period or simply deposited at a later time. Other imports include a red-burnished dipper juglet and a Levantine Painted Ware jug from a tomb at el-Lisht North dated to the mid-Twelfth Dynasty (Tomb 756).[881]

The surface debris near the late Middle Kingdom settlement produced imported Middle Minoan ware,[882] Cypriote ware,[883] Pan-Grave ware,[884] a fragment of Levantine Painted Ware[885] and Tell el-Yahudiyah ware (Figure 4.44 [31-33]).[886] The latter include remnants of piriform juglets paralleling those from Tell el-Dab'a Strata G-E/2,[887] a sherd decorated with a human arm and hand,[888] another with birds[889] and a third belonging to a hawk-shaped juglet, the shape of which has been assigned to the early Fifteenth Dynasty.[890] Other vessels of foreign fabric include large beakers and jars comparable to MBIIB shapes (Figure 4.44 [24-27]) as well as red-painted juglets with pointed bases (Figure

881 Dating is based on the associated Egyptian pottery assemblage. Arnold, Arnold and Allen, *E&L* 5 (1995), 17-20, fig. 2; Merrillees, *AJBA* 2 (1973), 53-57, figs 4-5; Bagh, *TeD* 23, 62, fig. 30 [b-c]; 'Juglet', *MMA Collection Online*.

882 Kemp and Merrillees, *Minoan Pottery*, 1-6, fig. 1, pls 1-3.

883 Arnold, in *Haus und Palast*, 19.

884 Arnold, in *Haus und Palast*, 19.

885 Kemp and Merrillees, *Minoan Pottery*, pl. 3 (first sherd at the top left); Bagh, *TeD* 23, 62, fig. 30 [d].

886 Also known as 'el-Lisht' ware. Arnold, Arnold and Allen, *E&L* 5 (995), 20.

887 Aston and Bietak's Levanto-Egyptian II Group I.2.2a. Arnold, Arnold and Allen, *E&L* 5 (995), 29-30; Kaplan, *Tell el Yahudiyeh*, fig. 25 [a]; Aston and Bietak, *TeD* 8, 152, 552-553, fig. 89.

888 Aston and Bietak's Levanto-Egyptian Vessels with Naturalistic Designs (Branch J). Aston and Bietak, *TeD* 8, 193; Smith, *Interconnections in the Near East*, fig. 48 [d].

889 Aston and Bietak, *TeD* 8, 200.

890 Aston and Bietak's Late Egyptian XV Group L.15.2. Aston and Bietak, *TeD* 8, 288, fig. 214; Kaplan, *Tell el Yahudiyeh*, fig. 123 [a].

4.44 [28-30]).[891] The majority of imports at the settlement are Syro-Palestinian store-jars (3.4% of the pottery refuse) with incurving slightly thickened rims (Figure 4.44 [2-3]), everted folded rims (Figure 4.44 [4-9]) and flaring thickened rims (Figure 4.44 [10-15]).[892] The incurving rim was a popular feature in MBIIA vessels whereas the flaring rim was common in the MBIIB-C period.[893] The earliest fragment of a Syro-Palestinian store-jar was uncovered between the first and second phase of House A3.3's construction (Figure 4.44 [21]), securely dating the sherd to Dynasty 13.[894] Also found was a jar handle with a sealing depicting, in deep relief, a falcon before a uraeus on a *nb*-basket above which sits a *wr*-bird.[895] As such designs in deep relief are common in Strata E/2-D/2 at Tell el-Dab'a,[896] the handle can be dated between the end of the Thirteenth and late Fifteenth Dynasty. As such, evidence from the settlement infers that a continuous supply of imported goods was available to el-Lisht's inhabitants from Dynasty 13 to 15.[897]

Imported ceramics were additionally unearthed within the settlement's burial shafts. The so-called dolphin jar of Shaft Tomb 879 can be generally described as a piriform juglet with a flat ring-base, loop-handle and a decorative layer depicting dolphins and birds (Figure 4.45).[898] Bourriau writes that the 'fabric, shape, technology and decoration all place the vase unequivocally within the ceramic traditions of Syria/Palestine'.[899] Similar decoration may be found on vases from MBIIB Tell Beit Mirsim[900] and MBIIA-B Sidon,[901] the latter of which is favoured as the place of manufacture by Bietak and Kopetzky.[902] NAA of the jug identified the fabric as Southern Levantine,[903] yet ambiguities surrounding the test process warrant different propositions for areas of manufacture.[904] Until further scientific analysis is carried out, the origin of the vessel should be attributed to the general region encompassing Sidon and Tell Beit Mirsim. The parallels in decoration also suggest that the juglet should be dated between the MBIIA-B and MBIIB periods. According to the tomb shaft's ceramic assemblage, Bourriau posits a deposition between the early Thirteenth Dynasty and Awibra Hor's reign.[905] F. Arnold, however, notes that Shaft 879 was dug from the floor level of House A1.3 before its last building phase, thereby dating the tomb to the early Second Intermediate

A.

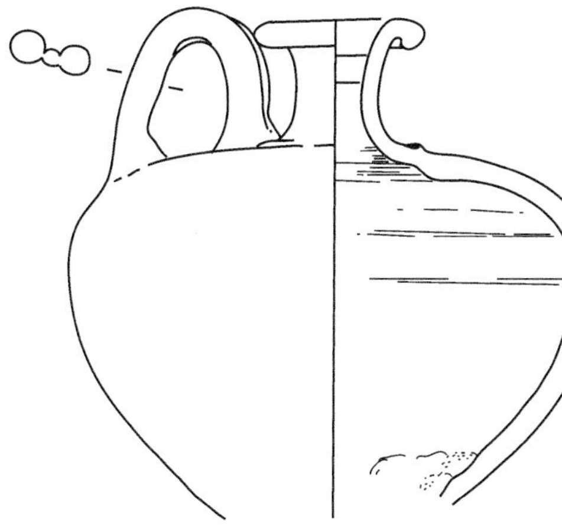

B.

Figure 4.45. The dolphin jar, its shape and decoration, Tomb 879, el-Lisht (not to scale). After Bourriau, in *Studies in Honour of William K. Simpson*, figs 2-3.

Period.[906] This is corroborated by four Tell el-Yahudiyah piriform juglets from the shaft that find parallels from Tell el-Dab'a's Strata F-E/3,[907] indicating that the tomb, its associated burial goods and the dolphin juglet should be dated between the late Thirteenth Dynasty and the early Second Intermediate Period.[908] So, it is possible to surmise that el-Lisht still had access to and a demand for foreign commodities well into the Second Intermediate Period.

4.3.6.4 Other

Seals with royal names and characteristic Middle Kingdom and Second Intermediate Period features were uncovered at el-Lisht.[909] Although not fully published, some reflect Levantine design influences, including:

- Two scarabs, one discovered beneath the right hand of a mummy in Pit 830 and the other from settlement debris featuring the Hathor symbol.[910] The motif is similarly found on scarabs from Tell el-Dab'a Strata E/3-D/3[911] and Tell el-Yahudiyah,[912] with the

891 Arnold, Arnold and Allen, *E&L* 5 (1995), 29, fig. 6.
892 Arnold, Arnold and Allen, *E&L* 5 (1995), 27-28, fig. 6.
893 Arnold, Arnold and Allen, *E&L* 5 (1995), 28.
894 Arnold, Arnold and Allen, *E&L* 5 (1995), 22-23.
895 Arnold, Arnold and Allen, *E&L* 5 (1995), 29, fig. 1.
896 See Mlinar's scarab group VIb. Mlinar, in *Scarabs of the Second Millennium BC*, 132-133; Bietak, *AJA* 88/4 (1984), 483-484, ill. 6.
897 Arnold, Arnold and Allen, *E&L* 5 (1995), 29, fig. 6.
898 For a detailed examination and further sources discussing the vase, see Bourriau, in *Studies in Honor of William K. Simpson* 1, 101-116, ns 1-3; Bietak and Kopetzky, in *Exploring the Longue Durée*, 7-34.
899 Bourriau, in *Studies in Honour of William K. Simpson*, 105.
900 Bourriau, in *Studies in Honour of William K. Simpson*, 107; Ben-Arieh, *Tell Beit Mirsim*, 93, fig. 2.61 [29].
901 Doumet-Serhal, in *Networking Patterns*, 12-15, fig. 13.
902 Bietak and Kopetzky, in *Exploring the Longue Durée*, 7-34.
903 McGovern et al., *BASOR* 296 (1994), 31-43.
904 See Chapter 4.2.2.8.
905 Bourriau, in *Studies in Honour of William K. Simpson*, 116.
906 Arnold, in *Haus und Palast*, 17.
907 Bourriau, in *Studies in Honor of W. K. Simpson*, 114, fig. 8; Bietak and Kopetzky, in *Exploring the Longue Durée*, 24-28, figs 10-13.
908 The date is also suggested in Bietak and Kopetzky, in *Exploring the Longue Durée*, 32.
909 Martin, in *Scarabs of the Second Millennium BC*, 103-106; Mace, *BMMA* 17/12.2 (1922), 16, fig. 22.
910 Ben-Tor's Design Class 10D2. Respectively, MMA 22.1.408 and MMA 15.3.325, at the Metropolitan Museum of Art. Ben-Tor, *Scarabs*, 49.
911 Ben-Tor, *Scarabs*, 101.
912 Naville and Griffith, *Mound of the Jew*, pl. 10 [34].

second closely paralleling a scarab from late MBA Tell el-'Ajjul;[913]

- Scarabs from the tomb of Nakht (Pit 468)[914] and settlement debris[915] depicting cross-hatched animals in deep relief. Two portray confronting cobras (MMA 15.3.181 and MMA 22.1.329). Based on the great number of Southern Levantine scarabs with such designs, the motifs are likely of Levantine origin;[916]

- A scarab with two cobras on either side of a kneeling figure holding a lotus.[917] Again, the large number of scarabs from the Levant with this motif points to its Levantine origins.[918] Similar designs appear on scarabs from MBA Jericho[919] and Tell el-'Ajjul;[920] and

- One cylinder seal from settlement debris.[921] The seal is designed with four columns comprising: (1) a kneeling figure with a short voluminous hairstyle, a large pointed nose, and a short detailed kilt;[922] (2) three human heads, each with a large nose and a short voluminous hairdo; (3) two seated caprids; and (4) three birds. The elements are typical of the MBA, particularly of cylinder seals from such sites as Ugarit, Alalakh and Qatna.[923]

While the scarabs indicate links with the Southern Levant during the MBIIB period, the cylinder seal signifies contact with the Northern Levant.

The evidence from el-Lisht offers Asiatic representations and products in both the royal and private spheres. Amenemhat I and Senwosret I featured illustrations of Asiatics in their pyramid complexes, the latter comprising bellicose portrayals, perhaps even a battle scene. Such representations indicate the royal ideological domination of foreigners, a domination and subjugation which is enhanced by the cemetery's Execration Texts. As products of cultic ritual, the texts were ultimately intended to benefit the state. No other evidence equals this negative treatment of Asiatics. In fact, the data implies that Asiatics were living, working and practicing their own religion at el-Lisht during the late Middle Kingdom. Perhaps this signifies an increase in foreigners in the area, or that these individuals, who were formerly depicted as subjugated enemies, were accorded with a greater freedom in expressing their ethnicity. Their products were certainly imported into the area along with pottery and sealings from Amenemhat I's reign to possibly Dynasty 15. This would imply the continuance of trade with the northeast throughout the Middle Kingdom until at least the early Second Intermediate Period. But, despite the increasing contact, the process was evidently gradual and not representative of a sudden influx or takeover.

4.3.7 Mit Rahina

Lat.Lon. 29°51'N 31°15'E

Refs Farag, *RdE* 32 (1980), 75-82; Posener, *JSSEA* 12/1 (1982), 7-8; Altenmüller and Moussa, *SAK* 18 (1991), 1-48; Dantong, *JAC* 14 (1999), 45-66; Marcus, *E&L* 17 (2007), 137-190.

Chron. Mid-Twelfth Dynasty (reign of Amenemhat II)

A pink granite block reused at Mit Rahina's temple of Ramesses II contains significant passages on mid-Twelfth Dynasty relations with foreigners.[924] Possibly from the Memphite temple of Ptah, the block preserves 40 columns of a longer inscription from Amenemhat II's daybook.[925] The text includes lists of donations to temples, chapels and festivals, as well as visits from foreign dignitaries and expeditions to foreign lands. Based on the difference in the width of column M28 and the frequent addition of Amenemhat II's titulary following this column, scholars have suggested that M1-27 record events dating to the last year of the co-regency of Senwosret I (Year 45) and Amenemhat II (Year 3), with the rest being of the latter's reign.[926] It is thus best to view the foreign relations as a reflection of Amenemhat II's administration, legitimising his reign and guaranteeing loyalty from Egyptian cults and foreign dignitaries.[927]

A translation of the most pertinent passages can be found in Appendix B.3. They record three main expeditions to the Levant:

- *Ḫnty-š:* The expedition was the first to be sent and the last to return. The term for travel, *mꜣꜥ*, in M7 is given a determinative of a ship, suggesting that the expedition travelled via a sea-route. Indeed, the army returned in two ships which are specifically *dp.t* and not *kbn.t* vessels.[928] Various natural and manufactured resources were obtained: metals; stones; fruits; and *ꜥš*-wood, the principal item of

913 Petrie, *Gaza* 4, pls 5 [38], 7 [155]; Ben-Tor, *Scarabs*, pl. 105 [43-44].
914 MMA 15.3.181. 'Scarab', *MMA Collection Online*.
915 MMA 20.1.28 and MMA 22.13.29. 'Scarab', *MMA Collection Online*.
916 Ben-Tor's Design Class 9B. Ben-Tor, *Scarabs*, 95-96, 174-176.
917 MMA 15.3.155. 'Scarab', *MMA Collection Online*.
918 Ben-Tor, *Scarabs*, 95-97, 176.
919 Ben-Tor, *Scarabs*, pl. 97 [20].
920 Petrie, *Gaza* 1, pl. 13 [52]; vol. 3, pl. 4 [147]; vol. 4, pl. 11 [397]; Ben-Tor, *Scarabs*, pl. 97 [24, 26, 30-31].
921 MMA 20.1.50. 'Cylinder Seal', *MMA Collection Online*.
922 Signs are preserved behind the figure's head and possibly represent a ⊙ *rꜥ* and a 𓆣 *ḫpr*.
923 Collon, *First Impressions*, 52-53 [202, 210]; Pfälzner, in *Beyond Babylon*, 228 [138]; Otto, *Klassisch-Syrischen Glyptik*, 113-115, 243-244, pls 4-5, 29.

924 Farag, *RdE* 32 (1980), 75.
925 Farag, *RdE* 32 (1980), 75; Posener, *JSSEA* 12/1 (1982), 7-8. Other possible fragments are published in Petrie, *Memphis* 1, 6-7, 17-18, pl. 5; Daressy, *ASAE* 4 (1903), 101-103.
926 Altenmüller and Moussa, *SAK* 18 (1991), 37-39; Marcus, *E&L* 17 (2007), 143; Dantong, *JAC* 14 (1999), 45-66; Obsomer, *Sésostris Ier*, 595-606.
927 Marcus, *E&L* 17 (2007), 143.
928 The passage can be interpreted in two ways: either the army left and returned in two ships, or the army only returned in two ships. Both cases warrant travel back and forth via a sea-route.

shipment.[929] The cargo contained 65 Asiatics and has been estimated to weigh approximately 12253kg, with 39000 litres of liquid,[930] a clear indicator of the efficiency and capability of Egyptian maritime trade. Due to the nature of these products, *H̱nty-š* is most likely located in the Northern Levant, perhaps on the modern Lebanese coast;[931]

- Turquoise Terraces of the Sinai: The despatch of this expedition is not preserved, but M13 includes terms for travel by foot with the determinative of 𓂻 indicating a land-based voyage. Turquoise is the main cargo transported with other fauna, minerals and aromatics acquired from the Sinai and possibly further afield.[932] The estimated total weight of cargo, 1050kg and 2238 litres, supports a land-based route;[933]

- *Ỉwꜣ(i)* and *Ỉꜣsy*: The third expedition journeyed to *Ỉwꜣ* intending to 'hack up' its *St.t*,[934] but details of its return add another locale, *Ỉꜣsy*.[935] The expedition was despatched in a ship, as the determinative 𓊛 suggests, but its second mention indicates that it travelled by foot (𓂻𓂻), offering another variant in the inscription. The imported cargo, the total of which has been estimated to be 50.5kg and 270-1620 litres,[936] includes metal weaponry, jewellery, minerals and *ꜥꜣm* household items.[937] The main cargo is 1554 *ꜥꜣm.w*, the number of which implies the expedition's return via a land route for easier and more efficient passage. Perhaps the order in which the expeditions were despatched is connected to the distance travelled, with the first sent being the furthest away.[938] If so, then the two settlements would be in the Levant, between the Sinai and *H̱nty-š*.[939] Despite this, some link *Ỉwꜣ(i)* with Ura (Asia Minor) and *Ỉꜣsy* with Alashiya (Cyprus),[940] which would suggest a foreign policy incorporating a geography much broader than previously theorised. Nevertheless, the expedition, especially to *Ỉwꜣ(i)*, was militaristic and specifically against the *St.t*.[941] As for the *ꜥꜣm* captives, the text indicates that they were transferred to *Sḫm-Ỉmn-m-ḥꜣ.t*, possibly as labourers.[942]

Amenemhat II's administration also hosted visits from foreign dignitaries. Delegations were received from [*Kꜣ*]*š*, *Wbꜣ.t-Sp.t*, the children of *St.t*'s rulers and *T̠mpꜣw*.[943] Each arrived voluntarily and respectfully,[944] bearing gifts and, in the case of the southern lands, *bꜣk.wt*, loosely translated as 'tribute'.[945] The *St.t*'s children arrived with 1002 *ꜥꜣm* Asiatics, perhaps as an attempt to stop the campaign on *Ỉwꜣ(i)* and *Ỉꜣsy*.[946] The third visit of the offering bearers of *T̠mpꜣw* could be from the Levant;[947] however lack of detail restricts toponymic analysis.

The delegations could be regarded as an attempt to show the foreigners' loyalty to the new pharaoh, providing a good example of the diplomacies officiated by Amenemhat II. Despite the text's fragmentary nature, the absence of any reference to Byblos or Byblite ships signals either a discord in relations with the city or the existence of trade alliances with another port such as Khnumhotep III's Ullaza.[948] As such, the Mit Rahina inscription reveals an Egyptian administration that was highly engaged in the Levant's political and commercial activities. As imported goods and captives were dispersed to temples and towns throughout Egypt, it is possible that the elite Egyptian echelon were aware of such relations and were, either directly or indirectly, in contact with the foreign.

929 M18-21.

930 Marcus, *E&L* 17 (2007), 150-154, tables 2-3.

931 Altenmüller and Moussa suggest that the list was written in chronological order with the dispatch of expeditions in *ꜣḫt* and their return in *šmw* (Altenmüller and Moussa, *SAK* 18 [1991], 28-29). If correct, then the voyage to *H̱nty-š* took the longest as it was the first to be sent, and the last to return. Perhaps this might also indicate its furthermost location in the Northern Levant.

932 M13-14. The aromatics were likely retrieved, directly or indirectly, from the Arabian Peninsula (Cohen, *Canaanites, Chronologies, and Connections*, 42, n. 50).

933 Marcus, *E&L* 17 (2007), 157, table 3.

934 M8, 16-18.

935 M16-18. Some have regarded *Ỉwꜣi* and *Ỉwꜣỉ* as distinct locales. Because the expedition to *Ỉwꜣi* returns before that of *H̱nty-š*, its order coincides with the expedition to *Ỉwꜣ*, despatched after that of *H̱nty-š*. Another factor that should be borne in mind is the nature of the text as a list recording court events, which would consequently contain expected inconsistencies in toponym spellings, particularly of foreign lands. For an interpretation that favours the two as different settlements, see Eder, *Die Ägyptischen Motive*, 185-186.

936 Marcus, *E&L* 17 (2007), tables 1, 3.

937 M16-18.

938 See n. 928.

939 Goedicke (*RdE* 42 [1991], 93, n. 32) equates *Ỉwꜣ(i)* with a toponym of the Execration Texts linked with Tyre. Gubel and Loffet connect it to Sinuhe's *Ỉꜣꜣ*, with *Ỉꜣsy* being a variant of the toponym *Ỉwꜣṯi* 'Ullaza' (*AHL* 34-35 [2011/2012], 82).

940 Redford, *Egypt, Canaan, and Israel*, 79, n. 47; Eder, *Die Ägyptischen Motive*, 191; Helck, *GM* 109 (1989), 27-30.

941 The translation as 'the *St.t* of *Ỉwꜣ*' or '*St.t*, namely *Ỉwꜣ*' is favoured here. Several have suggested that *St.t Ỉwꜣ* should be rendered as "*Ỉwꜣ* (located in) *St.t*' although grammatically the *nomen regens* is *St.t*. Alternatively, it may be *St.t(yw) Ỉwꜣ* '*St.t(yw)* of *Ỉwꜣ*'. For identifications of *St.t* as a geographical toponym, see Goedicke, *RdE* 42 (1991), 93, n. 31; Marcus, *E&L* 17 (2007), 144; Gubel and Loffet, *AHL* 34-35 (2011/12), 82. See also Chapter 7.3.2, Figure 7.9.

942 M16-18, 25-26.

943 Respectively, M11-12, M12-13 and M15.

944 That is, *ỉw(ỉ).t m wḏb-tp* 'coming with bowed-head'.

945 For more on the various meanings of this term, see Spalinger, *SAK* 23 (1996), 353-376.

946 M12-13. Bárta, *Sinuhe, the Bible, and the Patriarchs*, 115-116.

947 Goedicke, Gubel and Loffet associate *T̠mpꜣw* with *Tnpw* 'Tunip', identified with Tell Acharne in modern Syria (Goedicke, *RdE* 42 [1991], 91; Gubel and Loffet, *AHL* 34-35 [2011/2012], 82, 85).

948 See Chapter 4.3.1.2; Marcus, *E&L* 17 (2007), 173.

4.3.8 Saqqara

Lat.Lon. 29°52'N 31°13'E

Ref Posener, *Princes et Pays.*

Chron. Late Twelfth Dynasty[949]

Anthropomorphic clay statuettes, known as the Brussels figurines, were found buried adjacent to the north wall of Teti's pyramid at Saqqara. They are dated to late Dynasty 12, between the reigns of Senwosret III and Amenemhat III.[950] Simple in design, some of the figurines' heads feature a mushroom-like hairstyle,[951] similar to that of Asiatics from the Beni Hassan tombs of Khnumhotep I and Amenemhat (see Figures 4.48-50), and the statue from Area F/I, Tell el-Dab'a (see Figure 4.9). The hairstyle, along with traces of a beard on one figurine,[952] suggests that the statuettes textually and artistically represented Asiatics, in this case utilising the typical Asiatic phenotype. Appendix B.4 provides a translation of their texts regarding the Levant, which appear after lists pertaining to Nubia.

The Brussels figurines list a total of 58 *ḥḳꜣ* rulers,[953] one entry for the combined *ḥḳꜣ.w* 'rulers',[954] another for *wḥ.ywt* 'tribes', [955] two *wr/smsw n(.y) wḥ.ywt* 'great one/elder of the tribe',[956] one *wr/smsw* 'great one/elder',[957] one for the *sḳr.yw* 'smiters',[958] an entry for *ꜥꜣm* inhabitants of five locales[959] as well as one for the *Mntw* of *St.t.*[960] All inhabit 69 foreign lands.[961]

As there are more regions than rulers, some have identified a development from the Berlin bowls' tribal society to the Brussels texts' sedentary Levant.[962] Others find the differences to signal a change in Egyptian-Levantine relations with an increase in trade, administrative control or a greater awareness of the northeast.[963] The very nature of the texts does not allow for a critical appraisal of Egyptian-Levantine relations. Firstly, the possibility that the surviving figurines are only a small sampling of a lost or undiscovered corpora cannot be excluded,[964] thereby reducing the chance of reaching viable statistical conclusions. Secondly the addition or exclusion of a particular detail is heavily dependent on the surviving material and so little significance can be attributed to its absence/presence.[965] Lastly, the ritualistic purpose of burying these figurines as a possible means to protect the cemetery,[966] subdue foreigners or hinder rebellious action,[967] indicates that they cannot be used as evidence for an Egyptian hegemony over the Levant nor as a socio-political reflection of the situation in the northeast.[968] However, an undisputed observation is that the figurines reveal an informed knowledge of the geography and ruling aristocracy of the Levant,[969] implying that the late Twelfth Dynasty administration, which would have commissioned these rituals,[970] was concerned with foreign forces and perhaps perceived some to be antagonistic.

949 The late Second Intermediate Period sarcophagus of Abdu, in which the Levantine-inspired dagger of Nehmen was uncovered, is not examined here as it is assigned to Apophis's reign. For more, see Lacau, *Sarcophages antérieurs* 2, 86-87; Daressy, *ASAE* 7 (1906), 115-120; Schneider, *Ausländer in Ägypten* 2, 140-141; Arnold, in *Second Intermediate Period*, 210-213, pl. 37.

950 Posener, *Princes et Pays*, 15-17, 31-35; Ben-Tor, in *Essays on Ancient Israel*, 64-66. See also Chapter 4.6.1 for a discussion on the Berlin Bowls' Execration Texts and their dating.

951 Posener, *Princes et Pays*, frontispiece, figs 3-4, pls 1-2; Schiestl, *E&L* 16 (2006), 177.

952 Posener, *Princes et Pays*, pl. 1.

953 E1-49, E52-60.

954 E64.

955 E63.

956 E50-51.

957 E62.

958 E65.

959 F1-6.

960 F7.

961 F3 is included despite the missing 𓈉 determinative. A similar toponym, *Yiꜣm(w)t*, occurs in f9 and f13 of the Berlin Bowls Execration Texts. See Chapter 4.6.1; Appendix B.6.

962 See Chapter 4.6.1. Albright, *BASOR* 184 (1966), 26-35; Aharoni, *Land of the Bible*, 133; Redford, *Egypt, Canaan and Israel*, 91.

963 Posener, *Princes et Pays*, 45; Albright, *JPOS* 8 (1928), 224-225; van Seters, *Hyksos*, 80; Weinstein, *BASOR* 288 (1992), 12-13; Rainey, *BASOR* 295 (1994), 82-84.

964 Several figurines, both provenanced and unprovenanced, have been uncovered and dated to the Middle Kingdom, adding to a larger body of Execration Texts, deliberately broken pottery, and bound prisoner statues/figurines delineating the subjugation of a rival force. For more, see Posener, *Cinq figurines d'envoûtement*; Ritner, *Egyptian Magical Practice*, 111-180.

965 Posener writes that the appearance of the texts on fragmented bowls and figurines may further affect our interpretation, as a scribe could have written an Asiatic name or appellative on a bowl differently than on a figurine due to the available space (Posener, *Princes et pays*, 40-43). See also Cohen, *Canaanites, Chronologies, and Connections*, 48.

966 Arnold, *Tomb Architecture*, 16.

967 Montet, *Byblos et L'Égypte*, 275; Ahlström, *Ancient Palestine*, 169-171; Redford, *Egypt, Canaan and Israel*, 89; Cohen, *Canaanites, Chronologies, and Connections*, 48; Ritner, *Egyptian Magical Practice*, 141.

968 Cohen, *Canaanites, Chronologies, and Connections*, 48.

969 Dever, *BA* 50/3 (1987), 172; Posener, *Princes et pays*, 45; Cohen *Canaanites, Chronologies, and Connections*, 49.

970 As Ritner explains, 'to produce such an assemblage would require a canonical textual schema, distributed mostly from a single source, a staff of trained scribes, and detailed, current records of the names and parentage of rulers... only the state could meet these requirements' (Ritner, *Egyptian Medical Practice*, 141).

4.4 Middle Egypt

4.4.1 *Beni Hassan*

Lat.Lon. 27°56'N 30°53'E

Refs PM 4, 141-163; Newberry, *Beni Hasan*, vols 1-2; Garstang, *Burial Customs*; Kanawati and Woods, *Beni Hassan*; Arnold, in *Offerings to the Discerning Eye*, 17-31; Kanawati and Evans, *Beni Hassan* 1.

Chron. Twelfth Dynasty

Beni Hassan is located approximately 258km south of Cairo, on the east bank of the Nile. Part of the Sixteenth Upper Egyptian nome, the site features Old and Middle Kingdom tombs of the high-ranking elite, as well as shaft tombs of middle-ranking officials.[971] The rock-cut tombs of the Middle Kingdom belong to such officials as 'nomarchs of the Oryx nome' and 'overseers of the Eastern Desert'.[972] Excavated and published by Newberry and Garstang,[973] the tombs are currently being re-examined by the Australian Centre for Egyptology, Macquarie University.[974]

Two tombs ascribed to the period outside the chronological scope of this study include depictions of Asiatics. The tombs of Baqet III (Nr 15) and Khety (Nr 17) are of uncertain date, although scholars generally place them in the late Eleventh Dynasty with the latter probably completed in the early Twelfth Dynasty.[975] The tomb owners held the titles of 'count' and 'great overlord of the entire Oryx nome', and incorporated scenes of military activities on the east walls of their chapels, directly opposite the tombs' entrances.[976] As the scenes act as artistic precursors to later representations of Asiatics at Beni Hassan, they are examined here.

Baqet III's scene depicts Egyptian men protecting a fortress,[977] the surrounding troops consisting of yellow-skinned soldiers with short kilts (Figure 4.46).[978] The horizontal zigzag detailing on the latter's garments, their skin colour and, in some preserved instances, red hair, indicate that they are Asiatic.[979] The foreigners advance against the fortress and its coalition of Nubian and Egyptian forces, and are armed with weapons of close-combat and missile advantage (slings, axes, bows and throw-sticks). One also carries an Egyptian-type shield. A hand-to-hand combat is additionally pictured between a dark-skinned Nubian and a

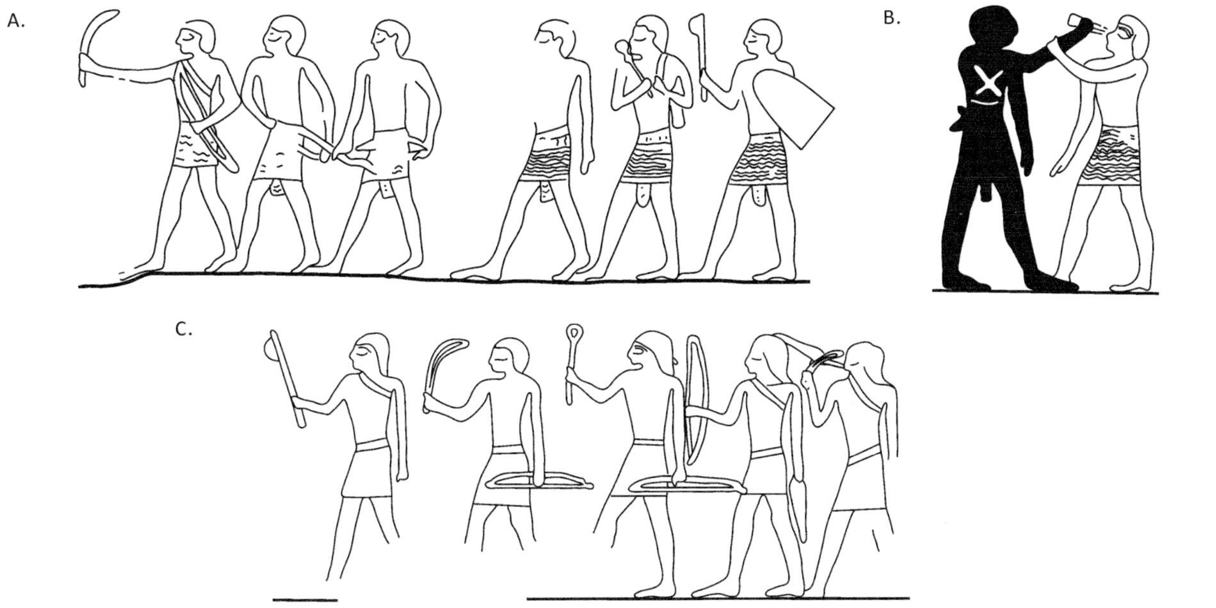

FIGURE 4.46. FOREIGN WARRIORS, EAST WALL, TOMB OF BAQET III (NR 15), BENI HASSAN. AFTER NEWBERRY, *BENI HASAN* 2, PL. 5.

971 Garstang, *Burial Customs*, 45-53, pls 3-4.

972 Garstang, *Burial Customs*, pls 3-4; Newberry, *Beni Hasan* 1, pl. 2; Kanawati and Woods, *Beni Hassan*, 6.

973 Garstang, *Burial Customs*; Newberry, *Beni Hasan*, 4 vols.

974 Kanawati and Woods, *Beni Hassan*, 1-2; Kanawati and Evans, *Beni Hassan* 1.

975 Willems and Schenkel suggest that the tombs were constructed during Amenemhat I's reign whereas Brovarski proposes a late Tenth to Eleventh Dynasty date. Willems, *JEOL* 28 (1983/1984), 83-84, 92-93, n. 26; Schenkel, *Frühmittelägyptische Studien*, 78-84; Brovarski, in *Egyptian Culture and Society*, 49-50, 55-56, 63. For the architectural sequence of the Beni Hassan tombs, see Hölzl, in *Sesto Congresso* 1, 279-283.

976 Khety is postulated to be Baqet III's son. Newberry, *Beni Hasan* 2, 5-7, pls 5, 15; Kanawati and Woods, *Beni Hassan*, 41, fig. 34.

977 Newberry, *Beni Hasan* 2, pl. 5; Schulman, *JSSEA* 12/4 (1982), 176-177.

978 Similar to those of the Asiatics depicted in the Eleventh Dynasty tomb of Intef (Jaroš-Deckert, *Asasif* 5, pl. 17, folding pls 1-3).

979 Personal examination; Newberry, *Beni Hassan* 2, 47; Brovarski, in *Egyptian Culture and Society*, 63.

yellow-skinned Asiatic, the former stabbing the latter in the eye (Figure 4.46B).[980]

The siege scene in Khety's tomb similarly incorporates an allied group attacking a fortress guarded by Egyptians (Figure 4.47A).[981] The attackers include Egyptians, Nubians as well as yellow-skinned warriors.[982] The latter wear elaborate kilts decorated with a detailed upper band and horizontal zigzags (Figure 4.47).[983] Items could be tucked into these bands (belts?), leaving the wearer free to carry additional weapons in his hands. The kilts and skin colour identify the warriors as Asiatics, their weapons similar to those of Baqet III's tomb[984] but with one different type of shield.

The Asiatics on the register occupying the top of the fortress carry shields with straight sides and triangular notches (Figure 4.47C), probably a development of the Asiatics' pointed, rectangular shields from Intef's Eleventh Dynasty siege scene.[985] Conversely, those on the bottom register closer to the gate of the fortress carry Egyptian-type shields and spears (Figure 4.47A).[986] Such variations may indicate different units among the Asiatics (troops specialised in combat versus siege techniques), or different areas of origin.[987] The division emphasises the Egyptian organisation of foreign troops on the battlefield, a quality befitting of Khety's role as 'overseer of the expedition'.

FIGURE 4.47. SIEGE SCENE AND FOREIGN WARRIORS, EAST WALL, TOMB OF KHETY (NR 17), BENI HASSAN. (A) KANAWATI AND WOODS, *BENI HASSAN*, FIG. 6. COURTESY OF THE AUSTRALIAN CENTRE FOR EGYPTOLOGY; (B-C) AFTER NEWBERRY, *BENI HASSAN* 2, PL. 15.

980 Although the melee is among other obvious close-combat skirmishes, the Nubian could be trying to pull the dagger out of the Asiatic's eye. In this case, it would be a sign of comradery rather than adversary. It should also be noted that Newberry's recording is slightly incorrect as the Asiatic is not unarmed but carries an object in his right hand (a dagger?). Personal examination; Newberry, *Beni Hasan* 2, pl. 15.

981 Newberry, *Beni Hasan* 2, pl. 15; Schulman, *JSSEA* 12/4 (1982), 177.

982 Personal examination; Brovarski, in *Egyptian Culture and Society*, 63-64, n. 261.

983 Personal examination.

984 The types of weapons are the same, but Khety provides additional details. For instance, one throw-stick is illustrated with a white-banded tip and striations across the shaft. Personal examination.

985 Jaroš-Deckert, *Asasif* 5, pl. 17; Schulman, *JSSEA* 12/4 (1982), 177, n. 68; Kanawati and Woods, *Beni Hassan*, pl. 74. Perhaps the shield is of the same type depicted on Obelisk Nr 163 from Serabit el-Khadim (Chapter 5.2.4.1, Figure 5.9). Schulman writes that the shield 'is certainly not carried by foreigners. The men carrying it in the Beni Hassan scene are clearly Egyptians'. Personal examination, however, confirms that the men carrying the shields are yellow-skinned and wear elaborate kilts, features typical of Asiatic representations. .

986 The shield emblem is distinctly a diamond-shaped symbol bordered by a dotted band. Although recorded with dark skin by Newberry, the two men are in fact painted with yellow skin and the same type of kilts worn by the other Asiatics. Personal examination.

987 Perhaps those with foreign weapons are newly migrated or new additions to the Egyptian army.

FIGURE 4.48. DETAILS FROM THE DECORATION ON THE EAST WALL, TOMB OF KHNUMHOTEP I (NR 14), BENI HASSAN. KANAWATI AND WOODS, *BENI HASSAN*, FIG. 5. COURTESY OF THE AUSTRALIAN CENTRE FOR EGYPTOLOGY.

4.4.1.1 Tomb of Khnumhotep I (Nr 14), reign of Amenemhat I

Like his predecessors, the 'great overlord of the Oryx nome' Khnumhotep I decorated the east wall of his early Twelfth Dynasty chapel with warfare scenes.[988] The east wall has been only partially published by Newberry as a number of selected details (Figure 4.48). Pertinent unpublished material includes the siege of a fortress on the northern end of the wall's lower registers.[989] The identity of this fortress's defenders is unclear, but Registers 2 and 3 (from the bottom) present Egyptians and Nubians attacking men atop the fortress. In Register 3, just behind a Nubian to the right of the fortress, is a row of five light-skinned individuals with red pointed beards and reddish-brown to black shoulder-length hair. They wear short kilts decorated with horizontal zigzags of blue, red and white, and carry slings and throw-sticks. At least three have necklaces with long pendants. Based on these details,[990] they are identified here as Asiatics.

Newberry's selection of details is copied from the southern end of Registers 1-3.[991] These include piles of dead bodies from Register 2 (Figure 4.48, bottom right) and a group of Libyans from Register 3 (Figure 4.48, centre).[992] The Libyans' inclusion is unique and may or may not be related to the siege scene;[993] however it adds yet another element of foreignness, further emphasising the tomb owner's significant role in foreign relations.

At the southern end of Register 1, directly beneath the fortress, is hand-to-hand combat amongst Egyptian men, hinting that the fortress was both attacked and defended by Egyptians. Published details of the register include Egyptian soldiers running towards the battlefield, followed by Egyptians carrying ammunition (Figure 4.48, top right). Behind them are four Asiatics (rather than Newberry's three) and an Egyptian archer (Figure 4.48, top left). A close inspection of the Asiatics reveals their colourful and intricate clothing. The first figure on the left wears a one-shouldered garment reaching just above the knees (Figure 4.49). The top half is designed with zigzags and chevrons of red, white and blue, while the bottom half is designed with horizontal zigzags and an elaborate blue hem. Faint traces of a detailed sash (?) draped over the left shoulder are discernible. As this Asiatic is the only foreigner wearing the distinctive garment, he is likely of higher rank. The second and fourth Asiatics wear kilts with horizontal zigzags of red, white and blue while the third's kilt bears stripes of the same colours. All four are depicted with colourful chest bands extending from the right shoulder to below the left arm, and wear multi-banded wristlets and anklets. They are armed with bows, throw-sticks, a dagger and a socketted weapon, similar in shape to the Levantine fenestrated eye-axe.[994] As the object in the second Asiatic's right hand curves outwards, it could

988 Newberry, *Beni Hasan* 1, 80, 84, pl. 47; Willems, *JEOL* 28 (1983/1984), 92.

989 Rabehl, *Grab des Amenemhet*, 177-181.

990 Their position on the register is the same as that of the Asiatics in Khety's siege scene, where a row of Asiatics follow a Nubian advancing towards the right side of the fortress. See Figure 4.47A-B.

991 Newberry, *Beni Hasan* 1, pl. 47.

992 Newberry, *Beni Hasan* 1, pls 45, 47.

993 The Libyans are not represented in a submissive state, their hands are untied and the men carry throw-sticks.

994 Features of this weapon include a wooden haft upon which a simple blade is mounted. The end is curved. Schulman, *JSSEA* 12/4 (1982), 178; Ward, *Egypt and the East Mediterranean*, 52-54; Maxwell-Hyslop, *Iraq* 11 (1949), 90-129.

also represent the Levantine scimitar (Figure 4.49).[995] The Asiatics' red hair is voluminous, coiffed and just above shoulder-length while their beards are thick, pointed and long. A similar beard, hairstyle and hair colour can be found on the warrior of Senwosret I's pyramid complex.[996]

An inscription on the chapel's west wall provides some historical background for the battle scene. It reads:

(5) *h3i.kw ḥnꜥ ḥm=f r im (m) ꜥḥꜥ.w n(.y) ꜥš 20 ꜥḥꜥ.n=f iw ḥr=s nw[...] dr.n=f sw m idbwy* (6)*Nḥs[.yw] 3r(.w) si(.w) St.tyw ḫr(.w) n.t(yw) ꜥb.w=f t3 ḫ3s.t...*

(5) I came down with his majesty there (in) 20 ships of *ꜥš*-wood, then he came upon it [...], then he expelled him from the Two Banks. (6)*Nḥs[.yw]* who had been driven away and who had perished and *St.tyw* who had fallen were of those whom he had united of the land and the foreign land...[997]

The text indicates state-controlled trade with the Levant for its timber during Amenemhat I's reign.[998] It also denotes that alongside Khnumhotep I are *St.tyw* Asiatics and *Nḥs[.yw]* Nubians who could have been involved in the battle.

If the text represents the same event on the east wall, then the two parties may be auxiliary forces employed by Egyptian royalty. This situation, combined with the sieges of Baqet III and Khety, would then mirror the circumstances described by Kay, where the king was allied with Asiatics and Nubians against Egyptian rebels from the Hare nome.[999]

Figure 4.49. Foreign warrior, east wall, tomb of Khnumhotep I (Nr 14), Beni Hassan (drawn from photograph).

4.4.1.2 Tomb of Amenemhat (Nr 2), reign of Senwosret I

The tomb of Amenemhat (Nr 2) likely dates to Senwosret I's reign, when the tomb owner was appointed as 'great overlord of the Oryx nome' and 'overseer of the great expedition'.[1000]

The battle scene

Like earlier tombs, the chapel's east wall preserves a battle scene, here arranged in two central registers.[1001] They are divided by a doorway into two halves: (1) the northern end, where the scene illustrates the siege of a fortress possibly protected by Egyptians, with more Egyptians and Nubians flanking the fortress on either side; and (2) the southern end, where the registers each have two opposing rows of armed men facing one another. It is uncertain which forces belong to whom or if the skirmish is connected to the scene on the northern end.[1002]

Three Asiatics are illustrated at the very right of the southern end (Figure 4.50). Like earlier representations, the individuals are bearded and have coiffed hair. They are dressed in short, patterned kilts of red, blue and white, yet the foremost Asiatic's kilt slightly varies in length and colour. The three are armed with throw-sticks, spears and a fenestrated eye-axe.[1003] As Amenemhat's biography reports expeditions to Nubia to 'overthrow' Senwosret's enemies,[1004] perhaps the scenes are connected to campaigns against Nubia[1005] in which Asiatics were Egyptian rather than Nubian allies.

The fair-skinned men

The decoration in the discussed tombs suggests that, by this time, Asiatic soldiers were in the service of the Oryx nome's rulers from at least the Eleventh Dynasty. A key artistic indicator that may be used as evidence for the depiction of foreigners among Egyptians is skin colour. Artists working in the tomb of Amenemhat seemingly utilised the same yellow of the skin of Asiatic soldiers for other men in scenes across the tomb's walls. These include:

- North wall, top register:[1006] from the left, the first (Plate 1a), second and fifth men partaking in hunting activities;
- North wall, second register:[1007] male dancers and clappers;

995 If correct, this would be the earliest representation of such swords in Egyptian art. See Hamblin, *Warfare in the Ancient Near East*, 66-71, fig. 2.

996 See Chapter 4.3.6.1 and Figure 4.43.

997 Hieroglyphic text and line numbers as transcribed by Newberry (*Beni Hasan* 1, pl. 44). Transliteration and translation are by the author.

998 The vessels were evidently used by the king himself.

999 See Chapter 4.4.3; Brovarski, in *Egyptian Culture and Society*, 65-66.

1000 Kanawati and Woods, *Beni Hassan*, 6, 21. For more on the tomb, see Newberry, *Beni Hasan* 1, 20-38; Rabehl, *Grab des Amenemhet*, passim.

1001 The top three registers contain wrestling scenes while the lowest register features pilgrimage voyages. Newberry, *Beni Hasan* 1, pls 14, 16; Kanawati and Woods, *Beni Hassan*, fig. 7.

1002 Schulman, *JSSEA* 12/4 (1982), 178.

1003 Unlike Newberry's drawing, the end of the axe is covered by the carrier's hand and so it is uncertain whether the wooden haft curves as in Khnumhotep I's scene (Figure 4.48). Personal examination.

1004 Newberry, *Beni Hasan* 1, 25-26.

1005 Kanawati and Woods, *Beni Hassan*, 69; Brovarski, in *Egyptian Culture and Society*, 65-66.

1006 Kanawati and Woods, *Beni Hassan*, fig. 20, pl. 25.

1007 Kanawati and Woods, *Beni Hassan*, fig. 20, pl. 52.

Figure 4.50. Foreign warriors, east wall, tomb of Amenemhat (Nr 2), Beni Hassan. Courtesy of the Australian Centre for Egyptology.

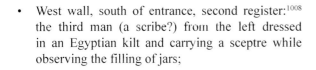

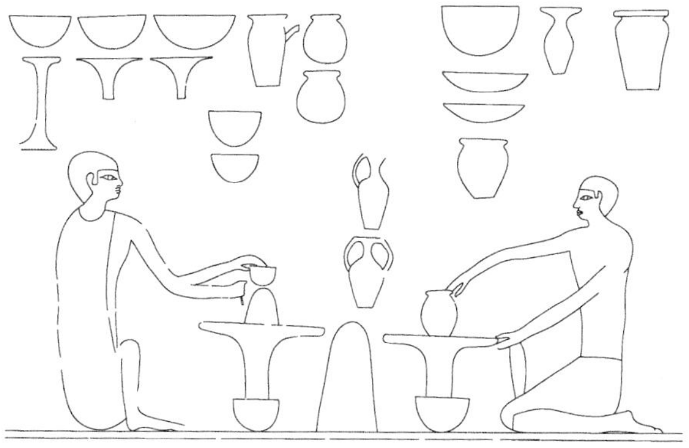

Figure 4.51. Potters at work, east wall, tomb of Amenemhat (Nr 2), Beni Hassan. Courtesy of the Australian Centre for Egyptology.

- West wall, south of entrance, second register:[1008] the third man (a scribe?) from the left dressed in an Egyptian kilt and carrying a sceptre while observing the filling of jars;
- West wall, south of entrance, fourth register:[1009] the fourth man from the right standing at the end of a papyrus boat;
- West wall, south of entrance, sixth register:[1010] the third man(?) from the right in a bread-making scene; and
- West wall, south of entrance, seventh register:[1011] all figures on the right end in a beer(?) making scene.

Based on skin colour, the men are tentatively identified as either Libyan or Asiatic, although the latter is favoured due to the greater number of Asiatics in earlier tombs (see Figure 4.55). The foreigners could be second generation Asiatics or of mixed Egyptian-Asiatic background. They are involved in mostly low-ranking daily activities such as hunting, bread-and-beer making and possibly scribal work. Some are also performers, a profession recorded for Asiatics in the later el-Lahun papyri.[1012] It is useful to note that darker-skinned individuals also feature in the tomb's scenes,[1013] possibly denoting Nubian descendents in the community. If correct, the men signify the assumption of Egyptian fashion and daily activities by peoples of foreign descent. Their inclusion in the tomb would also point to a foreign population residing in the Oryx nome during Senwosret I's reign.

Depiction of characteristic non-Egyptian ceramics

The northern end of the chapel's west wall, fourth register from the top, shows a series of workshop activities.[1014] The first one at the right depicts two potters at work, above which are examples of their craft (Figure 4.51). Two vessels between the opposing potters have handles. The top vessel is similar to a *ḫnm*-vessel but without the second smaller handle on its body. This, along with its more oblong shape, suggests that it is an EBIV/MBI dipper juglet with a flat base, as found in Megiddo[1015] or Tell 'Arqa.[1016] The vessel underneath has a narrower neck with two handles and also parallels Levantine forms.[1017] The two indicate knowledge of Levantine pottery by Egyptians,[1018] especially contemporary juglets, suggesting an increased influence of foreign technology and, considering the vessels' products as well as their use, foreign customs.

Depiction of organic products (?)

Among the south wall's piled offerings are four long black pods.[1019] Their shape is akin to that of acacia, tamarind or the carob plant (*Ceratonia siliqua*).[1020] While the former were common in the Middle Kingdom, carob is not indigenous to Egypt but was most probably imported from the Levant.[1021] If their identification as carob is correct, then the representation corroborates archaeological findings at el-Lahun,[1022] supporting the import of carob during the Middle Kingdom as well as its popularity and consumption by the elite. This consumption is not a new tradition as carob was included in offering lists and scenes of Old Kingdom tombs.

1008 Newberry, *Beni Hasan* 1, pl. 12; Kanawati and Woods, *Beni Hassan*, fig. 25.
1009 Newberry, *Beni Hasan* 1, pl. 12; Kanawati and Woods, *Beni Hassan*, fig. 25.
1010 Newberry, *Beni Hasan* 1, pl. 12; Kanawati and Woods, *Beni Hassan*, fig. 25.
1011 Newberry, *Beni Hasan* 1, pl. 12; Kanawati and Woods, *Beni Hassan*, fig. 25.
1012 Papyrus UC 32191. See Chapter 4.3.5.2, Appendix B.2.
1013 See, for example, the other hunters on the north wall's top register (Plate 1A). Kanawati and Woods, *Beni Hassan*, fig. 20, pl. 25.
1014 Newberry, *Beni Hasan* 1, pl. 11; Kanawati and Woods, *Beni Hassan*, pl. 120.
1015 Phase 3. Loud, *Megiddo* 2, pl. 17 [21].
1016 Thalmann, in *Bronze Age in the Lebanon*, fig. 5 [11].
1017 See, for example, the EBIV bi-handled jar from Byblos in Thalmann, in *Bronze Age in the Lebanon*, fig. 3 [4].
1018 Cohen-Weinberger and Goren, *E&L* 14 (2004), 82.
1019 Newberry, *Beni Hasan* 1, pl. 17.
1020 Personal communication with Naguib Kanawati.
1021 Gale et al., in *Ancient Egyptian Materials and Technology*, 338; Zohary, *Israel Journal of Plant Sciences* 50/1 (2002), 141-145.
1022 See Chapter 4.3.5.1; Gerner, in *Lahun Studies*, 88-89; Petrie, *Kahun*, 47, 50.

4.4.1.3 Tomb of Khnumhotep II (Nr 3), reign of Senwosret II

The tomb of Khnumhotep II (Nr 3) contains one of the most recognisable scenes of Asiatics in Egyptian Pharaonic history.[1023] The procession of foreigners is not, however, the only scene of pertinence. The north, south and west walls all feature subtle clues pointing to direct and indirect contact with Levantines, clues which are often overshadowed by the momentous visit of the Asiatics. Unlike former tombs, that of Khnumhotep II is marked by the complete absence of warfare and wrestling scenes, implying that Khnumhotep II was not responsible for such activities. In fact, he did not hold the title of 'great overlord of the Oryx nome' nor 'overseer of the expedition' but was instead 'overseer of the Eastern Desert'.[1024]

His duties as such are best reflected on the north wall (Plate 2). Two large scale figures of the tomb owner are illustrated, each occupying three registers: one is on the western end with Khnumhotep II aiming his bow east, and one is on the eastern end with Khnumhotep II facing west, carrying a staff. The feet of the first and head of the second figure share one register, that which pictures the Asiatic procession. The top two registers depict desert hunting activities and the bottom three registers are concerned with fowling, bull fighting, animal husbandry, offering bearers and the recording of a cattle-count. The placement of the Asiatics in between could, as Kamrin surmises, refer to their symbolic 'bridging the gap between the chaotic world above and the fully ordered world below'.[1025] Before analysing the contextual nuances of the scene, a study of the foreigners' procession is provided below (Figure 4.52).[1026]

The procession of foreigners

From the right, two Egyptians, the scribe Noferhotep and 'overseer of hunters' Khety, present a group of 15 *ʿ3m.w* to the eastern figure of Khnumhotep II. Noferhotep holds out a papyrus roll to the tomb owner, specifying:

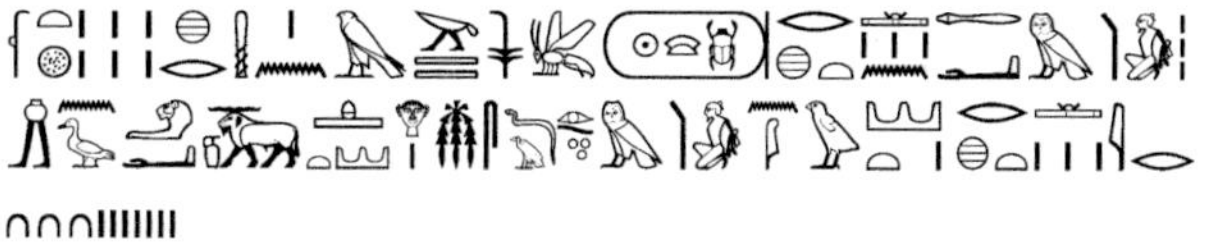

rnp.t-sp 6 ḫr ḥm n(.y) Ḥr.w sšm t3.wy nsw.t-bi.ty Ḫ3-ḫpr-Rʿ.w rḫ.t n(.y) ʿ3m.w ini.n[1027] *s3 ḥ3.ty-ʿ3 Ḫnm-ḥtp ḥr msdm.t m ʿ3m(.w) n(.y) Šw rḫ.t iry 37*

Year 6 under the majesty of Horus, uniter of the Two Lands, king of Upper and Lower Egypt, Khakheperra (Senwosret II). Number of *ʿ3m.w* whom the son of the count Khnumhotep brought on account of *msdm.t*, namely: *ʿ3m(.w)* of *Šw*,[1028] number amounting to 37.

The regnal year provides some historical validity to the event and indicates that it could have been part of a longer document, most possibly a register of Asiatics.[1029] The 'son of the count' is either Khnumhotep II or his son Khnumhotep III,[1030] but Khnumhotep II is not identified as 'son of a count' in his own tomb.[1031] Instead, Khnumhotep III is labelled as such on the eastern end of the north wall.[1032] He is also attested in his father's biography as 'sole companion', 'who brings what is useful' and 'entry of foreign lands'.[1033] Such roles would have allowed him to be in contact with foreigners or expeditions travelling across Egypt's borders.[1034] So the epithet, along with Khnumhotep III's other duties, supports the identification of the 'son of the count' with Khnumhotep III, who would accordingly be the one bringing the Asiatics to his father.

The text states that the purpose of the foreigners' visit concerns *msdm.t*, which may be translated as 'black eye-paint' or the mineral from which it was produced, galena (lead sulphide). Ore localities for galena span across several easterly regions such as the Eastern Desert and the Sinai, insinuating that the mineral was accessible to both Egyptians and their neighbours.[1035] Indeed, extant evidence supports its import from areas beyond Egypt.[1036] A principal ingredient in kohl, it was used in mortuary practices[1037] and medicinal remedies.[1038] If smelted into lead, products would include a range of metallic objects

1023 Kanawati and Evans, *Beni Hassan* 1, pls 42-48, 124, 128-129; Newberry, *Beni Hasan* 1, 59-72; Kamrin, *Monument and Microcosm*; Kamrin, *Cosmos of Khnumhotep II*; Rabehl, *Grab des Amenemhet*, 229-281.

1024 Newberry, *Beni Hasan* 1, 41-42; Aufrère, in *Egypt and Nubia*, 207-214.

1025 Kamrin, *JAEI* 1/3 (2009), 31.

1026 The following analysis is a revised form of an earlier publication by the author in *Beni Hassan* 1, 72-78.

1027 The verb could also be a passive perfective participle followed by a dative, *ini n* 'who were brought to'.

1028 *Šw* has been identified as *Šwtw* of the Execration texts, *R-šwt* of the Speos Artemidos, *Shaddu* of the Amarna letters and Sheth of Numbers 24:17. Geographical designates span from the east of the Jordan River (Moab, Gilead or the Transjordan) to the northern Sinai. For more, see Cohen, *JNES* 74/1 (2015), 23-24, table 1; Kamrin, *JAEI* 1/3 (2009), 24-25; Posener, *Princes et Pays*, 89-90; Helck, *Die Beziehungen Ägyptens*, 46, 50-51, 61-62; Aharoni, *Land of the Bible*, 46; Aḥituv, *Canaanite Toponyms*, 184; Redford, *Egypt, Canaan and Israel*, 87, n. 94; Thompson, *Historicity of the Patriarchal Narratives*, 123-125; Goedicke, *JARCE* 21 (1984), 210.

1029 Kessler, *SAK* 14 (1987), 150-151. For similar lists, see Chapter 4.3.5.2 and 4.6.3, Appendix B.2 and B.7.

1030 Khnumhotep II's son, Nakht, is already identified as a 'count' in his father's biography (Newberry, *Beni Hasan* 1, 63 [line 147]).

1031 Kamrin, *JAEI* 1/3 (2009), 25. Khnumhotep II was the son of the count Nehry.

1032 Also suggested in Kamrin, *JAEI* 1/3 (2009), 25; Franke, in *Middle Kingdom Studies*, 57-60.

1033 Newberry, *Beni Hasan* 1, 64 [151-160], pl. 26; Ward, *Index*, 101 [843]; Franke, in *Middle Kingdom Studies*, 57; Lloyd, in *Pharaonic Religion and Society*, 23.

1034 See also Khnumhotep III's biography in Dahshur, Chapter 4.3.1.2. A stela from Wadi Gasus, near the Red Sea, lists a Khnumhotep with similar titles who was probably involved in an expedition to the Sinai. If this Khnumhotep is the same as Beni Hassan's Khnumhotep III, then the individual was engaged in two ventures for acquiring minerals: the first dating to Year 1 of Senwosret II's reign and the second toYear 6 (Franke, in *Middle Kingdom Studies*, 59-60, fig. 1 [b]). For more on the findings near Wadi Gasus at Wadi/Mersa Gawasis, see Chapter 5.2.2.

1035 Ogden, in *Ancient Egyptian Materials and Technology*, 168-169; Forbes, *Ancient Technology* 8, 209-233; Lucas and Harris, *Ancient Egyptian Materials and Industries*, 83.

1036 See, for instance, the Mit Rahina text in Chapter 4.3.7 and Appendix B.3. Lead from non-Egyptian sources is attested in New Kingdom evidence, including the Annals of Thutmosis III and inorganic content of Egyptian make-up (samples dating between 2000 to 1200 B.C.). Redford, *Syria and Palestine*, 63-64, 72, 80, 88, 91, 93, 95-96, 139; Martinetto et al., *Nuclear Instruments and Methods in Physics Research B* 181 (2001), 744-748.

1037 A bag of eye-paint is among Khnumhotep II's list of offerings on the south wall of his chapel. Newberry, *Beni Hasan* 1, pl. 35; Kamrin, *JAEI* 1/3 (2009), 27.

1038 Kamrin, *JAEI* 1/3 (2009), 27; Manniche, *Ancient Egyptian Herbal*, 47.

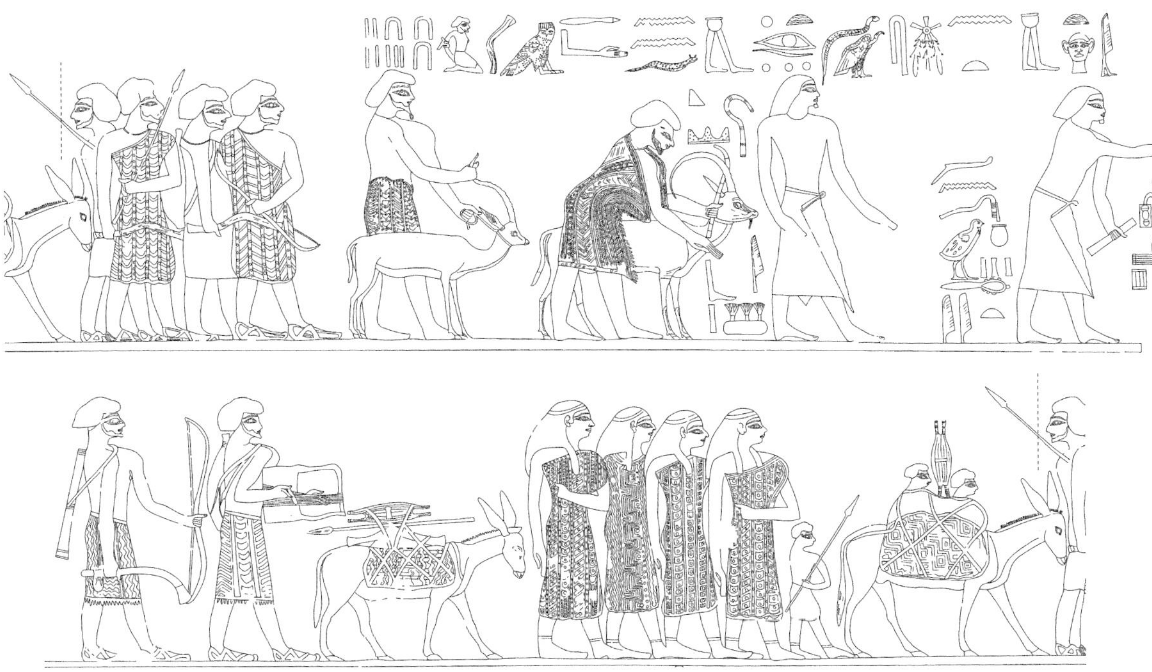

FIGURE 4.52. PROCESSION OF FOREIGNERS, NORTH WALL, TOMB OF KHNUMHOTEP II (NR 3), BENI HASSAN. COURTESY OF THE AUSTRALIAN CENTRE FOR EGYPTOLOGY.

including jewellery and figurines.[1039] MBA weapons also consist of a small percentage of lead and it is possible that Egyptian weapons similarly featured this mineral.[1040] Therefore, the product associated with the *ꜥ3m.w* could have been used for a variety of cultic and functional purposes in both its raw and processed forms. As it could be sourced from many regions, it is not particularly informative on the foreigners' homeland.[1041]

A second inscription above the group supports Noferhotep's text (Figure 4.52), reading *iyi.t ḥr ini.t msḏmt ini.n=f*[1042] *ꜥ3m 37* 'coming on account of the bringing of *msḏm.t*, he having brought: 37 *ꜥ3m*'. The determinative for *ꜥ3m* illustrates a man with a coiffed hairstyle and beard, similar to those of the men in the procession.[1043] The number of *ꜥ3m* in the text is also greater than those illustrated, a typical Egyptian practice where numbers in captions often do not agree with the number of figures portrayed. Instead, the scene represents 15 individuals: eight men, four women and three children (Figure 4.52).

All are depicted as Asiatics with yellow skin, large hooked noses and greyish-blue eyes.[1044] Their garments are patterned and brightly coloured in red, blue and white. The men and children have coiffed, mushroom-like hairstyles, whereas the women have long hair held in place by a white (silver?) headband.[1045]

The first foreigner and leader of the procession is barefoot. He is the only one to be given a label: *ḥk3 ḫ3s.t Ỉbš3* 'ruler of a foreign land, *Ỉbš3*' (Figure 4.52), offering the first recorded Middle Kingdom attestation of the title which, as discussed later, signals the individual's higher position amidst other non-Egyptian rulers.[1046] Further support for such a rank is the choice to employ this title rather than 'ruler of *Šw*', the toponym of Noferhotep's papyrus. His name is Northwest Semitic and has been equated with Abi-shai ('my father is a nobleman'),[1047] Abi-shar ('my father is king')[1048] and Abisharie ('my father is strong').[1049] Artistically distinct from the other men in his retinue, *Ỉbš3* wears a knee-length garment draped over one shoulder with the other bare but for a white detail (a pin?). Intricate patterns and fringing along the sides of the garment suggest a woollen textile.[1050] He holds in his left hand a banded, curved-stick with which he controls a Nubian ibex.[1051] His

1039 Ogden, in *Ancient Egyptian Materials and Technology*, 168; Brill, Barnes and Adams, *Recent Advances in Science and Technology of Materials* 3 (1974), 9-27.

1040 El-Morr and Pernot, *JAS* 38 (2011), 2616, 2618, 2622-2623, tables 4-6; Véron et al., *AHL* 34-35 (2011/2012), 68-78.

1041 Contra Franke, in *Middle Kingdom Studies*, 60.

1042 The verb could also be a relative form, *ini(.w)n=f* 'which they brought to him', the subject being the following 37 *ꜥ3m*. Goedicke refutes this, noting that the qualified word is feminine (Goedicke, *JARCE* 21 [1984], 206).

1043 The features are similar to the determinative used for Khnumhotep III's *M3ki*, ruler of *Kbny* (see Chapter 4.3.1.2 and Appendix B.1; Allen, *BASOR* 352 [2008], pl. 3).

1044 Kanawati and Woods, *Beni Hassan*, 71, pls 92-102.

1045 Newberry, *Beni Hasan* 1, pls 30-31; Shedid, *Felsgräber von Beni Hassan*, figs 101-104; Kanawati and Woods, *Beni Hassan*, pls 92-102.

1046 See Chapter 7.3.4.

1047 Goedicke, *JARCE* 21 (1984), 207; Saretta, *Egyptian Perceptions of West Semites*, 111, n. 280.

1048 Albright, *Vocalization*, 8.

1049 Schneider, *Ausländer in Ägypten* 1, 47.

1050 Saretta, *Egyptian Perceptions of West Semites*, 114.

1051 Shedid, *Beni Hassan*, fig. 103; Kanawati and Woods, *Beni Hassan*, pls 92-94; Shea, *BA* 44/4 (1981), 224. A staff with the same shape is portrayed on a sheath from a MBA deposit at Byblos (Temple of Obelisks). It is held at the right shoulder of a man riding an equid. See Chapter 6.3.3.1, Figure 6.16.

bent stance and extended right hand, palm open and facing down, symbolise his respect towards Khnumhotep II.[1052]

The second barefoot man in the group wears a banded kilt with a wavy waistline (Figure 4.52). He has a unique and unknown white object hanging at the tip of his beard that could perhaps be a jewelled adornment or a water (sweat?) droplet,[1053] and leads a Dorcas gazelle by rope. Since he remains distinct from both *Ỉbš3* as well as the men behind him, he is likely the second-in-command over the Asiatics.[1054]

To his left are four men in multi-strapped sandals and one-shouldered garments, two of which are patterned (Figure 4.52). The first carries a composite bow identifiable by its curved ends, the second and third have wooden throw-sticks, and the third and fourth are armed with spears.[1055] The second also carries a brown bag-shaped object on his back that resembles a leather gourd.[1056]

Following the men is a donkey bearing a red saddle bag out of which the heads of two Asiatic children are painted (Figure 4.52). Between them is an object, wide in its centre, with two protruding prongs at either ends. The item could be a skin bellow, although this typically has a single outlet pipe at one end,[1057] a small tent or container,[1058] a musical instrument, or a leather churning bag for the making of milk or butter (a qirbah/sqa).[1059]

A third child behind the donkey is in a short red kilt with red footwear and carries a spear (Figure 4.52).[1060] Despite remarks that the spear is 'an unusual weapon for a child',[1061] recent excavations at Sidon have uncovered a spearhead in a 12-17 year-old's burial of the MBIIA-B period, leading excavators to postulate that the weapon was a status marker.[1062] As such, the pictured weapon could represent the child's importance as an individual of high status.[1063]

Four women are next in the procession, all wearing patterned shin-length dresses, some one-shouldered, and red footwear (Figure 4.52).[1064] Behind them is a donkey on whose back is a throw-stick, a spear and the same unidentifiable object on the first donkey.

Two men at the back of the group are dressed in patterned kilts with fringed hems and multi-strapped sandals (Figure 4.52). With a bag-shaped object on his back, the first holds a lyre with a double set of strings. The instrument could be identified as a Levantine thin eastern lyre by its flat bottom edge and four to eight strings,[1065] the first of its kind in Egyptian art.[1066] The last figure is armed with a composite bow and quiver, as well as an axe with a curved end, its sockets and D-shaped head signifying that it is a MBIIA duckbill axe.[1067]

When compared to the texts, the Asiatics do not carry galena, but bring a lyre, animals, weapons and water skins. The variety of equipment brought by the Asiatics, alongside the inclusion of women and children, suggests that they were not captives or part of a trading caravan.[1068] While some have proposed that the foreigners had not yet procured the galena but were led to Beni Hassan for this vocational opportunity,[1069] others have theorised that they were employed to either manufacture or sell metal goods.[1070] Scholars have also suggested that the procession is a diplomatic envoy carrying gifts or tribute along with galena.[1071]

Amidst the many theories is the problematic identification of the foreigners as nomads.[1072] The ambiguities of the scene do not certify such a classification as details could be interpreted in many ways. For example, the metaphorical association of the gazelle and ibex with the desert can be interpreted as either the animals' capture in the desert as

1052 Kamrin, *JAEI* 1/3 (2009), 26.

1053 However, liquid is typically painted blue by Egyptian artists.

1054 The Epic of Kirta from Ugarit includes the summoning of 70 'captains' and 80 'chiefs', the former literally translated as 'bulls' while the latter are 'gazelles/wild deer' (*CAT* 1.15 IV.6-7 as translated in Parker, *Ugaritic Narrative Poetry*, 27, ns 81-82). Perhaps, then, the gazelle is symbolically related to the Asiatic's rank.

1055 As the paint along the spears' shafts is not preserved well, details for their identification as MBA socketted spears could not be ascertained.

1056 See Cohen, *JNES* 74/1 (2015), 21.

1057 Kamrin, *JAEI* 1/3 (2009), 26; Thompson, *Historicity of the Patriarchal Narratives*, 126; Nibbi, *Pot Bellows and Oxhide*, 33; Shea, *BA* 44/4 (1981), 222, 225-226; Redford, *Egypt, Canaan, and Israel*, 83.

1058 Kamrin, *JAEI* 1/3 (2009), 26-27, n. 71.

1059 A qirbah is commonly suspended from a tripod/branch or held at either ends, and then rocked back and forth. This churning process can produce a variety of dairy products such as butter and buttermilk (laban). Personal communication with Miral Lashien. For modern equivalents, see Richardson and Dorr, *Craft Heritage of Oman* 2, 373.

1060 Kanawati and Woods, *Beni Hassan*, pls 97-99.

1061 Kamrin, *JAEI* 1/3 (2009), 29.

1062 Doumet-Serhal, *NEA* 73/2-3 (2010), 118, fig. 8 [a-c]. See also Doumet-Serhal and Kopetzky, *AHL* 34-35 (2011/2012), 26; Doumet-Serhal, *Levant* 36 (2004), 108, figs 51-54, table 19. For a cylinder seal depicting a child with a spear, see Pittman, *Near Eastern Seals*, 67 [no. 57].

1063 For an interpretation suggesting that the child could either be a prince or guard, see Shea, *BA* 44/4 (1981), 227; Kamrin, *JAEI* 1/3 (2009), 29.

1064 Kanawati and Woods, *Beni Hassan*, pls 99-100.

1065 Lawergren, *BASOR* 309 (1998), 43, 47, fig. 1.

1066 Manniche, *Music and Musicians*, 37; Kamrin, *JAEI* 1/3 (2009), 27; Saretta, *Egyptian Perceptions of West Semites*, 127.

1067 Personal examination. See Mourad, in *Beni Hassan* 1, 76, pl. 128. For other illustrations of duckbill axes, see Gernez, *L'armement en metal*, 196; Matthiae, *Studi Eblaiti* 3 (1980), fig. 13. For more discussion on its identification, see Williams, *Second Intermediate Period*, 860; Dever, *BASOR* 288 (1992), 8; Weinstein, *BASOR* 288 (1992), 33-34; Bietak, *BASOR* 281 (1991), 49; Bietak, in *From Relative Chronology to Absolute Chronology*, 128-129.

1068 As suggested in Helck, *Die Beziehungen Ägyptens*, 41; Shea, *BA* 44/4 (1981), 219. Franke argues that the Asiatics were part of a mining expedition led by Khnumhotep III, and acted as nomadic guides (Franke, in *Middle Kingdom Studies*, 60). See also Kanawati and Woods, *Beni Hassan*, 71; Goedicke, *JARCE* 21 (1984), 206.

1069 Goedicke, *JARCE* 21 (1984), 206-207.

1070 Redford, *Egypt, Canaan, and Israel*, 83; Mazar, *Archaeology of the Land of the Bible*, 166; Kamrin, *JAEI* 1/3 (2009), 28.

1071 Aufrère, in *Egypt and Nubia*, 211; Kessler, *SAK* 14 (1987), 148.

1072 For their identification as nomads, see Albright, *Vocalization*, 8; Thompson, *History of the Patriarchal Narratives*, 123, n. 38; Wright, *Biblical Archaeology*, 46; Redford, *Egypt, Canaan, and Israel*, 83; Mazar, *Land of the Bible*, 166; Kamrin, *JAEI* 1/3 (2009), 28; Staubli, *Das Image der Nomaden*, 30-35; Schneider, *Ausländer im Ägypten* 2, 196-197; Goedicke, *JARCE* 21 (1984), 209. For more on the scholarly interpretations, see Cohen, *JNES* 74/1 (2015), 19-38, table 1.

offerings, or as of other cultic or royal significance.[1073] Both animals are indeed found in the Eastern Desert, but whether or not this is connected to the Asiatics' origin is uncertain. As only two are offered by barefoot men,[1074] a cultic association is most likely. Hence the Asiatics' nomadic lifestyle cannot be corroborated by the evidence. Still, the scene does illustrate the use of a textile easily patterned and coloured, such as wool,[1075] the employment of MBA weapons, a possible attribution of status to particular weapons, and knowledge in Near Eastern music and musical instruments. Hence, the Asiatics are very likely of a MBIIA culture fully or partially related to a sedentary lifestyle.

The texts stress that the Asiatics were brought specifically to Khnumhotep II for galena, which is not represented in the procession. Arguably, the donkeys could have carried the product, but the lack of any other textual or visual confirmation for its presence in such a detailed scene is highly questionable. It is more likely that the Asiatics were brought, not to trade in the mineral, but to procure and/or process it. Perhaps, the one 'who brings what is useful' accompanied the Asiatics to the one who controls the area from whence the useful is procured, that is, Khnumhotep II, 'overseer of the Eastern Desert'. Consequently, the Asiatics would settle in Beni Hassan to join expeditions to the Eastern Desert, in a diplomatic venture supported by the presence of their ruler, their armed men and even their possible animal offerings. Indeed, the scene suggests that the MBIIA Asiatics were not forcibly presented before Khnumhotep II but were honourably granted an audience with the elite of the Oryx nome, arriving peacefully in an event that was deemed significant enough to be recorded in Khnumhotep II's tomb. As such, it is not unfeasible that the foreigners were involved in a joint venture from which both parties would profit.[1076]

Contextually, the placement of the scene is also significant (Plate 2). Its inclusion on the north wall has been interpreted as either a celebration of the New Year Festival[1077] or a homage to the royal house.[1078] Above the eastern figure of Khnumhotep II is an inscription specifying the levying of cattle and dues (*inw*) from the Oryx nome and before him are scenes associated with such levying, yet the inclusion of a mythical creature in the desert landscape[1079] points to other fantastical, probably cultic, overtones to the wall's decoration. In fact, from top to bottom, the wall exhibits a variety of environments including the mystical, the desert, the marshlands and the floodplain.[1080] As Kamrin correctly states, the Asiatics are in the centre of the wall's composition, surrounded by the 'chaotic' desert above which is overpowered by Khnumhotep II and his sons, and the 'tamed' birds and cattle below which are controlled by Khnumhotep II's officials.[1081] Other Egyptian officials also present offerings to Khnumhotep II. Thus, the foreigners are artistically between the chaotic and the ordered,[1082] bordered at either end by the large figures of Khnumhotep II who visually and perhaps figuratively contains and controls their visit. The two Asiatics leading the procession are also dominating animals themselves, rendering the foreigners as tamers of wildlife and connecting them to the ordered realm.[1083] Nonetheless, the overarching beneficiary is Khnumhotep II who metaphorically receives an endless supply of products from all environments, including the foreign world. The depiction of this sphere in tomb decoration stresses the emerging role of Asiatics as bearers of 'worldly' goods and as providers of expertise and/or commodities, especially for the Egyptian elite.

The fair-skinned men

As in the tomb of Amenemhat, that of Khnumhotep II includes individuals painted using a lighter shade of colour than the male Egyptians. There are, in fact, two shades of a lighter colour. The first is a slightly darker yellow than that of the Asiatics on the north wall and the second is a lighter red, used for the sons of Khnumhotep II and other officials with blonde-red caps. Both could be of foreign descent,[1084] yet as the officials with caps appear in some cases with skin colour almost equivalent to that of the Egyptians,[1085] they are not listed here. Men with yellow skin can be found on the:

- North wall, fourth register from the top:  *im.y-r3 ḫtm.tyw Sn-ʿnḫ(.w)* 'overseer of sealers,[1086] Senankh(u)';[1087]

[1073] Both are presented as sacrificial offerings in rituals to Seth, and gazelles may have been sacrificed in funerary rituals in both Egypt and the Levant. Gazelle heads and ibex horns are also symbolic of royalty and divinity. Amiet, *La glyptique mésopotamienne archaique*, fig. 119A; de Miroschedji, in *Biblical Archaeology Today*, 213-215; Kamrin, *JAEI* 1/3 (2009), 30-31; Lilyquist, *Three Foreign Wives*, 159-161, figs 91 [g], 92 [a-d], 55; Cornelius, *Reshef and Ba'al*, 246-247.

[1074] Compare the Asiatics here with the Libyans of Khnumhotep I's tomb, who accompany numerous animals (Figure 4.48). Shea, *BA* 44/4 (1981), 225; Kamrin, *JAEI* 1/3 (2009), 30; Kanawati and Woods, *Beni Hassan*, fig. 5.

[1075] Saretta, *Egyptian Perceptions of West Semites*, 114, 131.

[1076] For a possibly similar case concerning the 'brother of the ruler of *Rṯnw*, *Ḫbddm*', see Chapter 5.2.4.1.

[1077] Kessler, *SAK* 14 (1987), 158-159.

[1078] Rabehl, *Grab des Amenemhet*, 241-250; Kamrin, *JAEI* 1/3 (2009), 29-30.

[1079] Kanawati and Woods, *Beni Hassan*, pl. 204.

[1080] Kamrin, *Monument and Microcosm*, 157-158.

[1081] Kamrin, *JAEI* 1/3 (2009), 31.

[1082] Kamrin, *JAEI* 1/3 (2009), 31.

[1083] Kamrin, *JAEI* 1/3 (2009), 31.

[1084] The first two female offering bearers on the third register of the south wall's west end (from the right) are depicted with a unique hairstyle with a low bun or short ponytail. Such a hairstyle is similar to that of the women of Amenemhat's tomb (west wall, south of entrance) and the Libyans of Khnumhotep I's chapel (Figure 4.48). The women, both household servants, could thus also be foreigners. See Newberry, *Beni Hasan* 1, pls 12, 35; Kanawati and Evans, *Beni Hassan* 1, pls 91b, 139.

[1085] These men are found on the north wall joining Khnumhotep II's hunt (the sons Khnumhotep, Netjernekhet, Nehry and Nekhet), the east wall above the lintel (the 'overseer of the treasury, Baqet') and the south wall (Khnumhotep II's sons and the 'overseer of the storehouse, Netjernekhet', the 'overseer of the storehouse, Khnumhotep' and the 'sealer, Khnumhotep'). Newberry, *Beni Hasan* 1, pls 30, 33, 35; Kanawati and Woods, *Beni Hassan*, figs 30-32; pls 19, 27, 29; Kanawati and Evans, *Beni Hassan* 1, pls 33-36, 67, 84b, 88b-89, 90b-91a, 93c-95a.

[1086] Ward, *Index*, 47 [367].

[1087] Ranke, *Personennamen* 1, 308 [14]; Kanawati and Evans, *Beni Hassan* 1, pl. 50b.

- North wall, fifth register from the top (Plate 1B): the first two men before Khnumhotep II, *wḥm(.w) Nḫti iri n Bkt* 'herald,[1088] Nekhti,[1089] born to Baqet' and *im.y-r3 ḫtm.t B3kt* 'overseer of the treasury,[1090] Baqet';[1091]

- South wall, bottom register (Plate 1C): the second man from the left, *im.y-r3 ʿḫnw.ty Ḫt.y* 'overseer of the inner chamber/chamberlain,[1092] Khety';[1093]

- West wall, south section, second register from the top:[1094] the man standing over (overseeing?) the building of a boat; and

- West wall, south section, bottom register: the first official from the left. The caption above is fragmentary, either belonging to him or the kneeling figure before him. It could read [...] *ḫtm.t* [...] *N*[*ḫt*] '[...] of sealers, [...] Ne[khet]'.[1095]

Compared with Amenemhat's tomb, the 'fair-skinned men' of Khnumhotep II do not partake in daily activities but are involved in managerial roles. Four of the six appear in a procession with the other two standing near, and possibly overseeing, Egyptians at work. The majority are connected to the treasury, five are overseers and one is a herald. Their identification as descendents of Asiatics is heightened by the drawing of a small clue on the south wall's 'fair-skinned man'. Here, the artist(s) outlined a larger, hooked nose in red[1096] but seemingly favoured a smaller form when the painting was completed. Perhaps the larger nose was reserved for the more alien Asiatics following *Ibš3*.[1097]

The inclusion of the men among the Egyptians mirrors their inclusion within the local community. Despite their skin colour and an early attempt of portraying distinct facial features, the men are otherwise Egyptian. They are given Egyptian names and titles, clothes, hairdos, beards, and an Egyptian staff. They have almost completely assumed the Egyptian culture, even attaining middle-ranking positions within the administration. Still, they are distinctly separated from the locals by their skin colour, an intentional artistic choice that illustrates their ethnicity in a decisively less stereotypical manner, representing their acculturation and creating an innovative artistic interpretation of mixed Egyptian-Asiatics.

FIGURE 4.53. POTTERS AT WORK, WEST WALL, TOMB OF KHNUMHOTEP II (NR 3), BENI HASSAN. COURTESY OF THE AUSTRALIAN CENTRE FOR EGYPTOLOGY.

Depiction of a characteristic non-Egyptian ceramic

At the southern end of the west wall, to the left of the second register, are two potters at work (Figure 4.53). Directly above the head of the seated potter is a bi-handled vessel with one handle extending from the body to the rim, and another, smaller, handle looped on the body.[1098] It has been identified as an EBIV/MBI dipper juglet,[1099] although these are not commonly found with the smaller handle. Instead, the vessel appears as a combination of two forms: (1) the Levantine juglet, with its narrower neck, long body and curved base; and (2) the Egyptian *ḫnm*-jug, with the handle meeting the rim and a smaller handle at the body. Such a combination could be either an artistic error, with the painter lacking in familiarity with the foreign ware, or a depiction of a true form mixing elements from both jugs, although such a vessel has not been found in the archaeological record. Nevertheless, the illustration hints at some contact between Levantines and Egyptians.

Depiction of organic products (?)

As in Amenemhat's tomb, the south wall of Khnumhotep II's chapel illustrates piled offerings among which are four long black pods (Figure 4.54). The pods may be identified as tamarind, acacia or carob. As mentioned above,[1100] carob was most probably imported from the Levant.[1101] Therefore, if the depicted items are carob, then their representation signals the import of this product to Beni Hassan.

[1088] Ward, *Index*, 89 [741].
[1089] Ranke, *Personennamen* 1, 212 (1).
[1090] Ward, *Index*, 47 [364].
[1091] Ranke, *Personennamen* 1, 90 [9]; Kanawati and Evans, *Beni Hassan* 1, pl. 54a.
[1092] Ward, *Index*, 14 [72]; Newberry, *Beni Hasan* 1, 47.
[1093] Ranke, *Personnenamen* 1, 277 (26).
[1094] Personal examination; Newberry, *Beni Hasan* 1, pl. 12; Kanawati and Evans, *Beni Hassan* 1, pls 25a, 26b.
[1095] Kanawati and Evans, *Beni Hassan* 1, pl. 28b.
[1096] Personal examination strongly points against the outline being a later addition. It should not be confused with a prominent reddish-brown dirt mark also near the outline of the nose.
[1097] For a similar differentiation in the representation of Egyptian-Levantines and foreign Levantines, see Chapter 5.2.4.1.
[1098] Newberry's original rendition does not include the smaller handle. Newberry, *Beni Hasan* 1, pl. 29.
[1099] This identification is based on Newberry's drawing of the scene (Newberry, *Beni Hasan* 1, pl. 29), as referenced in Arnold, Arnold and Allen, *E&L* 5 (1995), 18-20; Cohen-Weinberger and Goren, *E&L* 14 (2004), 82; Bietak, in *From Relative Chronology to Absolute Chronology*, 128-129.
[1100] See Chapter 4.4.1.2.
[1101] Gale et al., in *Ancient Egyptian Materials and Technology*, 338; Zohary, *Israel Journal of Plant Sciences* 50/1 (2002), 141-145.

Khnumhotep II's biography contains another reference for the use of an imported product:

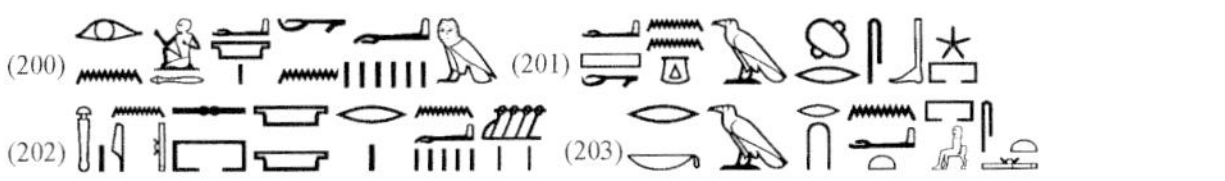

(200) *iri.n=i ꜥ3 n(.y) mḥ 6 m* (201) *ꜥš n(.y) Ng3w r sb3* (202) *tp n(.y) is ꜥ3.wy-r3 n(.y) mḥ 5 šsp 2* (203) *r k3r n(.y) ꜥ.t šps.t*

(200) I made a door of six cubits of (201) ꜥš-wood of *Ng3w* for the (202) first doorway of the tomb and a two-leaf door of five cubits and two palms (203) for the shrine of the splendid chamber.[1102]

Ng3w is thought to be located in the mountains of modern Lebanon.[1103] The reference supports the use of foreign commodities by the Egyptian elite.

4.4.1.4 Other

A wooden statuette from Shaft Tomb 181 has been described as that of a foreign woman and her child (Plate 3).[1104] The tomb has been assigned to Seidlmayer's *Stuffe* II which is tentatively dated between the reigns of Amenemhat I and Senwosret I.[1105] Bourriau assigns the statuette to the early Twelfth Dynasty and Do. Arnold to the first half of Dynasty 12.[1106] The artefact represents a woman wearing a long red sleeved garment with a V-shaped neckline and a probable zigzag pattern, as well as yellow footwear.[1107] Left foot forward and hands clasped at the chest, a material is wrapped around her shoulders, out of which is revealed the bold yellow-painted head of a child.[1108] The statuette's chin is slightly lifted, the face outlined with thick eyebrows, large eyes and ears, and a curved aquiline nose. The hair is black, tied back into a bun and styled with a slight angle at the back-centre of the head. Three bands hold the hairdo in place and circle a flattened area at the top of the head with a drilled hole (Plate 3c). Some have interpreted this as a fixture for now missing offerings,[1109] although Do. Arnold is correct in noting that female bearers typically balance offerings on the head with one hand and are rarely, if ever, carrying both a child on the back as well as offerings upon the head.[1110] She associates the hairstyle with those of the

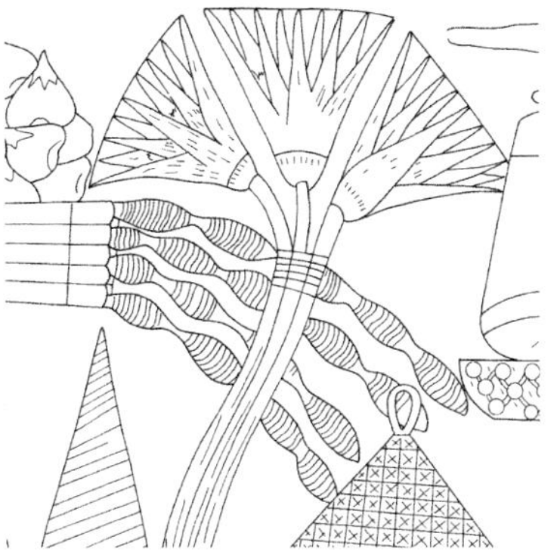

Figure 4.54. An offering of fruit, south wall, tomb of Khnumhotep II (NR 3), Beni Hassan. Courtesy of the Australian Centre for Egyptology.

women in Wekhhotep's tomb (C1),[1111] suggesting that the hole was a fixture for an ornamental comb or hairpiece.[1112]

The statuette's hairstyle is indeed similar to that of the women in Wekhhotep's tomb (C1), all having the same bun at the back.[1113] As the women are identified here as possible Delta inhabitants with Levantine ancestry,[1114] the same may be the case for the Beni Hassan statuette. The statuette is detailed with further atypical characteristics such as the pattern and colour of the garment, the shape of the nose and the colour of the child.[1115] As these features are commonly found in Middle Kingdom representations of Asiatics, it is possible to identify the statuette as a portrayal of a northeastern female. While male Egyptian-Levantines may be illustrated in the tombs of Amenemhat and Khnumhotep II, the statuette may be evidence for a female Asiatic in contact with the Middle Egyptians. Its deposition in a tomb connects the item with some cultic practice that consequently points to the role of the statuette, and perhaps the woman portrayed, in local funerary traditions.

Foreign commodities were additionally utilised in such traditions. Two coffins at the British Museum generally dated to Dynasty 12 have been assessed to be of the *Cedrus* species,[1116] corroborating Khnumhotep II's testimony of the timber's use for funerary elements.[1117] The coffins, as with the testimony, signify the import of Levantine cedar during the first half of the Middle Kingdom.

This import, together with the other evidence reviewed here from Beni Hassan, reflects considerable multifaceted

1102 Hieroglyphic text and line numbers as transcribed in Newberry, *Beni Hasan* 1, pl. 26; Kanawati and Evans, *Beni Hassan* 1, 35, pls 13b, 114. Transliteration and translation are by author.

1103 The toponym is noted in the Pyramid Texts as the dwelling of *Ḥ3i-t3w*. Allen locates it near modern Cairo in *Pyramid Texts*, 67 [T7 (PT 322)], 437. See also Aḥituv, *Canaanite Toponyms*, 150-151.

1104 The artefact is now at the National Museum of Scotland, Edinburgh (A.1911.260). Similar unprovenanced statuettes are at the Museum of Fine Arts, Boston (54.994) and the Metropolitan Museum of Art, New York (26.7.1407). Garstang, *Burial Customs*, 139-141, fig. 138; Bourriau, *Pharaohs and Mortals*, 108-109 [no. 97]; Arnold, in *Offerings to the Discerning Eye*, 17-31, figs 1-7; Wildung, *Le Moyen Empire*, 189, fig. 159; Hayes, *Scepter of Egypt* 2, 35, fig. 16.

1105 Seidlmayer, *Gräberfelder aus dem Übergang*, 217-231, fig. 95.

1106 Bourriau, *Pharaohs and Mortals*, 108; Arnold, in *Offerings to the Discerning Eye*, 19.

1107 Arnold, in *Offerings to the Discerning Eye*, 17-18; Garstang, *Burial Customs*, 140.

1108 Do. Arnold notes some light reddish paint around the woman's ears, possibly remnants of the colour used for her skin or hair (Arnold, in *Offerings to the Discerning Eye*, 17, n. 6).

1109 Bourriau, *Pharaohs and Mortals*, 108; Garstang, *Burial Customs*, 140.

1110 Arnold, in *Offerings to the Discerning Eye*, 22. A similar figurine at the Metropolitan Museum of Art (MMA 26.7.1407) represents a woman leading an animal while carrying a child on her back. She does not, however, carry offerings on her head (Hayes, *Scepter of Egypt* 2, 35, fig. 16).

1111 See Chapter 4.4.4.3 and Figure 4.59.

1112 Arnold, in *Offerings to the Discerning Eye*, 22-24, fig. 9 [b].

1113 See Chapter 4.4.4.3 and Figure 4.59.

1114 See Chapter 4.4.4.3.

1115 See Chapter 4.3.6.1 and Figure 4.39.

1116 EA 41572 is dated between the late Eleventh and early Twelfth Dynasty while EA 32051 is assigned to Dynasty 12 or 13. Davies, in *Egypt, the Aegean and the Levant*, 147.

1117 See Chapter 4.4.1.3. Khnumhotep I also mentions the use of cedar, although this is in association with ships and possibly royalty (see Chapter 4.4.1.1).

TOMB		BAQET III	KHETY	KHNUMHOTEP I	AMENEMHAT
CONTEXT	Reign	11th Dynasty (?)	late 11th Dynasty (?)	Amenemhat I	Senwosret I
	Titles	overlord of the entire Oryx nome	overlord of the entire Oryx nome, overseer of the expedition	great overlord of the Oryx nome	great overlord of the Oryx nome, overseer of the great expedition
	Wall	east wall	east wall	east wall	east wall
SETTLEMENT		fortress in elevation	fortress in elevation	fortress in elevation	fortress in elevation
ATTACKERS	Egyptian	✓	✓	✓	✓
	Asiatic	✓	✓	✓	✓
	Nubian	✓	✓	✓	✓
DEFENDERS	Egyptian	✓	✓	✓	✓
	Asiatic	-	-	(?)	-
	Nubian	✓	(?)	(?)	(?)
ASIATIC WARRIORS	Number	15 + x	10	9 + x	3
	Hair	short	short	short, long, coiffed	coiffed
		reddish-brown, black	reddish-brown, black	red, reddish-brown, black(?)	reddish-brown
		no beards	no beards	long, pointed beards	short to long, pointed beards
	Skin	yellow	yellow	yellow	yellow
	Eyes	black	black (?)	greenish-grey	brownish-black
	Clothes	short detailed kilts	short detailed kilts	short detailed kilts, detailed one-shoulder garment, wristlets, anklets, necklace	short detailed kilts, wristlets (?)
	Weapons	bows, axes, throw-sticks, shields, slings	bows, axes, throw-sticks, shield, slings, spears	bows, eye-axe, throw-sticks, dagger, slings, sickle-sword (?)	eye-axe (?), throw-sticks, spears

FIGURE 4.55. BATTLE SCENES AT BENI HASSAN: SIMILARITIES AND DIFFERENCES.

relations between northeasterners and the elite of the Sixteenth Upper Egyptian nome. Such relations evidently began with the employment of foreign mercenaries within the Egyptian army. The tombs of Baqet III, Khety, Khnumhotep I and Amenemhat illustrate sieges involving a multi-ethnic army, the Asiatics appearing as auxiliaries fighting alongside Egyptians and Nubians (Figure 4.55).[1118] Developments across the scenes are noticeable.[1119] At first, Asiatics can only be identified by their kilts and skin colour as armoury, facial features and hairstyles otherwise render them indistinguishable from Egyptians. Khety's artist added distinct shields as well as two separate groups of Asiatics. Khnumhotep I's artist(s) portrayed them with Asiatic adornments, beards and weapons, introducing the EBIV/MBI Levantine fenestrated eye-axe and perhaps a scimitar. He also illustrated different units of Asiatics, possibly including a foreigner of higher rank. Such units are absent in Amenemhat's tomb, where the least number of Asiatic warriors are represented but where depictions of 'fair-skinned men' and EBIV/MBI pottery occur. Although the homogeneity of the battle scenes has placed their historical validity in question,[1120] the tomb owners, as 'great overlords of the Oryx nome' and, at least for Khety and Amenemhat, as 'overseers of the expedition', could very well have been involved in managing Middle Egyptian troops.[1121]

In fact, the evidence suggests that the nomarchs of Beni Hassan were supporting the king's quests. The nome's position in proximity to the Fifteenth Upper Egyptian nome would have been of strategic importance to the king(s). As the inscriptions of Kay[1122] and Khnumhotep I relay, the king(s) took a personal interest in calming any rebellion by enlisting the help of the Oryx nome's elite and amassing troops from and beyond Egypt. Consequently, an influx of Asiatic and Nubian mercenaries into the region is likely. As their depictions are first attested in Eleventh Dynasty tomb(s), the foreigners appear to be in the nomarchs' service for approximately a century before the arrival of *Ibš3*'s people. However, a reduction in their significance as auxiliary forces is observable in Amenemhat's tomb, where only three Asiatic soldiers are portrayed. Instead, the outcome of such consistent Egyptian-Asiatic relations surfaces in the artistic repertoire.

The growing familiarity between Egyptians and Levantines may have resulted in the illustration of Levantine pottery as well as the acculturated 'fair-skinned' Asiatics who were employed within the Egyptian community. Moreover, the Egyptian artists attempted to depict facets

1118 Newberry, *Beni Hasan* 1, pl. 47; vol. 2, pls 5, 15.
1119 Rabehl, *Grab des Amenemhet*, 306-307.
1120 Brovarski, in *Egyptian Culture and Society*, 63; Schulman, *JSSEA* 12/4 (1982), 176, 180.

1121 Schulman, *JSSEA* 12/4 (1982), 176.
1122 See Chapter 4.4.3.

of contemporary Levantine culture, first painting objects of the EBIV/MBI period and then those of the MBIIA. Hence, it is in this social context that *Ἰbšꜣ*'s visit must be taken into account. The scene may have been unique in its details, particularly of the women and children, but it is not 'rare' in the sense that it was the only point of direct contact between the inhabitants of the Oryx nome and Levantines. What the earlier tombs inform us is that Asiatics already shared militaristic relations with Beni Hassan's nomarchs. These relations developed under Senwosret I, when the depiction of foreign commodities and possibly peoples of foreign descent arose, until they were completely absent under Senwosret II's reign. As an alternative, Beni Hassan's last decorated rock-cut tomb featured a scene engaging Asiatics in a different role associated more with trade than with warfare, a role which is also indirectly insinuated by the portrayal and presence of foreign products in Beni Hassan's tombs. It is, then, not surprising that Khnumhotep III continued such relations, recording his own voyage to a foreign land in search for 'what is useful'.[1123]

4.4.2 Bersha, Deir el-

Lat.Lon. 27°45'N 30°54'E

Refs PM 4, 179-181; Newberry, *El-Bersheh;* Blackman, *JEA* 2/1 (1915), 13-14.

Chron. Late Twelfth Dynasty

Deir el-Bersha, the capital of the Hare nome (Fifteen), is situated on the east bank of the Nile, south of Beni Hassan. Archaeological investigations were carried out and published by Newberry,[1124] and, since 2002, have been conducted by Leuven University.[1125]

4.4.2.1 Tomb of Djehutyhotep, reign of Senwosret III

The tomb of Djehutyhotep, 'treasurer of the king of Lower Egypt' and 'great overlord of the Hare nome, entry of all foreign lands',[1126] was probably completed during Senwosret III's reign.[1127] The chapel's west wall depicts the treasurer presiding over a series of activities.[1128] The lower register's caption features a disputed passage written above a row of cattle being brought to Djehutyhotep. It reads:

[...] *kꜣ.w Rṯnw/r-ṯnw m ṯnw* [...*ḥ*...] *i̓yi̓.n=ṯn šꜥ ḫnd=ṯn smw ḳḳ=ṯn šnw* [...]*w sꜣ=ṯn nfr n ḥꜥw=ṯn w*[...] *ḳmꜣ*[*=ṯn*...] *pḥ.w=ṯn snb*[*=ṯn*]
[...] cattle of *Rṯnw*/numbering in quantity [...] you have come on sand so that you tread on pastures, you feed on herbage [...] your back is good for your body [...] your form [...] your ends, healthy are your [...].

Despite Blackman's contentions,[1129] the above text would argue against the reading of 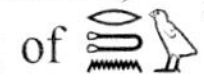 as *Rṯnw*. Based on the absence of a determinative for a foreign land, the glyphs' inclusion in a sequence of clauses concerned with cattle rather than the foreign, and the overall fragmentary nature of the passage, a reading as *r-ṯnw* 'numbering' is favoured.[1130] Although Djehutyhotep, as 'entry of all foreign lands', would have been able to access foreign imports and commodities, there are no other indications from his tomb for such trade.[1131] Moreover, the accompanying depiction of Egyptians escorting the animals supports their identification as local rather than imported cattle.

4.4.2.2 Organic products

A less contentious marker for trade is the material used for coffins from Deir el-Bersha. Following the scientific analysis of 36 coffins from the British Museum, it was concluded that, out of the seven wooden coffins from Deir el-Bersha, six were of cedar (*Cedrus* sp.).[1132] They are from the second half of Dynasty 12 and belong to officials with such titles as 'chief of physicians', 'overseer of the house' and 'overseer of the expedition'.[1133] The cedar may have been either directly or indirectly transported to Deir el-Bersha from the Levant, although the latter is a more likely scenario. Its use by officials of various positions attests to the timber's popularity and the administration's access to foreign products in Dynasty 12.

1123 See Chapter 4.3.1.2.
1124 Newberry, *El-Bersheh* 1.
1125 Willems, *Deir el-Bersha* 1; Willems et al., *E&L* 19 (2009), 293-331. For a complete list of published materials, see 'Publications Dayr al-Barsha Project', *Dayr al-Barsha Project*. Excavations have also been carried out by the Museum of Fine Arts, Boston, the results of which are published in Brovarski et al., *Bersheh Reports* 1.
1126 Newberry, *El-Bersheh* 1, 6-7, pl. 16.
1127 The chapel includes cartouches of Amenemhat II, Senwosret II and Senwosret III, possibly signalling the expanse of the tomb owner's career beginning under Amenemhat II. Newberry, *El-Bersheh* 1, 3, pl. 5; Willems, *JEOL* 28 (1983/1984), 83-84, n. 26. For a different opinion, see Blumenthal, *AOF* 4 (1976), 35-62.
1128 Newberry, *El-Bersheh* 1, pls 12, 18.
1129 Blackman, *JEA* 2/1 (1915), 13-14.
1130 As in Newberry's original translation (*El-Bersheh* 1, 14, 29). Attestations that the term *šꜥ* 'sand' are connected to the environment of *Rṯnw* is tentative while the tense of the verb *i̓yi̓.n=ṯn* as a present perfect *sḏm.n=f* may have been used to refer to the distance travelled from the cattle's original location and not necessarily 'to draw a comparison between the hard life of these cattle in Syria, and their present luxurious existence in Egypt' (Wilson, in *Ancient Near Eastern Texts*, 230, n. 11).
1131 See Appendix A.3 for comments regarding the official's statuette at Megiddo.
1132 Davies, in *Egypt, the Aegean and the Levant*, 146-147.
1133 Davies, in *Egypt, the Aegean and the Levant*, 147.

4.4.3 *Hatnub*

Lat.Lon. 27°33'N 31°00'E

Refs PM 4, 237-239; Anthes, *Hatnub;* Shaw, *Hatnub.*

Chron. Late Eleventh or early Twelfth Dynasty

Texts from the alabaster quarry at Hatnub explore the 'reign' of Nehry and his sons, Kay and Djehutynakht, nomarchs of the Fifteenth Upper Egyptian nome.[1134] Although much debate has circulated around the inscriptions' date,[1135] the palaeographic and archaeological evidence point to a historic situation prior to Amenemhat I's reign, most likely between Nebtawyra and Amenemhat I.[1136] They are included here to show the importance of Asiatics in the formation of a politically stable Twelfth Dynasty. Specifically mentioning Asiatics are Inscriptions Nr 16 and Nr 25.

Inscription of Kay, Nr 16 (Nehry I [?], Year 5)[1137]

(5) ... *ink iri* [...]*y=s m Šd.yt-š3 iw nn rmṯ.t ḥnˁ=i* (6) *wpw-ḥr šmsw.w=i Mḏ3.w W3w3.t Nḥ[sy(?)...ˁ3]m.w* (7) *Šmˁw t3 Mḥw sm3.w r=i iyi.kw sp m-ˁ rw(d.t ?)* [...] (8) *niw.t=i r ḏr=s ḥnˁ=i n nhw=s* ...
(5) ... It is I who acted (as) its [fortress][1138] in *Šd.yt-š3*, when there were no people with me (6) except my retainers, the *Mḏ3.w*, *W3W3.t*, *Nḥ[sy?...ˁ3]m.w*, (7) Upper Egypt and Lower Egypt being united against me. I emerged, the affair being a success [...] (8) my entire city with me without her loss ...

Inscription of Nehry, Nr 25 (Nehry I [?], Year 7)[1139]

...(14) *bni ṯḥn.t n.t t3 mi ḳd=f Mḏ3.w ˁ3m.w* [...]*s* (15) *Nḥs.yw(?) mr.t=f ˁḳ* [...] *Nḥri msi n Kmi m3ˁ-ḫrw ˁnḫ* (16) *ḏ.t r nḥḥ* ...
... (14) the faience of the land is sweet like his form,[1140] the *Mḏ3.w*, *ˁ3m.w* [...] (15)*Nḥs.yw* (?) are his serfs (?) [...] *Nḥri*, born to *Kmi*, (16) justified for all eternity ...

The Hatnub texts note a major conflict between vizier Nehry's followers and royal forces,[1141] with the former boasting of victories against the pharaoh. Inscriptions Nrs 16 and 25 reveal that the nameless king had rallied Egyptians from across the land, as well as foreigners from Nubia and Asia in a bid which, as history informs us, helped Amenemhat I emerge as victor. Accordingly, Asiatics would have established significant political relations by working for the king as auxiliary allies.[1142] Such relations would have also developed between the soldiers themselves as the Asiatics would have fought side-by-side with Nubians and Egyptians against the local rebels. By siding with the winning faction, it is very possible that such relations extended into Dynasty 12.

4.4.4 *Meir*

Lat.Lon. 27°27'N 30°45'E

Refs PM 4, 250-253; Blackman, *Meir*, vols 2-3, 6.

Chron. Twelfth Dynasty

The governors of the Fourteenth Upper Egyptian nome of el-Qusiya are buried at Meir. Their tombs date from the early Sixth to the Twelfth Dynasty with the construction of large rock-cut tombs ending under Amenemhat III. First excavated and recorded by Blackman,[1143] the tombs are currently being re-recorded by the Australian Centre for Egyptology, Macquarie University.[1144]

4.4.4.1 Tomb of Wekhhotep (B2), reign of Senwosret I

Wekhhotep, son of Senbi,[1145] was most likely the second royally-appointed nomarch to build his tomb at Meir (B2).[1146] His chapel's east wall depicts Wekhhotep

[1134] Anthes, *Hatnub*, 32-62 [nos. 14-26]; Redford, *Egypt, Canaan, and Israel*, 73; Shaw, *Hatnub*, 147-155.

[1135] Propositions favour one of four historical settings: (a) the transition between the Tenth and Eleventh Dynasties, a period of unification under Nebhepetra Montuhotep II (Anthes, Faulkner, Brovarski and Blumenthal); (b) the transition between the Eleventh and Twelfth Dynasties, from the Montuhoteps to the Amenemhats (Willems, Redford and Peden); (c) the tumultuous reign of Amenemhat I (Grajetzki and Gerstermann); and (d) the events following Amenemhat I's assassination (Schenkel). For more, see Anthes, *Hatnub*, 91-96; Faulkner, *JEA* 30 (1944), 61-63; Brovarski, in *Egyptian Culture and Society*, 31-85; Blumenthal, *AOF* 4 (1976), 35-62; Willems, *JEOL* 28 (1983/1984), 80-102; Willems, *Historical and Archaeological Aspects*, 79-86; Redford, *Egypt, Canaan, and Israel*, 73, n. 8; Redford, *JARCE* 23 (1986), 129; Peden, *Graffiti of Pharaonic Egypt*, 21; Grajetzki, *Middle Kingdom*, 110; Gerstermann, *ZÄS* 135 (2008), 1-16; Schenkel, *Frühmittelägyptische Studien*, 84-95.

[1136] The uncertainties surrounding the transition between Nebtawyra and Amenemhat I seems a likely historical situation for mounting tension, rebellion and the existence of several claims to the throne, such as Nehry I's of the Hatnub graffiti. Willems, *JEOL* 28 (1983/1984), 101-102; Redford, *Egypt, Canaan, and Israel*, 73, n. 8; Redford, *Pharaonic King-Lists*, 15; Callender, in *Ancient Egypt*, 145.

[1137] Hieroglyphic text and line numbers as transcribed by Anthes (*Hatnub*, 36 [no. 16]). Transliteration and translation are by the author.

[1138] Following Anthes and Redford. Shaw translates it as 'rear-guard'. Anthes, *Hatnub*, 37; Redford, *Egypt, Canaan, and Israel*, 73; Shaw, *Hatnub*, 148.

[1139] Hieroglyphic text and line numbers as transcribed by Anthes (*Hatnub*, 57 [no. 25]). Transliteration and translation are by the author.

[1140] Or 'sweetness and faience/brightness of the entire land', as translated by Shaw (*Hatnub*, 153).

[1141] As suggested by 'the sore dread of the Palace', or the royal house in Inscription Nr 24. Shaw, *Hatnub*, 152; Redford, *Egypt, Canaan, and Israel*, 73; Anthes, *Hatnub*, 57-58; Faulkner, *JEA* 30 (1944), 62; Grajetzki, *Middle Kingdom*, 110.

[1142] See Chapter 4.4.1 for Beni Hassan depictions in support of these relations.

[1143] Blackman, *Meir*, 6 vols.

[1144] Kanawati, *Meir* 1; Kanawati and Evans, *Meir* 2.

[1145] Blackman, *Meir* 2, 1-3, pls 10-12.

[1146] Grajetzki, *Middle Kingdom*, 108, fig. 23.

FIGURE 4.56. EAST WALL, TOMB OF WEKHHOTEP (B2), MEIR. AFTER BLACKMAN, *MEIR* 3, PL. 3.

and his wife standing alongside two female attendants (Figure 4.56). The one to the left carries a chest(?) and is identified by Blackman as a 'Aam-slave'.[1147] The fragmentary text above her, , may conversely be read as .[1148] No other delineating features designate her as an Asiatic, yet if Blackman's reconstruction is correct, it may reveal the employment of foreign women in elite Middle Egyptian households.

4.4.4.2 Tomb of Wekhhotep (B4), reign of Amenemhat II

Wekhhotep, son of Wekhhotep, features two possible references to Asiatics in his tomb (B4).[1149] Both appear on the north wall of his chapel's outer room in a scene picturing a large seated figure of the tomb owner inspecting cattle. The second register of the scene's west end portrays the official Wekhemsaf followed by two individuals forcibly ushered in a rendering of accounts scene (Figure 4.57).[1150] The register is very fragmentary and it is only possible to delineate a few of their features. Both have long, slightly pointed beards and, while the head of the foremost is damaged, the hairstyle of the second is shoulder-length and voluminous at the back, curving inwards at the shoulder.[1151] Such features point to the individuals' foreign origin and are akin to those of Amenemhat's Asiatics at Beni Hassan,[1152] supporting their identification as Asiatics by Blackman.[1153] Surviving captions accompanying the men read (1) [...]*ḫ3-wšb* '[...] khawesheb'; and (2) [... *ir.y-*ʿ].*t n*(.*y*) *iḥw* '[...hall-keeper] of the cattle-pen'.[1154] The individuals have Egyptian names and titles and, if their identification is correct, can be viewed as evidence for the acculturation of Levantines during Amenemhat II's reign. Their inclusion in a rendering of accounts scene denotes their middle-rank occupation as well as their subservience to Wekhhotep.

The second reference to Asiatics is found on the eastern end of the north wall's lowest register. The scene illustrates a row of cattle being led by at least two herdsmen. One is represented as an emaciated figure with curly hair leaning on a staff[1155] and the second is more rotund, his facial details missing (Figure 4.58). Following the latter and towards the east of the wall is a fragmentary inscription relaying *k3.w n.w* ʿ*3m.w ini.n* [...*m*...] 'cattle of ʿ*3m.w* which have been brought from [...]'. Their distinction as 'cattle of ʿ*3m.w*' does not necessarily point to the animals' Levantine origin[1156] but rather to their ownership by Asiatics. Whether or not these cattle belonged to [...]khawesheb and the '[hall-keeper] of the cattle-pen',[1157] the evidence suggests that Wekhhotep was responsible for Levantines residing in the region as well as their commodities.

4.4.4.3 Tomb of Wekhhotep (C1), reign of Senwosret III

The tomb of nomarch Wekhhotep (C1) is assigned to the reign of Senwosret III or Amenemhat III[1158] and contains rare scenes of women involved in a variety of activities typically attributed to men.[1159] The female bearers on the north wall are of particular interest (Figure 4.59). The inscriptions on the lower two registers indicate that the offerings are from the Delta region,[1160] so it is possible to surmise that some of the women, if not all of them, are also from the Delta. Eight of these women, one in each of the lower two registers and at least four in the upper register, are represented with a distinctive hairstyle designed with a slight bulb-like protrusion at the back of the head, much like a bun. The style, likened to a cap-like turban by Do. Arnold,[1161] could also include a fillet, a smaller wedge-shaped protrusion(s) from the head, and/or a ponytail. Blackman notes slight traces of red for the woman's hair in the lowest register.[1162] One woman on the south wall

1147 Blackman, *Meir* 2, 15, pl. 5 [2].

1148 Blackman, *Meir* 2, 15.

1149 Blackman, *Meir* 3, 1, pls 3-4.

1150 Blackman, *Meir* 3, pl. 3.

1151 The details are clearer in Blackman's earlier recordings (Blackman, *Meir* 3, pl. 3).

1152 See Chapter 4.4.1.2 and Figure 4.50. The shoulder-length hairstyle of the second man contests suppositions that the two individuals are Bedja herdsmen. See n. 1155; Blackman, *Meir* 2, 18, n. 1; vol. 3, 13; Schneider, *Ausländer im Ägypten* 2, 190, 329; Staubli, *Das Image der Nomaden*, 26-30.

1153 Blackman, *Meir* 3, 6, 11-12.

1154 Ward, *Index*, 59 [475].

1155 Identified as a Bedja herdsman, a Medjay herdsman, an Eastern Desert nomad, an Asiatic or a malnourished Egyptian. The figure's characteristics heavily feature in depictions of individuals across the tombs of Meir, mostly of men leading cattle and/or leaning on staffs. See Blackman, *Meir* 1, 32, fig. 8, pls 9-10, 20 [1], 25 [2-3], 26 [1], 30 [1], 31 [1]; vol. 2, 13-19, pls 19 [1], 22, 29, 30 [1]; vol. 3, 11-13, pls 3-4, 6, 11, 19-20; Staubli, *Das Image der Nomaden*, 26-30; Schneider, *Ausländer im Ägypten* 2, 190; Zibelius-Chen, *SAK* 36 (2007), 395; Arnold, in *Second Intermediate Period*, 196; Liszka, *Medjay and Pangrave*, 241-244.

1156 Blackman theorises that the cattle 'would have been obtained either by a foray, such as that of Sesostris III, or by traffic' (Blackman, *Meir* 3, 13). Scholars following this theory include Saretta, *Egyptian Perceptions of West Semites*, 153; David, *Pyramid Builders*, 192; Giveon, in *Hommages à François Daumas* 1, 279-284.

1157 Blackman, *Meir* 3, 13.

1158 Blackman, *Meir* 6, 13; Blackman, *Meir* 1, 17-18; Grajetzki, *Middle Kingdom*, 109.

1159 Wekhhotep's dedication to Hathor as 'priest of the mistress of heaven' and el-Qusiya's role as cultic centre for the goddess may have influenced the decoration. Blackman, *Meir* 6, 8, 35, pls 13, 17.

1160 Blackman, *Meir* 6, 19-21, pl. 18.

1161 Arnold, in *Offerings to the Discerning Eye*, 24.

1162 Blackman, *Meir* 6, 19.

FIGURE 4.57. DETAIL, NORTH WALL, TOMB OF WEKHHOTEP (B4), MEIR. COURTESY OF THE AUSTRALIAN CENTRE FOR EGYPTOLOGY.

FIGURE 4.58. DETAIL, NORTH WALL, TOMB OF WEKHHOTEP (B4), MEIR. COURTESY OF THE AUSTRALIAN CENTRE FOR EGYPTOLOGY.

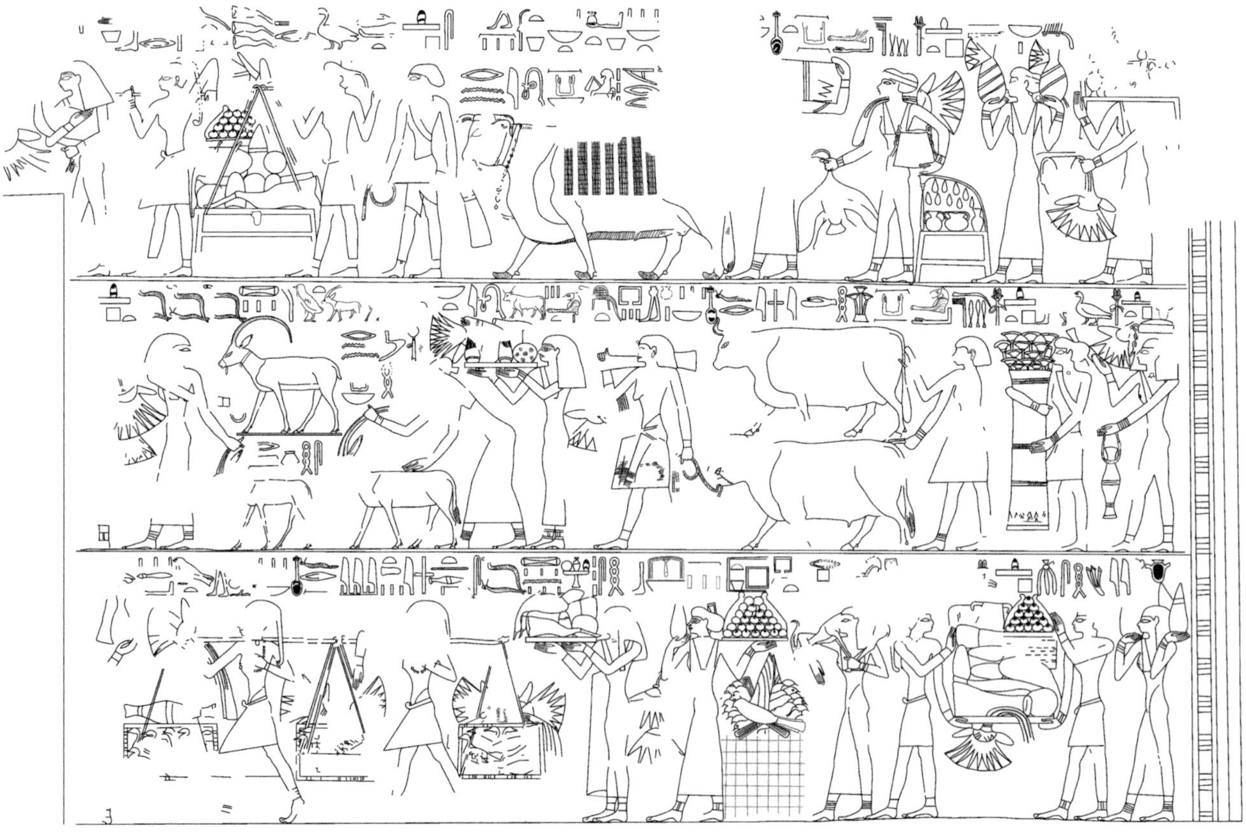

FIGURE 4.59. NORTH WALL, TOMB OF WEKHHOTEP (C1), MEIR. AFTER BLACKMAN, *MEIR* 1. PL. 18.

and two more on the east wall, north of the entrance, also appear to share this hairstyle.[1163]

Otherwise dressed as Egyptians, the hairdo and remaining colour signal an atypical representation most possibly associated with a foreign phenotype. While the red hair colour could be attributed to Libyans and Asiatics, a few of the objects carried by the women point to the northeast. The hairstyle has been connected to that of women from EBA Syria and Mesopotamia,[1164] yet, as the style is not contemporaneous with the tomb's dating, the women's origins cannot be verifiably sought in this region. Do. Arnold suggests that the women are Egyptian but, due to the scene's cultic associations, the hairstyle may have been copied from 'third millennium heirlooms in the temple treasures'.[1165] Although possible, it is questionable why such an archaism of foreignness would be featured in the tomb. Another proposition may be offered, relying on an early Thirteenth Dynasty stela picturing a woman with a similar hairdo labelled as a *ʿ3m.t*.[1166]

The last woman in the uppermost register supports a table on her shoulders (Figure 4.59). Within her left hand is a large bi-handled jar, and the first vessel on the table (from the left) is a small, bi-handled globular vessel. Similar globular handled jars can be found on the table before the second woman in this register. The shape of such vessels points to Levantine manufacture, with parallels stemming from EBIV/MBI Megiddo,[1167] Tell Beit Mirsim[1168] and Tell 'Arqa.[1169] Do. Arnold further suggests that the vessels are of metal, resembling the silver cups of the Tod Treasure.[1170] The other 'atypical' women carry a variety of objects including baskets, jars, lotus stems, birds as well as trays laden with fruit (fig?) and other foods. So, other than the Levantine-style vessels, the women are carrying characteristic Egyptian products that are usually presented to a tomb owner.

Key pieces of evidence that may help with the women's identification are their: (1) 'atypical' hairstyle which is shared by a *ʿ3m.t* on a Dynasty 13 stela; (2) red, non-Egyptian, hair colour; (3) Egyptian clothing; (4) accompaniment by a variety of Egyptian and EBIV/MBI Levantine items; (5) accompaniment by inscriptions detailing goods brought from the Delta; and (6) accompaniment by Egyptian women presenting offerings, as is customary in an Egyptian nomarch's tomb. Based on these pointers, the women are most likely from the Delta, possibly of Levantine or mixed Egyptian-Levantine ancestry. By adopting local traditions and customs, the women may have chosen to partake in the bringing of offerings to el-Qusiya's nomarch, presenting a myriad of local goods and foreign commodities possibly imported via a Delta trading hub like Tell el-Dab'a. In view of the Levantine population in the Delta at this time, such a scenario is highly likely, offering support for the acculturation of northeasterners living in Egypt.[1171] It also presents an intriguing case for the depiction of these female Egyptian-Levantines who are not entirely illustrated as Egyptian women and not completely portrayed as Asiatics.[1172] Instead, they are presented as a deviation from such stereotypical representations with the artist(s) customising their portrayal to form a variant artistic manifestation of the women's identity. Of importance is that this identity, at least at the time of the wall scenes' completion, was not fully synonymous with the identity of the artist(s) at Meir. That is, the women were not artistically 'accepted' as typical Egyptians.

This is similar to other Asiatics at Meir who are portrayed with a mixture of Egyptian and non-Egyptian elements. The men in Tomb B4 have Egyptian names and titles but are given foreign physical characteristics while the woman in B2, following Blackman's reading of her caption, is textually rather than artistically designated as a foreigner. Such a mixture of elements is likely synonymous with the individuals' mixed ethnic identity. Significantly, this identity did not hinder the Asiatics' participation in Egyptian activities and professions: they remained part of the tomb's repertoire of scenes and so were most likely an accepted part of Meir's community in the Twelfth Dynasty.

4.4.5 Rifeh, Deir

Lat.Lon. 27°06'N 31°10'E

Refs PM 5, 1-4; Petrie, *Gizeh and Rifeh*; Hamilton, *JSS* (2009), 51-79.

Chron. Second Intermediate Period

The southernmost point identified here as part of Middle Egypt is the site of Deir Rifeh, located approximately 10km south of Asyut. Deir Rifeh's Cemetery S consists of burials bearing elements of the distinct Pan-Grave culture.[1173] The burials also included Egyptian pottery which, based on a comparison with pottery from the Memphite region, Bourriau dates to the second half of Dynasty 13.[1174] Scarabs with the *ʿnrʿ* and *rḏi-rʿ* formulae as well as the name of *Šši* additionally attest to the site's occupation during the Second Intermediate Period.[1175] A few pieces from Deir Rifeh point to access to Levantine and/or Levantine-influenced products:

1163 Blackman, *Meir* 6, pls 10-11.
1164 Arnold, in *Offerings to the Discerning Eye*, 28-29, fig. 10.
1165 Arnold, in *Offerings to the Discerning Eye*, 29.
1166 See Chapter 4.6.8 and Figure 4.68.
1167 Guy, *Megiddo*, pls 101 [16], 102 [2, 13].
1168 Albright, *AASOR* 13 (1931/1932), pl. 3 [10].
1169 Thalmann, in *Bronze Age in the Lebanon*, pl. 6 [15-16].
1170 See Chapter 4.5.11.2. Arnold, in *Offerings to the Discerning Eye*, 24.

1171 See Chapter 4.2.2.10. A similar case of female offering bearers from the Delta can be found in Papyrus Boulaq 18/2 (Chapter 4.5.3).
1172 For a suggested depiction of male Egyptian-Asiatics, see Chapter 4.4.1.2-4.4.1.3.
1173 These include oval burial pits, Nubian pottery, intricate beadwork and leather wrist-guards. Petrie, *Gizeh and Rifeh*, 20.
1174 Bourriau, in *Studies on Ancient Egypt*, 44.
1175 Petrie, *Gizeh and Rifeh*, pls 13E [4], 23 [2, 9, 11].

FIGURE 4.60. BUTTON-SHAPED SEAL AMULET (UC 51354) WITH PSEUDO-HIEROGLYPHS, DEIR RIFEH. AFTER HAMILTON, *JSS* 54 (2009), FIG. 2.

- Tell el-Yahudiyah ware: Petrie's publication only includes outlines of the vessels from which it is possible to distinguish a cylindrical jug similar to that from Tell el-Maskhuta but with a flatter base,[1176] biconical jugs akin to those from Tell el-Yahudiyah (Grave 16),[1177] a wheel-made globular vessel paralleling those from Tell el-Dab'a Stratum E/1,[1178] and fragments of Piriform 2a jugs such as those from Tell el-Dab'a Strata E/2-D/2.[1179] The vessels were apparently uncovered in three Pan-Grave burials (Graves 59, 66 and 73) yet their precise context is not recorded.[1180] Their forms indicate that Tell el-Yahudiyah ware was imported into Deir Rifeh during Dynasty 15, most possibly from the Delta;

- Button-shaped seal amulet (Figure 4.60): The seal was reportedly not recovered from a Pan-Grave burial but its exact context is unknown.[1181] It was found alongside 79 small beads forming a necklace with which the seal was worn.[1182] The seal is decorated with two *ʿnḫ* symbols flanking five pseudo-hieroglyphic characters recently identified as Proto-Alphabetic signs dating paleographically to the MBA.[1183] Hamilton tentatively reads the signs as *l/w qn ḥz* 'for/and Cain, the Seer'.[1184] If correct, the inscription points to either Levantines in Deir Rifeh or their influence on locals. Indeed, the Proto-Alphabetic characters not only signal growing contact with the Levant, they also imply the presence of literate individuals knowledgeable in reading this early linear script within Egypt. Whether or not these individuals were present at Deir Rifeh is uncertain.

While the Tell el-Yahudiyah jugs provide evidence for trade relations between Deir Rifeh and the Fifteenth Dynasty, the seal may signal direct contact between the site and MBA Levantines. Regarding the Pan-Grave material, this would denote a connection between the Nubians and Levantines. In fact, the ceramic links with the north have led to a proposition that the southerners at Deir Rifeh formed a garrison controlling trade for the dynasties of the Delta.[1185] Mostagedda, on the opposite side of the Nile and with greater material parallels with southern Egyptian ceramic traditions, would have monitored trade for the Thebans along the east bank of the Nile.[1186] The examined evidence hints that a political or trading agreement could hve been possibly fostered between the Hyksos and the inhabitants buried at Deir Rifeh, perhaps to ensure continued trade with the regions further south. However, it does not suggest that such an agreement was encumbered by a heavy militaristic presence.

1176 Aston and Bietak's Late Egyptian L.12.1 or L.12.2. Redmount, *On an Egyptian/Asiatic Frontier*, fig. 157; Aston and Bietak, *TeD* 8, 265.
1177 Aston and Bietak's Late Egyptian L.8.1. Petrie, *Hyksos and Israelite Cities*, pl. 8 [38]; Aston and Bietak, *TeD* 8, 240-254, fig. 176.
1178 Aston and Bietak's Late Egyptian L.9.4. For references to more parallels from across Egypt see Aston and Bietak, *TeD* 8, 254-257, 499-507, fig. 186, pls 99 [559-561], 100 [564], 101 [567-568], 102 [575-576].
1179 Generally assigned to Aston and Bietak's Late Egyptian L.1. The base of one vessel could also belong to a biconical jug. Aston and Bietak, *TeD* 8, 206-211, 392-450, figs 138-141, pls 35-67.
1180 Petrie, *Gizeh and Rifeh*, pl. 26 [92-94].
1181 Hamilton, *JSS* 54 (2009), 51-52, n. 3.
1182 Hamilton, *JSS* 54 (2009), pl. 1.
1183 Hamilton, *JSS* 54 (2009), 51-79, figs 1-2, pls 1-2.
1184 Hamilton, *JSS* 54 (2009), 56-69, fig. 3.
1185 Hamilton, *JSS* 54 (2009), 43-48; Bourriau, in *Studies on Ancient Egypt*, 190; Bourriau, in *Second Intermediate Period*, 22-23.
1186 See Chapter 4.5.8. Bourriau, in *Second Intermediate Period*, 22-23; Bourriau, in *Studies on Ancient Egypt*, 43-48.

4.5 Upper Egypt

4.5.1 Abydos

Lat.Lon. 26°11'N 31°55'E

Refs PM 5, 39-105; Lange and Schäfer, *Grab und Denksteine*, vols 1-2, 4; Garstang, *El-Arábah*; Randall-MacIver and Mace, *El Amrah*, 92, 98, pl. 54 [13]; Peet, *Abydos* 2, 57-58, 68-69, pl. 13 [8]; Peet, *Stela of Sebek-Khu;* Petrie, *Tombs of the Courtiers*, 6, pl. 5 [28]; Garstang, *JEA* 14/1 (1928), 46-47; Sethe, *Ägyptische Lesestüke*, 82 [12-15]; Kitchen, *JEA* 47 (1961), 10-18; Hein and Satzinger, *Stelen des Mittleren Reiches* 1, 162-167; vol. 2, 79-86, 87-93, 111-127; Kitchen, *Catalogue* 1, 14-22, 64-67; vol. 2, pls 1-2, 45; Baines, in *Form und Mass*, 43-61; Simpson, *Inscribed Material*, 40-41, fig. 67, pl. 8 [d]; Satzinger and Stefanović, in *From Illahun to Djeme*, 241-245.

Chron. Twelfth Dynasty to Second Intermediate Period

Approximately 430km south of Cairo is the Eighth Upper Egyptian nome encompassing the sacred site of Abydos. Utilised as a burial ground from the Predynastic period to the Middle Kingdom, when a planned settlement also developed,[1187] Abydos was a place of pilgrimage for many Egyptians. Some officials and pharaohs of the Middle Kingdom and Second Intermediate Period chose to be buried there.[1188] Stelae, small chapels, statues and other cultic equipment were also erected by Egyptians buried elsewhere in dedication to Osiris.[1189] Evidence pertaining to Asiatics is largely derived from such stelae, providing a significant insight into their religious affiliations and relations with Egyptians.[1190]

4.5.1.1 The stelae

42 stelae and one shrine (grouped here as the 'Abydos stelae') refer to Asiatics and/or Levantine affairs and date from the beginning of Dynasty 12 to at least the early Second Intermediate Period. As only a few name pharaohs, some are assigned on stylistic grounds to either the Twelfth or Thirteenth Dynasty, with the rest dated generally to either the Middle Kingdom or the early Second Intermediate Period.[1191] Translations are provided in Appendix B.5, while bibliographic references and further comments regarding the context and depiction of individuals are summarised in Figure B.2.

Representing Asiatics

Among over 80 instances of individuals of Asiatic ancestry, only 10 names may be of Semitic origin[1192] while the rest are either simply *ꜥꜣm* or derived from the Egyptian. Individuals of unknown origin feature the element *Kpn*/*Kbn* for Byblos in their names.[1193] Pictorially, individuals labelled *ꜥꜣm* are depicted as Egyptians seated, kneeling or standing, their colour uncertain due to the stelae's greyscale publications. Where coloured photographs are presented, no colour is preserved for the Asiatic men. A few bear offerings such as ox legs (E.207.1900 and CG 20571), lotus stems (E.207.1900 and CG 20550), fowl (E.207.1900 and CG 20550) as well as baskets or vessels (CG 20158, CG 20164 and CG 20550). Three appear to be engaged in daily activities such as pouring beer, grinding grain and sowing seed (E.30).

The stelae support the Asiatics' acceptance of Egyptian traditions. Most descendents are shown with Egyptian names, titles and dress, taking part in daily activities and rituals. Two stelae owners are also of Asiatic descent (CG 20650 and ÄS 160), indicating that such individuals assumed Egyptian religious obligations by dedicating their stelae at Abydos. Familiarity with Egyptian deities is apparent through the utilisation of offering formulae expressing their devotion to Osiris, Anubis, Geb and Hapy.

Other seemingly Egyptian stelae owners (bar the bellicose Louvre C1, CG 20539 and Manchester 3306) did not represent the *ꜥꜣm.w* negatively. They included them in their lists of household members and, in effect, recognised them as proficient officials of their households. Moreover, the Egyptians acknowledged and recorded the genealogies of individuals of foreign descent, highlighting that the *ꜥꜣm.w* had become well-integrated within Egyptian society, and that the Egyptians themselves were well-acquainted with these foreigners' ancestry. This act of recording genealogy reflects a level of care in preserving the memory of an

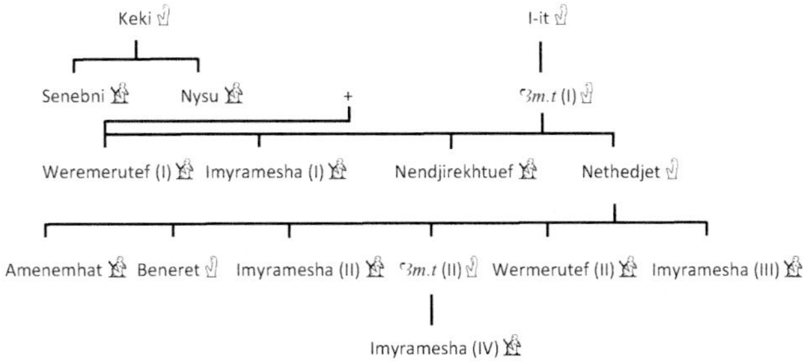

FIGURE 4.61. GENEALOGY OF ASIATICS IN ÄS 160.

1187 PM 5, 39-105; Richards, *Society and Death*, 129-131; Grajetzki, *Middle Kingdom*, 95-97; Adams, *NARCE* 158/189 (1992), 1-9; Wegner, *JARCE* 35 (1998), 1-44; Wegner, *MDAIK* 57 (2001), 281-308.

1188 Richards, *Society and Death*, 131-136, 169-172; Ayrton, Currelly and Weigall, *Abydos* 3, 11-34; Wegner, *E&L* 10 (2000), 83-125; Wegner, *Senwosret III*; Wegner, in *Archaism and Innovation*, 103-168; Grajetzki, *Middle Kingdom*, 95-97.

1189 Grajetzki, *Middle Kingdom*, 95.

1190 The following is a revised examination of the evidence from Abydos by the author, which originally appeared in *BACE* 24 (2013), 31-58.

1191 For more on the dating criteria, see Bennett, *JEA* 27 (1941), 77–82; Franke, *JEA* 89 (2003), 39–57; Ilin-Tomich, *ZÄS* 138 (2011), 20-34.

1192 *Ꞽbnr* (CG 20140), *ꜥbd* (CG 20161), *ꜥꞽ* (CG 20296), *Kbšty* (CG 20441), *ꜥꜣḳ* (CG 20753), *Ḳdmnt* (E.60.1926), *Gbgb* and his mother *Ꞽmꞽ* (Rio de Janeiro 627), as well as *Ꞽ-bꞽ* and *Twty* (Rio de Janeiro 680).

1193 CG 20086, CG 20224 and CG 20678. Another unprovenanced stela of the early Thirteenth Dynasty thought to be from Abydos, Rio de Janeiro 630 [2422], also contains the name. Kitchen, *Catalogue* 1, 34-37; vol. 1, pls 11-12. See Figure 7.10.

Asiatic's descent. Perhaps it signifies their acceptance, their importance within society, or even that decorum necessitated the appellation to signal their foreignness. In all cases, it appears that having an Asiatic background was not shunned. In the two examples of Asiatics dedicating stelae, their ancestry was not concealed, as the term *ꜥꜣm* was not employed for derogatory purposes, it simply labelled the origins of individuals living among Egyptians. Moreover, it was not an imperative identifier, for a small number of people with Semitic names, and presumably Semitic origins, did not have the term appended to their entries.

Asiatics in the Egyptian community

Stelae from the reign of Amenemhat III to the mid-Thirteenth Dynasty represent Asiatics as members of the typical Egyptian household. The attested examples signify that their numbers remained steadily the same but with a slight increase during Dynasty 13. They were employed as an 'overseer of a storehouse' (CG 20296), 'hall-keepers' (CG 20296 and ÄS 160) as well as 'butlers' (CG 20231, E.207.1900 and ÄS 160), and took part in Egyptian daily activities such as brewery, cooking and agricultural work (CG 20296 and E.30). Their participation in cultic rituals is also attested (E.30) as is their association with such individuals as the 'overseer of a storehouse' (Rio de Janeiro 627), 'overseer of the law-court' (ÄS 99), 'sealer of the king of Lower Egypt' (CG 20140) and 'major-domo of the great house' (Marseille 227).

Further notes can be offered when stelae of the general Middle Kingdom and Second Intermediate Period are examined. Additional professions of Asiatics include a 'carrier of provisions' (CG 20164), a 'steward' (CG 20650), a 'retainer' (Penn Museum 69-29-56), an 'overseer of the military' (CG 20650) and 'overseers of craftsmen' (Rio de Janeiro 680). In two attestations, Egyptians are custodians of Asiatics (CG 20103 and CG 20392) while in one stela, Asiatic women of successive generations are wives, the title 'lady of the house' signifying their role (CG 20650).

Asiatic women are also among other lists of household members. They are represented in at least three stelae as concubines or secondary wives apparently married to Egyptian men (CG 20125, CG 20441, ÄS 160 and ÄS 169). Egyptians(?) with an Asiatic sister (CG 20281) and brother (CG 20753) are mentioned, yet neither has their parentage specified. In one stela, five generations of Asiatic descendents are additionally recorded (ÄS 160; Figure 4.61).[1194] As the last three generations feature persons with Egyptian names, it may be surmised that the family had resided in Egypt for at least three generations. Asiatic relatives of Egyptians are recorded in 11 other stelae.

The number of attested Asiatic men and women is almost the same: approximately 51% of Asiatics are male and 49% are female. While it is important to note the fragmentary nature of the evidence[1195] and the possibility that the excavated data only concerns a small percentage of the entire population,[1196] such findings differ considerably from the 90% male and 10% female attestations calculated for Asiatics in el-Lahun's papyri.[1197] Perhaps this may be explained by the fragility of the papyri compared to the stelae, or that each body originates from a different context and textual genre.

Levantines and Egyptian foreign affairs

Five stelae concern contacts between the Egyptian administration and Levantines. Four relate to the Egyptian army, three of which note possible military encounters (Louvre C1, CG 20539 and Manchester 3306) while one presents an 'overseer of the expedition' as an Asiatic (CG 20650), and the fifth addresses commercial relations (EA 428).

The stela of general[1198] Nesumontu (Louvre C1) records how the Egyptians led successful attacks against fortresses housing the *Ỉwn.tyw*, *Mnṯ.tyw* and *Ḥr.yw-šꜥ* foreigners. Although these have been equated with settlements in the Levant,[1199] their exact location is not specified in the text. As such, they could have been within Egypt, the Eastern Desert or the Sinai region,[1200] the attacks not particularly informative on Amenemhat I's foreign policies in the Levant.

Another stelae addressing military action is that of Montuhotep (CG 20539). Here, only the epithet of the general represents bellicosity over the *Ḥr.yw-šꜥ* and *St.(t)yw* during Senwosret I's reign.

The third stelae mentioning evident clashes is that of Khusobek which, unlike the others, recounts his personal encounter against one *ꜥꜣm* in an event which transpired following Senwosret III's visit to the Levant (Manchester 3306). Apparently, Senwosret III and Khusobek marched[1201] northwards towards *St.t* specifically to overthrow the *Mnṯ.tyw*. The expedition reached *Skmm* then turned back, perhaps due to an unsuccessful military venture,[1202] although no explanation is clearly given. The

1194 Although previously postulated to be three generations (Hein and Satzinger, *Stelen des Mittleren Reiches* 2, 82; Schneider, *Ausländer in Ägypten* 2, 79, 308), a re-reading of the text suggests that the repetition of names relates to different individuals of five generations.

1195 Clarke, *Antiquity* 47 (1973), 16; Renfrew and Bahn, *Archaeology*, 54-72.

1196 O'Connor, in *Population Growth*, 81-3; Baines and Eyre, *GM* 61 (1983), 65-7; Baines and Lacovara, *JSA* 2 (2002), 12; Richards, *Society and Death*, 66.

1197 See Chapter 4.3.5.2. Petrik, in *From Illahun to Djeme*, 213.

1198 For a statue of Nesumontu as 'the very great general of the entire land', see Wildung, *MDAIK* 37 (1981), 503-507; Cohen, *Canaanites, Chronologies, and Connections*, 38, n. 39.

1199 Kemp, in *Ancient Egypt*, 143; Redford, *Egypt, Canaan and Israel*, 77, 82; Cohen, *Canaanites, Chronologies, and Connections*, 38; Bárta, *Sinuhe, the Bible, and the Patriarchs*, 105.

1200 Cohen, *Canaanites, Chronologies, and Connections*, 38. For more on the term *ẖnr.wt*, see Quirke, *RdE* 39 (1988), 83-106.

1201 Both *spr* and *wḏꜣ* (line C.1) are determined by 𓂻, most probably indicating that the army travelled by foot (Wells, *War in Ancient Egypt*, 133-134).

1202 Some have posited that the king led an unsuccessful siege against

lack of specificity could relate to the text's focus on the official's own contribution to the expedition amplifying Khusobek's personal achievements and perspective.[1203] Therefore, the first lines set the scene, purposely overlooking the pharaoh's exploits while only noting that *Skmm* and *Rṯnw* 'fell'[1204] following his return trip to the Residence. Then, the text relays how Khusobek courageously and victoriously fought a *ꜥꜣm* in a clash between the groups. Khusobek's account indicates that the Egyptian army travelled through the Levant up to *Skmm*, near *Rṯnw*, demonstrating Senwosret III's political interests in this region and the often violent nature of Egyptian-Levantine relations during Dynasty 12. Despite the bellicose relations, a *ꜥꜣm* descendent was still able to reach the position of an 'overseer of the expedition' (CG 20650), signalling the acceptance of Asiatics not only within Egyptian society and administration but also in the military. Such an acceptance is of great social and political significance, and attests to changing attitudes and perceptions to those from foreign lands.

Different perceptions are also attested in the fifth stela which hints at trade with the Northern Levant (EA 428). Evidently, a 'hall-keeper of (goods from) *Kpny*' is listed, highlighting that relations with Byblos would have been quite frequent to warrant this appointment in the mid-Thirteenth Dynasty.[1205] Indeed, the toponym for Byblos occurs in three instances as part of women's names,[1206] signifying knowledge of and reverence for the 'lady of Byblos', Baalat-Gebel. Such reverence may have been influenced by commercial contacts with the port city as developed by such individuals as the 'hall-keeper of (goods from) *Kpny*', whose inclusion in a treasurer's list of officials associates trade with elite members of the administration.

4.5.1.2 Other

A few finds at Abydos denote contact with the Levantine culture. An example is a bronze anchor axe-head from Twelfth Dynasty Tomb 51(?).[1207] The weapon is a precursor to the EBIV to MBIIA fenestrated eye and duckbill shapes, with two open sockets and a knob in the centre.[1208] Parallels

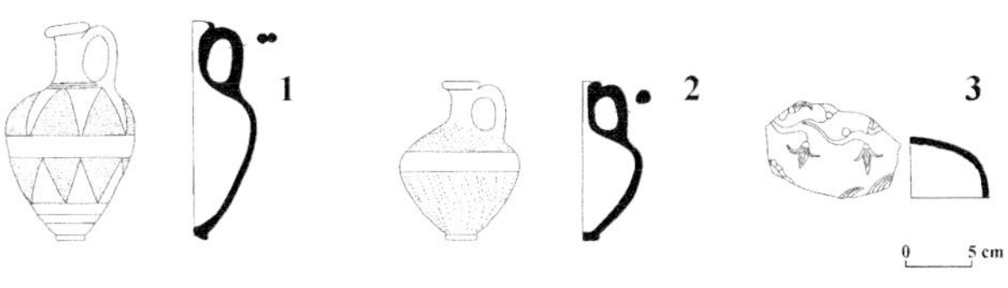

FIGURE 4.62. SELECTED CERAMICS, ABYDOS. AFTER KAPLAN, *TELL EL YAHUDIYEH*, FIGS 33 [B], 97 [B], 126 [I].

derive from such Northern Levantine sites as Ur (Middle to Late Akkadian Period),[1209] Tell Qarqur (EBIV)[1210] and Byblos (MBIIA),[1211] as well as a First Intermediate Period tomb at Helwan.[1212] The axe-head may be an imported, perhaps prestige, item from the Northern Levant.

Tell el-Yahudiyah vessels were also uncovered in Second Intermediate Period tombs (Figure 4.62).[1213] A piriform jug was found in Tomb B13, its parallels stemming from Tell el-Dab'a Strata F-E/2,[1214] a biconical jug was recovered from Tomb D21 with similar ware from Tell el-Dab'a Strata E/2-D/1,[1215] and Seventeenth Dynasty Tomb D11 yielded a fragment of a vessel's shoulder decorated with lotus petals.[1216] Thus, the Tell el-Yahudiyah ware can be stylistically dated to the late Thirteenth to Fifteenth Dynasties, indicating some relations between Abydos and the north.

Sealings of Dynasty 14 royals were additionally found in the necropolis.[1217] These include those of Sekhaenra (*nṯr nfr Sḫꜥ-n-Rꜥ.w* 'the good god, Sekhaenra'),[1218] *ꜥꜣmw* (*sꜣ Rꜥ.w ꜥꜣmw dỉ(.w)*

Skmm, despite the lack of details and the identification of the toponym as a region rather than a fortified settlement. Goedicke, *E&L* 7 (1998), 35; Bárta, *Sinuhe, the Bible, and the Patriarchs*, 127-128.

1203 Baines, in *Form und Mass*, 59-61.

1204 A militaristic meaning of the term interprets it as 'to withstand' an attack or 'to fall' upon or ambush the Egyptians, both usages being uncommon in earlier military narratives. Delia writes that the return of the Egyptians might have been either an act of retreat, with the Egyptians falling prey to a surprise attack, or a military strategy, with the king luring the Asiatics to attack (Delia, *Senwosret III*, 119). See also Baines, in *Form und Mass*, 51 [ee]; Goedicke, *E&L* 7 (1998), 35; Cohen, *Canaanites, Chronologies, and Connections*, 47.

1205 For a similar case, see Quirke, *RdE* 51 (2000), 229-230.

1206 See Figure 7.9.

1207 Petrie notes that the axe was uncovered in Tomb 30b, yet the plate labels it as part of Tomb 51's assemblage (Petrie, *Tombs of the Courtiers*, 6, pl. 5 [28]). In another report, Sebelien places the artefact in Tomb 51 (Sebelien, *Ancient Egypt* [1924], 6-15).

1208 Maxwell-Hyslop, *Iraq* 11 (1949), 118-119; Tubb, *Iraq* 44/1 (1982), 1; Gernez, in *Proceedings of the 4th International Congress*, 131; Gernez, *L'armament en métal*, 203-206.

1209 Gernez, *L'armament en métal*, 204; Woolley, *Ur* 2, pl. 224 [U. 9687]; Tubb, *Iraq* 44/1 (1982), 1-2.

1210 Gernez, *L'armament en métal*, 204; Dornemann, in *Tell Qarqur*, figs 189-190; Dornemann, in *Proceedings of the 6th International Congress* 2, 141.

1211 The context does not provide a clear date for the axe, but based on the accompanying cartouche of Noferhotep, a *terminus post quem* of the Thirteenth Dynasty or MBIIA is suggested. A mould for casting anchor axes was also uncovered at Byblos (Dunand, *Byblos* 1, 197, pl. 96 [3070]; vol. 2, 20, fig. 17).

1212 Saad, *Royal Excavations*, 173, pl. 88.

1213 Two further vessels were unearthed in Tombs D114 and E10, both of which included material of the Eighteenth Dynasty. The New Kingdom settlement also contained Tell el-Yahudiyah fragments. See Peet and Loat, *Abydos* 3, pl. 12 [4]; Garstang, *El-Arábah*, 28-29, pl. 17; Eriksson, *Late Bronze Age Cyprus*, 172-173; Aston and Bietak, *TeD* 8, 556; Kaplan, *Tell el Yahudiyeh*, 80-81, figs 13 [e], 87 [b], 133 [v].

1214 Aston and Bietak's Levanto-Egyptian Type L.3.1c. Peet, *Abydos* 2, 57-58, 68-69, pl. 13 [8]; Kaplan, *Tell el Yahudiyeh*, fig. 33 [b]; Aston and Bietak, *TeD* 8, 152-169, figs 102, 104.

1215 Aston and Bietak's Levanto-Egyptian Type L.5.3a. Randall-MacIver and Mace, *Abydos*, 92, 98, pl. 54 [13]; Aston and Bietak, *TeD* 8, 231, figs 162-164, 167.

1216 Aston and Bietak's Levanto-Egyptian Vessels with Naturalistic Designs. The excavation report does not include a full corpus of items uncovered in the tomb, restricting further analysis on its suggested date. Aston and Bietak, *TeD* 8, 200, 376-381; Kaplan, *Tell el Yahudiyeh*, fig. 126 [i].

1217 Ryholt also lists a scarab for *Kꜣrḥ*, although this remains unpublished. Ryholt, *Political Situation*, 363-364.

1218 The published line drawing of the scarab does not warrant the precise identification of some glyphs, and so the transcription presented is a reconstruction. Mariette, *Monuments d'Abydos*, 538 [1391]; Newberry, *Antiquités Égyptienne*, 11 [36042], pl. 1

ʿnḫ 'son of Ra, *ʿꜣmw*, given life'),[1219] Ipeq ( *sꜣ nsw.t smsw Ỉpḳ* 'king's eldest son, Ipeq')[1220] and eight naming Maaibra *Ššỉ*.[1221]

A Near Eastern adornment has additionally been recovered from Tomb 1008.[1222] The silver torque was found around the neck of a young female along with other jewellery. No items from the grave signify the deceased's foreign ancestry: she was buried in a supine, extended position in a tomb assigned to the Middle Kingdom.[1223] As with the torques at Mostagedda[1224] and the aforementioned axe, the Abydos torque may be a prestige item or status signifier.

Another artefact designating contact is an ivory sphinx from Shaft Tomb 477. Based on two peg holes, the artefact is likely a fixture, perhaps for a box or a piece of furniture. It has been identified as a representation of either Senwosret I or *Ḫyꜣn*[1225] and features the forepart of a sphinx holding the head of an Egyptian[1226] between its paws. The sphinx's head is crowned with a *nemes* headdress and a uraeus, and exhibits large ears, almond-shaped eyes slanting in towards an aquiline, curved nose, and straight, thick lips. Such characteristics, especially of the nose, have led scholars to identify the sphinx with an Asiatic.[1227] However, there is no comparative material for this,[1228] and the context also does not allow for a concrete date as excavation reports have not been fully published. Similarly, accompanying objects from 477 as well as the two adjoining shafts, 476 and 478, have been assigned to the Middle Kingdom and Second Intermediate Period, with notes of secondary usage and disturbed contexts.[1229] In fact, the context only conclusively points to the shaft's construction for a middle- or high-ranking individual(s).

With the available material, the identification of the sphinx as a representation of a Twelfth Dynasty king or Hyksos ruler cannot be verified. It is worthy of note that the shape of the nose and eyes is more akin to northeastern characteristics,[1230] but rather than classifying such features as those of an Asiatic king, perhaps they can be viewed as an artistic hybrid, mixing Egyptian royal symbols with Asiatic elements. Subsequently, it may not necessarily depict a pharaoh's own mixed ancestry; it could signify an attempt by an artist, not necessarily of the royal workshop, to portray the king with a more heterogeneous character, probably by or for multi-ethnic followers. In view of the Asiatic population in Egypt, as well as their presence amongst varying levels of society as witnessed in the stelae, such an attempt is more likely to have occurred during the late Twelfth Dynasty to Second Intermediate Period.

The available archaeological material at Abydos implies that contact with the Levant and the northern dynasties was meagre and mostly commercial in nature. The imported artefacts are largely related to middle- or high-ranking individuals, adding a possible prestige function for some foreign items. The Tell el-Yahudiyah vessels as well as the scarabs point to continued Second Intermediate Period contact with the north and the ivory sphinx indicates probable influences on Pharaonic art. Such reflections agree with the data gathered from the stelae, suggesting that at least the middle to high echelons of the Egyptian population at Abydos were familiar with some aspects of Levantine culture.

Combined, the Abydos texts as well as the archaeological material attest to a slight increase in the number of Asiatics during Dynasty 13 and the early Second Intermediate Period. Abydos was certainly accessible to Asiatics, a few of whom dedicated their own stelae at the site following popular Egyptian traditions. They were employed within the administration, holding titles related to private households as well as the local administration and workforce. Some may have also resided in Egypt, adopting Egyptian cultural elements without abandoning their own. Further, Egyptians accepted their foreign lineage and did not represent them in a derogatory manner. Despite records of conflict beyond the borders, the situation within Egypt marks mutual relations. Asiatic descendents were recognised for their contributions and were most probably encountered on a daily basis and in typical situations, especially by the elite. The elite apparently also controlled trade with the north, particularly the Northern Levant, during Dynasty 13. Therefore, the evidence from Abydos supports the rising status of the Asiatic population, who were not only acknowledged for their contributions to Egyptian society, but were also allowed to visit the sacred site of Abydos and, like devoted Egyptians, commemorate their pilgrimage to the site.

[36042]; Ryholt, *Political Situation*, 40-50, 359-360; Ben-Tor, *Scarabs*, 58-59.

1219 Mariette, *Monuments d'Abydos*, 538 [1391]; Newberry, *Antiquités Égyptienne*, 11 [36040], pl. 1 [36040].

1220 Brunton, *Qau and Badari* 3; Mariette, *Monuments d'Abydos*, 539 [1394]; Martin, *Egyptian Administrative and Private-Name Seals*, 16-18 [127-169], pls 31 [16-45], 32 [1-10], 38 [33], 42A [21-22].

1221 Newberry, *Antiquités Égyptienne*, 8 [36030], 9 [36031, 36033], 10 [36035], pl. 1 [36030-36031, 36033, 36035]; Mariette, *Monuments d'Abydos*, 536 [1382], 538 [1391]; Ryholt, *Political Situation*, 368.

1222 Frankfort, *JEA* 16/3 (1930), 219, pl. 37.

1223 Frankfort, *JEA* 16/3 (1930), 219.

1224 See Chapter 4.5.8.

1225 British Museum Nr 54678. Garstang, *JEA* 14/1 (1928), 46-47; Säve-Soderbergh, *JEA* 37 (1951), 66; Bourriau, *Pharaohs and Mortals*, 136-138.

1226 The captive could also be a Nubian. Marée, in *Pharaohs*, 426 [97].

1227 Garstang, *JEA* 14/1 (1928), 46-47.

1228 Bourriau refers to a Berlin statue of Senwosret I with a similar headdress and facial features. While these elements are similar to those of the ivory sphinx, Bourriau correctly notes that the nose and the slant of the eyes are different. The comparison of the nose with that of the king's personification of Lower Egypt on the base of his thrones does not provide close parallels to the sphinx's characteristics. Bourriau, *Pharaohs and Mortals*, 136-138 with references.

1229 Bourriau, *Pharaohs and Mortals*, 137-138; Garstang, *JEA* 14/1 (1928), 46-47.

1230 For example, the eyes of the wooden statuette from Dahshur and the Asiatics' noses in Khnumhotep II's tomb, Beni Hassan. See Figures 4.34, 4.52; Booth, *Role of Foreigners*, 22.

4.5.2 Aswan

Lat.Lon. 24°05'N 32°54'E

Refs PM 7, 221-224; de Morgan et al., *Catalogue* 1, 38 [166], 48 [7].

Chron. Twelfth to Thirteenth Dynasty

North of the First Cataract is Aswan, the First Upper Egyptian nome. Its granite quarries reveal a large concentration of graffiti, signalling heavy exploitation throughout Pharaonic history.[1231] Many are dated to Dynasty 12, the texts written by either quarrymen, expedition members or other travellers.[1232] Two graffiti refer to Asiatics:[1233]

A. 

...(1) ḥtp ḏỉ nsw.t Ỉꜣb.tt H̱nm.w ꜥnḳ.t ḏỉ=sn pr.t-ḫrw t ḥnḳ(.t) kꜣ.w ꜣpd.w n kꜣ (2) n(.y) ỉr.y [sš(r)?] Sbk-wr mꜣꜥ-ḫrw nb ỉmꜣḫ (3) msi n Ỉ-tỉ mꜣꜥ.t-ḫrw nb.t ỉmꜣḫ
(4) sn=f Nḫ.t-[...]w-(5) ỉmn.y mꜣꜥ-ḫrw ỉri n Ỉ-tỉ mꜣꜥ(.t)-ḫrw
(6) ỉr.y ꜥ.t n(.y) ꜥ.t ḥnḳ.t Nb-swmn.w mꜣꜥ-ḫrw
ꜥnḫ(.w) n(.y) nỉw(.t)(?) (7) Ỉmny mꜣꜥ-ḫrw sn=f ꜥnḫ(.w) n(.y) nỉw(.t)(?) Ỉmny (8) msi n Ỉ-tỉ mꜣꜥ(.t)-ḫrw
ỉt=f (ỉ)mꜣḫ.y (?) Rn=f-ꜥnḫ-nḫn mꜣꜥ-ḫrw (9) ỉri n Kkw mꜣ.t-ḫrw
mw.t=f nb.t pr(.w) Ỉ-ty mꜣꜥ.t-ḫrw ỉri.t n Ꜥꜣm.t mꜣꜥ(.t)-ḫrw
(10) mw.t n(.y) Ꜥꜣm.t ỉri.t n Pnt[...] mꜣꜥ.t-ḫrw
sn.t=f Kkw mꜣꜥ.t-ḫrw ỉri.t n Ỉ-tỉ mꜣꜥ(.t)-ḫrw
(11) sn=f ỉm.y-rꜣ ꜥẖn.wty n(.y) ḥnḳ.t Ỉmny mꜣꜥ-ḫrw ỉri n [...]pw-n-pr-ḥḏ 12 Ỉ-y mꜣꜥ-ḫrw ...

(1) An offering which the king gives and Satet, Khnum and Anukis: may they give an invocation offering of bread, beer, beef and fowl for the *kꜣ* (2) of the keeper of [linen?],[1234] Sobekwer,[1235] justified, possessor of reverence, (3) born to I-ti,[1236] justified, possessor of reverence;
(4) his brother (5)Nekhet[...]uimeny, justified, born to I-ti, justified;
(6) hall-keeper of the kitchen,[1237] Nebsumenu,[1238] justified; citizen(?),[1239] (7)Imeny, justified, his brother, citizen(?), Imeny,[1240] (8) born to I-ti, justified;
his father, the honoured one (?), Renefankhnekhen, justified, (9) born to Keku, justified;
his mother, lady of the house, I-ty, justified, born to *Ꜥꜣm.t*, justified;
(10) mother of *Ꜥꜣm.t*, born to *Pnt*[...],[1241] justified;
his sister, Keku,[1242] justified, born to I-ti, justified;
(11) his brother, chamberlain of the kitchen, Imeny, justified, born to [...]puenperhedj 12 I-y, justified ...

B. 

Ꜥꜣm.t Ỉsmꜣꜣ
Ꜥꜣm.t Ỉsmꜣꜣ[1243]

Hieratic Grafitti A[1244] for Sobekwer invokes an offering to local Egyptian gods. Sobekwer's title is uncertain and he is represented as a standing individual with no delineating features. The graffiti lists Sobekwer's household members, recording the children of his mother, I-ti, 'lady of the house', born to *Ꜥꜣm.t*. I-ti appears in another unprovenanced stela, Musée Guimet C 12, along with her daughter and son Imeny, who similarly feature in Graffiti A.[1245] The stela has been assigned to early Dynasty 13[1246] and so Sobekwer's text may also date to this period.

Middle Kingdom Graffiti B[1247] belongs to the 'major-domo' Iuseneb who lists the *Ꜥꜣm.t Ỉsmꜣꜣ* as a household member. As she is the only individual with no apparent familial relation, she may have been Iuseneb's wife or concubine.

The graffiti demonstrate the social mingling between Egyptians and Levantines. The Asiatic women had relations with Egyptians and, as Graffiti A signifies, their children were raised as Egyptians and employed within the administration. Furthermore, the texts denote that Asiatics like Sobekwer were travelling to the very south of Egypt during early Dynasty 13. They could record their visits and foreign ancestry in the Egyptian manner, use the hieratic script, and show reverence to Egyptian gods.

1231 De Morgan et al., *Catalogue* 1; Engelbach, *Obelisks*; Klemm and Klemm, *Stones and Quarries*; Peden, *Graffiti of Pharaonic Egypt*, 37-39.
1232 Peden, *Graffiti of Pharaonic Egypt*, 37-39.
1233 Letters ascribed by the author. Transcription after de Morgan, *Catalogue* 1, 38 [166], 48 [7]. Transliteration and translation are by the author.
1234 Title as translated in Schneider, *Ausländer in Ägypten* 2, 24; Ward, *Index*, 66 [544].
1235 Ranke, *Personennamen* 1, 303 [27].
1236 Ranke, *Personennamen* 1, 49 [17].
1237 Ward, *Index*, 57 [458].
1238 Ranke, *Personennamen* 1, 186 [8].
1239 The title is read as 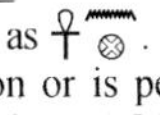. It may have been erroneously transcribed in its publication or is perhaps a case of scribal misrendering of signs. Ward, *Index*, 74 [604]; Schneider, *Ausländer in Ägypten* 2, 24; de Morgan. *Catalogue* 1, 38 [166].
1240 Ward, *Index*, 31 [13].
1241 Not attested in Ranke, *Personennamen*. Perhaps the name is derived from a Semitic word such as *benet* 'daughter' or *banah* 'to build'.
1242 Ranke, *Personennamen* 1, 349 [8].
1243 The name is not attested in Ranke, *Personennamen* and could be derived from the Semitic. Schneider, *Ausländer in Ägypten* 2, 24.
1244 De Morgan et al., *Catalogue* 1, 38 [166].
1245 Her daughter is given the title 'lady of the house' in the stela. Schneider, *Ausländer in Ägypten* 2, 67.
1246 Schneider, *Ausländer in Ägypten* 2, 24, 67.
1247 De Morgan et al., *Catalogue* 1, 48 [7].

4.5.3 Dra' Abu el-Naga'

Lat.Lon. 25°44'N 32°27'E

Refs Mariette, *Papyrus Boulaq*; Scharff, *ZÄS* 57 (1922), 51-68.

Chron. Mid-Thirteenth Dynasty (reign of Sobekhotep II or Khendjer)

The necropolis of Dra' Abu el-Naga' is located on the west bank at Thebes in the Fourth Upper Egyptian nome. A tomb uncovered during Mariette's excavation in 1860 revealed two documents known as Papyrus Boulaq 18 on the tomb's floor:[1248] (1) a larger manuscript, termed henceforth as Papyrus Boulaq 18/1; and (2) a smaller manuscript, Papyrus Boulaq 18/2.[1249] The tomb is thought to have belonged to a 'scribe of the main enclosure, Noferhotep', whose name and title appear on several grave goods.[1250] An individual with the same name and title is mentioned in Papyrus Boulaq 18/2, providing a possible link between the tomb owner and the papyri.[1251] The documents may have been included in the burial assemblage as a confirmation of the tomb owner's scribal practice for the afterlife.[1252]

The manuscripts were written by at least two different individuals, perhaps Noferhotep and another recording Noferhotep's scribal activities.[1253] They feature the names of a king Sobekhotep as well as a vizier Ankhu, who is otherwise attested under Khendjer's rule, providing a date of the first half of Dynasty 13 for the papyri.[1254] Papyrus Boulaq 18/1 refers to a regnal Year 3 while Papyrus Boulaq 18/2 mentions Year 5.[1255] As such, the named king has been identified as either Sobekhotep II[1256] or Sobekhotep III,[1257] but arguments noting the differences between the family of the latter and the royal family in Papyrus Boulaq 18/1 suggest that this manuscript concerns events during Sobekhotep II's Year 3.[1258] Accordingly, the reference to Year 5 of Papyrus Boulaq 18/2 should be allocated to either Sobekhotep II or his successor, Khendjer.[1259] This agrees with a recent redating of the tomb's assemblage to the late Middle Kingdom,[1260] providing support for the papyri's composition during Dynasty 13.

Papyrus Boulaq 18/1 relays the daily accounts associated with the king's visit to the Theban Residence.[1261] It contains lists of royal individuals and officials, references to offerings for Montu at Medamud, a report on the visit of a *Mḏꜣ.y* delegation and subsequent feasts at the palace. Attestations to Asiatics are found among a list of 62 officials invited to such a feast in the *wꜣḫ.y*-hall for the Festival of Montu.[1262] The Asiatics are:[1263]  *smsw hꜣy.t ꜥꜣm* 'elder of the portal,[1264] *ꜥꜣm*'; and 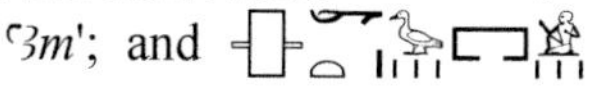 ...  *im.y-ḫt sꜣ.w pr.w... Nḥy sꜣ ꜥꜣm* 'police official ...[1265] Nehy's[1266] son, *ꜥꜣm*'.[1267]

Papyrus Boulaq 18/2 records the accounts of an estate related to a high-ranking official, possibly the vizier Ankhu who frequently appears in the document.[1268] One entry reads:[1269]  *iwi.t mniw ṯsm.w(?) Snb=f m iyi ḥr mḥ.ty m-ꜥ.w sš wr n ṯꜣ.ty Rs-snb(.w) ini.n=f m-ꜥ.w sr pn ḥr mḥ.ty tp [n(.y)] ꜥꜣm.t [...] 1[8] (?)* 'arrival of the herdsman of hounds(?), Senbef and the coming from the north with the chief scribe to the vizier Ressencb(u). He has brought with this nobleman from the north: *ꜥꜣm.t* [...] numbering 1[8]'. Fragments following the entry feature at least two Asiatic women supplying *bꜣk.w*,[1270] one by the name of Iunofer offering *dꜣbw* 'figs'[1271] and the other of uncertain name bringing *šbb* 'kneading dough'.[1272]

The two documents refer to the employment of Asiatics by the elite. Papyrus Boulaq 18/1 provides evidence for two Asiatic men working in security and advisory roles within the inner palace of the king's Theban Residence while Papyrus Boulaq 18/2 cites the delivery of products by Asiatic women from the north. Both confirm the presence of Asiatics within Thebes during the first half of Dynasty 13, demonstrating that such individuals were acquainted with high-ranking officials of the administration.

1248 Cairo 6139. The papyri were seemingly found next to a *rishi* coffin, the existence of which has been questioned. Mariette, *Boulaq* 2; Miniaci and Quirke, *Egitto e Vicino Oriente* 31 (2008), 13, 18-20, 24; Miniaci and Quirke, *BIFAO* 209 (2009), 341. For references discussing the papyri, see Spalinger, *SAK* 12 (1985), 179, n. 1.

1249 Neither papyrus is fully published.

1250 Quirke, *Administration*, 10.

1251 Quirke, *Administration*, 10-12.

1252 Quirke, *Administration*, 11.

1253 Quirke, *Administration*, 10-12.

1254 Quirke, *Administration*, 11-12.

1255 Quirke, *Administration*, 12-13.

1256 Quirke, *Administration*, 12-13; von Beckerath, *JNES* 17/4 (1958), 266-268.

1257 Hayes, *JNES* 12/1 (1953), 38-39.

1258 Von Beckerath, *JNES* 17/4 (1958), 268; Quirke, *Administration*, 12.

1259 Quirke, *Administration*, 13.

1260 Miniaci and Quirke, *BIFAO* 209 (2009), 357.

1261 Scharff, *ZÄS* 57 (1922), 51-68, pls 1**-24**; Quirke, *Administration*, 17-24.

1262 Columns XXXVII-XXXIX. Scharff, *ZÄS* 57 (1922), pls 18**-19**; Schneider, *Ausländer in Ägypten* 2, 35-36.

1263 Transcriptions are based on Scharff, *ZÄS* 57 (1922), pls 18**-19**. Transliterations and translations are by the author.

1264 Quirke, *Administration*, 87-89; Ward, *Index*, 152 [1309].

1265 Ward, *Index*, 54 [431].

1266 Ranke, *Personennamen* 1, 207 [15].

1267 An *im.y-ḫ.t Nḥy* is attested in two further instances in Papyrus Boulaq 18/1 and can perhaps be associated with this *ꜥꜣm*. See Papyrus Boulaq 18/1, XLV2,11 and XLVI,2 as transcribed in Scharff, *ZÄS* 57 (1922), pl. 23**. See also Chapter 4.5.10 for an individual with the same name and title.

1268 Mariette, *Boulaq* 2, pls 47-55; Quirke, *Administration*, 196.

1269 Column 2, ll.14-7. Transcription is based on Quirke, *Administration*, 197 and Mariette, *Boulaq* 2, pl. 49. Transliterations and translations are by the author.

1270 Columns 2, l.6. Mariette, *Boulaq* 2, pl. 55 [b]; Quirke, *Administration*, 197.

1271 Column 2, l.6. Mariette, *Boulaq* 2, pl. 55 [b]; Quirke, *Administration*, 202, n. 27.

1272 Quirke cautiously reads the name as either Rehut or Tjehut. Column 3, l.2. Mariette, *Boulaq* 2, pl. 55[a]; Quirke, *Administration*, 202, n. 27.

4.5.4 *Edfu, Tell*

Lat.Lon. 24°57'N 32°50'E

Refs PM 5, 200-205; Moeller and Farout, *EA* 31 (2007), 14-17; Marée, *British Museum Studies in Ancient Egypt and Sudan* 12 (2009), 31-92; Moeller, *The Oriental Institute News and Notes* 206 (2010), 3-8; Moeller and Marouard, *E&L* 11 (2011), 87-121; Moeller, *NEA* 75/2 (2012), 116-125.

Chron. Twelfth to Fifteenth / Seventeenth Dynasty

A main settlement in the Second Upper Egyptian nome, Tell Edfu preserves stratigraphical layers dating across the Pharaonic period. Excavations by the Institut français d'archéologie orientale, Cairo, and the Oriental Institute, Chicago, have revealed extensive remains of a Middle Kingdom and Second Intermediate Period settlement and cemetery site near the remaining Ptolemaic temple of Horus.[1273] A large administrative complex was also found, offering significant evidence on relations between Upper and Lower Egypt. As the excavations are ongoing, publications are preliminary. Nonetheless, they provide pertinent data on Egyptian-Levantine contacts.

4.5.4.1 *Stela*

The southwestern end of Tell Edfu features the tomb of Sixth Dynasty nomarch Isi.[1274] Reused in the Middle Kingdom, the tomb may have been the centre of a local cult dedicated to the official.[1275] Stelae uncovered within the tomb and cemetery mention Isi in their offering formulae, indicating that the nomarch was possibly attributed with divine status.[1276] One stela unearthed in his mastaba, in a niche of Room J's south wall, features [1277] *Pꜣ-ꜥꜣm*.[1278] The stela is dedicated by *wꜥb*-priest Ptahhotep and has been stylistically dated to the late Thirteenth or 'Sixteenth' Dynasty.[1279] *Pꜣ-ꜥꜣm*'s name is curiously written on the right hand side of the bottom register near an uninscribed space. As such, it could either belong to an unillustrated figure or to that of an Egyptian pictured above, offering a vessel to a seated Ptahhotep and his wife. The name *Pꜣ-ꜥꜣm* is found in Papyrus Brooklyn 35.1446[1280] as well as el-Lahun's UC 32124,[1281] both of the late Middle Kingdom.[1282] The inclusion of *Pꜣ-ꜥꜣm* on the stela suggests that an individual of Asiatic descent was in close contact with, and possibly working for, a *wꜥb*-priest in Tell Edfu during the late Thirteenth Dynasty.

4.5.4.2 *Administrative complex*

An administrative complex was recently uncovered along the eastern side of Tell Edfu's Old Kingdom enclosure wall (Figure 4.63).[1283] Thus far, excavations have revealed a compound with two large columned halls, their stratigraphical sequences assigned from the Twelfth Dynasty to the early Second Intermediate Period. The halls were subsequently abandoned and dismantled, after which large silos were constructed during Dynasty 17.[1284] The southern columned hall seems to have been deserted before the northern columned hall, which continued in activity until the second half of Dynasty 13.[1285] Finds displaying contact with the north are explored below.

Characteristic non-Egyptian ceramics

An accumulation of discarded objects along the sides of the southern columned hall's final occupation layer (US 2079 and 2280) featured two fragmentary vessels of Levantine Painted Ware.[1286] One is a bichrome long-necked jug with a black criss-cross design and bands of red and black, similar to a jug from MBIIA Tomb 235 at Tell Nami.[1287] The second is a dipper juglet with horizontal red band zones, parallels for which can be found at such MBIIA sites as Aphek, Megadim and Khargi.[1288] A foundation trench of a silo (405) dug into late Middle Kingdom levels revealed further fragments of a vessel decorated with a red spiral motif.[1289] Bagh suggests it could belong to a long-necked jug such as that from MBIIA Megadim, or a handle-less jar similar to a vessel from MBIIA Majdalouna.[1290] The stylistic details as well as the vessels' find-spots support Moeller's dating of the Levantine Painted Ware to the late Twelfth or beginning of the Thirteenth Dynasty.[1291]

Reports mention the discovery of ceramics with Levantine fabrics as well as Nubian Pan-Grave bowls and cooking pots from the southern columned hall's late Middle

1273 Henne, *Tell Edfou (1921-1922)*; Henne, *Tell Edfou (1923 et 1924)*; PM 5, 200; Michalowski et al., *Tell Edfou 1938*, vols 1-2; Moeller and Marouard, *E&L* 11 (2011), 87-121; Moeller, *NEA* 75/2 (2012), 116-125; Moeller, *JARCE* 46 (2010), 81-111. Annual reports may be accessed online at the *Tell Edfu Project*.

1274 Ibrahim, *ASAE* 33 (1933), 132-134.

1275 Grajetzki, *Middle Kingdom*, 88.

1276 Grajetzki, *Middle Kingdom*, 88; PM 5, 201-202.

1277 The could be a for *Pꜣw-ꜥꜣm* however this name is not attested elsewhere. Other strange features of the stela, such as a reversed *f* in the offering formula or the placement of an offering stand atop a mat rather than the reverse, support a misrendering of signs. See Marée, *British Museum Studies in Ancient Egypt and Sudan* 12 (2009), 51.

1278 Warsaw 141.266. Marée, *British Museum Studies in Ancient Egypt and Sudan* 12 (2009), 51, fig. 11.

1279 Marée, *British Museum Studies in Ancient Egypt and Sudan* 12 (2009), 51.

1280 Verso, 58. See Chapter 4.6.3 and Appendix B.7; Hayes, *Papyrus*, pl. 11.

1281 Line ii.8. See Chapter 4.3.5.2 and Appendix B.2; Collier and Quirke, *Letters*, 58-59.

1282 Another instance is found on a fragment of an unprovenanced stela. (Edwards, *JEA* 51 [1965], 27 [6], pl. 12 [1]; Schneider, *Ausländer in Ägypten* 2, 13). See also Ranke, *Personennamen* 1, 102 [21] for a New Kingdom attestation.

1283 Moeller and Marouard, *E&L* 11 (2011), 87-121; Moeller, *NEA* 75/2 (2012), 116-125.

1284 Moeller and Marouard, *E&L* 11 (2011), 91-97.

1285 Moeller and Marouard, *E&L* 11 (2011), 93-100.

1286 Moeller and Marouard, *E&L* 11 (2011), 107; Moeller, *The Oriental Institute News and Notes* 206 (2010), 7, fig. 12; Bagh, *TeD* 23, 64.

1287 Bagh, *TeD* 23, 64, fig. 51 [d]; Moeller, *The Oriental Institute News and Notes* 206 (2010), 7, fig. 12.

1288 Bagh, *TeD* 23, 28, 64, figs 2 [c], 37 [e, g], 52 [h], 74 [g]; Saidah, *Berytus* 41 (1993/1994), pl. 11 [2].

1289 Moeller and Farout, *EA* 31 (2007), 15; Bagh, *TeD* 23, 64.

1290 Bagh, *TeD* 23, 64.

1291 Bagh, *TeD* 23, 64, n. 201.

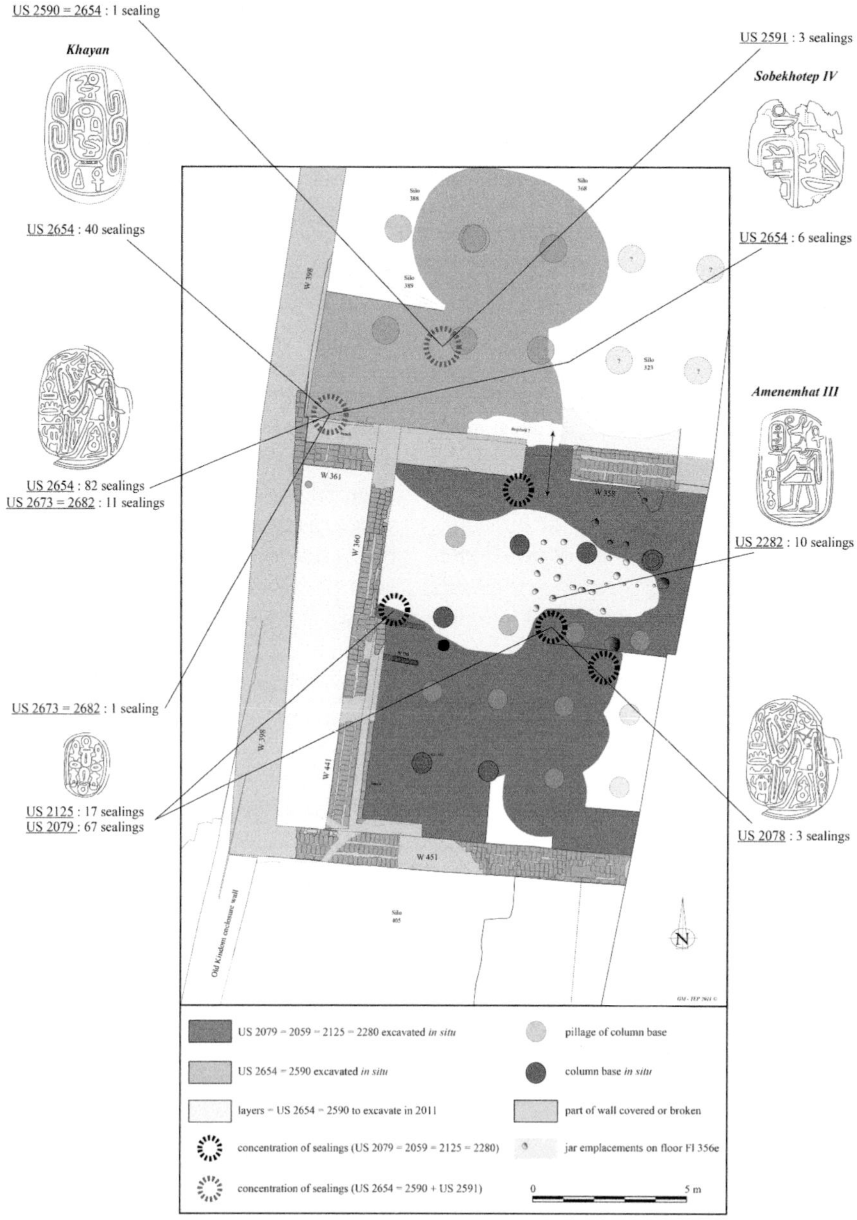

Figure 4.63. Plan of the southern and northern columned halls of the administrative complex with noted concentrations of sealings, Tell Edfu. Moeller and Marouard, *E&L* 11 (2011), fig. 7. Courtesy of Nadine Moeller and Gregory Marouard.

Kingdom layers.[1292] Imports from the Levant and the north are, however, rare and are only represented by Levantine Painted Ware and northern Marl C zirs.[1293]

Scarab seal impressions

Over 1400 seal impressions have been uncovered in the columned halls, some of which bear non-Egyptian designs.[1294] A common motif decorating 123 impressions is that of a standing male figure carrying a lotus flower (Figure 4.63).[1295] While the figure wears an Egyptian loincloth and is represented in a typical Egyptian stance, the crossed bands on the chest and the palaeography of hieroglyphs before him resemble Levantine elements akin to those on scarabs from, for example, Tell el-'Ajjul.[1296] Some have suggested that the scarab used for the sealings was made in the Southern Levant,[1297] although it is similarly possible that it was manufactured in an Egyptian workshop influenced by Levantine art forms, like that of Tell el-Dab'a. Moeller writes that the individual using this scarab could have been linked to such a workshop.[1298]

1292 The northern hall's abandonment layer also included Nubian cooking pots. Moeller, 'Tell Edfu – The 2007 Season', 5; Ayers, *E&L* 11 (2011), 115-116; Moeller and Ayers, in *Nubian Pottery*, 101-114.

1293 Personal communication with Natasha Ayers.

1294 Moeller, *NEA* 75/2 (2012), 118.

1295 Moeller, *NEA* 75/2 (2012), 121-123, fig. 14; Moeller and Marouard, *E&L* 11 (2011), 103, 110, fig. 12 [3: 2654.s.1).

1296 Ben-Tor's Design Class 10A. Moeller and Marouard, *E&L* 11 (2011), 110; Moeller, *NEA* 75/2 (2012), 121; Ben-Tor, *Scarabs*, 148; Ben-Tor, *IEJ* 47/3 (1997), 181, fig. 10.

1297 Moeller and Marouard, *E&L* 11 (2011), 103, 110; Moeller, *NEA* 75/2 (2012), 121.

1298 Moeller, *NEA* 75/2 (2012), 122.

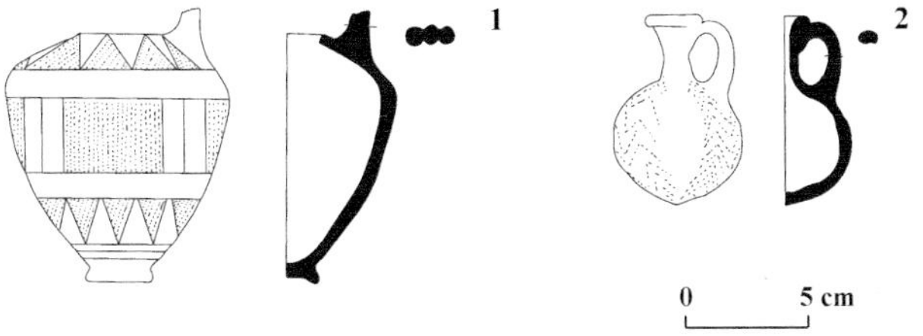

FIGURE 4.64. SELECTED CERAMICS, TELL EDFU. AFTER KAPLAN, *TELL EL YAHUDIYEH*, FIGS 17 [E], 25 [B].

He could be identified as an official from the workshop's centre, travelling to Edfu where the seal was used.[1299] Another possibility is that he could have sealed the items at the workshop, and then the products were sent to Edfu.[1300] A further scenario is that the items were sealed at Edfu after the scarab was received as a traded item or gift.[1301] The first two propositions are favoured based on the context of the seal impressions as described below.

The majority of seal impressions portraying the standing figure (82 instances) were unearthed in the northern columned hall's abandonment layer (US 2654) in a dense deposit along the western side of the room (Figure 4.63).[1302] Their back-types show impressions of round pegs, wooden material, baskets and fabric, indicating that the original scarab sealed a variety of commodities.[1303] The same deposit included 40 royal-name seal impressions of *Ḫy3n*.[1304] The back-types denote that the seals were likewise impressed onto wooden items, round pegs and fabric.[1305] Because the two types of seals are both numerous and in the same context, it is highly likely that they were created and deposited within a relatively short period of time. Thus, it has been postulated that deposit US 2654 comprised the refuse from a delivery of products imported from the Fifteenth Dynasty administration.[1306]

The published evidence makes a strong case for assigning the northern hall's abandonment layer to the early Second Intermediate Period.[1307] The Egyptian ceramic corpus shows affinities to mid-Thirteenth Dynasty and early Second Intermediate Period forms.[1308] Moreover, contexts US 2654 and US 2591 yielded sealings of Sobekhotep IV along with the impressions of *Ḫy3n* and the standing figure (Figure 4.63).[1309] This suggests that the reigns of Sobekhotep IV and *Ḫy3n* were close to one another, consequently placing *Ḫy3n* in the first half of Dynasty 15.[1310] Hence, the scarab seal impressions provide evidence of direct contact, most likely related to trade and diplomacy, between the early Fifteenth Dynasty and the Second Upper Egyptian nome.[1311]

4.5.4.3 *Other*

Earlier excavations at Tell Edfu yielded fragments of Tell el-Yahudiyah ware. Although their precise context is uncertain, their presence is worthy of mention in view of the postulated trade connections with Lower Egypt. The fragments include those of a piriform jug (Figure 4.64 [1]) decorated with three zones, the uppermost and lowermost with triangles and the central zone with rectangles.[1312] Such decoration is similar to those of Tell el-Yahudiyah jugs from Buhen[1313] and a MBIIA tomb at Tell el-'Ajjul.[1314] A wheel-made globular vessel[1315] (Figure 4.64 [2]) with parallels from Tell el-Yahudiyah[1316] was also found, its shape and decoration pointing to the Fifteenth Dynasty.[1317]

The findings shed light on relations between Upper Egypt and the north. While northern commodities reached the site during the late Twelfth or early Thirteenth Dynasty, individuals of Asiatic descent, such as *P3-ʿ3m*, may have been residing in the region from the late Thirteenth Dynasty. This period, or shortly thereafter, witnessed the import of products from the early Hyksos regime. Therefore, the evidence implies peaceful and commercial relations between Tell Edfu's officials and a Levantine-(influenced) culture from the late Twelfth or early Thirteenth Dynasty to the early Fifteenth Dynasty.

1299 Moeller, *NEA* 75/2 (2012), 122.
1300 Moeller, *NEA* 75/2 (2012), 122.
1301 Moeller, *NEA* 75/2 (2012), 122.
1302 Moeller, *NEA* 75/2 (2012), 121; Moeller and Marouard, *E&L* 11 (2011), 103, 110, fig. 7.
1303 Moeller and Marouard, *E&L* 11 (2011), 103; Moeller, *NEA* 75/2 (2012), 122, chart 3.
1304 Ben-Tor's Design Class 7B3. Moeller and Marouard, *E&L* 11 (2011), 100, 109-110, figs 7, 11 [1: 2654.s.18, 19, 35, 45, 75; 1: 2590.s.1, 3]; Moeller, *NEA* 75/2 (2012), 121; Ben-Tor, *Scarabs*, 92, 106, pl. 43 [5, 8].
1305 Moeller, *NEA* 75 /2 (2012), 123, chart 4.
1306 Moeller and Marouard, *E&L* 11 (2011), 103; Moeller, *NEA* 75/2 (2012), 123.
1307 Moeller, *NEA* 75/2 (2012), 93-106.
1308 Moeller, *NEA* 75/2 (2012), 99; Ayers, in Moeller and Marouard, *E&L* 11 (2011), 115-117, fig. 16.
1309 Moeller and Marouard, *E&L* 11 (2011), passim.
1310 The excavators note that the two rulers may be contemporaneous (Moeller and Marouard, *E&L* 11 [2011], 107). Ben-Tor writes that scarabs bearing cartouches of Thirteenth Dynasty kings are in most cases of contemporary date (Ben-Tor, *Scarabs*, 38-39, n. 127). Yet, she provides a footnote remarking on New Kingdom posthumous examples of Sobekhotep IV's seals. The king's seal impressions at Edfu, or the commodities to which they were attached, may have also been circulated for some time following his reign. As such, while the context points to the late Thirteenth Dynasty, it does not necessarily correlate Sobekhotep IV's reign with that of *Ḫy3n*. The context does, however, suggest that *Ḫy3n*'s reign should be placed in the early Fifteenth Dynasty to coincide with the ceramic evidence of the northern hall's abandonment layer. See Chapter 2.3; Porter, *GM* 239 (2013), 75-80; Forstner-Müller and Rose, in *Nubian Pottery from Egyptian Cultural Contexts*, 184.
1311 Moeller and Marouard further theorise that the sealings could represent cultic relations, perhaps donations to the temple of Horus at Tell Edfu. Moeller and Marouard, *E&L* 11 (2011), 106-107.
1312 Unpublished vessel from the Cairo Museum (JE 46743). Aston and Bietak's Levanto-Egyptian II Type I.2.1a. Merrillees, *Trade and Transcendence*, 67; Kaplan, *Tell el Yahudiyeh*, fig. 25 [b]; Aston and Bietak, *TeD* 8, 33, 144, figs 87, 99.
1313 Aston and Bietak, *TeD* 8, 144, fig. 87.
1314 Tomb 303b. Aston and Bietak, *TeD* 8, 144; Petrie, *Gaza* 3, 7, pl. 38 [60M5]; Kaplan, *Tell el Yahudiyeh*, fig. 77 [b].
1315 Stockholm MM 979. Aston and Bietak's Late Egyptian IX L.9.5a. Kaplan, *Tell el Yahudiyeh*, fig. 17 [e]; Aston and Bietak, *TeD* 8, 257, figs 187, 189.
1316 See Figure 4.29 [8].
1317 Aston and Bietak, *TeD* 8, 254-257, 552.

4.5.5 Hol, Wadi el-

Lat.Lon. 25°53'N 32°28'E

Ref. Darnell et al., *AASOR* 59 (2005), 64-124.[1318]

Chron. Late Twelfth to early Thirteenth Dynasty

Approximately halfway on a path cutting through the Qena Bend and along a route connecting Thebes with Hou, Abydos and the Western Desert oases, is Wadi el-Hol.[1319] The strategic route was accessed by military personnel, trading caravans and other individuals as evident by the graffiti left behind from the Predynastic to early Islamic periods.[1320] Most texts date between the Middle to early New Kingdom, with many assigned to the late Twelfth and early Thirteenth Dynasties.[1321] Four of these inscriptions are connected to a Levantine culture, two of which are Egyptian texts and two are linear scripts of a Northwest Semitic language.

4.5.5.1 Egyptian texts

The hieratic inscriptions date palaeographically and onomastically to the late Twelfth Dynasty.[1322] The first (A)[1323] is written within an incised border or, as epigraphers suggest, a ship's sail and mast.[1324] Based on associated texts with repeated names and titles, the inscription may be approximately dated to Amenemhat III's reign.[1325] Pertinently in the inscription is the *im.y-r3 mšꜥ n(.y) ꜥ3m.w Bbi* 'overseer of the expedition of *ꜥ3m.w*,[1326] Bebi'.[1327] The title is otherwise attested in el-Lahun's P Berlin 10004, also dated to Amenemhat III's reign.[1328] While the determinative in P Berlin 10004 was transcribed with only a seated male figure,[1329] the determinative here has both male and female figures, leading scholars to infer that the expedition included soldiers and their families.[1330] There is some evidence of women partaking in missions,[1331] so the presence of this determinative may not necessarily relate only to the *ꜥ3m* men's wives. Inscription A does indicate that Bebi was responsible for a host of foreigners, insinuating a bureau specifically for the organisation of *ꜥ3m* men and women. Related officials in the inscription, such as a 'royal messenger' and 'courier',[1332] suggest that the expedition was probably arranged by the Residence for relaying communiqués. Thus, Inscription A indicates the passage of a specialised group of Asiatics through Wadi el-Hol and under the auspices of the king, most possibly Amenemhat III.

The second inscription (B) is positioned near the first and could also be assigned to the same period.[1333] It reads: *Msy msi n Nb.t-Kpn* 'Mesy,[1334] born to Nebet-*Kpn*'.[1335] The Egyptian name referring to Baalat-Gebel, the Byblite goddess related to Hathor, signifies an awareness of the Northern Levantine city and its pantheon.[1336]

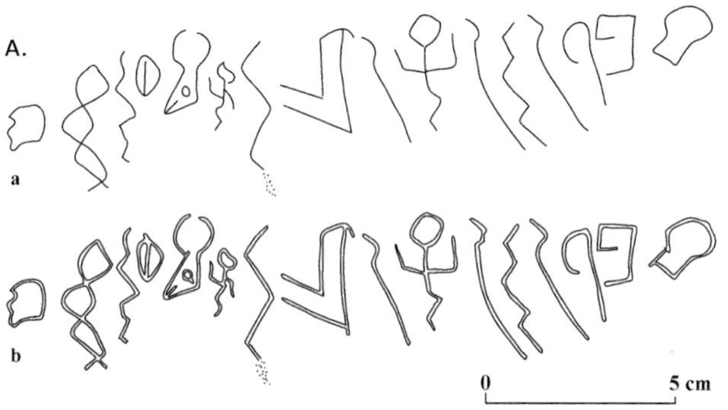

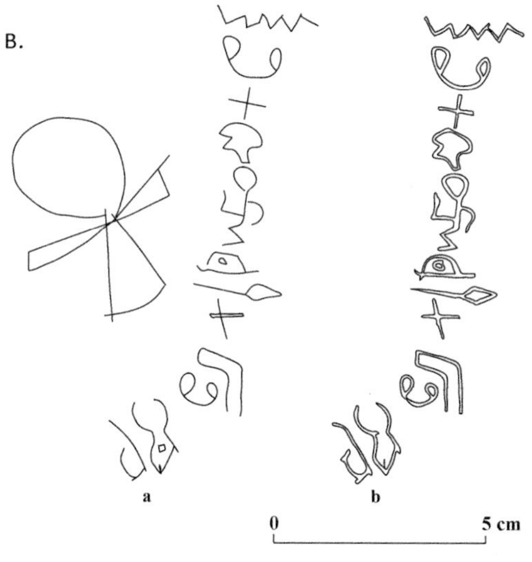

FIGURE 4.65. PROTO-ALPHABETIC INSCRIPTIONS A AND B, WADI EL-HOL. (A) INSCRIPTION A; (B) INSCRIPTION B. AFTER DARNELL, *AASOR* 59 (2005), FIG. 16.

1318 For more references on the palaeography, translation and significance of the Proto-Alphabetic texts at Wadi el-Hol, see Hamilton, *Origins of the West Semitic Alphabet*, 324, 327-328; Goldwasser, *E&L* 16 (2006), 146-150.
1319 The Wadi is along the Farshut Road. Darnell, *Theban Desert Road Survey* 1, 89, fig. 1; Darnell et al., *AASOR* 59 (2005), 73-74, fig. 1.
1320 Darnell et al., *AASOR* 59 (2005), 74.
1321 Darnell et al., *AASOR* 59 (2005), 74.
1322 Darnell et al., *AASOR* 59 (2005), 89.
1323 The complete publication of the inscriptions is in preparation. As such, the letters allocated to the inscriptions here are not as classified by epigraphers.
1324 Darnell et al., *AASOR* 59 (2005), 89.
1325 Darnell et al., *AASOR* 59 (2005), 89, 102-106, figs 23-27.
1326 Ward, *Index*, 29 [206].
1327 Ranke, *Personennamen* 1, 95 [16]; Darnell et al., *AASOR* 59 (2005), 88-89, fig. 21.
1328 See Chapter 4.3.5.2 and Appendix B.2. Kaplony-Heckel, *Handschriften* 1, 3 [4].
1329 See Appendix B.2; Kaplony-Heckel, *Handschriften* 1, 3 [4].
1330 Darnell et al., *AASOR* 59 (2005), 88.
1331 Darnell et al., *AASOR* 59 (2005), n. 7; Darnell, *Theban Desert Road Survey* 1, 119 [9].
1332 Darnell et al., *AASOR* 59 (2005), 89.
1333 Darnell et al., *AASOR* 59 (2005), 89.
1334 For a similar name, see Ranke, *Personennamen* 1, 164 [18].
1335 Ranke, *Personennamen* 1, 189 [17]; Darnell et al., *AASOR* 59 (2005), 88-89, fig. 22.
1336 See Chapter 4.3.5.2 and Appendix B.2 for UC 32196, a papyrus of Amenemhat IV's reign in which the 'lady of *Kpny*' is mentioned. See also Figure 7.9.

4.5.5.2 Proto-Alphabetic texts

Two Proto-Alphabetic inscriptions are located in an area closest to the main route (Section C).[1337] Inscribed on rock surfaces of good quality, in prominent locations and surrounded by Egyptian texts dating from the Middle Kingdom to Second Intermediate Period, the Proto-Alphabetic writings could generally be assigned to the MBIIA.[1338] They are written from right-to-left utilising signs derived from lapidary hieratic and hieroglyphic traditions (Figure 4.65A)[1339] with one of the inscriptions additionally bearing an adjoined *ꜥnḫ* symbol (Figure 4.65B). The horizontal inscription includes 16 letters (*r b l(?) n m n h n p m h(?) a š(?) m ḫ r*) and the vertical inscription has 12 (*m ṯ t r h(?) ꜥ w t p ṯ(?) a l*).[1340] Some speculative attempts have been made to decipher the texts,[1341] but only two words, Semitic *rb* 'chief' at the beginning of the horizontal inscription and the name of Levantine deity *al* 'El' at the end of the vertical inscription, have been accepted.[1342] On palaeographic and orthographic grounds, scholars have suggested a reliance on early Middle Kingdom prototypes and thus view the texts as two of the earliest recorded linear Semitic writings.[1343] Another interpretation views them as evidence for the reproduction of the Proto-Alphabetic script developed by illiterates in the Sinai.[1344]

The evidence does not allow for the inscriptions' precise dating, but it indicates that the writers were (a) Northwest Semitic; (b) knowledgeable in hieroglyphic and hieratic traditions; (c) knowledgeable in Egyptian religious symbols (i.e. the *ꜥnḫ* sign); (d) inscribing in an area heavily frequented by couriers and military personnel during the Middle Kingdom and Second Intermediate Period; and (f) inscribing in an area frequented by specialised Asiatics during late Dynasty 12. The Proto-Alphabetic inscriptions denote that literate Levantines, well-acquainted with the Egyptian language and religion, chose to mimic the Egyptians by leaving behind their own informal writings. They were not uneducated but, so far as the evidence suggests, were possibly specialists voyaging through a well-travelled route well within Egyptian territory.

1337 Darnell et al., *AASOR* 59 (2005), 75.

1338 Darnell et al., *AASOR* 59 (2005), 75, 86. For a different dating, see Sass, in *D'Ougarit à Jérusalem*, 193-203.

1339 Darnell et al., *AASOR* 59 (2005), 75-85.

1340 The transliteration follows Darnell et al., *AASOR* 59 (2005), 75-85.

1341 See, for example, Altschuler, *ANES* 39 (2002), 201-204; Wimmer and Wimmer-Dweikat, *GM* 180 (2001), 107-112.

1342 Darnell et al., *AASOR* 59 (2005), 85-86.

1343 Darnell et al., *AASOR* 59 (2005), 86-91; Hamilton, *Origins of the West Semitic Alphabet*, 295-296.

1344 Goldwasser contends that the inscriptions were by illiterates with little to no access to a papyri hieratic (Goldwasser, *E&L* 16 [2006], 146-147, 150-151). See Chapter 5.2.4.2.

4.5.6 Karnak

Lat.Lon. 25°43'N 32°40'E

Refs Helck, *MDAIK* 24 (1969), 194-200; Debono, *Cahiers de Karnak* 7 (1982), 380, pl. 1.

Chron. Mid-Thirteenth to early Fifteenth Dynasty

Specific data relating to Asiatics or the Hyksos from the period under examination is absent from Karnak, a temple precinct and Middle Kingdom settlement of the Fourth Upper Egyptian nome. Only circumstantial evidence, such as conflagration layers dating before the beginning of Dynasty 18 and statements referring to problematic foreigners and an impoverished city,[1345] hint at possible conflict. A stela of Sobekhotep IV uncovered in the Hypostyle Hall at the Karnak Temple conveys the king's dedication to Amun and Thebes.[1346] It also includes a reference to imports:

(10) *[ỉw wḏ.n ỉty] ꜥnḫ(.w) wḏꜣ(.w) s(nb.w) ỉri.t n=f sbꜣ n(.y) mḥ 10 mꜣw.t m ꜥš nfr n(.y) Ḫnty-š m ꜥꜣ.wy-rꜣ* (11)*bꜣk(.w) m nbw ḥḏ [ḥm.t ḥsmn ...] sꜣtw wꜥb m wꜣḏ.yt n.t ḥw.t-nṯr tn ḥnꜥ ỉri.(y)t n=f ꜥꜣ sn.wy-n.w* (12)*[ḥw.t]-nṯr [tn] m ꜥš mꜣꜥ nfr [n(.y) Ḫnty-š m ꜥꜣ.wy-rꜣ bꜣk(.w) m nbw ḥḏ ḥm.t ḥsmn m pr.w] Sbk-ḥtp m pr.w ỉmn(.w)*

(10) [It is the case that the sovereign], may he live, prosper and be healthy, commanded the building of a door of 10 cubits for him, made with the good *ꜥš*-wood of *Ḫnty-š* with a two-leaf door (11) worked in gold, silver, [copper and bronze ...] a pure floor in the columned hall of this temple with a second door (12) of [this temple] built for him in the true and good *ꜥš*-wood [of *Ḫnty-š* with a two-leaf door worked in gold, silver, copper and bronze, within the temple] of Sobekhotep, the temple of Amun.[1347]

The passage notes the import of *ꜥš*-wood from *Ḫnty-š*.[1348] The product is prized for its *nfr* 'good' and *mꜣꜥ* 'true' qualities. It additionally implies the pharaoh's access to the imported item and the continuance of Thirteenth Dynasty trade relations with the Northern Levant.

The settlement to the east of the temple of Amun's sacred lake additionally yielded Tell el-Yahudiyah

1345 Redford, *JSSEA* 11/4 (1981), 253-255; Vernus, *ASAE* 68 (1982), 129-135; Vernus, *RdE* 40 (1989), 145-161. Unearthed in Karnak were also fragments, likely of a gateway, featuring an inscription with Asiatic toponyms as well as offering bearers. Possibly relating to an expedition to the Northern Levant, the fragments have been dated to either the New Kingdom (perhaps Amenhotep I's reign) or the Middle Kingdom. Due to the uncertain dating, they are not examined here. For more, see Redford, *JAOS* 99/2 (1979), 270-287; le Saout, *Karnak* 8 (1987), 325-338.

1346 Helck, *MDAIK* 24 (1969), 194-198; Helck, *Historisch-biographische Texte* 2, 31-34.

1347 Transcription as in Helck, *MDAIK* 24 (1969), pl. 1. Transliteration and translation are by the author.

1348 As also in the Mit Rahina inscription. See Chapter 4.3.7 and Appendix B.3.

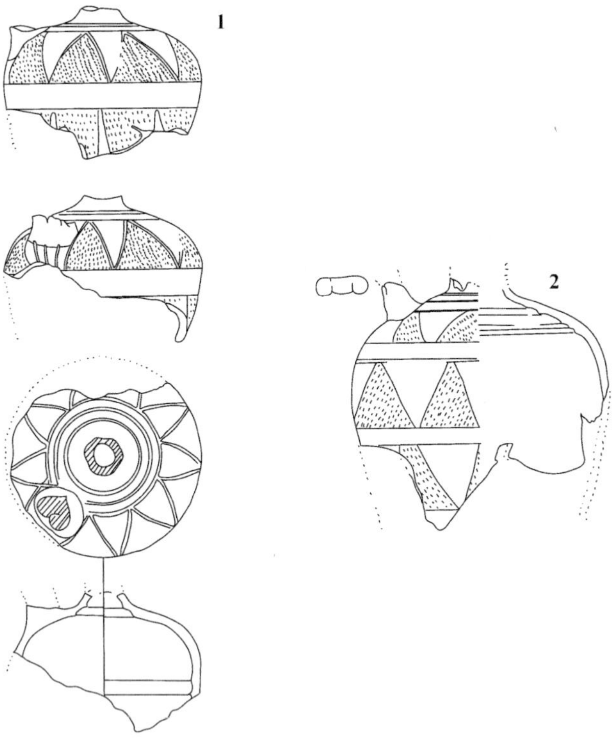

FIGURE 4.66. SELECTED CERAMICS, KARNAK (NOT TO SCALE). AFTER DEBONO, *KARNAK* 8, 128.

ware.[1349] Two fragments of piriform vessels have been published:[1350] L.S.868 with two or three zones of decoration (Figure 4.66 [1]), its closest parallels deriving from Tell el-Dab'a Strata F-E/2[1351] and Kumba, Sudan; and L.S.939 with three zones of decoration (Figure 4.66 [2]) that is also similar to a vessel from Kumba.[1352] Aston and Bietak stylistically classify these types of vessels as MBIIA or early MBIIB wares imported into Egypt between the mid-Thirteenth and early Fifteenth Dynasties.[1353]

The stela and Tell el-Yahudiyah vessels indicate the import of Levantine commodities for sacred and residential use. While Northern Levantine cedar was employed in temple architecture, the settlement's Tell el-Yahudiyah ware signifies the possible use of Levantine products for daily activities. It is therefore possible to deduce some commercial relations between Karnak and the Levant during the mid-Thirteenth and early Fifteenth Dynasties.

4.5.7 *Medamud, Nag' el-*

Lat.Lon. 25°44'N 32°42'E

Refs PM 5, 145; Bisson de la Roque, *Médamoud* 1, 67, fig. 37.

Chron. Mid-Twelfth Dynasty

Approximately five km north of Karnak is the temple of Montu at Nag' el-Medamud. The temple was extensively rebuilt by Senwosret III with further renovations added by Thirteenth Dynasty kings.[1354] A broken slab dating to Senwosret III's reign records   [...] *ḫ3s.t St.t ini.w=sn iʿb(.w)* *[r] ʿḥ nsw.t bi.ty Ḫʿ-[k3.w]-Rʿ.w* '[...] the foreign land of *St.t*, their products are presented [to] the palace of the king of Upper and Lower Egypt, Kha[kau]ra (Senwosret III)'.[1355] The text may refer to a diplomatic visit by Asiatics from *St.t*,[1356] where the imported products are distributed to temples throughout Egypt, perhaps including the temple of Montu. Due to the fragmentary nature of the inscription, only relations between Senwosret III's administration and Asiatics from *St.t* may be deduced.

Another fragment, perhaps of a gateway, is assigned between the reigns of Senwosret III and Sobekemsaf, and is decorated with bound and kneeling figures, four of whom are preserved.[1357] An accompanying block portrays the king's legs in a smiting stance with a captive before his feet, so the bound figures could have originally faced this aggressive king. Of the surviving reliefs, no distinctive facial elements can be observed; however, hieroglyphs in between the figures read  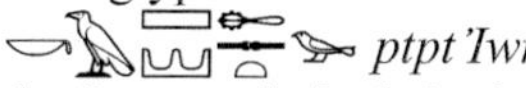 *ptpt Ꞽwn.tyw* [...] *ẖr.t K3š ẖsi.t* 'trampling the *Ꞽwn.tyw* [...], defeating the miserable *K3š*'. Hence, the fragments denote the portrayal of foreigners as subjugated enemies. Their inclusion in the temple increases the scene's *topos* as an attempt to show the king as a strong protector and controller of foreign lands and people.

[1349] They were originally identified as and with Pan-Grave pottery fragments. Lauffray, *Karnak d'Egypte*, 205.

[1350] Debono, *Cahiers de Karnak* 7 (1982), 380, pl. 1; Debono, *Cahiers de Karnak* 8 (1985), 121-122.

[1351] Aston and Bietak's Levanto-Egyptian III Type I.3.2a. Aston and Bietak, *TeD* 8, 152-169, 353-358, figs 105, 108, pls 10-14.

[1352] Aston and Bietak's Levanto-Egyptian II Type I.2.2f and I.2.2g. Aston and Bietak, *TeD* 8, 152, figs 94-96; Kaplan, *Tell el Yahudiyeh*, figs 26 [a], 27 [b].

[1353] Aston and Bietak, *TeD* 8, 553, figs 252-253.

[1354] PM 5, 145.

[1355] Bisson de la Roque, *Médamoud (1926)* 1, 67, fig. 27; Delia, *Senwosret III*, 121.

[1356] Perhaps similar to that which is mentioned in the Mit Rahina text. See Chapter 4.3.7 and Appendix B.3.

[1357] Bisson de la Roque, *Médamoud (1929)* 1, 96-97, fig. 87, pl. 10.

4.5.8 *Mostagedda*

Lat.Lon. 27°05'N 31°23'E

Refs PM 5, 6; Brunton, *Mostagedda*.

Chron. Fifteenth Dynasty

Mostagedda is located around 10km south of Asyut on the east bank of the Nile, opposite Deir Rifeh.[1358] Excavated and published by the British Museum Expedition,[1359] two main types of burials were unearthed: those adhering to Egyptian traditions; and those with elements assigned to the Pan-Grave culture.[1360] Based on the latter's degree of 'Egyptianisiation' as well as the Egyptian ceramic corpus, Bourriau identifies two archaeological phases before the Eighteenth Dynasty, both of which display increasingly close ceramic links with Upper Egypt.[1361] Williams further refines the chronology by dividing it into four, rather than two, phases from the beginning of the Fifteenth to the early Eighteenth Dynasty.[1362] The material culture of the earliest phase varies from that of nearby Deir Rifeh, leading Bourriau to suggest that Mostagedda dates slightly later than Deir Rifeh,[1363] although the differences could also be related to the status of buried individuals.[1364] Very few finds from Mostagedda attest to contact with a Levantine culture. However, because of the site's theorised strategic importance, they are listed here:

- Tell el-Yahudiyah vessel: One cylindrical jug was uncovered in Tomb 3146 with parallels from Tell el-Dab'a Stratum E/1.[1365] The tomb was assigned to Williams's Group B (early-to-mid Hyksos Age 2), despite its rectangular shape;[1366]

- Scarabs (Figure 4.67): Six scarabs from Egyptian burials and two from late Second Intermediate Pan-Grave tombs exhibit Levantine designs, including two pairs of oblong scrolls,[1367] paired scrolls united at the base along with a Levantine-style *k3* glyph,[1368] cobras confronted with animals,[1369] lions,[1370] a crocodile,[1371] a sphinx,[1372] and a standing individual with the head of a mythical figure;[1373]

- Adornment: Two oval graves, one of an adolescent (3170)[1374] and the other of an elderly female (3120),[1375] each yielded a silver torque around the neck of the deceased. Like those from Abydos and el-Lahun, the Mostagedda torques are of thick wire with hammered, coiled ends.[1376] Grave 3120 has been assigned to the beginning of the Fifteenth Dynasty,[1377] while the oval shape of Grave 3170 infers a date in the early Second Intermediate Period. Accompanying funerary equipment for both graves points to their use by Pan-Grave individuals.

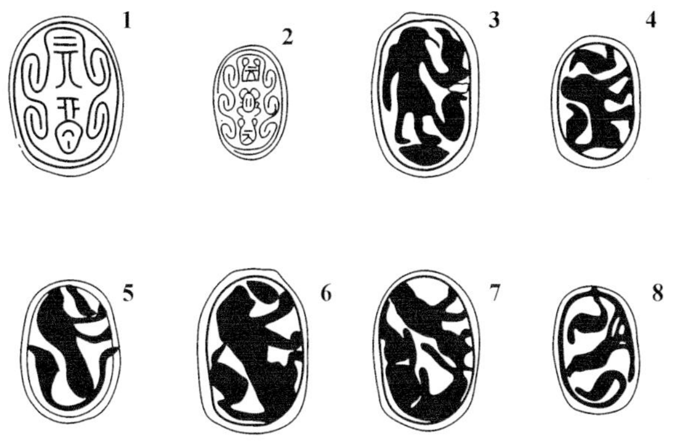

Figure 4.67. Selected scarabs, Mostagedda (not to scale). After Brunton, *Mostagedda*, pl. 69 [15-16, 32-37].

Due to the similarities between Mostagedda's ceramic corpus and that of Upper Egypt, Bourriau postulates that Mostagedda's Pan-Grave group, including mercenaries,[1378] safeguarded Theban commercial interests along the Nile. On the other hand, the inhabitants at/near Deir Rifeh would have served the Hyksos.[1379] The above evidence suggests further trade relations between Mostagedda and the north, hinting that the Pan-Grave and Egyptian cultures were not completely cut off from Levantine and Levantine-influenced products. In fact, as the latter occur in funerary

1358 See Chapter 4.4.5.

1359 Brunton, *Mostaggeda*.

1360 For example, oval and circular burial pits, Nubian pottery, and leatherworks (Brunton, *Mostaggeda*, passim).

1361 Bourriau, in *Studien zur altÄgyptischen Keramik* (Mainz, 1981), 28, figs 3-4; Bourriau, in *Studies on Ancient Egypt*, 44-45. For problems with the Egyptianisiation theory, see de Souza, *BACE* 24 (2013), 109-126.

1362 Williams, *Second Intermediate Period*, 196-199.

1363 Bourriau, in *Hyksos*, 167-168.

1364 Bourriau, in *Ancient Egypt*, 190.

1365 Aston and Bietak's Late Egyptian XII L.12.2d (Cylindrical II). Brunton, *Mostagedda*, 117, pl. 72 [60]; Aston and Bietak, *TeD* 8, 265, 513-515, figs 199, 201, pl. 107 [600-601].

1366 The rectangular shape of tombs has been argued to date to a later phase of the Second Intermediate Period. Williams, *Second Intermediate Period*, 197; de Souza, *BACE* 24 (2013), table 1.

1367 Ben-Tor's Design Class 7B2(ii). Brunton, *Mostagedda*, 127, pl. 69 [15]; Ben-Tor, *Scarabs*, 29, n. 86, pl. 16 [16].

1368 Ben-Tor's Design Class 7B3. Brunton, *Mostagedda*, pl. 69 [16]; Ben-Tor, *Scarabs*, 92.

1369 Ben-Tor's Design Class 9C3 and 9C5. Brunton, *Mostagedda*, pl. 69 [33, 37]; Ben-Tor, *Scarabs*, 95-96.

1370 Ben-Tor's Design Class 9E. Brunton, *Mostagedda*, pl. 69 [34-36]; Ben-Tor, *Scarabs*, 97.

1371 Ben-Tor's Design Class 9D. Brunton, *Mostagedda*, pl. 69 [36]; Ben-Tor, *Scarabs*, 97.

1372 Ben-Tor's Design Class 9F. Brunton, *Mostagedda*, pl. 69 [33]; Ben-Tor, *Scarabs*, 97.

1373 Ben-Tor's Design Class 10A. Brunton, *Mostagedda*, pl. 69 [32]; Ben-Tor, *Scarabs*, 98.

1374 Brunton, *Mostagedda*, 118, pl. 65 [18].

1375 Brunton, *Mostagedda*, 116, pl. 65 [16].

1376 Brunton, *Mostagedda*, 129. See Chapters 4.3.5.1 and 4.5.1.2.

1377 Bourriau, in *Studien zur altÄgyptischen Keramik*, 37, fig. 3 [7]. Williams's Group A (early-to-mid Hyksos Age 1; Williams, *Second Intermediate Period*, 196) and de Souza's Stage 2 (de Souza, *BACE* 24 [2013], table 1).

1378 Only 11 out of the 107 tombs at Mostagedda had weapons, signalling that the individuals at the site were not all associated with a militaristic profession (that is, assuming that weapons in a tomb point to the interred's occupation as a soldier, which is not always the case). See Liszka, *Medjay and Pangrave*, 491-509, table 21.

1379 Liszka, *Medjay and Pangrave*, 23; Bourriau, in *Studies on Ancient Egypt*, 46; Bourriau, in *Ancient Egypt*, 190; Bourriau, in *Second Intermediate Period*, 23.

contexts, a certain symbolic significance was attributed to the items, denoting some cultural influence from the north. Such influence was not restricted to trade but, in reference to the torques, could be status signifiers. Unlike prior suppositions, the data supports contact between the Pan-Grave and Levantine cultures at Mostagedda during Dynasty 15, although it was seemingly only occurring to a limited degree.

4.5.9 Rizaiqat, el-

Lat.Lon. 25°36'N 32°28'E

Refs PM 5, 161-162; Priese, *Ägyptische Museum*, 58 [37]; Martin, *Altägyptischen Denkmäler* 1, 97-100.

Chron. Thirteenth Dynasty to early Second Intermediate Period

Opposite Tod on the west bank of the Nile lies the cemetery of el-Rizaiqat. Two stelae reportedly from the site refer to Asiatics in the region.[1380] Both date between Dynasty 13 and the early Second Intermediate Period.[1381] The references are provided below.

Stela of Montuhotep (Berlin 22.708)[1382]

ꜥ3m.t S3.t-Ḥw.t-ḥr

ꜥ3m.t Sat-Hathor[1384]

Stela of Montusewew (Bremen 4558)[1383]

ꜥ3m.t [...*ḥr*...]

ꜥ3m.t [...*ḥr*...]

The similarities between the two stelae, including palaeography of signs, selection of depicted offerings and individuals, as well as the name of Montuhotep's and Montusewew's mother (Benenet), implies that the two individuals were kin,[1385] possibly creating their stelae in the same workshop. Berlin 22.708 shows Montuhotep standing before offerings. His body is coloured red yet his face is left unpainted and thus chalk-white. Between his legs is a mummiform figure with the translated label written behind Montuhotep's lower body. Some have suggested that the figure is of Montuhotep's deceased wife,[1386] but it is also possible that she is a deceased daughter. Bremen 4558 represents a similar case in which the woman, a *ꜥ3m.t*, is mummiform in shape.[1387] She stands behind Montusewew who, like Montuhotep, is illustrated with his body painted red and his face left uncoloured. Both stelae owners have shoulder-length hair and a long beard.

The portrayal of the *ꜥ3m.t* women denotes that they had accepted Egyptian fashion and funerary customs. While the white faces of the men may be reflective of a connection to Osiris, they could also indicate their foreign origin, much like the 'fair-skinned men' at Beni Hassan.[1388] If so, the stelae could belong to brothers of Asiatic descent. If they were not of Asiatic descent, they were evidently related to Asiatic individual(s),[1389] providing evidence for marital relations involving acculturated Asiatic women during the Thirteenth Dynasty or early Second Intermediate Period.

4.5.10 Tjauti, Gebel

Lat.Lon. 26°11'N 31°55'E

Ref. Darnell, *Theban Desert Road Survey* 1, 56-58.

Chron. Thirteenth Dynasty

Gebel Tjauti is situated on the west side of the Qena Bend, on a path connecting Thebes with Hou and Abydos.[1390] Inscriptions at the site attest to the route's use by military personnel and traders throughout the Predynastic to Coptic periods.[1391] Second Intermediate Period towers on the path north of western Thebes also indicate its strategic significance.[1392] Three rock graffiti inscribed on the Gebel Tjauti Inscription Shelf (Sections 17-18) present Asiatics.[1393] The texts are stylistically similar, suggesting that they were carved around the same time or by the same person.[1394] They are written from right to left and have been dated paleographically and onomastically to the Thirteenth Dynasty:[1395]

14. 

im.y-ḫt s3-pr.w ꜥ3m

Police official,[1396] *ꜥ3m*

15. 

im.y-ḫt Nḥy s3 ꜥ3m

Attendant,[1397] Nehy's[1398] son, *ꜥ3m*

1380 Both were bought at Luxor but attributed to el-Rizaiqat. PM 5, 162; Martin, *Altägyptischen Denkmäler* 1, 97.

1381 For further comments regarding the stelae's date, see Priese, *Ägyptische Museum*, 58 [37]; Martin, *Altägyptischen Denkmäler* 1, 97-100; Schneider, *Ausländer in Ägypten* 2, 29-30.

1382 Transcription as in Priese, *Ägyptische Museum*, 58 [37]; Schneider, *Ausländer in Ägypten* 2, 29. Transliteration and translation are by the author.

1383 Transcription as in Martin, *Altägyptischen Denkmäler* 1, 97-100; Schneider, *Ausländer in Ägypten* 2, 30. Transliteration and translation are by the author.

1384 Ranke, *Personennamen* 1, 291 [14].

1385 Martin, *Altägypt-ischen Denkmäler* 1, 98; Schneider, *Ausländer in Ägypten* 2, 29-30.

1386 Schneider, *Ausländer in Ägypten* 2, 29; Priese, *Ägyptische Museum*, 58 [37]; Wildung, in *Pharaonen und Fremde*, 137.

1387 Martin, *Altägyptischen Denkmäler*, 97-100.

1388 See Chapters 4.4.1.2, 4.4.1.3 and Plate 1.

1389 Although the woman's name in Bremen 4558 is damaged, it may be the same as that of Berlin 22.708. If so, perhaps the two are the same individual.

1390 The path is along the Alamat Tal road. Darnell, *Theban Desert Road Survey* 1, 5, fig. 1.

1391 Darnell, *Theban Desert Road Survey* 1, 5-10.

1392 Darnell, *Theban Desert Road Survey* 1, 9.

1393 Darnell, *Theban Desert Road Survey* 1, 56-58, pls 2, 7 [a-b], 16 [a-b], 32 [c-d], 33 [a-b].

1394 Darnell, *Theban Desert Road Survey* 1, 56.

1395 Transcriptions as presented in Darnell, *Theban Desert Road Survey* 1, 56-58. Transliterations and translations are by the author.

1396 Ward, *Index*, 54 [431].

1397 Ward, *Index*, 54 [429].

1398 Ranke, *Personennamen* 1, 207 [15].

16. 
im.y-ḫt ꜥꜣm sꜣ im.y-rꜣ ḥm.tyw Rn-snb(.w)
Attendant, ꜥꜣm's son, overseer of metalworkers,[1399] Renseneb(u)[1400]

Sharing ꜥꜣm's title and name is an *im.y-ḫt sꜣ-pr.w Nḥy sꜣ ꜥꜣm* attested in the Thirteenth Dynasty Papyrus Boulaq 18/1.[1401] It is probable that the two are the same person, thereby supporting a Thirteenth Dynasty date for the inscriptions. As ꜥꜣm in Papyrus Boulaq 18/1 was a 'police official', then it is also possible that Inscriptions 14-15 refer to the same official, with that in Inscription 16 being ꜥꜣm's son. Like the texts at Wadi el-Hol,[1402] the graffiti at Gebel Tjauti imply that Asiatics passed through the desert route, perhaps on an expedition. Their security roles further emphasise Asiatics' employment in the administration. Moreover, as Inscriptions 14-16 combine hieroglyphic and hieratic elements, they highlight the Asiatics' knowledge of both Egyptian scripts.

4.5.11 Tod

Lat.Lon. 25°35'N 32°32'E

Refs PM 5, 167-169; Bisson de la Roque, *Tôd*; Bisson de la Roque, *Le Trésor de Tôd;* Bisson de la Roque, Contenau and Chapouthier, *Le Trésor de Tôd*; Helck, in *Ägypten, Dauer und Wandel*, 45-52; Barbotin and Clère, *BIFAO* 91 (1991), 1-32; Redford, *JSSEA* 17/1 (1987), 35-57; Pierrat, *BSFE* 130 (1994), 18-28; Menu, *BSFE* 130 (1994), 29-45.

Chron. Early Twelfth Dynasty

Tod is located on the east bank of the Nile, 25km south of Thebes. Dating from at least the Fifth Dynasty to the Ptolemaic Dynasty and possibly restored by Senwosret I are the remains of the temple of Montu.[1403]

4.5.11.1 Inscription of Senwosret I (?)

Upon the west face of the rear wall, south of the axial doorway of the temple, is an inscription assigned to Senwosret I's reign or, more securely, to the rule of a king named 'Senwosret'.[1404] Pertinent passages are as follows:[1405]

(x+3) 
[... *Iwn.tyw*...]
[... *Iwn.tyw*...]

(x+26) 
... *m bꜣk.t ḫꜣs.tyw smn.tyw*[1406] *ḫns.w [tꜣ.w]* ...
... and the labour of the foreigners and the emissaries who travel across [the lands]...

(x+32) 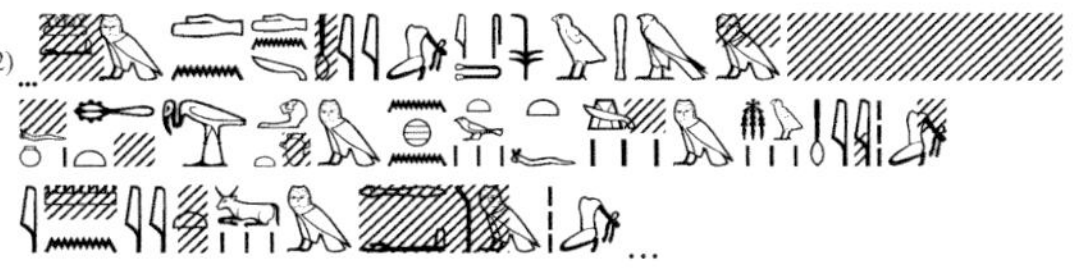
...[*šꜣꜥ*][1407] *m dndn [ḫr.]wy isṯ sw ḥm Ḥr.w*[1408] *m* [...]*=f n.w ḫ.t dšr(.w) ḥꜣ.ty[-ib] m nḫn.t=f nm.t msi.w ḫr.wy i[mn].y[t] m [ꜥꜣm.w]* ...
... [beginning] with the slaughter of the enemy while he, the majesty of Horus was [...] of the body, furious in his youth, the slaughterhouse was the children of the enemy, the daily offerings were the [*ꜥꜣm.w*] ...

(x+35) 
... [...] *ḥr wbd ꜥꜣ(mw?)*...[1409]
... [...] upon burning the *ꜥꜣ(mw?)*...

(x+36) 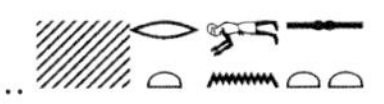
... [...]*r.t ḥr n(.y) St.t*[1410]
... [...] the falling of *St.t*

(x+37) 
[*Nḥs*]*.yt ꜥꜣm.t ḥr s.t n.t nb* [...][1411]
[The *Nḥs.yt*] and *ꜥꜣm.t* (speak) about the lady of the lord [...]

The fragmentary inscription begins with an encomium (x+1-13), perhaps with mythological undertones, followed by a recount of the king's journey to a temple where rites are then officiated (x+14-26). A direct speech by the king intervenes with a description of the temple's ruin (x+26-29), the punishment of local and foreign enemies (x+30-38) and the king's temple renovations and festivities (x+50-63). The account closes with a second-person eulogy directed to the king (x+64-66).[1412]

The text coordinates religious and political material to express the roles and responsibilities of the pharaoh.[1413] In the references to Asiatics, it is possible to discern two key representations. The first (x+26) mentions foreign labour with a determinative illustrating a seated, bound captive with the coiffed, possibly mushroom-shaped, hairstyle

1399 Ward, *Index*, 38 [281].
1400 Ranke, *Personnenamen* 1, 222 [26].
1401 See Chapter 4.5.3.
1402 See Chapter 4.5.5.
1403 For more on recent excavations, see the project's website ('Tod', *Institut français d'archéologie orientale, Caire*).
1404 Buchberger proposes a New Kingdom date, but a Middle Kingdom context is more accurate. Only the names of a Senwosret are identified in the fragmentary text. Based on Senwosret I's extensive additions to the temple of Montu as well as his policies, the inscription's dedication by this king is most likely. Helck, in *Ägypten, Dauer und Wandel*, 45-52; Redford, *JSSEA* 17/1 (1987), 37, 44-45; Barbotin and Clère, *BIFAO* 91 (1991), 1-3; Obsomer, *Le Muséon* 122 (1999), 265-266; Buchberger, in *Von Reichlich Ägyptischem Verstande*, 15-21.
1405 Transcriptions as presented in Buchberger, in *Von Reichlich Ägyptischem Verstande*, fig. 3; Redford, *JSSEA* 17/1 (1987), figs 1-2. Transliterations and translations are by the author.
1406 See Redford, *JSSEA* 17/1 (1987), 49, n. 41.
1407 Barbotin and Clère, *BIFAO* 91 (1991), 24, n. 117.
1408 Barbotin and Clère, *BIFAO* 91 (1991), 24, n. 118.
1409 Barbotin and Clère, *BIFAO* 91 (1991), 25, n. 127; Redford, *JSSEA* 17/1 (1987), 43.
1410 Or *ḫr.n St.t* 'the *St.t* have fallen'. The toponym is suggested by Barbotin and Clère, *BIFAO* 91 (1991), 25, n. 128.
1411 Barbotin and Clère, *BIFAO* 91 (1991), 25, n. 129.
1412 Redford theorises that the king's speech is before the court in *JSSEA* 17/1 (1987), 44. For similar divisions of the text's narrative, see Barbotin and Clère, *BIFAO* 91 (1991), 28-29.
1413 The inscription has been described as an early *Königsnovelle*. Helck, in *Ägypten, Dauer und Wandel*, 49; Muhlestein, *JESHO* 51 (2008), 189.

of Asiatics. This may either reflect the employment of foreigners or the placement of foreign captives in service for the temple. It also indicates the appeal, and perhaps exotic nature, of foreign labour in Egypt, implying the presence of Asiatics as far south as Tod. The second portrayal (x+32, x+35-37) is of bellicose activity against rebels, Asiatics and Nubians, the reason for which is described in lines x+26-x+32 and assumed to be the devastation of the southern temples.[1414] Placing the blame on foreigners is likely a royally-instigated *topos* portrayal of the king inscribed on what was believed to be sacred walls.[1415] The ideological representation of the *other* is therefore heightened, emphasising the king's sacrosanct duty to pacify foreigners.[1416]

4.5.11.2 The Tod treasure

Four copper chests were uncovered beneath the stone foundations of the temple of Montu,[1417] two of which are incised with the name of Amenemhat II.[1418] The chests were buried neatly in pure sand in the temple's Middle Kingdom corridor pavement, supporting their purposeful deposition at one time.[1419] The stratigraphy does not eliminate the possibility of a burial following Amenemhat II's reign,[1420] so scholars have assigned the chests to various epochs in the Middle and New Kingdoms.[1421] However, analyses of the objects within the chests support a date contemporary to Amenemhat II's rule.

The chests contained raw and manufactured imported products. Some are complete while others show signs of deliberate damage.[1422] This 'treasure' comprised gold objects (one cup, two fleurettes and 10 ingots), silver objects (jewellery, a mirror, figurines, pendants, a holster and more than 150 cups and bowls), copper objects (four boxes with nails and two shafts), products of lapis lazuli (cylinder, stamp and scarabs seals, pendants, plaques, beads, figurines and lumps), as well as small items of other minerals (carnelian, quartz, obsidian and amethyst).[1423]

The quality and quantity of assets within the chests point to their foreign origin. Lead isotope analysis on 53 silver samples suggests separate sources for the silver (the Taurus Mountains and the Aegean).[1424] The lapis lazuli indicates a Central Asian origin, a provenance confirmed by Porada's study on the treasure's seals which showed some stylistic similarities to those from Eastern Iran and possibly Afghanistan.[1425] Two cylinder seals bear Mesopotamian influences assigned to the Third Dynasty of Ur and the First Dynasty of Isin.[1426] Northern Levantine elements are additionally reflected in the designs of a few seals[1427] and pieces of jewellery,[1428] with Lilyquist stressing a northern origin for the granulated gold set on one of the silver bracelets.[1429] The shape of the silver vessels has parallels across Anatolia, the Northern Levant and Crete[1430] while a metrological analysis of the ingots proposed a similarity with a Near Eastern standard of weight.[1431] Therefore, the Tod treasure collects an assortment of valuable products imported from a number of sources across the Eastern Mediterranean and the Northern Levant.

The placement of such a medley of imported items could be either functional or ritualistic. A functional purpose would entail the chests' burial as a means for safekeeping.[1432] The items could have been donated to the temple's treasury and then, after accumulation, packed and (re-)buried in the chests.[1433] The chests may have also been offered as a ritualistic donation to Montu.[1434] Based on the inscriptions of Amenemhat II's cartouche as well as the specific mention of the ruler's relation to Montu,[1435] the latter proposition is favoured. Still, it remains questionable as to how the treasure was amassed. Many theories have been proposed, such as the chests' connection to tribute or booty or a Northern Levantine ruler's dispatch of goods collected over a period of time.[1436]

The Mit Rahina inscription offers further insight.[1437] Recording imported commodities from expeditions during Amenemhat II's reign, the text references the dispersal of products across Egypt and names the temple of Montu at

1414 Redford, *JSSEA* 17/1 (1987), 36-44, 46; Redford, *Egypt, Canaan and Israel*, 75-76.

1415 See Barbotin and Clère, *BIFAO* 91 (1991), 30.

1416 For more on the historicity of the text, see Muhlestein, *JESHO* 51 (2008), 191-193.

1417 Bisson de la Roque, *Tôd*, 113-121; Bisson de la Roque, *Le Trésor de Tôd*, 11; Bisson de la Roque, Contenau and Chapouthier, *Le Trésor de Tôd*, 7.

1418 CG 70502 of the Cairo Museum and E. 15128 of the Louvre Museum. Bisson de la Roque, *Le Trésor de Tôd*, 2-11, pls 1-2; Bisson de la Roque, Contenau and Chapouthier, *Le Trésor de Tôd*, 7-9.

1419 Bisson de la Roque, *Le Trésor de Tôd*, 10-11; Bisson de la Roque, Contenau and Chapouthier, *Le Trésor de Tôd*, 7; Lilyquist, *BASOR* 290-291 (1993), 35; Pierrat, *BSFE* 130 (1994), 19, 22-23.

1420 Pierrat, *BSFE* 130 (1994), 22-23; Lilyquist, *BASOR* 290-291 (1993), 35.

1421 For instance, see Bisson de la Roque, Contenau and Chapouthier, *Le Trésor de Tôd*, 15-35; Kemp and Merrillees, *Minoan Pottery*, 290-296; Porada, in *Societies and Languages*, 285-303; Laffineur, *Aegeum* 2 (1988), 17-30; Warren and Hankey, *Aegean Bronze Age Chronology*, 131-134; Pierrat, *BSFE* 130 (1994), 20-23, and references.

1422 The silver cups, for example, appear to be intentionally crushed. Bisson de la Roque, *Le Trésor de Tôd;* Bisson de la Roque, Contenau and Chapouthier, *Le Trésor de Tôd*; Kemp and Merrillees, *Minoan Pottery*, 295; Marcus, *E&L* 17 (2007), 158.

1423 Marcus, *E&L* 17 (2007), 158; Bisson de la Roque, *Le Trésor de Tôd;* Bisson de la Roque, Contenau and Chapouthier, *Le Trésor de Tôd.*

1424 Menu, *BSFE* 130 (1994), 41-42.

1425 Porada, in *Societies and Languages*, 285-303.

1426 Porada, in *Societies and Languages*, 285-303.

1427 Porada, in *Societies and Languages*, 285-303.

1428 Lilyquist, *BASOR* 290-291 (1993), 35-36.

1429 Lilyquist, *BASOR* 290-291 (1993), 36.

1430 Maxwell-Hyslop, *Anatolian Studies* 45 (1995), 243-250; Warren and Hankey, *Aegean Bronze Age Chronology*, 131-134.

1431 Laffineur, *Aegeum* 2 (1988), 23-24.

1432 Kemp and Merrillees, *Minoan Pottery*, 295-296; Porada, in *Societies and Languages*, 292; Pierrat, *BSFE* 130 (1994), 22-23; Maxwell-Hyslop, *Anatolian Studies* 45 (1995), 243-244; Kantor, in *Chronologies in Old World Archaeology*, 20.

1433 Porada, in *Societies and Languages*, 292; Kemp and Merrillees, *Minoan Pottery*, 295-296.

1434 Kemp and Merrillees, *Minoan Pottery*, 295-296; Montet, *Kêmi* 16 (1962), 91-96; Marcus, *E&L* 17 (2007), 160.

1435 Marcus, *E&L* 17 (2007), 158-160; Lilyquist, *BASOR* 290-291 (1993), 35-36; Pierrat, *BSFE* 130 (1994), 22-23.

1436 Bisson de la Roque, Contenau and Chapouthier, *Le Trésor de Tôd*, 32; Maxwell-Hyslop, *Anatolian Studies* 45 (1995), 250; Vandier, *Syria* 18 (1937), 174-182.

1437 See Chapter 4.3.7 and Appendix B.3.

Tod as one receiver of Amenemhat II's endowment.[1438] Marcus provides some correlations between the products from *Ḫnty-š* and those of the Tod chests, including 23kg of silver in the text compared to an estimated 13 to 18kg in the treasure, or the *ꜥ3m* seal as well as other minerals mentioned from *Ḫnty-š*.[1439] Despite the parallels between the two, linking the Mit Rahina text with the Tod treasure remains circumstantial.[1440] Nonetheless, the text hints that such items of quality and quantity were most likely products of trade, possibly from a Northern Levantine source with access to a wide-range of products. It also supports the ritualistic function of the treasure as an endowment to Montu. As for who dedicated the chests, the inscriptions naming Amenemhat II,[1441] combined with the stylistic date of the seals as well as the Mit Rahina text, suggest that Amenemhat II donated the treasure to a temple that was restored by his father.[1442]

It is clear that the treasure's deposition was purposeful and possibly symbolic, hence the assortment of products should be seen in the same light. The administration would have surely known the value of the items within the chests, notwithstanding the silver chests themselves. The collection featured products from the north and the northeast, ideologically reflecting the pharaoh's access to these areas and his ability to extract valuable resources for his godly patrons.[1443] It additionally denotes the administration's duty to appease the gods with imported luxury products,[1444] effectually implying the king's attempt to ritualistically ensure the continuance of successful trading expeditions. Therefore, the treasure represents the importance of maintaining continued trade relations with the Levant during the early Twelfth Dynasty, not only for commercial reasons but also for the maintenance of the pharaoh's prestige in the worldly and heavenly spheres.

1438 M9-10. See Chapter 4.3.7 and Appendix B.3.
1439 Marcus, *E&L* 17 (2007), 158.
1440 Marcus, *E&L* 17 (2007), 158.
1441 It is rare for endowments to be buried only with inscriptions of former rulers. Lilyquist, *BASOR* 290-291 (1993), 35.
1442 Pierrat, *BSFE* 130 (1994), 22-24; Lilyquist, *BASOR* 290-291 (1993), 35-36; Marcus, *E&L* 17 (2007), 158-160; Wastlhuber, *Die Beziehungen zwischen Ägypten und der Levante*, 100-101, 151-152, 180-181.
1443 Marcus, *E&L* 17 (2007), 160.
1444 Wastlhuber, *Die Beziehungen zwischen Ägypten und der Levante*, 180-181.

4.6 Selected Literary Texts and Unprovenanced Artefacts

4.6.1 *Berlin Execration Bowls*

Ref. Sethe, *Ächtung feindlicher Fürsten.*

Chron. Mid-late Twelfth Dynasty

The Berlin bowls constitute one of the largest corpora of Middle Kingdom Execration Texts. The hieratic texts are written on 289 broken red ceramics purchased in Luxor and now in Berlin.[1445] They are thought to derive from one of the graves of the west Theban necropolis.[1446] Sethe originally assigned the vessels to the Eleventh Dynasty or the end of the EB IV/MB I period.[1447] The dating altered with Posener's publication of the Saqqara figurines, after which the Berlin bowls were accordingly placed in the late Twelfth Dynasty or MBIIA period, around a generation before the Saqqara texts.[1448] Cohen notes an unpublished evaluation of the bowls' physical characteristics by Do. Arnold, writing that they are typical of the first half of the Twelfth Dynasty, between the reigns of Senwosret I and Amenemhat II.[1449] A dating of the texts to the mid-late Twelfth Dynasty is favoured here. Like the Saqqara figurines, the bowls feature a rebellion formula followed by lists of individuals and groups. These include Egyptians, Nubians, Libyans and Asiatics. Entries regarding the latter are provided in Appendix B.6.

The collected sherds specifically name 29 rulers governing a sum of 14 lands (e1-30). One entry is listed for the combined rulers of *Yisipi* (e31) and four more toponyms are recorded in the entries for the *ꜥ3m.w* inhabitants (f1-21), thereby bringing the total of foreign lands to 19.[1450] The texts add the *ḥnk.w* 'acquaintances' of each ruler, as well as the *nḫt.w* 'strong men', *wt n.w nmt.t* 'quick men', *sm3.w* 'allies' and *dmḏ.yw* 'assemblies' of the *ꜥ3m.w* inhabitants (g1-4). The *Mntw* of *St.t* are also mentioned (g5).

The ratio between rulers and regions has led scholars to interpret the texts as a portrayal of a tribal Levantine society.[1451] However, their nature and function as well as the medium upon which they are written,[1452] warn against forming such conclusions. The texts were most likely associated with ritualistic purposes.[1453] Their red

1445 Sethe *Ächtung feindlicher Fürsten*, 5-7.
1446 Sethe, *Ächtung feindlicher Fürsten*, 5-7.
1447 Sethe, *Ächtung feindlicher Fürsten*, 18, 21.
1448 See Chapter 4.3.8 and Appendix B.4. For a review of the various proposed dates, see Thompson, *Historicity of the Patriarchal Narratives*, 98-113. See also Redford, *Egypt, Canaan and Israel*, 88; Ben-Tor, in *Essays on Ancient Israel*, 64-65; Cohen, *Canaanites, Chronologies, and Connections*, 16-17.
1449 Cohen, *Canaanites, Chronologies, and Connections*, 16-17, n. 14.
1450 The lands not mentioned in the list naming particular rulers are *Kpny*, *ꞽw3ti*, *Yꞽ3m(w)t*, *Dmitiw* and *St.t*. *Yꞽ3m(w)t* is mentioned twice, but is counted here as one.
1451 Sethe, *Ächtung feindlicher Fürsten*, 43-45; Albright, *BASOR* 184 (1966), 26-35; Aharoni, *Land of the Bible*, 133; Redford, *Egypt, Canaan and Israel*, 91.
1452 See Chapter 4.3.8 and Appendix B.4. Posener, *Princes et pays*, 40-43; Cohen, *Canaanites, Chronologies, and Connections*, 48.
1453 For a greater discussion, see Cohen, *Canaanites, Chronologies, and*

colour and broken fragments suggest that the bowls were deliberately broken in ceremonial execration rites as, for instance, Ritner's 'Breaking the Red Pots' ritual.[1454] This infers that the ceremony itself may have influenced the selection of rulers, which was heavily reliant on the scribes' resources as well as the quality and quantity of the ceramics employed.

An additional clue that the ratio between rulers and regions could be suggestive of various interpretations comes from the entry for *Šwtw* (e4-e6). Three rulers are listed in the Berlin texts but the same toponym occurs in the Brussels figurines as an Upper *Šwtw* and a Lower *Šwtw*, each with a different ruler.[1455] As no such divisions are written for the toponyms in the Berlin bowls, the inclusion of several rulers for one foreign land may simply be due to scribal choice.

As such, the Berlin bowls cannot be considered as a notation on the foreigners' social structure or as a definitive reflection on the political situation in the Levant.[1456] Yet, they do imply the presence of Egyptian records on the geography and ruling elite of Levantine regions. Such records highlight Twelfth Dynasty interests in Levantine politics as well as the ideological subjugation of foreigners for the benefit of Egyptian prosperity and security.

4.6.2 Instructions of Amenemhat I

Refs Helck, *Lehre Amenemhets I.*; Adrom, *Lehre des Amenemhet.*

Chron. Early Twelfth Dynasty (reign of Senwosret I)

The Instructions of Amenemhat I follow the teachings of Amenemhat I to his son, Senwosret I, after a possible attempted assassination on the former king. Preserved on several papyri, tablets and ostraca of the New Kingdom,[1457] the text includes the accomplishments of Amenemhat I as well as the duties imparted upon his son. Current consensus assigns it to Senwosret I's reign, following the posited assassination of Amenemhat I in Year 30 and his son's rise to the throne.[1458]

One portrayal of foreigners appears in the didactic text and presents Amenemhat I's success in overpowering non-Egyptians:[1459]

(12) *ꞽw ḳnb.n(=ꞽ) mꜣꞽ.w ꞽnꞽ.n=ꞽ msḥ.w ꞽw ḏꞽ.n=ꞽ Wꜣwꜣ.yw ꞽnꞽ.n=ꞽ Mḏꜣ.yw ꞽm ḏꞽ.n=ꞽ ꞽrꞽ.y=ꞽ ḥr St.tyw ḥr šm.t ṯsm.w*

(12) I have subjugated lions and I have caught crocodiles. I have placed/suppressed[1460] the *Wꜣwꜣ.yw* and I have caught the *Mḏꜣ.yw*. I caused that the *St.tyw* do the walk of the dogs.

The composer equates lions with *Wꜣwꜣ.yw*, crocodiles with *Mḏꜣ.yw* and *St.tyw* with dogs. Such a *topos* representation places foreigners on par with animals.[1461] They are wild, resilient and, as elements of nature, must be pacified by the king.

4.6.3 Papyrus Brooklyn 35.1446

Ref. Hayes, *Papyrus Brooklyn.*

Chron. Mid-Thirteenth Dynasty (reign of Sobekhotep III)

In the late nineteenth century, fragments of a papyrus originally over two metres in length were purchased in Egypt.[1462] Papyrus Brooklyn 35.1446, which is thought to be from Thebes,[1463] features entries concerning administrative lists, letters, decrees and deeds, the majority of which are connected to the *ẖnr.t wr* 'main enclosure'.[1464] Palaeographically, the entries on the recto have been dated to the late Twelfth and Thirteenth Dynasties, from around Amenemhat III's reign to either Sobekhotep II or III. Those on the verso are attributed to Sobekhotep III's reign,[1465] primarily due to the inclusion of the king's nomen[1466] and decrees addressed to Ankhu, a vizier in Khendjer's administration[1467] who is also attested in Papyrus Boulaq 18.[1468]

Connections, 48; Redford, *Egypt, Canaan and Israel*, 89; Ritner, *Egyptian Medical Practice*, 136-153.

1454 Ritner, *Egyptian Medical Practice*, 144-147.

1455 Appendix B.4, E52-E53. See also Alt, *ZDPV* 64 (1941), 37; Thompson, *Historicity of the Patriarchal Narratives*, 115-116.

1456 Helck infers that the numerous rulers may belong to several generations (Helck, *Die Beziehungen Ägyptens*, 67). Thompson also mentions the differences with texts of the Berlin bowls that name certain locales with varying numbers of rulers (Thompson, *Historicity of the Patriarchal Narratives*, 113-117). See also Cohen, *Canaanites, Chronologies, and Connections*, 48; Rainey, in *Archaeological and Historical Studies* 1, 289-292.

1457 Griffith, *ZÄS* 34 (1896), 35-51; Helck, *Lehre Amenemhets I*; Adrom, *Lehre des Amenemhet.*; Quirke, *Egyptian Literature*, 129.

1458 Another proposition dates the text to the period of their co-regency. Posener, *Littérature et politique*, 61-86; Simpson, in *Ancient Egyptian Literature*, 438, n. 20; Grajetzki, *Middle Kingdom*, 33; Cohen, *Canaanites, Chronologies, and Connections*, 37; Lichtheim, *Ancient Egyptian Literature* 1, 136.

1459 Papyrus Sallier II, 12. Transcription follows Adrom, *Lehre des Amenemhet*, 68-70. Transliteration and translation are by the author.

1460 Adrom, *Lehre des Amenemhet*, 69. Ostraca Petrie 77 and Malinine contain *dꜣr.n=ꞽ* 'I subdued', the more frequently translated version as in Lichtheim, *Ancient Egyptian Literature* 1, 137.

1461 Posener, *Littérature et politique*, 63, 78-79; Cohen, *Canaanites, Chronologies and Connections*, 37, ns 35-36.

1462 Hayes, *Papyrus Brooklyn*, 5-6.

1463 Hayes originally theorised that the papyrus came from a tomb in Thebes, probably that of 'Senebtisy, in whose favor the texts on the verso were drawn up' (Hayes, *Papyrus Brooklyn*, 16-17). Menu suggests a deposition similar to that of Papyrus Boulaq 18, in a tomb of a scribe (Menu, *Égypte Nilotique et Méditerranéenne* 5 [2012], 23). The entries all apparently concern the Theban region, supporting an Upper Egyptian provenance for the papyrus.

1464 For the *ẖnr.t*, see Quirke, *RdE* 39 (1988), 83-106; Quirke, *Titles and Bureaux*, 94-95.

1465 Hayes, *Papyrus Brooklyn*, 11-16.

1466 Hayes, *Papyrus Brooklyn*, 111-112, 124, pls 9, 13.

1467 Hayes, *Papyrus Brooklyn*, 13, 73-74.

1468 See Chapter 4.5.3.

The verso enumerates a list of household members associated with Senebtysy, the subject of Insertions A-C. Two of these (A and B) concern Senebtysy's inheritance from her husband[1469] and the third (C), inserted last, labels the list with  *nꜣ pw rmṯ.t=s m ꜣw.t ḏ(r).t* 'her people, being generous gifts, are these', followed by a regnal date.[1470] The meaning of 'her people' has been interpreted as a reference to either Senebtysy's workers[1471] or ancestors,[1472] although their domestic occupations make the first proposition more likely. The list is presented in Appendix B.7 and is divided into four columns: (1) 'A' identifies the individuals; (2) 'B' contains their given names; (3) 'C' marks their occupation; and (4) 'D' records their designation as male, female or child.

The list comprises approximately 98 entries, 84 of which are wholly or partially preserved. Out of these, 79 have identifiable names. Based on the use of *ꜥꜣm* or *ꜥꜣm.t*, 45 individuals are certainly of Asiatic descent. Around 15.6% are adult males, 64.4% are adult females, 11% are male infants and 9% are female infants. Asiatics with non-Egyptian names account for approximately 78%. The majority are in column 'A' with column 'B' providing their Egyptian nicknames; however, one child, Ankhu, seems to have a given name identifying his foreign origins.[1473] All other Asiatic children, along with three adults, have names most possibly derived from the Egyptian.[1474]

From the remaining 34 workers, two seemingly have Semitic names.[1475] The rest are from the Egyptian, a marker which Hayes has used to identify their Egyptian ancestry.[1476] However, only 25 of the 32 are specifically labelled as *ḥm-nsw.t* or *ḥm.t*. If we are to take this appellation as an ethnic signifier, which is not always the case,[1477] then the remaining seven partially preserved entries do not necessarily have to belong to Egyptians. Notations of Asiatics with both Egyptian names and nicknames do exist in the list,[1478] thereby rendering the incomplete seven as individuals of unknown ancestry. Therefore, 57% of individuals are Asiatic, 2.5% are possibly Asiatic, 31.6% are labelled as *ḥm-nsw.t* or *ḥm.t* and 8.9% are of unknown origin.

The Asiatic population is involved in several daily activities. Men are connected to the preparation of foods ('cooks' and 'brewers') as well as the positions of 'major-domo' and 'tutor'. Women work with textiles ('weavers' and 'warpers'[?] of *šsr* and *ḥꜣ.tyw* cloth) and as 'labourers'. Their specialty in cloth-making signals a possible appreciation of Levantine textile methods and, perhaps, the Asiatic women's specific employment for such handiwork.[1479] No entries in column 'C' are present for any children, indicating that they were too young to work and/or were still dependent upon their parent(s). So, it appears that Senebtysy's 'people' included a large number of Asiatic descendents employed in numerous domestic positions, most likely in Senebtysy's own household.

Hayes expands on this point, suggesting that the Asiatics were slaves.[1480] Consequently, their presence in an Upper Egyptian household emphasises the 'brisk trade in Asiatic slaves'.[1481] While their Semitic names suggest that they had recently migrated into Egypt,[1482] there is no evidence for their treatment as slaves or their purposeful capture for servitude. They are only labelled as 'generous gifts' in the fragmentary Insertion C, perhaps denoting that they were sent to Upper Egypt for vocational opportunities as immigrants. Furthermore, they are listed alongside the individuals labelled as *ḥm-nsw.t* and *ḥm.t*, they retain references of their parentage, and they are generally classified by the term *rmṯ.t* which is otherwise commonly utilised to refer to Egyptians. They are not segregated as a 'possessed' or subjugated group nor are they specifically designated as captives. Therefore, their identification as 'slaves' (a term that is in itself heavily loaded with more modern historical connotations) is not warranted.

Still, the Asiatics of Papyrus Brooklyn 35.1446 indicate a rise in the number of Levantine workers employed by Upper Egyptians, stressing that the Upper Egyptian household was well-acquainted with Asiatics of all ages, sexes and professions during Sobekhotep III's reign.

4.6.4 Papyrus Leiden I.344 (Admonitions of Ipuwer)

Refs Gardiner, *Admonitions*; Enmarch, *Dialogue of Ipuwer*; Enmarch, *World Upturned*.

Chron. Middle Kingdom

The Admonitions of Ipuwer are preserved on the *recto* of Ramesside Papyrus Leiden I.344.[1483] The orthography and language reflect a late Middle Kingdom style[1484] whereas the contents may date between the First and Second Intermediate Periods. Gardiner first identified the text as a Twelfth Dynasty composition.[1485] Others following him

1469 Hayes, *Papyrus Brooklyn*, 87, 111-123, pls 13-14.

1470 As reconstructed by Hayes, the king named is Sobekhotep III. Hayes, *Papyrus Brooklyn*, 123-124, pls 8-10.

1471 Hayes, *Papyrus Brooklyn*, 111-125.

1472 Menu, *Égypte Nilotique et Méditerranéenne* 5 (2012), 23.

1473 Line 58.

1474 Children: Lines 8, 24, 30-31, 34, 36, 58. Adults: Lines 6-7, 61.

1475 Lines 64 and 88.

1476 Hayes, *Papyrus Brooklyn*, 90-92; Helck, *Die Beziehungen Ägyptens*, 77-81.

1477 The term *ḥm* or *ḥm.t* is related more to status and position rather than ethnicity. Menu has recently argued that all individuals on the list are of Asiatic descent (Menu, *Égypte Nilotique et Méditerranéenne* 5 [2012], 26-29; Menu, *Droit et Cultures* 64 [2012], 51-68).

1478 Two notations of adults labelled *ꜥꜣm.t* have both Egyptian names and nicknames (lines 7 and 61).

1479 See also Saretta, *Egyptian Perceptions of West Semites*, 136-137. Saretta proposes that the Asiatics may have been considered as 'cheap labour'.

1480 Hayes, *Papyrus Brooklyn*, 99.

1481 Hayes, *Papyrus Brooklyn*, 99.

1482 Hayes, *Papyrus Brooklyn*, 99; Albright, *JAOS* 74 (1954), 222-223.

1483 The verso contains hymns to a deity written in a different style. Gardiner, *Admonitions*, 1; Enmarch, *Dialogue of Ipuwer*, 1.

1484 Gardiner, *Admonitions*, 2-4; Enmarch, *World Upturned*, 18-24; Thompson, *Historicity of the Patriarchal Narratives*, 138, n. 120; Enmarch, in *Ramesside Studies*, 169-175.

1485 Gardiner, *Admonitions*, 18; Gardiner, *Egypt of the Pharaohs*, 109.

include Spiegel and Ward, the latter of whom depends on this date for his reconstruction of First Intermediate Period events.[1486] Conversely, some propose a late Dynasty 13 date based on the use of certain Middle Kingdom terms.[1487] Although this has received criticism,[1488] scholars remain cautious, setting the text in the general Middle Kingdom.[1489] Because of the questionable date, the Admonitions are only used here as a Middle Kingdom source for the *topos* representation of Asiatics.

While the beginning and end of the text are not preserved, the main body follows Ipuwer's laments to the 'lord of all', either the king or a deity.[1490] The Admonitions emphasise the contrast between chaos and order, describing an anarchic Egypt where norms of life are upturned by calamity and a lack of security. The portrayal is often contradictory and littered with the repetitive use of hyperbole.[1491] Generally the realm sees lower classes assuming positions of wealth and power, allies becoming enemies and Egypt's ideological enemies becoming neighbours. This upper class perspective finds the spread of foreigners as part of the chaotic, topsy-turvy land lacking in efficient border control. Key passages on this situation can be found in Appendix B.8.

The Admonitions of Ipuwer have been used as evidence for foreigners invading the Delta as well as a mutiny by Asiatic mercenaries against the state.[1492] Van Seters also argued for the text's Second Intermediate Period date as an expression of the tumultuous Hyksos period.[1493] Yet, one must consider the text's use of the 'lament' genre that highlights a flurry of chaos to display the consequences of a weak government.[1494] The destabilised administration apparently results in a land teeming with foreigners (1.9, 3.1-2) who mostly amass in the Delta (4.8), a region in need of security (1.4).[1495] Northerners mentioned in the Admonitions[1496] include the *Pḏ.tyw*, a threatening group who occur as outsiders and as rebel mercenaries (3.1-2, 14.14-15.1), and *St.tyw*, who are knowledgeable in Egyptian affairs (15.1). An entry for the *ꜥꜣm.w* may have also been written, but is not completely preserved (14.12).

Some similarities between the Admonitions and the Prophecies of Noferty exist. The ideological portrayal of how foreigners entered Egypt (lack of border security) and their apparent destination (the Delta) is the same in both.[1497] The depiction of foreigners as the cause of escalating chaos in the marshlands seems to be a literary device used in the texts' 'order versus chaos' motif.[1498] The fragmentary Admonitions infer that the foreigners in the north are formidable,[1499] some being knowledgeable in Egyptian affairs. Perhaps they also reflect the composer's concern for an escalated Asiatic presence in the Delta or, if the reversal should be considered the norm, they may inadvertently portray the necessity for effective border patrol, particularly near the Delta region.

Information on foreign relations is offered in 3.6-8, notably the significance of trade with *Kpny*. The Northern Levantine city is represented as a source for *ꜥš*-timber of which a continued supply was necessary for cultic processes, such as one involving mummification or coffin production. This inclusion amidst the laments denotes the administration's duty to ensure that such valuable products were constantly and consistently imported but probably only for the upper classes of society.

Overall, the Admonitions of Ipuwer characterise Asiatics[1500] in two ways. The first is their portrayal as a threat, their spread in Egypt being a force of chaos. Subsequently, the management of Asiatic immigration symbolises the ideological control of chaos. The second represents the Levant as a source of precious commodities with ongoing trade corresponding to a successful administration. Thus, the Admonitions express the state's ideological control of foreign affairs for security and trade, the ultimate benefactors of which were most likely the elite.

1486 Spiegel, *Reformbewegungen*; Ward, *Egypt and the East Mediterranean*, 21, 57. See also Redford, *Egypt, Canaan and Israel*, 63, 66-67; Redford, *Pharaonic King-Lists*, 144, n. 69.

1487 Van Seters, *JEA* 50 (1964), 13-23; van Seters, *Hyksos*, 103-120; Quirke, *Egyptian Literature*, 140.

1488 Ward, *Egypt and the East Mediterranean*, 21, ns 78-79; Redford, *Pharaonic King-Lists*, 144, n. 69; Thompson, *Historicity of the Patriarchal Narratives*, 138, n. 120.

1489 The Admonitions refer to a 'majesty' (15.3) and a 'Residence' (2.11), suggesting a composition either at the end of the Old Kingdom or the Middle Kingdom. The latter date is more likely considering the text's style. Thompson, *Historicity of the Patriarchal Narratives*, 138, n. 120; Enmarch, *World Upturned*, 24; Albright, *BASOR* 179 (1965), 40-41; Lichtheim, *Ancient Egyptian Literature* 1, 149-150; Simpson, *Literature of Ancient Egypt*, 188-189.

1490 Enmarch, *World Upturned*, 30-31; Williams, in *Seed of Wisdom*, 29-30.

1491 For instance, the presence of fine linen in line 7.11-12 contrasts with its absence in 10.3-10.6. Lichtheim, *Ancient Egyptian Literature* 1, 149.

1492 See Redford, *Egypt, Canaan and Israel*, 67; Gardiner, *Admonitions*, 91.

1493 Van Seters, *Hyksos*, 103-120; van Seters, *JEA* 50 (1964), 13-23.

1494 Enmarch, *World Upturned*, 36-38.

1495 Line 3.13 has been translated by Gardiner as 'Lo, every foreign country comes (?). That is our water! That is our happiness' (Gardiner, *Admonitions*, 34), insinuating that the foreigners may be in Egypt in search for water. Despite the similarities with the Prophecies of Noferty (see Chapter 4.6.5) and the Instructions for Merikara (see n. 1497), the hieroglyphic text is open to several interpretations. Quirke, for example, translates the passage as 'that is, when every land is our loyal subject, that is our flourishing' (Quirke, *Egyptian Literature*, 142).

1496 For comments regarding the groups, see van Seters, *JEA* 50 (1964), 15-16.

1497 Another text with a similar treatment of foreigners is the First Intermediate Period Instructions to Merikara. The didactic piece describes the Delta as a divided region with a large *Pḏ.tyw* population infiltrating the Delta because of lax border control. Unlike the Admonitions, the Instructions connect the *Pḏ.tyw* with the *ꜥꜣm.w*, clarifying their northeastern origins. While the composition has been paleographically dated to either the First Intermediate Period or the early Twelfth Dynasty, the majority of scholars agree that its contents date to the First Intermediate Period. As such, it is not examined here in detail. For more on the Instructions to Merikara, see Golénischeff, *Les papyrus hiératiques*; Scharff, *Lehre für König Merikarê*; Lichtheim, *Ancient Egyptian Literature* 1, 97-109; Ward, *Egypt and the East Mediterranean*, 22; Burkard, *Textkritische Untersuchungen*, 6; Seibert, *Charakteristik: Untersuchungen* 1, 88; Thompson, *Historicity of the Patriarchal Narratives*, 139-142.

1498 See Chapter 4.6.5 for a discussion on the Prophecies of Noferty.

1499 Enmarch, *World Upturned*, 206.

1500 In fact, the two characterisations can be applied to the representations of other foreigners and foreign lands in the Admonitions, excluding the *Mḏꜣ.yw*.

4.6.5 Prophecies of Noferty

Ref. Helck, *Prophezeiung des Nfr.tj*.

Chron. Early Twelfth Dynasty

Preserved on several New Kingdom sources, the literary 'Prophecies of Noferty' follow the sage Noferty in King Snoferu's court.[1501] As he recounts, several chaotic events would arise and be brought to an end by an 'Imeny', or Amenemhat I.[1502] The reflection on Amenemhat persuaded scholars to read the piece as political propaganda, purposed to legitimise and promote Amenemhat's reign.[1503] The text was then assigned to the reign of Amenemhat I or that of Senwosret I.[1504] The Prophecies indeed endorse Amenemhat, and it is in this ideological setting that the representations of Asiatics should be studied. Pertinent extracts are in Appendix B.9.

The Prophecies speak of a time when the *ꜥ3m.w* and *St.tyw* of the east entered Egypt. Widespread devastation ensued due to their need for water (lines 35, 68).[1505] At a time of civil unrest, the *ꜥ3m.w* met no resistance.[1506] Noferty describes the foreigners as terrorising the people instead of being terrorised by the king (line 19). Such a reversal of the orderly is then repaired by Amenemhat, who re-instilled fear in the *ꜥ3m.w*. The historicity of the Prophecies as a reflection of early Dynasty 12 events[1507] is decreased by this *topos* of 'order versus chaos', as well as the composer's intention to abet Amenemhat. Perhaps, the *ꜥ3m.w*'s representation as strong enemies[1508] was employed to enhance the need for the reconstructed Walls-of-the-Ruler,[1509] but it also remains possible that the *ꜥ3m.w* were stronger by the time of Amenemhat. In both cases, the Prophecies of Noferty note the presence of *ꜥ3m.w* in the Delta, emphasising Amenemhat's ideological role to protect Egypt's permeable borders.[1510]

[1501] In line 10, Noferty is described as 'lector-priest of Bastet... a noble/rich man of greater possessions than any equal of his'. Hence, his upper class status, combined with his Delta origins, make him the most suitable character to describe the influence of the Asiatics on this region to the king. Lichtheim, *Ancient Egyptian Literature* 1, 139; Simpson, *Literature of Ancient Egypt*, 214. For the sources recording the text, see Quirke, *Egyptian Literature*, 139; Helck, *Prophezeiung des Nfr.tj*, 1-2.

[1502] Quirke, *Egyptian Literature*, 135-140.

[1503] Posener, *Littérature et politique*, 21-60; Cohen, *Canaanites, Chronologies, and Connections*, 36-37; Younis, *GM* 195 (2003), 97-108. For more on the problems on interpreting such texts as propagandistic, see Quirke, *Egyptian Literature*, 47-51.

[1504] Posener, *Littérature et politique*, 46; Ward, *Egypt and the East Mediterranean World*, 64-65; Thompson, *Historicity of the Patriarchal Narratives*, 142; Simpson, *Literature of Ancient Egypt*, 214; Cohen, *Canaanites, Chronologies and Connections*, 36; Williams, in *The Seed of Wisdom*, 22.

[1505] Also noted in the Instructions for Merikara, lines 91-92, 99. See n. 1497.

[1506] For similarities with the Admonitions of Ipuwer, see Chapter 4.6.4.

[1507] Ward, *Egypt and the East Mediterranean*, 64-65; Thompson, *Historicity of the Patriarchal Narratives*, 142-143.

[1508] The *ꜥ3m.w* travel in strength (line 17-19), are well-provisioned and, as Redford remarks, acquainted with the art of siege warfare (lines 30-37). Redford, *Egypt, Canaan and Israel*, 69.

[1509] Amenemhat I was indeed active in the eastern Delta region, not only constructing the Walls-of-the-Ruler, but also adding to the temple of Bastet at Bubastis (Berman, *Amenemhat I*, 122).

[1510] Like Amenemhat I, further east and approximately 100 years earlier, Shusin of Ur is known to have 'built the fortress of mar.tu which keeps the Tidnum away' (Ungnad, in *Reallexikon* 2, 144). Akkadian sources situate *mar.tu* and *tidnum* (or Amurru) west of the Euphrates in the Northern Levant. Roux, *Ancient Iraq*, 175, n. 26; Cohen, *Canaanites, Chronologies, and Connections*, 38, n. 38; Saretta, *Egyptian Perceptions of West Semites*, 61-62.

4.6.6 Stela Louvre C 21

Ref. Gayet, *Stèles de la XIIe dynastie*, 3, pl. 11.

Chron. Twelfth Dynasty

Stela Louvre C 21 presents evidence on the influence of Asiatics in Egypt. The unprovenanced item dates to the Twelfth Dynasty and belongs to the 'steward' Senwosret.[1511] One of his family members is named as: (5)  (5) *sn.t=f Sn.t-ꜥ3m.t iri.t n Ḥtp.t m3ꜥ.t-ḫrw* "(5) his sister, Senet-*ꜥ3m.t*,[1512] born to Hotepet, justified'. Her name can be literally translated as 'she who resembles a/the *ꜥ3m.t* woman',[1513] thereby showing that Asiatics were considered to be physically distinct from Egyptians. It also insinuates that the term *ꜥ3m.t* need not necessarily be associated with negative connotations. It can be utilised to describe the unique physical characteristics and perhaps attractiveness of a woman otherwise of apparent Egyptian origin.

4.6.7 Stela Moscow I.1.a.5349 (4161)

Refs Hodjash and Berlev, *Reliefs and Stelae*, 77-79 [34].

Chron. Late Twelfth to early Thirteenth Dynasty

A stela of unknown provenance at the Pushkin Museum of Fine Arts, Moscow, features a number of Asiatics.[1514] Dated between the late Twelfth and early Thirteenth Dynasty, the stela is for the 'hall-keeper and butler' Senwosret.[1515] He is pictured seated before an offering table facing four women of his immediate family. Below him are three horizontal registers, the first two each illustrating five kneeling men and the third portraying eight kneeling women. The bottom two registers contain Asiatics, their entries presented in Appendix B.10.

The two registers depict three or five male[1516] and eight female Asiatics. In comparison to the individuals not identified by the *ꜥ3m* element, this amounts to 11/20 or 13/20 of Senwosret's household members. Most Asiatics are given an Egyptian name with the possibility of one bearing a name with Semitic origins (F3) and another

[1511] Gayet, *Stèles de la XIIe dynastie*, 3, pl. 11; Schneider, *Ausländer in Ägypten* 2, 65-66.

[1512] Ranke, *Personennamen* 1, 262 [22] (Louvre C 21 is listed as the sole reference for this name).

[1513] Schneider, *Ausländer in Ägypten* 2, 70.

[1514] The stela is postulated to be from Abydos, the owner possibly residing near el-Lisht or Thebes. Hodjash and Berlev, *Egyptian Reliefs and Stelae*, 77-79 [34]; Schneider, *Ausländer in Ägypten* 2, 59.

[1515] Hodjash and Berlev, *Egyptian Reliefs and Stelae*, 77-78.

[1516] E4 and E5 may be Asiatic, although they are not specifically designated as such.

FIGURE 4.68. DETAIL, STELA MUSÉE JOSEPH DÉCHELETTE, ROANNE NR 163. AFTER MEULENAERE, *CdE* 40 (1985), FIG. 1 (DRAWN FROM PHOTOGRAPH).

denoting worship of the lady of Byblos (F6).[1517] Artistically, all Asiatics are portrayed as Egyptians with no particular features delineating them as foreigners. Even the men's skin colour is noted to be red, the same colour used for the other men represented on the stela.[1518] Hence, the item provides a good example of (1) the number of Asiatics in Egyptian households, here outnumbering the seemingly Egyptian members; and (2) the representation of Asiatics as Egyptians, the only marker for their ethnicity being the term *ꜥ3m* or *ꜥ3m.t*.

4.6.8 Stela Musée Joseph Déchelette, Roanne Nr 163

Refs Meulenaere, *CdE* 40 (1985), 75-84, fig. 1.

Chron. Thirteenth Dynasty

Stela Musée Joseph Déchelette, Roanne Nr 163, offers a unique case of an Asiatic represented differently from her Egyptian counterparts. Postulated to come from Abydos, it is for the 'overseer of the treasury', Senebsuma.[1519] The stela is typologically and palaeographically assigned to Dynasty 13[1520] and illustrates a standing woman in the bottom left corner (Figure 4.68). She is labelled as *ꜥ3m.t=f mr.yt=f Snb-ḥḳ3* 'his *ꜥ3m.t*, his beloved, Senebheqa'.[1521] Sporting a long, one-shouldered garment reaching the shin, Senebheqa wears her hair with a slight bob-like protrusion at the back of the head resembling a bun held in place by two wedge-shaped nodules. The wedge-like pieces and bun are akin to those of Wekhhotep's offering bearers at Meir,[1522] while the garment is styled like the Asiatic women's dresses in Khnumhotep II's tomb at Beni Hassan.[1523] Senebheqa's foreignness is emphasised by the ethnonym *ꜥ3m.t*, her hairstyle and her dress, but her name and facial features are Egyptian.

The Asiatic appears in a sequence of individuals who, in the register above, stand before the 'overseer of the storehouse and treasury', Heriwah. In front of her is the 'butler of the beer-pantry', Werenheqa and behind her is the 'lady of the house', Henut. The suffix pronoun in *ꜥ3m.t=f mr.yt=f* could refer to either Heriwah[1524] or Werenheqa. While Henut is 'lady of the house', Senebheqa is visually more prominent,[1525] appearing in front of Henut and larger than the individuals before her. Her epithet as 'his beloved' further delineates her status as an important individual within the household.[1526] Therefore, the stela provides a representation of a respected Asiatic with mixed attributes in a household of officials from the middle to high echelons of Egyptian society.

4.6.9 Tale of Sinuhe

Refs Gardiner, *Notes on Sinuhe*; Koch, *Sinuhe*.

Chron. Twelfth Dynasty (reign of Senwosret I)

The Tale of Sinuhe is preserved on five papyri of the Middle Kingdom and Eighteenth Dynasty, and over 30 ostraca of the New Kingdom.[1527] The text situates its events in the rule of Amenemhat I and his successor, dating its composition to or after Senwosret I's reign.[1528] It follows the Egyptian Sinuhe who, after the attempted assassination of Amenemhat I, flees Egypt and takes refuge in the Levant where he establishes himself as a ruler. Years later, he returns to Egypt at the behest of the succeeding pharaoh, Senwosret I. Appendix B.11 contains the most relevant passages pertaining to Sinuhe's experience in the Levant. Significant notations may be extracted from each of the selected passages, a summary of which is presented below:

- R1-R2: Sinuhe's title is recorded as 'administrator of the estates of the sovereign of the lands of the *St.tyw*'. Whether this title was assigned to the character before his travels or after his return, it emphasises the portrayal of foreign lands as subordinate to Egypt;

- B11-19: The passage follows Sinuhe's flight.[1529] He journeys north from Itjtawy to *Ng3w*, crossing

1517 See Figure 7.10.
1518 Hodjash and Berlev, *Egyptian Reliefs and Stelae*, 77.
1519 Gabolde, *Catalogue*, 35-38; de Meulenaire, *CdE* 60 (1985), 77-80, fig. 1; Schneider, *Ausländer in Ägypten* 2, 70.
1520 Gabolde, *Catalogue*, 35-38; de Meulenaire, *CdE* 60 (1985), 77-80.
1521 The name is not attested in Ranke, *Personennamen*. However, it is clearly derived from the Egyptian.
1522 The offering bearers have a slightly more voluminous bun. See also the hairdo of the statuette from Beni Hassan. Chapters 4.4.1.4 and 4.4.4.3, Figure 4.59; Plate 3.
1523 No details, however, are present. Chapter 4.4.1.3, Figure 4.52.
1524 Schneider, *Ausländer in Ägypten* 2, 70; Gabolde, *Catalogue*, 36-37, n. 8.
1525 Gabolde, *Catalogue*, 36-37, n. 8.
1526 Perhaps she is a concubine or second wife. Gabolde, *Catalogue*, 36-37, n. 8.
1527 Koch, *Erzählung des Sinuhe*; Gardiner, *Story of Sinuhe*, 2-8; Baines, *JEA* 68 (1982), 32, n. 7; Quirke, *Egyptian Literature*, 58.
1528 Baines, in *Study of the Ancient Near East*, 355; Thompson, *Historicity of the Patriarchal Narratives*, 132, n. 85.
1529 The reasons for Sinuhe's flight have been discussed in detail in Goedicke, *RdE* 35 (1984), 95-103; Morschauser, *JARCE* 37 (2000),

a body of water and travelling past a quarry until he reaches the Walls-of-the-Ruler. The latter are described as an enclosure specifically built to repel the *St.tyw* and *Nmi.w-šꜥ*. The significance of efficient border control with northeastern lands is insinuated;

- B19-23: Beyond the limits of Egyptian border control,[1530] Sinuhe almost experiences death;

- B23-28: Sinuhe is rescued by the *St.tyw*. They have cattle, water and milk, as well as some knowledge in Egyptian affairs;

- B28-31: As a commodity, Sinuhe passes through several lands and heads towards *Kpn* until he reaches *Ḳdm*, where a ruler of Upper *Rtnw*, *ꜥmwsꜣnnši*, summons him. None of the foreign lands are given determinatives associated with cities;

- B31-36: *ꜥmwsꜣnnši* has considerable knowledge in Egyptian affairs. Other Egyptians are also in Upper *Rtnw*;

- B45-75: Sinuhe's Hymn to Senwosret I refers to the newly appointed king as a suppressor and crusher of the foreign, namely the *Pḏ.tyw*, *St.tyw* and *Nmi.w-šꜥ*. The bellicose treatment of Asiatics evidently accentuates the portrayal of a strong, subjugating pharaoh, although relations with the southern lands appear to be more violent than those with the north;

- B75-81: *ꜥmwsꜣnnši* endows Sinuhe with power, offering him his daughter in marriage as well as the best piece of his land;

- B81-85: *Iꜣꜣ* is described as a flat land fertile with foods and animals. It is most possibly in a region where elevation permits the production of honey as well as the growth of olive trees, fig trees and vineyards. The most plausible location for *Iꜣꜣ* is in the Beqa' valley of modern Lebanon;[1531]

- B85-92: Sinuhe is treated well and offered bread, wine, meat, fowl, cattle and a variety of dairy dishes;

- B92-99: Many years are spent in Upper *Rtnw* during which contact frequently occurs with Egyptians travelling to and from Itjtawy. The *St.tyw* appear as enemies of Sinuhe and the conglomeration of 'the rulers of foreign lands';

- B99-109: Sinuhe is a strong commander in *ꜥmwsꜣnnši*'s army, again symbolising Egyptian superiority;

- B109-146: Sinuhe duels with a formidable warrior from Upper *Rtnw*,[1532] representing the Egyptian perception of Levantine battles on the field, with tent encampments and one-on-one sparring. Despite the mention of tents, the warrior from Upper *Rtnw* is also from a place with a gate and walls. The *Pḏ.tyw* are associated with the Delta and the *ꜥꜣm.w* are the inhabitants of Upper *Rtnw*;

- B174-176: The pharaoh sends gifts to rulers of Upper *Rtnw*, specifying diplomatic Egyptian-Levantine relations;

- B197-198: The pharaoh's decree to Sinuhe points to the importance of an interment following Egyptian elite traditions. The description of funerary customs associated with Asiatics or, more correctly, non-elite ways, signifies the importance of burying Sinuhe according to his Egyptian traditions and status;

- B219-223: Sinuhe's reply to the pharaoh mentions a list of three toponyms whose rulers are to be brought before the king. *Rtnw*'s relationship with the pharaoh is equated with that of dogs (loyalty and submissiveness), stressing Egyptian dominance in foreign diplomatic matters;

- B238-245: Sinuhe leaves *Iꜣꜣ*, transferring his possessions and responsibilities to his eldest son. Assisted by the *St.tyw*, he travels south to the Ways-of-Horus and enters Egyptian domain, noting the king's gifts for the *St.tyw*;

- B264-266: Sinuhe appears before the royal family. The queen and children are taken aback by his foreign appearance.[1533]

The Tale of Sinuhe has been the subject of much research. Its historicity has been debated, with some identifying it as a literary composition[1534] and others as a text inspired by historical events.[1535] Its literary ingenuity has been appreciated, the grammatical and thematic elements

187-198; Obsomer, in *Le Muséon* 112 (1999), 207-271.

1530 Goedicke proposes that Sinuhe passed through Tell el-Maskhuta (*Ptn*) and Lake Timsah or the Bitter Lakes (*Kmwr*) on his journey (Goedicke, *CdE* 67 [1992], 28-29).

1531 Mourad, *GM* 238 (2013), 78-81, fig. 1. Other propositions include the Ghab, 'Akkar and Jezreel plains. See Gubel and Loffet, *AHL* 34-35 (2011/2012), 82, 86-87; Aḥituv, *Canaanite Toponyms*, 65, n. 72; Goedicke, *CdE* 67 (1992), 67, 40; Green, *CdE* 58 (1983), 38-59.

1532 Goedicke, *JARCE* 21 (1984), 197-201; King, *JBL* 106/4 (1987), 580-585.

1533 Goedicke suggests that the queen reacted as such because Sinuhe was her relative and possibly her brother (Goedicke, in *From Illuhun to Djeme*, 59).

1534 See Baines, *JEA* 68 (1982), 31-44; Foster, *JNES* 39/2 (1980), 89-117; Loprieno, *Topos and Mimesis*, 41-59; Parkinson, *Tale of Sinuhe*, 25-26.

1535 See Wilson, in *Ancient Near Eastern Texts*, 18; Barns, *JEA* 53 (1967), 13-14; Helck, *Die Beziehungen Ägyptens*, 40-41; Rainey, *BASOR* 295 (1994), 82; Rainey, *IOS* 2 (1972), 369-408; Rainey, in *Archaeological and Historical Studies* 1, 281.

explored.[1536] Nonetheless, it remains conjectural if the text, in its entirety, is fictional.[1537] Undoubtedly, its account of Egypt, with the death of Amenemhat I, the rule of his successor and the description of the marshlands and the Walls-of-the-Ruler, sets a historical framework familiar to the Egyptian audience.[1538] Across Egypt's borders, scholars have postulated that the text enters into the fictional realm of the *other*.[1539]

Nevertheless, there are some indications that the Levantine geography, topography and, to a limited extent, society, as depicted in the story may be based on some fact.[1540] Attested in other Twelfth Dynasty sources are the toponyms *Kpn*,[1541] Upper *Rtnw*[1542] or simply *Rtnw*,[1543] as well as *Ḳdm* and *Ꜣꜣ*.[1544] Similarly, Semitic-sounding names like *Mki*[1545] and *Fnḫ.w*[1546] are found elsewhere, with the construction of the name of the ruler in Sinuhe, *ꜥmwsꜣnnši* following that of other Levantine rulers.[1547] The relations between *ꜥmwsꜣnnši* and other MBA Levantines with the Egyptians is also corroborated by numerous textual and archaeological sources explored in this study.[1548]

Thus, if the composer(s) of Sinuhe's tale embedded such factual elements within the text, perhaps other features are also inspired by historical details. It should, however, be stressed that Sinuhe's character development was maintained as the tale's focal point. The description of foreign lands and groups is subordinate to and dependent on Sinuhe's own experiences. This explains why, for instance, the *St.tyw* are portrayed as both helpers and enemies.[1549] It also justifies Sinuhe's position in Asiatic society: fleeing Egypt as a middle class man, he was able to achieve high rank in the Levant,[1550] his superiority in leadership and military prowess representing the pharaoh's dominance over the northeast while ensuring Sinuhe's fulfilment of Egyptian precepts.[1551] Despite the years spent in the Levant, the Egyptian homeland, language, customs and mortuary practices remained favoured.[1552] Sinuhe's appearance in the royal court also resulted in shrieks of either fear or ridicule,[1553] necessitating the removal of the foreign from Sinuhe and his reinstatement into Egyptian society.[1554] As such, the Egyptian remained the norm, preferred and perhaps considered superior to the *other*.

With this in mind, the text's portrayal of Levantine society can be assessed. Firstly, debate has fuelled over whether Sinuhe's Asiatics were semi-nomadic or settled.[1555] The tale is particularly vague on the subject, its analysis open to many interpretations.[1556] There are the *Pḏ.tyw* in Egypt who are against the marsh-dwellers and the *Nmi.w-šꜥ* who are crushed at the border.[1557] Not much is written on the *St.tyw*, except that they frequently appear near Egyptian borders.[1558] The Asiatics in Upper *Rtnw*, identified as *wḥ.yt*, *ꜥꜣm.w* and *rmṯ.t*, are only mentioned in relation to Sinuhe rather than a particular city.[1559] In fact, designations for cities or towns are not utilised in the story. There are only instances of the strong man's *sꜣ* 'gate' and *inb.wt* 'walls' which stand in contrast to his *imꜣ(w)* 'tent' and *ꜥfꜣ.y* 'encampment', the latter two in a military context where warriors would be removed from their residence.[1560] The only detailed portrayal of a foreign land is that of *Ꜣꜣ* which, with its vineyards, plantations and honey production, supports a locale with a settled population.[1561] However, *Ꜣꜣ* was inhabited by Sinuhe, who himself originates from a sedentary society. Therefore, such ambiguities hinder reaching a sound conclusion on the Levantines' mode of subsistence and emphasise that the central focus of the tale is not on the Levant, but on Sinuhe.

Secondly, the text offers some details on the Asiatics' local affairs. Sinuhe is described as a ruler of *Ꜣꜣ*, subordinate to the overarching ruler of Upper *Rtnw*, *ꜥmwsꜣnnši*. The latter

1536 For example, Baines, *JEA* 68 (1982), 31-44; Foster, *JNES* 39/2 (1980), 89-117; Foster, *Thought Couplets*; Collier, in *Ancient Egyptian Literature*, 531-553; Parkinson, *Poetry and Culture*, 125-126, 150-153; Dotson, *Studia Antiqua* 8/1 (2010), 47-53. For more see Parkinson, *Tale of Sinuhe*, xviii-xx, 21-26.

1537 Greig, in *Studies in Egyptology*, 336-342; Purdy, *ZÄS* 104 (1977), 112-127; Assmann, in *Ancient Egyptian Literature*, 59-65.

1538 See, for instance, Posener, *Littérature et politique*, 87-115; Morschauser, *JARCE* 37 (2000), 192, 198; Goedicke, *RdE* 35 (1984), 95-103; Goedicke, in *From Illahun to Djeme*, 55-60. For the utilisation of a historical framework in New Kingdom texts, see Manassa, in *Opening the Tablet Box*, 245-269.

1539 Barocas, *L'Antico Egitto*, 200; Loprieno, in *Mysterious Lands*, 38, 40; O'Connor, in *Never Had the Like Occurred*, 169-170; Moers, in *Narratives of Egypt*, 171-174.

1540 As also argued in Mourad, *GM* 238 (2013), 70-72.

1541 See Chapter 6.3.3.

1542 Sinuhe B31.

1543 Sinuhe B100, B222.

1544 For more on the toponyms, see Mourad, *GM* 238 (2013), 78-81.

1545 Sinuhe B219. The name is attested as *Mꜣki* in Khnumhotep III's biography, *Mkiy* in E37 (toponym) and E62 of the Saqqara Execration Texts, and *Mki* in el-Lahun's P Berlin 10002. See Chapters 4.3.1.2, 4.3.8 and 4.3.5.2, respectively, and Figure 7.10.

1546 Sinuhe B221. *Wb* 1, 577.

1547 See, for example E14, E22, E41, E49, E54 and E57 of the Saqqara Execration Texts (Chapter 4.3.8 and Appendix B.4), or the name of a Fourteenth Dynasty king *ꜥꜣmw* (Figure 1.2; Ryholt, *Political Situation*, 364-366).

1548 See, for example, the Mit Rahina inscription (Chapter 4.3.7) and Khnumhotep III's biography (Chapter 4.3.1.2), or the finds at Tell el-Dab'a (Chapter 4.2.2) and el-Lahun (Chapter 4.3.5).

1549 Sinuhe B24-28, B97-99, B245.

1550 Sinuhe B78-81, B85-92, B99-109, B129-B146.

1551 Moers, in *Narratives of Egypt*, 173-174.

1552 Sinuhe B31, B238-242. O'Connor, in *Never Had the Like Occurred*, 169-170; Pérez-Accino, in *Narratives of Egypt*, 192-193.

1553 Sinuhe B265-266.

1554 Sinuhe was washed and anointed, his hair cut and combed and the foreign clothes replaced with fine Egyptian linen (Sinuhe B279-295). O'Connor, in *Never Had the Like Occurred*, 170; Baines, *JEA* 68 (1982), 43; Cohen, *Canaanites, Chronologies, and Connections*, 39, n. 43.

1555 Supporters of a pastoral Levant see a cultural group 'largely undifferentiated as to economic or societal function' (Redford, *BASOR* 301 [1996], 78), whereas others find an MBIIA society with an 'organized settlement with well developed military and political consciousness' (Rainey, *IOS* 2 [1972], 378). See also Redford, *Egypt, Canaan and Israel*, 86-87; Bárta, *Sinuhe, the Bible, and the Patriarchs*, 41-43; Rainey, *BASOR* 295 (1994), 82-84; Rainey, in *Archaeological and Historical Studies* 1, 282-289; Cohen, *Canaanites, Chronologies, and Connections*, 18-19.

1556 Cohen, *Canaanites, Chronologies, and Connections*, 18-19.

1557 Sinuhe B17-18, B52, B60-61, B63, B71-73, B121-122.

1558 Sinuhe B24-28, B245.

1559 Sinuhe B85, B93-94, B104, B113, B130, B141.

1560 Sinuhe B115-116, B145-146. Redford, *Egypt, Canaan and Israel*, 86; Rainey, *BASOR* 295 (1994), 83.

1561 Sinuhe B81-92, B241; Rainey, in *Archaeological and Historical Studies* 1, 286. For an opposing view, see Redford, *BASOR* 301 (1996), 79.

controls his territory through marital ties[1562] and military force,[1563] his army equipped with bows, daggers, axes and javelins.[1564] Fighting amongst the variant groups in *Rtnw* could transpire and be settled by duels.[1565] Additionally, rulers either within *Rtnw* or in the surrounding regions share a common enemy, the *St.tyw*, against whom they advance as a conglomeration of *ḥḳ3.w ḫ3s.wt*,[1566] an expression similar to the *ḥḳ3 ḫ3s.t* of Khnumhotep II's tomb at Beni Hassan and the later *ḥḳ3 ḫ3s.wt*.[1567] The Asiatics are involved in farming, horticulture, hunting and animal husbandry, their diet featuring an assortment of vegetables, grains, fruits, meats and dairy products.[1568] Thus, the Asiatics are not portrayed as a chaotic force. They are well-organised and betray a 'quasi-Egyptian' society.[1569]

Thirdly, there are several insights regarding Egyptian-Levantine relations. These include gift-exchange, trade and letter-correspondence.[1570] Egyptians could possibly travel unhindered through *Ί33* and Upper *Rtnw*,[1571] pointing to Senwosret I's diplomatic relations with Levantine regions. Asiatic rulers are also informed of Egyptian affairs; the *mtn* of the *St.tyw* as well as *ˁmws3nnši* recognise Sinuhe, the latter enjoying the company of other Egyptians.[1572] Peaceful dealings are evident with the *St.tyw*, who assist Sinuhe's journeys on the northern border of Egypt, exchanging products and people at the Walls-of-the-Ruler.[1573] Rulers of the Levant, *Mki* from *Ḳdmi*, *Ḫnty.w-š* of *Ḫnty-kšw* and *Mnws* from the two flat lands of the *Fnḫ.w*, could also visit Egypt.[1574] Still, the bellicose treatment of foreigners appears in instances concerning Senwosret I,[1575] heightening the segments' representation of Egyptian dominance. Interestingly, the *ˁ3m.w* are not treated negatively. It is the *St.tyw*, *Pḏ.tyw* and *Nmi.w-šˁ* who attract Egyptian antagonism. However, wherever points of contact occur between the Egyptian and Asiatic, it is the Egyptian that emerges as the stronger, orderly force. As such, the border between the two, represented by the Walls-of-the-Ruler and Ways-of-Horus,[1576] must be efficient and watchful, protecting Egypt from the beyond.

Overall, Sinuhe portrays diplomatic and peaceful Egyptian-Levantine relations. The king mostly ignores the internal politics of the Levant, unless it impacts the interests or security of Egypt. The text further provides important data on the similarities and differences between the representations of the Egyptian and the foreign, placing the former as the dominant power. Nonetheless, it demonstrates that the Egyptians were knowledgeable about their northeasterly neighbours who generally lived in comfort, much like the Egyptians.

1562 Sinuhe B78-79.
1563 Sinuhe B99-101.
1564 Sinuhe B105, B127-129, B134-140.
1565 Sinuhe B108-146; Goedicke, *JARCE* 21 (1984), 203-210.
1566 Sinuhe B98-B99; Foster, *JSSEA* 12/2 (1982), 84-85. Senwosret I, like Sinuhe and those loyal to him, also subdues the *St.tyw* (Sinuhe B18, B71-75).
1567 See Chapter 4.4.1.3 and Figure 4.52. See also Chapter 7.3.4 for more on the titles.
1568 Sinuhe B81-92, B241.
1569 Moers, in *Narratives of Egypt*,171-173. Moers infers that this representation is a literary device to assist the Egyptian audience in conceptualising a foreign land. While this is certainly possible, the attempt to 'humanise' Egypt's neighbours does not solely have to be regarded as literary or fictional. It could merely be a less bellicose treatment of non-Egyptians.
1570 Sinuhe B174-178, B204-205, B244-B246.
1571 Sinuhe B34 and perhaps B94-95.
1572 Sinuhe B24-26, B34.
1573 Sinuhe B24-28, B263-266; Thompson, *Historicity of the Patriarchal Narratives*, 133.
1574 Sinuhe B219-222. For more on the rulers, see Green, *CdE* 58 (1983), 38-59. Schneider postulates that their names are in fact titles of rulers, *Mki* being for Semitic *mlk* 'king', *Ḫnty.w-š* for Luwian *ḫantawattis* 'ruler' and *Mnws* for Hurrian <'a>múnənəš 'sovereign' (Schneider, *E&L* 12 [2002], 257-272).
1575 Sinuhe B45-75, B223.
1576 Sinuhe B17-19, B242-244.

4.7 Conclusions

Chapter 4 gathered data from 36 sites in Egypt: 13 in the Delta region; eight in the Memphite region; five in Middle Egypt; and 10 in Upper Egypt (see Figure 4.1). Nine additional unprovenanced artefacts were selected for their significance. The following presents a summary of the findings along with observations regarding the development of Egyptian-Levantine relations and the rise of the Hyksos.

4.7.1 The first half of the Twelfth Dynasty – Amenemhat I to II

Pertinent data from the first half of the Twelfth Dynasty, or the reigns of Amenemhat I to II, is primarily associated with royal activities. The beginning of Dynasty 12 was evidently troubled with major conflicts involving Asiatics. The tombs of Baqet, Khety and Khnumhotep I at Beni Hassan, and the Hatnub graffiti note that Asiatic and Nubian warriors were allied with Egyptians to secure royal power. Apparently, different divisions or units of Asiatics were involved in close-combat and siege attacks. One Asiatic is possibly portrayed as the leader of his unit, indicating the organisation of Asiatic troops and the presence of high-ranking Levantines. Such individuals most likely joined forces with the Egyptians at the behest of the king who, as Khnumhotep I's biography relays, personally visited Middle Egypt to quell the opposition. The military alliance consequently led to an influx of foreigners into Middle Egypt.

As the first king of a new dynasty, Amenemhat I was possibly involved in other security initiatives. Nesumontu's stela at Abydos (Louvre C1) suggests that, at the end of his reign, the king was associated with attacks on fortresses of the *Ỉwn.tyw*, *Mnṯw.tyw* and *Ḥr.yw-šꜥ*. Despite their ideological and literary connotations, the Prophecies of Noferty and the Tale of Sinuhe also mention the construction of the Walls-of-the-Ruler along the northeastern Egyptian borders. The royally-instigated walls were seemingly built to manage the flow of goods and peoples, and control the number of *ꜥꜣm.w* and *St.tyw* in the Delta.

Evidently Amenemhat I was, at least in the didactic text to his son, successful in restraining the 'dog-like' *St.tyw*. This negative treatment continues in the decorative programme of Senwosret I's mortuary temple at el-Lisht, where Asiatics are depicted in subjugated positions. The inscription from Tod's temple of Montu, which may also be of this king's reign, similarly represents belligerent activity against Asiatics with a mention of foreign labour. References to Senwosret I in other media, such as Montuhotep's stela at Abydos (CG 20539) or the Tale of Sinuhe, follow suit, noting the pharaoh's prowess in crushing Asiatics. The latter text repeats the association of Asiatics with dogs, highlighting their metaphoric submissiveness. However it, and all aforementioned examples, occurs in royally-instigated texts, royal funerary complexes or instances directly mentioning the king's office. They portray a *topos*

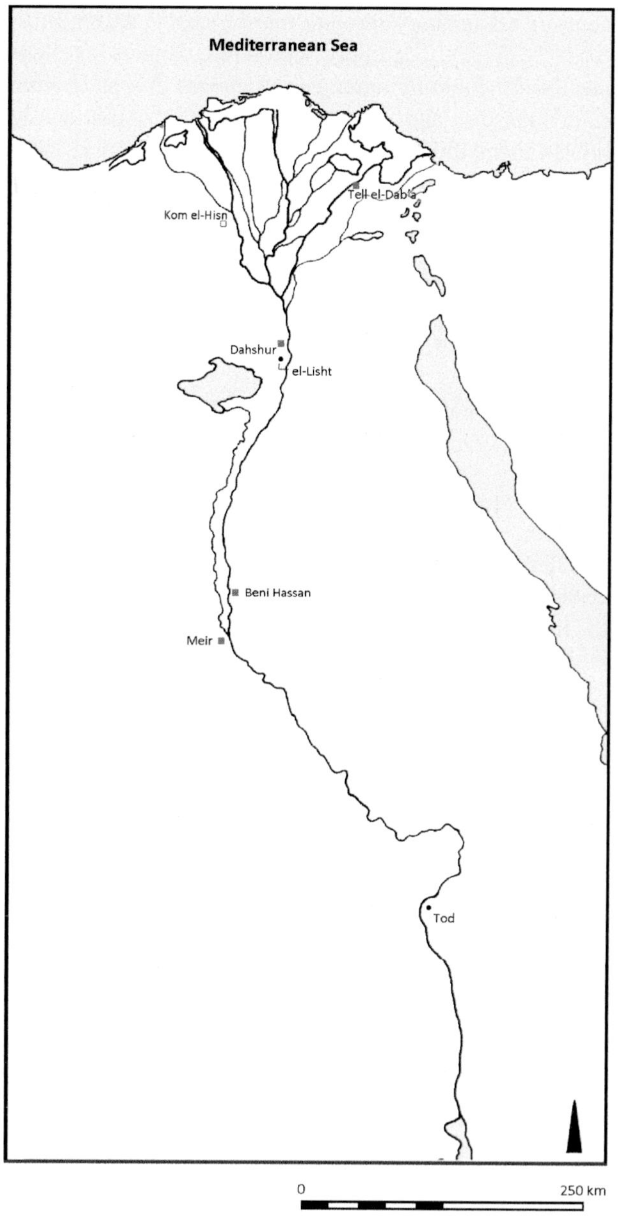

FIGURE 4.69. EGYPTIAN SITES WITH EVIDENCE OF CONTACT WITH THE LEVANTINE DURING THE FIRST HALF OF DYNASTY 12.

- • Presence of Levantine(-influenced) commodities
- ■ Presence of Levantine individuals and commodities
- □ Presence of Levantine individuals and commodities (?)

representation reaffirming the king's duty to protect Egypt's borders from chaotic foreigners. Although some military activity may have occurred, the Asiatics' negative treatment cannot be confirmed by any other non-royal sources.

In contrast to this bellicose ideological treatment of foreigners, the tombs at Beni Hassan and the Hatnub graffiti indicate that the Egyptian administration was allied with Asiatics. Khnumhotep I's biography at Beni Hassan mentions that the king travelled in ships of cedar, a small hint that trade with the Northern Levant had resumed during Amenemhat I's reign. Such trade is supported by the archaeological evidence from Tell el-Dab'a, the only site in the eastern Delta to reveal evidence from this period. Locally-made cooking pots were unearthed, indicating that Asiatics may have resided in the Delta region. Additionally, imported Syro-Palestinian store-jars and Levantine Painted Ware dipper juglets were found, attesting to commerce with the Northern Levant, particularly Byblos. Similar dipper juglets and store-jars are depicted in the tombs of Sobeknakht and Rehuerdjersen at el-Lisht, as well as Amenemhat's tomb at Beni Hassan. The scenes portray Egyptian men working with the jars, suggesting access to imported commodities and knowledge of Levantine pottery-making technologies. Meir's tomb of Wekhhotep (B2) as well as Beni Hassan's Shaft Tomb 181 and Amenemhat's chapel contain further representations of Egyptian-Asiatics in low- to middle-ranking positions. They provide evidence for the artistic mixture of Egyptian elements with such Asiatic characteristics as a lighter skin-tone for men or a foreign hairstyle and dress for females, pointing to local artists' attempts to portray the individuals' mixed heritage. While Asiatics were working in Middle Egypt, the Tale of Sinuhe notes Egyptians travelling to the Levant, especially the Northern Levant, where diplomatic relations were officiated. Gift-exchange, trade, letter-correspondence and envoys could ensure that both Egyptian and Levantine parties were well-versed in each other's languages, social hierarchy and geography.

Egyptian-Levantine relations under the following king, Amenemhat II, were of the same nature. Excerpts from his daybook verify gift-exchange between the Egyptian administration and Levantine rulers, as well as the reception of delegations in Egypt. The Mit Rahina text refers to assaults on fortresses at *Iwꜣ(i)* and *Ꜣsy*, the main outcome of which was the capture of Asiatics who were then transferred to an Egyptian town. This situation finds parallels with the aforementioned inscription from Tod, where foreign labour is associated with a temple district. The Tod temple also yielded a treasure containing an assortment of imported products. Assigned here to Amenemhat II's reign, the collection supports attestations in the Mit Rahina text for large-scale sea-borne trade with the Northern Levant (*Ḫnty-š*).

While such evidence signals the diplomatic and often bellicose nature of relations between the Egyptian administration and the Levantine elite, the evidence from non-royal tombs denotes a growing Egyptian-Asiatic community. At Dahshur, at least one Asiatic descendent was supplied with a possible false door, indicating his employment within the Egyptian administration as well as his adoption of Egyptian funerary traditions. The tomb of Wekhhotep (B4) at Meir also specifies Middle Egyptian nomarchs' continued employment of Asiatics residing in the region.

Thus, the evidence from the first half of the Twelfth Dynasty points to close Egyptian-Levantine alliances which helped secure the establishment of Dynasty 12. Asiatic presence can be traced at Tell el-Dab'a, Dahshur, Beni Hassan and Meir while sites bearing evidence only of access to Levantine products are el-Lisht and Tod (Figure 4.69). Border control along the northeast, as well as the planned settlement at Tell el-Dab'a, was royally instigated to manage the flow of goods and peoples. Trade with the Northern Levant, particularly Byblos and *Ḫnty-š*, was the most active. Once imported, commodities were evidently sent to administrative and temple complexes of the royalty and the elite. It is, then, no surprise that these same institutions and their neighbouring regions first feature the presence of Asiatic individuals as warriors under Amenemhat I, then as warriors, captives, officials, and delegates seeking trade and/or diplomacy under Senwosret I and Amenemhat II.

4.7.2 The second half of the Twelfth Dynasty

Most of the sites with evidence for contact during the first half of the Twelfth Dynasty continue to bear signs of Egyptian-Levantine relations in the second half. Evidence for individuals of Asiatic descent is found at Tell el-Dab'a, Beni Hassan, and Meir, but is newly attested at el-Lahun, el-Lisht, Abydos and Wadi el-Hol, supporting the spread of Asiatics to the south of Egypt (Figure 4.70). The burials at Kom el-Hisn, possibly of acculturated Asiatics, may also be assigned to the general Twelfth Dynasty. Sites producing only Levantine products include Dahshur, Kom Rabi'a, Deir el-Bersha and Tell Edfu.

Senwosret II's reign is represented by evidence from only one tomb, albeit a very significant one. The tomb of Khnumhotep II at Beni Hassan verifies diplomatic relations between Levantines and the Middle Egyptian elite. Like that of Amenemhat, it provides evidence for the presence of Egyptian-Asiatics, the 'fair-skinned' men, who were now employed in managerial roles. Furthermore, such Levantine commodities as *ꜥš*-wood and, perhaps, carob, are represented, indicating the elite's access to Northern Levantine products.

The connection between the Beni Hassan elite and the Levant apparently continued in Senwosret III's reign. A fragmentary inscription from the tomb of Khnumhotep III at Dahshur recounts dealings with Levantines. The official evidently travelled to *Rmnn* for cedar when, following some mishaps with rulers of *Kbny* and *Wꜣṯi*/*Wꜣiṯ*, letter-correspondence with the Egyptian king ensued. The text is not without bias, highlighting the pharaoh's ideological control over foreigners. Therefore, as with the texts from the first half of the Twelfth Dynasty, royalty was still in control over the foreign domain. Adding to this portrayal of royal might are Princess Mereret's pectoral from Dahshur, el-Lahun's Hymns of Senwosret III and the smiting scene from Montu's temple at Nag' el-Medamud. Whether from Khnumhotep III's voyage or another, Senwosret III's pyramid complex was inevitably supplied with ships of cedar, confirming trade with the Northern Levant. Other imports are attested textually as products of the *St.t* at the temple of Montu at Nag' el-Medamud, and archaeologically as imported ceramics from a temple at Tell el-Dab'a.

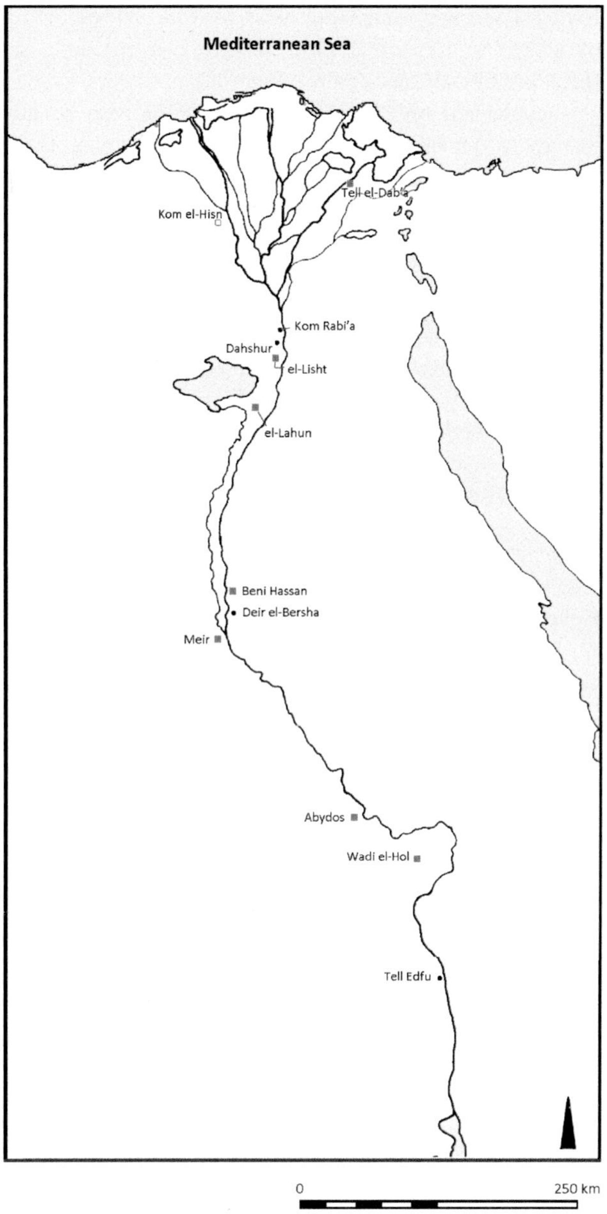

FIGURE 4.70. EGYPTIAN SITES WITH EVIDENCE OF CONTACT WITH THE LEVANTINE DURING THE SECOND HALF OF DYNASTY 12.

- • Presence of Levantine(-influenced) commodities
- ■ Presence of Levantine individuals and commodities
- □ Presence of Levantine individuals and commodities (?)

Khnumhotep III was not the only Egyptian to encounter Asiatics during Senwosret III's reign. Two stelae at Abydos (CG 20296 and Rio de Janeiro 627) record Asiatic descendents in Egyptian households. A papyrus from el-Lahun, Papyrus Berlin 10050, refers to Asiatics in service of Senwosret II's valley temple. The tomb of Wekhhotep (C1) at Meir also portrays Egyptian-Asiatic females bringing imported and local offerings from the Delta. Further, Khusobek's stela at Abydos mentions his experiences in the military, noting the king's involvement in a skirmish at *Skmm*. This mission is evidently the last recorded military expedition against the Levant.

Evidence from Amenemhat III's reign is largely similar in nature to that of former periods. Trade with the Levant is confirmed by the Syro-Palestinian store-jars in his pyramid complex. A number of Asiatics residing in Egypt are also observed in texts dating to his rule, including two stelae from Abydos representing Egyptian-Asiatics partaking in Egyptian activities and duties (CG 20231 and E.207.1900), and at least seven papyri from el-Lahun. They list Asiatic retainers, dancers, singers and other workers at the temples and settlement. They further point to the presence of institutions for the coordination of relations between Asiatics and the local population. As some Asiatics bear Semitic names, it is likely that Levantines were still migrating into Egypt at this time.

Significant developments are noticeable in the ideological treatment of these foreigners. The last attested smiting scene against Asiatics occurs on a pectoral from Princess Mereret's tomb at Dahshur. Dating to Amenemhat III's reign, it is also the only recorded portrayal of this pharaoh's negative treatment of Asiatics. The second half of the Twelfth Dynasty also marks the appearance of numerous groups of Execration Texts that were ritually buried for magical protection or empowerment against rebellious Egyptians and foreigners. Uncovered in funerary contexts at Saqqara, el-Lisht and perhaps Thebes, the texts reveal the administration's awareness of the geography and ruling aristocracy of the Levant, and signal concern over defiant forces within and beyond Egypt's borders.

The following two pharaohs, Amenemhat IV and Sobeknoferu, are only attested in a limited number of representations. In this chapter, only one text definitively dates to Amenemhat IV's reign, and is a papyrus from el-Lahun that refers to Hathor as 'lady of *Kpny*'.

The rest of the evidence for the second half of the Twelfth to the very beginning of the Thirteenth Dynasty cannot be assigned to a particular reign. It agrees with the above in the number, status and treatment of Levantines in Egypt. Texts from el-Lahun, Abydos, Wadi el-Hol and an unprovenanced stela (Moscow I.1.a.5349) list Asiatics in a variety of positions. They are household members, attendants, priests, workmen, temple staff and, perhaps, officials in the vizierate. The majority have Egyptian names and are often represented alongside Egyptian officials. Consequently, their literacy in the Egyptian hieroglyphic and hieratic scripts is highly likely, and indeed inferred in the earliest Proto-Alphabetic texts at Wadi el-Hol. Positions such as those of the 'scribe of the *ꜥ3m.w*' and 'overseer of the expedition of *ꜥ3m(.w)*' denote the administration's continued management of intercultural relations within the community.

Such relations are evident by the Levantine influences on the Egyptian populace. Individuals of apparent Egyptian descent are attested with names referring to an Asiatic resemblance or the goddess of Byblos. Levantine commodities were uncovered in elite tombs as: cedar coffins at Dahshur and Deir el-Bersha, an axe-head from Abydos, as well as Northern Levantine wine in an Egyptian vessel at Dahshur. Furthermore, the elite of Tell Edfu's administrative complex received such imports as Levantine Painted Ware and Lower Egyptian zirs.

The zirs suggest that Levantine products were distributed across Egypt from a northern location, most likely Tell el-Dab'a. The archaeological evidence at Tell el-Dab'a points to the presence of a heterogeneous Egyptian-Levantine population residing in the region, supporting the evidence from other Egyptian sites for the acculturation of Asiatics. Some residents were of the middle to high social echelons and evidently constructed tombs and houses carrying Northern Levantine features. Imported ceramics also indicate direct trade links with the coastal Northern Levant.

Apparently, relations with Levantines were intensifying throughout the second half of Dynasty 12. Major changes are evident with the royal treatment of Asiatics: the last recorded militaristic expedition (Senwosret III), the last artistic bellicose representation (Amenemhat III); and a new need for Execration Texts emphasising Egyptian interests in foreign lands and security. The latter possibly occurred during or shortly after the records of Khnumhotep III and Khusobek from Senwosret III's reign concerning foreign affairs and the maintenance of efficient and secure commercial links with the Levant. These links would have been of utmost importance for the persistent flow of goods which archaeologically occur mainly as Northern Levantine prestige items in funerary, administrative and religious contexts of the ruling elite. The demand for these items possibly influenced the growing settlement at Tell el-Dab'a which also featured Egyptian-Levantines bearing Northern Levantine cultural elements, whose power and wealth possibly developed due to their management of commerce with the Levant. The origins of other Levantines across Egypt are harder to ascertain. The available evidence suggests that some were new immigrants, apparently settling in areas with already-established Asiatic communities for possible commercial and vocational opportunities, and many were of acculturated and mixed Egyptian-Levantine ancestry.

4.7.3 The Thirteenth Dynasty

The early Thirteenth Dynasty witnessed the growing significance of Tell el-Dab'a as a hub of cultural and commercial activity. A large Egyptian-style administrative complex was constructed in Area F/I, its rooms producing Levantine design scarabs as well as a cylinder seal, possibly locally-made, illustrating Egyptian and Levantine elements that may be connected to the myth of Baal. The seal corroborates a find from Tell el-Habwa I which refers to a high official with the 'Baal' element in his name (*ʿpr-Bʿꜣr*). Tombs in the complex's courtyard at Tell el-Dab'a likely belonged to elite Levantines with goods reflecting Northern Levantine features. Scattered between the courtyard's plundered tombs were also fragments of a statue bearing hybrid Egyptian-Asiatic characteristics. The combination of artistic elements is similar to those of a sphinx figurine from Abydos, mirroring hybridised and mixed Egyptian items and Levantine archaeological finds at Tell el-Dab'a as well as the heterogeneous ancestry of the growing Asiatic community within Egypt. It is likely that the two items are a response to this community's increased influences on the elite who, whether of Asiatic ethnicity or not, were cleverly represented with Egyptian and Asiatic features.

The statue at Tell el-Dab'a was, however, intentionally damaged, the complex in which it appears suddenly abandoned. The Mayor's Residence at Tell Basta, which is architecturally very similar to Tell el-Dab'a's complex, was also abandoned and burnt.[1577] Moreover, a conflagration layer of a slightly earlier date was uncovered at Tell el-Dab'a's A/II Strata H and G/4-1.[1578] Evidently, the Delta region was experiencing some turmoil during the early Thirteenth Dynasty. As there is no major change in the material culture of the subsequent phases or an evident interruption in commercial ties, the turbulence was likely due to shifting political alliances. Significantly, the elite of Tell el-Dab'a, Tell el-Habwa I and Tell Basta were not buried in Memphis. Therefore, it is perhaps at this juncture that the Memphite rulers began to lose their control of the Delta, paving the way for the rise of the Fourteenth and Fifteenth Dynasties.

Following the intermission, settlements developed in Tell el-Dab'a F/I c and A/II G/4-1. Levantine imports and locally-made Levantine shapes mostly parallel Northern Levantine forms, although some are also similar to Southern Levantine vessels. The MBA ceramics increased in number, signalling a rise in trade relations, demand for foreign wares, or an influx of peoples. The material culture reveals adherence to both Egyptian and Levantine customs, but the latter are more noticeable in funerary traditions.

The concluding stages of F/I c and A/II G/3-1 are represented by a crisis leading to a high mortality rate. This marks the second point in the Thirteenth Dynasty where regional instability can be determined. Unlike the first juncture in the early Thirteenth Dynasty, the following phase at Tell el-Dab'a and, in fact, other regions in Egypt, witnessed major developments.

The mid-Thirteenth Dynasty is marked by the re-organisation of settlement plots, the appearance of a new settlement, and the construction of a sacred precinct at Tell el-Dab'a A/II, where a large temple (III) was built following Northern Levantine architectural traditions.

1577 In an early publication, Bietak connects the abandonment of Tell el-Dab'a's complex of Stratum d/1 with that of Tell Basta's administrative building, suggesting that both were perhaps influenced by the establishment of Nehsy's kingdom. This theory was later abandoned in favour of the proposition that the complex housed the Thirteenth Dynasty king Sihornedjheritef. As discussed in Chapter 4.2.2.3, the connection between this Thirteenth Dynasty king and the complex of Stratum d/1 is uncertain. See Bietak, *Avaris and Piramesse*, 294.

1578 The left door jamb fragments that name *ʿpr-Bʿꜣr* from Tell el-Habwa I were also damaged by fire. The report is not clear as to how or when the fragments may have been burnt. See Chapter 4.2.4.1; Abd el-Maksoud, *Tell el-Heboua*, 271.

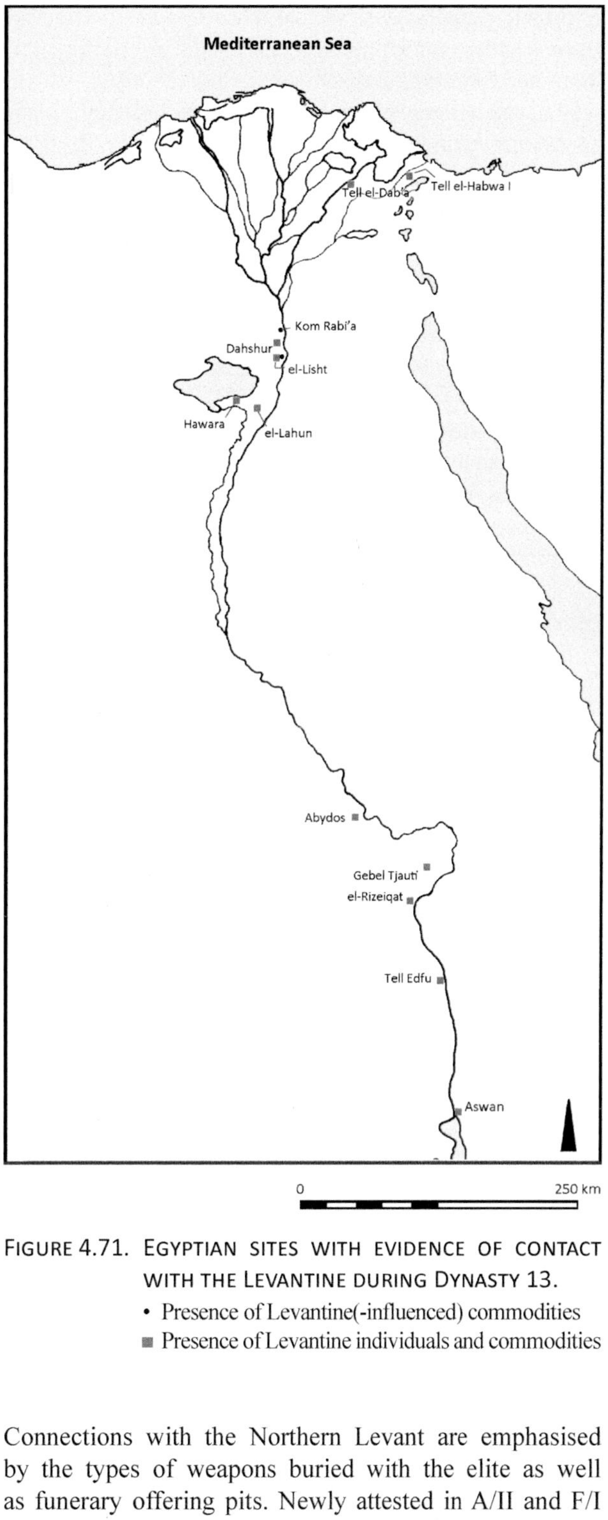

FIGURE 4.71. EGYPTIAN SITES WITH EVIDENCE OF CONTACT WITH THE LEVANTINE DURING DYNASTY 13.
• Presence of Levantine(-influenced) commodities
■ Presence of Levantine individuals and commodities

Connections with the Northern Levant are emphasised by the types of weapons buried with the elite as well as funerary offering pits. Newly attested in A/II and F/I are attendant burials denoting social differentiation. The introduction of large tri-partite houses in F/I similarly attest to greater social divisions. As the material culture indicates a continuance of the same heterogeneous Egyptian-Levantine elements, the developments should not be associated with an invading, external force. Instead, they symbolise a freedom to express ethnicity, wealth, status and religion. Possibly a response to socio-political shifts in the region, this expression could theoretically legitimise the power and independence of an emerging dynasty. The independence continued into the second half of the Thirteenth Dynasty with the renovation of Temple III, the construction of new temples inspired by Egyptian and Levantine architecture, as well as the first recorded occurrence of infant burials in Syro-Palestinian store-jars.

While these developments were taking place at Tell el-Dab'a, Asiatics across Egypt remained socially active. Their presence has been traced in (Figure 4.71):

- Dahshur: the graffiti of Senwosret III's pyramid;
- El-Lisht: a statue of an Egyptian-Asiatic official and a statuette of a possible Levantine cultic figure;
- El-Lahun: Levantine organic products, a torque and a Proto-Alphabetic text;
- Hawara: an official's fragmentary tomb inscription naming an Asiatic worker;
- Abydos: stelae dedications recording Egyptian-Asiatic household members and officials, one of which belonged to Asiatics living in Egypt for six generations;
- Gebel Tjauti: graffiti left by Asiatic military personnel and officials;
- El-Rizeiqat: stelae recording Asiatics;
- Tell Edfu: a stela listing an Asiatic household member;
- Aswan: graffiti left by an Asiatic individual;
- Dra' Abu el-Naga': Papyrus Boulaq 18 mentioning Egyptian-Asiatic officials in the Theban administration as well as Asiatic offering bearers from the Delta; and
- Papyrus Brooklyn 35.1446: a lengthy list of Asiatics probably residing in the region of Thebes.

The representations suggest that the individuals were of mixed Egyptian-Asiatic ancestry. An exception is Stela Musée Joseph Déchelette, Roanne Nr 163, which depicts a female Asiatic with an Egyptian name but a foreign hairstyle and dress, and the Dahshur graffiti which were arguably composed by Asiatics themselves. This may be explained by the aforementioned 'freedom of expression' which is also observable in el-Lisht's cultic statuette. While individuals of Asiatic descent still appear in low to middle class positions, a greater number are attested in higher positions within the Egyptian administration. Evidently, Asiatics had an established and respected community within Egyptian society, holding positions of some power from which they may have been able to steer social, political, and commercial relations.

Egyptians continued to have access to northern and Levantine commodities which were found in occupation levels as well as funerary contexts. A tomb at Tell Basta yielded a scarab of Nehsy and tombs at Abydos contained Tell el-Yahudiyah ware, a torque, and scarabs of Fourteenth Dynasty kings. Vessels from occupation levels were collected from el-Lisht, el-Lahun and Kom Rabi'a, the majority of the latter ascertained to be of Northern Levantine origins. This data agrees with two texts of the mid-Thirteenth Dynasty, the first from Abydos listing an official responsible for products from *Kpny*, and the second a stela of Sobekhotep IV referring to the utilisation of *ʿš*-wood from *Ḫnty-š* in temple architecture.

Therefore, it is evident that Dynasty 13 witnessed significant socio-political developments associated with Asiatics. Firstly, two main tumultuous intervals affected the first half of the dynasty. Initially only administrative centres appear to be affected but, when the general population suffered from a high mortality rate, the elite at Tell el-Dab'a responded by constructing the largest documented MBA temple as well as new and re-organised settlement plots. Architectural and funerary symbols of wealth and status became more prevalent, reflecting strong connections with Northern Levantine customs. Secondly, a 'freedom of expressing' this ethnic identity is clear. Finds across Egypt indicate that Levantines could practice their religion and wear distinctly non-Egyptian dress. Thirdly, an increasing differentiation in social echelons is attested. Levantines are represented as an elite group at Tell el-Dab'a, palatial officials, administrative officials, treasurers and military personnel. There were also butchers, retainers, cooks, musicians and weavers. The Asiatics intermingled with the Egyptians, with greater numbers of Asiatic wives and concubines. Judging by their names, a few may have been newly migrated from the Levant, but the majority seem to be descendents of acculturated Levantines, some living in Egypt for over a century. While these developments took place, trade with the Levant continued and intensified. Ties with the Southern Levant formed but relations with the Northern Levant were more dominant. Northern Levantine commodities remained prized by the Egyptian and Levantine elite, and an office is attested within the Egyptian administration for the management of products from Byblos. No definitive textual evidence for such offices has yet surfaced for Tell el-Dab'a's elite. However, this chapter has argued that they themselves were of Northern Levantine ancestry. This perhaps helped form continued alliances with Northern Levantine rulers, which may have inevitably led to the rise of the Hyksos.

4.7.4 The first half of the Fifteenth Dynasty

The first half of the Fifteenth Dynasty marks the complete establishment of Tell el-Dab'a as the commercial capital of the Delta. Excavations have revealed two areas with administrative complexes: R/III, where a seal impression of *Ḫy3n* was found; and F/II, where a large palatial complex is still being unearthed. The F/II compound features a plethora of Levantine(-inspired) wares, a storage and workshop quarter, magazines comprising imported goods, a large hall with ritualistic offering pits notably yielding decapitated human hands, and a courtyard for cultic assemblies with offering pits filled with local, Memphite, and imported ceramics. Seal impressions bear the names of Thirteenth Dynasty kings, Fifteenth Dynasty ruler *Ḫy3n*, and a ruler of *Rṯnw* whose name is lost. The latter impression, along with one other seal, depicts Near Eastern elements, as does an Akkadian cuneiform tablet unearthed nearby. All point to the compound's use by elite officials practicing Levantine customs while trading with the Levant, Memphis/Fayum, the Egyptian Oases, Nubia, Mesopotamia and Cyprus.

Heightened prosperity is indicated by developments in other sectors. Temples were constructed and renovated in A/II and F/I, their architecture borrowing from Egyptian, Southern and Northern Levantine traditions. Ritual banqueting is evident by the many offering pits filled with ceramics for storing, preparing and serving food. Settlements rapidly expanded in A/II, F/I and A/V and more tombs are detected, retaining the same burial architecture and forms of funerary goods as those found in previous phases. Further subtle developments in the material culture are observed: a local Tell el-Yahudiyah ware industry surfaced, producing new Levantine-inspired styles; local scarab workshops gained popularity; local pottery workshops began to produce distinct types of pottery or creoles influenced by MBA shapes; and imported Cypriote as well as Nubian wares are more prominent in occupation levels. Consequently, a growing regionalisation or 'Nilotisation' is discernible.

Tell el-Dab'a's population apparently increased and, as a result, new industries and places of worship were established. The site's administration was not only able to efficiently manage the industries and construction projects, it also ensured the consistent import of foreign goods. Trade with the Northern Levant continued, that with the Southern Levant increased, and emerging links with Nubia, the Mediterranean and Mesopotamia are witnessed. Such progress stresses regional stability, prosperity as well as an independence from Egyptian hegemony. Interestingly, Stager's 'port power' model of Levantine trade can be applied to these findings. It follows that the power of a trading centre, such as Tell el-Dab'a, in a decentralised system, like the Second Intermediate Period, could be exercised through economic ties in a heterogeneous and integrated network of market exchange.[1579]

Evidence suggests that, once Tell el-Dab'a's own stability was established, its rulers turned focus to the Delta (Figure 4.72). New settlements emerged with Levantine or, more precisely, Egyptian-Levantine, material traits. They are situated at Tell el-Habwa I and Tell el-Maskhuta, both strategically positioned on land-based routes leading to the Levant. Tell el-Habwa most likely supplied Tell el-Dab'a's growing

1579 Stager, in *Archaeology of Israel*, 625-638; Stager, in *MBA in the Levant*, 353-362. See also Cohen, in *Exploring the Longue Durée*, 69-75.

population with grains and foods, while Tell el-Maskhuta was possibly a trading settlement controlling the flow of goods through the Wadi Tumilat, guaranteeing land-based access to the Sinai, the Southern Levant and perhaps even the Red Sea. The data thereby supports these two sites being new initiatives by the Fifteenth Dynasty to manage an 'integrated network' of local and regional trade, and warrant its population's wealth and independence.

Tombs with Levantine(-influenced) ceramics, weapons, scarabs and equid burials point to other Egyptian-Levantine settlements in the Delta. These are found at Tell Farasha, Inshas, Tell el-Yahudiyah and probably el-Khata'na and Tell el-Sahaba (Figure 4.72). Perhaps the increased prosperity of Tell el-Dab'a attracted Egyptian-Levantines to settle in the eastern Delta.

Fifteenth Dynasty trade with other regions is supported by the discovery of a few Levantine(-influenced) goods. Within the Memphite region, Tell el-Yahudiyah ware is attested at el-Harageh, el-Lahun and el-Lisht, Syro-Palestinian store-jars are found at Kom Rabi'a and el-Lisht, and Levantine design scarabs and seals occur at el-Lisht. The Upper Egyptian sites of Abydos, Karnak and Tell Edfu also yielded northern commodities.

Between Upper Egypt and Memphis, only two sites included products of the north, Deir Rifeh and Mostagedda. As discussed in the chapter, some propose that Deir Rifeh was a Fifteenth Dynasty garrison while Mostagedda was under Seventeenth Dynasty control. The examined evidence includes: from Deir Rifeh, Tell el-Yahudiyah ware as well as a button-shaped seal amulet inscribed with Proto-Alphabetic signs; and from Mostagedda, Tell el-Yahudiyah ware, silver torques and Levantine design scarabs. All except for the amulet come from burials, suggesting that they were of funerary significance, perhaps related to status. Whether or not the sites were garrisons under two separate hegemonies, they both evidently had access to Levantine and Fifteenth Dynasty products, hinting at trade with the Delta.

Therefore, the first half of the Fifteenth Dynasty was involved in stabilising the internal security at Tell el-Dab'a and strengthening the city's 'port power' and commercial ties. Administrative complexes with magazines, a reception hall and spaces for ritual banqueting were set up. Population numbers increased, the material culture reflecting a continuance and development of mixed Egyptian-Levantine traits. Demand for commodities, ceramics and scarabs secured the popularity of emerging local industries. Trade links with Memphis and Upper Egypt were limited, but products were still being transported throughout Egypt. New initiatives secured strategic posts in the eastern Delta, emphasising the importance of commerce and trade for the prosperity of Tell el-Dab'a. Clearly, the city's rulers were interested in opening new avenues of trade via land and sea. Perhaps, in the course of securing commercial alliances, some conflict took place. F/II's decapitated hands and its magazines' conflagration

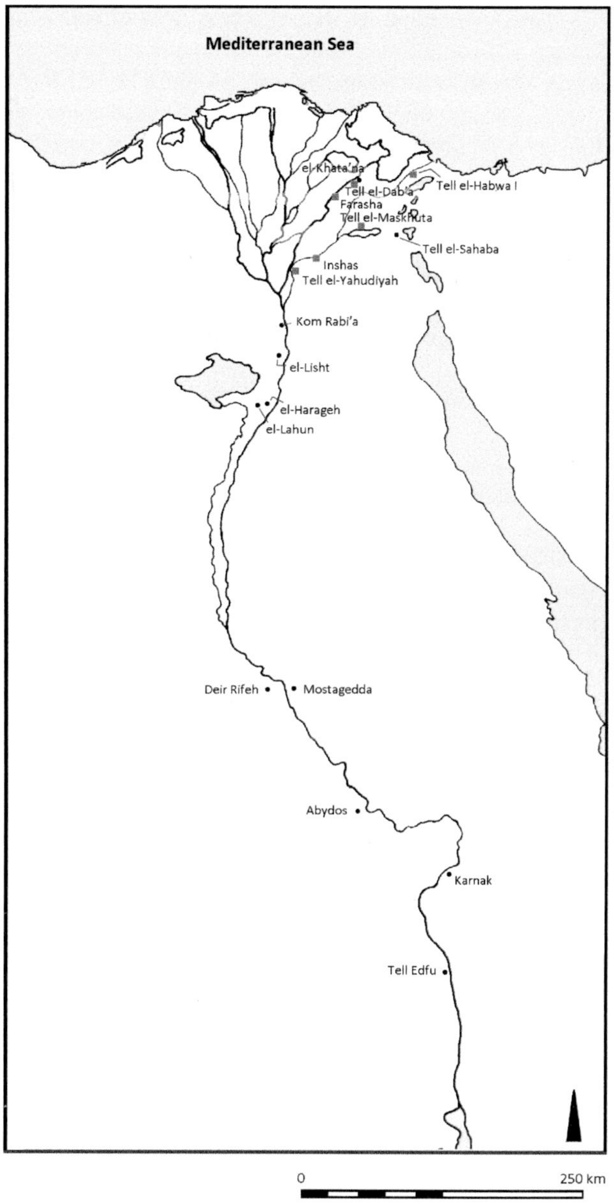

FIGURE 4.72. EGYPTIAN SITES WITH EVIDENCE OF CONTACT WITH THE LEVANTINE DURING THE FIRST HALF OF DYNASTY 15.

• Presence of Levantine(-influenced) commodities

■ Presence of Levantine individuals and commodities

layer hint that the first half of Dynasty 15 was not without qualms. On the whole, however, the establishment of the Fifteenth Dynasty was apparently peaceful. No evidence supports an invasion of a completely foreign race. Instead, the general populace as well as the elite seem to be of the same mixed culture as that of earlier periods: the creole populace was of heterogeneous character and the elite mostly followed Northern Levantine traditions. What distinctly surfaces during the Fifteenth Dynasty is the Hyksos's escalating control of the Delta as well as the elite's complete economic and commercial independence. These two factors ensured the dynasty's stability, security and affluence.

5. Between Egypt and the Levant: The Eastern Desert

'... the Eastern Desert formed an unavoidable
bridge linking the Nile to the Red Sea... the
Egyptians knew that the Eastern Desert, a
forbidding and otherwise frightening place,
was a repository of valuable caches of mineral
wealth, which were irresistible draws for them.'
Sidebotham, Hense and Nouwens, *Red Land*, 27.

5.1 Introduction

The Eastern Desert presents a periphery zone connecting Egypt with the Levant in the north and other African and Arabian lands further south. Rich in mineral deposits and other organic products, the area was constantly visited by Egyptians throughout its history. While ideologically under the king's auspices, the Eastern Desert cannot be considered Egyptian terrain, although control of the mines ensured the procurement of valuable commodities for the Egyptian state. Titles such as 'overseer of the Eastern Desert'[1] suggest the establishment of an organised administrative division specifically for the management of expeditions to the east.

This chapter gathers published evidence for Middle Kingdom and early Second Intermediate Period contact between Levantines and Egyptians at the Eastern Desert. Sites are divided into: (1) Mount Sinai and the Red Sea coast; and (2) the Southeastern Desert. For the sites' geographical location, see Figure 5.1. As in Chapter 4, each site includes its location by Latitude and Longitude, a list of selected references and its temporal placement within the Egyptian chronology. The chapter concludes with a review of the data, noting the nature of contact between Egyptians and Levantines, the origins of and evidence for Levantine groups, and the development of Egyptian-Levantine relations.

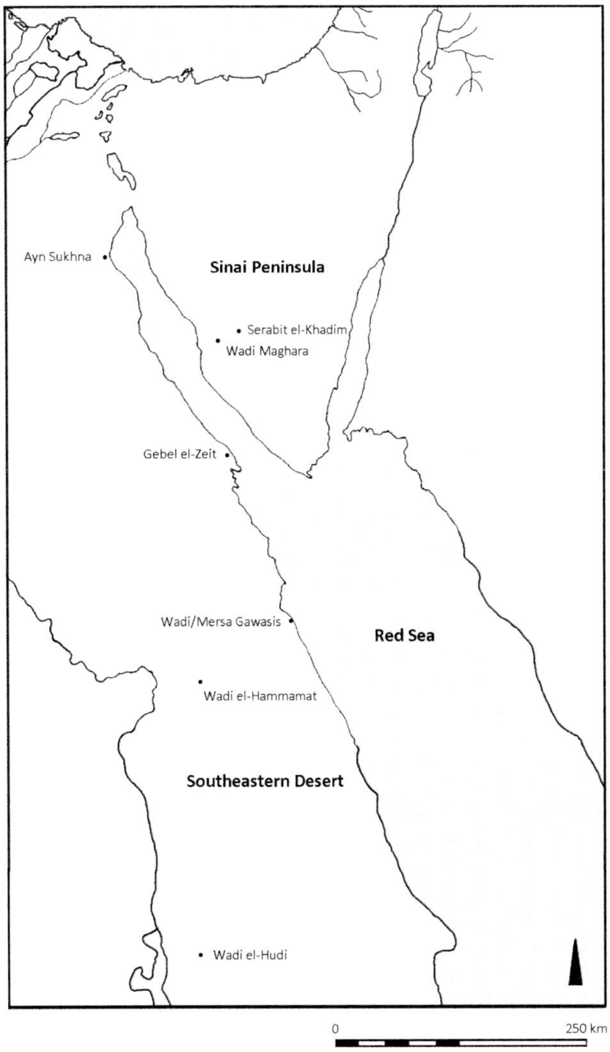

FIGURE 5.1. EXAMINED SITES IN THE EASTERN DESERT.

[1] See Chapters 4.4.1.1 and 4.4.1.3 for individuals who held this title. For more, see Ward, *Index*, 44 [340]; Aufrère, in *Egypt and Nubia*, 207-214.

5.2 Mount Sinai and the Red Sea Coast

5.2.1 *Ayn Sukhna*

Lat.Lon. 29°36'N 32°20'E

Refs Tallet, *British Museum Studies in Ancient Egypt and Sudan* 18 (2012), 147-168; Pomey, in *Red Sea in Pharaonic Times*, 35-52.

Chron. Twelfth Dynasty to early Second Intermediate Period

Ayn Sukhna is located almost 120km east of Memphis, on the west coast of the Red Sea's Gulf of Suez. Since 2001, excavations by the Institut français d'archéologie orientale and the University of Paris-Sorbonne[2] have uncovered Old and Middle Kingdom remains principally at: (1) sector 'Kom 14', where a temporary camp with hearths, workshops and other installations were found near the coast;[3] (2) Middle Kingdom metal workshops;[4] and (3) 10 storage galleries cut into the mountainside.[5] Inscriptions on the mountain's rock face and within the galleries point to the site's connection with the Sinai Peninsula, relating Ayn Sukhna with Pharaonic expeditions purposed to obtain turquoise, copper and possibly bronze.[6] Excavators believe that Ayn Sukhna acted as a point of arrival and departure for seafaring expeditions along the Red Sea, especially those on route to the Sinai mines.[7]

Two Middle Kingdom boats used in such voyages were found dismantled and neatly stored in Galleries G2 and G9.[8] The boats were each around 14-15m long and assembled using Egyptian shipbuilding methods but with Lebanese cedar (*Cedrus libani*).[9] An exact date for their construction is unknown, yet radiocarbon dating on timber samples indicates that they were stored at the end of the Middle Kingdom or the Second Intermediate Period.[10] Following their deposition, the boats were exposed to fire, as evidenced by their charred remains, leading excavators to infer that they were deliberately destroyed during the Second Intermediate Period.[11] Reasons for this assumption are not provided although, if correct, the destruction could signal the intentional and violent termination of expeditions along the Red Sea. The planks of cedar show the Egyptians' preference for the timber in the construction of seafaring ships, offering evidence for trade with the Northern Levant during the Middle Kingdom.

5.2.2 *Gawasis, Wadi / Mersa (Saww)*

Lat.Lon. 26°33'N 34°02'E

Refs Sayed, *RdE* 29 (1977), 150-173; Bard and Fattovich (eds), *Harbor of the Pharaohs*; Bard and Fattovich, *JAEI* 2/3 (2010), 1-13; Bard and Fattovich, in *Offerings to the Discerning Eye*, 33-38.

Chron. Twelfth Dynasty to Second Intermediate Period

Wadi/Mersa Gawasis is on the west coast of the Red Sea, around 378km south of Ayn Sukhna.[12] Investigations by Sayed, Bard and Fattovich uncovered a harbour with adjoined storage and administrative facilities dating from the Old to New Kingdoms (Figures 5.2-5.3).[13] The Twelfth Dynasty witnessed the occupation of the eastern and western terraces, as well as the harbour.[14] Lack of monumental permanent architecture indicates the site's temporary habitation. This is also marked by encampments at the top and southern slope of the western terrace.[15] Other parts of the terrace, including galleries cut into the coral reef, were utilised as storage facilities, administrative quarters, wood workshops and food processing areas.[16]

Finds from the storage areas and wood workshops of Galleries or Caves 1-3 (Figure 5.2) include Lebanese cedar hull planks, deck planks, a strake reused as a work bench and other small fragments.[17] A production area in front of the caves consisted of fire pits with charcoal, samples of which also include Lebanese cedar, oak and pine from the Northern Levant.[18] Cedar objects such as the strake[19] and a wooden spoon from an administrative

2 Abd el-Raziq, Castel, Tallet, in *Proceedings of the Ninth International Congress* 1, 61-68; Defernez, *CCE* 7 (2004), 59-89; Tallet, *British Museum Studies in Ancient Egypt and Sudan* 18 (2012), 147-168; Tallet, in *Navigated Spaces*, 33-37; Abd el-Raziq et al., in *Red Sea in Pharaonic Times*, 3-20.

3 Abd el-Raziq et al., in *Red Sea in Pharaonic Times*, 8-10.

4 Abd el-Raziq et al., in *Red Sea in Pharaonic Times*, 7-8; Abd el-Raziq et al., *Ayn Soukhna* 2.

5 Abd el-Raziq et al., in *Red Sea in Pharaonic Times*, 5-6; Tallet, *British Museum Studies in Ancient Egypt and Sudan* 18 (2012), 149-150; Tallet, in *Navigated Spaces*, 33-35.

6 Tallet, *British Museum Studies in Ancient Egypt and Sudan* 18 (2012), 148-149; Abd el-Raziq et al., in *Red Sea in Pharaonic Times*, 4-5; Abd el-Raziq et al., *Les inscriptions d'Ayn Soukhna*, MIFAO 122 (Cairo, 2002).

7 Tallet, *British Museum Studies in Ancient Egypt and Sudan* 18 (2012), 149; Abd el-Raziq et al., in *Red Sea in Pharaonic Times*, 4-5.

8 Tallet, *BSFE* 165 (2006), 10-31; Pomey, in *Red Sea in Pharaonic Times*, 35-52; Tallet, *British Museum Studies in Ancient Egypt and Sudan* 18 (2012), 150, fig. 10.

9 Abd el-Raziq et al., in *Red Sea in Pharaonic Times*, 5; Tallet, *British Museum Studies in Ancient Egypt and Sudan* 18 (2012), 150; Tallet, in *Navigated Spaces*, 35.

10 Around 1700 BC. Tallet, in *Navigated Spaces*, 35.

11 Tallet, in *Navigated Spaces*, 35.

12 Wadi Gawasis is at the mouth of the harbour, Mersa Gawasis (Figure 5.2), and around 2km north of Wadi Gasus. Sayed, in *Archaeology of Ancient Egypt*, 1060.

13 Sayed, *RdE* 29 (1977), 140-178; Bard and Fattovich (eds), *Harbor of the Pharaohs*; Bard and Fattovich, 'Mersa/Wadi Gawasis 2007-2008'; Bard and Fattovich, *JAEI* 2/3 (2010), 1-13; Bard and Fattovich, in *Offerings to the Discerning Eye*, 33-38; Bard and Fattovich, *Newsletter di Archeologia CISA* 1 (2010), 7-35; Bard, Fattovich and Ward, 'Mersa/Wadi Gawasis 2010-2011'.

14 Bard and Fattovich, in *Harbor of the Pharaohs*, 242.

15 Bard and Fattovich, in *Offerings to the Discerning Eye*, 33; Bard and Fattovitch, in *Harbor of the Pharaohs*, 240; Bard and Fattovich, *JAEI* 2/3 (2010), 4, 9.

16 Bard and Fattovich, *JAEI* 2/3 (2010), 4-9.

17 Bard and Fattovich, *JAEI* 2/3 (2010), 5-7; Bard et al., in *Harbor of the Pharaohs*, 62-66, 70-71; Ward, in *Harbor of the Pharaohs*, 137-139, 146-148; Gerisch, in *Harbor of the Pharaohs*, 185-186, table 12.

18 Gerisch, in *Harbor of the Pharaohs*, 173-181, table 6; Gerisch, in Bard, Fattovich and Ward, 'Mersa/Wadi Gawasis 2010-2011'; Bard and Fattovich, *JAEI* 2/3 (2010), 9.

19 Bard and Fattovich, *JAEI* 2/3 (2010), 7.

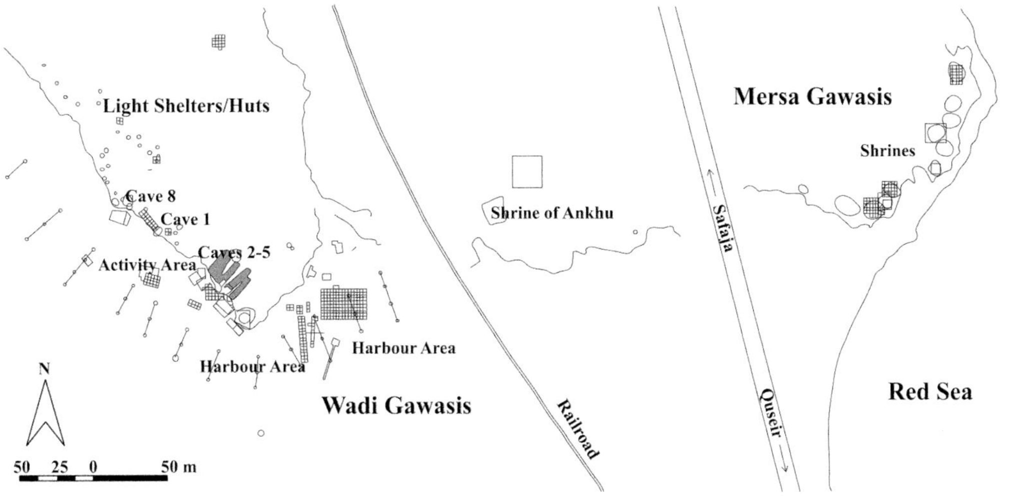

Figure 5.2. Site plan, Wadi/Mersa Gawasis. After Bard and Fattovich, *JAEI* 2/3 (2010), fig. 2.

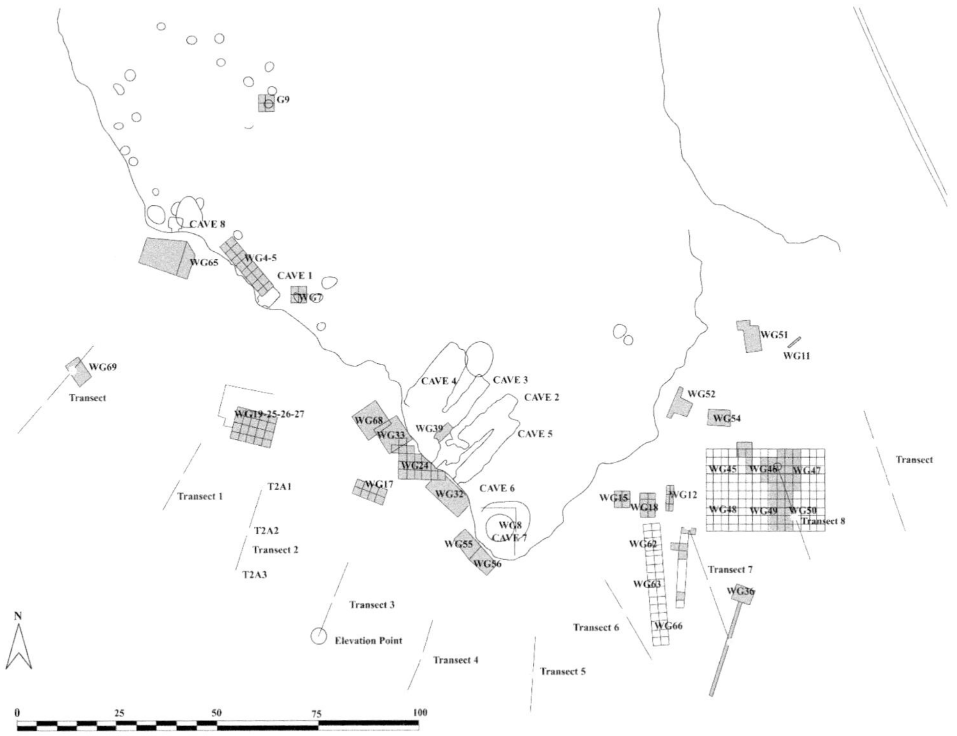

Figure 5.3. Excavation units on the western terrace, Wadi Gawasis. After Bard and Fattovich, *JAEI* 2/3 (2010), fig. 4.

area outside Cave 8[20] attest to the timber's functional reuse. From the overall wood samples, Lebanese cedar appears to be one of the most commonly used timbers alongside acacia and sycamore from Egypt.[21] In relation to the site's function as a harbour, it is possible that cedar was essential for the construction of seafaring ships. Consequently, its importation[22] was significant for the continuance of trade along the Red Sea.

The strong timber was not the only imported product from the Levant. Fragments of Syro-Palestinian store-jars have been found in at least three excavation units across the site: (1) an area outside the caves of the western terrace (WG 31, SU 1) where a piece of Lebanese cedar, rope fragments, hearths and pottery dating between the Second Intermediate Period and the early Eighteenth Dynasty were uncovered;[23]

20 Bard and Fattovich, *Newsletter di Archeologia CISA* 1 (2010), 27.

21 Gerisch, in *Harbor of the Pharaohs*, 175, 185; Gersich, in 'Mersa/Wadi Gawasis 2010-2011', 19.

22 A stela at Mersa/Wadi Gawasis for Senwosret I's vizier, Intefoker, describes how the ships were constructed at Qift (Coptos) and transported to Gawasis, where they were reassembled. So, the timber would have been transported from the Northern Levant to the Delta and then south to Coptos before being taken to Mersa/Wadi Gawasis. Sayed, *RdE* 29 (1977), 170-171, pl. 16; Sayed, in *Egyptology* 1, 433.

23 Wallace-Jones and Imbrenda, in Bard, Fattovich and Ward, 'Mersa/Wadi Gawasis 2010-2011'; Bard et al., in *Harbor of the Pharaohs*, 72-73.

(2) a beach near the harbour (WG 47), which yielded one sherd of a handle in a storage area with Egyptian jars belonging to the late Twelfth to early Thirteenth Dynasty, and one cooking pot of Nile E fabric from the eastern Delta;[24] and (3) near the edge of the harbour below Cave 8 (WG 69) in an area utilised as a refuse for broken pottery throughout Dynasty 12.[25] The three contexts point to the utilitarian and non-elite use of the Syro-Palestinian store-jars between the Twelfth Dynasty and Second Intermediate Period which, as WG 47's pottery insinuates, were most likely imported via the eastern Delta, perhaps Tell el-Dab'a.[26] It should be noted that wares from southern lands, such as South Arabia and Nubia, were more abundant than these northern fabrics, possibly signalling the presence of Nubians or local inhabitants alongside the Egyptians.[27] The presence of Levantines cannot, however, be substantiated by the current excavated material. Nevertheless, the existence of Levantine ceramics and timbers signals an active flow of trade in utilitarian goods, some of which were necessary for maintaining the very function of the site as a trading harbour.

5.2.3 Maghara, Wadi

Lat.Lon. 28°54'N 33°22'E

Refs PM 7, 339-345; Petrie, *Sinai;* Gardiner and Peet, *Inscriptions of Sinai* 1, pl. 11; Černy, *Inscriptions of Sinai* 2, 67-68.

Chron. Twelfth Dynasty

Wadi Maghara is located in the southwestern Sinai Peninsula. Explorations include those by Lepsius (1845),[28] Petrie (1904-5)[29] and Valbelle (1987).[30] Findings consist of an Old Kingdom settlement as well as inscriptions mainly dating from the Old to Middle Kingdoms,[31] the latter assigned to the reign of Amenemhat III,[32] Amenemhat IV[33] and the general Middle Kingdom period.[34] Wadi Maghara

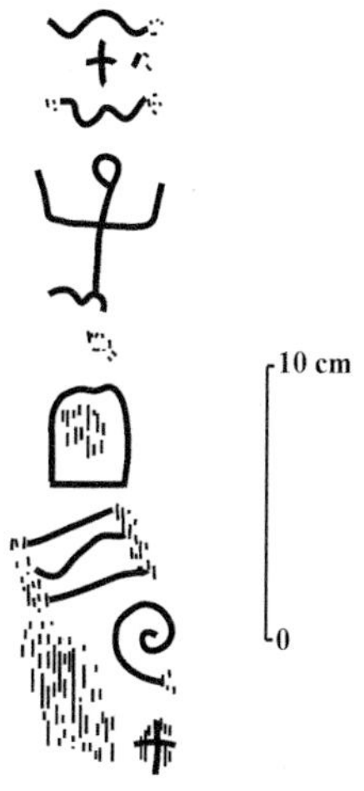

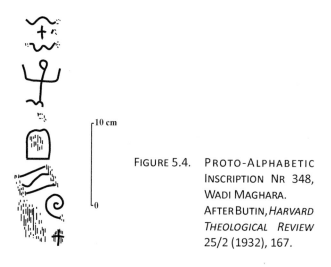

FIGURE 5.4. PROTO-ALPHABETIC INSCRIPTION NR 348, WADI MAGHARA. AFTER BUTIN, *HARVARD THEOLOGICAL REVIEW* 25/2 (1932), 167.

was mostly exploited for its turquoise ores with a possibility of copper manufacturing at the settlement.[35] Data relating to Egyptian-Levantine contact includes:

- Inscription Nr 24-24a: Two fragments of a commemorative stela for the 'remover of scorpions', Iti, that date to Year 2 of Amenemhat III's reign.[36] Among the list of named individuals is *ꜥ3m Ỉw=s-n=i* 'ꜥ3m Iuseni'.[37] A seated figure at the bottom of the fragment acts as a determinative for the name, although its larger scale indicates that it could also artistically represent the individual's identity.[38] It portrays a man with a long pointed beard, a throw-stick in his hands and a somewhat coiffed hairstyle. A drawing immediately behind the neck, similar to (V19) may also be related to the figure;[39]

- Proto-Alphabetic inscription Nr 348 (Figure 5.4): The exact context of the inscription is unknown but it may have been engraved onto a rock-face.[40] Sass identifies 10 characters of the fragmentary vertical text (*m ? š t m h b ꜥ l t*) and leaves it untranslated[41] while Butin reads eight letters for *št mhbꜥlt* '[...]sht, cherished of Baalat'.[42] In both renditions, the final six characters are the same, suggesting that the inscription possibly featured the Levantine goddess Baalat. Due to the uncertain location of the text, its exact date cannot be ascertained;

24 Wallace-Jones, in Bard and Fattovich, 'Mersa/Wadi Gawasis 2007-2008'; Bard and Fattovich, *JAEI* 2/3 (2010), 9-10.

25 Bard and Fattovich, *JAEI* 2/3 (2010), 9; Wallace-Jones, in Bard and Fattovich, *Newsletter di Archeologia CISA* 1 (2010), 19.

26 It is possible that Minoan sherds from the site, a Middle Minoan IB White Banded Kamares sherd and a Middle Minoan IIIA Fine Buff Crude Ware sherd, were similarly transported from the Delta. Wallace-Jones, in 'Mersa/Wadi Gawasis 2007-2008'; Bard and Fattovich, *JAEI* 2/3 (2010), 8-9.

27 Bard and Fattovich, *JAEI* 2/3 (2010), 11-12; Wallace-Jones, in 'Mersa/Wadi Gawasis 2007-2008'; Manzo, in Bard and Fattovich, *Newsletter di Archeologia CISA* 1 (2010), 19-21; Manzo, *British Museum Studies in Ancient Egypt and Sudan* 18 (2012), 76; Manzo, in *Navigated Spaces*.

28 Mumford, in *Archaeology of Ancient Egypt*, 1071.

29 Petrie, *Sinai*.

30 Chartier-Raymond, *CRIPEL* 10 (1988), 13-22.

31 Chartier-Raymond, *CRIPEL* 10 (1988), 13-22; Petrie, *Sinai*, 51-53; Gardiner and Peet, *Inscriptions of Sinai* 1, pls 1 [1a, 2, 4], 2 [5, 7], 3 [7], 4 [6], 5 [8], 6 [10], 8 [14, 16]; Černy, *Inscriptions of Sinai* 2, 24-29; Shaw, *Antiquity* 68 (1994), 114-115.

32 Nrs 23-32. Gardiner and Peet, *Inscriptions of Sinai* 1, pls 10 [23, 25, 29], 11 [24, 24a, 26, 27], 12 [28, 32], 13 [30], 14 [31]; Černy, *Inscriptions of Sinai* 2, 66-71 [Nrs 23-32].

33 Nrs 33-35. Gardiner and Peet, *Inscriptions of Sinai* 1, pls 11 [35], 12 [33-34]; Černy, *Inscriptions of Sinai* 2, 71-72 [Nrs 33-35].

34 Nrs 36-43. Gardiner and Peet, *Inscriptions of Sinai* 1, pls 12 [43], 13 [37-42], 14 [36]; Černy, *Inscriptions of Sinai* 2, 72-73 [Nrs 36-42].

35 Tools, copper slag, ore chips, ingot moulds and crucible fragments were uncovered at the site. Petrie, *Sinai*, 51-53; Mumford, in *Archaeology of Ancient Egypt*, 1075; Shaw, *Antiquity* 68 (1994), 115.

36 See also Nr 23 for a reference to the same individual. Gardiner and Peet, *Inscriptions of Sinai* 1, pl. 11 [24-24a]; Černy, *Inscriptions of Sinai* 2, 67-68 [Nrs 23-24a].

37 Ranke, *Personennamen* 1, 15 [4].

38 Černy, *Inscriptions of Sinai* 2, 68. For a similar use of a determinative, see Obelisk Nr 163 from Serabit el-Khadim (Chapter 5.2.4.1; Figure 5.9).

39 Perhaps the figure and symbol are a garbled writing of the title *ir.y-ꜥ.t n.y md.t* 'hall-keeper of the stable'. Ward, *Index*, 59 [479].

40 Sass, *Genesis of the Alphabet*, 16.

41 Sass, *Genesis of the Alphabet*, 16-17, figs 23-26.

42 Butin, *Harvard Theological Review* 25/2 (1932), 130-203.

- Inscription Nr 32: A text dated after Amenemhat III's Year 20.[43] Among a list of expedition members is the 'interpreter Nehy'[44] whose expertise may have been necessitated for contacting locals or other foreigners involved in the venture.

Despite the uncertain date of Nr 348, the hieroglyphic inscriptions imply that Asiatics were working alongside Egyptians at Wadi Maghara during Amenemhat III's reign. Based on the Egyptian name of the foreigner in Nr 24-24a, he was most likely not a local inhabitant of the Sinai but possibly accompanied the expedition from Egypt. He, along with his Egyptian associates, would have then required an interpreter such as Nehy of Nr 32 to communicate with the locals and/or other foreigners in the area.

5.2.4 Serabit el-Khadim

Lat.Lon. 29°02'N 33°28'E

Refs PM 7, 345-366; Petrie, *Sinai*; Gardiner and Peet, *Inscriptions of Sinai* 1; Černy, *Inscriptions of Sinai* 2; Beit-Arieh, *BA* 45/1 (1982), 13-18; Beit-Arieh, *Levant* 17 (1985), 89-116; Sass, *Genesis of the Alphabet*, 10-45; Valbelle and Bonnet, *Sanctuaire d'Hathor*; Hamilton, *Origins of the West Semitic Alphabet*, 332-389.

Chron. Twelfth to Fifteenth Dynasty (?)

Serabit el-Khadim is around 18km northeast of Wadi Maghara. The site was exploited for its turquoise and copper mines since the Chalcolithic period.[45] With the resumption of mining activity in the Sinai following the First Intermediate Period, the site was visited by Egyptian expeditions, some of which were involved in building a rock-cut temple in honour of Hathor, 'lady of *Mfk3.t*', and Sopdu.[46] Perhaps initially a shrine instigated by Amenemhat I,[47] the temple was renovated throughout the Middle Kingdom's Twelfth Dynasty and the New Kingdom's Eighteenth to Twentieth Dynasties.[48] Its remains, as well as other finds from the surrounding region, were uncovered by, for instance, Petrie,[49] Albright,[50] Beit-Arieh[51] and, more recently, Valbelle.[52] Evidence for Egyptian-Levantine relations mainly stems from Egyptian texts, although some data may be extracted from Proto-Alphabetic inscriptions.

5.2.4.1 *Egyptian texts*

A total of 29 Egyptian texts written on stelae, statues, an altar and wall inscriptions refer to Asiatics and/or Levantine toponyms (Appendix B.12, Figure B.3). Of those of known context, only one was found in Mine C (Nr 54), the rest being from several sections of the Hathor Temple. One dates to Senwosret III's reign, 19 or 20 are to Amenemhat III's, three are to Amenemhat IV's and five are of the general Middle Kingdom period. Details regarding their specific context, the portrayal of Asiatics and bibliographic references can be found in Figure B.3. The figure includes further instances of Asiatics that are only represented artistically. Translations of the inscriptions are provided in Appendix B.12. The texts represent: (1) individual Asiatics; (2) groups of Asiatics; and (3) toponyms of Asiatic lands not associated with particular Asiatics.

Individual Asiatics

There are 34 instances of Asiatic individuals of varying status, including those clearly within the Egyptian administration and those whose origins are more obscure. Three references can be ascribed to low- or middle-ranking officials with such titles as 'hall-keeper' (Nr 85) and 'major-domo' (Nr 112). They occur in lists of expedition members dating mainly to the reigns of Senwosret III and Amenemhat III.

13 inscriptions belong to high-ranking officials. Eight are for Imenyseshenen who is known as the 'sealer of the king of Lower Egypt' as well as 'deputy of the chief steward' (Nrs 93-99 and 402; Figure 5.6). His foreign origins are indicated by the presence of a pointed beard on his representation in Nr 95 (Figure 5.7) as well as his mother's designation as *ꜥ3m.t*. As her name is of Egyptian origin, she was probably either a first or second generation immigrant to Egypt. Accordingly, Imenyseshenen would have been raised in Egypt, an inference supported by Nr 98 in which he is described as the foster-child of Amenemhat III and a pupil of Horus. His high status and connection to royalty is further enforced by his inscribed name on a statuette of Amenemhat III's daughter, Princess Neithikret (Nr 98).

Another high official is the '(chief) chamberlain of the treasury', *ꜥ3m* or Ptahwer, who occurs in four inscriptions most possibly of Amenemhat III's reign (Nrs 54, 108-109 and 414; Figure 5.5). His identification as an Asiatic is solely based on Nr 414 in which Ptahwer is his 'beautiful name' whereas *ꜥ3m* is his true name. No mention of his foreign origins can be extrapolated from Nrs 54, 108 or 109, highlighting that Asiatics may not necessarily be represented as foreigners in Egyptian texts. His association with the treasury may have contributed to his involvement in expeditions to the northeast as implied by epithets in Nr 54 signalling exploratory missions to foreign lands.[53]

[43] Gardiner and Peet, *Inscriptions of Sinai* 1, pl. 12 [32]; Černy, *Inscriptions of Sinai* 2, 70-71 [Nr 32].

[44] An 'overseer of the *Imn.w*' is also listed, the determinative of *Imn.w* possibly being that of a foreign land. Gardiner and Peet, *Inscriptions of Sinai* 1, pl. 12 [32]; Černy, *Inscriptions of Sinai* 2, 70.

[45] Thompson, *Sinai and the Negev*, 24-29; Beit-Arieh, *Tel Aviv* 7 (1980), 45-64; Beit-Arieh, *Levant* 17 (1985), 92; Černy, *Inscriptions of Sinai* 2, 14-24, 38-41.

[46] Černy, *Inscriptions of Sinai* 2, 33-38.

[47] Černy, *Inscriptions of Sinai* 2, 35-36.

[48] Černy, *Inscriptions of Sinai* 2, 33-38.

[49] Petrie, *Sinai*.

[50] Albright, *BASOR* 109 (1948), 5-20.

[51] Beit-Arieh, *IEJ* 29 (1979), 256-257; Beit-Arieh, *BA* 45/1 (1982), 13-18; Beit-Arieh, *Levant* 17 (1985), 89-116; Beit-Arieh, in *Egypt, Israel, Sinai*, 57-67.

[52] Valbelle and Bonnet, *Sanctuaire d'Hathor*.

[53] For example, the inscription's mention of 'boundaries of the foreign lands', the 'mysterious valleys' and the 'total end of the unknown'.

FIGURE 5.5. INSCRIPTION NR 108, SERABIT EL-KHADIM. AFTER GARDINER AND PEET, *INSCRIPTIONS OF SINAI* 1, PL. 33.

FIGURE 5.6. INSCRIPTION NR 94, SERABIT EL-KHADIM. AFTER GARDINER AND PEET, *INSCRIPTIONS OF SINAI* 1, PL. 33.

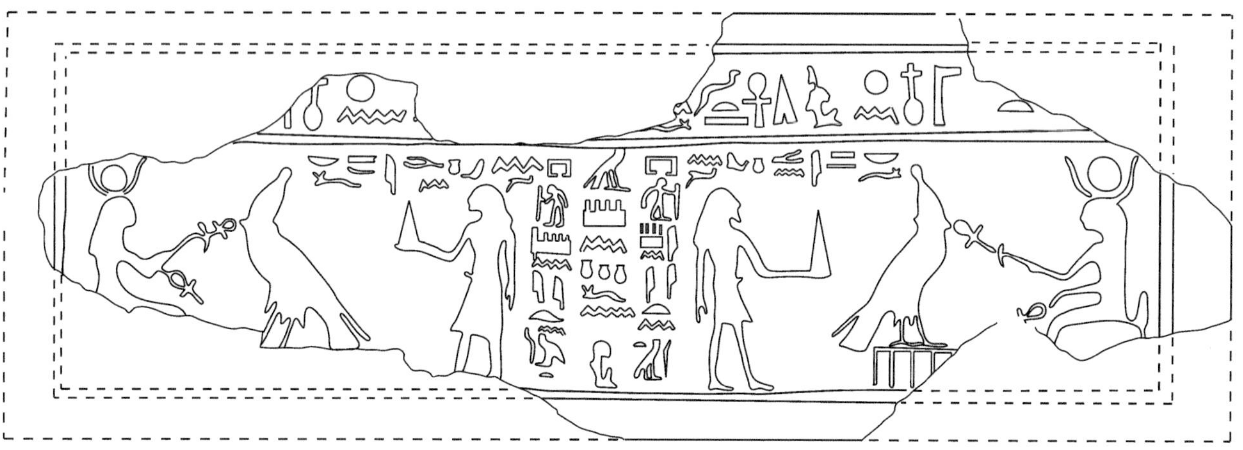

FIGURE 5.7. INSCRIPTION NR 95, SERABIT EL-KHADIM. AFTER GARDINER AND PEET, *INSCRIPTIONS OF SINAI* 1, PL. 30.

Duties of a religious nature are associated with the Asiatic 'senior chief lector priest', Werkherephemut (Nr 123). A high priest of Memphis, the official was involved in sending rations and offerings to the Hathor Temple during Amenemhat IV's reign. The text does not reveal whether he visited the temple. Nonetheless, his attainment of such a position stresses Asiatics' ability to hold powerful and influential religious roles.

Thus far, 16 out of the 34 references have been assigned to six Asiatics: three are low- to middle-ranking officials and three are of high status. Their Egyptian names, titles, epithets and relations advocate their accompaniment with the Egyptian expeditions to Serabit el-Khadim and/or their employment within Egypt. Therefore, they are most likely not inhabitants of Serabit el-Khadim. The Asiatics, namely the high officials, would not have been involved in mining duties but in the management of labourers, coordination of activities and, in reference to Wekherephemut, the distribution of temple offerings.

The remaining references concern those with foreign names and/or depictions. Four such instances specifically mention the 'brother of the ruler of *Rṯnw*, *Ḫbdd*(*m*)' (Nrs 85, 87, 92 and 112). He is textually represented in three inscriptions in a list of expedition members (Nrs 85, 92 and 112, south face).[54] A further two inscriptions artistically portray him as a foreigner: Nr 87 illustrates him in a row of officials with a coiffed hairdo (Figure 5.8); and Nr 112 (west face) shows him with a similar hairstyle while riding a donkey, the items he carries probably denoting his status

54 Goldwasser (*JAEI* 4/3 [2012], 14-17), following Sass (*Genesis of the Alphabet*, 143), proposes that the west and south faces of Nr 92 were inscribed by one who mixed the Egyptian and Proto-Alphabetic signs, probably a 'Canaanite' in *Ḫbdd*(*m*)'s group. Due to the script's poor workmanship and erroneous renderings of hieroglyphs which Goldwasser and Sass associate with the Proto-Alphabetic script, the stela could thus be evidence of an Asiatic's knowledge in the Egyptian and Proto-Alphabetic scripts. While the theory is attractive, it remains reliant on a fragmentary and weathered stela. For instance, the 'poor workmanship' of the signs is described in opposition to the east face's 'upper 10% quality-scale of hieroglyphs in Sinai', despite the latter being only around a quarter preserved. Yet, if correct, the theory would not only suggest the presence of bilingual Levantine scribes in the Sinai, it would also validate a Middle Kingdom date for the Proto-Alphabetic script. See Goldwasser, *E&L* 22-23 (2012/2013), 354.

(Figure 5.11).[55] A parallel may be found on a dagger from Byblos which portrays a donkey-rider carrying a staff across the shoulder while wearing a banded kilt.[56] This 'donkey-rider' portrayal is repeated in three other inscriptions that may also be attributed to *Ḫbdd(m)* (Nrs 103, 115 and 405; Figures 5.10, 5.12-13), one of which preserves his yellow skin colour and red-banded kilt (Nr 405). All representations of *Ḫbdd(m)* emphasise his foreign origins which, based on his name and portrayal as a 'donkey-rider',[57] point to the Levantine elite. Further, his inclusion in expedition lists dating from at least Year 4 to 25 of Amenemhat III's reign infers continued diplomatic relations between the king and the ruler of *Rṯnw*.

Artistically, *Ḫbdd(m)* or the 'donkey-rider' is never the solely depicted foreigner (Figures 5.10-5.13). He is accompanied by one or two individuals who, where captions are present, have Semitic-sounding names (Nrs 103, 112, 115 and 405). One is also described as the son of *Ḫbdd(m)* (Nr 112). Preserved characteristics show these individuals with coiffed hairstyles, multi-banded kilts and foreign products such as a Syro-Palestinian store-jar (Nr 112; Figure 5.11). Some also carry spears or axes, possibly of the duckbill shape, indicating their ability to remain armed in Serabit el-Khadim. Their 'flanking' of the donkey heightens the status of the 'donkey-rider', suggesting that they may have acted as his personal guard. Nr 115 also seems to associate six men from *Rṯnw* with the donkey-rider, increasing the number of his entourage. Therefore, it is observed that these individuals accompanied *Ḫbdd(m)* and could have been of the same origin.

However, was *Ḫbdd(m)* from the Sinai region? Disregarding the location of *Rṯnw*,[58] a significant clue that *Ḫbdd(m)* travelled from Egypt to Serabit el-Khadim occurs in Nr 87 (west face). As Černy reconstructs it, an official notes that '... [my forces arrived] complete in their entirety, there never occurred any loss among them...'.[59] This is followed by two registers listing the officials, one of whom is *Ḫbdd(m)*. Hence, the text indicates that he was part of the expedition from Egypt rather than the brother of a ruler in the Sinai who had developed relations with the visiting Egyptians.[60] Consequently, similar journeys to Serabit el-Khadim involving *Ḫbdd(m)* would have consisted of Egyptians as well as his armed entourage. Reasons for his presence there are unknown but could be related to: (a) overseeing Asiatic personnel from his place of origin; (b) developing or mediating relations with locals at Serabit el-Khadim; or (c) overseeing the quarrying of minerals to be transported to *Rṯnw* via Egypt. Considering *Ḫbdd(m)*'s high status as well as his frequent visitation to the area across a period of at least 20 years, a combination of all three suggestions is likely. Effectually, this proposition infers that the *Rṯnw* royal was visiting or perhaps residing in Egypt as his base of trading operations for at least 20 years. It also points to Amenemhat III's involvement in a significant trading and diplomatic venture with a ruler of *Rṯnw*.

FIGURE 5.8. DETAIL, WEST FACE, INSCRIPTION NR 87, SERABIT EL-KHADIM. AFTER GARDINER AND PEET, *INSCRIPTIONS OF SINAI* 1, PL. 24.

FIGURE 5.9. OBELISK NR 163, SERABIT EL-KHADIM. AFTER GARDINER AND PEET, *INSCRIPTIONS OF SINAI* 1, PL. 51.

Such an interpretation implies the presence of other Asiatics from the Levant at Serabit el-Khadim. Obelisk Nr 163 features three references to individuals with Semitic-sounding names, [...]*ỉ-ꜣšỉ* and his two sons. Two of their determinatives are depicted with a coiffed hairstyle and a pointed beard and all three carry duckbill(?) axes and rectangular-shaped shields (Figure 5.9), perhaps of the same type as those of Khety's Asiatics at Beni Hassan.[61] The

[55] As also proposed in Goldwasser, *E&L* 22-23 (2012/2013), 367.
[56] See Chapter 6.3.3.1 and Figure 6.16.
[57] Staubli, *Nomaden im Alten Israel*, 100-107; Stadelmann, in *Timelines* 2, 302.
[58] Černy attests that the Sinai is part of *Rṯnw*, although this is not definitive. Černy, *ArOr* 7 (1935), 389. See Chapter 7.3.2 for more on the toponym.
[59] Černy, *Inscriptions of Sinai* 2, 95 [87].
[60] Hoffmeier notes a personal communiqué with Bietak who posits that *Ḫbdd(m)* and his brother were travelling from Avaris (Hoffmeier, in *Peoples of the Eastern Desert*, 115-116, n. 20).
[61] See Chapter 4.4.1, Figure 4.47.

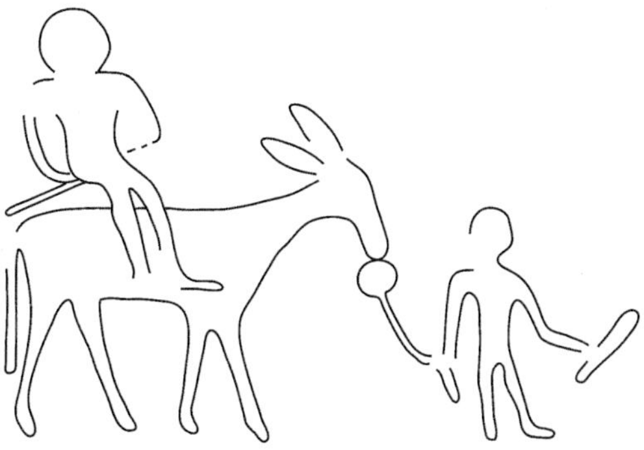

Figure 5.10. Detail, west face, Inscription Nr 103, Serabit el-Khadim. After Černy, *ArOr* 7 (1935), fig. 3.

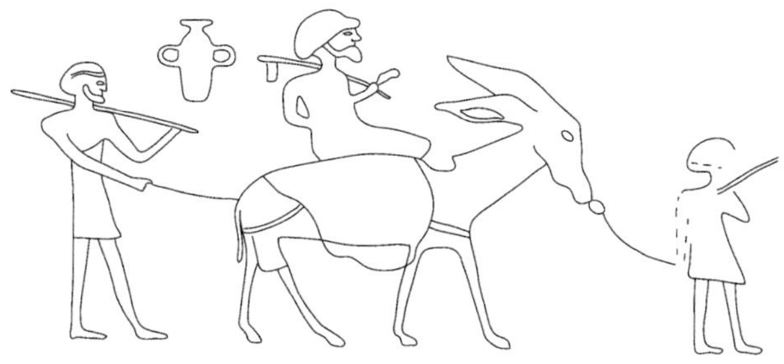

Figure 5.11. Detail, west face, Inscription Nr 112, Serabit el-Khadim. After Goldwasser, *E&L* 22-23 (2012/2013), fig. 2.

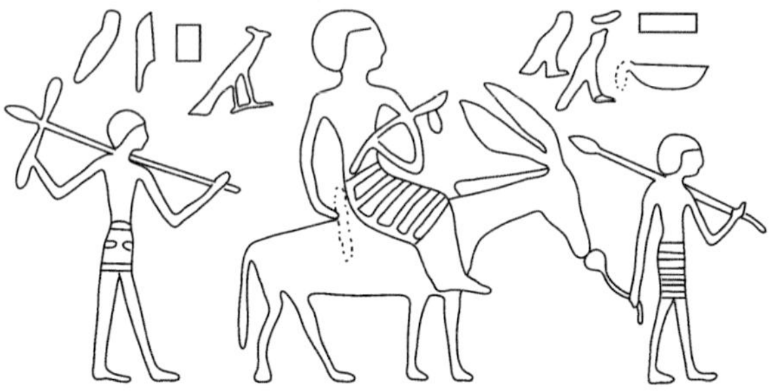

Figure 5.12. Detail, southeast face, Inscription Nr 405, Serabit el-Khadim. After Gardiner and Peet, *Inscriptions of Sinai* 1, pl. 85.

Figure 5.13. Detail, west face, Inscription Nr 115, Serabit el-Khadim. After Gardiner and Peet, *Inscriptions of Sinai* 1, pl. 39.

use of hieroglyphs indicates knowledge of the Egyptian language yet the individuals' names and artistic depictions suggest that they were not yet fully integrated within Egyptian society. As the only other representations of Asiatics with foreign names and dress belong to *Ḫbdd*(*m*) and his entourage, it is likely that the obelisk was for an Asiatic from the Levant, either a recent migrant or perhaps part of *Ḫbdd*(*m*)'s group. It is also possible that the obelisk belonged to an individual from the Sinai, but this would represent the only reference to local inhabitants, rendering origins from further afield more likely.

Overall, the 34 references to Asiatics at Serabit el-Khadim, and potentially the three in Nr 163, represent foreigners travelling from Egypt to the Eastern Desert. They include six individuals from the Egyptian administration, three of whom were associated with the management of activities, as well as *Ḫbdd*(*m*) and his retinue, who were most likely on a diplomatic venture. Markers of foreign ethnicity are more noticeable in the latter, indicating the acculturation of those within the Egyptian administration. No Asiatic is treated negatively. They were noted for their contributions to the expeditions, highlighting the cooperative nature of relations between Egyptians and Asiatic descendents.

The presence of Egyptians alongside Asiatics implies the existence of intercultural relations. Such relations would have been mediated not only by such elite personnel as *Ḫbdd*(*m*), but also by a number of interpreters referenced in the Middle Kingdom inscriptions. At least one is known for an expedition by Amenemhat II (Nr 83), 13 are on Amenemhat III's missions (Nrs 85, 88, 92, 94, 100, 105, 112 and 133) and 15 appear in other Middle Kingdom inscriptions (Nrs 133, 136, 141, 143, 153, 412 and 510-511).[62] None specify the interpreters' exact origins, their Egyptian names not necessarily reflective of their ethnicity, and it is uncertain if they were interpreting for the foreign Asiatics and/or the local population. However, their frequent occurrence signifies the importance of effective communication between the various cultures. Their tasks as mediators would also primarily require knowledge in Egyptian and foreign languages, implying that the Middle Kingdom kings employed multilingual officials to promote their diplomatic relations.

[62] For their translations, see Černy, *Inscriptions of Sinai* 2, 17, passim.

Groups of Asiatics

Five inscriptions dating from the reigns of Amenemhat III to Amenemhat IV list groups of Asiatics. Two represent them as *ꜥ3m* numbering 10 (Nr 85) and 20 (Nr 110), the latter specifically from *Ḥ3mi*. The remaining texts record them as men from *Rṯnw*, their numbers ranging from six (Nr 115) to 20 (Nr 120). One inscription also refers to 10 *Rṯnw* men as *ḫ3s.tyw* (Nr 114), listing them among 209 other members which brings their contribution to around 4.8% of the entire expedition. Nr 120 mentions 20 Asiatics among 200 Egyptian workers,[63] or 10% of the expedition. From such numbers, Černy concludes that the Asiatics were not employed as miners but as mediators.[64] While this is possible, the groups' small numbers indicates that they could also be specialists associated with mining, mineral processing and/or diplomatic relations. At least one party of *Rṯnw* men is connected with the brother of *Rṯnw*'s ruler and so it is likely that other *Rṯnw* groups were similarly travelling from Egypt to Serabit el-Khadim at the behest of *Ḫbdd(m)*. The inclusion of *ꜥ3m* groups from regions perhaps not within *Rṯnw* supports the Egyptians' alliance with Asiatics from various locales, subsequently providing further evidence for peaceful foreign relations during the late Twelfth Dynasty.

Toponyms of Asiatic lands not associated with particular Asiatics

Two toponyms not associated with particular Asiatics occur: *St.t* (Nrs 54, 91, 121 and 411) and *Rṯnw* (Nr 136). While Nrs 91 and 136 are fragmentary, the rest appear in connection to officials' ability to travel to distant regions to acquire valuable commodities. Nr 411 includes such items as turquoise and lapis-lazuli, the former derived from the Eastern Desert but the latter from much further afield. As with the representations of individual Asiatics and groups of foreigners, the toponyms are portrayed in a positive light, benefitting the Egyptian officials who visited them for peaceful trade ventures.

5.2.4.2 *Proto-Alphabetic texts*

The literature on Serabit el-Khadim's Proto-Alphabetic texts is filled with discussion and debate.[65] As a thorough examination is not possible here, a general overview is provided to highlight the texts' significance, with a selection of inscriptions that reflect intercultural relations. Over 30 inscriptions originate from the site: 20 were discovered at and around the entrance of Mine M, one was within the mine, five were near or within Mine L and four were found within the Hathor Temple.[66] Several individual examples were recorded near other mines and outside the Hathor Temple, as well as along the site's plateau.[67] They are inscribed on walls, stelae, stelaform panels, statuettes and other fragments of such items.[68]

Scholars have questioned the date of the texts, their language, translation, script and the identity of their scribes.[69] Current consensus agrees that the texts are of a Northwest Semitic speaking population. Chronological hypotheses generally span the period between the Middle and New Kingdoms for their origins.[70] However, following the discovery of the inscriptions in Wadi el-Hol,[71] scholars now favour a Middle Kingdom, MBIIA date for the texts.[72] It is agreed that their script is influenced by the Egyptian but it is uncertain whether it was the hieroglyphic and/or hieratic that inspired its creation. The Proto-Alphabetic texts from Wadi el-Hol, which are arguably earlier than those at Serabit el-Khadim, imply that both Egyptian scripts were used, thereby inferring that the scribes were literate in the hieroglyphic and hieratic traditions.[73]

Goldwasser contends that the Proto-Alphabetic script was invented in the Sinai by Semitic illiterates who visually imitated hieroglyphic inscriptions that they encountered.[74] Negating the postulated earlier date of the Wadi el-Hol texts, she asserts that the creators were miners who, separated from the Egyptian population and without free access to the Hathor Temple, invented the written system to satisfy their spiritual yearnings.[75] The script was then learned by elite Levantines at Serabit el-Khadim.[76] Goldwasser does not explicitly link the creators with a local population,

63 Černy, *ArOr* 7 (1935), 385.

64 Or, 'perhaps even as hostages against the annoyance of various kinds which were to be expected from surrounding tribes' (Černy, *ArOr* 7 [1935], 385).

65 See, for example, Gardiner, *JEA* 3 (1916), 1-16; Gardiner, *JEA* 48 (1962), 45-48; Albright, *BASOR* 110 (1948), 12-13; Albright, *Proto-Sinaitic Inscriptions*, passim; Butin, *Harvard Theological Review* 25/2 (1932), 130-137, 202-203; Cross, *BASOR* 134 (1954), 15-24; Sass, *Genesis of the Alphabet*, 141-144, passim; Sass, *Revue Internationale de l'Orient Ancien* 2 (2004/2005), 147-166; Hamilton, *Origins of the West Semitic Alphabet*, 320-321, passim; Lam, in *Inventions of Writing*, 189-195; Goldwasser, *E&L* 16 (2006), 121-160; Goldwasser, *JAEI* 4/3 (2012), 9-22; Goldwasser, in *Culture Contacts*, 251-316; Rollston, 'The Probable Inventors of the First Alphabet'; Simons, *Rosetta* 9 (2011), 16-40.

66 Petrie, *Sinai*, 129-132, pls 138-141; Starr and Butin, *Studies and Documents* 6, 31-42, pls 9-11; Beit-Arieh, *BA* 45/1 (1982), 13-18; Sass, *Genesis of the Alphabet*, 8-9; Hamilton, *Origins of the West Semitic Alphabet*, 332-389.

67 Hamilton, *Origins of the West Semitic Alphabet*, 332-389; Sass, *Genesis of the Alphabet*, 10-45.

68 Hamilton, *Origins of the West Semitic Alphabet*, 332-389; Sass, *Genesis of the Alphabet*, 10-45.

69 See references in n. 65 above, as well as May, *BA* 8/4 (1945), 93-99; Siegel, *AJSL* 49/1 (1932), 46-52; Leibovitch, *Le Muséon* 76 (1963), 201-203.

70 For more discussion on the dating, see the following with their listed references: Sass, *Genesis of the Alphabet*, 134-144; Sass, *Revue Internationale de l'Orient Ancien* 2 (2004/2005), 193-203; Hamilton, *Origins of the West Semitic Alphabet*, 299-307, 400-401; Goldwasser, *E&L* 16 (2006), 133; Simons, *Rosetta* 9 (2011), 24-27. For an archaeological perspective, see Beit-Arieh, *Levant* 17 (185), 116; Beit-Arieh, in *Egypt, Israel, Sinai*, 57-67.

71 See Chapter 4.5.5.2; Darnell et al., *AASOR* 59 (2005), 64-124.

72 Hamilton, *Origins of the West Semitic Alphabet*, 299-307, 400-401; Goldwasser, *E&L* 16 (2006), 133; Simons, *Rosetta* 9 (2011), 29-30; Lam, in *Inventions of Writing*, 189-190.

73 See Chapter 4.5.5.2; Darnell et al., *AASOR* 59 (2005), 64-124; Hamilton, *Origins of the West Semitic Alphabet*, 290-294. For a counterargument, see Goldwasser, *E&L* 16 (2006), 135, 150-151; Goldwasser, in *Culture Contacts*, 273-274.

74 Goldwasser, in *Culture Contacts*, 267-284; Goldwasser, *E&L* 16 (2006), 133-152; Goldwasser, *JAEI* 4/3 (2012), 13-19; Goldwasser *E&L* 22-23 (2012/2013), 363.

75 Goldwasser, *E&L* 16 (2006), 151-152; Goldwasser, in *Culture Contacts*, 267-268, 290.

76 Goldwasser, *JAEI* 4/3 (2012), 14-19; Goldwasser, *E&L* 16 (2006), 143-144.

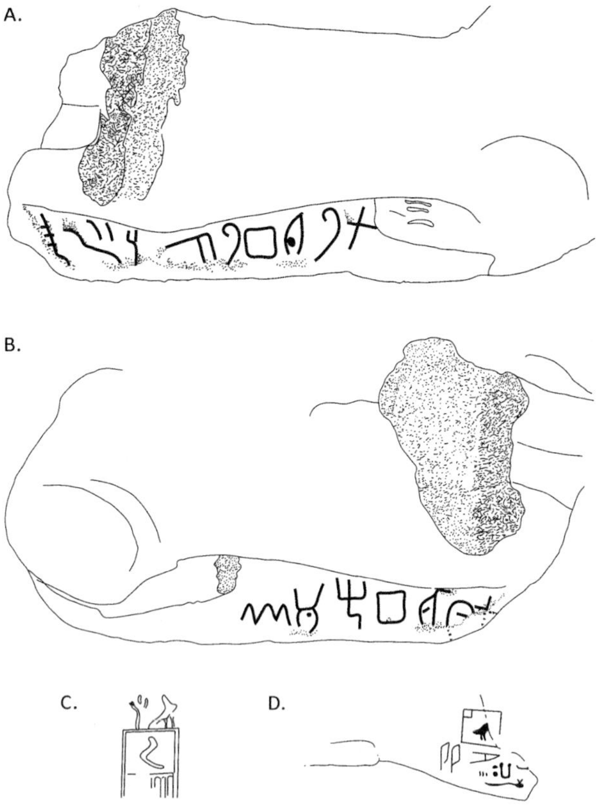

FIGURE 5.14. PROTO-ALPHABETIC INSCRIPTION NR 345, SERABIT EL-KHADIM (NOT TO SCALE).
(A-B) AFTER HAMILTON, *ORIGINS OF THE WEST SEMITIC ALPHABET*, FIG. A.7.
(C-D) AFTER SASS, *GENESIS OF THE ALPHABET*, FIG. 2.

yet argues that the Proto-Alphabet script remained with (semi-)nomadic marginal populations for almost 600 years.[77] Counterarguments state that the inventors were sophisticated members of the Levantine elite who had close ties with the Egyptian administration.[78] In support of the rebuttal are: a lack of archaeological data for a local population settled at Serabit el-Khadim; the absence of evidence for the Asiatics' separation from Egyptians; the location of a number of texts within the Hathor Temple; and the evidence for Asiatics and Egyptians working, travelling and presenting offerings together at Serabit el-Khadim. Because of the Proto-Alphabetic texts' anomalous dates, their questioned translations and their rarity,[79] a conclusive argument regarding the identity of the scribes cannot yet be reached. If the Wadi el-Hol texts are taken into account, then the evidence would lean in favour for the literacy of the scribes.

Whether the inventors were literate or illiterate, Goldwasser agrees that some Levantines at Serabit el-Khadim were possibly knowledgeable in both Egyptian and Proto-Alphabetic scripts. Moreover, all theories rely on the site being a 'melting-pot' of cultures.[80] Other than the script itself, the evidence that best reflects intercultural contact is the texts':

- Distribution: All texts were uncovered in the same or near areas where Egyptian inscriptions were found, including the Hathor Temple and the mines.[81] This would indicate that, if a MBIIA date for the texts is accepted, the areas were frequented and/or mined by both populations at the same time;

- Medium: Four texts from the Hathor Temple were inscribed on statuettes carved in the Egyptian fashion. Nr 345 is of a reclining sphinx wearing a possible *nemes* headdress (Figure 5.14).[82] The remaining three, a block statuette (Nr 346; Figure 5.15) and two busts (Nrs 347 and 347a; Figure 5.16), follow Twelfth Dynasty sculptural forms.[83] Despite their crude carving, the items signify the Levantines' attempts to mesh Egyptian religious dedications with their unique Semitic script. Perhaps the Proto-Alphabetic texts on stelae and stelaform panels also reflect such attempts;

- Deities: A Levantine deity identified in such expressions as *lbʿlt* and *mhbʿlt* is Baalat, the goddess synonymous with Hathor.[84] Her recurrence in the texts mirrors the Egyptians' dedications to Hathor in the hieroglyphic inscriptions.[85] The presence of four Proto-Alphabetic texts at the Hathor Temple additionally supports the goddess's worship by the Levantines. Apparently, Egyptians and Levantines were employing the one sacred space for their religious dedications, presenting similar sculptural artefacts to mark their devotion to Hathor/Baalat within and outside the temple. Although mere conjecture, perhaps some areas of the Hathor Temple served as a centre for intercultural mingling, where the Egyptians and Levantines came together to share in their worship of this goddess.

Another Proto-Alphabetic inscription portrays Ptah as a large figure holding a *wꜣs*-sceptre while standing on a platform within a shrine (Nr 351;

77 Goldwasser, *E&L* 16 (2006), 153; Goldwasser, in *Culture Contacts*, 284-287.
78 Rollston, 'The Probable Inventors of the First Alphabet'.
79 For more on other Proto-Alphabetic Texts, see Sass, *Genesis of the Alphabet*; Hamilton, *Origins of the West Semitic Alphabet*; Hamilton, 'From the Seal of a Seer', 1-24. To these should be added the newly-discovered texts at Timna (Wadi Arabah) published in Colless, *Antiquo Oriente* 8 (2010), 75-96.

80 For example, Albright, *BASOR* 110 (1948), 13; Sass, *Genesis of the Alphabet*, 143; Goldwasser, *E&L* 16 (2006), 151.
81 Sass suggests that it is because of the similarities in distribution that the Proto-Alphabetic texts could not have been inscribed by locals (Sass, *Genesis of the Alphabet*, 143).
82 The artefact was originally attributed to Hatshepsut's reign (Černy, *Inscriptions of Sinai* 2, 202), but recent arguments convincingly date the sphinx to the late Middle Kingdom. See Sass, *Genesis of the Alphabet*, 12-14, 135-139, figs 1-8; Hamilton, *Origins of the West Semitic Alphabet*, 333-335, fig. A.7.
83 Sass, *Genesis of the Alphabet*, 14-16, 139, figs 11-22; Hamilton, *Origins of the West Semitic Alphabet*, 335-338, figs A.8-11.
84 Gardiner, *JEA* 3 (1916), 1-16; Goldwasser, *E&L* 16 (2006), 128, n. 41.
85 See, for example, the translations of Inscriptions Nrs 54, 93-95, 97-98 in Appendix B.13; Černy, *Inscriptions of Sinai* 2, 41-42.

Figure 5.17).[86] Whether the inscriber worshipped Ptah or was merely emulating Egyptian inscriptions in the area,[87] Ptah's inclusion alongside a Proto-Alphabetic text highlights the influence of Egyptian art on the Levantine scribe;

- Two scripts on one artefact: Sphinx Nr 345 offers a unique case where a Proto-Alphabetic text is written beneath hieroglyphs (Figure 5.14). On the left of its base, the sphinx contains a Proto-Alphabetic inscription with an identifiable *lbʿlt* 'for Baalat'.[88] Between the paws are unclear hieroglyphs,[89] and on the right shoulder is *mr.y Ḥw.t-Ḥr.w* [*nb.t*] *Mfkꜣ.t* 'beloved of Hathor, [lady] of *Mfkꜣ.t*' above a Proto-Alphabetic *mhbʿlt* 'beloved of Baalat'.[90] Evidently, the two texts are almost synonymous. Goldwasser also posits that the hieroglyphic inclusion of *m* instead of *Ḥr.w* within the enclosure for Hathor's name is 'typically Canaanite writing'.[91] The two scripts could have been written by the same implement as evident by the thickness and depth of the inscribed characters.[92] In such a case, the sphinx could indicate a bilingual Levantine purposely relating Hathor with Baalat in this dedication to the goddess.

5.2.4.3 *Other*

Little archaeological evidence attests to a settlement at Serabit el-Khadim.[93] Ceramic remains near the Hathor Temple include late Twelfth to early Thirteenth Dynasty Egyptian pottery.[94] Additionally, a few unpublished sherds of Tell el-Yahudiyah juglets were uncovered,[95] pointing to the use of Levantine(-influenced) products at the site.

The evidence at Serabit el-Khadim emphasises the occurrence of Egyptian-Levantine relations from at least Senwosret III's reign. The Egyptian texts point to the presence of Asiatics from mixed backgrounds and various echelons of society. They were low- to middle -ranking officials of the Egyptian household, high officials of the Egyptian treasury, bands of personnel from Levantine regions, and royalty from *Rṯnw*. Those within the Egyptian administration and priesthood were represented as acculturated individuals whereas those from abroad retained a portrayal of foreignness. While the

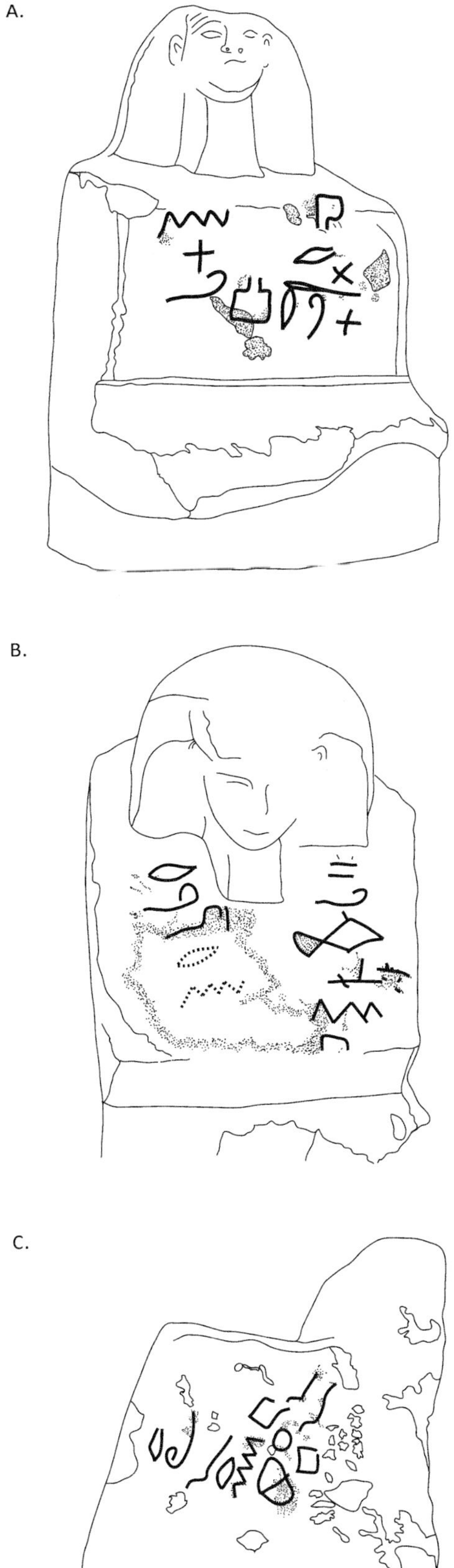

Figure 5.15. Proto-Alphabetic Inscription Nr 346, Serabit el-Khadim (not to scale). After Hamilton, *Origins of the West Semitic Alphabet*, fig. A.9.

86 Sass, *Genesis of the Alphabet*, 20, 137-138, figs 32, 37-39; Hamilton, *Origins of the West Alphabet*, 343-344, fig. A.14.
87 For examples, see Gardiner and Peet, *Inscriptions of Sinai* 1, pls 41 [126], 47 [124-125], 51 [140]; Valbelle and Bonnet, *Sanctuaire d'Hathor*, 40, figs 52-53.
88 Sass, *Genesis of the Alphabet*, 12.
89 Sass writes that this is the name of a Twelfth Dynasty king, although published photos are unclear (Sass, *Genesis of the Alphabet*, 139).
90 Sass, *Genesis of the Alphabet*, 12-14.
91 Goldwasser, *E&L* 16 (2006), 135, n. 86.
92 The assessment is based on the photographic publication of the sphinx (Butin, *Harvard Theological Review* 25/2 [1932], pl. 10).
93 Petrie, *Sinai*, 67, figs 83-84; Černy, *Inscriptions of Sinai* 2, 48-50; Chartier-Raymond et al., *CRIPEL* 16 (1994), 59-61; Bloxam, *JSA* 6/2 (2006), 291.
94 Bourriau, *CRIPEL* 18 (1996), 21, 24, 31.
95 Giveon, *Stones of Sinai*, 61.

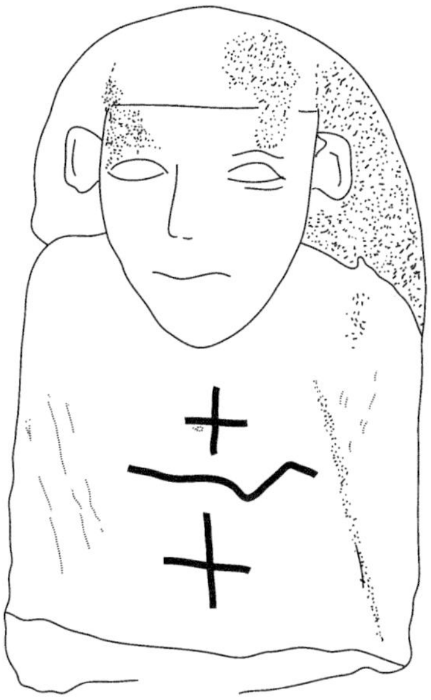

FIGURE 5.16. PROTO-ALPHABETIC INSCRIPTION NR 347, SERABIT EL-KHADIM. AFTER HAMILTON, *ORIGINS OF THE WEST SEMITIC ALPHABET*, FIG. A.11.

FIGURE 5.17. PROTO-ALPHABETIC INSCRIPTION NR 351, SERABIT EL-KHADIM. AFTER HAMILTON, *ORIGINS OF THE WEST SEMITIC ALPHABET*, FIG. A.14.

Egyptian inscriptions refer to multilingual interpreters of uncertain origins, the evidence from the Proto-Alphabetic texts suggests that bilingual Levantines were also in the area. Perhaps the two groups were one and the same or influenced each other, creating a hub of cross-cultural learning. The Proto-Alphabetic texts additionally reflect other influences by the Egyptian culture, ranging from the appropriation of Egyptian artistic forms to inspirations on Levantine religious expression. The Egyptian, Egyptian-Asiatic and Levantine populations all worshipped Hathor, ensuring their monumental and written dedications to this goddess. As such, Serabit el-Khadim offers a unique case where the various groups were able to gather and work together in an environment which was foreign to many of them. While the Levantines acquired several intellectual, artistic and perhaps religious influences from the Egyptians, the latter textually and artistically approached the northeasterners positively and inclusively, ensuring the continuance of peaceful ventures at Serabit el-Khadim.

5.2.5 Zeit, Gebel el-

Lat.Lon. 27°57'N 33°28'E (Site 2)

Refs Castel and Soukiassian, *BIFAO* 85 (1985), 285-293; Castel and Soukiassian, *BSFE* 112 (1988), 37-53; Castel and Soukiassian, *Gebel el-Zeit* 1; Régen and Soukiassian, *Gebel el Zeit* 2, 138; *25 ans de découvertes archéologiques*, 56 [37-38], 57 [40].

Chron. Second Intermediate Period

The west coast of the Red Sea includes a galena mining site, Gebel el-Zeit, south of Ayn Sukhna. Excavations by the Institut français d'archéologie orientale unearthed two areas: Site 1, with mines, encampments and a sanctuary; and Site 2, with mine-shafts, shelters and votive structures.[96] Unique inscriptions from Dynasty 13 kings Nebnun and his successor Siwesekhtawy as well as the Sixteenth Dynasty ruler Bebiankh signal late Middle Kingdom and Second Intermediate Period activity.[97]

Excavators note the discovery of MBA juglets and scarabs at Site 2.[98] One of the vessels is a hawk-shaped figural Tell el-Yahudiyah juglet with parallels from Tell el-Dab'a's Strata E/1-D/2,[99] another is a biconical juglet like those of Tell el-Dab'a's Strata D/3-D/2,[100] and two are red-burnished juglets (one piriform and the other ovoid).[101] A scarab displaying cobras confronting a mythical figure is also influenced by MBIIB-MBIIC Levantine designs and can thus be assigned to Dynasty 15.[102] The presence of these Levantine-influenced products emphasises continued trade relations with the north during the Second Intermediate Period at Gebel el-Zeit. Their deposition by Levantines themselves remain uncertain.[103]

96 Mey, *MDAIK* 36 (1980), 299-318; Castel and Soukiassian, *BIFAO* 85 (1985), 285-293; Castel and Soukiassian, *BSFE* 112 (1988), 37-53; Castel and Soukiassian, *Gebel el-Zeit* 1; Régen and Soukiassian, *Gebel el Zeit* 2.

97 Castel and Soukiassian, *BIFAO* 85 (1985), 285-293; Ryholt, *Political Situation*, 78, 159.

98 Castel and Soukiassian, *Gebel el-Zeit* 1, 138; Castel and Soukiassian, *BSFE* 112 (1988), 45.

99 Aston and Bietak's Late Egyptian Type Group L.15.2. Aston and Bietak, *TeD* 8, 288, 524, fig. 214, pls 111 [634], 112 [635-640]; *25 ans de découvertes archéologiques*, 56 [37].

100 Aston and Bietak's Late Egyptian Type Group L.5.3. Aston and Bietak, *TeD* 8, 231, 470, fig. 163, pl. 80; *25 ans de découvertes archéologiques*, 56 [38].

101 *25 ans de découvertes archéologiques*, 56 [38].

102 *25 ans de découvertes archéologiques*, 57 [40].

103 Bomann and Young suggest that the Asiatics of the Sinai mines may have extracted galena at Gebel el-Zeit (Bomann and Young, *JEA* 80 [1994], 31).

5.3 Southeastern Desert

5.3.1 Hammamat, Wadi el-

Lat.Lon. 25°55'N 33°20'E

Refs PM 7, 328-337; Couyat and Montet, *Ouâdi Hammâmât*, 40, 48-51, pls 5, 13-14; Gasse, *BIFAO* 87 (1987), 207-218.

Chron. Twelfth and Seventeenth Dynasties

Almost midway between the Red Sea coast and Qift (Coptos) is Wadi el-Hammamat, where gold and *bekhen*-stone were quarried.[104] The site features hieroglyphic inscriptions of Old to New Kingdom mining operations.[105] Well represented are Eleventh and Twelfth Dynasty kings, although texts point to continued quarrying activities in Dynasty 13 under Sobekhotep IV[106] and Dynasty 17 under a Sobekemsaf Sekhemrawadjkhaw.[107]

Four texts refer to Asiatics, three are epithets and one represents an Asiatic individual (Figure 5.18). The latter was first assigned to Sobekemsaf I of the early Seventeenth Dynasty[108] and then reclassified to Sobekemsaf II, who may be of the early[109] or mid-late Seventeenth Dynasty.[110] As the exact date remains uncertain, the inscription is only included to indicate Asiatic presence in Upper Egypt during the Second Intermediate Period. The texts are translated below.[111]

Inscription Nr 47 (Senwosret III, Year 14)

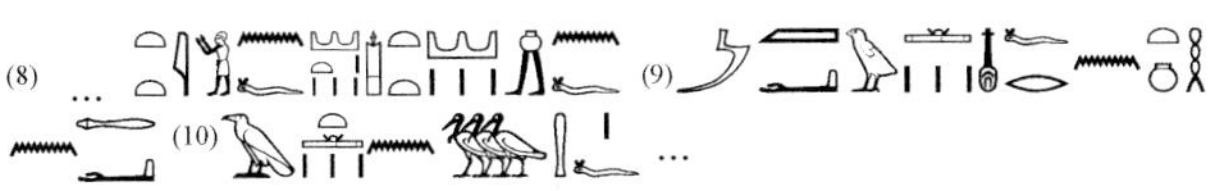

(8) ... *titi n=f ḥꜣs.wt Ꞽwn.t(y)w ini n=f* (9) *mꜣꜥ.w nfr(.w) n(.y) Tḥnw n* (10)*ꜥꜣ.t n(.y) bꜣ.w ḥm=f* ...

(8) ... the one who tramples the foreign lands of the *Ꞽwn.t(y)w* for him; the one who brings (9)the fine products of the *Tḥnw* through (10)the greatness of the power of his majesty ...

Inscription Nr 43 (Amenemhat III, Year 2)

(7) ... *sḫi Nḥs(.yw) wn tꜣ ꜥꜣm(.w)* (8) *hbhb ḫꜣs.t nb.t spd-ḥr m mšꜥ=f nb* ...

(7) ... the one who smites the *Nḥs(.yw)* and opens the land of the *ꜥꜣm(.w)*, (8) the one who traverses every foreign land, alert in each of his expeditions...

Inscription Nr 17 (Amenemhat III, Year 19)

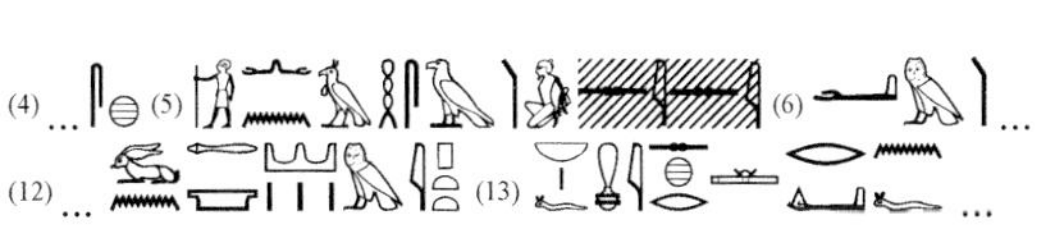

(4) ... *sḫi* (5) *Nḥs.ty(w)* [*sisi*] (6) *ꜥꜣm(.w)* ...
(12) ... *wn ꜥꜣ ḫꜣs.wt m ipt* (13)*nb=f mi sḫr rḏi(.w) n=f* ...

(4) ... the one who smites (5) the *Nḥs.ty(w)*; the one who [hurries][112] (6) the *ꜥꜣm(.w)*; (12)... the one who opens the door of the foreign lands for the counting (13)of his lord according to the plan which had been given to him...

Inscription Nr 23-24 (Sobekemsaf)

(13) *im.y-rꜣ sḫ.ty ꜥꜣm*
(13) Overseer of fieldworkers,[113] *ꜥꜣm*[114]

Khuy's inscription mentions the *Ꞽwn.tyw* and Libyan goods while those of Amenemhat III's reign group the *ꜥꜣm.w* with the *Nḥs.yw* alongside connotations of opening the lands for possible trade. The Dynasty 12 inscriptions are thus

NR	DATE	INSCRIPTION FOR...	ASIATIC(S)	REFERENCES
47	Senwosret III Year 14	steward of the storehouse of the controller of works, Khuy	*Ꞽwn.tyw*	Couyat and Montet, *Ouâdi Hammâmât*, 49-51, pl. 14
43	Amenemhat III Year 2	overseer of the infantry, inspector of retainers, Amenemhat	*ꜥꜣm.w*	Couyat and Montet, *Ouâdi Hammâmât*, 48-49, pl. 13
17	Amenemhat III Year 19	retainer of the ruler of the first battalion, Hetepi	*ꜥꜣm(.w)*	Couyat and Montet, *Ouâdi Hammâmât*, 40, pl. 5
23-24	Sobekemsaf	(Sobekemsaf's expedition)	*ꜥꜣm*	Gasse, *BIFAO* 87 (1987), pls 39-42

FIGURE 5.18. EGYPTIAN TEXTS AT WADI EL-HAMMAMAT REPRESENTING ASIATICS, WITH NOTATIONS ON THEIR DATE AND BIBLIOGRAPHICAL REFERENCES.

104 Shaw, *Antiquity* 68 (1994), table 1.
105 Couyat and Montet, *Ouâdi Hammâmât*; Goyon, *Ouadi Hammamat*.
106 Simpson, *MDAIK* 25 (1969), 154-158.
107 Gasse, *BIFAO* 87 (1987), 207-218.
108 Gasse, *BIFAO* 87 (1987), 207-218.
109 Polz, *Der Beginn des Neuen Reiches*, 45-50, table 2.
110 Ryholt, *Political Situation*, 170, table 28; Ryholt, *GM* 157 (1997), 75-76.
111 Transcriptions follow the references in Figure 5.18. Transliterations and translations are by the author.

112 The translation of this term follows *Wb* 4, 40; Leprohon, *JSSEA* 28 (2001), 136.
113 Ward, *Index*, 45 [347].
114 The name is read by Gasse as *Ḳmꜣw* (Gasse, *BIFAO* 87 [1987], 212, 216 [bb]), although the final letter *m* renders the reading *ꜥꜣm* more likely.

STELA	DATE	STELA FOR...	ASIATIC(S)	REFERENCES
143	Senwosret I	sealer of the king of Lower Egypt, Hor	*Ꞽwn.tyw* *St.t*	Rowe, *ASAE* 39 (1939), 187-191, pl. 25; Sadek, *Wadi el-Hudi* 1, 84-88; vol. 2, pl. 23
17	Senwosret III Year 13	trustworthy sealer, Senbebu	*ꜥ3m* Senbebu	Fakhry, *Wadi el Hudi*, 35-38, fig. 29, pl. 14; Sadek, *Wadi el-Hudi* 1, 38-39; vol. 2, pl. 8

FIGURE 5.19. EGYPTIAN TEXTS AT WADI EL-HUDI REPRESENTING ASIATICS, WITH NOTATIONS ON THEIR DATE AND BIBLIOGRAPHICAL REFERENCES.

associated with the expeditions' primary purpose to exploit foreign lands, presenting the foreigners and their regions as sources of commodities. Conversely, the fourth inscription lists one Asiatic as part of an expedition, his inclusion signalling the employment of northerners within the Theban Dynasty during the Second Intermediate Period. Hence, while Asiatics had claimed power in the Delta, the south still contained Asiatics within its administration, representing them alongside Egyptians in a clearly non-belligerent manner.

5.3.2 Hudi, Wadi el-

Lat.Lon. 17°42'N 34°17'E

Refs PM 7, 319-320; Rowe, *ASAE* 39 (1939), 187-191, pl. 25; Fakhry, *Wadi el Hudi*, 35-38, fig. 29, pl. 14; Sadek, *Wadi el-Hudi* 1, 38-39, 84-88; vol. 2, pls 8, 23.

Chron. Twelfth Dynasty

Situated southeast of Aswan is Wadi el-Hudi, where minerals such as amethyst and barytes were mined.[115] Archaeological investigations were carried out by the Egyptian Topographical Survey[116] and Fakhry,[117] with a recent survey by Shaw and Jameson.[118] The site features Middle Kingdom mines and a settlement, the latter including a Twelfth Dynasty fort built between the reigns of Senwosret I and III.[119] Lines from two pertinent stelae are translated below (Figure 5.19):[120]

Stela Nr 143 (Senwosret I)

[(1)] *ꜥnḫ Ḥr.w ꜥnḫ msi.wt nb.ty ꜥnḫ msi.wt nsw.t bi.ty Ḫpr-k3-Rꜥ.w [s3] Rꜥ.w S-n-wsr.t nṯr nfr dn Ꞽwn.(ty)w* [(2)]*sni wsr.t imi.w St.t iti.y ꜥrf Ḥ3.w-nb.w ini ḏr.w rs.t* [(3)]*Nḥs.(y)wt sk tp.w 3b.(w)t ḫ3k.(w)t-ib wsḫ t3š pḏ nmt.t* [(4)]*sm3 nfr.w=f t3.wy nb [3].t sn[ḏ].w(=f) m ḫ3s.wt*[121] *sḫr.n šꜥt=f rs.t* [(5)]*[3k.]n btn.w=f n šꜥ.t ḥm=f sp[ḥ.n]=f [ḫ]ft.y=f...*

[(1)] The living Horus, life of births, the two-goddesses, life of births, king of Upper and Lower Egypt, Kheperkara, [son of] Re, Senwosret (I), the good god who kills the *Ꞽwn.t(y)w*, [(2)]who cuts the throats of those who are in the *St.t* lands, the sovereign who encloses the *Ḥ3.w-nb.w*,[122] who reaches the boundaries of the [(3)]*Nḥs.(y)wt* rebels,[123] who cuts the heads of the disaffected groups, who widens the boundary, who extends the stride, [(4)]whose perfection unites the two lands, lord of [striking power], (whose) respect is in foreign lands, whose knife has overthrown the rebels, [(5)]whose defiant ones [have perished] by the knife of his majesty, he who has lassoed his enemies ...

Stela Nr 17 (Senwosret III, Year 13)

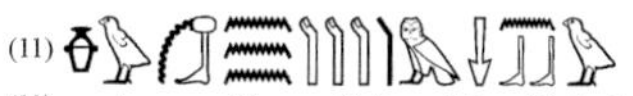

[(11)] *wdp.w wꜥb.w ḏbḥ.w ꜥ3m Snb-b-w*

[(11)] Butler,[124] pure of fingers, *ꜥ3m* Senbebu[125]

The stela of Hor (Nr 143) begins with a eulogy for Senwosret I, describing his prowess over foreign lands and people. Despite Wadi el-Hudi's situation to the south of Egypt, northern enemies such as the *Ꞽwn.tyw* and *Ḥ3.w-nb.w* as well as those in the *St.t* lands are included.[126] The text is ideological in nature, purposed to commemorate and idolise the reigning king's power over foreign lands.[127]

Conversely, Nr 17 includes a foreigner as part of an Egyptian household. The 'butler' Senbebu possesses the same name as his master, the 'trustworthy sealer' Senbebu.[128] It is likely that he was given this name following either his migration into Egypt or his employment by Senbebu. Whether or not the foreigner accompanied Senbebu to Wadi el-Hudi is uncertain.

Overall, the texts at Wadi el-Hudi offer two representations of Asiatics: (1) a *topos* portrayal as conveyed in a king's eulogy; and (2) a *mimetic* representation in an Egyptian's stela. The two display the effects of genre on the portrayal of Asiatics during Dynasty 12.

115 Shaw, *Antiquity* 68 (1994), 115-116, table 1; Sadek, *Wadi el-Hudi* 1, 100-105.
116 Rowe, *ASAE* 39 (1939), 187-194.
117 Fakhry, *Wadi el Hudi*.
118 Shaw and Jameson, *JEA* 79 (1993), 81-97.
119 Shaw and Jameson, *JEA* 79 (1993), 81-97; Shaw, *Antiquity* 68 (1994), 115, fig. 5.
120 Transcriptions follow the references in Figure 5.19. Transliterations and translations are by the author.
121 Sadek reads suffix-pronoun *sn* after this term [Sadek, *Wadi el-Hudi*, 85-86], however see Seyfried, *GM* 81 (1984), 60-63.
122 For more on this term and its association with people of the north, see Favard-Meeks, *SAK* 16 (1989), 39-63.
123 For more on this term, see Sadek, *Wadi el-Hudi*, 85-86; Ritner, *Egyptian Magical Practice*, 185; Ritner, *GM* 111 (1989), 85-95.
124 Ward, *Index*, 90 [755].
125 Ranke, *Personnenamen* 1, 315 [6].
126 Galán, *SAK* 21 (1994), 70-71.
127 For more on the stela's use of private and royal themes, see Galán, *SAK* 21 (1994), 65-79.
128 Also noticed by Fakhry in *Wadi el-Hudi*, 39 [17].

5.4 Conclusions

The chapter examined seven sites, two in Mount Sinai, three on the northern Red Sea coast, and two in the Southeastern Desert (see Figure 5.1). Most of the evidence is dated to Dynasty 12 but a few indications of Second Intermediate Period activity exist.

5.4.1 The Twelfth to the early Thirteenth Dynasty

All sites bar Gebel el-Zeit feature evidence of the Twelfth Dynasty (Figure 5.20). The earliest reference to Asiatics comes from Inscription Nr 143 at Wadi el-Hudi. The text's eulogy to Senwosret I is particularly belligerent against the *Ỉwn.tyw* and *St.t*, and clearly asserts the pharaoh's authority over the foreign. Three inscriptions are assigned to Senwosret III: one from Serabit el-Khadim, one from Wadi el-Hudi and one from Wadi el-Hammamat. While the latter provides a sequence of epithets directed towards controlling the *Ỉwn.tyw*'s lands, the first two contain references to individual Asiatics as expedition and household members. They have Egyptian names and most likely resided in Egypt.

The greatest number of inscriptions is assigned to Amenemhat III's reign. They include one from Wadi Maghara, 19-20 from Serabit el-Khadim and two from Wadi el-Hammamat. Only the latter two represent foreigners belligerently, referring to *ꜥ3m.w* in connection to their lands as doorways to commodities. The rest bear *mimetic* representations of Asiatics. Individuals possibly living and working in Egypt are depicted as members of households, expeditions and the treasury. They are represented as Egyptians and have Egyptian names but are identified by the ethnonym *ꜥ3m*. The foreign ancestry of one official, Ptahwer, is confirmed in one out of four of his inscriptions, emphasising that, by the second half of Dynasty 12, Egyptian-Asiatics were not always necessarily marked as foreigners.

Also mentioned are relatives of the ruler of *Rṯnw*, who are distinctly represented as Asiatics with their weaponry, clothing and hairstyle. As this chapter argued, they were involved in a diplomatic trading venture with Amenemhat III that witnessed their frequent voyage to Serabit el-Khadim from Egypt between, at least, Years 4 and 25 of the king's reign. Perhaps included in this venture are men from *Rṯnw*. Other Asiatic groups sent to the Sinai originate from such locations as *Ḥ3mi*.

The same situation is evident in Amenemhat IV's reign, during which three inscriptions were engraved at Serabit el-Khadim and, for the first time, an Egyptian-Asiatic occupied the office of high priest at Memphis. The Sinai emerged as a hub of intercultural activity where Egyptians, Egyptian-Levantines, non-local and, perhaps, local Levantines came together, their worship of Hathor/Baalat being a shared commonality. Such activity eventually resulted in the groups leaving behind inscriptional testimony in the hieroglyphic and Proto-Alphabetic form, emphasising cross-cultural influences in art, script and possibly religion.

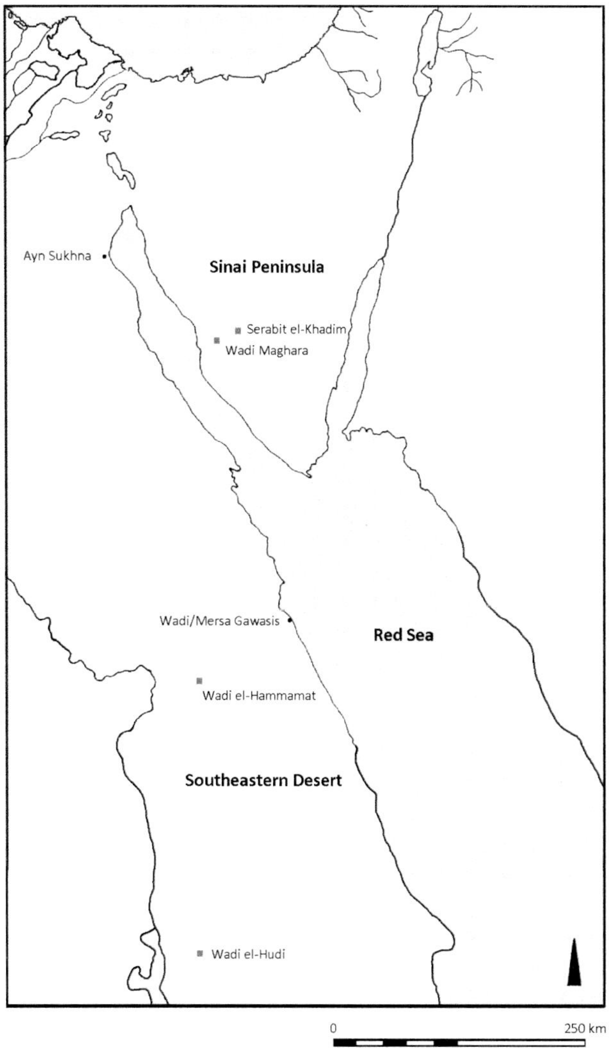

FIGURE 5.20 SITES IN THE EASTERN DESERT WITH EVIDENCE OF CONTACT WITH THE LEVANTINE DURING DYNASTY 12 TO EARLY DYNASTY 13.
- • Presence of Levantine(-influenced) commodities
- ■ Presence of Levantine individuals and commodities

The groups likely reached Mount Sinai via harbour sites. Perhaps they travelled in seafaring ships constructed of Lebanese cedar, similar to those at Ayn Sukhna and Wadi/Mersa Gawasis. The Northern Levantine timber was utilised in ship-building and recycled into functional pieces. The Northern Levant also supplied Wadi/Mersa Gawasis with other hard timbers such as oak and pine. These, along with Syro-Palestinian store-jars, attest to an active flow of trade in Levantine commodities during the Twelfth to early Thirteenth Dynasties.

5.4.2 The Thirteenth Dynasty to the Second Intermediate Period

The Thirteenth Dynasty to Second Intermediate Period witnessed a definite decrease in Egyptian-Levantine relations (Figure 5.21). The seafaring ships of Ayn Sukhna were apparently burnt and destroyed, and no inscriptions mentioning Asiatics were evidently carved at Mount Sinai. Nonetheless, a few fragments of Tell el-Yahudiyah ware from Serabit el-Khadim attest that some individuals still travelled to the area. Tell el-Yahudiyah vessels and a Levantine design scarab unearthed at Gebel el-Zeit also signify continued access to Fifteenth Dynasty items. Interestingly, a Seventeenth Dynasty inscription at Wadi el-Hammamat supports the inclusion of Egyptian-Asiatics in expeditions to the Eastern Desert. This would suggest that the fragmentation of Egypt in the Second Intermediate Period did not lead to a cessation of Levantine(-influenced) imports into Upper Egypt, nor to an apparent rise in ambivalence against Asiatic descendents in the area.

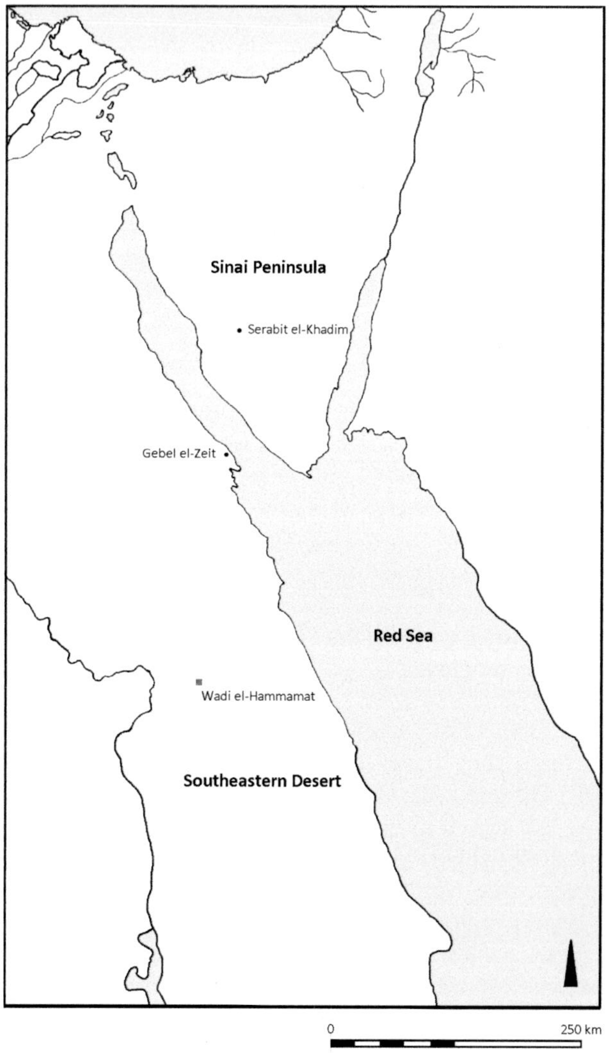

FIGURE 5.21 SITES IN THE EASTERN DESERT WITH EVIDENCE OF CONTACT WITH THE LEVANTINE DURING DYNASTY 13 TO THE SECOND INTERMEDIATE PERIOD.

- • Presence of Levantine(-influenced) commodities
- ■ Presence of Levantine individuals and commodities

6. Contact with the Egyptian in the Levant

'The Egyptian Middle Kingdom was a period when the men of the Nile looked beyond their narrow green carpet of god-given fertility to the variegated world beyond, a world that offered a new dimension of living and a veritable host of opportunities.'
MacDonald, *AJBA* 1/5 (1972), 98.

6.1 Introduction

Assessing the nature and extent of relations between Asiatics and the Twelfth to Fifteenth Dynasties necessitates an examination of the data from the Levant. The following chapter gathers evidence of contact and explores key areas that experienced interconnections with the Egyptian civilisation. Egyptian presence in the MBA Levant has generally been considered to be: (a) imperialistic, seeking political or economic dominance;[1] (b) diplomatic, seeking trade or commercial ties;[2] (c) watchful and intervenient, only when its political and/or commercial interests were in peril;[3] or (d) inconsequential and even non-existent in certain regions and particular periods.[4] Fifteenth Dynasty rulers have also been suggested to have had governing power over parts of the Levant, especially the south of modern Israel.[5]

While tracing Egyptian presence in the Levant relies on the Egyptian(-influenced) elements found across its sites, determining Hyksos relations is marred by the very fact that their culture is largely Levantine. Differentiating which markers represent contact with the Hyksos and which are Levantine is a difficult task that can lead to several misinterpretations. For instance, MBA fortification systems have been frequently attributed to the Hyksos, their use signalling Hyksos domination over the Levant.[6] However, recent studies have clearly shown that the so-called 'Hyksos fortifications' are Near Eastern in origin.[7] Similarly, some have considered Hyksos royal-name scarabs as evidence of their control,[8] but they can also be interpreted as items of trade. The most plausible means for ascertaining the relations between the Hyksos and the Levant would thereby require the identification of elements that are uniquely connected to the Hyksos. This chapter selects features related to the rulers' Egyptian and mercantile connections. It investigates contact with the Egyptian in the Levant, gathering data on Egyptian imports, Egyptian-influenced products and Egyptian(-influenced) customs.

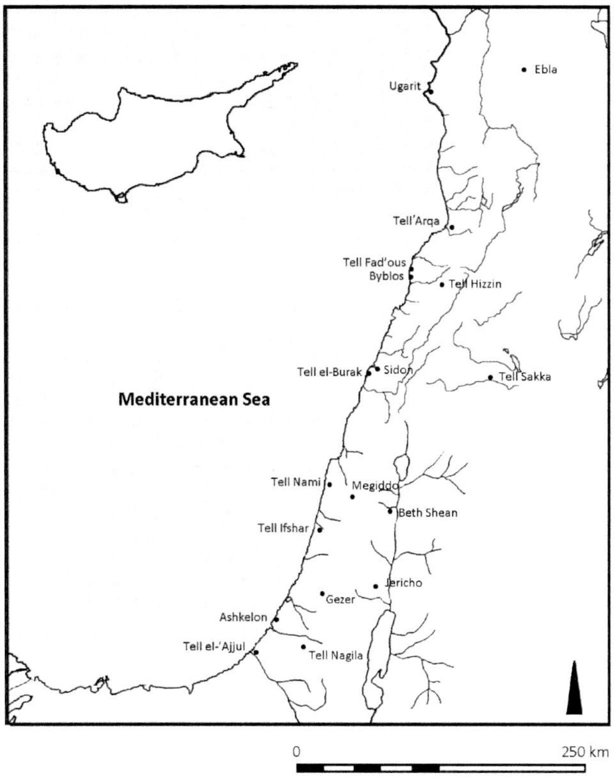

FIGURE 6.1. EXAMINED SITES IN THE LEVANT.

The chapter is classified into two main sections: sites in the Southern Levant and those in the Northern Levant (Figures 1.1, 6.1). Each site includes its location by Latitude and Longitude, a list of selected references and its temporal placement within the Egyptian as well as the Levantine chronology. Selected sites are those with significant, provenanced evidence of Egyptian-Levantine contact. Appendix A features a further selection of sites with artefacts utilised by scholars as evidence for Hyksos relations,

1 See, for example, Albright, *JPOS* 2 (1922), 110-138; Albright, *JPOS* 8 (1928), 223-256; Giveon, in *Egypt, Israel, Sinai*, 23-40; Mazar, *IEJ* 148 (1968), 65-97.
2 See, for example, Ward, *Orientalia* 30 (1961), 129-155; Weinstein, *BASOR* 217 (1975), 1-16; Flammini, *Tel Aviv* 37 (2010), 154-168; Cohen, *Canaanites, Chronologies, and Connections*.
3 See, for example, Ward, *Orientalia* 30 (1961), 129-155; Ward, *Egypt and the East Mediterranean*, 66-67; Gerstenblith, *Levant at the Beginning of the MBA*.
4 See, for example, Weinstein, *BASOR* 217 (1975), 12-13.
5 See, for example, Engberg, *Hyksos Reconsidered;* van Seters, *Hyksos*; Weinstein, *BASOR* 241 (1981), 1-28.
6 See, for example, Albright, *JPOS* 2 (1922), 123; Albright, *JPOS* 15 (1935), 224; Petrie, *Hyksos and Israelite Cities*, 3-10; Engberg, *Hyksos Reconsidered.*
7 See Burke, *MBA Fortification Strategies*.
8 See Chapter 2.2; Ben-Tor, *Scarabs*; Weinstein, *BASOR* 241 (1981), 1-28.

REGION	SITE	DATE	CONTEXT	DESIGN	REFERENCE(S)
SOUTHERN LEVANT	Aphek, Tell	late MBIIA to MBIIA-B	Phase 4: occupation	two Egyptian	Giveon, *Scarabs*, 44-46; Weinstein, *BASOR* 288 (1992), 35
	Aviv, Tell (Harbour)	late MBIIA to early MBIIB	tombs	mostly Levantine	Tufnell, *Scarab Seals* 2/1, 54-55; Weinstein, *BASOR* 217 (1975), 5-6
	Beit Mirsim, Tell	MBIIB to MBIIC	stratum E-D: occupation	royal (*Ykb*); mostly Levantine; Egyptian	Albright, *BASOR* 47 (1932), 8-10
	Beth Shemesh	early MBIIB	tombs	mostly Levantine	Grant, *Beth Shemesh*, 89
	Far'ah (N), Tell el-	late MBIIA to MBIIA-B	tombs	Egyptian and Levantine	Ben-Tor, *Scarabs*, 121
	Far'ah (S), Tell el-	MBIIB to MBIIC	tombs	mostly Levantine	Tufnell, *Scarab Seals* 2/1, 86-92; Ben-Tor, *Scarabs*, 155-156
	Fassuta	MBIIA-B	tombs	royal (Noferhotep I; heirloom?)	Gershuny and Aviam, *'Atiqot* 62 (2010), fig. 15
	Ginnosar	early MBIIB	tombs	mostly Levantine	Ben-Tor, *Scarabs*, 121
	Hazor	MBIIB	Strata 3, XVII: occupation and tomb	mostly Levantine; few Egyptian heirlooms	Tufnell, *Scarab Seals* 2/1, 56-57, fig. 17; Goldwasser, in *Hazor III-IV*, 339-345
	Kabri, Tell	late MBIIA to MBIIB	near and in burials	royal (*Ykbm*; late MBIIB context); mostly Levantine	Mizrachy, in *Tel Kabri*, 319-339
	Lachish	late MBIIB to LBA	tombs	royal (*ꜥ3mw* and *Šši*); mostly Levantine	Tufnell, *Lachish* 4, 92-123
	Nahariya	MBIIA to LBIA	Phase A; temple area	unpublished but for a Levantine-style scarab	Dothan, *IEJ* 6 (1956), 20, pl. 3 [d]
	Nami, Tell	MBA to LBA	occupation	Egyptian	Artzy, *IEJ* 41/1 (1991), 195-197, fig. 1
	Pella	MBIIB to LBA	tomb	royal (*Y3ꜥmw*, *Yꜥḳbhr*, Apophis, Kamose); mostly Levantine	Richards, *Scarab Seals*; Bourke and Eriksson, in *Timelines* 2, 339-348
	Rishon Lezziyon	MBIIA-B and MBIIB	tombs	mostly Levantine	Ben-Tor, *IEJ* 47/3 (1997), 162-189
	Safed	MBIIA-B	tomb	unpublished	Weinstein, *BASOR* 217 (1975), 4
	Shechem	MBIIB to LBA	occupation	mostly Levantine	Horn, *JNES* 21 (1962), 1-14; Horn, *JNES* 25 (1966), 48-56; Horn, *JNES* 32 (1973), 281-289
NORTHERN LEVANT	Alalakh	MBIIB to LBA	Level VII; occupation	Egyptian	Collon, *Seal Impressions from Tell Atchana*
	Hizzin, Tell	MBA	tomb	Egyptian	Personal communication with Hélène Sader
	Kamid el-Loz	MBIIB to MBIIC	occupation	Egyptian	Heinz and Linke, in *Materiality and Social Practice*
	Ruweise	early MBIIB	tombs	Egyptian	Guigues, *BMB* 2 (1938), 62-63

FIGURE 6.2. SOME LEVANTINE SITES BEARING SCARABS AND SEALINGS NOT DISCUSSED IN THE TEXT. THOSE WITH LEVANTINE DESIGNS ARE MARKED AS 'LEVANTINE' WHILE THOSE WITH EGYPTIAN DESIGNS ARE TERMED 'EGYPTIAN'.

along with a discussion regarding their ambiguities and, consequently, reasons for their omission here.

The chapter incorporates Tell el-Yahudiyah juglets of Egyptian origin. Some vessels are akin to shapes found solely in Egypt but only a handful have been chemically or petrographically analysed, the results pointing to Levantine as well as Egyptian fabrics. Due to the local production and most likely Levantine origin of Tell el-Yahudiyah ware,[9] only vessels that are scientifically of indisputable Egyptian origin are included here.

Imported stone vessels are also featured,[10] their material classification reliant on the terminology used by excavators. The most inconsistent identifications concern 'alabaster' and 'Egyptian alabaster'.[11] The latter refers to a stone containing the calcium carbonate 'calcite' that was used for Egyptian vessels.[12] 'Alabaster', however, contains the hydrated calcium sulphate 'gypsum' and was used for Levantine vessels.[13] The chapter favours the

9 Aston and Bietak, *TeD* 8, 551-552.

10 For more on imported Egyptian stone vessels, see Sparks, *Stone Vessels in the Levant*, 267-270.

11 See Sparks, *Stone Vessels in the Levant*, 4-5; Ben-Dor, *QDAP* 11 (1944), 93-112; Sparks, in *Cultural Interaction*, 51-66.

12 Sparks, *Stone Vessels in the Levant*, 5.

13 Sparks, *Stone Vessels in the Levant*, 5.

REGION	SITE	DATE AND CONTEXT	ITEM(S)	REFERENCE(S)
SOUTHERN LEVANT	'Ajjul, Tell el-	unknown / 'Stratum III'	three statues	(see Appendix A.1)
	Dan, Tell	unknown / secondary (Iron Age)	two statues	Maeir, *Jordan Valley during the MBA*, 34
	Gezer	unknown / secondary (LBA and Iron Age)	three statues	(see Appendix A.2)
	Hazor	unknown / secondary (Iron Age)	at least six statues	Ben-Tor, in *Confronting the Past*, 3-16
	Jo'ara	unknown	one statue	Giveon, *Impact of Egypt on Canaan*, 26
	Megiddo	secondary (LBA)	four fragments	(see Appendix A.3)
NORTHERN LEVANT	Adana	unknown	one statue	Ahrens, in *Intercultural Contacts in the Ancient Mediterranean*, 285-288
	Beirut	secondary	one sphinx	Dunand, *Syria* 9/4 (1928), 300-302
	Hizzin, Tell	unknown	two fragments	(see Appendix A.5)
	Neirab	unknown	one sphinx	Scandone-Matthiae, *RdE* 40 (1989), 125-129
	Qatna	MBA to LBA	two fragmentary statues; one sphinx	Du Mesnil du Buisson, *Syria* 9/1 (1928), 10-12, 17, pls 12, 14 [1]; du Mesnil du Buisson, *Qatna*, 45, pl. 4
	Ugarit	MBA to LBA	three or four fragmentary statues and sphinxes	(see Appendix A.6)
MESOPOTAMIA	Baghdad	unknown	one sphinx	*PM* VII, 396
ANATOLIA	Boğazköy	unknown	statuettes	Schaeffer, *Stratigraphie comparée*, 29, n. 3
	Yahşihan	secondary (late Antique)	one statue	Allen, *AJSL* 43 (1927), 294-296
CRETE	Knossos	secondary (late Minoan)	one statuette	Gill and Padgham, *ABSA* 100 (2005), 41-59

FIGURE 6.3. MEDITERRANEAN AND NEAR EASTERN SITES BEARING EGYPTIAN-STYLE STATUARY NOT DISCUSSED IN THE TEXT.

terms 'alabaster' where the stone is not identified in its publication(s), 'calcite-alabaster' for imported Egyptian vessels and 'gypsum-alabaster' for locally made vessels.[14]

Sites with meagre Egyptian or Egyptian-influenced artefacts have not been selected. This includes those with only stone vessels, scarabs, seal impressions or cylinder seals that could either be of Egyptian or, as several studies have proven, local manufacture, signifying the appropriation of Egyptian artistic traditions by Levantines. The popularity of seals and impressions is evident in Figure 6.2, which provides a list of some sites not discussed here but with scarabs and/or sealings of the studied MBIIA-MBIIB period.

Mention should also be made of Middle Kingdom statues unearthed in uncertain, often less-than-secure contexts. Although not included in this chapter, comments on some may be found in Appendix A. Discovered across Western Asia and the Mediterranean, the statues are of royal individuals and high officials (Figure 6.3). Some scholars propose that they were brought into the Levant during the Fifteenth Dynasty.[15] While this is likely, there is currently no evidence linking the statues with the Hyksos and it is equally possible that the artefacts were indirectly transported to the sites before the rise of the Hyksos, perhaps during the Middle Kingdom itself, to be later kept as luxury products or heirlooms until the time of deposition. Similarly, they could have been sent during the beginning of the Eighteenth Dynasty, when relations with Egypt had once again intensified.

The questionable nature of these finds represents just one problem inherent in the study of Egyptian elements in the Levant. The chronology and stratigraphy of Levantine sites have additionally been under fervent debate. Adding to this situation is, as mentioned in Chapter 1.5.1, the different cultural development of Levantine sites following the collapse of the EBA and the varying state of archaeological research across the Levant, with areas such as the Beqa' Valley of Lebanon or southern Israel receiving little attention. Until such problems are resolved, this chapter relies on the sites' most recent publications, chronological classifications and revisions. References to radiocarbon results and their synchronisations with the Egyptian relative chronology are additionally mentioned where applicable.

14 Terms proposed by others include 'travertine' and 'Egyptian alabaster' for the imported Egyptian variety. See Sparks, *Stone Vessels in the Levant*, 5; Ben-Dor, *QDAP* 11 (1944), 94-96; Klemm and Klemm, *GM* 122 (1991), 57-75; Klemm and Klemm, *Steine und Stein-Brüche*; Aston, *Ancient Egyptian Stone Vessels*, 43; Lilyquist, *Egyptian Stone Vessels*, 13.

15 See, for example, Helck, *Die Beziehungen Ägyptens*; Weinstein, *BASOR* 213 (1974), 49-57; Ahrens, in *Egypt and the Near East*, 21-40.

6.2 The Southern Levant: Israel, Jordan and the Palestinian Territories

6.2.1 'Ajjul, Tell el-

Lat.Lon. 31°22'N 34°27'E

Refs PM 7, 370-371; Petrie, *Gaza* 1-4; Mackay and Murray, *Gaza* 5; Petrie, *Shepherd Kings*; Tufnell, *BIA* 3 (1962), 1-37; Stewart, *Tell el 'Ajjūl*; Fischer and Sadiq, *E&L* 10 (2000), 211-226.

Chron. Thirteenth to Fifteenth Dynasty / Late MBIIA to MBIIC Period

Tell el-'Ajjul lies southwest of Ashkelon, around 1.8km from the Mediterranean coast.[16] Strategically positioned along an estuary, the site possibly had access to an ancient harbour allowing small vessels to reach the city.[17] Excavations by several researchers, such as Petrie[18] and, most recently, Fischer and Sadeq,[19] revealed EBIV cemeteries west and east of the tell,[20] a Courtyard Cemetery at the tell itself with MBIIA remains,[21] and other material from later periods.[22] The quality and quantity of evidence from the MBA and LBA suggest that the site reached its zenith during these periods. Based on Tell el-'Ajjul's location and remains, Kempinski has identified it with Sharuhen,[23] which has been widely accepted in the literature.[24]

The published remains and their contexts, as well as Petrie's excavation plans and stratigraphy, are confused and incomplete. Studies attempting to re-phase the site have reached various dates for its periods of occupation (Figure 6.4).[25] Recently, research identifying MBIIC-LBI material in Palace I and Stratum III has corroborated Albright's proposed dates.[26] As this monograph does not explore material from the MBIIC period, the following presents finds from below Stratum III, as well as newly discovered remains from Fischer and Sadeq's excavations. For further information on Egyptian finds from Strata III to II that have been used as evidence for Hyksos relations, see Appendix A.1.

6.2.1.1 Vessels

Stone vessels include Egyptian imports during the MBA. The earliest recorded vessel is a cylindrical calcite-alabaster jar from intramural Burial 2139 in Area GHJ, Level 817.[27] The burial was found underneath a wall of the Lower City, or Stratum III,[28] indicating a date prior to the MBIIC period and thus before the second half of the Fifteenth Dynasty. Preliminary publications of Fischer and Sadeq's excavations additionally mention a sherd of an Egyptian piriform jar. Of unknown fabric, the fragment was recovered from Horizon 8, a level in Trench 7 which has been preliminarily dated to the second half of the MBA.[29] Thus, it may attest to contact with the late Thirteenth to Fifteenth Dynasties.

STRATUM	PETRIE	ALBRIGHT	TUFNELL	KEEL
III	12th Dynasty (Palace II)	MBIIC late 15th Dynasty (Palace I)	MBIIB 12th to 15th Dynasty (Palace I)	MBIIB mid-13th to 15th Dynasty (Palace I)
II	15th Dynasty (Palace III-IV)	LBI 18th Dynasty (Palace II)	MBIIB - MBIIC 15th Dynasty (Palace II)	MBIIB - MBIIC mid-late 15th Dynasty (Palace II)
I	18th Dynasty (Palace V)	LBI 18th Dynasty (Palace III)	LBI 18th Dynasty (Palace III)	LBI 18th Dynasty (Fortress III)

FIGURE 6.4. PROPOSED CHRONOLOGIES FOR TELL EL-'AJJUL'S STRATA I-III. AFTER PETRIE, *GAZA* 1-4; ALBRIGHT, *AJSL* 55/4 (1938), 337-359; TUFNELL, *SCARAB SEALS* 2/1, 7-23; KEEL, *STEMPELSIEGEL-AMULETTE*, 105.

16 Burke, *MBA Fortification Strategies*, 230; Fischer and Sadeq, *E&L* 10 (2000), 212.
17 Fischer and Sadeq, *E&L* 10 (2000), 213, fig. 1.
18 Petrie directed excavations from 1930 to 1934 while Mackay and Murray continued archaeological exploration in 1938. Petrie, *Gaza* 1-4; Mackay and Murray, *Gaza* 5.
19 Fischer and Sadeq, *E&L* 10 (2000), 211-226; Fischer and Sadeq, *E&L* 12 (2002), 109-153.
20 Kenyon, in *Tell el 'Ajjūl*, 76-85; Fischer and Sadeq, *E&L* 10 (2000), 211.
21 Tufnell, *BIA* 3 (1962), 1-37; Fischer and Sadeq, *E&L* 10 (2000), 211.
22 Fischer and Sadeq, *E&L* 10 (2000), 212.
23 Kempinski, *IEJ* 24/3-4 (1974), 145-152.
24 Stewart, *Tell el 'Ajjūl*, 3; Bietak, *Avaris*, 60-63; Weinstein, *BASOR* 241 (1981), 8; Oren, in *Hyksos*, 253-283; Morris, *Architecture of Imperialism*, 51-53. For an alternate view, see Kopetzky, in *Bronze Age in the Lebanon*, 227.
25 Tufnell, *Scarab Seals* 2/1, 7-23; Albright, *AJSL* 55/4 (1938), 337-359; Daly, *Tell el-'Ajjul*, 231-261; Robertson, *MBA Tombs at Tell el Ajjul*, 113-166; Kempinski, *IEJ* 24/3-4 (1974), 147; Kopetzky, in *Bronze Age in the Lebanon*, 226.
26 For instance, chocolate-on-white ware, bichrome wheel-made ware, early Eighteenth Dynasty Marl zir forms as well as stone vessels of the New Kingdom. Sparks, *Stone Vessels in the Levant*, 205-206; Kopetzky, in *Bronze Age in the Lebanon*, 226-227.
27 Petrie, *Shepherd Kings*, pl. 19 [32]; Sparks, *Stone Vessels in the Levant*, 206, 314 [417].
28 Sparks, *Stone Vessels in the Levant*, 314 [417].
29 Fischer and Sadeq, *E&L* 12 (2002), 134.

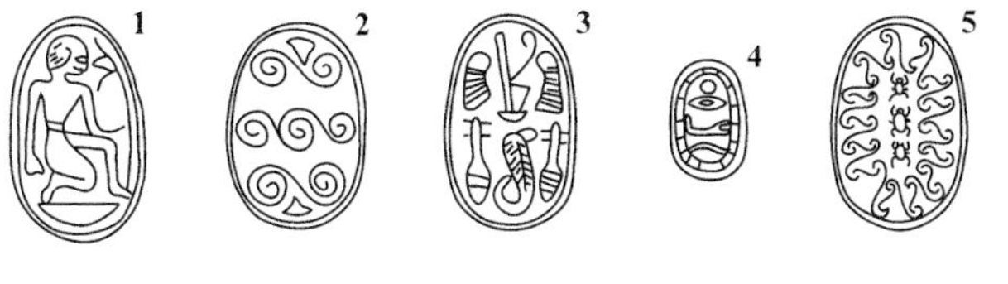

FIGURE 6.5. SELECTED SCARABS, TELL EL-'AJJUL (NOT TO SCALE). AFTER PETRIE, *GAZA* 2, PL. 7 [103-104, 6]; VOL. 3, PL. 4 [115-116].

6.2.1.2 Scarabs and seal impressions

Petrie's excavations uncovered over 1000 scarabs and seal impressions, the most unearthed at any site in the Southern Levant.[30] They feature designs bearing Levantine as well as Egyptian influences, the latter also representing the largest and most unique corpus of Egyptian design and royal-name scarabs. However, only a few from the Courtyard Cemetery can be more securely assigned to the MBIIA to MBIIB period.

Three display Levantine designs, two of which are from MBIIA Tomb 1406 (Figure 6.5 [1-2])[31] and one from early MBIIB Tomb 1410B (Figure 6.5 [3]).[32] Another tomb, 303, of the late MBIIA or MBIIA-B period contained two further scarabs, one of the *rḏi-rˤ* type (Figure 6.5 [4]) and the other with spirals enclosing three *ḫpr*-beetles (Figure 6.5 [5]).[33] Their late Middle Kingdom design[34] suggests that they were possibly imported.

Overall, the evidence is indicative of minimal trade relations with the Thirteenth and early Fifteenth Dynasties. Such a conclusion significantly affects the validity of claims regarding the influences of the so-called 'Kingdom of Sharuhen' on the rise of the Hyksos[35] and advises that, until further excavation is carried out, the extent of relations between Tell el-'Ajjul and the early Fifteenth Dynasty cannot be firmly ascertained.

30 Five design scarabs were collected in recent excavations. Two scarabs were found in Late Bronze Age strata, one in an MBIIC-LBI tomb and two in a phase dated to the MBIIC. Fischer and Sadeq, *E&L* 10 (2000), 217-218, fig. 7 [1-2]; Fischer and Sadeq, *E&L* 12 (2002), 131-134; Mlinar, in Fischer and Sadeq, *E&L* 12 (2002), 143-151, fig. 29.

31 The tomb belongs to Tufnell's Group 4. Petrie, *Gaza* 2, pl. 7 [103-104]; Tufnell, *BIA* 3 (1962), 19, fig. 7 [1-2].

32 The tomb belongs to Tufnell's Group 5. Petrie, *Gaza* 2, pl. 7 [106]; Tufnell, *BIA* 3 (1962), 19, fig. 7 [3]; Ben-Tor, *Scarabs*, 120-121.

33 Petrie, *Gaza* 3, 7, pl. 4 [115-116]; Tufnell, *'Atiqot* 14 (1980), fig. 3 [5-6]; Stewart, *Tell el 'Ajjūl*, 11; Weinstein, *BASOR* 217 (1975), 4.

34 Ben-Tor, *Scarabs*, 118, n. 574.

35 Oren, in *Hyksos*, 253-255.

6.2.2 Ashkelon

Lat.Lon. 31°40'N 34°33'E

Refs Stager, Schloen and Master (eds), *Ashkelon* 1; Stager and Voss, *Eretz-Israel* 30 (2011), 119*-126*; Stager and Voss, in *TeD* 8, 559-575.

Chron. Late Twelfth to Fifteenth Dynasty / MBIIA to MBIIC Period

Positioned on the Mediterranean coast south of Tel Aviv is Ashkelon, the largest known ancient seaport in the Southern Levant.[36] Its MBA occupation is marked by a thriving fortified, urban settlement and seaport.[37] Ceramics imported from Crete, Cyprus and the Northern Levant highlight Ashkelon's role in the MBA Mediterranean Sea trade.[38] Evidence of relations with Egypt can be tracked across several strata throughout the MBIIA to MBIIC periods. Material assigned between Dynasty 12 and early Dynasty 15 is examined here.[39]

6.2.2.1 Phase 14: Mid-MBIIA Period

Ashkelon's North Tell features an MBA sandstone causeway leading into the settlement's earliest Gate 1 (Figure 6.6).[40] Extending over the causeway and cut into the bedrock is a fosse lined with black ash (the Moat Deposit).[41] This ash lining contained over 45 seal impressions made almost entirely by scarabs bearing late Twelfth to early Thirteenth Dynasty Egyptian designs.[42] Although not all published,[43] the sealings were reportedly used on such products as a knobbled box or chest,[44] perhaps imported from Egypt. NAA and petrographic tests reportedly confirm that the sealings are of both Levantine and Egyptian clays,[45] signifying their impression at Egyptian and local administrative units. Ben-Tor identifies Tell el-Dab'a as the most likely Egyptian administrative centre, proposing small-scale trade with MBIIA Ashkelon.[46]

Ceramics from outside Gate 1 support this proposition. The Moat Deposit contained one rim of a Marl C, Type 4

36 Stager, Schloen and Master (eds), *Ashkelon* 1.

37 For an examination of the fortification, see Burke, *MBA Fortification Strategies*, 237-243, figs 61-66.

38 Stager, in *MBA in the Levant*, 353-362.

39 Not included is the Egyptian pottery from Phase 10 (MBIIC) representing the largest corpus of Egyptian finds at Ashkelon (3.45% of the complete ceramic corpus by rim fraction) that suggests increased contact with late Dynasty 15. For more, see Stager and Voss, *Eretz-Israel* 30 (2011), 123-125; Stager and Voss, in *TeD* 8, 572-574.

40 Stager and Voss, *Eretz-Israel* 30 (2011), 120*.

41 Stager and Voss, *Eretz-Israel* 30 (2011), 120*; Stager, in *MBA in the Levant*, 353.

42 Stager, in *MBA in the Levant*, 353.

43 Bell is reportedly preparing the sealings for publication. For an image of one of the sealings, see Stager, in *MBA in the Levant*, 353, fig. 1. For further comments regarding some designs, see Ben-Tor, *Scarabs*, 69, 135, ns 345, 647.

44 Stager, in *MBA in the Levant*, 353.

45 Stager, in *MBA in the Levant*, 353; Ben-Tor, *Scarabs*, 118, n. 570. To the author's knowledge, the results of the analysis have not been published.

46 Ben-Tor, *Scarabs*, 118.

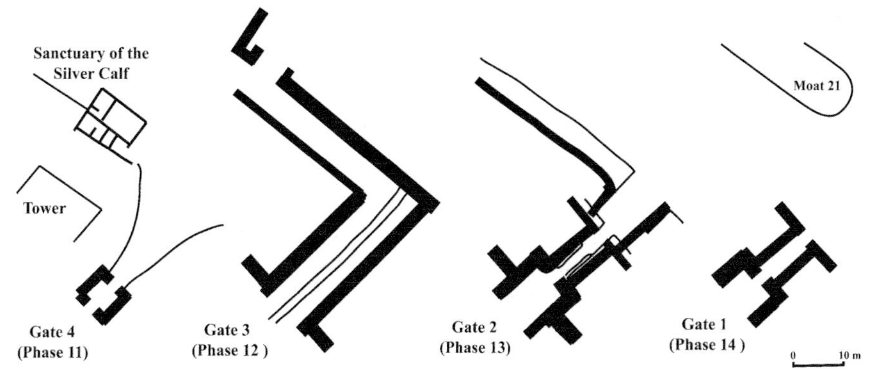

FIGURE 6.6. CITY GATES AND MOAT, ASHKELON. AFTER STAGER AND VOSS, *ERETZ ISRAEL* 30 (2011), FIG. 1.

Egyptian zir as well as a Marl C-1 store-jar.[47] The two vessels are comparable to ceramics from Tell el-Dab'a's Strata G/4-3 (early Dynasty 13).[48] Layer 166 of the courtyard in front of Gate 1's outer entrance yielded three more fragments of Egyptian pottery.[49] Two are of Marl C-1 store-jars and the third is a Marl C ringstand.[50] The latter finds parallels with ringstands from Tell el-Dab'a's G/4-3.[51] By rim fragment calculations, the Egyptian pottery adds up to almost 0.18% out of the entire ceramic repertoire at Ashkelon.[52]

6.2.2.2 *Transitional Phase 13 to 12: Late MBIIA to MBIIA-B Period*

No Egyptian imports have been reported in Phase 13 and Phase 12 contexts. But, during the construction of Phase 12's Gate 3, Phase 13's Gate 2 was buried and covered with a fill of sandstone, ash and clay.[53] The fill over the gate's barrel-vaulted chamber contained one sherd of a Type 4 or 5 Egyptian zir of Marl C fabric, offering a date in the first half of Dynasty 13.[54] Another Egyptian Marl C vessel from the fill over Gate 2's inner courtyard finds parallels with vessels from Tell el-Dab'a's Strata G/1-3 to D/3.[55]

6.2.2.3 *Phase 11: MBIIB Period*

A major structural modification and reduction in size from Phase 12's Gate 3 to Phase 11's Gate 4 denotes a shift in the entryway's function.[56] The rampart of the pedestrian Gate 4 now led to the so-called 'Sanctuary of the Silver Calf' (Figure 6.6),[57] the route containing the following scattered ceramics of Egyptian fabrics: (a) three cooking pots of Nile E-2 fabric, one at the footgate and two along the route;[58] (b) four fragments of Egyptian Marl C, Type 5 zirs along the route;[59] and (c) one fragment of a biconical(?) Tell el-Yahudiyah juglet composed of Nile silt from the Sanctuary's Room 5.[60] All vessels find parallels from Tell el-Dab'a's Strata E/2-D/3 (Dynasty 15).[61]

Chamber tombs within the necropolis additionally contained Egyptian imports. While the tombs were in use throughout the MBA, excavators have been able to ascribe particular deposits to Phase 11, a few of which preserved Tell el-Yahudiyah ware.[62] Petrographic analysis on some reportedly revealed the use of Egyptian fabrics for:[63] (a) one biconical juglet from Chamber Tomb 5 similar to juglets from Tell el-Dab'a's E/2;[64] and (b) four biconical juglets from Chamber Tomb 11 including two biconical juglets with parallels from Tell el-Dab'a's E/2-D/3,[65] and one biconical and one piriform vessel comparable to those from E/1-D/3.[66] Evidently, the imported Tell el-Yahudiyah ware provides further correlations with Dynasty 15.

Out of the entire ceramic repertoire from Phase 11, 2.45% has been calculated to be of Egyptian origin.[67] In contrast

47 Stager and Voss, *Eretz-Israel* 30 (2011), 120*-121*, pl. 1 [3].
48 Stager and Voss, *Eretz-Israel* 30 (2011), 120*-121*; Bietak et al., *E&L* 18 (2008), 49-52, fig. 2 [8, 16].
49 Stager and Voss, *Eretz-Israel* 30 (2011), 121*, pl. 1 [1-2].
50 Stager and Voss, *Eretz-Israel* 30 (2011), 121*, pl. 1 [1-2].
51 Stager and Voss, *Eretz-Israel* 30 (2011), 121*-122*.
52 Stager and Voss, *Eretz-Israel* 30 (2011), 125*.
53 Stager and Voss, *Eretz-Israel* 30 (2011), 122*.
54 The sherd was found in Layer 185, Square 85. Stager and Voss, *Eretz-Israel* 30 (2011), 122*, pl. 1 [5].
55 The vessel was found in Layer 40. Stager and Voss, *Eretz-Israel* 30 (2011), 122*, pl. 1 [4].
56 Stager and Voss, *Eretz-Israel* 30 (2011), 122*; Burke, *MBA Fortification Strategies*, 242-243.
57 Stager and Voss, *Eretz-Israel* 30 (2011), 122*; Burke, *MBA Fortification Strategies*, 242-243.
58 Respectively, from Layer 99, Mudbrick Floor 103, Southern Revetment Wall 97 and Street 117. Cooking pots of the same shape (Ashkelon's Type CP7) are common in Phase 11 and, discounting the three Egyptian imports, are all locally made. Stager and Voss, *Eretz-Israel* 30 (2011), 122*, pl. 1 [7-8]; Bietak et al., *E&L* 18 (2008), 52, fig. 5 [6, 12].
59 Three were collected from Street 90 and one from Street 117. Stager and Voss, *Eretz-Israel* 30 (2011), 122*-123*, pl. 1 [9]; Bietak et al., *E&L* 18 (2008), 52, fig. 6 [14, 16].
60 Aston and Bietak's Late Egyptian Type Group L.5 (Biconical III). Stager and Voss, *Eretz-Israel* 30 (2011), 123*; Stager and Voss, in *TeD* 8, 572, fig. 7 [41]; Bietak et al., *E&L* 18 (2008), 52, fig. 5 [3, 9].
61 Stager and Voss, *Eretz-Israel* 30 (2011), 122*-123*; Bietak et al., *E&L* 18 (2008), 52, figs 5 [3, 6], 6 [14]; Aston and Bietak, *TeD* 8, 231.
62 Stager and Voss, in *TeD* 8, 565, 570-572, figs 6-7.
63 To the author's knowledge, the results of the tests have not been published but are mentioned in Stager and Voss, in *TeD* 8, 559-575.
64 Grid 50, Square 48, Layer 487. Aston and Bietak's Late Egyptian Type Group L.2.2 (Biconical I). Stager and Voss, in *TeD* 8, 570, fig. 6 [34]; Aston and Bietak, *TeD* 8, 211, 450, figs 149, 153, pl. 67 [383].
65 Grid 50, Square 47, Layer 315. Aston and Bietak's Late Egyptian Type Group L.2.2 (Biconical I) and Group L.5 (Biconical III). Stager and Voss, in *TeD* 8, 570, fig. 7 [36, 38]; Aston and Bietak, *TeD* 8, 211, 221-231, 450, figs 149, 153, pl. 67 [383].
66 Layer 311. Aston and Bietak's Late Egyptian Type Group L.1.3 (Piriform 2a) and Group L.5 (Biconical III). Stager and Voss, in *TeD* 8, 570-572, fig. 7 [37, 39]; Aston and Bietak, *TeD* 8, 206, 221-231, 435-438, figs 141, 147, pls 58 [332], 59 [334-338].
67 By rim fragment calculations. Stager and Voss, *Eretz-Israel* 30

to Phase 14's 0.18%, the Egyptian imports appear in more varied forms and contexts. Phase 14's Egyptian corpus is represented by storage containers along the entrance of Gate 1 whereas Phase 11's repertoire contains storage containers and vessels for food preparation at the entrance of its gate through to the sanctuary.[68] Phase 11 also marks the first instance of imported Tell el-Yahudiyah juglets which were not only found at the sanctuary, but also within funerary contexts. Albeit influenced by Levantine designs, the juglets provide an added function for imported Egyptian goods at Ashkelon.

Therefore, it is possible to discern continuous trade relations between Egypt and Ashkelon. The material from Phase 11 denotes small-scale trade with the late Twelfth or early Thirteenth Dynasty. A reduction occurs across Phases 12 and 13, or the second half of the Thirteenth Dynasty, followed by renewed and heightened contact during the Hyksos Period. While no Egyptian pottery has been found in the site's domestic quarters, the range of Fifteenth Dynasty imports implies direct cross-cultural contact. Individuals from Ashkelon may have visited Egypt, bringing back Egyptian-made MBA cooking pots, or those of mixed Egyptian-Levantine ancestry could have sailed to Ashkelon. Perhaps, after delivering a shipment of goods from, for instance, Tell el-Dab'a, the traders visited the Sanctuary of the Silver Calf to offer homage, leaving some of their wares behind.

6.2.3 Beth Shean / Hosn, Tell el-

Lat.Lon. 32°29'N 35°32'E

Refs PM 7, 376-380; Rowe, *Scarabs*, 3 [10], 56-57 [214b], pls 1 [10], 6 [214b]; Mazar and Mullins (eds), *Beth Shean* 2; Maeir and Mullins, in *TeD* 8, 577-589.

Chron. Late Thirteenth to Fifteenth Dynasty / MBIIB to MBIIC Period

Beth Shean lies west of the Jordan River, near frequented routes linking highland Jordan with the coastal Mediterranean plain.[69] Excavations in Area R by the University Museum of the University of Pennsylvania (1921-1933)[70] and the Hebrew University of Jerusalem (1983, 1989-1996)[71] unearthed remains of an EBIII settlement, minor EBIV/MBI finds and no MBIIA evidence except for some tombs in the surrounds.[72] The site was reoccupied during the MBIIB as a small domestic settlement.[73] Data on Egyptian relations are presented below according to the Hebrew University's stratigraphical designations, R-5 and R-4.[74]

6.2.3.1 Stratum R-5: MBIIB Period

Stratum R-5 represents the most fragmentary MBA stratum at Beth Shean.[75] Egyptian remains were recovered from both occupation debris as well as funerary contexts. The beaten-earth surface's occupation debris of Locus 10547, Stratum R-5b, produced a scarab with a scroll and three decorative hieroglyphs (Figure 6.7 [1]).[76] Brandl typologically connects it to Mlinar's Type IIIb of the Early Tell el-Dab'a workshop (Strata F-E/2) dating to the late Thirteenth or early Fifteenth Dynasty Egypt.[77] Two other scarabs found in occupation debris (Loci 10544 and 10316) are likely of Levantine origin: one displays meaningless hieroglyphs, and one bears addorsed cobras, with lotus flowers on the back (Figure 6.7 [2-3]).[78] Therefore, R-5's occupation debris retained three scarabs, one of possible Egyptian origin and two from Levantine workshops influenced by such Egyptian elements as lotus flowers and hieroglyphs.

Egyptian influence is also evident in gypsum-alabaster fragments. The base of a small jar or ovoid bottle was collected from the floor of an open area (Locus 10574) and assigned to Stratum R-5c (Figure 6.8 [5]).[79] Another vessel, a globular stone vase, was found on a plaster floor (Figure 6.8 [8]).[80] Prototypes of both forms occur in Twelfth Dynasty Egypt.[81]

Of Area R's graves, two burials produced Egyptian imports.[82] A child's burial (Burial 38201) yielded four

(2011), 125*.

68 Stager and Voss, *Eretz-Israel* 30 (2011), 125*.

69 Mazar, in *Egypt, Canaan and Israel*, 156-157; Sparks, *Stone Vessels in the Levant*, 227.

70 Rowe, *Beth-Shan*; Rowe, *Four Canaanite Temples* 1; Fitzgerald, *Four Canaanite Temples* 2; Fitzgerald, *Beth-Shan Excavations*; Oren, *Northern Cemetery*. For more publications, see Mullins, in *Beth Shean* 2, 23.

71 Mazar and Mullins (eds), *Beth Shean* 2.

72 For instance, Tomb 92 of the Northern Cemetery consisted of EBIV/MBI grave goods with evidence of later reuse for Roman burials. A frit design scarab bearing Egyptian glyphs has been linked to the tomb, yet its date of deposition remains uncertain. Mazar and Mullins, in *Beth Shean* 2, 12-13; Oren, *Northern Cemetery*, 61-67; Mazar, in *Beth Shean*, 199-200; Cohen, *'Atiqot* 59 (2008), 11*-20*, 195-196; Maeir, *Jordan Valley during the MBA*, 49; Weinstein, *BASOR* 217 (1975), 2.

73 Mazar and Mullins, in *Beth Shean* 2, 13-17.

74 The following Stratum R-3 of the MBIIC period coincides with approximately the end of the Fifteenth Dynasty and is not examined here. It is linked with the University Museum's Level XA. Mazar and Mullins, in *Beth Shean* 2, 16; Maeir, in *Beth Shean* 2, 263-264, 279-282; Maeir and Yellin, in *Tel Beth Shean* 2, 563; Brandl, in *Beth Shean* 2, 590-593; Clamer, in *Beth Shean* 2, 629-630; Rowe, *Scarabs*, 24 [89], 35 [132], 48 [180], 73 [277], 104 [436], 105 [441]; Oren, *Northern Cemetery*, figs 33, 51, 73; Ben-Tor, *Scarabs*, 139, 143, 171, n. 698.

75 Stratum R-5 is equivalent to the revised University Museum's Level XI. Mazar and Mullins, in *Beth Shean* 2, 12-13, table 1.1; Mullins, in *Beth Shean* 2, 25-27; Mullins and Mazar, in *Beth Shean* 2, 48-49.

76 Brandl, in *Beth Shean* 2, 583-584, fig. 8 [1], photo 8 [1].

77 Brandl, in *Beth Shean* 2, 584; Mlinar, in *Scarabs of the Second Millennium BC*, 120.

78 Brandl, in *Beth Shean* 2, 584-586, fig. 8 [2-3], photo 8 [2-3].

79 Clamer, in *Beth Shean* 2, 631, fig. 10 [1.5].

80 Locus 88326. Clamer, in *Beth Shean* 2, 631-632, fig. 10 [1.8].

81 Clamer, in *Beth Shean* 2, 631-632.

82 Two drop-shaped bottles were each uncovered in R-5's infant jar burials 28333 and 10342. A third was found in the Northern Cemetery's Tomb 42 of the MBIIC-LBI period. While it has been argued that the bottles are based on Egyptian forms, no Egyptian parallels are known. Moreover, preliminary petrographic analysis on the fabric of the bottle from Burial 10342 points to its local origin. See Maeir, in *Beth Shean* 2, 282, photo 4 [68-69], pls 16 [10], 17 [4]; Maeir and Yellin, in *Beth Shean* 2, 563.

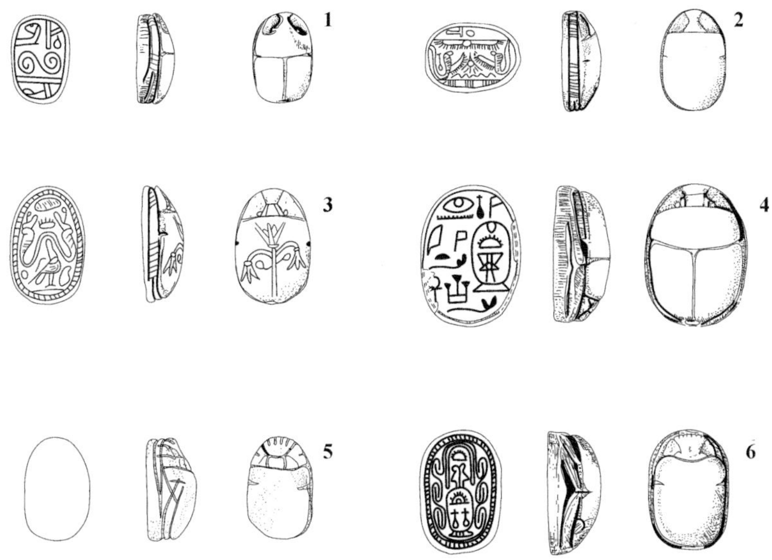

FIGURE 6.7. SELECTED SCARABS, BETH SHEAN (NOT TO SCALE). AFTER BRANDL, IN *BETH SHEAN* 2, FIG. 8 [1-7].

gold earrings as well as MBIIB pottery vessels.[83] Near the deceased's left arm were two calcite-alabaster vessels (Figure 6.8 [1-2]), one a cylindrical jar and the other a miniature shouldered jar, paralleling Twelfth to early Eighteenth Dynasty vessels.[84] An amethyst scarab mounted on a gold ring was also found near the body, its fine workmanship and material suggesting Egyptian manufacture.[85] Such a combination of Egyptian imports with gold jewellery represents the child's elite status[86] and indicates the funerary significance of Egyptian goods, perhaps as prestige markers, during the MBIIB period.

Burial 1822 reportedly contained scarabs with hieroglyphs.[87] One scarab bears such Levantine elements as meaningless signs along with two scrolls.[88] A second contained hieroglyphs reading *nb nfr Ḫpr-ḫˁ-Rˁ.w* 'the good lord, Kheperkhara (Senwosret II)', its back also incised with a crosshatched design.[89] While some have dated the latter scarab to the early Twelfth Dynasty, Ben-Tor strongly argues that the back type is of Levantine origin,[90] the scarab thereby being a royal-name scarab bearing mixed Levantine and Egyptian influences.

6.2.3.2 Stratum R-4: Late MBIIB Period

Stratum R-4 is marked by the site's continued domestic occupation.[91] Locus 105225, the stone bedding of a R-4b street, contained a scarab inscribed with *nṯr nfr Ḫˁ-sḫm-Rˁ.w iri n it nṯr Ḥ3-ˁnḫ=f* 'the good god, Khasekhemra (Noferhotep I), born to the god's father, Haankhef' (Figure 6.7 [4]).[92] The genealogical royal-name scarab is most likely of Egyptian origin, exported during Noferhotep I's reign.[93] As no MBIIA levels were found at the settlement, the scarab would have been in circulation for some time, and perhaps across various centres, before its final deposition.

A piriform Tell el-Yahudiyah juglet was discovered in an unclear, R-4b context, possibly a foundation trench.[94] The vessel is typologically similar to juglets of the MBIIB period and, for instance, those from Tell el-Dab'a's Strata E/2-D/2 (Dynasty 15).[95] Instrumental NAA deduced that it is of Egyptian origin,[96] and so the juglet may be used as evidence for imports from Fifteenth Dynasty Egypt.

The following phase R-4a contained two objects of Egyptian influence.[97] The first is a plain scarab, of either Egyptian or Levantine origin, deposited in an accumulation (Locus 58117) (Figure 6.7 [5]).[98] The second is a scarab retrieved from the makeup of an R-3 floor (Locus 78327b)

83 Mazar and Mullins, in *Beth Shean* 2, 15-16, fig. 1 [5]; Mullins and Mazar, in *Beth Shean* 2, 50.

84 Mazar and Mullins, in *Beth Shean* 2, 15-16, fig. 1 [5]; Clamer, in *Beth Shean* 2, 627-629, figs 10 [1.1-1.2], photos 10 [1a-1b].

85 Mazar and Mullins, in *Beth Shean* 2, 15-16, fig. 1 [5]; Brandl, in *Beth Shean* 2, 586-587, fig. 8 [4], photo 8 [4].

86 Mazar and Mullins, in *Beth Shean* 2, 15-16; Mullins and Mazar, in *Beth Shean* 2, 50.

87 Rowe, *Scarabs*, 3 [10], 56-57 [214b], pls 1 [10], 6 [214b].

88 Rowe, *Scarabs*, 56-57 [214b], pl. 6 [214b].

89 Rowe, *Scarabs*, 3 [10], pl. 1 [10].

90 Ben-Tor, *Scarabs*, 137-138, 151, n. 662.

91 Stratum R-4 corresponds to the University Museum's Level XB. Mullins and Mazar, in *Beth Shean* 2, 52-60, 72-85.

92 Brandl, in *Beth Shean* 2, 587-589, fig. 8 [5], photo 8 [5].

93 Brandl, in *Beth Shean* 2, 589.

94 Aston and Bietak's Late Egyptian I Type Group L.1.3 (Piriform 2a). Maeir, in *Beth Shean* 2, 290, photo 4 [81], pl. 10 [19]; Maeir and Mullins, in *TeD* 8, 585, fig. 5 [2]; Aston and Bietak, *TeD* 8, 206, figs 141, 147.

95 Aston and Bietak, *TeD* 8, 206, 394-438, figs 141, 147, pls 36-59.

96 Maeir and Mullins, in *TeD* 8, 585; Maeir and Yellin, in *Beth Shean* 2, 562.

97 A fragmentary bird-shaped Tell el-Yahudiyah vessel has also been recorded as an import by excavators. While no scientific analyses have yet been made on its fabric, parallels from the Levant have been petrographically confirmed to be of local origin. As such, it too may be of local manufacture. To this may be added two unpublished drop-shaped gypsum-alabaster alabastra and one conical alabastron. The vessels are assigned to Level XB or XA and, based on the material, are also locally made. For the Tell el-Yahudiyah fragment, see Maeir, in *Beth Shean* 2, 284-285, 291, photo 4 [75-76], pl. 30 [19]; Maeir and Mullins, in *TeD* 8, 584-585, fig. 5 [1]; Stager and Moss, in *TeD* 8, 567, fig. 4; Kaplan, *Tell el Yahudiyeh*, 43. For the stone vessels, see Sparks, *Stone Vessels of the Levant*, 101-103, 351 [882], 353 [906], 357 [953].

98 Brandl, in *Beth Shean* 2, 589-590, fig. 8 [6], photo 8 [6].

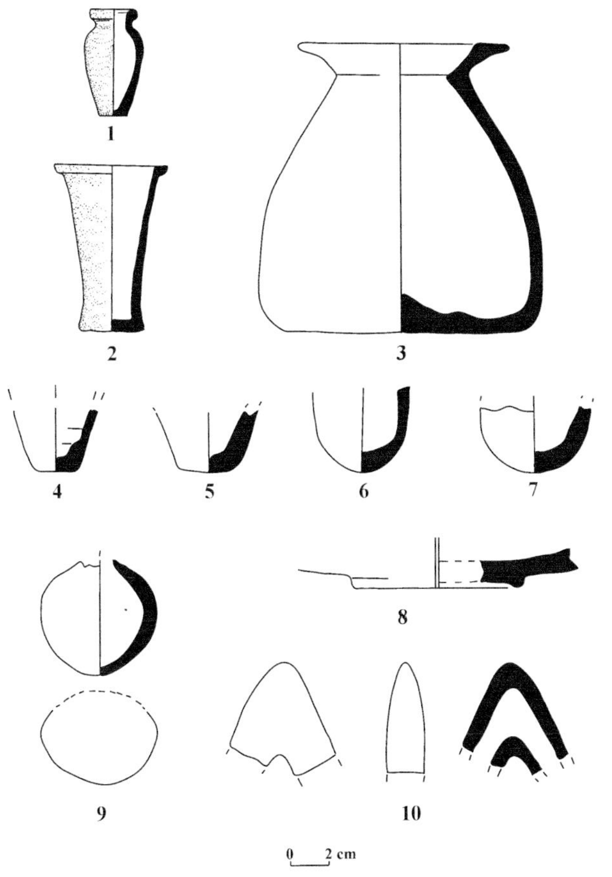

FIGURE 6.8. SELECTED STONE VESSELS, BETH SHEAN. AFTER CLAMER, IN *BETH SHEAN* 2, FIG. 10 [1].

and bears meaningless hieroglyphs signalling its local origin (Figure 6.7 [6]).[99]

Like Stratum R-5, R-4 contained both Egyptian imports as well as locally-made scarabs displaying Egyptian influences. Despite the assortment of goods, only the piriform Tell el-Yahudiyah juglet definitively indicates contemporaneous trade with Dynasty 15. Combined with items from Stratum R-5, the juglet, calcite-alabaster vessels and, perhaps, the scarab from Stratum R-5b, demonstrate Beth Shean's access to Egyptian goods imported from the late Thirteenth to the Fifteenth Dynasties during the MBIIB period. Their quantities indicate that individuals from Egypt were most likely not present at the site. Nonetheless, inhabitants at Beth Shean were evidently familiar with Egyptian(-influenced) products.

99 Brandl, in *Beth Shean* 2, 589-590, fig. 8 [7], photo 8 [7].

6.2.4 *Gezer / Jazari, Tell*

Lat.Lon. 31°53'N 34°57'E

Refs PM 7, 374-375; Macalister, *Gezer* 1-3.

Chron. Second Intermediate Period / MBIIB to MBIIC Period

Gezer is strategically situated along a route from the coastal plain to the highlands of Israel.[100] Stratigraphical data for the settlement and its MBA tombs is somewhat lacking and confused while a complete repertoire of finds, particularly from the Palestine Exploration Fund's excavations, is unpublished.[101] Examples of contextual uncertainties are apparent in reports on Gezer's Egyptian statuettes, presented in Appendix A.2. The current work directed by Ortiz and Wolff may shed more light on Gezer's MBA occupation.[102] Until then, pertinent material only occurs as 'alabaster' and faience vessels, as well as scarabs.

6.2.4.1 *'Alabaster' and faience vessels*

The tomb of Cave 15.I includes mixed EBA and MBA burials.[103] An MBIIA deposit in the cave's first chamber yielded an 'alabaster' vessel of possible Twelfth Dynasty origin (Figure 6.9 [1]).[104] One other Egyptian-style vessel is a bluish-green, round-based faience bottle (Figure 6.9 [2]) from Tomb 3, a burial of the 'Second Semitic Period' (the Thirteenth to Eighteenth Dynasties) with MBA weaponry as well as scarabs bearing early MBIIB features (see below).[105] The bottle's shape is akin to an Egyptian vessel from Tomb 7196 at Badari,[106] evidently of the Second Intermediate Period, as well as a bottle from an MBIIC tomb at Jericho.[107] If Tomb 3's dating to the MBIIB or MBIIC period is correct, the vessel may be considered as an item influenced by late Thirteenth to early Eighteenth Dynasty faience workshops.[108]

100 Ortiz, in *Bible and Archaeology*, 468-469.

101 For excavation reports, see Macalister, *Gezer*, 3 vols; Dever, Lance and Wright, *Gezer* 1; Dever, *Gezer* 2; Dever, Lance and Wright, *Gezer* 4. For a treatment on the history of excavations at the site, see Finkelstein, *Tel Aviv* 29/2 (2002), 262-296. For responses to Finkelstein's article, see Dever, *Tel Aviv* 30/2 (2003), 259-282; Hardin and Seger, in *Confronting the Past*, 51-60. See also Weinstein's comments on Macalister's stratigraphy (Weinstein, *BASOR* 213 [1974], 55).

102 Ortiz, in *Bible and Archaeology*, 469.

103 Macalister, *Gezer* 1, 86-93; Weinstein, *BASOR* 217 (1975), 4.

104 Another 'alabaster' vessel was apparently found in the cave; however its context is not mentioned. Macalister, *Gezer* 1, 90; vol. 3, pls 21 [1], 22 [2]; Weinstein, *BASOR* 217 (1975), 4.

105 As the pottery from Gezer's Tomb 3 is not published, the burial's date cannot be confirmed. The recorded artefacts do, however, imply an MBIIB date. Macalister, *Gezer* 1, 303-304, fig. 160 [9].

106 Brunton, *Qau and Badari* 3, 11-12, pl. 21 [7196].

107 Kenyon, *Jericho* 2, fig. 238 [7].

108 The item may have been imported, but studies have supported the presence of MBA faience workshops in the Southern Levant, indicating that the bottle could be a product of such a workshop. Other faience vessels from the site are recorded, but Macalister makes no mention of their context. Sagona, *ZDPV* 96/2 (1980), 101-120; Macalister, *Gezer* 2, 336-339; vol. 3, pl. 211.

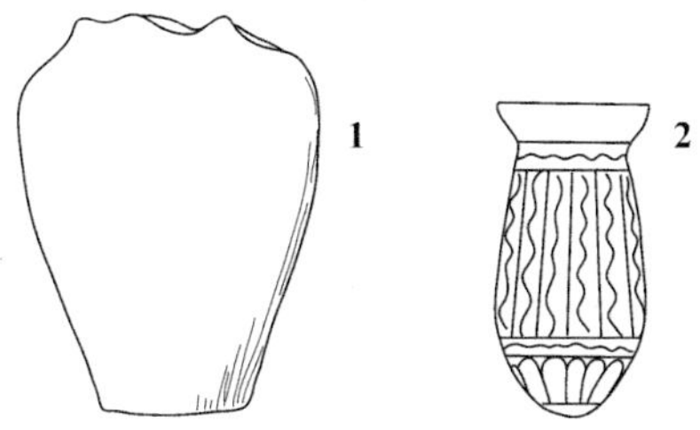

FIGURE 6.9. SELECTED STONE VESSELS, GEZER (NOT TO SCALE). AFTER MACALISTER, *GEZER* 1, FIG. 160 [9]; VOL. 3, PL. 21 [1].

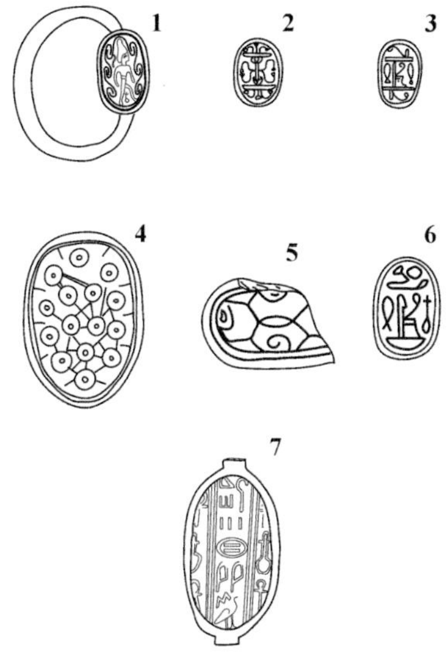

FIGURE 6.10. SELECTED SCARABS, GEZER (NOT TO SCALE). AFTER MACALISTER, *GEZER* 1, FIG. 160 [10-13, 15]; VOL. 3, PL. 204B [16].

6.2.4.2 Scarabs

Gezer's collection of sealings displaying Middle Kingdom and Second Intermediate Period designs has been utilised as proof for MBIIA and MBIIB relations with Dynasties 12-15.[109] An examination of the published evidence reveals that the majority of scarabs assigned to Macalister's 'Second Semitic Period' are of unpublished or uncertain contexts. As their date and manner of deposition cannot be confirmed, the scarabs have not been analysed here. However, it should be noted that the group includes a scarab of *Šši*,[110] and a Middle Kingdom or Second Intermediate Period scarab of official Imeny.[111]

Of the scarabs from known contexts, only a small number may be examined.[112] These include one scarab inscribed with *ḥḳꜣ ḫꜣs.wt Ḫyꜣn* 'ruler of foreign lands, *Ḫyꜣn*' from the top of the inner wall of Gezer's fortification at the north end of trench 3 (Figure 6.10 [7]).[113] The wall is thought to be of MBIIB-C construction,[114] providing a possible date for the scarab's deposition. As *Ḫyꜣn*'s position within Dynasty 15 is not verified, the scarab's context does not necessarily imply a correlation with his reign. It alternatively points to the flow of Fifteenth Dynasty products from Lower Egypt to Gezer during the MBIIB-C period.

The only other tomb with scarabs possibly of the MBIIB to MBIIC is Tomb 3. As aforementioned, the tomb is assigned to the 'Second Semitic Period', its published material ascribing to an MBIIB or MBIIC date (see above).[115] The scarabs' designs bear features of Ben-Tor's Early and Late Palestinian Series. Early MBIIB elements include the sign of union (*smꜣ tꜣ.wy*) (Figure 6.10 [2]),[116] 'L-shaped' red crowns addorsed on a *nb* sign (Figure 6.10 [3, 6])[117] and concentric circles (Figure 6.10 [4]).[118] Elements common in the Early and Late Palestinian Series are the standing figure bordered by six oblong scrolls (Figure 6.10 [1])[119] and 'L-shaped' red crowns (Figure 6.10 [3, 6]).[120] Based on the designs' popularity in the Levant, the scarabs are most likely of Levantine origin.[121] The red-crowns, sign of union and concentric circles are, however, inspired by Egyptian designs.

Tomb 3's scarabs, as well as the 'alabaster' and faience vessels, support the presence of Egyptian artistic influences on funerary items in Gezer. The faience vessel, in particular, suggests that such influences were possibly concurrent with the Second Intermediate Period. Further support surfaces in the scarabs of *Šši* and *Ḫyꜣn* which, despite their uncertain contexts, imply relations with Lower Egypt during the Second Intermediate Period. However, the extent of Egyptian contact with Gezer appears limited to commercial and artistic influences.

109 Macalister, *Gezer* 2, 314-319; vol. 3, pls 202a, 203-205a, 206-207 [1-11]; Macalister, *PEQ* 37 (1905), 314-316; Giveon, in *Egypt, Israel, Sinai*, 25-26, 28, 30; Ben-Tor, *Scarabs*, 155-163, 166-172, 174-182; Ben-Tor, *BASOR* 294 (1994), 14.

110 The scarab was reportedly 'found on the same day and on the same level, a short distance from the spot where the vase was deposited' (Macalister, *PEQ* 40 [1908], 287-289, pl. 4 [17]). The vase here refers to a vessel from a trench in the Central Valley assigned to the Second Semitic Period.

111 Martin, *Egyptian Administrative and Private-Name Seals*, 21 [209].

112 Other scarabs with recorded contexts include a steatite scarab from IV.18's cistern, another from an infant burial in III.16, two scarabs from III.17 and a scarab from underneath the foundations of a structure at the north end of IIIa.27, 28 (Macalister, *Gezer* 2, 314-319). A description of the scarabs' find-spots and their associated material is not included in Macalister's report, so their ascription to the Second Semitic Period cannot be confirmed. For provenanced scarabs with Egyptian-inspired designs from the late MBIIC to LBI period, see Seger, *BASOR* 221 (1976), 133-140.

113 Macalister, *Gezer* 2, 316, pl. 204b [16]; Giveon, *JEA* 51 (1965), 204.

114 Burke, *MBA Fortification Strategies*, 261-262.

115 Macalister, *Gezer* 1, 303-304, fig. 160.

116 Ben-Tor's Design Class 3A1. Macalister, *Gezer* 1, fig. 160 [11]; Ben-Tor, *Scarabs*, 159-160, n. 756.

117 Ben-Tor's Design Class 3B3a and 3B3d. Macalister, *Gezer* 1, fig. 160 [15]; Ben-Tor, *Scarabs*, 129, 162-163.

118 Ben-Tor's Design Class 4. Macalister, *Gezer* 1, fig. 160 [13]; Ben-Tor, *Scarabs*, 168-169, n. 805.

119 Ben-Tor's Design Class 7B2 and 10A1. Macalister, *Gezer* 1, fig. 160 [10]; Ben-Tor, *Scarabs*, 172-173, 178-179.

120 Ben-Tor's Design Class 3B3d. Macalister, *Gezer* 1, fig. 160 [12]; Ben-Tor, *Scarabs*, 163.

121 Ben-Tor, *Scarabs*, 129, 159-160, 162-163, 168-169, 172-173, 178-179.

6.2.5 *Ifshar, Tell / Hefer*

Lat.Lon. 32°22'N 34°54'E

Refs Marcus et al., *E&L* 18 (2008), 203-219; Marcus, Porath and Paley, *E&L* 18 (2008), 221-244; Marcus, in *Radiocarbon*, 182-208.

Chron. Twelfth Dynasty / MBIIA Period

Tell Ifshar is located on a probably navigable river in the southern coastal plain of Israel.[122] Three areas (A, B and C) expose a fortified settlement occupied from the EBI to the Byzantine period.[123] MBIIA levels, which are principally represented at Area C, have been divided into eight main phases (A-H) spanning the entire MBIIA period.[124] Phases A-C revealed Middle Kingdom pottery.[125]

6.2.5.1 *Phase A*

Two sub-phases have been identified in Phase A: Phase A 'early' and Phase A 'late'.[126] The latter is characterised by the final deposits and fill before Phase B[127] and revealed three Egyptian sherds: (1) a rim and shoulder of a Marl C-1 jar typologically akin to Twelfth or Thirteenth Dynasty Egyptian zir rims (Figure 6.11 [1]);[128] (2) a rim and neck of a Marl A-4 bottle, with parallels from the reigns of Amenemhat II to Senwosret III (Figure 6.11 [2]);[129] and (3) a body sherd of a Marl C-2 jar which has been assigned between late Senwosret I and Amenemhat III (Figure 6.11 [3]).[130] The first two sherds were respectively found in the make-up of Phase B floors and the third comes from Pit L754.[131] Together, they denote trade with Upper and Lower Egypt during the first half of Dynasty 12, a synchronism that is supported by recent radiocarbon dating results on material from the phase.[132]

6.2.5.2 *Phase B*

Phase B is characterised by a large public or elite Mittelsaalhaus complex.[133] Its precise function remains unclear but its monumental scale, the use of such architectural elements as cedar supporting beams, the presence of ceramic imports from the Northern Levant as well as painted vessels of most likely elite character, imply that the complex was of administrative and/or ritual significance.[134] One room to the building's southeast[135] produced the greatest number of Middle Kingdom sherds belonging to a minimum of four and a maximum of seven Egyptian vessels. They include:[136] a reconstructed burnished globular jar of marl clay similar to those of the first half of the Twelfth Dynasty (Figure 6.11 [4]);[137] the rim and shoulder of a Marl C-2 globular jar, similar to the third sherd discussed above under Phase A (Figure 6.11 [5]);[138] the rim and upper body of a Marl C-1 zir of the Twelfth or early-mid Thirteenth Dynasty (Figure 6.11 [6]);[139] and the base of a Marl C-1 zir paralleling those of the Twelfth Dynasty to the first half of the Thirteenth Dynasty (Figure 6.11 [7]).[140]

The Egyptian pottery supports relations between Tell Ifshar and Egypt during the first half of Dynasty 12. Such contact is verified by the chronological correlations offered by radiocarbon dating results,[141] linking Tell Ifshar's Phase B with the early-mid Twelfth Dynasty (see Figure 6.26).

6.2.5.3 *Phase C*

Phase B's complex was destroyed by a conflagration then rebuilt, with minor modifications, in Phase C1.[142] After its renovation in Phase C2, the building was again burnt and destroyed.[143] Either from Phase C2 or earlier is the upper body of a Marl C-1 bag-shaped jar from the south of the excavated complex, (Figure 6.11 [8]) its shape typical of jars from the end of the Twelfth to the Thirteenth Dynasty.[144] Also retrieved south of the complex is a complete Marl A-3 bottle from within Phase C's destruction phase (Figure 6.11 [9]).[145] While no close parallels for the vessel are found in Egypt, Do. Arnold proposes that it is of the Twelfth Dynasty, dating approximately between the end of Amenemhat III's reign to that of Senwosret III.[146] A recent analysis of its shape and decoration agrees with this dating.[147]

---

122 Marcus, in *Radiocarbon*, 185.

123 Paley and Porath, *IEJ* 29/3-4 (1979), 236-239; Paley and Porath, *IEJ* 30/3-4 (1980), 217-219; Paley and Porath, *IEJ* 32/1 (1982), 66-67; Paley, Porath and Stieglitz, *IEJ* 32/4 (1982), 259-261; Paley, Porath and Stieglitz, *IEJ* 33/3-4 (1983), 264-266; Paley, Porath and Stieglitz, *IEJ* 34/4 (1984), 276-278; Paley and Porath, *IEJ* 35/4 (1985), 299-301; Paley and Porath, in *Hyksos*, 369-378. For more publications, see Marcus, Porath and Paley, *E&L* 18 (2008), 221-244.

124 Marcus, in *Radiocarbon*, 185; Marcus et al., *E&L* 18 (2008), 205.

125 Marcus et al., *E&L* 18 (2008), 205.

126 Marcus, in *Radiocarbon*, 185.

127 Marcus, in *Radiocarbon*, 185, fig. 15 [2].

128 Marcus et al., *E&L* 18 (2008), 206, fig. 2 [1].

129 Marcus et al., *E&L* 18 (2008), 207, fig. 2 [2].

130 Marcus et al., *E&L* 18 (2008), 207, fig. 2 [3].

131 Marcus et al., *E&L* 18 (2008), 206.

132 Marcus, in *Radiocarbon*, 198, tables 15.3-15.4.

133 Marcus, in *Radiocarbon*, 188, fig. 15 [2]; Marcus, Porath and Paley, *E&L* 18 (2008), 226-228.

134 Marcus, in *Radiocarbon*, 188; Marcus, Porath and Paley, *E&L* 18 (2008), 226-228.

135 Marcus et al., *E&L* 18 (2008), 207.

136 Marcus et al., *E&L* 18 (2008), 207.

137 The fabric is Marl DAN E3, which has not been classified in the Vienna System. It is of Upper Egyptian origin. Marcus et al., *E&L* 18 (2008), 205, 207-209, fig. 3 [1].

138 The rim type parallels those deriving from Amenemhat III's reign and later. Marcus et al., *E&L* 18 (2008), 209-210, fig. 3 [2].

139 Marcus et al., *E&L* 18 (2008), 207, 210, fig. 3 [3].

140 Marcus et al., *E&L* 18 (2008), 207-210, fig. 3 [4].

141 Marcus, in *Radiocarbon*, 198, tables 15.3-15.4.

142 Marcus, in *Radiocarbon*, 188, fig. 15 [2].

143 Marcus, in *Radiocarbon*, 188.

144 Marcus et al., *E&L* 18 (2008), 210-211, fig. 4 [1].

145 For the history of research on the vessel, see Marcus et al., *E&L* 18 (2008), 203-205, 211-213, fig. 4 [2]. While Marcus assigns the bottle to either Phase C or E in *E&L* 18 (2008), 211-212, a recent publication of his supports its Phase C context following a reanalysis of the stratigraphy (Marcus, in *Radiocarbon*, 188).

146 Bietak, in *High, Middle or Low?*, 96; Bietak, *BASOR* 287 (1981), 54; Weinstein, *BASOR* 288 (1992), 34-35; Paley and Porath, in *Hyksos*, 373.

147 Marcus et al., *E&L* 18 (2008), 211-213.

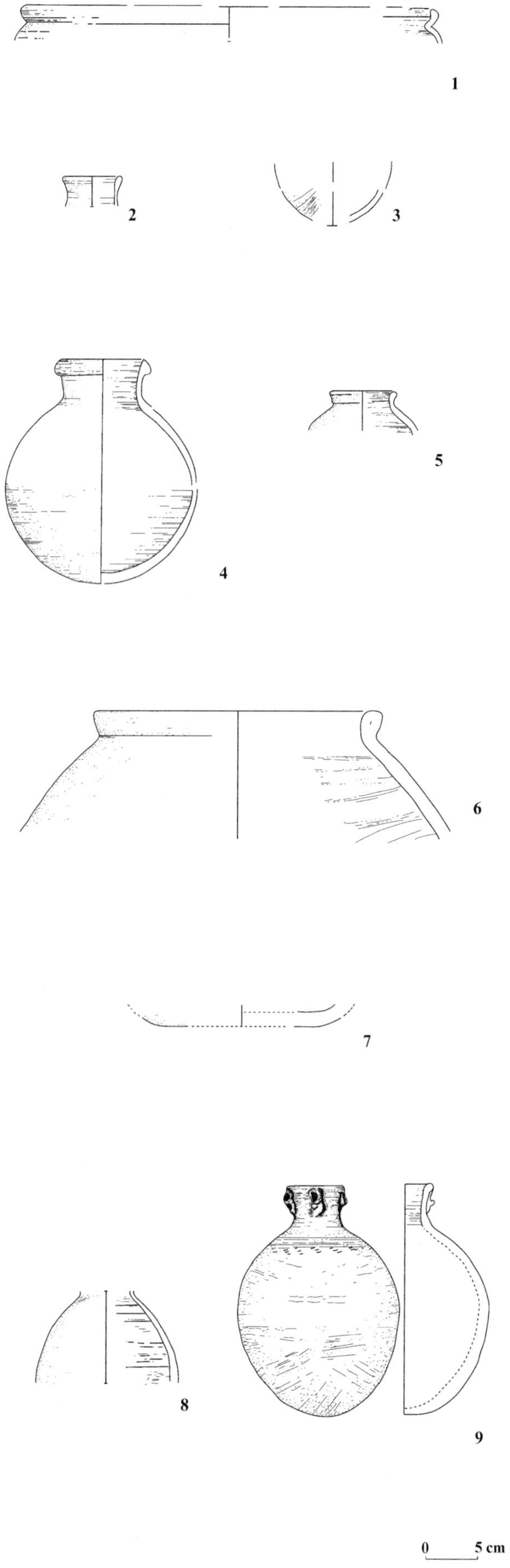

FIGURE 6.11. SELECTED CERAMICS, TELL IFSHAR. AFTER MARCUS ET AL., *E&L* 18 (2008), FIGS 2-4.

Overall, Phases A to C contained a minimum of eight and a maximum of 12 imported vessels.[148] The Marl A and C fabrics reflect trade with Upper and Lower Egyptian workshops exporting storage containers such as bottles, jars and zirs. Imported goods are higher in number during the later phases, particularly Phase B. This could point to an increase in trade, but it may also be linked with the construction of a new monumental complex in Area C. The rise in Egyptian imports is also correlated with imported goods from the Southern and Northern Levant, denoting a trade network circulating Levantine and Egyptian goods across the Mediterranean coast.[149] While Tell Ifshar's Egyptian assemblage is reportedly the largest thus far found in the Southern Levant,[150] it is only but a fraction of the entire ceramic assemblage at the site.[151] Therefore, the evidence implies only some trade with Egypt between Phases A-C of MBIIA Tell Ifshar and the first three quarters of the Twelfth Dynasty.

6.2.6 Jericho / Sultan, Tell el-

Lat.Lon. 31°51'N 35°27'E

Refs PM 7, 373; Kenyon, *Jericho* 1-3; Marchetti, *Isimu* 2 (1999), 305-312; Marchetti, in *Synchronisation of Civilizations*; Nigro, in *Tell es-Sultan/Jericho.*

Chron. Thirteenth to Fifteenth Dynasty / Late MBIIA or MBIIA-B to MBIIC Period

Jericho is located almost 10km from the Dead Sea, within southern Jordan. Excavations at the site have uncovered an occupation spanning almost the entire MBA period.[152] Publications of the tell's tombs and settlement are not without complications and faults,[153] yet the available material includes a significant number of scarabs, seal impressions, faience and stone vessels. They are discussed below chronologically utilising Kenyon's divisions of MBIIB tombs into Groups I-III, later revisions of these divisions, as well as stratigraphical phases determined by the recent University of Rome explorations.

6.2.6.1 Late MBIIA or MBIIA-B Period (Kenyon's Group I; University of Rome's Phase IVa)

Two tombs likely of the late MBIIA or transitional MBIIA-B period yielded Egyptian-influenced material.[154]

148 Marcus et al., *E&L* 18 (2008), 213.
149 Marcus et al., *E&L* 18 (2008), 215-216.
150 Marcus et al., *E&L* 18 (2008), 213.
151 The assemblage has been published in preliminary form in Marcus, Porath and Paley, *E&L* 18 (2008), 221-244.
152 Garstang, *PEQ* 62 (1930), 123-132; Garstang, *PEQ* 63 (1931), 186-191; Garstang, *AAALiv* 19 (1932), 3-22, 35-54; Kenyon, *PEQ* 84 (1952), 62-82; Kenyon, *PEQ* 86 (1954), 45-63; Kenyon, *PEQ* 87 (1955), 108-128; Kenyon, *PEQ* 88 (1956), 67-82; Kenyon, *Jericho*, 5 vols, Marchetti, in *Synchronisation of Civilisations* 2, 295-321; Marchetti and Nigro, *Jericho*; Nigro, in *Tell es-Sultan/Jericho*, 1-40.
153 For a summary, see Maeir, *Jordan Valley during the MBA*, 57-61.
154 Wright, *Antiquity* 40 (1966), 149; Wright, *JAOS* 91 (1971), 290; Weinstein, *BASOR* 217 (1975), 7; Tufnell, *Scarab Seals* 2/1, 59;

Phase 3 of Tomb B48 contained two drop-shaped vessels of 'alabaster' (Figure 6.13 [1-2])[155] and seven scarabs,[156] one of which displays a single line thread on its lower part and a sign of union on its upper part indicating its likely Egyptian manufacture (Figure 6.12 [2]).[157] Another tomb of Phase 1, Tomb A34, held a gypsum-alabaster drop-shaped alabastron which can be attributed to a Levantine workshop.[158]

The University of Rome's recent excavations unearthed another tomb, D.641, assigned to Stratum IVa-2.[159] The tomb held two scarabs, one bearing a *sꜣ* hieroglyph paralleling designs of Middle Kingdom scarabs,[160] and another displaying a reclining lion with a possible fish (Figure 6.12 [22]).[161] The latter has been translated as *ꜥḏ mr Rḫꜥ* 'administrator of Jericho';[162] however, the lion motif is very common in the MBIIB Levantine series, and should not be construed as a phonogram.[163] Arguably, the scarab is of Levantine production.

Therefore, only two scarabs from this period could be Egyptian imports, the rest of the material being of Levantine or uncertain origin but undoubtedly inspired by Egyptian designs.

6.2.6.2 MBIIB Period (Kenyon's Groups II-III; University of Rome's Phase IVb)

Calcite-alabaster vessels occur in three tombs from Group II: Tomb J54 with one drop-shaped alabastron (Figure 6.13 [3]);[164] Tomb D9 comprising four drop-shaped alabastra and one cylindrical jar (Figure 6.13 [4-6]);[165] and Tomb J14 containing three drop-shaped alabastra, three cylindrical jars and one ridge-necked alabastron (Figure 6.13 [7-13]).[166] To these may be added a drop-shaped alabastron from a Stratum IVb fill between Fortress A1 and House A2.[167] Gypsum-alabaster vessels are more common, with Group II tombs producing over 26 vessels.[168] As only a small number of the stone vessel corpus is generally designated as 'alabaster',[169] more than half of the stone vessels from Group II are evidently of Levantine origin.

The following Group III marks a further divide between calcite-alabaster and gypsum-alabaster vessels. The latter represents over 85% of alabasters from Group III tombs in comparison to less than 3% of calcite-alabaster vessels.[170] Apparently, Levantine-made stone vessels became more popular or more accessible during this phase.[171]

Two tombs assigned to the last phase of Group III, Tombs B51 and J20, contained flat-based faience bottles.[172] The bottles are decorated with a pair of parallel and wavy lines bordering a central zigzag design atop petals. The design is otherwise only attested at Tell el-Far'ah South,[173] hinting at the bottles' Levantine manufacture.

Private- and royal-name scarabs are few.[174] Tomb G37 of Group II contained a scarab reading *ir.y-ꜥ.t n(.y) ḏꜣd.w Pn.wy* 'hall-keeper of the audience hall,[175] Penwy' (Figure 6.12 [15]).[176] From Group III tombs are two scarabs, one from Tomb B35 naming Thirteenth Dynasty king *Ḫꜥ-ḥtp-Rꜥ.w* 'Khahotepra (Sobekhotep V)' (Figure 6.12 [20]),[177] and another from Tomb B3 with *ḫtm.ty bi.ty im.y-rꜣ pr.w wr Nm.ty-m-wsḫ.t* 'sealer of the king of Lower Egypt, chief steward,[178] Nemtyemweskhet'

Ward and Dever, *Scarab Seals* 3, 69-70. Beck and Zevulun date all deposits from the two tombs to the MBIIB (Beck and Zevulun, *BASOR* 304 [1996], 70).

155 Kenyon, *Jericho* 2, 208-209, 221-222, fig. 100 [2-3]; Sparks, *Stone Vessels in the Levant*, 381-382 [1246], 383 [1270].

156 Kenyon, *Jericho* 2, 208-209, 221; Kirkbride, in *Jericho* 2, 595-597, fig. 282 [2-8].

157 Ben-Tor's Design Class 6A1. Kirkbride, in *Jericho* 2, fig. 282 [3]; Ben-Tor, *Scarabs*, 138, n. 664.

158 Kenyon, *Jericho* 1, 353, 366, fig. 144 [1]; Sparks, *Stone Vessels in the Levant*, 234, 351 [884].

159 Marchetti, in *Synchronisation of Civilisations*, 295-321; Nigro, in *Exploring the Longue Durée*, 361-376. Maeir dates the tomb to the early MBIIB and argues for the entire phase's early MBIIB date (Maeir, *Jordan Valley during the MBA*, 58-59).

160 Ben-Tor's Design Class 3A3. Nigro, in *Exploring the Longue Durée*, 372, fig. 22; Marochetti, in *Synchronisation of Civilisations*, fig. 9 [b]; Ben-Tor, *Scarabs*, 16-17.

161 Ben-Tor's Design Class 9E. Nigro, in *Exploring the Longue Durée*, 372, fig. 23; Marochetti, in *Synchronisation of Civilisations*, fig. 9 [b]; Ben-Tor, *Scarabs*, 146-147, 177.

162 Nigro, in *Exploring the Longue Durée*, 372-373.

163 Ben-Tor, *Scarabs*, 177; Maeir, *Jordan Valley during the MBA*, 34-35, 58-59.

164 Kenyon, *Jericho* 2, fig. 100 [11]; Sparks, *Stone Vessels in the Levant*, 288 [111].

165 Kenyon, *Jericho* 2, 283, fig. 100 [16-18]; Sparks, *Stone Vessels in the Levant*, 288 [109], 290 [131, 138], 291 [147], 313 [407].

166 Kenyon, *Jericho* 2, fig. 154 [1-3, 5, 10, 12, 16]; Sparks, *Stone Vessels in the Levant*, 288 [110], 291 [139-140], 292 [162], 311 [385], 312 [398], 313 [408].

167 Marochetti, *Isimu* 2 (1999), 305-312, figs 2-3. Nigro suggests that the item was part of the funerary assemblage of a disturbed burial (Nigro, in *Tell es-Sultan/Jericho*, 33, n. 55, fig. 51).

168 Kenyon, *Jericho* 1, 313, 326, 338, figs 118 [1-11], 187 [10]; vol. 2, 241, 257, 267, figs 100 [5-6, 8-14], 154 [9, 11]; Sparks, *Stone Vessels in the Levant*, 344 [809], 351 [885-891], 353 [910-911], 355 [937-938], 361 [1002], 363 [1018-1019], 364-365 [1037-1038], 366 [1055-1058], 367 [1059], 370 [1094-1095], 371 [1101-1102].

169 Kenyon, *Jericho* 2, 208-209, 221-222, figs 100 [1, 4, 15], 154 [4, 14]; Sparks, *Stone Vessels in the Levant*, 382 [1247], 383 [1270-1271], 384 [1284], 388 [1344].

170 The remaining vessels are termed simply as of 'alabaster'. Kenyon, *Jericho* 1, 349, 366, 381, 402, figs 118 [12-16], 171 [1-2, 5-6]; vol. 2, 353, figs 100 [20-24], 171 [3-5, 7, 9, 11-12, 14-16], 179 [1-5, 7-11, 14-22, 24]; Sparks, *Stone Vessels in the Levant*, 233-234, 344 [811-812], 352 [892-898], 353 [912-915], 353 [916-921], 354-355 [927-931], 356 [939-942], 357 [954], 358 [963-964], 363 [1020-1023], 365 [1040-1045], 367 [1060-1062, 1066-1068], 368 [1071-1074], 377 [1188], 378 [1195-1196], 382 [1248-1251, 1256-1257], 383 [1264-1265, 1273-1275], 387 [1337], figs 81-82.

171 Some have proposed that Jericho had a gypsum-alabaster workshop. See Sparks, *Stone Vessels in the Levant*, 234-235.

172 Kenyon, *Jericho* 2, figs 171 [1], 179 [12-13]; Sagona, *ZDPV* 96/2 (1980), 103, fig. 1 (8-10).

173 Sagona, *ZDPV* 96/2 (1980), 103, fig. 2 [9].

174 Contested scarabs which have been read as that of Intef V (Group II Tomb G37) and Maaibra (Group III-V Tomb B51) are not included due to their ambiguous glyphs. For a discussion on the scarabs, see Bietak, *AJA* 88/4 (1984), 483; Bietak, *BASOR* 281 (1991), 55; Ward, *AJA* 91/4 (1987), 521-522.

175 Ward, *Index*, 61 [496].

176 The name here follows Martin's translation (Martin, *Egyptian Administrative and Private-Name Seals*, 42 [475], pl. 5 [20]). See also Kirkbride, in *Jericho* 2, fig. 286 [14]. For a similar name, see Ranke, *Personennamen* 1, 133 [6].

177 Kirkbride, in *Jericho* 2, fig. 292 [13].

178 Ward, *Index*, 72 [141], 170 [1472].

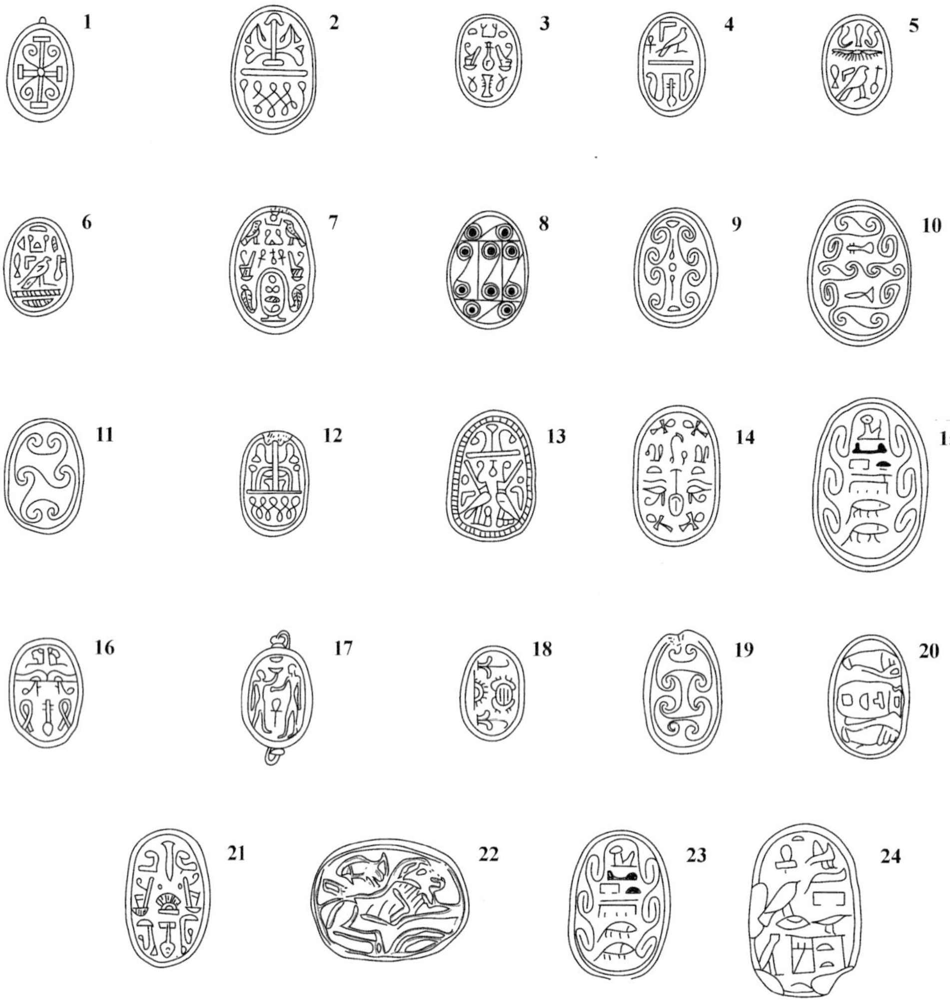

FIGURE 6.12. SELECTED SCARABS, JERICHO (NOT TO SCALE). AFTER KIRKBRIDE, IN *JERICHO* 2, FIGS 282-284, 286, 288, 290, 292-293; NIGRO, IN *EXPLORING THE LONGUE DURÉE*, FIG. 23; MARTIN, *EGYPTIAN ADMINISTRATIVE AND PRIVATE-NAME SEALS*, PLS 5 [20], 20 [14].

(Figure 6.12 [24]).[179] The settlement produced four MBIIB jar handle seal impressions inscribed with 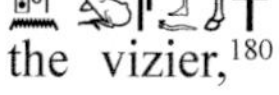 *sš n(.y) ṯ3.ty Snb=f wḥm ꜥnḫ* 'scribe of the vizier,[180] Senbef, repeating life'.[181] The funerary epithet at the end of the impressions suggests that the original seal was not intended for sealing jars. As Ben-Tor writes, Senbef was most likely a Twelfth Dynasty official whose sealings had no connection with the official's duties.[182] Perhaps the seal was utilised by another individual as a property marker or for decorative purposes. Because of their rarity in the scarab repertoire, the same may be the case with the other private- and royal-name scarabs from Tombs G37, B35 and B3. The artefacts were probably Egyptian items indirectly imported into Jericho and then used as amulets or status identifiers.

The vast majority of design scarabs bear Levantine characteristics. Egyptian designs include interlocking scrolls,[183] paired oblong scrolls,[184] the *sm3 t3.wy* sign of union,[185] *wḏ3.t* eyes,[186] a lion's forepart,[187] concentric circles[188] and a single-line thread (Figure 6.12).[189] Of the tombs with calcite-alabaster vessels, Tomb D9 contained

179 The name here follows Ben-Tor's translation (Ben-Tor, *BASOR* 294 [1994], 14). See also Martin, *Egyptian Administrative and Private-Name Seals*, 33 [354], pl. 20 [14]; Kirkbride, in *Jericho* 2, fig. 293 [12]; Ranke, *Personennamen* 1, 69 [19].

180 Ward, *Index*, 167 [1449].

181 One jar handle was uncovered in Room 17 and three others were in Room 44C. Two further jar handles with the same seal impression were uncovered in uncertain contexts. Rowe, *Scarabs*, 235, pl. 26 [S5]; Martin, *Egyptian Administrative and Private-Name Seals*, 121 [1574], pl. 15 [8]; Ranke, *Personennamen* 1, 314 [5]; Ben-Tor, *BASOR* 294 (1994), 14.

182 Ben-Tor, *BASOR* 294 (1994), 10-11.

183 Ben-Tor's Design Class 2B. Kirkbride, in *Jericho* 2, figs 283 [17], 284 [2], 286 [4]; Ben-Tor, *Scarabs*, 124, n. 595.

184 Ben-Tor's Design Class 7B3ii. Kirkbride, in *Jericho* 2, fig. 286 [14]; Ben-Tor, *Scarabs*, 143.

185 Ben-Tor's Design Class 3A1. Kirkbride, in *Jericho* 2, fig. 286 [3]; Ben-Tor, *Scarabs*, 125.

186 Ben-Tor's Design Class 3B4. Kirkbride, in *Jericho* 2, fig. 286 [8, 16]; Ben-Tor, *Scarabs*, 131.

187 Ben-Tor's Design Class 3B7. Kirkbride, in *Jericho* 2, figs 286 [6], 293 [5]; Ben-Tor, *Scarabs*, 132.

188 Ben-Tor's Design Class 4. Kirkbride, in *Jericho* 2, fig. 282 [10]; Ben-Tor, *Scarabs*, 136.

189 Ben-Tor's Design Class 6A1. Kirkbride, in *Jericho* 2, figs 282 [3], 286 [3]; Ben-Tor, *Scarabs*, 138.

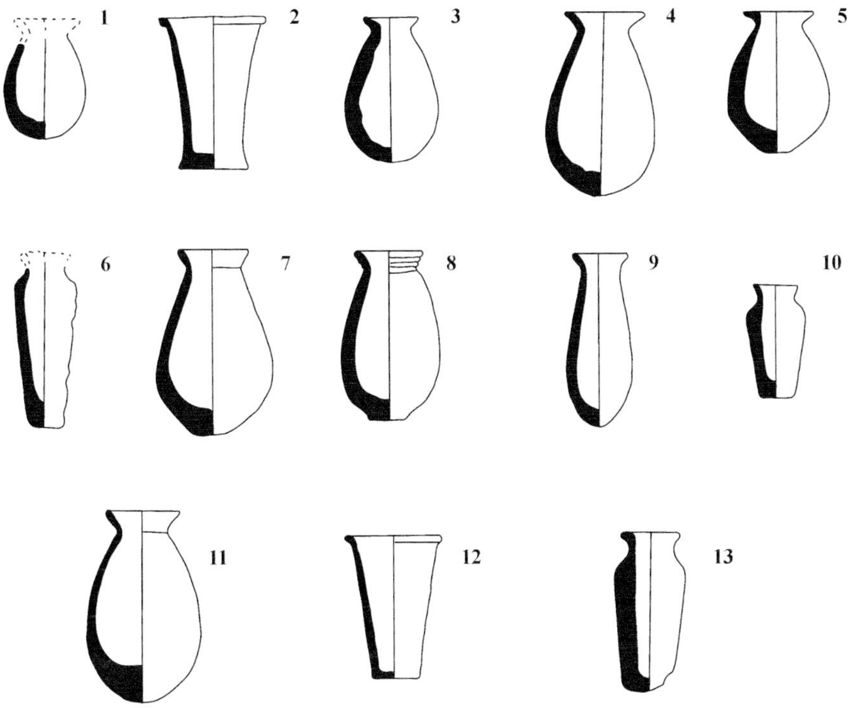

Figure 6.13. Selected stone vessels, Jericho (not to scale). After Kenyon, *Jericho* 2, figs 100 [2-3, 11, 16-18], 154 [1-3, 5, 10, 12, 16].

one scarab displaying interlocking scrolls of Egyptian origin,[190] while Tomb J14 produced an amethyst scarab with a Levantine design (Figure 6.12 [17]).[191] Ben-Tor suggests that the scarab was imported with a blank base and then engraved locally.[192]

In contrast to scarab designs from Group II burials, those from Group III contained a limited number of Egyptian elements such as interlocking scrolls[193] or a sedge plant (Figure 6.12 [18-19]).[194] Hence, like the stone vessels, scarabs displaying Levantine characteristics became either in greater demand or availability to Jericho's inhabitants during Group III's MBIIB phase.

Overall, the evidence clearly shows that Egyptian imports trickled into Jericho from the late MBIIA or transitional MBIIA-B period predominantly in the form of scarabs, when Egyptian influences on locally made stone vessels and scarabs are also apparent. During the beginning of the MBIIB, calcite-alabaster vessels and scarabs of most possible Egyptian origin increase in number and variety but are outnumbered by their locally produced counterparts. The difference in the percentage between Egyptian-influenced and Egyptian-made items widens throughout the MBIIB. Evidently, Levantine workshops were producing Egyptian-influenced items that were either more popular or more accessible to the locals than Egyptian imports. Some artisans also seemingly had access to Egyptian materials as, for example, an amethyst which was modified to display local designs. Nonetheless, a few Egyptian scarabs and calcite-alabaster vessels did reach the site, signalling Jericho's continued access to Egyptian products during the MBIIB.

6.2.7 Megiddo / Mutasallim, Tell el-

Lat.Lon. 32°35'N 35°11'E

Refs PM 7, 380-381; Loud, *Megiddo* 2; Guy, *Megiddo Tombs*; Kenyon, *Levant* 1 (1969), 25-60; Tufnell, *Levant* 5 (1973), 69-82.

Chron. Twelfth to Fifteenth Dynasty / MBIIA to MBIIC Period

Megiddo is strategically positioned southwest of the Jezreel plain on an easily navigable route from the coast to the Jordan Valley.[195] Although excavations have unearthed wide exposures of the site's MBA material culture,[196] various problems related to methodology and stratigraphy as well as ceramic and architectural sequences have surfaced.[197] Tel Aviv University's renewed excavations

190 Kirkbride, in *Jericho* 2, fig. 284 [2].
191 Kirkbride, in *Jericho* 2, fig. 288 [13].
192 Ben-Tor, *Scarabs*, 149.
193 Ben-Tor's Design Class 2B. Kirkbride, in *Jericho* 2, fig. 291 [3]; Ben-Tor, *Scarabs*, 159, n. 753.
194 Ben-Tor's Design Class 3B5. Kirkbride, in *Jericho* 2, fig. 290 [10]; Ben-Tor, *Scarabs*, 164.

195 Davies, *Megiddo*, 1.
196 Schumacher, *Tell el-Mutesellim* 1; Watzinger, *Tell el-Mutesellim* 2; Lamon and Shipton, *Megiddo* 1; Loud, *Megiddo* 2; Guy, *Megiddo Tombs*; Harrison, *Megiddo* 3.
197 For a discussion of the problems, see Kenyon, *Eretz-Israel* 5 (1958), 51*-60*; Kenyon, *Levant* 1 (1969), 25; Müller, *ZDPV* 86 (1970), 50-86; Hallote, in *Archaeology of Israel*, 199-214.

continue to clarify these issues,[198] yet a cautious approach is necessary for material from EBIV/MBI to MBIIB strata uncovered during earlier excavations (Strata XV-XI). The Egyptian evidence from these levels is presented in two main bodies: stone vessels and scarabs. Ambiguous artefacts are discussed in Appendix A.3.

6.2.7.1 Stone vessels

Only four 'alabaster' vessels were retrieved from MBIIA and MBIIB contexts.[199] They include two calcite-alabaster vessels, one a body sherd, possibly from a jar, collected near the MBIIA Tomb 4010 of Stratum XIII.[200] The other, a flask with a convex base, comes from Tomb 3095 of MBIIB Stratum XII.[201] Of the same stratum are an 'alabaster' dipper juglet from tomb 4099[202] and a gypsum-alabaster drop-shaped alabastron from Tomb 3111.[203] The vessels specify the import and imitation of Egyptian products between the MBIIA and MBIIB periods, the uses of which are associated with funerary practices.

6.2.7.2 Scarabs and seal impressions

The earliest scarab is from Tomb 3143 of MBIIA Stratum XIV.[204] It is designed with hieroglyphs in both horizontal and vertical settings (Figure 6.14 [1]), which points to its Levantine origin, although its early date suggests otherwise.[205] Stratum XIII tombs 3109, 3125 and 5090 of the MBIIA also contained scarabs[206] displaying Levantine designs such as three vertical panels with glyphs (Figure 6.14 [2]),[207] and red crowns addorsed on a *nb* sign (Figure 6.14 [3]).[208] Kenyon dates two further tombs of Stratum XII to an earlier phase: MBIIA Tomb 5106 with one scarab bearing interlocked spirals of a most possible late Middle Kingdom origin (Figure 6.14 [4]);[209] and

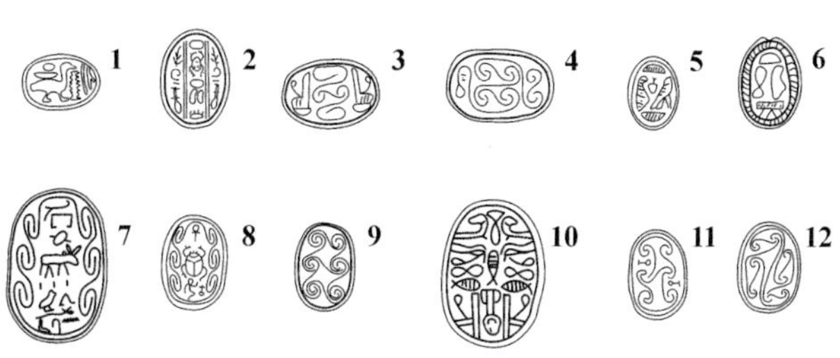

Figure 6.14. Selected scarabs, Megiddo (not to scale). After Loud, *Megiddo* 2, pls 149-150.

transitional MBIIA-B Tomb 3087 containing two scarabs with pseudo-hieroglyphs of a likely Levantine origin (Figure 6.14 [5-6]).[210] Thus, the majority of scarabs from these early phases show Levantine characteristics, albeit those influenced by Egyptian designs.[211] In view of this, Tufnell remarks on the overall rarity of scarabs in MBIIA graves,[212] advising that contact with the Egyptian was minor.

An increase in the number of scarabs occurs in the following Strata XII and XI of the MBIIB period.[213] Again, the majority are decorated with Levantine characteristics.[214] Only a small number may be assigned an Egyptian origin. These include a private-name scarab from Stratum XII's Tomb 5067 inscribed with *im.y-r3 pr.w ḥsb iḥ.w Ἰw=f-snb* 'steward of reckoning cattle,[215] Iufseneb' (Figure 6.14 [7]),[216] which could be an heirloom of late Middle Kingdom origin.[217] Another from Stratum XII Tomb 4099 bears a child hieroglyph that is also suggestive of its Egyptian manufacture (Figure 6.14 [8]).[218] Similarly, the interlocking spirals of a scarab from Tomb 2135 point to Egypt (Figure 6.14 [9]).[219]

From Stratum XI are Tombs 3085 and 3110, each of which produced a scarab displaying Middle Kingdom interlocking scrolls (Figure 6.14 [11-12]).[220] Tomb 3080

198 Finkelstein, Ussishkin and Halpern, *Megiddo*, vols 3-5.

199 These do not include two 'alabaster' vessels from Tombs 42 and 56. While classified by Guy as MBA vessels, the tombs contain LBA material and so their dating cannot be confirmed. Similarly, a faience jar decorated with wavy bands mimicking the striations of calcite-alabaster was found in Tomb 912B. The tomb had both MBIIA as well as LBII objects. For the 'alabaster' vessels, see Guy, *Megiddo Tombs*, 186, fig. 184 [1-2], pls 107 [17], 114 [7]; Sparks, *Stone Vessels in the Levant*, 295 [192-193]. For the faience jar, see Guy, *Megiddo Tombs*, 188, fig. 185 [1], pl. 130 [15]; Weinstein, *BASOR* 217 (1975), 2.

200 Loud identifies the sherd as of a bowl. Loud, *Megiddo* 2, pl. 258 [2]; Sparks, *Stone Vessels in the Levant*, 338 [735]; Weinstein, *BASOR* 217 (1975), 2, n. 13.

201 The tomb is assigned to Kenyon's MBII Group F. Loud, *Megiddo* 2, pl. 258 [3]; Kenyon, *Levant* 1 (1969), 34; Sparks, *Stone Vessels in the Levant*, 308 [351].

202 The tomb is assigned to Kenyon's MBII Group A. Loud, *Megiddo* 2, pl. 258 [4]; Kenyon, *Levant* 1 (1969), 28-31; Sparks, *Stone Vessels in the Levant*, 387 [1340].

203 The tomb is assigned to Kenyon's MBII Group D. Loud, *Megiddo* 2, pl. 258 [5]; Kenyon, *Levant* 1 (1969), 31; Sparks, *Stone Vessels in the Levant*, 352 [901].

204 Loud, *Megiddo* 2, pl. 149 [1]; Tufnell, *Levant* 5 (1973), 71, fig. 3 [126].

205 Ben-Tor, *Scarabs*, 126; Ben-Tor, *BASOR* 294 (1994), 11.

206 Loud, *Megiddo* 2, pl. 149 [3-6].

207 Ben-Tor's Design Class 3E1. The scarab is from Tomb 3109. Loud, *Megiddo* 2, pl. 149 [3]; Ben-Tor, *Scarabs*, 135, pl. 57 [21].

208 Ben-Tor's Design Class 3B3a. The scarab is from Tomb 5090. Loud, *Megiddo* 2, pl. 149 [5]; Ben-Tor, *Scarabs*, 129, pl. 53 [32].

209 Ben-Tor's Design Class 2B. Loud, *Megiddo* 2, pl. 149 [48]; Tufnell, *Levant* 5 (1973), fig. 1 [6]; Kenyon, *Levant* 1 (1969), 26; Ben-Tor, *Scarabs*, 124.

210 Ben-Tor's Design Class 3A3. Loud, *Megiddo* 2, pl. 149 [15-16]; Tufnell, *Levant* 5 (1973), fig. 1 [3, 7]; Kenyon, *Levant* 1 (1969), 28; Ben-Tor, *Scarabs*, 126, pl. 51 [7].

211 Not included here are contexts comprising MBIIA material as well as later LBA objects, such as Tombs 24 and 912B. One seal impression on a loom weight is also assigned to Stratum XIIIB, yet its design is not clear on its published photograph. See Guy, *Megiddo Tombs*, 48-50, 69-72, pls 105-106, 131 [1-14], 164 [1].

212 Tufnell, *Levant* 5 (1973), 73.

213 Note that some of the tombs attributed to these strata have been assigned to Kenyon's Phases MBII A-D, possibly of the early MBIIB period. Loud, *Megiddo* 2, pls 149 [8-57], 150; Kenyon, *Levant* 1 (1969), 28-30.

214 Ben-Tor, *Scarabs*, 156.

215 Ward, *Index*, 25 [160].

216 Ranke, *Personennamen* 1, 16 [1]; Loud, *Megiddo* 2, pl. 149 [32]; Tufnell, *Levant* 5 (1973), fig. 1 [51]; Martin, *Egyptian Administrative and Private Name Seals*, 13 [85], pl. 8 [2]; Ben-Tor, *BASOR* 294 (1994), 14.

217 Ben-Tor's Design Class 7B3ii. Ben-Tor, *Scarabs*, 143.

218 Loud, *Megiddo* 2, pl. 149 [41]; Tufnell, *Levant* 5 (1973), fig. 1 [13]; Ben-Tor, *Scarabs*, 143.

219 Ben-Tor's Design Class 2B. Loud, *Megiddo* 2, pl. 149 [8]; Tufnell, *Levant* 5 (1973), fig. 3 [129]; Ben-Tor, *Scarabs*, 124.

220 Ben-Tor's Design Class 7B. Loud, *Megiddo* 2, pl. 150 [75, 92]; Tufnell, *Levant* 5 (1973), fig. 2 [55, 59]; Ben-Tor, *Scarabs*, 143.

additionally contained one scarab with *wḏ3.t* eyes and a distinct Thirteenth Dynasty back type (Figure 6.14 [10]).[221]

The number of scarabs possibly of Egyptian origin increases between the MBIIA and MBIIB periods. Most notable is the private-name scarab of Iufseneb which is a definite Middle Kingdom import, though the circumstances through which it reached Megiddo are unknown. The increase in both Egyptian and Levantine designs from MBIIA to MBIIB contexts highlights the growing popularity of scarabs. The same is apparent from the stone vessels which are similarly of more varied forms and material in the MBIIB. Despite these observations, the Megiddo evidence does not stress direct relations with Egypt. It is more likely that the site's strategic position offered its inhabitants access to trade routes and goods from Egypt as well as Levantine workshops influenced by Egyptian art.

6.2.8 Nagila, Tell

Lat.Lon. 31°30'N 34°45'E

Refs Amiran and Eitan, *Archaeology* 18/2 (1965), 113-123.

Chron. Second Intermediate Period / MBIIB to MBIIC Period

Southeast of Ashkelon is the settlement of Tell Nagila. A detailed publication of excavations has not yet been produced, but reports note four or five strata dating to the MBIIB-C period (VII-XI), as well as a MBIIB-C tomb south of the tell (Tomb DT 2).[222] Settlement finds purportedly include faience and 'alabaster' bottles. From Amiran and Eitan's preliminary report, it is possible to identify: (1) a drop-shaped alabastron with a grooved neck,[223] its shape suggesting a Middle Kingdom origin;[224] and (2) two white faience bottles with slightly pointed and decorated bases,[225] showing affinities with vessels from MBIIB-C Tell el-Far'ah South and Jericho.[226]

Tomb DT 2's published scarabs display such designs as a Hathor symbol (Figure 6.15 [1]),[227] an antelope (Figure 6.15 [2]),[228] convoluted coils (Figure 6.15 [3]),[229] a cross pattern (Figure 6.15 [4]),[230] and misrendered signs

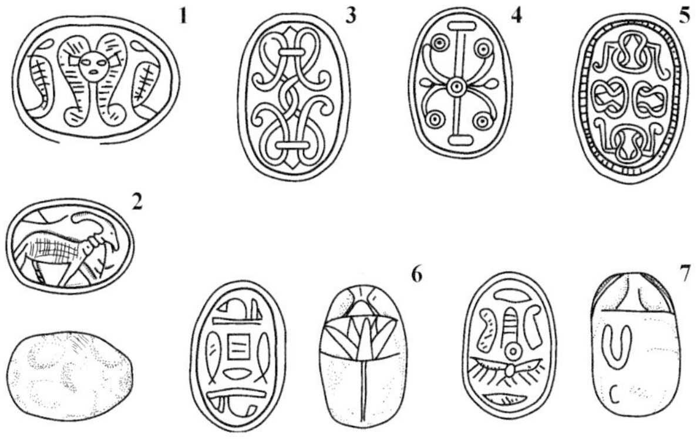

Figure 6.15. Selected scarabs, Tell Nagila (not to scale). After Amiran and Eitan, *Archaeology* 18/2 (1965), fig. 15 (drawn from photographs).

(Figure 6.15 [6-7]).[231] All are plausibly of Levantine origin. Only the cross pattern and convoluted coils may be Egyptian imports, yet the designs are known to have been imitated by Levantine artisans.[232] Thus, the published scarabs cannot certainly point to the import of Egyptian products, but denote Egyptian artistic influences on Levantine workshops.

Overall, the published material only indicates indirect links between the MBIIB-C Tell Nagila and Second Intermediate Period Egypt.

221 Ben-Tor's Design Class 3B4 and 3B7. Loud, *Megiddo* 2, pl. 150 [70]; Tufnell, *Levant* 5 (1973), fig. 2 [67]; Ben-Tor, *Scarabs*, 131-132, n. 638.
222 Amiran and Eitan, *BIES* 28 (1964), 193-203; Amiran and Eitan, *Archaeology* 18/2 (1965), 113-123.
223 Amiran and Eitan, *Archaeology* 18/2 (1965), 123, fig. 16.
224 Sparks, in *Cultural Interaction*, 59.
225 Amiran and Eitan, *Archaeology* 18/2 (1965), 123, fig. 16.
226 Petrie, *Beth Pelet* 1, pl. 9 [39]; Kenyon, *Jericho* 1, fig. 205 [16].
227 Ben-Tor's Design Class 10D2. Amiran and Eitan, *Archaeology* 18/2 (1965), fig. 15 [1]; Ben-Tor, *Scarabs*, 181-182.
228 Ben-Tor's Design Class 9B. Amiran and Eitan, *Archaeology* 18/2 (1965), fig. 15 [2]; Ben-Tor, *Scarabs*, 175.
229 Ben-Tor's Design Class 6B1. Amiran and Eitan, *Archaeology* 18/2 (1965), fig. 15 [3]; Ben-Tor, *Scarabs*, 139.
230 Ben-Tor's Design Class 5. Amiran and Eitan, *Archaeology* 18/2 (1965), fig. 15 [4]; Ben-Tor, *Scarabs*, 137.
231 Ben-Tor's Design Class 3A3. Amiran and Eitan, *Archaeology* 18/2 (1965), fig. 15 [6-7]; Ben-Tor, *Scarabs*, 126, 160.
232 Ben-Tor, *Scarabs*, 137, 139, 169-170.

6.3 The Northern Levant: Lebanon and West Syria

6.3.1 'Arqa, Tell

Lat.Lon. 34°31'N 36°02'E

Refs Charaf, in *Interconnections in the Eastern Mediterranean*, 295-297, pl. 2 [5-6]; Kopetzky, *AHL* 26-27 (2007/2008), 23; Kopetzky, *TeD* 20, 165.

Chron. Mid-Twelfth to Fifteenth Dynasty / Late MBIIA to MBIIC Period

Tell 'Arqa is located in the coastal 'Akkar Plain of modern Lebanon. Excavations have unearthed a fortified settlement of which only a section has been explored.[233] A small number of Egyptian ceramics have thus far been identified from its late MBIIA to MBIIC Level 13.[234] Three fragmentary vessels were found in loci of a late MBIIA room in a large building:[235] (1) fragments of a base belonging to a Type 3 Egyptian zir akin to those of the mid-Twelfth to mid-Thirteenth Dynasty;[236] (2) the upper part of a Marl C-1 jar with a corrugated neck, the low position of the first ridge beneath its rim paralleling forms of the mid-Thirteenth to mid-Fifteenth Dynasty; [237] and (3) the rim and neck of a third Marl C jar with a slightly narrower corrugated neck that also finds similarities to jars from the mid-Thirteenth to mid-Fifteenth Dynasty.[238]

The Egyptian ceramics indicate contact with the Middle Kingdom and/or the early Second Intermediate Period. While the precise function of their contexts cannot yet be determined, they were evidently collected from occupation levels, indicating that the site's inhabitants received and utilised Egyptian storage containers for non-funerary purposes.

233 Thalmann, *Tell Arqa* 1; Thalmann, *NEA* 73/2-3 (2010), 86-101.

234 As mentioned in the introduction (Chapter 1.5.2), the tripartite division of the MBA (MBIIA, MBIIB and MBIIC) does not completely apply to the archaeological sites in modern Lebanon. Thalmann has favoured the attribution of Level 14/Phase N to the 'MBI' while Level 13/Phase M is to the 'MBII'. For more on the chronology and comparative stratigraphy of sites in Lebanon, see Charaf, in *Archaeology of the Levant*, 434-437, table 29.1.

235 Loci 02/301 and 02/308. The room is beneath a LBIA tower of Level 12. Charaf, in *Interconnections in the Eastern Mediterranean*, 295; Kopetzky, *AHL* 26-27 (2007/2008), 23; Kopetzky, *TeD* 20, 165.

236 Kopetzky, *AHL* 26-27 (2007/2008), 23; Kopetzky, *TeD* 20, 264-265, pls 14, 39, 76, 113, 161.

237 Charaf, in *Interconnections in the Eastern Mediterranean*, 295-297, pl. 2 [5]; Forstner-Müller and Kopetzky, in *Interconnections in the Eastern Mediterranean*, 147, fig. 6 [3].

238 Charaf, in *Interconnections in the Eastern Mediterranean*, 297, pl. 2 [6].

6.3.2 Burak, Tell el-

Lat.Lon. 33°29'N 35°20'E

Refs Kamlah and Sader, *BAAL* 12 (2008), 17-34; Sader and Kamlah, *NEA* 73/2-3 (2010), 130-141; Sader, in *Interconnections in the Eastern Mediterranean*, 177-186.

Chron. Middle Kingdom / MBIIA Period

Tell el-Burak is situated on the Mediterranean coast near Sidon.[239] A joint expedition by the American University of Beirut and the University of Tübingen has identified an MBA site represented by a monumental fortified building or 'palace'.[240] Two archaeological phases have been discerned. The first, based on preliminary radiocarbon results, is dated to the beginning of the MBA,[241] and the second is of the MBIIA period.[242] The structure yielded a few finds, indicating that it was either never inhabited or only utilised for a short period of time. One such find is an unpublished scarab from Room 1 displaying an antelope with legs bent inwards under the body, above which is a *ꜥnḫ* sign.[243] The design finds a very close parallel with a scarab of Mlinar's Type II from a Tell el-Dab'a tomb of Strata G/1-3 (Tomb 4).[244] The parallel suggests that the Tell el-Burak scarab could be an Egyptian import, perhaps from Thirteenth Dynasty Tell el-Dab'a.

The filling of the structure's Room 10 between Occupational Phases 1 and 2 has preserved wall paintings displaying Egyptian influences (Plate 4). These influences are most apparent in the methods utilised for the preparation of the paintings and the represented motifs. The employed techniques included covering the walls with two layers of plaster, the outer being of smooth white lime plaster, and then painting red sketch drawings and guidelines using brushes.[245] Such techniques, particularly of the red sketch drawings, are inspired by Egyptian artistic methods for preparing mudbrick walls to receive paintings.[246] After the

239 Sader, in *Interconnections in the Eastern Mediterranean*, 177.

240 The function of the building is not entirely clear. A connection to the Sidonian kingdom is highly likely, with excavators postulating the building's possible defensive purpose or connection to the management of maritime trade. A funerary function or a connection with ancestral worship is also likely. Personal communication with Hélène Sader; Sader, in *Interconnections in the Eastern Mediterranean*, 177-186; Finkbeiner and Sader, *BAAL* 5 (2001), 173-194; Kamlah and Sader, *BAAL* 7 (2003), 145-173; Kamlah and Sader, *BAAL* 12 (2008), 32; Sader and Kamlah, *NEA* 73/2-3 (2010), 130-141.

241 Kamlah and Sader, *BAAL* 12 (2008), 25-27.

242 Ceramics from the second phase suggest a short time span from Occupational Phase 1. Kamlah and Sader, *BAAL* 12 (2008), 25-27.

243 Personal communication with Hélène Sader.

244 Ben-Tor's Design Class 9B. Ben-Tor, *Scarabs*, 95, pl. 30 [2]; Mlinar, in *Scarabs of the Second Millennium BC*, 116, fig. 5 [1]. Personal examination of a photograph provided by Hélène Sader. See also Figure 6.24 [20] for another parallel from Sidon, although from MBIIB Phase 6.

245 Kamlah and Sader, *BAAL* 12 (2008), 30.

246 Sader notes that the method of applying plaster derives from Egyptian and local traditions (personal communication with Hélène Sader). Red guidelines are also attested at other sites such as Ebla and Qatna in modern Syria. See Smith, *Egyptian Sculpture and Painting*,

walls were prepared, the scenes were painted with such pigments as red ochre, lime white, vegetal black and, significantly, Egyptian blue, which could have been either imported from Egypt or reproduced on site.[247]

As for the paintings themselves, the only uncovered preserved scenes are on the south and east walls. They feature geometric as well as figurative motifs.[248] The section left of the entrance is divided into two registers by a frieze of three horizontal rows bordered in black (Plate 4A). The middle row is decorated with circles filled with red lozenges[249] while the upper and lower rows are each decorated with rectangular blocks of red and blue. The blocks are further divided by five vertical strips of black-white-black in a manner reminiscent of the Egyptian banded frieze. While the latter commonly borders the entire wall, the Tell el-Burak frieze separates the wall's registers. It would thus seem that the artist(s) had appropriated an Egyptian motif for use in a non-Egyptian way.

The same is the case with one figurative element. The upper register to the left of Room 9's entrance depicts at least two black dogs wearing red collars (Plate 4A). One dog is clearly shown, its muzzle open and forelegs stretched, as if in a hunting stance. Sader observes that the dog is portrayed in the same manner and even the same red collar as that of Khnumhotep II's dog from the north wall of his Beni Hassan tomb.[250] Other figurative elements that have been linked to Egyptian parallels are a standing goat leaning its forelegs on a tree, a type of red kilt worn by the portrayed men (Plate 4B), the acacia branches and leaves painted on the floor and ceiling(?) of Room 10, and the chequered design of the floor.[251] While these designs are attested in Egypt, they cannot be specifically identified as uniquely Egyptian: the goat's stance is common across the Mediterranean,[252] the winding tree being distinctive in form; the preserved red kilts and chequered design are too fragmentary to provide an accurate comparison; and the acacia plant is known to have grown in the Levant[253] and so could represent local trees. Thus, until more of Room 10's paintings are uncovered, the inspiration behind these designs remains uncertain.

Nonetheless, some painting tools and preparation techniques are clearly influenced by Egyptian prototypes. The banded frieze and the hunting dogs also display striking counterparts in Egyptian wall scenes, but they were evidently modified for the room's unique scene. So, it is likely that the artist(s) were not Egyptian but knowledgeable in Egyptian designs. The evidence additionally suggests that they were trained in Egyptian art either indirectly by non-Egyptian artisans teaching Egyptian techniques or directly by Egyptian artists. The representation of the hunting dogs would in fact favour the latter. Hence, the wall paintings at Tell el-Burak may represent direct Egyptian influences. Together with the imported scarab, they offer evidence for contact between the MBIIA site and the Middle Kingdom.

6.3.3 Byblos / Jbeil

Lat.Lon. 34°08'N 35°38'E

Refs PM 7, 386-392; Montet, *Byblos et l'Égypte*; Dunand, *Byblos* 1-5.

Chron. Twelfth to Fifteenth Dynasty / MBIIA to MBIIC Period

The EBA and MBA periods at the coastal city of Byblos are represented by a wealth of data reflecting a thriving harbour city with strong links to Cyprus, the Aegean, Mesopotamia and Egypt.[254] Since at least the First Egyptian Dynasty, intermittent contact with Egypt contributed to the city's growing association with cedar wood and its products, as well as its reverence to Baalat-Gebel, a goddess equated with Hathor, lady of Byblos. Poorly excavated, Byblos's stratigraphy does not take into account the site's topographic features or contemporaneous stratigraphic phases.[255] The publication of contextual data is also lacking in detail, creating difficulties in determining artefacts' chronological attributions.[256] The inadequate excavation methods have further complicated dating such artefacts as the MBA or LBA pseudo-hieroglyphic texts,[257] or scarabs bearing MBIIB to MBIIC Levantine designs.[258] Due to these chronological qualms, the following presents pertinent Egyptian(-influenced) material that is generally agreed to belong to the MBA. The evidence occurs in: (1) cultic buildings; and (2) the royal tombs.

247; Brysbaert, *E&L* 12 (2002), 100-101; Pfälzner, in *Archäologie und Geschichte*, 99; Robins, *Art of Ancient Egypt*, 27; Kanawati and Woods, *Artists of the Old Kingdom*, 39-40; di Ludovico and Ramazzotti, in *Proceedings of the 7th International Congress* 2, 291.

247 Kamlah and Sader, *BAAL* 12 (2008), 30.

248 Kamlah and Sader, *BAAL* 12 (2008), 30, figs 7, 15; Sader and Kamlah, *NEA* 73/2-3 (2010), fig. 13.

249 For similar lozenges, see those inlaid along the border of a pendant from Royal Tomb II at Byblos (Chapter 6.3.3.2, Figure 6.18).

250 In fact, the dog appears on the same register as that of Khnumhotep II's Asiatics (Plate 2). Sader and Kamlah, *NEA* 73/2-3 (2010), 138, fig. 13; Sader, in *Interconnections in the Eastern Mediterranean*, 182; Kamlah and Sader, *BAAL* 12 (2008), 32.

251 Kamlah and Sader, *BAAL* 12 (2008), 32; Sader, in *Interconnections in the Eastern Mediterranean*, 182; Sader and Kamlah, *NEA* 73/2-3 (2010), 138.

252 Bushnell, in *Postgraduate Cypriot Archaeology*, 65-76.

253 Gale et al., in *Ancient Egyptian Materials and Technology*, 335.

254 For a recent overview on Byblos and its trade relations, see Aubet, *Commerce and Colonization*, 201-265.

255 Dunand, *Byblos* 1, 6-10; Negbi and Moskowitz, *BASOR* 184 (1966), 22.

256 For more on the problems in the excavations and their publications, see Saghieh, *Byblos*; Burke, *MBA Fortification Strategies*, 192, n. 4.

257 For more on the texts, see Dunand, *Byblia Grammata*; Dhorme, *Syria* 25 (1946-1948), 1-35; Dunand, *BMB* 30 (1978), 51-59; Mendenhall, *Syllabic Inscriptions*; Sass, *Genesis of the Alphabet*, 74, 86-87, ns 48, 58; Hoch, *JSSEA* 20 (1990), 115-124; Colless, *ANES* 30 (1992), 55-102; Hoch, *JARCE* 32 (1995), 59-65; Woudhuizen, *UF* 39 (2007), 689-756; Best and Rietveld, *UF* 42 (2010), 15-40.

258 Dunand, *Byblos* 1, pls 127 [2835], 128 [2443], 129 [1227], 130 [1400]. The scarabs' uncertain dating has led Ben-Tor to note that Byblos did not receive Egyptian imports or produce Egyptian-influenced products during the Second Intermediate Period (Ben-Tor, in *Synchronisation of Civilisations*, 246, n. 20; Ben-Tor, *Scarabs*, 188, n. 265).

A.

B.

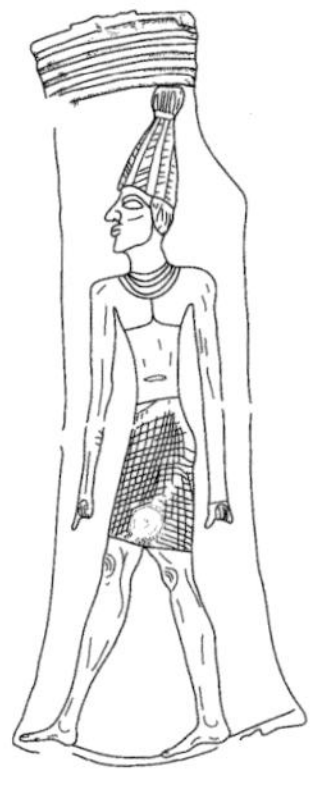

FIGURE 6.16. DECORATION ON (A) SHEATH AND (B) DAGGER HANDLE, TEMPLE OF OBELISKS, BYBLOS (NOT TO SCALE) (DRAWN FROM PHOTOGRAPHS).

6.3.3.1 The cultic buildings

The Temple of Obelisks, is recognised as an MBA building and features a small sanctuary of 26 obelisks.[259] One preserves the inscription (1) (2) (1) *mry Ḥr.w-šꜥ=f-Rꜥ.w ḥꜣ.ty-ꜥ n(.y) Kpny ꜣIbšmw wḥm ꜥnḫ* (2) *ḫtm.ty nsw=f Kwkwn sꜣ Rtt mꜣꜥ-ḫrw* '(1) beloved of Horshafra, count of *Kpny*,[260] *ꜣIbšmw*, repeating life; (2) the seal-bearer of his king, *Kwkwn*, son of *Rtt*, justified'.[261] Following the Egyptian tradition of honorific transposition, the epithet *mry Ḥr-šꜥ=f-Rꜥ.w* should be placed after *ꜣIbšmw*'s name,[262] but the engraver(s) did not follow this custom, suggesting the obelisk's local manufacture. The title *ḫtm.ty nsw=f* was also used instead of the Egyptian *ḫtm.ty bi.ty*.[263] Perhaps the term *bi.ty*, 'king of Lower Egypt', was not applicable as there was no such king in Byblos. Its replacement with *nsw=f* could instead refer to a local title translated to the Egyptian.

The temple additionally produced a bas-relief fragment displaying an individual seated on an Egyptian-style stool, possibly with lion legs.[264] Before him is the restored inscription: (1) (2) (1)[...*Sḫm-ḫꜥ-Rꜥ.w Nfr-*]*ḥtp* [...] (2) [...] *Rꜥ.w-Ḥr.w-ꜣḫ.ty di=f* [*dw*]*ꜣ*[*.t=f*] *Rꜥ.w rꜥ nb ḥꜣ.ty-ꜥ n*(*.y*) *Kpn ꜣIntn wḥm* [*ꜥnḫ*] *iri n ḥꜣ.ty-ꜥ* [*Ryn mꜣꜥ-ḫrw*] '(1)[... Sekhemkhara Noferhotep (Noferhotep I)...]; (2) [...] Ra-Horakhty, that he may give [his praise] (to) Ra every day, the count of *Kpn*, *ꜣIntn*,[265] repeating [life], born to the count,[266] [*Ryn*, justified]'.[267] If the restoration is correct, the relief offers a chronological synchronism between Noferhotep I and *ꜣIntn*,[268] denoting the latter's use of the title *ḥꜣ.ty-ꜥ n*(*.y*) *Kpn* during Dynasty 13. Ryholt notes that the title shows *ꜣIntn*'s subordination to Noferhotep I and Flammini suggests that *ꜣIntn* is paying homage to the Egyptian king.[269] But, not enough of the text survives to assess the exact nature of political relations between the two individuals.

The floor of the courtyard and cella of the Temple of Obelisks yielded eight foundation deposits of artefacts buried either for safekeeping or as offerings.[270] Some artefacts bearing Egyptian influences include: small human figurines (e.g. women wearing the Hathoric wig[271] and a child with a finger to the mouth);[272] deities (e.g. Bes[273] and Hathor);[274] and animals (e.g. hippos,[275] a crocodile,[276] felines,[277] hedgehogs,[278] baboons,[279] and a sphinx).[280] Panels with Egyptian signs, such as crocodiles, baboons and *wḏꜣ.t* eyes, were also found.[281] Possibly imported are a headed pendant seal, the base inscribed with *im.y-rꜣ pr.w Wsir ꜥnḫ-nfr* 'steward of Osiris,[282] Ankhnofer',[283] and a private-name scarab naming *S-*(*n*)*-wsr.t* 'Senwosret'.[284] Also of interest is a dagger and sheath of gold, ivory and silver (Figure 6.16).[285] The sheath is decorated on each side with a figure riding

259 Dunand, *Byblos* 2, 643, 651, fig. 707; Dunand, *Byblos. Its History, Ruins and Legends*, 50-54.

260 Ward, *Index*, 107 [882].

261 Dunand, *Byblos* 2, pl. 32 [2]; Montet, *Kêmi* 16 (1962), 89-90, fig. 5.

262 Ryholt, *Political Situation*, 89.

263 Ryholt, *Political Situation*, 89.

264 Personal examination of the relief, currently exhibited at the National Museum of Beirut, Lebanon. Dunand, *Byblos* 1, 197-198, pl. 30 [3065]; Montet, *Kêmi* 1 (1928), 90-93, figs 8-9.

265 Ward, *Index*, 107 [882].

266 Ward, *Index*, 104 [864].

267 Many glyphs are now unidentifiable. The reconstruction is based on Dunand, *Byblos* 1, 197-198, pl. 30 [3065]; Montet, *Kêmi* 1 (1928), 90-93, figs 8-9. Transliteration and translation are by the author.

268 Montet, *Kêmi* 1 (1928), 92-93; Kitchen, *Orientalia* 36 (1967), 44-52.

269 Ryholt, *Political Situation*, 87; Flammini, *Tel Aviv* 37 (2010), 159.

270 Dunand, *Byblos* 2, 643-651, pls 90-141; Seeden, *Standing Armed Figurines*.

271 Dunand, *Byblos* 2, pls 94 [15372], 99 [15366].

272 Dunand, *Byblos* 2, pl. 97 [15312].

273 Dunand, *Byblos* 2, pl. 95 [15377].

274 Dunand, *Byblos* 2, pl. 164 [12166].

275 Dunand, *Byblos* 2, pls 99 [15142], 100 [15121, 15124-15125], 101 [15138-15139], 102 [15140, 15153, 15156].

276 Dunand, *Byblos* 2, pl. 102 [15156].

277 Dunand, *Byblos* 2, pls 103 [15228, 15244, 15236, 15303], 104 [15241].

278 Dunand, *Byblos* 2, pl. 107 [15288, 15294, 15297].

279 Dunand, *Byblos* 2, pl. 108 [15178, 15194, 15220, 15306].

280 Dunand, *Byblos* 2, pl. 116 [14499].

281 Dunand, *Byblos* 2, pl. 95 [15462-15463].

282 Ward also translates it as 'overseer of the temple of Osiris' (Ward, *Index*, 23 [146]).

283 Ranke, *Personennamen* 1, 65 [3]; Martin, *Egyptian Administrative and Private-Name Seals*, 31 [392], pls 43 [3], 47B [8-9]; Dunand, *Byblos* 2, pl. 95 [15378].

284 Ranke, *Personennamen* 1, 279 [1]. The illegible title has been transliterated by Dunand as *nb nḫn* (Dunand, *Byblos* 2, 860, pl. 134 [16746]) and by Martin as *wꜣḥ* (?) *kꜣ* (Martin, *Egyptian Administrative and Private-Name Seals*, 98 [1259], pl. 33 [42]).

285 Dunand, *Byblos* 2, pls 114 [5], 117 [14443], 118 [14442].

an equid before a row of animals and bearers, while the dagger's hilt portrays a standing figure in a short kilt and an *3tf*-like crown. The individuals are illustrated in the Egyptian profile-view,[286] but the stance of some animals, such as the antelope and attacking lion, borrows from the Near Eastern tradition.[287]

Another cultic structure, the Syrian Temple, yielded the so-called 'Montet Jar'.[288] The jar's contents portray Egyptian, Mesopotamian and Levantine traits.[289] Egyptian finds were of Old Kingdom to early Middle Kingdom date.[290] They include: amulets and pendants of a female head, an ibis and baboons; Egyptian-style cylindrical, barrel, ring and spheroid beads; and a large collection of scarabs and seals.[291] While some favour a later date for the jar,[292] Ward and Tufnell present a compelling case for its EBIV/MBI to MBIIA date.[293] The Egyptian items may have arrived at Byblos through 'trade, barter, booty or as personal souvenirs'.[294] The jar's contents were possibly also collected over time and then later deposited at the temple.

6.3.3.2 The royal tombs

Around 20 rock-cut tombs were discovered, nine of which are classified as tombs of Byblos's royalty.[295] Of these, three were found intact (Tombs I-III), one was plundered in modern times (Tomb IV), and five were looted in antiquity (Tombs V-IX).[296] Tombs I-IV and VI-IX are dated to the MBA while Tomb V contained Iron Age finds. Most tombs feature a rock-cut shaft leading to a burial chamber containing the funerary equipment. Such architecture may reflect Egyptian influences, yet the lack of comparable royal tombs in the area restricts assessing when the architectural elements were first used in the Levant.

Tomb I

Tomb I's chamber yielded one calcite-alabaster flask with a convex base and a small 'alabaster' jar.[297] The sarcophagus contained a necklace with amethyst beads,[298] an amethyst scarab mounted on a gold ring,[299] fragments of a gold *wsḫ* collar,[300] and the soles of a pair of silver sandals postulated to be in the Egyptian style.[301] An obsidian and gold cylindrical jar was also found.[302] Two cartouches on either side of the top of its lid belong to 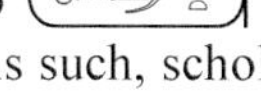 *Nj-M3ˁ.t-Rˁ.w* 'Nimaatra (Amenemhat III)'. As such, scholars have correlated the tomb's date with Amenemhat III's reign,[303] despite the fact that the cartouche only provides a *terminus post quem*. The buried individual was evidently provided with prestigious Egyptian items within his tomb and sarcophagus, most of which are personal adornments, insinuating that the elite may have worn Egyptian regalia.

Tomb II

The same case is observable in Tomb II. Egyptian-style adornments include a gold *wsḫ* collar,[304] an amethyst bead,[305] amethyst scarabs mounted on gold rings and a bracelet,[306] a gold amulet representing two female Hathor(?) figures,[307] fragments of a pair of silver Egyptian-style(?) sandals at the feet of the interred,[308] and two gold uraei probably belonging to now-lost diadems.[309] The tomb also produced a pectoral depicting a falcon flanked by two opposing seated individuals, each with an *3tf*-crown and a mace (Figure 6.17).[310] The thick-set, disproportionate, legs of the figures could indicate either a late Middle Kingdom date or local manufacture.

Another jewellery piece found on the body of the buried individual is a pendant portraying a lozenge-filled border surrounding a *ḫpr* beetle, a falcon and a cartouche naming *Ypšmw-ib* (Figure 6.18).[311] Due to the glyphs' substandard carving and multi-directional layout,[312] a Levantine origin is proposed,[313] suggesting that locals were knowledgeable in Egyptian art and language. Another locally made object is a gold belt decorated with a central *ˁnḫ* sign and the repeated symbols 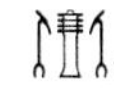,[314] signalling the adoption of hieroglyphs in local elite fashion. Other Egyptian-style products of uncertain origin are a silver mirror with a

286 Hansen, *AJA* 73/3 (1969), 282-283.
287 Hansen, *AJA* 73/3 (1969), 282-283.
288 Montet, *Byblos et l'Égypte*, 127-139.
289 Tufnell and Ward, *Syria* 43 (1966), 165-241.
290 Tufnell and Ward, *Syria* 43 (1966), 187-188, 196, 200-204, 220-225.
291 Tufnell and Ward, *Syria* 43 (1966), 165-241, figs 2-5, pls 13-14, 16.
292 Albright, *BASOR* 184 (1966), 27; O'Connor, *World Archaeology* 6/1 (1974), 33; O'Connor, *JSSEA* 15 (1987), 38-40; Kemp and Merrillees, *Minoan Pottery*, 44-46.
293 Tufnell and Ward, *Syria* 43 (1966), 165-241; Ward, *Berytus* 26 (1978), 37-53; Ward, *AJA* 91/4 (1987), 509-512; Ben-Tor, in *Ancient Egyptian and Mediterranean Studies*, 1-17.
294 Tufnell and Ward, *Syria* 43 (1966), 225.
295 Montet, *Byblos et l'Égypte*. Several more burials have been identified in recent times, some near the vicinity of the royal tombs, but no archaeological excavations have yet been carried out. See Frost, *BAAL* 5 (2001), 197; Frost, *AHL* 15 (2002), 76. See also Salles, in *Biblo*, 49-71.
296 Montet, *Byblos et l'Égypte*, 18-26.
297 Montet, *Byblos et l'Égypte*, 159 [612-613]; Virolleaud, *Syria* 3 (1922), 277-278, pls 62 [1-2], 66 [2]; Sparks, *Stone Vessels in the Levant*, 308 [344], 388 [1354].
298 Montet, *Byblos et l'Égypte*, 169 [623]; Virolleaud, *Syria* 3 (1922), 286.
299 Montet, *Byblos et l'Égypte*, 171 [640], pl. 96 [640]; Virolleaud, *Syria* 3 (1922), 286, pl. 65.
300 Montet, *Byblos et l'Égypte*, 167 [621-622], 169 [623], pl. 96 [621-622]; Virolleaud, *Syria* 3 (1922), 287, pl. 65 [5].
301 Montet, *Byblos et l'Égypte*, 173 [650], pl. 101 [650]; Virolleaud, *Syria* 3 (1922), 284, fig. 5 [13].
302 Montet, *Byblos et l'Égypte*, 155-157 [610], 169 [623]; pls 88-89 [610]; Virollaud, *Syria* 3 (1922), 284-285, pl. 67 [1]; Sparks, *Stone Vessels in the Levant*, 382.
303 See Montet, *Byblos et l'Égypte*, 285; Albright, *BASOR* 176 (1964), 39; Kitchen, *Orientalia* 36 (1967), 40, 48, 53; Hansen, *AJA* 73/3 (1969), 282; Nigro, in *Interconnections in the Eastern Mediterranean*, 160-161, table 2.
304 Montet, *Byblos et l'Égypte*, 167 [620], pl. 95 [620].
305 Montet, *Byblos et l'Égypte*, 169 [625].
306 Montet, *Byblos et l'Égypte*, 170 [636], 171 [641-642], pls 96 [641-642], 97 [636].
307 Montet, *Byblos et l'Égypte*, 185-186 [707], pl. 94 [707].
308 Montet, *Byblos et l'Égypte*, 173 [651], pl. 101 [651].
309 Montet, *Byblos et l'Égypte*, 172 [647-648], pl. 98 [647-648].
310 Montet, *Byblos et l'Égypte*, 162-164 [617], pl. 93 [617].
311 Montet, *Byblos et l'Égypte*, 165-166 [618], pl. 97 [618]; Dunand, *Byblos. Its History, Ruins and Legends*, 68-69.
312 The name is read from right to left as if in two horizontal lines. The cartouche, however, is facing the opposite direction.
313 Smith, *AJA* 73/3 (1969), 279.
314 Montet, *Byblos et l'Égypte*, 171-172 [644], pl. 98 [644].

FIGURE 6.17. PECTORAL, ROYAL TOMB II, BYBLOS (DRAWN FROM PHOTOGRAPH).

FIGURE 6.18. PECTORAL, ROYAL TOMB II, BYBLOS (DRAWN FROM PHOTOGRAPH).

papyriform handle,[315] a gold spoon with the arm shaped as a bird's head,[316] a similar gold and silver spoon,[317] a small bronze papyriform column,[318] two bronze and one gold papyriform cup,[319] as well as two fragments of a drop-shaped 'alabaster' jar.[320]

Tomb II contained three additional inscribed items. The first, a bronze Levantine scimitar sword, was retrieved from the right hand of the buried individual.[321] Neatly incised texts on both faces of the sword are (1) (2) (1) *ḥ3.ty-ʿ n(.y) Kpny Ypšmw-ib wḥm ʿnḫ* (2) *iri n ḥ3.ty-ʿ Ibšmw m3ʿ-ḫrw* '(1) count of *Kpny*,[322] *Ypšmw-ib*, repeating life, (2) born to the count,[323] *Ibšmw*, justified'. Each glyph is well-executed, yet the neck of the *ḥ3.ty* sign in (1) is decorated with a disproportionately lengthened neck, a beak-like nose and no ears, indicating that the inscription was likely produced locally.[324]

The second inscribed item is a cylindrical jar of grey stone.[325] The shape may be dated to the late Twelfth or Thirteenth Dynasty,[326] which is supported by the mention of a ruler on its lid: *ḥm.w ʿnḫ(.w) nṯr nfr s3 Rʿ.w Imn-m-ḥ3.t ʿnḫ(.w) ḏ.t* 'offerings: may the good god, son of Ra, Amenemhat live, may he live eternally'. The vessel is evidently an imported item from the reign of an Amenemhat.

The third inscribed artefact is an obsidian and gold chest.[327] Its lid is inscribed with *ʿnḫ(.w) nṯr nfr nb t3.wy nsw.t bi.ty M3ʿ.t-ḫrw-Rʿ.w mry Tm nb Iwn di(.w) ʿnḫ mi Rʿ.w ḏ.t* 'may the good god, lord of the two lands, king of Upper and Lower Egypt, Maatkherura (Amenemhat IV), beloved of Atum, lord of Heliopolis, live. May he be given life like Ra, eternally'. The cartouche has been used to correlate the tomb's date with Amenemhat IV's reign;[328] however, it only supplies a *terminus post quem*.

Following Montet's MBIIA dating of the tombs, Tomb I would belong to *Ibšmw*, contemporary of Amenemhat III, and Tomb II would belong to his son, *Ypšmw-ib*, contemporary of Amenemhat IV.[329] A familial relation between the individuals buried in the two tombs is highly likely considering that they share a passageway. However, chronological correlations with Amenemhat III and IV cannot be proven by each tomb's respective finds. While it is possible that the two Twelfth Dynasty kings each sent gifts to the rulers of Byblos, it is equally likely that the items were heirlooms or that the Byblite elite received them at the same time, perhaps as gifts from later Egyptian rulers or as looted items.

Tombs III-IV and VI-IX

Meagre finds from Tombs III-IX include:

- Tomb III: a *wsḫ* collar,[330] amethyst scarabs mounted on gold jewellery[331] and a calcite-alabaster conical alabastron;[332]

315 Montet, *Byblos et l'Égypte*, 161 [616], pls 92-93 [616].
316 Montet, *Byblos et l'Égypte*, 185 [705], pl. 103 [705].
317 Montet, *Byblos et l'Égypte*, 185 [706], pl. 103 [706].
318 Montet, *Byblos et l'Égypte*, 184 [699], pl. 105 [699].
319 Montet, *Byblos et l'Égypte*, 184-185 [700-702], pls 104 [700], 105 [701-702].
320 Montet, *Byblos et l'Égypte*, 195 [785], fig. 86; Sparks, *Stone Vessels in the Levant*, 292 [154].
321 Montet, *Byblos et l'Égypte*, 174-177 [653], pls 99-100.
322 Ward, *Index*, 107 [882].
323 Ward, *Index*, 104 [864].
324 Personal examination of the artefact currently at the National Museum of Beirut, Lebanon.
325 Montet, *Byblos et l'Égypte*, 159 [614], pl. 91, fig. 70; Sparks, *Stone Vessels in the Levant*, 315 [436].
326 Ahrens, *JAEI* 4/2 (2012), 1-2.
327 Montet, *Byblos et l'Égypte*, 157-159 [611], pls 88-90 [611].
328 For references, see n. 303.
329 For references, see n. 303.
330 Montet, *Byblos et l'Égypte*, 166-167 [619], pls 95-96 [619].
331 Montet, *Byblos et l'Égypte*, 170 [639], 171 [643], fig. 76, pls 92 [639], 96 [643].
332 Montet, *Byblos et l'Égypte*, 196 [786], pl. 118 [786]; Sparks, *Stone Vessels in the Levant*, 297 [221].

- Tomb IV:[333] an 'alabaster' drop-shaped vessel and other 'alabaster' fragments, two of which belong to one vessel inscribed with ⸗ *[...] n k3 n(.y) ir.y-pˁ.t ḥ3.ty-ˁ ḥḳ3 ḥḳ3.w ḥ3.ty-ˁ n(.y) Kpn[y...] tn wḥm ˁnḫ nb im3ḫ '[...] for the k3 of the nobleman, the count,[334] ruler of rulers, count of Kpny,[335] [...]tn, repeating life, possessor of reverence';[336]

- Tomb VI: an 'alabaster' drop-shaped vessel along with a faience cup;[337]

- Tomb VII: a ḥs faience vase with glyphs reading ⸗ ḥḳ3 ḫ3s.wt 'ruler of foreign lands' (Figure 6.19),[338] as well as amethyst beads and pieces;[339]

- Tomb VIII: a blue faience cup and 'alabaster' fragments;[340] and

- Tomb IX:[341] calcite-alabaster drop-shaped alabastra, a calcite-alabaster flask, a conical faience vessel with ⸗ ḥ3.ty-ˁ n(.y) Kpny 'Ib 'count of Kpny, Ib', and a ḥs-faience vase with ⸗ 'Ibšmw wḥm ˁnḫ [...] 'Ibšmw, repeating life [...]'.[342]

As most of the tombs were plundered, the quantity of finds should not be regarded as a decrease in contacts or Egyptian influence. In fact, the remaining items are similar in type to those of Tombs I-II, being predominantly cosmetic vessels and personal adornments. The calcite-alabaster and amethyst artefacts could be Egyptian imports, whereas the inscribed pieces of Tombs IV and IX are probably local due to their inclusion of titles and names of Byblos's elite.

A note on the tombs' date

Since the tombs' publication, scholars have agreed with Montet's dating: Tomb I was assigned to Amenemhat III's reign; Tomb II to Amenemhat IV; Tomb III to the early Thirteenth Dynasty; and Tombs IV and VI-IX were dated to the early Second Intermediate Period.[343] Yet, the dating of Tombs I and II are not certain and no inscription from the tombs specifically connects a Byblite ruler with

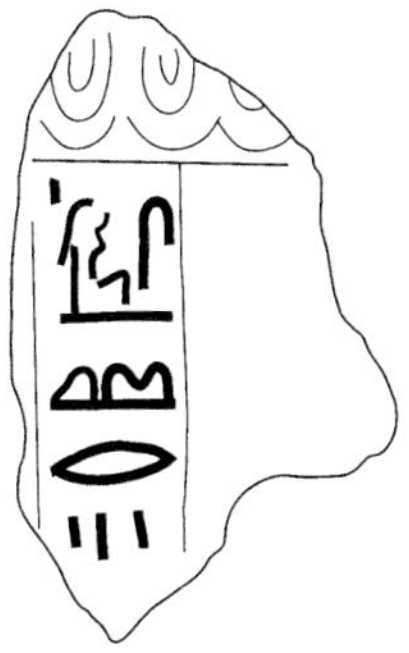

FIGURE 6.19. FRAGMENT OF A FAIENCE VASE, ROYAL TOMB VII, BYBLOS. AFTER MONTET, *BYBLOS ET L'ÉGYPTE*, FIG. 94.

an Egyptian king. Some have correctly noted that the published Levantine ceramics, metal vessels and jewellery forms argue for placing Tombs I-III to the late MBIIA or MBIIB period, and Tombs IV and VI-IX between the MBIIB and MBIIC periods.[344] Recently, Kopetzky identified three vessels from photographs in Montet's publication as of Egyptian origin. One jar from either Tombs I, II or III bears characteristics of a mid-Thirteenth to Fifteenth Dynasty zir type[345] while the other two vessels, possibly from Tombs IV or VI-IX, are of Fifteenth to early Eighteenth Dynasty shapes.[346] Such evidence warns that the traditional dating of the tombs cannot be accepted. Evidently, late MBIIA to MBIIC artefacts and Thirteenth to Fifteenth Dynasty imports were deposited in the burials, implying contact between Egypt and Byblos after the MBIIA. Hence, Tombs I-II are cautiously assigned here to the MBIIA, Tomb III is to the late MBIIA to MBIIB and Tombs IV, VI-IX are to the MBIIB to MBIIC period.

6.3.3.3 Other

Based on similarities in names, one fragmentary hieroglyphic stela of unknown context may be linked with individuals mentioned on Tomb II's scimitar. It reads:[347]

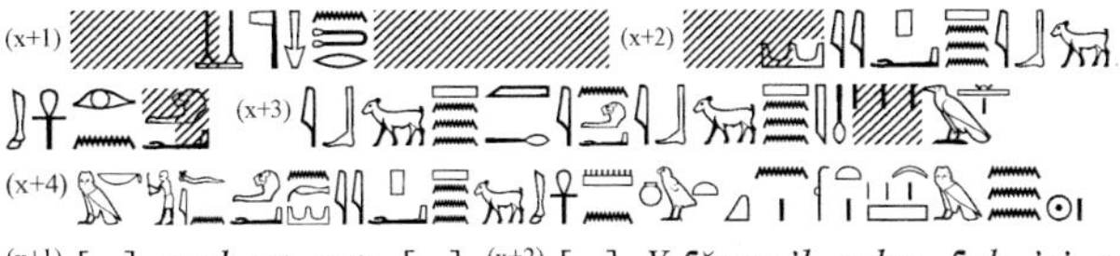

(x+1) [...] mnḫ.wt snṯr [...] (x+2) [...] Ypˁšmw-ib wḥm ˁnḫ iri n [ḥ3.ty-ˁ] (x+3) 'Ibšmw m3ˁ-ḫrw in ḥ3.ty-ˁ 'Ibšmw m3ˁ-ḫrw [...] (x+4) mki=f in ḥ3.ty-ˁ n(.y) Kp(n) Ypˁšmw-ib wḥm ˁnḫ mn.wt (?) kn (?) rnp.t 2 3bd 1 šmw sw 1

333   Three scarabs are attributed to the tomb but are of uncertain context. Montet, *Byblos et l'Égypte*, 197-199, fig. 88; Montet, *Syria* 8 (1927), 85-92, figs 1-2, 7; Martin, *Egyptian Administrative and Private-Name Seals*, 19 [174a], 105 [1354], pls 17 [19], 19 [14].

334   Ward, *Index*, 104 [864].

335   Ward, *Index*, 107 [882].

336   Montet, *Byblos et l'Égypte*, 196 [787], pl. 117 [787]; 199 [788]; Montet, *Kêmi* 16 (1962), 95, fig. 6; Sparks, *Stone Vessels in the Levant*, 292 [155], 338 [733].

337   Montet, *Byblos et l'Égypte*, 207 [820-821], pl. 122 [820].

338   Montet, *Byblos et l'Égypte*, 208 [826], fig. 94.

339   Montet, *Byblos et l'Égypte*, 209 [831], 210 [836], pl. 121 [831, 836].

340   Montet, *Byblos et l'Égypte*, 210 [843-845].

341   The items were found removed from their original context, possibly by looters, and may have belonged to connecting Tomb VIII. Dunand, *Byblos. Its History, Ruins and Legends*, 67.

342   Ward, *Index*, 107 [882]; Montet, *Byblos et l'Égypte*, 211 [846-848], 212 [852-853], pls 122 [846-848], 123 [852-853]; Sparks, *Stone Vessels in the Levant*, 208 [345], 292 [156-157].

343   Montet, *Byblos et l'Égypte*, 285-286. See n. 303.

344   Tufnell, *Berytus* 18 (1969), 5-33; Dever, in *Magnolia Dei*, 11, 27, n. 69; Gerstenblith, *Levant at the Beginning of the MBA*, 38-41, 103; Ward, *AJA* 91/4 (1987), 528-529; Lilyquist, *BASOR* 290-291 (1993), 41-44; Ben-Tor, in *Bilder als Quellen*, 182-183.

345   Montet, *Byblos et l'Égypte*, pl. 124 (back row, fourth vessel from the left); Kopetzky, in *Bronze Age in the Lebanon*, 225.

346   The jars could also be from the 'Tombeau de particuliers'. Montet, *Byblos et l'Égypte*, pl. 124 (back row, third vessel from the left; third row, fourth vessel from the left); Kopetzky, in *Bronze Age in the Lebanon*, 225.

347   Transcription either follows the figure or the text as presented in Montet, *Kêmi* 17 (1964), fig. 5; Kitchen, *BMB* 20 (1967), 149-153. Transliterations and translations are by the author.

(x+1) [...] clothes, incense [...] (x+2) [...]*Ypʿšmw-ib*, repeating life, born to [the count], (x+3) *Ỉbšmw*, justified. It is the count *Ỉbšmw*, justified [...], (x+4) it is he who protects. It is the count of *Kp(n)*, *Ypʿšmw-ib*, repeating life, who fully completed(?), year 2, month 1 of *šmw*, day 1.

Hoch identifies the use of hieratic in the text which, if contemporaneous with Tomb II, would infer that MBIIA scribes were trained in both hieroglyphic and hieratic scripts.[348] The inscription additionally implies the utilisation of the Egyptian calendar in Byblos.[349]

Other private tombs of the MBA yielded Egyptian-style scarabs.[350] A tomb outside one of the city's gates, beneath a rampart, produced two scarabs. One of lapis-lazuli is inscribed with  *wʿr(.tw) ʿꜣ n(.y) niw.t Mrw-nfr wḥm ʿnḫ* 'chief administrator of a city,[351] Merunofer,[352] repeating life'.[353] The second scarab reads  *it-nṯr Mnt(w)-m-ḥꜣ.t* 'god's father,[354] Montuemhat'.[355] The scarabs are most likely late Middle Kingdom imports or heirlooms. They were found alongside a jar identified as an Egyptian zir of the first half of Dynasty 13[356] while the rampart itself has been assigned to the MBIIB-C,[357] suggesting that the tomb is of this period or slightly earlier.

Worthy of mention are six scarabs and one cylinder sealing bearing the names of rulers with the title 'count of Byblos'.[358] The sealing comes from Alalakh and follows the style of the Northern Levantine Green Jasper Workshop.[359] The text on the sealing has been recently deciphered as *ḥꜣ.ty-ʿ n(.y) Kpn Nḥsiʿn[ḫ mꜣʿ-ḫrw mry] Stḫ nb Rb[n]w[n]* 'count of *Kpn*, *Nḥsiʿn[ḫ]*, justified, beloved of Seth, lord of *Rb[n]w[n]*'.[360] If correct, the sealing denotes a Byblite ruler's reverence to Seth or his Levantine equivalent. Of the six unprovenanced scarabs, three name *Ỉntn*,[361] one is for *Ỉbšmw*,[362] one is for *Rynty*[363] and one is for *Kꜣin*.[364] An offering formula evoking Hathor, lady of Byblos, is also inscribed on the latter.[365] Based on the scarabs' style and design, Ben-Tor ascribes four to the royal Egyptian workshop (two scarabs for *Ỉntn*, one for *Ỉbšmw* and another for *Kꜣin*) and two to the early Tell el-Dab'a scarab workshop (one for *Ỉntn* and the other for *Rynty*).[366] She suggests that the Egyptian title was awarded by the Egyptian administration, noting that a cartouche's inclusion for some names would be peculiar if Egyptian-made.[367]

Such a peculiarity has led to much discussion on the Byblites' use of Egyptian titles. Some perceive them as a reflection of Egyptian domination, either through direct administrative control or indirect administrative representation, with the titles being awarded by the Egyptian king.[368] Another suggestion is that the rulers recognised themselves as 'governors' but were not necessarily viewed as such by the Egyptians.[369] The Byblites may have also simply adopted the titles after years of Egyptian contact and influence.[370] A similar argument identifies the titles, as well as the Egyptian and Egyptian-influenced artefacts, as evidence for elite emulation[371] and a patron-client relationship.[372]

There are few markers from Byblos directly referencing Middle Kingdom pharaohs and none that can definitively determine an Egyptian administrative presence. An indirect or unofficial administrative representation is possible, but unlikely in view of the use of the term *nsw* on the abovementioned obelisk and the cartouches bordering local rulers' names. Extra-Byblite references, such as to *Mꜣki* of Khnumhotep III's biography[373] or the *lugal* 'king' in texts from Mari and Drehem,[374] also argue against the Byblite rulers' subordination to the pharaohs. The title *ḥꜣ.ty-ʿ n.y Kpny* was more likely bestowed by the Byblites themselves, in most cases from father to son. The particular use of this label instead of the Egyptian *ḥkꜣ* is potentially due to close relations between Egypt and Byblos, as well

348 Hoch, *JARCE* 32 (1995), 63-64.

349 Hoch translates a pseudo-hieroglyphic text (Stela L) to also feature an Egyptian-style date (Hoch, *JARCE* 32 [1995], 61-62).

350 Other sealings from Byblos bear Egyptian and Levantine designs as well as private and royal names, such as that of Thirteenth Dynasty king Ibiaw, but are of uncertain context and date. See Dunand, *Byblos* 2, pls 98-101; Martin, *Egyptian Administrative and Private-Name Seals*, 67 [813], 103 [1319], pls 10 [36], 16 [31]; Ryholt, *Political Situation*, 89-90, 353.

351 Ward, *Index*, 84 [698].

352 Ranke, *Personnenamen* 1, 152 [5].

353 Dunand, *BMB* 17 (1964), 32, pl. 3 [2]; Martin, *Egyptian Administrative and Private-Name Seals*, 47 [551a], pl. 15 [32].

354 Ward, *Index*, 69 [570e].

355 Dunand translated the name as *Ỉmn-m-ḥꜣ.t* 'Amenemhat' (Dunand, *BMB* 17 [1964], 32, pl. 3 [2]). The translation here follows Martin, *Egyptian Administrative and Private-Name Seals*, 48 [564], pl. 24 [3]; Ranke, *Personnenamen* 1, 154 [7].

356 Dunand, *BMB* 17 (1964), 32, pl. 2 [1-2]; Kopetzky, *AHL* 26-27 (2007/2008),26.

357 Burke, *MBA Fortification Strategies*, 196-197.

358 A seventh scarab has no parallels and so cannot be connected to MBA designs. Ben-Tor, in *Bilder als Quellen*, 177-180.

359 Collon argues for a Byblite place of manufacture for seals of this group (in *Insight Through Images*, 57-70), Keel suggests two areas of origin (in *Stempelsiegel aus Palästina/Israel* 2, 211-280) while Teissier argues for multiple centres of production across the Levant (Teissier's Group C; Teissier, *Syro-Palestinian Cylinder Seals*, 15, 20-22). See also Boschloos, *JAEI* 6/4 (2014), 36-7.

360 Wimmer, *Levant* 37 (2005), 127-132; Flammini, *Tel Aviv* 37 (2010), 160. Perhaps the toponym *Rb[n]w[n]* is associated with the name Lebanon.

361 Martin, *Egyptian Administrative and Private-Name Seals*, 25-26 [261-263], pls 9 [19], 16 [18], 32 [14]; Newberry, *JEA* 14/1 (1928), 109, figs 1-2; Ben-Tor, in *Bilder als Quellen*, 177-178, pl. 23 [1].

362 Martin, *Egyptian Administrative and Private-Name Seals*, 14 [105], pl. 32 [13].

363 Martin, *Egyptian Administrative and Private-Name Seals*, 66-67 [810], pl. 30 [11].

364 Martin, *Egyptian Administrative and Private-Name Seals*, 129 [1689], pl. 20 [37]. Ben-Tor transliterates the name as *Ỉn* or *Ỉntn* in *Bilder als Qeullen*, 177.

365 Martin, *Egyptian Administrative and Private-Name Seals*, 129 [1689], pl. 20 [37]; Ben-Tor, in *Bilder als Qeullen*, 177.

366 Ben-Tor, in *Bilder als Quellen*, 177-180.

367 Ben-Tor, in *Bilder als Qeullen*, 179-181.

368 Montet, *Byblos et l'Égypte*, 92; Albright, *BASOR* 176 (1964), 42; Helck, *Die Beziehungen Ägyptens*, 64; Redford, *Egypt, Canaan, and Israel*, 97; Ben-Tor, in *Bilder als Quellen*, 179.

369 Ryholt, *Political Situation*, 86-90.

370 Ward, *Orientalia* 30 (1961), 134-137.

371 Ahrens, in *Intercultural Contacts in the Ancient Mediterranean*, 291-293, 300-301; Flammini, *Tel Aviv* 37 (2010), 154-168.

372 Flammini, *Tel Aviv* 37 (2010), 154-168.

373 See Chapter 4.3.1.2.

374 Kitchen, *Orientalia* 36 (1967), 39-54; Albright, *BASOR* 99 (1945), 9-18; Flammini, *Tel Aviv* 37 (2010), 156.

as Egyptian influences on the city.[375] A patron-client relationship is marred by the indefinite chronological synchronism of the Byblites with Egyptian kings. That is, while patronage vies that 'by linking themselves to the most prestigious elite of the time, the rulers of Byblos were substantially well positioned in the local system of inter-elite relationships',[376] the revised tombs' dating advises that the 'most prestigious elite of the time' may not have been the pharaohs. Hence, *ḥ*ꜥ*.ty-*ꜥ *n.y Kpny* is most likely a literal translation of a local title that emerged following direct contact with the Egyptian culture over successive generations. Perhaps, the Byblites knew of the term *ḥḳ*ꜣ but regarded the designation *ḥ*ꜥ*.ty-*ꜥ *n.y Kpny* as a more fitting expression for their administrative roles.

The same may also explain other Egyptian influences at Byblos. The Temple of Obelisks adapts an Egyptian symbol in its architecture while the temple deposits reflect the use of Egyptian artefacts for cultic purposes. The temple inscriptions, stela and other inscribed funerary goods note a local scribal tradition experienced in the hieroglyphic and, perhaps, hieratic scripts. Knowledge and use of the Egyptian calendar, epithets and titles signify a high understanding and appreciation of the Egyptian culture and administration. Similarly, the deposition of Egyptian(-influenced) items of personal adornment within elite tombs indicates local knowledge of Egyptian art, emphasising the adoption of Egyptian regalia. The Byblite elite represented themselves in their monuments, tombs and temples to be closely affiliated with the Egyptian culture and its symbols of authority, royalty and power. However, the fact that they mixed elements of this culture with Levantine traits insinuates the appropriation of Egyptian traditions for the benefit of the Levantine city and its maritime connections rather than its subordination to an Egyptian dynasty.

Despite the weakened state of the Thirteenth Dynasty, Byblos still had access to Egyptian goods until at least the beginning of the Fifteenth Dynasty. Like the elite of Tell el-Dab'a, its rulers utilised a hybrid Egyptian-Levantine representation, worshipped Egyptian as well as Levantine gods including Seth and Hathor, and used the Egyptian script to commemorate their own monumental activities. The reference to *ḥḳ*ꜣ *ḫ*ꜣ*s.wt* on Tomb VII's vase may even indicate some connection to the *ḥḳ*ꜣ *ḫ*ꜣ*s.wt* of Egypt. At the very least, one may suggest maritime links between the rulers of Byblos and the Hyksos, links which would explain the late Thirteenth and Fifteenth Dynasty finds at the site, warranting the Byblite rulers' continued affiliation with the Egyptian or, more specifically, a hybrid Egyptian-Levantine culture.

375 As also recognised in Flammini, *Tel Aviv* 37 (2010), 156.
376 Flammini, *Tel Aviv* 37 (2010), 164.

6.3.4 Ebla / Mardikh, Tell

Lat.Lon. 35°52'N 37°02'E

Refs Matthiae, *Syria* 46 (1969), 1-43, figs 1-3, pls 1-2; Matthiae, *BA* 47/1 (1984), 18-32; Scandone-Matthiae, in *Wirtschaft und Gesellschaft*, 71, pl. 13 [3]; Matthiae, *CRAIBL* 139/2 (1995), 651-681; Scandone-Matthiae, in *Hyksos*, 415-427, figs 15 [4, 6-9, 11]; Scandone-Matthiae, in *Scarabs of the Second Millennium BC*, 195-201, figs 1-3, pls 1-2; Peyronel, in *Synchronisation of Civilisations*, 413, fig. 16.

Chron. Thirteenth to Fifteenth Dynasty / Late MBIIA to MBIIC Period

Northeast of Ugarit is the site of Ebla, the head of a MBA city-state.[377] The discovery of several items of Egyptian origin and influence has resulted in postulated ties with Egypt.[378] The objects are attributed to Mardikh IIIA2 (MBIIA) and Mardikh IIIB (MBIIA-B to MBIIC). Final reports on their contexts and a full assemblage of associated finds remain unpublished.

6.3.4.1 Mardikh IIIA2: Late MBIIA Period

Three elite tombs of possible royalty were found beneath the Western Palace (Area Q) and Temples B1-2 of Ebla's lower city.[379] The earliest tomb, the Tomb of the Princess, has been assigned to the end of Mardikh IIIA2, or the late MBIIA period.[380] Its owner was buried with 'alabaster' vessels of uncertain origin, and a necklace of amethyst beads.[381] The latter's material points to its possible Egyptian origin.[382]

6.3.4.2 Mardikh IIIB: MBIIA-B to MBIIC Period

Vessels

Another tomb beneath Palace Q is the Tomb of the Lord of the Goats. It contained several stone vessels, including a serpentine drop-shaped alabastron,[383] two calcite-alabaster conical alabastra,[384] and two calcite-alabaster

377 Matthiae, *AAS* 17 (1967), 25-43; Matthiae, *AAS* 18 (1968), 5-20; Matthiae, *AAS* 20 (1970), 55-72; Matthiae, *Akk* 17 (1980), 1-51; Matthiae, *CRAIBL* 139/2 (1995), 651-681; Matthiae, in *Hyksos*, 379-414; Matthiae, in *Proceedings of the 6th International Congress* 2, 3-26; Matthiae, in *Ebla and its Landscape*, 35-48.
378 Matthiae, in *Hyksos*, 397-398, 407; Scandone-Matthiae, in *Wirtschaft und Gesellschaft*, 67-73; Scandone-Matthiae, in *Egyptology* 2, 487-493; Scandone Matthiae, in *Hyksos*, 415-427.
379 Matthiae, *Akk* 17 (1980), 1-51.
380 Matthiae, *Akk* 17 (1980), 1-51; Nigro, in *Interconnections in the Eastern Mediterranean*, table 2.
381 Nigro, in *Interconnections in the Eastern Mediterranean*, 162.
382 Scandone-Matthiae, in *Wirtschaft und Gesellschaft*, 71; Matthiae, *BA* 47/1 (1984), 24.
383 Scandone-Matthiae, in *Wirtschaft und Gesellschaft*, 71, pl. 13 [3]; Sparks, *Stone Vessels in the Levant*, 259, 288 [101].
384 Scandone-Matthiae, in *Wirtschaft und Gesellschaft*, 71, pl. 13 [3]; Matthiae et al., *Ebla*, 501, 527 [462]; Sparks, *Stone Vessels in the Levant*, 259, 295 [188], 297 [222].

drop-shaped alabastra,[385] all bearing Middle Kingdom and Second Intermediate Period forms.[386] A MBA silver bowl decorated with a *ʿnḫ* sign was also found,[387] its decoration signalling that Levantine artists had some knowledge of hieroglyphs which they used for artistic purposes.

Scarabs, a seal and seal impressions

Three scarabs from Mardikh IIIB contexts were found.[388] A waste deposit atop the ruins of the MBIIA Archaic Palace's north wing produced one scarab (Figure 6.20 [2]).[389] Its base is designed with a continuous oblong scroll bordering a cartouche with the signs *nfr* and *kꜣ*.[390] Parallels derive from late Middle Kingdom scarabs at Kahun,[391] Nubt[392] and Mirgissa,[393] supporting its Egyptian origin. The second scarab surfaced from one of Palace E's excavation trenches and displays a 'S' scroll (Figure 6.20 [1]) akin to scarab designs from Second Intermediate Period Egyptian contexts as well as MBIIB to MBIIC Levantine contexts.[394] Although its place of manufacture cannot be determined, the design is originally Egyptian. The third scarab comes from a room in the eastern units south of the Western Rampart (Figure 6.20 [3]).[395] The excavator describes the base's fish-bone design as of Second-Intermediate Period origin, yet its Levantine manufacture is also possible.[396] Thus, of the published scarabs, one could be of Egyptian origin and two show Egyptian influences.

Such influences are also evident on sealings. A seal from the debris of a private home adjacent to Temple B1 (temple of Reshef) illustrates columns of a repeated *ʿnrʿ* formula on either side of a scene with human figures, branches, a winged falcon-headed sphinx and a cobra (Figure 6.20 [4]).[397] The hieroglyphs and cobra are clearly inspired by Egyptian prototypes, but have been combined with Near Eastern elements in this locally produced specimen.

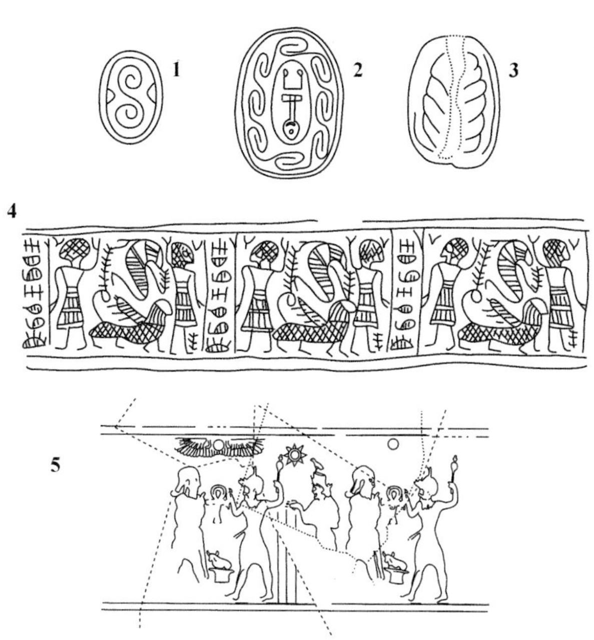

FIGURE 6.20. SELECTED SCARABS AND SEALS, EBLA (NOT TO SCALE). AFTER SCANDONE-MATTHIAE, IN *SCARABS OF THE SECOND MILLENNIUM BC*, FIGS 1-3; PEYRONEL, IN *SYNCHRONISATION OF CIVILIZATIONS* 3, FIG. 16; MATTHIAE, *EBLA*, FIG. 7, PL. 12 [ILL. 6].

Another seal is preserved on impressions on the shoulders of jars from the Western Palace and the area of Temple B1.[398] The impressions portray Prince Maratewari, son of Indilimma, the last king of MBIIB Ebla, receiving a stylised *ʿnḫ* sign as a gift of life from Haddad (Figure 6.20 [5]).[399] Otherwise decorated with Northern Levantine iconography of the Aleppo style, the seal's representation of the Egyptian sign as a symbol for life not only reflects the glyph's adoption by Levantine artists, it also denotes an understanding of the Egyptian meaning conveyed by the sign.

Other

The Tomb of the Lord of the Goats contained a ceremonial mace.[400] Its handle features a cylinder decorated with two seated baboons, palms up in adoration, flanking hieroglyphs reading *Ḥtp-ib-rʿ.w* 'Hotepibra'. The *ḥtp* sign is unusually mounted upside down with only one of its phonetic complements (*t*) present. The *ib* glyph is also slightly askew. Scandone-Matthiae and Matthiae have explained the glyphs' positioning as a result of their restoration by Levantine craftsmen.[401] Ryholt adds that the glyphs could have belonged to another item and were then mounted onto the mace.[402] The detailed and neat incisions per hieroglyph suggest that the signs are Egyptian-made,[403] but the mace itself has no

385 Scandone-Matthiae, in *Wirtschaft und Gesellschaft*, 71, pl. 13 [2]; Sparks, *Stone Vessels in the Levant*, 259, 292 [158-159].

386 Sparks also identifies a breccia jar to be a probable Old Kingdom heirloom. Sparks, *Stone Vessels in the Levant*, 52, 259.

387 Nigro, in *Interconnections in the Eastern Mediterranean*, 166, fig. 14.

388 A fourth was collected from the surface of the tell. It is designed with a myriad of hieroglyphs that are indicative of its late MBA Levantine origin. Ben Tor's Design Class 3A3, 3B3d and 3B4. Scandone-Matthiae, in *Scarabs of the Second Millennium BC*, 195, fig. 1 [4]; Ben-Tor, *Scarabs*, 126-131, 160-163.

389 Scandone-Matthiae, in *Scarabs of the Second Millennium BC*, 196, fig. 2 [3]; Matthiae, *CRAIBL* 139/2 (1995), 678; Matthiae, in *Confronting the Past*, 101, fig. 14.

390 Ben-Tor's Design Class 3D and 7A2. Ben-Tor, *Scarabs*, 21-22, 27-28.

391 Ben-Tor, *Scarabs*, pl. 15 [40]; Petrie, Brunton and Murray, *Lahun* 2, pl. 65 [354].

392 Ben-Tor, *Scarabs*, pl. 12 [20]; Petrie and Quibell, *Naqada and Ballas*, pl. 80 [63]; Scandone-Matthiae, in *Scarabs of the Second Millennium BC*, fig. 2 [4].

393 Ben-Tor, *Scarabs*, pl. 16 [2]; Gratien, *CRIPEL* 22 (2001), fig. 3 [7A-35].

394 Ben-Tor's Design Class 2A. Scandone-Matthiae, in *Scarabs of the Second Millennium BC*, 196, fig. 2 [1]; Ben-Tor, *Scarabs*, 74, 159, pls 32 [16, 19-20, 27, 29], 75 [1-5].

395 Peyronel, in *Synchronisation of Civilisations* 3, 413, fig. 16.

396 Peyronel, in *Synchronisation of Civilisations* 3, 413.

397 Scandone-Matthiae, in *Scarabs of the Second Millennium BC*, 197, fig. 3 [1].

398 Matthiae, *Syria* 46 (1969), 1-43, figs 1-3, pls 1-2; Matthiae, *Ebla in the Amorite Dynasties*, fig. 7, pl. 12 [ill. 16]; Matthiae, in *Cultures in Contact*, 106-107, fig. 12.

399 Matthiae, in *Cultures in Contact*, 106-107.

400 Matthiae, *BA* 47/1 (1984), 27-28; Scandone-Matthiae, in *Hyksos*, 417-420, fig. 15 [5].

401 Matthiae, *BA* 47/1 (1984), 28; Scandone-Matthiae, in *Hyksos*, 418.

402 Ryholt, *BASOR* 311 (1998), 4.

403 Ryholt, *BASOR* 311 (1998), 4. Lilyquist writes that the hatching in the

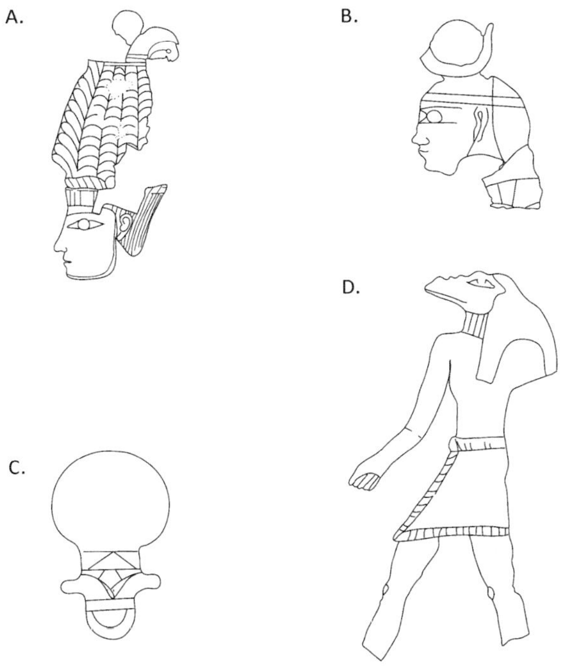

FIGURE 6.21. IVORY PLAQUES, NORTHERN PALACE, EBLA (NOT TO SCALE). AFTER MATTHIAE, PINNOCK AND SCANDONE-MATTHIAE, *EBLA*, 476-477 (DRAWN FROM PHOTOGRAPHS).

exact Egyptian parallels.[404] The third elite tomb beneath the Western Palace, the Tomb of the Cisterns, produced a similar mace, its handle comprising a cylinder decorated with lozenges resembling that of a Byblite knife handle.[405] Consequently, the mace from the Tomb of the Lord of the Goats could justifiably be of Levantine manufacture.[406]

The reading 'Hotepibra' has been associated with Hotepibra *ꜥ3mw/Ḳm3w*-Sihornedjheritef of early Dynasty 13, primarily because of the closeness in date between his reign and the Tomb of the Lord of the Goats.[407] Connections between the so-called Asiatic king and the Eblaite dynasty have also been proposed.[408] Disregarding the issues in identifying this king as an Asiatic,[409] the association of 'Hotepibra' with *ꜥ3mw/Ḳm3w*-Sihornedjheritef is uncertain.[410] 'Hotepibra' could be linked to Amenemhat I's throne name or Thirteenth Dynasty king 'Sihotepibra', bearing in mind the possibility that the glyphs were restored and the 's' may have been lost.[411] Additionally, the hieroglyphs are not encircled by a cartouche nor paired with a title or epithet;[412] only the baboons' posture signals that they are of significance. Therefore, the mace cannot definitively point to direct relations between Ebla and *ꜥ3mw/Ḳm3w*-Sihornedjheritef's reign. Nonetheless, it does evince three key points: it reflects the fusion of Egyptian and Levantine characteristics, as well as Egyptian hieroglyphs; its artistic elements indicate wealth; and its deposition in an elite tomb demonstrates a relation to Levantine funerary customs. Accordingly, the mace is likely a marker of prestige and status.

Another significant find occurs in a room within the Northern Palace (P).[413] Ivory plaques were discovered on the floor, possibly detached from a piece of furniture such as a bed-head or a throne.[414] They represent a variety of detailed figures, some of which emulate the Egyptian style. For example, one male head is shown in profile with an *3tf*-crown (Figure 6.21A),[415] two others wear the double feather crown,[416] a female is adorned with horns and a sun-disk (Figure 6.21B), and a lotiform panel is preserved (Figure 6.21C).[417] Two additional antithetic fragments represent a falcon-headed figure, whereas another inlay preserves the full body of a crocodile-headed individual (Figure 6.21D).[418] Such Egyptian elements are manifestations of royalty and divinity. The Levantine artist(s) who crafted the inlays was thereby well-versed in Egyptian symbolism and art. The choice to pair the inlays with a piece of palatial furniture further highlights the association of Egyptian art with Eblaite elitism and power.

This association is supported by the other finds from Ebla. From the late MBIIA, burials of the ruling elite included Egyptian imports and imitations with an apparent rise in number during the second half of the MBA. Contexts of administrative function, such as a unit near the Western Rampart as well as the Northern and Western Palaces, yielded items of mixed Egyptian-Levantine artistic styles, some of which bear symbols of royalty and divinity. While exact contextual data on the scarabs and *ꜥnrꜥ* cylinder seal is not yet published, the objects' presence in occupation levels suggests that another echelon of Eblaite society could have had access to Egyptian-influenced products. Whether these products were locally made or imported from another Levantine centre is unclear, yet it is evident that Egyptian symbols were adapted by Levantines, signalling the Eblaite elite's representation of their own nobility and status through Egyptian iconography.

ib sign points to its Levantine origin (*BASOR* 290-291 [1993], 46).

404 Ryholt, *BASOR* 311 (1998), 4.

405 Matthiae, *BA* 47/1 (1984), 27; Nigro, in *Interconnections in the Eastern Mediterranean*, 164-165, fig. 12; Montet, *Byblos et l'Égypte*, 180, pl. 102 [655].

406 As also inferred in Lilyquist, *BASOR* 290-291 (1993), 46; Ryholt, *BASOR* 311 (1998), 4.

407 Matthiae, *BA* 47/1 (1984), 25, 28; Scandone-Matthiae, in *Hyksos*, 417-420; Bietak, *BASOR* 281 (1991), 49.

408 Matthiae, *BA* 47/1 (1984), 25, 28; Scandone-Matthiae, in *Hyksos*, 417-420.

409 See Chapter 4.2.2.3, n. 78, for attestations of this name and for further discussion.

410 Ryholt, *BASOR* 311 (1998), 4.

411 Ryholt, *BASOR* 311 (1998), 4; Bietak, *BASOR* 281 (1991), 49 n. 22.

412 Ryholt, *BASOR* 311 (1998), 4.

413 There is some confusion in the literature regarding the find-spot. Ahrens writes that the ivories are from a room 'close to the throne room' (in *Intercultural Contacts in the Ancient Mediterranean*, 298) while Akkermans and Schwartz report that they are from the throne room itself (*Archaeology of Syria*, 300). Matthiae's recent publication is followed here (Matthiae, in *Beyond Babylon*, 37). See also Scandone-Matthiae, in *Hyksos*, 420.

414 Scandone-Matthiae, in *Hyksos*, 420; Matthiae, in *Beyond Babylon*, 37.

415 Scandone-Matthiae, in *Hyksos*, 420, fig. 15 [6]; Matthiae, in *Beyond Babylon*, 37, fig. 9; Ahrens, in *Intercultural Contacts in the Ancient Mediterranean*, fig. 5.

416 Scandone-Matthiae, in *Hyksos*, 420.

417 Scandone-Matthiae, in *Hyksos*, 420, fig. 15 [7]; Akkermans and Schwartz, *Archaeology of Syria*, 300, fig. 9 [7].

418 Scandone-Matthiae, in *Hyksos*, 420-421, fig. 15 [8, 11].

6.3.5 *Fad'ous, Tell / Kfar'abida*

Lat.Lon. 34°13'N 35°39'E

Refs Genz et al., *BAAL* 13 (2009), 78; Genz et al., *BAAL* 14 (2010), 247-249, 252, 265, figs 10, 12, pls 4 [2], 5 [5], 13; Genz, *Berytus* 53-54 (2010/2011), 116-118, figs 7 [3], 14 [1-2].

Chron. Late Twelfth to Thirteenth Dynasty / Late MBIIA or MBIIA-B Period

North of Byblos is the coastal site of Tell Fad'ous.[419] The tell's MBA settlement has been preliminarily suggested to be of rural rather than maritime nature, dedicated to agricultural and fishing activities.[420] The existence of regional and Egyptian imports indicates that at least some inhabitants had access to high-value commodities.[421] The Egyptian material occurs in contexts assigned to Area II Phase VI or the late MBIIA to transitional MBIIA-B period:

- Tomb 736: A hemispherical cup with a round base was found, parallels of which are attested at Tell el-Dab'a.[422] The form is typical of the Middle Kingdom and Second Intermediate Period.[423] Unlike Egyptian examples, the Tell Fad'ous/Kfar'abida cup does not show signs of knife-trimming on its base and its fabric is of local clay.[424] Thus the cup is likely a local imitation of an Egyptian food/drink receptacle.

  The tomb's owner, a female, also had a scarab on one of her right hand fingers.[425] Its base is designed with a paired scroll border encapsulating symmetrical *wḏ3.t* eyes and a *nbw* sign (Figure 6.22).[426] The border's vertical setting is akin to late Middle Kingdom examples.[427] The *wḏ3.t* design gains popularity towards the late Middle Kingdom and is found on scarabs displaying both Egyptian and Levantine characteristics.[428] Therefore, the exact origin of the scarab cannot be ascertained.[429] The designs, however, are suggestive of a date in the late Twelfth to Thirteenth Dynasty,[430] agreeing with that offered by radiocarbon tests on samples from the tomb.[431]

- Context 1707: A pit, possibly for storage, contained a late Middle Kingdom carinated bowl with a spout.[432]

- Context 531: A pit, perhaps for storage,[433] yielded a globular cooking pot akin to late Twelfth Dynasty vessels, as well as body sherds of an Egyptian zir.[434]

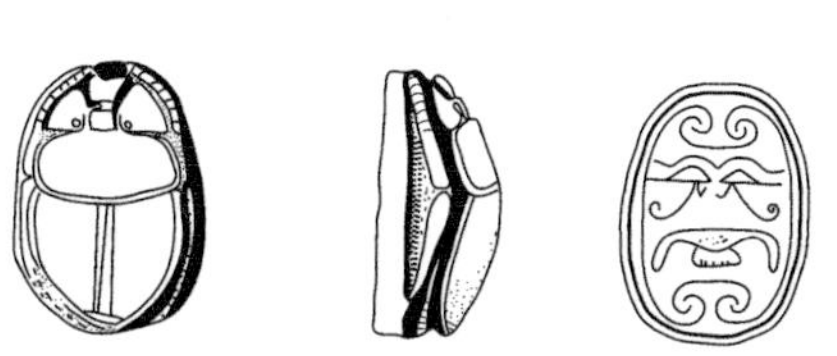

FIGURE 6.22. SCARAB, TELL FAD'OUS (NOT TO SCALE). AFTER GENZ ET AL., *BAAL* 14 (2010), PL. 13.

The Egyptian vessels' shapes point to their use for storing, preparing and serving food, indicating some degree of Egyptian influence over local customs. Similarly, the locally made Egyptian-type cup from Tomb 736 highlights the existence of such influences on local pottery workshops. This cup, together with the scarab, signify the use of Egyptian(-influenced) items for local funerary traditions. For a site that was apparently rural, the variety of such Egyptian finds emphasises that Tell Fad'ous was in contact with Egypt during the late MBIIA or MBIIA-B period. The site's excavator suggests that the items first arrived at Byblos and were then transported overland to Tell Fad'ous, but whether or not Egyptians visited the site cannot be verified by the present evidence.[435] Nonetheless, it is clear that its inhabitants were receiving, using and modifying Egyptian products of the contemporary late Twelfth to Thirteenth Dynasty.

419 Genz and Sader, *BAAL* 11 (2007), 7-16; Genz and Sader, *BAAL* 12 (2008), 149-159; Genz et al., *BAAL* 13 (2009), 71-123; Genz et al., *BAAL* 14 (2010), 241-274; Genz et al., *E&L* 20 (2010), 183-205; Genz, *NEA* 73/2-3 (2010), 102-113; Genz, *Berytus* 53-54 (2010/2011), 115-132.

420 Personal communication with Hermann Genz; Genz, *Berytus* 53-54 (2010/2011), 118; Genz and Sader, *BAAL* 11 (2007), 15; Genz and Sader, *BAAL* 12 (2008), 158; Genz, *NEA* 73/2-3 (2010), 111-112; Pederson, *BAAL* 11 (2007), 17-23; Pederson, *Skyllis* 12/1 (2012), 6-7, 9.

421 Genz, *E&L* 20 (2010), 201.

422 Genz et al., *BAAL* 14 (2010), 249, pl. 4 [2]; Genz, *Berytus* 53-54 (2010/2011), 116, fig. 7 [3]; Tufnell, *Berytus* 18 (1969), fig. 2 [2-4]; Czerny, in *MBA in the Levant*, 133-134; Aston, *TeD* 12, 62-66.

423 Czerny, in *MBA in the Levant*, 133-134; Genz et al., *BAAL* 14 (2010), 249; Genz, *Berytus* 53-54 (2010/2011), 116; Aston, *TeD* 12, 62-66.

424 Genz et al., *BAAL* 14 (2010), 249; Genz, *Berytus* 53-54 (2010/2011), 116-117.

425 Genz et al., *BAAL* 14 (2010), 247-249, figs 10, 12, pl. 13.

426 Respectively, Ben-Tor's Design Classes 7B1ii, 3B4 and 3B. Genz et al., *BAAL* 14 (2010), 265, pl. 13; Ben-Tor, *Scarabs*, 19, 28, 142, 131.

427 Ben-Tor, *Scarabs*, 19, 28, 131, 142, pl. 16 [10-15].

428 Ben-Tor, *Scarabs*, 17, 131.

429 This has also been surmised in Genz et al., *BAAL* 14 (2010), 265.

430 Genz et al., *BAAL* 14 (2010), 265.

431 Genz et al., *BAAL* 14 (2010), 267-268, figs 28-29.

432 Genz et al., *BAAL* 14 (2010), 252, pl. 5 [5]; Genz, *Berytus* 53-54 (2010/2011), 116, 118, fig. 14 [1]; Aston, *TeD* 12, 90-91.

433 Genz et al., *BAAL* 13 (2009), 78; Genz, *Berytus* 53-54 (2010/2011), 116.

434 Personal examination granted by Hermann Genz; Genz, *Berytus* 53-54 (2010/2011), 118, fig. 14 [2]; Czerny, in *MBA in the Levant*, 138, fig. 23.

435 Personal communication with Hermann Genz.

6.3.6 *Sakka, Tell*

Lat.Lon. 33°26'N 36°27'E

Ref. Taraqji, *BSFE* 144 (1999), 35-41, figs 9-12.

Chron. Thirteenth to early Fifteenth Dynasty / Late MBIIA to MBIIB Period

Excavations at Tell Sakka in western Syria have uncovered a large public building, possibly a palace.[436] The structure is attributed to the site's Level 4 of the late MBIIA to MBIIB period.[437] The floor of a major columned hall yielded fragments of wall paintings.[438] Although partially published, the paintings imbue several Egyptian aspects. One fragment pictures two bearded men (Figure 6.23A).[439] They are shown in Egyptian profile-view but their clothing and hairstyle are not of the Egyptian style. Another fragment depicts a head, also in profile-view, wearing a white headband decorated with a cobra, an *ꜣtf*-crown and ram horns (Figure 6.23B).[440] Remnants of an arc above the head suggest that the figure could be standing in a niche-like structure such as a shrine. Taraqji identifies the figure as either a deity or a royal, noting the adaptation of Egyptian status markers by Tell Sakka's elite.[441] A third unpublished fragment reportedly illustrates women wearing colourful ornamented garments inspired by Egyptian female dress.[442]

Tell Sakka's paintings clearly reflect Egyptian inspirations,[443] but the presence of fragments displaying Near Eastern motifs suggests other Levantine influences.[444] The customisation of the Egyptian elements with local details implies that the artists were not Egyptian, although they were knowledgeable in Egyptian art, particularly Egyptian symbols of power and divine authority.

A.

B.

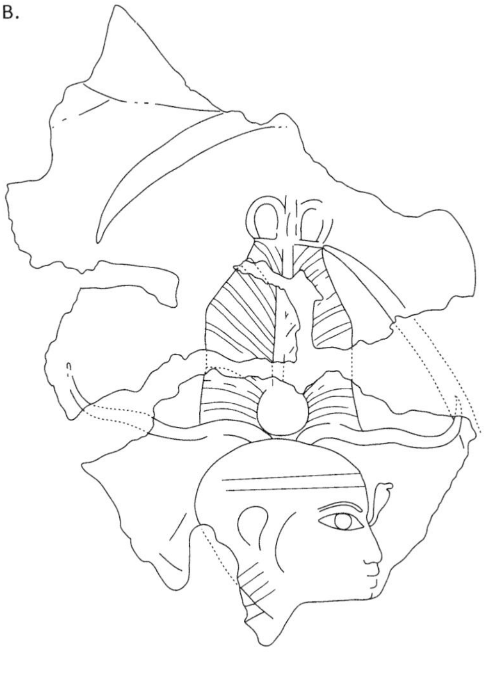

Figure 6.23. Wall paintings, Tell Sakka (not to scale). (a) After Taraqji, *BSFE* 144 (1999), figs 9-10; (b) After Taraqji, in *Beyond Babylon*, fig. 70 (drawn from photograph).

436 Taraqji, *BSFE* 144 (1999), 27-43.

437 Taraqji's MBII period (Taraqji, *BSFE* 144 [1999], 35, 40). Bietak proposes an MBIIB date relying on the MBIIB types of Tell el-Yahudiyah ware uncovered in the palace (Bietak, in *Synchronisation of Civilisations* 3, 279, n. 97).

438 Taraqji, *BSFE* 144 (1999), 36-37; Taraqji, in *Beyond Babylon*, 128. The excavation report does not comment on the painting technique or whether there were any traces of red guidelines or sketches. To the author's knowledge, no analysis has been done on its pigments.

439 Taraqji, *BSFE* 144 (1999), 37-39, fig. 9.

440 Taraqji, *BSFE* 144 (1999), 39, fig. 10; Taraqji, in *Beyond Babylon*, 128, fig. 70 [a].

441 Taraqji, *BSFE* 144 (1999), 39; Taraqji, in *Beyond Babylon*, 128-129.

442 Taraqji, *BSFE* 144 (1999), 39; Taraqji, in *Beyond Babylon*, 128-129.

443 Taraqji, *BSFE* 144 (1999), 39-40; Taraqji, in *Beyond Babylon*, 128-129.

444 Taraqji, *BSFE* 144 (1999), 39, fig. 11; Taraqji, in *Beyond Babylon*, fig. 70 [b]; Bietak, in *Synchronisation of Civilisations* 3, 279; Akkermans and Schwartz, *Archaeology of Syria*, fig. 9 [20].

6.3.7 Sidon

Lat.Lon. 33°32'N 35°22'E

Refs Doumet-Serhal, *Levant* 36 (2004), 89-154; Taylor, *Levant* 36 (2004), 155-158; Mlinar, *AHL* 20 (2004), 61-64; Doumet-Serhal, *BAAL* 10 (2006), 131-165; Forstner-Müller and Kopetzky, *AHL* 24 (2006), 52-62; Doumet-Serhal, *AHL* 24 (2006), 34-47; Loffet, *AHL* 24 (2006), 78-84; Doumet-Serhal, *BAAL* 13 (2009), 7-69; Mlinar, *AHL* 29 (2009), 23-45; Bader et al., *AHL* 29 (2009), 23-45; Loffet, *AHL* 34-35 (2011/2012), 104-138; Kopetzky, *AHL* 34-35 (2011/2012), 163-172.

Chron. Twelfth to early Fifteenth Dynasty / MBIIA to MBIIC Period

Eight MBA strata have been identified at the College Site, Sidon. Levels 1-3 contained MBIIA burials and offering deposits, and Levels 4-8 featured MBIIA-B to MBIIC cultic structures, burials and funerary deposits.[445] The site's position on the coast possibly supplied links to a trade network spanning the east Mediterranean region.[446] Egyptian(-influenced) artefacts occur across all MBA phases and are presented below according to their stratigraphy, with the exclusion of MBIIC Levels 7-8.[447] As publications are preliminary, the nature and function of several contexts cannot yet be determined. Some relevant material also remains unpublished, including Egyptian scarabs as well as a large number of Egyptian ceramics of Twelfth to Fifteenth Dynasty forms from occupation deposits.[448]

6.3.7.1 Level 1: MBIIA Period

Level 1 burials were found in a fine sand deposit raised over the EBA settlement.[449] The tombs' construction and equipment suggest that this phase was possibly used by the elite.[450] Five published tombs contain Egyptian(-influenced) items. Of these, Burial 12 yielded three scarabs with scrolls ending in lotus flowers, paralleling scarabs from the first half of Dynasty 12 (Figure 6.24 [1-2]).[451] Burial 74 also yielded a scarab displaying interlocking scrolls and hieroglyphic symbols (Figure 6.24 [3]),[452] and Burial 74-75 contained a scarab portraying a *nbw* sign surmounted by two confronting red crowns (Figure 6. 24 [4]).[453] Both scarabs have parallels in Egypt and the Levant, but are more akin to late Middle Kingdom examples.[454] The fourth tomb, Burial 78, included two scarabs displaying geometric motifs,[455] a third with a lotiform design,[456] and a fourth with a *s3* hieroglyph (Figure 6.24 [5]).[457] All are likely early Middle Kingdom imports.[458] The fifth tomb, Burial 13, contained a handmade globular Marl C jar comparable to Twelfth Dynasty vessels dating from the reign of Senwosret I to late Dynasty 12.[459] Based on the finds from these burials, Doumet-Serhal has preliminarily correlated Level 1 with the first half of Dynasty 12.[460]

6.3.7.2 Level 2: MBIIA Period

Level 2 is defined by burials within the sandy deposit that overlays EBA structures.[461] Scarabs with features indicative of their Egyptian origin were retrieved from three tombs (Burials 42, 45 and 55) (Figure 6.24 [6-7]). The bases display such designs as a central motif ending with a lotus on either side,[462] and double horizontal bows connected by central lines.[463] An imported amethyst scarab was additionally collected from Burial 55.[464]

The ceramic repertoire consists of two complete vessels indicating trade with Upper and Lower Egypt during the second half of the Twelfth Dynasty. One is a globular Marl C-1 zir that was found in a secondary context as a burial container (Burial 24) . The zir is of rim Type 3 dating from the period post-Senwosret II to the middle of Dynasty 13.[465] The second vessel is a globular Marl A-2 jar that was recovered from atop a burial. It exhibits similarities to jars dating between the reigns of Senwosret I and III.[466] Three other fragments of zirs have additionally been reported from Level 2, although their contexts are not published.[467]

---

445 Doumet-Serhal, *BAAL* 3 (1998/1999), 181-224; Doumet-Serhal, *BAAL* 4 (2000), 75-122; Doumet-Serhal, *BAAL* 5 (2001), 153-172; Doumet-Serhal, *BAAL* 6 (2002), 179-210; Doumet-Serhal, *BAAL* 7 (2003), 175-207; Doumet-Serhal, *BAAL* 8 (2004), 47-82; Doumet-Serhal, *BAAL* 10 (2006), 131-135; Doumet-Serhal, *BAAL* 13 (2009), 7-69; Doumet-Serhal, *Levant* 36 (2004), 89-154.

446 Doumet-Serhal, *AHL* 24 (2006), 34-47; Doumet-Serhal, in *Networking Patterns*, 9-19; Doumet-Serhal, in *Cultures in Contact*, 132-141.

447 Doumet-Serhal, in *Bronze Age in the Lebanon*, 24.

448 Doumet-Serhal and Kopetzky are currently working on clarifying the levels' correlations with the Egyptian chronology. X-ray spectrometry analyses carried out on some sherds verify their Egyptian origin. Personal communication with Claude Doumet-Serhal and Karin Kopetzky; Griffiths and Ownby, *AHL* 24 (2006), 63-77.

449 Doumet-Serhal, in *Bronze Age in the Lebanon*, 17.

450 Doumet-Serhal, *AHL* 24 (2006), 35.

451 Ben-Tor's Design Class 1E and 2A. Doumet-Serhal, *BAAL* 5 (2001), 164; Doumet-Serhal, *AHL* 18 (2003), 10, fig. 12; Mlinar, *AHL* 20 (2004), 63; Ben-Tor, *Scarabs*, 10-13.

452 Ben-Tor's Design Class 2B. Doumet-Serhal, *BAAL* 13 (2009), 22; Loffet, *AHL* 34-35 (2011/2012), 109; Ben-Tor, *Scarabs*, 124.

453 Ben-Tor's Design Class 3B6. Loffet, *AHL* 34-35 (2011/2012), 110; Ben-Tor, *Scarabs*, 132.

454 Ben-Tor, *Scarabs*, pls 4 [28, 54, 56-57], 8 [45-46, 48-50].

455 Ben-Tor's Design Class 1B. Loffet, *AHL* 34-35 (2011/2012), 111; Ben-Tor, *Scarabs*, 10.

456 Ben-Tor's Design Class 1E. Loffet, *AHL* 34-35 (2011/2012), 112; Ben-Tor, *Scarabs*, 10-11.

457 Loffet classifies the scarab as of the 'omega' class (*AHL* 34-35 [2011/2012], 112), which appears after the beginning of the MBIIB. Vanessa Boschloos has confirmed that the scarab bears the *s3* hieroglyph (personal communication), supporting the tomb's assignment to Phase 1. The scarab is therefore of Ben-Tor's Design Class 3A3 (Ben-Tor, *Scarabs*, 15-17).

458 Personal communication with Claude Doumet-Serhal and Vanessa Boschloos.

459 Doumet-Serhal, *Levant* 36 (2004), 94; Doumet-Serhal, *AHL* 24 (2006), 39, fig. 8; Bader, *AHL* 18 (2003), 31-34, fig. 1.

460 Doumet-Serhal, *AHL* 18 (2003), 9.

461 Doumet-Serhal, *AHL* 24 (2006), 36.

462 Ben-Tor's Design Class 1E and 5. Doumet-Serhal, *BAAL* 8 (2007), 54; Doumet-Serhal, in *Networking Patterns*, 21 [23]; Ben-Tor, *Scarabs*, 10-12, 23-24, pls 1 [48-50], 12 [45].

463 Ben-Tor's Design Class 1B. Doumet-Serhal, *BAAL* 8 (2007), 55-56; Mlinar, *AHL* 29 (2009), 23-24; Ben-Tor, *Scarabs*, 122.

464 Doumet-Serhal, *BAAL* 8 (2007), 60.

465 Bader, *AHL* 18 (2003), 34-36, fig. 4; Doumet-Serhal, *AHL* 24 (2006), 39, fig. 9; Bader et al., *AHL* 29 (2009), 79-83; Forstner-Müller, Kopetzky and Doumet-Serhal, *AHL* 24 (2006), 55.

466 Doumet-Serhal, *AHL* 24 (2006), 39, fig. 13; Forstner-Müller and Kopetzky, *AHL* 24 (2006), 60-62, figs 1-3.

467 Doumet-Serhal, *AHL* 24 (2006), 39.

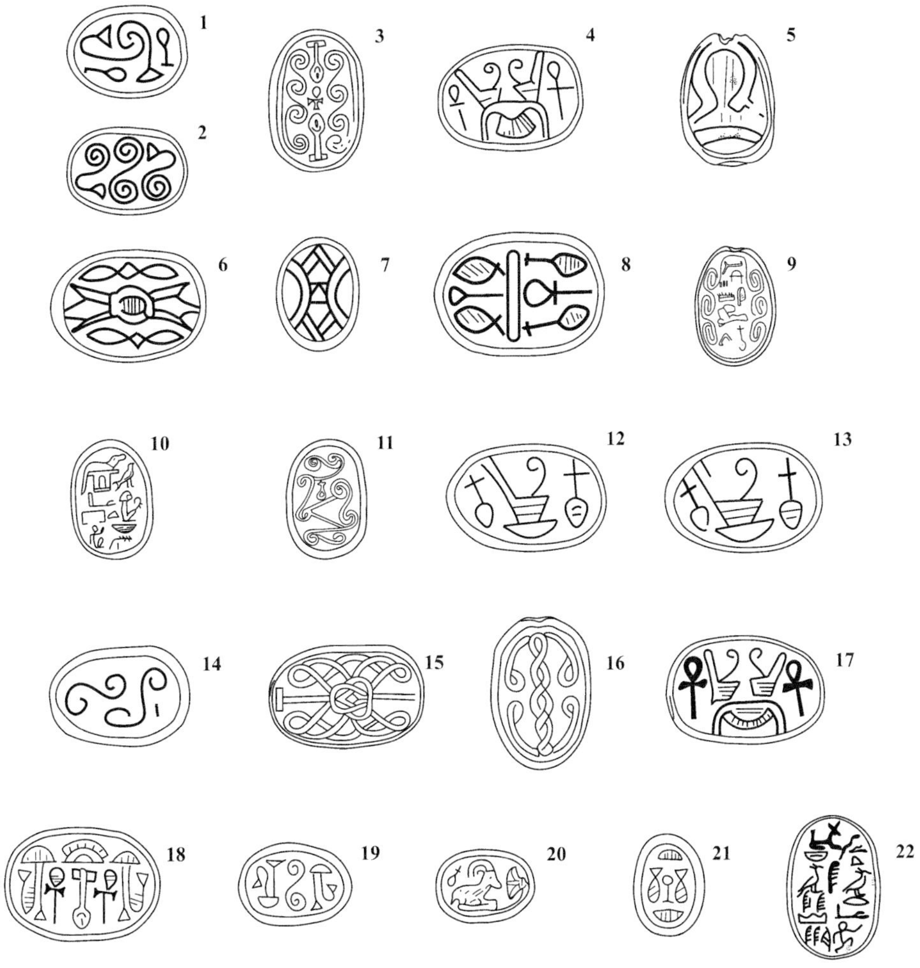

FIGURE 6.24. SELECTED SCARABS, SIDON (NOT TO SCALE).
AFTER LOFFET, *AHL* 34-35 (2011/2012), 105-106, 109-113, 116-119; DOUMET-SERHAL, IN *NETWORKING PATTERNS*, 21-22; MLINAR, *AHL* 20 (2004), 61-63; MLINAR, *AHL* 29 (2009), 23-24; GUBEL AND LOFFET, *AHL* 34-35 (2011/2012), 79 (DRAWN FROM PHOTOGRAPHS).

6.3.7.3 Level 3: MBIIA Period

The last stratum within the sandy deposit is Level 3. Burial 10 contained a scarab that can almost definitively be identified as an import. The base is divided into two rows, one depicting a lotus flanked by stylised *s3* signs, and the other a *ʿnḫ* sign with two *nfr* symbols (Figure 6.24 [8]).[468] Parallels from el-Lahun[469] and Uronarti[470] suggest that the scarab is of Thirteenth Dynasty date.

19 sherds of Egyptian fabric have also been noted by the excavator, 12 of which reportedly belonged to zirs and seven to small globular jars and long corrugated jars.[471] Details on their contexts and fabrics have not yet been published, but they have been used to synchronise Level 3 with Thirteenth Dynasty Egypt.[472] The date agrees with that assigned to the scarab from Burial 10.

6.3.7.4 Level 4: MBIIA-B Period

Level 4 represents the first occupation layer above the sandy deposit. Burial 29 yielded the site's earliest recorded attestation of a private-name scarab.[473] The item bears interlinked oblong scrolls bordering *ỉm.y-r3 mḏ.wt Ỉmn-(m)-ḥ3(.t)-nfr-ỉw* 'overseer of cattle-pens,[474] Amenemhatnoferiu' (Figure 6.24 [9]).[475] The scarab has been stylistically dated to Dynasty 12[476] and is most likely an import. Although it is possible that it was made for the individual interred in Burial 29, a few cases of private-name scarabs from Levantine tombs have exact parallels in Egypt, suggesting that the Sidon scarab was more likely retrieved from its original Egyptian context and then transported to the Levant.[477] Scarabs displaying Levantine

468 Ben-Tor's Design Class 1E and 3A3. Doumet-Serhal, *Levant* 36 (2004), 92, 112, table 14; Mlinar, *AHL* 20 (2004), 62-63; Ben-Tor, *Scarabs*, 10-12, 16-17, pls 1 [14], 7 [19, 28-29].
469 Petrie, Brunton and Murray, *Lahun* 2, pls 64 [274], 65 [337].
470 Reisner, *Kush* 3 (1955), fig. 13 [316, 323-344].
471 Doumet-Serhal, *AHL* 24 (2006), 39.
472 Doumet-Serhal, *AHL* 24 (2006), 39; Doumet-Serhal, *AHL* 20 (2003), 13.
473 Doumet-Serhal, *BAAL* 7 (2003), 184; Loffet, *AHL* 34-35 (2011/2012), 105-106.
474 Ward, *Index*, 30 [216].
475 The name is not attested in Ranke, *Personennamen*, but is clearly of Egyptian origin. For similar names, see Ranke, *Personennamen* 1, 28 [8-13].
476 Loffet, *AHL* 34-35 (2011/2012), 105.
477 For more on private-name scarabs in Levantine contexts, see

characteristics such as meaningless hieroglyphs have also been found in Burials 20, 22 and 95,[478] demonstrating the manufacture of scarabs for local funerary traditions.

Over 50 sherds of Egyptian Marl C clay come from Level 4's cultic occupation deposits,[479] the highest number thus far uncovered in the Levant. The majority are from zirs with rim Type 3 that date after Senwosret II's reign until the mid-Thirteenth Dynasty.[480] Other sherds belong to globular medium-sized jars with parallels from post-Senwosret I's reign to the mid-Thirteenth Dynasty, bag-shaped medium-sized jars akin to late Twelfth to mid-Fifteenth Dynasty forms, as well as large jars with corrugated necks paralleling vessels from the Twelfth to mid-Fifteenth Dynasty.[481] A jar with a rolled rim was also found, its rare form similar to a late Twelfth to early Thirteenth Dynasty jar from Elephantine.[482] As all vessels are suitable for the transport of commodities, they signify Sidon's access to a variety of Dynasty 13 goods.

6.3.7.5 Level 5: Early-mid MBIIB Period

The second occupation layer produced scarabs with MBIIB Levantine characteristics, including stylised *s3* signs with decorative elements,[483] misrendered hieroglyphs,[484] and a cross pattern.[485] Burial 104 produced a private-name scarab with features typical of the late Middle Kingdom.[486] Its base reads *Sbk-wr ir.y ꜥ.t nb im3ḫ* 'Sobekwer,[487] hall-keeper,[488] possessor of reverence' (Figure 6.24 [10]). As with Burial 29's scarab from Level 4, that of Burial 104 was possibly collected from an Egyptian context and then transported to Sidon. Other imported scarabs displaying Egyptian designs include (Figure 6.24 [12-17]): one from Burial 69 with a late Middle Kingdom design of interlocking scrolls;[489] three from Burial 1 stylistically dating to the first half of Dynasty 12, two of which bear a red crown atop a *nb* sign[490] and one showing a scroll pattern;[491] one from Burial 4 with a convoluted coil comparable to designs of the late Twelfth to Thirteenth Dynasty;[492] and one from Burial 67 portraying a central cable with encompassed coils paralleling a scarab of Mlinar's Type III from Thirteenth Dynasty Tell el-Dab'a.[493] Hence, overall, the scarabs include Twelfth Dynasty heirlooms, Thirteenth Dynasty imports, a Levantine imitation influenced by Egyptian designs, and Levantine-made scarabs.

One 'alabaster' vessel was retrieved from Burial 69.[494] No classification of its material has been reported, but its shape is similar to unguent containers from Tell el-Dab'a Strata F-E/1.[495] Burial 4 contained two further items of interest. The first is a medium-sized Marl C jar stylistically assigned to the Twelfth and Thirteenth Dynasties,[496] and the second is a hemispherical cup with a broad red band at the rim with signs of knife-trimming at the base.[497] While such features parallel those of Egyptian cups,[498] the Sidon cup was produced on a fast wheel, its fabric of Levantine origin.[499] According to its cup index, the vessel's form can be dated to the mid-Thirteenth Dynasty.[500] Its presence denotes Egyptian influences on local potters as well as locals' knowledge of contemporary Egyptian pottery techniques.

6.3.7.6 Level 6: MBIIB Period

Level 6 deposits produced scarabs and stone vessels. Two scarabs from Burial 102 are of imported materials (amethyst and rock crystal) and so could be from Egypt.[501] Published scarabs from Burials 83 and 100 are incised with characteristics such as two red crowns surmounting a *nbw* sign,[502] floral motifs combined with hieroglyphic

Ben-Tor, *BASOR* 294 (1994), 7-22.

478 Doumet-Serhal, *BAAL* 6, 190; Doumet-Serhal, *BAAL* 13, 26-27; Loffet, *AHL* 18, 26-28; Loffet, *AHL* 34-35 (2011/2012), 114.

479 Doumet-Serhal, *AHL* 24 (2006), 39; Forstner-Müller, Kopetzky and Doumet-Serhal, *AHL* 24 (2006), 52-59.

480 Doumet-Serhal, *AHL* 24 (2006), 39; Forstner-Müller, Kopetzky and Doumet-Serhal, *AHL* 24 (2006), 54-55, fig. 5.

481 Doumet-Serhal, *AHL* 24 (2006), 39; Forstner-Müller, Kopetzky and Doumet-Serhal, *AHL* 24 (2006), 52-54, figs 2-3; Kopetzky, *AHL* 34-35 (2011/2012), 166-168.

482 Forstner-Müller, Kopetzky and Doumet-Serhal, *AHL* 24 (2006), 54-55, fig. 4; Kopetzky, *AHL* 34-35 (2011/2012), 166, fig. 4 [2].

483 Ben-Tor's Design Class 3A3. Doumet-Serhal, *BAAL* 13 (2009), 30-31; Loffet, *AHL* 34-35 (2011/2012), 113-115; Ben-Tor, *Scarabs*, 126.

484 Ben-Tor's Design Class 3A3. Doumet-Serhal, *BAAL* 13 (2009), 31; Loffet, *AHL* 34-35 (2011/2012), 114-115; Ben-Tor, *Scarabs*, 126.

485 Ben-Tor's Design Class 5. Doumet-Serhal, *BAAL* 13 (2009), 32; Loffet, *AHL* 34-35 (2011/2012), 122; Ben-Tor, *Scarabs*, 137-138.

486 Doumet-Serhal, *BAAL* 13 (2009), 32; Loffet, *AHL* 34-35 (2011/2012), 106.

487 Ranke, *Personennamen* 1, 303 [27].

488 An unprovenanced scarab bears the same name and title. Ward, *Index*, 54 [452]; Martin, *Egyptian Administrative and Private-Name Seals*, 108 [1391], pl. 41 [30].

489 Vanessa Boschloos suggests that the scarab is a late Middle Kingdom import (personal communication). Ben-Tor's Design Class 2B. Doumet-Serhal, *BAAL* 13 (2009), 31; Loffet, *AHL* 34-35 (2011/2012), 109; Ben-Tor, *Scarabs*, 124, 139, 143.

490 Ben-Tor's Design Class 3B3a. Doumet-Serhal, *Levant* 36 (2004), 135; Taylor, *Levant* 36 (2004), 155-156, fig. 1; Mlinar, *AHL* 20 (2004), 61-62; Ben-Tor, *Scarabs*, 129-130.

491 Ben-Tor's Design Class 1B and 1E. Doumet-Serhal, *Levant* 36 (2004), 135; Taylor, *Levant* 36 (2004), 155-156; Mlinar, *AHL* 20 (2004), 61-62; Ben-Tor, *Scarabs*, 122.

492 Ben-Tor's Design Class 6B2. Doumet-Serhal, *Levant* 36 (2004), 131, table 25; Taylor, *Levant* 36, 157, fig. 1; Mlinar, *AHL* 20 (2004), 62; Ben-Tor, *Scarabs*, 139.

493 Ben-Tor's Design Class 6C3. Doumet-Serhal, in *Networking Patterns*, 22 [24]; Ben-Tor, *Scarabs*, 90-91, 140, pls 15 [17], 30 [9, 17], 38 [11].

494 Doumet-Serhal, in *Cultures in Contact*, 134, fig. 2; Doumet-Serhal, *BAAL* 13 (2009), fig. 46. The image in the latter is incorrectly captioned as an 'alabaster' vase from Burial 102.

495 Doumet-Serhal, *BAAL* 13 (2009), 41-42; Forstner-Müller, *TeD* 16, pls 84a [9,5426], 216a [5,2273].

496 Doumet-Serhal, *AHL* 24 (2006), 39, fig. 14; Kopetzky, *TeD* 20, 157-159, fig. 47, pls 12, 37.

497 Doumet-Serhal, *Levant* 36 (2004), 130, 139, table 25, fig. 73 [S/1735]; Forstner-Müller and Kopetzky, in *Interconnections in the Eastern Mediterranean*, 150, fig. 8.

498 Forstner-Müller and Kopetzky, in *Interconnections in the Eastern Mediterranean*, 150, fig. 8.

499 Forstner-Müller and Kopetzky, in *Interconnections in the Eastern Mediterranean*, 150; Doumet-Serhal, *Levant* 36 (2004), 130, table 25.

500 Forstner-Müller and Kopetzky, in *Interconnections in the Eastern Mediterranean*, 150, fig. 8.

501 Doumet-Serhal, *BAAL* 13 (2009), 39-40; Loffet, *AHL* 34-35 (2011/2012), 122.

502 Ben-Tor's Design Class 3B2c and 3B6. Doumet-Serhal, *BAAL* 13 (2009), 39; Loffet, *AHL* 34-35 (2011/2012), 116; Ben-Tor, *Scarabs*, 130, 132.

FIGURE 6.25. CYLINDER SEAL, SIDON. AFTER DOUMET-SERHAL, *AHL* 34-35 (2011/2012), FIGS 4-7.

symbols or scrolls,[503] a recumbent caprid smelling a lotus flower,[504] and stylised *wḏꜣ* signs (Figure 6.24 [18-21]).[505] While the scarab depicting the latter is likely of Levantine manufacture,[506] the other designs could be of either Egyptian origin or inspiration. Both cases indicate that scarabs continued to be part of the funerary assemblage.

Egyptian influence is also apparent on a cylinder seal from Burial 100 (Figure 6.25). The seal is incised with schematic Mesopotamian and Levantine motifs as well as a few Egyptian elements such as a hawk wearing an Egyptian crown, a *ꜥnḫ* symbol and a *ḏd* pillar.[507] Doumet-Serhal notes the Egyptian-influenced postures of two depicted individuals.[508] Indeed, each is represented with one leg raised, arms reaching forward, palm up, in a dance step reminiscent of the Egyptian layout dance.[509] The arms, however, are crossed in a manner comparable to that of dancers depicted in Twelfth Dynasty tombs[510] or on other 'Egyptianised' MBA cylinder seals.[511] The cylinder, with its use of Egyptian motifs, provides evidence for the appropriation of Egyptian artistic elements and their modification to suit local artistic styles.

Burial 102 yielded three stone vessels not yet published in detail. One of these is a steatite container which, based on its material, could be of Egyptian or Levantine origin.[512] Another is a piriform faience jar with a thick everted rim comparable to Middle Kingdom and Second Intermediate Period vessels.[513] The third is a haematite piriform jar with a flat top for which no exact contemporary Levantine parallels have yet been found.[514] Based on the rarity of Burial 102's piriform jars in MBIIB contexts, an Egyptian origin is possible.

From a cultic context comes one scarab found on a floor near MBIIB burials and ovens used for cultic meals.[515] Some have dated the scarab to the late Twelfth Dynasty[516] while others assign it to the late MBIIA and MBIIB periods.[517] Extensive damage on the scarab's side and back restricts a typological confirmation and lack of parallels limit further refinements on its date of manufacture. Its base is engraved with *Ḏdkꜣrꜥ mry Stḫ*[518] *nb Ꞽꜣy* '*Ḏdkꜣrꜥ*[519] beloved of Seth, lord of *Ꞽꜣy*' (Figure 6.24 [22]).[520] Based on the orthography of hieroglyphs, Loffet writes that the scarab was produced locally.[521] Knowledge of the Egyptian script is apparent in the well-drawn signs and the use of correct Egyptian grammar. Further, the inclusion of an Egyptian deity's name signals that the inhabitants of *Ꞽꜣy*, or at least *Ḏdkꜣrꜥ*, revered Seth.[522] The scarab marks the only near definite case of Levantines producing private-name scarabs in the MBIIB.

Overall, all discussed levels at Sidon contain evidence of contact with Egypt. Beginning with the first MBIIA phase at the site, a few valuable Twelfth Dynasty goods are attested. A steady flow of imports continued into

503 Ben-Tor's Design Class 1E and 3A3. Loffet, *AHL* 34-35 (2011/2012), 116-118.
504 Ben-Tor's Design Class 9B. Loffet, *AHL* 34-35 (2011/2012), 118-119; Ben-Tor, *Scarabs*, 95, 122-123, 126, 146-147.
505 Ben-Tor's Design Class 3A3. Loffet, *AHL* 34-35 (2011/2012), 113; Ben-Tor, *Scarabs*, 126.
506 Ben-Tor, *Scarabs*, 126.
507 Doumet-Serhal, *AHL* 34-35 (2011/2012), 95-99, figs 4-9.
508 Doumet-Serhal, *AHL* 34-35 (2011/2012), 97.
509 Kinney, in *Behind the Scenes*, 65, figs 2, 9-10, 15, 21, pl. 42.
510 For instance, one of the dancers depicted on the north wall of Amenemhat's tomb, Beni Hassan. Newberry, *Beni Hasan* 1, pl. 13; Kanawati and Woods, *Beni Hassan*, pl. 52.
511 Ben-Tor, *Tel Aviv* 36 (2009), 27; Doumet-Serhal, *AHL* 34-35 (2011/2012), 97.
512 Doumet-Serhal, *BAAL* 13 (2009), 39-40; Doumet-Serhal, in *Cultures in Contact*, 134, fig. 2.
513 Doumet-Serhal, in *Cultures in Contact*, fig. 3; Doumet-Serhal, *BAAL* 13 (2009), 42, fig. 48; Aston, *Ancient Egyptian Stone Vessels*; Petrie, *Gaza* 3, pl. 26 [9]; Dunand, *Byblos* 2, pl. 203 [9361]; Sparks, *Stone Vessels in the Levant*, 52-53, 317 [459-461].
514 Similar vessels are attested from later contexts. Doumet-Serhal, *BAAL* 13 (2009), 42, fig. 48a; Doumet-Serhal, in *Cultures in Contact*, 134, fig. 3; Sparks, *Stone Vessels in the Levant*, 52-53, 316 [449-453]; Petrie, *Gaza* 3, pl. 36 [7-8]; vol. 4, pl. 38 [46]; Mackay and Murray, *Gaza* 5, pl. 20 [51].
515 Doumet-Serhal, in *Cultures in Contact*, 135.
516 Goldwasser, *E&L* 16 (2006), 123.
517 Loffet, *AHL* 24 (2006), 81-83.
518 The sign could also refer to Baal.
519 Loffet translates the name as Semitic 'Sadok-Re' (Loffet, *AHL* 24 [2006], 78). The name could also be related to the Egyptian Djedkara, although this is written differently. For the Egyptian spelling, see Ranke, *Personnenamen* 1, 412 [17].
520 For more on the toponym, see Mourad, *GM* 238 (2013), 69-84. It has been connected to Sinuhe's *Ꞽꜣꜣ* and utilised as evidence of the latter's existence and proximity to Sidon (Loffet, *AHL* 24 [2006], 78-84; Gubel and Loffet, *AHL* 34-35 [2011/2012], 79, 86). See Chapter 4.6.9 for the Tale of Sinuhe.
521 Loffet, *AHL* 24 (2006), 79-80.
522 Goldwasser, *E&L* 16 (2006), 123.

MBIIA Levels 2-3 with a slight rise in Egyptian ceramics specifically for the transport of commodities, some from Upper Egypt. Level 4 contained the greatest number of Egyptian sherds, the majority of which belonged to storage containers. A number of rare Egyptian forms also occur, pointing to unique relations between MBIIA-B Sidon and Egypt. This variety of imports proposes that Sidon was likely directly trading with Dynasty 13.

Contacts continue into the MBIIB Levels 5-6, developing into locally made imitations and adaptations of Egyptian styles. Egyptian pottery was mimicked, the private-name scarab tradition was modified for a Levantine individual, and artistic elements were fused for locally produced sealings. The Levantines were utilising Egyptian language, art and pottery styles for their own commercial and funerary needs. While such influences were growing, Egyptian imports were still incoming, although, as the present evidence suggests, at a reduced scale. Therefore, it is clear that Sidon sustained relations with Egypt from the Twelfth to the first half of the Fifteenth Dynasty.

6.4 Conclusions

This chapter has investigated a total of eight Southern Levantine sites and seven Northern Levantine sites (see Figure 6.1). Egyptian material from three or more stratigraphical phases at Ashkelon, Tell Ifshar and Sidon have provided correlations with the Egyptian chronology indicating that, contrary to earlier theories, the Southern Levant had some contact with Egypt in the Twelfth Dynasty while the Northern Levant continued its relations with the Thirteenth to Fifteenth Dynasties. Based on the preliminary publications of these sites, chronological synchronisations with Egypt and Tell el-Dab'a are suggested in Figure 6.26.

6.4.1 The MBIIA Period and the early to mid-Twelfth Dynasty

Only four sites provide evidence for contact with the first half of the Twelfth Dynasty: (1) Tell Ifshar; (2) Megiddo; (3) Sidon; and (4) Byblos (Figure 6.27). The Southern Levantine site of Tell Ifshar contained a number of fragments derived from Upper and Lower Egypt in its administrative complex. Megiddo yielded one scarab, possibly imported, from a burial. Also in a funerary context are other imported scarabs at Sidon where an additional small globular Egyptian jar was collected from a Level 1 tomb. While finds from Byblos are of questionable context, the Temple of Obelisks as well as a few temple deposits, such as the Montet jar, can be assigned to the first half of the Twelfth Dynasty. The obelisks are of Egyptian inspiration and cultic deposits include a myriad of small but valuable Egyptian goods. Unlike other finds from the Levant, the deposits collect items of the First Intermediate Period to the early Middle Kingdom, hinting at ongoing contact between Byblos and Egypt from the very beginning of the MBA.

Thus, Egyptian imports from the first half of Dynasty 12 are scarce. Scarabs are imbued with a funerary, cultic and most likely elite significance, vessels for storage and transportation occur in an administrative context, and 'heirloom' artefacts and figurines are found in a cultic setting. Therefore, the early to mid-Twelfth Dynasty appears to have shared predominantly small-scale commercial relations with sites on easily navigable trade routes. Items of prestige occur in the Northern Levant, especially Byblos, where Egyptian influence is most apparent.

6.4.2 The MBIIA Period and the mid-Twelfth to early Thirteenth Dynasty

Sites yielding evidence of contact with the mid-Twelfth to early Thirteenth Dynasty are: (1) Ashkelon; (2) Gezer; (3) Tell Ifshar; (4) Megiddo; (5) Sidon; and (6) Byblos (Figure 6.28). Tell Ifshar features only two imported vessels, the reduction in number possibly due to the destruction of the site's administrative complex. Ashkelon yielded greater evidence for contact, producing local and imported sealings, a zir, a ringstand and several store-jars

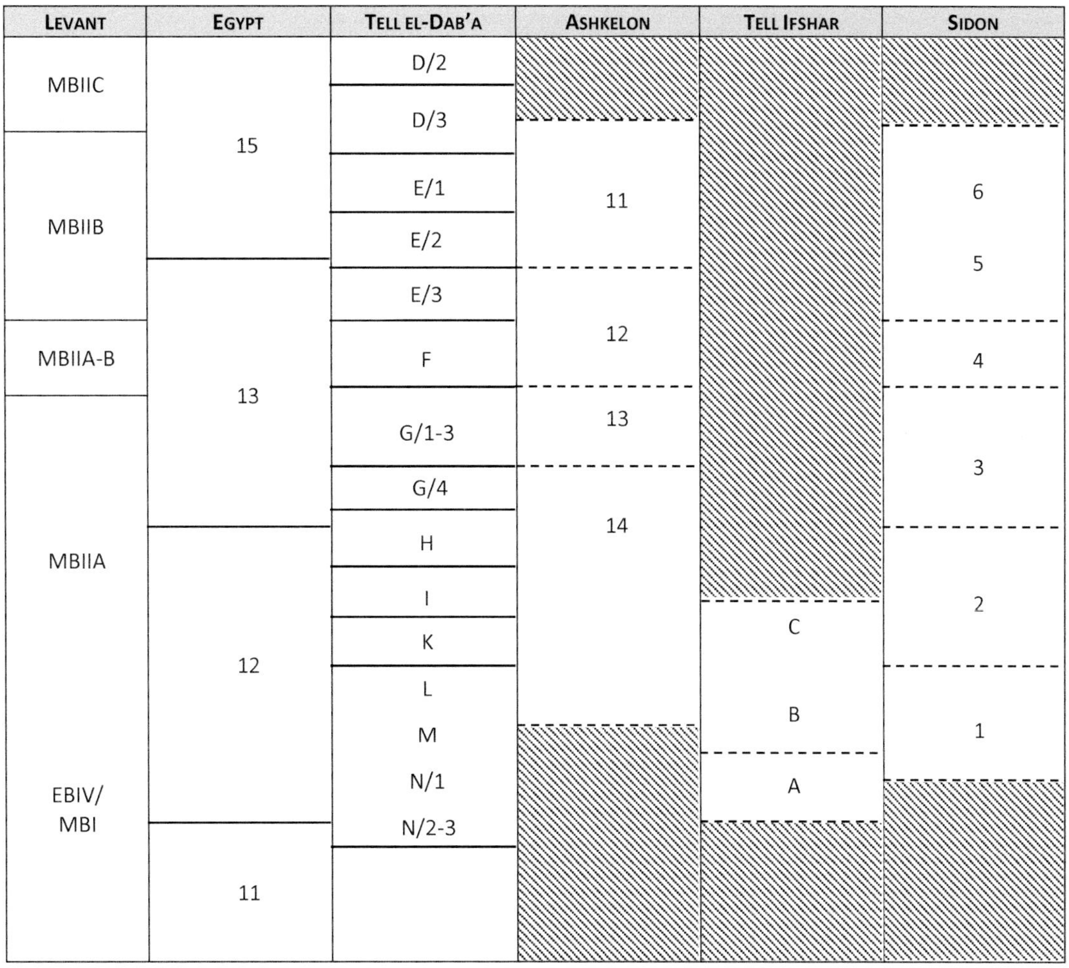
Levant
Egypt
Tell el-Dab'a
Ashkelon
Tell Ifshar
Sidon
MBIIC
MBIIB
MBIIA-B
MBIIA
EBIV/
MBI
15
13
12
11
D/2
D/3
E/1
E/2
E/3
F
G/1-3
G/4
H
I
K
L
M
N/1
N/2-3
11
12
13
14
C
B
A
6
5
4
3
2
1

Figure 6.26. Chronological correlations between selected Levantine sites, Egypt and Tell el-Dab'a, based on Egyptian material in the Levant. Cross-hatched inserts represent phases either not examined in the text, or for which no Egyptian material exists.

at/near the settlement's gate. Burials at Gezer and Megiddo contained stone vessels while Gezer additionally held scarabs bearing Egyptian designs. Sidon again consisted of scarabs in burials, but the burials also contained Egyptian storage and transport vessels from Upper and Lower Egypt, one of which was used secondarily as a jar burial. Royal Tombs I-II of Byblos included a variety of valuable Egyptian imports such as incised stone vessels, bodily adornments and scarabs, as well as precious, locally made and engraved items showing Egyptian influence.

The evidence thus suggests a continuation in Egyptian and Levantine relations which, like the first half of the Twelfth Dynasty, point to commercial relations with sites positioned on trade routes. Imported ceramics are mostly for storage and transportation, and are deposited in contexts alluding to trade (e.g. Ashkelon's gateway) or funerary significance (e.g. Sidon's jar burial). The finds are slightly more numerous in funerary contexts as Egyptian items began to be imitated by local artisans. Artefacts produced by workshops supplying Byblos betray the greatest Egyptian influence, revealing knowledge in Egyptian hieroglyphs, titles, epithets and artistic motifs. The evidence indicates that such objects, alongside prestigious imports, were initially connected to elite individuals. Apparently, Byblite ruling officials represented themselves as Levantine rulers wearing and utilising Egyptian elements of power, authority and prestige.

6.4.3 The late MBIIA to early MBIIB Period and the Thirteenth Dynasty

A marked increase in relations between the late MBIIA and early MBIIB is clear. Sites with attested Egyptian and Egyptian-influenced items include: (1) Tell el-'Ajjul; (2) Ashkelon; (3) Jericho; (4) Megiddo; (5) Tell el-Burak; (6) Sidon; (7) Tell Sakka; (8) Byblos; (9) Tell Fad'ous; (10) Tell 'Arqa; and (11) Ebla (Figure 6.29). To these may be added sites where only scarabs and impressions were found, such as Tell Aphek, Tel Aviv, Beth Shemesh, Tell el-Far'ah (N), Fassuta, Ginnosar, Tell Kabri, Rishon Lezziyon, Safed and Nahariya in the Southern Levant, and Ruweise in the Northern Levant (Figures 6.2, 6.29).

Evidence for contact with the Egyptian culture appears in varied forms and contexts:

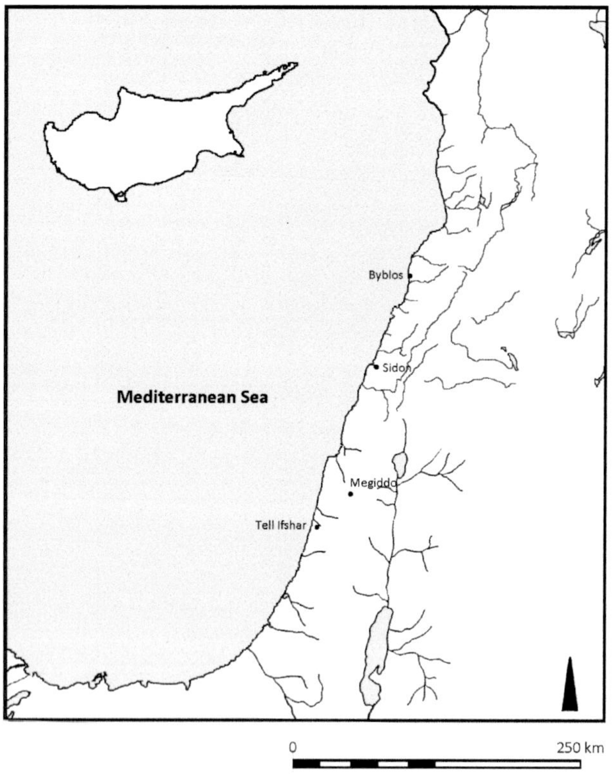

FIGURE 6.27 SITES IN THE LEVANT WITH EVIDENCE OF CONTACT WITH THE EGYPTIAN DURING THE MBIIA AND THE EARLY TO MID-TWELFTH DYNASTY.
• Presence of Egyptian(-influenced) commodities/elements

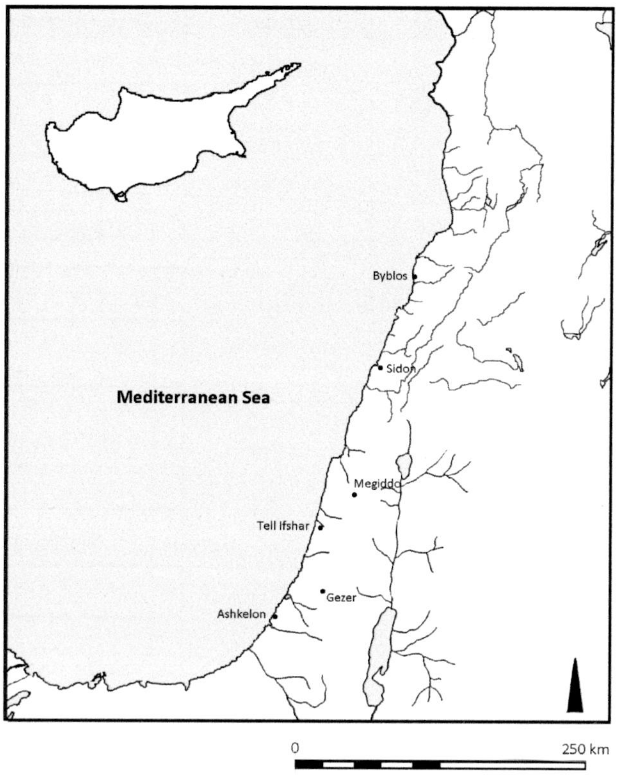

FIGURE 6.28 SITES IN THE LEVANT WITH EVIDENCE OF CONTACT WITH THE EGYPTIAN DURING THE MBIIA AND THE MID-TWELFTH TO EARLY THIRTEENTH DYNASTY.
• Presence of Egyptian(-influenced) commodities/elements

- Stone vessels occur in burials. The imported variety is at Tell el-'Ajjul, Megiddo and Byblos while those of local or uncertain origin are at Megiddo, Jericho, Sidon and Ebla;

- Scarabs and seal impressions are predominantly from funerary contexts. They are also attested in occupation levels at, for instance, Tell el-Burak and Tell Aphek. Designs are more prominently of Levantine or local origin, especially at sites where only scarab seals remain as items of Egyptian influence. The earliest recorded instances of Egyptian royal- and private-name scarabs also occur. They include three Twelfth Dynasty private-name scarabs, two at Sidon in MBIIA-B and early MBIIB burials and a third in an early MBIIB burial at Megiddo, as well as one royal-name scarab of Noferhotep I in a MBIIA-B tomb at Fassuta. Such items are most likely heirlooms, supporting an association of imported Egyptian goods with prestige and value;

- Imported vessels of Lower Egyptian fabrics come from Ashkelon, Sidon, Tell Fad'ous and Tell 'Arqa. Ashkelon's gate retained two sherds of storage and transport vessels. Ceramics of the same function were retrieved from Sidon's cultic and funerary deposits, late MBIIA occupation loci at Tell 'Arqa, and a pit at Tell Fad'ous. The latter site uniquely contained Egyptian pottery for preparing and serving food, the first of such finds in the MBA. The site preserved an imported cooking pot and a carinated bowl as well as a locally-made Egyptian-style cup in a burial. A similar cup of local fabric was unearthed in a slightly later tomb at Sidon;

- Small prestige or high-value items were collected from elite burials at Byblos and Ebla;

- Egyptian-influenced wall paintings adorn the Northern Levantine palaces of Tell el-Burak and Tell Sakka, the former possibly of an earlier date.

The evidence suggests both direct and indirect contact with Egypt. Indirect contact is represented by Egyptian-influenced, Levantine-made, objects. These are mostly found in burials, in the form of scarabs and stone vessels. Scarabs continued to be imported but local workshops began to produce a variety of Levantine design scarabs imitating Egyptian motifs. An increase in their popularity and demand has been attributed to direct relations with Asiatics in the Delta.[523] However, the evidence suggests that it is more likely related to scarabs' earlier use by the elite in funerary and cultic contexts. A rise in demand would consequently warrant the establishment of local

[523] Ben-Tor, *BASOR* 294 (1994), 11; Ben-Tor, *JAEI* 1/1 (2009), 1-7.

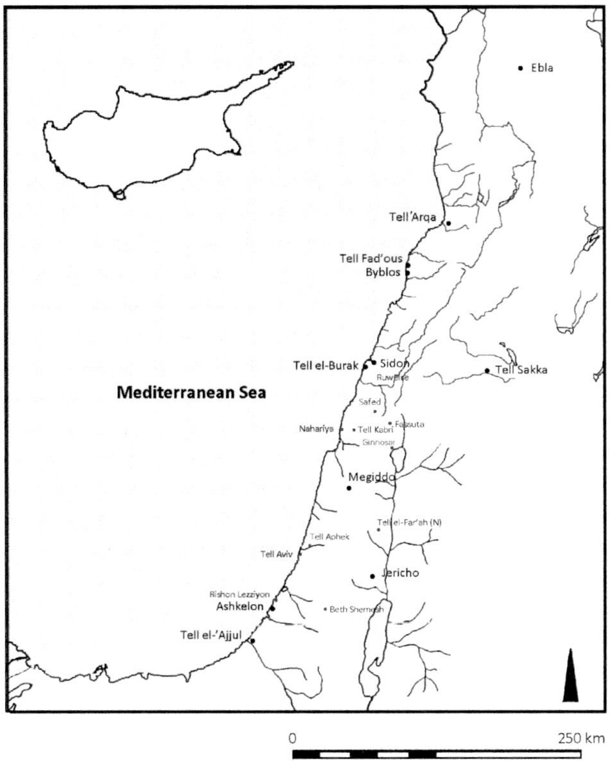

FIGURE 6.29 SITES IN THE LEVANT WITH EVIDENCE OF CONTACT WITH THE EGYPTIAN DURING THE LATE MBIIA TO EARLY MBIIB AND THE THIRTEENTH DYNASTY.
• Presence of Egyptian(-influenced) commodities/elements
· Presence of scarabs and/or seals (see Figure 7.2)

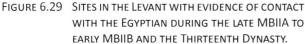

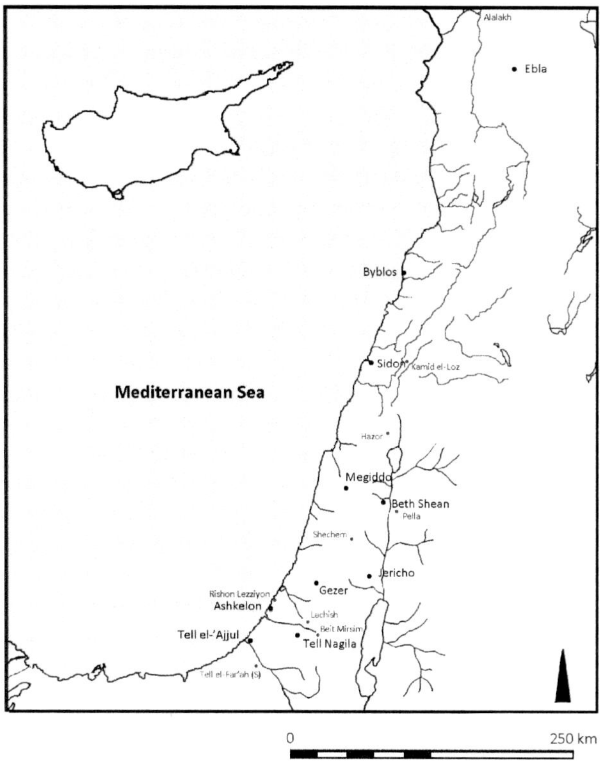

FIGURE 6.30 SITES IN THE LEVANT WITH EVIDENCE OF CONTACT WITH THE EGYPTIAN DURING THE MBIIB TO MBIIB-C AND THE EARLY FIFTEENTH DYNASTY.
• Presence of Egyptian(-influenced) commodities/elements
· Presence of scarabs and/or seals (see Figure 7.2)

markets specialised in imitations and/or the supply of imports. So, what was first only accessible to the elite as imported prestige items would have been later popularised by local workshops, retaining its connection with funerary traditions and becoming associated with amuletic significance. This also explains why Middle Kingdom Egyptian royal- and private-name scarabs appear in secondary burial contexts as heirlooms. It is also similarly reflected by the establishment of local workshops skilled in the production of Egyptian-style stone and faience vessels.

The presence of local Egyptian-style cups at Tell Fad'ous and Sidon may hint at a local ceramic workshop knowledgeable in Egyptian pottery-making techniques. Yet, as they remain the only recorded examples of their kind and both date to different periods, the cups likely indicate direct contact with Egyptians. As with other ceramics from Tell Fad'ous, the vessels suggest that non-elite individuals were using Egyptian-style ceramics for preparing and cooking foods, denoting Egyptian influence as well as the possibility that individuals of Egyptian ancestry were in the area. Their deposition in tombs emphasises a funerary significance, and it is probable that they are a remnant of a funerary ritual tradition. The vessels additionally mark a significant development in the nature of relations between Egypt and the Levant. Together with other imported ceramics, they corroborate the continuation of trade relations with Lower Egypt. Worthy of note is that all sites with imported commodities are along the coast, indicating that they were transported via maritime-based trade. The majority are also situated in the Northern Levant.

Northern Levantine sites further reflect influences from Egypt on monumental art in the form of wall paintings. Symbols of power and divinity were appropriated by Tell Sakka's artists whereas typical Egyptian artistic techniques and motifs were applied on Tell el-Burak's walls, although these may be of an earlier MBIIA date. Both sites betray paintings with mixed Egyptian-Levantine characteristics, indicating local artisans' knowledge and use of Egyptian artistic traditions. They additionally suggest a link between such traditions, elitism and palatial architecture.

Therefore, the late MBIIA to early MBIIB period witnessed new and continued Egyptian influences. Small, high-value, Egyptian adornments remained in tombs of the elite, especially those of the Northern Levant. Imported scarabs and stone vessels were deposited in funerary and occupation levels, and trade relations were concentrated at coastal Levantine sites, where only Lower Egyptian vessels are attested. Egyptian-inspired objects, formerly reserved as luxury items of the elite, became more common as local markets likely supplied a growing demand for scarabs and stone vessels. The period also observed the first recorded instances of royal- and private-name scarabs in secondary funerary contexts, Egyptian ceramics for serving and preparing food, Egyptian-style local ceramics, and possibly the appropriation of Egyptian artistic traditions in Northern Levantine palatial wall paintings. Combined, the evidence insinuates that the elite of coastal cities retained control of maritime commerce with Egypt, possibly distributing imported items to markets trading with local scarab and stone workshops. The effects of such trade may have resulted in Egyptian influences on the daily life of non-elite individuals near harbour cities like Byblos and Ashkelon, which could have feasibly received Egyptian and Egyptian-Levantine travellers, and/or newly imported technologies.

6.4.3 The MBIIB to MBIIB-C Period and the Fifteenth Dynasty

Egyptian-Levantine relations continued to develop in the MBIIB to MBIIB-C period. Contact with Egyptian cultural elements is attested at (1) Tell el-'Ajjul; (2) Tell Nagila; (3) Ashkelon; (4) Gezer; (5) Jericho; (6) Beth Shean; (7) Megiddo; (8) Sidon; (9) Byblos; and (10) Ebla (Figure 6.30). Some sites only include sealings, such as Beit Mirsim, Tell el-Far'ah (S), Hazor, Lachish, Pella, Rishon Lezziyon and Shechem in the Southern Levant, as well as Alalakh and Kamid el-Loz in the Northern Levant (Figures 6.2, 6.30).

As with the late MBIIA to early MBIIB period, the evidence includes:

- Stone vessels, which are mostly found in burials at Beth Shean, Jericho, Byblos, Sidon and Ebla. A few were collected from occupation levels at Beth Shean and Jericho. As for the vessels' origin, some are imported (Beth Shean, Jericho and Ebla), some are locally made (Beth Shean, Jericho and Byblos), and a few are of uncertain material (Tell Nagila, Byblos and Sidon). Faience vessels are further attested at such sites as Gezer and Tell Nagila (uncertain origin) as well as Jericho (locally made);

- Scarabs and seal impressions in funerary contexts. Scarabs bearing Egyptian designs are far less common in burials as locally made sealings are attested in greater numbers. Egyptian private-name scarabs in funerary contexts come from Jericho and Byblos, their Middle Kingdom form suggesting an heirloom function. Royal-name scarabs likewise feature in burials as, for instance, that of Sobekhotep IV at Jericho or Senwosret II at Beth Shean. A tomb at Sidon also contained a cylinder seal with mixed Egyptian-Levantine elements;

- Scarabs and seal impressions in occupation and cultic contexts. Egyptian and Levantine features are found on cylinder seals from administrative, cultic and perhaps domestic contexts at Ebla. Other Egyptian and Levantine design scarabs were retrieved from the site's occupation levels. They also occur at Beth Shean's settlement. Jar sealings made with a Middle Kingdom private-name scarab were unearthed at Jericho and royal-name scarabs were found in late MBIIB occupation contexts at, for instance, Beth Shean (Noferhotep I) and Gezer (*Ḫyꜣn*). A cultic deposit at Sidon produced a unique locally-made private-name scarab inscribed with hieroglyphs. The earliest provenanced example of its kind, the scarab signals local knowledge in the Egyptian script and the appropriation of an Egyptian administrative custom. It can perhaps be compared to the unprovenanced sealings of Byblite rulers;

- Imported Egyptian ceramics from (1) Tell el-'Ajjul; (2) Ashkelon; (3) Beth Shean; and (4) Byblos. The Tell el-'Ajjul fragment was from a level of uncertain function, those at Ashkelon were collected around its footgate and sanctuary, and the two vessels from Beth Shean and Byblos were found in burials. They belong to a piriform jar (Tell el-'Ajjul), zirs (Ashkelon and Byblos), Tell el-Yahudiyah ware (Ashkelon and Beth Shean), and cooking pots (Ashkelon). A decrease in imported vessels between the late MBIIA to early MBIIB period and the MBIIB to MBIIB-C period is evident, though it may be related to the state of archaeological research at these four sites. The gate at Ashkelon, for instance, had altered its function by this stage and so goods could have been transported via another route, and the absence of evidence from Sidon could be explained by a known lack of publications which are, however, forthcoming;

- High-value items from funerary contexts, including an imported amethyst ring from Beth Shean and a mace and silver vessel with a *ꜥnḫ* sign at Ebla. The mace was most likely produced locally but utilised Egyptian imported hieroglyphic inlays; and

- Egyptian-influenced ivory inlays possibly adorning a furniture piece from a palace at Ebla. The inlays reflect local knowledge and use of Egyptian motifs related to royalty and divinity, coinciding with their elite and palatial context.

The Southern and Northern Levant both present evidence for relations with Egypt. The most popular items are stone vessels and sealings. Various sites along trade routes were evidently continued to be supplied with Egyptian heirlooms, imports and imitations, as well as Levantine-made items. The growing need for local workshops and, consequently, the increasing economic power of these markets, possibly led to the formation of new trade links across the Levant. Items such as locally made royal- and private-name scarabs imply gradually evolving markets. The locally made, private-name scarab at Sidon emphasises that locals were knowledgeable and literate in the Egyptian script. Instead of mimicking the Egyptian text as in other Levantine-design scarabs, the scarab was utilised to identify a particular Levantine individual in the Egyptian manner. Although the artefact surfaced in a cultic context, one may question the reason for its manufacture. Was it simply an item of prestige, or was it for sealing items traded with others literate in hieroglyphs? Perhaps the presence of scarabs belonging to rulers of Byblos suggests that Levantines had adopted an Egyptian administrative tradition to promote their own commercial dealings in the Levant and, perhaps, Egypt. The private-name scarab would then coincide with the proposed development of a trade network comprising regions across the Levant and Egypt.

Despite this development, maritime trade continued, seemingly at a reduced scale. Vessels for storage and transportation were imported, while those for cooking and serving occur at Ashkelon, perhaps in relation to the site's sanctuary. Imported Tell el-Yahudiyah ware is additionally attested for the first time, surfacing in funerary and cultic contexts. The ruling class also evidently still had some control over trade relations. High-value items in their tombs and the ivory inlays at Ebla's palace support their utilisation of Egyptian motifs for power and prestige. However, the prestige items are mostly of local manufacture, perhaps signalling decreased trade with Egypt or limited access to imported prestige items.

Overall, the evidence points to continued trade links with Egypt. From the early MBIIA, commodities were imported mostly into coastal cities where seals, stone vessels and other prestige items are found in elite funerary contexts and cultic areas. The mid-MBIIA witnessed workshops beginning to appropriate elements of the Egyptian culture for locally-made imitations, and hybrid products that mixed Egyptian artistic motifs and script(s) with Levantine items. They initially supplied the elite, who possibly later promoted scarab and stone-vessel workshops in the region during the late MBIIA and early MBIIB.

Throughout the MBIIB, these items became more common in occupation deposits, hinting at their growing popularity. While Levantine designs were more popular, some market demand remained for Egyptian imports which were possibly supplied by a ruling class that accordingly maintained trade links across the Levant. Other Egyptian influences, however, are more regionally concentrated: Egyptian and Egyptian-style vessels for cooking and serving foods are found at Ashkelon, Sidon and Tell Fad'ous, all three sites strategically positioned near harbours; the use of the Egyptian script to record Levantine names and matters is only attested at Sidon and Byblos, as is reverence to a deity equivalent to Seth; and Egyptian artistic motifs were adapted for the monumental and palatial complexes at Byblos, Ebla and Tell Sakka. Evidently, direct contact with the Egyptian culture is greater in the Northern Levant, where the elite adopted Egyptian symbols of power and divine authority. The one site that is represented in all discussed phases is Byblos. Other significant sites with a concentration of evidence across the examined period are Ashkelon and Sidon. Therefore, it seems reasonable to conclude that relations with Egypt were predominantly of maritime nature. Controlled by the elite, they became largely influential for the development of local and regional markets. The period of greatest contact and influence is the late MBIIA to early MBIIB period which significantly coincides with the Thirteenth Dynasty and the rise of Hyksos rule.

Section 3: Observations and Findings

7. Representing Asiatics and the Levant

'The land is cast to pain through the
sustenance
of the *St.tyw* who pervade the land.
It is the enemies who will arise in the east.
It is the *ꜥ3m.w* who will descend to Egypt.'
Prophecies of Noferty, 31-33.

7.1 Introduction

In the course of examining the rise of the Hyksos, much discussed textual and artistic evidence was analysed anew. Artefacts were re-translated and reassessed according to their socio-political and geographical contexts, providing significant data on the changing Egyptian ideology of the *other*. This chapter offers observations on the nature and development of Egyptian textual and artistic representations of Asiatics and the Levant. The plethora of this evidence is divided into the following contextual categories, each discussed in the first section of this chapter:

- Category 1: Inscriptions and texts from royal and administrative complexes;
- Category 2: Royal funerary complexes;
- Category 3: Temples and religious texts;
- Category 4: Non-royal settlements and occupation levels;
- Category 5: Non-royal graffiti;
- Category 6: Non-royal cemeteries and tombs of officials; and
- Category 7: Literary pieces.

The discussion is followed by a succinct overview of specific terms relating to the Levant and Levantines, as well as a review of shifting artistic elements in Egyptian portrayals of Asiatics.

7.2 Context and Genre: Interpreting the Evidence 'Between the Lines'

7.2.1 Category 1: Inscriptions and texts from royal and administrative complexes

Category 1 comprises royal inscriptions and texts from administrative complexes. Due to their administrative function, the belligerent portrayal of the *other* is reduced as events are likely connected to historical occurrences. Representations from the examined period are rare: one is ascribed to Dynasty 12 and two are from Dynasty 13 (Figure 7.1).

As a daybook of activities relating to Amenemhat II's administration, the Mit Rahina text indicates both peaceful and bellicose events in the Levant. These mainly involve the state-controlled dispatch of expeditions for the acquisition of natural and manufactured resources. While the greatest quantity of cargo was retrieved from the Northern Levantine coast (*Ḫnty-š*), other areas such as the Sinai were apparently frequented. A great number of captives and labourers were acquired from areas targeted by warfare, and a minority are listed amongst the returned cargo from diplomatic trade missions.

State-controlled contact with the Northern Levant continued into the Thirteenth Dynasty, as insinuated by a cylinder seal from an early Thirteenth Dynasty level at Tell el-Dab'a (F/I d/1). The seal expresses Levantine-influences not only on local workshops but also on local religion. Utilising Egyptian and Levantine elements, its proposed depiction of the myth of Baal supports the deity's worship in the Delta. It also signals that such myths may have been acceptable forms of cross-cultural communication by the administration.

Further pointing to the heterogeneity of Lower Egypt is Papyrus Boulaq 18 in which Asiatic women are listed among offering bearers from the Delta. No expeditions to the Levant are purported; however Asiatics within the administration are noted to have been invited to a palatial dinner. This signifies a major development in the role and status of Asiatics, for while they were received as guests from the Levant during Amenemhat II's reign, they were now within the administration itself, received as Egyptian officials and offering bearers in Upper Egypt.

DYNASTY	RULER	SITE	FEATURE(S)	CHAPTER
12	Amenemhat II	Mit Rahina	- Military expeditions: *St.t, Ỉꜣsy* and *Ỉwꜣ* - Trade expeditions to Sinai and *Ḫn.ty-š* - Reception of guests from *St.t* and *Ṯmpꜣw*	4.3.7
13	(early)	Tell el-Dab'a F/I d/1	- Cylinder seal depicting Baal (?)	4.2.2.3
	Sobekhotep II or Khendjer	Dra' Abu el-Naga'	- Papyrus Boulaq 18/1: *ꜥꜣm* officials - Papyrus Boulaq 18/2: *ꜥꜣm.wt* offering bearers from Delta	4.5.3

FIGURE 7.1. CATEGORY 1: INSCRIPTIONS AND TEXTS FROM ROYAL AND ADMINISTRATIVE COMPLEXES.

DYNASTY	RULER	SITE	FEATURE(S)	CHAPTER
12	Amenemhat I	El-Lisht	- Mortuary temple: fragment of Asiatic woman and child	4.3.6.1
	Senwosret I	El-Lisht	- Mortuary temple: smiting scene; Asiatic ruler as enemy; Asiatic warrior; captives	4.3.6.1
	Senwosret III	Dahshur	- Pectoral, tomb of Mereret: griffins seizing Asiatics	4.3.1.3
	Amenemhat III	Dahshur	- Pectoral, tomb of Mereret: smiting the *St.tyw*	4.3.1.3
13	-	Dahshur	- Tomb of Nebhoteptikhered: Asiatic statuette	4.3.1.4

FIGURE 7.2. CATEGORY 2: ROYAL FUNERARY COMPLEXES.

DYNASTY	RULER	SITE	FEATURE(S)	CHAPTER
12	Senwosret I	Tod	- Temple inscription: punishment of *Ỉwn.tyw*(?), *ꜥꜣm.w* and *St.t*	4.5.11.1
	Senwosret III	El-Lahun	- Hymn to Senwosret III: slaughters and instils fear in *Pḏ.tyw* and *Ỉwn.tyw*	4.3.5.2
		Nag' el-Medamud	- Temple slabs: offering products of *St.t*; trampling the *Ỉwn.tyw*	4.5.7
		Serabit el-Khadim	- Inscription: *ꜥꜣm* expedition member	5.2.4.1
	Senwosret III - Amenemhat III	El-Lahun	- El-Lahun papyri: *ꜥꜣm.w* individuals	4.3.5.2
	Amenemhat III	Serabit el-Khadim	- Inscriptions: *ꜥꜣm* expedition members; brother of the ruler of *Rṯnw*; men from *Rṯnw*	5.2.4.1
	Amenemhat IV	Serabit el-Khadim	- Inscriptions: *ꜥꜣm* expedition members; *ꜥꜣm* chief lector priest; men from *Rṯnw*	5.2.4.1
	-	El-Lisht	- Execration Texts	4.3.6.2
		Saqqara	- Execration Texts	4.3.8
		-	- Execration Texts (Berlin)	4.6.1
		Serabit el-Khadim	- Inscriptions: Asiatic expedition members; products of *St.t*	5.2.4.1
13	Sobekhotep IV	Karnak	- Temple stela: *ꜥš*-wood of *Ḫn.ty-š* employed for cultic architectural elements	4.5.6

FIGURE 7.3. CATEGORY 3: TEMPLES AND RELIGIOUS TEXTS.

7.2.2 Category 2: Royal funerary complexes

The second category encompasses representations from royal tombs and funerary complexes (Figure 7.2). They date from the reigns of Amenemhat I to III, and the Thirteenth Dynasty. Portrayals possibly include warfare scenes in the mortuary temples of the first two kings of Dynasty 12, and a smiting scene in Senwosret I's tomb. More diverse representations are attested in late Dynasty 12. Asiatics remain illustrated as subdued and conquered elements in two pectorals from Princess Mereret's tomb; however, one is presented in a more peaceful stance as a statuette from Princess Nebhoteptikhered's tomb.

The bellicose nature of depictions may be explained by their funerary context. Deposited in the eternal resting place of royalty, the items and scenes would necessitate the presentation of Pharaonic strength and success in maintaining order for the hereafter. All preserved bellicose instances betray a *topos* representation. The introduction of representations with Asiatics as less chaotic elements and the absence of negative portrayals from Dynasty 13 may signal changing royal, social and political prerogatives.

DYNASTY	RULER	SITE	FEATURE(S)	CHAPTER
13 - SIP	-	El-Lahun	- El-Lahun papyri: *ꜥ3m.w* individuals	4.3.5.2
		El-Lisht	- Settlement debris (?): statuette of cultic figure	4.3.6.2

FIGURE 7.4. CATEGORY 4: NON-ROYAL SETTLEMENTS AND OCCUPATION LEVELS.

DYNASTY	RULER	SITE	FEATURE(S)	CHAPTER
12	Amenemhat I (?)	Hatnub	- Inscriptions: *ꜥ3m.w* allies with king (?)	4.4.3
	Amenemhat I	Abydos	- Stela Louvre C1: destroying the *Ꞽwn.tyw*, *Mnṯ.tyw* and *Ḥr.yw-š*	4.5.1.1
	Senwosret I	Abydos	- Stela CG 20539: pacifying and instilling fear in *Ḥr.yw-š* and *St.tyw*	4.5.1.1
		Wadi el-Hudi	- Stela: Senwosret I kills *Ꞽwn.tyw*, *St.tyw* and rebels	5.3.2
	Senwosret III	Dahshur	- Pyramid complex: graffiti of Asiatics	4.3.1.4
		Abydos	- Stela Manchester 3306: battle against *Rṯnw*, *Skmm* and a *ꜥ3m*	4.5.1.1
		Abydos	- Stelae: *ꜥ3m* officials and household members	4.5.1.1
		Wadi el-Hammamat	- Inscriptions: trampling *Ꞽwn.tyw*; opening the land of the *ꜥ3m*; *ꜥ3m* expedition member	5.3.1
	Amenemhat III	Abydos	- Stelae: *ꜥ3m* officials and household members	4.5.1.1
		Wadi Maghara	- Inscription: *ꜥ3m* expedition member	5.2.3
		Serabit el-Khadim	- Inscriptions: *ꜥ3m* expedition members	5.2.4.1
	-	Abydos	- Stelae: *ꜥ3m* officials and household members	4.5.1.1
12-13	-	Wadi el-Hol	- Inscriptions: *ꜥ3m* individual; Egyptian(?) with name Nebet-*Kpn*	4.5.5.1
		Aswan	- Inscriptions: *ꜥ3m* expedition and household members	4.5.2
13	Sobekhotep III	-	- Papyrus Brooklyn 35.1446: *ꜥ3m* individuals and workers	4.6.3
	-	Abydos	- Stelae: *ꜥ3m* officials and household members	4.5.1.1
		Gebel Tjauti	- Inscriptions: *ꜥ3m* officials	4.5.10
SIP	-	El-Rizeiqat	- Stelae: *ꜥ3m* household members	4.5.9

FIGURE 7.5. CATEGORY 5: NON-ROYAL INSCRIPTIONS AND GRAFFITI.

7.2.3 Category 3: Temples and religious texts

Portrayals of Asiatics assigned to Category 3 are embedded in religious, cosmic and ideological principles (Figure 7.3). Royally-instigated examples from Dynasty 12 focus on the subjugation of forces threatening Egypt, emphasising the king's dominion over foreign lands, peoples and resources. Texts from the reigns of Senwosret I and III note the king's punishment of *Ꞽwn.tyw* and *Pḏ.tyw*. Belligerent action against *ꜥ3m.w* is further mentioned in the Tod inscription. The action of punishing an entire foreign group is narrowed in the Execration Texts to only focus on the rebels and rebellious actions of Levantines. Underscoring the state's knowledge in foreign aristocracy, geography and affairs, the Execration Texts note the persistent ideological requirement to ritually protect Egypt from foreign forces. As with the representations of Category 2, the shift in representation, in this case being from an entire foreign group to particular rebels, may point to socio-political changes.

These changes are further highlighted by a rise in the number of *mimetic* and diplomatic texts from Senwosret III's reign. Firstly are instances representing foreign lands as sources of commodities, with the pharaoh offering foreign products of *St.t* and *Ḫnty-š* to Egyptian temples, some of which were used in the construction of cultic architectural elements. Secondly are the many attestations of individuals of Asiatic descent working or offering homage to Egyptian temples. These include Asiatic door-keepers, attendants, singers, dancers and priests in service of el-Lahun's temples, expedition members travelling to Serabit el-Khadim, and a senior chief lector priest sending temple offerings to Serabit el-Khadim. While some of these individuals are of mixed Egyptian-Levantine ancestry, the men from *Rṯnw*, a few of whom were of Levantine royalty, were also commemorated in lists of expedition members at Serabit el-Khadim's Hathor Temple. Hence, the evidence suggests that, at least from Senwosret III's reign, Levantines and Egyptian-Levantines were represented as active participants in Egyptian religious customs and temple activities.

DYNASTY	RULER	SITE	FEATURE(S)	CHAPTER
12	Amenemhat I	El-Lisht	- Wall scene fragments: Levantine ceramics	4.3.6.1
		Beni Hassan	- Tomb of Khnumhotep I: Asiatic warriors; ships of *ʿš*-wood	4.4.1.1
	Amenemhat I - Senwosret I	Beni Hassan	- Statuette of Asiatic woman	4.4.1.4
	Senwosret I	Beni Hassan	- Tomb of Amenemhat: Asiatic warriors; Levantine ceramics; 'fair-skinned men'; carob(?)	4.4.1.2
		Meir	- Tomb of Wekhhotep (B2): *ʿ3m*(?) servant	4.4.4.1
	Amenemhat II	Dahshur	- False door (?) fragments belonging to Asiatic	4.3.1.1
		Meir	- Tomb of Wekhhotep (B4): Asiatic officials; cattle of *ʿ3m.w*	4.4.4.2
	Senwosret II	Beni Hassan	- Tomb of Khnumhotep II: procession of *ʿ3m.w*; Levantine-influenced ceramics; 'fair-skinned men'; *ʿš*-wood for tomb; carob(?)	4.4.1.3
	Senwosret III	Dahshur	- Biography of Khnumhotep III: relations with *W3ṯi/W3iṯ*, Byblos and *ʿ3m.w*	4.3.1.2
		Meir	- Tomb of Wekhhotep (C1): Asiatic(?) bearers from Delta	4.4.4.3
	-	El-Lisht	- Filling of Tomb 499: statue base for a *ʿ3m*	4.3.6.2
13	-	Hawara	- Tomb of Imenysenebnebwy: *ʿ3m* butler	4.3.3
		Tell el-Habwa I	- Door jamb fragments of nobleman and count *ʿpr-Bʿ3r*	4.2.4.1
		Tell el-Dab'a F/I d/2-c	- Statue fragments: 'hybrid' artistic elements	4.2.2.3
		Tell Edfu	- Stela of Ptahhotep: *ʿ3m* individual	4.5.4.1
13-SIP	-	Abydos	- Shaft Tomb 477: ivory sphinx with 'hybrid' artistic elements	4.5.1.2

FIGURE 7.6. CATEGORY 6: NON-ROYAL CEMETERIES AND TOMBS OF OFFICIALS.

7.2.4 *Category 4: Non-royal settlements and occupation levels*

The Levant and Levantines are represented in very few textual and artistic evidence from non-royal settlements and occupation levels, all of which date to the Thirteenth Dynasty and the Second Intermediate Period (Figure 7.4). Levantine individuals are mentioned in undated papyri from el-Lahun's settlement as members of the community, one of whom apparently had a statue fashioned in his honour while another worked in the vizierate. A statuette from el-Lisht supports the existence of Asiatics or artists influenced by Levantine designs living in Memphis. Possibly a cultic figure, the statuette may represent a freedom to express Levantine religious and/or cultic beliefs in an area largely recognised for its Egyptian cults.

7.2.5 *Category 5: Non-royal inscriptions and graffiti*

Sources belonging to Category 5 (Figure 7.5) are divided into hostile and peaceful/diplomatic representations. The former primarily date between the reigns of Amenemhat I and Senwosret III. They include military skirmishes against foreigners, who are commonly identified in bellicose portrayals by the terms *Ꞽwn.tyw*, *Mnṯ.tyw*, *Ḥr.yw-š* and *St.tyw*. The last militaristic campaign is ascribed to Senwosret III's reign, after which most texts refer to Egyptian-Asiatics working and residing in Egypt. This indicates that the second half of Dynasty 12 witnessed: (a) a noticeable increase of Asiatics in Egypt; (b) a development from state-instigated inscriptions to those naming the responsible official; (c) an increase in the interest and perhaps responsibility of non-royals over foreigners; and (d) a rise in the number of Egyptian-Levantine relations. The last notation is supported by inscriptions recording the 'opening' of the land of the *ʿ3m*, bringing products from foreign lands, as well as names and titles concerned with Byblos, its goddess and its commodities. The Egyptians evidently held a certain respect towards individual Levantines: they recorded their ancestry; depicted them as equal household and family members; and honoured their contributions. They did not represent them negatively, but instead portrayed them as a part of Egyptian society.

7.2.6 *Category 6: Non-royal cemeteries and tombs of officials*

References in non-royal tombs and cemeteries mainly occur in elite contexts (Figure 7.6). They consist of depictions of Levantine commodities, lands and individuals. Representations of Levantine goods include ceramics, a Levantine-influenced handled vessel, *ʿš*-wood, and possibly carob. They date from the reigns of Amenemhat I to Senwosret III. Levantine toponyms are portrayed as sources of these commodities as well as peoples.

Individuals from the Levant are represented to be of two origins: those from across the borders of Egypt and those living in Egypt. Representations depend on the responsibilities of the tomb owner and the extent to which he fulfilled these duties. For instance, the overseers of the Oryx nome and its army depict activities concerning the nome's mercenaries. So, Asiatics are represented as

DYNASTY	RULER	SITE	FEATURE(S)	CHAPTER
12	Senwosret I	-	- Instructions of Amenemhat I: *St.tyw* as dogs	4.6.2
			- Tale of Sinuhe: Walls-of-the-Ruler repel *St.tyw* and *Nmi.w-šꜥ*; *St.tyw* helpful at border; *St.tyw* against rulers of *Rṯnw*; *ꜥꜣm.w* assist Sinuhe; ruler of Upper *Rṯnw* bestows land, power and daughter to Sinuhe	4.6.9
			- Prophecies of Noferty: *ꜥꜣm.w* terrorising Egyptians; strangers in the Delta; *St.tyw* across the land; *ꜥꜣm.w* slaughtered but controlled by Amenemhat I and the Walls-of-the-Ruler	4.6.5
-	-	-	- Admonitions of Ipuwer: *Pḏ.tyw* adversaries; *St.tyw* informed of Egyptian affairs; foreigners in the Delta	4.6.4

FIGURE 7.7. CATEGORY 7: LITERARY PIECES.

warriors, possibly allies, in the tombs of Khnumhotep I and Amenemhat. Scenes of the foreigners also display correct details of their equipment, denoting a certain care in representing contemporary MBA culture. None of the examined attestations present a hostile treatment towards Asiatics in Egypt, indicating that the elite were not obliged to represent foreigners with the same royal ideological principles displayed in Categories 1-3. However, the negative portrayal of Levantines in the biography of Khnumhotep III is affected by these principles. This may be explained by the fact that the described events occur beyond the borders of Egypt and concern state-controlled expeditions, or that the tomb is located in Memphis.

Individuals of mixed Egyptian-ancestry are illustrated from the early Twelfth Dynasty, their background arguably represented in art as a combination of elements relating to Egyptian and Asiatic portrayals. Examples include the 'fair-skinned men' of Beni Hassan and the women of Wekhhotep's tomb at Meir (C1). They are also textually distinguished through the use of the term *ꜥꜣm*. The mixture of Egyptian and Levantine elements is also found in the Thirteenth Dynasty, when attestations newly occur in the Delta region and Upper Egypt. Hybridised representations are affiliated with individuals of higher rank and items reflecting power or authority (e.g. a life-size statue and possibly a sphinx). Such developments denote an increase in the number, geographical spread and rank of Asiatic individuals across Egypt.

7.2.7 Category 7: Literary pieces

Literary pieces mentioning Asiatics are clustered in the reign of Senwosret I (Figure 7.7). The Prophecies of Noferty is the most hostile, describing the *ꜥꜣm.w* and *St.tyw* as strong and fearsome enemies destabilising the Delta. This theme is similarly explored in the Admonitions of Ipuwer. On a lesser scale, the Instructions of Amenemhat I mention the animalistic traits of Asiatics and their inferior subordinate status. The Tale of Sinuhe alternatively offers variant representations of Asiatics as friendly foreigners helping and assisting Egyptians abroad, or as enemies threatening Egypt's security. Sinuhe's different portrayals are more a reflection of the literary role played by foreigners in the development of his character, and should not be solely construed as a commentary on the treatment of Asiatics in Egyptian society. Nonetheless, they do impart some knowledge on foreign lands, customs and peoples. The tale, as well as the other literary pieces, contains underlying threads of ideology affecting the overall characterisation of foreigners. This is enhanced by *topos* elements supporting and glorifying the king as protector of his people.

7.3 Textual Representations

7.3.1 *Terms relating to Levantine ancestry and ethnicity*

Collected textual representations include nine terms linked to Levantine ancestry and ethnicity. Comments on the nature and development of each are presented below. For information regarding the sources, their respective sites and chapter references, refer to Figure 7.8.

ꜥ3m(.w) / ꜥ3m.(w)t

The term is the most frequently attested, and the only one to be represented from the early Middle Kingdom to the Second Intermediate Period. Early Twelfth Dynasty sources mostly represent *ꜥ3m(.w)/ꜥ3m.(w)t* as an ethnic signifier for individuals within the Levant or directly from the Levant. It is also used as a negative connotation portraying strong enemies of the state that are terrorised

TERM	DYNASTY	SOURCE	SITE	CHAPTER
ꜥ3m(.w) / ꜥ3m.(w)t	Late 11-12	Inscription Nr 16*	Hatnub	4.4.3
		Inscription Nr 25	Hatnub	4.4.3
	12 (Senwosret I)	tomb of Wekhhotep (B2)*	Meir	4.4.4.1
		Tale of Sinuhe	-	4.6.9
	12 (Senwosret I?)	Inscription	Tod	4.5.11.1
	Early 12	Prophecies of Noferty	-	4.6.5
	12 (Senwosret II)	tomb of Khnumhotep II	Beni Hassan	4.4.1.3
	12 (Amenemhat II)	block	Mit Rahina	4.3.7
		tomb of Wekhhotep (B4)*	Meir	4.4.4.2
	12 (Senwosret III)	UC 32191	El-Lahun	4.3.5.2
		P Berlin 10050	El-Lahun	4.3.5.2
		Rio de Janeiro 627	Abydos	4.5.1.1
		Manchester 3306	Abydos	4.5.1.1
		Inscription Nr 81	Serabit el-Khadim	5.2.4.1
		Inscription Nr 17	Wadi el-Hudi	5.3.2
	12 (Amenemhat III)	P Berlin 10066	El-Lahun	4.3.5.2
		P Berlin 10047	El-Lahun	4.3.5.2
		P Berlin 10081C	El-Lahun	4.3.5.2
		CG 20231	Abydos	4.5.1.1
		E.207.1900	Abydos	4.5.1.1
		Inscription Nr 24-24a	Wadi Maghara	5.2.3
		Inscription Nr 85	Serabit el-Khadim	5.2.4.1
		Inscription Nr 93	Serabit el-Khadim	5.2.4.1
		Inscription Nr 95	Serabit el-Khadim	5.2.4.1
		Inscription Nr 98	Serabit el-Khadim	5.2.4.1
		Inscription Nr 110	Serabit el-Khadim	5.2.4.1
		Inscription Nr 112	Serabit el-Khadim	5.2.4.1
		Inscription Nr 43	Wadi el-Hammamat	5.3.1
		Inscription Nr 17	Wadi el-Hammamat	5.3.1
	12 (Amenemhat III ?)	UC 32168, UC 32269	El-Lahun	4.3.5.2
		Inscription A	Wadi el-Hol	4.5.5.1
	12 (Amenemhat IV)	P Berlin 10010	El-Lahun	4.3.5.2
		Inscription Nr 123	Serabit el-Khadim	5.2.4.1
	12 (Amenemhat IV ?)	UC 32058	El-Lahun	4.3.5.2
	12	Execration Texts	Saqqara	4.3.8
		Execration Texts	-	4.6.1
	12-13	UC 32295	El-Lahun	4.3.5.2
		P Berlin 10244	El-Lahun	4.3.5.2
		UC 32151B	El-Lahun	4.3.5.2
		UC 32167	El-Lahun	4.3.5.2
		P Berlin 10391	El-Lahun	4.3.5.2
		UC 32201	El-Lahun	4.3.5.2
		UC 32286	El-Lahun	4.3.5.2
		UC 32130	El-Lahun	4.3.5.2
		UC 32101H	El-Lahun	4.3.5.2
		UC 32127	El-Lahun	4.3.5.2
		UC 32143B	El-Lahun	4.3.5.2
		UC 32143E	El-Lahun	4.3.5.2
		UC 32147G	El-Lahun	4.3.5.2
		Inscription B	Aswan	4.5.2
	Late 12-13	ÄS 99	Abydos	4.5.1.1
		ÄS 186	Abydos	4.5.1.1
		Stela Moscow I.1.a.5349	-	4.6.7
	13 (Khendjer)	Liverpool E.30	Abydos	4.5.1.1

FIGURE 7.8. TERMS RELATING TO LEVANTINE ANCESTRY AND ETHNICITY RECORDED IN STUDIED TEXTS (1/2).

by the king, as in the Inscription of Tod or the Prophecies of Noferty. The term is further utilised to describe a group of mercenaries allied with the king in the Hatnub graffiti.

Sources from the second half of the Twelfth Dynasty include *ʿ3m(.w)/ʿ3m.(w)t* as an ethnic marker for individuals within Egypt who are newly migrated or of mixed Egyptian-Levantine heritage. The first secure identification for this use is from the reign of Senwosret III. This period also witnessed the last recorded instance of the term's use in a specific militaristic expedition (Khusobek's stela; Manchester 3306), and its appearance in the ritualistic Execration Texts.

Individuals represented as *ʿ3m(.w)/ʿ3m.(w)t* became increasingly attested in the late Twelfth and the Thirteenth Dynasties. Their specific area of origin is rarely specified and appears to be affiliated to many regions within

Term	Dynasty	Source	Site	Chapter
ʿ3m(.w)* / *ʿ3m.(w)t *(continued)*	13	ÄS 143	Abydos	4.5.1.1
		CG 20281	Abydos	4.5.1.1
		Roanne Nr 163	-	4.6.8
	Mid-13	tomb of Imenysenebnebwy	Hawara	4.3.3
		P Boulaq 18/2	Dra' Abu el-Naga'	4.5.3
		P Brooklyn 35.1446	-	4.6.3
	13 (?)	Marseille 227	Abydos	4.5.1.1
	Middle Kingdom	P Leiden I.344 (Admonitions of Ipuwer)*	-	4.6.4
	13-early SIP	Berlin 22.708	El-Rizeiqat	4.5.9
		Bremen 4558	El-Rizeiqat	4.5.9
	(?)	CG 20103	Abydos	4.5.1.1
		CG 20114	Abydos	4.5.1.1
		CG 20119	Abydos	4.5.1.1
		CG 20158	Abydos	4.5.1.1
		CG 20164	Abydos	4.5.1.1
		CG 20227	Abydos	4.5.1.1
		CG 20392	Abydos	4.5.1.1
		CG 20520	Abydos	4.5.1.1
		CG 20549	Abydos	4.5.1.1
		CG 20550	Abydos	4.5.1.1
		CG 20571	Abydos	4.5.1.1
		Rio de Janeiro 680	Abydos	4.5.1.1
Fnḫ.w	12 (Senwosret I)	Tale of Sinuhe	-	4.6.9
Ỉwn.tyw	12 (Amenemhat I)	Louvre C1	Abydos	4.5.1.1
	12 (Senwosret I)	Inscription Nr 143	Wadi el-Hudi	5.3.2
	12 (Senwosret III)	Inscription Nr 47	Wadi el-Hammamat	5.3.1
	12 (Amenemhat III)	UC 32157	El-Lahun	4.3.5.2
	(?)	block	Nag' el-Medamud	4.5.7
Pd.tyw* / *Pḏ.tyw	12 (Senwosret I)	Tale of Sinuhe	-	4.6.9
	12 (Amenemhat III)	UC 32157	El-Lahun	4.3.5.2
	Middle Kingdom	P Leiden I.344 (Admonitions of Ipuwer)	-	4.6.4
Mnṯ.tyw* / *Mntw	12 (Amenemhat I)	Louvre C1	Abydos	4.5.1.1
	12 (Senwosret III)	tomb of Khnumhotep III	Dahshur	4.3.1.2
		Manchester 3306	Abydos	4.5.1.1
	12	Execration Texts	Saqqara	4.3.8
		Execration Texts	-	4.6.1
Nmi.w-šʿ	12 (Senwosret I)	Tale of Sinuhe	-	4.6.9
Ḥ3.w-nb.w	12 (Senwosret I)	Inscription Nr 143	Wadi el-Hudi	5.3.2
Ḥr.yw-šʿ	12 (Amenemhat I)	Louvre C1	Abydos	4.5.1.1
	12 (Senwosret I)	CG 20539	Abydos	4.5.1.1
St.tyw	12 (Amenemhat I)	tomb of Khnumhotep I	Beni Hassan	4.4.1.1
	12 (Senwosret I)	Tale of Sinuhe	-	4.6.9
		CG 20539	Abydos	4.5.1.1
		Instructions of Amenemhat I	-	4.6.2
	12 (Amenemhat II)	block*	Mit Rahina	4.3.7
	Early 12	Prophecies of Noferty	-	4.6.5
	12 (Amenemhat III)	pectoral	Dahshur	4.3.1.3
		UC 32157	El-Lahun	4.3.5.2
	Middle Kingdom	P Leiden I.344 (Admonitions of Ipuwer)	-	4.6.4

Figure 7.8. Terms relating to Levantine ancestry and ethnicity recorded in studied texts (2/2).
* Uncertain reading.

the Levant. The term is typically complemented by an individual's name and title, and is also attested as a personal name.

Fnḫ.w

The group is only represented once in the Tale of Sinuhe, where its ruler is summoned to appear before the pharaoh. Peaceful relations between Egypt and the *Fnḫ.w* are implied, although the utilisation of ideological principles refers to the *Fnḫ.w* ruler as subordinate to the Egyptian king.

ꞽwn.tyw

Attestations are mainly dated between the reigns of Amenemhat I and III. All portrayals negatively represent the group: Amenemhat I's official must destroy (*ssḥ*) its fortresses; Senwosret I kills (*dn*) its people; and the group is struck with dread (*ḥwi*) and trampled (*titi*, *ptpt*) by an official of Senwosret III (Inscription Nr 47), as well as the king himself in el-Lahun's Hymn to Senwosret III. The bellicose attestations can all be assigned to royal, royally-instigated and royally-controlled offices, proposing that the group only had dealings with the Egyptian state across the borders of Egypt.

Pd.tyw / Pḏ.tyw

The *Pd.tyw/Pḏ.tyw* are represented in three Middle Kingdom sources: (1) the Tale of Sinuhe, where they are attacked by Senwosret I and placed in the Delta; (2) the Hymn to Senwosret III, where they flee from the king's slaughter; and (3) the Admonitions of Ipuwer, where they must be driven away from the Delta. The *topos* representations thus note that the *Pd.tyw/Pḏ.tyw* had entered the Delta during the Twelfth Dynasty.

Mnṯ.tyw / Mntw

Representations are derived from the Twelfth Dynasty. The earliest is from the reign of Amenemhat I noting the destruction (*ssḥ*) of the *Mnṯ.tyw/Mntw* fortresses. Other references of the second half of Dynasty 12 associate the *Mnṯ.tyw/Mntw* with the land of *St.t*. They are mentioned in the biography of Khnumhotep III, who must trample (*ptpt*) the group, Khusobek's stela in which the king intends to overthrow (*sḫr.t*) them, and in the Execration Texts. The group is seemingly involved in militaristic skirmishes with the Egyptians, and so can perhaps be identified as a warrior class in the northeast.

Nmi.w-šꜥ

The group is only attested in the Tale of Sinuhe. As the story records, Senwosret I and the Walls-of-the-Ruler were 'made' to crush (*ptpt*) them.

Ḥꜣ.w-nb.w

The *Ḥꜣ.w-nb.w* occur in one inscription from Wadi el-Hudi, in which Senwosret I apparently encloses (*ꜥrf*) or surrounds the group.[1]

Ḥr.yw-šꜥ

The term is attested in the early Twelfth Dynasty. Two stelae at Abydos (Louvre C1 and CG 20539) portray the group as one that is destroyed (*ssḥ*) and pacified (*sgrḥ*).

St.tyw

St.tyw is the second most frequently attested term, but one which is only found in Middle Kingdom texts. Early representations provide various treatments of the *St.tyw*. They 'fell' (*ḫr*) due to Amenemhat I's actions in Khnumhotep I's biography, but it is unclear whether they were the enemy or ally of the king. They appear as both friend and foe in the Tale of Sinuhe, assisting Sinuhe at the border of Egypt and receiving rewards from Senwosret I. Senwosret I and his Walls-of-the-Ruler also repelled (*ḫsf*) them from Egypt while the *ḥḳꜣ.w ḫꜣs.wt* opposed their movements. Sinuhe's varying treatment may be explained by the characterisation of the *St.tyw* as a means to support the character's progression, as well as the ideological influences when referring to the reigning king.

The remaining representations are bellicose in nature: the vizier Montuhotep is provided with an epithet to pacify (*sḥtp*) them; they are forced to do the 'dog-walk' in the Instructions of Amenemhat I; the Mit Rahina text mentions an expedition to destroy (*ḫbꜣ*) their fortresses; they pervade Egypt in the Prophecies of Noferty and know the state of the land in the Admonitions of Ipuwer; Senwosret III restrains them; and Amenemhat III smites them (*sḳr*) on a pectoral from Princess Mereret's tomb.

Their exact origin, however, is not specified. They are commonly represented near the borders of Egypt and as traders across the Walls-of-the-Ruler. Their knowledge of Egyptian affairs is significant, as is their predominantly negative portrayals following the reign of Amenemhat II. More of their relations with Egypt may be revealed from the use of the toponym, *St.t*, which likely refers to the land which they inhabited. This toponym, as well as several others, is examined in the following section.

[1] For more on the *Ḥꜣ.w-nb.w*, see Favard-Meeks, *SAK* 16 (1989), 39-63.

7.3.2 Toponyms

Excluding those listed in the Execration texts, 21 Levantine toponyms may be assigned to the Middle Kingdom and early Second Intermediate Period. Their attestations are provided in Figure 7.9. The toponyms can be divided into those of the Eastern Desert, the Southern Levant, the Northern Levant and those of unidentifiable location.

Eastern Desert

Four toponyms may be securely located in the Eastern Desert. Three of these are preserved in the Tale of Sinuhe as areas through which the character traversed after crossing the Egyptian border. They include *Ptn*, *Ng3w* and *Kmwr*. The fourth toponym, *Ḫt.yw-Mfk3.t/Mfk3.t* or 'Turquoise Terraces', is recorded in the Mit Rahina text as well as four of the examined inscriptions at Serabit el-Khadim. Natural and mineral resources from the Sinai as well as Western Asia were retrieved by an expedition to the site. The toponym's connection with Hathor is also inferred by the Serabit el-Khadim texts, where a temple to the goddess remains.

Southern Levant

None of the toponyms can be definitively identified with Southern Levantine cities, yet circumstantial evidence related to three toponyms may signal their location in this region. Based on the order of dispatched and returned expeditions in the Mit Rahina inscription, the two fortresses of *3sy* and *Iw3(i)* may arguably be situated between *Ḫt.yw-Mfk3.t* and *Ḫnty-š*, or the Sinai and the Northern Levant. The two toponyms are militaristically targeted by Amenemhat II's soldiers, who return to Egypt with over 1500 Asiatics, offering one means of Levantine migration into Egypt. Another bellicose expedition is represented in Khusobek's stela (Manchester 3306) where Senwosret III and his army were sent to the region of *Skmm*, which has been connected to the Southern Levantine Shechem.

If these toponyms' location in the Southern Levant is correct, then relations with the region would be twofold. It is a target of military skirmishes, and it is a source of Levantine migrants. However, as the evidence is circumstantial, relations between the Southern Levant and Egypt cannot be conclusively assessed from the region's toponyms.

Northern Levant

The greatest number of attestations are assigned to Northern Levantine toponyms which, unlike those of the Eastern Desert and the Southern Levant, can be securely dated from the early Twelfth to the mid-Thirteenth Dynasty. They are mostly related to peaceful and diplomatic relations, and as areas of significant commercial interest.

The earliest are dated to Senwosret I's reign and occur in the Tale of Sinuhe. They include: (1) *I33*,[2] bestowed to Sinuhe as a fruitful flat land frequented by Egyptians travelling to and from the Egyptian Residence; (2) *Ḫnty-kšw*, whose ruler is sent on a diplomatic expedition to the Residence, his subordination being expressively noted; (3) *Ḳdm(i)*,[3] which housed Sinuhe for one and a half years; and (4) *Kbny* (Byblos), which was Sinuhe's intended destination.

Amenemhat II's Mit Rahina daybook lists an expedition, possibly seaborne, to *Ḫnty-š*. A small number of Asiatics returned with the expedition, offering another method of Levantine migration into Egypt. Numerous natural and manufactured commodities were retrieved, the greatest in weight being ꜥš-wood. The timber is again represented as a Levantine resource in the inscription of Khnumhotep II mentioning *Ng3w*, as well as the inscription of Khnumhotep III. Assigned to Senwosret III's reign, the latter biography records three Northern Levantine toponyms: *Iw3ṯi/W3iṯ* (Ullaza), *Rmnn* (Lebanon?) and *Kbny*. Khnumhotep III's expedition docked first at the latter site, negotiated with its ruler and then journeyed to *Iw3ṯi/W3iṯ*.

References dated to the mid-Thirteenth Dynasty support Egypt's continued commercial and political relations with the Northern Levant. Cedar wood of *Ḫnty-š* is recorded in Sobekhotep IV's reign, a hall-keeper of goods from *Kbny* is attested during the mid-Thirteenth Dynasty, and a block from the Byblite Temple of Obelisks refers to Noferhotep I alongside *Kbny*'s count.

Despite such diplomatic relations, the toponyms *I33*, *Iw3ṯi* and *Kbny* are among the Execration Texts, highlighting the importance of securing productive and continuous relations from rebellious action. This significance is further emphasised by the Admonitions of Ipuwer, which notes the lack of journeys to Byblos as a sign of reigning chaos.

Northern Levantine toponyms additionally shed light on cross-cultural influences. Within Egypt, several individuals of seemingly Egyptian origin and Egyptian-Asiatic descent are given the name Nebet-*Kbn* from at least Amenemhat III's reign. Literally translated as the 'lady of Byblos', the name emphasises knowledge of and reverence to the Levantine deity within Egypt. This is further supported by the mention of Hathor as 'lady of *Kbn*' in el-Lahun papyrus UC 32196. In the Levant, toponyms are used in locally-produced texts. A MBIIB scarab from Sidon records the 'lord of *I3y*' and an MBA obelisk, scimitar and several stelae from Byblos utilise *Kpny* to refer to the site and its rulers.

The toponymic evidence indicates that Egypt shared close relations of commercial, cultural and religious nature with the Northern Levant. Relations were predominantly peaceful, lasting from the early Twelfth Dynasty to at least the mid-Thirteenth Dynasty. Rulers, officials, and individuals evidently had knowledge of Northern Levantine toponyms, denoting the influences of such relations across geographical borders and social hierarchies.

[2] For the toponym's identification as one in the Northern Levant see Mourad, *GM* 238 (2013), 78-81.

[3] For the toponym's identification as one in the Northern Levant see Mourad, *GM* 238 (2013), 72-77.

TOPONYM	DATE	SOURCE	SITE	CHAPTER
Ỉ3 / Ỉ3y	12 (Senwosret I)	Tale of Sinuhe	-	4.6.9
	12	Execration Texts	Saqqara	4.3.8
	12	Execration Texts	-	4.6.1
	(?) / MBIIB	scarab	Sidon	6.3.7.6
Ỉ3sy	12 (Amenemhat II)	block	Mit Rahina	4.3.7
Ỉw3(ỉ)	12 (Amenemhat II)	block	Mit Rahina	4.3.7
(Ỉ)w3ṯi / W3ỉṯ	12 (Senwosret III)	tomb of Khnumhotep III	Dahshur	4.3.1.2
	12	Execration Texts	Saqqara	4.3.8
	12	Execration Texts	-	4.6.1
Ptn	12 (Senwosret I)	Tale of Sinuhe	-	4.6.9
Ng3w	12 (Senwosret I)	Tale of Sinuhe*	-	4.6.9
	12 (Senwosret II)	tomb of Khnumhotep II	Beni Hassan	4.4.1.3
Rmnn	12 (Senwosret III)	tomb of Khnumhotep III	Dahshur	4.3.1.2
	Middle Kingdom	P Leiden I.344 (Admonitions of Ipuwer)*	-	4.6.4
Rṯnw / Rṯ(n)w / (R)ỉṯinw	12 (Senwosret I)	Tale of Sinuhe (Upper *Rtnw*)	-	4.6.9
	12 (Senwosret III)	tomb of Khnumhotep III*	Dahshur	4.3.1.2
		Manchester 3306	Abydos	4.5.1.1
	12 (Senwosret III)	Inscription Nr 85	Serabit el-Khadim	5.2.4.1
		Inscription Nr 87	Serabit el-Khadim	5.2.4.1
		Inscription Nr 92	Serabit el-Khadim	5.2.4.1
		Inscription Nr 112	Serabit el-Khadim	5.2.4.1
		Inscription Nr 114	Serabit el-Khadim	5.2.4.1
		Inscription Nr 115	Serabit el-Khadim	5.2.4.1
		Inscription Nr 120	Serabit el-Khadim	5.2.4.1
		Inscription Nr 136	Serabit el-Khadim	5.2.4.1
	Early 13	scarab*	Tell el-Dab'a F/I d/1	4.2.2.3
	15	seal impression	Tell el-Dab'a F/II d	4.2.2.5
Hb3y	12 (Senwosret III)	tomb of Khnumhotep III	Dahshur	4.3.1.2
Ḥ3mỉ	12 (Amenemhat III)	Inscription Nr 110	Serabit el-Khadim	5.2.4.1
Ḫnty-š	12 (Amenemhat II)	block	Mit Rahina	4.3.7
	13 (Sobekhotep IV)	stela	Karnak	4.5.6
Ḫnty-kšw	12 (Senwosret I)	Tale of Sinuhe	-	4.6.9
Ḫt.yw-Mfk3.t / Mfk3.t	12 (Amenemhat II)	block	Mit Rahina	4.3.7
	12 (Amenemhat III)	Inscription Nr 93	Serabit el-Khadim	5.2.4.1
		Inscription Nr 97	Serabit el-Khadim	5.2.4.1
		Inscription Nr 94	Serabit el-Khadim	5.2.4.1
		Inscription Nr 98	Serabit el-Khadim	5.2.4.1
Skmm	12 (Senwosret III)	Manchester 3306	Abydos	4.5.1.1
	12	Execration Texts	Saqqara	4.3.8
St.t	12 (Senwosret I)	Inscription Nr 143	Wadi el-Hudi	5.3.2
	12 (Senwosret I?)	Inscription	Tod	4.5.11.1
	12 (Senwosret III)	tomb of Khnumhotep III	Dahshur	4.3.1.2
		Manchester 3306	Abydos	4.5.1.1
		block	Nag' el-Medamud	4.5.7
	12 (Amenemhat II)	block	Mit Rahina	4.3.7
	12 (Amenemhat III)	Inscription Nr 54	Serabit el-Khadim	5.2.4.1
		Inscription Nr 121	Serabit el-Khadim	5.2.4.1
		Inscription Nr 411	Serabit el-Khadim	5.2.4.1
	12	Execration Texts	Saqqara	4.3.8
		Execration Texts	-	4.6.1
Šw	12 (Senwosret II)	tomb of Khnumhotep II	Beni Hassan	4.4.1.3
Ḳdm(ỉ)	12 (Senwosret I)	Tale of Sinuhe	-	4.6.9
Kbn(y) / Kpn(y)	12 (Senwosret I)	Tale of Sinuhe	-	4.6.9
	12 (Senwosret III)	tomb of Khnumhotep III	Dahshur	4.3.1.2
	12 (Amenemhat III ?)	Inscription A	Wadi el-Hol	4.5.5.1
	12 (Amenemhat IV)	UC 32196	El-Lahun	4.3.5.2
	12	Execration Texts	Saqqara	4.3.8
		Execration Texts	-	4.6.1
	12-13 (?) / MBIIA	scimitar, Royal Tomb II	Byblos	6.3.3.2
	Late 12-13	Stela Moscow I.1.a.5349	-	4.6.7

FIGURE 7.9. LEVANTINE TOPONYMS RECORDED IN STUDIED TEXTS (1/2).

TOPONYM	DATE	SOURCE	SITE	CHAPTER
Kbn(y) / Kpn(y) (continued)	13 (Noferhotep I) / MBA	block	Byblos	6.3.3.1
	Mid-13	EA 428	Abydos	4.5.1.1
		CG 20086	Abydos	4.5.1.1
	Middle Kingdom	P Leiden I.344 (Admonitions of Ipuwer)	-	4.6.4
	(?)	CG 20224	Abydos	4.5.1.1
		CG 20678	Abydos	4.5.1.1
	(?) / MBA	obelisk	Byblos	6.3.3.1
		stela	Byblos	6.3.3.3
Kmwr	12 (Senwosret I)	Tale of Sinuhe	-	4.6.9
Ṯmp3w	12 (Amenemhat II)	block	Mit Rahina	4.3.7

FIGURE 7.9. LEVANTINE TOPONYMS RECORDED IN STUDIED TEXTS (2/2). TOPONYMS IN THE EXECRATION TEXTS ARE NOT INCLUDED, UNLESS MENTIONED ELSEWHERE.
* Uncertain reading.

Unidentifiable location

Five toponyms cannot be securely attributed to a particular region: (1) *Ḫ3mi*, the place of origin of a group of *ꜥ3m.w* in Serabit el-Khadim; (2) *Šw*, from which the procession of Asiatics in the tomb of Khnumhotep II evidently came; (3) *Ṯmp3w*, from which a delegation visited Amenemhat II bearing a gift of lead; (4) *Rṯnw*, with attestations dating from the Twelfth to the Fifteenth Dynasties; and (5) *St.t*, which occurs in Twelfth Dynasty texts.

As with the *St.tyw*, *St.t* is mainly portrayed in bellicose situations, although a few references are of less belligerent nature. The people of *St.t* are to have their throats cut in an inscription at Wadi el-Hudi, the land is destroyed in the Tod inscription, its fortresses targeted in Amenemhat II's daybooks and obstructed in Khnumhotep III's epithet. The *Mnṯ.tyw* are additionally related to the toponym. Products were also possibly imported from *St.t*, as evident in texts at Nag' el-Medamud and Serabit el-Khadim.

Rṯnw, on the other hand, is attested in only one bellicose portrayal. It has been situated by scholars in the Southern Levant and/or the Northern Levant, with one associating it with the Litani River.[4] The collected evidence implies a Northern Levantine location. Firstly, its earliest attestation for the examined period is in the Tale of Sinuhe featuring the ruler of Upper *Rtnw*. This character appears to have some control over the region of *Ḳdm(i)* and *Ꜣ3* which are to be located in the Northern Levant. Therefore, a connection between Upper *Rtnw* and the Northern Levant could be extrapolated. Secondly, and if its reconstruction is correct, Khnumhotep III's expedition to Ullaza and Byblos is noted as one to *Rtnw* for the bringing of cedar. Thirdly, glyphs on a scarab ring from an early Thirteenth Dynasty tomb at Tell el-Dab'a can be interpreted to read *ḥḳ3 n(.y) Rṯnw*. As the tomb features Northern Levantine goods and elements, the scarab may have belonged to an individual either of Northern Levantine descent or influenced by Northern Levantine traditions. So, the *ḥḳ3 n(.y) Rtnw* could be from the Northern Levant. However, *Rṯnw*'s only bellicose portrayal in Khusobek's stela (Manchester 3306) suggests that it was near *Skmm*. If *Skmm* is to be identified with Shechem (see above), then *Rtnw* would have also encompassed the northern region of the Southern Levant. Therefore, the attestations warn against forming any definitive conclusions regarding *Rtnw*'s identified location.

Nonetheless, the significance of *Rṯnw* should not be underestimated. Its aristocracy had close diplomatic ties with Amenemhat III, travelling with Egyptian expeditions to Serabit el-Khadim for a period of at least 20 years. Political relations between Tell el-Dab'a and *Rtnw* are further insinuated by a seal impression from an early Fifteenth Dynasty administrative complex at Tell el-Dab'a, which clearly reads *ḥḳ3 n(.y) Rṯnw*. As mentioned in Chapter 2.2, this title is also attributed to late Hyksos king Apophis. Thus, it is evident that the Hyksos were linked to *Rṯnw* and possibly even originated from this region. In fact, *Rṯnw*'s ruling elite shared diplomatic relations with Egypt from the very early Twelfth Dynasty, their attestations first placing them in the Levant, then in Egyptian expeditions to Serabit el-Khadim, and finally as rulers in the Delta region.

7.3.3 Personal names

Section 2 featured over 200 names belonging to individuals of Asiatic descent (Figure 7.10), bar those of Levantine rulers in the Execration Texts. A non-Egyptian origin is identified for a minimum of 68 names. Common elements are: *ꜥpr* with the name of a Levantine deity such as Baal or Reshef; *ꜥmw*, orthographically different from the Egyptian *ꜥ3mw*; *ib*, represented by a calf; and *skr*, possibly from the Semitic stem *škr* 'reward, favour'.[5] The ethnic marker *ꜥ3m* is also attested as a personal name: it is found in *ꜥ3m*, *ꜥ3m.w*, *ꜥ3m.t*, *P3-ꜥ3m*, *Ỉmnty-ꜥ3m.t* and possibly *S3.t-ꜥ3m*. The name may have been attributed to an individual by an Egyptian, especially if it derives from the Egyptian language.

Around 68% of the names are of Egyptian origin, a third of which are coupled with those of non-Egyptian derivation. These secondary Egyptian names were likely bestowed to Asiatics upon their migration into Egypt or their employment by Egyptian households. Individuals

[4] Gardiner, *Onomastica* 1, 142-149; Helck, *Die Beziehungen Ägyptens*, 266-268; Green, *CdE* 58 (1983), 56; Goedicke, *CdE* 67 (1998), 35, n. 2; Gubel and Loffet, *AHL* 34-35 (2011/2012), 84.

[5] Albright, *JAOS* 74/4 (1954), 227-228; Hayes, *Papyrus Brooklyn*, 95-96, Posener, *Syria* 34/1 (1957), 149.

with only Egyptian names are most likely descendents of such Asiatics residing in Egypt. They had adopted names associated with local deities, the reigning pharaoh, and/or their employer(s). Egyptian gods featured in the Asiatics' names are Ptah, Ra, Maat, Mut (which could also be identified as a Levantine deity), Khnum, Hathor and Sobek. Names including the elements Imeny and Senwosret may also refer to the nomens of kings Amenemhat and Senwosret. Such elements signify the Asiatics' assumption of Egyptian customs, language and religion.

7.3.4 Titles of officials

A clear indicator of Levantines' acceptance in Egyptian society is their variety of titles. The evidence points to Asiatics in state administrative positions, such as those of the vizierate and treasury, palatial complexes, temple precincts, military and security offices, local governments, specialised crafts, labour work and household ranks. Added to these are titles referring to rulers of Levantine lands. The following section provides an overview of the titles, with further information on their attestations, dates and respective chapters organised in Figure 7.11.

State administrative positions

Titles relating to state administrative positions include those of the vizierate, the treasury and the Residence. Only one uncertain title may be assigned to the vizierate: it is attested in the Middle Kingdom el-Lahun papyrus UC 32143E and refers to the [...*tp*] *ṯ3.t* '[...member] of the vizierate'.

Five titles belong to positions within the treasury, three date to the Twelfth Dynasty and two are of the Thirteenth Dynasty. The Dynasty 12 titles are from the tomb of Khnumhotep II, where one 'fair-skinned man' is listed as *im.y-r3 ḫtm.t* 'overseer of the treasury' and another is an *im.y-r3 ḫtm.tyw* 'overseer of sealers'. Inscriptions 58, 108 and 109 at Serabit el-Khadim additionally record a *im.y-r3 ʿḫnw.ty wr n.y pr ḥḏ* 'chief chamberlain of the treasury'. Thirteenth Dynasty titles occur in the Delta region. They include the *idn.w n.y im.y-r3 ḫtm.t* 'deputy of the overseer of the treasury' from a scarab at Tell el-Dab'a and the *ḫtm.ty bi.ty* 'sealer of the king of Lower Egypt' from a door fragment at Tell el-Habwa I.

The title *idn.w n.y im.y-r3 pr.w wr* 'deputy of the chief steward' may also be included in this division. It occurs in three inscriptions of Amenemhat III's reign at Serabit el-Khadim.

Palatial complexes

Four titles are associated with palatial complexes. The earliest is from the reign of Amenemhat III when an Asiatic *im.y-r3 iḫ.wt nb.wt n.y nsw.t* 'overseer of all property of the king' is recorded at Serabit el-Khadim. During the Thirteenth Dynasty, the titles *ir.y-ʿ.t ʿḥ* 'hall-keeper of the palace' and *smsw h3y.t* 'elder of the portal' are bestowed to individuals of Asiatic descent.

Temple precincts

Titles connected to temple precincts are assigned between the reigns of Senwosret III and Amenemhat IV. All relate to positions in the Memphite Region, and include *ir.y ʿ3 n.y ḥw.t-nṯr* 'door-keeper of a temple', *mty n.y s3* 'controller of a phyle', *ḫb* 'dancer', *ḫtm.ty nṯr* 'god's sealer' and *šmʿw* 'singer'. One Asiatic attained the title of high priest of Memphis, *s3b ḫr.y-ḥb.t ḥr.y-tp ḥm-nṯr sš* 'senior chief lector-priest, god's servant, scribe', stressing the Levantines' ability to reach prominent Egyptian religious positions.

Military and security offices

Asiatics with military and security titles mostly date to Dynasty 13. The title *im.y-ḫt s3.w pr.w* 'police official' is bestowed to an Asiatic in Papyrus Brooklyn 18/1 and at Gebel Tjauti. In Aswan, a Thirteenth Dynasty inscription may include the *ʿnḫ.w n.y niw.t* 'citizen, officer of the city regiment'. A further title refers to the *im.y-r3 mšʿ* 'overseer of the army/expedition', indicating that Asiatics were able to hold positions of significant military power. Interestingly, all offices occur at Upper Egyptian sites.

Local government

Offices are represented by three titles of the Twelfth Dynasty and three of later date. The tomb of Wekhhotep (B4) at Meir captions an individual of possible Asiatic descent with *ir.y ʿ.t n.y iḥw* 'hall-keeper of the cattle-pen'. A 'fair-skinned man' in the tomb of Khnumhotep II is also identified by a caption reading *wḥm.w* 'herald'. Another title is that of the *im.y-r3 šnʿ.w* 'overseer of a storehouse' from a stela at Abydos.

In the Thirteenth Dynasty, an Asiatic was bestowed with the position of *ḥ3.ty-ʿ smr wʿ.ty* 'count, sole companion' at Tell el-Habwa I. This presents one of the highest ranks in the Middle Kingdom local administration, evidently indicating that Asiatics were well-received in the Egyptian state. The data suggests that they even continued to be employed in the local governments of the Seventeenth Dynasty, as indicated by the title *im.y-r3 sḫ.ty* 'overseer of fieldworkers' belonging to an individual of Asiatic origin.

One other title may be assigned to the local government. It is inscribed on a statue-base of uncertain date from el-Lisht and is of the *im.y-r3 iḥ.w* 'overseer of cattle'.

Specialised crafts

A connection between Asiatic individuals and crafts is inferred in the use of the title *im.y-r3 ḥm.wt* 'overseer of craftsmen' on an Abydos stela. Asiatics were further involved in two main specialised crafts during Dynasty 13: metalwork (*im.y-r3 ḥm.tyw* 'overseer of coppersmiths') and textile fabrication (*sḫ.ty ḥ3.tyw/sšr* 'weaver of *ḥ3.tyw/sšr*-cloth' and *d3 ḥ3.tyw/sšr* 'warper(?) of *ḥ3.tyw/sšr*-cloth'). Another title associated with textiles comes from Aswan and may be read as *ir.y sšr* 'keeper of linen'.

Labour work

Although not commonly identified as professions assigned by administrative institutions, four expressions are associated with the physical labour of Asiatic descendents: (1) *itḥ inr.w* 'stone-hauler' from Amenemhat III's reign; (2) *ḥsb* 'workman' from the Middle Kingdom; and Thirteenth Dynasty (3) *šnᶜ* 'labourer' and (4) *ṯ.t k3.t* 'labourer (female)'.

Household ranks

Titles also reflect the roles and responsibilities of household members and workers. Those which are household administrative titles include: *im.y-r3 ᶜḫnw.ty* 'chamberlain', which occurs in Senwosret II's reign; *im.y-ḫt* 'attendant', which is attested in Dynasty 13 inscriptions; *ir.y-ᶜ.t* 'hall-keeper', which occurs from Senwosret III's reign to Dynasty 13; *ḥr.y-pr.w* 'major-domo', which is noted in two texts each respectively dated to Amenemhat III and Dynasty 13; and *wdp.w* 'butler', a position held by several Asiatics from the reign of Senwosret III to Dynasty 13.

Other positions within the household are dated from Senwosret III's reign to the mid-Thirteenth Dynasty, and record the *ᶜfty* 'brewer', *psy* 'cook', *nb.t pr.w* 'lady of the house', *sf.ty* 'butcher' and *šdi* 'tutor'.

Rulers of Levantine lands

Hieroglyphic titles of rulers of Levantine lands are found in texts of the early Twelfth to Fifteenth Dynasties. Those of the Twelfth Dynasty predominantly occur as titles in elite and royal Egyptian texts, whereas those of the Thirteenth to Fifteenth Dynasty mostly include titles from elite and royal items produced in Egypt and the Levant.

The earliest references to these rulers are in the Tale of Sinuhe. The text mentions the *ḥk3 n.y Rtnw ḥr.t* 'ruler of Upper *Rtnw*', a toponym that is associated in the tale with other areas in the Northern Levant. Sinuhe joins this ruler and others in the region, the *ḥk3.w ḫ3s.wt* 'rulers of foreign lands', in a conglomeration opposed to the movements of the *St.tyw*. The Tale of Sinuhe shows that the *ḥk3 n.y Rtnw ḥr.t*, who possibly ruled over Northern Levantine land, was among the *ḥk3.w ḫ3s.wt*.

The next attestation is found in the Mit Rahina text, in which the children of the *ḥk3.w n.w St.t* 'rulers of *St.t*' diplomatically visit Amenemhat II's court. A delegation naming a *ḥk3 ḫ3s.t* 'ruler of the foreign land' is recorded during Senwosret II's reign in Khnumhotep II's tomb, offering the only recorded use of this title in Dynasty 12. The ruler heads a procession of *ᶜ3m.w* from *Šw* yet he is not identified as a *ḥk3 n.y Šw* 'ruler of *Šw*'. The formula, *ḥk3 n.y GN*,[6] was indeed used in other texts of the Middle Kingdom, such as the Mit Rahina text (*ḥk3 n.w St.t*), the biography of Khnumhotep III (*ḥk3 n.y Kbny*), inscriptions at Serabit el-Khadim (*ḥk3 n.y Rtnw*) and the Execration Texts. The specific use of *ḥk3 ḫ3s.t* hints that this title expressed different and possibly more senior duties.

Between the late Twelfth to Thirteenth Dynasties, rulers of Levantine lands began to employ Egyptian titles. The Byblites referred to themselves as *ḥ3.ty-ᶜ n.y Kpny* 'count of *Kpny*' or simply *ḥ3.ty-ᶜ* 'count'. The titles continued in use until the MBIIB-C period, when the further titles of *ir.y-pᶜ.t* 'nobleman' and *ḥk3 ḥk3.w* 'ruler of rulers' are attested. As discussed in Chapter 6.3.3.3, the use of Egyptian titles in Byblos is most likely explained by the close relations between Egypt and Byblos and the many Egyptian influences on the Northern Levantine site, with the titles most possibly being direct translations of local ranks. This same reasoning may also be applied to the MBIIB Sidon scarab with *nb T3y* 'ruler of *T3y*'.

One further title from Byblos, *ḥk3 ḫ3s.wt* 'ruler of foreign lands', is written on a *ḥs*-vase from Royal Tomb VII. Cautiously dated to the MBIIB-C period, or the Thirteenth and Fifteenth Dynasties, it represents the only example for the title's use on a vessel from the examined period. The remaining attestations belong to sealings of Hyksos kings at Tell el-Dab'a, Tell el-Yahudiyah, Edfu and Gezer.

In regards to the *ḥk3 ḫ3s.wt* and its related titles, the examined evidence indicates: (a) the existence of political affiliations between the *ḥk3 n.y Rtnw ḥr.t* and other *ḥk3.w ḫ3s.wt*, the former joining the latter with a common aim during the early Twelfth Dynasty; (b) the difference between the *ḥk3 n.y GN* and the *ḥk3 ḫ3s.t* possibly being one of rank; (c) the diplomatic relations of a *ḥk3 ḫ3s.t* and a *ḥk3 n.y Rtnw ḥr.t* (as part of the *ḥk3.w ḫ3s.wt*) with Egypt; (d) possible relations between a *ḥk3 ḫ3s.wt* and the Egyptian-influenced Byblos during the MBIIB-C period; and (e) the title's use by early Fifteenth Dynasty rulers. The title thereby appears to be affiliated with high-ranking individuals who acted as representatives of rulers of several allied lands, or peoples, in political and diplomatic roles.[7]

Consequently, this affiliation sheds light on the reason for the adoption of the title *ḥk3 ḫ3s.wt* by the rulers of Dynasty 15. It is possible that the Hyksos favoured it as the most suitable expression for their commercial and mercantile initiatives, particularly with the establishment and stabilisation of Dynasty 15 as an independent hegemony. In fact, all provenanced and contemporary attestations of the title appear in administrative complexes within Egypt alongside other imported goods, and in elite contexts in the Levant. Such an association between use and purpose is not marred by Ryholt's observation that the last Fifteenth Dynasty rulers are not attested with the title.[8] The different programmes of the later Hyksos could theoretically warrant other titulary representation.

[6] 'Ruler of a Geographical Name'.

[7] Goldwasser writes that the title may refer to rural Levantine rulers in *E&L* 22-23 (2012/2013), 368.

[8] Ryholt describes the title as a 'petty' one for Levantine chieftains (*Political Situation*, 123-125, 303-304).

7.4 Artistic Representations

7.4.1 Artistic elements

Artistic representations of Asiatics can be found from the very beginning of Amenemhat I's reign to the Thirteenth Dynasty. Figure 7.12 presents a brief layout of pertinent representations utilising artistic elements typically associated with Asiatics, along with chapter references. These elements include facial features, hairstyles, skin colour, clothing and jewellery, foreign equipment, and unique stances and/or activities.

Facial features

Asiatic men and women can be illustrated with large, hooked noses. The men are usually shown with a pointed beard which may either be short or long, extending from ear to ear. Eyes tend to be large and almond-shaped, and are attested as black, brown or greyish-greenish blue.

Hairstyles

Male hair strands could be thick and wiry, or groomed. The colour is predominantly black, although some men are shown with red hair. From the early Twelfth Dynasty until the reign of Amenemhat II, a popular hairstyle for men is the coiffed and voluminous design, reaching just above shoulder-length. A tuft at the front may also be styled. The hair at the back is voluminous, either shaved perpendicular to the neck or curved inwards at an angle. The mushroom-like coiffed hairstyle is first recorded in Senwosret II's reign and continued in use until at least the Thirteenth Dynasty.[9] A rarer Middle Kingdom male hairstyle is the longer, shoulder-length hair depicted on a pectoral dating to Senwosret III's reign.

Women are portrayed with two main hairstyles. The first is illustrated as long, below shoulder-length, hair in Amenemhat I's pyramid complex and the tomb of Khnumhotep II. The women in the latter also wear white (silver?) headbands. The second hairstyle is characterised by a bulb-like protrusion, akin to a bun. This protrusion can be held in place with headbands, fillets, or wedge-shaped objects. The design occurs from early Dynasty 12 to Dynasty 13. As with men's hair, women are usually portrayed with black hair, but traces of red have been found on the women of Wekhhotep's tomb (C1) and a statuette at Beni Hassan.

Skin colour

Where the colour is preserved, Asiatic men could be painted with a yellow or a lighter yellow-brown skin colour. Women, as in other representations of Egyptian females, have a lighter yellow skin tone.

Clothing and jewellery

Foreign dress for men includes multi-banded, multi-coloured or detailed kilts, often with fringing along the bottom. Those of higher status are depicted with long tight-fitting garments draped over one shoulder. They are also multi-coloured, detailed, and often with fringing along the hem. Jewellery could consist of necklaces, either long or short, with pendants, banded wristlets, detailed anklets, and possible toggle-pins. Some men of Khnumhotep II's procession are illustrated wearing black strapped sandals and one sports an object hanging at the tip of his beard.

Women are also shown with long non-Egyptian garments. The dresses are either sleeved or draped over one shoulder, and are often detailed with red, blue and white designs. Some women additionally wear boot-like shoes, which appear to be painted yellow or red.

Foreign equipment

Weapons are the most frequently attested goods carried by Levantines. The tomb of Khnumhotep I records Asiatics with bows, throw-sticks, a dagger, a fenestrated eye-axe and a possible scimitar. During Senwosret I's reign, similar weapons are depicted along with spears. The following pharaoh's rule features a development in the type of Asiatic axe, with the depiction of the duckbill form and the newly attested composite bow. Asiatics could also carry rectangular shields, some with triangular notches at the edges.

Weapon-like objects and staffs are carried by individuals of high status, signifying their function as status markers. Well-attested is a staff with a slight curve at one end. First illustrated in Khnumhotep II's tomb, the staff continues to be associated with elite Asiatics during Amenemhat III's reign and probably in the Thirteenth Dynasty. It is similarly carried by a donkey-rider at Byblos. Another marker of status is an axe, which is represented between the reigns of Senwosret III and Amenemhat III.

Other goods are shown with the Asiatics. Those in Khnumhotep II's tomb lead animals (donkeys, a Nubian ibex and a gazelle) and carry such objects as a musical instrument, possible water-skins and two unidentifiable items. Handled vessels are represented in the tomb of Wekhhotep (C1) as well as Inscription Nr 112 at Serabit el-Khadim.

[9] Do. Arnold's suggestion (in *Second Intermediate Period*, 195-196) that 'the hairstyle of the Beni Hasan Aamu is unmistakably different from the "mushroom type" of the pectoral (dating to Amenemhat III) and related attestations' is not entirely correct. The Asiatics depicted in Khnumhotep II's tomb are in fact shown with different styles of the mushroom-like hair design. *Ibš3*'s hair is curving in at the back, that of the second-in-command is slightly longer, and the other men have their hair either cut perpendicular at the back or curved inwards. These variations most likely reflect artistic choice rather than markers of different ethnic identities.

Unique stances and/or activities

While Asiatics are shown in numerous instances partaking in typical Egyptian activities, some illustrations represent them in uncommon stances. Between the reigns of Amenemhat I and Senwosret, two women are depicted with an infant wrapped at the back. As mentioned in Chapter 4.3.6.1, this position is rarely utilised for Egyptians before the New Kingdom with several examples attributed to foreigners.

Other Twelfth Dynasty illustrations have Asiatic men shown as warriors freely carrying their weapons in battle scenes and processions. However, some depictions picture them as bound or subjugated prisoners in determinatives for Levantine peoples, a procession of captives, and smiting scenes. Despite the association of Asiatic men with war and the warrior class, the procession in Khnumhotep II's tomb and the inscriptions at Serabit el-Khadim uniquely portray elite and armed Asiatics in non-bellicose situations, either presented before a nobleman of the Oryx nome or as expedition members. The latter includes repeated motifs of an elite donkey rider with his retinue.

Thirteenth Dynasty to Second Intermediate Period attestations are few in number. Tell el-Dab'a's cylinder seal is the first portrayal to associate a smiting figure with Levantine elements possibly related to the myth of Baal. While this presents a Levantine-influenced figure in a cosmic context, the ivory sphinx from Abydos depicts a human-headed sphinx likely with mixed Egyptian-Asiatic elements. Apparently, representations were continually developing to adapt to the changing status and position of individuals of Asiatic descent.

7.4.2 Artistic differentiation of Asiatics and mixed Egyptian-Asiatics

Asiatics were portrayed in two key ways: (1) as individuals from the Levant; and (2) as individuals of mixed Egyptian-Asiatic heritage. This study has argued that artists first attempted to distinguish the two groups at Beni Hassan. The earliest depictions of individuals of mixed ancestry are in Amenemhat I's tomb (Senwosret I's reign), when the artist(s) were probably faced with the dilemma of distinguishing Asiatic warriors from Asiatics residing in the region. As neither of the two were correlated with ethnonyms such as *ꜥꜣm*, another identifier may have been required. The apparent artistic solution was to portray Asiatics living in Egypt with Egyptian dress, hairstyles, and facial features, but with a lighter, yellow, skin colour.

This artistic innovation of the 'fair-skinned men' continued to be utilised in Senwosret II's reign in Khnumhotep II's tomb. The warriors were no longer portrayed but the tomb did include a procession of Asiatics that were both textually and artistically represented as those from a foreign land. The 'fair-skinned men', however, were supplied with Egyptian names, titles, dress, hairstyles and facial features. A small red outline of a larger hooked nose on one of the men can be identified, indicating a possible artist's error in utilising the features of the procession's Asiatics with those living in Egypt. Perhaps, the inclusion of such features would have made the latter appear too foreign and so a more subtle but distinct lighter skin colour was favoured.

Another artistic dilemma was possibly met by the artists of Wekhhotep's tomb (C1) during Senwosret III's reign. Women of likely mixed Egyptian-Asiatic ancestry were to be depicted as offering bearers. As women in Egyptian art typically have a light yellow skin colour, the postulated solution of the Beni Hassan artists would not have sufficed. As such, other features, namely the women's hairstyles and goods, were possibly amended to express their mixed identity.

Evidence dating from Amenemhat III to the Thirteenth Dynasty indicates that a more standardised method of depicting foreigners arose. Individuals from the Levant were still shown with foreign features but those of mixed ancestry were mostly textually identified with the term *ꜥꜣm*, particularly in funerary stelae. A few cases still employed hybridised Egyptian-Asiatic elements, but all date to Dynasty 13. They include graffiti possibly drawn by Asiatics themselves and representations associated with the elite. As argued in Chapter 4.7, the evident use of mixed Egyptian-Asiatic features in art may correspond to a growing Asiatic community's influences on the elite as well as a certain 'freedom of expressing' a Levantine ethnic identity.

7.5 Conclusions

The overview of textual and artistic representations of Asiatics has revealed significant developments in the Egyptians' treatment of foreigners from the early Middle Kingdom to the early Fifteenth Dynasty. The Asiatic population was represented as individuals of Asiatic descent and individuals from the Levant. Asiatics from abroad were portrayed in both bellicose and peaceful representations. Royal ideological principles at first dominated the foreigners' portrayals in the examined Categories 2-3 while those in Categories 1, 5-7 bear only traces of these ideological influences. The cosmic and royal subjugation of the *other* gradually diminished in representations until Dynasty 13, when no attestations are found to negatively portray Asiatics.

Levantines are shown to enter Egypt by land and sea as war captives, travellers on and from diplomatic expeditions (particularly the elite), and allied warriors. The Northern Levant also appears to be most frequently referenced. Within Egypt, Asiatics intermingled with the local population, adopting Egyptian names, titles, dress and religious customs. They were treated as effective and significant members of the Egyptian community and were employed in a range of state, palatial, religious, and local government positions. From the mid-Twelfth to the Thirteenth Dynasties, they held high ranks in the capital's vizierate, treasury, military and temple precincts. One also became a nobleman in the Delta. Their growing number and power at first saw Egyptian artists experimenting with ways to portray them in artistic and textual sources. Then, between the reigns of Senwosret III and Amenemhat III, the term *ꜥ3m* became favoured. The use of this term was not a derogative delineator but simply a marker of their ethnicity. During Dynasty 13, hybridised elements bearing Asiatic features were mostly associated with elite Asiatics or items displaying royal or religious significance. This 'freedom to express' Asiatic customs thus became more prominent, signifying the growing power and influences of the Asiatic elite and the Levantine community on the Egyptians. It also signifies that their ethnic identity had become more prominent, perhaps in response to shifting socio-political situations.

Interestingly, few representations specifically date to Dynasties 14-15. In consideration of the available evidence, there are several attestations that are generally classified to be of Second Intermediate Period date, at least some of which could have been created during the Hyksos period. Furthermore, several contextual categories have not been found in the archaeological record and were possibly not even produced during the Hyksos period. These include Categories 1-3 and 7 relating to portrayals in royally-instigated Pharaonic inscriptions, funerary complexes, temple and religious texts, and literary pieces. Many of these items are also preserved on papyri which, considering the wet environment of the Delta, may not have been favourable for preservation. The categories of evidence are, however, supplanted by the archaeological evidence which notes trade, Levantine burials, and temples with Levantine features.

Therefore, the results emphasise the growing Egyptian acceptance of Levantines who gradually rose in power and political authority, especially in the Delta. This likely influenced the ideology of the distant and dangerous as indicated by the late Twelfth Dynasty's employment of less bellicose illustrations. The Egyptian view of the ethnic *other* was evidently not a stagnant and racially motivated concept, but a flexible one swayed by changing socio-political circumstances.[10] The Asiatic community was acknowledged by Egyptian royalty, the Egyptian elite and the general Egyptian community as a flourishing and noteworthy component of Egyptian society and politics. This Egyptian acceptance consequently led to Levantine influences on Egyptian life and, eventually, Egyptian politics. As such, it was not only the number and power of Asiatics in Egypt that may have supported the Fifteenth Dynasty takeover. The Egyptians' acceptance of Asiatics could have also been an essential ingredient in the Hyksos rulers' final claim to sovereignty.

[10] As also observed in Saretta, *Egyptian Perceptions of West Semites*.

NAME	TITLE(S)	DYNASTY	SOURCE	SITE	CHAPTER
ꜣpim	-	12 (A III)	Inscription Nr 405	Serabit el-Khadim	5.2.4.1
ꜥꜣ[...]*	ḥḳꜣ n.y Rṯnw	15	seal impression	Tell el-Dab'a F/II d	4.2.2.5
ꜥꜣm	ꜥfty	12 (S III)	CG 20296	Abydos	4.5.1.1
	ir.y-ꜥ.t	12 (A III)	Inscription Nr 85	Serabit el-Khadim	5.2.4.1
	ḥḳꜣ n.y Y-iꜥnḳ	12	Execration Texts	-	4.6.1
	-	12 (?)	CG 20125	Abydos	4.5.1.1
	-	13 (So. IV?)	ÄS 204	Abydos	4.5.1.1
	idn.w n.y im.y-rꜣ sḏꜣ.wt	Mid-13	scarab	Tell el-Dab'a A/II F	4.2.2.4
	smsw hꜣy.t	Mid-13	P Boulaq 18/1	Dra' Abu el-Naga'	4.5.3
	im.y-ẖt sꜣ.w pr.w	Mid-13	P Boulaq 18/1	Dra' Abu el-Naga'	4.5.3
	im.y-ẖt sꜣ.w pr.w	13	Inscription 14	Gebel Tjauti	4.5.10
	im.y-ẖt	13	Inscription 15	Gebel Tjauti	4.5.10
	im.y-rꜣ sẖ.ty	17 (Sobm.)	Inscription Nrs 23-24	Wadi el-Hammamat	5.3.1
	-	(?)	CG 20062	Abydos	4.5.1.1
	-	(?)	CG 20520	Abydos	4.5.1.1
	šmsw	(?)	U. Penn. Museum 69-29-56	Abydos	4.5.1.1
ꜥꜣm.t	-	Mid-12	false door (?) fragment	Dahshur	4.3.1.1
	-	12 (?)	CG 20421	Abydos	4.5.1.1
	-	12 (?)	ÄS 169	Abydos	4.5.1.1
	-	12-15	statue base	El-Lisht	4.3.6.2
	-	13	ÄS 160	Abydos	4.5.1.1
	nb.t pr.w	13	Inscription A	Aswan	4.5.2
	-	(?)	CG 20028	Abydos	4.5.1.1
	nb.t pr.w	(?)	CG 20650	Abydos	4.5.1.1
ꜥꜣmw / ꜥꜣ-ḥtp-Rꜥ.w	-	14	scarab	Abydos	4.5.1.2
	-	14 / late MBIIB-LBA	scarab	Lachish	6.1
	-	14 / (?)	scarabs	Tell el-'Ajjul	6.2.1.2
ꜥꜣmw[...] / Wr-n=i	-	Mid-13	P Brooklyn 35.1446	-	4.6.3
ꜥꜣḳ	-	(?)	CG 20753	Abydos	4.5.1.1
ꜥbd	-	(?)	CG 20161	Abydos	4.5.1.1
ꜥpr	im.y-rꜣ ḥm.wt	(?)	Rio de Janeiro 680	Abydos	4.5.1.1
ꜥpr-Bꜥꜣr	ir.y-pꜥ.t ḥꜣ.ty-ꜥ ẖtm.ty bi.ty smr wꜥ.ty im.y-rꜣ ẖtm.t	13	false door (?) jamb	Tell el-Habwa I	4.2.4.1
ꜥpr-Ršpw	ꜥfty	Mid-13	P Brooklyn 35.1446	-	4.6.3
ꜥmwsꜣnnši	ḥḳꜣ n.y Rtnw ḥr.t	12 (S I)	Tale of Sinuhe	-	4.6.9
ꜥn[...i] / Nb-m-mr-ḳis	sẖ.ty ḥꜣ.tyw	Mid-13	P Brooklyn 35.1446	-	4.6.3
ꜥnẖ.w	-	12 (?)	CG 20421	Abydos	4.5.1.1
	-	Late 12-13	Stela Moscow I.1.a.5349	-	4.6.7
ꜥnẖ.w / Pꜣ-ꜥꜣm	-	Mid-13	P Brooklyn 35.1446	-	4.6.3
ꜥnẖ.w-snb.w	-	Mid-13	P Brooklyn 35.1446	-	4.6.3
ꜥnẖy[t...]	-	12-13	UC 32130	El-Lahun	4.3.5.2
ꜥnt[...] / 'Iw=n-r-tꜣ-n	ḏꜣ ḥꜣ.tyw	Mid-13	P Brooklyn 35.1446	-	4.6.3
ꜥẖiꜣ.t=f / Km.tn=i	-	12-13	UC 32167	El-Lahun	4.3.5.2
ꜥẖtmr / Ḥnw.t=i-pw-wꜣḏ.t	ḏꜣ ḥꜣ.tyw	Mid-13	P Brooklyn 35.1446	-	4.6.3
[ꜥ]k[...] / [...nf]r.t-n[...]	sẖ.ty ḥꜣ.tyw	Mid-13	P Brooklyn 35.1446	-	4.6.3
ꜥḳbi / Rs-snb-wꜣḥ	ḏꜣ ḥꜣ.tyw	Mid-13	P Brooklyn 35.1446	-	4.6.3
ꜥḳbtw	-	Mid-13	P Brooklyn 35.1446	-	4.6.3
Wꜣḥ-kꜣ	-	(?)	CG 20549	Abydos	4.5.1.1
Wp-wꜣ.wt-ḥtp	-	Late 12-13	ÄS 186	Abydos	4.5.1.1
Wr-mr.wt-r=f	ir.y-ꜥ.t wdp.w	13	ÄS 160	Abydos	4.5.1.1
	-	13	ÄS 160	Abydos	4.5.1.1
Wr-n-Ptḥ	-	13 (?)	Marseille 227	Abydos	4.5.1.1
Wr-nb	-	13	ÄS 143	Abydos	4.5.1.1
Wr-ẖrp-ḥm(.wt)	sꜣb ẖr.y-ḥb.t ḥr.y-tp ḥm-nṯr sš	12 (A IV)	Inscription Nr 123	Serabit el-Khadim	5.2.4.1
Yꜣꜥmw / Nb.w-wsr-Rꜥ.w	-	14 / MBIIB-LBA	scarab	Pella	6.1
Yꜥḳbhr	-	14	scarab	Tell el-Yahudiyah	4.2.13.3
	-	14 / MBIIB-LBA	scarab	Pella	6.1
Yiy[...]	itḥ inr.w	12 (A III)	UC 32168; UC 32269	El-Lahun	4.3.5.2

FIGURE 7.10. NAMES OF INDIVIDUALS OF LEVANTINE ANCESTRY RECORDED IN STUDIED TEXTS (1/5).

NAME	TITLE(S)	DYNASTY	SOURCE	SITE	CHAPTER
Ypšmw-ỉb	-	12-13 (?) / MBIIA	pendant, Royal Tomb II	Byblos	6.3.3.2
	ḥꜣ.ty-ꜥ n.y Kpny	12-13 (?) / MBIIA	scimitar, Royal Tomb II	Byblos	6.3.3.2
	-	(?) / MBA	stela	Byblos	6.3.3.3
***Ykb*(*m*)** / *Sḫ-ꜥ-n-rꜥ.w*	-	14	scarab	Tell el-Yahudiyah	4.2.13.3
	-	14	scarab	Abydos	4.5.1.2
	-	14 / MBIIB-C	scarab	Tell Beit-Mirsim	6.1
	-	14 / late MBIIB	scarab	Tell Kabri	6.1
	-	14 / (?)	scarab	Tell el-'Ajjul	6.2.1.2
Ỉ-y	*ỉm.y-rꜣ*	(?)	CG 20650	Abydos	4.5.1.1
Ỉ-ꜥrꜣ	[...]	12 (A III)	P Berlin 10021	El-Lahun	4.3.5.2
Ỉ-tỉ	*nb.t pr.w*	13	Inscription A	Aswan	4.5.2
Ỉyỉ-m-ḥtp	-	(?)	CG 20158	Abydos	4.5.1.1
Ỉyỉ-nfr	-	Late 12-13	Stela Moscow I.1.a.5349	-	4.6.7
Ỉꜥsbtw / *Ỉmn*[*.tyw*]	*šdỉ*	Mid-13	P Brooklyn 35.1446	-	4.6.3
Ỉw-nfr	-	Late 12-13	Stela Moscow I.1.a.5349	-	4.6.7
Ỉw=s-n=ỉ	-	12 (A III)	Inscription Nr. 24-24a	Wadi Maghara	5.2.3
Ỉw-Snb	-	12 (?)	CG 20421	Abydos	4.5.1.1
Ỉb	*ḥꜣ.ty-ꜥ n.y Kpny*	13-15 / MBIIB-C	vessel, Royal Tomb IX	Byblos	6.3.3.2
***Ỉbỉ*[...*mꜥ*]** / *Snb-nb=f*	-	Mid-13	P Brooklyn 35.1446	-	4.6.3
Ỉbnr	-	12 (A III)	CG 20140	Abydos	4.5.1.1
Ỉbšꜣ	*ḥkꜣ ḫꜣs.t*	12 (S II)	tomb of Khnumhotep II	Beni Hassan	4.4.1.3
Ỉbšmw	*ḥꜣ.ty-ꜥ*	12-13 (?) / MBIIA	scimitar, Royal Tomb II	Byblos	6.3.3.2
	-	13-15 / MBIIB-C	vessel, Royal Tomb IX	Byblos	6.3.3.2
	ḥꜣ.ty-ꜥ n.y Kpny	(?) / MBA	obelisk	Byblos	6.3.3.1
	ḥꜣ.ty-ꜥ n.y Kpny	(?) / MBA	stela	Byblos	6.3.3.3
Ỉpnwỉrw	-	12 (A III ?)	Inscription Nr 115	Serabit el-Khadim	5.2.4.1
Ỉpḳ	-	14	scarab	Abydos	4.5.1.2
Ỉm.y-rꜣ-mšꜥ	*ỉr.y-ꜥ.t ꜥḥ*	13	ÄS 160	Abydos	4.5.1.1
	-	13	ÄS 160	Abydos	4.5.1.1
	-	13	ÄS 160	Abydos	4.5.1.1
	-	13	ÄS 160	Abydos	4.5.1.1
Ỉmỉ	-	12 (S III)	Rio de Janeiro 627	Abydos	4.5.1.1
Ỉmỉ-skr*(*t*)*w / *Snb-*[*S-n*]*-wsr.t*	*sḫ.ty ḥꜣ.tyw*	Mid-13	P Brooklyn 35.1446	-	4.6.3
Ỉmmw	-	Late 12-13	Stela Moscow I.1.a.5349	-	4.6.7
Ỉmny	*ỉr.y-ꜥ.t*	12 (S III)	CG 20296	Abydos	4.5.1.1
	*ꜥnḫ.w n.y nỉw.t**	13	Inscription A	Aswan	4.5.2
	ỉm.y-rꜣ ỉḥ.w	12-15	statue base	El-Lisht	4.3.6.2
Ỉmny-sšn=n/ Ỉmny	*ḫtm.ty nṯr ỉdn.w ỉm.y-rꜣ pr.w wr*	12 (A III)	Inscription Nr 93	Serabit el-Khadim	5.2.4.1
	ỉdn.w ỉm.y-rꜣ pr.w wr	12 (A III)	Inscription Nr 97	Serabit el-Khadim	5.2.4.1
	ỉdn.w ỉm.y-rꜣ pr.w wr	12 (A III)	Inscription Nr 94	Serabit el-Khadim	5.2.4.1
	ỉdn.w ỉm.y-rꜣ pr.w wr	12 (A III)	Inscription Nr 95	Serabit el-Khadim	5.2.4.1
	ỉdn.w ỉm.y-rꜣ pr.w wr	12 (A III)	Inscription Nr 96	Serabit el-Khadim	5.2.4.1
	ỉm.y-rꜣ ỉḫ.wt nb.wt n.y nsw.t ḫtm.ty nṯr ỉdn.w ỉm.y-rꜣ pr.w wr	12 (A III)	Inscription Nr 98	Serabit el-Khadim	5.2.4.1
	ỉdn.w ỉm.y-rꜣ pr.w wr	12 (A III ?)	Inscription Nr 402	Serabit el-Khadim	5.2.4
Ỉmnty-ꜥꜣm.t	-	13	ÄS 160	Abydos	4.5.1.1
Ỉmn[...]	-	12-13	P Berlin 10244	El-Lahun	4.3.5.2
Ỉmn[...] *ḫn.t* / *Ỉꜣy*	*ḫb*	12 (A III)	UC 32191	El-Lahun	4.3.5.2
Ỉnỉ	-	Late 12-13	Stela Moscow I.1.a.5349	-	4.6.7
Ỉntn	*ḥꜣ.ty-ꜥ n.y Kpn*	13 (No. I) / MBA	block	Byblos	6.3.3.1
Ỉrsỉ*	*ꜥfty*	13 (Khen.)	Liverpool E.30	Abydos	4.5.1.1
Ỉhnm	-	MK	Inscription Nr 163	Serabit el-Khadim	5.2.4.1
Ỉsmꜣꜣ	-	12-13	Inscription B	Aswan	4.5.2
Ỉšr / *Wr-ỉnỉ.t=f*	*sḫ.ty* [...]	Mid-13	P Brooklyn 35.1446	-	4.6.3
Ỉ-šrỉ	-	12-13	UC 32127	El-Lahun	4.3.5.2
Ỉḳr	*ḥsb*	12-13	UC 32201	El-Lahun	4.3.5.2
Ỉt	-	12 (A III)	Inscription Nr 54	Serabit el-Khadim	5.2.4.1
	-	12 (A III)	Inscription Nr 108	Serabit el-Khadim	5.2.4.1

FIGURE 7.10. NAMES OF INDIVIDUALS OF LEVANTINE ANCESTRY RECORDED IN STUDIED TEXTS (2/5).

NAME	TITLE(S)	DYNASTY	SOURCE	SITE	CHAPTER
Ỉt	-	(?)	CG 20227	Abydos	4.5.1.1
(continued)	-	(?)	CG 20227	Abydos	4.5.1.1
Ỉt-nfr.w / ꜥꜣm.t	-	12 (A III)	Inscription Nr 93	Serabit el-Khadim	5.2.4.1
	-	12 (A III)	Inscription Nr 96	Serabit el-Khadim	5.2.4.1
	-	12 (A III)	Inscription Nr 98	Serabit el-Khadim	5.2.4.1
Ỉdwtw */ Nb[...]*	*sḥ.ty ḥꜣ.tyw*	Mid-13	P Brooklyn 35.1446	-	4.6.3
Bꜣkt	*im.y-rꜣ ḫtm.t*	12 (S II)	tomb of Khnumhotep II	Beni Hassan	4.4.1.3
	nb.t pr.w	(?)	CG 20650	Abydos	4.5.1.1
Bꜥꜣtwy */ Wꜣḥ-rs-snb(.w)*	*ṯ.t kꜣ.t*	Mid-13	P Brooklyn 35.1446	-	4.6.3
Bb=i	-	(?)	CG 20441	Abydos	4.5.1.1
Bnn	-	Late 12-13	Stela Moscow I.1.a.5349	-	4.6.7
Bnr.t	-	13	ÄS 160	Abydos	4.5.1.1
Pꜣ-ꜥꜣm	-	12-13	UC 32124	El-Lahun	4.3.5.2
	-	Late 13	Warsaw 141.266	Edfu	4.5.4.1
Pnt [...]	-	13	Inscription A	Aswan	4.5.2
Psꜣ	-	Late 12-13	Stela Moscow I.1.a.5349	-	4.6.7
Ptḥ-ꜥꜣ.t	-	(?)	CG 20164	Abydos	4.5.1.1
Ptḥ-wr	*im.y-rꜣ ꜥḫnw.ty wr n.y pr ḥḏ*	12 (A III)	Inscription Nr 54	Serabit el-Khadim	5.2.4.1
	ḫtm.ty nṯr im.y-rꜣ ꜥḫnw.ty wr n.y pr ḥḏ	12 (A III)	Inscription Nr 108*	Serabit el-Khadim	5.2.4.1
	ḫtm.ty nṯr im.y-rꜣ ꜥḫnw.ty wr n.y pr ḥḏ	12 (A III)	Inscription Nr 109	Serabit el-Khadim	5.2.4.1
	ḫtm.ty nṯr im.y-rꜣ ꜥḫnw.ty wr n.y pr ḥḏ	12 (A III ?)	Inscription Nr 414	Serabit el-Khadim	5.2.4.1
Mꜣꜥ.t	-	13	CG 20281	Abydos	4.5.1.1
Mꜣꜥ-ib-rꜥ.w / ***Šši***	-	14	scarab	Tell el-Maskhuta	4.2.9.4
	-	14	scarabs	Tell el-Yahudiyah	4.2.13.3
	-	14	scarab	Abydos	4.5.1.2
	-	14	scarab	Deir Rifeh	4.4.5
	-	14 / late MBIIB-LBA	scarab	Lachish	6.1
	-	14 / (?)	scarabs	Tell el-'Ajjul	6.2.1.3
	-	14 / (?)	scarab	Gezer	6.2.5.3
Mꜣki	*ḥkꜣ n.y Kbny*	12 (S III)	tomb of Khnumhotep III	Dahshur	4.3.1.2
Mꜥšy	-	12-13	UC 32167	El-Lahun	4.3.5.2
Mw.t	-	Late 12-13	Stela Moscow I.1.a.5349	-	4.6.7
	-	Late 12-13	Stela Moscow I.1.a.5349	-	4.6.7
Mmi[...]	-	12-13	UC 32130	El-Lahun	4.3.5.2
Mnw-nfr	*wḏp.w*	Mid-13	tomb of Imenysenebnebwy	Hawara	4.3.3
Mnws	*(ḥkꜣ)*	12 (S I)	Tale of Sinuhe	-	4.6.9
Mnḥmi	*sḥ.ty ḥꜣ.tyw*	Mid-13	P Brooklyn 35.1446	-	4.6.3
Mri	*sf.ty*	12 (S III)	P Berlin 10050	El-Lahun	4.3.5.2
Mḥy	-	12 (A III)	Inscription Nr 93	Serabit el-Khadim	5.2.4.1
Mki	*(ḥkꜣ)*	12 (S I)	Tale of Sinuhe	-	4.6.9
N.t-ḥḏ	-	(?)	CG 20549	Abydos	4.5.1.1
N.t-ḥḏ.t	-	13	ÄS 160	Abydos	4.5.1.1
Nb-swmn.w	-	12 (A III)	E.207.1900	Abydos	4.5.1.1
*Nb.t-**Kbn***	-	Late 12-13	Stela Moscow I.1.a.5349	-	4.6.7
Nfr-iw	-	(?)	CG 20119	Abydos	4.5.1.1
	-	(?)	CG 20227	Abydos	4.5.1.1
Nfr-iw[...]	-	12-13	UC 32101H	El-Lahun	4.3.5.2
Nfr-mw.t=f	-	Late 12-13	Stela Moscow I.1.a.5349	-	4.6.7
Nfr-mni.t	-	Late 12-13	Stela Moscow I.1.a.5349	-	4.6.7
Nn-ḏi-rḫ.tw=f	-	13	ÄS 160	Abydos	4.5.1.1
Nhꜣi	*im.y-rꜣ mšꜥ*	(?)	CG 20650	Abydos	4.5.1.1
Nḥy-n=i	-	12-13	UC 32127	El-Lahun	4.3.5.2
Nḥsi *ꜥnḫ*	*ḥꜣ.ty-ꜥ n.y Kpn*	(?) / MBA	seal impression	Alalakh	6.3.3.3
Nḥsy (?)	*(sꜣ nsw.t smsw)*	14	scarabs	Tell Basta	4.2.1
	(sꜣ Rꜥ.w)	14	stelae	Tell el-Habwa I	4.2.4
	(sꜣ Rꜥ.w)	14	door jamb (?) fragment	Tell el-Dab'a	4.2.2
	(sꜣ Rꜥ.w)	14	block	Tell el-Dab'a	4.2.2
	(sꜣ Rꜥ.w)	14	usurped statue	Tell el-Muqdam	4.2.10
Nḫ.t-[...]w-imn.y	-	13	Inscription A	Aswan	4.5.2
Nḫti	*wḥm(.w)*	12 (S II)	tomb of Khnumhotep II	Beni Hassan	4.4.1.3
Nṯr-m-mr	-	13 (?)	Marseille 227	Abydos	4.5.1.1
Rꜣ-in[.t] / Snb-ḥ[nw.t]=s	*sḥ.ty ḥꜣ.tyw*	Mid-13	P Brooklyn 35.1446	-	4.6.3

FIGURE 7.10. NAMES OF INDIVIDUALS OF LEVANTINE ANCESTRY RECORDED IN STUDIED TEXTS (3/5).

NAME	TITLE(S)	DYNASTY	SOURCE	SITE	CHAPTER
Rwꜣ	-	12 (A III)	Inscription Nr 81	Serabit el-Khadim	5.2.4.1
Rn=f-snb(.w)	*wdp.w*	12 (A III)	E.207.1900	Abydos	4.5.1.1
Rn=s-snb(.w)	-	(?)	CG 20549	Abydos	4.5.1.1
Rn-snb(.w)	*ỉm.y-ẖt ỉm.y-rꜣ ḥm.tyw*	13	Inscription 16	Gebel Tjauti	4.5.10
*Rn-snb(.w)**	-	13 (?)	Marseille 227	Abydos	4.5.1.1
Rḥ.wy / Kꜣ(=ỉ)-pw-nb=ỉ	*ḏꜣ šsr*	Mid-13	P Brooklyn 35.1446	-	4.6.3
Rs-snb(.w) / Rn=f-rs(.w)	-	Mid-13	P Brooklyn 35.1446	-	4.6.3
Rs[...]	-	12-13	UC 32130	El-Lahun	4.3.5.2
R[...] / Ỉw-n-sỉ[...]	-	Mid-13	P Brooklyn 35.1446	-	4.6.3
Hꜣỉmmỉ	*sḫ.ty ḥꜣ.tyw*	Mid-13	P Brooklyn 35.1446	-	4.6.3
Hyibỉrw / *[Nḥ]-n=ỉ-m-ḫꜣs.t*	*šnꜥ*	Mid-13	P Brooklyn 35.1446	-	4.6.3
Hrw-nfr	-	12 (S III)	Rio de Janeiro 627	Abydos	4.5.1.1
Ḥyỉwr[...]	-	Mid-13	P Brooklyn 35.1446	-	4.6.3
Ḥw[...]	-	Mid-13	P Brooklyn 35.1446	-	4.6.3
Ḥp.w	*wdp.w*	(?)	CG 20571	Abydos	4.5.1.1
Ḥr-ỉ[...]	-	12-13	UC 32130	El-Lahun	4.3.5.2
Ḥrỉ	-	(?)	CG 20549	Abydos	4.5.1.1
Ḥtp.wy	-	(?)	CG 20549	Abydos	4.5.1.1
Ḥtp.t	-	12 (S III)	CG20296	Abydos	4.5.1.1
Ḫyꜣn	*ḥḳꜣ ḫꜣs.wt*	Early 15	seal impression	Tell el-Dab'a R/III	4.2.2.2
	ḥḳꜣ ḫꜣs.wt	15	seal impressions	Tell el-Dab'a F/II c/1	4.2.2.5
	ḥḳꜣ ḫꜣs.wt	15	scarabs	Tell el-Yahudiyah	4.2.13.3
	ḥḳꜣ ḫꜣs.wt	15	seal impressions	Edfu	4.5.4.2
	ḥḳꜣ ḫꜣs.wt	15 / MBIIB-C	scarab	Gezer	6.2.4.2
Ḫꜥ-wsr-rꜥ.w	-	14	scarab	Abydos	4.5.1.2
Ḫꜥ-ḫpr-Rꜥ.w [...]	*[...tp] ṯꜣ.t*	12-13	UC 32143E	El-Lahun	4.3.5.2
Ḫꜥ-[...]-Rꜥ.w/[...] pw	*ḫb*	12 (A III)	UC 32191	El-Lahun	4.3.5.2
Ḫbdd(m)	*(sn n.y ḥḳꜣ Rṯnw)*	12 (A III)	Inscription Nr 85	Serabit el-Khadim	5.2.4.1
	(sn n.y ḥḳꜣ Rṯnw)	12 (A III)	Inscription Nr 87	Serabit el-Khadim	5.2.4.1
	(sn n.y ḥḳꜣ Rṯnw)	12 (A III)	Inscription Nr 92	Serabit el-Khadim	5.2.4.1
	(sn n.y ḥḳꜣ Rṯnw)	12 (A III)	Inscription Nr 112	Serabit el-Khadim	5.2.4.1
Ḫnw [...]	-	12-13	UC 32130	El-Lahun	4.3.5.2
H̱nm[..w...]	-	12-13	UC 32151B	El-Lahun	4.3.5.2
Ḫntỉ-wr	*wdp.w*	12 (A III)	CG 20231	Abydos	4.5.1.1
Ḫnty.w-š	*(ḥḳꜣ)*	12 (S I)	Tale of Sinuhe	-	4.6.9
H̱t.y	*ỉm.y-rꜣ ꜥẖnw.ty*	12 (S II)	tomb of Khnumhotep II	Beni Hassan	4.4.1.3
S-n-wsr.t	*ỉr.y ꜥꜣ n(.y) ḥw.t-nṯr*	12 (S III)	P Berlin 10050	El-Lahun	4.3.5.2
	šmsw	12 (A III)	P Berlin 10033	El-Lahun	4.3.5.2
	šmꜥw	12 (A III)	P Berlin 10047	El-Lahun	4.3.5.2
	šꜥmỉ (?)	12 (A III)	CG 20140	Abydos	4.5.1.1
	-	12-13	UC 32151B	El-Lahun	4.3.5.2
	-	12-13	P Berlin 10106	El-Lahun	4.3.5.2
	-	Late 12-13	Stela Moscow I.1.a.5349	-	4.6.7
S-n-wsr.t-snb	*šmꜥw*	12 (A III)	P Berlin 10066	El-Lahun	4.3.5.2
S-nfrw	-	13 (?)	Marseille 227	Abydos	4.5.1.1
Sꜣ-Ỉp	*mty n(.y) sꜣ*	Mid-12	false door (?) fragment	Dahshur	4.3.1.1
Sꜣ-nfr	*ḥr.y-pr.w*	12 (A III)	Inscription Nr 112	Serabit el-Khadim	5.2.4.1
*Sꜣ.t-ꜥꜣm**	-	12-13	UC 32276	El-Lahun	4.3.5.2
Sꜣ.t-Ḥw.t-ḥr	-	13 - early SIP	Berlin 22.708	El-Rizeiqat	4.5.9
Sꜣ.t-H̱nmw	-	13 (?)	Marseille 227	Abydos	4.5.1.1
Sw[rꜥ...]	*ỉtḥ ỉnr.w*	12 (A III)	UC 32168, UC 32269	El-Lahun	4.3.5.2
Sw[...]ỉ / ꜥnḫ.w-snb(.w)	*psy*	Mid-13	P Brooklyn 35.1446	-	4.6.3
Sbk-ỉry	-	13 (Khen.)	Liverpool E.30	Abydos	4.5.1.1
	-	13 (Khen.)	Liverpool E.30	Abydos	4.5.1.1
Sbk-ꜥꜣ	-	(?)	CG 20549	Abydos	4.5.1.1
Sbk-wr	*ỉr.y sšr**	13	Inscription A	Aswan	4.5.2
Sbk-nḫ.t	*ỉm.y-rꜣ šnꜥ.w*	12 (S III)	CG 20296	Abydos	4.5.1.1
	-	12 (S III)	CG 20296	Abydos	4.5.1.1
	-	13	ÄS 143	Abydos	4.5.1.1
Sbk-ḥtp	-	(?)	CG 20550	Abydos	4.5.1.1
Smkn	*ḥḳꜣ ḫꜣs.wt*	15 (?)	scarab	Tell el-Yahudiyah	4.2.13.3
Sn-ꜥnḫ(.w)	*ỉm.y-rꜣ ḫtm.tyw*	12 (S II)	tomb of Khnumhotep II	Beni Hassan	4.4.1.3
Sn-bwbw	-	12-13	UC 32130	El-Lahun	4.3.5.2
Sn-nw.t	*pr.t n.t r=s*	Mid-13	P Brooklyn 35.1446	-	4.6.3

FIGURE 7.10. NAMES OF INDIVIDUALS OF LEVANTINE ANCESTRY RECORDED IN STUDIED TEXTS (4/5).

NAME	TITLE(S)	DYNASTY	SOURCE	SITE	CHAPTER
Sn.t-Sbk	-	12 (?)	ÄS 169	Abydos	4.5.1.1
Snb.ty=fy	-	12 (?)	CG 20421	Abydos	4.5.1.1
Snb.ty=sy	-	Mid-13	P Brooklyn 35.1446	-	4.6.3
	-	Mid-13	P Brooklyn 35.1446	-	4.6.3
Snb-imny-nb-it	-	13 (Khen.)	Liverpool E.30	Abydos	4.5.1.1
Snb-b-w	*wdp.w*	12 (S III)	Inscription Nr 17	Wadi el-Hudi	5.3.2
Snb-r-ꜣw	-	12 (?)	CG 20421	Abydos	4.5.1.1
*Snb-rẖ.w**	-	13 (?)	Marseille 227	Abydos	4.5.1.1
Snb-rs-snb(.w)	*psy*	Mid-13	P Brooklyn 35.1446	-	4.6.3
Snb-ḥḳꜣ	-	13	Roanne Nr 163	-	4.6.8
Snbỉ	-	(?)	CG 20392	Abydos	4.5.1.1
Snb [...]-snb / [...ꜥỉ]	*ẖb*	12 (A III)	UC 32191	El-Lahun	4.3.5.2
Snt[..ṯ...]-ẖpr-snb/ [...]sḥtp	*ẖb*	12 (A III)	UC 32191	El-Lahun	4.3.5.2
Skr */ Nb-rḏi=s*	-	Mid-13	P Brooklyn 35.1446	-	4.6.3
Skr*[wp...] / Mr.t-nb*	*ḏꜣ šsr*	Mid-13	P Brooklyn 35.1446	-	4.6.3
Skrtw */ Wr-ꜥt-n=i-nbw*	*sẖ.ty ḥꜣ.tyw*	Mid-13	P Brooklyn 35.1446	-	4.6.3
Skrtw */ Sn[b...]*	*sẖ.ty sšr*	Mid-13	P Brooklyn 35.1446	-	4.6.3
Sty-rꜣ	*šmsw*	12 (A III)	P Berlin 10081C	El-Lahun	4.3.5.2
Sḏꜣ[...]	-	12-13	UC 32130	El-Lahun	4.3.5.2
Šꜣꜥ*	-	Late 12-13	ÄS 186	Abydos	4.5.1.1
Špr */ Snb-ḥnw.t=s*	*sẖ.ty ḥꜣ.tyw*	Mid-13	P Brooklyn 35.1446	-	4.6.3
Šmštw */ Snb-ḥnw.t[...]*	*ḏꜣ ḥꜣ.tyw*	Mid-13	P Brooklyn 35.1446	-	4.6.3
Škꜣm	-	12 (A III)	Inscription Nr 405	Serabit el-Khadim	5.2.4.1
Šd.ty	-	12 (A III)	P Berlin 10047	El-Lahun	4.3.5.2
Ḳꜣ-sn.w	-	(?)	CG 20114	Abydos	4.5.1.1
Ḳwi[...] / Rs-snb(.w)	*ḥr.y-pr.w*	Mid-13	P Brooklyn 35.1446	-	4.6.3
Ḳdmni	-	Late 12	E.60.1926	Abydos	4.5.1.1
Kwkwn	*ẖtm.ty nsw=f*	(?) / MBA	obelisk	Byblos	6.3.3.1
Kbšty	-	(?)	CG 20441	Abydos	4.5.1.1
Km.n=i / Spdw-m-mr=i	-	12-13	UC 32167	El-Lahun	4.3.5.2
Kms	-	Late 12	E.60.1926	Abydos	4.5.1.1
Kms[...]	-	12-13	UC 32130	El-Lahun	4.3.5.2
Kni	-	MK	Inscription Nr 163	Serabit el-Khadim	5.2.4.1
Kkw	-	13	Inscription A	Aswan	4.5.2
Kkbi	-	12 (A III)	Inscription Nr 112	Serabit el-Khadim	5.2.4.1
Gbgb	-	12 (S III)	Rio de Janeiro 627	Abydos	4.5.1.1
Twty	*im.y-rꜣ n.y ḥm.wt*	(?)	Rio de Janeiro 680	Abydos	4.5.1.1
Twtwit */ ꜥnẖ.w-m-ḥs.wt*	*ḥr.y-pr.w*	Mid-13	P Brooklyn 35.1446	-	4.6.3
Ṯnꜥtisi */ Pt=i-mn.ti*	*šnꜥ*	Mid-13	P Brooklyn 35.1446	-	4.6.3
*Di-sbk-m-ḥꜣ.t**	*ḥḳꜣ n.y Rṯnw**	Early 13	scarab*	Tell el-Dab'a F/I d/1	4.2.2.3
Diꜣihitw */ Mn-ḥs[.wt]*	-	Mid-13	P Brooklyn 35.1446	-	4.6.3
Ddmwtw*...*.*	-	Mid-13	P Brooklyn 35.1446	-	4.6.3
*Ḏfꜣ-snb**	-	Late 12-13	ÄS 186	Abydos	4.5.1.1
Ḏḏ.t	-	Late 12-13	ÄS 99	Abydos	4.5.1.1
Ḏdkꜣrꜥ	*nb ꜣꜣy*	(?) / MBIIB	scarab	Sidon	6.3.7.6
[...] / Iḥꜣ[.y]	*šnꜥ*	Mid-13	P Brooklyn 35.1446	-	4.6.3
*[...]i-**ꜣši***	-	MK	Inscription Nr 163	Serabit el-Khadim	5.2.4.1
[...]ꜥm [...bnwy]	-	12-13	UC 32167	El-Lahun	4.3.5.2
[...wnꜥ..] / Nfr.t	*ḏꜣ šsr*	Mid-13	P Brooklyn 35.1446	-	4.6.3
[..].t-pw-Ptḥ	*nb.t pr.w*	(?)	CG 20650	Abydos	4.5.1.1
[...]tn	*ir.y-pꜥ.t ḥꜣ.ty-ꜥ ḥḳꜣ ḥḳꜣ.w ḥꜣ.ty-ꜥ n.y Kpn[y]*	13-15 / MBIIB-C	vessel fragments, Royal Tomb IV	Byblos	6.3.3.2
[...ḥr...]	-	13-early SIP	Bremen 4558	El-Rizeiqat	4.5.9
[...] ẖpr-ḥr-sḥb / [...i]m-ẖꜣ[...]	*ẖb*	12 (A III)	UC 32191	El-Lahun	4.3.5.2
[...]ki[...]	-	12-13	UC 32151B	El-Lahun	4.3.5.2

FIGURE 7.10. NAMES OF INDIVIDUALS OF LEVANTINE ANCESTRY RECORDED IN STUDIED TEXTS (5/5). NAMES IN THE EXECRATION TEXTS ARE NOT INCLUDED UNLESS MENTIONED ELSEWHERE.

* Uncertain reading.

Notes: Names likely of non-Egyptian origin are in bold.

A: Amenemhat	S: Senwosret	Khen: Khendjer	So.: Sobekhotep
No.: Noferhotep	Sobm.: Sobekemsaf	MK: Middle Kingdom	SIP: Second Intermediate Period

TITLE	TRANSLATION	DYNASTY	SOURCE	SITE	CHAPTER
im.y-rꜣ	overseer	(?)	CG 20650	Abydos	4.5.1.1
im.y-rꜣ iḥ.w	overseer of cattle	12-15	statue base	El-Lisht	4.3.6.2
im.y-rꜣ iḫ.wt nb.wt n.y nsw.t	overseer of all property of the king	12 (A III)	Inscription Nr 98	Serabit el-Khadim	5.2.4.1
im.y-rꜣ ꜥḫnw.ty	chamberlain	12 (S II)	tomb of Khnumhotep II	Beni Hassan	4.4.1.3
im.y-rꜣ ꜥḫnw.ty wr n.y pr ḥḏ	chief chamberlain of the treasury	12 (A III)	Inscription Nr 54	Serabit el-Khadim	5.2.4.1
		12 (A III)	Inscription Nr 108	Serabit el-Khadim	5.2.4.1
		12 (A III)	Inscription Nr 109	Serabit el-Khadim	5.2.4.1
im.y-rꜣ mšꜥ	overseer of the expedition/army	(?)	CG 20650	Abydos	4.5.1.1
im.y-rꜣ ḥm.wt	overseer of craftsmen	(?)	Rio de Janeiro 680	Abydos	4.5.1.1
im.y-rꜣ ḥm.tyw	overseer of coppersmiths	13	Inscription 16	Gebel Tjauti	4.5.10
im.y-rꜣ ḫtm.t	overseer of the treasury, treasurer	12 (S II)	tomb of Khnumhotep II	Beni Hassan	4.4.1.3
		13	false door (?) jamb	Tell el-Habwa I	4.2.4.1
im.y-rꜣ ḫtm.tyw	overseer of sealers	12 (S II)	tomb of Khnumhotep II	Beni Hassan	4.4.1.3
im.y-rꜣ sḫ.ty	overseer of fieldworkers	17 (Sobm.)	Inscription Nr 23-24	Wadi el-Hammamat	5.3.1
im.y-rꜣ šnꜥ.w	overseer of a storehouse	12 (S III)	CG 20296	Abydos	4.5.1.1
im.y-ḫt	attendant	13	Inscription 15	Gebel Tjauti	4.5.10
			Inscription 16	Gebel Tjauti	4.5.10
im.y-ḫt sꜣ.w pr.w	police official	Mid-13	P Boulaq 18/1	Dra' Abu el-Naga'	4.5.3
		13	Inscription 14	Gebel Tjauti	4.5.10
ir.y-ꜥ.t	hall-keeper	12 (S III)	CG 20296	Abydos	4.5.1.1
		12 (A III)	Inscription Nr 85	Serabit el-Khadim	5.2.4.1
		13	ÄS 160	Abydos	4.5.1.1
*ir.y ꜥ.t n.y iḥw**	hall-keeper of the cattle-pen	12 (A II)	tomb of Wekhhotep (B4)	Meir	4.4.4.2
ir.y-ꜥ.t ꜥḥ	hall-keeper of the palace	13	ÄS 160	Abydos	4.5.1.1
ir.y ꜥꜣ n.y ḥw.t-nṯr	door-keeper of a temple	12 (S III)	P Berlin 10050	El-Lahun	4.3.5.2
ir.y pꜥ.t	nobleman	13-15 / MBIIB-C	vessel fragments, Royal Tomb IV	Byblos	6.3.3.2
	nobleman	(?) / MBA	stela	Byblos	6.3.3.3
*ir.y sšr**	keeper of linen	13	Inscription A	Aswan	4.5.2
itḥ inr.w	stone-hauler	12 (A III)	UC 32168, UC 32269	El-Lahun	4.3.5.2
idn.w n.y im.y-rꜣ pr.w wr	deputy of the chief steward	12 (A III)	Inscription Nr 93	Serabit el-Khadim	5.2.4.1
			Inscription Nr 97	Serabit el-Khadim	5.2.4.1
			Inscription Nr 98	Serabit el-Khadim	5.2.4.1
idn.w n.y im.y-rꜣ ḫtm.t	deputy of the overseer of the treasury	Mid-13	scarab	Tell el-Dab'a A/II F	4.2.2.4
ꜥfty	brewer	12 (S III)	CG 20296	Abydos	4.5.1.1
		13 (Khen.)	Liverpool E.30	Abydos	4.5.1.1
		Mid-13	P Brooklyn 35.1446 (x 1)	-	4.6.3
*ꜥnḫ.w n.y niw.t**	citizen, officer of the city regiment	13	Inscription A	Aswan	4.5.2
wḥm.w	herald	12 (S II)	tomb of Khnumhotep II	Beni Hassan	4.4.1.3
wdp.w	butler	12 (S III)	Inscription Nr 17	Wadi el-Hudi	5.3.2
		12 (A III)	CG 20231	Abydos	4.5.1.1
			E.207.1900	Abydos	4.5.1.1
		Mid-13	tomb of Imenysenebnebwy	Hawara	4.3.3
		13	ÄS 160	Abydos	4.5.1.1
		(?)	CG 20571	Abydos	4.5.1.1
psy	cook	Mid-13	P Brooklyn 35.1446 (x 2)	-	4.6.3
mty n.y sꜣ	controller of a phyle	Mid-12	false door (?) fragment	Dahshur	4.3.1.1
nb Ꞽꜣy	ruler of *Ꞽꜣy*	(?) / MBIIB	scarab	Sidon	6.3.7.6
nb.t pr.w	lady of the house	Mid-13	CG 20086	Abydos	4.5.1.1
		13	Inscription A	Aswan	4.5.2
		(?)	CG 20650	Abydos	4.5.1.1
			CG 20650	Abydos	4.5.1.1
ḥꜣ.ty-ꜥ	count	12-13 (?) / MBIIA	scimitar, Royal Tomb II	Byblos	6.3.3.2
		13	false door (?) jamb	Tell el-Habwa I	4.2.4.1
		13 (No. I) / MBA	block	Byblos	6.3.3.1
		(?) / MBA	stela	Byblos	6.3.3.3
ḥꜣ.ty-ꜥ n.y Kpny	count of *Kpny*	12-13 (?) / MBIIA	scimitar, Royal Tomb II	Byblos	6.3.3.2
		13 (No. I) / MBA	block	Byblos	6.3.3.1

FIGURE 7.10. EGYPTIAN TITLES OF INDIVIDUALS OF LEVANTINE ANCESTRY RECORDED IN STUDIED TEXTS (1/2).

TITLE	TRANSLATION	DYNASTY	SOURCE	SITE	CHAPTER
ḥ3.ty-ʿ n.y Kpny *(continued)*	count of *Kpny*	13-15 / MBIIB-C	fragments, Royal Tomb IV	Byblos	6.3.3.2
		13-15 / MBIIB-C	vessel, Royal Tomb IX	Byblos	6.3.3.2
		(?) / MBA	obelisk	Byblos	6.3.3.1
			stela	Byblos	6.3.3.3
			seal impression	Alalakh	6.3.3.3
ḥm-nṯr	god's-servant	12 (A IV)	Inscription Nr 123	Serabit el-Khadim	5.2.4.1
ḥr.y-pr.w	major-domo, domestic servant	12 (A III)	Inscription Nr 112	Serabit el-Khadim	5.2.4.1
		Mid-13	P Brooklyn 35.1446 (x 3)	-	4.6.3
ḥsb	workman	12-13	UC 32201	El-Lahun	4.3.5.2
ḥḳ3 n.y Kbny	ruler of *Kbny*	12 (S III)	tomb of Khnumhotep III	Dahshur	4.3.1.2
ḥḳ3 n.y Rṯnw	ruler of *Rṯnw*	12 (A III)	Inscription Nr 85	Serabit el-Khadim	5.2.4.1
			Inscription Nr 87	Serabit el-Khadim	5.2.4.1
			Inscription Nr 92	Serabit el-Khadim	5.2.4.1
			Inscription Nr 112	Serabit el-Khadim	5.2.4.1
		Early 13	scarab*	Tell el-Dab'a F/I d/1	4.2.2.3
		15	seal impression	Tell el-Dab'a F/II d	4.2.2.5
ḥḳ3 n.y Rṯnw ḥr.t	ruler of Upper *Rṯnw*	12 (S I)	Tale of Sinuhe	-	4.6.9
ḥḳ3 ḥḳ3.w	ruler of rulers	13-15 / MBIIB-C	vessel fragments, Royal Tomb IV	Byblos	6.3.3.2
ḥḳ3 ḫ3s.t	ruler of the foreign land	12 (S II)	tomb of Khnumhotep II	Beni Hassan	4.4.1.3
ḥḳ3 ḫ3s.wt	ruler of foreign lands	13-15 / MBIIB-C	vessel, Royal Tomb VII	Byblos	6.3.3.2
		Early 15	seal impression	Tell el-Dab'a R/III	4.2.2.2
		15	seal impressions	Tell el-Dab'a F/II c/1	4.2.2.5
			scarab	Tell el-Yahudiyah	4.2.13.3
			scarab	Tell el-Yahudiyah	4.2.13.3
			seal impressions	Edfu	4.5.4.2
		15 / MBIIB-C	scarab	Gezer	6.2.4.2
ḥḳ3.w n.w St.t	rulers of *St.t*	12 (A II)	block	Mit Rahina	4.3.7
ḥḳ3.w ḫ3s.wt	rulers of foreign lands	12 (S I)	Tale of Sinuhe	-	4.6.9
ḫb	dancer	12 (A III)	UC 32191	El-Lahun	4.3.5.2
ḫtm.ty bi.ty	sealer of the king of Lower Egypt	13	false door (?) jamb	Tell el-Habwa I	4.2.4.1
ḫtm.ty nsw=f	sealer of his king	(?) / MBA	obelisk	Byblos	6.3.3.1
ḫtm.ty nṯr	god's sealer	12 (A III)	Inscription Nr 93	Serabit el-Khadim	5.2.4.1
			Inscription Nr 108*	Serabit el-Khadim	5.2.4.1
			Inscription Nr 109	Serabit el-Khadim	5.2.4.1
			Inscription Nr 98	Serabit el-Khadim	5.2.4.1
s3b ḫr.y-ḥb.t ḥr.y-tp	senior chief lector priest	12 (A IV)	Inscription Nr 123	Serabit el-Khadim	5.2.4.1
sf.ty	butcher	12 (S III)	P Berlin 10050	El-Lahun	4.3.5.2
smr wʿ.ty	sole companion	13	false door (?) jamb	Tell el-Habwa I	4.2.4.1
smsw h3y.t	elder of the portal	Mid-13	P Boulaq 18/1	Dra' Abu el-Naga'	4.5.3
sḫ.ty ḥ3.tyw	weaver of *ḥ3.tyw*-cloth	Mid-13	P Brooklyn 35.1446 (x 9)	-	4.6.3
sḫ.ty sšr	weaver of *sšr*-cloth	Mid-13	P Brooklyn 35.1446 (x 1)	-	4.6.3
sḫ.ty [...]	weaver [...]	Mid-13	P Brooklyn 35.1446	-	4.6.3
sš	scribe	12 (A IV)	Inscription Nr 123	Serabit el-Khadim	5.2.4.1
šʿmi (?)	(?)	12 (A III)	CG 20140	Abydos	4.5.1.1
šmʿw	singer	12 (A III)	P Berlin 10066	El-Lahun	4.3.5.2
			P Berlin 10047	El-Lahun	4.3.5.2
šmsw	retainer, guard	12 (A III)	P Berlin 10033	El-Lahun	4.3.5.2
			P Berlin 10081C	El-Lahun	4.3.5.2
		(?)	U. Penn. Museum 69-29-56	Abydos	4.5.1.1
šnʿ	labourer	Mid-13	P Brooklyn 35.1446 (x 3)	-	4.6.3
šdi	tutor	Mid-13	P Brooklyn 35.1446 (x 1)	-	4.6.3
ṯ.t k3.t	labourer (?)	Mid-13	P Brooklyn 35.1446 (x 1)	-	4.6.3
d3 ḥ3.tyw	warper(?) of *ḥ3.tyw*-cloth	Mid-13	P Brooklyn 35.1446 (x 5)	-	4.6.3
d3 šsr	warper(?) of *šsr*-cloth	Mid-13	P Brooklyn 35.1446 (x 4)	-	4.6.3
[...*tp*]* *ṯ3.t*	[...member] of the vizierate	12-13	UC 32143E	El-Lahun	4.3.5.2

FIGURE 7.11. EGYPTIAN TITLES OF INDIVIDUALS OF LEVANTINE ANCESTRY RECORDED IN STUDIED TEXTS (2/2). TITLES IN THE EXECRATION TEXTS ARE NOT INCLUDED.

* Uncertain reading.

Notes: All translations of titles are based on those in Ward, *Index*.

A: Amenemhat S: Senwosret Khen: Khendjer Sobm.: Sobekemsaf
No.: Noferhotep MK: Middle Kingdom SIP: Second Intermediate Period

DYNASTY	SOURCE	SITE	FACE	HAIR	SKIN	CLOTHES	EQUIPMENT	STANCE AND/OR ACTIVITY	CHAPTER
A I	Pyramid complex	El-Lisht	hooked nose	woman with long hair	yellow	-	-	infant wrapped at back	4.3.6.1
	Tomb of Khnumhotep I	Beni Hassan	pointed beards; greenish-grey eyes	red to black; above shoulder-length; coiffed	yellow	kilts and long one-shouldered garment; red, blue and white detail; necklaces with pendants; chest bands; banded wristlets and anklets	bows; throw-sticks; dagger; fenestrated eye-axe; scimitar*	warriors	4.4.1.1
A I-S I	Shaft Tomb 181	Beni Hassan	thick eyebrows; curved nose	black; bulb-like protrusion (bun?); headbands	yellow	long-sleeved garment; red with possible detail; yellow footwear	-	infant wrapped at back	4.4.1.4
S I	Pyramid complex	El-Lisht	pointed beard	slightly bulbous at back centre, angular at back; shaved at neck	-	-	-	relation to smiting scene	4.3.6.1
	Pyramid complex	El-Lisht	pointed beard	slightly bulbous at back centre, angular at back; shaved at neck	-	-	-	bound; procession of foreigners	4.3.6.1
	Pyramid complex	El-Lisht	pointed beards	red; tuft at front	yellow-brown	-	spear*, shield*	attacking from fortress*	4.3.6.1
S I	Tomb of Amenemhat (warriors)	Beni Hassan	pointed beards; brownish-black eyes	black; above shoulder-length; coiffed	yellow	kilts; red, blue and white detail	throw-stick; spear; fenestrated eye-axe	warriors	4.4.1.2
	Tomb of Amenemhat ('fair-skinned men')	Beni Hassan	-	-	yellow	-	-	-	4.4.1.2
A II	Tomb of Wekhhotep (B4)	Meir	pointed beards	shoulder-length; voluminous at back	-	-	-	-	4.4.4.2
S II	Tomb of Khnumhotep II (procession)	Beni Hassan	hooked noses; greyish-blue eyes; men with short beards, one with an unidentified object	black; men with mushroom-like hair; women with long hair and headbands	yellow	men with kilts, long one-shouldered garment and sandals; women with long one-shouldered garments and red footwear; all red, blue and white detail with fringes	composite bows; spears; duckbill axe; curved staff as status marker; animals; lyre; gourds(?); unknown object	procession bringing goods	4.4.1.3
	Tomb of Khnumhotep II ('fair-skinned men')	Beni Hassan	red outline of hooked nose	-	yellow	-	-	-	4.4.1.3
S III	Tomb of Khnumhotep III	Dahshur	pointed beards	mushroom-like	-	-	axes as status markers	determinative of *Mꜣki*: kneeling and bound	4.3.1.2
	Pectoral	Dahshur	pointed beards	black; shoulder-length	yellow	loincloths	-	kneeling, hand raised	4.3.1.3
S III	Tomb of Wekhhotep (C1)	Meir	-	red; bulb-like protrusion (bun ?); fillet; small wedge-shaped protrusions	-	-	handled vessels	procession of offering-bearers from Delta	4.4.4.3
A III	Pectoral	Dahshur	pointed beards	black mushroom-like	yellow	kilts; red and blue detail	curved staffs; daggers*	kneeling, armed, hands raised	4.3.1.3
	Inscription Nr 87	Serabit el-Khadim	-	coiffed; above shoulder-length	-	kilt	-	-	5.2.4.1

DYNASTY	SOURCE	SITE	FACE	HAIR	SKIN	CLOTHES	EQUIPMENT	STANCE AND/OR ACTIVITY	CHAPTER
A III	Inscription Nr 103	Serabit el-Khadim	-	-	-	-	unidentified objects	donkey rider and driver	5.2.4.1
	Inscription Nr 95	Serabit el-Khadim	pointed beard	-	-	-	-	-	5.2.4.1
	Inscription Nr 112	Serabit el-Khadim	-	slightly voluminous at back	-	kilts	weapon*; axe and staff(?) as status marker; bi-handled jar	donkey rider and driver	5.2.4.1
	Inscription Nr 405	Serabit el-Khadim	-	black	yellow	kilts; red detail	spears; staff; axe as status marker	donkey rider, driver and guard	5.2.4.1
	Inscription Nr 115	Serabit el-Khadim	-	-	-	-	weapons*; axe as status marker	donkey rider, driver and guard	5.2.4.1
12	Brussels figurines	Saqqara	short beards	coiffed	-	-	-	-	4.3.8
12 -13	Obelisk Nr 163	Serabit el-Khadim	pointed beards	coiffed	-	-	duckbill axes; shields	-	5.2.4.1
Early 13	Cylinder seal	Tell el-Dab'a F/I d/1	-	long fillet	-	-	duckbill axe; mace	[association with Baal myth(?)]	4.2.2.3
13	Statue	Tell el-Dab'a F/I d/2-c	-	red; mushroom-like	yellow	long garment (either Egyptian or Levantine style); red, blue and white detail with fringes*	curved staff*	-	4.2.2.3
	Statuette	Dahshur	short, pointed beard	black; above shoulder-length	-	kilt	-	-	4.3.1.4
	Stela Roanne Nr 163	-	-	bulb-like protrusion (bun?); small wedge-shaped protrusions	-	long one-shouldered garment	-	-	4.6.8
13 (?)	Pyramid complex of S III: graffiti	Dahshur	-	voluminous yet straight to round and coiffed	-	long one-shouldered garment; detail with fringes	-	-	4.3.1.4
13-SIP	Ivory sphinx	Abydos	hooked nose; almond-shaped eyes	*nemes* headdress and uraeus	-	-	-	-	4.5.1.2

FIGURE 7.12. SELECTED ARTISTIC PORTRAYALS OF INDIVIDUALS OF LEVANTINE ANCESTRY OR INFLUENCE WITH A SUMMARY OF OBSERVED FEATURES AND UNIQUE STANCES.

* Unclear detail.

Notes: A: Amenemhat S: Senwosret SIP: Second Intermediate Period

8. Rulers of Foreign Lands

'... unexpectedly, from the regions of the East,
invaders of obscure race marched
in confidence of victory against our land.
By main force they easily seized it,
without striking a blow.'
Manetho, *Aegyptiaca*, frg. 42, 1.75-1.76.

8.1 Introduction

This study set out to explore how Egyptian-Levantine connections during the Middle Kingdom and the early Second Intermediate Period influenced and affected the rise of Dynasty 15. Three main aims were presented: (1) investigate how the Hyksos were able to form an independent state by assessing Egyptian-Levantine relations; (2) explore the origins of the Fifteenth Dynasty; and (3) reanalyse Egyptian-Levantine relations, particularly the status and role of Levantines and their representation.

The first section navigated scholarly opinion on the origins and accession of the Hyksos, perusing Egyptian and modern understandings of the concept of ethnicity and the Levantine *other*. The second section analysed the evidence holistically, tracing Asiatics across four major regions in Egypt (Chapter 4), intercultural contact in the periphery Eastern Desert (Chapter 5), and contact with the Egyptian culture in the Southern and Northern Levant (Chapter 6). Findings on the nature and development of Egyptian-Levantine relations, or Aim 3, were provided in each chapter's conclusions, noting major shifts and occurrences concerned with the origins and rise of the Hyksos (Aims 1 and 2). Aim 3 was further addressed in the third section's Chapter 7, which offered an overview of observations on representations of Asiatics and the Levant, and the changing Egyptian view of the Levantine *other*.

Overall findings in direct reference to Aims 1 and 2 are offered in this chapter. It includes a reappraisal of the rise of the Hyksos, as well as comments on ethnic markers delineating the dynasty's origins. This is followed by final remarks on the limitations encountered in this research as well as possible areas for further study.

8.2 Origins and Rise of the Hyksos

8.2.1 Rise of the Fifteenth Dynasty

A main objective of this monograph was to investigate how the Hyksos were able to establish their Fifteenth Dynasty. Three models were identified in the literature: (1) invasion; (2) gradual infiltration and peaceful takeover; and (3) gradual infiltration and violent takeover.

Chapter 4 concluded that there is little concrete, contextual and contemporary evidence for the invasion model. There was no sudden or radical change in the material culture of the eastern Delta or the Memphite capital. The developments in ceramic typology as well as scarab and seal use reflect the outcome of socio-political shifts including growing regionalisation, as well as continuous and consistent cultural interactions, specifically in Tell el-Dab'a where hybridised and creole qualities surfaced. The establishment of settlements in the eastern Delta were explained as new initiatives of an emerging dynasty solidifying its control, whereas the expansion of Tell el-Dab'a was clarified as an indication of the site's prosperity and appeal for individuals from across the borders and across Egypt. Further, there is no evidence for an Egyptian antagonism against a foreign Levantine force that dates specifically to the early Fifteenth Dynasty, and neither is there support for a Levantine antagonism against the Egyptian culture.

The evidence instead favours a gradual infiltration. The Twelfth Dynasty was secured following the help of Levantine warriors, which created a hub of intercultural contact in Middle Egypt that later led to diplomatic relations between the Egyptian and Levantine elite. Trade mainly flowed with the Northern Levant, where the site of Byblos evinces the most evidence for Egyptian influence. Relations intensified during the second half of Dynasty 12 from which comes the last recorded military skirmishes and the last bellicose representations of Asiatics. The data emphasises the increasing number of Asiatics and acculturated Egyptian-Asiatics from a range of professions across Egypt. It additionally highlights the development of diplomatic contact with rulers of the Levant, a region that became frequently represented as a source of commodities and trade. The Levantine elite were even involved in an expeditionary venture with Egyptians in the Eastern

Desert that spanned over 20 years. The demand for and persistence of such relations possibly resulted in Tell el-Dab'a's rising importance as a commercial hub, its elite gradually acquiring power and wealth, their material culture showing greatest affinities with Northern Levantine elements. These affinities correspond with the evidence from the Levant, particularly sites along trade routes, with Byblos again displaying the greatest Egyptian influences.

The Thirteenth Dynasty is marked by further shifts. Two main events, both during the first half of the dynasty, suggest the Memphite rulers' loss of control over the Delta's elite. The first is represented by the abandonment of Tell Basta's Mayor's Residence and the intentional destruction of an official's statue at Tell el-Dab'a. The second event resulted in major developments at Tell el-Dab'a that signal a demonstrable freedom of expressing ethnicity and status which may be associated with an emerging dynasty's legitimisation of power and independence. Again, this elite class betrayed mostly Northern Levantine cultural elements. The acculturated and newly migrated Asiatics also display a freedom of expressing ethnic identity, and appear in various roles and administrative positions pointing to their continued presence across Egypt. Apparently, the developments in the north did not affect commercial relations with the Levant, as trade with the Northern Levant continued while links developed with the Southern Levant. Direct contact with Egypt can mostly be identified at Northern Levantine sites while the elite of Levantine coastal cities controlled maritime commerce with Egypt.

The growing wealth and independence of the elite at Tell el-Dab'a eventuated into an independent Fifteenth Dynasty represented by Tell el-Dab'a's established stability. This stability likely appealed to immigrants searching for security and vocational opportunities from the Levant as well as Egypt. The population increased, its settlement expanded, and new local industries and places of worship were set up, all expressing cultural elements of diverse Egyptian, Southern and Northern Levantine origin. Initiatives were likely undertaken to manage local and regional trade, assuring the dynasty's 'port power', commercial links, prosperity and independence. Such initiatives probably encountered some conflict, but the rise of the dynasty was, overall, peaceful. Finds from administrative complexes at Tell el-Dab'a and Edfu attest to Hyksos trade with Memphis/Fayum, the Egyptian Oases, Nubia, Mesopotamia, Cyprus and the Levant. Sporadic finds across Egypt and the Eastern Desert also support the spread of Levantine(-influenced) goods, although their numbers are more indicative of trade with Dynasty 15 rather than political dominance. Southern and Northern Levantine sites similarly had access to Egyptian products but at a reduced scale, perhaps relating to Dynasty 15's independence, its consequent limited access to high-quality Egyptian exports, and/or its initiatives to secure internal stability and sovereignty.

8.2.2 Ethnicity and ethnic markers

Utilising a minimalist approach to ethnicity, evidence that could possibly delineate a Levantine ethnic identity was gathered and examined along with observations on which marked trade or cultural influence, and which justifiably expressed the presence of Asiatics and/or the Hyksos. In reference to the Hyksos and their people, the following ethnic markers are represented by the evidence.

A common name

Two terms are connected to the Hyksos: the ethnonym *ꜥꜣm* and the title *ḥḳꜣ ḫꜣs.wt*. The ethnonym was in use throughout the examined period, initially representing Asiatics from beyond the borders of Egypt and, from the second half of the Twelfth Dynasty, those of Levantine ancestry. Either newly migrated or of mixed Egyptian-Levantine heritage, they originated from various regions in the Levant. Evidently, and as previous scholars have argued, *ꜥꜣm* was employed to refer to the Levantine ethnicity of the Fifteenth Dynasty's rulers and people. Based on the ethnonym alone, the Hyksos and their people could accordingly be from a range of Levantine regions and/or Egyptian-Levantines.

One of the unique features of Dynasty 15 is its rulers' use of the title *ḥḳꜣ ḫꜣs.wt*. The title was apparently connected to high-ranking rulers acting as representatives of allied people for political and diplomatic pursuits. As seen in Chapter 4, the Hyksos were particularly interested in opening new avenues of trade, securing strategic posts in the eastern Delta that could give access to land-based and sea-based trade routes. The title's association with diplomacy could have advantageously demonstrated the duties of the Hyksos as the leading representatives of a wide integrated trading network.

Common cultural elements

Chapter 4 argued that the early Fifteenth Dynasty's general populace at Tell el-Dab'a were of mixed origins. They expressed Egyptian, Southern Levantine and Northern Levantine cultural elements, eventually forming architectural, funerary and ceramic features that combined the Levantine with the Egyptian (hybrid qualities) and created new and distinctive components (creole qualities). The unique cultural interaction at Tell el-Dab'a from the late Twelfth to the Fifteenth Dynasties indicates that any attempt to pinpoint one ethnic origin for Dynasty 15's general populace would be ineffective as its cultural elements are of numerous derivation, largely influenced and inspired by the immediate eastern Delta and Egyptian environment. Levantines across Egypt, and from the very beginning of the Twelfth Dynasty, experienced all three processes of cultural interaction described in Chapter 3.5. They were hybridised in textual and artistic representations, acculturated in the adoption of Egyptian elements, and perhaps creolised due to their reciprocal socio-political and cultural interactions in the lead-up to Hyksos rule.

The evidence for the early Fifteenth Dynasty elite and ruling class of Tell el-Dab'a, and thus the Hyksos, expresses more affinities to Northern Levantine customs. The elite employed Northern Levantine architectural and funerary symbols of power, as well as cultic and religious customs, maintaining continued commercial links with the Northern Levant. The creole and hybrid character of their populace influenced their own employment of Egyptian traditions in funerary, administrative, occupational and cultic contexts. The Northern Levantine rulers similarly utilised Egyptian expressions of authority, with Sidon and Byblos presenting the only cases for the Levantine use of the Egyptian script. The two sites and others in their region, such as Tell el-Burak and Tell Fad'ous, also offer further elements of significance that are shared with Tell el-Dab'a's elite: the creation of hybrid artistic and ceramic forms; the appropriation of Egyptian titulary that best reflects an official's duty; and the utilisation of the epithet 'beloved of Seth', which may denote a shared reverence to the deity and/or his Levantine equivalent. These, combined with the other observed links in the material culture with the Northern Levant from the Middle Kingdom through to the Fifteenth Dynasty, suggest that the early Fifteenth Dynasty elite of Tell el-Dab'a had close political and commercial ties with Northern Levantine rulers. Whether or not this is associated with the Northern Levantine identity of the Hyksos remains inconclusive. Nevertheless, the assertion that the Hyksos and their people are of sole Southern Levantine ethnicity is not supported by the evidence.

A link with a Levantine land

The land with the most possible connections with the Hyksos is *Rṯnw*. From the second half of Dynasty 12, the toponym was utilised in texts noting close diplomatic ties between its rulers, the Egyptian elite and Tell el-Dab'a. Such ties evidently led to at least one *Rṯnw* royal frequenting Egypt for over 20 years. In view of the supported gradual infiltration of the Hyksos, perhaps these *Rṯnw* elite resided in Tell el-Dab'a from Dynasty 12, maintaining relations with its officials until early Dynasty 15. Theoretically, it is feasible to deduce that the early Hyksos, as the later Apophis, were of elite ancestry from *Rṯnw*, a toponym that was here cautiously linked with the Northern Levant and the northern region of the Southern Levant.

The three markers of a common name, common cultural elements, and a link with a Levantine land all infer the same observations regarding Dynasty 15's origins: the Hyksos elite had close relations with the Northern Levant, possibly stemming from the area; and the general population were of more varied Northern Levantine, Southern Levantine and Egyptian ancestry.

8.3 A Final Glance

8.3.1 An overview of the research

The rise of the Hyksos was due to a gradual infiltration of Northern and Southern Levantines across the Middle Kingdom and the early Second Intermediate Period. The Levantines entered Egypt as captives, warriors, expedition members and individuals searching for vocational, diplomatic and commercial opportunities. Escalating trade with the Levant for prized and prestigious commodities developed a lucrative and strategically positioned hub of cultural activity at Tell el-Dab'a, the officials of which became more powerful and affluent as significant ties with the Northern Levant were maintained. Following internal conflict in the Delta, perhaps related to this increasing power and/or other political shifts in Dynasty 13, the Northern Levantine-influenced elite gradually began to secede from Thirteenth Dynasty rule, first securing the site's internal security and affluence, and then assuring regional stability and control, with initiatives focussed on securing provisions and maintaining commerce. On the whole, the examined evidence suggests that the Hyksos dynasty was a result of the Egyptian rulers' own persistent relations with the Levant from the very beginning of Dynasty 12 to the Second Intermediate Period.

8.3.2 Research limitations and prospective areas of research

Three research limitations were encountered: (1) the lack of complete and recent publications of excavations; (2) the lack of recent archaeological research in the Delta, southern Israel, and significant areas of modern Lebanon; and (3) the ambiguities in the chronology of individual sites, regions and periods. Further archaeological research would add to this study's findings, especially in illuminating the vague Fourteenth Dynasty and its relations to the Hyksos. While necessary for the scope of this work, the selection of contextual and provenanced evidence could be enhanced by an examination of other unprovenanced or non-contemporaneous material, such as scarabs or late Fifteenth Dynasty texts. An analysis of Hyksos policies and alliances during the second half of Dynasty 15, and the supposed expulsion of the Hyksos, could also provide insight into the origins of the dynasty and its links to Levantine targets of Seventeenth to early Eighteenth Dynasty campaigns by the Egyptians. Another area of prospective research is the role of Nubia and its relations with Dynasty 15, and whether the rare Middle Kingdom ascription of the title *ḥḳꜣ ḫꜣs.wt* to its rulers agrees with observations for the Levantine 'rulers of foreign lands'.

8.3.3 A new light on Manetho

The results of this study denote that, when read anew, sources such as Manetho's history can be interpreted from a different perspective. So, perhaps Manetho's writings can be re-interpreted as follows:

'From the regions of the east', an elite group of Northern Levantines entered Tell el-Dab'a and Egypt as allies and diplomats, and formed vocational and commercial opportunities with the Egyptians. After some internal socio-political conflicts, the elite 'seized' independence from their city, Tell el-Dab'a. They assumed the title *ḥḳꜣ ḫꜣs.wt*, and established and secured their Fifteenth Dynasty by developing its commercial ties and promoting a hub of cross-cultural contact. 'Without striking a blow', these Hyksos rose to power, creating a unique dynasty that later beleaguered the Egyptians and continued to fascinate ancient and modern historians alike.

Select Bibliography

A

Abd el-Maksoud, M., 'Un monument du roi *'AA-SḤ-R' NḤSY* à Tell-Haboua (Sinaï Nord)', *ASAE* 69 (1983), 1-3.

Abd el-Maksoud, M., 'Excavations on "The Ways of Horus": Tell Heboua North Sinai (1986-1987)', in *The Archaeology, Geography and History of the Egyptian Delta in Pharaonic Times. Proceedings of Colloquium Wadham College 29-31 August, 1988*, DE Special Number 1 (Oxford, 1989), 173-192.

Abd el-Maksoud, M., *Tell Heboua (1981-1991). Enquête archéologique sur la deuxième péreiode intermédiaire et la Nouvel Empire à l'extrémité orientale du Delta* (Paris, 1998).

Abd el-Maksoud, M. and Valbelle, D., 'Tell Héboua-Tjarou. L'apport de l'épigraphie', *RdE* 56 (2005), 1-44.

Abd el-Raziq, M., Castel, G., Tallet, P., 'L'exploration archéologique du site d'Ayn Soukhna (2001-2004)', in *Proceedings of the Ninth International Congress of Egyptologists*, vol. 1, OLA 150 (Leuven, 2007), 61-68.

Abd el-Raziq et al., *Les inscriptions d'Ayn Soukhna*, MIFAO 122 (Cairo, 2002).

Abd el-Raziq, M. et al., *Ayn Soukhna*, vol. 2: *Les ateliers métallurgiques du Moyen Empire*, FIFAO 66 (Cairo, 2011).

Abd el-Raziq, M. et al., 'The Pharaonic Site of Ayn Soukhna in the Gulf of Suez 2001-2009 Progress Report', in P. Tallet and S. Mahfouz (eds), *The Red Sea in Pharaonic Times. Recent Discoveries along the Red Sea Coast. Proceedings of the Colloquium held in Cairo/Ayn Soukhna 11th-12th January 2009* (Cairo, 2012), 3-20.

Abrahams, R. D., 'About Face. Rethinking Creolization', in R. Baron and A. C. Cara (eds), *Creolization as Cultural Creativity* (Jackson, 2011), 285-305.

Adam, S., 'Recent Discoveries in the Eastern Delta', *ASAE* 55 (1958), 301-324.

Adam, S., 'Report on the Excavations of the Department of Antiquities at 'Ezbet Rushdi', *ASAE* 56 (1959), 207-226.

Adams, M. D., 'Community and Societal Organization in Early Historic Egypt. Introductory Report on 1991-92 Fieldwork Conducted at the Abydos Settlement Site', *NARCE* 158/189 (1992), 1-9.

Adrom, F., *Die Lehre des Amenemhet*, BiAe 19 (Turnhout, 2006).

Aharoni, Y., *The Land of the Bible: A Historical Geography*, trans. A. F. Rainey (London, 1967).

Aharoni, Y., *The Archaeology of the Land of Israel: From the Prehistoric Beginnings to the End of the First Temple Period*, trans. A. F. Rainey (Philadelphia, 1982).

Ahrens, A., 'Strangers in a Strange Land? The Function and Social Significance of Egyptian Imports in the Northern Levant during the 2nd Millennium BC', in K. Duistermaat and I. Regulski (eds), *Intercultural Contacts in the Ancient Mediterranean. Proceedings of the International Conference at the Netherlands-Flemish Institute in Cairo, 25th to 29th October 2008*, OLA 202 (Leuven, Paris and Walpole, 2011), 285-307.

Ahrens, A., 'A "Hyksos Connection?" Thoughts on the Date of Dispatch of Some of the Middle Kingdom Objects found in the Northern Levant', in J. Mynářova (ed.), *Egypt and the Near East – the Crossroads. Proceedings of an International Conference on the Relations of Egypt and the Near East in the Bronze Age. Prague, September 1-3, 2010* (Prague, 2011), 21-40.

Ahrens, A., 'News From an Old Excavation: Two Hitherto Unnoticed Measure Capacity Signs on an Egyptian Stone Vessel of the Middle Kingdom From Royal Tomb II at Byblos', *JAEI* 4/2 (2012), 1-4.

Aḥituv, S., *Canaanite Toponyms in Ancient Egyptian Documents* (Jerusalem, 1984).

Ahlström, G. W., *The History of Ancient Palestine from the Paleolithic Period to Alexander's Conquest*, JSOT-Suppl. 146 (Sheffield, 1993).

Akkermans, P. and Schwartz, G. M., *The Archaeology of Syria: From Complex Hunter-Gatherers to Early Urban Societies (c. 16,000-300 BC)* (Cambridge, 2003).

Albright, W. F., 'Palestine in the Earliest Historical Record', *JPOS* 2 (1922), 110-138.

Albright, W. F., 'The Egyptian Empire in Asia in the 21st Century, B.C.', *JPOS* 8 (1928), 223-256.

Albright, W. F., 'The Excavation of Tell Beit Mirsim. I A: The Bronze Age Pottery of the Fourth Campaign', *AASOR* 13 (1931/1932), 55-127.

Albright, W. F., 'The Fourth Joint Campaign of Excavation at Tell Beit Mirsim', *BASOR* 47 (1932), 3-17.

Albright, W. F., *The Vocalization of the Egyptian Syllabic Orthography*, American Oriental Series 5 (New Haven, 1934).

Albright, W. F., 'Palestine in the Earliest Historical Period', *JPOS* 15 (1935), 193-234.

Albright, W. F., 'The Chronology of a South Palestinian City, Tell el-'Ajjul', *AJSL* 55/4 (1938), 337-359.

Albright, W. F., 'An Indirect Synchronism between Egypt and Mesopotamia, cir. 1730 B. C.', *BASOR* 99 (1945), 9-18.

Albright, W. F., 'Exploring in Sinai with the University of California African Expedition', *BASOR* 109 (1948), 5-20.

Albright, W. F., 'The Early Alphabetic Inscriptions from Sinai and their Decipherment', *BASOR* 110 (1948), 6-22.

Albright, W. F., *The Archaeology of Palestine* (London, 1949).

Albright, W. F., 'Northwest-Semitic Names in a List of Egyptian Slaves from the Eighteenth Century B. C.', *JAOS* 74/4 (1954), 222-233.

Albright, W. F., 'The Eighteenth-Century Princes of Byblos and the Chronology of Middle Bronze', *BASOR* 176 (1964), 38-46.

Albright, W. F., 'Further Light on the History of Middle-Bronze Byblos', *BASOR* 179 (1965), 38-43.

Albright, W. F., 'Remarks on the Chronology of Early Bronze IV – Middle Bronze IIA in Phoenicia and Syria-Palestine', *BASOR* 184 (1966), 26-35.

Albright, W. F., *The Proto-Sinaitic Inscriptions and Their Decipherment* (Cambridge, 1966).

Allen, J. P., *The Ancient Pyramid Texts* (Atlanta, 2005).

Allen, J. P., 'The Historical Inscription of Khnumhotep at Dahshur: Preliminary Report', *BASOR* 352 (2008), 29-39.

Allen, J. P., 'The Second Intermediate Period in the Turin King-List', in M. Marée (ed.), *The Second Intermediate Period (Thirteenth-Seventeenth Dynasties). Current Research, Future Prospects* (Leuven, Paris and Walpole, 2010), 1-10.

Allen, S. J., 'Funerary Pottery in the Middle Kingdom: Archaism or Revival?', in D. P. Silverman, W. K. Simpson and J. Wegner (eds), *Archaism and Innovation: Studies in the Culture of Middle Kingdom Egypt* (New Haven and Philadelphia, 2009), 319-339.

Allen, S. J., 'Pyramid Ware', in R. Schiestl and A. Seiler (eds), *Handbook of the Pottery of the Egyptian Middle Kingdom*, vol. 2: *The Regional Volume*, ÖAW: Denkschriften der Gesamtakademie 72 (Vienna, 2012), 185-195.

Allen, T. G., 'A Middle Kingdom Egyptian Contact with Asia Minor', *AJSL* 43 (1927), 291-296.

Allon, N., 'Seth is Baal – Evidence from the Egyptian Script', *E&L* 17 (2007), 15-22.

Alt, A., 'Herren und Herrensitze Palästinas im Anfang des zweiten Jahrtausends v. Chr.', *ZDPV* 64 (1941), 21-39.

Altenmüller, H. and Moussa, A. M., 'Die Inschrift Amenemhets II. Aus dem PtahTempel von Memphis. Ein Vorbericht', *SAK* 18 (1991), 1-48.

Altschuler, E., 'A Gloss on One of the Wadi el-Hol Inscriptions', *ANES* 39 (2002), 201-204.

Amiet, P., *La glyptique mésopotamienne archaique* (Paris, 1980).

Amiran, R., *Ancient Pottery of the Holy Land* (Jerusalem, 1969).

Amiran, R. and Eitan, A., 'Two Seasons of Excavations at Tell Nagila (1962-1963) / (1962-1963)', *BIES* 28 (1964), 193-203.

Amiran, R. and Eitan, A., 'A Canaanite-Hyksos City at Tell Nagila', *Archaeology* 18/2 (1965), 113-131.

Amiran, R. and Ilan, O., *Early Arad*, vol. 2: *The Chalcolithic and Early Bronze IB Settlements and the Early Bronze II City-Architecture and Town Planning, Sixth to Eighteenth Seasons of Excavations, 1971-1978, 1980-1984* (Jerusalem, 1996).

Anthes, R., *Die Felseninschriften von Hatnub* (Leipzig, 1929).

Antonaccio, C. M., '(Re)defining Ethnicity: Culture, Material Culture, and Identity', in T. Hodos and S. Hales (eds), *Material Culture and Social Identity in the Ancient Mediterranean* (Cambridge, 2010), 32-53.

Arnold, Di., 'The Private Tombs North of the Senwosret III Pyramid Complex, Dahshur', *Heilbrunn Timeline of Art History* (2000), http://www.metmuseum.org/toah/hd/dapt/hd_dapt.htm (accessed 22/12/2012).

Arnold, Di., *The Pyramid Complex of Senwosret III at Dahshur. Architectural Studies* (New York, 2002).

Arnold, Di., *Middle Kingdom Tomb Architecture at Lisht*, Metropolitan Museum of Art Egyptian Expedition 28 (New York, 2008).

Arnold, Do., 'Keramikbearbeitung in Dahschur 1976-1981', *MDAIK* 38 (1982), 25-65.

Arnold, Do., 'Image and Identity: Egypt's Eastern Neighbours, East Delta People and the Hyksos', in M. Marée (ed.), *The Second Intermediate Period (Thirteenth-Seventeenth Dynasties). Current Research, Future Prospects* (Leuven, Paris and Walpole, 2010), 183-221.

Arnold, Do., 'Foreign and Female', in S. H. D'Auria (ed.), *Offerings to the Discerning Eye: An Egyptological Medley in Honour of Jack A. Josephson* (Leiden and Boston, 2010), 17-31.

Arnold, Do., Arnold, F. and Allen, S. J., 'Canaanite Imports at Lisht, the Middle Kingdom Capital of Egypt', *E&L* 5 (1995), 13-32.

Arnold, F., 'Settlement Remains at Lisht-North', in M. Bietak (ed.), *Haus und Palast im Alten Ägypten*, ÖAW: Denkschriften der Gesamtakademie 14 (Vienna, 1996), 13-21.

Artzy, M., 'Notes and News: Nami Land and Sea Project, 1985-1988', *IEJ* 40/1 (1990), 73-76.

Artzy, M., 'Notes and News: Nami Land and Sea Project, 1989', *IEJ* 41/1 (1991), 194-197.

Artzy, M. and Marcus, E. S., 'The MBIIA Coastal Settlement at Tel Nami', *Michmanim* 5 (1991), 5*-16*.

Ashmawy Ali, A., 'Tell el-Yahudiya: New Information from Unpublished Excavations', *E&L* 20 (2010), 31-42.

Assmann, J., 'Kulturelle und Literarische Texte', in A. Loprieno (ed.), *Ancient Egyptian Literature. History & Forms* (Leiden, 1996), 59-65.

Aston, B. G., *Ancient Egyptian Stone Vessels: Materials and Forms*, SAGA 5 (Heidelberg, 1994).

Aston, D. A., 'Ceramic Imports at Tell el-Dab'a during the Middle Bronze IIA', in M. Bietak (ed.), *The Middle Bronze Age in the Levant. Proceedings of an International Conference on MBIIA Ceramic Material. Vienna, 24th-26th of January 2001*, ÖAW: Denkschriften der Gesamtakademie 26 (Vienna, 2002), 43-87.

Aston, D. A., 'New Kingdom Pottery Phases as Revealed through Well-Dated Tomb Contexts', in M. Bietak (ed.), *The Synchronisation of Civilisations in the Eastern Mediterranean in the Second Millennium B.C.*, vol. 2: *Proceedings of the SCIEM 2000 – EuroConference, Haindorf 2nd of May-7th of May 2001*, CCEM 4 (Vienna, 2003), 135-162.

Aston, D. A., 'Review of McGovern, P. E., *The Foreign Relations of the 'Hyksos'. A Neutron-Activation Study of Middle Bronze Age Pottery from the Eastern Mediterranean* (Oxford, 2000)', *JEA* 90 (2004), 233-237.

Aston, D. A., *Tell el-Dab'a*, vol. 12: *A Corpus of Late Middle Kingdom and Second Intermediate Period Pottery*, 2 parts, Untersuchungen der Zweigstelle Kairo des Österreichischen Archäologischen Instituts 23 (Vienna, 2004).

Aston, D. A. and Bader, B., 'Fishes, Ringstands, Nudes and Hippos – A Preliminary Report on the Hyksos Palace Pit Complex L81 OF', *E&L* 19 (2009), 19-89.

Aston, D. A. and Bietak, M., *Tell el Dab'a*, vol. 8: *The Classification and Chronology of Tell el-Yahudiya Ware*, Untersuchungen der Zweigstelle Kairo des Österreichischen Archäologischen Institutes 12 (Vienna, 2012).

Aubet, *Commerce and Colonization in the Ancient Near East* (New York, 2013).

Aufrère, S. H., 'The Deserts and the Fifteenth and Sixteenth Upper Egyptian Nomes during the Middle Kingdom', in R. Friedman (ed.), *Egypt and Nubia. Gifts of the Desert* (London, 2002), 207-214.

Al-Ayedi, A. R., *Tharu: The Starting Point on the "Ways of Horus"* (PhD Dissertation, University of Toronto, 2000).

Ayers, N., 'Appendix II: Selection of Pottery found in the Administrative Building Complex at Tell Edfu', in Moeller and Marouard, *E&L* 11 (2011), 112-119.

Ayrton, E., Currelly, C. and Weigall, A., *Abydos*, vol. 3 (London, 1904).

B

Badawy, A., 'The Civic Sense of Pharaoh and Urban Developments in Ancient Egypt', *JARCE* 6 (1967), 103-109.

Bader, B., 'The Egyptian Jars from Sidon in their Egyptian Context', *AHL* 18 (2003), 31-37.

Bader, B., 'A Tale of Two Cities: First Results of a Comparison Between Avaris and Memphis', in M. Bietak and E. Czerny (eds), *The Synchronisation of Civilisations in the Eastern Mediterranean in the Second Millennium B.C.*, vol. 3: *Proceedings of the SCIEM 2000-2nd EuroConference Vienna, 28th of May-1st of June 2003*, CCEM 9 (Vienna, 2007), 249-267.

Bader, B., 'Avaris and Memphis in the Second Intermediate Period in Egypt (*ca.* 1770-1550/40 BC)', in J. M. Córdoba et al. (eds), *Proceedings of the 5th International Congress of the Archaeology of the Ancient Near East. Madrid, April 3-8 2006* (Madrid, 2008), 207-223.

Bader, B., *Tell el-Dab'a*, vol. 19: *Auaris und Memphis im Mittleren Reich und in der Hyksoszeit. Vergleichsanalyse der materiellen Kultur*, Untersuchungen der Zweigstelle Kairo des Österreichischen Archäologischen Instituts 31 (Vienna, 2009).

Bader, B., 'Contacts between Egypt and Syria-Palestine as seen in a Grown Settlement of the Late Middle Kingdom at Tell el-Dab'a/Egypt', in J. Mynářová (ed.), *Egypt and the Near East – the Crossroads. Proceedings of an International Conference on the Relations of Egypt and the Near East in the Bronze Age, Prague, September 1-3, 2010* (Prague, 2011), 41-72.

Bader, B., 'Traces of Foreign Settlers in the Archaeological Record of Tell el-Dab'a', in K. Duistermaat and I. Regulski (eds), *Intercultural Contacts in the Ancient Mediterranean. Proceedings of the International Conference at the Netherlands-Flemish Institute in Cairo, 25th to 29th October 2008*, OLA 202 (Leuven, Paris and Walpole, 2011), 137-158.

Bader, B., 'Cultural Mixing in Egyptian Archaeology: The 'Hyksos' as a Case Study', in W. P. van Pelt (ed.), *Archaeological Review from Cambridge* 28/1 (2013), 257-286.

Bader, B. et al., 'An Egyptian Jar from Sidon in its Egyptian Context. Some Fresh Evidence', *AHL* 29 (2009), 79-83.

Bagh, T., 'Painted Pottery at the Beginning of the Middle Bronze Age: Levantine Painted Ware', in M. Bietak (ed.), *The Middle Bronze Age in the Levant. Proceedings of an International Conference on MBIIA Ceramic Material. Vienna, 24th-26th of January 2001*, ÖAW: Denkschriften der Gesamtakademie 26 (Vienna, 2002), 89-101.

Bagh, T., *Tell el-Dab'a*, vol. 23: *Levantine Painted Ware from Egypt and the Levant*, ÖAW: Denkschriften der Gesamtakademie 71 (Vienna, 2013).

Bagwell, L. S. and Bernheim, B. D., 'Veblen Effects in a Theory of Conspicuous Consumption', *The American Economic Review* 86/3 (1996), 349-373.

Baines, J., 'Interpreting Sinuhe', *JEA* 68 (1982), 31-44.

Baines, J., 'The Stela of Khusobek: Private and Royal Military Narrative and Values', in J. Osing and G. Dreyer (eds), *Form und Mass: Beiträge zur Literatur, Sprache und Kunst des alten Ägypten. Festschrift für Gerhard Fecht zum 65. Geburtstag am 6. Februar 1987* (Wiesbaden, 1987), 43-61.

Baines, J., 'Contextualizing Egyptian Representations of Society and Ethnicity', in J. S. Cooper and G. M. Schwartz (eds), *The Study of the Ancient Near East in the Twenty-First Century: The William Foxwell Albright Centennial Conference* (Indiana, 1996), 339-384.

Baines, J. and Eyre, C., 'Four Notes on Literacy', *GM* 61 (1983), 65-96.

Baines, J. and Lacovara, P., 'Burial and the Dead in Ancient Egyptian Society: Respect, Formalism, Neglect', *JSA* 2 (2002), 5-36.

Baines, J. and Malek, J., *The Cultural Atlas of Ancient Egypt* (New York, 2000).

Baker, J. L., *The Funeral Kit. Mortuary Practices in the Archaeological Record* (Walnut Creek, 2012).

Bakir, A. M., 'Slavery in Pharaonic Egypt', *ASAE* 45 (1947), 135-143.

Ballard, R., 'Race, Ethnicity and Culture', in M. Holborn (ed.), *New Directions in Sociology* (Omskirk, 2002), 93-124.

Barbotin, C. and Clère, J. J., 'L'inscription de Sésostris Ier à Tôd', *BIFAO* 91 (1991), 1-32.

Bard, K. A. and Fattovich, R. (eds), *Harbor of the Pharaohs to the Land of Punt. Archaeological Investigations at Mersa/Wadi Gawasis, Egypt, 2001-2005* (Naples, 2007).

Bard, K. A. and Fattovich, R., 'Synthesis', in K. A. Bard and R. Fattovich (eds), *Harbor of the Pharaohs to the Land of Punt. Archaeological Investigations at Mersa/Wadi Gawasis, Egypt, 2001-2005* (Naples, 2007), 239-253.

Bard, K. A. and Fattovich, R., 'Mersa/Wadi Gawasis 2007-2008', *Archaeogate Egittologia: Articoli e News* (2008), http://www.archaeogate.org/egittologia/article/974/9/mersawadi-gawasis-mission-2007-2008-kathryn-a-bard-and.html#23 (accessed 13/03/2013).

Bard, K. A. and Fattovich, R., 'Mersa/Wadi Gawasis 2009-2010', *Newsletter di Archeologia CISA* 1 (2010), 7-35.

Bard, K. A. and Fattovich, R., 'Spatial Use of the Twelfth Dynasty Harbor at Mersa/Wadi Gawasis for the Seafaring Expeditions to Punt', *JAEI* 2/3 (2010), 1-13.

Bard, K. A. and Fattovich, R., 'Recent Excavations at the Ancient Harbor of *SAWW* (Mersa/Wadi Gawasis) on the Red Sea', in S. H. D'Auria (ed.), *Offerings to the Discerning Eye: An Egyptological Medley in Honour of Jack A. Josephson* (Leiden and Boston, 2010), 33-38.

Bard, K. A., Fattovich, R. and Ward, C., 'Mersa/Wadi Gawasis 2010-2011', *Archaeogate Egittologia: Articoli e News* (2012), http://www.archaeogate.org/egittologia/article/1506/1/mersawadi-gawasis-2010-2011-report-by-kathryn-a-bard-bo.html (accessed 13/03/2013).

Bard, K. A. et al., 'Excavations', in K. A. Bard and R. Fattovich (eds), *Harbor of the Pharaohs to the Land of Punt. Archaeological Investigations at Mersa/Wadi Gawasis, Egypt, 2001-2005* (Naples, 2007), 38-90.

Barns, J. W. B., 'Sinuhe's Message to the King. A Reply to a Recent Article', *JEA* 53 (1967), 6-14.

Barocas, C., *L'Antico Egitto* (Rome, 1978).

Bárta, M., *Sinuhe, the Bible, and the Patriarchs* (Prague, 2003).

Barth, F., 'Introduction', in F. Barth (ed.), *Ethnic Groups and Boundaries. The Social Organization of Culture Difference* (Boston, 1969), 9-38.

Battle, I. and Tous, J., *Carob tree. Ceratonia siliqua L.*, Promoting the Conservation and Use of Underutilized and Neglected Crops 17 (Rome, 1997).

Beck, P., 'The Pottery of the Middle Bronze Age IIA at Tell Aphek', *Tel Aviv* 2 (1975), 45-85.

Beck, P. and Zevulun, U., 'Back to Square One', *BASOR* 304 (1996), 64-75.

von. Beckerath, J., 'Notes on the Viziers 'Ankhu and 'Iymery in the Thirteenth Egyptian Dynasty', *JNES* 17/4 (1958), 263-268.

von Beckerath, J., *Untersuchungen zur politischen Geschichte der Zweiten Zwischenzeit in Ägypten* (Glückstadt, 1964).

Beit-Arieh, I., 'Sinai Survey', *IEJ* 29 (1979), 256-257.

Beit-Arieh, I., 'A Chalcolithic Site near Serabit el-Khadim', *Tel Aviv* 7 (1980), 45-64.

Beit-Arieh, I., 'New Discoveries at Serabit el-Khadem', *BA* 45/1 (1982), 13-18.

Beit-Arieh, I., 'Serâbīt el-Khâdim: New Metallurgical and Chronological Aspects', *Levant* 17 (1985), 89-116.

Beit-Arieh, I., 'Canaanites and Egyptians at Serabit el-Khadim', in A. F. Rainey (ed.), *Egypt, Israel, Sinai: Archaeological and Historical Relationships in the Biblical Period* (Jerusalem, 1987), 57-67.

Ben-Arieh, S., *Bronze and Iron Age Tombs at Tell Beit Mirsim*, Israel Antiquities Authority Reports 23 (Jerusalem, 2004).

Ben-Dor, I., 'Palestinian Alabaster Vases', *QDAP* 11 (1944), 93-112.

Ben-Tor, A., 'Do the Execration Texts reflect an Accurate Picture of the Contemporary Settlement Map of Palestine?', in Y. Amit et al. (eds), *Essays on Ancient Israel in its Near Eastern Context. A Tribute to Nadav Na'aman* (Winonan Lake, 2006), 63-87.

Ben-Tor, A., 'The Sad Fate of Statues and the Mutilated Statues of Hazor', in S. Gitin, J. E. Wright and J. P. Dessel (eds), *Confronting the Past: Archaeological and Historical Essays on Ancient Israel in Honor of William G. Dever* (Winona Lake, 2006), 3-16.

Ben-Tor, A., 'A Decorated Jewellery Box from Hazor', *Tel Aviv* 36 (2009), 5-67.

Ben-Tor, D., 'The Historical Implications of Middle Kingdom Scarabs found in Palestine bearing Private Names and Titles of Officials', *BASOR* 294 (1994), 7-22.

Ben-Tor, D., 'The Relations between Egypt and Palestine in the Middle Kingdom as reflected by Contemporary Canaanite Scarabs', *IEJ* 47/3 (1997), 162-189.

Ben-Tor, D., 'The Absolute Date of the Montet Jar Scarabs', in L. H. Lesko, *Ancient Egyptian and Mediterranean Studies in Memory of William A. Ward* (Providence, 1998), 1-17.

Ben-Tor, D., 'Egyptian-Levantine Relations and Chronology in the Middle Bronze Age: Scarab Research', in M. Bietak (ed.), *The Synchronisation of Civilisations in the Eastern Mediterranean in the Second Millennium B.C.*, vol. 2: *Proceedings of the SCIEM 2000 EuroConference Haindorf, 2nd of May-7th of May 2001*, CCEM 4 (Vienna, 2003), 239-248.

Ben-Tor, D., 'Second Intermediate Period Scarabs from Egypt and Palestine: Historical and Chronological Implications', in M. Bietak and E. Czerny (eds), *Scarabs of the Second Millennium BC from Egypt, Nubia, Crete and the Levant: Chronological and Historical Implications. Papers of a Symposium, Vienna, 10th-13th January 2002*, ÖAW: Denkschriften der Gesamtakademie 35 (Vienna, 2004), 27-42.

Ben-Tor, D., *Scarabs, Chronology, and Interconnections. Egypt and Palestine in the Second Intermediate Period*, OBO 27 (Friburg, 2007).

Ben-Tor, D., 'Scarabs of Middle Bronze Age Rulers of Byblos', in S. Bickel et al. (eds), *Bilder als Quellen. Images as Sources. Studies on Ancient Near Eastern Artefacts and the Bible Inspired by the Work of Othmar Keel* (Fribourg, 2007), 177-188.

Ben-Tor, D., 'Can Scarabs Argue for the Origin of the Hyksos?', *JAEI* 1/1 (2009), 1-7.

Ben-Tor, D., 'Sequences and Chronology of Second Intermediate Period Royal-Name Scarabs, based on Excavated Series from Egypt and the Levant', in M. Marée (ed.), *The Second Intermediate Period (Thirteenth-Seventeenth Dynasties). Current Research, Future Prospects* (Leuven, Paris and Walpole, 2010), 91-108.

Ben-Tor, D., 'Egyptian-Canaanite Relations in the Middle and Late Bronze Ages as Reflected by Scarabs', in S. Bar, D. Kahn and J. J. Shirley (eds), *Egypt, Canaan and Israel: History, Imperialism, Ideology and Literature. Proceedings of a Conference at the University of Haifa, 3-7 May 2009*, Culture and History of the Ancient Near East 52 (Leiden and Boston, 2011), 23-43.

Ben-Tor, D., Allen, S. J. and Allen, J. P, 'Seals and Kings', *BASOR* 315 (1999), 47-74.

Bennett, C., 'Growth of the *ḥtp-dj-nsw* Formula in the Middle Kingdom', *JEA* 27 (1941), 77–82.

Bennett, C., 'The Structure of the Seventeenth Dynasty', *GM* 149 (1997), 25-32.

Bennett, C., 'The Genealogical Chronology of the Seventeenth Dynasty', *JARCE* 39 (2002), 123-155.

Bennett, C., 'Genealogy and the Chronology of the Second Intermediate Period', *E&L* 16 (2007), 231-244.

Berman, L. M., *Amenemhet I* (PhD Dissertation, Yale University, 1985).

Berry, J. W., 'Conceptual Approaches to Acculturation', in K. M. Chun, P. B. Organista and G. Marin (eds), *Acculturation: Advances in Theory, Measurement, and Applied Research* (Washington, 2003), 17-37.

Best, J. and Rietveld, L., 'Structuring Byblos Tablets *c* and *d*', *UF* 42 (2010), 15-40.

Bietak, M., 'Vorläufiger Bericht über die erste und zweite Kampagne der österreichischen Ausgrabungen auf Tell Ed-Dab'a im Ostdelta Ägyptens (1966, 1967)', *MDAIK* 23 (1968), 79-114.

Bietak, M., *Tell el-Dab'a*, vol. 2: *Der Fundort im Rahmen einer archäologisch-geographischen Untersuchung über das ägyptische Ostdelta*, Untersuchungen der Zweigstelle Kairo des Österreichischen Archäologischen Instituts 1 (Vienna, 1975).

Bietak, M., 'Problems of Middle Bronze Age Chronology: New Evidence from Egypt', *AJA* 88/4 (1984), 471-485.

Bietak, M., *Avaris and Piramesse: Archaeological Exploration in the Eastern Nile Delta*, Proceedings of the British Academy 45 (London, 1986).

Bietak, M., 'Canaanites in the Eastern Nile Delta', in *Egypt, Israel, Sinai: Archaeological and Historical Relationships in the Biblical Period* (Jerusalem, 1987), 41-55.

Bietak, M., 'Servant Burials in the Middle Bronze Age Culture of the Eastern Nile Delta', *Eretz Israel* 20 (1989), 30-43.

Bietak, M., 'The Middle Bronze Age of the Levant – A New Approach to Relative and Absolute Chronology', in P. Åström (ed.), *High, Middle or Low? Acts of an International Colloquium on Absolute Chronology held at the University of Gothenberg, 20-22 August 1987*, vol. 3 (Gothenberg, 1989), 78-120.

Bietak, M., 'Der Friedhof in einem Palastgarten aus der Zeit des späten mittleren Reiches und andere Forschungsergebnisse aus dem östlichen Nildelta (Tell el-Dab'a 1984-1987)', *E&L* 2 (1991), 47-75.

Bietak, M., 'Egypt and Canaan during the Middle Bronze Age', *BASOR* 281 (1991), 27-72.

Bietak, M., 'Die Chronologie Ägyptens und der Beginn der Mittleren Bronzezeit-Kultur', *E&L* 3 (1992), 29-37.

Bietak, M., *Avaris: The Capital of the Hyksos. Recent Excavations at Tell el-Dab'a* (London, 1996).

Bietak, M., 'The Center of Hyksos Rule: Avaris (Tell el-Dab'a)', in E. D. Oren (ed.), *The Hyksos: New Historical and Archaeological Perspectives* (Philadelphia, 1997), 87-139.

Bietak, M., 'The King and the Syrian Weather God on Egyptian Seals of the Thirteenth Dynasty', in Z. Hawass, S. Bedier and K. Daoud (eds), *Studies in Honor of Ali Radwan*, Supplément aux ASAE 34 (Cairo, 2005), 201-212.

Bietak, M., 'The Predecessors of the Hyksos', in J. S. Gitin, E. Wright and J. P. Dessel (eds), *Confronting the Past: Archaeological and Historical Essays on Ancient Israel in Honor of William G. Dever* (Winona Lake, 2006), 285-293.

Bietak, M., 'Towards a Middle Bronze Age Chronology', in P. Matthiae et al. (eds), *From Relative Chronology to Absolute Chronology: The Second Millennium BC in Syria-Palestine (Rome 29th November – 21st December 2001)* (Rome, 2007), 121-146.

Bietak, M., 'Bronze Age Paintings in the Levant: Chronological and Cultural Considerations', in M. Bietak and E. Czerny (eds), *The Synchronisation of Civilisations in the Eastern Mediterranean in the Second Millennium B.C.*, vol. 3: *Proceedings of the SCIEM 2000-2nd EuroConference Vienna, 28th of May-1st of June 2003*, CCEM 9 (Vienna, 2007), 269-300.

Bietak, M., 'Houses, Palaces and Development of Social Structure in Avaris', in M. Bietak, E. Czerny and I. Forstner-Müller (eds), *Cities and Urbanism in Ancient Egypt. Papers from a Workshop in November 2006 at the Austrian Academy of Sciences*, ÖAW: Denkschriften der Gesamtakademie 60 (Vienna, 2010), 11-68.

Bietak, M., 'From Where Came the Hyksos and Where Did They Go?', in M. Marée (ed.), *The Second Intermediate Period (Thirteenth-Seventeenth Dynasties). Current Research, Future Prospects* (Leuven, Paris and Walpole, 2010), 139-181.

Bietak, M., 'The Palace of thc Hyksos Khayan at Avaris', in P. Matthiae et al. (eds), *Proceedings of the 6th International Congress on the Archaeology of the Ancient Near East (2-11 May 2008) in Rome*, vol. 2: *Excavations, Surveys and Restorations: Reports on Recent Field Archaeology in the Near East* (Wiesbaden, 2010), 99-109.

Bietak, M. and Dorner, J., 'Der Tempel und die Siedlung des Mittleren Reiches bei ʿEzbet Ruschdi. Grabungsvorbericht 1996', *E&L* 8 (1998), 9-40.

Bietak, M. and Forstner-Müller I., 'Eine palatiale Anlage der frühen Hyksoszeit (Area F/II). Vorläufige Ergebnisse der Grabungskampagne 2006 in Tell el-Dab'a', *E&L* 16 (2006), 61-76.

Bietak, M. and Forstner-Müller, I., 'Der Hyksos-Palast bei Tell el-Dab'a. Zweite und Dritte Grabungskampagne (Frühling 2008 und Frühling 2009)', *E&L* 19 (2009), 91-119.

Bietak, M., Forstner-Müller, I. and Herbich, T., 'Discovery of a New Palatial Complex in Tell el-Dab'a in the Delta: Geophysical Survey and Preliminary Archaeological Verification', in Z. A. Hawass and J. Richards (eds), *The Archaeology and Art of Ancient Egypt. Essays in Honor of David B. O'Connor*, vol. 1, ASAE 36 (Cairo, 2007), 119-125.

Bietak, M., Forstner-Müller, I. and Mlinar, C., 'The Beginning of the Hyksos Period at Tell el-Dab'a: A Subtle Change in Material Culture', in P. M. Fischer (ed.), *Contributions to the Archaeology and History of the Bronze and Iron Ages in the Eastern Mediterranean. Studies in Honour of Paul Åström*, Österreichisches Archäologisches Institut Sonderschriften Band 39 (Vienna, 2001), 171-181.

Bietak, M. and Kopetzky, K., 'The Dolphin Jug: A Typological and Chronological Assessment', in J. D. Schloen (ed.), *Exploring the Longue Durée: Essays in Honor of Lawrence E. Stager* (Winona Lake, 2009), 7-34.

Bietak, M. et al., 'Synchronisation of Stratigraphies: Ashkelon and Tell el-Dab'a', *E&L* 18 (2008), 49-60.

Bietak, M. et al., 'Report on the Excavations of a Hyksos Palace at Tell el-Dab'a/Avaris (23rd August-15th November 2011', *E&L* 22-23 (2012/2013), 17-53.

Binder, S., *Gold of Honour in New Kingdom Egypt*, ACE: Studies 8 (Oxford, 2008).

Bisson de la Roque, F., *Tôd, 1934 à 1936* (Cairo, 1937).

Bisson de la Roque, F., *Le Trésor de Tôd, nos. 70501-754, Catalogue générale des antiquités égyptiennes de Musée du Caire* (Cairo, 1950).

Bisson de la Roque, F., Contenau, G. and Chapouthier, F., *Le Trésor de Tôd*, DFIFAO 11 (Cairo, 1953).

Bisson de la Roque, M., *Rapport sur les fouilles de Médamoud (1926)*, vol. 1 (Cairo, 1927).

Bisson de la Roque, M., *Rapport sur les fouilles de Médamoud (1929)*, vol. 1 (Cairo, 1930).

Blackman, A. M., 'An Indirect Reference to Sesostris III's Syrian Campaign in the Tomb-Chapel of "Ḏḥwty-ḥtp" at El-Bersheh', *JEA* 2/1 (1915), 13-14.

Blackman, A. M., *The Rock Tombs of Meir*, 6 vols (London, 1914-1953).

Bloxam, E., 'Miners and Mistresses: Middle Kingdom Mining on the Margins', *JSA* 6/2 (2006), 277-303.

Blumenthal, E., 'Die Datierung der *Nḥri*-Graffiti von Hatnub. Zur Stellung der ägyptischen Gaufürsten im frühen Mittleren Reich', *AOF* 4 (1976), 35-62.

Bomann, A. and Young, R., 'Preliminary Survey in the Wadi Abu Had, Eastern Desert, 1992', *JEA* 80 (1994), 23-44.

Booth, C., *The Hyksos Period in Egypt* (Princes Risborough, 2005).

Booth, C., *The Role of Foreigners in Ancient Egypt: A Study of Non-Stereotypical Artistic Representations*, BAR International Series 1426 (Oxford, 2005).

Borchardt, L., 'Der zweite Papyrusfund von Kahun und die zeitliche Festlegung des Mittleren Reiches der ägyptischen Geschichte', *ZÄS* 37 (1899), 89-103.

Borchardt, L., *Statuen und Statuetten von Königen und Privatleuten*, 5 vols (Berlin, 1911-1936).

Boschloos, V., 'The Middle Bronze Age "Green Jasper Seal Workshop": New Evidence from the Levant and Egypt', *JAEI* 6/4 (2014), 36-37.

Bou-Assaf, Y. M., 'Organisation architectural à Byblos (Liban) au Bronze Ancien', in M. Bietak and E. Czerny (eds), *The Bronze Age in the Lebanon: Studies on the Archaeology and Chronology of Lebanon, Syria and Egypt*, ÖAW: Denkschriften der Gesamtakademie 50 (Vienna, 2008), 52-60.

Bourke, S. J. and Eriksson, K. O., 'Pella in Jordan, Royal Name Scarabs and the Hyksos Empire: A View from the Margins', in E. Czerny et al. (eds), *Timelines. Studies in Honour of Manfred Bietak*, vol. 2, OLA 149 (Leuven, Paris and Dudley, 2006), 339-348.

Bourriau, J., 'Nubians in Egypt during the Second Intermediate Period. An Interpretation based upon the Egyptian Ceramic Evidence', in Do. Arnold (ed.), *Studien zur altÄgyptischen Keramik* (Mainz, 1981), 25-41.

Bourriau, J., 'Cemetery and Settlement Pottery of the Second Intermediate Period to Early New Kingdom', *BES* 8 (1986/1987), 47-59.

Bourriau, J., *Pharaohs and Mortals. Egyptian Art in the Middle Kingdom* (Cambridge, New York, 1988).

Bourriau, J., 'Canaanite Jars from New Kingdom Deposits at Memphis, Kom Rabi'a', *Eretz Israel* 21 (1990), 18-26.

Bourriau, J., 'Relations between Egypt and Kerma during the Middle and New Kingdoms', in W. Davies (ed.), *Egypt and Africa: Nubia from Prehistory to Islam* (London, 1991), 129-144.

Bourriau, J., 'Observations on the Pottery of Serabit el-Khadim', *CRIPEL* 18 (1996), 19-32.

Bourriau, J., 'The Dolphin Vase from Lisht', in P. der Manuelian (ed.), *Studies in Honor of William K. Simpson*, vol. 1 (Boston, 1996), 101-116.

Bourriau, J., 'Beyond Avaris: The Second Intermediate Period in Egypt Outside the Eastern Delta', in E. D. Oren (ed.), *The Hyksos: New Historical and Archaeological Perspectives*, University Museum Monograph 96 (Philadelphia, 1997), 159-182.

Bourriau, J., 'Some Archaeological Notes on the Kamose Texts', in A. Leahy and J. Tait (eds), *Studies on Ancient Egypt in Honour of H. S. Smith*, Occasional Publications 13 (London, 1999), 43-48.

Bourriau, J., 'The Second Intermediate Period (c.1650-1550 BC)', in I. Shaw (ed.), *The Oxford History of Ancient Egypt* (Oxford, 2000), 172-206.

Bourriau, J., 'The Relative Chronology of the Second Intermediate Period: Problems in linking Regional Archaeological Sequences', in M. Marée (ed.), *The Second Intermediate Period (Thirteenth-Seventeenth Dynasties). Current Research, Future Prospects* (Leuven, Paris and Walpole, 2010), 11-37.

Bourriau, J. and Gallorini, C., 'Memphis: Pottery from Memphis, Kom Rabi'a', in R. Schiestl and A. Seiler (eds), *Handbook of the Pottery of the Egyptian Middle Kingdom*, vol. 2: *The Regional Volume*, ÖAW: Denkschriften der Gesamtakademie 72 (Vienna, 2012), 107-130.

Brandl, B., 'Canaanite and Egyptian Scarabs from Area R', in A. Mazar and R. A. Mullins (eds), *Excavations at Tel Beth Shean 1989-1996*, vol. 2: *The Middle and Late Bronze Age Strata in Area R* (Jerusalem, 2007), 582-605.

Brill, R. H., Barnes, I. L. and Adams, B., 'Lead Isotopes in Some Ancient Egyptian Objects', *Recent Advances in Science and Technology of Materials* 3 (1974), 9-27.

van den Brink, E. C. M., *Tombs and Burial Customs at Tell el-Dab'a and their Cultural Relationship to Syria-Palestine during the Second Intermediate Period*, Veröffentlichungen der Institute für Afrikanistik und Ägyptologie der Universität Wien 23 (Vienna, 1982).

van den Brink, E. C. M., van Wesemael, B. and Dirksz, P., 'A Geo-Archaeological Survey in the North-Eastern Nile Delta, Egypt; the First Two Seasons, a Preliminary Report', *MDAIK* 43 (1987), 7-31.

Brovarski, E., et al., *Bersheh Reports*, vol 1: *Report of the 1990 Field Season of the Joint Expedition of the Museum of Fine Arts, Boston* (Boston, 1992).

Brovarski, E., 'The Hare and Oryx Nomes in the First Intermediate Period and Early Middle Kingdom', in A. Woods, A. McFarlane and S. Binder (eds), *Egyptian Culture and Society: Studies in Honour of Naguib Kanawati* (Cairo, 2010), 31-85.

Brunton, G., *Qau and Badari*, vol. 3 (London, 1930).

Brunton, G., *Mostagedda and the Tasian Culture* (London, 1937).

Brysbaert, A., 'Common Craftsmanship in the Aegean and East Mediterranean Bronze Age: Preliminary Technological Evidence with Emphasis on the Painted Plaster from Tell el-Dab'a, Egypt', *E&L* 12 (2002), 95-107.

Buchberger, H. W., 'Sesostris I. und die Inschrift von et-Tôd? Eine philologische Anfrage', in K. Zibelius-Chen and H. W. Fischer-Elfert (eds), *Von Reichlich Ägyptischem Verstande: Festschrift für Waltraud*

Guglielmi zum 65 Geburstag (Wiesbaden, 2006), 15-21.

Bunimovitz, S., 'The Middle Bronze Age Fortifications in Palestine as a Social Phenomon', *Tel Aviv* 19 (1992), 221-234.

Burkard, G., *Textkritische Untersuchungen zu ägyptischen Weisheitslehren des Alten und Mittleren Reiches*, ÄgAb 34 (Wiesbaden, 1977).

Burke, A. A., *"Walled Up to Heaven": The Evolution of Middle Bronze Age Fortification Strategies in the Levant*, SAHL 4 (Winona Lake, 2008).

Bursche, A., 'Archaeological Sources as Ethnical Evidence – The Case of the Eastern Vistula Mouth', in P. Graves-Brown et al. (eds), *Cultural Identity and Archaeology: The Construction of European Communities* (London, 1996), 228-237.

Bushnell, L., 'The Wild Goat-and-Tree Icon and its Special Significance for Ancient Cyprus', in G. Papantoniou (ed.), *Postgraduate Cypriot Archaeology. Proceedings of the Fifth Annual Meeting of Young Researchers on Cypriot Archaeology, Department of Classics, Trinity College, Dublin, 21-22 October 2005*, BAR International Series 1803 (Oxford, 2008), 65-76.

Butin, R. F., 'The Protosinaitic Inscriptions', *The Harvard Theological Review* 25/2 (1932), 130-203.

C

Callender, G., 'The Middle Kingdom Renaissance (c.2055-1650 BC)', in I. Shaw (ed.), *The Oxford History of Ancient Egypt* (Oxford, 2000), 137-171.

Callot, O., *Les sanctuaires de l'acropole d'Ougarit, les temples de Baal et de Dagan*, Ras Shamra – Ougarit 19 (Lyon, 2011).

Cartwright, C., Granger-Taylor, H. and Quirke, S., 'Lahun Textile Evidence in London', in S. Quirke (ed.), *Lahun Studies* (Reigate, 1998), 92-111.

Castel, G. and Soukiassian, G., 'Dépôt de steles dans le sanctuaire du Nouvel Empire au Gebel Zeit', *BIFAO* 85 (1985), 285-293.

Castel, G. and Soukiassian, G., 'Les mines de galena pharaoniques du Gebel el-Zeite (Egypte)', *BSFE* 112 (1988), 37-53.

Castel, G. and Soukiassian, G., *Gebel el-Zeit*, vol. 1: *Les Mines de Galène (Egypte, IIe millénaire av. J.-C.)*, FIFAO 35 (Cairo, 1989).

Černy, J., 'Semites in Egyptian Mining Expeditions to Sinai', *ArOr* 7 (1935), 384-389.

Černy, J., *The Inscriptions of Sinai*, vol. 2: *Translations and Commentary* (London, 1955).

Charaf, H., 'Arqa and its Regional Connections Redux', in *Interconnections in the Eastern Mediterranean. Lebanon in the Bronze and Iron Ages. Proceedings of the International Symposium Beirut 2008*, BAAL Hors-Série 6 (Beirut, 2009), 295-309.

Charaf, H., 'The Northern Levant (Lebanon) during the Middle Bronze Age', in M. L. Steiner and A. E. Killebrew (eds), *The Oxford Handbook of the Archaeology of the Levant c. 8000-332 BCE* (Oxford, 2013), 434-450.

Chartier-Raymond, M., 'Notes sur Maghara (Sinaï)', *CRIPEL* 10 (1988), 13-22.

Chartier-Raymond, M. et al., 'Les sites miniers pharaoniques de Sud-Sinaï. Quelques notes et observations de Terrain', *CRIPEL* 16 (1994), 31-77.

Chavalas, M. W., *The Ancient Near East: Historical Sources in Translation* (Oxford, 2006).

Chehab, M., 'Chroniques', *BMB* 9 (1949/1950), 107-117.

Chehab, M., 'Relations entre l'Égypte et la Phénicie des origins à Oun-Amoun', in W. A. Ward (ed.), *The Role of the Phoenicians in the Interaction of Mediterranean Civilizations. Papers Presented at the American University of Beirut* (Beirut, 1968), 1-8.

Chehab, M., 'Noms de personnalités égyptiennes découvertes au Liban', *BMB* 22 (1969), 1-48.

Chehab, M., 'Découvertes phéneciennes au Liban', in *Atti del I Congresso Internazionale di Studi Fenici e Punici 1979* (Rome, 1983), 165-172.

Clamer, C., 'The Stone Vessels', in A. Mazar and R. A. Mullins (eds), *Excavations at Tel Beth Shean 1989-1996*, vol. 2: *The Middle and Late Bronze Age Strata in Area R* (Jerusalem, 2007), 626-638.

Clarke, D., 'Archaeology: The Loss of Innocence', *Antiquity* 47 (1973), 6-18.

Clédat, J., 'Deux monuments nouveaux de Tell el-Maskhoutah', *RT* 32 (1910), 40-42.

Cohen, A., 'Introduction: The Lesson of Ethnicity', in A. Cohen (ed.), *Urban Ethnicity* (London, 1974), ix-xxiv.

Cohen, M., 'A Middle Bronze Age IIA-B Tomb at Bet She'an', *'Atiqot* 59 (2008), 11*-20*, 195-196.

Cohen, R. and Toninato, P., 'The Creolization Debate: Analysing Mixed Identities and Cultures', in R. Cohen and P. Toninato (eds), *The Creolization Reader: Studies in Mixed Identities and Cultures* (London and New York, 2010), 1-21.

Cohen, S. L., *Canaanites, Chronologies, and Connections: The Relationship of Middle Bronze IIA Canaan to Middle Kingdom Egypt*, SAHL 3 (Indiana, 2002).

Cohen, S. L., 'Continuities and Discontinuities: A Reexamination of the Intermediate Bronze Age-Middle Bronze Age Transition in Canaan', *BASOR* 354 (2009), 1-13.

Cohen, S. L., 'Cores, Peripheries, and Ports of Power: Theories of Canaanite Development in the Early Second Millennium B.C. E.', in J. D. Schloen (ed.), *Exploring the Longue Durée in Honor of Lawrence E. Stager* (Winona Lake, 2009), 69-75.

Cohen, S. L., 'Interpretive Uses and Abuses of the Beni Hasan Tomb Painting', *JNES* 74/1 (2015), 19-38.

Cohen-Weinberger, A. and Goren, Y., 'Levantine-Egyptian Interactions during the 12th to the 15th Dynasties based on the Petrography of the Canaanite Pottery from Tell el-Dab'a', *E&L* 14 (2004), 69-100.

Cole, D. P., *Shechem*, vol. 1: *The Middle Bronze Age Pottery* (Winona Lake, 1984).

Collard, M. and Wood, B., 'How Reliable are Human Phylogenetic Hypotheses?', *Proceedings of the National Academy of Sciences of the United States of America* 97 (2000), 5003-5006.

Colless, B. E., 'The Byblos Syllabary and the Proto-Alphabet', *ANES* 30 (1992), 55-102.

Colless, B. E., 'Proto-Alphabetic Inscriptions from the Wadi Arabah', *Antiquo Oriente* 8 (2010), 75-96.

Collier, M., 'The Language of Literature: On Grammar and Texture', in A. Loprieno (ed.), *Ancient Egyptian Literature. History & Forms* (Leiden, 1996), 531-553.

Collier, M. and Quirke, S. (eds), *The UCL Lahun Papyri: Letters*, BAR International Series 1083 (Oxford, 2002).

Collier, M. and Quirke, S. (eds), *The UCL Lahun Papyri: Religious, Literary, Legal, Mathematical and Medical*, BAR International Series 1209 (Oxford, 2004).

Collier, M. and Quirke, S. (eds), *The UCL Lahun Papyri: Accounts*, BAR International Series 1471 (Oxford, 2006).

Collon, D., *The Seal Impressions from Tell Atchana/Alalakh*, AOAT 27 (Neukirchen-Vluyn, 1975).

Collon, D., 'The Green Jasper Cylinder Seal Workshop', in M. Kelly-Buccellati, P. Matthiae and M. Van Loon (eds), *Insight Through Images. Studies in Honor of Edith Porada*, Bibliotheca Mesopotamica 21 (Malibu, 1986), 57-70.

Collon, D., *First Impressions. Cylinder Seals in the Ancient Near East* (London, 1987).

Collon, D., 'New Seal Impressions from Tell el-Dab'a', in E. Czerny et al. (eds), *Timelines. Studies in Honour of Manfred Bietak*, vol. 2, OLA 149 (Leuven, Paris and Dudley, 2006), 97-101.

Collon, D., Lehmann, M. and Müller, S. E. M., 'Tell el-Dab'a Sealings 2009-2011', *E&L* 22-23 (2012/2013), 95-104.

Contenau, G., 'Mission archéologique à Sidon (1914)', *Syria* 1 (1920), 108-154.

Cooke, W. D., 'W. F. Petrie and the Weavers Waste', *Archaeological Textiles Newsletter* 17 (1993), 13-14.

Cornelius, I., *The Iconography of the Canaanite Gods Reshef and Ba'al. Late Bronze and Iron Age I Periods (c 1500 – 1000 BCE)*, OBO 140 (Freiburg, 1994).

Couyat, J. and Montet, P., *Les inscriptions hiéroglyphiques et hiératiques du Ouâdi Hammâmât*, MIFAO 34 (Cairo, 1912).

Creasman, P. P., *The Cairo Dahshur Boats* (M. A. Thesis, Texas A&M University, 2005).

Cross, F. M., 'The Evolution of the Proto-Canaanite Alphabet', *BASOR* 134 (1954), 15-24.

Czerny, E., *Tell el Dab'a*, vol. 9: *Eine Plansiedlung des frühen Mittleren Reiches*, Untersuchungen der Zweigstelle Kairo des Österreichischen Archäologischen Instituts 15 (Vienna, 1999).

Czerny, E., 'Egyptian Pottery from Tell el-Dab'a as a Context for Early MBIIA Painted Ware', in M. Bietak (ed.), *The Middle Bronze Age in the Levant. Proceedings of an International Conference on MBIIA Ceramic Material in Vienna, 24th-26th of January 2001*, ÖAW: Denkschriften der Gesamtakademie 26 (Vienna, 2002), 133-142.

D

Daly, R. L., *Kings of the Hyksos, Tell el-'Ajjul in the Bichrome Ware Period: A Comparative Stratigraphical Analysis* (PhD Dissertation, University of Utah, 1994).

Danelius, E., 'Shamgar Ben 'Anath', *JNES* 22/3 (1963), 191-193.

Dantong, G., 'The Inscription of Amenemhet II from Memphis: Transliteration, Translation, and Comment', *JAC* 14 (1999), 45-66.

Daressy, G., 'Notes et Remarques', *RT* 16 (1870), 123-134.

Daressy, G., 'Inscriptions hiéroglyphiques trouvées dans le Caire', *ASAE* 4 (1903), 101-109.

Daressy, G., 'Un poignard du temps des rois pasteurs', *ASAE* 7 (1906), 115-120.

Darnell, J. C., *Theban Desert Road Survey in the Egyptian Western Desert*, vol. 1: *Gebel Tjauti Rock Inscriptions 1-45 and Wadi el-Ḥôl Rock Inscriptions 1-45*, OIP 119 (Chicago, 2002).

Darnell, J. C. et al., 'Two Early Alphabetic Inscriptions from the Wadi el-Ḥôl: New Evidence for the Origin of the Alphabet from the Western Desert of Egypt', *AASOR* 59 (2005), 64-124.

David, R., 'Religious Practices in a Pyramid Workmen's Town of the Twelfth Dynasty', *BACE* 2 (1991), 33-40.

David, R., *The Pyramid Builders of Ancient Egypt. A Modern Investigation of Pharaoh's Workforce* (London and New York, 1996).

Davies, G. I., *Cities of the Biblical World. Megiddo* (Cambridge, 1986).

Davies, W. V., 'Ancient Egyptian Timber Imports. An Analysis of Wooden Coffins in the British Museum', in W. V. Davies and L. Schofield (eds), *Egypt, the Aegean and the Levant: Interconnections in the Second Millennium B.C.* (London, 1995), 146-156.

Debono, F., 'Rapport préliminaire sur les resultants de l'étude des objets de la fouille des installations du Moyen Empire et "Hyksos" a l'est du lac sacré de Karnak', *Cahiers de Karnak* 7 (1982), 377-383.

Debono, F., 'Rapport de cloture sur les résultats et études des objets du sondage à l'est du lac sacré de Karnak', *Cahiers de Karnak* 8 (1985), 121-131.

Defernez, C., 'La céramique d'Ayn Soukhna: observations préliminaires', *CCE* 7 (2004), 59-89.

Delia, R. D., *A Study of the Reign of Senwosret III* (PhD Dissertation, Columbia University, 1980).

Desroches-Noblecourt, Ch., 'Fouilles en Egypte 1948-1949', *BSFE* 1 (1949), 12-13.

Dever, W. G., *Gezer*, vol. 2: *Report of the 1967-1970 Seasons in Fields I and II* (Jerusalem, 1974).

Dever, W. G., 'MBIIA Cemeteries at 'Ain es-Sâmiyeh and Sinjil', *BASOR* 217 (1975), 23-35.

Dever, W. G., 'The Beginning of the Middle Bronze Age in Palestine', in F. M. Cross, W. E. Lemke and P. D. Miller (eds), *Magnolia Dei. The Mighty Acts of God. Essays on the Bible and Archaeology in Memory of G. Ernest Wright* (Garden City, 1976), 1-38.

Dever, W. G., 'Archaeological Sources for the History of Palestine: The Middle Bronze Age: The Zenith of the Urban Canaanite Era', *BA* 50/3 (1987), 149-177.

Dever, W. G., 'Tell el-Dab'a and Levantine Middle Bronze Age Chronology: A Rejoinder to Manfred Bietak', *BASOR* 281 (1991), 73-79.

Dever, W. G., 'The Chronology of Syria-Palestine in the Second Millennium B.C.E. A Review of Current Issues', *BASOR* 288 (1992), 1-52.

Dever, W. G., 'Visiting the Real Gezer: A Reply to Israel Finkelstein', *Tel Aviv* 30/2 (2003), 259-282.

Dever, W. G., 'Ethnicity and the Archaeological Record: The Case of Early Israel', in D. R. Edwards and C. T. McCollough (eds), *The Archaeology of Difference. Gender, Ethnicity, Class and the 'Other' in Antiquity. Studies in Honor of Eric M. Meyers*, ASOR 60-61 (Boston, 2005), 49-66.

Dever, W. G., Lance, H. and Wright, G. E., *Gezer*, vol. 1: *Preliminary Report of the 1964-1966 Seasons* (Jerusalem, 1970).

Dever, W. G., Lance, H. and Wright, G. E., *Gezer*, vol. 4: *The 1969-1971 Seasons in Field VI, the "Acropolis"* (Jerusalem, 1986).

Dhorme, E., 'Déchiffrement des inscriptions pseudo-hiéroglyphiques de Byblos', *Syria* 25 (1946-1948), 1-35.

Di Biase-Dyson, C., *Characterisation across Frontiers: Foreigners and Egyptians in the Late Egyptian Stories from Linguistic and Literary Perspectives* (PhD Dissertation, Macquarie University, 2008).

Di Biase-Dyson, C., *Foreigners and Egyptians in the Late Egyptian Stories: Linguistic, Literary and Historical Perspectives* (Leiden, 2013).

Dijkstra, M., 'The So-called 'Ăḥiṭūb-Inscription from Kahun (Egypt)', *ZDPV* 106 (1990), 51-56.

Dodson, A., 'The Tombs of the Kings of the Thirteenth Dynasty in the Memphite Necropolis', *ZÄS* 114 (1987), 36-44.

Dodson, A., 'On the Internal Chronology of the Seventeenth Dynasty', *GM* 120 (1991), 33-38.

Dodson, A., 'Review: Ryholt, K.S.B. – The Political Situation in Egypt during the Second Intermediate Period, c. 1800-1550 B.C.', *BiOr* 57/1-2 (2000), 48-52.

Dornemann, R. H., 'Seven Seasons of ASOR Excavations at Tell Qarqur, Syria, 1993-1999', in N. Lapp (ed.), *Preliminary Excavation Reports and Other Archaeological Investigations: Tell Qarqur, Iron I Sites in the North-Central Highlands of Palestine* (Boston, 2003), 1-142.

Dornemann, R. H., 'Current Thoughts on the Transition from Early Bronze Age to Middle Bronze Age at Tell Qarqur', in P. Matthiae (ed.), *Proceedings of the 6th International Congress of the Archaeology of the Ancient Near East*, vol. 2: *Excavations, Surveys and Restorations: Reports on Recent Field Archaeology in the Near East* (Wiesbaden, 2010), 139-150.

Dothan, M., 'The Excavations at Nahariyah. Preliminary Report (Seasons 1954/55)', *IEJ* 6 (1956), 14-25.

Dotson, C., 'A Portrait of Ancient Egyptian Common Life: The Cycle of Order and Chaos in *The Tale of Sinuhe*', *Studia Antiqua* 8/1 (2010), 47-53.

Doumet-Serhal, C., 'First Season of Excavation at Sidon: Preliminary Report', *BAAL* 3 (1998/1999), 181-224.

Doumet-Serhal, C., 'Second Season of Excavation at Sidon: Preliminary Report', *BAAL* 4 (2000), 75-122.

Doumet-Serhal, C., 'Third Season of Excavation at Sidon: Preliminary Report', *BAAL* 5 (2001), 153-172.

Doumet-Serhal, C., 'Fourth Season of Excavation at Sidon: Preliminary Report', *BAAL* 6 (2002), 179-210.

Doumet-Serhal, C., 'Fifth Season of Excavation at Sidon: Preliminary Report', *BAAL* 7 (2003), 175-207.

Doumet-Serhal, C., 'Weapons from the Middle Bronze Age Burials at Sidon', *AHL* 18 (2003), 38-57.

Doumet-Serhal, C., 'Sixth and Seventh Seasons of Excavation at Sidon: Preliminary Report', *BAAL* 8 (2004), 47-82.

Doumet-Serhal, C., 'Warrior Burial 27 at Sidon', *AHL* 20 (2004), 21-29.

Doumet-Serhal, C., 'Sidon (Lebanon): Twenty Middle Bronze Age Burials from the 2001 Season of Excavation', *Levant* 36 (2004), 89-154.

Doumet-Serhal, C., 'Eighth and Ninth Season of Excavation (2006-2007) at Sidon – Preliminary Report', *BAAL* 10 (2006), 131-135.

Doumet-Serhal, C., 'Sidon: Mediterranean Contacts in the Early and Middle Bronze Age, Preliminary Report', *AHL* 24 (2006), 34-47.

Doumet-Serhal, C., 'The Kingdom of Sidon and its Mediterranean Connections', in C. Doumet-Serhal (ed.), *Networking Patterns of the Bronze and Iron Age Levant. The Lebanon and Its Mediterranean Connections* (Beirut, 2008), 1-70.

Doumet-Serhal, C., 'The British Museum Excavation at Sidon: Markers for the Chronology of the Early and Middle Bronze Age in Lebanon', in M. Bietak and E. Czerny (eds), *The Bronze Age in the Lebanon: Studies on the Archaeology and Chronology of Lebanon, Syria and Egypt*, ÖAW: Denkschriften der Gesamtakademie 50 (Vienna, 2008), 11-44.

Doumet-Serhal, C., 'Tenth, Eleventh and Twelfth Season of Excavation (2008-2010) at Sidon', *BAAL* 13 (2009), 7-69.

Doumet-Serhal, C., 'Sidon during the Bronze Age: Burials, Rituals and Feasting Grounds at the "College Site" ', *NEA* 73/2-3 (2010), 114-129.

Doumet-Serhal, C., 'A Decorated Box from Sidon', *AHL* 34-35 (2011/2012), 93-103.

Doumet-Serhal, C., 'Tracing Sidon's Mediterranean Networks in the Second Millennium B.C.: Receiving, transmitting, and assimilating. Twelve Years of British Museum Excavations', in J. Aruz, S. B. Graff, and Y. Rakic (eds), *Cultures in Contact. From Mesopotamia to the Mediterranean in the Second Millennium B.C.* (New York, 2013), 132-141.

Doumet-Serhal, C. and Kopetzky, K., 'Sidon and Tell el-Dab'a: Two Cities – One Story. A Highlight on Metal Artefacts from the Middle Bronze Age Graves', *AHL* 34-35 (2011/2012), 9-52.

Doxey, D. M., *Egyptian Non-Royal Epithets in the Middle Kingdom: A Social and Historical Analysis* (Leiden, 1998).

Driver, G. R., *Semitic Writing: From Pictograph to Alphabet* (3rd edition, London, 1976).

Dunand, M., 'Les Égyptiens a Beyrouth', *Syria* 9/4 (1928), 300-302.

Dunand, M., *Fouilles de Byblos*, vols 1-5 (Paris, 1939-1973).

Dunand, M., *Byblia Grammata. Documents et recherché sur le développement de l'écriture en Phénicie* (Beirut, 1945).

Dunand, M., 'Rapport préliminaire sur les fouilles de Byblos en 1962', *BMB* 17 (1964), 29-35.

Dunand, M., *Byblos. Its History, Ruins and Legends* (Jbeil, 1973).

Dunand, M., 'Nouvelles inscriptions pseudo-hiéroglyphiques découvertes à Byblos', *BMB* 30 (1978), 51-59.

Dussaud, R., 'Nouveaux renseignements sur la Palestine et la Syrie vers 2000 avant notre ère', *Syria* 8/3 (1927), 216-233.

E

Eder, C., *Die Ägyptischen Motive in der Glyptik des Östlichen Mittelmeerraumes zu Anfang des 2. Jts.v. Chr.*, OLA 71 (Leuven, 1995).

Edwards, I. E. S., 'Lord Dufferin's Excavations at Deir El-Baḥri and the Clandeboye Collection', *JEA* 51 (1965), 16-28.

Eigner, D., 'Der ägyptische Palast eines asiatischen Königs', *JÖAI* 56 (1985), 19-25.

Eisler, R., *Die Kenitischen Weihinschriften der Hyksoszeit im Bergbaugebiet der Sinaihalbinsel und einige andere unerkannte Alphabetdenkmäler aus der Zeit der 12.-18. Dynastie* (Freiburg, 1919).

Eller, J. D. and Coughlan, R. M., 'The Poverty of Primordialism: The Demystification of Ethnic Attachments', *Ethnic and Racial Studies* 16/2 (1993), 183-201.

Engberg, R. M., *The Hyksos Reconsidered*, SAOC 18 (Chicago, 1939).

Engelbach, R., *Harageh* (London, 1923).

Engelbach, R., *The Problem of the Obelisks, From a Study of the Unfinished Obelisk at Aswan* (London, 1923).

Enmarch, R., *The Dialogue of Ipuwer and the Lord of All* (Oxford, 2005).

Enmarch, R., *World Upturned: Commentary and Analysis of The Dialogue of Ipuwer and the Lord of All* (Oxford, 2008).

Enmarch, R., 'The Reception of a Middle Egyptian Poem: *The Dialogue of Ipuwer and the Lord of All* in the Ramesside Period and Beyond', in M. Collier and S. R. Snape (eds), *Ramesside Studies in Honour of K. A. Kitchen* (Bolton, 2011), 169-175.

Eriksen, T. H., 'Creolization in Anthropological Theory and in Mauritius', in C. Stewart (ed.), *Creolization. History, Ethnography, Theory* (Walnut Creek, 2007), 153-177.

Eriksson, K. O., *The Creative Independence of Late Bronze Age Cyprus*, CCEM 10 (Vienna, 2007).

Erman, A. and Grapow, H., *Wörterbuch der Aegyptischen Sprache*, 7 vols (Berlin, 1926-1971).

F

Fakhry, A., *The Inscriptions of the Amethyst Quarries at Wadi el Hudi* (Cairo, 1952).

Farag, S., 'Une Inscription Memphite de la XIIe Dynastie', *RdE* 32 (1980), 75-82.

Farid, S., 'Preliminary Report on the Excavations of the Antiquities Department at Tell Basta (Season 1961)', *ASAE* 58 (1964), 85-98.

Faulkner, R. O., 'The Rebellion in the Hare Nome', *JEA* 30 (1944), 61-63.

Faulkner, R. O., *A Concise Dictionary of Middle Egyptian* (Oxford, 1962).

Favard-Meeks, C., 'Le Delta Egyptien et la mer jusqu'd la foundation d'Alexandrie', *SAK* 16 (1989), 39-63.

Fearon, J., 'Ethnic and Cultural Diversity by Country', *Journal of Economic Growth* 8/2 (2003), 195-222.

Finkbeiner, U. and Sader, H., 'The Tell el-Burak Archaeological Project: A Preliminary Report on the 2001 Season', *BAAL* 5 (2001), 173-194.

Finkelstein, I., 'Middle Bronze Age 'Fortifications': A Reflection of Social Organization and Political Formations', *Tel Aviv* 19 (1992), 201-220.

Finkelstein, I., 'Gezer Revisited and Revised', *Tel Aviv* 29/2 (2002), 262-296.

Finkelstein, I., Ussishkin, D. and Halpern, B. (eds), *Megiddo*, vols 3-5 (Tel Aviv, 2000, 2006, 2013).

Fiore-Marochetti, E., 'Inscribed Blocks from Tomb Chapels at Hawara', *JEA* 86 (2000), 43-50.

Fischer, H. G., 'The Nubian Mercenaries of Gebelein during the First Intermediate Period', *Kush* 9 (1961), 44-56.

Fischer, P. M. and Sadeq, M., 'Tell el-ᶜAjjul 1999. A Joint Palestinian-Swedish Field Project: First Season Preliminary Report', *E&L* 10 (2000), 211-226.

Fischer, P.M. and Sadeq, M., 'Tell el-ᶜAjjul 2000. Second Season Preliminary Report', *E&L* 12 (2002), 109-153.

Fitton, L., Hughes, M. and Quirke, S., 'Northerners at Lahun', in S. Quirke (ed.), *Lahun Studies* (Reigate, 1998), 112-140.

Fitzgerald, G. M., *The Four Canaanite Temples of Beth-Shan*, vol. 2: *The Pottery* (Philadelphia, 1930).

Fitzgerald, G. M., *Beth-Shan Excavations 1921-1923: The Arab and Byzantine Levels* (Philadelphia, 1931).

Flammini, R., 'Elite Emulation and Patronage Relationships in the Middle Bronze: The Egyptianized Dynasty of Byblos', *Tel Aviv* 37 (2010), 154-168.

Forbes, D., 'The Others', *KMT* 16/1 (2005), 66-73.

Forbes, R. J., *Studies in Ancient Technology*, vol. 8 (Leiden, 1974).

Forstner-Müller, I., 'Tombs and Burial Customs at Tell el-Dab'a in Area A/II at the End of the MBIIA Period (Stratum F)', in M Bietak (ed.), *The Middle Bronze Age in the Levant. Proceedings of an International Conference on MBIIA Ceramic Material in Vienna, 24th-26th of January 2001*, ÖAW: Denkschriften der Gesamtakademie 26 (Vienna, 2002), 163-184.

Forstner-Müller, I., 'The Colonization/Urbanization of the Tell Area A/II at Tell el-Dab'a and its Chronological Implications', *E&L* 17 (2007), 83-95.

Forstner-Müller, I., 'A New Scimitar from Tell el-Dab'a', *AHL* 26-27 (2007/2008), 207-211.

Forstner-Müller, I., *Tell el Dab'a*, vol. 16: *Die Gräber des Areals A/II von Tell el-Dab'a*, Untersuchungen der Zweigstelle Kairo des Österreichischen Archäologischen Instituts 28 (Vienna, 2008).

Forstner-Müller, I., 'Providing a Map of Avaris', *EA* 34 (2009), 10-13.

Forstner-Müller, I., 'Tombs and Burial Customs at Tell el-Dab'a during the Late Middle Kingdom and the Second Intermediate Period', in M. Marée (ed.), *The Second Intermediate Period (Thirteenth-Seventeenth Dynasties). Current Research, Future Prospects* (Leuven, Paris and Walpole, 2010), 127-138.

Forstner-Müller, I., 'Settlement Patterns at Avaris: A Study on Two Cases', in M. Bietak, E. Czerny and I. Forstner-Müller (eds), *Cities and Urbanism in Ancient Egypt. Papers from a Workshop in November 2006 at the Austrian Academy of Sciences*, ÖAW: Denkschriften der Gesamtakademie 60 (Vienna, 2010), 103-123.

Forstner-Müller, I. and Kopetzky, K., 'An Upper Egyptian Import at Sidon', *AHL* 24 (2006), 60-62.

Forstner-Müller, I. and Kopetzky, K., 'Egypt and Lebanon: New Evidence for Cultural Exchanges in the First Half of the 2nd Millennium B.C.', in *Interconnections in the Eastern Mediterranean. Lebanon in the Bronze and Iron Ages. Proceedings of the International Symposium Beirut 2008*, BAAL Hors-Série 6 (Beirut, 2009), 143-157.

Forstner-Müller, I. and Rose, P., 'Nubian Pottery at Avaris in the Second Intermediate Period and the New Kingdom: Some Remarks', in I. Forstner-Müller and P. Rose (eds), *Nubian Pottery from Egyptian Cultural Contexts of the Middle and Early New Kingdom. Proceedings of a Workshop held at the Austrian Archaeological Institute at Cairo, 1-12 December 2010* (Vienna, 2012), 181-212.

Forstner-Müller, I. and Rose, P., 'Grabungen des österreichischen archäologischen Instituts Kairo in Tell el-Dab'a/Avaris: Das Areal R/III', *E&L* 22-23 (2012/2013), 53-64.

Forstner-Müller, I., Kopetzky, K. and Doumet-Serhal, C., 'Egyptian Pottery of the Late 12th and 13th Dynasty from Sidon', *AHL* 24 (2006), 52-59.

Forstner-Müller, I., et al., 'Geophysical Survey 2007 at Tell el-Dab'a', *E&L* 17 (2007), 97-106.

Forstner-Müller, I., et al., 'Preliminary Report on the Geophysical Survey at Tell el-Dab'a/Qantir in Spring 2008', *E&L* 18 (2008), 87-106.

Forstner-Müller, I., et al., 'Report on the Excavations at Tell el-Dab'a 2011', *Tell el-Dab'a Homepage*, http://www.auaris.at/ (accessed 01/09/2012), 1-14.

Foster, J. L., 'Sinuhe: The Ancient Egyptian Genre of Narrative Verse', *JNES* 39/2 (1980), 89-117.

Foster, J.L., 'Cleaning up Sinuhe', *JSSEA* 12/2 (1982), 81-85.

Foster, J. L., *Thought Couplets in The Tale of Sinuhe. Verse Text and Translation*, Münchener Ägyptologische Untersuchungen 3 (Frankfurt am Mein and New York, 1993).

Franke, D., 'The Career of Khnumhotep III. of Beni Hasan and the So-called "Decline of the Nomarchs" ', in S. Quirke (ed.), *Middle Kingdom Studies* (New Malden, 1991), 51-65.

Franke, D., 'The Middle Kingdom Offering Formulas – A Challenge', *JEA* 89 (2003), 39–57.

Franke, D. 'The Late Middle Kingdom (Thirteenth to Seventeenth Dynasties): The Chronological Framework', *JEH* 1/2 (2008), 267-287.

Frankfort, H., 'The Cemeteries of Abydos: Work of the Season 1925-26: II. Description of Tombs', *JEA* 16/3 (1930), 213-219.

Frost, H., 'The Necropolis, Trench and Other Ancient Remains. A Survey of the Byblian Seafront', *BAAL* 5 (2001), 195-217.

Frost, H., 'Byblos: The Lost Temple, the Cedars and the Sea. A Marine Archaeological Survey', *AHL* 15 (2002), 57-77.

Fuscaldo, P., *Tell el-Dab'a*, vol. 10: *The Palace District of Avaris. The Pottery of the Hyksos Period and the New Kingdom (Areas H/III and H/VI)*, 2 parts, Untersuchungen der Zweigstelle Kairo des Österreichischen Archäologischen Instituts 16 (Vienna, 2000).

G

Gabolde, M., *Catalogue des antiquités égyptiennes du Musée Joseph Déchelette* (Roanne, 1990).

Galán, J. M.,'The Stela of Hor in Context', *SAK* 21 (1994), 65-79.

Gale, R. et al., 'Wood', in P. T. Nicholson and I. Shaw (eds), *Ancient Egyptian Materials and Technology* (Cambridge, 2000), 334-371.

Galling, K., 'Berichte: Archäologisch-historische Ergebnisse einer Reise in Syrien und Libanon im Spätherbst 1952', *ZDPV* 69 (1953), 88-93.

Gallorini, C., *Incised Marks on Pottery and Other Objects from Kahun: Systems of Communication in Egypt during the Late Middle Kingdom* (PhD Dissertation, University College London, 1998).

Gallorini, C., 'A Cypriote Sherd from Kahun in Context', in D. Aston et al. (eds), *Under the Potter's Tree. Studies on Ancient Egypt Presented to Janine Bourriau on the Occasion of her 70th Birthday*, OLA 204 (Leuven, Paris and Walpole, 2011), 397-415.

Gardiner, A. H., *Notes on the Story of Sinuhe* (Paris, 1916).

Gardiner, A. H., 'The Egyptian Origin of the Semitic Alphabet', *JEA* 3/1 (1916), 1-16.

Gardiner, A. H., 'The Defeat of the Hyksos by Kamose: The Carnavron Tablet, No. I', *JEA* 3 (1916), 95-110.

Gardiner, A. H., *Late Egyptian Stories*, BiAe 1 (Brussels, 1932).

Gardiner, A. H., *Ancient Egyptian Onomastica* 1 (Oxford, 1947).

Gardiner, A. H., *Egypt of the Pharaohs. An Introduction* (London, Oxford and New York, 1961).

Gardiner, A. H., 'Once Again the Proto-Sinaitic Inscriptions', *JEA* 48 (1962), 45-48.

Gardiner, A. H., *The Admonitions of an Egyptian Sage from a Hieratic Papyrus in Leiden (Pap. Leiden 344 recto)* (Hildesheim, 1969).

Gardiner, A. H. and Peet, T. E., *The Inscriptions of Sinai*, vol. 1: *Introduction and Plates* (London, 1917).

Garstang, J., *El-Arábah: A Cemetery of the Middle Kingdom Survey of the Old Kingdom Temenos Graffiti from the Temple of Sety* (London, 1901).

Garstang, J., *The Burial Customs of Ancient Egypt as illustrated by Tombs of the Middle Kingdom* (London, 1907).

Garstang, J., 'An Ivory Sphinx from Abydos (British Museum, No. 54678)', *JEA* 14/1 (1928), 46-47.

Garstang, J., 'Jericho. Sir. Charles Marston's Expedition of 1930', *PEQ* 62 (1930), 123-132.

Garstang, J., 'The Walls of Jericho. The Marston-Melchett Expedition of 1931', *PEQ* 63 (1931), 186-191.

Garstang, J., 'Jericho: City and Necropolis', *AAALiv* 19 (1932), 3-22, 35-54.

Gasse, A., 'Une expédition au Ouādi Hammāmāt sous le règne de Sebekemsaf Ier', *BIFAO* 87 (1987), 208-218.

Gates, M., 'The Palace of Zimri-Lim at Mari', *BA* 47/2 (1984), 70-87.

Gautier, J. and Jéquier, G., *Mémoire sur les fouilles de Licht*, MIFAO 6 (Cairo, 1902).

Gayet, E., *Musée du Louvre. Stèles de la XIIe dynastie*, Bibliothèque de l'Ecole des Hautes Etudes 68 (Paris, 1886).

Gee, J., 'Overlooked Evidence for Sesostris III's Foreign Policy', *JARCE* 41 (2004), 23-31.

Geertz, C., 'The Integrative Revolution: Primordial Sentiments and Civil Politics in the New States', in C. Geertz (ed.), *Old Societies and New States* (New York, 1963), 105-157.

Genz, H., 'Middle Bronze Age Pottery from Baalbek', in M. van Ess (ed.), *Baalbek/Heliopolis. Results of Archaeological and Architectural Research 2002-2005*, BAAL Hors-Série 4 (Beirut, 2008), 127-149.

Genz, H., 'Recent Excavations at Tell Fadous-Kfarabida', *NEA* 73/2-3 (2010), 102-113.

Genz, H., 'Middle Bronze Age Pottery from Tell Fadous – Kfarabida, Lebanon', *Berytus* 53-54 (2010/2011), 115-132.

Genz, H. and Sader, H., 'Excavations at the Early Bronze Age site of Tell Fadous-Kfarabida. Preliminary Report on the 2007 Season of Excavations', *BAAL* 11 (2007), 7-16.

Genz, H. and Sader, H., 'Tell Hizzin: Digging Up New Material from an Old Excavation', *BAAL* 12 (2008), 183-201.

Genz, H. and Sader, H., 'Middle Bronze Age Pottery from Tell Hizzin, Lebanon', *Berytus* 53-54 (2010/2011), 133-146.

Genz, H. and Sader, H., 'Excavations at Tell Fadous-Kfarabida. Preliminary Report on the 2008 Season of Excavations', *BAAL* 12 (2008), 149-159.

Genz, H. et al., 'Excavations at Tell Fadous-Kfarabida. Preliminary Report on the 2009 Season of Excavations', *BAAL* 13 (2009), 71-123.

Genz, H. et al., 'Excavations at Tell Fadous-Kfarabida. Preliminary Report on the 2010 Season of Excavations', *BAAL* 14 (2010), 241-274.

Genz, H. et al., 'A Middle Bronze Age Burial from Tell Fadous-Kfarabida, Lebanon', *E&L* 20 (2010), 183-205.

Gerisch, R., 'Identification of Charcoal and Wood', in K. A. Bard and R. Fattovich (eds), *Harbor of the Pharaohs to the Land of Punt. Archaeological Investigations at Mersa/Wadi Gawasis, Egypt, 2001-2005* (Naples, 2007), 170-188.

Gerisch, R., 'Wood Anatomical Identifications and Vegetation Studies', in K. A. Bard, R. Fattovich and C. Ward, 'Mersa/Wadi Gawasis 2010-2011', *Archaeogate Egittologia: Articoli e News* (2012), http://www.archaeogate.org/egittologia/article/1506/1/mersawadi-gawasis-2010-2011-report-by-kathryn-a-bard-bo.html (accessed 13/03/2013), 19-23.

Germer, R., 'The Plant Material found by Petrie at Lahun and Some Remarks on the Problems of identifying Egyptian Plant Names', in S. Quirke (ed.), *Lahun Studies* (Reigate, 1998), 84-91.

Gernez, G., *L'armement en métal au Proche et Moyen-Orient. Des origines à 1750 av. J.-C.*, 2 vols (PhD Dissertation, Université de Paris 1 Panthéon-Sorbonne, 2007).

Gernez, G., 'Metal Weapons and Cultural Transformations', in H. Kühne, R. Czichon and F. Janoscha Kreppner (eds), *Proceedings of the 4th International Congress on the Archaeology of the Ancient Near East, Berlin, March 29th-April 3rd, 2004* (Wiesbaden, 2008), 125-146.

Gershuny, L. and Aviam, M., 'Middle Bronze Age Tombs at Fassuṭa', *'Atiqot* 62 (2010), 17-49.

Gerstenblith, P., *The Levant at the Beginning of the Middle Bronze Age*, ASOR Dissertation Series 5 (Winona Lake, 1983).

Gestermann, L., 'Die Datierung der Nomarchen von Hermopolis aus dem frühen Mittleren Reich – eine Phantomdebate?', *ZÄS* 135 (2008), 1-15.

Geva, S., *Tell Jerishe. The Sudenik Excavations of the Middle Bronze Age Fortifications*, Qedem 15 (Jerusalem, 1982).

Geyer, J., *Mythology and Lament: Studies in the Oracles About the Nations* (Cornwall, 2004).

Giddy, L., *The Survey of Memphis*, vol. 2: *Kom Rabi'a: The New Kingdom and Post-New Kingdom Objects* (London, 1999).

Giddy, L. and Jeffreys, D. G., 'Memphis, 1990', *JEA* 77 (1991), 1-6.

Gill, D. and Padgham, J., ''One Find of Capital Importance': A Reassessment of the Statue of User from Knossos', *ABSA* 100 (2005), 41-59.

Gilmore, G. H., 'The Composition of the Kahun Metals', in R. David (ed.), *Science in Egyptology. Proceedings of the 'Science in Egyptology' Symposia* (Manchester, 1986), 447-462.

Giveon, R., 'A Sealing of Khyan from the Shephela of Southern Palestine', *JEA* 51 (1965), 202-204.

Giveon, R., *The Stones of Sinai Speak* (Tokyo, 1978), 61.

Giveon, R., *The Impact of Egypt on Canaan. Iconographical and Related Studies*, OBO 20 (Göttingen and Friburg, 1978).

Giveon, R., 'Some Egyptological Considerations Concerning Ugarit', in G. D. Young (ed.), *Ugarit in Retrospect. Fifty Years of Ugarit and Ugaritic* (Winona Lake, 1981), 55-58.

Giveon, R., 'Cattle Administration in Middle Kingdom Egypt and Canaan', in *Hommages à François Daumas*, vol. 1 (Montpellier, 1986), 279-284.

Giveon, R., 'The Impact of Egypt on Canaan in the Middle Bronze Age', in A. F. Rainey (ed.), *Egypt, Israel, Sinai* (Tel Aviv, 1987), 23-40.

Giveon, R., *Scarabs from Recent Excavations in Israel*, OBO 83 (Friburg, 1988).

Goedicke, H., *Re-used Blocks from the Pyramid of Amenemhet I at Lisht* (New York, 1971).

Goedicke, H., 'A New Hyksos Inscription', *JSSEA* 7/4 (1977), 10-12.

Goedicke, H., 'Sinuhe's Duel', *JARCE* 21 (1984), 197-201.

Goedicke, H., 'Abi-Sha(i)'s Representation in Beni Hasan', *JARCE* 21 (1984), 203-210.

Goedicke, H., 'The Riddle of Sinuhe's Flight', *RdE* 35 (1984), 95-103.

Goedicke, H., *The Quarrel of Apophis and Seqenenre* (San Antonio, 1986).

Goedicke, H., 'Egyptian Military Actions in "Asia" in the Middle Kingdom', *RdE* 42 (1991), 89-94.

Goedicke, H., 'Where did Sinuhe stay in "Asia"? (Sinuhe B 29-31)', *CdE* 67 (1992), 28-40.

Goedicke, H., 'Khu-u-Sobek's Fight in 'Asia' ', *E&L* 7 (1998), 33-37.

Goedicke, H., 'The Building Inscription from Tell el-Dab'a of the Time of Sesostris III', *E&L* 12 (2002), 187-190.

Goedicke, H., 'Who Was Sinuhe?', in E. Bechtold, A. Gulyás and A. Hasznos (eds), *From Illahun to Djeme. Papers Presented in Honour of Ulrich Luft*, BAR International Series 2311 (Oxford, 2011), 55-60.

Goldwasser, O., 'Some Egyptian Finds from Hazor: Scarabs, Scarab Impressions and a Stele Fragment', in Y. Yadir et al. (eds), *Hazor III-IV. An Account of the Third and Fourth Seasons of Excavations 1957-1958 (Text)* (Jerusalem, 1989), 339-345.

Goldwasser, O., 'Canaanites Reading Hieroglyphs. Horus is Hathor? – The Invention of the Alphabet in Sinai', *E&L* 16 (2006), 121-160.

Goldwasser, O., 'The Advantage of Cultural Periphery: The Invention of the Alphabet in Sinai (circa 1840 B.C.E.)', in R. Sheffy and G. Toury (eds), *Culture Contacts and the Making of Cultures. Papers in Homage to Itamar Even-Zohar* (Tel Aviv, 2011), 251-316.

Goldwasser, O., 'The Miners who invented the Alphabet – A Response to Christopher Rollston', *JAEI* 4/3 (2012), 9-22.

Goldwasser, O., 'Out of the Mists of the Alphabet - Redrawing the "Brother of the Ruler of Retjenu" ', *E&L* 22-23 (2012/2013).

Golénischeff, W., *Les papyrus hiératiques nos. 1115, 1116A et 1116B de l'Ermitage impérial à St-Petersburg* (St. Petersburg, 1916).

Gordon, M. M., *Assimilation in American Life: The Role of Race, Religion, and National Origin* (Oxford, 1964).

Goren, Y., 'Review of McGovern P. E., *The Foreign Relations of the "Hyksos"* ', BAR International Series 888 (Oxford, 2000), *BiOr* 60/1-2 (2003), 105-109.

Górka, K. and Rzepka, S., 'Infant Burials or Infant Sacrifices? New Discoveries from Tell el-Retaba', *MDAIK* 67 (2011), 93-100.

Goyon, G., *Nouvelles inscriptions du Ouadi Hammamat* (Paris, 1957).

Grajetzki, W., *Two Treasurers of the Late Middle Kingdom*, BAR International Series 1007 (Oxford, 2001).

Grajetzki, W., *Harageh. An Egyptian Burial Ground for the Rich, around 1800 BC* (London, 2004).

Grajetzki, W., *The Middle Kingdom of Ancient Egypt: History, Archaeology and Society* (London, 2006).

Grajetzki, W., *Tomb Treasures of the Late Middle Kingdom. The Archaeology of Female Burials* (Phildelphia, 2014).

Grant, E., *Beth Shemesh (Palestine): Progress of the Haverford Archaeological Expedition. A Report of the Excavations made in 1928* (Haverford, 1929).

Gratien, B., 'Scellements et contrescellements au Moyen Empire en Nubie l'apport de Mirgissa', *CRIPEL* 22 (2001), 47-69.

Green, A. R. W., *The Storm-God in the Ancient Near East* (Winona Lake, 2003).

Green, M., 'The Syrian and Lebanese Topographical Data in the Story of Sinuhe', *CdE* 58 (1983), 38-59.

Greig, G. S., 'The *sḏm=f* and *sḏm.n=f* in the Story of Sinuhe and the Theory of the Nominal (Emphatic) Verbs', in S. Israelit-Groll (ed.), *Studies in Egyptology presented to Miriam Lichtheim* (Jerusalem, 1990), 336-342.

Griffith, F. L., 'The Millingen Papyrus', *ZÄS* 34 (1896), 35-51.

Griffith, F. L., *Hieratic Papyri from Kahun and Gurob (Principally of the Middle Kingdom): Text* (London, 1898).

Griffiths, D. and Ownby, M., 'Assessing the Occurrence of Egyptian Marl C Ceramics in Middle Bronze Age Sidon', *AHL* 24 (2006), 63-77.

Gubel, E. and Loffet, H., 'Qedem and the Land of Iay', *AHL* 34-35 (2011/2012), 79-92.

Guigues, P. E., 'Lébé'a, Kafer-Ğarra, Qraye nécropoles de la région sidonienne (suite)', *BMB* 2 (1938), 27-72.

Gundlach, R., *Die Zwangsumsiedlung auswärtiger Bevölkerung als Mittel ägyptische Politik bis zum Ende des Mittleren Reiches* (Stuttgart, 1994).

Guy, P. L. O., *Megiddo Tombs*, OIP 33 (Chicago, 1938).

H

Habachi, L., 'Khatâ'na-Qantîr: Importance', *ASAE* 52 (1954), 443-562.

Habachi, L., *Tell Basta*, Supplément aux ASAE 22 (Cairo, 1957).

Habachi, L., *The Second Stela of Kamose and His Struggle Against the Hyksos Ruler and His Capital* (Glückstadt, 1972).

Hall, T. D. and Chase-Dunn, C., 'The World-Systems Perspective and Archaeology: Forward into the Past', *Journal of Archaeological Research* 1 (1993), 121-143.

Hallote, R. S., 'Tombs, Cult, and Chronology: A Reexamination of the Middle Bronze Age Strata of Megiddo', in S. R. Wolff (ed.), *Studies in the Archaeology of Israel and Neighboring Lands in Memory of Douglas L. Esse*, SAOC 59 (Chicago, 2001), 199-214.

Hamada, A. and el-Amir, M., 'Excavations at Kom el-Ḥisn 1943', *ASAE* 46 (1947), 101-141.

Hamada, A. and Farid, S., 'Excavations at Kom el-Ḥisn Season 1945', *ASAE* 46 (1947), 195-235.

Hamada, A. and Farid, S., 'Excavations at Kom el-Ḥisn: Third Season 1946', *ASAE* 48 (1948), 299-325.

Hamada, A. and Farid, S., 'Excavations at Kom el-Ḥisn: Fourth Season 1947', *ASAE* 50 (1950), 367-390.

Hamblin, W. J., *Warfare in the Ancient Near East to 1600BC. Holy Warriors at the Dawn of History* (London and New York, 2006).

Hamilton, G. J., *The Origins of the West Semitic Alphabet in Egyptian Scripts*, The Catholic Biblical Quarterly Monograph Series 40 (Washington, 2006).

Hamilton, G. J., 'A Proposal to Read the Legend of a Seal-Amulet from Deir Rifa, Egypt as an Early West Semitic Alphabetic Inscription', *JSS* 54 (2009), 51-79.

Hamilton, G. J., 'From the Seal of a Seer to an Inscribed Game Board: A Catalogue of Eleven Early Alphabetic Inscriptions Recently Discovered in Egypt and Palestine', *The Bible and Interpretation* (2010), http://www.bibleinterp.com/articles/seal357910.shtml (accessed 13/03/2013), 1-24.

Hansen, D. P., 'Mendes 1964', *JARCE* 6 (1965), 31-39.

Hansen, D. P., 'Some Remarks on the Chronology and Style of Objects from Byblos', *AJA* 73/3 (1969), 281-284.

Hardin, J. W. and Seger, J.D., 'Gezer Rectified: The Dating of the South Gate Complex', in J. S. Gitin, E. Wright and J. P. Dessel (eds), *Confronting the Past: Archaeological and Historical Essays on Ancient Israel in Honor of William G. Dever* (Winona Lake, 2006), 51-60.

Hari, R., 'Une Reine Enigmatique: Nebou-Hotepti', *BSEG* 4 (1980), 45-48.

Harrison, T. P., *Megiddo*, vol. 3: *Final Report on the Stratum VI Excavations*, OIP 127 (Chicago, 2004).

Hayes, W. C., 'Notes on the Government of Egypt in the Late Middle Kingdom', *JNES* 12/1 (1953), 31-39.

Hayes, W. C., *The Scepter of Egypt*, vols 1-2 (New York, 1953-1959).

Hayes, W. C., *A Papyrus of the Late Middle Kingdom in the Brooklyn Museum (Papyrus Brooklyn 35.1446)* (2nd reprint, Brooklyn, 1972).

Hein, I., 'Die Fundpositionen zweier syrischer Siegelabformungen aus Tell el-Dab'a', in E. Czerny et al. (eds), *Timelines. Studies in Honour of Manfred Bietak*, vol. 2, OLA 149 (Leuven, Paris and Dudley, 2006), 135-148.

Hein, I., 'Area A/IV', *Tell el-Dab'a Homepage*, http://www.auaris.at/html/areal_a4.html, (accessed 22/03/2012).

Hein, I. and Jánosi, P., *Tell el Dab'a*, vol. 11: *Areal A/V. Siedlungsrelikte der Späten 2. Zwischenzeit*, Untersuchungen der Zweigstelle Kairo des Österreichischen Archäologischen Instituts 21 (Vienna, 2004).

Hein, I. and Mlinar, C., 'Kat Nr. 22', in M. Bietak and I. Hein (eds), *Pharaonen und Fremde. Dynastien im Dunkel. Katalogue der 194* (Vienna, 1994), 97.

Hein, I. and Satzinger, H., *Stelen des Mittleren Reiches*, 2 vols, Corpus Antiquitatum Aegyptiacum Kunsthistorisches Museum Wien Lieferung 4 and 7 (Mainz am Rhein, 1989-1993).

Heinz, M. and Linke, J., 'Hyperculture, Tradition and Idenitity: How to communicate with Seals in Times of Global Action. A Middle Bronze Age Seal Impression from Kamid el-Loz', in J. Maran and P. W. Stockhammer (eds), *Materiality and Social Practice. Transformative Capacities of Intercultural Encounters* (Oxford, 2012), 185-190.

Helck, H. W., 'Eine Stele Sobekhoteps IV. aus Karnak', *MDAIK* 24 (1969), 194-198.

Helck, H. W., *Der Text der 'Lehre Amenemhets I. für seinen Sohn'* (Wiesbaden, 1969).

Helck, H. W., *Die Prophezeiung des Nfr.tj* (Wiesbaden, 1970).

Helck, H. W., *Die Beziehungen Ägyptens zu vorderasien im 3. und 2. Jahrausend v. Chr.* (2nd edition, Wiesbaden, 1971).

Helck, H. W., 'Ägyptische Statuen im Ausland – ein Chronologisches Problem', *UF* 8 (1976), 101-115.

Helck, H. W., 'Politische Spannungen zu Beginn des Mittleren Reiches', in *Ägypten, Dauer und Wandel: Symposium anlässlich des 75 jährigen Bestehens des Deutsches Archäologischen Instituts Kairo, am 10. und 11. Oktober 1982*, DAIAK Sonderschrift 18 (1985), 45-52.

Helck, H. W., 'Ein Ausgreifen des Mittleren Reiches in den zypriotischen Raum?', *GM* 109 (1989), 27-30.

Helck, H. W., *Historisch-biographische Texte der 2. Zwischenzeit und neue Texte der 18. Dynastie* (Wiesbaden, 1995).

Helck, W. and Otto, E., *Lexikon der Ägyptologie* II (Wiesbaden, 1977).

Henne, H., *Rapport sur les fouilles de Tell Edfou (1921-1922)*, FIFAO 1.2 (Cairo, 1924).

Henne, H., *Rapport sur les fouilles de Tell Edfou (1923 et 1924)*, FIFAO 3.2 (Cairo, 1925).

Herbich, T. and Forstner-Müller, I., 'Small Harbours in the Nile Delta: The Case of Tell el-Dab'a', *Études et travaux* 26 (2013), 258-272.

Hill, M., 'Relief of a Foreigner throwing a Spear', in N. Thomas (ed.), *The American Discovery of Ancient Egypt* (Los Angeles, 1995), 153.

Hoch, J. E., 'The Byblos Syllabary: Bridging the Gap between Egyptian Hieroglyphs and Semitic Alphabets', *JSSEA* 20 (1990), 115-124.

Hoch, J. E., 'Egyptian Hieratic Writing in the Byblos Pseudo-Hieroglyphic Stele L', *JARCE* 32 (1995), 59-65.

Hodjash, S. and Berlev, O., *The Egyptian Reliefs and Stelae in the Pushkin Museum of Fine Arts, Moscow* (Leningrad, 1982).

Hoffman, M. A., *Egypt Before the Pharaohs* (New York, 1979).

Hoffmeier, J. K., *Israel in Egypt: The Evidence for the Antiquity of the Exodus Tradition* (New York and Oxford, 1996).

Hoffmeier, J. K., 'Aspects of Egyptian Foreign Policy in the 18th Dynasty in Western Asia and Nubia', in G. N. Knoppers and A. Hirsch (eds), *Egypt, Israel, and the Ancient Mediterranean World. Studies in Honor of Donald B. Redford* (Leiden and Boston, 2004), 121-141.

Hoffmeier, J. K., ' 'The Walls of the Ruler' in Egyptian Literature and the Archaeological Record: Investigating Egypt's Eastern Frontier in the Bronze Age', *BASOR* 343 (2006), 1-20.

Hoffmeier, J. K., 'Sinai in Egyptian, Levantine and Hebrew (Biblical) Perspectives', in H. Barnard and K. Duistermaat (eds), *The History of the Peoples of the Eastern Desert* (California, 2013), 105-131.

Holladay, J. S., Jr., *Cities of the Delta*, vol. 3: *Tell El-Maskhuṭa. Preliminary Report on the Wadi Tumilat Project 1978-1979*, ARCE Reports 6 (Malibu, 1982).

Holladay, J. S. Jr., 'The Eastern Nile Delta during the Hyksos and Pre-Hyksos Periods: Toward a Systemic/Socioeconomic Understanding', in E. D. Oren (ed.), *The Hyksos: New Historical and Archaeological Perspectives*, University Museum Monograph 96 (Philadelphia, 1997), 183-247.

Hölzl, C., 'The Rock-tombs of Beni Hasan: Architecture and Sequence', in *Sesto Congresso Internazionale di Egittologia Atti*, vol. 1 (Turin, 1992), 279-283.

Horn, S. H., 'Scarabs from Schechem', *JNES* 21/1 (1962), 1-14.

Horn, S. H., 'Scarabs and Scarab Impressions from Shechem II', *JNES* 25/1 (1966), 48-56.

Horn, S. H., 'Scarab and Scarab Impressions from Shechem III', *JNES* 32/3 (1973), 281-289.

Horváth, Z., 'Temple(s) and Town at El-Lahun. A Study of Ancient Toponyms in the el-Lahun Papyri', in D. P. Silverman, W. K. Simpson and J. Wegner (eds), *Archaism and Innovation: Studies in the Culture of*

Middle Kingdom Egypt (New Haven and Philadelphia, 2009), 171-203.

Horváth, Z., 'El-Lahun Survey Project: The Archaeological Mission of the Museum of Fine Arts', *Bulletin du Musèe Hongrois des Beaux-Arts* 110-111 (2009), 186-190.

Hourany, Y., المجهول والمهمل من تاريخ الجنوب اللبناني (جبل عاملة) من سجلات الفراعنة لالف الثاني ق.م (*The Unknown and the Neglected History of Southern Lebanon [Mount 'Amilat] from the Pharaonic Records to the Second Millennium B.C.*) (Beirut, 1999).

Hutchinson, J. and Smith, A. D., 'Introduction', in J. Hutchinson and A. D. Smith (eds), *Ethnicity* (Oxford and New York, 1996), 3-14.

I

Ibrahim, R., 'Rapport sur un mastaba découvert à Edfu en 1932-1933', *ASAE* 33 (1933), 132-134.

Ilin-Tomich, A., 'Two Notes on Middle Kingdom Annals', *Lingua Aegyptia* 18 (2010), 119-129.

Ilin-Tomich, A., 'Changes in the *ḥtp-dj-nsw* Formula in the Late Middle Kingdom and the Second Intermediate Period', *ZÄS* 138 (2011), 20-34.

J

Jaroš-Deckert, B., *Grabung im Asasif 1963-1970*, vol. 5: *Das Grab des Jnj-jtj.f: Die Wandmalereien der XI. Dynastie*, AV (Mainz am Rhein, 1984).

Jeffreys, D. G. and Giddy, L., 'Memphis, 1988', *JEA* 75 (1989), 1-12.

Jenkins, R., *Rethinking Ethnicity. Arguments and Explorations* (2nd edition, London, 2008).

Jidejian, N., *Lebanon. A Mosaic of Cultures* (Yarze, 2001).

Jones, J., *Textiles in Early Egyptian Funerary Contexts. Analysis of the Epigraphic and Archaeological Evidence* (PhD Dissertation, Macquarie University, 2011).

Jones, S., *The Archaeology of Ethnicity. Constructing Identities in the Past and Present* (London and New York, 1997).

Junker, H., 'Vorlaufiger Bericht über die zweite Grabung der Akademie Wissenschaften in Wien auf der vorgeschichtlichen Siedlung Merimde-Benisalame vom 7. Februar bis 8. April 1930', *Anzeiger der Akademie der Wissenschaften in Wien* 66 (1926), 156-248.

K

Kamal, A. B., 'Rapport sur le nécropole d'Arabe-el-Borg', *ASAE* 3 (1902), 80-84.

Kamlah, J. and Sader, H., 'The Tell el-Burak Archaeological Project. Preliminary Report on the 2002 and 2003 Seasons', *BAAL* 7 (2003), 145-173.

Kamlah, J. and Sader, H., 'The Tell el-Burak Archaeological Project: Preliminary Report on the 2005 and 2008 Seasons', *BAAL* 12 (2008), 17-34.

Kamp, K. A. and Yoffee, N., 'Ethnicity in Ancient Western Asia during the Early Second Millennium B. C.: Archaeological Assessments and Ethnoarchaeological Prospectives', *BASOR* 237 (1980), 85-104.

Kamrin, J., *Monument and Microcosm: The 12th Dynasty Tomb Chapel of Khnumhotep II at Beni Hasan* (PhD Dissertation, University of Pennsylvania, 1992).

Kamrin, J., *The Cosmos of Khnumhotep II at Beni Hasan* (New York, 1998).

Kamrin, J., 'The Aamu of Shu in the Tomb of Khnumhotep II at Beni Hassan', *JAEI* 1/3 (2009), 22-36.

Kanawati, N., *The Cemetery of Meir*, vol. 1: *The Tomb of Pepyankh the Middle*, ACE: Reports 31 (Oxford, 2012).

Kanawati, N. and Evans, L., *The Cemetery of Meir*, vol. 2: *The Tomb of Pepyankh the Black*, ACE: Reports 34 (Oxford, 2014).

Kanawati, N. and Evans, L., *Beni Hassan*, vol. 1: *The Tomb of Khnumhotep II*, ACE: Reports 36 (Oxford, 2014).

Kanawati, N. and Woods, A., *Artists of the Old Kingdom. Techniques and Achievements* (Cairo, 2009).

Kanawati, N. and Woods, A., *Beni Hassan: Art and Daily Life in an Egyptian Province* (Cairo, 2010).

Kantor, H. J., 'The Relative Chronology of Egypt and its Foreign Correlations before the Late Bronze Age', in R. W. Ehrich (ed.), *Chronologies in Old World Archaeology* (Chicago and London, 1954), 1-46.

Kaplan, M. F., *The Origin and Distribution of Tell el Yahudiyeh Ware*, SMA 62 (Gothenburg, 1980).

Kaplony-Heckel, U., *Ägyptische Handschriften*, vol. 1 (Wiesbaden, 1971).

Keel, O., 'Die Ω-Gruppe. Ein Mittelbronzezeitlicher Stempelsiegel-Typ mit erhabenem Relief aus Anatolien-Nordsyrien und Palästina; Die Jaspis Skarabäen des 17. Jahrhunderts v. Chr.; Zar Identifikation des

Falkenköpfigen auf den Skarabäen der ausgehenden 13. und der 15. Dynastie', in O. Keel, H. Keel-Leu and S. Schroer (eds), *Stempelsiegel aus Palästina/Israel*, vol. 2, OBO 88 (Freiburg, 1989), 211-280.

Keel, O., *Corpus der Stempelsiegel-Amulette aus Palästina/Israel*, OBO 10 (Freiburg, 1995).

Kemp, B. J., 'An Incised Sherd from Kahun, Egypt', *JNES* 36/4 (1977), 289-292.

Kemp, B. J., *Ancient Egypt: Anatomy of a Civilization* (2nd edition, London and New York, 2006).

Kemp, B. J. and Merrillees, R. S., *Minoan Pottery in Second Millennium Egypt* (Mainz am Rhein, 1980).

Kemp, B. J. and Vogelsang-Eastwood, G., *The Ancient Textile Industry at Amarna* (London, 2001).

Kempinski, A., 'Tell el-ʿAjjul – Beth-Aglayim or Sharuḥen?', *IEJ* 24 (1974), 146-152.

Kempinski, A., 'Some Observations on the Hyksos (XVth) Dynasty and its Canaanite Origins', in S. Israelit-Groll (ed.), *Pharaonic Egypt. The Bible and Christianity* (Jerusalem, 1985), 129-137.

Kenyon, K. M., 'Excavations at Jericho, 1952', *PEQ* 84 (1952), 62-82.

Kenyon, K. M., 'Excavations at Jericho, 1954', *PEQ* 86 (1954), 45-63.

Kenyon, K. M., 'Excavations at Jericho, 1955', *PEQ* 87 (1955), 108-128.

Kenyon, K. M., 'Excavations at Jericho, 1956', *PEQ* 88 (1956), 67-82.

Kenyon, K. M., 'Some Notes on the Early and Middle Bronze Age Strata at Megiddo', *Eretz-Israel* 5 (1958), 51*-60*.

Kenyon, K. M., *Excavations at Jericho*, 5 vols (London, 1960-1965).

Kenyon, K. M., *Amorites and Canaanites* (London, 1966).

Kenyon, K. M., 'The Middle and Late Bronze Age Strata at Megiddo', *Levant* 1 (1969), 25-60.

Kenyon, K. M., 'Tombs of the Intermediate Early Bronze – Middle Bronze Age at Tell el-'Ajjul', in J. R. Stewart, *Tell el 'Ajjūl. The Middle Bronze Age Remains*, SMA 38 (Göteborg, 1974), 76-85.

Kenyon K. M. and Holland, T. A., *Excavations at Jericho*, vol. 4: *The Pottery Type Series and Other Finds* (Jerusalem and London, 1982).

Kessler, D., 'Die Asiatenkarawane von Beni Hassan', *SAK* 14 (1987), 147-165.

King, J. R., 'The Joseph Story and Divine Politics: A Comparative Study of a Biographic Formula from the Ancient Near East', *JBL* 106/4 (1987), 577-594.

Kinney, L. J., 'Music and Dance', in A. McFarlane and A.-L. Mourad (eds), *Behind the Scenes. Daily Life in Old Kingdom Egypt*, ACE: Studies 10 (Oxford, 2012), 53-71.

Kirby, C. J., Orel, S. E. and Smith, S. T., 'Preliminary Report on the Survey of Kom el-Hisn, 1996', *JEA* 84 (1998), 23-26.

Kirkbride, D., 'Scarabs', in K. M. Kenyon, *Excavations at Jericho*, vol. 2: *The Tombs excavated in 1955-58* (Jerusalem, 1965), 580-655.

Kitchen, K. A., 'An Unusual Stela from Abydos', *JEA* 47 (1961), 10-18.

Kitchen, K. A., 'Amenysonb in Liverpool and the Louvre', *JEA* 48 (1962), 159-160.

Kitchen, K. A., 'Byblos, Egypt, and Mari in the Early Second Millennium B.C.', *Orientalia* 36 (1967), 39-54.

Kitchen, K. A., 'An Unusual Egyptian Text from Byblos', *BMB* 20 (1967), 149-153.

Kitchen, K. A., 'Early Canaanites in Rio De Janeiro and a "Corrupt" Ramesside Land-Sale', in S. Israelit-Groll (ed.), *Studies in Egyptology: Presented to Miriam Lichtheim*, vol. 2 (Jerusalem, 1990), 635-645.

Kitchen, K. A., *Catalogue of the Egyptian Collection in the National Museum, Rio de Janeiro*, 2 vols (Warminster, 1990).

Kitchen, K. A., 'Non-Egyptians recorded on Middle Kingdom Stelae in Rio de Janeiro', in S. Quirke (ed.), *Middle Kingdom Studies* (New Malden, 1991), 87-90.

Klemm, D. and Klemm, R., 'Calcit-Alabaster oder Travertin?', *GM* 122 (1991), 57-75.

Klemm, D. and Klemm, R., *Steine und Stein-Brüche im Alten Ägypten* (Berlin and Heidelberg), 1993.

Klemm, R. and Klemm, D., *Stones and Quarries in Ancient Egypt* (London, 2008).

Knapp, A. B., *The History and Culture of Ancient Western Asia and Egypt* (Belmont, 1988).

Koch, R., *Die Erzählung des Sinuhe*, BiAe 17 (Bruxelles, 1990).

Kopetzky, K., 'The Dipper Juglets of Tell el-Dab'a. A Typological and Chronological Approach', in M. Bietak (ed.), *The Middle Bronze Age in the Levant. Proceedings of an International Conference on MBIIA Ceramic Material in Vienna, 24th-26th of January 2001*, ÖAW: Denkschriften der Gesamtakademie 26 (Vienna, 2002), 227-244.

Kopetzky, K., 'Typologische Bemerkungen zur Siedlungskeramik von A/V-p/19', in I. Hein and P. Jánosi, *Tell el-Dab'a*, vol. 11: *Areal A/V. Siedlungsrelikte der Späten 2. Zwischenzeit*, Untersuchungen der Zweigstelle Kairo des Österreichischen Archäologischen Instituts 21 (Vienna, 2004), 237-335.

Kopetzky, K., 'The MBIIB-Corpus of the Hyksos Period at Tell el-Dab'a', in M. Bietak and E. Czerny (eds), *The Bronze Age in the Lebanon: Studies on the Archaeology and Chronology of Lebanon, Syria and Egypt*, ÖAW: Denkschriften der Gesamtakademie 50 (Vienna, 2008), 195-241.

Kopetzky, K., 'Pottery from Tell Arqa found in Egypt and its Chronological Considerations', *AHL* 26-27 (2007/2008), 17-58.

Kopetzky, K., *Tell el Dab'a*, vol. 20: *Die Chronologie der Siedlungskeramik der Zweiten Zwischenzeit aus Tell el Dab'a*, 2 parts, Untersuchungen der Zweigstelle Kairo des Österreichischen Archäologischen Instituts 32 (Vienna, 2010).

Kopetzky, K., 'The Egyptian Corpus of Middle Bronze Age Layers of Sidon', *AHL* 34-35 (2011/2012), 163-172.

von Koppen, F. and Radner, R., 'Ein Tontafelfragment aus der diplomatischen Korrespondenz der Hyksosherrscher mit Babylonien', in Bietak and Forstner-Müller, *E&L* 19 (2009), 91-119.

von Koppen, F. and Lehmann, M., 'A Cuneiform Sealing from Tell el-Dab'a and its Historical Context', *E&L* 22-23 (2012/2013), 91-94.

Kramer, S. N., *Sumerian Mythology. A Study of Spiritual and Literary Achievement in the Third Millennium B.C.* (revised edition, Philadelphia, 1972).

Krauss, R., 'Zur Problematik der Nubienpolitik Kamoses sowie Hyksosherrschaft in Oberägypten', *Orientalia* 62/2 (1993), 17-29.

L

Labib, P., *Die Herrschaft der Hyksos in Ägypten und ihr Sturz* (Glückstadt, 1936).

Lacau, P., *Sarcophages antérieurs au Nouvel Empire* 2 (Cairo, 1904).

Lacau, P., 'Une stèle du roi "Kamosis" ', *ASAE* 39 (1939), 245-271.

Lacovara, P., 'Egypt and Nubia during the Second Intermediate Period', in E. D. Oren (ed.), *The Hyksos: New Historical and Archaeological Perspectives*, University Museum Monograph 96 (Philadelphia, 1997), 69-86.

Laffineur, R., 'Réflections sur le trésor de Tôd', *Aegeum* 2 (1988), 17-30.

Lam, J., 'The Invention and Development of the Alphabet', in C. Woods (ed.), *Visible Language. Inventions of Writing in the Ancient Middle East and Beyond*, OIMP 32 (Chicago, 2010), 189-195.

Lamon, R. S. and Shipton, G. M., *Megiddo*, vol. 1: *Seasons of 1925-1934, Strata I-IV*, OIP 42 (Chicago, 1939).

Lange, K. and Schäfer, H., *Grab und Denksteine des Mittleren Reichs im Museum von Kairo*, vols 1-2, 4 (Cairo, 1902-1908).

Lansing, A. and Hayes, W. C., 'The Egyptian Expedition: The Excavations at Lisht', *BMMA* 28/11.2 (1933), 4-38.

Larkman, S. J., 'Human Cargo: Transportation of Western Asiatic People during 11th and 12th Dynasty', *JSSEA* 34 (2007), 107-113.

Lauffray, J., *Karnak d'Egypte. Domaine du divin. Dix ans de recherché archéologiques et de travaux de maintenance en cooperation avec l'Égypte* (Paris, 1979).

Lawergren, B., 'Distinctions among Canaanite, Philistine, and Israelite-Lyres, and their Global Lyrical Contexts', *BASOR* 309 (1998), 41-68.

Leibovitch, M. J., 'The Date of the Protosinaitic Inscriptions', *Le Muséon* 76 (1963), 201-203.

Leprohon, R., 'Remarks on Private Epithets Found in the Middle Kingdom Wadi Hammamat Graffiti', *JSSEA* 28 (2001), 124-146.

Lichtheim, M., *Ancient Egyptian Literature: A Book of Readings*, 3 vols (London, 1975-1980).

Lilyquist, C., 'Granulation and Glass: Chronological and Stylistic Investigations at Selected Sites, ca. 2500-1400 B.C.E', *BASOR* 290-291 (1993), 29-94.

Lilyquist, C., *Egyptian Stone Vessels: Khian through Tuthmosis IV* (New York, 1995).

Lilyquist, C., *The Tomb of Three Foreign Wives of Tuthmosis III* (New York, 2003).

Liszka, K., *"We Have Come to Serve Pharaoh": A Study of the Medjay and Pangrave as an Ethnic Group and as Mercenaries from c. 2300BCE until c.1050 BCE* (PhD Dissertation, University of Pennsylvania, 2012).

Liverani, M., *Prestige and Interest. International Relations in the Near East ca. 1600-1100 B.C.* (Padua, 1990).

Lloyd, A. B., 'The Great Inscription of Khnumhotep II at Beni Hassan', in A. B. Lloyd (ed.), *Studies in Pharaonic Religion and Society in Honour of J. Gwyn Griffiths* (London, 1992), 21-36.

Loffet, H. C., 'The Sidon Scaraboid S/3487', *AHL* 24 (2006), 78-84.

Loffet, H. C., 'The Sidon Scarabs', *AHL* 34-35 (2011/2012), 104-138.

Loprieno, A., *Topos und Mimesis: Zum Ausländer in der ägyptischen Literatur*, ÄA 48 (Wiesbaden, 1988).

Loprieno, A., 'Travel and Fiction in Egyptian Literature', in D. O'Connor and S. Quirke (eds), *Mysterious Lands* (London, 2003), 31-51.

Loud, G., *Megiddo*, vol. 2: *Seasons of 1935-1939*, OIP 62 (Chicago, 1948).

Lucas, A. and Harris, J., *Ancient Egyptian Materials and Industries* (London, 1989).

Lucy, S., 'Ethnic and Cultural Identities', in M. Diaz-Andrew et al. (eds), *The Archaeology of Identity. Approaches to Gender, Age, Status, Ethnicity and Religion* (London, 2005), 86-109.

di Ludovico, A. and Ramazzotti, M., 'White, Red and Black. Technical Relationships and Stylistic Perceptions between Colours, Lights and Places', in R. Matthews and J. Curtis (eds), *Proceedings of the 7th International Congress on the Archaeology of the Ancient Near East. 12 April – 16 April 2010, The British Museum and UCL, London*, vol. 2: *Ancient & Modern Issues in Cultural Heritage, Colour & Light in Architecture, Art & Material Culture, Islamic Archaeology* (Wiesbaden, 2010), 287-301.

Luft, U., 'Asiatics in Illahun: A Preliminary Report', in *Sesto Congresso Internazionale di Egittologia Atti*, vol. 2 (Turin, 1993), 291-297.

Luft, U., 'Toponyms at Lahun', in S. Quirke (ed.), *Lahun Studies* (Reigate, 1998), 1-41.

M

Macalister, R. A. S., 'Second Quarterly Report on the Excavation of Gezer', *PEQ* 35 (1903), 7-50.

Macalister, R. A. S., 'Thirteenth Quarterly Report on the Excavation of Gezer', *PEQ* 37 (1905), 309-327.

Macalister, R. A. S., 'Nineteenth Quarterly Report on the Excavation of Gezer', *PEQ* 40 (1908), 272-290.

Macalister, R. A. S., *The Excavation of Gezer, 1902-1905 and 1907-1909*, 3 vols (London, 1912).

MacDonald, J., 'Egyptian Interests in Western Asia to the End of the Middle Kingdom: An Evaluation', *AJBA* 1/5 (1972), 72-98.

MacDonald, B., 'Tell el-Maskhuṭa', *BA* 43/1 (1980), 49-58.

Mace, A. C., 'Excavations at Lisht', *BMMA* 17/12.2 (1922), 4-18.

Mackay, E. J. H. and Murray, M. A., *Ancient Gaza*, vol. 5 (London, 1952).

Maeir, A. M., 'Hyksos Miscellanea', *DE* 14 (1989), 61-68.

Maeir, A. M., 'The Middle Bronze Age II Pottery', in A. Mazar and R. A. Mullins (eds), *Excavations at Tel Beth Shean 1989-1996*, vol. 2: *The Middle and Late Bronze Age Strata in Area R* (Jerusalem, 2007), 242-389.

Maeir, A. M., *'In the Midst of the Jordan'. The Jordan Valley during the Middle Bronze Age (Circa 2000-1500 BCE). Archaeological and Historical Correlates*, ÖAW: Denkschriften der Gesamtakademie 64 (Vienna, 2010).

Maeir, A. M. and Mullins, R. A., 'The Tell el-Yahudiyah Ware from Tel Beth-Shean', in D. A. Aston and M. Bietak, *Tell el Dab'a*, vol. 8: *The Classification and Chronology of Tell el-Yahudiya Ware*, Untersuchungen der Zweigstelle Kairo des Österreichischen Archäologischen Institutes 12 (Vienna, 2012), 577-589.

Maeir, A. and Yellin, J., 'Instrumental Neutron Activation Analysis of Selected Pottery from Tel Beth-Shean and the Central Jordan Valley', in A. Mazar and R. A. Mullins (eds), *Excavations at Tel Beth Shean 1989-1996*, vol. 2: *The Middle and Late Bronze Age Strata in Area R* (Jerusalem, 2007), 554-571.

Maguire, L. C., *Tell el-Dab'a*, vol. 21: *The Cypriot Pottery and its Circulation in the Levant*, Untersuchungen der Zweigstelle Kairo des Österreichischen Archäologischen Instituts 33 (Vienna, 2009).

Manassa, C., 'Defining Historical Fiction in New Kingdom Egypt', in S. C. Melville and A. L. Slotsky (eds), *Opening the Tablet Box. Near Eastern Studies in Honor of Benjamin R. Foster*, Culture and History of the Ancient Near East 42 (Leiden, 2010), 245-269.

Manniche, L., *An Ancient Egyptian Herbal* (London, 1989).

Manniche, L., *Music and Musicians in Ancient Egypt* (London, 1991).

Manzo, A., 'Nubian Pottery and Ceramics from Southern Regions of the Red Sea', in K. A. Bard and R. Fattovich, 'Mersa/Wadi Gawasis 2009-2010', *Newsletter di Archeologia CISA* 1 (2010), 19-21.

Manzo, A., 'From the Sea to the Deserts and Back: New Research in Eastern Sudan', *British Museum Studies in Ancient Egypt and Sudan* 18 (2012), 75-106.

Manzo, A., 'Nubians and the Others on the Red Sea: An Update on the Exotic Ceramic Materials from the Middle Kingdom Harbour of Mersa/Wadi Gawasis, Red Sea, Egypt', in D. A. Agius et al. (eds), *Navigated Spaces, Connected Places. Proceedings of Red Sea Project V Held at the University of Exeter 16-19 September 2010*, BAR International Series 2346 (Oxford, 2013).

al-Maqdissi et al., 'Rapport Préliminaire sur les activités de la mission syro-française de Ras Shamra-Ougarit en 2005 et 2006 (65e et 66e campagnes)', *Syria* 84 (2007), 33-55.

Maragioglio, V. and Rinaldi, C., 'Note pulla piramide di Ameny 'Aamu' ', *Orientalia* 37 (1968), 325-338.

Marchetti, N., 'A Middle Bronze II Alabastron from Tell es-Sultan/Jericho and a Syro-Palestinian Class of Alabaster Vessels', *Isimu* 2 (1999), 305-312.

Marchetti, N., 'A Century of Excavations on the Spring Hill at Tell es-Sultan, Ancient Jericho: A Reconstruction of its Stratigraphy', in M. Bietak (ed.), *The Synchronisation of Civilisations in the Eastern Mediterranean in the Second Millennium B.C.*, vol. 2: *Proceedings of the SCIEM 2000 – EuroConference, Haindorf 2nd of May-7th of May 2001*, CCEM 4 (Vienna, 2003), 295-321.

Marchetti, N. and Nigro, L., 'Cultic Activities in the Sacred Area of Ishtar at Ebla during the Old-Syrian Period: the *Favissae* F.5327 and F.5238', *JCS* 49 (1997), 1-44.

Marchetti, N. and Nigro, L., 'The *Favissa* F.5238 in the Sacred Area of Ishtar and the Transition from the Middle Bronze I to the Middle Bronze II at Ebla', in M. Lebeau, K. Van Lerberghe and G. Voet (eds), *Languages and Cultures in Contact. At the Crossroads of Civilizations in the Syro-Mesopotamian Realm*, OLA 96 (Leuven, 1999), 245-287.

Marchetti, N. and Nigro, L., (eds), *Excavations at Jericho, 1998. Preliminary Report on the Second Season of Excavations and Surveys at Tell es-Sultan, Palestine*, Quaderni di Gerico 2 (Rome, 2000).

Marcus, E. S., 'Venice on the Nile? On the Maritime Character of Tell el-Dab'a/Avaris', in E. Czerny et al. (eds), *Timelines. Studies in Honour of Manfred Bietak*, vol. 2, OLA 149 (Leuven, Paris and Dudley, 2006), 187-190.

Marcus, E. S., 'Amenemhet II and the Sea: Maritime Aspects of the Mit Rahina (Memphis) Inscription', *E&L* 17 (2007), 137-190.

Marcus, E. S., 'Correlating and Combining Egyptian Historical and Southern Levantine Radiocarbon Chronologies at Middle Bronze Age IIa Tel Ifshar, Israel', in A. J. Shortland and C. B. Ramsey (eds), *Radiocarbon and the Chronologies of Ancient Egypt* (Oxford, 2013), 182-208.

Marcus, E. S. and Artzy, M., 'A Loom Weight from Tel Nami with a Scarab Seal Impression', *IEJ* 45/2 (1995), 136-149.

Marcus, E. S., Porath Y. and Paley, S. M., 'The Early Middle Bronze Age IIa Phases at Tel Ifshar and their External Relations', *E&L* 18 (2008), 221-244.

Marcus, E. S. et al., 'The Middle Kingdom Egyptian Pottery from Middle Bronze IIa Tel Ifshar', *E&L* 18 (2008), 203-219.

Marée, M., 'Forepart of a Sphinx holding a Captive (Cat Number 97)', in C. Ziegler (ed.), *The Pharaohs* (London, 2002).

Marée, M., 'Edfu under the Twelfth to Seventeenth Dynasties: The Monuments in the National Museum of Warsaw', *British Museum Studies in Ancient Egypt and Sudan* 12 (2009), 31-92.

Mariette, A., *Les papyrus egyptiens du Musée de Boulaq*, vol. 2 (Paris 1872).

Mariette, A., *Catalogue général des monuments d'Abydos découverts pendant les fouilles de cette ville* (Paris, 1880).

Martin, G., *Egyptian Administrative and Private-Name Seals Principally of the Middle Kingdom and Second Intermediate Period* (Oxford, 1971).

Martin, G., 'The Toponym Retjenu on a Scarab from Tell el-Dab'a', *E&L* 8 (1998), 109-112.

Martin, G., 'Seals and Seal Impressions from the Site of Lisht: The Middle Kingdom and Second Intermediate Period Material', in M. Bietak and E. Czerny (eds), *Scarabs of the Second Millennium BC from Egypt, Nubia, Crete and the Levant: Chronological and Historical Implications. Papers of a Symposium, Vienna, 10th-13th January 2002*, ÖAW: Denkschriften der Gesamtakademie 35 (Vienna, 2004), 103-106.

Martin, K., *Die Altägyptischen Denkmäler*, vol. 1: *Mit einem Beitrag von Eva Martin-Pardey* (Mainz, 1991).

Martinetto, P., et al., 'Synchrotron X-ray Micro-Beam Studies of Ancient Egyptian Make-up', *Nuclear Instruments and Methods in Physics Research B* 181 (2001), 744-748.

Maspero, G., 'Monument égyptiens du Musée de Marseille', *RT* 13 (1890), 113-126.

Maspero, G., *History of Egypt, Chaldea, Syria, Babylonia, and Assyria*, vol. 1 (London, 1901).

Matthiae, P., 'Mission archéologique de l'Université de Rome à Tell Mardikh', *AAS* 17 (1967), 25-43.

Matthiae, P., 'Mission archéologique de l'Université de Rome à Tell Mardikh (1966)', *AAS* 18 (1968), 5-20.

Matthiae, P., 'Empreintes d'un cylinder paléosyrien de Tell Mardikh', *Syria* 46 (1969), 1-43.

Matthiae, P., 'Mission archéologique de l'Université de Rome à Tell Mardikh: Rapport sommaire sur la quatrième et la cinquième campagnes, 1967 et 1968', *AAS* 20 (1970), 55-72.

Matthiae, P., *Ebla in the Period of the Amorite Dynasties and the Dynasty of Akkad: Recent Archaeological Discoveries at Tell Mardikh (1975)* (Malibu, 1979).

Matthiae, P., 'Fouilles à Tell Mardikh-Ebla, 1978: Le Bâtiment Q et la nécropole princière du Bronze Moyen', *Akk* 17 (1980), 1-51.

Matthiae, P., 'Sulle asce fenestrate del "Signore dei capridi" ', *Studi Eblaiti* 3 (1980), 53-62.

Matthiae, P., 'New Discoveries at Ebla: The Excavation of the Western Palace and the Royal Necropolis of the Amorite Period', *BA* 47/1 (1984), 18-32.

Matthiae, P., 'Les dernières découvertes d'Ébla en 1983-1986', *CRAIBL* 131/1 (1987), 135-161.

Matthiae, P., 'High Old Syrian Royal Statuary from Ebla', in B. Hrouda, S. Kroll and P. Z. Spanos (eds), *Von Uruk Nach Tuttul: Eine Festschrift für Eva Strommenger. Studien und Aufsätze von Kollegen und Freuden* (Munich, 1992), 111-128.

Matthiae, P., 'Fouilles à Ébla en 1993-1994: Les palais de la ville basse nord', *CRAIBL* 139/2 (1995), 651-681.

Matthiae, P., 'Ebla and Syria in the Middle Bronze Age', in E. D. Oren (ed.), *The Hyksos: New Historical and Archaeological Perspectives*, University Museum Monograph 96 (Philadelphia, 1997), 379-414.

Matthiae, P., 'The Archaic Palace at Ebla: A Royal Building between Early Bronze Age IVB and Middle Bronze Age I', J. S. Gitin, E. Wright and J. P. Dessel (eds), *Confronting the Past: Archaeological and Historical Essays on Ancient Israel in Honor of William G. Dever* (Winona Lake, 2006), 85-103.

Matthiae, P., 'Furniture Inlay', in J. Aruz, K. Benzel and J. M. Evans (eds), *Beyond Babylon: Art, Trade, and Diplomacy in the Second Millennium B.C.* (New York, 2008), 37.

Matthiae, P., 'Recent Excavations at Ebla, 2006-2007', in P. Matthiae (ed.), *Proceedings of the 6th International Congress of the Archaeology of the Ancient Near East*, vol. 2: *Excavations, Surveys and Restorations: Reports on Recent Field Archaeology in the Near East* (Wiesbaden, 2010), 3-26.

Matthiae, P., 'A Long Journey. Fifty Years of Research on the Bronze Age at Tell Mardikh/Ebla', in P. Matthiae and N. Marchetti (eds), *Ebla and its Landscape. Early State Formation in the Ancient Near East* (Walnut Creek, 2013), 35-48.

Matthiae, P., 'Ebla: Recent Excavation Results and the Continuity of Syrian Art', in J. Aruz, S. B. Graff and Y. Rakic (eds), *Cultures in Contact. From Mesopotamia to the Mediterranean in the Second Millennium B.C.* (New York, 2013), 96-111.

Matthiae, P. et al., *Ebla: alle origini della civilità urbana. Trent'anni di scavi in Siria dell'Università di Roma La Sapienza* (Milan, 1995).

Maxwell-Hyslop, K. R., 'A Note on the Anatolian Connections of the Tôd Treasure', *Anatolian Studies* 45 (1995), 243-250.

Maxwell-Hyslop, R., 'Western Asiatic Shaft-hole Axes', *Iraq* 11 (1949), 90-129.

May, H., 'Moses and the Sinai Inscriptions', *BA* 8/4 (1945), 93-99.

Mays, S., 'Biodistance Studies using Craniometric Variation in British Archaeological Skeletal Material', in M. Cox and S. Mays (eds), *Human Osteology in Archaeology and Forensic Science* (London, 2000), 277-288.

Mazar, A., *The Archaeology of the Land of the Bible: 10,000-586 B.C.E.* (New York, 1992).

Mazar, A., 'Chapter 3 Appendix 1. A Note on the Middle Bronze Age Burials in Area M', in A. Mazar and R. A. Mullins (eds), *Excavations at Tel Beth Shean 1989-1996*, vol. 2: *The Middle and Late Bronze Age Strata in Area R* (Jerusalem, 2007), 199-200.

Mazar, A., 'The Egyptian Garrison Town at Beth-Shean', in S. Bar, D. Kahn and J. J. Shirley (eds), *Egypt, Canaan and Israel: History, Imperialism, Ideology and Literature. Proceedings of a Conference at the University of Haifa, 3-7 May 2009*, Culture and History of the Ancient Near East 52 (Leiden and Boston, 2011), 155-189.

Mazar, A. and Mullins, R. A., 'Introduction and Overview', in A. Mazar and R. A. Mullins (eds), *Excavations at Tel Beth Shean 1989-1996*, vol. 2: *The Middle and Late Bronze Age Strata in Area R* (Jerusalem, 2007), 1-22.

Mazar, B., 'The Middle Bronze Age in Palestine', *IEJ* 18 (1968), 65-97.

McGovern, P. E., *The Foreign Relations of the "Hyksos". A Neutron Activation Study of Middle Bronze Age Pottery from the Eastern Mediterranean*, BAR International Series 888 (Oxford, 2000).

McGovern, P. E. et al., 'The Archaeological Origin and Significance of the Dolphin Vase as determined by Neutron Activation Analysis', *BASOR* 296 (1994), 31-43.

Mendenhall, G. E., *The Syllabic Inscriptions from Byblos* (Beirut, 1985).

Menu, B., 'Le papyrus du Brooklyn Museum n° 35.1446 et l'immigration syro-palestinienne sous le Moyen Empire', *Égypte Nilotique et Méditerranéenne* 5 (2012), 19-30.

Menu, B., 'Onomastique et statut des immigrés syro-palestiniens dans l'Égypte du Moyen Empire', *Droit et Cultures* 64 (2012), 51-68.

Mercer, A. B., *The Pyramid Texts* (New York, London and Toronto, 1952).

Merrillees, R. S., 'Syrian Pottery from Middle Kingdom Egypt', *AJBA* 2 (1973), 51-59.

Merrillees, R. S., *Trade and Transcendence in the Bronze Age Levant*, SMA 39 (Guttenberg, 1974).

Merrillees, R. S., 'El-Lisht and Tell el-Yahudiyah Ware in the Archaeological Museum of the American University in Beirut', *Levant* 10 (1982), 75-98.

Merrillees, R. S., 'The Relative and Absolute Chronology of the Cypriote White Painted Pendent Line Style', *BASOR* 326 (2002), 1-9.

du Mesnil du Buisson, R., 'Compte rendu sommaire d'une mission à Tell el-Yahoudiyé', *BIFAO* 29 (1929), 155-178.

de Meulenaire, H., 'Les monuments d'un haut dignitaire de la 13e dynastie', *CdE* 60 (1985), 75-84.

Mey, P., 'Installations Rupestres du Moyen et du Nouvel Empire au Gebel Zeit (près de Râs Dib) sur la Mer Rouge', *MDAIK* 36 (1980), 299-318.

Michalowski, K. et al., *Tell Edfou 1938, Fouilles Franco-Polonaises*, vols 1-2 (Cairo, 1938-1950).

Midant-Reynes et al., 'Kom el-Khilgan. A New Site of the Predynastic Period in Lower Egypt. The 2002 Campaign', in S. Hendrickx et al. (eds), *Egypt at its Origins. Studies in Memory of Barbara Adams*, OLA 138 (Louvain, 2004), 465-486.

Miniaci, G. and Quirke, S., 'Mariette at Dra Abu el-Naga and the Tomb of Neferhotep: A Mid 13th Dynasty Rishi Coffin (?)', *Egitto e Vicino Oriente* 31 (2008), 1-25.

Miniaci, G. and Quirke, S., 'Reconceiving the Tomb in the Late Middle Kingdom. The Burial of the Accountant of the Main Enclosure Neferhotep at Dra Abu al-Naga', *BIFAO* 209 (2009), 339-383.

de Miroschedji, P., 'Cult and Religion in the Chalcolithic and Early Bronze Age', in A. Biran and J. Aviram (eds), *Biblical Archaeology Today, 1990. Proceedings of the Second International Congress on Biblical Archaeology, Jerusalem, June-July 1990* (Jerusalem, 1993), 208-220.

Mizrachy, Y., 'Glyptic Finds. I. Scarabs and Seals', in A. Kempinski (ed.), *Tel Kabri. The 1986-1993 Excavation Seasons*, Tel Aviv University Institute of Archaeology Monograph Series 20 (Tel Aviv, 2002), 319-339.

Mlinar, C., 'The Scarabs from the Excavations of 1999 and 2000 at Tell el-'Ajjul', in P. M. Fischer and M. Sadeq, 'Tell el-'Ajjul 2000. Second Season Preliminary Report', *E&L* 12 (2002), 143-151.

Mlinar, C., 'The Scarab Workshops of Tell el-Dab'a', in M. Bietak and E. Czerny (eds), *Scarabs of the Second Millennium BC from Egypt, Nubia, Crete and the Levant: Chronological and Historical Implications. Papers of a Symposium, Vienna, 10th-13th January 2002*, ÖAW: Denkschriften der Gesamtakademie 35 (Vienna, 2004), 107-140.

Mlinar, C., 'Sidon. Scarabs from the 2001 Season of Excavation: Additional Notes', *AHL* 20 (2004), 61-64.

Mlinar, C., 'Palästinensische Skarabäen aus einem Grab der frühen Hyksoszeit in Tell el-Dab'a', in E. Czerny et al. (eds), *Timelines. Studies in Honour of Manfred Bietak*, vol. 2, OLA 149 (Leuven, Paris and Dudley, 2006), 213-247.

Mlinar, C., 'Scarabs from Sidon', *AHL* 29 (2009), 24-42.

Moeller, N., 'Tell Edfu – The 2007 Season', http://www.telledfu.org/annual-reports (accessed 14/04/2013).

Moeller, N., 'The 2009 Season at Tell Edfu, Egypt. Latest Discoveries', *The Oriental Institute News and Notes* 206 (2010), 3-8.

Moeller, N., 'Tell Edfu: Preliminary Report on Seasons 2005-2009', *JARCE* 46 (2010), 81-111.

Moeller, N., 'Unsealing Tell Edfu, Egypt: Who was a Local Official and Who Was Not?', *NEA* 75/2 (2012), 116-125.

Moeller, N. and Ayers, N., 'Nubian Pottery Traditions during the 2nd Millennium BC at Tell Edfu', in I. Forstner-Müller and P. Rose (eds), *Nubian Pottery from Egyptian Cultural Contexts of the Middle Kingdom and Early New Kingdom. Proceedings of a Workshop held at the Austrian Archaeological Institute at Cairo, 1-12 December 2010* (Vienna, 2012), 101-114.

Moeller, N. and Farout, D., 'Tell Edfu: Uncovering a Provincial Capital', *EA* 31 (2007), 14-17.

Moeller, N. and Marouard, G., 'Discussion of Late Middle Kingdom and Early Second Intermediate History and Chronology in Relation to the Khayan Sealings from Tell Edfu', *E&L* 11 (2011), 87-121.

Moers, G., 'Travel as Narrative in Egyptian Literature', in G. Moers (ed.), *Definitely: Egyptian Literature. Proceedings of the Symposium 'Ancient Egyptian Literature. History and Forms', Los Angeles, March 24-26, 1995*, Lingua Aegyptia Studia Monographica 2 (Göttingen, 1999), 43-61.

Moers, G., 'Broken Icons: The Emplotting of Master-Narratives in the Ancient Egyptian *Tale of Sinuhe'*, in F. Hagen et al. (eds), *Narratives of Egypt and the Ancient Near East. Literary and Linguistic Approaches*, OLA 189 (Leuven, Paris and Walpole, 2011), 165-176.

Montet, P., 'Un Egyptien, roi de Byblos, sous la XIIe dynastie étude sur deux scarabées de la collection de Clereq', *Syria* 8 (1927), 85-92.

Montet, P., *Byblos et L'Égypte: Quatre campaigne de fouilles a Gebeil 1921-1922-1923-1924* (Paris, 1928).

Montet, P., 'Notes et documents: Pour servir à l'histoire des relations entre l'Égypte et la Syrie II - Nouvelles traces des égyptiens à Byblos', *Kêmi* 1 (1928), 83-93.

Montet, P., 'La stele l'an 400 retrouvè', *Kêmi* 4 (1933), 191-215.

Montet, P., 'Note sur les inscriptions de Sanousrit-ankh', *Syria* 15 (1934), 131-133.

Montet, P., 'Notes et documents: Pour servir à l'histoire des relations entre l'ancienne Égypte et la Syrie', *Kêmi* 13 (1954), 63-76.

Montet, P., 'Notes et documents pour server à l'histoire des relations entré l'Égypte et la Syrie XII, depot d'offrandes à Byblos et à Tod', *Kêmi* 16 (1962), 91-96.

Montet, P., 'Notes et documents pour server à l'histoire des relations entré l'Égypte et la Syrie XIII - Quatre nouvelles inscriptions hiéroglyphiques de Byblos', *Kêmi* 17 (1964), 61-68.

Moorey, P. R. S., 'Where did They Bury the Kings of the IIIrd Dynasty of Ur', *Iraq* 46/1 (1984), 1-18.

Morenz, L. D., 'Die bisher ältesten Belege für den Libanon in zwei frühen ägyptischen Texten', *OLP* 31 (2005), 25-35.

de Morgan, J. et al., *Catalogue des monuments et inscriptions de l'Égypte antique*, vol. 1: *De la frontière de Nubie a Kom Ombo* (Vienna, 1894).

de Morgan, J., *Fouilles à Dahchour*, 2 vols (Vienna, 1895-1903).

el-Morr, Z. and Pernot, M., 'Fabrication Techniques of the Socketed Spearheads from Middle Bronze Age Byblos', *BAAL* 13 (2011), 215-228.

el-Morr, Z. and Pernot, M., 'Middle Bronze Age Metallurgy in the Levant: Evidence from the Weapons of Byblos', *JAS* 38 (2011), 2613-2624.

Morris, E. F., *The Architecture of Imperialism: Military Bases and the Evolution of Foreign Policy in Egypt's New Kingdom*, Problem der Ägyptologie 22 (Leiden and Boston, 2005).

Morschauser, S., 'What Made Sinuhe Run: Sinuhe's Reasoned Flight', *JARCE* 37 (2000), 187-198.

Mourad, A.-L., 'Siege Scenes of the Old Kingdom', *BACE* 22 (2011), 135-158.

Mourad, A.-L., 'Remarks on Sinuhe's Qedem and Yaa', *GM* 238 (2013), 69-84.

Mourad, A.-L., 'Asiatics and Abydos: From the Twelfth Dynasty to the Early Second Intermediate Period', *BACE* 24 (2013), 31-58.

Mourad, A.-L., 'The Procession of Asiatics', in N. Kanawati and L. Evans, *Beni Hassan*, vol. 1: *The Tomb of Khnumhotep II*, ACE: Reports 36 (Oxford, 2014), 72-78.

Muhlestein, K., 'Royal Executions: Evidence bearing on the Subject of Sanctioned Killing in the Middle Kingdom', *JESHO* 51 (2008), 181-208.

Muhlestein, K., 'Levantine Thinking in Egypt', in S. Bar, D. Kahn and J. J. Shirley (eds), *Egypt, Canaan and Israel: History, Imperialism, Ideology and Literature. Proceedings of a Conference at the University of Haifa, 3-7 May 2009*, Culture and History of the Ancient Near East 52 (Leiden and Boston, 2011), 190-233.

Müller, U., 'Kritische Bemerkungen zu den Straten XIII bis IX in Megiddo', *ZDPV* 86 (1970), 50-86.

Müller, V., 'Offering Practices in the Temple Courts of Tell el-Dab'a and the Levant', in M. Bietak (ed.), *The Middle Bronze Age in the Levant. Proceedings of an International Conference on MBIIA Ceramic Material in Vienna, 24th-26th of January 2001*, ÖAW: Denkschriften der Gesamtakademie 26 (Vienna, 2002), 269-295.

Müller, V., *Tell el Dab'a*, vol. 17: *Opferdeponierungen in der Hyksoshauptstadt Auaris (Tell el-Dab'a) vom späten mittleren Reich bis zum frühen neuen Reich*, 2 parts, Untersuchungen der Zweigstelle Kairo des Österreichischen Archäologischen Instituts 29 (Vienna, 2008).

Mullins, R. A., 'Reflections on Levels XI-IX of the University Museum Excavations', in A. Mazar and R. A. Mullins (eds), *Excavations at Tel Beth Shean 1989-1996*, vol. 2: *The Middle and Late Bronze Age Strata in Area R* (Jerusalem, 2007), 23-38.

Mullins, R. A. and Mazar, A., 'The Stratigraphy and Architecture of the Middle and Late Bronze Ages: Strata R-5-R-1a', in A. Mazar and R. A. Mullins (eds), *Excavations at Tel Beth Shean 1989-1996*, vol. 2: *The Middle and Late Bronze Age Strata in Area R* (Jerusalem, 2007), 39-239.

Mumford, G., 'Wadi Maghara', in K. A. Bard (ed.), *Encyclopedia of the Archaeology of Ancient Egypt* (London, 1999), 1071-1076.

Myres, J. L., 'Excavations in Cyprus in 1894', *Journal of Hellenic Studies* 17 (1897), 134-173.

N

Naville, E., *The Store-City of Pithom and the Route of the Exodus* (London, 1888).

Naville, E., *The Shrine of Saft el-Henneh and the Land of Goshen* (London, 1889).

Naville, E., *Bubastis (1887-1889)* (London, 1891).

Naville, E., *Ahnas el Medineh (Heracleopolis Magna)* (London, 1894).

Naville, E., *The XIth Dynasty Temple at Deir el-Bahari*, vol. 1 (London, 1907).

Naville, E. and Griffith, F. L., *The Mound of the Jew and the City of Onias. The Antiquities of Tell el-Yahudiyeh* (London, 1890).

Negbi, O. and Moskowitz, S., 'The "Foundation Deposits" or "Offering Deposits" of Byblos', *BASOR* 184 (1966), 21-26.

Newberry, P. E., *El-Bersheh*, vol. 1: *The Tomb of Tehuti-hetep* (London, 1895).

Newberry, P. E., *Beni Hasan*, 4 vols (London, 1893-1900).

Newberry, P. E., *Catalogue général des antiquités Égyptienne du Musée du Caire N° 36001-37521* (London, 1907).

Newberry, P. E., *Scarabs. An Introduction to the Study of Egyptian Seals and Signet Rings* (London, 1908).

Newberry, P. E., 'Miscellanea', *JEA* 14/1 (1928), 109-111.

Nibbi, A., *Ancient Egyptian Pot Bellows and Oxhide Ingot Shape* (Oxford, 1987).

Nigro, L., 'A Human Sacrifice Associated with a Sheep Slaughter in the Sacred Area of Ishtar at MBI Ebla?', *JPR* 11-12 (1998), 22-36.

Nigro, L., 'Results of the Italian-Palestinian Expedition to Tell es-Sultan: At the Dawn of Urbanization in Palestine', in L. Nigro and H. Taha (eds), *Tell es-Sultan/Jericho in the Context of the Jordan Valley. Site Management, Conservation and Sustainable Development* (Rome, 2006), 1-40.

Nigro, L., 'Towards a Unified Chronology of Syria and Palestine. The Beginning of the Middle Bronze Age', in P. Matthiae et al. (eds), *From Relative Chronology to Absolute Chronology: the Second Millennium B.C. in Syria-Palestine* (Rome, 2007), 365-389.

Nigro, L., 'The Built Tombs on the Spring Hill and the Palace of the Lords of Jericho (*ʿḏmr Rḫʿ*) in the Middle Bronze Age', in J. D. Schloen (ed.), *Exploring the Longue Durée in Honor of Lawrence E. Stager* (Winona Lake, 2009), 361-376.

Nigro, L., 'The Eighteenth Century BC Princes of Byblos and Ebla and the Chronology of the Middle Bronze Age', in *Interconnections in the Eastern Mediterranean. Lebanon in the Bronze and Iron Ages. Proceedings of the International Symposium Beirut 2008*, BAAL Hors-Série 6 (Beirut, 2009), 159-175.

Nordström, H. and Bourriau, J., 'Ceramic Technology: Clays and Fabrics', in Do. Arnold and J. Bourriau (eds), *An Introduction to Ancient Egyptian Pottery* (Mainz am Rhein, 1993), 147-19.

Nougayrol, J., et al., *Ugaritica* 5 (Paris, 1962).

O

O'Connor, D., 'A Regional Population in Egypt to circa 600 BC', in B. Spooner (ed.), *Population Growth: Anthropological Implications* (Cambridge, 1972), 78-100.

O'Connor, D., 'Political Systems and Archaeological Data in Egypt', *World Archaeology* 6/1 (1974), 15-38.

O'Connor, D., 'The Chronology of Scarabs of the Middle Kingdom and the Second Intermediate Period', *JSSEA* 15 (1987), 1-41.

O'Connor, D., 'The Hyksos Period in Egypt', in E. D. Oren (ed.), *The Hyksos: New Historical and Archaeological Perspectives* (Philadelphia, 1997), 45-67.

O'Connor, D., 'Egypt's Views of "Others" ', in J. Tait (ed.), *'Never had the Like Occurred': Egypt's View of its Past* (London, 2003), 155-185.

Obsomer, C., 'La Date de Nésou-Montou (Louvre C1)', *RdE* 44 (1993), 103-140.

Obsomer, C., *Sésostris Ier. Étude chronologique et historique du Règne*, Connaissance de l'Egypte Ancienne 5 (Brussels, 1995).

Obsomer, C., 'Sinouhé l'Égyptien et les Raisons de son Exil', *Le Muséon* 122 (1999), 207-271.

Ogden, J., 'Metals', in P. T. Nicholson and I. Shaw (eds), *Ancient Egyptian Materials and Technology* (Cambridge, 2006), 148-176.

Orel, S. E., 'A Reexamination of the 1943-1952 Excavations at Kom el-Ḥisn, Egypt', *GM* 179 (2000), 39-49.

Oren, E. D., *The Northern Cemetery at Beth Shan* (Philadelphia and Leiden, 1973).

Oren, E. D., 'The Hyksos Enigma – Introductory Overview', in E. D. Oren (ed.), *The Hyksos: New Historical and Archaeological Perspectives* (Philadelphia, 1997), xix-xxvi.

Oren, E. D., 'The "Kingdom of Sharuhen" and the Hyksos Kingdom', in E. D. Oren (ed.), *The Hyksos: New Historical and Archaeological Perspectives* (Philadelphia, 1997), 253-283.

Ortiz, S. M., 'Gezer', in D. Master (ed.), *The Oxford Encyclopedia of the Bible and Archaeology* (Oxford, 2013), 468-474.

Otto, A., *Entstehung und Entwicklung der Klassisch-Syrischen Glyptik* (Berlin, 1999).

Ownby, M. F., *Canaanite Jars from Memphis as Evidence for Trade and Political Relationships in the Middle Bronze Age* (PhD Dissertation, University of Cambridge, 2010).

Ownby, M. F., 'The Importance of Imports: Petrographic Analysis of Levantine Pottery Jars in Egypt', *JAEI* 4/3 (2012), 23-29.

Ownby, M. F., 'Les relations économiques entre l'Égypte et le Levant durant l'age du Bronze Moyen', *Égypte, Afrique et Orient* 65 (2012), 33-38.

Ownby, M. F. and Bourriau, J., 'The Movement of Middle Bronze Age Transport Jars. A Provenance Study Based on Petrographic and Chemical Analysis of Canaanite Jars from Memphis, Egypt', in P. S. Quinn (ed.), *Interpreting Silent Artefacts. Petrographic Approaches to Archaeological Ceramics* (Oxford, 2009), 173-189.

Ownby, M. F. and Smith, L. M. V., 'The Impact of Changing Political Situations on Trade between Egypt and the Near East: A Provenance Study of Canaanite Jars from Memphis, Egypt', in K. Duistermaat and I. Regulski (eds), *Intercultural Contacts in the Ancient Mediterranean. Proceedings of the International Conference at the Netherlands-Flemish Institute in Cairo, 25th to 29th October 2008*, OLA 202 (Leuven, Paris and Walpole, 2011), 267-284.

P

Paice, P., Holladay, J. S. Jr. and Brock, E. C., 'The Middle Bronze Age/Second Intermediate Period Houses at Tell El-Maskhuta', in M. Bietak (ed.), *Haus und Palast im Alten Ägypten*, Denkschriften der Gesamtakademie 14 (Vienna, 1996), 159-173.

Paley, S. M. and Porath, Y., 'Notes and News: The Regional Project in 'Emeq Hefer', *IEJ* 29/3-4 (1979), 236-239.

Paley, S. M. and Porath, Y., 'Notes and News: The Regional Project in 'Emeq Hefer', *IEJ* 30/3-4 (1980), 217-219.

Paley, S. M. and Porath, Y., 'Notes and News: The 'Emeq Hefer Archaeological Research Project', *IEJ* 32/1 (1982), 66-67.

Paley, S. M. and Porath, Y., 'Notes and News: The 'Emeq Hefer Archaeological Research Project', *IEJ* 35/4 (1985), 299-301.

Paley, S. M. and Porath, Y., 'Early Middle Bronze Age IIa Remains at Tel el-Ifshar, Israel: A Preliminary Report', in E. D. Oren (ed.), *The Hyksos: New Historical and Archaeological Perspectives*, University Museum Monograph 96 (Philadelphia, 1997), 369-378.

Paley, S. M., Porath, Y. and Stieglitz, R. R., 'Notes and News: The 'Emeq Hefer Archaeological Research Project', *IEJ* 32/4 (1982), 259-261.

Paley, S. M., Porath, Y. and Stieglitz, R. R., 'Notes and News: The 'Emeq Hefer Archaeological Research Project', *IEJ* 33/3-4 (1983), 264-266.

Paley, S. M., Porath, Y. and Stieglitz, R. R., 'Notes and News: The 'Emeq Hefer Archaeological Research Project', *IEJ* 34/4 (1984), 276-278.

Palumbo, G., ' 'Egalitarian' or 'Stratified' Society? Some Notes on Mortuary Practices and Social Structure at Jericho in EB IV', *BASOR* 267 (1987), 43-59.

Parker, S. B. (ed.), *Ugaritic Narrative Poetry* (Atlanta, 1997).

Parkinson, R. B., 'Individual and Society in Middle Kingdom Literature', in A. Loprieno (ed.), *Ancient Egyptian Literature. History & Forms* (Leiden, 1996), 137-155.

Parkinson, R. B., *The Tale of Sinuhe and Other Ancient Egyptian Poems 1940-1640 B.C.* (Oxford, 1997).

Parkinson, R. B., *Poetry and Culture in Middle Kingdom Egypt: A Dark Side to Perfection* (London and New York, 2002).

Parr, P. E. (ed.), *The Levant in Transition. Proceedings of a Conference held at the British Museum on 20-21 April 2004*, PEFA 9 (London, 2009).

Peden, A. J., *The Graffiti of Pharaonic Egypt: Scope and Roles of Informal Writings (c. 3100-332 BC)* (Leiden, 2001).

Pederson, R. K., 'The Underwater Survey at Tell Fadous – Kfarabida', *BAAL* 11 (2007), 17-23.

Pederson, R. K., 'Emerging Maritime Paradigms for Bronze Age in Lebanon', *Skyllis* 12/1 (2012), 5-10.

Peet, T. E., *The Cemeteries of Abydos*, vol. 2: *1911-1912* (London, 1914).

Peet, T. E., *The Stela of Sebek-Khu. The Earliest Record of an Egyptian Campaign in Asia* (Manchester, 1914).

Peet, T. E. and Loat, W. L. S., *The Cemeteries of Abydos*, vol. 3: *1912-1913* (London, 1913).

Perdu, O., 'Khnemet Nefer Hedjet: Une Princesse et deux Reines du Moyen Empire', *RdE* 29 (1977), 68-85.

Pérez-Accino, J.-R., 'Text as Territory: Mapping Sinuhe's Shifting Loyalties', in F. Hagen et al. (eds), *Narratives of Egypt and the Ancient Near East. Literary and Linguistic Approaches*, OLA 189 (Leuven, Paris and Walpole, 2011), 177-194.

Petrie, W. M. F., *Tanis*, vol. 1: *1883-4* (2nd edition, London, 1889).

Petrie, W. M. F., *Kahun, Gurob and Hawara* (London, 1890).

Petrie, W. M. F., *Illahun, Kahun and Gurob 1889-90* (London, 1891).

Petrie, W. M. F., *The Royal Tombs of the First Dynasty 1900*, vol. 1 (London, 1900).

Petrie, W. M. F., 'The Hyksos', *Man* 6 (1906), 113-114.

Petrie, W. M. F., *Hyksos and Israelite Cities* (London, 1906).

Petrie, W. M. F., *Memphis*, vol. 1 (London, 1906).

Petrie, W. M. F., *Researches in Sinai* (London, 1906).

Petrie, W. M. F., *Gizeh and Rifeh* (London, 1907).

Petrie, W. M. F., *Heliopolis, Kafr Ammar, and Shurafa* (London, 1915).

Petrie, W. M. F., *Prehistoric Egypt* (London, 1920).

Petrie, W. M. F., *Tombs of the Courtiers and Oxyrhynkhos* (London, 1925).

Petrie, W. M. F., *Beth Pelet*, vol. 1 (London, 1930).

Petrie, W. M. F., *Ancient Gaza*, vols 1-4 (London, 1931-1934).

Petrie, W. M. F., *City of Shepherd Kings* (London, 1952).

Petrie, W. M. F. and Quibell, J. E., *Naqada and Ballas* (London, 1896).

Petrie, W. M. F., Brunton, G. And Murray, M. A., *Lahun*, vol. 2 (London, 1923).

Petrie, W. M. F., Mackay, E. and Murray, M. A., *City of the Shepherd Kings and Ancient Gaza*, vol. 5 (London, 1951).

Petrik, M., 'Foreign Groups at Lahun during the Late Middle Kingdom', in E. Bechtold, A. Gulyàs and A. Hasznos (eds), *From Illahun to Djeme: Papers*

Presented in Honour of Ulrich Luft, BAR International Series 2311 (2011), 211-226.

Peyronel, L., 'Late Old Syrian Fortifications and Middle Syrian Re-Occupation on the Western Rampart at Tell Mardikh-Ebla', in M. Bietak and E. Czerny (eds), *The Synchronisation of Civilisations in the Eastern Mediterranean in the Second Millennium B.C.*, vol. 3: *Proceedings of the SCIEM 2000-2nd EuroConference Vienna, 28th of May-1st of June 2003*, CCEM 9 (Vienna, 2007), 403-422.

Pfälzner, P., 'Cylinder Seal and Modern Impression: Columns of Animals and Symbols', in J. Aruz, K. Benzel and J. M. Evans (eds), *Beyond Babylon: Art, Trade, and Diplomacy in the Second Millennium B.C.* (New York, 2008), 228.

Pfälzner, P., 'Between the Aegean and Syria: The Wall Paintings from the Royal Palace of Qatna', in D. Bonatz et al. (eds), *Fundstellen. Gesammelte zur Archäologie und Geschichte Altvorderasiens ad Honorem Hartmut Kühne* (Wiesbaden, 2008), 95-118.

Philip, G., *Tell el-Dab'a*, vol. 15: *Metalwork and Metalworking Evidence. The Late Middle Kingdom and the Second Intermediate Period*, Untersuchungen der Zweigstelle Kairo des Österreichischen Archäologischen Instituts 26 (Vienna, 2006).

Phinney, J. S., 'Ethnic Identity and Acculturation', in K. M. Chun, P. B. Organista and G. Marin (eds), *Acculturation: Advances in Theory, Measurement, and Applied Research* (Washington, 2003), 63-81.

Pierrat, G., 'Á propos de la date et de l'origine du trésor de Tôd', *BSFE* 130 (1994), 18-28.

von Pilgrim, C., *Elephantine*, vol. 18: *Untersuchungen in der Stadt das Mittleren Reiches und der Zweiten Zwischenzeit* (Mainz, 1996).

Pittmann, H., *Ancient Art in Miniature: Near Eastern Seals from the Collection of Martin and Sarah Cherkasky* (New York, 1987).

Polz, D., *Der Beginn des Neuen Reiches zur Vorgeschichte einer Zeitenwende*, Sonderschriften DAIAK 31 (Berlin, 2007).

Pomey, P., 'Ship Remains at Ayn Soukhna', in P. Tallet and S. Mahfouz (eds), *The Red Sea in Pharaonic Times. Recent Discoveries along the Red Sea Coast. Proceedings of the Colloquium held in Cairo/Ayn Soukhna 11th-12th January 2009* (Cairo, 2012), 35-52.

Porada, E., 'Remarks on the Tôd Treasure in Egypt', in M. A. Dandamayev et al. (eds), *Societies and Languages of the Ancient Near East: Studies in Honor of I. M. Diakonoff* (Warminster, 1982), 285-303.

Porada, E., 'The Cylinder Seal from Tell el-Dab'a', *AJA* 88 (1984), 485-488.

Porter, B. and Moss, R., *Topographical Bibliography of Ancient Egyptian Hieroglyphic Texts, Reliefs and Paintings* (Oxford, 1927-52; 2nd edition J. Málek, 1960-).

Porter, R. M., 'The Second Intermediate Period according to Edfu', *GM* 239 (2013), 75-80.

Posener, G., *Princes et Pays d'Asie et de Nubie. Textes Hiératiques sur des figurines d'envoûtement du Moyen Empire* (Brussels, 1940).

Posener, G., 'Les Asiatiques en Égypte sous les XIIe et XIIIe dynasties (À propos d'un livre recent)', *Syria* 34/1 (1957), 145-163.

Posener, G., *Littérature et politique dans l'Égypte de la XII' dynastie* (Paris, 1969).

Posener, G., 'A New Royal Inscription of the XIIth Dynasty', *JSSEA* 12/1 (1982), 7-8.

Posener, G., *Cinq figurines d'envoûtement* (Cairo, 1987).

Priese, K. H., *Ägyptische Museum / [herausgegeben von] Staatliche Museen zu Berlin* (Mainz, 1991).

Purdy, S., 'Sinuhe and the Question of Literary Types', *ZÄS* 104 (1977), 112-127.

Q

Quack, J. F., '*kftȝw* and *iȝśy*', *E&L* 6 (1996), 75-81.

Quirke, S., 'A Reconsideration of the Term *ḫnrt*', *RdE* 39 (1988), 83-106.

Quirke, S., *The Administration of Egypt in the Late Middle Kingdom: The Hieratic Documents* (New Malden, 1990).

Quirke, S., 'Review of Loprieno, Antonio, Topos und Mimesis. Zum Ausländer in der ägyptischen Literatur', *DE* 16 (1990), 89-95.

Quirke, S., 'Royal Power in the 13th Dynasty', in S. Quirke (ed.), *Middle Kingdom Studies* (New Malden, 1991), 123-139.

Quirke, S., 'Six Hieroglyphic Inscriptions in University College Dublin', *RdE* 51 (2000), 223-251.

Quirke, S., *Egyptian Literature 1800 BC: Questions and Readings* (London, 2004).

Quirke, S., *Title and Bureaux of Egypt 1850-1700 BC* (London, 2004).

Quirke, S., *Lahun. A Town in Egypt 1800 BC, and the History of its Landscape* (London, 2005).

R

Rabehl, S. M., *Das Grab des Amenemhet (Jmnjj) in Beni Hassan oder Der Versuch einer Symbiose* (PhD Dissertation, Ludwig-Maximilians-Universität München, 2006).

Rainey, A. F., 'The World of Sinuhe', *IOS* 2 (1972), 369-408.

Rainey, A. F., 'Review: Remarks on Donald Redford's "Egypt, Canaan, and Israel in Ancient Times" ', *BASOR* 295 (1994), 81-85.

Rainey, A. F., 'Sinuhe's World', in A. M. Maeir and P. D. Miroschedji (eds), *"I Will Speak the Riddles of Ancient Times". Archaeological and Historical Studies in Honour of Amihai Mazar on the Occasion of his Sixtieth Birthday*, vol. 1 (Winona Lake, 2006), 277-299.

Randall-MacIver, D. and Mace, A. C., *El Amrah and Abydos 1899-1901* (London, 1902).

Ranke, H., *Die Ägyptischen Personennamen*, 3 vols (Glückstadt, 1935-1977).

Reali, Ch., 'The Seal Impressions from 'Ezbet Rushdi, Area R/III of Tell el-Dab'a: Preliminary Report', *E&L* 22-23 (2012/2013), 67-74.

Redford, D. B., 'The Hyksos in History and Tradition', *Orientalia* 39 (1970), 1-52.

Redford, D. B., 'A Gate Inscription from Karnak and Egyptian Involvement in Western Asia during the Early 18th Dynasty', *JAOS* 99/2 (1979), 270-287.

Redford, D. B., 'Interim Report on the Excavations at East Karnak (1979 and 1980 Seasons)', *JSSEA* 11/4 (1981), 244-262.

Redford, D. B., 'Egypt and Western Asia in the Old Kingdom', *JARCE* 23 (1986), 125-143.

Redford, D. B., *Pharaonic King-Lists, Annals and Day-Books: A Contribution to the Study of the Egyptian Sense of History*, SSEA Publication 4 (Mississauga, 1986).

Redford, D. B., 'The Tod Inscription of Senwosret I and Early 12th Dynasty Involvement in Nubia and the South', *JSSEA* 17/1 (1987), 35-57.

Redford, D. B., *Egypt, Canaan, and Israel in Ancient Times* (Princeton, 1992).

Redford, D. B., 'A Response to Anson Rainey's "Remarks on Donald Redford's *Egypt, Canaan, and Israel in Ancient Times"* ', *BASOR* 301 (1996), 77-81.

Redford, D. B., *The Wars in Syria and Palestine of Thutmose III* (Leiden, 2003).

Redmount, C. A., *On an Egyptian/Asiatic Frontier: An Archaeological History of the Wadi Tumilat* (PhD Dissertation, University of Chicago, 1989).

Redmount, C. A., 'Ethnicity, Pottery, and the Hyksos at Tell El-Maskhuta in the Egyptian Delta', *BA* 58/4 (1995), 182-190.

Redmount, C. A., 'Pots and Peoples in the Egyptian Delta: Tell El-Maskhuta and the Hyksos', *JMA* 8/2 (1995), 61-89.

Régen, I. and Soukiassian, G., *Gebel el Zeit*, vol. 2: *Le matériel inscrit. Moyen Empire – Nouvel Empire* (Cairo, 2008).

Reisner, G. A., *The Development of the Egyptian Tomb Down to the Accession of Cheops* (Cambridge, 1936).

Reisner, G. A., 'Clay Sealings of Dynasty XIII from Uronarti Fort', *Kush* 3 (1955), 26-69.

Renfrew, C. and Bahn, P., *Archaeology: Theories, Methods and Practices* (London, 2008).

Richards, F. V., *Scarab Seals from a Middle to Late Bronze Age Tomb at Pella in Jordan*, OBO 117 (Göttingen, 1992).

Richards, F. V., *The Anra Scarabs. An Archaeological and Historical Approach*, BAR International Series 919 (Oxford, 2001).

Richards, J., *Society and Death in Ancient Egypt: Mortuary Landscapes of the Middle Kingdom* (Cambridge, 2005).

Richardson, N. and Dorr, M. S., *The Craft Heritage of Oman*, vol. 2 (Dubai, 2003).

Ricke, H., 'Der 'Hohe Sand' in Heliopolis', *ZÄS* 71 (1935), 107-111.

Ritner, R. K., 'So-called 'Pre-dynastic Hamster-headed' Figurines in London and Hanover', *GM* 111 (1989), 85-95.

Ritner, R. K., *The Mechanics of Ancient Egyptian Magical Practice*, SAOC 54 (Chicago, 1993).

Ritner, R. K, 'Egypt and the Vanishing Libyan: Institutional Responses to a Nomadic People', in J. Szuchman (ed.), *Nomads, Tribes, and the State in the Ancient Near East.*

Cross-Disciplinary Perspectives, OIS 5 (Chicago, 2009), 43-56.

Ritner, R. K. and Moeller, N., 'The Ahmose 'Tempest Stela', Thera and Comparative Chronology', *JNES* 73/1 (2014), 1-19.

Robertson, B. M., *The Chronology of the Middle Bronze Age Tombs at Tell el Ajjul* (PhD Dissertation, University of Utah, 1999).

Robins, G., *The Art of Ancient Egypt* (Cairo, 2008).

Rollston, C., 'The Probable Inventors of the First Alphabet: Semites functioning as rather High Status Personnel in a Component of the Egyptian Apparatus', *ASOR Blog* (2010), http://asorblog.org/?p=427 (accessed 13/03/2013).

Roux, G., *Ancient Iraq* (3rd edition, London, 1992).

Rowe, A., *The Topography and History of Beth-Shan* (Philadelphia, 1930).

Rowe, A., *A Catalogue of Egyptian Scarabs, Scaraboids, Seals and Amulets in the Palestine Archaeological Museum*, Imprimerie de l'Institut français d'archéologie orientale (Cairo, 1936).

Rowe, A., 'Three New Stelae from the South-Eastern Desert', *ASAE* 39 (1939), 187-194.

Rowe, A., *The Four Canaanite Temples of Beth-Shan*, vol. 1: *The Temple and Cult Objects* (Philadelphia, 1940).

Rowlands, M., Larsen, M. and Kristiansen, K. (eds), *Centre and Periphery in the Ancient World* (Cambridge, 1987).

Royce, A. P., *Ethnic Identity: Strategies of Diversity* (Bloomington, 1982).

Ryholt, K. S. B., *The Political Situation in Egypt during the Second Intermediate Period c. 1800-1550 BC*, Carsten Niebuhr Institute Publications 20 (Copenhagen, 1997).

Ryholt, K. S. B., 'Some Notes on an Inscription Dated to the Reign of Sobkemsaf Sekhemrewadjkhaw', *GM* 157 (1997), 75-76.

Ryholt, K. S. B., 'Hotepibre, a Supposed Asiatic King in Egypt with Relations to Ebla', *BASOR* 311 (1998), 1-6.

Rzepka, S. et al., 'Tell el-Retaba. Season 2007', *PAM* 19 (2007), 143-151.

Rzepka, S. et al., 'Tell el-Retaba 2007-2008', *E&L* 19 (2009), 241-280.

Rzepka, S. et al., 'Tell el-Retaba, Season 2011', *PAM* 23/1 (2011), 87-108.

Rzepka, S. el al., 'Tell el-Retaba from the Second Intermediate Period to the Late Period. Results of the Polish-Slovak Archaeological Mission, Seasons 2011-2012', *E&L* 24 (2014), 39-120.

S

Saad, Z., *Royal Excavations at Sakkara and Helwan*, Supplément aux ASAE 3 (Cairo, 1947).

Sabbahy, L. K., 'Comments on the Title ḫnmt-nfr-ḥḏt', *SAK* 23 (1996), 349-352.

Sadek, A. I., *The Amethyst Mining Inscriptions of Wadi el-Hudi*, 2 vols (Warminster, 1980-1985).

Sader, H., 'Palace Architecture in Tell el-Burak – Lebanon: Some Evidence for Egyptian Mesopotamian Levantine Interconnections', in *Interconnections in the Eastern Mediterranean. Lebanon in the Bronze and Iron Ages. Proceedings of the International Symposium Beirut 2008*, BAAL Hors-Série 6 (Beirut, 2009), 177-185.

Sader, H., 'Tell Hizzin: Location, Identification and History', in P. Matthiae et al. (eds), *Proceedings of the 6th International Congress on the Archaeology of the Ancient Near East (2-11 May 2008) in Rome*, vol. 2: *Excavations, Surveys and Restorations: Reports on Recent Field Archaeology in the Near East* (Wiesbaden, 2010), 636-650.

Sader, H. and Kamlah, J., 'Tell el-Burak: A Middle Bronze Age Site from Lebanon', *NEA* 73/2-3 (2010), 130-141.

Saghieh, M., *Byblos is the Third Millennium B.C.: A Reconstruction of the Stratigraphy and a Study of the Cultural Connections* (Warminster, 1983).

Sagona, C., 'Middle Bronze Faience Vessels from Palestine', *ZDPV* 96/2 (1980), 101-120.

Saidah, R., 'Beirut in the Bronze Age: The Kharji Tombs', *Berytus* 41 (1993/1994), 137-210.

Salles, J.-F., 'La mort à Byblos: Les nécropoles', in E. Acquaro et al. (eds), *Biblo. Una città e la sua cultura* (Rome, 1994), 49-71.

Santley, R., Yarborough, C. and Hall, B., 'Enclaves, Ethnicity, and the Archaeological Record at Matacapan', in R. Auger et al. (eds), *Ethnicity and Culture. Proceedings of the Eighteenth Annual Chacmioul Conference of the Archaeological Association of the University of Calgary* (Canada, 1987), 85-100.

le Saout, F., 'Un magasin à onguents de Karnak et le problème du nom de Tyr: Mise au point', *Karnak* 8 (1987), 325-338.

Saretta, P., *Egyptian Perceptions of West Semites in Art and Literature during the Middle Kingdom* (PhD Dissertation, University of New York, 1997).

Sartori, N., 'Die Siegel aus Areal F/II in Tell el-Dab'a erster Vorbericht', *E&L* 19 (2009), 281-292.

Sass, B., *The Genesis of the Alphabet and its Development in the Second Millennium B.C.*, ÄAT 13 (Wiesbaden, 1988).

Sass, B., 'The Genesis of the Alphabet and its Development in the Second Millennium B.C.: Twenty Years Later', *De Kêmi à Birīt Nāri: Revue Internationale de l'Orient Ancien* 2 (2004/2005), 147-166.

Sass, B., 'Wadi el-Hol and the Alphabet', in C. Roche (ed.), *D'Ougarit à Jérusalem: Recueil d'études épigraphiques et archéologiques offerts à Pierre Bordreuil* (Paris, 2008), 193-203.

Satzinger, H. and Stefanović, D., 'The Domestic Servant of the Palace *rn-snb*', in E. Bechtold, A. Gulyàs, A. Hasznos (eds), *From Illahun to Djeme: Papers Presented in Honour of Ulrich Luft*, BAR International Series 2311 (Oxford, 2011), 241-245.

Säve-Söderbergh, T., 'The Hyksos Rule in Egypt', *JEA* 37 (1951), 53-71.

el-Sawi, A., *Excavations at Tell Basta. Report of Seasons 1967-1971 and Catalogue of Finds* (Prague, 1979).

Sayed, A. M., 'Discovery of the Site of the 12th Dynasty Port at Wadi Gawasis on the Red Sea Shore', *RdE* 29 (1977), 140-178.

Sayed, A. M., 'Wadi Gasus', in K. A. Bard (ed.), *Encyclopedia of the Archaeology of Ancient Egypt* (London, 1999), 1060-1062.

Sayed, A. M., 'The Land of Punt: Problems of the Archaeology of the Red Sea and the Southeastern Delta', in Z. A. Hawass (ed.), *Egyptology at the Dawn of the Twenty-First Century. Proceedings of the Eighth International Congress of Egyptologists Cairo, 2000*, vol. 1 (Cairo, 2003), 432-439.

Scandone-Matthiae, G., 'Les relations entre Ébla et l'Égypte au IIIème et au IIème millénaire avant J.-C', in H. Waetzoldt and H. Hauptmann (eds), *Wirtschaft und Gesellschaft von Ebla* (Heidelberg, 1988), 67-73.

Scandone-Matthiae, G., 'Un Sphinx d'Amenemhat III au Musée d'Alep', *RdE* 40 (1989), 125-129.

Scandone-Matthiae, G., 'The Relations between Ebla and Egypt', in E. D. Oren (ed.), *The Hyksos: New Historical and Archaeological Perspectives*, University Museum Monograph 96 (Philadelphia, 1997), 415-427.

Scandone-Matthiae, G., 'Les rapports entre Ebla et l'Égypte à l'Ancien et au Moyen Empire', in Z. A. Hawass (ed.), *Egyptology at the Dawn of the Twenty-First Century. Proceedings of the Eighth International Congress of Egyptologists Cairo, 2000*, vol. 2 (Cairo, 2003), 487-493.

Scandone-Matthiae, G., 'Les scarabées d'Ebla', in M. Bietak and E. Czerny (eds), *Scarabs of the Second Millennium BC from Egypt, Nubia, Crete and the Levant: Chronological and Historical Implications. Papers of a Symposium, Vienna, 10th-13th January 2002*, ÖAW: Denkschriften der Gesamtakademie 35 (Vienna, 2004), 195-201.

Schaeffer, C., 'Les fouilles Minet el-Beida et de Ras Shamra (campagne du printemps 1929). Rapport sommaire', *Syria* 10 (1929), 285-297.

Schaeffer, C., 'Les fouilles de Minet-el-Beida et de Ras-Shamra. Troisième campagne (printemps 1931): Rapport sommaire', *Syria* 13 (1932), 1-27.

Schaeffer, C., 'Les fouilles de Minet-el-Beida et de Ras-Shamra. Quatrième campagne (printemps 1932): Rapport sommaire', *Syria* 14 (1933), 93-127.

Schaeffer, C., 'Les fouilles de Ras-Shamra. Cinquième campagne (printemps 1933): Rapport sommaire', *Syria* 15 (1934), 105-136.

Schaeffer, C., 'Les fouilles de Ras Shamra-Ugarit. Sixième campagne (printemps 1934): Rapport sommaire', *Syria* 16 (1935), 141-176.

Schaeffer, C., 'Les fouilles de Ras Shamra-Ugarit. Septième campagne (printemps 1935)', *Syria* 17 (1936), 105-148.

Schaeffer, C., 'Les fouilles de Ras Shamra-Ugarit. 8e campagne (printemps 1936)', *Syria* 18 (1937), 125-154.

Schaeffer, C., 'Les fouilles de Ras Shamra-Ugarit. Neuvième campagne (printemps 1937)', *Syria* 19 (1938), 193-255, 314-334.

Schaeffer, C., *The Cuneiform Texts of Ras Shamra-Ugarit* (London, 1939).

Schaeffer, C., *Ugaritica*, vols 1-4, 6-7 (Paris, 1939-1978).

Schaeffer, C., *Stratigraphie compare et chronologie de l'Asie occidentale (IIIe et IIe millénaires)* (London, 1948).

Schaeffer, C., Montet, P. and Virollaud, C., 'Les fouilles de Ras-Shamra. Cinquième campagne (printemps 1933). Rapport sommaire', *Syria* 15/2 (1934), 105-136.

Scharff, A., 'Ein Rechnungsbuch des königlichen Hofes aus der 13. Dynastie', *ZÄS* 57 (1922), 51-68.

Scharff, A., 'Briefe aus Illahun', *ZÄS* 59 (1924), 20-51.

Scharff, A., *Der historische Abschnitt der Lehre für König Merikarê*, SBAW 8 (1936).

Schenkel, W., *Frühmittelägyptische Studien* (Bonn, 1962).

Schiestl, R., 'Some Links between a Late Middle Kingdom Cemetery at Tell el-Dab'a and Syria-Palestine: The Necropolis of F/I, Strata d/2 and d/1 (= H and G/4)', in M. Bietak (ed.), *The Middle Bronze Age in the Levant. Proceedings of an International Conference on MBIIA Ceramic Material in Vienna, 24th-26th of January 2001*, ÖAW: Denkschriften der Gesamtakademie 26 (Vienna, 2002), 329-352.

Schiestl, R., 'The Statue of an Asiatic Man from Tell el-Dab'a, Egypt', *E&L* 16 (2006), 173-185.

Schiestl, R., 'Tomb Types and Layout of a Middle Bronze IIA Cemetery at Tell el-Dab'a, Area F/1. Egyptian and Non-Egyptian Features', in M. Bietak and E. Czerny (eds), *The Bronze Age in the Lebanon: Studies on the Archaeology and Chronology of Lebanon, Syria and Egypt*, ÖAW: Denkschriften der Gesamtakademie 50 (Vienna, 2008), 243-256.

Schiestl, R., *Tell el Dab'a*, vol. 18: *Die Palastnekropole von Tell el-Dab'a. Die Gräber des Areals F/I der Straten d/2 und d/1*, Untersuchungen der Zweigstelle Kairo des Österreichischen Archäologischen Instituts 30 (Vienna, 2009).

Schmitz, B., *Untersuchungen zum Titel s3-njswt 'Konigsohn'* (Bonn, 1976).

Schneider, T., 'Die semitischen und ägyptischen Namen der syrischen Sklaven des Papyrus Brooklyn 35.1446 Verso', *UF* 19 (1987), 255-282.

Schneider, T., *Asiatische Personennamen in ägyptischen Quellen des Neuen Reiches*, OBO 114 (Gottingen, 1992).

Schneider, T., *Ausländer in Ägypten während des Mittleren Reiches und der Hyksoszeit*, 2 vols, ÄAT 42 (Wiesbaden, 1998, 2003).

Schneider, T., 'Sinuhes Notiz über die Könige: Syrisch-anatolische Herrschertitel in ägyptischer Überlieferung', *E&L* 12 (2002), 257-272.

Schneider, T., 'Foreign Egypt: Egyptology and the Concept of Cultural Appropriation', *E&L* 8 (2003), 155-161.

Schneider, T., 'The Relative Chronology of the Middle Kingdom and the Hyksos Period (Dyns. 13-17)', in E. Hornung, R. Krauss, and D. A. Warburton (eds), *Ancient Egyptian Chronology* (Leiden and Boston, 2006), 168-196.

Schneider, T., 'Foreigners in Egypt. Archaeological Evidence and Cultural Context', in W. Wendrich (ed.), *Egyptian Archaeology* (Oxford, 2010), 143-163.

Schulman, A. R., 'The Battle Scenes of the Middle Kingdom', *JSSEA* 12/4 (1982), 165-183.

Schulz, R., 'Block Statue', in W. Wendrich (ed.), *UCLA Encyclopedia of Egyptology*, http://digital2.library.ucla.edu/viewItem.do?ark=21198/zz002b24rf (accessed 30/08/2013).

Schumacher, G., *Tell el-Mutesellim*, vol. 1 (Leipzig, 1908).

Schwartz, G. M. and Nichols, J. J. (eds), *After Collapse: The Regeneration of Complex Societies* (Tucson, 2006).

Schwemer, D., 'The Storm-Gods of the Ancient Near East: Summary, Synthesis, Recent Studies. Part II', *JANER* 8/1 (2008), 1-44.

Sebelien, J., 'Early Copper and its Alloys', *Ancient Egypt* (1924), 6-15.

Seeden, H., *The Standing Armed Figurines in the Levant*, Prähistorische Bronzefunde I.1 (Munich, 1980).

Seger, J. D., 'Reflections on the Gold Hoard from Gezer', *BASOR* 221 (1976), 133-140.

Seibert, P., *Die Charakteristik: Untersuchungen zu einer altägyptischen Sprechsitte und ihren Ausprägungen in Folklore und Literature*, vol. 1: *Philologische Bearbeitung der Bezeugungen*, ÄA 17 (Wiesbaden, 1967).

Seidlmayer, S., *Gräberfelder aus dem Übergang vom Alten zum Mittleren Reich* (Heidelberg, 1990).

Seiler, A., 'Hebua I. Second Intermediate Period and Early New Kingdom Pottery', *CCE* 5 (1997), 23-30.

Seiler, A., *Tradition und Wandel: Die Keramik als Spiegel der Kulturentwicklung Thebens in der Zweiten Zwischenzeit*, Sonderschriften DAIAK 32 (Mainz, 2005).

Seiler, A., 'The Second Intermediate Period in Thebes: Regionalism in Pottery Development and its Cultural Implications', in M. Marée (ed.), *The*

Second Intermediate Period (Thirteenth-Seventeenth Dynasties). Current Research, Future Prospects (Leuven, Paris and Walpole, 2010), 39-53.

van Seters, J., 'A Date for the "Admonitions" in the Second Intermediate Period', *JEA* 50 (1964), 13-23.

van Seters, J., *The Hyksos: A New Investigation* (New Haven, 1966).

Sethe, K., *Urkunden der 18. Dynastie*, vol. 2 (Leipzig, 1906).

Sethe, K., *Ägyptische Lesestücke* (Leipzig, 1924).

Sethe, K., *Die Ächtung feindlicher Fürsten, Völker und Dinge auf altägyptischen Tongefässcherben des Mittleren Reiches*, Abhandlungen der preussichen Akademie der Wissenschaften Phil-Hist Klasse No. 5 (Berlin, 1926).

Sethe, K., *Urkunden des Alten Reichs* (Leipzig, 1933).

Seyfried, K.-J., 'Zur Inschrift des Hor (Wadi el Hudi Nr. 1 (143))', *GM* 81 (1984), 55-66.

Shaw, I., 'Pharaonic Quarrying and Mining: Settlement and Procurement in Egypt's Marginal Regions', *Antiquity* 68 (1994), 108-119.

Shaw, I., *The Oxford History of Ancient Egypt* (3rd edition, Oxford, 2003).

Shaw, I., *Hatnub: Quarrying Travertine in Ancient Egypt* (London, 2010).

Shaw, I. and Jameson, R., 'Amethyst Mining in the Eastern Desert: A Preliminary Survey at Wadi el-Hudi', *JEA* 79 (1993), 81-97.

Shea, W. H., 'Artistic Balance among the Beni Hasan Asiatics', *BA* 44/4 (1981), 219-228.

Shedid, A. G., *Die Felsgräber von Beni Hassan in Mittelägypten*, ZBA 16 (Mainz am Rhein, 1994).

Shils, E. A., 'Center and Periphery: Essays in Macrosociology', in *Selected Papers of Edward Shils* (Chicago, 1957), 111-126.

Shirley, J. J., 'Crisis and Restructuring of the State. From the Second Intermediate Period to the Advent of the Ramesses', in J. C. Moreno Garcia (ed.), *Ancient Egyptian Administration* (Leiden and Boston, 2013), 521-606.

Shortland, A. J. and Ramsey, C. B. (eds), *Radiocarbon and the Chronologies of Ancient Egypt* (Oxford, 2013).

van Siclen III, C. C., 'The Mayors of Basta in the Middle Kingdom', in S. Schoske (ed.), *Akten des vierten Internationalen Ägyptologen Kongresses München 1985*, vol. 4, SAK Beihefte 4 (Hamburg, 1988), 187-194.

van Siclen III, C. C., 'Remarks on the Middle Kingdom Palace at Tell Basta', in M. Bietak (ed.), *Haus und Palast im Alten Ägypten*, ÖAW: Denkschriften der Gesamtakademie 14 (Vienna, 1996), 239-246.

Sidebotham, S. E., Hense, M. and Nouwens, H. M., *The Red Land. The Illustrated Archaeology of Egypt's Eastern Desert* (Cairo, 2008).

Siegel, J. L., 'The Date and Historical Background of the Sinaitic Inscriptions', *AJSL* 49/1 (1932), 46-52.

Simons, F., 'Proto-Sinaitic – Progenitor of the Alphabet', *Rosetta* 9 (2011), 16-40.

Simpson, W. K., 'The Hyksos Princess Tany', *CdE* 34 (1959), 233-239.

Simpson, W. K., 'The Dynasty XIII Stela from the Wadi Hammamat', *MDAIK* 25 (1969), 154-158.

Simpson, W. K., *The Terrace of the Great God at Abydos: The Offering Chapels of Dynasties 12 and 13* (New Haven and Philadelphia, 1974).

Simpson, W. K., 'Mentuhotep, Vizier of Sesostris I, Patron of Art and Architecture', *MDAIK* 47 (1991), 331-340.

Simpson, W. K., *Inscribed Material from the Pennsylvania Yale Excavations at Abydos*, Publications of the Pennsylvania-Yale Expedition to Egypt 6 (New Haven and Philadelphia, 1995).

Simpson, W. K., 'Belles Lettres and Propaganda', in A. Loprieno (ed.), *Ancient Egyptian Literature: History and Forms* (Leiden, 1996), 435-443.

Simpson, W. K., *The Literature of Ancient Egypt: An Anthology of Stories, Instructions, Stelae, Autobiographies, and Poetry* (3rd edition, Yale, 2003).

Singer-Avitz, L., 'The Middle Bronze Age Pottery from Areas D and P', in D. Ussishkin (ed.), *The Renewed Archaeological Excavations at Lachish (1973-1994)*, vol. 3, Tel Aviv Monograph Series 22 (Tel Aviv, 2004), 900-965.

Smith, A. D., *The Ethnic Revival. Themes in the Social Sciences* (Cambridge, 1981).

Smith, H. S. and Smith, A., 'A Reconsideration of the Kamose Texts', *ZÄS* 103 (1976), 48-76.

Smith, S. T., *Wretched Kush: Ethnic Identities and Boundaries in Egypt's Nubian Empire* (London and New York, 2003).

Smith, S. T., 'Ethnicity and Culture', in T. Wilkinson (ed.), *The Egyptian World* (London and New York, 2007), 218-241.

Smith, W. S., 'Influence of the Middle Kingdom of Egypt in Western Asia, especially in Byblos', *AJA* 73/3 (1969), 277-281.

Smith, W. S., *Interconnections in the Ancient Near East: A Study of the Relationships between the Arts of Egypt, the Aegean, and Western Asia* (New Haven, 1965).

Smith, W. S., *A History of Egyptian Sculpture and Painting in the Old Kingdom* (New York, 1978).

Snape, S. R., *Liverpool University Delta Survey: Archaeological Fieldwork at Tell Yehud, Gheyta*, vol. 2 (Liverpool, 1997).

de Souza, A., 'The "Egyptianisation" of the Pan-Grave Culture: A New Look at an Old Idea', *BACE* 24 (2013), 109-126.

Spalinger, A. J., 'Notes on the Day Summary of P. Bulaq 18 and the Intradepartmental Transfers', *SAK* 12 (1985), 179-241.

Spalinger, A. J., 'From Local to Global: The Extension of an Egyptian Bureaucratic Term to the Empire', *SAK* 23 (1996), 353-376.

Spalinger, A. J., 'Orientations on *Sinuhe*', *SAK* 25 (1998), 311-339.

Spalinger, A. J., 'Review: The Political Situation in Egypt during the Second Intermediate Period, c. 1800-1550 B.C., by K. S. B. Ryholt ', *JNES* 60/4 (2001), 296-300.

Sparks, R., 'Egyptian Stone Vessels in Syro-Palestine during the Second Millennium B.C. and their Impact on the Local Stone Vessel Industry', in G. Bunnens (ed.), *Cultural Interaction in the Ancient Near East. Papers Read at a Symposium at the University of Melbourne, Department of Classics and Archaeology (29-30 September 1994)*, Abr-Nahrain Supplement Series 5 (Louvain, 1996), 51-66.

Sparks, R., *Stone Vessels in the Levant*, PEFA 8 (Leeds, 2007).

Spiegel, J., *Soziale und Weltansschauliche Reformbewegungen in alten Ägypten* (Heidelberg, 1950).

Stadelmann, R., 'Riding the Donkey: A Means of Transportation for Foreign Rulers', in E. Czerny et al. (eds), *Timelines. Studies in Honour of Manfred Bietak*, vol. 2, OLA 149 (Leuven, Paris and Dudley, 2006), 301-304.

Stager, L. E., 'Port Power in the Early and the Middle Bronze Age: The Organization of Maritime Trade and Hinterland Production', in S. R. Wolff (ed.), *Studies in the Archaeology of Israel and Neighboring Lands in Memory of Douglas L. Esse*, SAOC 59 (Chicago, 2001), 625-638.

Stager, L. E., 'The MBIIA Ceramic Sequence at Tel Ashkelon and its Implications for the 'Port Power' Model of Trade', in M. Bietak (ed.), *The Middle Bronze Age in the Levant. Proceedings of an International Conference on MBIIA Ceramic Material. Vienna, 24th-26th of January 2001*, ÖAW: Denkschriften der Gesamtakademie 26 (Vienna, 2002), 353-362.

Stager, L. E. and Voss, R. J., 'Egyptian Pottery in Middle Bronze Age Ashkelon', *Eretz-Israel* 30 (2011), 119*-126*.

Stager, L. E. and Voss, R. J., 'A Sequence of Tell el Yahudiya Ware from Ashkelon', in D. A. Aston and M. Bietak, *Tell el Dab'a*, vol. 8: *The Classification and Chronology of Tell el-Yahudiya Ware*, Untersuchungen der Zweigstelle Kairo des Österreichischen Archäologischen Institutes 12 (Vienna, 2012), 559-576.

Stager, L. E., Schloen, D. J. and Master, D. M. (eds), *Ashkelon*, vol. 1: *Introduction and Overview (1985-2006). Final Reports of the Leon Levy Expedition to Ashkelon* (Winona Lake, 2008).

Starr, R. F. and Butin, R. F., *Studies and Documents*, vol. 6: *Excavations and Protosinaitic Inscriptions at Serabit el-Khadem* (London, 1936).

Staubli, T., *Das Image der Nomaden im Alten Israel und in der Ikonographie seiner sesshaften Nachbarn*, OBO 107 (Freiburg, 1991).

Stewart, C., 'Syncretism and its Synonyms: Reflections on Cultural Mixture', *Diacritics* 29/3 (1999), 40-62.

Stewart, C., 'Creolization, Hybridity, Syncretism, Mixture', *Portuguese Studies* 27/1 (2011), 48-55.

Stewart, J. R., *Tell el 'Ajjūl. The Middle Bronze Age Remains*, SMA 38 (Göteborg, 1974).

Stiebing, W. H., 'Hyksos Burials in Palestine: A Review of the Evidence', *JNES* 30 (1971), 110-117.

Stockhammer, P. W., 'Conceptualizing Cultural Hybridization in Archaeology', in P. W. Stockhammer (ed.), *Conceptualizing Cultural Hybridization: A Transdisciplinary Approach* (Berlin, 2012), 43-58.

Strauss, A. and Hubbe, M., 'Craniometric Similarities within and between Human Populations in Comparison with Neutral Genetic Data', *Human Biology* 82/3 (2010), 315-330.

Swelim, N. and Dodson, A., 'On the Pyramid of Ameny-Qemau and its Canopic Equipment', *MDAIK* 54 (1998), 319-334.

Szpakowska, K., *Daily Life in Ancient Egypt: Recreating Lahun* (Malden, Oxford and Carlton, 2008).

T

Tallet, P., 'Six campagnes archéologiques sur le site d'Ayn Soukhna, golfe de Suez', *BSFE* 165 (2006), 10-31.

Tallet, P., 'Ayn Sukhna and Wadi el-Jarf: Two Newly Discovered Pharaonic Harbours on the Suez Gulf', *British Museum Studies in Ancient Egypt and Sudan* 18 (2012), 147-168.

Tallet, P., 'A New Pharaonic Harbour in Ayn Sokhna (Gulf of Suez)', in D. A. Agius et al. (eds), *Navigated Spaces, Connected Places. Proceedings of Red Sea Project V Held at the University of Exeter 16-19 September 2010*, BAR International Series 2346 (Oxford, 2012), 33-37.

Taraqji, A. F., 'Nouvelles découvertes sur les relations avec l'Égypte à Tell Sakka et à Keswé, dans la region de Damas', *BSFE* 144 (1999), 27-43.

Taraqji, A. F., 'Wall Painting Fragments', in J. Aruz, K. Benzel and J. M. Evans (eds), *Beyond Babylon: Art, Trade, and Diplomacy in the Second Millennium B.C.* (New York, 2008), 128-129.

Tatlock, J. R., *How in Ancient Times They Sacrificed People: Human Immolation in the Eastern Mediterranean Basin with Special Emphasis on Ancient Israel and the Near East* (PhD Dissertation, University of Michigan, 2006), 112-114.

Taylor, J. H., 'Scarabs from the Bronze Age Tombs at Sidon (Lebanon)', *Levant* 36 (2004), 155-158.

Te Velde, H., *Seth, God of Confusion: A Study of His Role in Egyptian Mythology and Religion* (Leiden, 1967).

Teissier, B., *Egyptian Iconography on Syro-Palestinian Cylinder Seals of the Middle Bronze Age*, OBO 11 (Friburg, 1996).

Thalmann, J.-P., *Tell Arqa*, vol. 1: *Les niveaux de l'âge du Bronze*, Bibliothèque archéologique et historique 177 (Beirut, 2006).

Thalmann, J.-P., 'Tell Arqa et Byblos, essai de corrélation', in M. Bietak and E. Czerny (eds), *The Bronze Age in the Lebanon: Studies on the Archaeology and Chronology of Lebanon, Syria and Egypt*, ÖAW: Denkschriften der Gesamtakademie 50 (Vienna, 2008), 61-78.

Thalmann, J.-P., 'Tell Arqa: A Prosperous City during the Bronze Age', *NEA* 73/2-3 (2010), 86-101.

Thompson, T. L., *The Settlement of Sinai and the Negev in the Bronze Age*, Beihefte zum Tübinger Atlas des vorderen orients Reihe B (Geisteswissenschaften) 8 (Wiesbaden, 1975).

Thompson, T. L., *The Historicity of the Patriarchal Narratives: The Quest for the Historical Abraham* (Harrisburg, 2003).

Tietze, C. and Abd el-Maksoud, M., *Tell Basta. Ein Führer über das Grabungsgelände* (Potsdam, 2004).

Tomkins, H. G., 'Notes on the Hyksos or Shepherd Kings of Egypt', *JAIGB* 19 (1890), 182-199.

Trigg, A. B., 'Veblen, Bourdieu, and Conspicuous Consumption', *Journal of Economic Issues* 35/1 (2001), 99-115.

Tubb, J. N., 'A Crescentic Axehead from Amarna (Syria) and an Examination of Similar Axeheads from the Near East', *Iraq* 44/1 (1982), 1-12.

Tubb, J. N., *Peoples of the Past: Canaanites* (London, 1998).

Tufnell, O., 'The Courtyard Cemetery at Tell el-ᶜAjjul, Palestine', *BIA* 3 (1962), 1-37.

Tufnell, O., 'The Pottery from Royal Tombs I-III at Byblos', *Berytus* 18 (1969), 5-33.

Tufnell, O., 'The Middle Bronze Age Scarab-Seals from Burials on the Mound at Megiddo', *Levant* 5 (1973), 69-82.

Tufnell, O., 'Graves at Tell el-Yehudiyeh: Reviewed after a Life-Time', in R. Moorey and P. Parr (eds), *Archaeology in the Levant. Essays for Kathleen Kenyon* (Warminster, 1977), 76-101.

Tufnell, O., 'A Review of the Contents of Cave 303 at Tell el-'Ajjul', *'Atiqot* 14 (1980), 37-48.

Tufnell, O., *Studies on Scarab Seals*, vol. 2: *Scarabs and Their Contribution to History in the Early Second Millennium B.C.*, vol. 1 (Warminster, 1984).

Tufnell, O. and Ward, W. A., 'Relations between Byblos, Egypt and Mesopotamia at the End of the Third

Millenium B.C.: A Study of the Montet Jar', *Syria* 43 (1966), 165-241.

Tufnell, O. et al., *Lachish (Tell ed-Duweir)*, vol. 4: *The Bronze Age* (London, New York and Toronto, 1958).

U

Ungnad, A., 'Datenlisten', in *Reallexikon der Assyriologie*, vol. 2 (Berlin, 1938), 131-194.

V

Valbelle, D. and Bonnet, C., *Le Sanctuaire d'Hathor maîtresse de la turquoise* (Paris, 1996).

Vandier, J., 'Á propos d'un depot de provenance asiatique trouvé à Tôd', *Syria* 18 (1937), 174-182.

Veblen, T., *The Theory of the Leisure Class* (New York, 1899).

Vernus, P., 'La stèle du roi Sekhemsankhtaouyrê Neferhotep Iykhernofert et la domination Hyksôs (Stèle Caire JE 59635)', *ASAE* 68 (1982), 129-135.

Vernus, P., 'La stèle du pharaon *MNṮW-ḤTPI* à Karnak: Un nouveau témoignage sur la situation politique et militaire au début de la D.P.I.', *RdE* 40 (1989), 145-161.

Véron, A. et al., 'Origin of Copper used in Bronze Artefacts from Middle Bronze Age Burials in Sidon: A Synthesis from Lead Isotope Imprints and Chemical Analyses', *AHL* 34-35 (2011/2012), 68-78.

Vila, A., 'Un ritual d'envoûtement au Moyen Empire', in M. Sauter (ed.), *L'Homme, hier et aujourd'hui. Recueil d'études en homage à André Leroi-Gourhan* (Paris, 1973), 625-639.

Virolleaud, C., 'Découverte a Byblos d'un hypogée de la douziéme dynastie égyptienne', *Syria* 3 (1922), 273-290.

Voss, B. L., *The Archaeology of Ethnogenesis. Race and Sexuality in Colonial San Francisco* (Berkeley, 2008).

W

Wade, P., 'Rethinking Mestizaje: Ideology and Lived Experience', *Journal of Latin American Studies* 37 (2005), 239-257.

Waddell, W. G., *Manetho* (2nd edition, London, 1971).

Wallace-Jones, S., 'Pottery', in K. A. Bard and R. Fattovich, 'Mersa/Wadi Gawasis 2007-2008', *Archaeogate Egittologia*: *Articoli e News* (2008), http://www.archaeogate.org/egittologia/article/974/9/mersawadi-gawasis-mission-2007-2008-kathryn-a-bard-and.html#23 (accessed 13/03/2013).

Wallace-Jones, S., 'Pottery', in K. A. Bard and R. Fattovich, 'Mersa/Wadi Gawasis 2009-2010', *Newsletter di Archeologia CISA* 1 (2010), 17-19.

Wallace-Jones, S. and Imbrenda, M., 'Pottery', in K. A. Bard, R. Fattovich and C. Ward, 'Mersa/Wadi Gawasis 2010-2011', *Archaeogate Egittologia*: *Articoli e News* (2012), http://www.archaeogate.org/egittologia/article/1506/1/mersawadi-gawasis-2010-2011-report-by-kathryn-a-bard-bo.html (accessed 13/03/2013).

Wallerstein, I., 'World System versus World-Systems: A Critique', *Critique of Anthropology* 11 (1991), 169-194.

Wapnish, P., 'Middle Bronze Equid Burials at Tell Jemmeh and a Reexamination of a Purportedly "Hyksos" Practice', in E. D. Oren (ed.), *The Hyksos: New Historical and Archaeological Perspectives* (Philadelphia, 1997), 335-367.

Warburton, D., *Egypt and the Near East: Politics in the Bronze Age*, Civilisations du Proche-Orient Serie 4: Histoire-Essais 1 (Paris, 2001).

Ward, C., *Sacred and Secular: Ancient Egyptian Ships and Boats*, Archaeological Institute of America Monographs 5 (Philadelphia, 2000).

Ward, C., 'Ship Timbers: Description and Preliminary Analysis', in K. A. Bard and R. Fattovich (eds), *Harbor of the Pharaohs to the Land of Punt. Archaeological Investigations at Mersa/Wadi Gawasis, Egypt, 2001-2005* (Naples, 2007), 135-150.

Ward, W. A., 'Egypt and the East Mediterranean in the Early Second Millennium B. C.', *Orientalia* 30 (1961), 22-45, 129-155.

Ward, W. A., 'Relations between Egypt and Mesopotamia from Prehistoric Times to the End of the Middle Kingdom', *JESHO* 7/1 (1964), 1-45.

Ward, W. A., 'Relations between Egypt and Mesopotamia from Prehistoric Times to the End of the Middle Kingdom (Concluded)', *JESHO* 7/2 (1964), 121-135.

Ward, W. A., *Egypt and the East Mediterranean World 2200-1900 B.C.: Studies in Egyptian Foreign Relations during the First Intermediate Period* (Beirut, 1971).

Ward, W. A., 'A New Chancellor of the Fifteenth Dynasty', *OLP* 6/7 (1976), 589-594.

Ward, W. A., 'The *Hiw*-Ass, the *Hiw*-Serpent, and the God Seth', *JNES* 37/1 (1978), 23-34.

Ward, W. A., 'Scarabs from the Montet Jars', *Berytus* 26 (1978), 37-53.

Ward, W. A., 'Remarks on Some Middle Kingdom Statuary found at Ugarit', *UF* 11 (1979), 799-807.

Ward, W. A., *Index of Egyptian Administrative and Religious Titles of the Middle Kingdom* (Beirut, 1982).

Ward, W. A., 'Scarab Typology and Archaeological Context', *AJA* 91/4 (1987), 507-532.

Ward, W. A. and Dever, W. G., *Studies on Scarab Seals*, vol. 3: *Scarab Typology and Archaeological Context. An Essay on Middle Bronze Age Chronology* (San Antonio, 1994).

Wardini, E., *A Dictionary of Lebanese Place-Names (Mount Lebanon and North Lebanon)* (Beirut, 2008).

Warner, D., *The Archaeology of Canaanite Cult. An Analysis of Canaanite Temples from the Middle and Late Bronze Age in Palestine* (Lexington, 2008).

Warren, P., 'Minoan Crete and Pharaonic Egypt', in W. V. Davies and L. Schofield (eds), *Egypt, the Aegean and the Levant. Interconnections in the Second Millennium BC* (London, 1995), 1-18.

Warren, P. and Hankey, V., *Aegean Bronze Age Chronology* (Bristol, 1989).

Wastlhuber, C., *Die Beziehungen zwischen Ägypten und der Levante während der 12. Dynastie – Ökonomie und Prestige in Außenpolitik und Handel* (PhD Dissertation, Universität München, 2011).

Watelin, L., *Excavations at Kish*, vol. 4 (Paris, 1934).

Watzinger, C., *Tell el-Mutesellim*, vol. 2 (Leipzig, 1929).

Way, K. C., *Donkeys in the Biblical World. Ceremony and Symbol* (Winona Lake, 2011).

Weeks, K. R., 'Art, Word, and the Egyptian World View', in K. R. Weeks (ed.), *Egyptology and the Social Sciences. Five Studies* (Cairo, 1979), 50-81.

Wegner, J., 'Excavations at the Town of Enduring-are-the-Places-of-Khakaure-Maa-Kheru-in-Abydos. A Preliminary Report on the 1994 and 1997 Seasons', *JARCE* 35 (1998), 1-44.

Wegner, J., 'The Organization of the Temple *NFR-K3* of Senwosret III at Abydos', *E&L* 10 (2000), 83-125.

Wegner, J., 'The Town of *Wah-sut* at South Abydos: 1999 Excavations', *MDAIK* 57 (2001), 281-308.

Wegner, J., *The Mortuary Temple of Senwosret III at Abydos*, Publications of the Pennsylvania-Yale Expedition to Egypt 8 (New Haven and Philadelphia, 2007).

Wegner, J., 'The Tomb of Senwosret III at Abydos: Considerations on the Origins and Development of the Royal Amduat-Tomb', in D. P. Silverman, W. K. Simpson and J. Wegner (eds), *Archaism and Innovation: Studies in the Culture of Middle Kingdom Egypt* (New Haven and Philadelphia, 2009), 103-168.

Weinstein, J. M., 'A Statuette of the Princess Sobeknefru at Tell Gezer', *BASOR* 213 (1974), 49-57.

Weinstein, J. M., 'Egyptian Relations with Palestine in the Middle Kingdom', *BASOR* 217 (1975), 1-16.

Weinstein, J. M., 'The Egyptian Empire in Palestine: A Reassessment', *BASOR* 241 (1981), 1-28.

Weinstein, J. M., 'Egypt and the Middle Bronze IIC/Late Bronze IA Transition in Palestine', *Levant* 23 (1991), 105-115.

Weinstein, J. M., 'The Chronology of Palestine in the Early Second Millennium B.C.E.', *BASOR* 288 (1992), 27-46.

Weinstein, J. M., 'Reflections on the Chronology of Tell el-Dab'a', in W. V. Davis and L. Schofield (eds), *Egypt, the Aegean and the Levant* (London, 1995), 84-90.

Wells, J. W., *War in Ancient Egypt* (PhD Dissertation, The John Hopkins University, 1995).

Wenke, R. J., et al., 'Kom el-Hisn: Excavation of an Old Kingdom Settlement in the Egyptian Delta', *JARCE* 25 (1988), 5-34.

Wildung, D., 'Ein Würfelhocker des Generals Nes-Month', *MDAIK* 37 (1981), 503-507.

Wildung, D., *L'âge d'Or de l'Égypte: Le Moyen Empire* (Friburg, 1984).

Wildung, D., 'Kat. 97', in M. Bietak and I. Hein (eds), *Pharaonen und Fremde. Dynastien im Dunkel. Katalogue der 194* (Vienna, 1994), 137.

Wildung, D., *Ägypten 2000 v. Chr.: Die Geburt des Individuums* (Munich, 2000).

Willems, H., 'The Nomarchs of the Hare Nome and Early Middle Kingdom History', *JEOL* 28 (1983/1984), 80-102.

Willems, H., *Deir el-Bersha*, vol. 1: *The Rock Tombs of Djehutinakht (17K84/1), Khnumnakht (17K84/2), and Iha (17K84/3) with an Essay on the History and Nature of Nomarchical Rule in the Early Middle Kingdom* (Leuven, 2007).

Willems, H., *Historical and Archaeological Aspects of Egyptian Funerary Culture. Religious Ideas and Ritual Practice in Middle Kingdom Elite Cemeteries* (Leiden, 2014).

Willems, H. et al., 'An Industrial Site at al-Shaykh Sa'īd/ Wādī Zabayda', *E&L* 19 (2009), 293-331.

Williams, B., *Archaeology and Historical Problems of the Second Intermediate Period* (PhD Dissertation, University of Chicago, 1975).

Williams, R. J., 'Literature as a Medium of Political Propaganda in Ancient Egypt', in W. McCullough (ed.), *The Seed of Wisdom: Essays in Honour of T. J. Meek* (Toronto, 1964), 14-30.

Wilson, J. A., 'The Egyptian Middle Kingdom at Megiddo', *AJSL* 58/3 (1941), 225-236.

Wilson, J. A., 'Egyptian Myths, Tales, and Mortuary Texts', in J. Pritchard (ed.), *Ancient Near Eastern Texts: Relating to the Old Testament* (3rd edition, Princeton and New Jersey, 1969).

Wimmer, S. J., 'Byblos vs. Ugarit: The Alalakh Seal Impression 194 Once Again', *Levant* 37 (2005), 127-132.

Wimmer, S. J. and Wimmer-Dweikat, S., 'The Alphabet from Wadi el-Hol – A First Try', *GM* 180 (2001), 107-112.

Winkler, E. M. and Wilfing, H., *Tell el Dab'a*, vol. 6: *Anthropologische Untersuchungen an den Skelettresten der Kampagnen 1966-69, 1975-80, 1985*, Untersuchungen der Zweigstelle Kairo des Österreichischen Archäologischen Institutes 9 (Vienna, 1991).

Winlock, H. E., *The Rise and Fall of the Middle Kingdom in Thebes* (New York, 1947).

Wodzińska, A., 'Tell el-Retaba. Ceramic Survey, 2007', *PAM* 19 (2007), 152-160.

Wodzińska, A., 'Imported Vessels found in Tell el Retaba – Signs of Egypt International Contacts', *JAEI* 4/4 (2012), 45-46.

Wodzińska, A., 'Tell el-Retaba 2011: The Pottery', *PAM* 23/1 (2011), 109-116.

Woolley, L., *Ur Excavations*, vol. 2: *The Royal Cemetery. A Report on the Predynastic and Sargonid Graves Excavated Between 1926 and 1931* (London and Philadelphia, 1934).

Woolley, L., *Alalakh: An Account of the Excavations at Tell Atchana in the Hatay, 1937-1949* (Oxford, 1955).

Woudhuizen, F. C., 'On the Byblos Script', *UF* 39 (2007), 689-756.

Wright, G. E., 'Review of Kathleen M. Kenyon: Excavations at Jericho II', *Antiquity* 40 (1966), 149-150.

Wright, G. E., 'The Archaeology of Palestine from the Neolithic through the Middle Bronze Age', *JAOS* 91 (1971), 276-293.

Wright, G. R. H., *Biblical Archaeology* (London, 1962).

Wright, G. R. H., 'Tell el-Yehūdīyah and the Glacis', *ZDPV* 84 (1968), 1-17.

Wright, G. R. H., *Ancient Building in South Syria and Palestine* (Leiden, 1985).

Y

Yacoub, F., 'Excavations at Tell Farasha', *ASAE* 65 (1983), 175-176.

Yadin, Y., *Hazor. The Head of all those Kingdoms* (London, 1972).

Yon, M., *The Royal City of Ugarit on the Tell of Ras Shamra* (Winona Lake, 1998).

Younis, S. A., 'Itj-towy and the Prophecies of Neferti', *GM* 195 (2003), 97-108.

Z

Zane, N. and Mal, W., 'Major Approaches to the Measurement of Acculturation among Ethnic Minority Populations: A Content Analysis and an Alternative Empirical Strategy', K. M. Chun, P. B. Organista and G. Marin (eds), *Acculturation: Advances in Theory, Measurement, and Applied Research* (Washington, 2003), 39-60.

Zibelius-Chen, K., 'Die Medja in altägyptischen Quellen', *SAK* 36 (2007), 391-405.

Zohary, D., 'Domestication of the Carob (Ceratonia siliqua L.), *Israel Journal of Plant Sciences* 50/1 (2002), 141-145.

Zurins, J., 'Equids Associated with Human Burials in Third Millennium B. C. Mesopotamia: Two Complementary Facets', in R. H. Meadow and H.-P. Uerpmann (eds), *Equids in the Ancient World* (Wiesbaden, 1986), 164-193.

.Other

25 ans de découvertes archéologiques sur les chantiers de l'IFAO 1981-2006 (Cairo, 2007).

'Block of Relief', *The Metropolitan Museum of Art Collection Online*, http://www.metmuseum.org/collections/search-the-collections/100009602?img=1 (accessed 22/12/2012).

'Cylinder Seal', *The Metropolitan Museum of Art Collection Online*, http://www.metmuseum.org/collections/search-the-collections/100014833?img=1, (accessed 22/12/2012).

'Fragment from an Egyptian Vessel decorated with the Image of an Eastern Foreigner', *The Metropolitan Museum of Art Collection Online*, http://www.metmuseum.org/Collections/search-the-collections/100014704 (accessed 22/12/2012).

'Fragment from a Battle Scene depicting a Foreigner throwing a Spear and holding a Distinctive Shield', *The Metropolitan Museum of Art Collection Online*, http://www.metmuseum.org/Collections/search-the-collections/100000361 (accessed 22/12/2012).

'Fragments depicting a Group of Foreigners including a Child', *The Metropolitan Museum of Art Collection Online*, http://www.metmuseum.org/Collections/search-thecollections/100001960?rpp=60&pg=5&ft=lisht&pos=285 (accessed 22/12/2012).

'Juglet', *The Metropolitan Museum of Art Collection Online*, http://www.metmuseum.org/Collections/search-the-collections/100002229 (accessed 22/12/2012).

'Publications Dayr al-Barsha Project', *Dayr al-Barsha Project*, http://www.dayralbarsha.com/node/12 (accessed 14/01/2013).

'Relief Fragment: Foreigner with Feather in His Hair and Nubian', *The Metropolitan Museum of Art Collection Online*, http://www.metmuseum.org/Collections/search-thecollections/100001963?rpp=60&pg=5&ft=lisht&pos=287 (accessed 22/12/2012).

'Scarab', *The Metropolitan Museum of Art Collection Online*, http://www.metmuseum.org/Collections/search-the-collections/100019059 and http://www.metmuseum.org/Collections/search-the-collections/100001725 (accessed 22/12/2012).

'Scarab', *The Metropolitan Museum of Art Collection Online*, http://www.metmuseum.org/Collections/search-the-collections/100003214, (accessed 22/12/2012).

'Scarab', *The Metropolitan Museum of Art Collection Online*, http://www.metmuseum.org/Collections/search-the-collections/100002217, (accessed 22/12/2012).

'Scarab', *The Metropolitan Museum of Art Collection Online*, http://www.metmuseum.org/Collections/search-the-collections/100001689, (accessed 22/12/2012).

'Scarab', *The Metropolitan Museum of Art Collection Online*, http://www.metmuseum.org/Collections/search-the-collections/100003225, (accessed 22/12/2012).

'Statuette of King', *The Metropolitan Museum of Art Collection Online*, http://www.metmuseum.org/collections/search-the-collections/100014651?img=1 (accessed 22/12/2012).

The Synchronization of Civilizations in the Eastern Mediterranean in the 2nd Millennium BC, http://www.oeaw.ac.at/sciem2000/index.html (accessed 30/11/2012).

Tell Edfu Project, http://www.telledfu.org/annual-reports (accessed 14/04/2013).

Tell el-Dab'a homepage, http://www.auaris.at/html/bibliographie_en.html (accessed 20/02/2012).

Titriş Höyük Archaeological Project, http://www3.uakron.edu/titris/OuterExc.htm (accessed 01/04/2012).

'Tod', *Institut français d'archéologie orientale, Caire*, http://www.ifao.egnet.net/archeologie/tod/ (accessed 5/03/2013).

Appendix A. Ambiguous Data from the Levant

A.1 'Ajjul, Tell el- (see Chapter 6.2.1)

The incomplete and unclear publications of finds excavated at Tell el-'Ajjul have led to a range of proposed dates for the site's stratigraphy (see Figure 6.4). Petrie originally proposed that Stratum I and Palace V are correlated with the Eighteenth Dynasty, Stratum II, Palace III and Palace IV are to the Fifteenth Dynasty, and Stratum III and Palace II are to the Twelfth Dynasty.[1] Albright's re-analysis ascribes Palace I and Stratum III to the MBIIC, and Strata II-I to the LBI period.[2] Another proposition assigns Palace I and Stratum III to the MBIIB (the Thirteenth to Fifteenth Dynasties), Palace II and Stratum II to the MBIIB and MBIIC period (the Fifteenth Dynasty) and Palace III and Stratum I to the LBA (Eighteenth Dynasty).[3] The imprecise nature of the published material does not allow for an exact dating of the deposition of all finds per stratum. The issue is further confused with the lack of secure and datable find-spots for the recovered Egyptian(-influenced) items. In consequence, the material has been subjected to different interpretations regarding the site's relations with Egypt and, more specifically, the Hyksos. The following are some finds from Strata III and II that have been utilised by scholars as evidence for Hyksos relations with Tell el-'Ajjul.

Statuettes

Three Egyptian statuettes were retrieved, two of which are uninscribed fragments.[4] One is noted to be from Building EW, its level uncertain,[5] while the context of the second is unknown.[6] The third statuette was recorded among the contents of Burial 21 in a grain pit of the Lower City's House AN.[7] The block statuette is carved in a common Middle Kingdom style dating after the mid-Twelfth Dynasty with head, hands and feet protruding from a tight-fitting cloak enclosing the seated body.[8] An inscription at the front of the statue has been transcribed as  *im3ẖ(.y)* [*ẖ*]*r Ptḥ-Skr im.y-r3 s3 H̱nt.yw-k3* 'the honoured before Ptah-Sokar, the overseer of a phyle,[9] Khentiuka'.[10] The Lower City is correlated with Stratum III which, following Petrie, corresponds to the Twelfth Dynasty.[11] Tufnell, however, dates the stratum to the MBIIB period (between the late Thirteenth and early Fifteenth Dynasty)[12] whereas Albright suggests an MBIIB-C or MBIIC date (late Fifteenth Dynasty).[13] Whether Tell el-'Ajjul was visited by Khentiuka or the latter's statuette was acquired from an Egyptian context and secondarily deposited at Tell el-'Ajjul cannot be ascertained. Questions regarding its stratum's date restrict its use as evidence for Egyptian-Levantine relations, yet the statue's significance is reflected by its funerary context. Interred in an apparent Levantine burial, it represents the locals' knowledge and appreciation of Egyptian culture.

Vessels

Tell el-'Ajjul produced 290 MBA and LBA stone vessels, the largest number recorded at any Southern Levantine site, with around 80% originating in Egypt.[14] The vessels ascribe to a variety of forms including plates, carinated bowls, zoomorphic bowls, drop-shaped alabastra, conical alabastra, dipper juglets, small piriform jars, pilgrim flasks, footed jars and cylindrical juglets.[15]

Stratum III produced at least 36 calcite-alabaster vessels, over 70% of which were uncovered in tombs.[16] Small serpentine and haematite piriform jars were also found in both settlement and funerary contexts, providing rare instances of Egyptian cosmetic vessels in the Levant.[17] Other rare Egyptian imports are a fish-shaped jar from a pit pre-dating Stratum II[18] and a fragmentary handle formed as an Egyptian figure and a cobra (Area E, Level 760).[19] Kopetzky additionally identifies Marl zir rims from Wall MT and Room OH, although these have been attributed to early Eighteenth Dynasty forms.[20]

1 Petrie, *Gaza* 1-4.
2 Albright, *AJSL* 55/4 (1938), 337-359; Sparks, *Stone Vessels in the Levant*, 205-206.
3 Sparks, *Stone Vessels in the Levant*, 147; Tufnell, *Scarab Seals* 2/1, 7-23.
4 Petrie, *Gaza* 3, 8, pls 16 [49], 17; vol. 4, 12, pl. 40 [107].
5 Petrie, *Gaza* 4, 12, pl. 40 [107].
6 Petrie, *Gaza* 3, 8, pls 16 [49], 17.
7 Petrie, *Gaza* 1, 5, 8, pls 21 [99], 22; Weinstein, *BASOR* 213 (1974), 54-55.
8 Schulz, in *Encyclopedia of Egyptology*, 1-10.
9 Ward, *Index*, 43 [328].
10 Ranke, *Personennamen* 1, 273 [12-13]. As the statuette's hieroglyphs are unclear in the publication's photograph, the transcription here follows Ward's translation, *im.y-r3 s3 H̱nt.yw-k3*. In this case, both the title and name can be found in other Middle Kingdom examples. The text has otherwise been read as *im.y-r3 s3 ẖnt.y Ḥr.w-k3* 'the overseer of the phyle at the fore, Horuka' (Ward, *Index*, 43 [328]), the title and name both unattested.

11 Petrie, *Gaza* 1, 3.
12 Tufnell, *Scarab Seals* 2/1, 7-23.
13 Albright, *AJSL* 55/4 (1938), 342, 348-351.
14 The majority of vessels are made of imported Egyptian calcite-alabaster. Other materials include basalt, limestone/marble, serpentine and gypsum-alabaster. Sparks, *Stone Vessels in the Levant*, 206, fig. 70.
15 Petrie, *Gaza* 1, pls 24-25; vol. 2, pls 21-23; vol. 3, 11, 15; vol. 4, 38-39; Petrie, *Shepherd Kings*, pls 19-20.
16 Petrie, *Gaza* 1, pls 24 [2], 25 [9, 11-12, 14, 25, 27, 38-39, 66]; vol. 3, pl. 26 [21-22]; vol. 4, pls 22 [242-244], 23-24, 38 [5, 22, 29, 35, 46], 39 [53, 58, 60-61, 66]; Petrie, *Shepherd Kings*, pls 19 [1, 4-5, 24-25, 30, 32, 34, 38], 20 [43]; Sparks, *Stone Vessels in the Levant*, 287 [89-91], 289 [125], 290 [133], 293 [169-174], 296 [211], 299 [243-247], 300 [264-266], 301 [273, 276-278], 302 [281, 288], 303 [296], 312 [393, 401-402], 314 [417-419], 315 [431-433], 329 [606], 337 [720].
17 Sparks, *Stone Vessels in the Levant*, 207.
18 Petrie, *Shepherd Kings*, pl. 20 [43]; Sparks, *Stone Vessels in the Levant*, 207, 329 [606].
19 Petrie, *Gaza* 4, pl. 23; Sparks, *Stone Vessels in the Levant*, 207, 337 [720].
20 Kopetzky, in *Bronze Age in the Lebanon*, 226.

Around 40 calcite-alabaster vessels were unearthed in Stratum II contexts, 38% of which were found in tombs.[21] A rare serpentine bowl with duck-and-cobra-shaped handles was also discovered (Area H, Level 771).[22] A few vessels are of New Kingdom shapes, indicating that some Stratum II contexts date to the LBI period.

Scarabs and seal impressions

Tell el-'Ajjul yielded the largest corpus of scarabs and seal impressions from the Southern Levant. Due to the sheer number, their complete analysis is beyond this study.[23] Thus only some comments are hereto offered.

Royal-name seals and impressions referring to rulers of the Twelfth to Fifteenth Dynasties occur in the settlement and its tombs. Although many are of uncertain context,[24] some have been assigned to the settlement's stratigraphic levels. Stratum III yielded scarabs of Noferhotep I,[25] a Sihotepibra,[26] *Šši*,[27] *ˁmw*[28] and Sekhaenra.[29] Stratum II produced a scarab of *Šši*[30] and Apophis[31] as well as a bead with the name of Amenemhat III from grain pit AT.[32]

Private-name scarabs are additionally attested, yet the majority are from unrecorded contexts.[33] One scarab is listed for Room DN, Stratum III, and is inscribed with *ir(.w) wḥm(.t) Mr.y-Ptḥ-B3s(tt)* 'maker of furniture-legs,[34] Meryptahbastet'.[35] Three scarabs are from Stratum II: the first is from an unclear context and reads *Ysinn 'Ysinn'*;[36] Room AN contained the second with *sš wr n(.y) im.y-r3 ḫtm.t Nḥs(y) m3ˁ-ḫrw* 'chief scribe of the overseer of the treasury,[37] Nehsy,[38] justified';[39] and Room AC held the third with *ḫtm.ty bi.ty smr wˁ.ty im.y-r3 ḫtm.t Snbi* 'sealer of the king of Lower Egypt, sole friend, overseer of the treasury,[40] Senbi'.[41] As the rooms' functions remain unknown, the scarabs' use cannot be determined. But, based on the titles associated with the treasury on the scarabs of Rooms AN and AC, a relation to imported commodities is conceivable.

The vast number of scarabs at Tell el-'Ajjul has led to the supposition that the site was under the control of Dynasty 15.[42] However, reliance on the scarabs alone does not allow for such an interpretation. Second Intermediate Period royal- and private-name scarabs surface in Stratum III with late Fifteenth Dynasty royal-name scarabs in Stratum II. While it's tempting to date the strata based on the scarabs, the site's problematic chronology as well as the methods and publication of its early excavations restrict any correlation between the scarab evidence and the development of relations with Egypt during the Second Intermediate Period.

Comments

While Albright's dating implies minimal contact during the period of the Hyksos's rise to power, others who have assigned Strata III to II to earlier dates have argued for significant contacts with the Hyksos.[43] If their chronology is accepted, the rise of the Hyksos would coincide with Stratum III comprising Khentiuka's statuette, at least 36 calcite-alabaster vessels and numerous scarabs, all evidence of significant and most likely direct contact with an Egyptian(-influenced) culture. This contact would then have intensively continued throughout the Fifteenth Dynasty, reflecting close ties between the Hyksos and Tell el-'Ajjul which, as the above evidence shows, are seemingly related more with trade than political or cultural control.[44] But, following Albright's dating, the material

21 The number includes a calcite-alabaster vessel uncovered in the Courtyard Cemetery's Tomb 1416 of Stratum II. The tomb is assigned to Tufnell's Group 6 which is given a MBIIC or LBI date. Petrie, *Gaza* 1, pl. 25 [2, 8, 16-17, 24, 36-37]; vol. 2, pls 22 [7, 22, 26-28], 23 [32, 45]; vol. 4, pls 11 [108], 22 [246-247], 28 [28, 31], 38 [1, 7, 14, 18, 37], 39 [51, 55, 59, 72], 41 [122]; Petrie, *Shepherd Kings*, pl. 19 [3, 7, 12, 17, 21, 26]; Sparks, *Stone Vessels in the Levant*, 281 [19], 282 [29], 283 [40], 287 [93-95], 289-290 [126-127], 293-294 [175-177], 296 [203, 212-213], 297 [214-215], 299 [249], 301 [272], 302 [289], 303 [290, 298], 304 [305], 308 [352], 309 [358, 369], 312 [394], 314 [420], 317-318 [467-468, 482], 319 [487-488], 321 [521], 323 [537-540], 332 [657-658], 336 [710].

22 Sparks, *Stone Vessels in the Levant*, 207, 283 [40]; Petrie, *Gaza* 4, pl. 22 [247].

23 For more on the site's scarabs and seal impressions, see Keel, *Stempelsiegel-Amulette*, 106-525; Tufnell, *Scarab Seals* 2/1, 92-106; Richards, *Anra Scarabs*, 130-131; Ben-Tor, *Scarabs*, passim.

24 These include scarabs bearing the names of Senwosret I and II, Amenemhat III, Noferhotep I, *Šši*, Sekhaenra, *ˁmw*, Aahotepra, Apophis and a cylinder seal of Amenemhat III. Petrie, *Gaza* 1, pl. 14 [123, 143-145, 148]; vol. 2, pls 7 [77], 8 [123, 145], vol. 3 [37]; vol. 4, pls 5 [3, 17, 61], 7 [231, 268], 9 [352], 11 [465]; Mackay and Murray, *Gaza* 5, pl. 9 [1]; Petrie, *Shepherd Kings*, pl. 9 [1-9].

25 Petrie, *Gaza* 3, pl. 3 [16].

26 Petrie, *Gaza* 4, pl. 5 [124].

27 Petrie, *Gaza* 3, pl. 3 [9]; vol. 4, pls 8-9 [274].

28 Petrie, *Gaza* 1, pl. 14 [144]; vol. 3, [106]; vol. 4, pl. 5 [26].

29 Petrie, *Gaza* 2, pl. 3 [92].

30 Petrie, *Gaza* 4, pl. 7 [215].

31 Petrie, *Gaza* 1, pl. 13 [2, 44].

32 Petrie, *Gaza* 1, pl. 13 [43].

33 See Petrie, *Gaza* 3, pl. 3 [16, 33]; vol. 4, 4, pls 5 [1, 12], 9 [310]; Mackay and Murray, *Gaza* 5, 7, pl. 9 [2]; Martin, *Egyptian Administrative and Private-Name Seals*, 67 [811], 73-74 [915a], 75 [932], 83 [1064], 102 [1309], 127-128 [1665], pls 8 [7], 11 [10], 12 [23], 26 [12], 292 [23], 42b [6]; Ben-Tor, *BASOR* 294 (1994), 12-13.

34 Ward, *Index*, 67 [558].

35 Petrie, *Gaza* 1, 7, pl. 13 [67]. The name is unattested in Ranke, *Personennamen*. Its translation follows Martin, *Egyptian Administrative and Private-Name Seals*, 52 [614], pl. 20 [39].

36 The name is unattested in Ranke, *Personennamen*. Petrie, *Gaza* 1, 7, pl. 13 [45]; Martin, *Egyptian Administrative and Private-Name Seals*, 29 [306], pl. 27 [25].

37 Ward, *Index*, 159 [1371].

38 Ranke, *Personnenamen* 1, 209 [4].

39 Petrie, *Gaza* 1, 7, pl. 13 [26]; Martin, *Egyptian Administrative and Private-Name Seals*, 66 [799], pl. 11 [15].

40 Ward, *Index*, 171 [1476].

41 Ranke, *Personnenamen* 1, 313 [23]; Petrie, *Gaza* 1, 7, pl. 13 [23]; Martin, *Egyptian Administrative and Private-Name Seals*, 120 [1554], pl. 22 [8].

42 Kempinski, *IEJ* 24/3-4 (1997), 328; Weinstein, *BASOR* 241 (1981), 8.

43 See, for instance, Oren, in *Hyksos*, 253-255.

44 Ben-Tor additionally emphasises that 'the archaeological evidence at Tell el-'Ajjul... reflect a typical, albeit affluent Canaanite town that differs considerably from the typical eastern Delta cultural sphere reflected in the material culture found in this region... It can therefore be concluded that the "Kingdom of Avaris"... did not extend into southern Palestine' (Ben-Tor, *Scarabs*, 193). Trade rather than political hegemony is also suggested by Holladay, in

from Stratum III and II would reflect heightened contacts from the second half of the Fifteenth Dynasty, after the Hyksos had already established their reign. Nevertheless, the varying chronological propositions agree on one point: Tell el-'Ajjul had some relations with the Fifteenth Dynasty. But, to connect the questionable evidence with a political hegemony extending from the Delta to Tell el-'Ajjul is problematic. Renewed excavations by Fischer and Sadeq at the site have, thus far, not recovered conclusive evidence for close political alliances with the early Hyksos rulers. Thus, until such evidence is found, it is best to approach the data from Tell el-'Ajjul with caution.

Hyksos, 204-208; Richards, *Anra Scarab*, 161; Ben-Tor, in *Scarabs of the Second Millennium BC*, 39.

A.2 Gezer / Jazari, Tell (see Chapter 6.2.4)

Three Egyptian statuettes utilised as evidence for Egyptian-Levantine contact during the MBIIB-C period were uncovered at Gezer. These are:

- A kneeling figure for 'the butler of the chamber, Heqaib' from an ash-pit on the western side of the tell. The statuette was assigned to Macalister's First Semitic Period corresponding to the EBA and the first half of the MBA.[45] No other material from the find-spot has been published and so the date of its context cannot be verified;

- A fragment of a shabti apparently for the 'citizen, Deduamun' from the Central Valley, with an inscription dated to the Thirteenth Dynasty.[46] Macalister writes that the piece was found in 'fifth stratum debris' or the level dated to the Third Semitic Period (Iron Age I-II);[47]

- The base of a statuette incised with the name of Princess Sobeknofru, the daughter of either Senwosret I or Amenemhat III.[48] The text offers a *terminus post quem* of Dynasty 12, but the context suggests a later date of deposition. The statuette was found in Locus 5062.1 of Field VI, Area NE5, as one of several stones used for the west face of LBII Wall 5061, its associated pottery being of the MBII to LBII period.[49] Excavators have preliminarily classified the locus to Stratum 6 of Field VI, or the LBIIB period.[50]

The uncertain contexts and secondary use of the statuettes denote that none of the three artefacts can be listed as definite imports of the Twelfth to Fifteenth Dynasties. While some have remarked that there are no reasons why the statuettes cannot be used as evidence for Middle Kingdom contacts,[51] the ambiguities regarding the statues' deposition and date are significant rationales against forming any conclusive remarks regarding Middle Kingdom contacts at Gezer. It is only possible to note that the statuettes are of Twelfth to, perhaps, Thirteenth Dynasty origin and, possibly between the MBA and LBII periods, reached Gezer.

45 Macalister, *Gezer* 2, 311-312, fig. 450.
46 Macalister, *Gezer* 2, 312-313.
47 Macalister, *PEQ* 35 (1903), 36-37.
48 Weinstein, *BASOR* 213 (1974), 49-57.
49 Weinstein, *BASOR* 213 (1974), 51.
50 Weinstein, *BASOR* 213 (1974), 51.
51 Teissier, *Syro-Palestinian Cylinder Seals*, 4, n. 21; Giveon, in *Egypt, Israel, Sinai*, 26; Muhlestein, in *Egypt, Canaan and Israel*, 193.

A.3 Megiddo / Mutasallim, Tell el- (see Chapter 6.2.7)

Four fragments of Twelfth Dynasty statuettes were found in secondary contexts at Megiddo. One is uninscribed and was collected from among rubble supporting the pavement outside LBA Temple 2048,[52] and three were incorporated within Temple 2048's platform wall.[53] Of the latter, two are uninscribed busts[54] while the third preserves the lower half of a seated figure with a hieroglyphic inscription naming a 'great overlord of the [Hare nome]', Djehutyhotep, son of Kay and S[...].[55] The official's name, titles, and lineage all equate with those of Djehutyhotep, 'treasurer of the king of Lower Egypt', whose tomb is located at Deir el-Bersha.[56] Dating to the reign of Senwosret III, some have identified Djehutyhotep as a resident of Megiddo, leading to the notion that the site was under Egyptian control during the Twelfth Dynasty.[57] A caption in Djehutyhotep's tomb supposedly reading *Rṯnw* provided further advocacy for this theory. However, as the toponym's presence has been refuted in this work,[58] no other direct evidence exists to support the possibility of Djehutyhotep's presence at Megiddo. Further, the statuette is from a context assigned to Stratum VII or the LBA,[59] and so it remains uncertain when and how it reached the site. As such, none of the statuettes from Megiddo can be used as concrete evidence for relations with Egypt during the Twelfth to Fifteenth Dynasties.

52 Loud, *Megiddo* 2, pl. 267 [6]; Wilson, *AJSL* 58/3 (1941), 226.
53 Loud notes that the temple's foundations are no earlier than Stratum VIII (LBA). Loud, *Megiddo* 2, pls 265-266; Wilson, *AJSL* 58/3 (1941), 226.
54 Loud, *Megiddo* 2, pl. 266 [2-3].
55 Loud, *Megiddo* 2, pl. 265; Wilson, *AJSL* 58/3 (1941), 227, pls 1-3.
56 Newberry, *El-Bersheh* 1, 6-7, pl. 16. See Chapter 4.4.2.1.
57 Wilson, *AJSL* 58/3 (1941), 225-236; Tufnell, *Levant* 5 (1973), 82; Davies, *Megiddo*, 41; Giveon, in *Egypt, Israel, Sinai*, 23-40.
58 See Chapter 4.4.2.1.
59 Loud, *Megiddo* 2, pl. 265; Wilson, *AJSL* 58/3 (1941), 226.

A.4 Nami, Tell

A settlement at Tell Nami on the southern Carmel coast revealed four main areas, D, D1, G and O, dating to the MBIIA, LBIIB and, possibly, the LBIIA period.[60] MBIIA remains were primarily found in Area D featuring several buildings, storerooms and an open courtyard.[61] A large room in one of the storerooms was sealed by a layer of charcoal, ash and burnt mudbrick, suggesting that the final MBIIA phase was marked by its destruction and the collapse of its roof by fire.[62] The room was then later robbed in the LBA.[63] The room's floor revealed such items as a bronze statue fragment, a spearhead and a loom weight with a scarab seal impression.[64] The latter's context beneath Locus 420 (remains of a robbed stone surface) obscures its date of deposition.[65] It could belong to the last phase of MBIIA occupation or the following LBA layer when the floor was robbed.[66] Despite this ambiguity, the loom weight has been used as evidence for MBIIA contact with Egypt.[67]

The correlation is based on the weight's seal impression displaying two red crowns atop a *nbw* sign flanked by two *ʿnḫ* symbols.[68] Parallels for the design are found at the late Twelfth to mid-late Thirteenth Dynasty Egyptian sites of el-Lahun and Uronarti.[69] They also occur at late MBIIA(?) to MBIIB Megiddo, and MBIIB Jericho and Gibeon.[70] Marcus and Artzy write that 'Given the absence of MBIIB occupation at Tel Nami, our weight may only be attributed to either the LBIIA or LBIIB'.[71] Nevertheless, they conclude that the object indicates 'contact with, and/or orientation towards, Egyptian culture during the Middle Bronze IIA Age'.[72] Indeed, the seal's impression on a Levantine object reflects a non-Egyptian custom,[73] denoting a mesh of Egyptian and Levantine practices. However, the weight's uncertain context restricts any further comments regarding chronological or cultural relations between Egypt and Tell Nami.[74] So, the current evidence does not conclusively specify Egyptian-Levantine contacts at Tell Nami during the MBIIA.

60 Artzy, *IEJ* 40/1 (1990), 73-76; Artzy and Marcus, *Michmanim* 5 (1991), 5*-16*; Artzy, *IEJ* 41/1 (1991), 194-197.
61 Artzy, *IEJ* 41/1 (1991), 195-197, fig. 1.
62 Artzy, *IEJ* 41/1 (1991), 196.
63 Marcus and Artzy, *IEJ* 45/2 (1995), 136.
64 Artzy, *IEJ* 41/1 (1991), 196-197; Cohen, *Canaanites, Chronologies, and Connections*, 89.
65 Marcus and Artzy, *IEJ* 45/2 (1995), 136.
66 Marcus and Artzy, *IEJ* 45/2 (1995), 136.
67 Marcus and Artzy, *IEJ* 45/2 (1995), 149; Ben-Tor, *Scarabs*, 118.
68 Ben-Tor's Design Class 3B3. Marcus and Artzy, *IEJ* 45/2 (1995), 138, 141-142; Ben-Tor, *Scarabs*, 18-19.
69 Marcus and Artzy, *IEJ* 45/2 (1995), 139, 142-143; Petrie, *Lahun* 2, pl. 64 [300]; Ben-Tor, *Scarabs*, 19, pl. 8 [41-50].
70 Marcus and Artzy, *IEJ* 45/2 (1995), 139-143; Ben-Tor, *Scarabs*, 80, 130, n. 401.
71 Marcus and Artzy, *IEJ* 45/2 (1995), 144.
72 Marcus and Artzy, *IEJ* 45/2 (1995), 149.
73 Marcus and Artzy, *IEJ* 45/2 (1995), 147-148.
74 As also surmised in Cohen, *Canaanites, Chronologies, and Connections*, 89.

A.5 Hizzin, Tell

Tell Hizzin lies southwest of Baalbek in the Beqa' Valley of modern Lebanon.[75] Excavations uncovered a settlement and cemetery intermittently used between the EBIV/ MBI and Roman periods.[76] The investigation and its finds were never published, yet the discovery of two Egyptian statuary fragments led to the site's mention in studies regarding Egyptian hegemony over the Levant.[77] Genz and Sader have recently published their preliminary results on the Tell Hizzin material, shedding light on these contested fragments as well as other MBA evidence.[78]

The Egyptian evidence reportedly includes two statue fragments as well as a *ꜥnrꜥ* scarab bearing a late Middle Kingdom to Fifteenth Dynasty design.[79] One of the fragments, of unknown context,[80] is the base of a statue with the legs of a standing figure.[81] An inscription in front of the feet offers the nomen and prenomen of Sobekhotep IV,[82] indicating that the statue represented this Thirteenth Dynasty king. The other fragment is most likely the back of a statue preserving an offering formula as well as the name of a count *Ḥp*[...] who has been identified as early Twelfth Dynasty [*Ḏfꜣ=i-*]*ḥpi* 'Djefaihapi', count of Asyut.[83] The fragment was collected from a level deep beneath a conflagration layer of a room filled with pithoi.[84] The latter ceramics are unfortunately missing and so a precise date for this layer cannot be determined.[85] Hence, neither of the two Egyptian fragments can be assigned to a MBA context. Until further excavations at the tell occur, the extent of relations between Egypt and Tell Hizzin remains unknown.

A.6 Ugarit / Ras Shamra

The coastal site of Ugarit is located in modern Syria. The MBA is marked by large multiple graves in its first phase and an urban settlement in its second and third phases.[86] Certain monuments of the latter phases, or Level II, including the temples of Dagan and Baal, as well as the 'North Palace', have recently been assigned to the MBIIC or LBI period.[87] The refinement in the dating of Level II structures warns that other contexts may similarly be attributed to the end of the MBA or beginning of the LBA.

Several Egyptian items from Level II have been utilised as evidence for relations between Ugarit and the Middle Kingdom; however the objects were either mostly retrieved from late MBA contexts or display late MBA, particularly MBIIC, forms. This late date, along with contextual ambiguities, indicates that the material cannot be definitively utilised to show relations between the Levant and the Egyptian Middle Kingdom to early Second Intermediate Period.

Such material includes several pieces of Middle Kingdom statues and sphinxes. One of these is the lower half of a seated statue, its base inscribed with 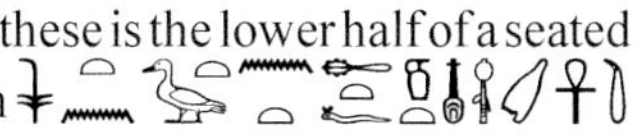 *sꜣ.t nsw.t n.t ẖ.t=f Ḫnm.t-nfr-ḥḏ ꜥnḫ.ti* 'the king's daughter of his body, Khnumetnoferhedj, may she live'.[88] As the princess's name is attested during the Middle Kingdom,[89] several propositions for her identity have been offered. She has been equated with the daughter of Amenemhat II and wife of Senwosret II, her sister Itaweret or Senwosret III's wife,[90] all signifying that she was most likely a Twelfth Dynasty princess. Her statue was retrieved from Locus CH near the temple of Dagan, at the base of Level II.[91] Its position led Ward to infer that the context is contemporary with the Twelfth Dynasty,[92] contrary to Helck's assumption that the statue was deposited during the Hyksos period.[93] Schaeffer, however, suggested that the statue was deliberately mutilated during a hostile event.[94] As this event is associated with the end of the MBA or the beginning of the LBA,[95] the statue could have been imported at any time between the MBIIA and the LBI.

---

75 Genz and Sader, *BAAL* 12 (2008), 183.

76 Genz and Sader, *BAAL* 12 (2008), 184-185; Chehab, *BMB* 9 (1949/1950), 109; Chehab, in *Studi Fenici e Punici*, 167.

77 Galling, *ZDPV* 69 (1953), 90.

78 Genz and Sader, *BAAL* 12 (2008), 183-201; Sader, in *Archaeology of the Ancient Near East* 2, 636-650; Genz and Sader, *Berytus* 53-54 (2010/2011), 133-146.

79 Personal communication with Hélène Sader; personal examination of a photograph of the scarab; Genz and Sader, *BAAL* 12 (2008), 134-135; Chehab, in *Role of the Phoenicians*, 4-5, pls 3 [c], 6 [a]; Chehab, *BMB* 22 (1969), 22 28, pl. 4 [1-2]; Genz and Sader, *BAAL* 12 (2008), 186-187, figs 5, 7.

80 The statue was brought to Chehab by an antiquities dealer who informed him that it came from Tell Hizzin (Genz and Sader, *BAAL* 12 [2008], 184).

81 Genz and Sader, *BAAL* 12 (2008), fig. 5; Chehab, in *Role of the Phoenicians*, pl. 6 [a].

82 Chehab, in *Role of the Phoenicians*, pl. 6 [a]; Montet, *Kêmi* 13 (1954), 76; Genz and Sader, *BAAL* 12 (2008), 184, fig. 5.

83 Genz and Sader, *BAAL* 12 (2008), 185, fig. 7; Chehab, in *Role of the Phoenicians*, pl. 3 [c]; Ahrens, in *Intercultural Contacts in the Ancient Mediterranean*, 300, n. 40.

84 Genz and Sader, *BAAL* 12 (2008), 185; Chehab, in *Atti del I Congresso Internazionale*, 167.

85 Genz and Sader, *BAAL* 12 (2008), 185, 187.

86 Schaeffer, *Syria* 10 (1929), 285-297; Schaeffer, *Syria* 13 (1932), 1-27; Schaeffer, *Syria* 14 (1933), 93-127; Schaeffer, *Syria* 15 (1934), 105-136; Schaeffer, *Syria* 16 (1935), 141-176; Schaeffer, *Syria* 17 (1936), 105-148; Schaeffer, *Syria* 18 (1937), 125-154; Schaeffer, *Syria* 19 (1938), 193-255, 314-334; Schaeffer, *Ugaritica*, vols 1-4, 6-7; Nougayrol et al., *Ugaritica* 5.

87 Yon, *City of Ugarit*, 16.

88 Schaeffer, *Syria* 13 (1932), 20, pl. 14 [1]; Schaeffer, *Ugaritica* 4, 212, fig. 19; Nigro, in *From Relative to Absolute Chronology*, 370, fig. 2.

89 Sabbahy, *SAK* 23 (1996), 349-352; Ward, *UF* 11 (1979), 801.

90 Sabbahy, *SAK* 23 (1996), 350; Ward, *UF* 11 (1979), 801; Perdu, *RdE* 29 (1977), 68-85.

91 Schaeffer, *Syria* 13 (1932), 20; Schaeffer, *Syria* 16 (1935), pl. 36; Ward, *UF* 11 (1979), 801-802.

92 Ward, *UF* 11 (1979), 802.

93 Helck, *UF* 8 (1976), 101-115.

94 Schaeffer, *Cuneiform Texts*, 13; Yon, *City of Ugarit*, 16-18.

95 Schaeffer, *Cuneiform Texts*, 13; Yon, *City of Ugarit*, 18.

Another statuette is the lower half of a triad of an official and two female family members.[96] The official is represented as the 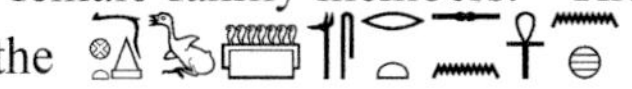 *im.y-rꜣ niw.t mr ṯꜣ.ty S-n-wsr.t-ʿnḫ* 'the overseer of the pyramid-town, vizier,[97] Senwosretankh(u)'.[98] The statuette's artistic and textual features point to a late Twelfth or Thirteenth Dynasty date.[99] It was found in the vicinity of Khnumetnoferhedj's statue.[100] Lack of further details on its context restricts the statuette's use as a marker for Egyptian-Ugaritic relations.

Fragments of Amenemhat III's sphinx(es), numbering either one or two in the literature, were also collected with other statue pieces at the entrance of the temple of Baal (Locus AM).[101] Like Khnumetnoferhedj's statue, the fragmentary state of the sphinxes has led Schaeffer to remark that they were intentionally damaged,[102] creating some uncertainty regarding their date of deposition. Additionally, the temple was in use from at least the MBIIC-LBI period until the late LBA.[103] Hence, the context cannot validate the sphinxes' arrival at Ugarit during Amenemhat III's reign[104] or the MBA.

Likewise, little can be determined from the reported scarabs.[105] Some were evidently found in tombs, others in a votive sanctuary, and a number from unknown contexts. Those from tombs that are dated to the late MBA, namely Tombs 54, 56 and 57, each have one published scarab, although Tomb 57 contained one other scarab of unknown design.[106] The published scarabs display elements of either Levantine or Egyptian origin, such as reclining lions[107] or a Horus falcon with the  sign.[108] Tombs assigned to Level II yielded scarabs of uncertain origin bearing, for instance, the *ʿnrʿ* formula,[109] a standing figure with a falcon's head,[110] and concentric circles.[111] Schaeffer additionally reported an amethyst scarab, possibly of Egyptian origin, but does not provide a drawing or details of its context.[112] So, the insufficient publication of Ugarit's scarab repertoire does not allow for comments on which were imported and which were local. Yet, the inhabitants of Ugarit had evidently adapted the use of scarabs with Egyptian-influenced designs for funerary purposes during the late MBA.

These scarabs provide evidence for contact between Egypt and Ugarit at the end of the MBA, most possibly the late MBIIB or MBIIC period. Because the majority of these small items are from tombs, the Egyptian(-influenced) products were apparently of funerary significance. As for the statuettes, most were retrieved from or adjacent to the acropolis's temples, their precise contexts and dates of deposition remaining uncertain. Therefore, the extent of MBA relations between Ugarit and Egypt cannot be clarified with the available evidence. It is clear that Egyptian items and artistic influences had reached the coastal city by the end of the MBA, possibly as a product of trade, but none of the available data can specifically point to Egyptian diplomatic or political relations with Ugarit.

---

96 Schaeffer, *Syria* 15 (1934), 113, pl. 14; Schaeffer, *Ugaritica* 4, 217, figs 22-23; Montet, *Syria* 15 (1934), 131-133.

97 Ward, *Index*, 31 [225].

98 Ranke, *Personennamen* 1, 279 [4].

99 Ward, *UF* 11 (1979), 803-805.

100 Schaeffer, *Syria* 15 (1934), 113-114.

101 Schaeffer, *Syria* 14 (1933), 120, pl. 15; Schaeffer, *Ugaritica* 4, 223, fig. 25; Schaeffer, *Syria* 16 (1935), pl. 36; Helck, *UF* 8 (1976), 104, n. 39; Ward, *UF* 11 (1979), 802-803; Giveon, in *Ugarit in Retrospect*, 57.

102 Schaeffer, *Cuneiform Texts*, 13; Yon, *City of Ugarit*, 16-18.

103 Yon, *City of Ugarit*, 16-18; al-Maqdissi et al., *Syria* 84 (2007), 36-37.

104 A cylinder seal naming Amenemhat III was purchased and apparently noted to have come from Ugarit. No other contextual data can confirm its provenance. Giveon, in *Ugarit in Retrospect*, 57.

105 Schaeffer, *Syria* 13 (1932), pl. 11 [2]; Schaeffer, *Syria* 14 (1933), 114; Schaeffer, *Syria* 15 (1934), 113-114; Schaeffer, *Syria* 16 (1935), 153; Schaeffer, *Syria* 19 (1938), fig. 14; Schaeffer, *Cuneiform Texts*, pl. 5; Schaeffer, *Ugaritica* 1, figs 59, 113; Schaeffer, *Ugaritica* 2, fig. 21, pls 12, 16. For a brief summary, see Richards, *Anra Scarab*, 124-125; Teissier, *Syro-Palestinian Cylinder Seals*, 1, n. 2.

106 Schaeffer, *Syria* 19 (1938), 220, 241, 246, fig. 14.

107 Ben-Tor's Design Class 9E. Schaeffer, *Syria* 19 (1938), fig. 14 [9569]; Ben-Tor, *Scarabs*, 177.

108 Ben-Tor's Design Class 3A4. Schaeffer, *Syria* 19 (1938), fig. 14 [9871]; Ben-Tor, *Scarabs*, 160-161.

109 Ben-Tor's Design Class 3C. Schaeffer, *Syria* 13 (1932), pl. 11 [2]; Ben-Tor, *Scarabs*, 165-166.

110 Ben-Tor's Design Class 10A2. Schaeffer, *Syria* 13 (1932), pl. 11 [2]; Ben-Tor, *Scarabs*, 178-180.

111 Ben-Tor's Design Class 4. Schaeffer, *Syria* 13 (1932), pl. 11 [2]; Ben-Tor, *Scarabs*, 168-169.

112 Schaeffer, *Syria* 14 (1933), 114.

Appendix B. Translations

Introduction

The section presents the transcription, transliteration and translation of lengthy excerpts from hieroglyphic and hieratic texts examined in Section 2, Chapters 4-6. As with the shorter texts provided within the chapters, only pertinent material has been selected for translation.

Each translation is assigned a number along with entries referring to its provenance (*Prov.*), date (*Chron.*) and associated chapter (*Chapter*).

Transliterations and translations are all by the author, unless otherwise specified. References from which hieroglyphic transcriptions were retrieved can be found under *Ref(s)* or in a table at the end of the translation. The entry *Ref(s)* also includes any further works relied upon in the process of translating these works.

The following notations have been utilised for all the translations in this section as well as in the monograph:

///	lacuna of damaged hieroglyphs
[...]	lacuna of damaged text in transliteration and translation
[ ]	suggested reconstruction of lacuna
( )	addition to or clarification of orthography and grammar
●	Egyptian scribe's punctuation marks (verse points)

Names of postulated non-Egyptian origin have also been kept in transliteration.

B.1 Inscription of the Tomb of Khnumhotep III

Prov. Dahshur

Ref. Allen, *BASOR* 352 (2008), 29-39, pls 1-8.[1]

Chron. Mid-Twelfth Dynasty (reign of Senwosret III)

Chapter 4.3.1.2

1R 

ir.y-pꜥ.t ḥꜣ.ty-ꜥ ḫtm.ty bi.ty smr wꜥ.ty n(.y) mr.wt im.y-rꜣ pr.w wr H̱nm-ḥtp(.w) pri=k m rwt mḥ.tt ꜥḥꜥ=k imi=s wr is

Nobleman, count, seal-bearer of the king of Lower Egypt, sole companion, (worthy) of love, chief steward, Khnumhotep. May you come out of the northern gate and stand in it as a great one.

2H 

ḥtp di [nsw.t Ptḥ pr.t-ḫrw t ḥnḳ.t kꜣ(.w) ꜣpd(.w) n kꜣ n(.y) ir.y-pꜥ.t ḥꜣ.ty-ꜥ ḫtm.ty bi.ty smr] wꜥ.ty mḥ-ib nsw.t m ḏr St.t m ptpt Mnṯ(y)w im.y-rꜣ pr.w wr H̱nm-ḥtp(.w) nb imꜣḫ

An offering which the [king] gives and [Ptah: an invocation offering of bread, beer, beef and fowl for the *kꜣ* of the nobleman, count, seal-bearer of the king of Lower Egypt], sole [companion], confidant of the king in obstructing *St.t* and trampling the *Mnṯ(y)w*, chief steward, Khnumhotep, possessor of reverence.

1C1-2 

ḏd in im.y-rꜣ mšꜥ n(.y) sḳd.w

Speaking by the overseer of the expedition of sailors:

1C2-3 

pḥ [pw iri(.y) r Rṯnw r ini.t] ꜥš n(.y) dmi [n(.y) Wꜣṯi]

[What was done was to] reach [*Rṯnw* to bring] *ꜥš*-wood of the harbour [of *Wꜣṯi*]

1C4-5 ... 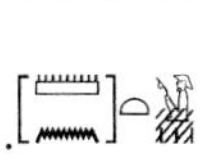

...[Mn]t.(y)w

... [*Mn*]*t.*(*y*)*w*

1D1-2 

hꜣi.t pw [ir ...]

[What was done] was to descend...

---

[1] The section divisions follow Allen's preliminary reconstruction. The transliteration and translation are also reliant on Allen, *BASOR* 352 (2008), 32-37, pls 1-8. Lacuna of missing hieroglyphs are not reflective of actual lacuna measurements.

1D2-3 

[*t3 s*]*m3 n*(.*y*) *K*[*b*]*ny pri.t pw* [*ir...*]

[the landing place] of *K*[*b*]*ny*, [what was done] was to ascend...

1D4-2A2 

[*pw*] *iri.n im.y-r3 mšʿ n*(.*y*) *sḳd.w* [*r pr.w-ḥḳ3*] *n*(.*y*) *Kbny M3*[*k*]*i*

What the overseer of the expedition of sailors did [was to (enter) the palace of the ruler] of *Kbny*, *M3*[*k*]*i*

2A2-3 

ḏd.in=f n=f ptr st (*i*)*n i*[*w*]*=k r dmir n*(.*y*) *W*[*3ṯi*]

Then he said to him: 'What is it, are you towards the harbour of *W*[*3ṯi*]?'

2A4-B4 

[*ḏd.n n=f im.y-r3 mšʿ n*(.*y*) *sḳd.w*] *iṯi gr.t* [*nṯr ʿ3*] *nsw.t-bi.ty S-ḥtp-ib-Rʿ.w m3ʿ-ḫrw idb.wy b3k n=f ḫ3s*[.*t nb.t rḏi.n*] *M3ki* [*n*(.*y*) *Kbny*] *mni=n r Kbny*

[The overseer of the expedition of sailors said to him]: 'Now, after the [great god], king of Upper and Lower Egypt, Sihotepibra (Senwosret III), justified, took possession of the two banks, [every] foreign land worked for him and *M3ki* [of *Kbny*] had let us moor at *Kbny*'

2B4 

sḏm.n=f ḏd.w Mnt.(*y*)*w*

for he had heard that which the *Mnt.*(*y*)*w* had said[2]

2P8-10 

ḏ[...] *m W3*[*ṯi*] *rḏi.in* [*ḥ*]*ḳ3* [*pf n*(.*y*) *Kbny M3ki* ...] *ḥnʿ ʿ3m 100 rḏi*(.*w*) *n=s*[*n*][3]

[...] from *W3*[*ṯi*]. Then [that] ruler [of *Kbny*, *M3ki* ...] gave/let... with 100 *ʿ3m*, they having been given to [them]

2C1-D3 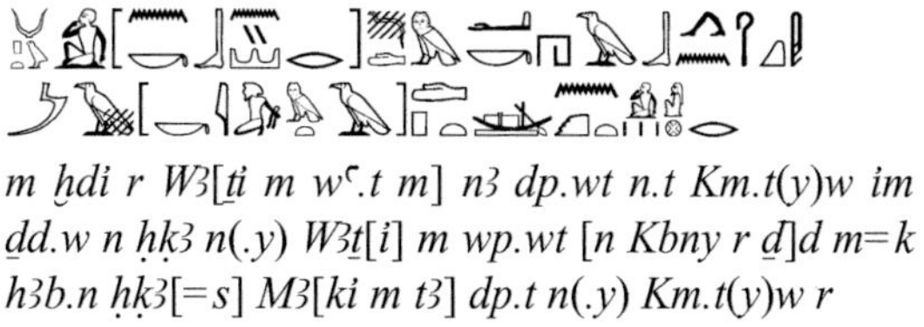

m ḫdi r W3[*ṯi m wʿ.t m*] *n3 dp.wt n.t Km.t*(*y*)*w im ḏd.w n ḥḳ3 n*(.*y*) *W3ṯ*[*i*] *m wp.wt* [*n Kbny r ḏ*]*d m=k h3b.n ḥḳ3*[*=s*] *M3*[*ki m t3*] *dp.t n*(.*y*) *Km.t*(*y*)*w r*

to travel north to *W3*[*ṯi* in one of] the ships of the Egyptian-speakers[4] there, who speak to the ruler of *W3ṯ*[*i*] with a message [from *Kbny*] saying: 'Behold, [her] (*Kbny*'s) ruler *M3ki* has sent word via the ship of the Egyptian-speakers to

2D4-5 

[...]*t=k nb.t rḏi*[...]*n msw m Hb3y w...*

[...] all/every [...] give [...] children of *Hb3y*[5]...

3A1-4 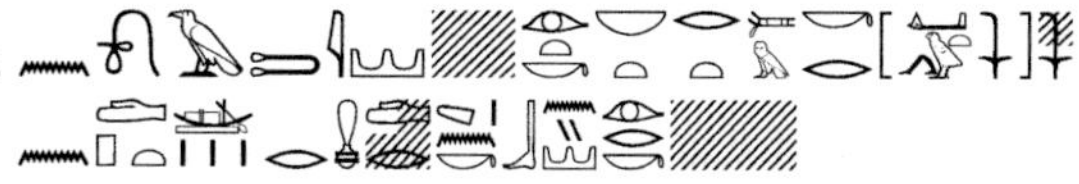

n W3ṯi [...] *iri.t=k nb.t r tm=k r*[*ḏi iwi.t n*]*n n*(.*y*) *dp.wt r dmi*[*r*] *n*(.*y*) *Kbny irr=k* [...]

to *W3ṯi* [...] all you can do to not [let] those ships [return] to the harbour of *Kbny*. You do [...]

3A5-B5 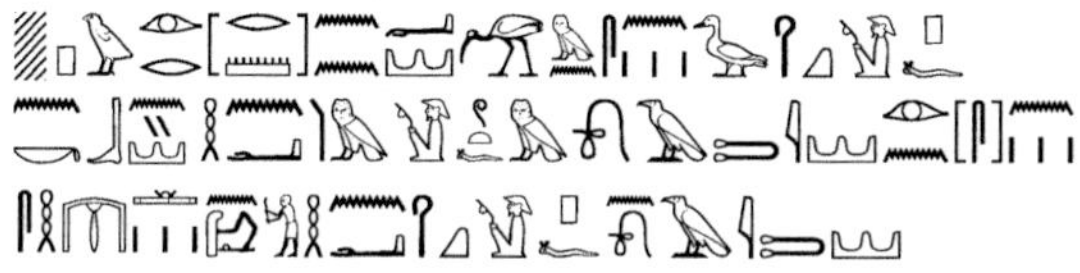

[...] *pw ir* [*Rm*]*nn gmi.n=sn s3 ḥḳ3 pf n*(.*y*) *Kbny ḥnʿ ʿ3m 100 tf m W3ṯi iri.n=*[*s*]*n sḫ n ʿḥ3 ḥnʿ ḥḳ3 pf n*(.*y*) *W3iṯ*

[...] was done to [*Rm*]*nn*, they had found the son of that ruler of *Kbny* with those 100 *ʿ3m* at *W3ṯi*, and they had made a plan to fight with that ruler of *W3iṯ*

3P1-4 

[...*sn ...w...*] *ʿ.wy=sn* [...*ḥḳ3*] *pf n*(.*y*) *Kbny* [...] *iri.in=f mḏ3.t ḥr* [...]

[... they/them/their ...] their two arms [...] that ruler of *Kbny* [...] then he made a letter about [...]

3P6-10 

[...] *ḥr=k pw nfr mrr.w* [... *m...*]*f* [*mi md.t*] *mḏ3.t tn* [...*t* ...]*n wḏ-nsw.t ḏd n ḥḳ3* [... *m*]*d.t n.t mḏ3.t tn m3ʿ.t n=k r stp-*[*s3*...] *dp.wt* [...*ḥb*]*s ʿw.y=f sḫ pn n*(.*y*) *ir*[*r=k... t... n... i... ṯ..*.]

[...] that beautiful face of yours which [...] loves [... according to the speech of] this letter [...] the decree of the king spoken to the ruler [...] the speech of this letter which was despatched to you concerning the palace [...] the ships [...] his two arms cover that plan of [your] doing [...]

---

2 Or, as Allen translates it: *sḏm nf ḏd.w Mn.tyw* 'for those things that the Asiatic Bedouin said had been heard' (*BASOR* 352 [2008], 34, n. 10).

3 Or *rḏi.n=sn* 'they had given/let'.

4 For this translation, see Allen, *BASOR* 352 (2008), 34-35.

5 Following Allen's suggestion of a Middle Egyptian orthography representing the Semitic name *hbry* or *hbly*, the toponym may be related to the names of such modern locales as هابيل *Habeel* or حبالين *Ḥbaleen*, both in the district of modern Jbeil. See Wardini, *Lebanese Place-Names*, 199, 215.

3C1 

[ḥkꜣ pf n(.y) Wꜣṯ]i [n ḥm=f r ḏ]d in kꜣ=k nṯr nfr nb tꜣ.wy mrr.w [nṯr.w ḥss].w Spd.w nb ḫꜣs.wt Ḥw.t-Ḥr.w nb.t Kbny siꜣ=f [m] ḥm n(.y) stp-sꜣ [...]

[that ruler of *Wꜣṯi* to his majesty saying]: 'Your *kꜣ*, the good god, lord of the two lands, whom [the gods] love and whom Sopdu, lord of the foreign lands, and Hathor, lady of *Kbny*, [bless,] it will recognise in the majesty of the palace [...]'

3D2-4 

[...]r Rmnn [... W]ꜣiṯ ḥn[ꜥ ...] im r ḏꜣ.t ḥn(.w) wꜣḥ ḥr tꜣ ꜥꜣm wnn ḥr pgꜣ

[...] to *Rmnn* [... *W*]*ꜣiṯ* with [...] there to cross the brook/canal and set down upon the land of the *ꜥꜣm* and be on the entrance/mouth/battlefield[6]

ON4-5 

[...] spr [n]n n(.y) dp.[w]t [r] ẖnw m i[...] ḫdw im=sn r Kbny

[...] arrival of those ships [to] the palace with [...] travelling north in them to *Kbny*

ON5-OS5 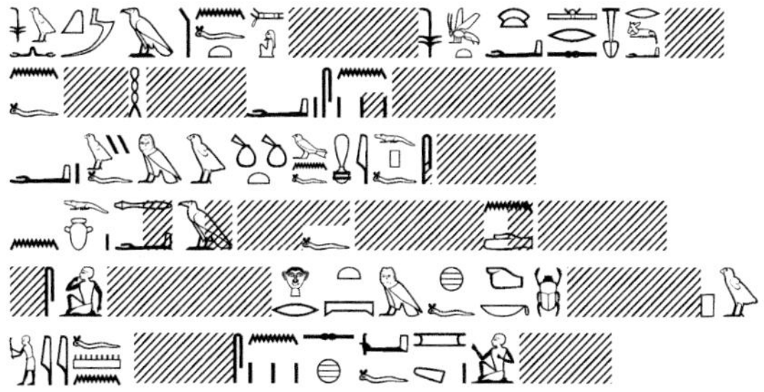

[...] sw n ḳmꜣ n=f Tm [...] nsw.t-bi.ty ḫꜥ r smꜣ r iwꜥ [...] n=f [...ḥ...] ꜥ.w=sn [...] ꜥ.wy=f m wgg.t n=f mi msḥ pf s[...] n ꜣd ib ꜥꜣ[...f ...n d ...]s [...] ḥr.t m ḫfꜥ=k ḫpr [...] pw ḥwy=f mn [...]=sn sḫ=f mr[.wt...]

[...] him, Atum has not created for himself [...] king of Upper and Lower Egypt who has appeared to unite and to inherit [...] to him [...] their arm [...] his two arms from that which is woeful, like that crocodile [...] of the aggressive, great [...] the sky in your grasp, become [...] he smites [...] them, seizing the underlings [...]

6 The latter translation is preferred by Allen in *BASOR* 352 (2008), 36.

B.2 El-Lahun Papyri

Prov. el-Lahun
Ref. See Figure B.1
Chron. Mid-Twelfth Dynasty to early Second Intermediate Period
Chapter 4.3.5.2
Figure B.1

P Berlin 10050 (Senwosret III, Year 6)

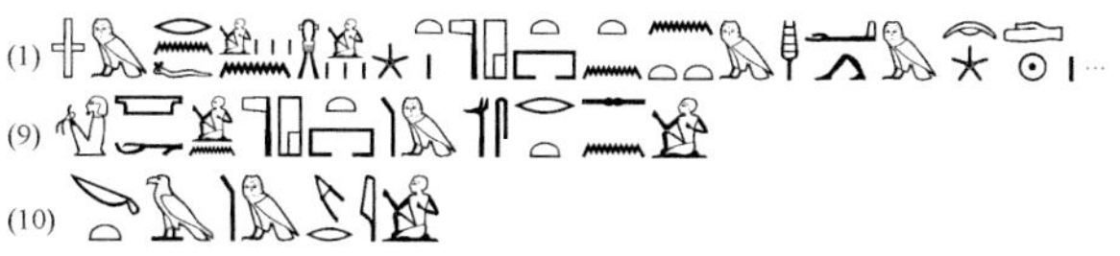

(1) *im.y-rn=f n(.y) sꜣ.w(t) wn.(w)t ḥw.t-nṯr tn n.tt m ꜥḥꜥ m ꜣbd ...*
(9) *iry ꜥꜣ n(.y) ḥw.t-nṯr ꜥꜣm S-n-wsr.t*
(10) *sf.ty ꜥꜣm Mri*
(1) List of phyles of the priesthood of this temple who are in attendance in the month...
(9) Door-keeper of a temple,[7] *ꜥꜣm* Senwosret[8]
(10) Butcher,[9] *ꜥꜣm* Meri[10]

UC 32157 (Senwosret III to Amenemhat III)

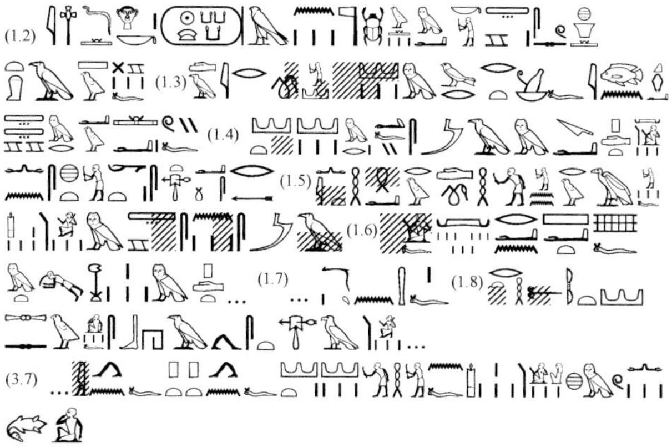

(1.2) inḏ-ḥr=k Ḫꜥ-kꜣ.w-Rꜥ.w Ḥr.w=n nṯr ḫpr.w mk tꜣ swsḫ tꜣš.w=f (1.3) dꜣir [ḫꜣs.wt] m wrr.t=f ink tꜣ.wy m r-ꜥ.w ꜥ.wy=f (1.4) ḫꜣs.t [...] ḫꜣs.wt m rmn(.wy)=fy smꜣ Pd.t(y)w nn sḫ.t ḫt sti šsr (1.5) n [it]ḥ rwd ḥwi.n nrw=f Iwn.t(y)w m tꜣ=sn smꜣ (1.6) [...]=f pḏ.t 9 rdi.n šꜥt=f mw.t ḫꜣ.w m Pd.t(yw) ... (1.7)... ns n(.y) ḥm=f (1.8) rtḥ St.t ṯs.w=f sbḥꜣ St.tyw...
(3.7) [iyi].n=f ptpt.n=f ḫꜣs.wt ḥwi.n=f Iwn.t(y)w ḥmw snd

(1.2) Hail to you Khakaura (Senwosret III), our Horus, divine of forms, protector of the land, extender of its boundaries, (1.3) who defeats [the foreign lands] with his crown, uniter of the two lands with the actions of his arms (1.4) [...] the foreign lands with his two arms, who slaughters the *Pd.t(y)w* without a blow of a thing (weapon), who shoots an arrow (1.5) without drawing the string, he whose dread has struck the *Iwn.t(y)w* in their land, he whose [...] slaughters (1.6) the 9 bows, he whose terror/massacre causes the death of thousands of *Pd.t(yw)* ... (1.7) ... the tongue of

7 Ward, *Index*, 62 [502].
8 Ranke, *Personennamen* 1, 279 [1].
9 Ward, *Index*, 149 [1286].
10 Ranke, *Personennamen* 1, 159 [22].

his majesty [(1.8)] is the restraint of *St.t* and it is his utterances which cause the *St.tyw* to flee...
[(3.7)] He has [come], having trampled the foreign lands, having struck the *Ἰwn.t(y)w* who are ignorant of fear ...

P Berlin 10033 (Amenemhat III, Year 15)

(3) 

(3) *šmsw* [...*ʿ3*]*m S-n-wsr.t*

(3) (Brought by the) retainer,[11] [*ʿ3*]*m* Senwosret

P Berlin 10066 (Amenemhat III, Year 18)

(3) 

(3) *ini.n šmʿw* (4)*ʿ3m S-n-wsr.t-snb*

(3) Brought by the singer,[12] (4) *ʿ3m* Senwosretseneb

P Berlin 10021 (Amenemhat III, Year 18)

(1) 

(1) *imi ini.t*... (3) *ʿ3m Ἰ-ʿr3 1 m wn.t rḥ.ty Ḥtpi*[...]

(1) Let... bring... (3) *ʿ3m Ἰ-ʿr3*[13] 1 from the *wn.t* and his dependant/son Hotepi[...]

P Berlin 10047 (Amenemhat III, middle of reign)

(4) 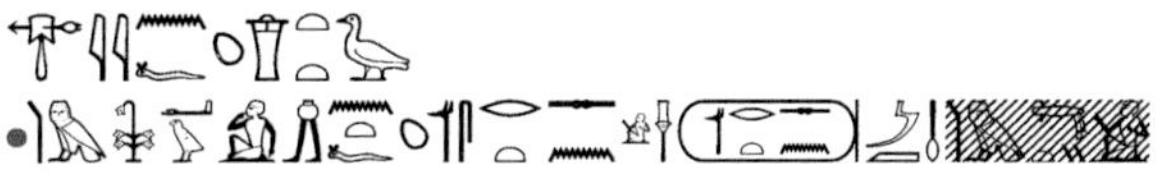

(4) *Sty-n=f s3 S3-B3st.t*

(8) *ʿ3m šmʿ.w Ἰni-it=f s3 S-n-wsr.t Sḫm-S-n-wsr.t m3ʿ-ḫrw* [*ʿ3m Šd.ty*]

(4) *Sty-n=f*'s[14] son Sabastet[15]

(8) *ʿ3m*, the singer, Initef's[16] son Senwosret of *Sḫm-S-n-wsr.t*, justified, and [*ʿ3m* Shedty][17]

P Berlin 10081C (Amenemhat III, Year 27)

(R3) 

(R3) *ini.n šmsw ʿ3m* [*Sty-r3*]

(R3) Brought by the retainer, *ʿ3m* [*Sty-r3*][18]

UC 32191 (Amenemhat III, Year 35)

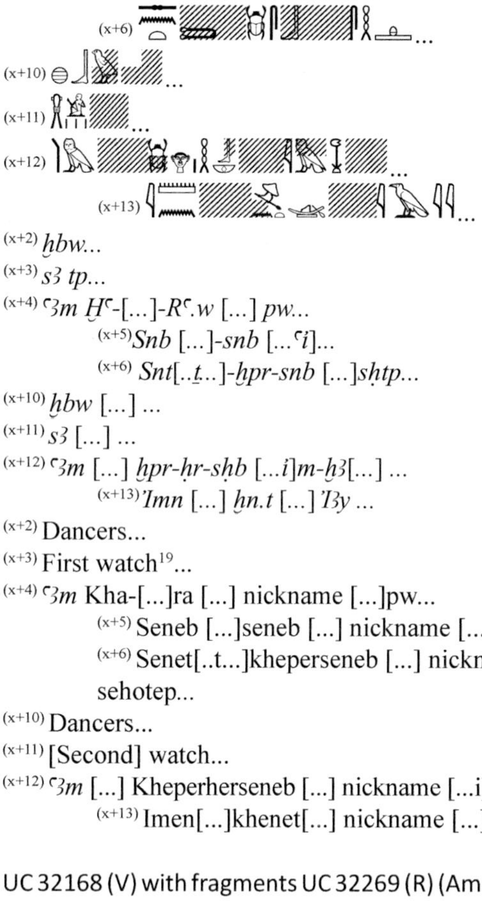

(x+2) *ḫbw*...

(x+3) *s3 tp*...

(x+4) *ʿ3m Ḫʿ*-[...]-*Rʿ.w* [...] *pw*...

(x+5)*Snb* [...]-*snb* [...*ʿi*]...

(x+6) *Snt*[..*t*..]-*ḫpr-snb* [...]*sḥtp*...

(x+10) *ḫbw* [...] ...

(x+11) *s3* [...] ...

(x+12) *ʿ3m* [...] *ḫpr-ḥr-sḫb* [...*i*]*m-ḫ3*[...] ...

(x+13)*Ἰmn* [...] *ḫn.t* [...] *Ἰ3y* ...

(x+2) Dancers...

(x+3) First watch[19]...

(x+4) *ʿ3m* Kha-[...]ra [...] nickname [...]pw...

(x+5) Seneb [...]seneb [...] nickname [...ai]...

(x+6) Senet[..t...]kheperseneb [...] nickname [...] sehotep...

(x+10) Dancers...

(x+11) [Second] watch...

(x+12) *ʿ3m* [...] Kheperherseneb [...] nickname [...i]mkha[...] ...

(x+13) Imen[...]khenet[...] nickname [...] Iay [...] ...

UC 32168 (V) with fragments UC 32269 (R) (Amenemhat III, Year 45)

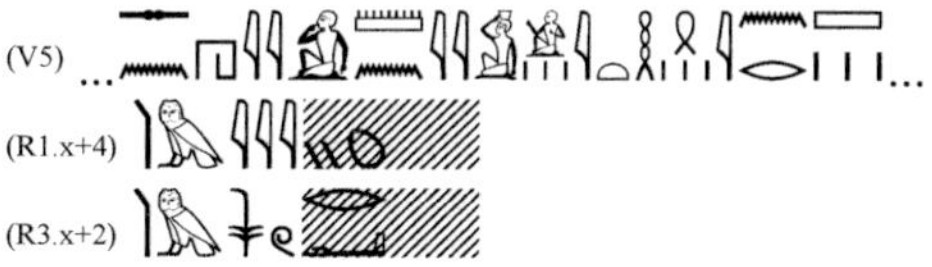

(V5) ... *snhy mny.w itḥ.w inr.w*...

(R1.x+4) *ʿ3m Yiy*[...]

(R3.x+2) *ʿ3m Sw*[*rʿ*...]

(V5) ...Register of enlisted workers: stone-haulers...

(R1.x+4) *ʿ3m* Yiy[...]

(R3.x+2) *ʿ3m* Su[ra...]

UC 32196 (Amenemhat IV)

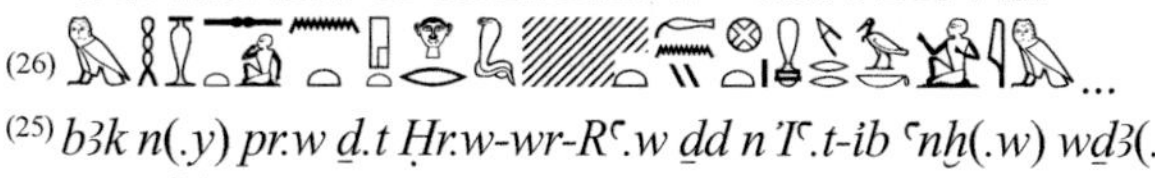

(25) *b3k n(.y) pr.w ḏ.t Ḥr.w-wr-Rʿ.w ḏd n Ἰʿ.t-ib ʿnḫ(.w) wḏ3(.w) s(nb.w)* (26) *m ḥs.t n.t Ḥw.t-ḥr* [*nb*].*t Kpny mi mrr b3k im*...

(25) The servant of the estate, Horuwerra speaks to Iatib, may he live, prosper and be healthy, (26) in the favour of Hathor, [lady] of *Kpny*, as the servant there wishes...

11 Ward, *Index*, 175 [1517].
12 Ward's 'musician' (*Index*, 175 [1514]).
13 Not attested in Ranke, *Personennamen*.
14 Not attested in Ranke, *Personennamen*.
15 Ranke, *Personennamen* 1, 281 [19].
16 A similar name, *Ἰn=f* is attested (Ranke, *Personennamen* 1, 10 [36]).
17 A similar name, *Šd.t* is attested (Ranke, *Personennamen* 1, 331 [33]).
18 Ranke, *Personennamen* 1, 322 [20].

19 Translation as suggested in Collier and Quirke, *Accounts*, 92-93.

P Berlin 10010 (Amenemhat III [?], Year 15)

ini.n sš n(.y) ꜥꜣm.w Sn.t sꜣ S-n-wsr.t-s[nb]
Brought by the scribe of the *ꜥꜣm.w*, Senet,[20] son of Senwosretseneb[21]

UC 32058 (Amenemhat IV [?]), Year 2)

(7) *im.t-pr iri.t n(.y) wꜥb ḥr sꜣ n(.y) Spd.w nb iꜣb.tt Wꜣḥ ...*
(9) *... nts rdi=s* (10) *n mry=s nb m nꜣy=s (n.y) ẖrd(.w) msi=s n=i iw=i ḥr rdi.t n=s pꜣ ꜥꜣm.w tp 4* (11) *rdi.n n=i pꜣy=i sn ḫtm.w kfꜣ-ib n(.y) ḫrp kꜣ.t ꜥnḫ-rn...*
(7) Deed of conveyance made by the *wꜥb*-priest in charge of a phyle of Sopdu, lord of the East, Wah ...
(9) ... It is she who may give (10) to any one she wishes of her children whom she bears/bore for me. I give her the four *ꜥꜣm.w* (11) given to me by my brother, the trustworthy sealer of the director of works, Ankhren...

UC 32295 ([?], Year 2+x)

(6) *...ꜥꜣm.t* [...]
(6) ...*ꜥꜣm.t* [...]

P Berlin 10244 a, c, d, e ([?], Year 9)

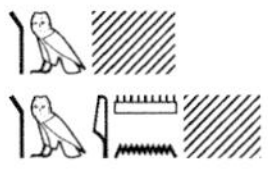

ꜥꜣm [...]
ꜥꜣm Imn[...]
ꜥꜣm [...]
ꜥꜣm Imen[...]

UC 32151B, (V) ([?], Year 24)

(x+4) [...] *im.y-rꜣ mšꜥ n(.y) ꜥꜣm* [...]
(x+5) *ꜥꜣm S-n-wsr.t* [...]
(x+6) [...]*ki*[...]
(x+7) *Ḫnm*[..*w*...]
(x+4) [...] overseer of the expedition of *ꜥꜣm*[22] [...]
(x+5) *ꜥꜣm* Senwosret[...]
(x+6) [...]ki[...]
(x+7) Khnum[..w...]

UC 32167 ([?], Year 29)

(4) *swn.t ḫr-ꜥ n im.y-rꜣ ḫtm.t Šps.t sꜣ Iḥy-snb wꜥr.t mḥ.tt...*
(7) *ꜥꜣm.t ꜥḥiꜣ.t=f Km.tn=i*
(8) *Km.n=i Spdw-m-mr=i*
(9) *Mꜥšy 2 ꜣbd 3*
(10) [...]*ꜥm* [...*bnwy*]
(4) Transfer deed of the assistant to the treasurer Shepset's son Ihyseneb of the northern administrative division...
(7) *ꜥꜣm.t* Akhiatef[23] Kemetni[24]
(8) Kemeni[25] Sopduemmeri[26]
(9) *Mꜥšy*[27] 2 years and 3 months
(10) [...]*ꜥm* [...*bnwy*]

P Berlin 10106

[...] *ꜥꜣm S-n-wsr.t* [...]
[...] *ꜥꜣm* Senwosret [...]

P Berlin 10391 a-e

[...] *ꜥꜣm.t*
[...] *ꜥꜣm.t*

UC 32124

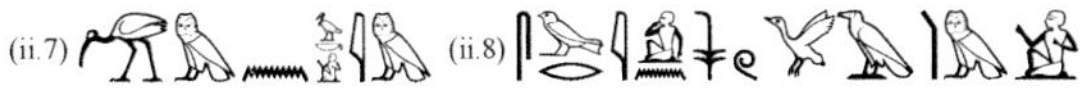

(ii.7) *gmi.n bꜣk im* (ii.8) *swri.n sw Pꜣ-ꜥꜣm*
((ii.7) The servant there found (ii.8) that *Pꜣ-ꜥꜣm* had drunk it

UC 32201

(6) ... *iw rdi.n=i n=f ḥsb 3*
(7) *im.y-rn=f iry*
(10) *ꜥꜣm n(.y) ḥw.t Iḳr*

20 Ranke, *Personennamen* 1, 296 [21].
21 Ranke, *Personennamen* 1, 279 [6].
22 Ward, *Index*, 29 [206].

23 Not attested in Ranke, *Personennamen*. Possibly not of Egyptian origin. See Ranke, *Personennamen* 1, 71 [2].
24 Ranke, *Personennamen* 1, 345 [24].
25 Ranke, *Personennamen* 1, 345 [10].
26 Ranke, *Personennamen* 1, 306 [19].
27 Not attested in Ranke, *Personennamen*. Possibly not of Egyptian origin.

(6) ... I have allocated for him 3 workmen
(7) List of them:
(10) ꜥ3m of the administrative district, *Ỉḳr*[28]

UC 32098D (V)

(1) 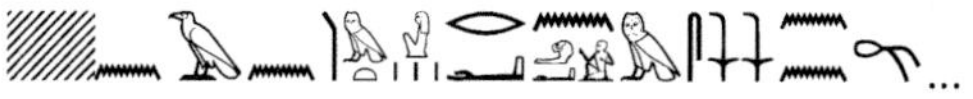

(1) [...] *n3 n(.y) ꜥ3m.wt rḏi n ḥ3.ty-ꜥ m snn...*
(1) [...] those *ꜥ3m.wt* given to the count in a document...

UC 32286

(5) ... 

(5) ...*ꜥ3m (?) ḥw.t ꜥn*[...]
(5) ...*ꜥ3m* (?) of the administrative district, *ꜥn*[...]

UC 32130

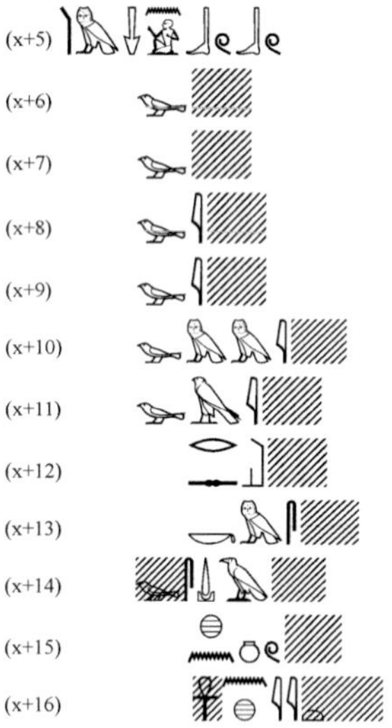

(x+5) *ꜥ3m Sn-bwbw*
(x+6) *šri(?)*[29] [...]
(x+7) *šri(?)* [...]
(x+8) *šri(?)* [...]
(x+9) *šri(?)* [...]
(x+10) *šri(?) mmi*[...]
(x+11) *šri(?) Ḥr-i*[...]
(x+12) *Rs*[...]
(x+13) *Kms*[...]
(x+14) [*šri(?)*] *Sḏ3*[...]
(x+15) *Ḫnw* [...]
(x+16) [ꜥ]*nḫy*[*t*...]
(x+5) *ꜥ3m* Senbubu[30]
(x+6) Minor(?) [...]
(x+7) Minor(?) [...]
(x+8) Minor(?) [...]
(x+9) Minor(?) [...]
(x+10) Minor(?) Memi[...]
(x+11) Minor(?) Hori[...]
(x+12) Res[...]
(x+13) Kemes[...]
(x+14) Minor(?) Sedja[...]
(x+15) Khenu [...]
(x+16) [A]nkhy[t...]

UC 32276

(F.x+6) 

(F.x+6) [...] *s3=f S3.t-ꜥ3m(?)* [...]
(F.x+6) [...] his son Sat-*ꜥ3m*(?) [...]

UC 32101 H (large fragment)

(x+7) 

(x+7) *ꜥ3m Nfr-iw*[...]
(x+7) *ꜥ3m* Noferiu[...]

UC 32127 (V)

(x+2) *ꜥ3m.t Nḥy-n=i ḥr mty n(.y) s3* [*M*...]
(x+3) *Ỉ-šri ini*
(x+4) [...]*g3w (?) ḥr ꜥ3m* [...]
(x+2) *ꜥ3m.t* Nehyeni[31] for controller of a phyle, [M...]
(x+3) Isheri,[32] brought
(x+4) [...]gaw (?), for *ꜥ3m* [...]

UC 32143B

(x+17) 

(x+17) *twt.w 1 ꜥ3m(?)* [...]
(x+17) 1 statue for *ꜥ3m*(?) [...]

UC 32143E

[...*tp*] *Ṯ3.t ꜥ3m Sn.t s3 Ḫꜥ-ḫpr-Rꜥ.w* [...]
[...] vizier staff (?) *ꜥ3m* Senet's son Khakheperra[33] [...]

UC 32147G (V)

ꜥ3m.t 12 (?)
ꜥ3m.t 12 (?)

[28] Translated as 'foundation' in Collier and Quirke, *Letters*, 105. It could also be the workman's name (Ranke, *Personennamen* 1, 47 [16]).

[29] Following Collier and Quirke who interpret the sparrow as a sign indicating minority in age (Collier and Quirke, *Accounts*, 51). It could otherwise point to minority in rank.

[30] For a similar name, see Ranke, *Personennamen* 1, 94 [25].

[31] Ranke, *Personennamen* 1, 207 [19].

[32] Not attested in Ranke, *Personennamen*.

[33] Ranke, *Personennamen* 1, 264 [17].

TEXT	DATE	CONTEXT	ASIATIC(S)	REPRESENTATION	REFERENCE(S)
P BERLIN 10050	S III Year 6	VT	2 x m	marked as attendees at work	Borchardt, *ZÄS* 37 (1899), 97-98; *Congresso*, 296
UC 32157	S III to A III	O, lot 55.1	3 groups: *Pd.tyw*, *ꞽwn.tyw*, *St.tyw*	in Hymns to Senwosret III	*Religious*, 16-19
P BERLIN 10033	A III Year 15	VT	1 x m	in recording temple activities; possibly delivered letter	Luft, *Archiv*, P 10033
P BERLIN 10066	A III Year 18	VT	1 x m	in recording temple activities; delivered letter	Luft, *Archiv*, P 10066
P BERLIN 10021	A III Year 18	VT	2 x m	as retrieved from *wn.t*-camp; possibly allocated to work	Luft, *Urkunden*, 43-48
P BERLIN 10047	mid-A III	VT	4 x m	marked as absent from work	Luft, *Urkunden*, 91-96
P BERLIN 10004	A III Year 21	VT	2 x m 1 x f	3 marked as allocated to work; an additional male with title 'overseer of the expedition of *ꜥꜣm.w*'	*Congresso*, 297
P BERLIN 10081C	A III Year 27	VT	1 x m	in recording temple activities; delivered letter	Luft, *Urkunden*, 105-107
UC 32191	A III Year 35	O, lot 41.1	5 x m	marked as attendees at local festival ('cloth of Khakheperra'), regional festival ('sailing of Hathor') and national festival (festivals of Sokar and Nebkauhor)	*Accounts*, 92-95
P BERLIN 10002	A III Year 36	VT	7 x m 2 x f	as singers for the Residence	*Congresso*, 292-295
P BERLIN 10071	A III Year 36	VT	1 x m	as singer sent to institution	*Congresso*, 296
P BERLIN 10228E, 10323A, 10111A	A III Year 37	VT	1 x m	in letter by overseer of sealers to nomarch Senwosret's son Khakheperraseneb requesting not to send Asiatics for work	*Congresso*, 297
UC 32168, UC 32269 (R)	A III Year 45	O, lot 6.21	2 x m	as stone-haulers; marked as attendees at work	*Accounts*, 56-59
UC 32196	A IV	O, lot 3.2	-	servant in favour of Hathor, lady of Byblos; otherwise of Egyptian ancestry	*Religious*, 48-49
P BERLIN 10010	(A III?) Year 15	VT	-	title related to Asiatics ('scribe of the *ꜥꜣm.w*'); otherwise of Egyptian ancestry	Kaplony-Heckel, *Handschriften* 1, 5 [8]
UC 32058	(A IV?) Year 2	O, lot 1.1	4 x m	as bestowed to Wah's wife in a deed of conveyance from Wah's brother Ankhren (possible connection to UC 32167 and UC 32295)	*Religious*, 104-105
UC 32295	(?) Year 2+x	O, lot 2.15	1 x f	fragmentary (possible connection to UC 32058 and UC 32167)	*Religious*, 122-123
P BERLIN 10244 A, C, D, E	(?) Year 9	VT	2 x m	fragmentary	Kaplony-Heckel, *Handschriften* 1, 133 [317]
UC 32151B (V)	(?) Year 24	O	3 x m	fragmentary; an additional male with title 'overseer of the expedition of *ꜥꜣm*'	*Accounts*, 264-265
UC 32167	(?) Year 29	O, lot 1.2	4 x f	as transferred to the treasurer's son (possible connection to UC 32058 and UC 32295)	*Religious*, 118-119
P BERLIN 10034	-	VT	1 x m	marked as absent from work	*Congresso*, 296; *AÄ* 2, 28
P BERLIN 10046	-	VT	? x m	as attendants of temple of Anubis	*Congresso*, 293
P BERLIN 10055	-	VT	2 x m	as *ḏꜣi*-priests; deliverers of *inw*-taxes to temple of Anubis	*Congresso*, 296
P BERLIN 10106	-	VT	1 x m	fragmentary	Kaplony-Heckel, *Handschriften* 1, 48 [88]
P BERLIN 10391 A-E	-	VT	1 x f	fragmentary	Kaplony-Heckel, *Handschriften* 1, 227 [576]
P BERLIN 10287	-	VT	4 x m	marked as attendees at work	*AÄ* 2, 29
UC 32124	-	O, lot 17.1	1 x m	reported by servant to have drunk honey	*Letters*, 58-59
UC 32201	-	O, lot 6.4	1 x m	in letter to overseer of the interior from Senbi informing him that the overseer had sailed south with three workmen and *ꜥꜣm*	*Letters*, 104-105
UC 32098D (V)	-	O	? x f	in fragmentary letter possibly involving land rights or inheritance	*Religious*, 106-107
UC 32286	-	O, lot 2.6	1 x m	as belonging to the administrative district *ꜥn*(?)	*Religious*, 120-121

FIGURE B.1. EL-LAHUN PAPYRI REPRESENTING ASIATICS AND LEVANTINE TOPONYMS (1/2).

TEXT	DATE	CONTEXT	ASIATIC(S)	REPRESENTATION	REFERENCE(S)
UC 32130	-	O, lot 6.18	12 x *ꜥ3m* (?)	fragmentary accounts document; 11 names following *ꜥ3m;* seven *šri*(?) could also be foreign	*Accounts,* 50-51
UC 32276	-	O	1 x m	fragmentary	*Accounts,* 132-133
UC 32101H	-	O	1 x m	fragmentary; possibly temple staff member	*Accounts,* 200-201
UC 32127 (V)	-	O	1 x m 2 x f	fragmentary	*Accounts,* 224-225
UC 32143B	-	O	1 x m (?)	fragmentary; possibly temple staff member; among list of statues given to temple staff	*Accounts,* 250-251
UC 32143E	-	O	1 x m	fragmentary	*Accounts,* 252-253
UC 32147G (V)	-	O	12 (?) x f	fragmentary	*Accounts,* 258-259

FIGURE B.1. EL-LAHUN PAPYRI REPRESENTING ASIATICS AND LEVANTINE TOPONYMS (2/2), WITH NOTATIONS ON THEIR DATE AND BIBLIOGRAPHICAL REFERENCES.

Notes: A: Amenemhat
S: Senwosret
VT: Rubbish heap north of the Valley Temple
O: Settlement occupation levels
m: male
f: female

Religious: Collier and Quirke, *Religious, Literary.*
Accounts: Collier and Quirke, *Accounts.*
Letters: Collier and Quirke, *Letters.*
Congresso: Luft, in *Sesto Congresso* 2.

B.3 Mit Rahina Daybook[34]

Prov. Mit Rahina
Refs Farag, *RdE* 32 (1980), 75-82; Posener, *JSSEA* 12/1 (1982), 7-8; Altenmüller and Moussa, *SAK* 18 (1991), 1-48; Dantong, *JAC* 14 (1999), 45-66; Marcus, *E&L* 17 (2007), 137-190.
Chron. Mid-Twelfth Dynasty (reign of Amenemhat II)
Chapter 4.3.7

Despatching armies (M7-8)

... mꜣꜥ mšꜥ ir Ḫnty-š [...] *s.t ḥꜣw tp wnw.t nb.t n.t bꜣk.t n nsw.t rdi r-ḫt n(.y) Sḫm-ꞽmn-m-ḥꜣ.t mꜣꜥ mšꜥ ḥnꜥ im.y-rꜣ mnfꜣ.t mšꜥ r ḫbꜣ St.t ꞽwꜣ*

... despatching of an expedition to *Ḫnty-š* [...] every service/duty of taxes for the king to be given under the authority of *Sḫm-ꞽmn-m-ḥꜣ.t*. Despatching of an expedition with the overseer of soldiers[35] and the expedition to hack up the *St.t* of *ꞽwꜣ*.

Offering of cultic objects (M9-10)

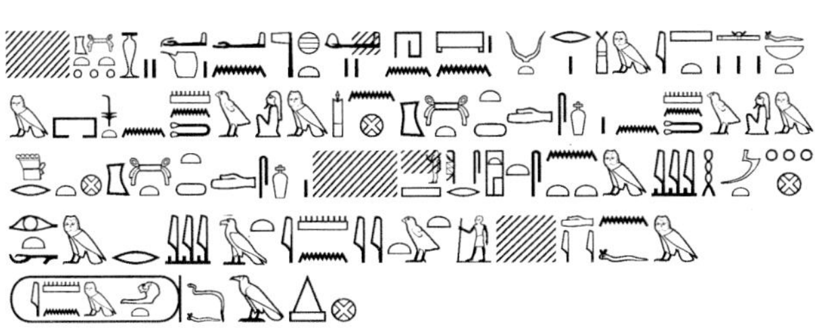

[...] *ḥm.t St.t ḥs(.t) 2 iꜥi 1 ꜥmn(.y) ḥ.t-nṯr 2 hn 1 n wpt rꜣ ꜥpr m iš.wt=f nb.(w)t m pr.w-nsw.t n Mnṯw m ꞽwn(i) ḥm.t St.t ds 1 n Mnṯw m Ḏr.t(i) ḥm.t St.t ds 1* [... *rp.wt?*] *šms(.t) r ḥw.t=s n.tt m Sḫ.t-Ḥmꜣ.t iri.t ḫt im.y-rꜣ sḫ.tyw ꞽmny twt* [...] *dy n=f m Ḏfꜣ-ꞽmn-m-ḥꜣ.t*

[...] *St.t* copper: 2 *ḥs.t*-jars; 1 hand-washing object; 2 arms of incense; 1 *hn*-box for the opening of the mouth ceremony, equipped with all its possessions from the king's palace. For Montu of Armant: Of *St.t* copper, 1 *ds*-vessel. For Montu of Tod: Of *St.t* copper, 1 *ds*-vessel; [... statue of female?] presented to her house/temple which is in *Sḫ.t-Ḥmꜣ.t*. The making (with) wood of a statue of the overseer of field-workers, Imeny [...], here it is in *Ḏfꜣ-ꞽmn-m-ḥꜣ.t*.

Visit(?) and goods from *Kꜣš* and of *Wbꜣ.t-Sp.t* (M11-12)

[...*Kꜣ*]*š n.w Wbꜣ.t-Sp.t ḥr bꜣk.wt=sn in(i).n=sn mꜥ=sn snṯr dbn 23752 ḥm.w dbn 24 ḥmꜣgt ḥkꜣ.t 1 25/32 wḏꜣ(.w) r-gs ḏꜥm dbn 1¾ (w)ḏꜣ(.w r-gs) wꜣḏ dbn 120 st(y) ḥkꜣ.t 11¾ šꜣsḫ ḥkꜣ.t 2¼ šꜣb.t ḥkꜣ.t ⅜ pḏ.t 4 šsr 20* [...*ti.w tp.w*] *ꜥꜣ.t nꜥꜥ.t 1 šsꜣ.wt ẖꜣr 280 nbs ẖꜣr 5 ḫt wrs 7 mšš ꜥꜣ 15 kꜣ 3 wnḏw 14 iꜣr.t 164 sr 1 sḏ 11 hbn(y) 1*

[...*Kꜣ*]*š* and of *Wbꜣ.t-Sp.t* with their *bꜣk.wt* (tribute?). They had brought with them: 23752 *dbn* of incense; 24 *dbn* of *ḥm.w*-stands(?); 1 25/32 *ḥkꜣ.t* and a remainder of carnelian; 1¾ *dbn* and a remainder of electrum; 120 *dbn* of malachite; 11¾ *ḥkꜣ.t* of yellow (Nubian) ochre; 2¼ *ḥkꜣ.t* of *šꜣsḫ*-plant; ⅜ *ḥkꜣ.t* of *šꜣb.t*-plant; 4 bows; 20 arrows; [...?] 1 block of undecorated precious stone; 280 sacks of *šsꜣ.wt*; 5 sacks of *nbs*-plant. Of wood: 7 headrests; 15 *mšš*-wooden rods. 3 bulls, 14 short-horned cattle, 164 wigs, 1 giraffe, 11 tails, 1 (log?) of ebony.

Visit and goods from *St.t* Asiatics (M12-13)

[...] *iw(i).t m wḏb tp msi.w ḥkꜣ.w n.w St.t in(i).n=sn ḥḏ dbn 220* [...*ꜥ.wt iri m wnḏ.w*] *5[6] ꜥꜣm 1002 ḏḥ.ti dbn 6 sš.w dbn 55*

[...] The coming with bowed-head of the children of the rulers of *St.t*. They brought: 220 *dbn* of silver; [...] 5[6 small cattle made as short-horned cattle]; 1002 *ꜥꜣm*; 6 *dbn* of lead; 55 *dbn* of white lead.

Return of army from Turquoise Terraces (M13-14)

spr mšꜥ mꜣꜥ Ḫt.y(w)-(M)fkꜣ.t in(i).n=sn (m)fkꜣ.t ḥkꜣ.t 14 13/32[36] *wḏꜣ(.w) (r)-gs ḫt ꜥwꜣ dbn 8700 biꜣ ḳis dbn 5570 ski-ḏꜣ.t ḥkꜣ.t 6* [... *ibn.w*] *ḳm 26 13/16 nṯr.(y)t ḥkꜣ.t 10 9/16*[37] *sbꜣ-š 8 šsꜣ.wt ẖꜣr 33*[38] *ḥḏ dbn 9¾ kꜣ 10 niꜣ.w-ib(.w) 3 nṯr.t 1*

Arrival of the expedition which was despatched to the Turquoise Terraces. They had brought: 14 13/32 *ḥkꜣ.t* and a remainder of turquoise; 8700 *dbn* of rotting (petrified?) wood; 5570 *dbn* of *ḳis*-mineral; 6 *ḥkꜣ.t* of *ski-ḏꜣ.t*; [...

[34] Hieroglyphic text as transcribed by Altenmüller and Moussa, *SAK* 18 (1991), folding plate. Lacuna of missing hieroglyphs are not reflective of actual lacuna measurements. Transliteration and translation are by the author, relying on Altenmüller and Moussa, *SAK* 18 (1991), 4-19; Dantong, *JAC* 14 (1999), 45-66; Marcus, *E&L* 17 (2007), 139-142; Wastlhuber, *Die Beziehungen zwischen Ägypten und der Levante*, 75-78; Obsomer, *Sésostris Ier*, 595-606.

[35] Or 'general of infantry' as in Ward, *Index*, 28 [194].

[36] 14 19/32 in Obsomer, *Sésostris Ier*, 598.

[37] 9/16 in Obsomer (*Sésostris Ier*, 598) and 10+x 1/16 in Wastlhuber (*Die Beziehungen zwischen Ägypten und der Levante*, 76).

[38] 41 in Marcus (*E&L* 17 [2007], 139) and Obsomer (*Sésostris Ier*, 598).

alum?]-*ḳ3m* 26$\frac{13}{16}$; 10$\frac{9}{16}$ *ḥḳ3.t* of natron; 8 stars of the lake (starfish?); 33 sacks of *šs3.wt*; 9¾ *dbn* of silver; 10 bulls; 3 young ibexes; 1 cheetah hide.

Visit and goods from *Ṯmp3w* (M15)

iw(i).t m wdb-tp ḥtp.yw[39] *n.w Ṯmp3w in(i).n=sn m-ʿ=sn dḥ.ty dbn 238¼*

The coming with bowed-head of the peaceful ones/ offering bearers of *Ṯmp3w*. They have brought with them: 238¼ *dbn* of lead.

Return of army from *Iw3(i)* and *I3sy* (M16-18)

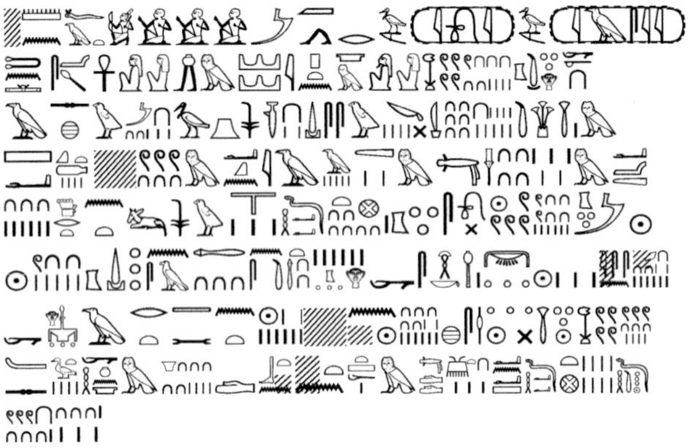

[...iwi.t mšʿ ḥnʿ im.y-r3] mnf3.t m3ʿ r ḫb3 Iw3i ḫb3 I3sy tn(w) sḳr(.w)-ʿnḫ in(i.w) m ḫ3s.ty iptn ʿ3m 1554 ḥsmn ḥr ḫt mib.t 10 3sḫ.w 33 b3gs.w 12 ḏ3ss.w 4¼ nm 79 tiḫ3 1 mšʿḳ.t 4[40] *[...x+]330 mʿḳ n i33 5 2 mšd 45*[41] *mʿb3 36 ḏr.t n.t iws.w 3 dḥʿʿ.t 61*[42] *ḥm.t sw3 dbn 646 ḥm.t m3 dbn 125 ḥsmn nstiw 30 nstit 26 ḥm.t ḥr ḫt sk 1 nbw dbn 3 i[s]s*[43] *n [tp] msḏr 38 ḫt ḥr ḥḏ 3r.(y)t ḏn.t 8 [...n] dbn 58 ḫswḏ dbn ¼ w3ḏ dbn 1734 3bw s3.t 4 ḫt ḥnw n(.y) ʿ3m 54 db.t n.t [ḫ]ntš 1 mšdd.t 13 ʿ n(.y) ʿš dḥʿʿ.t 8 dḥ.ty dbn 375*

[... the coming of the expedition and the overseer] of soldiers which were sent to hack up *Iw3i* and *I3sy*. Number of captives brought from these two foreign lands: 1554 *ʿ3m*. Of bronze and wood: 10 axes; 33 sickles; 12 daggers; 4¼ saws; 79 daggers; 1 chisel; 4 shoulder-blades/razors; [...x+]330; 2 *mʿḳ* with 5 rods; 45 *mšd*-weapons; 36 harpoons; 3 hands of balance; 61 six-spoked objects;[44] 646 *dbn* of copper scraps; 125 *dbn* of new copper. Of bronze: 30 spears; 26 javelins. Of copper and wood: 1 spear. Of gold: 3 *dbn*; 38 pieces of jewellery for the head and ear. Of wood and silver: 8 staffs with metal rings; [...] 58 *dbn*; ¼ *dbn* of *ḫswḏ*; 1734 *dbn* of malachite. Of ivory: 4 *s3.t*-tablets. Of wood: 54 household items of the *ʿ3m*; 1 chest for travelling (?); 13 combs; 8 *ʿš*-wood axles of six-spoked objects. Of lead: 375 *dbn*.

Return of army from *Ḫnty-š* (M18-21)

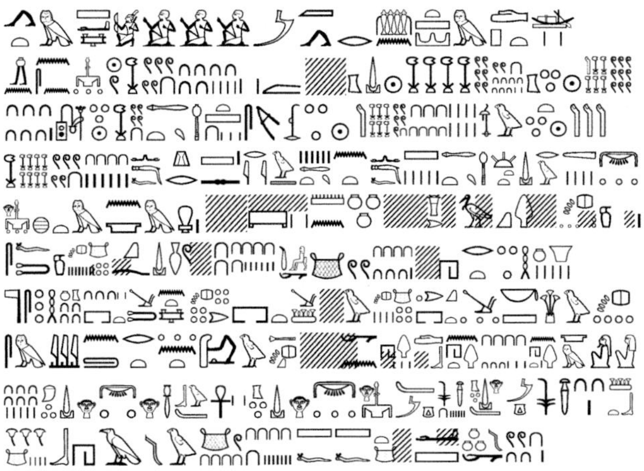

iw(i).t mšʿ m3ʿ(.w) r Ḫnty-š m dp.t 2[45] *in(i).n=sn ḥḏ dbn 1676½ [...] ḥsmn dbn 4882 ḥm.t dbn 15961 sš dbn 1410 ʿ3.t ḥḏ.t inr 13 (i)smr dbn 16588 ḥmw.t dbn 39556 nmḥf ḫr š 1 sr.yw-š 6 ʿ3.t n.t nmḥf inr 5*[46] *ʿ3.t ḥḏ.t km.t ḏ3r.w 4 nbw ḥr ḥḏ ḫtm n(.y) ʿ3m 1 [...] hn 2 mnw [...] b3ḳ [...] ḥḳ3.t [5...]*[47] *sft ḥḳ3.t 66⅜ (w)ḏ3(.w r-gs) hbn.t x+176 ti-šps ḫ3r 271 [...]hr.t ḥnw 5*[48] *sntr ḥnw 72 pr.t tntm ḥḳ3.t 8$\frac{1}{16}$ pr.t š3w ḥḳ3.t 55¾*[49] *pr.t kšw ḥḳ3.t 4 sm r.t n.t ʿḥ3.w ḥḳ3.t ¼ [...ḫt] nht x+3 d[3]b nht 73 nht 1 ʿ3m 65 ḥsmn ḥr nbw ḥr 3bw ʿnḫ 2 ḥsmn ḥr nbw ḥr ḥḏ m3gsw 16 ḥsmn ḥr 3bw m3gsw 21 š3b.t ḫ3r 4*[50] *bh3w ḫ3r 197 šfšf.t ḫ3r [...] ʿš 231*

The coming of the expedition which was sent to *Ḫnty-š* in 2 ships, they having brought: 1676½ *dbn* of silver; [...] 4882 *dbn* of bronze; 15961 *dbn* of copper; 1410 *dbn* of white lead; 13 blocks of precious white stone (marble?); 16588 *dbn* of emery; 39556 *dbn* of polishing sand; 1 block of dolerite from under the lake; 6 blocks of grinding stone; 5 blocks of hard dolerite; 4 blocks of precious white and black stone. Of gold and silver: 1 *ʿ3m*-seal; 2 [...] boxes; quartz [...]; moringa oil [...] *ḥḳ3.t* [...]; 66⅜ *ḥḳ3.t* and a remainder of oil; x+176 *hbn.t*-jars; 271 sacks of *ti-šps*-wood; [...] 5 *ḥnw*-vessels of [...]; 72 *ḥnw*-vessels of incense; 8$\frac{1}{16}$ *ḥḳ3.t* of *tntm*-fruit; 55¾ *ḥḳ3.t* of *š3w*-fruit; 4 *ḥḳ3.t* of *kšw*-fruit; ¼ *ḥḳ3.t* of a herb for the remedy of fighting (for wounds?); x+3 [...wood] sycamore; 73 (logs?) of fig-trees; 1 (log?) of sycamore; 65 *ʿ3m*. Of bronze, gold and ivory: 2 mirrors. Of bronze, gold and silver: 16 daggers. Of bronze and ivory: 21 daggers. 4 sacks of *š3b.t*-plant; 197 sacks of *bh3w*-plant; [...] sacks of *šfšf.t*-plant; 231 (logs?) of *ʿš*-wood.

Distribution of goods and rewards (M21-23, 25-26)

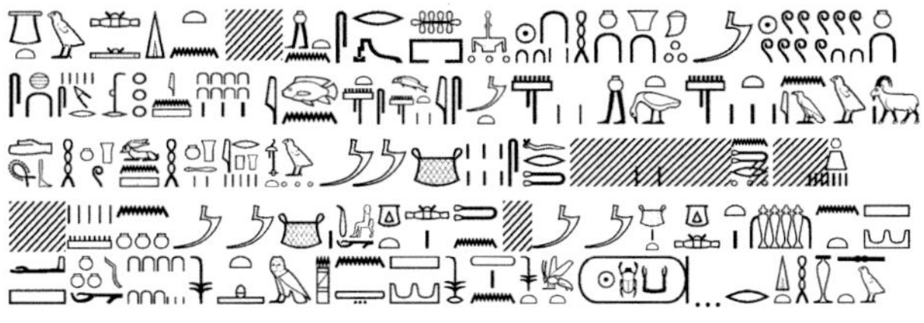

39 *ḫrw* 'nomads' in Altenmüller and Moussa, *SAK* 18 (1991), 12. The translation here follows Goedicke and Dantong (Goedicke, *RdE* 42 [1991], 90-91; Dantong, *JAC* 14 [1999], 61).

40 3 in Obsomer, *Sésostris Ier*, 599.

41 25 in Obsomer, *Sésostris Ier*, 599.

42 60 in Obsomer (*Sésostris Ier*, 599) and Altenmüller and Moussa (*SAK* 18 [1991], 15).

43 *i[b]s* in Obsomer, *Sésostris Ier*, 599.

44 Many have translated *dḥʿʿ.t* as a six-spoked wheel. Another suggestion is that it is a bridle-bit. For more see Ilin-Tomich, *Lingua Aegyptia* 18 (2010), 126-127.

45 10 in Goedicke, *RdE* 42 (1991), 90.

46 13 in Obsomer, *Sésostris Ier*, 599.

47 ⅝ in Dantong, *JAC* 14 (1999), 48.

48 7 in Obsomer, *Sésostris Ier*, 600.

49 54¾ in Obsomer, *Sésostris Ier*, 600.

50 3 in Obsomer, *Sésostris Ier*, 600.

[hieroglyphic text]

g3w.t di.t n [...] ini.t(w)=s r stp-s3 ḥd dbn 32 ḥnw 20 ḥm.t m3 dbn 920 nws 25 (i)smr-w-inr 83 in.t sḥ3.t 2 ism3.t 2 in.t dšr.t 3 ni3.w 1 d(3)b ḥnw 100 wnš ḥnw ᶜ3 2 irp hbn.t 5 ḥmw.t m3m3 6 sfrt [..2..s]nṯr ḥnw [... x]+7[51] [...x+]5 mnw m3m3 1 ti-šps 1

g3w.t (R)tnw [...] m3m3 g3w.t Ḫnty-š ᶜš 73 ḥtp-nsw.t m ᶜḥ n(.y) T3-š rsy iw n(.y) nsw.t-bi.ty Ḫpr-k3-Rᶜ.w...

rdi.t ḥs.wt [mr.(w)t 3ḥ.(w)t] nbw ḥbs (i)ḫ.t nb(.t) nfr.t ᶜ3(.t) wr.t n im.y-r3 mnf3.t n ḫrp nfr.w n nfr.w iyi.w ḥr ḥb3 ʾIw3i ʾ3sy mst.t Sḥm-ʾImn-m-ḥ3.t m skr.w-ᶜnḫ [...] ḫ3s.ty iptn snm.t ᶜ3m.t [n...skr(.w)-ᶜn]ḫ.w n msi.w-nsw.t n špss.w-nsw.t n ḫ3.tyw-ᶜḥ nsw.t ds=f...

Dues given to [...] it was brought to the palace: 32 *dbn* of silver; 20 *ḥnw*-vessels; 920 *dbn* of new copper; 25 sheets; 83 blocks of emery; 2 of *in.t*-and-*sḥ3.t*-textiles; 2 of *ism3.t*-textiles; 3 of red *in.t*-textiles; 1 ibex; 100 *ḥnw*-vessels of fig (fruit?); 2 large *ḥnw*-vessels of raisins; 5 *hbn.t*-vessels of wine; 6 *m3m3*-vessels of polishing sand; [...2..]; [x+]7 *ḥnw*-vessels of incense; [... x+]5; 1 *m3m3*-vessel of quartz; 1 (log) of *ti-šps*-wood.

Dues of (R)tnw: [...] *m3m3*-vessel. Dues of Ḫnty-š: 73 (logs?) of ᶜš-wood. Royal offerings in the palace of T3-š of the southern lake of the king of Upper and Lower Egypt, Kheperkara (Senwosret I)....

Giving of rewards, [serfs, fields], gold, clothes and every good and great thing to the overseer of soldiers, to the foreman of recruits[52] and to the recruits who came after hacking ʾIw3i and ʾ3sy and supplying Sḥm-ʾImn-m-ḥ3.t with captives [...] these 2 foreign lands; ᶜ3m.t food-supplies [of...captives] for the king's children, the king's nobles and the counts of the palace and of the king himself...

B.4 Brussel Figurines

Prov. Saqqara
Ref. Posener, *Princes et Pays*, 64-96, pl. 1a.
Chron. Late Twelfth Dynasty
Chapter 4.3.8

E1 [hieroglyphs]

ḥk3 n(.y) Ḥ3im ʾI-tim3ibi
Ruler of Ḥ3im,[53] ʾI-tim3ibi

E2 [hieroglyphs]

ḥk3 n(.y) ʾIsk3i Mwri
Ruler of ʾIsk3i,[54] Mwri

E3 [hieroglyphs]

ḥk3 n(.y) ʾIsinw Nk̠mwpᶜi
Ruler of ʾIsinw,[55] Nk̠mwpᶜi

E4 [hieroglyphs]

ḥk3 n(.y) Ḥ3mw Ytn-Hddw/Ytn-ᶜ3mp3-Hddw
Ruler of Ḥ3mw, Ytn-Hddw/Ytn-ᶜ3mp3-Hddw

E5 [hieroglyphs]

ḥk3 n(.y) Mkwtry ʾIbi3fi
Ruler of Mkwtry,[56] ʾIbi3fi

E6 [hieroglyphs]

ḥk3 n(.y) Skmimi ʾIbs-Hddw
Ruler of Skmimi,[57] ʾIbs-Hddw

E7 [hieroglyphs]

ḥk3 n(.y) Kni ʾI-Ṯp-Hddw
Ruler of Kni, ʾI-Ṯp-Hddw

E8 [hieroglyphs]

ḥk3 n(.y) Piḥ3wm ᶜprw-ᶜnw
Ruler of Piḥ3wm, ᶜprw-ᶜnw

E9 [hieroglyphs]

ḥk3 n(.y) ʾI-pk̠wm Ynky3w
Ruler of ʾI-pk̠wm,[58] Ynky3w

E10 [hieroglyphs]

ḥk3 n(.y) ᶜny ᶜ3imw
Ruler of ᶜny, ᶜ3imw

---

[53] Perhaps linked to Sinai Inscription Nr 110 and its Ḥ3mi (Gardiner and Peet, *Inscriptions of Sinai* 1, pl. 36 [110]). See Appendix B.11.
[54] Postulated to be Ashkelon. For a similar toponym, ʾIsk3nw, in e23-25 and f15 of the Berlin Bowls Execration Texts, see Appendix B.6.
[55] For a similar toponym, ʾIsinw, in e13-15 and f14 of the Berlin Bowls Execration Texts, see Appendix B.6.
[56] Postulated to be Migdol (Helck, *Die Beziehungen Ägyptens*, 52).
[57] Linked to the Skmm of Khusobek's stela and postulated to be Shechem. See Manchester 3306 (Chapter 4.5.1.1, Appendix B.5); Posener, *Princes et Pays*, 68; Baines, in *Form und Mass*, pl. 1; Ben-Tor, in *Essays on Ancient Israel*, 70-72.
[58] Postulated to be Aphek (Posener, *Princes et Pays*, 69).

---

[51] 8 in Dantong (*JAC* 14 [1999], 48) and Obsomer (*Sésostris Ier*, 600).
[52] Ward, *Index*, 134 [1150].

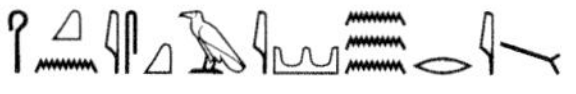

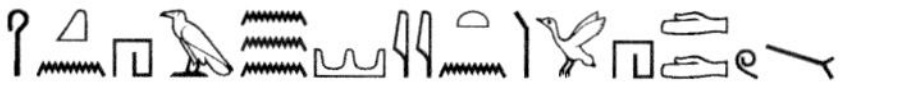

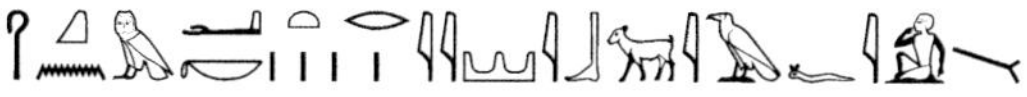

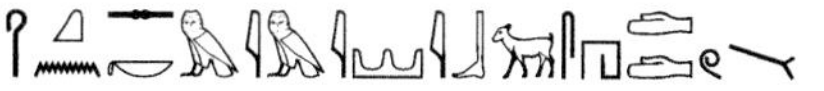

E11 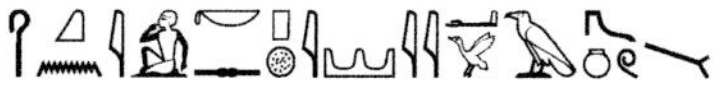
ḥḳ3 n(.y) Ỉ-kspi Yꜥp3nw
Ruler of *Ỉ-kspi*, *Yꜥp3nw*

E12 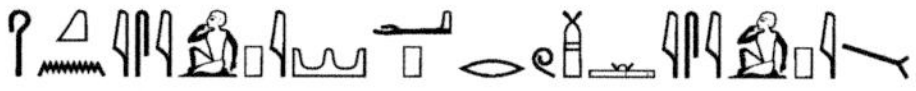
ḥḳ3 n(.y) Ỉsi-pi ꜥprw-isi-pi
Ruler of *Ỉsi-pi*,[59] *ꜥprw-isi-pi*

E13 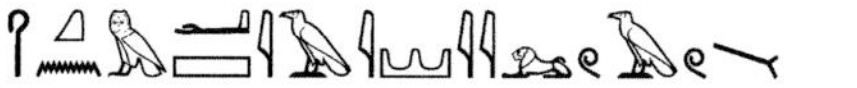
ḥḳ3 n(.y) Mši3i Yrw3w
Ruler of *Mši3i*,[60] *Yrw3w*

E14 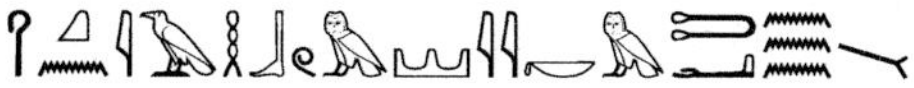
ḥḳ3 n(.y) Ỉ3ḥbwm Ykmṯꜥmw
Ruler of *Ỉ3ḥbwm*, *Ykmṯꜥmw*

E15 
ḥḳ3 n(.y) Ḥḏwi3i Gṯi
Ruler of *Ḥḏwi3i*,[61] *Gṯi*

E16 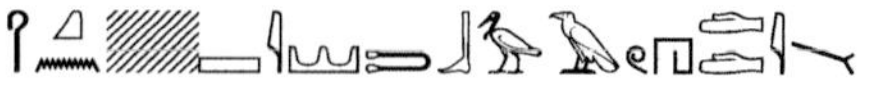
ḥḳ3 n(.y) [..]ši Ṯb3w-Hddi
Ruler of *[..]ši*, *Ṯb3w-Hddi*

E17 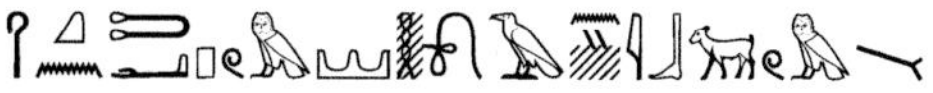
ḥḳ3 n(.y) Ṯꜥpwm [Ḫ]w3n[y...]ibwm
Ruler of *Ṯꜥpwm [Ḫ]w3n[y...]ibwm*

E18 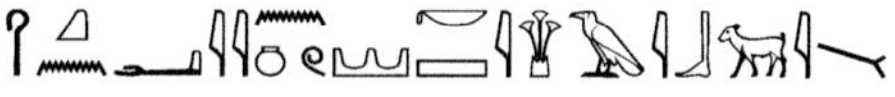
ḥḳ3 n(.y) ꜥynw Kšiḥ3ibi
Ruler of *ꜥynw*, *Kšiḥ3ibi*

E19 
ḥḳ3 n(.y) Ḏi3m Ynḏm-Hddw
Ruler of *Ḏi3m*, *Ynḏm-Hddw*

E20 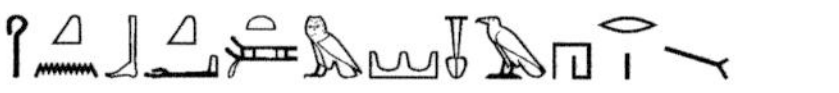
ḥḳ3 n(.y) Bḳꜥtm Sm3-Hr
Ruler of *Bḳꜥtm*,[62] *Sm3-Hr*

E21 
ḥḳ3 n(.y) Ỉ3iy 3w3-Hddi
Ruler of *Ỉ3iy*,[63] *3w3-Hddi*

E22 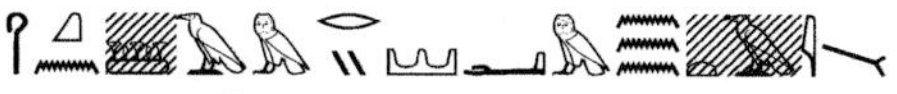
ḥḳ3 n(.y) [Š]3mry ꜥmw[t3]i
Ruler of *[Š]3mry*, *ꜥmw[t3]i*

E23 
ḥḳ3 n(.y) Mrḏḥky rs.t(y) Y[k]y3w
Ruler of southern *Mrḏḥky*, *Y[k]y3w*

E24 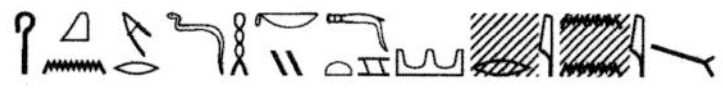
ḥḳ3 n(.y) Mrḏḥky mḥ.t(y) [R]i[nn]i
Ruler of northern *Mrḏḥky*,*[R]i[nn]i*

E25 
ḥḳ3 n(.y) ꜥs[...]3tm Y[..]3w
Ruler of *ꜥs[...]3tm*, *Y[..]3w*

E26 
ḥḳ3 n(.y) ꜥḫwmt Kiwrw
Ruler of *ꜥḫwmt*, *Kiwrw*

E27 
ḥḳ3 n(.y) Bwḏ3nw Ymwrw
Ruler of *Bwḏ3nw*, *Ymwrw*

E28 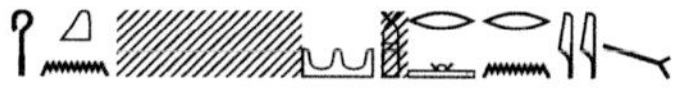
ḥḳ3 n(.y) [.... ꜥp]r-Rny
Ruler of *[...., ꜥp]r-Rny*

E29 
ḥḳ3 n(.y) Miši [Sḳ]3i
Ruler of *Miši*, *[Sḳ]3i*

E30 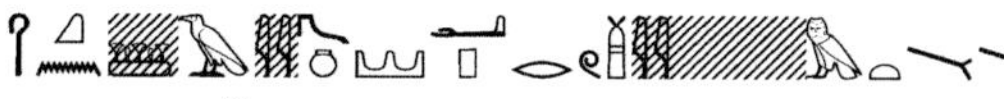
ḥḳ3 n(.y) [Š]3[y]nw ꜥprw-[y...]mt
Ruler of *[Š]3[y]nw*, *ꜥprw-[y...]mt*

E31 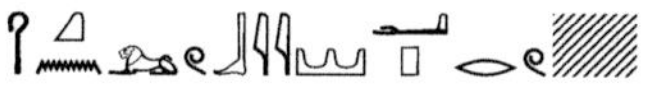
ḥḳ3 n(.y) Rwby ꜥprw-[...]
Ruler of *Rwby*, *ꜥprw-[...]*

E32 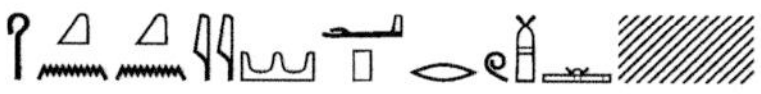
ḥḳ3 n(.y) Ḳny ꜥprw-[...]
Ruler of *Ḳny*, *ꜥprw-[...]*

E33 
ḥḳ3 n(.y) Ỉ-pwm rs.t(y) [...]
Ruler of southern *Ỉ-pwm* [...]

E34 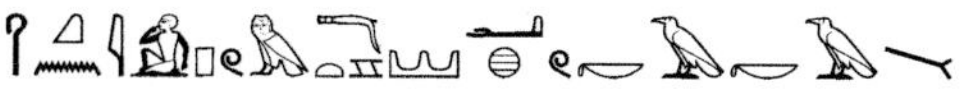
ḥḳ3 n(.y) Ỉ-pwm mḥ.t(y) ꜥḫwk3k3
Ruler of northern *Ỉ-pwm ꜥḫwk3k3*

E35 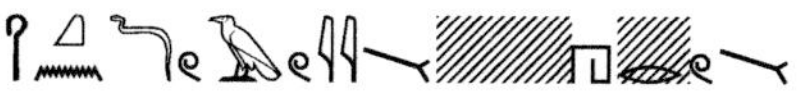
ḥḳ3 n(.y) Ḏw3wy [...]-H[r]w
Ruler of *Ḏw3wy*,[64] *[...]-H[r]w*

59 Postulated to be Achshaph (Posener, *Princes et Pays*, 70; Ben-Tor, in *Essays on Ancient Israel*, 75-76). For a similar toponym, *Yisipi*, in e31 and f21 of the Berlin Bowls Execration Texts, see Appendix B.6.

60 Postulated to be Misch'al (Helck, *Die Beziehungen Ägyptens*, 53).

61 Postulated to be Hazor (Posener, *Princes et Pays*, 73; Ben-Tor, in *Essays on Ancient Israel*, 74-75).

62 Postulated to be the Beqa' Valley (Aḥituv, *Canaanite Toponyms*, 65).

63 Postulated to be Sinuhe's *Ỉ3* (Aḥituv, *Canaanite Toponyms*, 65; Gubel and Loffet, *AHL* 34-35 [2011/2012], 81, 86).

64 Postulated to be Tyre (Posener, *Princes et Pays*, 82; Helck, *Die Beziehungen Ägyptens*, 56).

E36 
ḥḳ3 n(.y) Yʿnḳi [...]*i*
Ruler of *Yʿnḳi*,[65] [...]*i*

E37 
ḥḳ3 n(.y) Mkiy Šm[*š*...]
Ruler of *Mkiy*, *Šm*[*š*...]

E38 
ḥḳ3 n(.y) [...]*3ynw Ꞽrrti*
Ruler of [...]*3ynw*, *Ꞽrrti*

E39 
ḥḳ3 n(.y) Ḳhrmw rs.t(y) H[*m*]*y*
Ruler of southern *Ḳhrmw*, *H*[*m*]*y*

E40 
ḥḳ3 n(.y) Ḳhrmw mḥ.t(y) Yṯrkni
Ruler of northern *Ḳhrmw*, *Yṯrkni*

E41 
ḥḳ3 n(.y) [*Ṯ*]*w*[*3*]*w*[*d*]*nw ʿmwi3wbw*
Ruler of [*Ṯ*]*w*[*3*]*w*[*d*]*nw*, *ʿmwi3wbw*

E42 
ḥḳ3 n(.y) ʿf3[...]*i ʿmw*[...]
Ruler of *ʿf3*[...]*i*, *ʿmw*[...]

E43 
ḥḳ3 n(.y) Yb3y Šmšw-Ꞽpirim
Ruler of *Yb3y*,[66] *Šmšw-Ꞽpirim*

E44 
ḥḳ3 n(.y) Ry[*t*]*i* [...]*pʿi*[...]
Ruler of *Ry*[*t*]*i*,[67] [...]*pʿi*[...]

E45 
ḥḳ3 n(.y) 3wš3mm [...]
Ruler of *3wš3mm*[68] [...]

E46 
ḥḳ3 n(.y) [...]*3y* [...]*-Hddw*
Ruler of [...]*3y*, [...]*-Hddw*

E47 
ḥḳ3 n(.y) Ꞽbw3m [...]
Ruler of *Ꞽbw3m*, [...]

E48 
ḥḳ3 n(.y) Ꞽs[*n*]*nws Tiḫ3rsir*
Ruler of *Ꞽs*[*n*]*nws*, *Tiḫ3rsir*

E49 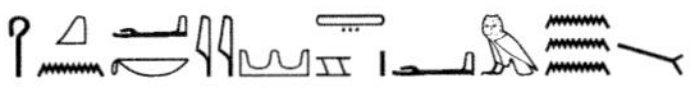
ḥḳ3 n(.y) ʿky T3ʿmw
Ruler of *ʿky*,[69] *T3ʿmw*

E50 
wr/smsw n(.y) wḥ.ywt n.(w)t Kwšw [...]*yi*
The great one/elder of the tribes of *Kwšw*, [...]*yi*

E51 
wr/smsw n(.y) wḥ.ywt n.(w)t Kwšw [...]*y*
The great one/elder of the tribes of *Kwšw*, [...]*y*

E52 
ḥḳ3 n(.y) Šwtw ḥr.t Šmwibw
Ruler of Upper *Šwtw*,[70] *Šmwibw*

E53 
ḥḳ3 n(.y) Šwtw ḫr.t Yk[...]*mw*
Ruler of Lower *Šwtw*, *Yk*[...]*mw*

E54 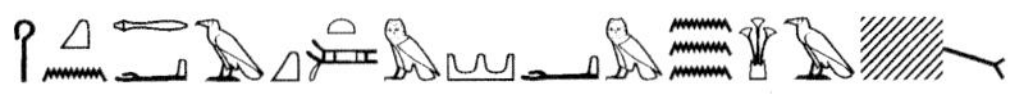
ḥḳ3 n(.y) ʿ3ḳtm ʿmwḥ3[...]
Ruler of *ʿ3ḳtm*,[71] *ʿmwḥ3*[...]

E55 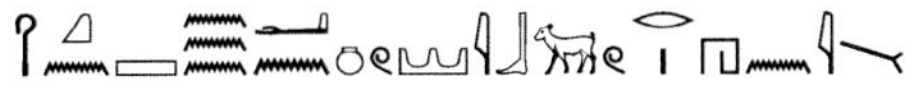
ḥḳ3 n(.y) Šmwʿnw Ꞽbwrhni
Ruler of *Šmwʿnw*, *Ꞽbwrhni*

E56 
ḥḳ3 n(.y) Ḳ3ḳ3m Ꞽbw[...]*i*
Ruler of *Ḳ3ḳ3m*, *Ꞽbw*[...]*i*

E57 
ḥḳ3 n(.y) [*Š*]*wsw Ykmṯmw*
Ruler of [*Š*]*wsw*, *Ykmṯmw*

E58 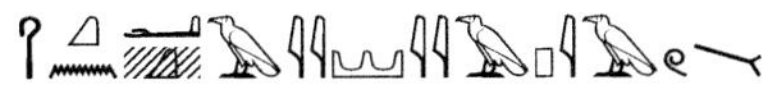
ḥḳ3 n(.y) ʿ[*ḳ*]*3y Y3pi3w*
Ruler of *ʿ*[*ḳ*]*3y*, *Y3pi3w*

E59 
ḥḳ3 n(.y) 3wsy [*Ḥ*]*w3*[*ny*]*ib*[...]
Ruler of *3wsy*, [*Ḥ*]*w3*[*ny*]*ib*[...]

65 For a similar toponym, *Yiʿnḳ*, in e1-3 of the Berlin Bowls Execration Texts, see Appendix B.6.

66 Postulated to be Ebla (Gee, *JARCE* 41 [2004], 30).

67 Postulated to be *Ri-du* or *Lu-te* of the Ebla tablets (Gee, *JARCE* 41 [2004], 30).

68 Although phonetically problematic, the name has been postulated to be Jerusalem (Posener, *Princes et Pays*, 86; Ben-Tor, in *Essays on Ancient Israel*, 68-70). For the same toponym in e27-28 and f48 of the Berlin Bowls Execration Texts, see Appendix B.6.

69 Postulated to be Acco (Posener, *Princes et Pays*, 87). Perhaps it is also connected to modern Kfar-'aqqa in North Lebanon (Wardini, *Lebanese Place-Names*, 254).

70 For the same toponym in e4-6 of the Berlin Bowls Execration Texts, see Appendix B.6.

71 For the same toponym in e22 and f12 of the Berlin Bowls Execration Texts, see Appendix B.6.

E60 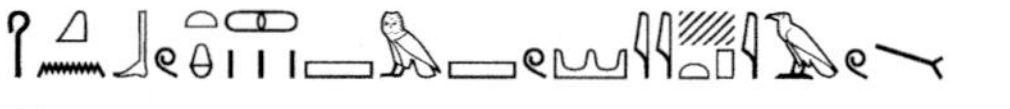
ḥḳ3 n(.y) Bwt-šmšw Y[..]*pti3w*
Ruler of *Bwt-šmšw*, *Y*[..]*pti3w*

E61 
wḥ.ywt n.(w)t ʿ3ḳti
Tribes of *ʿ3ḳti*

E62 
wr.w/smsw.w n.w Mkiy
Great ones/elders of *Mkiy*

E63 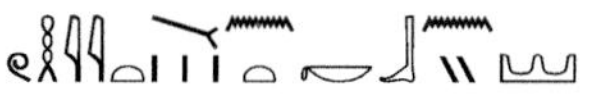
wḥ.ywt n.(w)t Kbny
Tribes of *Kbny*[72]

E64 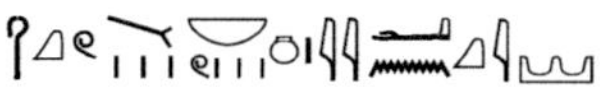
ḥḳ3.w nb.w n.w Yʿnḳi
All rulers of *Yʿnḳi*

E65 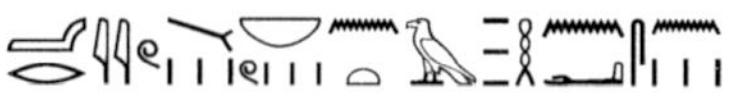
skr.yw nb.w n.t(y)w ḥnw=sn
All smiters[73] who are with them

F1 
ʿ3mw nb.w
All *ʿ3mw*

F2 
n.w ʾIw3ṯi
Of *ʾIw3ṯi*

F3 
n.w 3m(w)t
Of *3m(w)t*

F4 
n.w 3ḳḥi
Of *3ḳḥi*

F5 
n.w Dmitiw
Of *Dmitiw*[74]

F6 
n.w Ḫsswm
Of *Ḫsswm*

F7 
Mntw m St.t
Mntw of *St.t*

72 Identified as Byblos (Posener, *Princes et Pays*, 94).
73 The term possibly refers to non-Egyptian soldiers who have not been captured (Ritner, *Egyptian Magical Practice*, 141, n. 628).
74 For the same toponym in f16 of the Berlin Execration Texts, see Appendix B.6. See also Dussaud, *Syria* 8/3 (1927), 227-229.

B.5 Abydos Stelae and a Shrine

Prov. Abydos
Ref. See Figure B.2
Chron. Twelfth Dynasty to Second Intermediate Period
Chapter 4.5.1.1
Figure B.2

Stelae assigned to the Twelfth Dynasty

Louvre C1 (Amenemhat I, Year 24)[75]

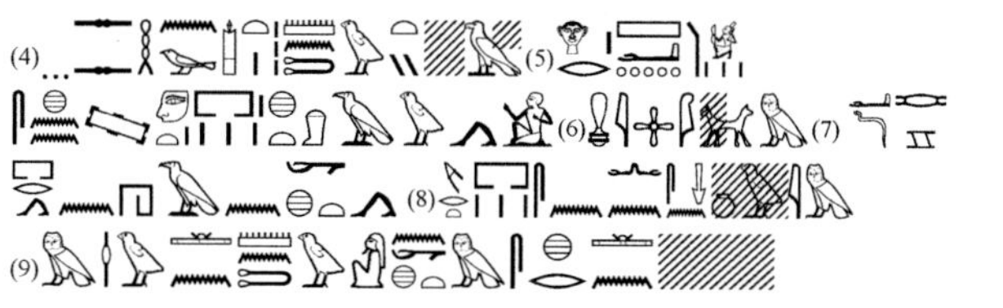

(4) ... *ssḥ.n(=i) ʾIwn.tyw Mnṯw.tyw* (5) *Ḥr.yw-šʿ sḫn.n(=i) ẖnr.wt ḫt3.w=i* (6) *mi wnš.wy m* (7) *ʿḏ pri.n(=i) h3.n(=i) ḫt* (8) *mr.wt=sn nn sn*[*w*] *im* (9) *m wḏ.n Mnṯw nḫ.t m sḫr n* [...]
(4) ... I destroyed the *ʾIwn.tyw*, *Mnṯw.tyw* and (5) *Ḥr.yw-šʿ*; I demolished the fortresses, I creeping up (6) like two jackals(?)[76] at the (7) edge of the cultivation; I came and went through their (8) streets, there being no equal therein, (9) as Montu had commanded the victory by the plan of [...]

CG 20539 (Senwosret I)

(10) ... *ḏd(.w) 3wr=f m ḫ3s.tyw sgrḥ(.w) n=f Ḥr.yw-šʿ sḥtp(.w)* (11) *St.(t)yw ḥr iri.wt=sn...*
(10) ... the one who puts his oppression/terror upon the foreigners; the one who pacifies the *Ḥr.yw-šʿ* for him; the one who pacifies the (11)*St.(t)yw* for their actions...

Cairo CG 20296 (Senwosret III)

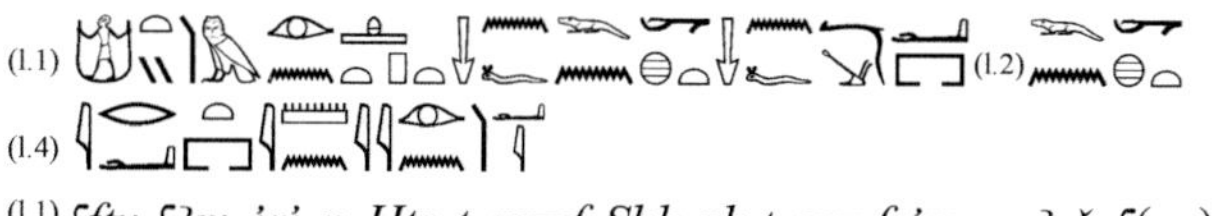

(1.1) *ʿfty ʿ3m iri n Ḥtp.t sn=f Sbk-nḫ.t sn=f im.y-r3 šnʿ(.w)*
(1.2) *Sbk-nḫ.t*
(1.4) *ir.y-ʿ.t ʾImny iri n ʿ3m ʿi*
(1.1) The brewer,[77] *ʿ3m* born to Hotepet; his brother (1.2) Sobeknakht;[78] his brother, overseer of a storehouse,[79]

75 The stela opens with the titulary of both Amenemhat I and Senwosret I, leading scholars to postulate a possible co-regency between the two. Some consequently assign the events to the period of co-regency, or Year 4 of Senwosret I's reign. See Breasted, *Ancient Records of Egypt* 1, 227; Posener, *Littérature et politique*, 54, 66; Wildung, *MDAIK* 37 (1981), 507; Obsomer, *RdE* 44 (1993), 103-140; Spalinger, SAK 25 (1998), 318.
76 Berman suggests 'wolves' in *Amenemhet I*, 109.
77 Ward, *Index*, 73 [595].
78 Ranke, *Personennamen* 1, 304 [15].
79 Ward, *Index*, 49 [381].

(1.2) Sobeknakht;
(1.4) the hall-keeper,[80] Imeny,[81] born to *ꜥꜣm ꜥỉ*[82]

Rio de Janeiro 627 [2419; Nr 1] (Senwosret III)

(55-57 [XV]) (58 [II])
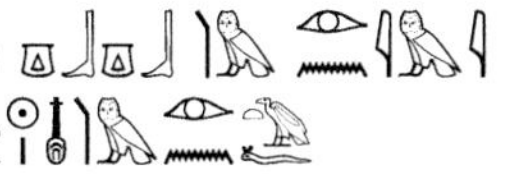

(55-57 [XV]) *Gbgb ꜥꜣm iri n ỉmi*
(58 [II]) *sꜣ=f Hrw-nfr ꜥꜣm iri n mw.t=f*
(55-57 [XV]) Gebgeb,[83] *ꜥꜣm* born to *ỉmi*;[84]
(58 [II]) His son Herunofer,[85] *ꜥꜣm*, born to his mother

Manchester 3306 (Senwosret III)

(c.1) (c.2) (c.3) (c.4) (c.5)
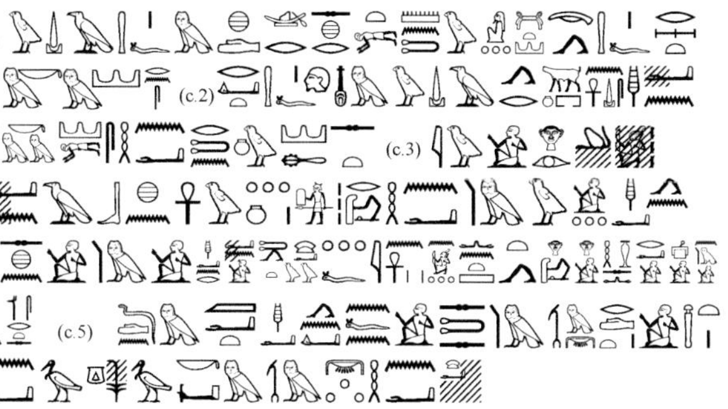

(c.1) *wḏꜣ ḥm=f m ḫdi r sḫr.t Mnṯw St.t spr ḥm=f r spꜣ.t Skmm rn=s* (c.2) *rdi.t ḥm=f tp-nfr m wḏꜣ r ḫnw ꜥnḫ(.w) (w)ḏꜣ(.w) s(nb.w) ꜥḥꜥ.n Skmm ḫr=s ḥnꜥ Rṯnw ḫsi.t* (c.3) *iw=i ḥr iri(.t) pḥ [mšꜥ ꜥḥ]ꜥ.n ꜣbḫ.n ꜥnḫ.w n.w mšꜥ r ꜥḥꜣ ḥnꜥ ꜥꜣm.w ꜥḥꜥ.n* (c.4) *sḫ.n=i ꜥꜣm ꜥḥꜥ.n rdi.n=i iṯi.tw ḫꜥ.w=f in ꜥnḫ 2 n(.y) mšꜥ nn tš.t ḥr ꜥḥꜣ ḥr=i ḥsi(.w) n rdi=i sꜣ=i n ꜥꜣm ꜥnḫ n(=i) S-n-wsr.t* (c.5) *ḏd.n(=i) m mꜣꜥ.t ꜥḥꜥ.n di.n=f n=i sṯs*[86] *m ḏꜥm r dr.t=i mtpn.t*[87] *ḥnꜥ bꜣgsw bꜣk(.w) m ḏꜥm ḥnꜥ ḥfꜥ[w ...]*[88]

(c.1) His majesty's proceeding in travelling northwards to overthrow the *Mnṯw* of *St.t*; his majesty's arrival at the district of *Skmm*,[89] its name; (c.2) his majesty's making a good start in proceeding to the Residence,[90] may it live, be prosperous and healthy. Then *Skmm* fell with the miserable *Rṯnw*,[91] (c.3) I acting as the army's rearguard. Then the soldiers of the army engaged to fight with the *ꜥꜣm.w*. (c.4) Then I hit the *ꜥꜣm* and I caused that his weapons be taken by two soldiers of the army, without desisting from fighting, my face was courageous[92] and I did not turn my back on the *ꜥꜣm*.
As Senwosret lives (for me), (c.5) I have spoken in truth. Then he gave me a staff of electrum for my hand, a sheath with a dagger worked with electrum and a handle [...].

Cairo CG 20231 (Amenemhat III)

(h)

(h) *wdp.w ꜥꜣm Ḫnti-wr*
(h) The butler,[93] *ꜥꜣm* Khentywer[94]

Fitzwilliam Museum E.207.1900 (Amenemhat III)

ꜥꜣm wdp.w Rn=f-snb
ꜥꜣm Nb-swmn.w
ꜥꜣm, the butler, Renefseneb;[95]
ꜥꜣm Nebsumenu[96]

Cairo CG 20140 (Amenemhat III)

(f)
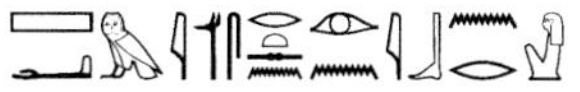

(f) *šꜥmi S-n-wsr.t iri n ỉbnr*
(f) *šꜥmi* (?),[97] Senwosret,[98] born to *ỉbnr*[99]

Cairo CG 20125 (Twelfth Dynasty [?])

(h.1) (h.2)

(h.1) *imꜣḫ Sḥtp-ib-Rꜥ.w mꜣꜥ-ḫrw*
(h.2) *ḥm.t=f ꜥꜣm mꜣꜥ(.t)-ḫrw*
(h.1) The revered Sehotepibra, justified;
(h.2) his wife, *ꜥꜣm*, justified

80 Ward, *Index*, 57 [452].
81 Ranke, *Personennamen* 1, 31 [13].
82 Perhaps the name is of foreign origin.
83 Rio 227 is cited as the only reference for this name in Ranke, *Personennamen* 1, 350 [22]. Kitchen prefers an Egyptian derivative, translating it as 'the lame' rather than a Semitic origin with relation to *gbꜥ* 'tall' (Kitchen, in *Studies in Egyptology* 2, 638-639, ns 20-21).
84 Possibly relating to the Semitic *ummi* 'my mother'. See Kitchen, in *Studies in Egyptology* 2, 638, n. 19; Schneider, *Ausländer in Ägypten* 2, 131; Schneider, *AsPN*, 20 [22]. For Egyptian attestations, see Ranke, *Personennamen* 1, 25 [17].
85 Ranke, *Personennamen* 1, 231 [4]; Kitchen, in *Middle Kingdom Studies*, 88.
86 The reading could also be *ꜥmꜥꜣ* 'throw-stick' or, as Goedicke suggests, *sṯn* 'support' (*E&L* 7 [1998], 36).
87 See *Wb* 2, 170 [6].
88 Garstang (*El-Arábah*, pl. 5) and Sethe (*Ägyptische Lesestüke*, 83 [15]) end the term with two quail chicks (Gardiner's G43), however the reading is uncertain. See also Baines, in *Form und Mass*, 52 [rr].
89 Postulated to be the city of Shechem, although the determinative as well as the preceding word point to a regional designate (Goedicke, *E&L* 7 [1998], 34-35; Aḥituv, *Canaanite Toponyms*, 173-174; Redford, *Egypt, Canaan and Israel*, 76; Thompson, *Historicity of the Patriarchal Narratives*, 132; Aharoni, *Land of the Bible*, 134; Ahlström, *History of Ancient Palestine*, 166; Cohen, *Canaanites, Chronologies, and Connections*, 46-47, n. 59). For a similar toponym, see E6 of the Saqqara Execration Texts (Appendix B.4).
90 For *ḫnw*'s identification as the Residence, see Baines, in *Form und Mass*, 51 [dd]. A different interpretation recognises *ḫnw* as the citadel at *Skmm*, with the ensuing *ꜥnḫ(.w) (w)ḏꜣ(.w) s(nb.w)* formula referring back to the majesty. However, in such a case the formula would typically follow *ḥm=f* rather than *ḫnw*. The term *ḫnw* is also used twice in other sections of the stela to refer to Egyptian men of the *ḫnw*, thereby most likely pointing to the Egyptian Residence rather than that of *Skmm*. For more, see Goedicke, *E&L* 7 (1998), 35; Gundlach, *Bevölkerung als Mittel ägyptische Politik*, 172.
91 Goedicke translates the expression as 'when *Skmm* withstood – it and *Rṯnw* will fall' (Goedicke, *E&L* 7 [1998], 35).
92 For this expression, see Baines, in *Form und Mass*, 52 [ll].
93 Ward, *Index*, 90-91 [755].
94 Ranke, *Personennamen* 1, 272 [5].
95 Ranke, *Personennamen* 1, 223 [17].
96 Ranke, *Personennamen* 1, 186 [8].
97 The title and term are not attested in Ward but see Ward, *Index*, 174 [1508].
98 Ranke, *Personennamen* 1, 279 [1].
99 Most possibly of Semitic origin (Schneider, *Ausländer in Ägypten* 2, 127-128).

Cairo CG 20421 (Twelfth Dynasty [?])

(4) *Snb.t(y)=fy msi n ꜥꜣm.t Sꜣ-Mntw* (5) *msi n [...p]ti-n(.y)-[kꜣ.w]=sn*
(6) *ꜥꜣm.t msi n Ḥpyw ꜥnḫ.w* (7) *msi n ꜥꜣm.t Snb-r-ꜣw msi n ꜥꜣm.t*
(8) *Iw-Snb msi n ꜥꜣm.t ꜥnḫ(.w) ḏ.t*
(4) Senebtyfy,[100] born to *ꜥꜣm.t*; Samontu,[101] (5) born to [...p]tiny[kau]sen;
(6) *ꜥꜣm.t*, born to Hepyu;[102] Ankhu,[103] (7) born to *ꜥꜣm.t*; Senebraw,[104] born to *ꜥꜣm.t*;
(8) Iuseneb,[105] born to *ꜥꜣm.t*; may he/they live eternally.

Vienna ÄS 169 (Twelfth Dynasty [?])

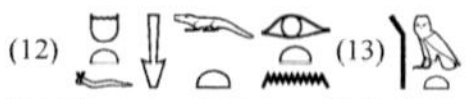

(12) *ḥm.t=f Sn.t-Sbk iri.t n* (13)*ꜥꜣm.t*
(12) His wife Senet-Sobek,[106] born to (13)*ꜥꜣm.t*

Stelae assigned to the late Twelfth to Thirteenth Dynasty

Fitzwilliam Museum E.60.1926

(4) *Kms iri n Ḳdmnt*
(4) Kemes,[107] born to *Ḳdmnt*[108]

Vienna ÄS 99

(12) *sꜣ.t=s ꜥꜣm.t Dd.t*
(12) Her daughter, *ꜥꜣm.t* Djedjet[109]

Vienna ÄS 186 (shrine)

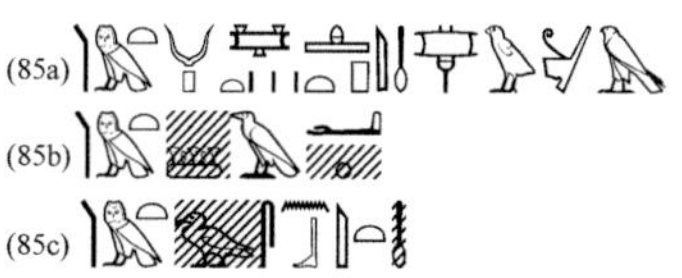

(85a) *ꜥꜣm.t Wp-wꜣ.wt-ḥtp mꜣꜥ(.t)-ḫrw nfw N(.y)-Ḥr.w*
(85b) *ꜥꜣm.t [Š]ꜣꜥ*
(85c) *ꜥꜣm.t [Ḏfꜣ]-snb, mꜣꜥ.t-ḫrw*
(85a) *ꜥꜣm.t* Wepwawethotep,[110] justified; sailor[111] Nyhoru;[112]
(85b) *ꜥꜣm.t* [Sh]aa;[113]
(85c) *ꜥꜣm.t* [Djefa]seneb,[114] justified

Stelae assigned to the Thirteenth Dynasty

Liverpool E.30 (Khendjer)

ꜥfty ꜥꜣm Ir[s?]i
ꜥꜣm Sbk-iry
ꜥꜣm.t Snb-imny-nb-it
ꜥꜣm Sbk-iry
The brewer, *ꜥꜣm* Ir[s?]i;
ꜥꜣm Sobekiry;[115]
ꜥꜣm.t Senebimenynebit;[116]
ꜥꜣm Sobekiry

Vienna ÄS 204 (Sobekhotep IV [?])

(11) *sn=f ꜥꜣm mꜣꜥ-ḫrw*
(11) His brother *ꜥꜣm*, justified

Vienna ÄS 143

(27) *ꜥꜣm.t Wr-nb*
(28) *ꜥꜣm.t Sbk-nḫ.t*
(27) *ꜥꜣm.t* Werneb;
(28) *ꜥꜣm.t* Sobeknekhet

Vienna ÄS 160

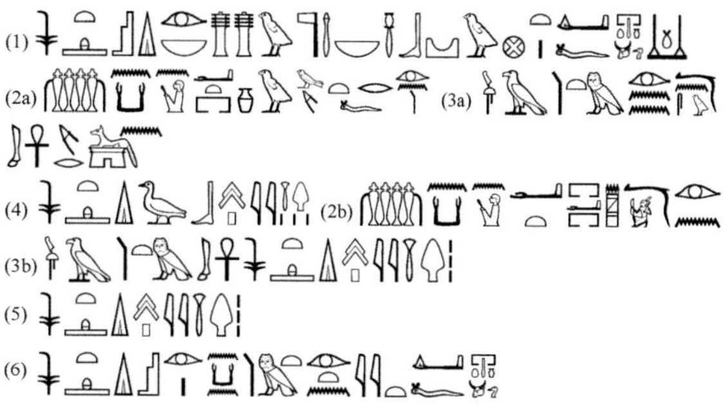

100 Ranke, *Personennamen* 1, 314 [23].
101 Ranke, *Personennamen* 1, 282 [7].
102 Ranke, *Personennamen* 1, 238 [8].
103 Ranke, *Personennamen* 1, 68 [6].
104 Ranke, *Personennamen* 1, 313 [13].
105 Ranke, *Personennamen* 1, 15 [22].
106 Ranke, *Personennamen* 1, 297 [2].
107 Ranke, *Personennamen* 1, 345 [16].
108 Most possibly of Semitic origin (Schneider, *Ausländer in Ägypten* 2, 166-167).
109 Ranke, *Personennamen* 1, 59 [4]; Schneider, *Ausländer in Ägypten* 2, 77.
110 Ranke, *Personennamen* 1, 77 [27].
111 Ranke, *Personennamen* 1, 99 [826].
112 The name is not attested in Ranke, *Personennamen*, but the second element is likely Egyptian. See Hein and Satzinger, *Stelen des Mittleren Reiches* 2, 115.
113 Ranke, *Personennamen* 1, 324 [20].
114 The name is not attested in Ranke, *Personennamen*, but the second element is Egyptian. See Hein and Satzinger, *Stelen des Mittleren Reiches* 2, 115.
115 Ranke, *Personennamen* 1, 303 [22].
116 The name, *Snb-Imn.y* is attested (Ranke, *Personennamen* 1, 312 [19]).

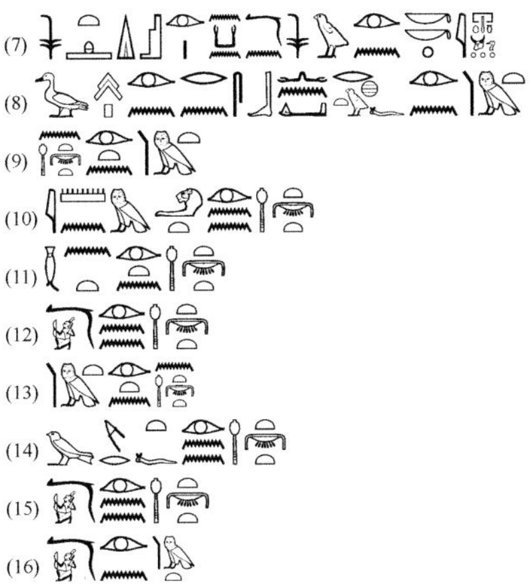

(1) *ḥtp ḏi nsw.t Wsir nb Ḏdw nṯr ꜥꜣ nb ꜣbḏw niw.t ḏi=f pr.t-ḫrw t ḥnḳ(.t) kꜣ(.w) ꜣpd(.w) šs(.wt) mnḫ.wt* (2a) *ḫnty.w n kꜣ n(.y) ir.y-ꜥ.t wdp.w Wr-mr.wt-r=f iri n* (3a) *ʾImnty-ꜥꜣm.t iri n Ny-sw wḥm(.w) ꜥnḫ mr n(.y) ʾInp.w*

(4) *ḥtp ḏi nsw.t Gb Ḥpy wꜣḏ.w imꜣ.w* (2b) *ḫnty.w n kꜣ n(.y) ir.y-ꜥ.t ꜥḥ ʾIm.y-rꜣ-mšꜥ iri n* (3b)*ʾImnty-ꜣm.t wḥm(.t) ꜥnḫ ḥtp ḏi nsw.t Ḥpy wꜣḏ.w imꜣ.w*

(5) *ḥtp ḏi nsw.t Ḥpy wꜣḏ.w imꜣ.w*

(6) *ḥtp ḏi nsw.t Wsir n kꜣ n(.y) ꜥꜣm.t iri.t n ʾI-it ḏi=s pr.t-ḫrw t ḥnḳ.t kꜣ(.w) ꜣpd(.w)*

(7) *ḥtp ḏi nsw.t Wsir n kꜣ n(.y) Ny-sw iri n Kki pr.t-ḫrw t ḥnḳ.t kꜣ.w ꜣpd.w*

(8) *Sꜣ-Ḥpi iri n Rn-S(n)b(.w) Nn-ḏi-rḫ.tw=f iri n ꜥꜣm.t*

(9) *N.t-ḥḏ.t iri.t n ꜥꜣm.t*

(10) *ʾImn-m-ḥꜣ.t iri n N.t-ḥḏ.t*

(11) *Bnr.t iri.t (n) N.t-ḥḏ.t*

(12) *ʾIm.y-rꜣ-mšꜥ iri n N.t-ḥḏ.t*

(13) *ꜥꜣm.t iri.t n N.t-ḥḏ.t*

(14) *Wr-mr.wt=f iri n N.t-ḥḏ.t*

(15) *ʾIm.y-rꜣ-mšꜥ iri n N.t-ḥḏ.t*

(16) *ʾIm.y-rꜣ-mšꜥ iri n ꜥꜣm.t*

(1) An offering which the king gives and Osiris, lord of Busiris, the great god, lord of the city Abydos: may he give an invocation offering of bread, beer, beef, fowl, (ointment) alabasters and clothes (2a) which are for the *kꜣ* of the hall-keeper and butler Wermerutef,[117] born to (3a) Imenty-*ꜥꜣm.t* and Nysu,[118] repeating life, beloved of Anubis.

(4) An offering which the king gives and Geb and Hapy, may he/she be prosperous and splendid; (2b) which are for the *kꜣ* of the hall-keeper of the palace,[119] Imyramesha,[120] born to (3b) Imenty-*ꜥꜣm.t*, repeating life, and an offering which the king gives and Hapy, may he/she be prosperous and splendid.

(5) An offering which the king gives and Hapy, may he/she be prosperous and splendid.

(6) An offering which the king gives and Osiris, for the *kꜣ* of *ꜥꜣm.t*, born to I-it:[121] may she give/be given an invocation offering of bread, beer, beef and fowl.

(7) An offering which the king gives and Osiris, for the *kꜣ* of Nysu, born to Keki:[122] (may he give/be given) an invocation offering of bread, beer, beef and fowl.

(8) Sahepi, born to Rense(ne)b(u); Nendjirekhtuef,[123] born to *ꜥꜣm.t;*

(9) Nethedjet,[124] born to *ꜥꜣm.t*;

(10) Amenemhat,[125] born to Nethedjet;

(11) Beneret,[126] born to Nethedjet;

(12) Imyramesha, born to Nethedjet;

(13) *ꜥꜣm.t*, born to Nethedjet;

(14) Wermerutef, born to Nethedjet;

(15) Imyramesha, born to Nethedjet;

(16) Imyramesha, born to *ꜥꜣm.t*

Cairo CG 20281

(g) 

(g) *sn.t=f ꜥꜣm.t Mꜣꜥ.t*

(g) His sister, *ꜥꜣm.t* Maat

British Museum EA 428 (mid-Thirteenth Dynasty)

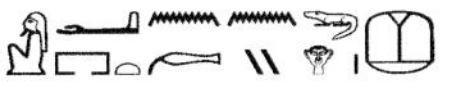

ir.y-ꜥ.t n(.y) Kpny Sbk-ḥr-ḥꜣb

Hall-keeper of (goods from) *Kpny*,[127] Sobekherhab

Cairo CG 20086 (mid-Thirteenth Dynasty)

(m) 

(m) *sn.t=f nb.t pr.w Nb.t-K(b)ny mꜣꜥ.t-ḫrw*

(m) His sister, lady of the house, Nebet-*K*(*b*)*ny*,[128] justified

Marseille 227 (Thirteenth Dynasty [?])

...  ...

... *ꜥꜣm S-nfrw ꜥꜣm.t* [*Snb*]*-rḫ.w ꜥꜣm Nṯr-m-mr ꜥꜣm Rn-*[*snb*(*.w*)] *ꜥꜣm.t Wr-n-Ptḥ ꜥꜣm.t Sꜣ.t-Ḫnmw* ...

...*ꜥꜣm* Senoferu;[129] *ꜥꜣm.t* [Seneb]rehu;[130] *ꜥꜣm* Netjeremer;[131] *ꜥꜣm* Ren[seneb(u)]; *ꜥꜣm.t* Werenptah;[132] *ꜥꜣm.t* Sat-Khnumu[133]...

---

117 The name is clearly derived from the Egyptian.

118 Ranke, *Personennamen* 1, 173 [12].

119 Ward, *Index*, 57 [459].

120 The name is not attested in Ranke, *Personennamen*, but derives from the Egyptian.

121 The similar name, *ʾIyit* is attested (Ranke, *Personennamen* 1, 11 [11]).

122 Ranke, *Personennamen* 1, 349 [1].

123 The name, *N-rḫ.tw=f* is attested (Ranke, *Personennamen* 1, 168 [19]).

124 Ranke, *Personennamen* 1, 181 [7].

125 Ranke, *Personennamen* 1, 28 [8].

126 Ranke, *Personennamen* 1, 97 [17].

127 Identified as Byblos. The title is also attested on an unprovenanced stela currently at University College Dublin (UC 1360). See Grajetzki, *Two Treasurers*, 27-28 [1.4]; Grajetzki, *Middle Kingdom*, 71; Quirke, *RdE* 51 (2000), 223-251; Quirke, *Titles*, 71.

128 Ranke, *Personennamen* 1, 189 [17].

129 Ranke, *Personennamen* 1, 315 [18].

130 Ranke, *Personennamen* 1, 313 [15].

131 Ranke, *Personennamen* 1, 214 [14].

132 Ranke, *Personennamen* 1, 81 [9].

133 Ranke, *Personennamen* 1, 292 [24].

Stelae broadly assigned between the Twelfth and Thirteenth Dynasties

Cairo CG 20028

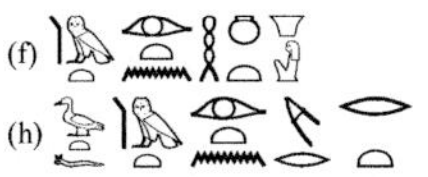

(f) *ꜥꜣm.t iri.t n Ḥnw.t*
(h) *sꜣ.t=f ꜥꜣm.t iri.t n Mrr.t*
(f) *ꜥꜣm.t*, born to Henut;
(h) His daughter *ꜥꜣm.t*, born to Mereret

Cairo CG 20062

(c) *ꜥꜣm iri n Mꜣꜥ.t mꜣꜥ-ḫrw*
(c) *ꜥꜣm*, born to Maat, justified

Cairo CG 20103

(d) *ꜥꜣm=f Ptḥ-wn=f (?)*
(d) His *ꜥꜣm*, Ptahwenef (?)[134]

Cairo CG 20114

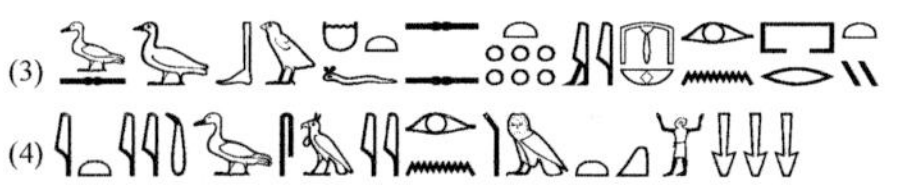

(3) *sꜣ=s Gbw ḥm.t=f Ss.t-iyi(.t)-ḥb iri n Pr.ty-*(4)*ityti sꜣ Snḥy iri n ꜥꜣm.t Ḳꜣ-sn.w*
(3) Her son, Gebu; his wife, Sesetiyitheb, born to Perty-(4)ityti,[135] son of Senehy,[136] born to *ꜥꜣm.t* Qasenu[137]

Cairo CG 20119

(n) [*ꜥꜣm*]*.t Nfr-iw*
(n) [*ꜥꜣm*]*.t* Noferiu[138]

Cairo CG 20158

(b) *ꜥꜣm.t 'Iyi-m-ḥtp*
(b) *ꜥꜣm.t* Iyiemhotep[139]

Cairo CG 20161

(c.29) *ꜥbd*
(c.29) *ꜥbd*[140]

Cairo CG 20164

(g) *ꜥꜣm.t Ptḥ-ꜥꜣ.t fꜣi(.t) dfꜣ.w n nb=s*
(g) *ꜥꜣm.t* Ptahaat,[141] the one who carries provisions for her lord

Cairo CG 20224

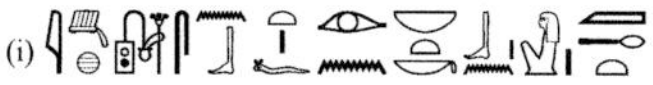

(i) *imꜣḫ(.w) sš Snb.t(y)=f(y) iri n Nb.t-Kbn mꜣꜥ(.t)-ḫrw*
(i) The revered, the scribe, Senebtyfy, born to Nebet-*Kbn*,[142] justified

Cairo CG 20227

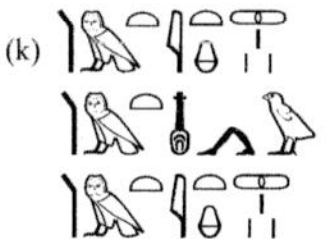

(k) *ꜥꜣm.t 'It*
ꜥꜣm.t Nfr-iw
ꜥꜣm.t 'It
(k) *ꜥꜣm.t* It;[143]
ꜥꜣm.t Noferiu;
ꜥꜣm.t It

Cairo CG 20392

(e.1) *ꜥꜣm=f Snbi*
(e.1) His *ꜥꜣm* Senbi

Cairo CG 20441

(a.2) *ḥm.t=f Kbšty sꜣ.t=f Bb=i*
(a.2) His wife, *Kbšty*;[144] her daughter, Bebi[145]

Cairo CG 20520

(i.1) *it n(.y) ẖrd ꜥꜣm mꜣꜥ-ḫrw*
(i.1) The father of the child,[146] *ꜥꜣm*, justified

134 Ranke, *Personennamen* 1, 139 [3]. Schneider reads the name as *Tpḥ-wn=f* in *Ausländer in Ägypten* 2, 37.
135 As the two halves of the name are on separate lines, they could be two separate individuals. See Schneider, *Ausländer in Ägypten* 2, 37.
136 Or *iri.n Pr.ty-ityti sꜣ=s Nḥy* 'born to Perty-ityti; her son Nehy'. See Schneider, *Ausländer in Ägypten* 2, 37; Mourad *BACE* 24 (2013), n. 32.
137 Ranke, *Personennamen* 1, 332 [17].
138 Ranke, *Personennamen* 1, 194 [7].
139 Ranke, *Personennamen* 1, 9 [2].
140 The name is of Northwest Semitic origin (Ranke, *Personennamen* 1, 60 [9]; Schneider, *Ausländer in Ägypten* 2, 139-140).
141 Ranke, *Personennamen* 1, 138 [18].
142 Ranke, *Personennamen* 1, 189 [17].
143 Ranke, *Personennamen* 1, 49 [5].
144 Most possibly of Akkadian or Amorite origin (Ranke, *Personennamen* 1, 344 [12]; Schneider, *Ausländer in Ägypten* 2, 168).
145 Ranke, *Personennamen* 1, 95 [16].
146 *'It-n-ẖrd* could also be the name of the individual. While the placement of *ꜥꜣm* after this rare name is uncommon, it is not unattested (see CG 20571 for an example).

Cairo CG 20549

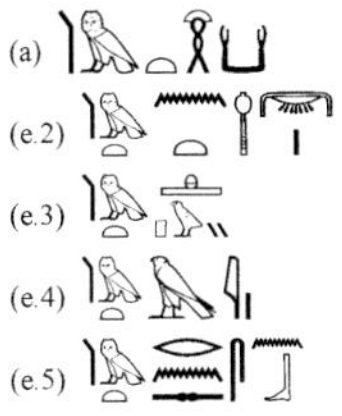

(a) ꜥꜣm.t *Wꜣḥ-kꜣ*
(e.2) ꜥꜣm.t *N.t-ḥd*
(e.3) ꜥꜣm.t *Ḥtp.wy*
(e.4) ꜥꜣm.t *Ḫri*
(e.5) ꜥꜣm.t *Rn=s-snb(.w)*
(a) *ꜥꜣm.t* (of?) Wahka;[147]
(e.2 *ꜥꜣm.t* Nethedj;[148]
(e.3) *ꜥꜣm.t* Hotepwy;[149]
(e.4) *ꜥꜣm.t* Hori;[150]
(e.5) *ꜥꜣm.t* Renesseneb(u)[151]

Cairo CG 20550

(a) *ꜥꜣm.t Sbk-ḥtp*
(c.4) *ꜥꜣm.t Sbk-ꜥꜣ*
(a) *ꜥꜣm.t* Sobekhotep;[152]
(c.4) *ꜥꜣm.t* Sobekaa[153]

Cairo CG 20571

(c.1) *wdp.w Ḥp.w ꜥꜣm*
(c.1) The butler, Hepu,[154] *ꜥꜣm*

Cairo CG 20650

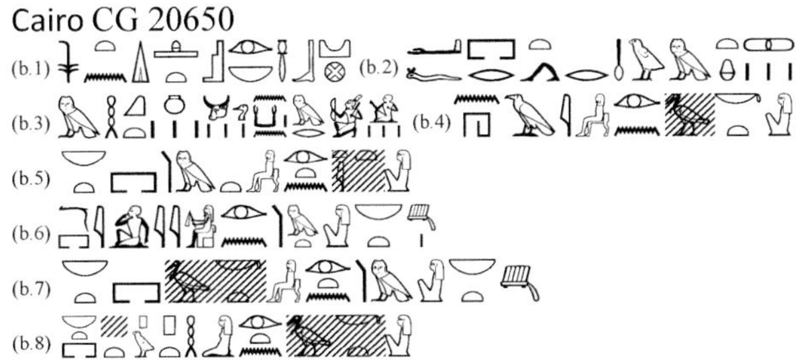

(b.1) *ḥtp-di-nsw.t Wsir nb ꜣbḏw* (b.2) *di=f pr.t-r-ḫrw(.t) m t*
(b.3) *m ḥnḳ.t kꜣ.w ꜣpd.w n kꜣ n(.y) im.y-rꜣ mšꜥ* (b.4) *Nḥꜣi iri n [Bꜣ]k.t*
(b.5) *nb.t pr.w ꜥꜣm.t iri.t n [Tit...]*
(b.6) *im.y-rꜣ pr.w Ꞽ-y iri n ꜥꜣm.t nb.t imꜣḫ*
(b.7) *nb.t pr.w [Bꜣk.t] iri.t n ꜥꜣm(.t) nb.t imꜣḫ*
(b.8 *nb.t pr.w [...].t-pw-Ptḥ iri.t n [Bꜣk.t]*
(b.9) *nb.t pr.w Snb=f iri.t n Ꞽ-ttw nb.t imꜣḫ*
(b.1) An offering which the king gives and Osiris, lord of Abydos:
(b.2) may he give invocation offerings of bread, (b.3) beer, beef and fowl to the *kꜣ* of the overseer of the expedition,[155]
(b.4) Nehai,[156] born to [Ba]ket;[157]
(b.5) Lady of the house, *ꜥꜣm.t*, born to [Tit...];
(b.6) Steward,[158] I-y,[159] born to *ꜥꜣm.t*, possessor of reverence;
(b.7) Lady of the house, [Baket], born to *ꜥꜣm.t*, possessor of veneration;
(b.8) Lady of the house, [..]tpuptah, born to [Baket];
(b.9) Lady of the house, Senebef, born to I-tetu, possessor of reverence.

CG 20678

(4) *im.y-rꜣ mr n(.y) Ꞽwn.t* (5) *Ꞽmb.w msi n nb.t pr.w Nb.t-Kpny mꜣꜥ.t-ḫrw nb.t imꜣḫ*
(4) The overseer of the canal of Denderah, (5) Imbu, born to the lady of the house, Nebet-*Kpny*, justified, possessor of reverence

Cairo CG 20753

(4) *sn=f ꜥꜣḳ mꜣꜥ-ḫrw*
(4) His brother, *ꜥꜣḳ*,[160] justified

Museum of Archaeology and Anthropology, University of Pennsylvania 69-29-56

šmsw ꜥꜣm mꜣꜥ-ḫrw
The retainer,[161] *ꜥꜣm*, justified

Rio de Janeiro 680 [Nr 21]

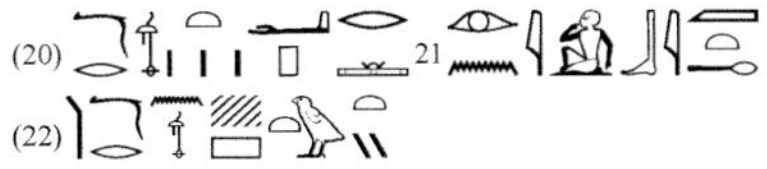

(20) *im.y-rꜣ ḥm.wt ꜥpr* [21]*iri n Ꞽ-bi mꜣ.t-ḫrw*
(22) *ꜥꜣm im.y-rꜣ n(.y) ḥm.wt Twty*
(20) Overseer of craftsmen,[162] *ꜥpr*,[163] (21)born to *Ꞽ-bi*,[164] justified;
(22) *ꜥꜣm*, overseer of craftsmen, *Twty*[165]

147 Ranke, *Personennamen* 1, 73 [23]. *ꜥꜣm.t* could either be a name or part of the *nomens regens* of a direct genitive in '*ꜥꜣm.t* of Wahka', as Wahka is also the name of the stela's dedicator.
148 Ranke, *Personennamen* 1, 181 [7].
149 Ranke, *Personennamen* 1, 260 [10].
150 Ranke, *Personennamen* 1, 251 [8].
151 Ranke, *Personennamen* 1, 224 [1].
152 Ranke, *Personennamen* 1, 305 [6].
153 Ranke, *Personennamen* 1, 303 [24].
154 Ranke, *Personennamen* 1, 238 [14].
155 Ward, *Index*, 29 [205].
156 Ranke, *Personennamen* 1, 207 [3].
157 Ranke, *Personennamen* 1, 92 [5].
158 Ward, *Index*, 21 [32].
159 Ranke, *Personennamen* 1, 7 [17].
160 The name is most possibly of Semitic origin (Ranke, *Personennamen* 1, 59 [6]; Schneider, *Ausländer in Ägypten* 2, 138, 143).
161 Ward, *Index*, 175 [1517].
162 Ranke, *Personennamen* 1, 38 [282].
163 Most possibly of Semitic origin (Ranke, *Personennamen* 1, 60 [12]; Kitchen, in *Middle Kingdom Studies*, 89; Kitchen, in *Studies in Egyptology*, 637-638; Schneider, *Ausländer in Ägypten* 2, 141).
164 Possibly of Semitic origin (Ranke, *Personennamen* 1, 20 [5-10]; Kitchen, in *Middle Kingdom Studies*, 89; Kitchen, in *Studies in Egyptology*, 638; Schneider, *Ausländer in Ägypten* 2, 125-126).
165 Most possibly of Semitic origin (Kitchen, in *Studies in Egyptology*, 636-637; Kitchen, in *Middle Kingdom Studies*, 88-89; Schneider,

STELA	DATE	STELA FOR...	ASIATIC(S)	REPRESENTATION	REFERENCE(S)
LOUVRE C1	A I Year 24	count, overseer of the expedition, Nesumontu	3 groups: *ỉwn.tyw*, *Mnṯw.tyw*, *Ḥr.yw-šꜥ*	text separated from main text describing Asiatics as destroyed targets	Sethe, *Ägyptische Lesestüke*, 82 [12-15]; Simpson, *Terrace*, pl. 14 [6.2]; Obsomer, *RdE* 44 (1993), 103-140
CG 20539	S I	vizier, treasurer, Montuhotep	3 groups: *Ḫꜣs.tyw*, *Ḥr.yw-š*, *St.(t)yw*	in a sequence of epithets concerning the bellicose treatment of foreigners	*Grab und Denk.* 2, 150-158; vol. 4, pl. 41; Simpson, *MDAIK* 47 (1991), 333
CG 20296	S III	overseer of tenant farmers, Seneb (Iunofert's father of Rio 627)	4 x m	in list of individuals (household members?)	*Grab und Denk.* 1, 309-310; *AÄ* 2, 40-41
RIO DE JANEIRO 627 [2419; NR 1]	S III	overseer of a storehouse, Senwosretiunofert	2 x m	as Egyptian; Gebgeb kneeling in a row of officials; Herunofer in list of individuals	Kitchen, *Catalogue* 1, 14-22; vol. 2, pls 1-2; *AÄ* 2, 68-69
MANCHESTER 3306	S III	great attendant of the city, Khusobek	2 groups: *Mnṯw* of *St.t*, *ꜥꜣm.w*	text separated from main text describing Asiatics as destroyed targets	Garstang, *El-Arábah*, 6, 32-34, pls 4-5; Peet, *Stela of Sebek-Khu*, 5, pls 1-2; Simpson, *Terrace*, pl. 31 [69.1]; Sethe, *Ägyptische Lesestüke*, 83 [8-15]
CG 20231	A III	scribe of the outer chamber, Senbi	1 x m	as Egyptian, seated among officials	*Grab und Denk.* 1, 250-252; vol. 4, pl. 18; *AÄ* 2, 39
E.207. 1900	A III	steward of divine offerings, Amenemhat, Nebwy	2 x m	as Egyptians; Rennefsenebu offering an ox leg; Nebsumenu carrying lotus stems and baskets of fowl	Garstang, *El-Arábah*, 33-34, pl. 6; Bourriau, *Pharoahs and Mortals*, 50-51 [39]
CG 20140	A III	sealer of the king of Lower Egypt, Iykhernofert	1 x m	as Egyptian, kneeling	*Grab und Denk.* 1, 165; vol. 4, pl. 13
CG 20125	12th Dyn. (?)	Senwosret	1 x f	in list of family relatives	*Grab und Denk.* 1, 147-148; vol. 4, pl. 11; *AÄ* 2, 38
CG 20421	12th Dyn. (?)	Senwosret	5 x m 1 x f	in list of individuals (household members?)	*Grab und Denk.* 2, 16-17; *AÄ* 2, 43-44
ÄS 169	12th Dyn. (?)	Kheperkara and Kuki	1 x f	as Egyptian, seated behind her husband, Werenhor, at an offering table	Hein and Satzinger, *Stelen des Mittleren Reiches* 2, 87-93; *AÄ* 2, 79-80
E.60.1926	late 12th Dyn.	steward, Sobekhotep Senebrau	1 x m	in list of individuals mostly of low status	Petrie, *Tombs of the Courtiers*, 11, pl. 29 [281]; Bourriau, *Pharaohs and Mortals*, 52-53 [41]
ÄS 99	late 12th - 13th Dyn.	overseer of a law-court, Khentykhety-hotep	1 x f	in list of individuals; daughter of Kui, wife of Khentykhetyhotep; seven siblings listed but with no identifiable foreign ancestry	Hein and Satzinger, *Stelen des Mittleren Reiches* 2, 28-32; *AÄ* 2, 77
ÄS 186	late 12th - 13th Dyn.	(shrine) of overseer of a half-gang of stone-masons, Hori	3 x f	in list of individuals; Nyhoru's title and name are written in the same rectangle as Wepwawethotep, perhaps signifying some relation	Hein and Satzinger, *Stelen des Mittleren Reiches* 2, 111-127; *AÄ* 2, 80
LIVERPOOL E.30	Khen.	regulator of a phyle, Imenyseneb	3 x m 1 x f	as Egyptians, straining liquid into a jar, pouring beer into a jar, grinding grain, sowing seed	Kitchen, *JEA* 47 (1961), 10-18; Kitchen, *JEA* 48 (1962), 159-160; Bourriau, *Pharaohs and Mortals*, 60-63 [48]; *AÄ* 2, 52
VIENNA ÄS 204	13th Dyn. (So. IV ?)	great attendant of the city, Sarerut	1 x m	in list of individuals (household members); as Egyptian, seated; described as a brother, but parentage is unclear; possibly connected to the individuals of Stela Turin 98 (1629) of So. IV's reign	Hein and Satzinger, *Stelen des Mittleren Reiches* 1, 162-167; *AÄ* 2, 77, 80-81
VIENNA ÄS 143	13th Dyn.	chamberlain of the private apartments, Titi and others	2 x f	in list of individuals (household members?)	Hein and Satzinger, *Stelen des Mittleren Reiches* 1, 68-74; *AÄ* 2, 78
VIENNA ÄS 160	13th Dyn.	hall-keeper and butler, Wermerutef; hall-keeper of the palace, Imyramesha	8 x m 4 x f	as Egyptians; stela of brothers of Asiatic descent; immediate family members of Asiatic descent; 20 individuals not directly linked to the family are listed, including a scribe of a sanctuary, an attendant of a chamber, an overseer of a hall, butlers and a *wꜥb*-priest	Hein and Satzinger, *Stelen des Mittleren Reiches* 2, 79-86; *AÄ* 2, 78-79
CG 20281	13th Dyn.	Rekhtyhotep	1 x f	as Egyptian, seated; probable connection to CG 20062	*Grab und Denk.* 1, 295-297; vol. 4, pl. 20; *AÄ* 2, 40

FIGURE B.2. ABYDOS STELAE REPRESENTING ASIATICS AND LEVANTINE TOPONYMS (1/2).

STELA	DATE	STELA FOR...	ASIATIC(S)	REPRESENTATION	REFERENCE(S)
BM EA 428	mid-13th Dyn.	treasurer, Senbi	-	title related to *Kpny*; otherwise of Egyptian ancestry	Peet, *Abydos* 2, 111, fig. 65, pl. 23 [3]; Grajetzki, *Two Treasurers*, 27-28 [1.4]
CG 20086	mid-13th Dyn.	deputy treasurer, Ibiau	-	in list of household members; name related to *K(b)ny*; otherwise of Egyptian ancestry	*Grab und Denk.* 1, 101-103
MARSEILLE 227	13th Dyn. (?)	major-domo of the great house, Renseneb	3 x m 3 x f	in list of individuals (household members?)	Maspero, *RT* 13 (1890), 116-117 [27]; Satzinger and Stefanović, in *From Illahun to Djeme*, 241-245; *AÄ* 2, 58
CG 20028	-	Keshu	2 x f	depiction of Mereret's daughter: as Egyptian; immediate family possibly of Asiatic ancestry	*Grab und Denk.* 1, 36-37; vol. 4, pl. 3; *AÄ* 2, 36
CG 20062	-	Panetyn	1 x m	as Egyptian, seated in a row of relatives (?); probable connection to CG 20281	*Grab und Denk.* 1, 75-77; vol. 4, pl. 6; *AÄ* 2, 37
CG 20103	-	Bedjetyn-shemaankhu	1 x m	as Egyptian, standing behind the son of the stela's owner; pronoun (*ʿ3m=f*) could refer to either the son or the father	*Grab und Denk.* 1, 125-127; *AÄ* 2, 37
CG 20114	-	Bedjetysenyseneb	2 x f	in list of family relatives	*Grab und Denk.* 1, 136-137; *AÄ* 2, 37
CG 20119	-	keeper of a property, Nehnen	1 x f (?)	as Egyptian, kneeling; reading uncertain	*Grab und Denk.* 1, 141-143; *AÄ* 2, 38
CG 20158	-	steward, Noferrudj	1 x f	as Egyptian, standing, carrying a basket and a jar hanging from a rope	*Grab und Denk.* 1, 185-186; *AÄ* 2, 38
CG 20161	-	(unknown)	1 x m	in list of individuals	*Grab und Denk.* 1, 189-191
CG 20164	-	Sobekhotep	1 x f	as Egyptian, kneeling, basket on her head	*Grab und Denk.* 1, 195-197; vol. 4, pl. 14; *AÄ* 2, 38-39
CG 20224	-	scribe of offerings, Senebtyfy	-	mother of Senebtyfy; name related to *Kbn*; otherwise of Egyptian ancestry	*Grab und Denk.* 1, 244
CG 20227	-	overseer of fields, Antyhotep	3 x f	in list of individuals (household members?)	*Grab und Denk.* 1, 246-247; *AÄ* 2, 39
CG 20392	-	steward of divine offerings, Sobekhotep	1 x m	in list of individuals (household members?)	*Grab und Denk.* 1, 388-389; vol. 4, pl. 28; *AÄ* 2, 41-42
CG 20441	-	(unknown)	2 x f	in list of household members; wife and daughter of Noferiu, member of the ruler's household	*Grab und Denk.* 2, 39
CG 20520	-	magnate of the southern tens, Nehy	1 x m	as Egyptian, seated before offering table	*Grab und Denk.* 2, 116-122; vol. 4, pl. 36; *AÄ* 2, 44-45
CG 20549	-	steward, Wahka	5 x f	*ʿ3m.t* as standing Egyptian, bringing offerings to Wahka; others as Egyptian girls with side-locks of youth	*Grab und Denk.* 2, 177-179; Simpson, *Terrace*, pl. 41 [32.1]; *AÄ* 2, 45
CG 20550	-	steward, Sobekaa	2 x f	as Egyptians; Sobekhotep standing, basket on head, jug and lotus in left hand; Sobekaa kneeling, basket on head, fowl in right hand	*Grab und Denk.* 2, 179-181; vol. 4, pl. 43; *AÄ* 2, 45-46
CG 20571	-	chamberlain of the bureau of the overseer of the treasury, Remnyankh	1 x m	as Egyptian, offering an ox leg	*Grab und Denk.* 2, 209-211; vol. 4, pl. 46; *AÄ* 2, 46
CG 20650	-	overseer of the expedition, Nehai	2 x m 4 x f	stela of Asiatic descendant; most, if not all, of the list of individuals are of Asiatic descent	*Grab und Denk.* 2, 284-285; *AÄ* 2, 46
CG 20678	-	steward of a storehouse, Senbi	-	as grandmother of Senbi; name possibly related to *Kpny*; otherwise of Egyptian ancestry	*Grab und Denk.* 2, 305; vol. 4, pl. 51
CG 20753	-	Renefankh	1 x m	in list of household members	*Grab und Denk.* 2, 387; vol. 4, pl. 58
U. PENN. MUSEUM 69-29-56	-	(fragment of cenotaph stela)	1 x m	in list of individuals (household members?); as Egyptian, seated	Simpson, *Inscribed Material*, 40-41, fig. 67, pl. 8 [d]; *AÄ* 2, 68
RIO DE JANEIRO 680 [NR 21]	-	member of the foremen, Karu	2 x m	*ʿpr* as Egyptian; name and title of *Twty* appear near figure of *ʿpr*	Kitchen, *Catalogue* 1, 64-67; vol. 2, pl. 45; *AÄ* 2, 69-70

FIGURE B.2. ABYDOS STELAE REPRESENTING ASIATICS AND LEVANTINE TOPONYMS (2/2), WITH NOTATIONS ON THEIR DATE AND BIBLIOGRAPHICAL REFERENCES.

Notes: A: Amenemhat — m: male
S: Senwosret — f: female
Khen: Khendjer — *Grab und Denk.*: Lange and Schäfer, *Grab und Denksteine*, vols 1-2.
So.: Sobekhotep — *AÄ*: Schneider, *Ausländer im Ägypten*.

B.6 Berlin Execration Bowls[166]

Prov. Unknown
Ref. Sethe, *Ächtung feindlicher Fürsten*, 45-59, pls 15-21.
Chron. Mid-late Twelfth Dynasty
Chapter 4.6.1

e1 

ḥḳ3 n(.y) Yiʿnḳ ʿ3m ḥnk.w nb.w n.t(y)w ḥnʿ=f
Ruler of *Yiʿnḳ*,[167] *ʿ3m*, and all acquaintances who are with him

e2 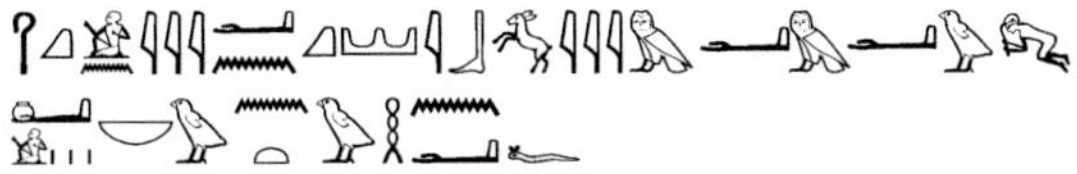

ḥḳ3 n(.y) Yiʿnḳ Ỉb-yimʿmʿw ḥnk.w nb.w n.t(y)w ḥnʿ=f
Ruler of *Yiʿnḳ*, *Ỉb-yimʿmʿw*, and all acquaintances who are with him

e3 

ḥḳ3 n(.y) Yiʿnḳ ʿk3m ḥnk.w nb.w n.t(y)w ḥnʿ=f
Ruler of *Yiʿnḳ*, *ʿk3m*, and all acquaintances who are with him

e4 

ḥḳ3 n(.y) Šwtw Ỉyi-bm ḥnk.w nb.w n.t(y)w ḥnʿ=f
Ruler of *Šwtw*,[168] *Ỉyi-bm*, and all acquaintances who are with him

e5 

ḥḳ3 n(.y) Šwtw Kwšr ḥnk.w nb.w n.t(y)w ḥnʿ=f
Ruler of *Šwtw*, *Kwšr*, and all acquaintances who are with him

e6 

ḥḳ3 n(.y) Šwtw Ṯb3nw ḥnk.w nb.w n.t(y)w ḥnʿ=f
Ruler of *Šwtw*, *Ṯb3nw*, and all acquaintances who are with him

e7 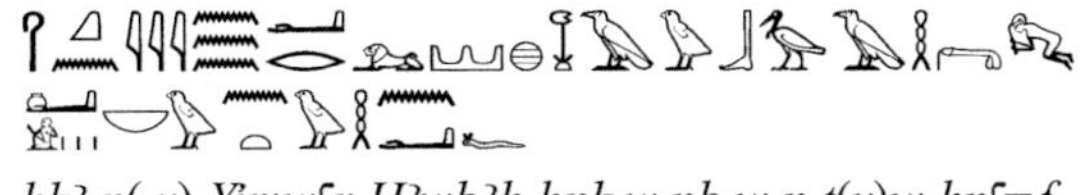

ḥḳ3 n(.y) Yimwʿr Ḫ3wb3ḥ ḥnk.w nb.w n.t(y)w ḥnʿ=f
Ruler of *Yimwʿr*, *Ḫ3wb3ḥ*, and all acquaintances who are with him

e8 

ḥḳ3 n(.y) Ḳhrmw ʿmwit3 ḥnk.w nb.w n.t(y)w ḥnʿ=f
Ruler of *Ḳhrmw*, *ʿmwit3*, and all acquaintances who are with him

e9 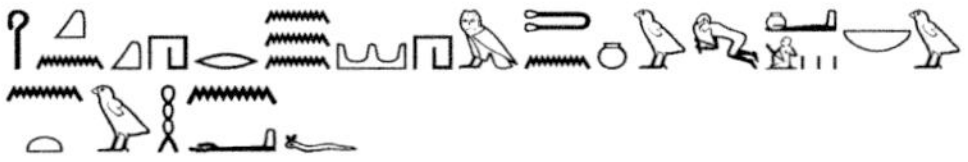

ḥḳ3 n(.y) Ḳhrmw Hmṯnw ḥnk.w nb.w n.t(y)w ḥnʿ=f
Ruler of *Ḳhrmw*, *Hmṯnw*, and all acquaintances who are with him

e10 

ḥḳ3 n(.y) Ḳhrmw ʿmwyikn ḥnk.w nb.w n.t(y)w ḥnʿ=f
Ruler of *Ḳhrmw*, *ʿmwyikn*, and all acquaintances who are with him

e11 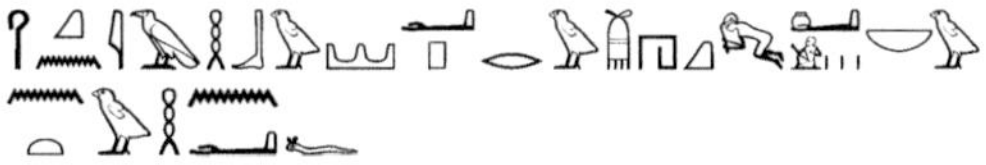

ḥḳ3 n(.y) Ỉ3ḥbw ʿprw-hḳ ḥnk.w nb.w n.t(y)w ḥnʿ=f
Ruler of *Ỉ3ḥbw*, *ʿprw-hḳ*, and all acquaintances who are with him

e12 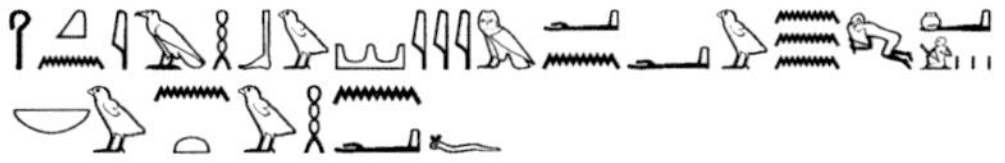

ḥḳ3 n(.y) Ỉ3ḥbw Yimʿnʿwmw ḥnk.w nb.w n.t(y)w ḥnʿ=f
Ruler of *Ỉ3ḥbw*, *Yimʿnʿwmw*, and all acquaintances who are with him

e13 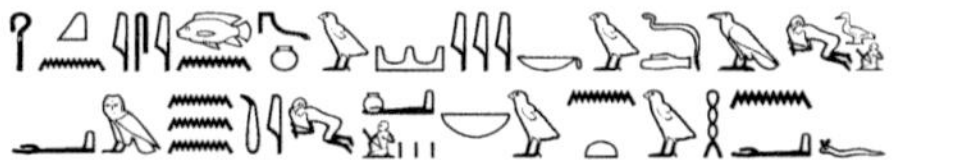

ḥḳ3 n(.y) Ỉsinw Yikwḏd3 s3 ʿmwti ḥnk.w nb.w n.t(y)w ḥnʿ=f
Ruler of *Ỉsinw*, *Yikwḏd3*'s son *ʿmwti*, and all acquaintances who are with him

e14 

ḥḳ3 n(.y) Ỉsinw ʿwḏwšnw ḥnk.w nb.w n.t(y)w ḥnʿ=f
Ruler of *Ỉsinw*, *ʿwḏwšnw*, and all acquaintances who are with him

e15 

ḥḳ3 n(.y) Ỉsinw M33mt ḥnk.w nb.w n.t(y)w ḥnʿ=f
Ruler of *Ỉsinw*, *M33mt*, and all acquaintances who are with him

e16 

ḥḳ3 n(.y) Ỉnhi3 [M3]k3m(?) ḥnk.w nb.w n.t(y)w ḥnʿ=f
Ruler of *Ỉnhi3*, [*M3*]*k3m*(?), and all acquaintances who are with him

Ausländer in Ägypten 2, 172; Schneider, *AsPN*, 243-244 [521]).

166 The variant spellings of toponyms inscribed on the different vessels are not included here but may be found in Sethe's publication.

167 For a similar toponym, *Yʿnḳi*, in E36 of the Saqqara Execration Texts, see Appendix B.4.

168 For the same toponym in E52-3 of the Saqqara Execration Texts, see Chapter 4.3.8, Appendix B.4.

e17 

ḥk3 n(.y) ꞽInhi3 Km3m ḥnk.w nb.w n.t(y)w ḥnᶜ=f
Ruler of *ꞽInhi3*, *Km3m*, and all acquaintances who are with him

e18 

ḥk3 n(.y) ꞽInhi3 3k̠ḥm ḥnk.w nb.w n.t(y)w ḥnᶜ=f
Ruler of *ꞽInhi3*, *3k̠ḥm*, and all acquaintances who are with him

e19 

ḥk3 n(.y) ꞽInhi3 Yipᶜnw ḥnk.w nb.w n.t(y)w ḥnᶜ=f
Ruler of *ꞽInhi3*, *Yipᶜnw*, and all acquaintances who are with him

e20 

ḥk3 n(.y) 3k̠hi Yik̠3d̠mw ḥnk.w nb.w n.t(y)w ḥnᶜ=f
Ruler of *3k̠hi*, *Yik̠3d̠mw*, and all acquaintances who are with him

e21 

ḥk3 n(.y) 3k̠hi Šmšwiri[m] ḥnk.w nb.w n.t(y)w ḥnᶜ=f
Ruler of *3k̠hi*, *Šmšwiri[m]*, and all acquaintances who are with him

e22 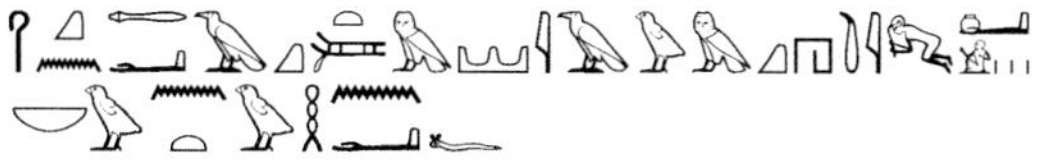

ḥk3 n(.y) ᶜ3ktm ꞽI3wmk̠hti ḥnk.w nb.w n.t(y)w ḥnᶜ=f
Ruler of *ᶜ3ktm*,[169] *ꞽI3wmk̠hti*, and all acquaintances who are with him

e23 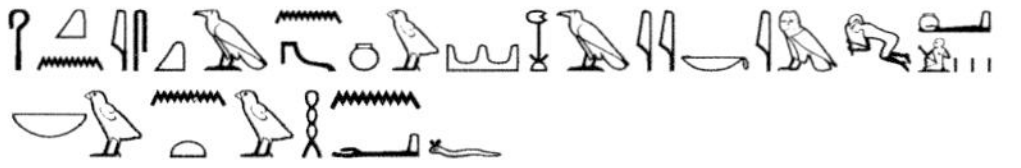

ḥk3 n(.y) ꞽIsk̠3nw H̱3ykim ḥnk.w nb.w n.t(y)w ḥnᶜ=f
Ruler of *ꞽIsk̠3nw*,[170] *H̱3ykim*, and all acquaintances who are with him

e24 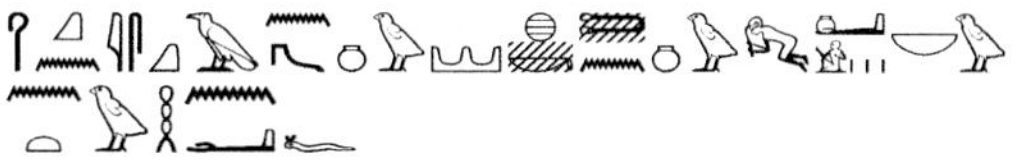

ḥk3 n(.y) ꞽIsk̠3nw H̱[kt̠]nw ḥnk.w nb.w n.t(y)w ḥnᶜ=f
Ruler of *ꞽIsk̠3nw*, *H̱[kt̠]nw*, and all acquaintances who are with him

e25 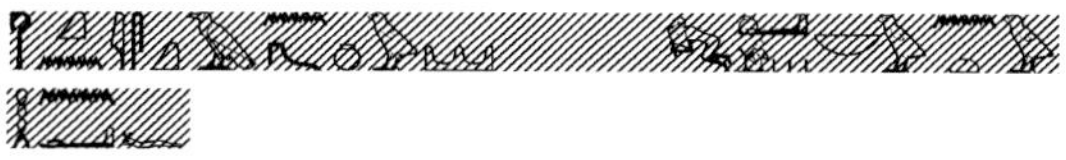

[*ḥk3 n(.y) ꞽIsk̠3nw... ḥnk.w nb.w n.t(y)w ḥnᶜ=f*]
[Ruler of *ꞽIsk̠3nw*, ..., and all acquaintances who are with him]

e26 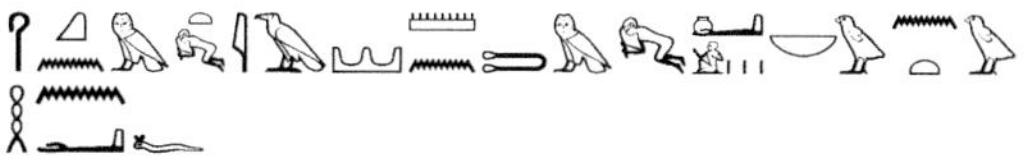

ḥk3 n(.y) M(w)ti3 Mnt̠m ḥnk.w nb.w n.t(y)w ḥnᶜ=f
Ruler of *M(w)ti3*, *Mnt̠m*, and all acquaintances who are with him

e27 

ḥk3 n(.y) 3wš3mm Yik̠3ᶜmw ḥnk.w nb.w n.t(y)w ḥnᶜ=f
Ruler of *3wš3mm*,[171] *Yik̠3ᶜmw*, and all acquaintances who are with him

e28 

ḥk3 n(.y) 3wš3mm Sṯnw ḥnk.w nb.w n.t(y)w ḥnᶜ=f
Ruler of *3wš3mm*, *Sṯnw*, and all acquaintances who are with him

e29 

ḥk3 n(.y) ᶜḥm(w)t [...]ksm3m ḥnk.w nb.w n.t(y)w ḥnᶜ=f
Ruler of *ᶜḥm(w)t*, [...]*ksm3m*, and all acquaintances who are with him

e30 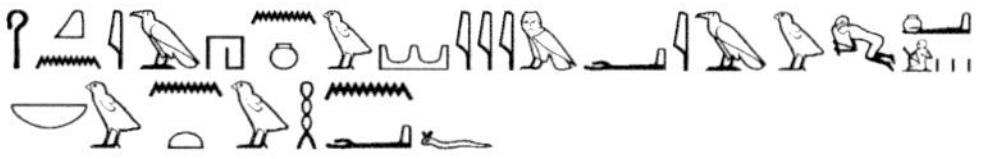

ḥk3 n(.y) ꞽI3hnw Yimᶜi3w ḥnk.w nb.w n.t(y)w ḥnᶜ=f
Ruler of *ꞽI3hnw*, *Yimᶜi3w*, and all acquaintances who are with him

e31 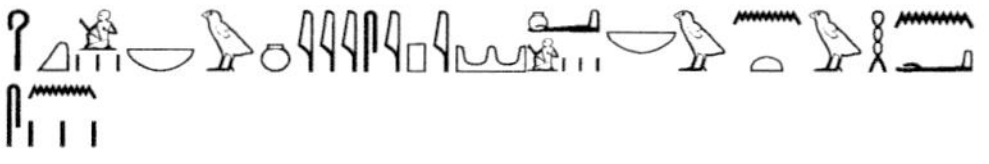

ḥk3.w nb.w n.w Yisipi ḥnk.w nb.w n.t(y)w ḥnᶜ=sn
All rulers of *Yisipi*,[172] and all acquaintances who are with them

f1 

ᶜ3m.w nb.w
All *ᶜ3m.w*

f2 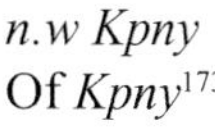

n.w Kpny
Of *Kpny*[173]

---

169 For the same toponym in E54 of the Saqqara Execration Texts, see Appendix B.4.

170 Postulated to be Ashkelon. For a similar toponym, *ꞽIsk̠3i*, in E2 of the Saqqara Execration Texts, see Appendix B.4.

171 Postulated to be Jerusalem (Ben-Tor, in *Essays on Ancient Israel*, 68-70). For the same toponym in E45 of the Saqqara Execration Texts, see, Appendix B.4.

172 Postulated to be Achshaph (Ben-Tor, in *Essays on Ancient Israel*, 75-76). For a similar toponym, *ꞽIsi-pi*, in E12 of the Saqqara Execration Texts, see Appendix B.4.

173 Identified as Byblos (Sethe, *Ächtung feindlicher Fürsten*, 55-56).

f3 
n.w Ỉwꜣṯi
Of *Ỉwꜣṯi*

f4 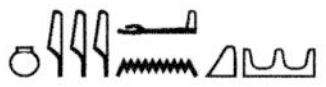
n.w Yiʿnḳ
Of *Yiʿnḳ*

f5 
n.w Šwtw
Of *Šwtw*

f6 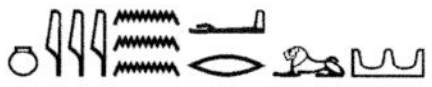
n.w Yimwʿr
Of *Yimwʿr*

f7 
n.w Ḳhrmw
Of *Ḳhrmw*

f8 
n.w Ỉꜣḥbw
Of *Ỉꜣḥbw*

f9 
n.w Yiꜣm(w)t
Of *Yiꜣm(w)t*

f10 
n.w Ỉnhiꜣ
Of *Ỉnhiꜣ*

f11 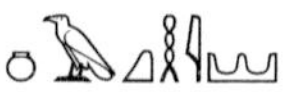
n.w ꜣḳḥi
Of *ꜣḳḥi*

f12 
n.w ʿꜣḳtm
Of *ʿꜣḳtm*

f13 
n.w Yiꜣm(w)t
Of *Yiꜣm(w)t*

f14 
n.w Ỉsinw
Of *Ỉsinw*

f15 
n.w Ỉsḳꜣnw
Of *Ỉsḳꜣnw*

f16 
n.w Dmitiw
Of *Dmitiw*[174]

f17 
n.w M(w)tiꜣ
Of *M(w)tiꜣ*

f18 
n.w ꜣwšꜣmm
Of *ꜣwšꜣmm*

f19 
n.w ʿẖm(w)t
Of *ʿẖm(w)t*

f20 
n.w Ỉꜣhnw
Of *Ỉꜣhnw*

f21 
n.w Yisipi
Of *Yisipi*

g1 
nḫt.w=sn
Their strong men

g2 
wt n.w nmt.t=sn
Their quick men

g3 
smꜣ.w=sn
Their allies

g4 
dmḏ.yw=sn
Their assemblies

g5 
Mntw m St.t
Mntw in *St.t*

174 For the same toponym in F5 of the Saqqara Execration Texts, see Appendix B.4. See also Dussaud, *Syria* 8/3 (1927), 227-229.

B.7 Papyrus Brooklyn 35.1446[175]

Prov. Unknown
Ref. Hayes, *Papyrus Brooklyn*, pls 8-13.
Chron. Mid-Thirteenth Dynasty (reign of Sobekhotep III)
Chapter 4.6.3

	A	B	C	D
1				
	ḥm-nsw.t Rn=s-snb(.w) s3 ꜥnḫ.w	*ḏd.w n=f Ḥdri*	*ḥr.y-pr(.w)*	
	King's servant, Renesseneb(u)'s son Ankhu	He is called Hedjeri	Major-domo	
2				
	ḥm.t Ỉ-y s3.t S3.t-gmi.n(=i)	*rn=s pw*	*nš.t*	
	Servant Iy's daughter Satgemini	It is her name	Hairdresser	
3				
	s3.t=s Rn-snb(.w)	*rn=s pw*	-	
	Her daughter Renseneb(u)	It is her name	-	
4				
	ḥm-nsw.t Ỉw=s-n=i s3 ꜥš3	*rn=f pw*	*ꜥḥ.wty*	
	King's servant Iuseni's son Asha	It is his name	Cultivator	
5				
	Ỉ-y s3 Ỉbw	*rn=f pw*	*ꜥḥ.wty*	
	Iy's son Ibu	It is his name	Cultivator	
6				
	ꜥ3m Snb-rs-snb(.w)	*rn=f pw*	*psy*	
	ꜥ3m Senebresseneb(u)[176]	It is his name	Cook[177]	
7				
	ꜥ3m.t Rḥ.wy	*ḏd.t n=s K3(=i)-pw-nb=i*	*d3 šsr*	
	ꜥ3m.t Rehwy[178]	She is called Kaipunebi[179]	Warper(?) of *šsr*-cloth[180]	
8				
	s3=s Nfw s3 Rs-snb(.w)	*ḏd.w n=f Rn=f-rs(.w)*	-	
	Her son, Nefu's son, Resseneb(u)[181]	He is called Renefres(u)[182]	-	
9				
	[*ꜥ3m ꜥ*]*pr-Ršpw*	[...]	*ꜥfty*	
	[*ꜥ3m ꜥ*]*pr*-Reshef[183]	[...]	Brewer[184]	
10				
	ꜥ3m.t H3immi	*ḏd.t n=s* [....*n*]	*sḫ.ty ḥ3.tyw*	
	ꜥ3m.t H3immi[185]	She is called [...n]	Weaver of *ḥ3.tyw*-cloth[186]	

175 The four columns mark an individual's: (A) name, (B) given name; (C) occupation; and (D) designation as male, female or child.

176 The name is not attested in Ranke, *Personennamen*. However, it is clearly derived from the Egyptian.

177 Ward, *Index*, 94 [787].

178 Ranke, *Personnenamen* 1, 225 [18]. Schneider proposes a Semitic origin for the name, although it is attested in the Egyptian (*UF* 19 [1987], 257-258).

179 The name is not attested in Ranke, *Personenamen*. However, it is clearly derived from the Egyptian. For similar names, see Ranke, *Personnenamen* 1, 339 [9-13].

180 The transcription of the first sign is questioned by Hayes. The translation as *d3* for 'warper' is also reached cautiously. The occupation appears to be associated with the manufacture or preparation of cloth. See Hayes, *Papyrus Brooklyn*, 105-106.

181 Ranke, *Personnenamen* 1, 226 [25].

182 Ranke, *Peronennamen* 1, 223 [16].

183 Postulated to be from the Semitic *ꜥpra-Ršpw* 'nurturer of Reshef', a theophoric name referring to the Levantine deity Reshef (Albright, *JAOS* 74/4 [1954], 225; Hayes, *Papyrus Brooklyn*, 94; Posener, *Syria* 34/1 [1957], 148. See also Ranke, *Personnenamen* 1, 60 [12-18]; Schneider, *UF* 19 [1987], 258-261).

184 Ward, *Index*, 73 [595].

185 Postulated to be from the Semitic *Hay'immī* 'where is my mother?' (Albright, *JAOS* 74/4 [1954], 225-227; Helck, *Die Beziehungen Ägyptens*, 79; Hayes, *Papyrus Brooklyn*, 94-95; Posener, *Syria* 34/1 [1957], 148-149; Schneider, *UF* 19 [1987], 261).

186 Ward, *Index*, 156 [1343].

11	*ʿ3m.t Mnḥmi* ʿ3m.t Mnḥmi[187]	*S[...tn]f* S[...tn]f	*sḫ.ty ḥ3.tyw* Weaver of *ḥ3.tyw*-cloth
12	*ʿ3m Sw[...]i* ʿ3m Sw[...]i	*dd.w n=f ʿnḫ.w-snb(.w)* He is called Ankhuseneb(u)[188]	*psy* Cook
13	*ʿ3m.t Skrtw* ʿ3m.t Skrtw[189]	*dd.t n=s Wr-ʿt-n=i-nbw* She is called Werateninebu[190]	*sḫ.ty ḥ3.tyw* Weaver of *ḥ3.tyw*-cloth
14	*ʾImi-skr(t)w* ʾImi-skr(t)w[191]	*Snb-[S-n]-wsr.t* Seneb[sen]wosret[192]	*[sḫ.ty] ḥ3.tyw* [Weaver] of *ḥ3.tyw*-cloth
15	*ʾIdwtw* ʾIdwtw[193]	*Nb[...]* Neb[...]	*[sḫ.ty ḥ3].tyw* [Weaver of *ḥ3*].*tyw*-cloth
16	*[S]krtw* [S]krtw	*Sn[b...]* Sen[eb...]	*sḫ.ty sšr* Weaver of *sšr*-cloth
17	*ʿ3m.t ʿḫtmr* ʿ3m.t ʿḫtmr[194]	*dd.t n=s Ḥnw.t=i-pw-w3d.t* She is called Henutipuwadjet[195]	*d3 ḥ3.tyw* Warper(?) of *ḥ3.tyw* -cloth
18	*ʿ3m Twtwit* ʿ3m Twtwit[196]	*dd.w n=f ʿnḫ.w-m-ḥs.wt* He is called Ankhuemhesut[197]	*ḥr.y-pr.w* Major-domo[198]
19	*ʿ3m Ḳwi[...]* ʿ3m Ḳwi[...]	*dd.w n=f Rs-snb(.w)* He is called Resseneb(u)	*ḥr.y-pr.w* Major-domo
20	*ḥm-nsw.t ʾIyi.tw[...]* King's servant Iyitu[...]	*rn=f pw* It is his name	*ḥr.y-pr.w* Major-domo
21	*ʿ3m.t Špr* ʿ3m.t Špr[199]	*dd.t n=s Snb-ḥnw.t=s* She is called Senebhenutes[200]	*sḫ.ty ḥ3.tyw* Weaver of *ḥ3.tyw*-cloth

187 Postulated to be from the Semitic *Munaḥḥima* '(such and such a God) shows mercy' (Albright, *JAOS* 74/4 [1954], 227; Helck, *Die Beziehungen Ägyptens*, 79; Hayes, *Papyrus Brooklyn*, 95; Posener, *Syria* 34/1 [1957], 149; Schneider, *UF* 19 [1987], 261-262).

188 The name is not attested in Ranke, *Personennamen*. However, it is clearly derived from the Egyptian.

189 Postulated to be from the Semitic stem *škr* 'reward/favour' (Albright, *JAOS* 74/4 [1954], 227-228; Helck, *Die Beziehungen Ägyptens*, 79; Hayes, *Papyrus Brooklyn*, 95-96; Posener, *Syria* 34/1 [1957], 149).

190 The name is not attested in Ranke, *Personennamen*. However, it is clearly derived from the Egyptian.

191 Postulated to be from the Semitic stems *škr* 'reward/favour' and *immi* 'my mother' (Albright, *JAOS* 74/4 [1954], 227-228; Helck, *Die Beziehungen Ägyptens*, 79; Hayes, *Papyrus Brooklyn*, 95-96).

192 See Ranke, *Personennamen* 1, 279 [1], 312 [15].

193 Postulated to be from the Semitic *aduttu* 'lady' (Albright, *JAOS* 74/4 [1954], 228; Helck, *Die Beziehungen Ägyptens*, 79; Hayes, *Papyrus Brooklyn*, 96; Posener, *Syria* 34/1 [1957], 149).

194 Postulated to be from the Semitic stems *'aḥātu* 'sister' and probably *mil(katu)* 'queen' (Albright, *JAOS* 74/4 [1954], 228-229; Helck, *Die Beziehungen Ägyptens*, 79; Hayes, *Papyrus Brooklyn*, 96; Posener, *Syria* 34/1 [1957], 149; Schneider, *UF* 19 [1987], 264).

195 The name is not attested in Ranke, *Personennamen*. However, it is clearly derived from the Egyptian.

196 Postulated to be from the Semitic *Dôdī-hu'at(u)* 'my beloved is he' (Albright, *JAOS* 74/4 [1954], 229; Helck, *Die Beziehungen Ägyptens*, 79; Hayes, *Papyrus Brooklyn*, 9; Posener, *Syria* 34/1 [1957], 149).

197 Ranke, *Personennamen* 1, 68 [10].

198 Ward, *Index*, 116 [977].

199 Postulated to be from the Semitic stem *špr* 'to be fair/beautiful' (Albright, *JAOS* 74/4 [1954], 229; Helck, *Die Beziehungen Ägyptens*, 79; Hayes, *Papyrus Brooklyn*, 96; Posener, *Syria* 34/1 [1957], 149).

200 See Ranke, *Personennamen* 1, 243 [29], 312 [15].

No.	Name	Alias	Title
22	*ꜥ3m.t Skr[wp...]* *ꜥ3m.t Skr[wp...]*	*ḏd.t [n]=s Mr.t-nb* She is called Meretneb[201]	*ḏ3 šsr* Warper(?) of *šsr*-cloth
23	*ꜥ3m.t ꞽšr* *ꜥ3m.t ꞽšr*[202]	*ḏd[.t n=s] Wr-ini.t=f* [She is] called Werinitef[203]	*sḫ.ty* [...] Weaver [...]
24	*s3.t=s Snb.t(y)=sy* Her daughter Senebtysy[204]	*[rn=s p]w* [It is her name]	- - -
25	*ꜥ3m.t ꜥn[...i]* *ꜥ3m.t ꜥn[...i]*	*ḏd.t n=s Nb-m-mr-ḳis* [She is called] Nebemmerqis[205]	*sḫ.ty [ḥ3.tyw]* Weaver of [*ḥ3.tyw*-cloth]
26	*ꜥ3m.t Šmštw* *ꜥ3m.t Šmštw*[206]	*ḏd.t n=s Snb-ḥnw.t[...]* She is called Senebhenut[...]	*ḏ3 ḥ3.tyw* Warper(?) of *ḥ3.tyw* -cloth
27	*ꜥ3m ꞽꜥsbtw* *ꜥ3m ꞽꜥsbtw*[207]	*ḏd.w n=f ꞽmn[.tyw]* He is called Imen[tyw]	*[šdi]* [Tutor][208]
28	*ḥm.t Wwi s3.t ꞽr.t* Servant Wewi's daughter Iret	*rn=s pw* It is her name	- - -
29	*ꜥ3m[.t D]i3ihitw* *ꜥ3m[.t D]i3ihitw*[209]	*ḏd.t n=s Mn-ḥs[.wt]* She is called Menhes[ut][210]	- - -
30	*s3.t=s [Ddmwtw...]* Her daughter [Dedmutu...][211]	*[rn=s pw]* [It is her name]	- - -
31	*s3=s ꜥnḫ(.w)-snb(.w)* Her son Ankhuseneb(u)	- - -	- - -
32	*ꜥ3m[.t] ꜥḫ[...]* *ꜥ3m[.t] ꜥḫ[...]*	- - -	[...]*ḥ3*[...] [...]ha[...]
33	*ꜥ3m[.t] ꞽ-tni* *ꜥ3m[.t] ꞽ-tni*[212]	*ḏd.t n=s Snb-ḥ[nw.t=s]* She is called Senebhe[nutes]	- - -

201 See Ranke, *Personnenamen* 1, 159 [2].

202 Postulated to be from the Semitic stem *ꜥšr* 'blessed/be prosperous' (Albright, *JAOS* 74/4 [1954], 229-231; Helck, *Die Beziehungen Ägyptens*, 79; Hayes, *Papyrus Brooklyn*, 97).

203 The name is not attested in Ranke, *Personennamen.* However, it is clearly derived from the Egyptian.

204 Ranke, *Personennamen* 1, 314 [25].

205 The name is not attested in Ranke, *Personennamen.* However, it is clearly derived from the Egyptian.

206 Postulated to be a theophoric name consisting of the Levantine deity *Šamaš* (Albright, *JAOS* 74/4 [1954], 231; Helck, *Die Beziehungen Ägyptens*, 80; Hayes, *Papyrus Brooklyn*, 97; Posener, *Syria* 34/1 [1957], 150).

207 Postulated to be from the Semitic stem *ꜥsb* 'herbage' (Hayes, *Papyrus Brooklyn*, 97; Albright, *JAOS* 74/4 [1954], 231; Helck, *Die Beziehungen Ägyptens*, 80; Posener, *Syria* 34/1 [1957], 150).

208 Ward, *Index*, 178 [1537].

209 See n. 196 above.

210 The name is not attested in Ranke, *Personennamen.* However, it is clearly derived from the Egyptian.

211 See Ranke, *Personennamen* 1, 401 [12-13].

212 Postulated to be from the Semitic, although derivation is uncertain (Albright, *JAOS* 74/4 [1954], 231; Helck, *Die Beziehungen Ägyptens*, 80; Hayes, *Papyrus Brooklyn*, 97).

34	*s3=s ꜥnḫ.w* Her son Ankhu[213]	*dd.w n=f Ḥdrw* He is called Hedjeru[214]	- - -
35	*ꜥ3m.t Bꜥ3twy* *ꜥ3m.t Bꜥ3twy*[215]	*dd.t n=s W3ḥ-rs-snb(.w)* She is called Wahresseneb(u)[216]	*t.t k3.t* Labourer(?)[217]
36	*s3.t=s Snb.t(y)=sy* Her daughter Senebt(y)sy	*rn=s pw* It is her name	- - -
37	*ꜥ3m.t ꜥkbi* *ꜥ3m.t ꜥkbi*[218]	*dd.t n=s Rs-snb-w3ḥ* She is called Ressenebwah[219]	*d3 ḥ3.tyw* Warper(?) of *ḥ3.tyw* -cloth
38	[*ḥm.t*] *Sš-ib s3.t Rn-snb(.w)* [Servant] Seshib's daughter Renseneb(u)	*rn=s pw* It is her name	*k3r(y).t* Gardener
39	[*s3.t*]*=s Ḥnw.t=i-pw* Her [daughter] Henutipu	*rn=s pw* It is her name	- - -
40	[...]*Ḥnw.t=i-pw s3.t Sn-nw.t* [...]Henutipu's daughter Sennut	*rn*[*=s p*]*w* [It is her] name	*pr.t n.t r=s* Make-up artist
41	[...]*ib-ꜥnḫ* [...]ibankh	*rn=f pw* It is his name	*ꜥḥ.wty* Cultivator
42	[...]*ḥs.wt* [...]hesut	*rn=f pw* It is his name	*ꜥḥ.wty* Cultivator
43	[...]*y*[*s3 Ḥtp*] [...]y['s son Hotep]	*rn=f pw Ry.t-rn=s-pw* It is his name, Rytrenespu	*k3r(y).t* Gardener
44	- - -	*rn=f pw* It is his name	- - -
45	[...*i*] [...i]	- - -	*šnꜥ* Labourer
46	[*ḥm-nsw.t*...] [King's servant...]	- - -	*tbw* Sandal-maker

213 Ranke, *Personennamen* 1, 68 [6].

214 Ranke, *Personennamen* 1, 261 [22].

215 Postulated to be a theophoric name referencing the Levantine deity Baal (Albright, *JAOS* 74/4 [1954], 231; Helck, *Die Beziehungen Ägyptens*, 80; Hayes, *Papyrus Brooklyn*, 97; Posener, *Syria* 34/1 [1957], 150; Schneider, *UF* 19 [1987], 271).

216 The name is not attested in Ranke, *Personennamen*. However, it is clearly derived from the Egyptian.

217 Ward, *Index*, 185 [1597].

218 Postulated to be from the Semitic stem *ꜥqb* 'to watch, protect' (Albright, *JAOS* 74/4 [1954], 231; Helck, *Die Beziehungen Ägyptens*, 80; Hayes, *Papyrus Brooklyn*, 97; Posener, *Syria* 34/1 [1957], 150).

219 The name is not attested in Ranke, *Personennamen*. However, it is clearly derived from the Egyptian. For a similar name, see Ranke, *Personennamen* 1, 226 [25].

47	*ꜥꜣm.t* [...*wnꜥ*..] *ꜥꜣm.t* [...*wnꜥ*..]	[*ḏd*].*t n=s Nfr.t* She is [called] Noferet[220]	*ḏꜣ šsr* Warper(?) of *šsr*-cloth
48	*ḥm.t Ḥnw.t=i-pw* [*sꜣ.t...sn*] Servant Henutipu['s daughter ...sen]	*ḏd.t n=s Nfr.t-ṯn.t*[*t*...] She is called Noferetjenet[t...]	- - -
49	*sꜣ=s* Her son	*Rn=f pw* It is his name	- - -
50	*ḥm-nsw.t Rs-snb*(*.w*) King's servant Resseneb(u)	*ḏd.w n=f* [...] He is called [...]	- - -
51	*ꜥꜣm ꜥꜣm.w*[...] *ꜥꜣm ꜥꜣm.w*[...]	*ḏd.w n=f Wr-n=i* He is called Wereni[221]	- - -
52	*ꜥꜣm.t R*[...] *ꜥꜣm.t* R[...]	*ḏd.t n=s Ỉw-n-si*[...] She is called Iunesi[...]	- - -
53	*ḥm-nsw.t Ỉ*[*r*...] King's servant I[r...]	*Rn=f pw* It is his name	- - -
54	*ḥm.t* [...] Servant [...]	*rn=s pw* It is her name	- - -
55	*ꜥꜣm.t* [ꜥ]*k*[...] *ꜥꜣm.t* [ꜥ]*k*[...]	*ḏd.t n=s* [...*nf*]*r.t-n*[...] She is called [...nof]ereten[...]	*sḫ.ty* [*ḥꜣ*].*tyw* Weaver of [*ḥꜣ*].*tyw*-cloth
56	[*ꜥꜣm.t*...] [*ꜥꜣm.t*...]	*ḏd.t n*[*=s*] *Ỉḥꜣ*[*.y*] [She] is called Iha[y][222]	*šnꜥ* Labourer[223]
57	*sꜣ.t=s Ḥw*[...] Her daughter Hu[...]	- - -	- - -
58	*sꜣ=s ꜥnḫ.w* Her son Ankhu	[*ḏd.w n=f*] *Pꜣ-ꜥꜣm* [He is called] *Pꜣ-ꜥꜣm*[224]	(*ms*) (child)
59	*ꜥꜣm.t ꜥnt*[...] *ꜥꜣm.t ꜥnt*[...]	[*ḏd.t n=s*] *Ỉw=n-r-tꜣ-n* [She is called] Iunertan[225]	*ḏꜣ ḥꜣ.tyw* Warper(?) of *ḥꜣ.tyw* -cloth
60	*ḥm.t Ỉyi-ti* Servant Iyiti	*ḏd.t n=s Bbi sꜣ.t Ỉyi.t* She is called Bebi's daughter Iyit	*sḫ.ty* [...] Weaver [...]

220 Ranke, *Personennamen* 1, 201 [10].
221 See Ranke, *Personennamen* 1, 81 [8].
222 Ranke, *Personennamen* 1, 44 [13].
223 Hayes's 'magazine employee' (*Papyrus Brooklyn*, 108).
224 See Figure 7.10 for other attestations of the name.
225 The name is not attested in Ranke, *Personennamen*. However, it is clearly derived from the Egyptian.

61	*ʿꜣm.t Rꜣ-in[.t]* *ʿꜣm.t* Rain[t][226]	*ḏd.t n=s Snb-ḥ[nw.t]=s* She is called Senebh[enut]es	*sẖ.ty ḥꜣ.tyw* Weaver of *ḥꜣ.tyw*-cloth
62	*ʿꜣm.t Hyibirw* *ʿꜣm.t Hyibirw*[227]	*ḏd.t n=s [Nḥ]-n=i-m-ḫꜣs.t* She is called Nehenimkhaset[228]	*šnʿ* Labourer
63	*sꜣ=s Ꞽbi[...mʿ]* Her son *Ꞽbi[...mʿ]*	*ḏd.w n=f Snb-nb=f* He is called Senebnebef[229]	- - -
64	[...]*ibʿꜣ* [...]*ibʿꜣ*	*ḏd.t n=s Nṯr=i-m-sꜣ=i* She is called Netjerimsai	*ḏꜣ ḥꜣ.tyw* Warper(?) of *ḥꜣ.tyw* -cloth
65	[...]*hꜣw* [...]hau	*rn=s pw* It is his name	*ḏꜣ šsr* Warper(?) of *šsr*-cloth
66	*sꜣ=s [Rs]-snb(.w)* Her son [Res]seneb(u)	*rn=f pw* It is his name	- - -
67	*ʿꜣm.t Skr* *ʿꜣm.t Skr*[230]	*ḏd.t n=s Nb-rḏi=s* She is called Nebredjies[231]	- - -
68	*ḥm-nsw.t Rs-snb(.w)* King's servant Resseneb(u)	*Rn=f pw* It is his name	*ḫr.y-pr.w* Major-domo
69	*ʿꜣm.t Ṯnʿtisi* *ʿꜣm.t Ṯnʿtisi*[232]	*ḏd.t n=s Pt=i-mn.ti* She is called Petimenti[233]	*šnʿ* Labourer
70	*ḥm.t Ḥtp.t* Servant Hotepet	*rn=s pw* It is her name	*ḏꜣ šsr* Warper(?) of *šsr*-cloth
71	*sꜣ=s ʿnḫ.w* Her son Ankhu	*rn=f pw* It is his name	- - -
72	[*ḥm-nsw.t Rs-snb(.w)*] [Servant Resseneb(u)]	[*ḏd.w n=f Bw-rḫ*] [He is called Burekh]	[*ʿḥ.wty*] [Cultivator]
73	- - -	[...*r*] [...r]	- - -

226 Ranke, *Personennamen* 1, 216 [16].

227 Postulated to be from the Semitic *Hayabilu* or *Ayya'abi-'ilu* 'where is my father, God?' (Albright, *JAOS* 74/4 [1954], 225-227; Helck, *Die Beziehungen Ägyptens*, 80; Hayes, *Papyrus Brooklyn*, 94-95; Posener, *Syria* 34/1 [1957], 150).

228 The name is not attested in Ranke, *Personennamen*. However, it is clearly derived from the Egyptian.

229 Ranke, *Personennamen* 1, 313 [11].

230 See n. 189 above.

231 Ranke, *Personennamen* 1, 191 [16].

232 Postulated to be from the Semitic, although derivation is uncertain (Albright, *JAOS* 74/4 [1954], 232; Helck, *Die Beziehungen Ägyptens*, 80; Hayes, *Papyrus Brooklyn*, 98; Schneider, *UF* 19 [1987], 277-279).

233 The name is not attested in Ranke, *Personennamen*. However, it is clearly derived from the Egyptian. See Ranke, *Personennamen* 1, 137 [18].

74	-	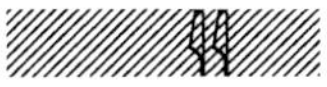	-	-
	-	[...*y*...]	-	
	-	[...y...]	-	
75		-	-	-
	[...*ḥnw.t=i-pw*]	-	-	
	[...henutipu]	-	-	
80		-	-	
	ꜥ3m.t Ḥyiwr[...]	-	-	
	ꜥ3m.t Ḥyiwr[...]	-	-	
81		-	-	
	ḥm-nsw.t Nfr-rw-ḥtp	-	-	
	King's servant Noferruhotep	-	-	
82		-	-	
	ḥm.t Iwy s3.t Mr[...]	-	-	
	Servant Iwy's daughter Mer[...]	-	-	
85		-	-	-
	[...*i*]*bi*	-	-	
	[...i]bi	-	-	
86		-	-	-
	[...]*nfw-m-ꜥn.tyw*	-	-	
	[...]nefuemantyu	-	-	
87		-	-	
	[*ꜥ3*]*m.t ꜥḳbtw*	-	-	
	[*ꜥ3*]*m.t ꜥḳbtw*[234]	-	-	
88		-	-	-
	[...*ṯ*]*nꜥt*[*r*]*ti*	-	-	
	[...*ṯ*]*nꜥt*[*r*]*ti*	-	-	

234 See n. 218 above.

B.8 Papyrus Leiden I.344 (Admonitions of Ipuwer)[235]

Prov. Unknown
Refs Gardiner, *Admonitions*, 19-92, pls 1-15; Enmarch, *Dialogue of Ipuwer*, 21, 27, 31, 55, 57, 67, 69-70, 81-82.
Chron. Middle Kingdom
Chapter 4.6.4

1.4

[T]dḥw.t ẖr.t ikm.w...

The Delta dwellers are with shields...

1.9

ḫ3s[.tyw] ḫpr(.w) m rmṯ.t m s.t nb...

The foreigners have become as people in every place...

3.1-2

[iw-m]s dšr.t ḫt t3 sp3.wt ḫb[3] Pḏ.tyw rw.ty iyi.ty n Km.t iw-ms spr.t(w) [...] nn ms wn rmṯ.t m s.t nb...

Lo, the desert covers the land, the nomes are ravaged and the *Pḏ.tyw* of abroad have come to Egypt. Lo, [...] was reached [...], [...] there are no people anywhere...

3.6-8

... n ms [ḫ]di.[t]w r [Kp]ny min ptr iri.ti=n r ʿš n sʿḥ.w=n ḳrs.tw [wʿb.w... m] ini.w=sn sdwḫ.tw [wr.w] m sft ir.y r mn m Kf[3].tyw n iyi.n=sn ...

... No one travels northwards to [*Kp*]*ny* today. What shall we do for *ʿš*-wood for our mummies, the products with which the [*wʿb*-priests are buried] and the oil with which the great ones are embalmed? From as far as *Kf*[*3*].*tyw*,[236] they do not come...

4.8

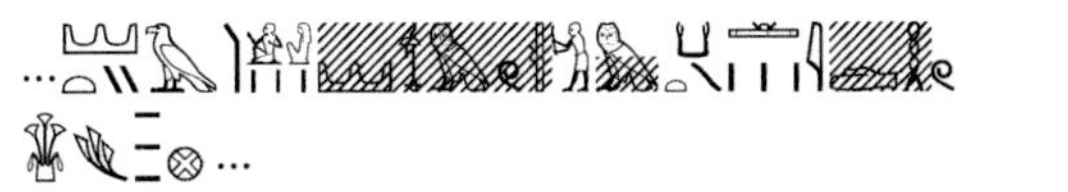

... ḫ3s.tyw [ḥmw] m k3.wt T[dḥ]w...

... The foreigners [are skilful] in the crafts of the Delta marshes...

14.10 -15.2

[... m-ḳ3b][237] *ir.y mi St.tyw [... n.ty...n=f] iw=tw ḥr sḫr.w ir.y ḳn=sn n=sn nn gmi.ntw n.ty r ʿḥʿ.w ḥr mkt st ḫt [...f]m.w*[238] *ʿḥ3 si nb ḥr sn.t=f mk=f ḥʿ.w=f in Nḥs.yw k3 iri=n mkt=n sʿš3 ʿḥ3[.ty...] r ḫsf Pḏ.tyw in iw=s m Tmḥ.yw k3 iri=n ʿn.w Mḏ3.yw nḏm.w ḥnʿ Km.t mi-m ir=f si nb ḥr sm3 sn=f ḏ3m.w ṯs=n n=n ḫpr.w m Pḏ.tyw w3.w r ḫb3 [ḫpr].t n=f im=f rḏi.t rḫ St.tyw sšm.w n(.y) t3 iw gr.t ḫ3s.tyw nb ẖr.t snḏ.w=f ...*

[... in the midst] thereof like the *St.tyw* [... for him]. One says: 'the situation thereof is finished for them, the one who will stand up for their protection not being found [...]*m.w*. Every man fights for his sister and protects himself. Is it the *Nḥs.yw*? Then let us make our protection and multiply fighters to drive away the *Pḏ.tyw*. Is it the *Tmḥ.yw*? Then let us turn back, as the *Mḏ3.yw* are well with Egypt. Yet, what is this, when every man kills his brother, the troops that we marshal for ourselves have changed into *Pḏ.tyw*, falling into plundering? What he has brought about through it is to let the *St.tyw* know the state of the land. Now, all foreigners are afraid of him/it...[239]

---

235 Transliterations and translations are reliant on Quirke, *Egyptian Literature*, 140-149.

236 Or *Rmnm Kf[3].tyw n iyi.n=sn* '*Rmnm* and *Kf[3].tyw*, they do not come'. Enmarch notes that the toponym *Rmnm* or *Rmnn* is not securely attested before Thutmosis III; however it does occur in the biography of Khnumhotep III. See Chapter 4.3.1.2, Appendix B.1; Morenz, *OLP* 31 (2005), 31; Quack, *E&L* 6 (1996), 81; Enmarch, *World Upturned*, 89.

237 Translated by Quirke as *pḫr iry mi...* 'its circuit like...' (Quirke, *Egyptian Literature*, 149).

238 Perhaps *ʿ3m.w* (Enmarch, *World Upturned*, 203-204) or, as suggested by Quirke, *ḏ3m.w* (*Egyptian Literature*, 149).

239 Redford translates the expression as: 'which indeed formerly all foreigners showed respect for' (*Egypt, Canaan and Israel*, 67).

B.9 Prophecies of Noferty[240]

Prov. Unknown
Ref. Helck, *Prophezeiung des Nfr.tj*, 16, 25-31, 52-57.
Chron. Early Twelfth Dynasty
Chapter 4.6.5

17-19 ...

... [iw]=f mḥi=f ḥr ḫpr.ty=sn m tꜣ iw=f sḫꜣ=f ḳni n(.y) Iꜣbt.t ḫpi ꜥꜣm.w m ḫpš.t=sn sh=sn ib.w [...] n.tyw ḥr šmw nḥm=sn ḥtr.w ḥr skꜣ ...

... He (Noferty) ponders on what will happen in the land. He remembers thc condition of the east, when the *ꜥꜣm.w* travelled in their strength terrorising the hearts [...] of those who are upon the harvest, carrying off those yoked upon the plough ...

29-30 ...

... iw ꜣpd.w ḏrḏry.(w)t [...] r msi.t m hꜣ.t n.t Tꜣ-mḥw iri.n=f sšw ḥr-gs.wy rmṯ.t stkn sw rmṯ.t n gꜣw

... strange bird(s) [...] will be born in the marshes of the Delta, having made a nest beside the people, while the people cause it to approach because of lack.

30-36

ḥdi (n)ḥmn (n)fꜣ n(.y) bw-nfr nꜣ n(.y) š.w kꜥh.w wn.yw ḫr wgs.w wbn.w ḥr rm.w ꜣpd.w bw-nfr nb rwi.w ptḫ m tꜣ n ḳsn.t m-ꜥ nfꜣ n(.y) ḏfꜣ.w St.tyw ht.yw-tꜣ
iw ḫr.w ḫpr(.w) ḥr Iꜣbt.t iw ꜥꜣm.w hꜣi.t(w) r Km.t
gꜣw.tw ḫnr.t ky r gs nn sḏm m ꜥwn=f
tw r isḳ mꜣḳ.t m grḥ tw r ꜥḳ ḫnr.wt tw r snb ḳdd m ir.ty=i sḏr.kw ḥr iw=i rs.kw
ꜥw.t ḫꜣs.t r swr ḥr itrw n.w Km.t
[s]ḳbb=sn ḥr wḏb.w=sn n gꜣw stri st

Those good things are utterly perished; those lakes and fish-ponds where the gutting of fish (took place?) overflow with fish and birds; all good is gone; the land is cast to pain through the sustenance of the *St.tyw* who pervade the land.
Enemies have arisen in the east, the *ꜥꜣm.w* have descended to Egypt.
The enclosure will be deprived, the other at the side without hearing from its plunderer;[241] one will hinder the latter at night; one will banish the sleep from my two eyes, I spending the night while being vigilant.
The small cattle of the foreign land will drink at the river of Egypt, they cooling off at its riverbanks because of the lack of that which drives them back.

62-65
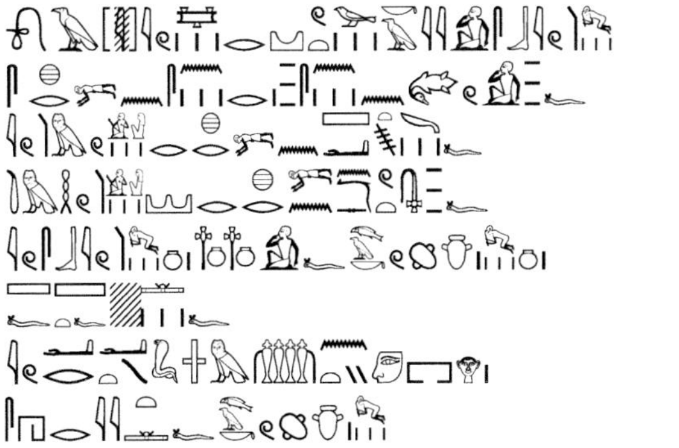
... wꜣ.yw r ḏw.t kꜣy(.w) sbi.w sḫr.n=sn rꜣ.w=sn n snḏ.w=f
iw ꜥꜣm.w r ḫr n šꜥ.t=f
Tmḥ.w r ḫr n nsw.t=f
iw sbi.w n ndnd=f hꜣk.w-ib n šfšf.yt=f
iw ꜥrꜥ.t im.t ḫnt.y ḥr shri.t (n)=f hꜣk.w-ib

... Those who fall into evil and those who plan rebellions: they have cast down their voices before his fear.
The *ꜥꜣm.w* will fall to his sword; the *Tmḥ.w* will fall to his flame;
the rebels before his wrath; the disaffected persons before his awe;
the uraeus which is in the Residence making content the disaffected persons for him.

66-70
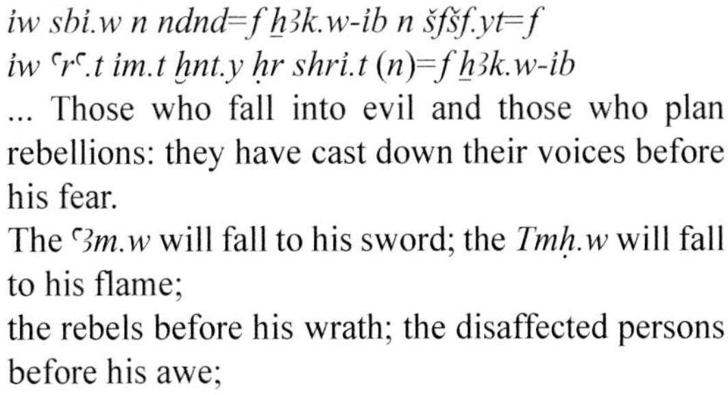
...

240 Hieroglyphic transcription follows Papyrus Hermitage 1116B.

241 Quirke translates it as *nn sḏmm n=f* '(he) who will not be heard' (*Egyptian Literature*, 137). Parkinson prefers 'without the guards hearing' (*Tale of Sinuhe*, 136).

tw r ḳd Ỉnb.w-Ḥḳꜣ ꜥnḫ(.w) wḏꜣ(.w) s(nb.w) nn rḏi.t hꜣi.y ꜥꜣm.w r Km.t
dbḥ=sn mw mi sḫr.w=s sšꜣy.w r rḏi.t swi ꜥ.wt=sn
iw mꜣꜥ.t r iyi.t r s.t=s i[sf.t] dr.(ty)=sy r rw.ty
ršy gmḥ.[ty=f(y) wn]n.ty=f(y) ḥr šms nsw.t ...
One will build the Walls-of-the-Ruler, may he live, be prosperous and healthy, not allowing the *ꜥꜣm.w* to descend to Egypt.
They will beg for water according to the manner of beseeching to allow that their small cattle drink.
It is order that will return to its place, [chaos] being driven out.
He who will witness and [be] in the following of the king will rejoice...

B.10 Stela Moscow I.1.a.5349 (4161)

Prov. Unknown
Ref. Hodjash and Berlev, *Reliefs and Stelae*, 77-79 [34].
Chron. Late Twelfth to early Thirteenth Dynasty
Chapter 4.6.7

E1 
ꜥꜣm [S-n]-wsr.t
ꜥꜣm Senwosret[242]

E2 
ꜥꜣm Ỉw-nfr
ꜥꜣm Iunofer[243]

E3 
ꜥꜣm Nfr-mni.t
ꜥꜣm Nofermenit[244]

E4 
sn=f Ỉmmw
His brother, Imemu[245]

E5 
sn=f ꜥnḫ.w
His brother, Ankhu[246]

F1 
ꜥꜣm.t Mw.t
ꜥꜣm.t Mut

F2 
ꜥꜣm.t Mw.t
ꜥꜣm.t Mut

F3 
ꜥꜣm.t Psꜣ
ꜥꜣm.t Psꜣ

F4 
ꜥꜣm.t Ỉni
ꜥꜣm.t Ini

F5 
[ꜥꜣm.t] Ỉyi-nfr
ꜥꜣm.t Iyinofer

F6 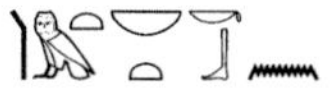
ꜥꜣm.t Nb.t-Kbn
ꜥꜣm.t Nebet-*Kbn*

F7 
ꜥꜣm.t Nfr-mw.t=f
ꜥꜣm.t Nofermutef

F8 
ꜥꜣm.t Bnn
ꜥꜣm.t Benen

242 Ranke, *Personennamen* 1, 279 [1].
243 Ranke, *Personennamen* 1, 15 [21].
244 The name is not attested in Ranke, *Personennamen* but see Ranke, *Personennamen* 1, 196 [21-22].
245 The name is not attested in Ranke, *Personennamen* but see Ranke, *Personennamen* 1, 26 [14-17].
246 Ranke, *Personennamen* 1, 68 [6].
247 Ranke, *Personennamen* 1, 147 [3].
248 The name is not attested in Ranke, *Personennamen*. Possibly of Semitic origin (Schneider, *Ausländer in Ägypten* 2, 147).
249 Ranke, *Personennamen* 1, 36 [13].
250 Ranke, *Personennamen* 1, 10 [5].
251 Ranke, *Personennamen* 1, 189 [17].
252 The name is not attested in Ranke, *Personennamen*, but see Ranke, *Personennamen* 1, 196 [20].
253 Ranke, *Personennamen* 1, 97 [15].

B.11 Tale of Sinuhe[254]

Prov. Unknown
Ref. Koch, *Sinuhe.*
Chron. Twelfth Dynasty (reign of Senwosret I)
Chapter 4.6.9

R1-R2 

ir.y-pʿ.t ḥ3.ty-ʿ s3b ʿḏ-mr ḏ3t.t ity m t3.w St.tyw [R2] *rḫ nsw.t m3ʿ mr.y=f šms*[.*w S3n*]*h.t ḏd=f*...

Nobleman, count, dignitary, administrator of the estates of the sovereign of the lands of the *St.tyw*,[255] true acquaintance of the king, his beloved, the retainer, Sinuhe. He says...

B11-19 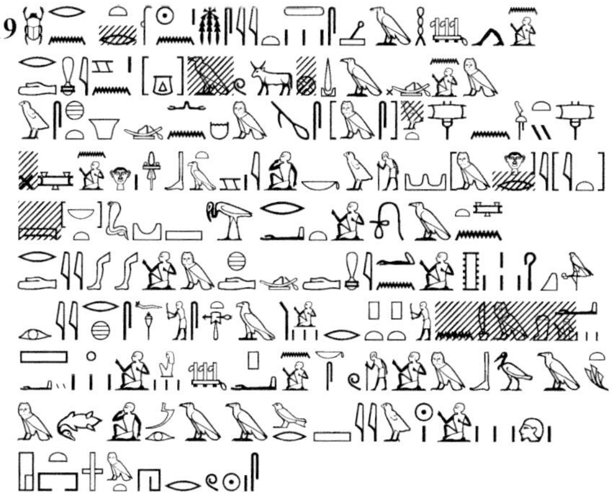

ḫpr.n t[*r*] *n*(.*y*) *ms.yt s3ḫ.n=i r dmi N*[*g*]*3w ḏ3i.n=i m wsḫ.t nn ḥm.w=s* [*m sw*].*t n*(.*y*) *imn.ty sw3.n=i ḥr i3b.tyw ikw* [*m ḥr.yt nb*].*t dw-dšr rdi.t=i w3.t n rd.wy=i m ḫdi dmi.n=i 'Inb.w-Ḥḳ3 iri.y r ḫsf St.tyw r ptpt* [*Nmi.w-šʿ*] *šsp.n=i ksw=i m b3.t m snḏ m33 wrš.yw tp ḥw.t im.yt hrw=s*

When the time of the evening meal had come, I had reached the quay of *N*[*g*]*3w*. I ferried in a barge without its rudder by means of the westerly wind and I crossed upon the east of the stone-quarry above the Mistress-of-the-Red-Mountain. Giving way for my two feet travelling north, I reached the Walls-of-the-Ruler which had been made to repel the *St.tyw* and crush the *Nmi.w-šʿ*. I took on a crouching position in a thicket from fear of being seen by the watchers atop the enclosure[256] who were on its duty.

B19-23 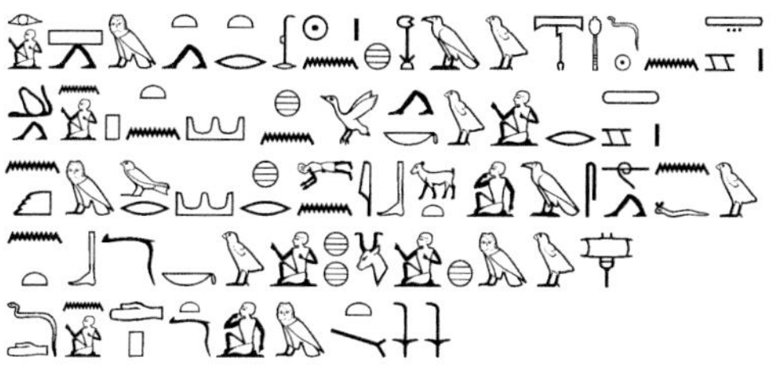

iri=i šm.t tr n ḫ3wy ḥḏ.n t3 pḥ.n=i Ptn ḥni.kw r iw n(.*y*) *Kmwr ḫr.n ib.t 3s.n=f w*(*i*) *ntb.kw ḫḫ=i ḥmw ḏd.n=i dp.t mwt nn*

I walked on at night time. At dawn I had reached *Ptn* and halted at the island of *Kmwr*. Thirst struck, it overtook me, I was parched, and my throat was dry. I said: 'This is the taste of death'.

B23-28 

ṯs.t(*n*)*=i ib=i s3k=i ḥʿw=i sḏm.n=i hrw nmi n*(.*y*) *mnmn.t gmḥ.n=i St.tyw si3.n wi mtn im p3 wnn ḥr Km.t ʿḥʿ.n rdi.n=f n=i mw psi n=i irt.t šm.n=i ḥnʿ=f n wḥ.w=f nfr iri.tn=sn*

I lifted my heart and gathered my body when I heard the sound of cattle's lowing and I caught sight of *St.tyw*, the leader there who had been in Egypt recognised me. Then he gave me water and boiled milk for me. I went with him to his people. That which they did was good.

B28-31 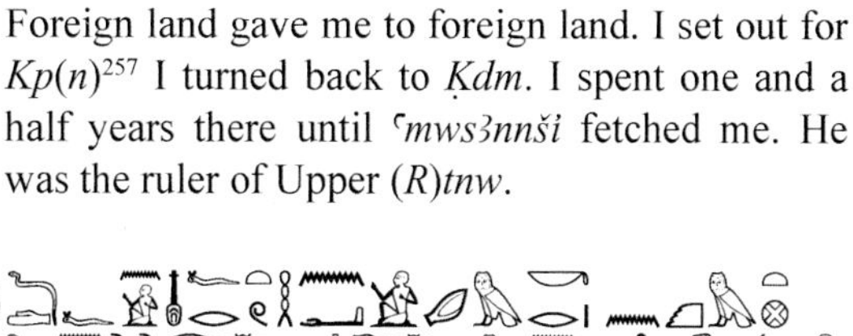

rdi.n wi ḫ3s.t n ḫ3s.t fḫ.n=i r Kp(*n*) *ḥsi.n=i r Ḳdm iri.n=i rnp.t wʿ gs im ini.n wi ʿmws3nnši ḥḳ3 pw n*(.*y*) (*R*)*tnw ḥr.t*

Foreign land gave me to foreign land. I set out for *Kp*(*n*)[257] I turned back to *Ḳdm*. I spent one and a half years there until *ʿmws3nnši* fetched me. He was the ruler of Upper (*R*)*tnw*.

B31-36 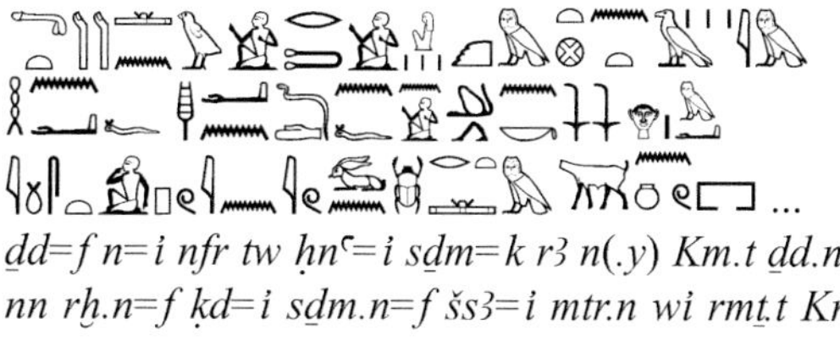 ...

ḏd=f n=i nfr tw ḥnʿ=i sḏm=k r3 n(.*y*) *Km.t ḏd.n=f nn rḫ.n=f ḳd=i sḏm.n=f šs3=i mtr.n wi rmṯt Km.t*

---

[254] The translation follows the 'R' and 'B' texts, relating to the two principal manuscripts Ramesside Papyrus Berlin 10499 (Twelfth Dynasty) and Papyrus Berlin 3022 (Middle Kingdom), respectively.

[255] Parkinson (*Tale of Sinuhe*, 27) translates the titles as 'Governor of the Sovereign's Domains in the Syrian lands' while Quirke (*Egyptian Literature*, 58) prefers 'governor and canal-cutter, sovereign in the lands of the Syrians'.

[256] R45 contains the term *inb* 'wall' (Koch, *Sinuhe*, 18).

[257] R53 contains the complete toponym *Kpny*, identified as Byblos (Koch, *Sinuhe*, 23).

n.tyw im ḥnꜥ=f ꜥḥꜥ.n ḏd.n=f n=i pḥ.n=k nn ḥr m išs.t pw in iw wn ḫpr.t m ẖnw ...

He said to me: 'You are well with me (because) you will hear the speech of Egypt'. He said this as he had known my character and he had heard of my wisdom, the Egyptians who were there with him having testified concerning me. Then he said to me: 'Why and how have you reached this (place)? Has something transpired in the Residence?'...

B45-75 ...

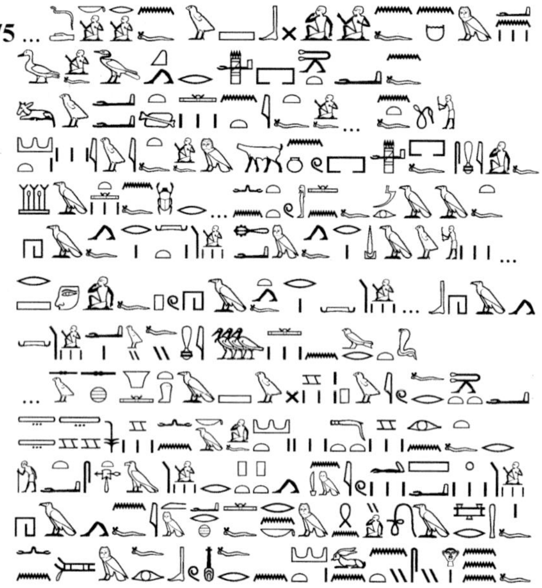

... ḏd.kw r=i n=f wšb=i n=f nḥmn sꜣ=f ꜥḳ(.w) r ꜥḥ iṯi.n=f iwꜥ.t n.t it=f ...
ntf dꜣir ḫꜣs.wt iw it=f m ẖnw ꜥḥ=f smi=f šꜣ.t n=f ḫpr ...
... nn twt n=f mꜣꜣ.t[w]=f hꜣi=f r Pḏ.tyw ḫꜥm=f r-ḏꜣ.w ...
... rš=f pw hꜣi.t=f r Pḏ.tyw ...
... bḥꜣ Pḏ.tyw ꜥ.wy=fy mibꜣ.w n wr.t ...
swsḫ tꜣš.w pw iw=f r iṯi.t tꜣ.w rs.yw nn kꜣ=f ḫꜣs.wt mḥ.tyt iri.nt(w)=f r [ḥ]w.t St.tyw r ptpt Nmi.w-šꜥ hꜣi n=f imi rḫ=f rn=k m šn.y wꜣ r ḥm=f nn tm=f iri bw-nfr n ḫꜣs.t wnn.ty=sy ḥr mw=f

... As for me, I said to him, answering him: 'Surely his son has entered the palace, he having taken the inheritance of his father...

... He was the suppressor of foreign lands when his father was within his palace, he reporting to him that whatever he ordered him came to pass...

... None resemble him when he is seen charging against the *Pḏ.tyw* and approaching the melee...

... His charging down against the *Pḏ.tyw* is his joy...

... The *Pḏ.tyw* flee from his two arms as before the power of the great one... He is one who extends the borders. He will take the southern lands without considering the northern lands. He was made to smite the *St.tyw* and crush the *Nmi.w-šꜥ*. Go down to him and let him know your name. Do not think of falling away from his majesty. He will not fail to do good for the foreign land which is loyal to him.

B75-81

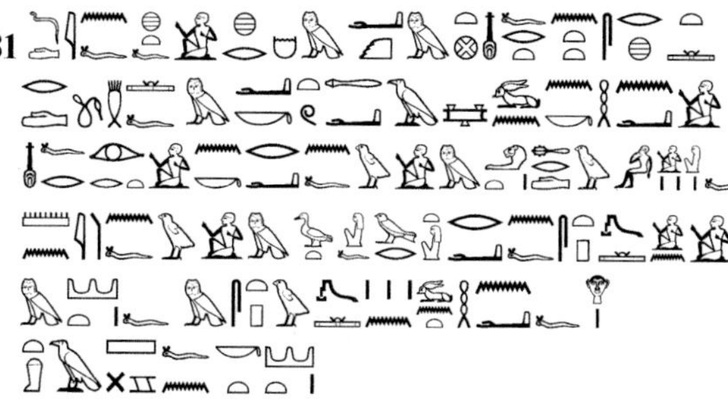

ḏd.in=f ḫft=i ḥr ḥm Km.t nfr.ti (n) n.tt s(y) rḫ.ti rwd=f m=k tw ꜥꜣ wnn=k ḥnꜥ=i nfr iri.t=i n=k rdi.n=f wi m ḥꜣ.t ẖrd.w=f mni.n=f wi m sꜣ.t=f wr.t rdi.n=f stp=i n=i m ḫꜣs.t=f m stp.w n(.y) wn.t ḥnꜥ=f ḥr tꜣš=f n k.t ḫꜣs.t

Then he said before me: 'Indeed, beautiful is Egypt because it knows that he flourishes. Behold, you are here and you will be with me. Good is what I will do for you'. He placed me at the head of his children and attached me to his eldest daughter. He let me choose for myself from his foreign land, from the choicest of what was for him on his border with another foreign land.

B81-85

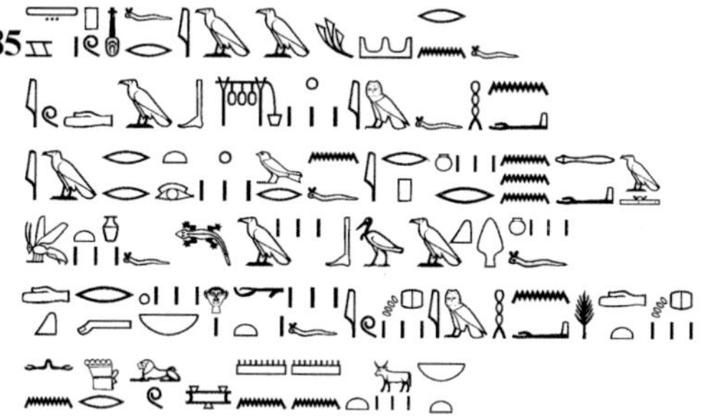

tꜣ pw nfr Iꜣꜣ rn=f iw dꜣb.w im=f ḥnꜥ iꜣrr.t wr n=f irp r mw ꜥꜣ bit=f ꜥšꜣ bꜣḳ.w=f dkr.w nb ḥr ḫt.w=f iw it im ḥnꜥ bd.t nn ḏr.w mnmn.t nb.t

It was a good land, *Iꜣꜣ* was its name. Figs were in it as well as grapes. It had more wine than water. Its honey was plentiful and its moringa oil abundant. All *dkr*-fruits were upon its trees. Barley was there as well as wheat, without a limit of any kind of cattle.

B85-92

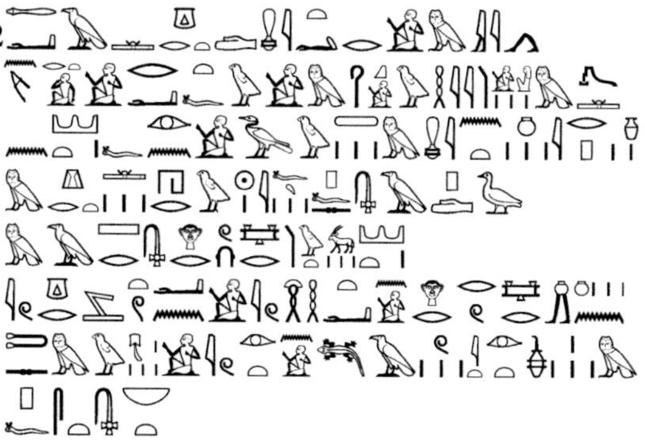

ꜥꜣ gr.t dmi.t r=i m iyi n mr.t=i rdi.t=f wi m ḥḳꜣ wḥ.y(t) m stp n(.y) ḫꜣs.t=f iri n=i ꜥḳ.w m min.t irp m ḥr.t hrw i(w)f psi ꜣpd m ꜣšr ḥr.w-r ꜥw.t ḫꜣs.t iw grg. tw n=i iw wꜣḥ.t(w) n=i ḥr.w-r inw ṯsm.w=i iw iri.t(w) n=i ꜥšꜣ.w irt.t m psi.t nb.t

Indeed, great was that which accrued to me because of the love for me. He placed me as ruler of a people with the choice of his foreign land. Loaves and wine were made for me daily, cooked meat, roasted fowl as well as cattle of the foreign land. One hunted for me and laid before me, besides the catch of my dogs. Many things were made for me and milk with everything cooked.

B92-99 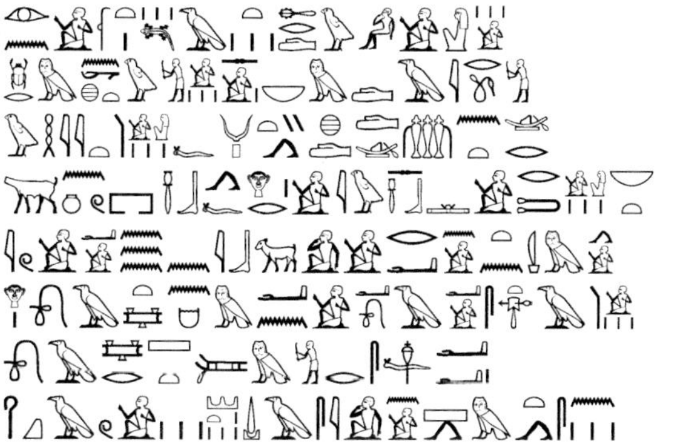

iri.n=i rnp.wt ꜥšꜣ.wt ḫrd.w=i ḫpr(.w) m nḫ.tw si nb m dꜣr wḥ.yt=f wpw.ty ḫdd ḫnti r ḫnw ꜣb=f ḥr=i iw sꜣb=i rmṯ.t nb.t iw=i di=i mw n ib rdi.n=i tnm ḥr wꜣ.t nḥm.n=i ꜥwꜣ(.w) St.tyw wꜣ r štm r sḫsf-ꜥ ḥkꜣ.w ḫꜣs.wt dꜣis.n=i šm.t=sn

I spent many years, my children becoming as strong men, each man controlling his people. The messenger who (always) travels northwards and southwards to the Residence, he stayed with me. I caused all people to tarry. I gave water to the thirsty, I placed the lost (back) upon the road and I rescued he who had been robbed. The *St.tyw* that had fallen to hostility to create opposition against the rulers of the foreign lands, I opposed their actions.

B99-109 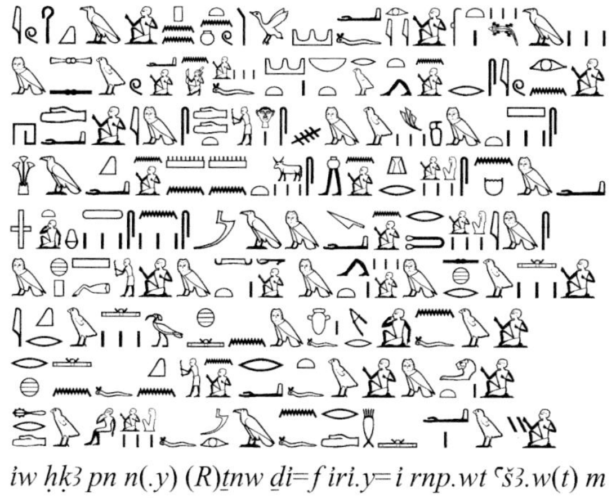

iw ḥkꜣ pn n(.y) (R)ṯnw di=f iri.y=i rnp.wt ꜥšꜣ.w(t) m ṯsw n mšꜥ=f ḫꜣs.t nb.t rwt.n=i r=s iw iri.n=i hd=i im=s dr.t ḥr smw(=s) ḫnm.wt=s ḥꜣḳ.n=i mnmn.t=s ini.n=i ḥr.yw=s nḥm wnm.t=sn smꜣ.n=i rmṯ.t im=s m ḫpš=i m pḏ.t=i m nmt.wt=i m sḫr.w=i iḳr.w ꜣḫ.n(=i) m ib=f mr.n=f wi rḫ.n=f ḳnn=i rdi.(n)t=f wi m ḥꜣ.t ḫrd.w=f mꜣ.n=f rwd ꜥ.wy=i

This ruler of (*R*)*ṯnw* made me spend many years as a commander in his army. Every foreign land which I advanced against, I achieved my prevailing over it, destroying (its) pastures and its wells. I captured its cattle and I carried off its inhabitants, taking away their food. I killed its people with my strong arm, my bow, my movements and my excellent plans. I was efficient in his heart. He loved me because he knew I was valiant. He placed me at the head of his children as he had seen the strength of my two arms.

B109-113 

iwi nḫ.t n(.y) (R)ṯnw mṯꜣ=f wi m imꜣ(w)=i pri.y pw nn sn.w=f dr.n=f s(y) r dr=s ḏd.n=f ꜥḥꜣ=f ḥnꜥ=i ḥmt.n=f ḥwi.t=f wi kꜣ.n=f ḥꜣḳ mnmn.t=i ḥr sḥ n(.y) wḥ.yt=f

A strong man of (*R*)*ṯnw*, who challenged me in my tent, came. He was a champion without equal who had subdued it in its entirety. He said he would fight with me, he intended to strike me and planned to capture my cattle under the council of his people.

B113-122 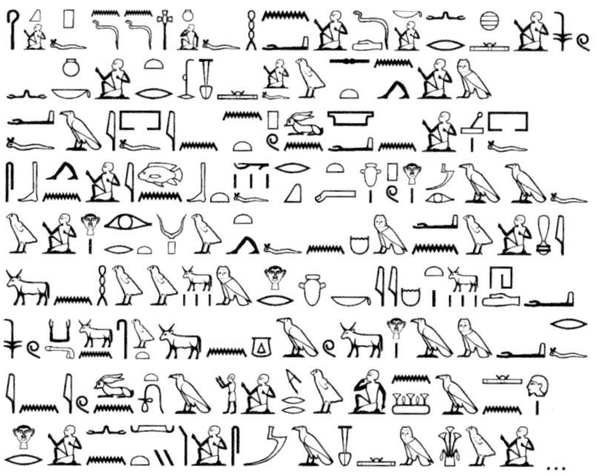

ḥkꜣ pf ndnd=f ḥnꜥ=i ḏd.ki n rḫ=i sw n ink tr smꜣ=f wstn=i m ꜥfꜣi=f in n.t pw wn.n=i sꜣ=f sb.n=i inb.wt=f rḳ.t-ib pw ḥr mꜣꜣ=f wi ḥr iri.t wpw.t=f nḥmn wi mi kꜣ n(.y) ḥww m-ḥr-ib ky ḥm.t hd sw kꜣ n ꜥw.t ngꜣw ḥr ꜣm r=f in-iw wn twꜣ.(w) mrr.w n šꜣ n tp-ḥr(.y) nn Pḏ.ty smꜣ m ꜣIdḥw...

That ruler, he consulted me and I said: 'I do not know him. It was not I who associated with him so that I could walk about in his encampment.' Is it the case that I have opened his gate and overstepped his walls? It is resentment upon seeing me do his commissions. It is I who is like a bull of cattle amidst another herd. The bull of the small cattle attacks him and the long-horned bull assails him. Is there a lowly man who is loved for ordering as a master? No *Pḏ.ty* associates with a man of the Delta marshes...

B129-131 

... ḥḏ.n tꜣ (R)ṯnw iyi.t ḏdb.n=s wḥ.yt=s sḥwy.n=s ḫꜣs.wt n.t gs sy kꜣ.n=s ꜥḥꜣ pn ...

... At dawn, the land of (*R*)*tnw* came, it had incited its people and assembled the foreign lands of its region for it had planned this fight...

B139-146 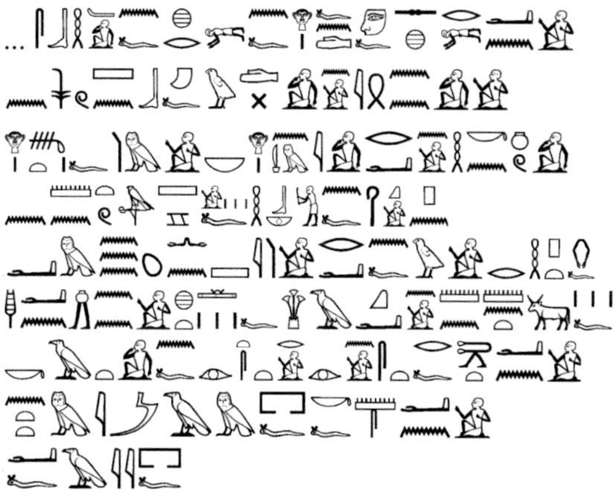

... *sbḫ.n=f ḫr.n=f ḥr fnḏ=f sḫr.n=i n sw (m) minb=f wdi.n=i išnn=i ḥr iꜣ.t=f ꜥꜣm nb ḥr nmi rḏi.n=i ḥkn.w n Mnt.w mr.w=f ḥb(.w) n=f ḥkꜣ pn ꜥmwsꜣnnši rḏi.n=f wi r ḥpt=f ꜥḥꜥ.n ini.n=i (i)ḫ.t=f ḥꜣḳ.n=i mnmn.t=f kꜣt.n=f iri.t st r=i iri.n=i st r=f iṯi.n=i n.tt m imꜣ(w)=f kf.n=i ꜥfꜣ.y=f...*

... He cried out and fell upon his nose. I threw him down with his axe and I uttered my war-cry on his back, every *ꜥꜣm* shouting. I gave praise to Montu while his subjects mourned for him. This ruler *ꜥmwsꜣnnši*, he gave me an embrace. Then, I carried off his possessions and I captured his cattle. That which he planned to do to me, I did to him. I took what was in his tent and I stripped his encampment...

B174-176 

... *wn.in ḥm=f hꜣb=f n=i ḫr ꜣw.t-ꜥ n.t ḫr nsw.t sꜣw=f ib n(.y) bꜣk im mi ḥkꜣ n(.y) ḫꜣs.t nb.t ...*

... Then his majesty sent me gifts of the king and satisfied the heart of this servant like any ruler of a foreign land...

B197-198 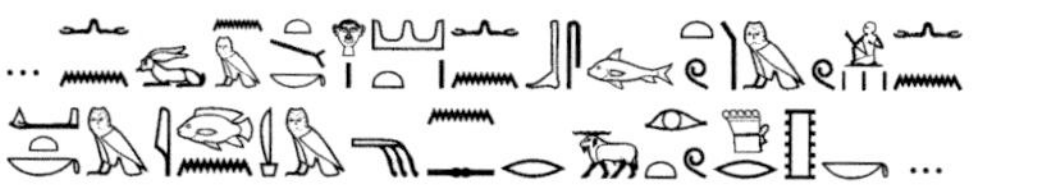

... *nn wn m(w)t=k ḥr ḫꜣs.t nn bs tw ꜥꜣm.w nn ḏi.t(w)=k m inm n(.y) sr iri.tw ḏri=k ...*

... You will not die upon a foreign land. The *ꜥꜣm.w* will not bury you; you will not be placed in sheep's skin when your enclosure is made...

B219-223 

wḏ gr.t ḥm=k rḏi.t ini.t=f Mki m Ḳdmi Ḫnty.w-š m Ḫnty-kšw Mnws m tꜣ.wy Fnḫ.w ḥkꜣ.w pw mtr.w rn.w ḫpr.w m mr.wt=k nn sḫꜣ (R)tnw n=k im=y sy mi.tt ṯsm.w=k

Now, may your majesty decree[258] to have brought to him *Mki* from *Ḳdmi*, *Ḫnty.w-š* from *Ḫnty-kšw* and *Mnws* from the two flat lands of the *Fnḫ.w*. They are rulers, renown of names, who have come into your affection, without mentioning (*R*)*tnw*, it is yours like your dogs.

B238-245 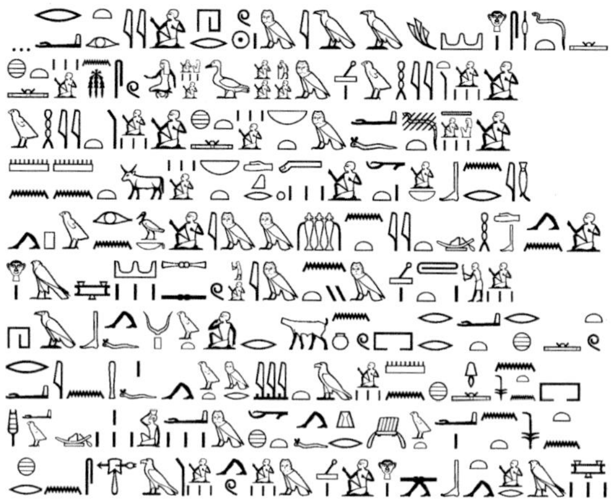

... *rḏi.t(w) iri.y=i hrw m Iꜣꜣ ḥr swḏ.t (i)ḫ.t=i n ms.w=i sꜣ=i smsw m-sꜣ wḥ.yt=i wḥ.yt=i (i)ḫ.t=i nb.t m-ꜥ=f ḏ.t=i mnmn.t=i nb.t dkr.w=i ḫt=i nb bnr iwi(.t) pw iri.n bꜣk im m-ḫnty.t ḥdb.n=i ḥr Wꜣ.wt-Ḥr.w ṯsw im n.ty m-sꜣ pḫr.t hꜣb=f wpw.t r ḫnw r rḏi.t rḫ.tw rḏi.in ḥm=f iwi.t im.y-rꜣ sḫ.tyw mnḫ n(.y) pr.w-nsw.t ꜥḥꜥ.w ꜣtp.w m-ḫt=f ḫr ꜣw.t-ꜥ n.t ḫr nsw.t n St.tyw iwi.w m-sꜣ=i ḥr sbi.t=i r Wꜣ.wt-Ḥr.w*

... I was allowed to spend a day in *Iꜣꜣ* transferring my possessions to my children, my eldest son in charge of my people. My people and all my things were with him, my serfs, all my cattle, my *dkr.w*-fruits and all my fruit trees. Then this servant returned south. I halted at the Ways-of-Horus. The commander there who was in charge of the frontier patrol sent a message to the Residence letting it be known. Then his majesty let the excellent overseer of the palace's fieldworkers come, followed by ships laden with the gifts of the king for the *St.tyw* that had come with me, leading me to the Ways-of-Horus.

B264-266 

... *ḏd.in ḥm=f n ḥm.t-nsw.t mt Sꜣ-nh.t iw.wi m ꜥꜣm ḳmꜣ n(.y) St.tyw wd=s sbḥ ꜥꜣ wr.t msi.w nsw.t m diw.t wꜥ.t ...*

... Then his majesty said to the king's wife: 'Here is Sinuhe, come as a *ꜥꜣm*, a product of the *St.tyw*'. She uttered a great cry and the king's children shrieked as one...

258 The clause may also be translated as 'May your majesty command', with *wḏ* being a subjunctive verb.

B.12 Egyptian Texts at Serabit el-Khadim[259]

Prov. Serabit el-Khadim
Ref. See Figure B.3
Chron. Middle Kingdom
Chapter 5.2.4.1
Figure B.3

Inscription 81 (Senwosret III)

(5) *ꜥꜣm Rwꜣ nb imꜣḫ*
(5) ꜥꜣm Rua,[260] possessor of reverence

Inscription Nr 85 (Amenemhat III, Year 4)

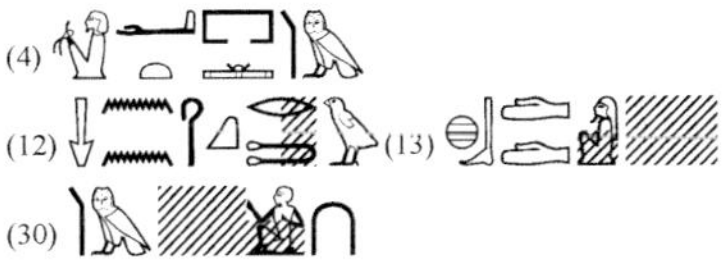

(4) *ir.y-ꜥ.t ꜥꜣm*
(12) *sn n(.y) ḥkꜣ Rṯ(n)w* (13)*Ḫbdd* [...]
(30) *ꜥꜣm* [...] *10*
(4) Hall-keeper,[261] *ꜥꜣm*
(12) Brother of the ruler of *Rṯ(n)w*, (13)*Ḫbdd*[262] [...]
(30) *ꜥꜣm* [...]: 10

Inscription Nr 87 (Amenemhat III, Year 5)

sn n(.y) ḥkꜣ n(.y) Rṯnw [...]
Brother of the ruler of *Rṯnw*, [...]

Inscription Nr 92 (Amenemhat III, Year 13)

(1-2) *sn n(.y) ḥkꜣ n(.y) Rṯnw Ḫbdd*
(1-2) Brother of the ruler of *Rṯnw, Ḫbdd*

Inscription Nr 93 (Amenemhat III, Year 15)

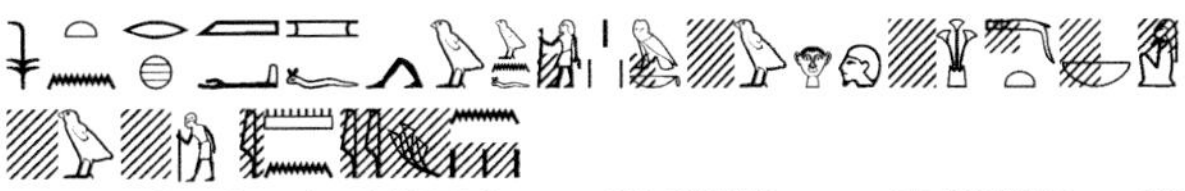

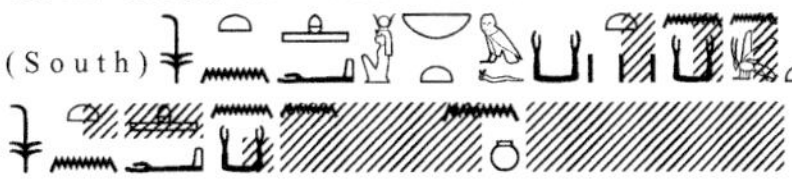

(West) (1)*ḥtp di nsw.t n [kꜣ n(.y)] ḫtm.ty nṯr idn.w* (2)*im.y-rꜣ pr.w wr Ỉ[mn.y-sšn]=n* (3)*iri n Ỉt-nfr.w ꜥꜣm(.t)* (4)*sn=f Mḥy sn=f ꜥnk ...*
(North) *rḫ nsw.t mꜣꜥ mr=f sꜣw* [...] *šd.t(y)* [...*s*...] *n m* [...*n*] *im.y-rꜣ pr.w wr*
rḫ nsw.t mꜣꜥ mr=f iwi.w n=f sr.w m k[...]*w ḥr.y-tp* [...] *mḥ.t nb* [...*idn.w im.y-rꜣ pw*] *wr* [*Ỉ*]*mn*[*.y-sšn*]*=n*
(South) *ḥtp di nsw.t Ḥw.t-Ḥr.w nb.t Mfkꜣ.t n kꜣ n(.y) ḫtm.ty bi.ty smr* [*wꜥ.ty ... r... t... ḥtp*] *di nsw.t n kꜣ* [*n(.y)... nw...*]
(West) (1) An offering which the king gives for the [*kꜣ*] of god's sealer,[263] deputy (2) of the chief steward,[264] Imenyseshenen,[265] (3) born to It-noferu,[266] *ꜥꜣm(.t)*; (4) his brother, Mehy;[267] his brother, Anek[268]...
(North) True acquaintance of the king, his beloved, gladdening [...], deputy of the chief steward,[269] true acquaintance of the king, his beloved, to whom the officials come [bowing], chief of [...] Lower Egypt, lord of [... deputy of the] chief, [Imenyseshen]en.
(South) An offering which the king gives and Hathor, lady of *Mfkꜣ.t*, for the *kꜣ* of the sealer of the king of Lower Egypt, [sole] companion [... an offering] which the king gives for the *kꜣ* [of...].

Inscription Nr 54 (Amenemhat III, Year 45)

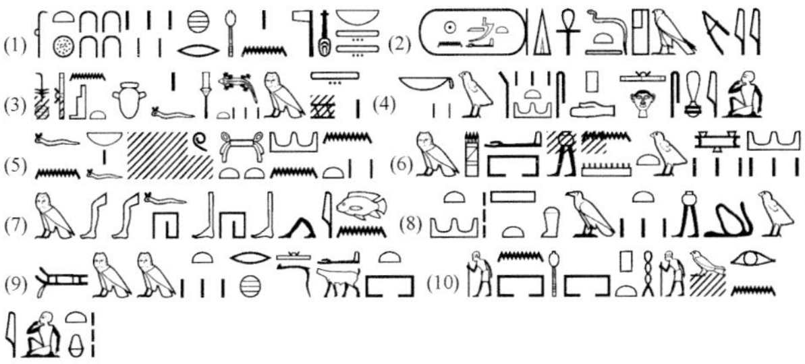

(1)*rnp.t-sp 45 ḫr ḥd n(.y) nṯr nfr nb tꜣ.wy* (2)*N(.y)-mꜣꜥ.t-Rꜥ.w di.(w) ꜥnḫ d.t mr.y Ḥw.t-Ḥr.w* (3)*rḫ nsw(.t) n(.y) s.t ib=f ḫrp ꜥšꜣ.t m tꜣ* (4)*Ky.wt spd ḥr smi=f* (5)*n nb=f* [...] *St.t n n.tyw* (6)*m ꜥḥ ini dr.w*[270] *ḫꜣs.wt* (7)*m rd.wy=f hbhb in.wt* (8)*štꜣ.wt ini pḥ.w* (9)*tmm.t rḫ im.y-rꜣ ꜥḫnw.ty* (10)*wr n(.y) pr ḥd Ptḥ-wr iri n Ỉt*
(1) Year 45 under the majesty of the good god, lord of the two lands, (2) Nimaatra (Amenemhat III), may he be given life eternally, beloved of Hathor, (3) acquaintance of the king, of his affection, controller of the multitudes in the

---

259 Transcriptions follow the line drawings in the figures or as presented in Gardiner and Peet, *Inscriptions of Sinai* 1.

260 Schneider postulates a possible Semitic origin for the name, linking it with *Yrwꜣw* of the Saqqara Execration Texts (E13; Appendix B.4; Schneider, *Ausländer in Ägypten* 2, 150). Ranke lists a couple of attestations in New Kingdom texts (Ranke, *Personennamen* 1, 220 [14]).

261 Ward, *Index*, 57 [452].

262 The name is most likely of non-Egyptian origin. Various interpretations have been suggested, including an Amorite personal name, *Ḫabi-Haddu(m)*, or *ḫābi'-dādu(m)* 'sheltering is the uncle'. A Hurrian-Egyptian origin has also been proposed, rendering it as *Ḫeba(t)-dāta* '(Hurrian goddess) Hebat has given'. For more, see Schneider, *Ausländer in Ägypten* 2, 156-157.

263 Ward, *Index*, 171 [1479].

264 Ward, *Index*, 70 [575].

265 The name is not attested in Ranke, *Personennamen*. However it is clearly derived from the Egyptian. For similar names, see Ranke, *Personennamen* 1, 31 [13], 297 [29].

266 Ranke, *Personennamen* 1, 49 [9].

267 Ranke, *Personennamen* 1, 163 [25-26].

268 Ranke, *Personennamen* 1, 69 [7].

269 Černy translates the sequence as '... his beloved, foster-child of the king of Upper Egypt, ward of [the king of Lower Egypt], pupil of Horus, lord [of the palace]...' (*Inscriptions of Sinai* 2, 101 [93]).

270 Ranke, *Personennamen* 1, 80 [54i]. Following Černy who corrects *ini Mntw* to *ini dr.w* (*Inscriptions of Sinai* 2, 80 [54]).

land of (4) *Ky.wt*/the (foreign) others, effective when he reports (5) to his lord, [...] *St.t* for he who is (6) in the palace, reaching the boundaries of the foreign lands (7) with his two feet, traversing the (8) mysterious valleys, reaching (9) the total end[271] of the unknown, (10) chief chamberlain of the treasury,[272] Ptahwer,[273] born to It.

Inscription Nr 108 (Amenemhat III, Year 45 [?])

(1) *imꜣḫ(.y) ḫr Ptḥ-Skr n kꜣ n(.y) [ḫtm.ty] nṯr* [...] (2)*im.y-rꜣ ꜥḫnw.ty wr [n(.y) pr]-ḥḏ Ptḥ-wr iri n ꞽIt*

(1) Honoured before Ptah-Sokar, for the *kꜣ* of the god('s) [sealer ...], (2) chief chamberlain of the treasury, Ptahwer, born to It.

Inscription Nr 109 (Amenemhat III, Year 45 [?])

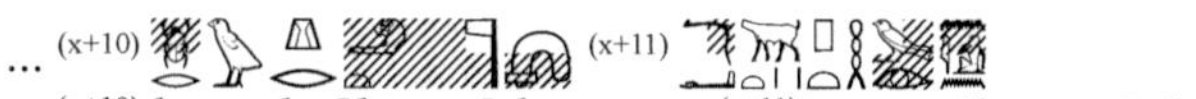

... (x+10) *ḫpr.w ḫr [ḥꜣ.ty...] ḫtm.ty nṯr* (x+11)*im.y-rꜣ ꜥḫnw.ty Ptḥ-wr [iri n] ꞽIn*[274]

... (x+10) which had never occurred before, [count...], god's sealer, (x+11) chief chamberlain of the treasury, Ptahwer, born to In.

Inscription Nr 97 (Amenemhat III, Year 10 + x)

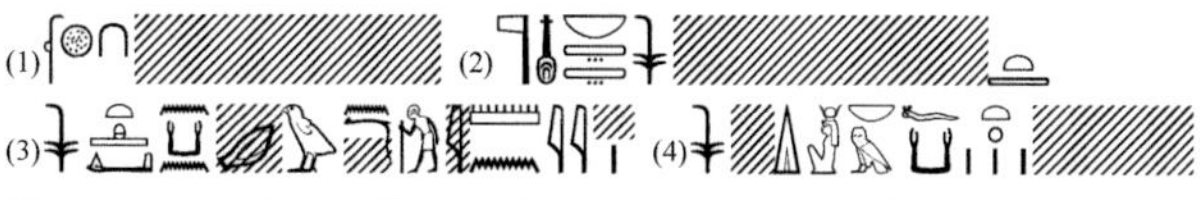

(1) *rnp.t sp 10* [...] (2) *nṯr nfr nb tꜣ.wy nsw* [...]*t*

(3) *ḥtp ḏi nsw.t n kꜣ n(.y) [idn].w n(.y) im.y-rꜣ [pr.w] wr [ꞽI]mn.y* [...] (4) *[ḥtp] ḏi nsw[.t] Ḥw.t-Ḥr.w nb(.t) Mfkꜣ.t* [...]

(1) Year 10 [+ x... of] (2) the good god, lord of the two lands, king [...].

(3)An offering which the king gives for the *kꜣ* of the [deputy] of the chief steward, Imeny[...].

(4) [An offering] which the king gives and Hathor, lady of *Mfkꜣ.t* [...]

Inscription Nr 94 (Amenemhat III)

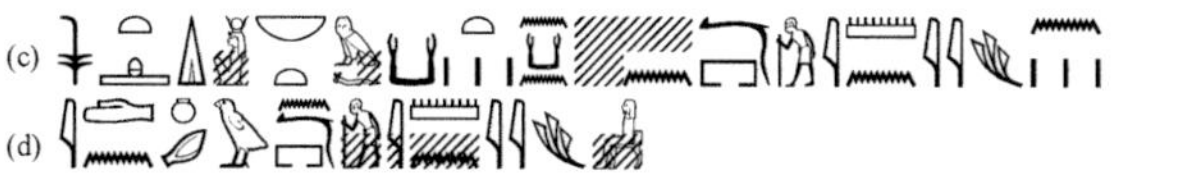

(c) *ḥtp ḏi nsw.t Ḥw.t-Ḥr.w nb.t Mfkꜣ.t n kꜣ n(.y) [idn.w] n(.y) im.y-rꜣ pr.w wr ꞽImn.y-sšn=n*

(d) *idn.w n(.y) im.y-rꜣ pr.w wr ꞽImn.y-sšn[=n]*

(c) An offering which the king gives and Hathor, lady of *Mfkꜣ.t*, for the *kꜣ* of the [deputy] of the chief steward, Imenyseshenen.

(d) Deputy of the chief steward, Imenyseshen[en].

Inscription Nr 95 (Amenemhat III)

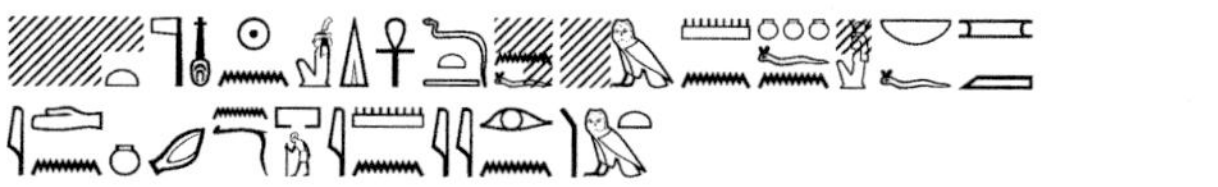

[...]*t nṯr nfr N(.y)-Mꜣꜥ.t-Rꜥ.w ḏi(.w) ꜥnḫ ḏ.t [iri.n=f st?] m mn.w=f n Ḥw.t-Ḥr.w nb=f mr mꜣꜥ idn.w n(.y) im.y-rꜣ pr.w wr ꞽImny iri n ꜥꜣm.t*

[...] the good god, Nimaatra (Amenemhat III), may he be given life eternally. He [made it?] as his monument for Hathor. One truly beloved of his lord, deputy of the chief steward, Imeny, born to *ꜥꜣm.t*.

Inscription Nr 96 (Amenemhat III)

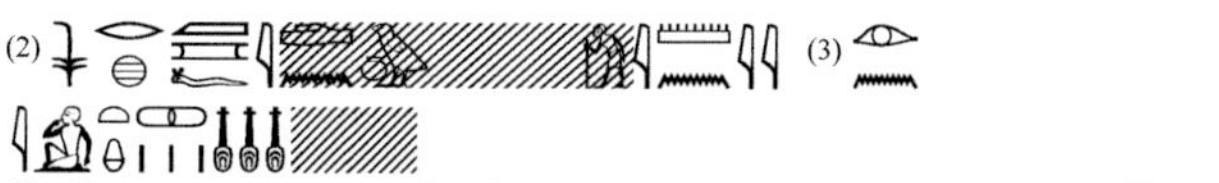

(2) *rḫ nsw.t mꜣꜥ mr=f i[dn.w n.y im.y-rꜣ pr.w wr] ꞽImny* (3) *iri n ꞽIt-nfr.w*

(2) True acquaintance of the king, his beloved [deputy of the chief steward], Imeny, (3) born to It-noferu

Inscription Nr 98 (Amenemhat III)

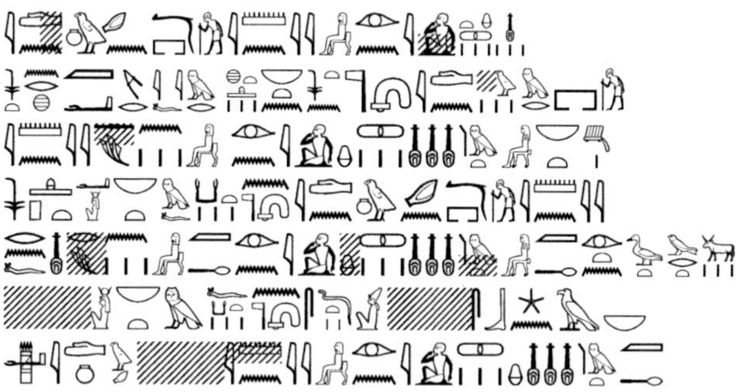

idn.w n(.y) im.y-rꜣ pr.w wr ꞽImny iri n ꞽIt-nfr.w

rḫ nsw.t mꜣꜥ mr.y=f im.y-rꜣ iḫ.wt nb.wt n(.y) nsw.t ḫtm.ty nṯr idn.w im.y-rꜣ pr.w wr ꞽImn.y-sšn=n iri n ꞽIt-nfr.w ꜥꜣm.t nb.t imꜣḫ

ḥtp ḏi nsw(.t) Ḥw.t-Ḥr.w nb.t Mfkꜣ.t n ḫtm.ty nṯr idn.w im.y-rꜣ pr.w wr ꞽImny rn=f nfr Sšn=n mꜣꜥ-ḫrw iri n ꞽIt-nfr.w ꜥꜣm[.t] mꜣꜥ(.t)-ḫrw iri.t n Sꜣ.t-wr.t

[ḥtp ḏi nsw(.t)] Ḥw.t-Ḥr.w nb.t Mfkꜣ.t n ḫtm.ty nṯr sḏt.y nsw(.t) [...]sbꜣ n(.y) Ḥr.w nb ꜥḥ idn.w [im.y-rꜣ pr.w wr ꞽImn]y iri n ꞽIt-nfr.w ꜥꜣm.t mꜣꜥ(.t)-ḫrw

Deputy of the chief steward, Imeny, born to It-noferu.

True acquaintance of the king, his beloved, overseer of all property of the king, god's sealer, deputy of the chief steward, Imenyseshenen, born to It-noferu, *ꜥꜣm.t*, possessor of reverence.

An offering which the king gives and Hathor, lady of *Mfkꜣ.t*, for the god's sealer, deputy of the chief steward, Imeny, his beautiful name is Seshenen, justified, born to It-noferu, *ꜥꜣm.t*, justified, born to Satweret.[275]

[An offering which the king gives and] Hathor, lady of *Mfkꜣ.t*, for the god's sealer, the foster-child of the king [...], pupil of Horus, lord of the palace, deputy [of the chief steward Imen]y, born to It-noferu, *ꜥꜣm.t*, justified.

271 Ranke, *Personennamen* 1, 80 [54].

272 Ward, *Index*, 16 [80].

273 Ranke, *Personennamen* 1, 139 [6].

274 Schneider suggests that the name may have been mistaken for [hieroglyphs] or [hieroglyphs] for *ꞽIt* (*Ausländer in Ägypten* 2, 72).

275 Ranke, *Personennamen* 1, 287 [28].

Inscription Nr 110 (Amenemhat III)

ꜥꜣm n Ḥꜣmi 20

ꜥꜣm from *Ḥꜣmi*:[276] 20

Inscription Nr 112 (Amenemhat III)

(West) ... 

(South) (2)  ...

(14) 

(West) ... *sn n(.y) ḥḳꜣ n(.y) Rṯnw Ḫbddm sꜣ=f Ḳḳbi*

(South) (2)*sn n(.y) ḥḳꜣ n(.y) Rṯnw Ḫbddm ...*

(14) *ḥr.y-pr.w ꜥꜣm Sꜣ-nfr*[...]

(West) ... Brother of the ruler of *Rṯnw*, *Ḫbddm*; his son, *Ḳḳbi*[277]

(South) (2) Brother of the ruler of *Rṯnw*, *Ḫbddm ...*

(14) Major-domo, *ꜥꜣm* Sanofer [...][278]

Inscription Nr 114 (Amenemhat III)

(24) 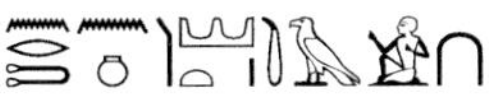

(24) *n Rṯnw ḫꜣs.ty 10*

(24) From *Rṯnw*: 10 foreigners

Inscription Nr 405 (Amenemhat III)

(Bottom right)  (Bottom left) 

(Bottom right) *Škꜣm* (Bottom left) *ꜣpim*

(Bottom right) *Škꜣm*;[279] (Bottom left) *ꜣpim*[280]

Inscription Nr 402 (Amenemhat III [?]), Year 15)

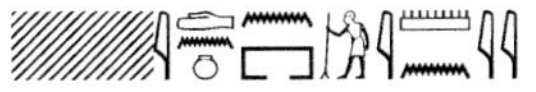

[...] *idn.w* [*im.y-rꜣ*] *pr.w wr ỉmn.y*

[...] deputy of the chief steward, Imeny

Inscription Nr 115 (Amenemhat III [?], Year 18

(Bottom centre)  (Bottom left) 

(Bottom centre) *(R)iṯinw 6* (Bottom left) *ỉpnwirw*

(Bottom centre) (Men from) *(R)iṯinw*: 6; (Bottom left) *ỉpnwirw*[281]

Inscription Nr 414 (Amenemhat III [?])

(3)  (4) 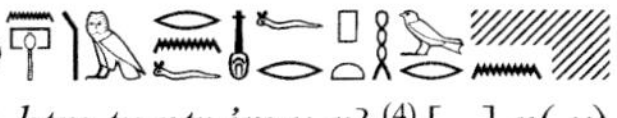

(3) *imꜣḫ(.y) Ptḥ-Skr n kꜣ n(.y) ḫtm.ty nṯr im.y-rꜣ* (4) [...] *n(.y) pr-ḥḏ ꜥꜣm rn=f nfr Ptḥ-wr* [...*n*...]

(3)Honoured before Ptah-Sokar, for the *kꜣ* of the god's sealer, (4)[...] chamberlain of the treasury,[282] *ꜥꜣm*, his beautiful name, Ptahwer[283] [...]

Inscription Nr 120 (Amenemhat A IV, Year 6)

...  ...

... *Rṯnw* 20 ...

... (men from) *Rṯnw*: 20 ...

Inscription Nr 121 (Amenemhat IV, Year 8)

(6) 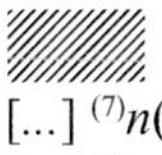 (7) 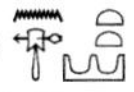 ...

(6) [...] (7)*n(.y) St.t ...*

(6) [...] (7)of *St.t ...*

Inscription Nr 123 (Amenemhat A IV)

(2)... 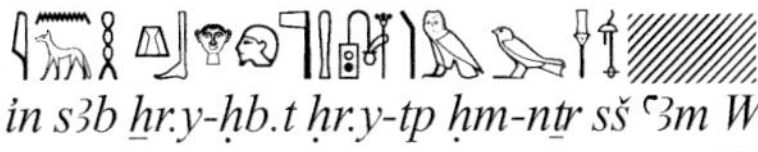

(2)... *in sꜣb ḥr.y-ḥb.t ḥr.y-tp ḥm-nṯr sš ꜥꜣm Wr-ḫrp-ḥm(.wt)* [...]

(2)... by the senior chief lector priest,[284] god's servant,[285] scribe,[286] *ꜥꜣm* Werkherephemut[287] [...]

Inscription Nr 136 (Middle Kingdom, (?) Year 11)

(6)  (7) 

(6) [...] (7) *Rṯnw m rs n(.y) mšꜥ=f ḥḳꜣ.w wr.w* [...]

(6) [...] (7) *Rṯnw* through the vigilance of his army, the great rulers [...]

Obelisk Nr 163 (Middle Kingdom)

(Face A) 

(Face B) 

(Face C) 

(Face A) [...]*i-ꜣši*

(Face B) [*sꜣ=f mr*]*=f Ḳni*

(Face C) [*sꜣ=f mr*]*=f ỉhnm*

(Face A) [...]*i-ꜣši*;[288]

(Face B) [his son], his [beloved], *Ḳni*;[289]

(Face C) [his son], his [beloved], *ỉhnm*[290]

276 Perhaps linked to *Hꜣim* of the Saqqara Execration Texts (E1). Posener, *Princes et Pays*, 64 [E1]. See Appendix B.4.

277 Postulated to derive from the Semitic language, either the Amorite *kbkb* or Akkadian *kakkabu*, both translated as 'star' (Saretta, *Egyptian Perceptions of West Semites*, 189-190, n. 540).

278 Ranke, *Personennamen* 1, 282 [22].

279 Postulated to derive from the Semitic *šaglum* 'gift' or to have some relation with the city of Shechem in the Southern Levant (Saretta, *Egyptian Perceptions of West Semites*, 188-189; Schneider, *Ausländer in Ägypten* 2, 162).

280 Postulated to derive from the Semitic or Amorite *rapi'um* 'he is a healer' or to be related with Apum, a city in the Northern Levant (Schneider, *Ausländer in Ägypten* 2, 123; Saretta, *Egyptian Perceptions of West Semites*, 189-190).

281 Although the name is fragmentary, perhaps the first half, *ỉpnw*, is derived from such Semitic roots as *ab* 'father' or *bn* 'son' while the second, *irw*, perhaps refers to the Canaanite deity El.

282 Ward, *Index*, 16 [84].

283 Ranke, *Personennamen* 1, 139 [6].

284 Ward, *Index*, 148 [1270].

285 Ward, *Index*, 108 [897].

286 Ward, *Index*, 156 [1346].

287 The apparent title of the high-priest of Memphis. Ranke, *Personennamen* 1, 81 [18]; Černy, *Inscriptions of Sinai* 2, 128 [123].

288 Postulated to derive from a Semitic language. For a range of possibilities from Akkadian, Hebraic and Arabic stems, see Schneider, *Ausländer in Ägypten* 2, 124.

289 The name can also be read as *Ḳin*. For the latter's derivation from a Semitic language, see Schneider, *Ausländer in Ägypten* 2, 163.

290 Postulated to derive from a Semitic language. For a range of

Inscription Nr 411 (Middle Kingdom)

(x+1) *[...w...] sbỉ.t* [...] *wḏ.yt* (x+2) *nb.t r St.t r ỉnỉ.t n=f mꜣꜥ.w nb(.w) nfr(.w) n(.y) ḫꜣs.t n(.y)* (x+3) *mfkꜣ.t ḫsb[ḏ] tfrr.t mnwr* (x+4) *ỉr.t[yw...] ỉm.y-rꜣ ꜥẖn.wty H̱ty-snb(.w) m[...f...]*

(x+1) [...] travel [...] (x+2) every expedition to *St.t* to bring for him all the beautiful products of the foreign land, of (x+3) turquoise, lapis lazuli, *tfrr.t*-stone,[291] *mnwr*-incense,[292] (x+4) *ỉr.tyw*-mineral[293] [...], chamberlain, Khetyseneb [...]

possibilities see Schneider, *Ausländer in Ägypten* 2, 132.

291 *Wb* 5, 300.

292 *Wb* 2, 79.

293 *Wb* 1, 116.

NR	DATE	CONTEXT	ASIATIC(S)	OCCUPATION	REPRESENTATION	REFERENCE(S)
81	S III	Seated statue, Hathor Temple (lesser Hanafiyah)	Rua	-	in list of individuals	*Sinai* 1, pl. 22; *Sinai* 2, 90
85	A III Year 4 (?)	North face of stela, Hathor Temple	*ʿ3m*	hall-keeper	in list of expedition members	*Sinai* 1, pl. 23; *Sinai* 2, 92-94
			Ḫbdd	brother of the ruler of *Rṯnw*		
			ʿ3m [...]: 10	-		
87	A III Year 5	West face of stela, Hathor Temple (old approach to cave)	*Ḫbdd(m)* (?)	brother of the ruler of *Rṯnw*	in list of expedition members, wearing knee-length kilt and coiffed hairstyle cut straight below the ear with a tuft at the front	*Sinai* 1, pl. 24; *Sinai* 2, 95
91	A III Year 8	East face of stela, Hathor Temple (portico court)	*St.t*	-	toponym illegible in *Sinai* 1, pl. 33	*Sinai* 1, pl. 33; *Sinai* 2, 99
92	A III Year 13	South face of stela, Hathor Temple (old approach)	*Ḫbdd*	brother of the ruler of *Rṯnw*	in fragmentary list of expedition members	*Sinai* 1, pl. 27; *Sinai* 2, 100
93	A III Year 15	Stela, Hathor Temple (Hanafiyah court)	Imenyseshenen	god's sealer, sealer of the king of Lower Egypt, deputy of the chief steward	as Egyptian among officials; inconclusive if two listed brothers are of the same mother; see Nrs 94-99 and 402	*Sinai* 1, pl. 28; *Sinai* 2, 100-101
103	A III Year 25	West face of stela, Hathor Temple (Hanafiyah court)	x 2	(donkey-rider and driver)	fragmentary; as donkey-rider holding a staff (?); donkey is led by another individual	*Sinai* 2, 107-108; *ArOr* 7, 386, fig. 3
54	A III Year 45	Rock stela, Mine C	Ptahwer	chief chamberlain of the treasury	with epithets concerned with travel to foreign lands; see Nrs 108-109 and 414	*Sinai* 1, pl. 18; *Sinai* 2, 80
			St.t	-		
108	A III Year 45 (?)	Block, Hathor Temple (shrine of kings)	Ptahwer	chief chamberlain of the treasury	as standing figure in knee-length kilt before offerings; no delineating facial features; see Nrs 54, 109 and 414	*Sinai* 1, pl. 33; *Sinai* 2, 112
109	A III Year 45 (?)	Fragment	Ptahwer	chief chamberlain of the treasury	very fragmentary; see Nrs 54, 108 and 414	*Sinai* 1, pl. 33; *Sinai* 2, 112
97	A III, Year 10 + x	Stela	Imeny[...]	deputy of the chief steward	fragmentary, possibly with list of members; see Nrs 93-96, 98-99 and 402	*Sinai* 1, pl. 26; *Sinai* 2, 104
94	A III	Wall inscription fragments c-d, Hathor Temple (cave)	Imenyseshenen	deputy of the chief steward	as seated figure before offering table; no delineating facial features except a beard; see Nrs 93, 95-99 and 402	*Sinai* 1, pls 29, 33; *Sinai* 2, 101-103
95	A III	Front of altar, Hathor Temple (cave)	Imeny	deputy of the chief steward	as two opposing figures offering coned objects to Horus and Hathor; no delineating facial features except a beard; see Nrs 93-94, 96-99 and 402	*Sinai* 1, pl. 30; *Sinai* 2, 103
96	A III	Stela, Hathor Temple (?)	Imeny	[deputy of the chief steward]	in stela seemingly dedicated by Egyptians; see Nrs 93-95, 97-99 and 402	*Sinai* 1, pl. 32; *Sinai* 2, 104
98	A III	Seated statuette	Imenyseshenen / Imeny	overseer of all property of the king, god's sealer, deputy of the chief steward	on statuette of princess perhaps dedicated by Imeny; described as foster-child of the king and pupil of Horus; see Nrs 93-97, 99 and 402	*Sinai* 1, pl. 33; *Sinai* 2, 104-105
99	A III	Door inscription (?), Hathor Temple	Imeny	(?)	no copy of the inscription exists; see Nrs 93-98 and 402	*Sinai* 2, 105
110	A III	Stela, Hathor Temple (portico court)	*ʿ3m* from *Ḥ3mi*: 20	-	in list of expedition members	*Sinai* 1, pl. 35A; *Sinai* 2, 112-113
112	A III	West face of stela, Hathor Temple (porch)	*Ḫbddm*	brother of the ruler of *Rṯnw*	as donkey-rider; carrying an axe and staff(?); hair coiffed and voluminous at back	*Sinai* 1, pl. 37; *Sinai* 2, 113-116; Goldwasser, *E&L* 22-23 (2012/2013), 353-358, figs 1-2
			Kkbi	(carrying offering?)	in knee-length kilt; carrying a spear(?) in left hand, steering a donkey by rope with the right; hair slightly voluminous at back, tied with fillet	

FIGURE B.3. EGYPTIAN TEXTS AT SERABIT EL-KHADIM REPRESENTING ASIATICS AND LEVANTINE TOPONYMS (1/2).

NR	DATE	CONTEXT	ASIATIC(S)	OCCUPATION	REPRESENTATION	REFERENCE(S)
112	A III	West face of stela (*continued*)	x 1	(leading donkey)	leading a donkey; hair slightly voluminous at back	
		South face of stela, Hathor Temple (porch)	*Ḫbddm*	brother of the ruler of *Rṯnw*	in list of expedition members	
			Sanofer	major-domo		
114	A III	South face of stela, Hathor Temple (sanctuary)	*ḫ3s.tyw* from *Rṯnw*: 10	-	in list of 209 expedition members	*Sinai* 1, pls 36, 38; *Sinai* 2, 116-118
405	A III	Southeast face of stela, (portico to Sopdu approach)	x 1	(donkey-rider)	with yellow skin and black hair; wearing a red-banded knee-length kilt; carrying an axe in the left hand and an unknown implement in the right	*Sinai* 1, pl. 85; *Sinai* 2, 205-206
			Šk3m	(leading donkey)	with yellow skin and black hair; wearing a red-banded knee-length kilt; carrying a spear in the left hand and leading the donkey by rope in the right	
			3pim	-	with yellow skin and black hair; wearing a red-banded short kilt; carrying a spear in the left hand and a throw-stick in the right	
402	A III (?) Year 15	Stela fragment, Hathor Temple (Sopdu hall)	Imeny[...]	deputy of the chief steward	fragmentary	*Sinai* 1, pl. 83; *Sinai* 2, 204
115	A III (?) Year 18	West face of stela, Hathor Temple (old approach)	x 1	(donkey-rider)	carrying an axe or staff	*Sinai* 1, pl. 39; *Sinai* 2, 118-119
			x 1	(leading donkey)	leading a donkey by a rope in the right hand	
			Ỉpnwirw	(driving donkey)	carrying a staff in the right hand	
			(Men from) *Rṯnw*: 6	-	in list of expedition members; number could include depicted men	
414	A III (?)	Stela, Hathor Temple (shrine of kings)	Ptahwer	chamberlain of the treasury	likely the same Ptahwer in Nrs 108-109	*Sinai* 1, pl. 86; *Sinai* 2, 210
120	A IV Year 6	North face of stela, Hathor Temple (portico court)	(Men from) *Rṯnw*: 20	-	in list of expedition members	*Sinai* 1, pl. 43; *Sinai* 2, 122-124
121	A IV Year 8	Stela	*St.t*	-	fragmentary; in sequence of epithets of the chief chamberlain of the treasury, Djef[...]	*Sinai* 1, pl. 48; *Sinai* 2, 124-125
123	A IV	Wall inscription, Hathor Temple	Werkherep-hemut	senior chief lector priest, god's servant, scribe	fragmentary; in list of rations for the temple of Hathor	*Sinai* 1, pl. 46; *Sinai* 2, 127-128
136	MK, (?) Year 11	West face of stela, Hathor Temple (shrine of kings)	*Rṯnw*	-	fragmentary	*Sinai* 1, pl. 49; *Sinai* 2, 135-137
163	MK	Obelisk	[...]*i-3ši*	-	names are each determined by a kneeling figure, two with a coiffed hairstyle and a long, thick beard; all carrying a square-shaped shield in the right hand and a duckbill(?) axe in the left	*Sinai* 1, pl. 51; *Sinai* 2, 147
			Ḳni	-		
			Ỉḫnm	-		
411	MK	East face of stela, Hathor Temple (portico court)	*St.t*	-	fragmentary; toponym seemingly encompasses a vast region from which products were brought	*Sinai* 1, pl. 86; *Sinai* 2, 208

FIGURE B.3. EGYPTIAN TEXTS AT SERABIT EL-KHADIM REPRESENTING ASIATICS AND LEVANTINE TOPONYMS (2/2), WITH NOTATIONS ON THEIR DATE, CONTEXT AND BIBLIOGRAPHICAL REFERENCES.

Notes: Activities of Asiatics represented pictorially are written in brackets under 'Occupation'.

A: Amenemhat — *Sinai* 1: Gardiner and Peet, *Inscriptions of Sinai* 1.
S: Senwosret — *Sinai* 2: Černy, *Inscriptions of Sinai* 2.
MK: Middle Kingdom — *ArOr* 7: Černy, *ArOr* 7 (1935), 384-389.

A. Detail, north wall, tomb of Amenemhat (Nr 2). Courtesy of the Australian Centre for Egyptology.

B. Detail, north wall, tomb of Khnumhotep II (Nr 3).

C. Detail, south wall, tomb of Khnumhotep II (Nr 3).

Plate 1. 'Fair skinned men', Beni Hassan.

Plate 2. North wall, tomb of Khnumhotep (Nr 3), Beni Hassan. Courtesy of the Australian Centre for Egyptology.

A.

B.

C.

Plate 3. Statuette of a foreign female, tomb of Weseri, Beni Hassan.
National Museums of Scotland, Edinburgh, A.1911.260. © National Museums Scotland.

A. SOUTH END OF THE SOUTHEASTERN WALL WITH A BLOCKED ENTRANCE TO ROOM 9.
IMAGE BY DANIELA ARNOLD.

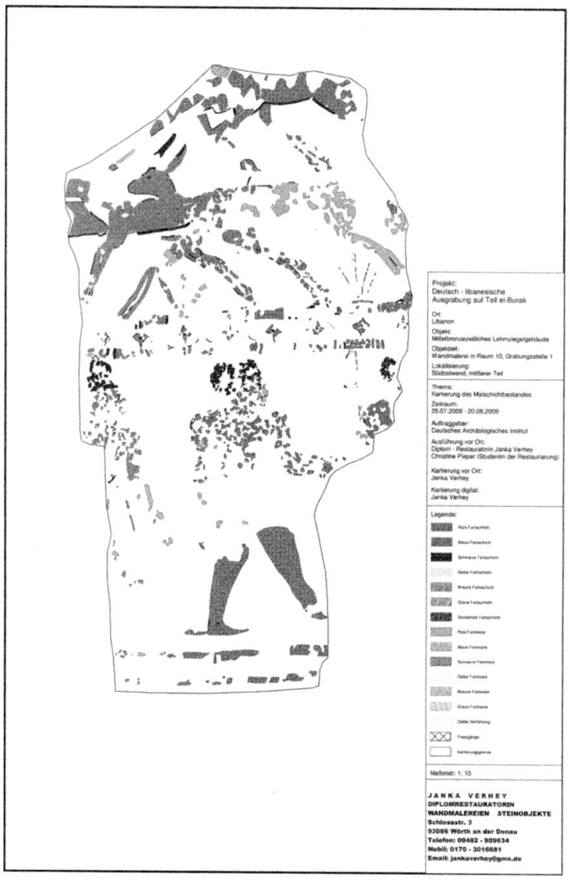

B. MIDDLE PART OF THE SOUTHEASTERN WALL. IMAGE BY JANKA VERHEY.

PLATE 4. WALL PAINTINGS, ROOM 10 OF COMPLEX, TELL EL-BURAK.
COURTESY OF HÉLÈNE SADER. © TELL EL-BURAK ARCHAEOLOGICAL PROJECT.